IB WORLD SCHOOLS YEARBOOK 2020

Editor: Jonathan Barnes

Acknowledgements

We are extremely grateful to those who have helped to compile this yearbook.

We also extend our warm gratitude to the many schools and colleges for providing us promptly and efficiently with the accurate information this yearbook contains.

Published in 2020 by John Catt Educational Ltd
15 Riduna Park, Station Road,
Melton, Woodbridge, Suffolk IP12 1QT, UK.
Tel: +44 (0) 1394 389850
Email: enquiries@johncatt.com
Website: www.johncatt.com

International Baccalaureate Organization (UK) Ltd
Peterson House
Malthouse Avenue
Cardiff Gate
Cardiff
Wales CF23 8GL
United Kingdom
Website: www.ibo.org

British Library Cataloguing in Publication Data.

ISBN: 978 1 912906 80 2

Designed and typeset by John Catt Educational Ltd.

IB WORLD SCHOOLS
YEARBOOK 2020

Contents

Message from Chair and Director General

Dear member of the IB community,
Last year we celebrated our anniversary, marking 50 years of impact and innovation in global education. The anniversary gave us the opportunity to reflect on our growth and achievements, and on our aims for the next 50 years.

Our commitment to IB schools is clear: we will continue to work together, with the same vision and passion, to deliver our shared mission of creating a better world through education; to grow our diverse community of schools; to increase access to excellent education for students of all backgrounds, everywhere; and to have a positive impact on the lives of millions worldwide.

To pursue this mission, we will deliver continuous improvement and excellence in our three core areas:

- **Teaching and learning** – development of philosophy-based curricula and programmes;
- **Services to schools** – authorisation, implementation, evaluation and professional development of teachers;
- **Assessment of students** – design, development and delivery of assessment.

We will do so by delivering to our three key strategic objectives (Innovation, Service and Community). We would like to share a selection of highlights in each of these areas:

Innovation – continuous educational innovation and improvement

- **The enhanced PYP** was successfully launched in October 2018, *providing flexibility for schools to teach a national curriculum (subject specific) alongside the PYP programme* of enquiry. Alongside other researched improvements for this age group, a *range of enhancements* have been designed – reflection as a core skill, taking action (including advocacy, social justice and social entrepreneurship) and a greater focus on multilingualism.
- **Standards and practices**: The *comprehensive review* of the standards, practices and requirements that schools follow to obtain their initial authorization and subsequent evaluations, is now complete and *ready for launch to the community in 2020*. One of the key changes is a focus on *continued development and innovation in schools* – a set of 'stretch' practices has been created to help schools continually refine and improve.

Service – excellent IB teaching and learning embedded in schools

- **More for less:** Since 2015, there has been *no increase to fees* other than inflation. In 2018, the IB announced a significant *incentive to continuum and multi-programme schools*, to reward the breadth of uptake of IB programmes in their schools. In 2019, we announced the *elimination of the candidate registry fee,* as well as *a reduction in the price of online Professional Development.*
- **Our digital publishing** vision is complete. The *Programme Resource Centre now contains 100% of all programme content.* Continuous improvement plans have resulted in *steadily increasing satisfaction levels.*
- **The IB World Schools Survey showed improvements in schools' ratings of the IB's performance** in authorization, evaluation, quality of workshops and with programme Communities.

Community – a stronger IB for a stronger IB community

- Our **50th Anniversary** celebrations showed the strength of our global community, who joined campaigns such as #weareIB, #GenerationIB and our alumni video campaign, which reached millions of people around the world, spreading the message of the IB's impact with a range of inspiring stories.
- We gained widespread **media coverage** for the IB in top tier publications and broadcasts such as Forbes, Tes, Newsweek, ITN Films, Channel NewsAsia, Cheddar, PBS NewHour, The Straits Times, Chinese Business Daily, Brainfeed Magazine, Education Journal Middle East and many others.
- We successfully launched the **Masters of Education (M.Ed.) programme** with the University of the People (UoPeople), offering a tuition-free online university degree to benefit teachers worldwide.
- We **engage with governmental and other educational bodies** to help grow and strengthen the IB community globally. Recent highlights include partnerships and projects with the governments of United Arab Emirates, Japan and South Korea.

We thank you, colleagues and partners in all our schools, for your continued commitment and dedication to our shared mission.

As we continue to grow, bringing excellent education to ever more students of all backgrounds across the world, we look forward to working with all our schools to making a better world through education as we proceed through the Fourth Industrial Revolution. Together, we will continue to develop, delivering continuous improvements in education, to develop the open-minded, independent thinkers who are citizens and leaders of tomorrow.

Siva Kumari – IB Director General
George Rupp – Chair of the IB Board of Governors

Introduction, How to use this Yearbook

The International Baccalaureate (IB) offers high quality programmes of international education to a worldwide community of schools, aiming to develop internationally minded people who, recognizing their common humanity and shared guardianship of the plant, help to create a better, more peaceful world.

The IB works alongside state and privately funded schools around the world that share the commitment to international education, to deliver these programmes.

Schools that have achieved the high standards required for authorization to offer one or more of the IB programmes are known as 'IB World Schools'. As of November 2019 there were 1,315 schools with 1,509 programmes in candidate status (637 PYP, 465 MYP, 355 DP, 52 CP).

The IB World Schools Yearbook is the official guide to schools authorized to offer the Primary Years Programme, the Middle Years Programme, the Diploma Programme and the Career-related Programme. It tells you where the IB World Schools are situated and what they offer, and provides up-to-date information about IB programmes and the IB organization.

This is an ideal reference for school administration, parents and education ministries worldwide as it:

- provides a comprehensive reference of IB World Schools for quick and easy access
- raises the profile of IB World Schools within their local community and beyond
- provides comprehensive information about IB programmes and the IB.

How to use this yearbook

The Yearbook has been designed to be as easy as possible to use and has been divided into five sections.

1. **General information** about the IB and its programmes.
2. **Comprehensive information** about IB World Schools presented in alphabetical order by school name, colour coded according to IB geographical region. In this section, schools have been given the opportunity to highlight their best qualities by creating an enhanced profile for their school.
3. **Directory information** about every IB World School that offers one or more of the IB programmes as of November 2019. The directory is ordered by IB region and contains general and contact information about each school. Information about the three IB regions is also given in this section. (Those schools that have elected to purchase a profile in the Yearbook will appear in capital letters in the directory.)
4. **Appendices** containing information and lists relevant to the IB. These include addresses of IB offices, location of IB World Schools, Diploma Programme subjects offered (in 2020), IB Associations around the world, university acknowledgement of the Diploma Programme and Career-related Programme and universities offering IB scholarships.
5. **Index** of all schools listed geographically and alphabetically by name.

Are you looking for a specific IB World School?

If you know the name of the school but are unsure of its location, turn to the index on p. 698 where you will find an alphabetic listing of all IB World Schools.

Are you looking for an IB World School in a specific country?

Look first in the directory section; this will give you the basic information about all the schools in each region. More detailed information can be found in the profiles section for those schools marked with capitalized letters.

The IB website, ibo.org, also contains the most up-to-date information on IB World Schools. A school search option is available from every page on the site for people wanting to find an IB World School.

IB Mission Statement

The International Baccalaureate aims to develop inquiring, knowledgeable and caring young people who help to create a better and more peaceful world through intercultural understanding and respect.

To this end the organization works with schools, governments and international organizations to develop challenging programmes of international education and rigorous assessment.

These programmes encourage students across the world to become active, compassionate and lifelong learners who understand that other people, with their differences, can also be right.

Déclaration de mission de l'IB

Le Baccalauréat International (IB) a pour but de développer chez les jeunes la curiosité intellectuelle, les connaissances et la sensibilité nécessaires pour contribuer à bâtir un monde meilleur et plus paisible, dans un esprit d'entente mutuelle et de respect interculturel.

À cette fin, l'IB collabore avec des établissements scolaires, des gouvernements et des organisations internationales pour mettre au point des programmes d'éducation internationale stimulants et des méthodes d'évaluation rigoureuses.

Ces programmes encouragent les élèves de tout pays à apprendre activement tout au long de leur vie, à être empreints de compassion, et à comprendre que les autres, en étant différents, puissent aussi être dans le vrai.

Declaración de principios de IB

El Bachillerato Internacional tiene como meta formar jóvenes solidarios, informados y ávidos de conocimiento, capaces de contribuir a crear un mundo mejor y más pacífico, en el marco del entendimiento mutuo y el respeto intercultural.

En pos de este objetivo, la organización colabora con establecimientos escolares, gobiernos y organizaciones internacionales para crear y desarrollar programas de educación internacional exigentes y métodos de evaluación rigurosos.

Estos programas alientan a estudiantes del mundo entero a adoptar una actitud activa de aprendizaje durante toda su vida, a ser compasivos y a entender que otras personas, con sus diferencias, también pueden estar en lo cierto.

About the IB

Pioneering a movement of international education since 1968, the International Baccalaureate (IB) is a non-profit foundation that offers four high quality and challenging educational programmes to students aged 3-19 years old. The four programmes focus on teaching students to think critically and independently, and how to inquire with care and logic. An IB education also prepares students to succeed in a world where facts and fiction merge in the news, and where asking the right questions is a crucial skill that will allow them to flourish long after they've left school. The organization is supported by IB teachers and coordinators who develop and promote the IB's curriculums in almost 5,000 schools globally every day, in more than 150 countries around the world.

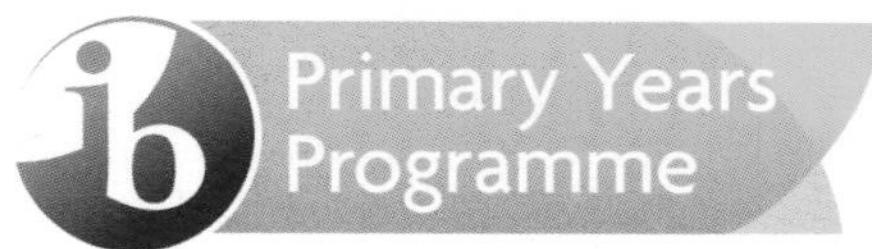

The **IB Primary Years Programme (PYP)**, for students aged 3 to 12, focuses on the development of the whole child as an inquirer, both in the classroom and in the world outside.

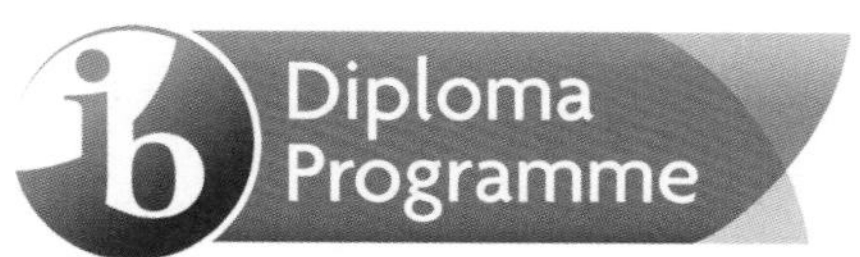

The **IB Diploma Programme (DP)**, for students aged 16 to 19, is an academically challenging and balanced programme of education with final examinations that prepares students for success at university and beyond.

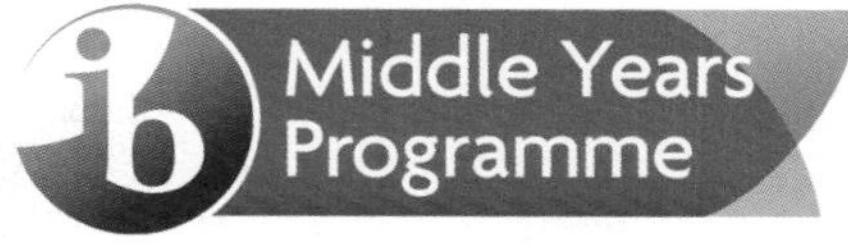

The **IB Middle Years Programme (MYP)**, for students aged 11 to 16, provides a framework of academic challenge that encourages students to embrace and understand the connections between traditional subjects and the real world, and become critical and reflective thinkers.

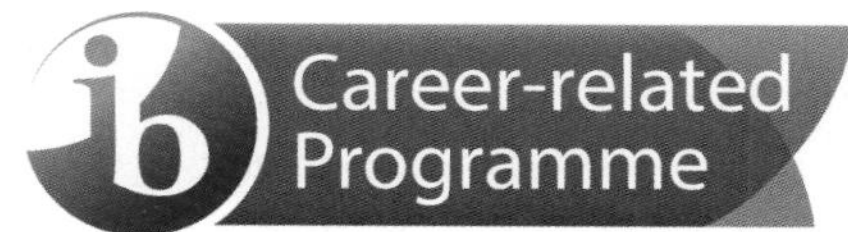

The **IB Career-related Programme (CP)**, for students aged 16 to 19, incorporates the vision and educational principles of the IB programmes into a unique offering specifically designed for students who wish to engage in career-related learning.

IB programmes are available to students in a wide variety of schools and from a range of cultural, ethnic and socio-economic backgrounds. IB World Schools form a worldwide community in which there is no such thing as a "typical" school.

Figure 1: Types of IB World Schools (Information correct as of November 2019)

	Charter	Private	State	State subsidized	Total
Africa, Middle East	4	904	298	51	1,257
Asia Pacific		797	132	12	941
Americas	127	762	2,067	29	2,985
Total	**131**	**2,463**	**2,497**	**92**	**5,183**

Does not include European Platform schools. Includes MYP Partner Schools.

IB World Schools:

- share the mission and commitment of the IB to quality, international education
- play an active and supporting role in the worldwide community of IB World Schools
- share their knowledge and experience in the development of IB programmes
- are committed to the professional development of teachers

Funding for IB programmes comes from the fees paid by IB World Schools, with additional income from workshops and publication sales. Donors provide support for development projects that cannot be implemented from the organization's budget.

Figure 2: IB World Schools
Total number of IB World Schools: 5,183 in 158 countries (as of November 2019).

Breakdown by regions

Africa, Europe, Middle East	97 countries	1,257 Authorized schools
Asia Pacific	28 countries	941 Authorized schools
Americas	33 countries	2,985 Authorized schools
Total	**158 countries**	**5,183 Authorized schools**

Does not include European Platform schools. Includes MYP Partner Schools.

Breakdown by programmes

	PYP	MYP	DP	CP	Total
Africa, Europe, Middle East	425	328	1,011	86	1,850
Asia Pacific	528	242	610	21	1,401
Americas	836	792	1,815	146	3,589
Total	**1,789**	**1,362**	**3,436**	**253**	**6,840**

*As of November 2019

Does not include European Platform schools nor MYP Partner Schools.

As of November 2019, the four IB programmes are taught in 158 countries.

Figure 3: Growth of the four IB Programmes

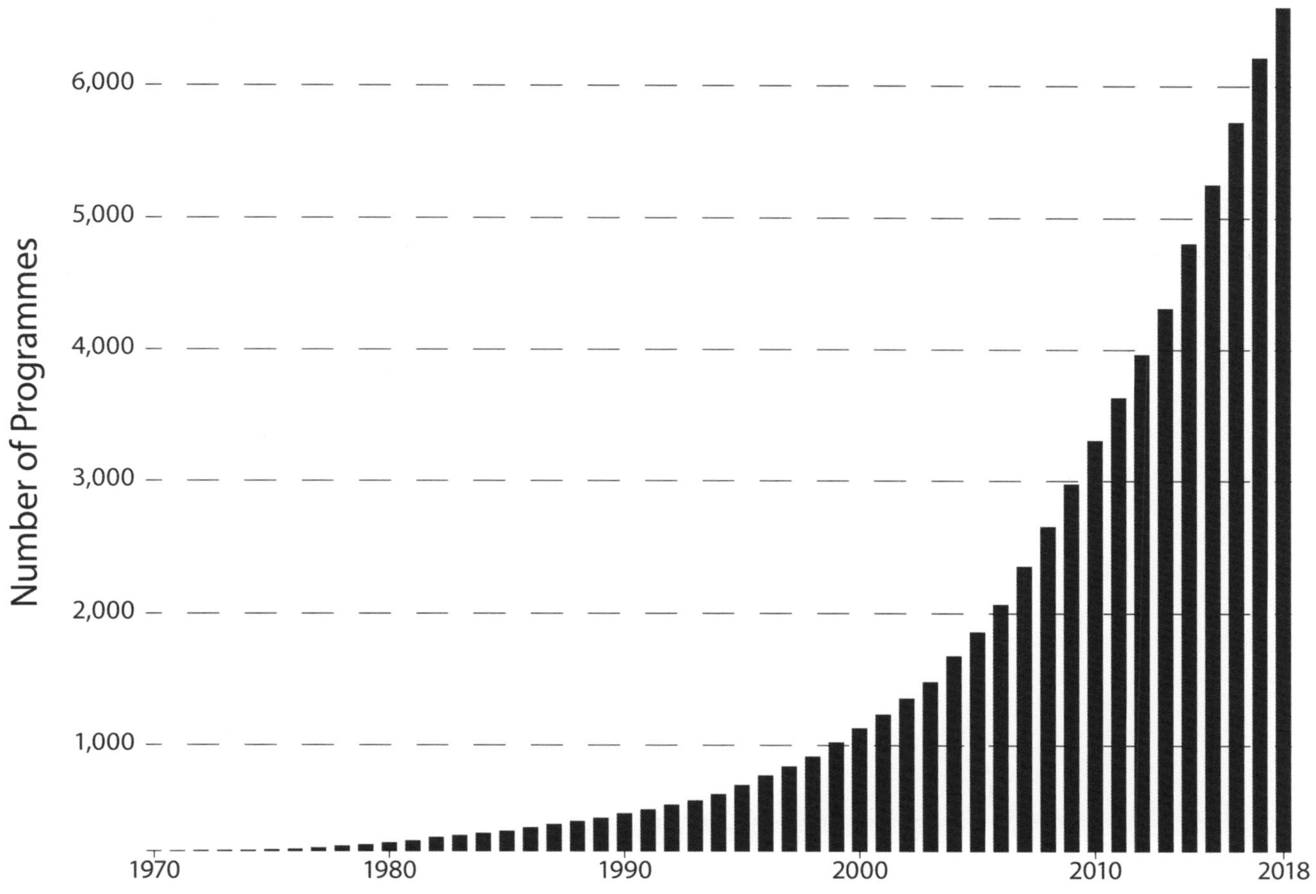

Does not include European Platform nor MYP Partner Schools

The IB Learner Profile

The aim of all IB programmes is to develop internationally minded people who, recognizing their common humanity and shared guardianship of the planet, help to create a better and more peaceful world

As IB learners we strive to be:

Inquirers	We nurture our curiosity, developing skills for inquiry and research. We know how to learn independently and with others. We learn with enthusiasm and sustain our love of learning throughout life.
Knowledgeable	We develop and use conceptual understanding, exploring knowledge across a range of disciplines. We engage with issues and ideas that have local and global significance.
Thinkers	We use critical and creative thinking skills to analyze and take responsible action on complex problems. We exercise initiative in making reasoned, ethical decisions.
Communicators	We express ourselves confidently and creatively in more than one language and in many ways. We collaborate effectively, listening carefully to the perspectives of other individuals and groups.
Principled	We act with integrity and honesty, with a strong sense of fairness and justice, and with respect for the dignity and rights of people everywhere. We take responsibility for our actions and their consequences.
Open-minded	We critically appreciate our own cultures and personal histories, as well as the values and traditions of others. We seek and evaluate a range of points of view, and we are willing to grow from the experience.
Caring	We show empathy, compassion and respect. We have a commitment to service, and we act to make a positive difference in the lives of others and in the world around us.
Risk-takers	We approach uncertainty with forethought and determination; we work independently and cooperatively to explore new ideas and innovative strategies. We are resourceful and resilient in the face of challenges and change.
Balanced	We understand the importance of balancing different aspects of our lives – intellectual, physical and emotional – to achieve well-being for ourselves and others. We recognize our interdependence with other people and with the world in which we live.
Reflective	We thoughtfully consider the world and own ideas and experience. We work to understand our strengths and weaknesses in order to support our learning and personal development.

IB Programmes

What is an International Baccalaureate (IB) education?

An IB education is unique because of its rigorous academic and personal standards. IB programmes challenge students aged 3 to 19 to excel not only in their studies but also in their personal growth.

We aspire to help schools develop well-rounded students, who respond to challenges with optimism and an open mind, are confident in their own identities, make ethical decisions, join with others in celebrating our common humanity and apply what they learn in real-world, complex and unpredictable situations.

Through our high-quality programmes of international education, we aim to inspire a quest for learning throughout life that is marked by enthusiasm and empathy.

Our vision is to offer all students an IB education that:

- focuses on learners – our student-centred programmes promote healthy relationships, ethical responsibility, and personal challenge
- develops effective approaches to teaching and learning – our programmes help students to develop the attitudes and skills they need for both academic and personal success
- works within global contexts – our programmes increase understanding of languages and cultures and explore globally significant ideas and issues
- explores significant content – our programmes offer a curriculum that is broad and balanced, conceptual and connected.

Informed by values described in the IB Learner Profile, IB learners strive to become inquirers, knowledgeable, thinkers, communicators, principled, open-minded, caring, risk-takers, balanced, and reflective. These attributes represent a broad range of human capacities and responsibilities that go beyond intellectual development and academic success.

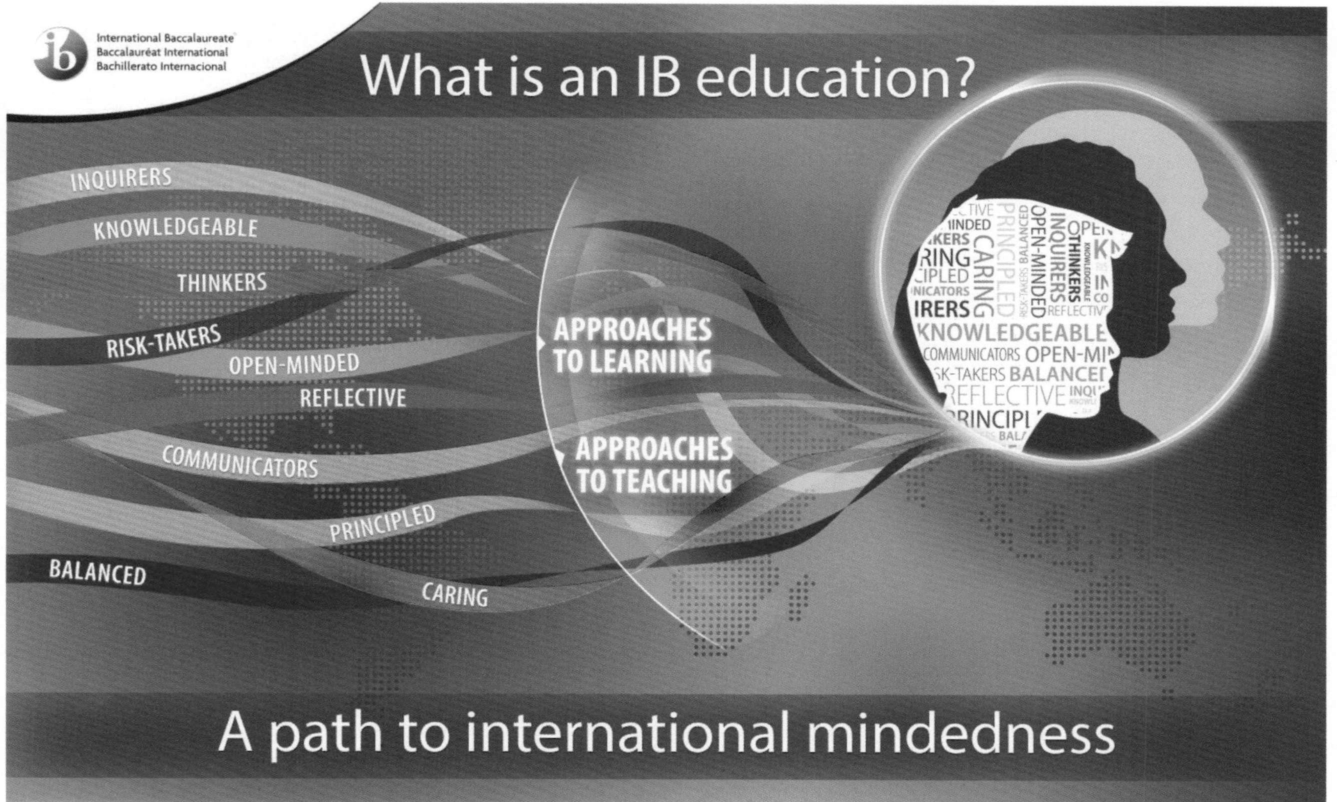

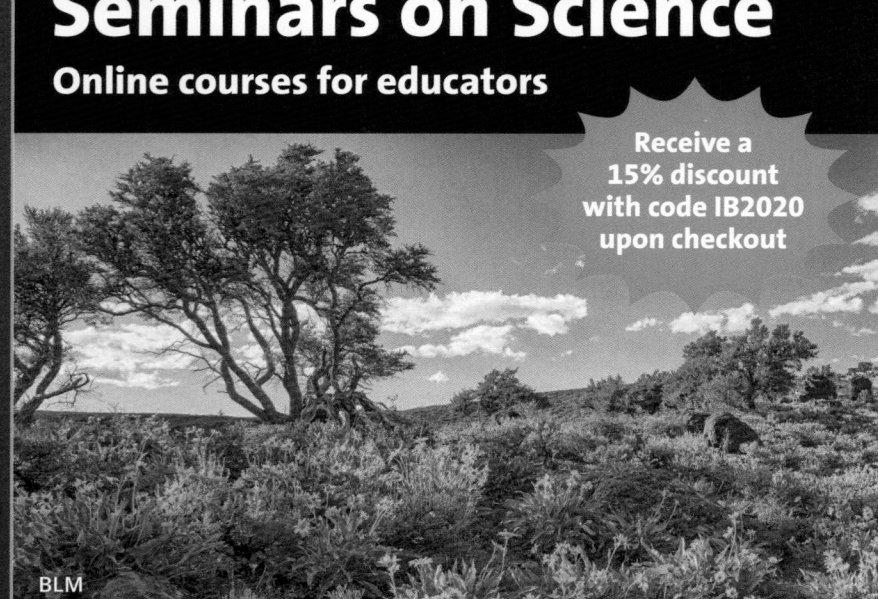

What is the IB Primary Years Programme (PYP)?

A transformative and caring approach that builds a lifelong love of learning

The PYP, for children from 3-12 years, is the start to a lifelong love of learning. It is a caring and thoughtful approach that nurtures the 'whole' child and gives them ownership of their studies from the very beginning.

PYP teachers consider each child's unique abilities and interests, to develop inquiry-based learning environments that build universal skills for life, like thinking, researching and cultural understanding. Children explore across and beyond subject boundaries through transdisciplinary inquiries, investigating big – and small – questions about what it means to be human in today's world. But the most important thing children get from the programme is an inquiring mind, the ability to find things out for themselves and take action to benefit their local community.

Key features of the PYP curriculum framework

Informed by research into how children learn, how educators teach, and the principles and practices of effective assessment, the PYP places a powerful emphasis on conceptual, inquiry-based learning.

Transdisciplinary learning

The PYP is designed to support transdisciplinary learning because it mirrors the natural way children learn. Guiding learning experiences through transdisciplinary themes, across and beyond the boundaries of subjects, teachers build on what children know – and their areas of interest – to help them relate to the world around them.

Figure 4: IB Primary Years Programme model

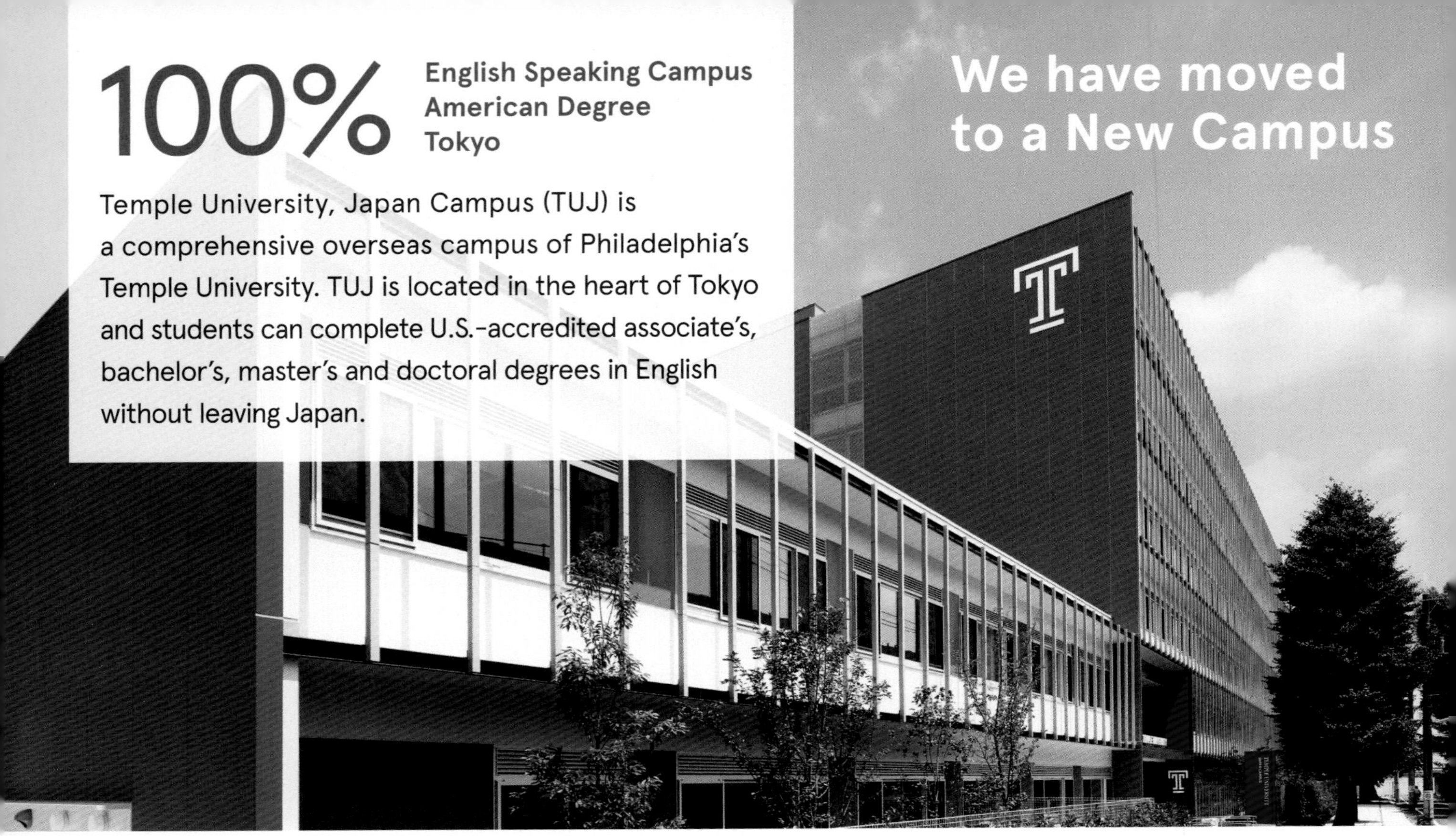

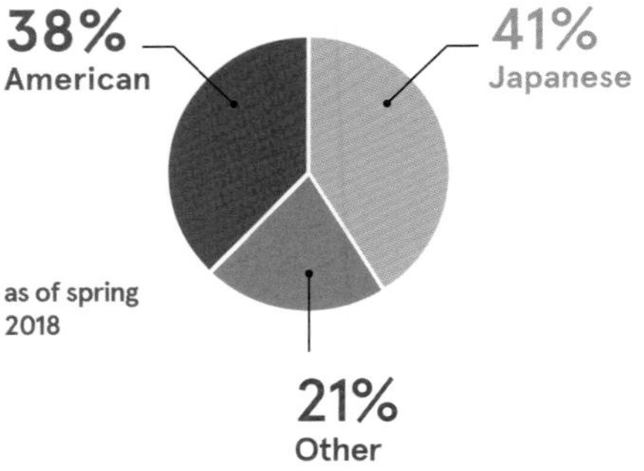

Transdisciplinary themes

- Who we are
- Where we are in place and time
- How we express ourselves
- How the world works
- How we organize ourselves
- Sharing the planet

Subject areas

- Arts
- Language
- Science
- Social studies
- Mathematics
- Personal, social and physical education

Agency

By encouraging agency (voice, choice and ownership), the PYP creates a culture where teachers can create relevant, authentic, challenging learning experiences and children develop a love of learning by finding things out for themselves.

Assessment

Assessment is ongoing in the PYP, deepening learning and providing opportunities for teachers to reflect on what their students know, what they understand and what they can do. Immediate, effective feedback and feed-forward helps children to self-monitor and adjust their learning experiences to gain confidence in their own abilities, increase well-being and build resilience.

The exhibition

In the PYP exhibition, children follow their passions to collaborate on an in-depth project, resulting in a community-wide celebration of their learning journey. Analysing, researching and proposing solutions to real world challenges and opportunities prepares them for success in the IB Middle Years Programme, or the next stage in their education.

PYP in the early years (3-6)

The PYP transdisciplinary framework is designed to provide authentic opportunities to strengthen key developmental skills and abilities in young children. Inquiring through play and exploration, young learners learn to self-regulate and build and test theories to make sense of the world around them.

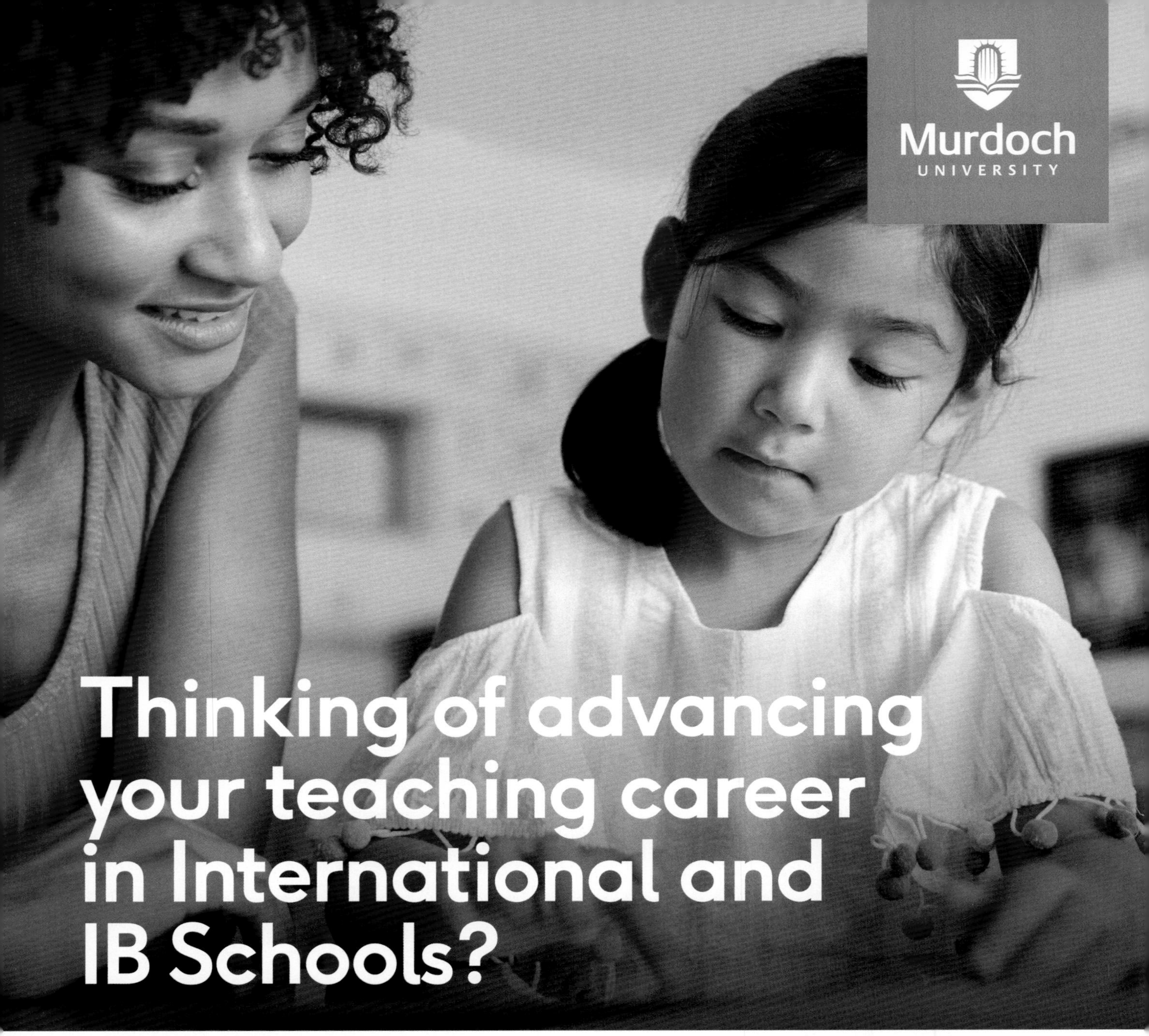
Murdoch
UNIVERSITY
Thinking of advancing your teaching career in International and IB Schools?

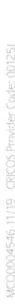

What is the IB Middle Years Programme?

The IB Middle Years Programme (MYP) is designed for students aged 11 to 16. It provides a framework of learning that encourages students to become creative, critical and reflective thinkers. The MYP emphasizes intellectual challenge, encouraging students to make connections between their studies in traditional subjects and the real world. It fosters the development of skills for communication, intercultural understanding and global engagement – essential qualities for young people who are becoming global leaders.

The MYP is flexible enough to accommodate national or local curriculum requirements. It builds upon the knowledge, skills and attitudes developed in the IB Primary Years Programme (PYP) and prepares students to meet the academic challenges of the IB Diploma Programme (DP) and the IB Career-related Programme (CP).

The IB Middle Years Programme:

- addresses holistically students' intellectual, social, emotional and physical well-being
- provides students opportunities to develop the knowledge, attitudes and skills they need in order to manage complexity and take responsible action for the future
- ensures breadth and depth of understanding through study in eight subject groups and interdisciplinary learning.
- requires the study of at least two languages (language of instruction and additional language of choice) to support students in understanding their own cultures and those of others.
- empowers students to participate in service within the community.
- helps to prepare students for further education, the workplace and a lifetime of learning.

The MYP consists of eight subject groups: language acquisition, language and literature, individuals and societies, sciences, mathematics, arts, physical and health education, and design. Student study is supported by a minimum of 50 hours of instruction per subject group in each academic year. In years 4 and 5, students have the option to take courses from six of the eight subject groups, which provides greater flexibility, with optional MYP eAssessments at the end of year 5 for schools that wish for their students to have externally validated results.

Figure 5: IB Middle Years Programme model

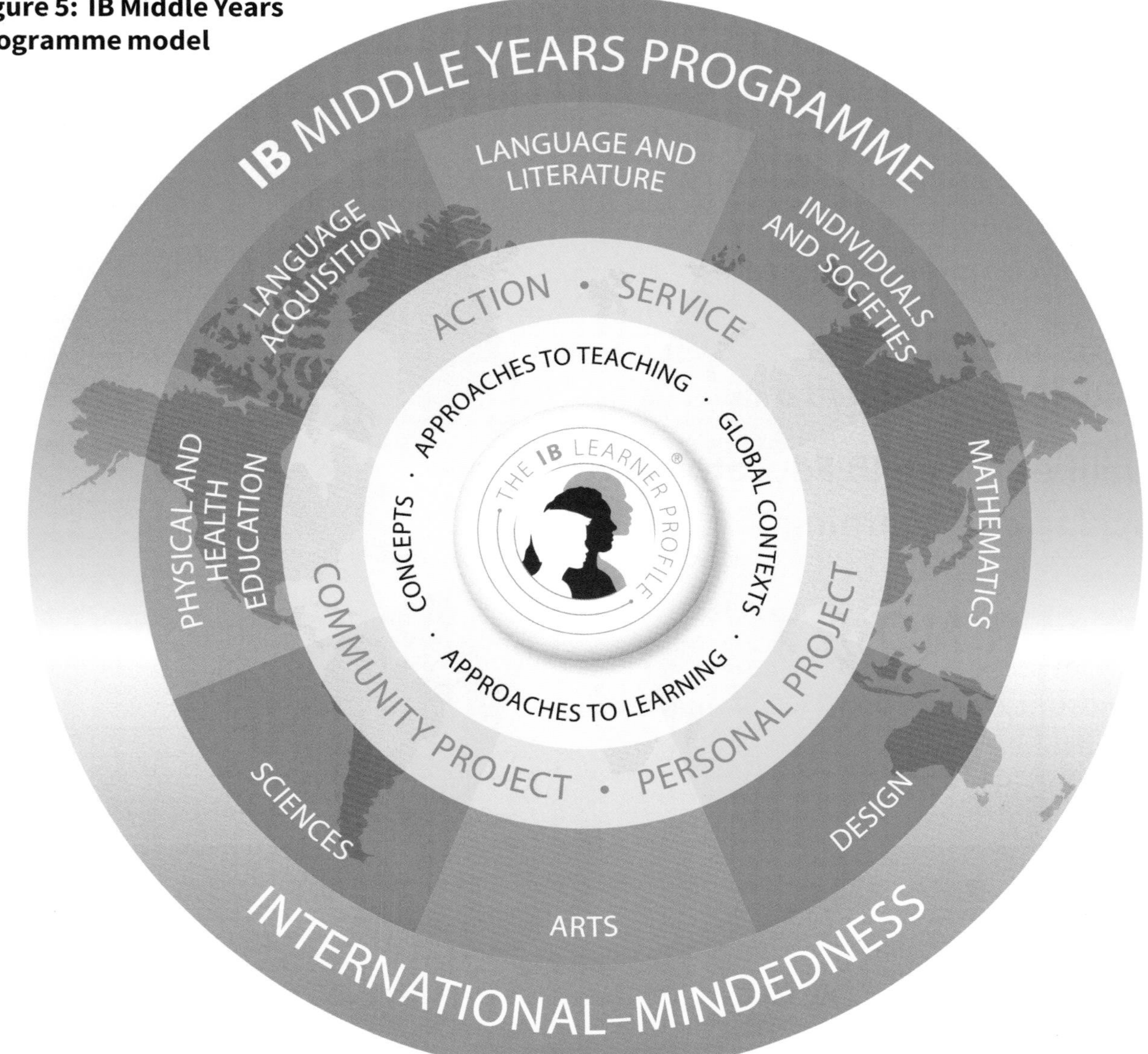

The MYP: a unique approach, relevant for a global society

The MYP aims to help students develop their personal understanding, their emerging sense of self and responsibility in their community. Using global contexts, MYP students explore human identity, global challenges and what it means to be internationally minded.

MYP teachers organize the curriculum with appropriate attention to:

- Teaching and learning in context
- Conceptual understanding
- Approaches to learning (ATL)
- Service as action
- Language and identity.

MYP projects

MYP projects provide students the opportunity to demonstrate what they have learned in the MYP. In schools that include MYP year 5, all students must complete the personal project. In programmes that include MYP years 4 or 5, schools may offer students the opportunity to do both the community project and the personal project. In schools that include MYP year 3 or 4, students must complete the community project.

- The community project encourages students to explore their right and responsibility to implement service as action in the community. Students may complete the community project individually or in small groups.
- Each student develops a personal project independently, producing a truly personal and creative piece of work that stands as a summative review of their ability to conduct independent work.

MYP assessment

The optional MYP eAssessment provides external evaluation for students in MYP year 5 (typically 15–16 years old) that leads to the internationally recognized IB MYP certificate and IB MYP course results.

MYP eAssessment represents a balanced, appropriately-challenging model that comprises examinations and coursework.

- Two-hour on-screen examinations in four subject groups (language and literature, sciences, mathematics, individuals and societies) and in interdisciplinary learning are individually marked by IB examiners.
- Portfolios of student work for four subject groups (language acquisition, physical and health education, arts, and design) are moderated by IB examiners to international standards.
- Long term personal project work is marked by school teachers and moderated by IB examiners to international standards.

These innovative assessments focus on conceptual understanding and the ability to apply knowledge in complex, unfamiliar situations. They offer robust and reliable assessment of student achievement in the MYP.

Registration for MYP eAssessment is highly flexible and can differ per candidate from a single subject to the full MYP certificate. IB World Schools can register their students for a variety of subjects, which provide the candidates with externally validated results. All candidates receive IB MYP course results; specific conditions apply for registration for the IB MYP certificate.

MYP eAssessments meet the General Conditions for Recognition established by England's Office of Qualifications and Examinations Regulation and is recognized by other national education systems as preparation for further study at the senior secondary level.

What is the IB Diploma Programme (DP)?

The IB Diploma Programme (DP) is an academically challenging and motivating curriculum designed to address the intellectual, social, emotional and physical well-being of students aged 16 to 19 and prepare them for success at university and life beyond.

To ensure both breadth and depth of knowledge and understanding, DP students must choose at least one subject from each of the six groups:

1. Studies in language and literature
2. Language acquisition
3. Individuals and societies
4. Sciences
5. Mathematics
6. The Arts

Students may choose either an arts subject from group 6 or a second subject from groups 1 to 5. In addition to disciplinary and interdisciplinary study, the DP features three core elements that broaden students' educational experience and challenge them to apply their knowledge and skills.

The DP core elements are:

- **The extended essay** is an independent, self-directed piece of research, finishing with a 4,000-word paper
- **The theory of knowledge (TOK) course** in which students reflect on the nature of knowledge and on how we know what we claim to know.
- **Creativity, activity, service (CAS)** is a project related to these three concepts.

The DP prepares students for effective participation in a rapidly evolving and increasingly global society as they:

- develop the skills and a positive attitude towards learning that will prepare them for higher education
- study at least two languages and increase understanding of cultures, including their own
- make connections across traditional academic disciplines and explore the nature of knowledge through the programme's unique theory of knowledge course
- undertake in-depth research into an area of interest through the lens of one or more academic disciplines in the extended essay
- enhance their personal and interpersonal development through creativity, activity and service

The Diploma Programme has gained recognition and respect from the world's leading universities.

Ten diploma courses can now be taken online by students in IB World Schools through Pamoja Education Ltd (www.pamojaeducation.com).

Figure 6: IB Diploma Programme model

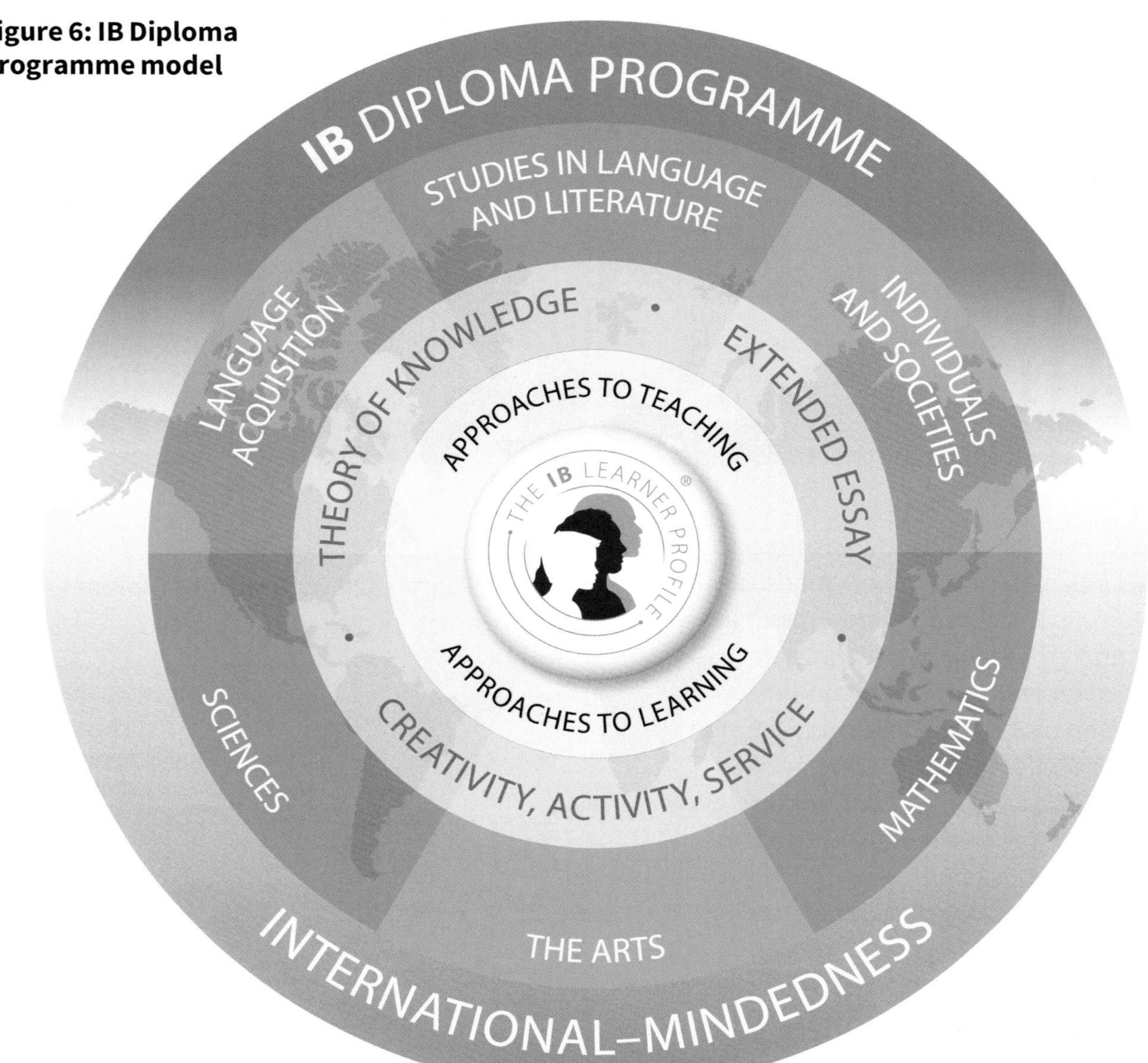

What is the IB Career-related Programme (CP)?

The IB Career-related Programme (CP) is designed for students aged 16 to 19. It incorporates the vision and educational principles of the IB into a unique programme specifically developed for students who wish to engage in career-related learning.

The CP's flexible educational framework allows schools to meet the needs, backgrounds and contexts of students. By engaging with a rigorous study programme that genuinely interests them, CP students gain transferable and lifelong skills in applied knowledge, critical thinking, communication and cross-cultural engagement.

The CP enables students to prepare for effective participation in an ever-changing world of work as they:

- consider new perspectives and other points of view
- engage in learning that makes a positive difference
- develop a combination of traditional academic skills and practical skills
- think critically and creatively in rapidly-changing and global workplaces
- communicate clearly and effectively
- work independently and in collaboration with others
- become self-confident, resilient and flexible.

The CP framework allows students to specialize in, and focus on a career-related pathway. CP students must complete at least two Diploma Programme courses alongside their selected career-related studies and the distinctive CP core, which is designed to connect academic courses and the career-related study and provide students with a combination of academic and practical skills.

The CP core

Personal and professional skills, designed for students to develop attitudes, skills and strategies to be applied to personal and professional situations and contexts now and in the future. It emphasizes skills development for the workplace, as these are transferable and can be applied in a range of situations.

Figure 7: IB Career-related Programme model

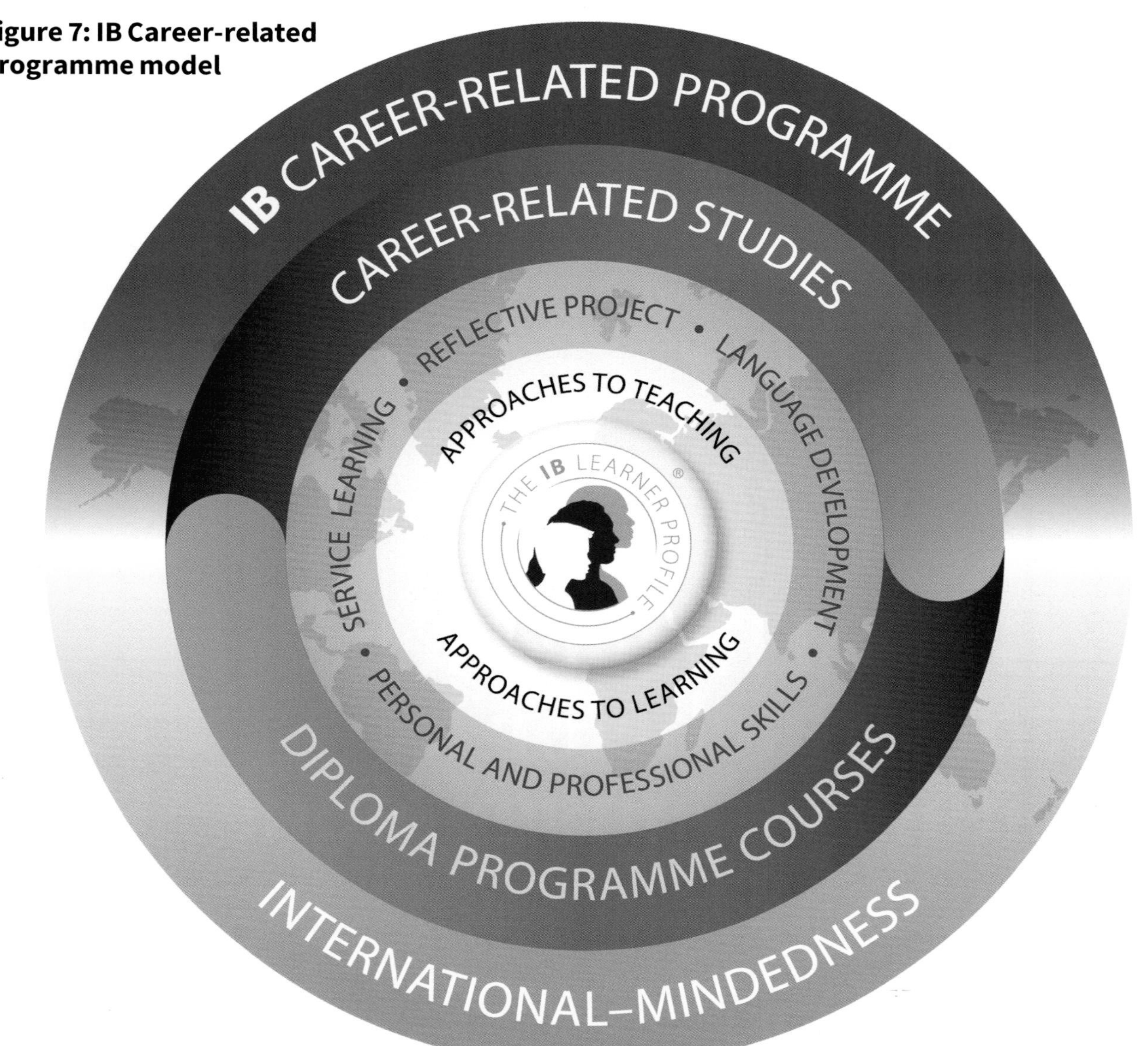

Service learning is the development and application of knowledge and skills towards meeting an identified and authentic community need. Through service learning, students develop and apply personal and social skills in real life situations.

Language development is a central tenet of an IB education that ensures students have access and are exposed to a second language in order to increase their understanding of the wider world and enhance their skillsets within a highly competitive global workforce.

The **reflective project** is an in-depth body of work submitted towards the end of the programme. Students identify, analyze, critically discuss and evaluate an ethical dilemma associated with an issue from their career-related studies. The project can be submitted in different formats including an essay, web page or short film. This work encourages students to engage in personal inquiry, action, and reflection, and to develop strong research and communications skills.

Assessment

CP students are assessed both internally by the school and externally by the IB. Diploma Programme courses within the CP framework are assessed in accordance with rigorous international standards.

Students take written examinations at the end of their courses, which are marked by external IB examiners. The marks awarded for each course range from 1 (lowest) to 7 (highest).

The reflective project is assessed by the school and moderated and graded by the IB (grades A to E with A being the highest). The school is also responsible for monitoring and confirming with the IB that students have completed requirements for service learning, personal and professional skills, and language development.

Through the CP's flexible framework schools create their own distinctive version of the programme. The IB collaborates with major providers of career-related qualifications to support schools who wish to offer the CP.

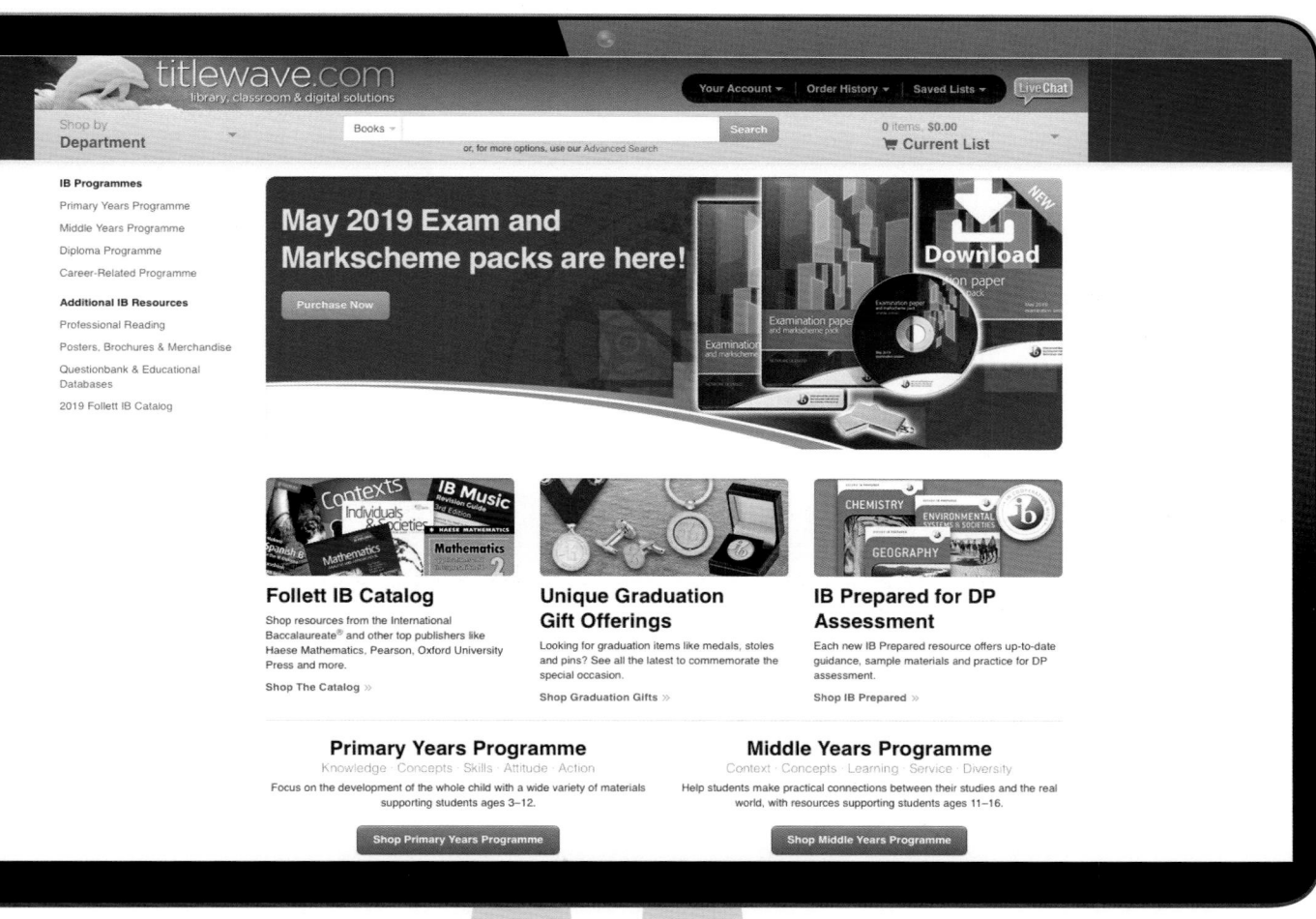

IB Recognition

The IB works with the higher education community to support IB students in getting the recognition they have earned, as well as to examine and further develop our programmes to make sure we continue to offer the best preparation for university studies and life beyond. The IB prepares students to thrive in an ever-evolving world by nurturing the skills and attitudes they need to lead happy and successful lives. The programmes are designed to be innovative from the ground up, which means they're always ready to match the educational needs of today.

Through our programmes, students develop:

- social, leadership and self-efficacy skills.
- critical thinking and problem-solving skills students need to thrive in the future.
- reasoning, communication and collaboration skills essential for teamwork.
- fluency in a second language and global cultural awareness, giving them an edge in our increasingly connected world.

A number of online resources focusing on recognition of IB programmes are available on **www.ibo.org**. These include information about IB programmes, research and evidence into the effectiveness of IB programmes, support in policy development, and information on where and how the IB is recognized around the world. The purpose is to increase understanding of the IB's aims and the unique aspects of each of its programmes, their assessment and the way they prepare students for further education.

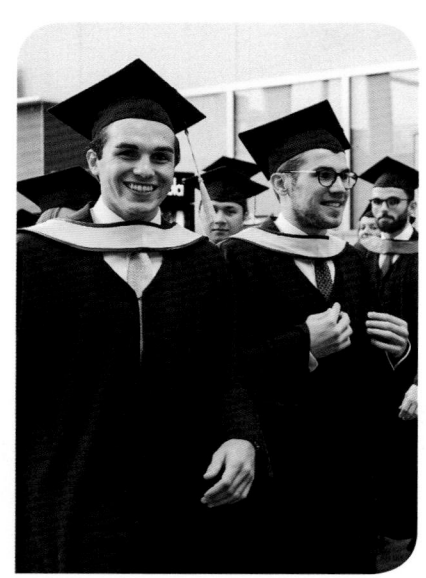

Research, Professional Development and Government

IB research

Research plays a central role in the development, quality assurance and assessment of IB programme outcomes. The IB commissions research to leading research institutions and universities around the world, and also conducts a small number of studies in-house.

The core of our work involves research on IB programmes. We conduct Outcomes research to investigate the impact of IB programmes on students, teachers and schools, and Curriculum research to support the development and review of all programme curriculum and pedagogy.

We also design, implement and maintain Quality assurance frameworks that inform the IB's service to schools and professional development. The Assessment research department (formally part of the Assessment Division) collects and analyses data to ensure assessments are well-grounded in current understanding of best practice. Lastly we coordinate research services such as the Jeff Thompson Research Award.

For more information on IB research, please visit **ibo.org/research**.

Professional development

Educators, school leaders and administrators are offered continuous support through plentiful IB professional development workshops and services. Development of a worldwide teaching and learning community committed to lifelong learning is an IB priority.

The IB offers a comprehensive calendar of workshops, webinars and conferences to help teachers and schools better understand and deliver our four IB programmes. Through this broad array of resources, IB educators are continuously challenged to reflect on and improve their teaching practices.

For more information, please consult **ibo.org/programmes/pd**

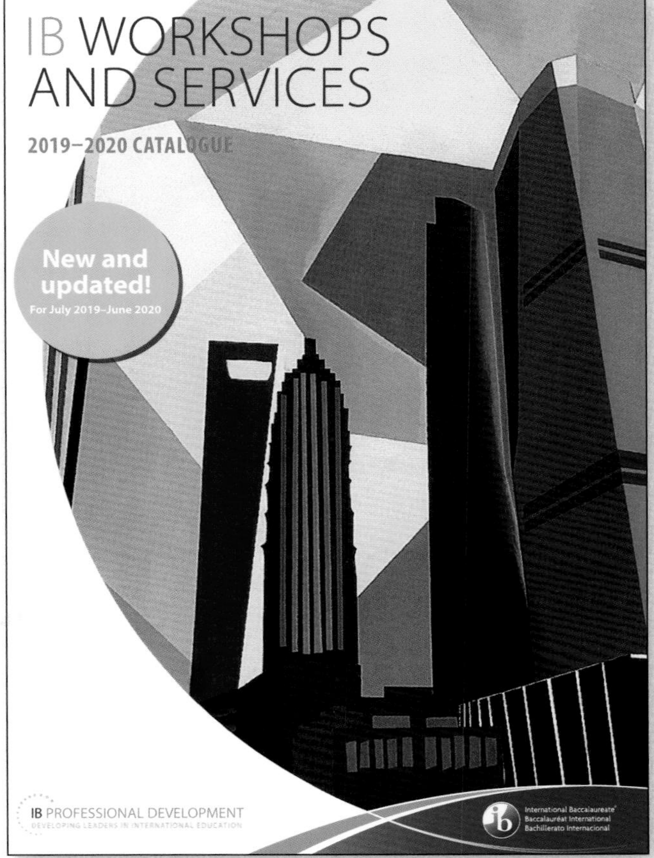

The IB and governments

Engaging regional and national governments is at the centre of the IB's commitment to diversity and inclusivity. We are defined by our values and those include pedagogical leadership and international-mindedness. There is a growing awareness among governments that education systems have to work in an international society, not just a national one. We engage with many governments, either to create more IB World Schools or to influence national education systems. Across the world, the IB is working hand-in-hand with regional and national governments to ensure state access to IB programmes.

The IB Around the World

We currently work with IB World Schools in 158 countries. All our jurisdictions have not-for-profit or charitable status with headquarters in Geneva, Switzerland. Our four global centres are in Washington, USA, The Hague, Netherlands, Cardiff, UK, and Singapore. We employ approximately 700 IB staff worldwide.

Our IB staff and educators work closely with prospective and candidate schools as well as existing IB World Schools. They are also responsible for creating and sustaining relationships with governments, international and national agencies, universities and other educational institutions, foundations and concerned individuals. Through its strategic goals, we are also promoting wider educational access.

Core services we provide include:
For prospective schools

- introductory or orientation workshops
- consultation, advice, and materials on application and authorization
- training workshops
- authorization visits.

For IB World Schools

- professional development programmes for new and experienced IB teachers
- regional conferences
- support via webinar
- online access to resources and support via My IB
- periodic evaluations of schools' IB programmes
- ongoing support throughout a school's IB journey.

For universities

- information on the philosophy, structure and requirements of the IB Diploma and Career-related Programmes
- access to the content and requirements of the IB Diploma and IB Career-related Programme curriculums and assessment
- research to demonstrate the effectiveness of IB programmes
- advice on establishing an IB recognition policy.

For governments

- advice on how to integrate IB programmes into state educational systems
- consultation regarding recognition of the IB Diploma.

Figure 8: IB Global Centres

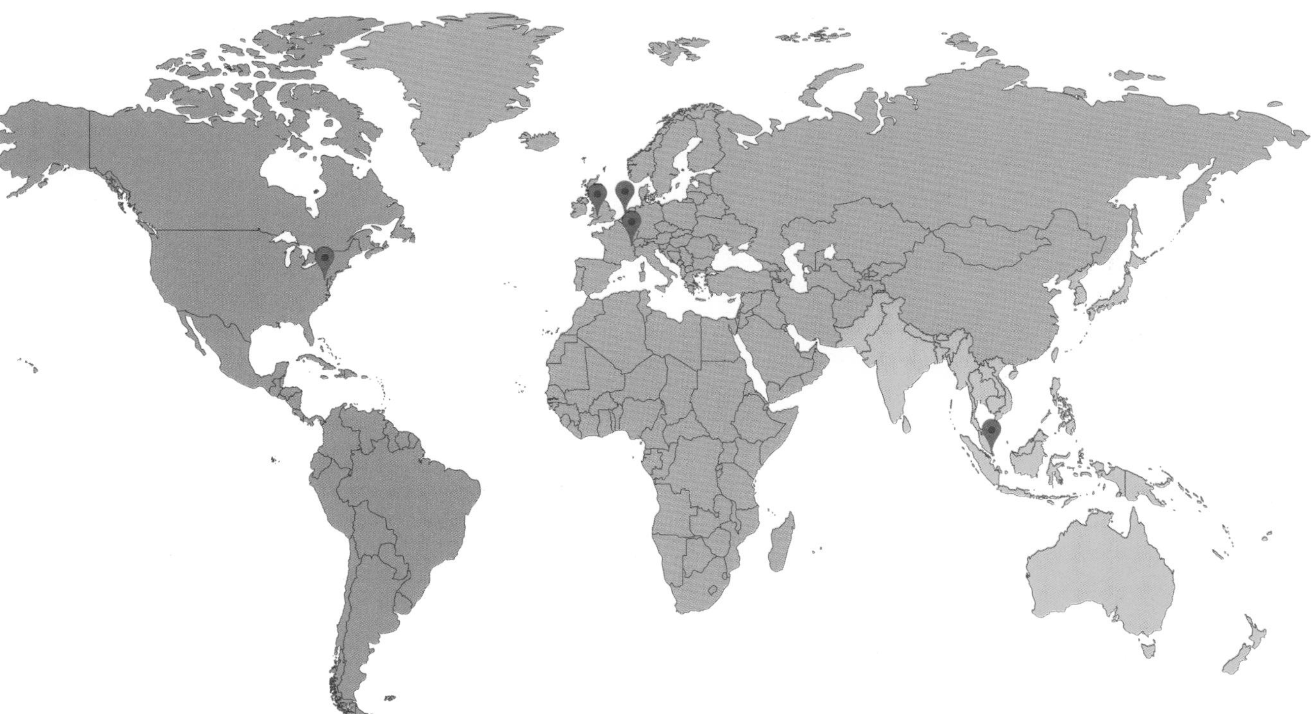

IB Global Centre, Washington DC

IB Global Centre, Cardiff
IB Global Centre, The Hague

IB Foundation Office, Geneva
IB Global Centre, Singapore

Promoting and Explaining IB Logos

The IB World School logo

IB World Schools may use the IB World School logo in connection with the programmes for which they are authorized.

The logo is a registered trademark to ensure that only schools that have achieved the high standards required by the IB are able to use it. The design uses the same core as the main IB logo. It is available for download from the digital toolkit on ibo.org in a wide variety of formats

IB programme logos

We have some unique logos representing each of the IB's four programmes. This is simply an extension of the IB brand that allows the IB and the extended community a more deliberate and distinct method of promoting each of the individual IB programmes. The programme logos draw on the core IB colours and attributes of the already recognized brand to ensure that all marques remain fully connected. Programme logos are offered in English, French and Spanish, and are available in various application styles for different backgrounds for both colour and black and white reproduction.

Using the IB World School and programme logos together

Programme logos must only be used to identify and support programme-related information and must always be accompanied by the trilingual IB World School logo. For convenience and correct application, we have created versions of the programme logos in combination with the trilingual schools logo. These combination logos are offered in English, French and Spanish and are available in various application styles for different backgrounds for both colour and black and white reproduction.

The IB Continuum logo

The IB Continuum logo is for use by IB World Schools offering three or more contiguous IB programmes.

An IB Continuum logo, with overlapping spheres connecting the Primary Years Programme (PYP), Middle Years Programme (MYP), Diploma Programme (DP) and Career-related (CP) Programme is available. This visual represents the alignment and articulation of IB programmes and the IB's philosophy of the continuum of international education

All of the materials described here are available to download at www.ibo.org/digital-toolkit.

IB Governance

IB Board of Governors

We are governed by a Board of Governors, whose members are appointed by the Board upon recommendation by the governance committee. Membership comprises a diversity of gender, culture and geography with experience from both the business and academic worlds. Board members, with the exception of the Chair, are volunteers and receive no payment for their time or work on the Board.

Members as of November 2019

Chair
Dr George Rupp, former President of the International Rescue Committee, Connecticut, USA.

Vice-chair
Dr Sijbolt Noorda, President of the Magna Charta Observatory, Bologna, Italy, and President of the Academic Cooperation Association, Brussels, Belgium

Members
Professor Amy Tsui, Professor Emerita in the Faculty of Education at The University of Hong Kong (HKU), Hong Kong.

Dr Coenraad Vrolijk, Regional CEO, Allianz, Geneva, Switzerland.

Mr David Walker, Founder, Kauri Capital, Singapore.

Ms Dianne Drew, Head of School, Dwight School, New York City, USA, Chair of the Heads Council

Mr Dominique Ledouble

Dr Jamelle Wilson, Dean of the School of Professional and Continuing Studies, University of Richmond, USA.

Mr Jon Kessler, President and CEO of HealthEquity, Utah, USA.

Dr Luis Rey Goñi, Director of Colegio de San Francisco de Paula, Seville, Spain.

Ms Maysa Jalbout, Leader in international development and philanthropy, and non-resident Fellow at the Brookings Institution in Washington DC. Resides in Dubai, United Arab Emirates.

Dr Nikki C. Woodson, Superintendent of Schools for the Metropolitan School District of Washington Township, Indiana, USA.

Dr Peter Hoeben, Chair of the Examining Board, The Hague, the Netherlands

Ms Sian Carr, Director of Education at Harrow International Schools, Shanghai, China.

Mr Steven Kim, Partner at Verdis Investment Management, Villanova, Pennsylvania, USA.

Chairs of the IB Board of Governors (formerly Council of Foundation)

1968-1981	John Goormaghtigh	Director of the European office of the Carnegie Endowment for International Peace.
1981-1984	Seydou Madani Sy	Rector of the University of Dakar, Senegal, and later minister for justice and special advisor to the president of Senegal.
1984-1990	Piet Gathier	Director General of secondary education, the Netherlands
1990-1996	Thomas Hagoort	International lawyer, USA
1996-1997	Bengt Thelin	Director General of education, Sweden
1997-2003	Greg Crafter	Former minister for education in South Australia, lawyer
2003-2009	Monique Seefried	Former Executive Director, Center for the Advancement and Study of International Education, USA
2009-2015	Carol Bellamy	Attorney, New York, USA
2015-present	George Rupp	former President of the International Rescue Committee

IB Directors General

Alec Peterson	1968-77
Gérard Renaud	1977-83
Roger Peel	1983-98
Derek Blackman	1998-1999
George Walker	1999-2006
Jeffrey Beard	2006-December 2013
Siva Kumari	January 2014-present

The IB Online

IB public website

The IB public website is often the first point of contact for many people who are new to our organization and community. Each year, over 24.5 million pages are viewed on ibo.org – it is the largest, most comprehensive and most widely used source of information about the IB.

Every IB World School is given its own page on ibo.org that is automatically created and maintained using data from our administrative website (My School – www.myschool.ibo.org). We encourage IB World Schools to link to their official page on our site to certify their relationship with the IB.

Features accessed from the website include:

- application forms to find out more and start the process of becoming an IB World School
- information, resources and links for IB coordinators, school leaders, educators, students, parents, universities, and policy-makers
- a "Find Workshops" function, supporting thousands of professional development opportunities, both around the world and online, for educators, coordinators, heads and administrators
- a "Find an IB World School" function, to enable quick and easy searching for authorized IB World Schools
- a rich variety of research on outcomes of IB programmes, curriculum research, assessment, and monitoring and evaluation
- links to all of the official IB social media accounts
- the IB blog is home to hundreds of engaging and inspiring stories from across the IB community of educators, students, alumni, and school leaders, plus opinion pieces from people in the wider field of education. Visit blogs.ibo.org
- an online store where you can purchase IB publications, resources and merchandise. Find the store at: www.follettibstore.com.

New applications available via My IB include:

- Three online communities – Heads Engage, programme communities and IBEN Engage – that replace the forums on the Online Curriculum Centre (OCC) as the place for educators to network and collaborate.
- The programme resource centre that replaces the resources on the OCC.
- A new IB Answers service that contains thousands of FAQs, multi-media content and real-time support.

Look out for more applications in the future; plus plenty of ongoing enhancements to the existing applications.

Heads of schools, IB programme coordinators, and members of the IB Educator Network (IBEN) were registered automatically with My IB and can log in using their My School and/or IBEN Central login credentials. All other IB educators can register themselves with My IB by clicking on the link **at the top left of www.ibo.org.**

IBIS

IBIS is the online administrative system used by IB coordinators in IB World Schools. IBIS allows coordinators to:

- register candidates, change registrations and produce reports about candidate registrations
- produce invoice/fees reports
- submit predicted grades and internal assessment marks
- receive examination results
- submit electronic forms
- access relevant guidance during an examination session
- upload candidate's coursework.

Explaining and Promoting IB Programmes

For schools that have achieved the high standards required for authorization, one of the many benefits is the designation as an IB World School and the use of the IB brand identity. This helps to reinforce the reputation and credibility of your school by associating with the globally recognized quality and values of the IB.

IB World Schools pages on the IB website

To increase the number of visitors to your page on ibo.org we automatically ensure that Google and other major search engines index your page regularly. We include your page in our own site search engine and the site A to Z index.

IB Digital toolkit

The IB digital toolkit is designed to provide IB World Schools with a wide range of free communications materials that can be used to present the IB and its programmes to stakeholders such as students, parents, teachers and school boards within your community as well as universities and government bodies.

- You will find:
- branding guidelines
- brochures, flyers and posters
- logos and programme models
- Powerpoint presentations to help schools explain and promote IB programmes to diverse audiences.
- videos and testimonials
- ‘alumni relations’ materials
- university recognition materials.

Visit www.ibo.org/digital-toolkit

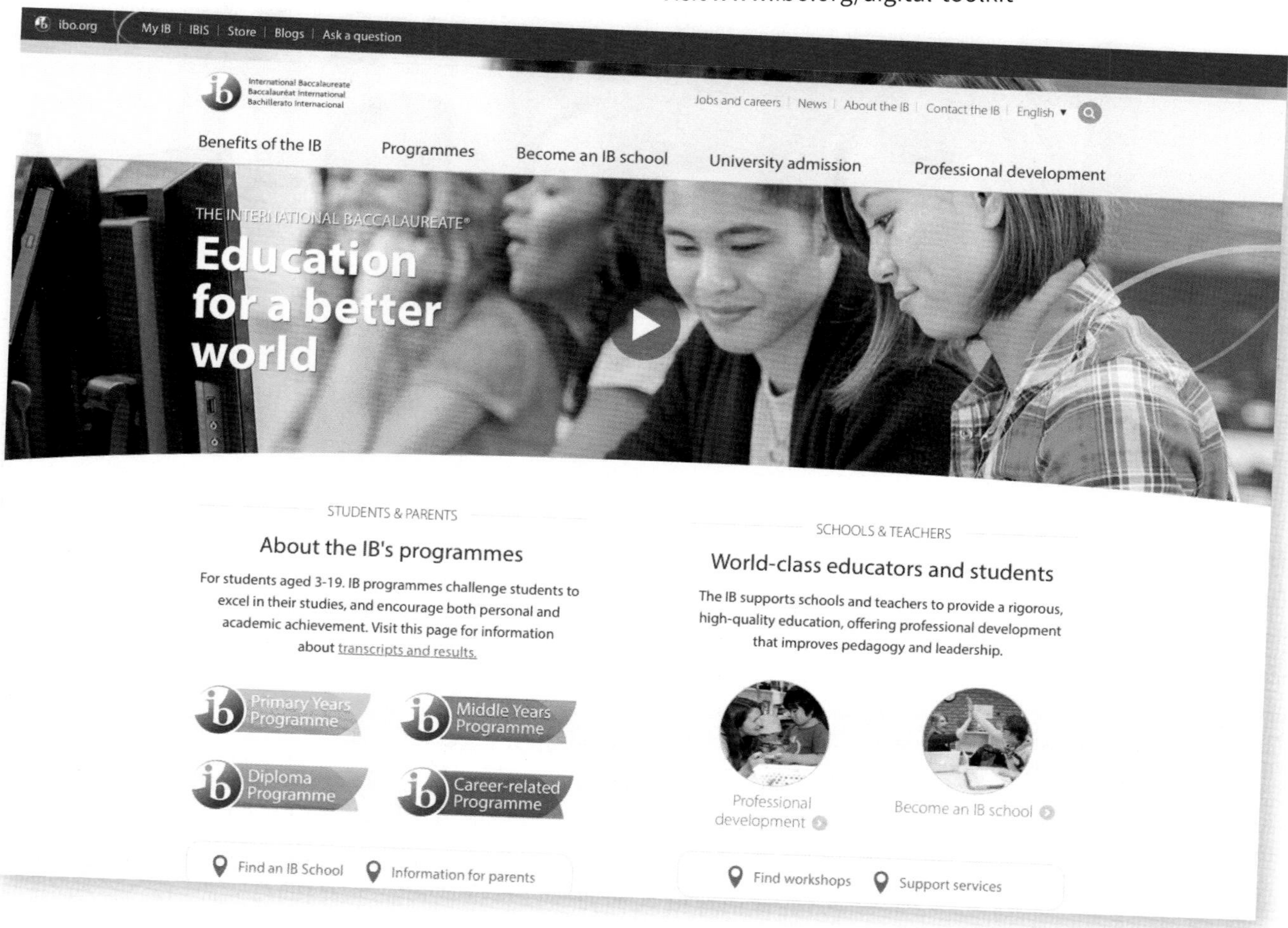

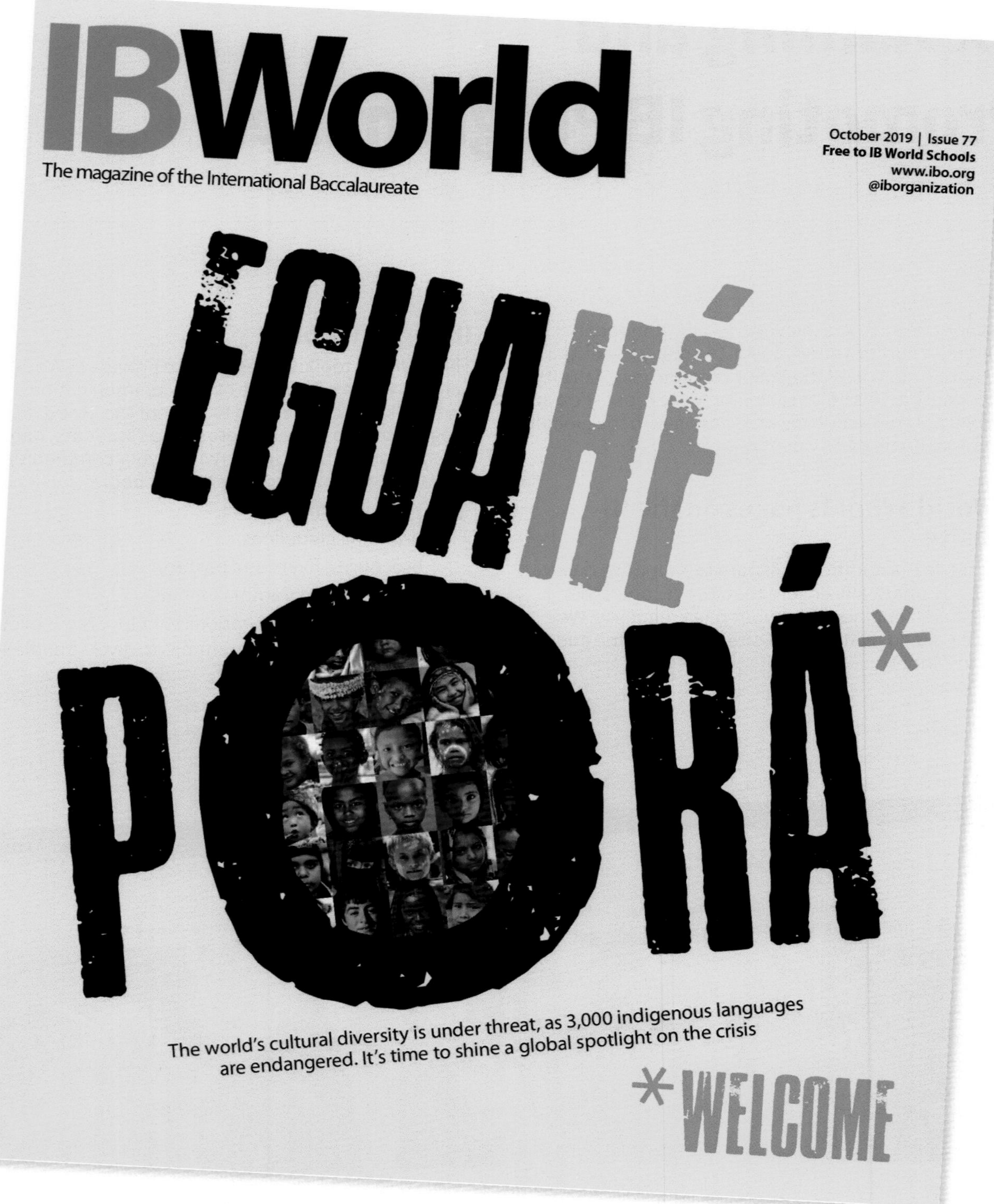

IB World magazine

Our official magazine is published once per year in October plus additional IB World digital stories published weekly on the IB blog. The magazine aims to share best practice and interesting stories from the ever widening IB community along with a variety of content from opinion makers and experts from the field of international education. The articles vary widely, from teachers writing about classroom experiences and students sharing their community, activity, service (CAS) projects to thought leadership articles about the role of international education.

All IB World Schools receive four complimentary copies of each edition. The magazine is also uploaded to ibo.org/news/ib-world/ making it possible for parents, students, teachers, board members and others who are interested in the IB to enjoy. The magazine is available in English and Spanish with key features also available online in French.

Support available

Information and supporting materials are available on the public website with the IB digital toolkit to help you promote your programmes. Alternatively, if you have any other questions, please contact the IB communications team by email at: communications@ibo.org.

IB Certificates in Teaching and Learning

Two distinct certification opportunities in teaching and learning are offered by a network of universities in coordination with the IB. Educators can choose from nearly 50 highly ranked universities in locations all around the world.

1. Choose the **IB certificate in teaching and learning** to examine principles and practices associated with the Primary Years, Middle Years and Diploma Programmes. These university courses of study help new and experienced educators develop themselves into reflective practitioners and teacher-researchers.
2. Pursue the **IB advanced certificate in teaching and learning research** to supplement IB experience with rigorous, systematic, investigative work in curriculum development, pedagogy and assessment.

The IB educator certificates can help you gain a rich learning experience, ongoing professional development and a career path leading to greater opportunities in the IB global community of schools. Your programme of study at an IB-recognized university will enable you to:

- improve the quality of your classroom teaching.
- demonstrate your deep understanding of student learning.
- enhance your competitive edge in the education job sector.
- interact with leading academics.
- demonstrate your commitment to continuous self-improvement and lifelong learning.
- establish a strong peer network for research and publishing consultation.
- gain access to IB community resources, including the IB's online Programme resource centre.

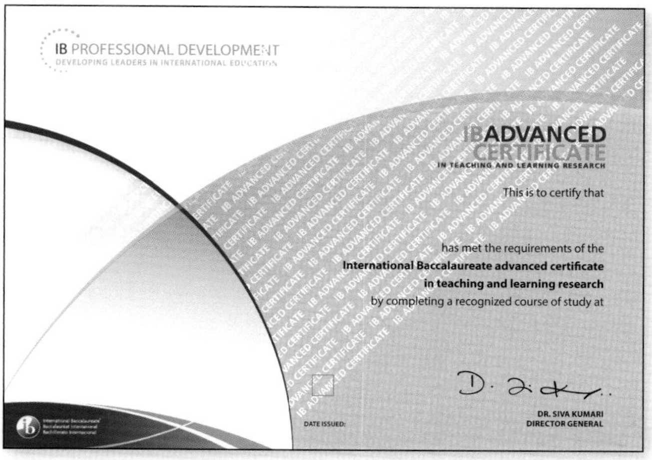

IB Certificates in Leadership

Certified IB leaders inspire and guide school communities as they implement and sustain IB programmes. IB certificates in leadership verify your understanding of principles and practices associated with leadership in an IB World School and in the IB community at large. Two distinct IB certificates in leadership development are offered by universities around the world.

1. The **IB certificate in leadership practice** is designed for aspiring educators and administrators who want to improve their leadership capabilities in an IB context. Through this programme, learn to refine your abilities to take on leadership responsibilities and to better understand your role in guiding a school through IB authorization and implementation
2. The **IB advanced certificate in leadership research** focuses on rigorous investigative work to give experienced leaders a more grounded understanding of IB leadership responsibilities and capabilities. Your training will include research within the context of IB leadership as well as deep reflection on your personal leadership practice.

Take the next step to becoming a certified IB educator or leader. Visit www.ibo.org/en/professional-development/professional-certificates for more information about the IB's partner universities, or contact pd.pathways@ibo.org.

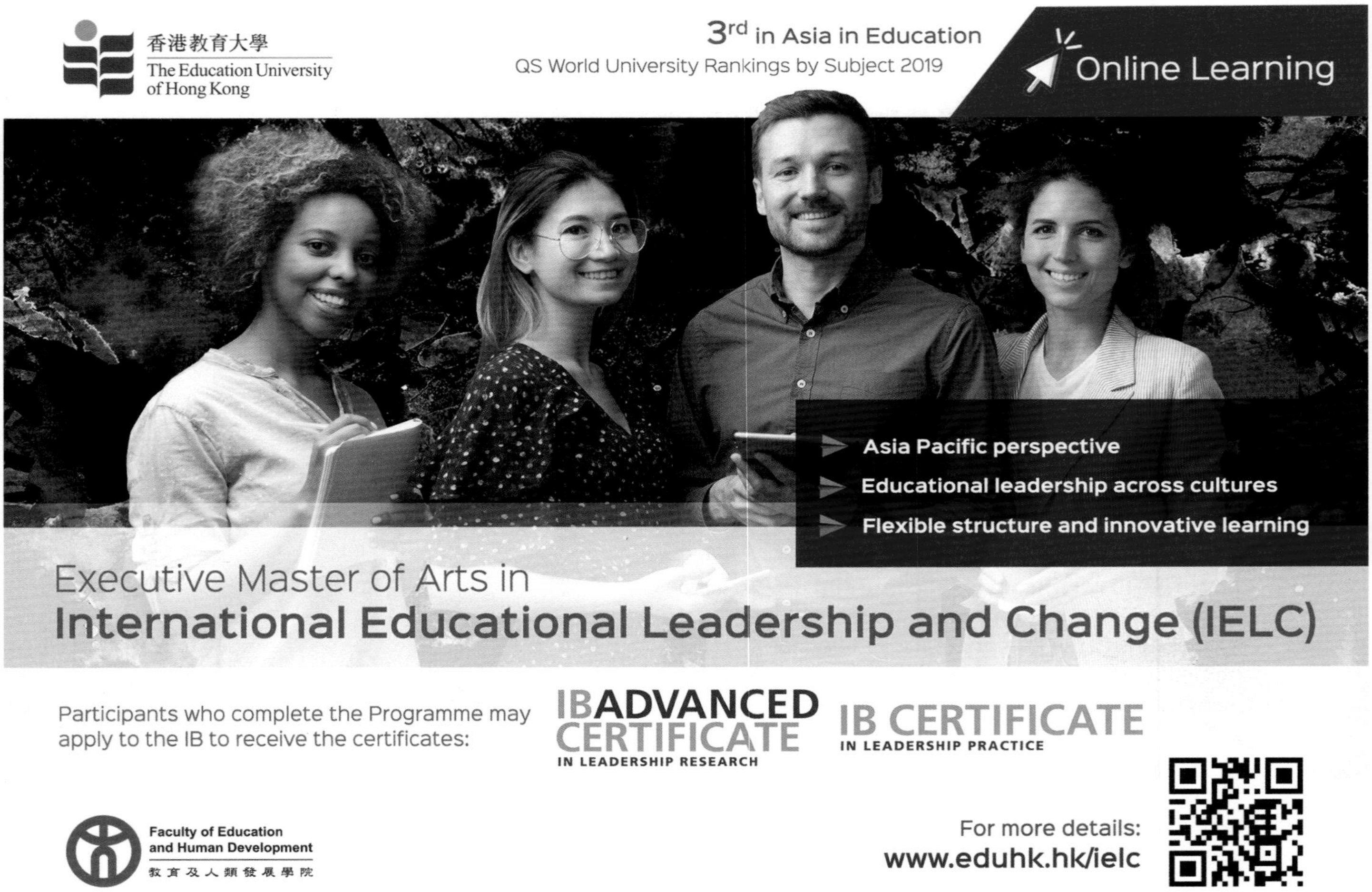
香港教育大學
The Education University of Hong Kong
3rd in Asia in Education
QS World University Rankings by Subject 2019
Online Learning
Asia Pacific perspective
Educational leadership across cultures
Flexible structure and innovative learning
Executive Master of Arts in
International Educational Leadership and Change (IELC)
Participants who complete the Programme may apply to the IB to receive the certificates:
IB ADVANCED CERTIFICATE IN LEADERSHIP RESEARCH
IB CERTIFICATE IN LEADERSHIP PRACTICE
Faculty of Education and Human Development
教育及人類發展學院
For more details:
www.eduhk.hk/ielc

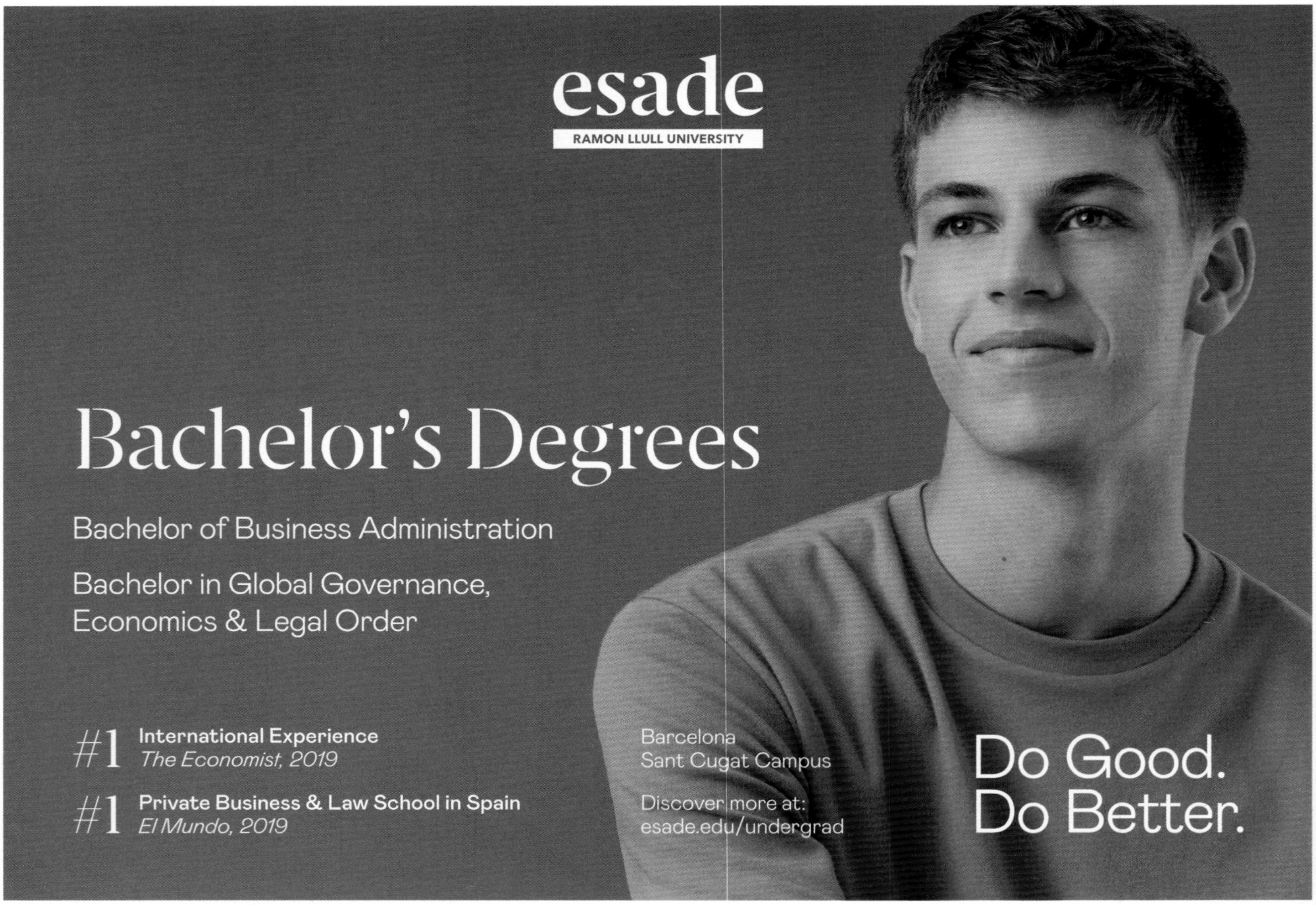
esade
RAMON LLULL UNIVERSITY
Bachelor's Degrees
Bachelor of Business Administration
Bachelor in Global Governance, Economics & Legal Order
#1 International Experience
The Economist, 2019
#1 Private Business & Law School in Spain
El Mundo, 2019
Barcelona
Sant Cugat Campus
Discover more at:
esade.edu/undergrad
Do Good.
Do Better.

IB World Schools

This section is divided into the three IB regions. Here you will find editorial from each region, including facts and figures, enhanced profiles of selected schools and a full directory of all IB World Schools in the region.

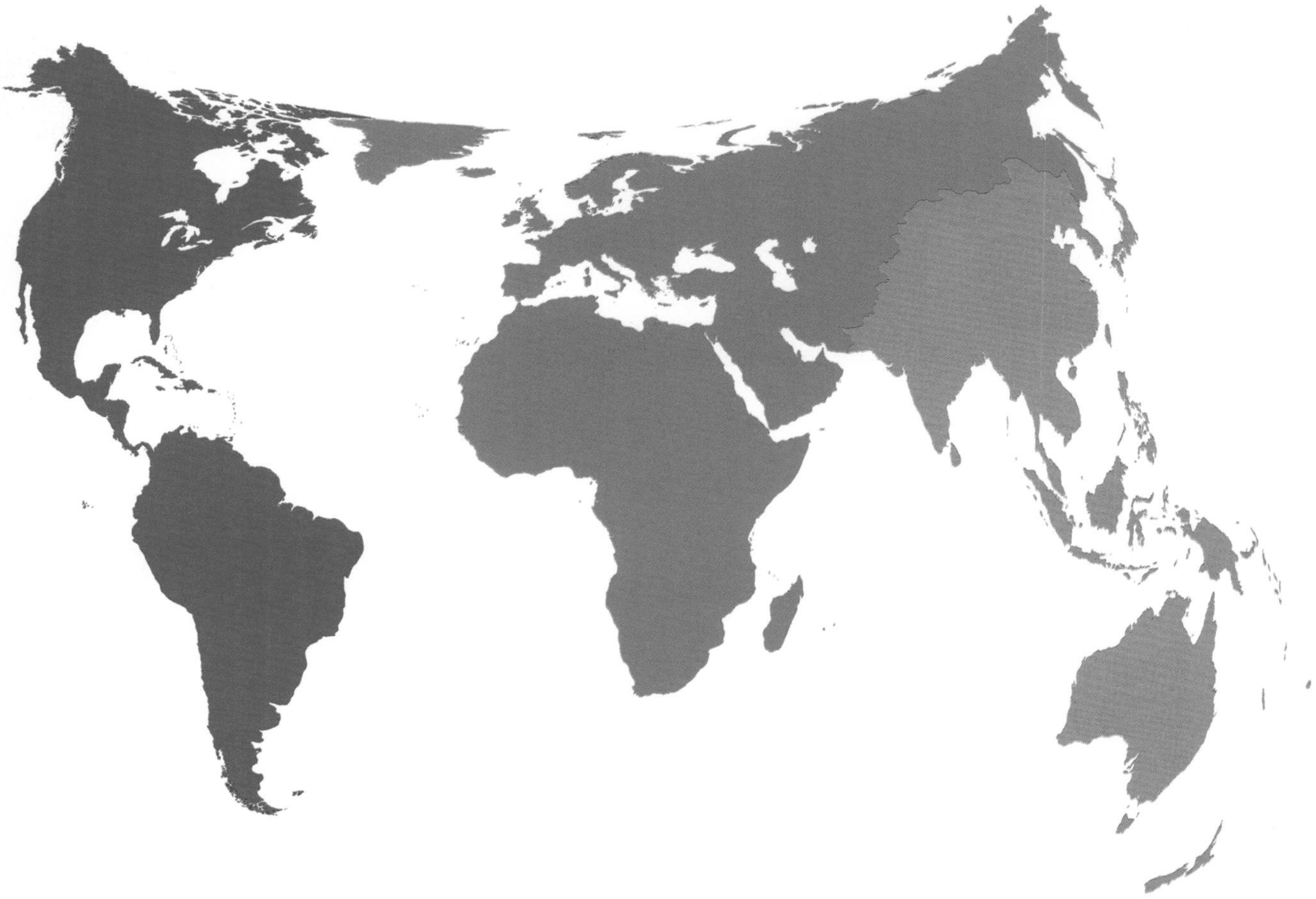

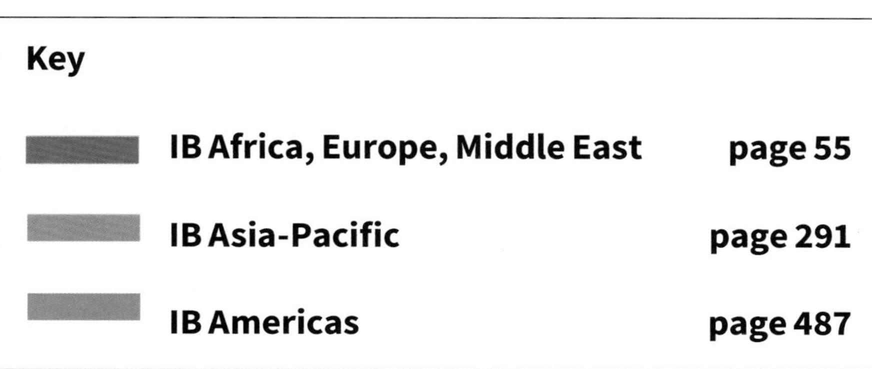

IB

AFRICA | EUROPE | MIDDLE EAST

Africa, Europe and Middle East

Some facts about this region

We serve 1,217 IB World Schools across Africa, Europe and Middle East (AEM). These schools offer 1,795 IB programmes and each school may teach more than one IB programme. Specifically, we have:

- 403 that offer the Primary Years Programme (PYP)
- 321 that offer the Middle Years Programme (MYP)
- 983 that offer the Diploma Programme (DP)
- 88 that offer the Career-related Programme (CP)

** Figures as of September 2019*

Recent developments in Africa, Europe and Middle East (AEM)

Africa

In February 2019 the IB hosted the second African Education Festival in Kenya. The event attracted IB and non IB educators from across the continent. The festival again highlighted the value of an IB education and its impact on the continent with speakers and panellists coming from varied backgrounds and included IB alumni.

With the growing awareness of the IB on the continent, ADvTECH, Africa's largest private education provider with 100 schools in South Africa, Botswana and Kenya has become the first group of schools in Southern Africa to adopt the Primary Years Programme in 7 of its flagship schools in South Africa. ENKO Education, a growing network of international schools in Africa also offers IB programmes in its schools in Cameroun, Ivory Coast, Senegal, Mozambique and set up the first IB schools in Mali and Burkina Faso.

Europe

The Career-related Programme (CP) continues its recognition advances in the region. The CP has gained recognition with hospitality providers in Switzerland, as part as an ongoing professional focus on industry pathways. This initiative allows CP students to enter major hospitality management institutions in the country.

In the UK, development of the CP continues with a further 10 schools starting to teach the programme in the 2019-2020 academic year. This has brought the total of CP schools in the UK up to almost 50. The CP meets a critical need in offering a flexible programme which bridges the academic-vocational divide and allows a student's

curriculum to be personalised. Although the CP was envisaged as a career focused programme many students have progressed to university and we are delighted that the summer of 2019 saw the first CP student gain acceptance to the University of Cambridge.

Spain continues to grow in all IB programmes. It is highlighted that Spain has reached 127 authorized schools from which 38 are either state or state-subsidized which will benefit from the new conversion scale of DP scores towards the national system for university access. Both state and private Spanish universities accept the IB diploma as an entrance qualification and welcome IB graduates from all over the world.

Following up on a successful project with the European Commission in Georgia on the Eastern Partnership Scholarship Programme, the IB Development & Recognition team is working on further recognition of IB programmes in the Eastern Partnership countries (Armenia, Azerbaijan, Belarus, Moldova and Ukraine). In the Republic of Moldova, the Ministry of Education, Culture and Research has recognized the IB Diploma as a valid entry qualification to higher education.

The IB continues taking part in various events such as the Moscow Education Fair, Didacta (Germany), BETT Show (UK), etc. In March 2020, the IB European Education Festival will be organised in Warsaw, Poland.

Portugal has welcomed the first state PYP candidate school in the country and there is an emerging interest from the Government to expand the PYP in more state primary schools.

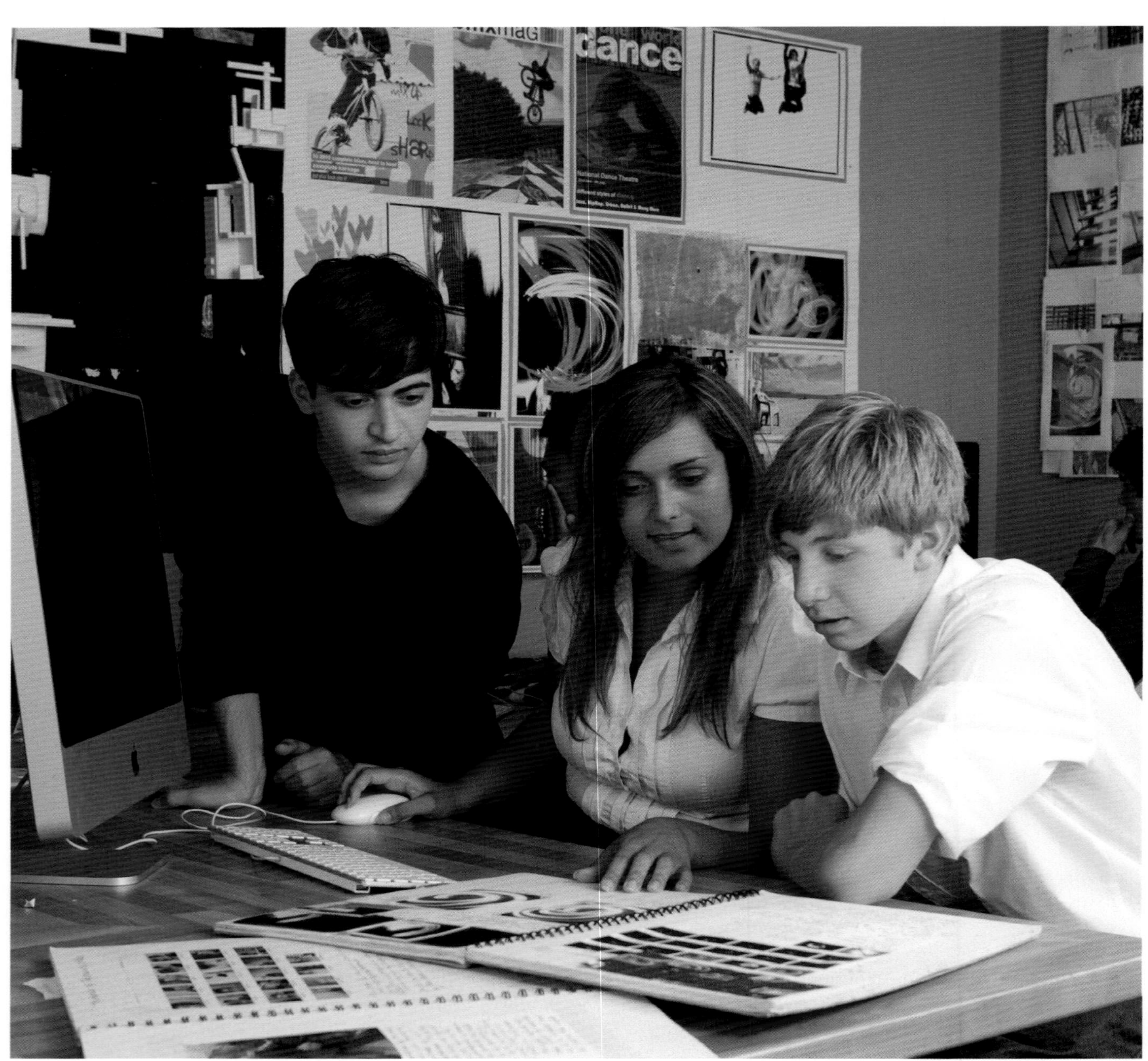

Middle East

The Ministry of education in Jordan has recognised the CP as an official qualification in Jordan and this makes the Diploma, Diploma courses and CP recognised in Jordan.

The parliament in Lebanon issued a decree of the equivalency of the IB DP and the Lebanese Baccalaureate allowing Lebanese students to pursue an IB education.

The Middle East Development & Recognition team continues working closely with the Ministry of Education in Qatar, Oman, and Egypt as well Kuwait and Saudi Arabia for the recognition of IB qualifications. These relationships have led to growth in these countries.

Pakistan

Recognition of IB programmes in Pakistan continues to develop at a steady pace, with ongoing discussions with the Inter Board Committee of Chairmen (IBCC).

The IB Educator Network (IBEN)

The IB Educator Network (IBEN) holds a critical position within the IB, by collaborating with IB educators from 164 countries who perform a variety of roles (e.g. workshop leader, consultant, school visit team leader, field representative, etc.) on behalf of the IB. With a peer-to-peer methodology, the IB Educator network allows the IB to make key achievements globally.

The IBEN department within the IB manages the network of educators, professionals who are highly experienced in IB pedagogy and leadership, by recruiting, training, and assigning them to events requested by other IB departments in support of school development (leading workshops, visiting and consulting schools, etc.). Research has shown that educators who belong to the IBEN have access to up-to-date resources prior to general launch of the documents, show greater commitment and engagement with the IB and their school, have greater opportunities to master core IB concepts, improve and practice andragogy and pedagogy, understand assessment strategies in depth and develop professional status.

The IB Educator Network is key in the development and growth of international mindedness and the IB mission.

Professional development

The IB offers diverse and engaging training events which allow educators to share best practice and network with colleagues across the region. Our goal is for PD to be available, affordable and of exceptional quality. Our face-to-face workshops are expanding to new locations each year and the range of online PD offerings continue to grow. All of our workshops are delivered by highly-qualified IB Educators that work in IB Schools throughout the world. Find which model of PD matches your schools needs and register via the ibo.org website.

- **Regional events** are held in a variety of venues in major cities throughout the region. They provide collaborative learning experiences, opportunities to network and share best practice with peers, bringing regional and global perspectives to a face-to-face learning environment. A wide variety of workshop titles are offered with new ones added each year. Subject-specific seminars, designed to help educators understand and implement the changes made to IB subject guides, are only available at these events. To broaden our reach, we work in cooperation with a network of authorized external PD providers. These can be identified by the "in cooperation with" logo.
- **In-school workshops** are on-demand IB training events that provide schools with the opportunity to meet professional development needs in their own school. They create a collaborative environment for teachers and staff, while eliminating or greatly reducing travel costs. In-school workshops are available to all IB schools, from those just starting candidacy or preparing for an evaluation.
- **Cluster events** are designed to take place at a host school with a minimum of two participating IB World Schools. They are a flexible solution to meet localized PD needs in the region.
- **Online workshops** offer the same content as face-to-face, serving as a cost-effective option for participants that don't require travel or time out of the classroom. The online environment promotes exchange between IB teachers living and working around the world. The learning platform promotes invaluable social and professional interaction.

Online professional development (PD) continues to offer engaging and high quality formal and informal online professional development products to IB teachers and leaders globally. The IB Workshop and resource guide includes almost 350 online workshop titles covering all IB programmes, enabling educators globally to engage in professional learning. Furthermore, an increasing number of these online workshops are now being offered in French and Spanish. Online workshops are scheduled throughout the year and can also be requested on demand through the IB website. Online PD has also launched free PD in the form of e learning resources and bite-sized nanoPD for teachers and the IB community worldwide, including the nanoPD series on "What is an IB education", the PYP Playlist and DP Maths elearning resource. Webinars address topics of interest for teachers and leaders of all programmes which can be accessed on the IB website under "Free Learning".

Online PD products continue to offer great opportunities for schools that are looking for a flexible and cost-effective way to offer their teachers relevant and innovative PD.

For more information on Professional Development, please visit www.ibo.org/pd

University recognition

The AEM Development & Recognition team continues their important mission to achieve recognition or clarify the status of IB programmes in each country where there is an IB World School and remains in contact with ministries and a large number of universities throughout the AEM region. A growing number of ministries have shown an interest in closer cooperation with the IB by signing a Memorandum of Understanding or similar agreements.

Associations of IB World Schools in Africa, Europe and Middle East

Many IB World Schools have chosen to form local associations with other IB World Schools at a national or sub-regional level. These non-profit associations provide a forum for school collaboration, informal gatherings and the exchange of good practice. Associations are often active in negotiating university and government recognition for IB programmes and can be an indispensable resource for schools discovering the IB for the first time. There are formal and/or informal associations for IB World Schools in the following countries:

Associations of IB World Schools with a cooperation and licence agreement

- Commonwealth of Independent States – The IB Schools Association of Commonwealth of Independent States (IBSA)
- Germany – Association of German International Schools (AGIS)
- Middle East – Middle East IB Schools Association (MEIBA)
- Morocco - Association des Ecoles du BI du Maroc (AEBIM)
- Netherlands – The Association of Dutch IB World Schools
- Spain – Asociacion de Colegios BI en Espana (ACBIE)
- Spain – Asociacion Ibérica de BI (ASIBI)
- Sweden – The Association of Swedish IB Schools (ASIB)
- United Kingdom – The IB Schools and Colleges Association (IBSCA)
- Italy – Association of IB World Schools in Italy
- Switzerland – Swiss Group of International Schools (SGIS)
- Greece – IB Schools in Greece Association
- Lebanon – Association of IB World Schools in Lebanon (chapter of MEIBA)
- Association of Eastern European Schools (ACES) – Eastern Europe

Other Associations of IB World Schools

- Denmark – The Danish Association of IB Schools
- Finland – Association of Finnish IB Schools (AFIB)
- Norway – Norwegian IB Schools (NIBS)
- Poland – IB Schools Association in Poland
- Portugal – IB Schools in Portugal Association
- Pakistan - Association of IB world schools in Pakistan (IBPAK)
- Turkey – Association of IB World Schools in Turkey
- Saudi Arabia – IB Association of Saudi Arabia
- UAE – Association of IB World Schools in the UAE (a chapter of MEIBA)

The IB Organization would like to inform all Associations of IB World Schools of the updated cooperation and licence agreement available on www.ibo.org. It is our hope that all IB candidate and authorized schools within the region will be able to be part of an association in the coming years.

IB research

1. Key findings from research in the Africa, Europe or the Middle East (AEM) region:
2. A study across five countries (**including Russia, the United Kingdom (UK) and Kenya**) explored student, teacher and parent experiences with the **PYP exhibition**—the culminating project of the PYP. Study participants found the exhibition to be a pivotal experience that helped students to develop critical thinking skills, international-mindedness and learner profile attributes. Additionally, parents valued the exhibition for fostering "real world" skills, such as independent inquiry and reflectiveness (Medwell et al 2017).
3. In **Spain**, researchers investigated the **impact and implementation of the MYP** in eight private schools, including examining the **integration** of the MYP and the local curriculum. Implementing the MYP alongside the local curriculum offered students and schools a number of benefits, particularly introducing concept-based learning, the learner profile and a more comprehensive assessment system. School heads and coordinators also believed the MYP helped to develop students' critical thinking, communication and research skills, and fostered positive shifts in teaching and learning (Valle et al 2017).
4. To explore the **alignment of the DP and Norway's upper secondary qualification (Vitnemål for Videregående Opplæring)**, researchers conducted a curriculum comparison of select subjects, and also examined the underpinning philosophies and approaches of both systems. The study found notable and substantial alignment between the DP and the Vitnemål for Videregående Opplæring. While the DP provides a wider breadth of knowledge, both educational programmes develop similar skills and content knowledge. This alignment indicates that IB World Schools in Norway are well equipped to

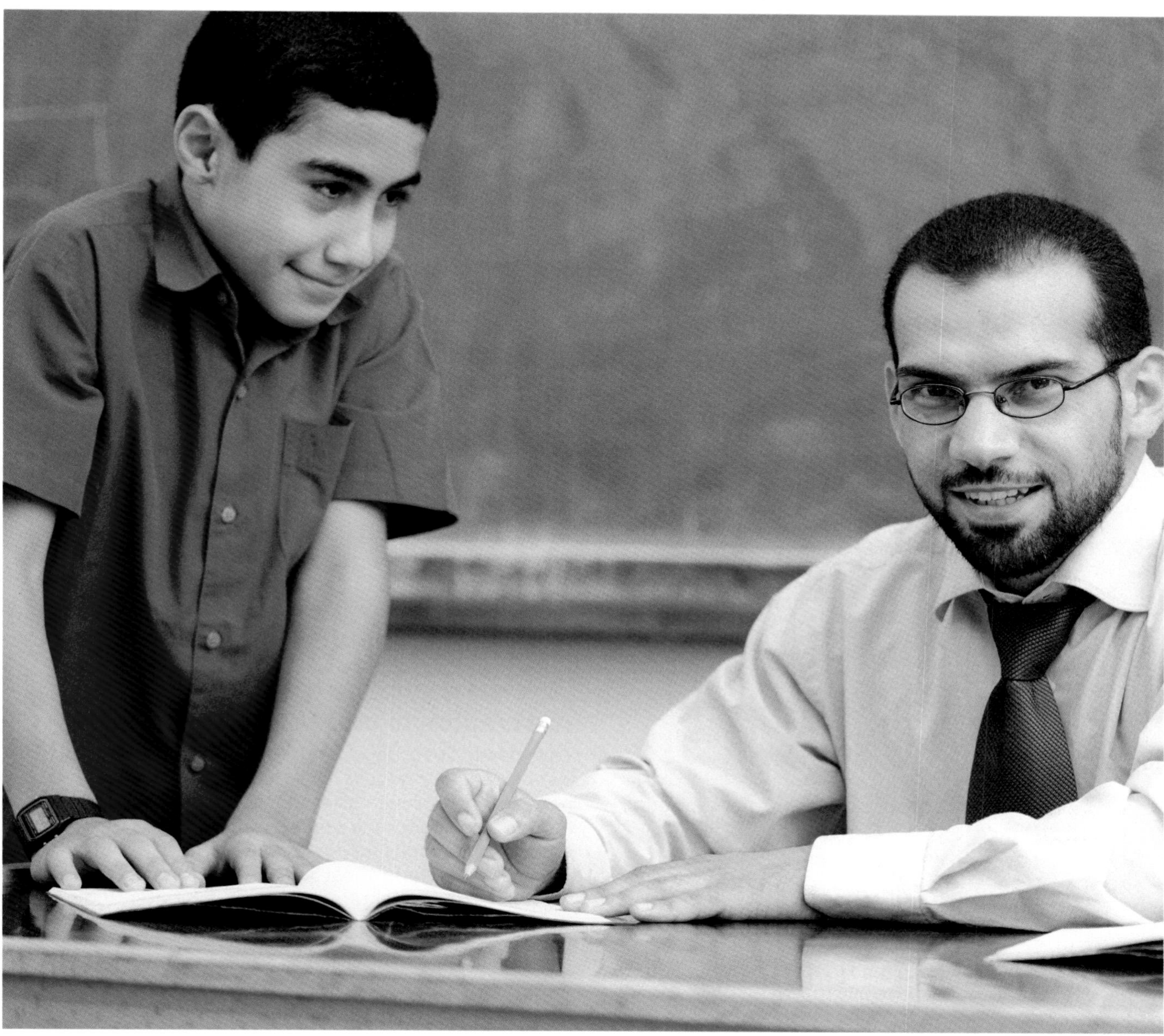

deliver the DP in a way that is compatible with the Norwegian system (UK NARIC 2019).

5. Researchers in **Turkey** investigated the **university outcomes** of DP graduates and their non-IB peers at Turkish universities. Compared to non-IB students, DP graduates generally had higher subject grades (in all subject areas examined), overall grade point averages (GPA) and graduation rates. DP alumni also reported feeling well-prepared for university studies, particularly with regard to English language skills and academic skills, such as writing and managing independent work (Ateşkan et al 2015).
6. A large-scale study that took place across two regions—Asia-Pacific and **Africa, Europe, Middle East**—explored the **impact of creativity, activity, service (CAS)** on DP students and schools. Coordinators, students, and alumni believed that CAS helps students to become better at "taking on new challenges", "learning to persevere", and "developing better interpersonal skills". Students also generally believed that CAS would have a positive impact on them post-DP in terms of preparing them for future life or studies (Hayden et al 2017).
7. A study in five **Eastern and Central European countries** explored components of the DP that support **academic persistence**. Analysis indicated that the DP fosters students' academic persistence to a higher degree than does the traditional education system. Fostering academic persistence has other benefits as well—in this study, IB students had higher academic achievement and were less likely to drop out of high school compared to similar non-IB students in Romania (Holman et al 2016).
8. To examine the higher education outcomes of students in

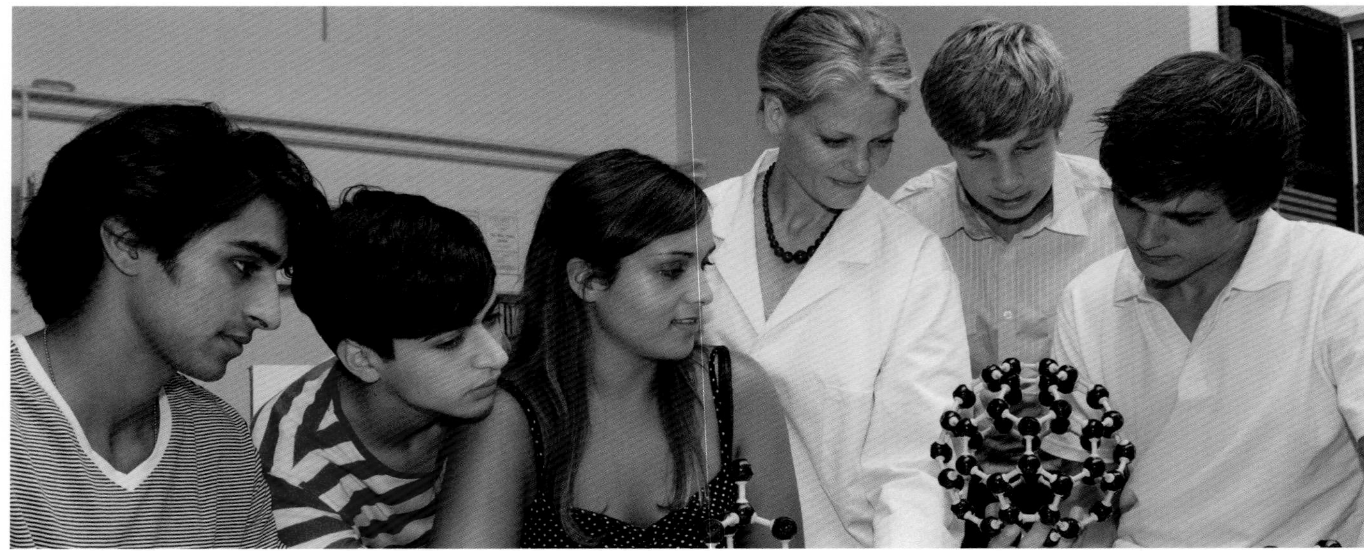

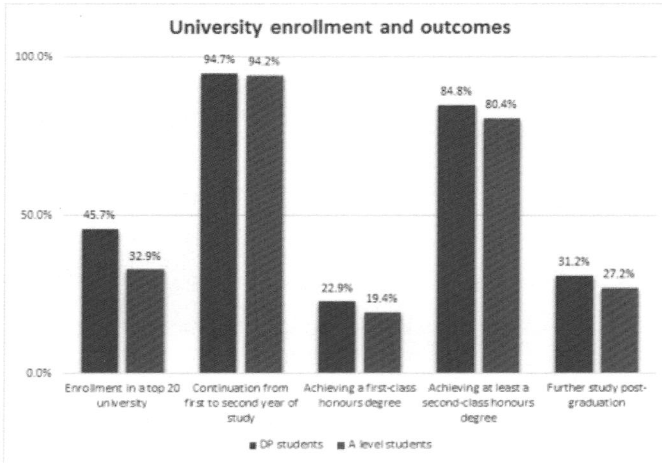

the **UK**, researchers explored the **university enrollment and achievement** of statistically matched groups of DP and A level students[1]. The study revealed that enrollment in the DP significantly increased a student's likelihood of attending a top 20 university in the UK (by 57%). Additionally, compared to their A level peers, DP students were significantly more likely to receive a first- or second-class honours degree and to enroll in further education after completing university (HESA 2016).

The IB Alumni Network

The IB Alumni Network is a resource for IB graduates around the world. The network links graduates from IB World Schools in 156 countries to support their future studies and careers. By connecting with the IB, former students have the opportunity to participate in research, support development efforts and speak at our events. These graduates are also supporting educators and parents in understanding the impact of an IB education from a student's perspective. To see how graduates are supporting IB programmes, visit ibo.org/programme-stories and connect with us at ibo.org/alumni.

AEM region in media 2019

Throughout 2019, the IB secured a steady stream of significant editorial coverage across the AEM region and was reported on in an increasing number of high quality media outlets. The quality and range of widespread coverage ensures that significant messaging and news about the IB, its programmes and, most importantly, its students are highlighted and celebrated. The total estimated audience reach of this coverage for the past calendar year (starting in January 2019) is 387,877,243. The coverage featured all four programmes; focussing on the important details of each programme as a single unit and the all-encompassing nature of an IB education. Notable media coverage across the AEM region includes: the Times Educational Supplement covering the elimination of student examination registration fees, The National's front page report on Diploma Programme results day 2019, EdArabia's exclusive interview with Joel Adams, curriculum manager at IB on the new digital society course and School Week's coverage by Headteacher Ryan Kelsall, which discusses why the UK doesn't need to reinvent the education wheel.

Contact

IB AEM Global Centre
Churchillplein 6
2517 JW, The Hague
the Netherlands

Main: +31.70.352.6000 | Fax: +31.70.352.6003
Web: http://www.ibo.org/about-the-ib/the-ib-by-region/ib-africa-europe-middle-east/

1 This study used propensity score matching to compare DP students with similar non-DP students. This statistical technique allows the researchers to better isolate and identify the impacts of the DP specifically, as the two groups are similar otherwise.

accadis International School Bad Homburg

(Founded 2004)

Head of School
Ms Janina Sparks

DP coordinator
Prof. Dr. Christoph Kexel

Status Private

Boarding/day Day

Gender Coeducational

Language of instruction
English, German

Authorised IB programmes
DP

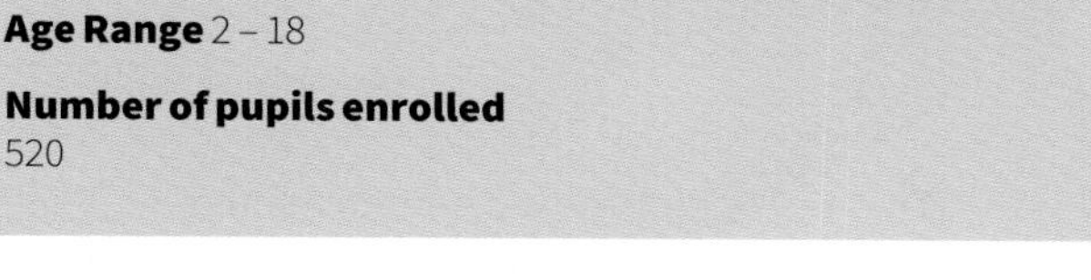

Age Range 2 – 18

Number of pupils enrolled
520

Fees
Preschool €3,360 – €4,560
Elementary School €8,040 – €9,480
Secondary School €11,100 – €16,800

Address
Norsk-Data-Strasse 5
61352 Bad Homburg | GERMANY

TEL +49 6172 9841 41

Email
info@accadis-isb.com

Website
www.accadis-isb.com

Our mission
accadis ISB aims to develop confident, knowledgeable and caring young people prepared to create a better future. We aim to build within each child a sense of responsibility, a love for learning, self-discipline, and respect for others. Challenging programs, combined with inter-cultural understanding and respect, enable our students to reach their potential and become compassionate and lifelong learners.

Who we are
accadis ISB is situated in Bad Homburg, a leafy town in the Taunus mountains, just north of Frankfurt am Main. We are a non for profit, lively, friendly and expanding bilingual co-ed school which currently has approximately 520 students from 2 – 18 years of age, representing over 53 nationalities. Privately owned, it is part of a family business with links to the nearby accadis University of Applied Sciences. The school has a bilingual concept, teaching some subjects in English and some in German. accadis ISB is an official IB World School since January 2016. accadis ISB is also accredited by Cambridge Assessment International Education to teach the two year IGCSE course in Grades 9 and 10.

Our students
The school provides a supportive and challenging environment where students are encouraged to become responsible and independent learners. accadis ISB caters for a wide range of students, and is both a “local” school for families who live nearby and also an international school for students who come to us from all over the world.

Our school
accadis ISB was founded in 2004 and is situated on a state of the art campus featuring several buildings connected with each other, its own sports hall, a well-equipped library, a Music and Drama room as well as two Science and two Art rooms. Special to our school is our designated IB Learning Suite for the IB Diploma students. Features such as modern smartboards, plenty of laptops and tablets for student use and 3D printing highlight the school’s strong focus on technology.

Acorns International School (AIS)

Head of School
Ameena Lalani

PYP coordinator
Evans Kimani

Status Private

Boarding/day Day

Gender Coeducational

Language of instruction
English

Authorised IB programmes
PYP

Age Range 18 months – 16 years

Number of pupils enrolled
500

Fees
$2,358 – $8,850

Address
Plot 328, Kisota Road
(Along) Northern Bypass, Kisaasi
Roundabout
Kampala | **UGANDA**

TEL +256 393 202 665

Email
admin@ais.ac.ug

Website
www.ais.ac.ug

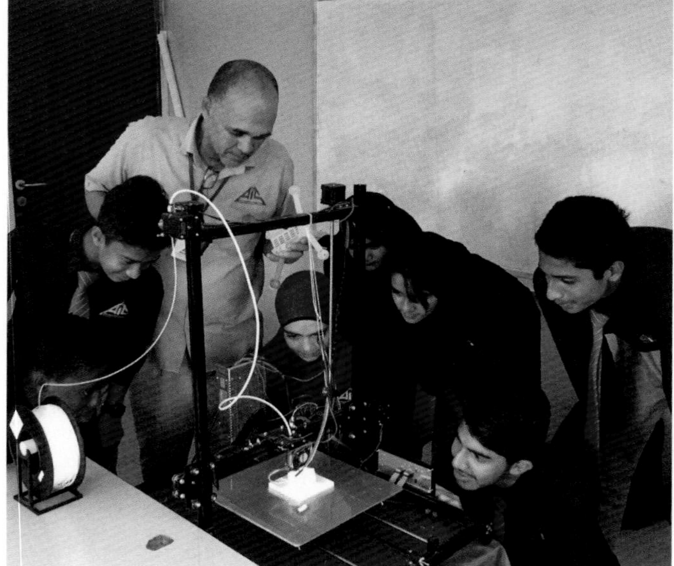

Encapsulating the adage, 'A tree with strong roots laughs at storms', Acorns International School (AIS) bears fruits that stand the test of time.

Nestled between the verdant folds of Kampala, the capital city of Uganda, AIS is sprawled over a 5-acre state-of-the-art, purpose-built campus, that nurtures the balance between academics and extracurriculars.

Over two decades in the field of education, we have grown to represent more than 50 nationalities. The AIS team strives to inspire and empower every student to achieve their personal best and become inquiring, knowledgeable, lifelong learners and pluralists who create a better and peaceful world, through intercultural understanding and respect.

Admissions are open throughout the academic year, subject to availability. We have a limit to the number of students per classroom, for uncompromised quality. This interface gives teachers an edge to assess each student's area of strength, and improvement. Teachers are supported in this process, with timely professional development sessions, to ensure growth and excellence. Through an open-door policy, we ensure that our main stakeholders, our parents, are full partners in the decision-making process and voice concerns not only of their children, but their own too.

The language of instruction is English, with French and Kiswahili as part of our dynamic curriculum. Through our engaging and rigorous, inquiry-based environment, students reach their full academic potential and become responsible, caring, multilingual, and culturally-literate global learners.

AIS is non-sectarian and co-educational institution, founded on strong partnerships between parents, teachers and learners.

A visit to AIS allows your family to experience the school in a relaxed environment, meet with the administration, as well as visit classrooms, science lab, performing arts room, library, swimming pool, auditorium, soccer fields and the basketball court.

AIS is an authorised International Baccalaureate (IB) Primary Years Programme (PYP) School and a *candidate school for the Middle Years Programme (MYP) and Diploma Programme (DP).

AIS accepts students from the age of 18 months, in the Early Childhood department (18 months – 5 years), to Primary Years Programme (Year 1 – Year 6), Middle Years Programme (Year 7 – Year 11), and Diploma Programme (Year 12 – 13) to be offered in academic year 2020-21.

It is always onwards and upwards for us, at AIS, and we would love for you to join us!

*Only schools authorized by the IB Organization can offer any of its four academic programmes: the Primary Years Programme (PYP), the Middle Years Programme (MYP), the Diploma Programme (DP), or the Career-related Programme (CP). Candidate status gives no guarantee that authorization will be granted.

Head of School
Mrs. Nicola Sparrow

Deputy Head of Curriculum
Mr. Tomas Duckling

DP coordinator
Mr. Esmond Tweedie

Status Private

Boarding/day Mixed

Gender Coeducational

Language of instruction
English

Authorised IB programmes
DP

Age Range 9 – 18

Number of pupils enrolled
375

Fees
Day: CHF35,100 – CHF78,700
Boarding: CHF70,500 – CHF115,500

Address
Avenue Centrale 61
1885 Chesières-Villars |
SWITZERLAND

TEL +41 (0)24 496 6177

Email
admissions@aiglon.ch

Website
www.aiglon.ch

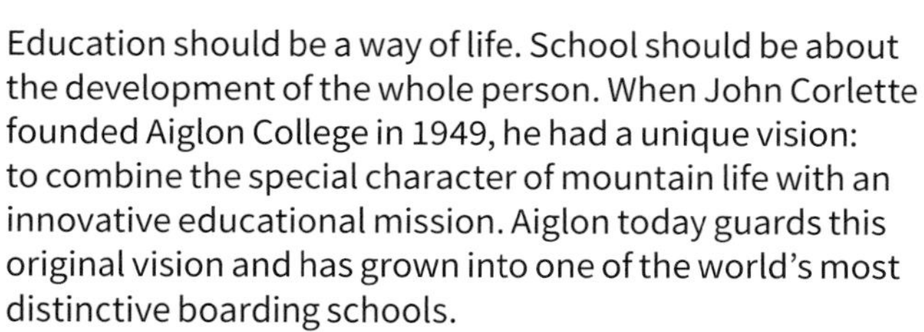

Education should be a way of life. School should be about the development of the whole person. When John Corlette founded Aiglon College in 1949, he had a unique vision: to combine the special character of mountain life with an innovative educational mission. Aiglon today guards this original vision and has grown into one of the world's most distinctive boarding schools.

Spirited, independent and a not-for-profit organisation, Aiglon's aim toward the balanced development of mind, body and spirit works to create a principle-driven environment where students and teachers alike are encouraged toward academic excellence, pursuit of physical challenge and the learning born through a deeply international culture.

Aiglon is an English-speaking school styled in the tradition of British education. Students follow the globally recognised IGCSE and International Baccalaureate (IB) programmes while simultaneously developing practical skills that integrate curriculum into all areas of life. The focused, individually tailored programme allows each student to access a unique course of study.

The school's professional College & Careers Counselling team works closely with each student to help them understand and succeed in the university application process. Through these efforts, our students have access to the world's top universities. This tailored programme encourages, develops and ultimately matches every student with a university that can continue developing their education.

The character of Aiglon students is forged on the mountain. Aiglon is located just beyond the ski resort village of Villars-sur-Ollon in French-speaking Switzerland, at 1,258m. Making use of our safe, alpine environment we enjoy an open-style campus and are just 250m from the ski resort's main lift. Central to its educational philosophy, the uniquely crafted expedition programme utilises Aiglon's location in the Swiss Alps to engage students in activities designed to develop their sense of challenge and responsibility in a highly practical environment.

In winter, students ski twice per week as part of the physical education programme. Beyond winter, students participate in a wide range of competitive and noncompetitive activities from football and swimming to yoga.

All the teaching staff play a key role in pastoral care and learning support at Aiglon. From their roles as Houseparents, Assistant Houseparents or as tutors, teachers are available to students 24/7. In this community relationship, students and teachers are able to connect in unique ways that enable young people to grow and better understand their purpose and role at Aiglon.

Our unique combination of academic excellence and the spirit of living life on the mountain ensure that an Aiglon education provides your child with everything needed to succeed.

(Founded 2012)

Director Fiyaz Ahmed

Primary School Principal
Sandra Kellec

Secondary School Principal
Colin Bibby

Secondary School Deputy Principal
Robert Henry

PYP coordinator
Rachel Poulton

Status Private

Boarding/day Day

Gender Coeducational

Language of instruction
English

Authorised IB programmes
PYP

Number of pupils enrolled
990

Fees
Day: AED24,000 – AED64,350

Address
Sheikh Ammar Road
Mowaihat 2
Ajman | **UNITED ARAB EMIRATES**

TEL +971 6 731 4444
FAX +971 6 731 4443

Email
school@ajmanacademy.com

Website
www.ajmanacademy.com

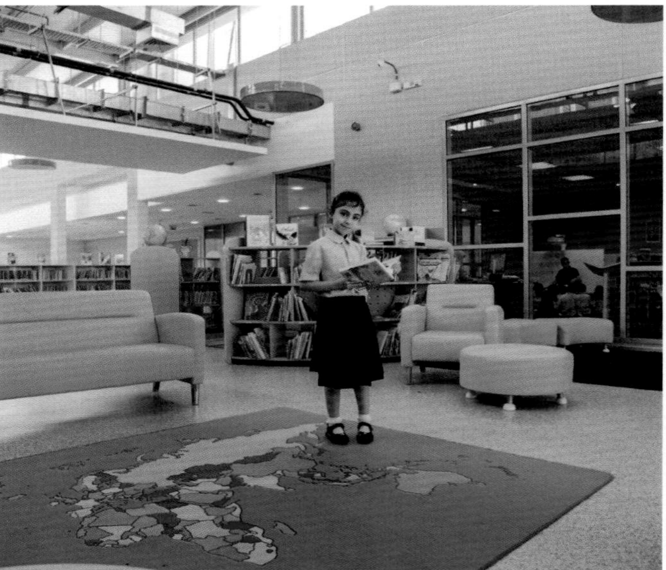

In this fast-moving world, it is the ability to become lifelong learners that help us be on top of every challenge and change. We eagerly learn, improve, and at the end of every day, we all succeed.

Welcome to Ajman Academy, a truly unique international school – where we embrace the values of respect, happiness, cooperation and positivity to lead your child on an incredible learning journey.

Ajman Academy is a dynamic IB World School community accredited to offer the IB Primary Years Programme to primary students and is a candidate school for Middle Years Programme in grades 6 to 8. We then offer IGCSE and AS/A levels for students from grade 9 to grade 12. Our focus is to create an inspirational, safe and supportive environment for your child to learn and develop.

We pride ourselves on our integration of technology into our learning environments, where our curriculum allows technology to support and enhance student learning.

Wireless network connectivity is available throughout our school, and all classrooms are resourced with interactive whiteboards or data projectors. We have a 1:1 iPad programme so that all our learners are equipped to actively engage in their own learning journey. We also ensure that our students develop a variety of transferable technological skills that can be utilised in an ever-changing workplace. A particular specialism of the school is its Artificial Intelligence programme that prepares students for the future by applying technology in an authentic manner.

As an IB World School, we provide language programmes in English and Arabic, celebrating and improving mother tongue in addition to developing English skills. All our teachers are committed to supporting the emotional and social well-being of students in their care. Our flexible learning spaces include well-resourced Libraries, Music, Art and Design Tech rooms, Science, Food and IT laboratory, as well as a 25m indoor swimming pool. As we encourage the importance of a healthy lifestyle, all our students participate in our Physical Education programme, and our school cafeterias have an emphasis on healthy choices.

Al Faris International School

مدارس الفارس العالمية
Al FARIS International School

Head of School/School Director
Mrs. Sahar Al Marzouki

PYP coordinator
Mrs. Rasha Ghraizi

MYP coordinator
Mrs. Salwa Ghandour

DP coordinator
Mrs. Farah Kiblawi

Status Private

Boarding/day Day

Gender Coeducational

Language of instruction
English

Authorised IB programmes
PYP, MYP, DP

Age Range 3 – 18

Number of pupils enrolled
2439

Address
Tawaan Area, Imam Saud Road
Khan Younes Street
Riyadh
9483 | SAUDI ARABIA

TEL +966 011 454 9358

Email
info@alfarisschools.com

Website
www.alfarisschool.com

Al Faris International School is a fully authorized IB World School in the PYP, MYP and DP Programmes. The school was established in 2004, is licensed by the Saudi Ministry of Education and certified by Cognia (formerly AdvancED). Diversity is reflected in the student and teacher profiles as well as the teaching methodology and resources.

Academics

Al Faris provides an enriching, challenging and supportive learning environment that allows each student to fulfill his/ her own individual potential. We have an experienced international staff including teachers from Saudi Arabia, the Middle East Region, South Africa, Asia, Europe and the USA.

Our curriculum meets international standards and includes the core subjects of English, math, sciences, social studies/ history as well as Arabic, French, computer studies, robotics, art, and physical education in a transdisciplinary learning framework for the PYP and disciplinary and interdisciplinary learning in the MYP and DP. Year 5 MYP students have the option to complete the MYP eAssessments.

We strive to give our students a comprehensive educational experience which will prepare them to be effective contributors in today's global arena as well as life-long learners. To this aim, we continuously keep informed of the latest educational programs and trends worldwide and implement those which we feel effective in order to give students the best in global education. Examples include the Lucy Calkins Writing Workshop and the Daily 5 Literacy Program. At the same time, we offer a strong Arabic language program as well as Islamic studies, thus maintaining the balance between our world outreach and our cultural heritage.

School Facilities

Facilities include interactive classrooms; state-of-the art computer and science labs; four libraries serving diverse grade levels; art rooms; an auditorium; drama rooms; sports facilities including a gymnasium; indoor and outdoor soccer courts; two indoor swimming pools; ballet and gymnastics rooms; spacious, shaded playgrounds; a school clinic and cafeterias.

Extracurricular Activities

Activities include sports, ballet and art. Students also participate in field trips and school trips abroad. Model United Nations (MUN) is offered for middle and high school students.

Our DP students are involved in many local community service activities as well as an ongoing support of the Azraq School through Helping Refugees in Jordan which includes regular student visits to take supplies and provide assistance.

Al Hussan International School Khobar

(Founded 1998)

School Head
Mr. Burhan Mazahreh

DP coordinator
Maria Faisal

Status Private

Boarding/day Day

Gender Coeducational

Language of instruction
English

Authorised IB programmes
DP

Age Range 3 – 18

Address
PO Box 297
Dammam
31411 | SAUDI ARABIA

TEL +966 13 858 7566
FAX +966 13 857 3874

Email
ahisk@alhussan.edu.sa

Website
international.alhussan.edu.sa

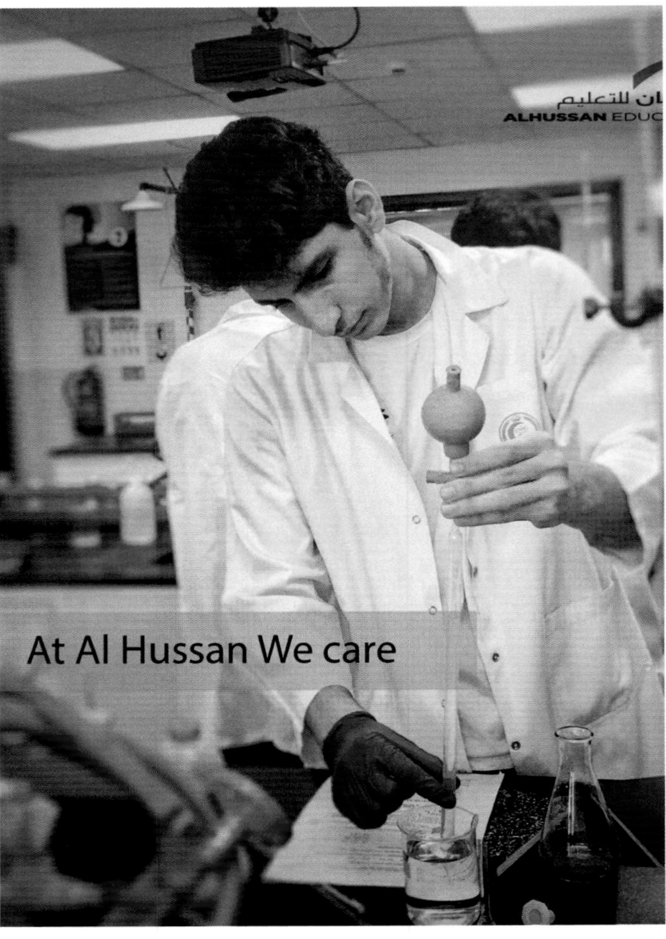

Al-Hussan International School (AHISK) is a private English language day school with 1,285 students, situated in three buildings in the city of Al-Khobar. The Pre-School-G2 Campus currently houses students in Pre-K to Grade 2. The Girls' and Boys' Section Campuses house Grades 3 to 12 respectively. The school provides the environment and the experiences which promote the moral, social and intellectual development of all its pupils. Every child is cherished and receives support and encouragement within a strong, caring community.

The school offers a well-rounded education through its provision of different programmes of instruction for students from Pre-K to Grade 12. We acknowledge that every child is born with unique potential, and we seek to develop each child's creativity, expand their horizons and prepare them to be responsible citizens and leaders. English is the language of instruction, with Arabic, French or Urdu offered as a second language and as a foreign language for non-native speakers. Islamic classes are offered to all students from KG to Grade 12.

AHISK strives to continually improve the quality of education it provides. We are accredited by AdvancED and a member of CIS. The Al Hussan curriculum is offered from KG to 12. Students have the option to sit for IGCSE O levels in Grade 10 and A levels or IB in Grades 11 and 12.

Courses on offer in the IB Diploma Programme are: English Literature, Arabic B, Arabic *ab-initio*, French B, French *ab-initio*, Business Management, Economics, Biology, ITGS, Chemistry, Physics, Computer Science, Math Studies, Mathematics and Visual Arts.

Our Vision
Leaders of Excellence in International Education

Our Mission
Al Hussan International School provides high quality education through a safe, stimulating, and multicultural environment to prepare leaders for a global society.

Our Beliefs
At AHISK, we believe:

1. all students can learn and realize their full potential.
2. a safe and stimulating environment promotes quality education.
3. in respecting cultural and individual differences.
4. all stakeholders share the responsibility for advancing our mission.
5. in preparing students to pursue further educational goals.
6. commitment to continuous improvement is imperative.

At AHISK we believe in preparing students to become well-rounded young people, ready to meet the challenges in an ever-changing world. This is done through our challenging programs of study and with the help of an experienced, extensively trained team of teachers. Our student body is very active and striving to make a change in their community. Our graduates are joining universities across the world, mainly in the Middle East, Far East, Canada and USA. We are proud of our family and we invite you to visit us and experience our loving and nurturing family ambiance.

(Founded 2003)

Director Dr. Fatma Odaymat

Head of Secondary Alpana Mukherjee

Head of Primary Dania Sadek

PYP coordinator Sandeepa Chavan

MYP coordinator Barbara Bilgre

DP coordinator Dorinda Tham

Status Private

Boarding/day Day

Gender Coeducational

Language of instruction English, French

Authorised IB programmes PYP, MYP, DP

Age Range 2 – 19

Number of pupils enrolled 550

Fees Day: US$6,300 – US$9,735

Address Boundry Road
East Legon
Accra | GHANA

TEL +233 (0)541 897254

Email communication@aris.edu.gh

Website www.aris.edu.gh

ARIS is one of the leading IB World Schools not just in Ghana but Africa as a whole, as it sets on a journey towards inclusion, collaboration, and innovation. The ARIS Educational Model is centered on our students' personalised learning, performance and experiences giving an ode to student agency as they take ownership of their learning.

Fully authorized with the IB Primary Years Programme, IB Middle Years Programme, and IB Diploma Programme, ARIS has inculcated the values of global citizenship and international-mindedness right from the early years to the point where we send our Golden Eagles out into the world. Our core values of collaboration and communication, believing in greatness in everyone and teamwork also shines through in our everyday efforts to inspire, empower and transform for a better, and more inclusive world.

ARIS is now a Candidate school to offer the fourth and final IB Career-related Programme (IBCP) which upon authorization will put us on the map as the first continuum school in Africa to offer all four IB Programmes. With the development and growth of our counseling and support department, ARIS is becoming highly inclusive in a fully integrated curriculum for students ranging across varying needs and abilities and prioritizes student wellbeing with the ARIS Wellbeing Model.

We strongly encourage our students to learn foreign languages, exposing them to different cultures and different linguistic systems, enabling an informed awareness of diversities and similarities in the global community. We currently offer Arabic, English, French, Spanish, Mandarin, German, Hindi, and Local Languages.

With over 50 nationalities, our students learn to recognize and grow from their cultural roots. We believe that intercultural understanding and interpersonal competencies are essential to modern life and that learning from others is an integral part of forming one's identity.

As an institution that highly encourages collaboration, we include parents of our community in the approaches to teaching and learning. Through applications and software such as ManageBac, Seesaw and School Stream, parents are given a constant update on the learning progress of their children and of all school activities.

ARIS is fortunate to have a highly professional and dynamic team of facilitators, who are committed to continuous professional development.

At ARIS, students are by all means at the center of all growth and development as we move towards more creativity and more innovation in order to prepare 21st-century learners for the future full of possibilities that await.

AMADEUS International School Vienna

(Founded 2012)

Head of School
Jeremy House

PYP coordinator
Kevin Osborne

MYP coordinator
Amanda Cornish

DP coordinator
Melanie Pages

Status Private

Boarding/day Mixed

Gender Coeducational

Language of instruction
English

Authorised IB programmes
PYP, MYP, DP

Age Range 3 – 18

Number of pupils enrolled
254

Fees
Day: €13,190 – €28,820
Boarding: €48,490 – €53,020

Address
Bastiengasse 36-38
1180 Vienna | **AUSTRIA**

TEL +43 1 470 30 37 00
FAX +43 1 470 30 37 99

Email
admissions@amadeus-vienna.com

Website
www.amadeus-vienna.com

"Where academic excellence meets passion" – The first of its kind in the heart of Europe, AMADEUS International School Vienna offers a unique blend of rigorous academics, innovative music and arts education, and optional boarding in superior facilities. The mission of the school is to create an internationally-minded community of happy, passionate and aspirational learners.

School

As a fully authorized International Baccalaureate Continuum School, AMADEUS follows the IB's rigorous internationally recognized programmes for Grades 1-12. AMADEUS also offers an Early Years Kindergarden Programme for ages 3-6. By creating an innovative and positive learning environment, the school engages students in inquiry-based learning that addresses real-life challenges and cultivates critical-thinking, problem-solving, and presentation skills. AMADEUS's student body and faculty are distinguished by its internationalism representing over 40 different nationalities. In order to best teach the qualities of global citizenship, the school recruits educators from around the world. An average class size of 18-20 students allows for a caring individualized approach to learning.

Music and Arts

AMADEUS's dynamic co-curricular arts enrichment programme emphasizes an exploratory learning approach in a variety of areas such as, editorial design, music production, and instrument lessons. Students also have the opportunity to participate in choir, orchestra, dance, drawing, painting, theatrical productions, and more. The AMADEUS Music and Arts Academy includes Foundation, Advanced, and Professional Programmes to challenge and nurture artists at all stages of growth. The Academy empowers students to become deeply proficient at their skill through intense study with distinguished instructors in their areas of expertise, practice, and performance opportunities.

Boarding

As the only international boarding school in Vienna, students are welcome from all around the world to engage in an educational experience that is inclusive, happy, and respectful of different cultures. AMADEUS has a strong sense of community that cultivates a supportive and caring environment while promoting a healthy lifestyle that emphasises nutritious food, physical exercise, social activities and overall well-being.

Location

The AMADEUS campus is just a tram ride away from the city center. Famous for its history, culture, and quality of life, the city of Vienna is named "the World's Most Livable City" by The Economist. Home to numerous universities and nearly a dozen international schools, Vienna is Austria's hub of international education and learning.

Empowering individuals to transform the world as architects of their own learning

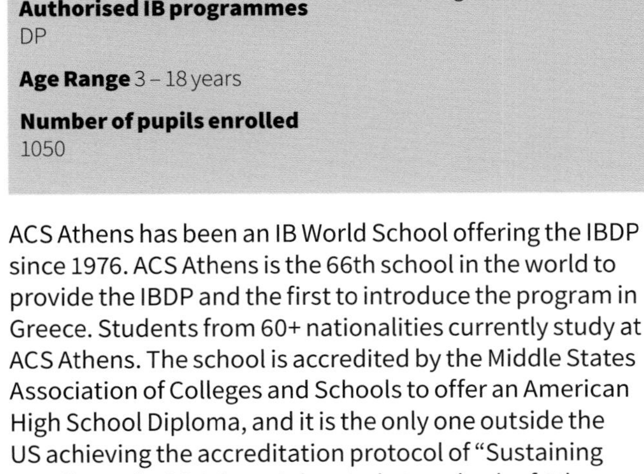

(Founded 1945)

Acting President
Dr Peggy Pelonis

DP coordinator
Dr Andreas Tsokos

Status Private

Boarding/day Day

Gender Coeducational

Language of instruction
English

Authorised IB programmes
DP

Age Range 3 – 18 years

Number of pupils enrolled
1050

Fees
€13,000 – €15,000

Address
129 Aghias Paraskevis Str.
Halandri
152 34 Athens | **GREECE**

TEL +30 210 639 3200
FAX +30 210 639 0051

Email
acs@acs.gr

Website
www.acs.gr

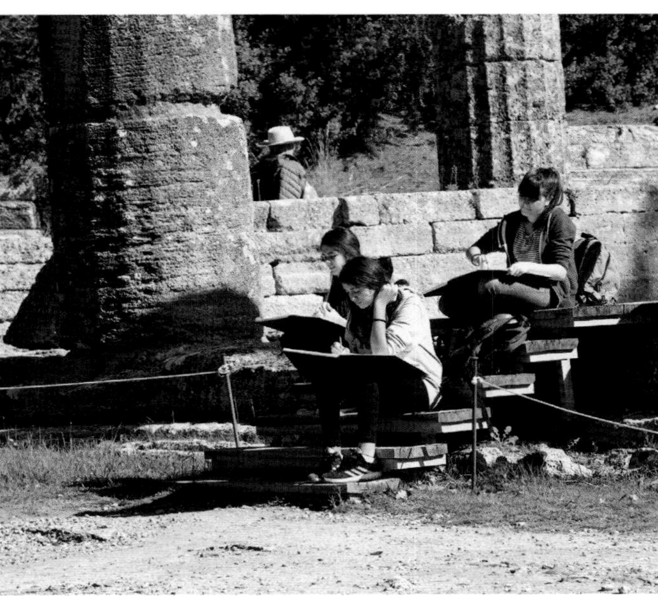

ACS Athens has been an IB World School offering the IBDP since 1976. ACS Athens is the 66th school in the world to provide the IBDP and the first to introduce the program in Greece. Students from 60+ nationalities currently study at ACS Athens. The school is accredited by the Middle States Association of Colleges and Schools to offer an American High School Diploma, and it is the only one outside the US achieving the accreditation protocol of "Sustaining Excellence." ACS Athens is located at a suburb of Athens on a privately owned enclosed campus consisting of five main buildings. The campus features a large swimming pool, a state-of-the-art theater and media studio, a soccer field, an indoor gymnasium with a climbing wall, indoor and outdoor basketball courts, and a fine arts suite.

About 60% of ACS Athens upper high school students choose the IB Diploma Programme (IBDP), and more than 87% of the non-IBDP students prefer a combination of IB, AP, and ACS Athens authentic courses. Full IBDP candidates at ACS Athens obtain a bilingual IB diploma, as well as an American High School Diploma when they complete the required courses successfully. ACS Athens has had a consistent average of 36 points, which is considerably higher than the average world score. Over 98% of ACS Athens graduates are admitted to top universities in the US, UK, Canada, the Netherlands, and elsewhere.

The extensive IB CAS program, including musical performances, participation in sports and service in hospitals, elderly care facilities, and refugee camps, broadens a student's education and perspectives and makes a student aware of real-life situations and concerns.

ACS Athens also embraces virtual learning, inaugurating its Virtual School in 2019-20, which offers mainstream and non-traditional high school accredited courses. Academic support through the Writing and Math Studios assists and enhances the writing and mathematical skills of each student. Furthermore, a comprehensive program for college applications offered by our Student Affairs department facilitates admission to the finest institutions around the world. ACS Athens follows a best-fit university approach, ensuring students identify universities and colleges that will best suit them academically and personally.

The fundamental principles of ACS Athens' mission statement and its educational philosophy are in direct alignment with the philosophy and mission statement of the IBO. ACS Athens student-centered environment aims toward high academic achievement, as well as providing a broader education to produce graduates with what the Ancient Greeks called "Morfosis", i.e., educated, cultured, compassionate, and caring individuals with Ethos.

American International School of Kuwait

المدرسة الأمريكية الدولية
American International School

(Founded 1991)

Superintendent David Botbyl

Director Samera Al Rayes

PYP coordinator Emma Wheatley

MYP coordinator Teri Kwiatkowski

DP coordinator Amel Limam

Status Private

Boarding/day Day

Gender Coeducational

Language of instruction English

Authorised IB programmes PYP, MYP, DP

Age Range 4 – 18

Number of pupils enrolled 2200

Fees
Pre-K KD3,867
KG KD2,650 (KG 1) – KD2,871 (KG 2)
Grades 1-4 KD3,867
Grades 5-8 KD4,086
Grades 9-12 KD4,531

Address
PO Box 3267, Salmiya
22033 | KUWAIT

TEL +965 1 843 247
FAX +965 256 33322

Email superintendent@ais-kuwait.org

Website www.ais-kuwait.org

The American International School Kuwait (AIS) is a private independent day school serving students from pre-kindergarten through grade 12. AIS is an IB World School that is fully authorized for the Primary Years, Middle Years and Diploma Programmes. It has a rigorous academic programme within a nurturing learner-centered environment.

The ethnic diversity of the Middle East layered with the complexity of an otherwise international student and staff body provides a stimulating and endlessly fascinating environment in which we live the IB Learner Profile. The school has grown steadily since it opened and currently houses international students from around fifty countries across the world.

The school has an outstanding extracurricular program that offers a wide-variety of activities in sports and the creative arts. AIS students strive for balance and take part in a wide range of athletics and activities through the NESAC of which AIS is a full member. AIS also participates fully in KASAC, our local activities and athletics conference.

Our learning spaces are well designed to provide essential facilities and services for an inviting and welcoming learning environment.

The school facility includes two gymnasia, several outdoor sports areas, music and theater spaces, strength training and aerobics rooms, as well as a 1200 seat auditorium. The walled campus includes over one hundred teaching spaces that surround two interior courts. Our Learning Commons offers a collaborative space for student inquiry, instructional coaching, and collaboration and houses a library with a large fiction, non-fiction, and Arabic collection.

Upon graduation, our students proudly enter many of the world's most respected and top-rated universities in the United States, Canada and the United Kingdom, poised to be contributors and difference-makers in the world.

AIS Kuwait inspires students to become critical thinkers and contributing world citizens through rigor and balance in a nurturing educational environment.

American School of The Hague

(Founded 1953)

Director
J. Courtney Lowe Ed.D.

DP coordinator
Victor Ferreira

Status Private

Boarding/day Day

Gender Coeducational

Language of instruction
English

Authorised IB programmes
DP

Age Range 3 – 18 years

Number of pupils enrolled
1220

Fees
€14,400 – €22,500

Address
Rijksstraatweg 200
2241BX Wassenaar |
NETHERLANDS

TEL +31 70 512 1060

FAX +31 70 511 2400

Email
admissions@ash.nl

Website
www.ash.nl

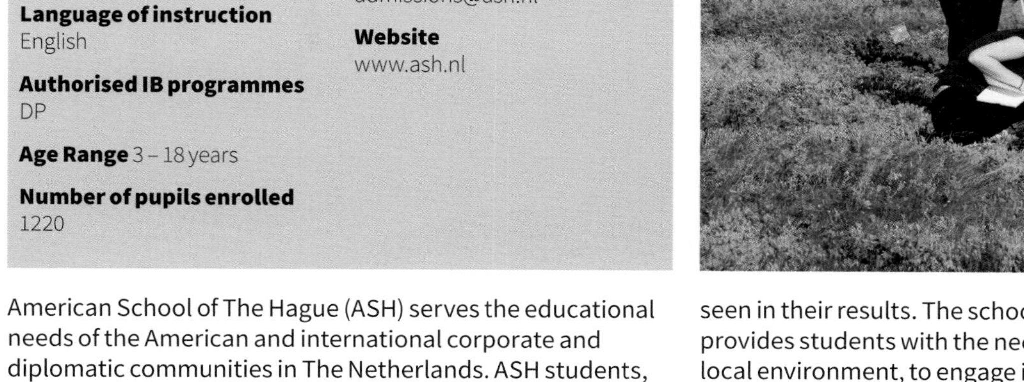

American School of The Hague (ASH) serves the educational needs of the American and international corporate and diplomatic communities in The Netherlands. ASH students, ages 3-18, represent up to 80 nationalities at any one time with 28% of the student body being American and 14% being host country, Dutch nationals.

While the school reflects an American educational philosophy, the diverse backgrounds of the students foster teaching and learning in the context of international understanding and global citizenship. ASH has a rigorous academic program. The High School curriculum emphasizes preparation for university studies in North America, Europe and students' home countries around the world. All students may earn an IB Diploma in addition to a US High School Diploma. IB Diploma Programme offerings include both standard and higher level courses across the curriculum. Students may choose the IB Diploma Programme (IB), or combine IB courses with Advanced Placement (AP) or regular curriculum subjects to earn IB certificates in subject specialties. A variety of IB language courses – including mother tongue tutorials – are available. Students who choose the IB Diploma Programme continue to achieve an excellent success rate, and ASH consistently posts scores higher than the world average. The school prides itself in engaging students in active learning at all levels and accessibility to highly academic classes remain an ASH hallmark as can be seen in their results. The school's unique IB group IV project provides students with the necessary conditions, using the local environment, to engage in STEM for three days in the field. The project has become a model for emulation by schools around the globe.

In addition, ASH students move with confidence to new schools throughout the world, and on average 98% of each graduating class enters university. The academic program includes a wide range of fine and applied arts courses, with a curriculum that is technologically competitive throughout the disciplines. A full athletic program and extra-curricular activities are an important part of student life and the school boasts several gyms, soccer and baseball fields and basketball courts. Athletic teams in ten sports travel throughout Europe competing with other international schools. ASH sponsors The Hague International Model United Nations, a major event for many ASH High School students and which counts more than 3500 international participants. The arts program offers individual and group instruction and performance opportunities in vocal and instrumental music, movement and theatre, and the ASH Jazz Band is well known throughout Europe. The two campus locations have spacious classrooms, specialized teaching areas, and multiple science and multi-media labs. ASH accepts applications at all grade levels throughout the year. For more information, visit www.ash.nl or follow ASH on social media.

Amman Baccalaureate School

مـــــدرسة البكالوريـــــا – عمـــــان
Amman Baccalaureate School

(Founded 1981)

Principal
Mr. Joss Williams

PYP coordinator
Ms Noura Dissy

MYP coordinator
Ms Dina Katafago

DP coordinator
Ms Jwan Kolaghassi

CP coordinator
Ms Gill Deesi

Status Private

Boarding/day Day

Gender Coeducational

Language of instruction
English, Arabic

Authorised IB programmes
PYP, MYP, DP, CP

Age Range 4 – 18

Number of pupils enrolled
1180

Address
Al Hijaz Street, Dabouq
PO Box 441 Sweileh 11910
Amman | **JORDAN**

TEL +962 6 5411191
FAX +962 6 5412603

Email
info@abs.edu.jo

Website
www.abs.edu.jo

The Amman Baccalaureate School (ABS) is a private, fee-paying day school, licensed by the Jordanian Ministry of Education. It is coeducational and prepares its students for the International Baccalaureate Diploma and Career-related Programme and courses as school leaving qualifications. In addition to providing an academic education of high quality, the school attaches considerable importance to creative, physical and community service activities, and offers a wide and developing range of facilities and opportunities in these areas.

ABS was founded in 1981 with the aim of providing a bilingual education that would meet, in quality and breadth, the highest international standards, whilst remaining firmly rooted in the Arab heritage. At the same time, the school has increasingly attracted students from the international community who wish to take advantage of the opportunity offered in the Middle Years School (MYP) and the IB College (Diploma Programme/Career-related Programme) to pursue an education in English that, nonetheless, sustains close contact with the culture of the host country.

The Amman Baccalaureate School is a school where modern educational theory and practice are implemented and enthusiastically embraced. In its officially recognised role as a 'pioneer school', ABS pilots new material, methods and approaches, and so paves the way for other schools to follow. Emphasis on bilingualism at every stage promotes knowledge of different cultures, traditions and values, and this fosters openness, understanding and tolerance.

Aligned with the School's vision to be "recognised as a leading pioneer school", ABS piloted the World Academy of Sport (WAoS) Athlete Friendly Education Centre (AFEC) accreditation in 2015 and the Council of International School's International Protocol accreditation in 2017. Both accreditations were deemed a huge success. ABS was re-accreditated by WAoS AFEC in 2018.

The ABS has a unique curriculum model for a bilingual (Arabic/English) Primary Years Programme (PYP) and is amongst a select few schools worldwide to offer all four IB Programmes (PYP, MYP, DP, CP).

Involvement with each and every student as an individual is a guiding principle at ABS. The 1:6 teacher to student ratio allows this principle to be a reality. This compares very favourably with institutions of similar academic standing, nationally and internationally. ABS teachers are qualified and trained educators, coming from open-minded and global backgrounds.

Amman Baccalaureate School also offers an international section for Grades 6-12. This section is for those students that do not have the level of Arabic to cope with an ABS bilingual education, but wish to benefit from our outstanding holistic educational experience.

Anatolia High School

(Founded 1886)

President
Dr. Panos Vlachos

MYP coordinator
Elisavet Exidaveloni

DP coordinator
Anna Billi Petmeza

Status Private, Non-Profit

Boarding/day Mixed

Gender Coeducational

Language of instruction
English (DP), Greek (MYP)

Authorised IB programmes
MYP, DP

Address
PO Box 21021
60 John Kennedy Avenue
555 35 Pylea | **GREECE**

TEL +30 2310 398 200
FAX +30 2310 327 500

Email
info@anatolia.edu.gr

Website
www.anatolia.edu.gr/highschool

Since its founding in 1886, the name of Anatolia has been synonymous with educational innovation and achievement. Located in Thessaloniki, Greece, Anatolia College is a private, non-profit, international learning community imbued with the best ideals of Greek and American education, and one of the very few institutions in the world today that offers education from pre-K all the way to graduate studies, through its various academic divisions.

The IB Middle Years Programme commenced in the Fall of 2013 at the freshman level and has now been introduced into grades 7 to 10 illustrating Anatolia's commitment to providing a curriculum meaningfully linked to the social, cultural and natural environment the students live in. Anatolia MYP students that follow the Greek curriculum in grades 11 and 12 have achieved a very high success rate in the entrance exams for Greek universities.

First introduced at Anatolia High School in 1997, the IBDP is open to students from all schools and nationalities. Classes at Anatolia are kept small to facilitate a more individualized approach to teaching from its well-qualified staff. The large variety of subjects offered at the DP level allows students to tailor their program of study to their particular strengths and interests. Anatolia IBDP graduates have been accepted at top universities around the world.

Across Anatolia's 50-acre campus of great natural beauty, one finds a residence hall for students wishing to stay on campus, a refectory, two modern libraries, science and computing laboratories, a Green Education Center, a Fabrication Lab, a music room, two theaters, a conference center, a multi-use gym and an open-air track & field court.

An extensive extracurricular program allows students to discover or develop their talent, while a comprehensive scholarship program ensures that worthy students may enroll at Anatolia, regardless of financial circumstance.

Anglo European School

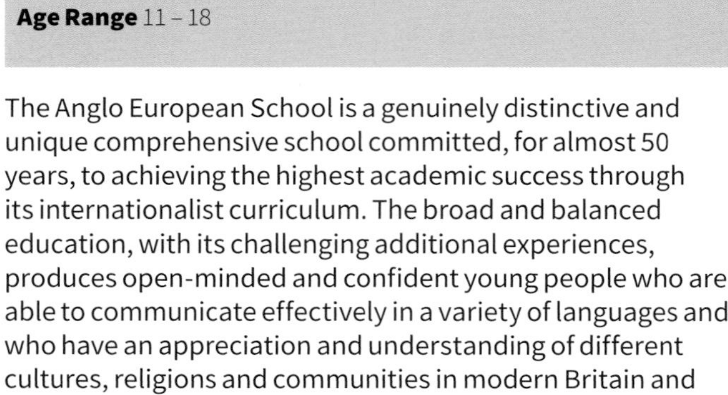

(Founded 1973)

Headteachers
Mr David Barrs & Mrs Jody Gee

DP coordinator
Mr Stuart Newton

CP coordinator
Mr Ben Knights

Status State

Boarding/day Day

Gender Coeducational

Language of instruction
English

Authorised IB programmes
DP, CP

Age Range 11 – 18

Number of pupils enrolled
1465

Address
Willow Green
Ingatestone
Essex
CM4 0DJ | UK

TEL 01277 354018

Email
admissions@aesessex.co.uk

Website
www.aesessex.co.uk

The Anglo European School is a genuinely distinctive and unique comprehensive school committed, for almost 50 years, to achieving the highest academic success through its internationalist curriculum. The broad and balanced education, with its challenging additional experiences, produces open-minded and confident young people who are able to communicate effectively in a variety of languages and who have an appreciation and understanding of different cultures, religions and communities in modern Britain and beyond.

The Sixth Form is outstanding and has been awarded the highest Ofsted grades for over 20 years. In 1977 Anglo European School was the first UK state school to offer the International Baccalaureate Diploma and in 2010 became the first UK state school to offer the IB Career Programme. It also provides the opportunity to study A Levels or A Levels with selected parts of the IB Diploma. All students also study a language ranging from introductory level, which assumes no prior knowledge, up to more advanced courses in the A Level and IB Diploma Routes. Eight languages are taught: Arabic, French, German, Italian, Japanese, Mandarin, Russian and Spanish. We believe that this gives an unrivalled opportunity for each student to combine qualifications in a way which best suits their needs and makes them stand out in the global employment marketplace.

Situated in Ingatestone, with excellent rail and road connections, local children are joined by children from Essex, Suffolk, Hertfordshire, London and abroad who value its internationalist philosophy based on the mission of the International Baccalaureate. This diversity provides a rich education which prepares succeeding generations of students for the world they will live and work in, whatever their background or ability. It really is an education fit for the 21st Century.

A remarkable feature of the school is its visits and exchanges programme. Over 700 students every year take part in the exchange programmes and extended study visits in Europe, China and Japan. Sixth Form students also have the opportunity to undertake international work experience in Madrid, Frankfurt and Paris, visit the United Nations in Geneva and to do voluntary community work in Lesotho.

This is a caring, principled but purposeful school which is confident in its ambition and passionate about its mission. It is a school which is determined to ensure that an education within an international dimension is compatible with high academic success and outstanding personal development for all its students whatever their background or ability.

(Founded 2010)

Principal
Ms. Janette Wakileh

PYP coordinator
Ms. Nour Maroun

DP coordinator
Ms. Yasmine Haddadin

Status Private

Boarding/day Day

Gender Coeducational

Language of instruction
English, Arabic

Authorised IB programmes
PYP, DP

Age Range 3 – 18

Number of pupils enrolled
600

Address
Khalda, Taqi al-Din al-Subki
Amman | **JORDAN**

TEL +962 6 5335 301
FAX +962 6 5333 753

Email
info@ais.edu.jo

Website
www.ais.edu.jo

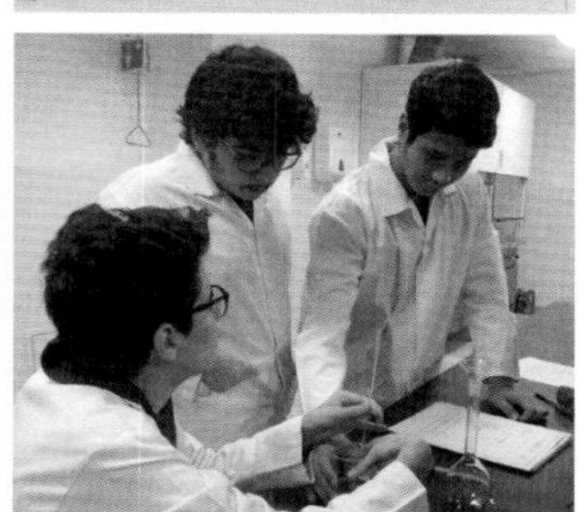

Asamiah International School (AIS) is an IB; co-educational, bilingual school offering children from KG to Grade 12 IB PYP Curriculum (KG and grades 1-5) as well as the DP for grades 11 and 12. The school is easily accessible to parents and visitors with state-of-the-art facilities. We emulate comfortably and proudly alongside the best IB schools in the country; this is reflected on our students' outstanding characteristics and remarkable results. We are also proud of our alumni who receive prompt acceptance at the best universities worldwide.

AIS aims to develop inquiring, self-confident, independent, productive, respectful and caring lifelong learners who seek to make their societies a better place and who are willing to transfer their knowledge to community service and social development.

At AIS, we aim to provide every learner with the finest education possible through vibrant and engaging teaching approaches that are deeply stemmed from the IB pedagogy and practices. Our learners are thus enabled and challenged to become independent learners who acquire their personal knowledge through the five approaches to learning (ATL skills): Communication, social, thinking, self-management and research skills. Hence, our school is equipped with various facilities that help students enjoy and learn the necessary skills.

The after-school activities are designed to complement the school programs and provide students with an opportunity to acquire extra-curricular skills. They include a wide variety of choices such as athletics, basketball, football, mixed martial arts, photography, robotics, gaming, design, drama and dance classes, arts, individual & group music instrument lessons, languages in addition to our yearly enriching summer camps.

At AIS, we prepare children for the real world. We make our learners ready to meet the future with confidence and to contribute positively to their local and global society. Our educators work hard to ensure that the best possible quality of education is at the service of our dear learners.

To complete our journey, AIS is an MYP candidate School. Preparing for MYP has enriched our conceptual-based curricula, teaching and learning approaches making the learning process linked to life and globally – oriented. We teach in compliance with the 21st century demands, and what is more essential is that we instill cultural diversity and international-mindedness in order for students to learn to embrace differences.

To put a closure to the IB journey, our DP students are encouraged to leave a tangible impact in their community by serving and taking actions to create novel solutions to apparent local conflicts through their DP/CAS projects which are set to align with the UN 17 sustainable development goals (SDGs) to benchmark a better society; a better world.

Ashcroft Technology Academy

Head of School
Mr Douglas Mitchell

DP coordinator
Joseph Anson

Status State

Boarding/day Day

Gender Coeducational

Language of instruction
English

Authorised IB programmes
DP

Age Range 11 – 18

Number of pupils enrolled
1261

Address
100 West Hill
London
London
SW15 2UT | UK

TEL +44 (0)208 877 0357
FAX +44 (0)208 877 0617

Email
joseph.anson@
ashcroftacademy.org.uk

Website
www.atacademy.org.uk

Ethos

The Sixth Form at Ashcroft Technology Academy is an exceptional place to learn. Students and staff have worked together to create a culture of aspiration and success. Our students enjoy their time at the Sixth Form and are given superb support and guidance, which combined with excellent teaching, enables our students to excel.

Academic

Students leave our sixth form articulate, confident, accomplished and ambitious young adults who understand the importance of rigour and high standards. Underpinning our proven track record of success is a team of highly motivated, hard working and qualified staff who have an unreserved belief in the ability and potential of young people to succeed. Our IB results are outstanding: in 2019 our average score was 36.7 points and the average grade per subject was 5.8. Each year a number of students achieve over 40 points, allowing them to take places at the very best universities in the UK and abroad such as Cambridge, Edinburgh and the Universidad Carlos III.

Outside the Classroom

The extracurricular provision at the Academy is virtually unrivalled. Every member of staff at the Academy runs a club or society, providing our students with a wealth of enrichment opportunities. Advanced Collective Orchestra, Debating Society and Model UN have been particularly popular with IB students. Students attend a range of workshops, lectures and conferences both within and outside of school. The Academy offers a range of leadership opportunities, from House Captains to the Head Student Team. Furthermore, students who display a particular passion for a subject may also apply for our scholarship, receiving up to £500 to put towards an opportunity to develop in that field. Examples include pre-med courses or university summer schools.

Location and Facilities

Ashcroft Technology Academy has a superb location in South West London. Waterloo station is just 15 minutes away by train and we are located adjacent to the A3 and East Putney underground station. Facilities are exceptional; our purpose built Sixth Form Centre has a university style study area, classrooms designed for Sixth Formers and a Sixth Form exclusive annex to our main school library. Additional to our excellent existing resources, the Academy boast 10 state-of-the-art science laboratories, a sixth form Art Studio and two professional quality fitness suites.

Benjamin Franklin International School

(Founded 1986)

Head of School
Mr. Colin Boudreau

DP coordinator
Laura Blair

Status Private

Boarding/day Day

Gender Coeducational

Language of instruction
English

Authorised IB programmes
DP

Age Range 3 – 18

Fees
Day: €11,000 – €16,830

Address
Martorell i Pena 9
08017 Barcelona, Catalonia |
SPAIN

TEL +34 93 434 2380

Email
info@bfischool.org

Website
www.bfischool.org

The Benjamin Franklin International School (BFIS) is an independent, coeducational, IB world school, which offers an English-language, college-preparatory program from Nursery through Grade 12 for students of all nationalities. Founded in 1986, the school offers a differentiated, American curriculum, fully accredited with strong academic programs, including learning support, service learning and foreign languages. BFIS offers three diploma programmes: American High School Diploma, International Baccalaureate (IB) Diploma, and Spanish High School Bachillerato Certificate. BFIS is a truly international school with 700 students, representing more than 50 different nationalities and cultural heritages.

As an American International school, the curriculum is rooted in US standards, such as Common Core for Math and English Language Arts, Next Generation Science Standards, and the C3 Framework for Social Studies Standards. The school believes that a meaningful curriculum needs to connect teaching and learning to the world and bring out the best in each student. Students must be active participants at the center of the learning process and must be given the opportunities, instruction, guidance and support to discover their interests, pursue their passions, and develop the skills and knowledge they need to thrive and reach their full potential.

Standards are delivered through an inquiry-based approach to teaching and learning with a focus on innovation and technology through a wide 1:1 program, makerspace, and robotics. The school promotes meaningful uses of integrated technology to develop critical thinking skills and support continuous inquiry. In addition to the academic programs, BFIS has developed a robust social-emotional approach to create a supportive environment for all students and help them to strengthen their social-emotional skills, such as self-esteem, confidence, resilience or problem-solving, which will place them on a path for long-term success in all areas of life.

BFIS IB results have always exceeded the IB worldwide average scores and the school's pass rate is very close to 100%. The significant achievements of BFIS students in such a challenging academic program have gained them entry into a range of competitive colleges and universities worldwide.

BFIS has three campuses with sports courts, playground spaces, several science labs, cafeteria, two libraries, a makerspace, a computer lab, and auditorium for 350 people. In 2016, the school inaugurated a new Elementary building and in September 2020 a new Middle School building will be open to students.

INSPIRATIONAL Box Hill School

(Founded 1959)	**Fees from** Day: £17,985 Weekly Boarding: £28,350 Full Boarding: £34,950 International Study Centre Boarding £41,250
Headmaster Cory Lowde	
DP coordinator Julian Baker	
Status Private	
Boarding/day Mixed	**Address** London Road Mickleham Dorking, Surrey RH5 6EA | UK
Gender Coeducational	
Language of instruction English	
Authorised IB programmes DP	**TEL** 01372 373382
Age Range 11 – 18	**Email** registrar@BoxHillSchool.com
Number of pupils enrolled 425	**Website** www.boxhillschool.com

Box Hill School is a co-educational day, weekly and full boarding school for girls and boys aged 11-18. We are a founding member of Round Square, a global network of schools that share a passion for learning through experience and character education, basing its educational philosophy on the teachings of educationalist Kurt Hahn. We follow this philosphy and its IDEALS of Internationalism, Democracy, Environmentalism, Adventure, Leadership and Service underpin our school ethos and values.

The school is located just 40 minutes from central London, in the heart of the beautiful Surrey Hills. Easily accessible and just 30 minutes from Heathrow Airport and 25 minutes from Gatwick Airport.

Academic – The Curriculum

Our focus is on achieving the best academic outcome for each student and ensuring each student fulfils their full potential. They are encouraged, nurtured and challenged in all that they do. It is important to us that we produce well-rounded, resilient and confident young people, who achieve academic success.

The school offers a dedicated Lower School for Years 7, 8 and 9, which follows the intentions of the National Curriculum but broadens its scope to guarantee that courses are constructed to suit the abilities and interests of our students. In the Middle School we provide a wide range of GCSE's and (I) GCSE's and in the Sixth Form we offer our students the choice of the International Baccalaureate Diploma Programme (IBDP) or an A Level course.

In our International Study Centre we offer a range of courses for overseas students including: the one year Pre-IB Diploma course (intensive), one year Pre-Sixth Form Science, Technology & Mathematics Study Programme, Pre-boarding preparation courses and a 2 week Summer Pre-School English course.

Co-Curricular

At Box Hill School, we provide our pupils with a wide range of co-curricular options to develop their interests and gain life skills.

All students participate in our activities programme, consisting of over 60 options, timetabled during the school day three afternoons a week. These range from team sports with weekly fixtures, through to high ropes, chess and debating clubs.

The school is also actively involved in the Duke of Edinburgh's Award Scheme which runs in parallel to our programme of expeditions, all designed to encourage outdoor education.

As a Round Square school there are also opportunities for pupils to participate in global and regional conferences, exchange programmes and overseas community service projects.

Boarding

The Independent School's Inspectorate report, 2019 stated *"They (the students) enjoy school and thrive in the nurturing and supportive environment provided by the excellent pastoral care system and family atmosphere in boarding and day houses."*

Boarding life is structured around 6 boarding houses, where pupils are placed according to age and gender, with a mix of nationalities and cultures. They benefit from a diverse and varied activities programme, including weekly weekend trips all designed to develop interests, maximise the use of campus facilities and spend time with friends in a home-from-home environment.

BRADFIELD COLLEGE

(Founded 1850)

Headmaster
Dr Christopher Stevens

DP coordinator
Kirstie Parker

Status Private

Boarding/day Mixed

Gender Coeducational

Language of instruction
English

Authorised IB programmes
DP

Age Range 13 – 18

Number of pupils enrolled
815

Fees
Day: £31,080
Boarding: £38,850

Address
Bradfield
Berkshire
RG7 6AU | UK

TEL 0118 964 4516

Email
admissions@bradfieldcollege.org.uk

Website
www.bradfieldcollege.org.uk

Set in the village of Bradfield amidst unspoilt Berkshire countryside, Bradfield College enjoys a well-established reputation for being one of the country's leading co-educational, independent schools through its provision of academic excellence and a well-rounded education.

The College welcomes pupils from Britain and overseas and provides challenge and choice for all. We offer a personalised programme of study that is inspired by expert, passionate and engaging teaching and focuses on providing an education for life. We are acutely aware of the global community in which pupils will live and work when they leave the security and dynamism of Bradfield.

The Bradfield Sixth Form aims to provide an outstanding all-round education to prepare young people for success in a rapidly changing world. We care about the individual and pride ourselves in the warmth of a community in which young people feel happy and valued. We aim to foster an environment of high expectations in which all our students are encouraged to believe in themselves, to be inquisitive, to be resilient and to show ambition both within and beyond the classroom.

The IB Diploma Programme focuses on the education of the whole person whilst also seeking to provide an international perspective. This is very much in line with Bradfield's own education for life ethos and values. The IBDP emphasises the importance of Language, Science and Mathematics, as well as the Arts and Individuals and Societies. At the core of the curriculum model, Theory of Knowledge, Creativity, Activity and Service and Approaches to Teaching and Learning, both inside and outside of the classroom are all elements that Bradfield views as essential to an all-round education. We offer an unrivalled sports and co-curricular programme for all our pupils which ensures that every individual has the opportunity to develop valuable skills, wherever their interests lie. The need to complete the Extended Essay sits perfectly with Bradfield's drive towards creating independently-minded and curious young men and women by the end of the Sixth Form. In short, the IB Diploma and Bradfield fit perfectly together.

brains/
INTERNATIONAL SCHOOLS

DP coordinator
Michael Harvey

Status Private

Boarding/day Day

Gender Coeducational

Language of instruction
English

Authorised IB programmes
DP

Address
Calle Salvia, N° 48
28109 Alcobendas, Madrid |
SPAIN

TEL +34 91 650 43 00

Email
michael@colegiobrains.com

Website
www.colegiobrains.com

The founding of Brains International Schools was an innovative and challenging educational project started in Madrid in 1979. Four decades have since passed; during which time, Brains Schools have earned a reputation for excellence in bilingual education.

Brains International Schools offers a fully international Diploma Programme for both Spanish and international students alike. We pride ourselves on our uniquely diverse range of subject-language combinations, which we are able to offer from our multi-lingual teaching team from all over the world.

Taking full advantage of Spanish and English as official IB languages, students may choose to study subjects in either of these two languages, allowing truly bilingual programmes to be achieved through all of the six subject areas which make up the Diploma Programme.

At Brains we appreciate and value the distinct backgrounds and interests of our students, and we aim to provide them with the appropriate study programmes for the futures which they may be seeking. Accordingly, we strive to provide a wide choice of subjects at both standard and high level, enabling students to hand pick the diploma that best suits them.

The Diploma Programme is currently taught at our Madrid campus, which is situated in the northern part of the city within easy reach from all areas of Madrid by our school bus service or local transport. We offer students an excellent range of academic and technological facilities at this site, in addition to outstanding sporting and extra curricula opportunities, which fully support the educational service we aim to provide at Brains International Schools.

Brains International Schools are currently following the process of authorisation and implementation of PYP, MYP and DP across all our sites, as we strive to provide an excellent international education through an IB continuum of programmes.

Brentwood School

(Founded 1557)

Headmaster
Mr Michael Bond

DP coordinator
Mr Rob Higgins

Status Private

Boarding/day Mixed

Gender Coeducational

Language of instruction
English

Authorised IB programmes
DP

Age Range 3 – 18

Number of pupils enrolled
1620

Fees
Day: £19,800
Boarding: £38,799

Address
Middleton Hall Lane
Brentwood
Essex
CM15 8EE | UK

TEL 01277 243243
FAX 01277 243299

Email
headmaster@brentwood.essex.sch.uk

Website
www.brentwoodschool.co.uk

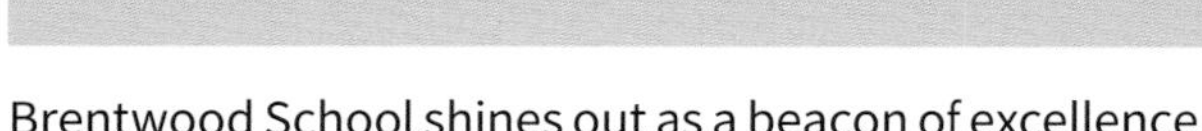

Brentwood School shines out as a beacon of excellence.

Academically, we sit comfortably alongside the best day and boarding schools in the country, and we enjoy an unparalleled local reputation.

Our pupils are happy individuals who thrive on the high standards which are expected of them. They benefit from state-of-the-art facilities, set in the heart of Brentwood in Essex, and are surrounded by 75 acres of green playing fields and gardens. Our close proximity to London is especially helpful for international families looking to place their children in a safe UK location but within easy reach of the Capital.

To quote our latest ISI Inspectorate report (2019), rating us excellent in every possible area: *"The school's focus on growth mindsets and the attributes of an effective learner through the Brentwood (IB) Learner Profile has contributed significantly to this highly successful outcome..."*

We offer full and weekly boarding for 13 to 18 year olds in comfortable houses where experienced husband and wife teams ensure the best possible care for all the boarders.

We celebrate a 463-year history and take our heritage seriously. We are a Christian School and our pupils are expected to have self-respect, to exhibit pride in their appearance and embrace values such as courtesy, consideration for others, kindness, looking after each other, honour, courage, sportsmanship, duty and selflessness.

"The cultural diversity of the school is highly valued by pupils, who demonstrate exceptional tolerance for all members of their community" ISI Inspection report, 2019

Our vast and exciting co-curricular programme enjoys national prominence.

Our pupils achieve excellent academic standards that rank among some of the best in the country and consistent high grades are achieved by all pupils. They work exceptionally hard and are supported by highly professional and inspiring teachers who offer dedicated Oxbridge mentoring. 70% of offers are from Russell Group / UK Top 20 universities (90% for IB Diploma students). 70% of our students were admitted to their first choice university (85% for IB Diploma).

A five year average of 36 points (equal to AAA at A Level), puts Brentwood among the top IB schools in the UK and the world. More than a quarter of our students consistently achieve 40 points or more and our recent cohorts have taken up places at top universities across the globe including Oxford, Imperial College, London; WWU Munster, SciencesPo Paris, UCLA, and The London School of Economics & Political Science.

We offer an enviable range of subjects including Dance, Food Science, Chinese *ab initio* and Global Politics, as well as more usual subjects like Physics, History, English, Mathematics, Psychology and Economics.

Our IB Diploma cohort has increased noticeably in the last two years. More than two-thirds of our IB students are from the UK, with one-third international.

A flourishing Old Brentwoods community keeps thousands of alumni connected across the globe.

Bromsgrove School

(Founded 1553)

Headmaster
Peter Clague

DP coordinator
Michael Thompson

Status Private

Boarding/day Mixed

Gender Coeducational

Language of instruction
English

Authorised IB programmes
DP

Age Range 13 – 18

Number of pupils enrolled
1300

Fees
Day: £17,085
Weekly Boarding: £25,335
Boarding: £38,220

Address
Worcester Road
Bromsgrove
Worcestershire
B61 7DU | UK

TEL +44 (0)1527 579679

Email
admissions@bromsgrove-school.co.uk

Website
www.bromsgrove-school.co.uk

FLAIR, DISCIPLINE, ACADEMIC RIGOUR

Set in 100 acres of beautiful parkland, Bromsgrove School caters for 1300 pupils with over 400 pupils in the hugely popular sixth form. Main intake is at ages 7, 11, 13 and 16, with international pupils joining at any of these stages.

Bromsgrove takes girls and boys between the ages of 7 and 18 in the hope of nurturing compassionate people who change the world for the better. International Baccalaureate and A level results place Bromsgrove in the first division. These impressive results combined with a massive sporting and extra-curricular programme means that at Bromsgrove breadth and quality are not mutually exclusive.

Life at Bromsgrove is dynamic. Great boarding schools offer pupils a home, not a place to sleep after work. People, not systems, must come first. The houses are different, as boarding houses in the best schools should be, but there are core values and structures shared by all. Houseparents are resident in the boarding houses with their own families. They are academic staff and are supported by a housemother. Bromsgrove boarders see family life going on around them. Each house has a dedicated tutor team, doing day and evening duties on a rota basis. Support, encouragement and trust are the watchwords.

A mix of over 50 different nationalities makes Bromsgrove vibrant. Bromsgrove School has an active International Students Department with full-time teachers who provide pastoral and academic support, specialising in the particular needs of the international pupils in the school. The department focuses lessons on the development of English language skills. International pupils are prepared for internationally recognised tests of English as an Additional Language. Bromsgrove results are outstanding: the IB Diploma average score was 37.5 in 2019.

Bromsgrove offers a unique weekend programme, covering a huge range of timetabled options from exclusively academic sessions to school trips. All staff work Saturday and the Sunday boarders' programme is extensive.

Admission for international students is by entrance test and, where possible, interview. Prospective pupils and their families are encouraged to visit. The Admissions Director has an extensive programme of international visits each year and will always try to meet prospective pupils in their own countries when she visits.

Bryanston School

(Founded 1928)

Headmaster
Mr M Mortimer

DP coordinator
Jo Strange

CP coordinator
Rose Ings

Status Private

Boarding/day Mixed

Gender Coeducational

Language of instruction
English

Authorised IB programmes
DP, CP

Age Range 13 – 18

Number of pupils enrolled
687

Fees
Day: £32,547
Boarding: £39,693

Address
Blandford Forum
Dorset
DT11 0PX | UK

TEL 01258 484633
FAX 01258 484661

Email
admissions@bryanston.co.uk

Website
www.bryanston.co.uk/ib

At Bryanston we aim to develop well-balanced 18-year-olds, ready to go out into the wider world, to lead happy and fulfilling lives and to contribute, positively and generously; an aim that is reflected in the principles of the IB, making it a natural fit at Bryanston. In 2019 our fifth cohort of IB Diploma pupils passed with an average score of 32.

Set in 400 acres of Dorset countryside, Bryanston offers a wide range of facilities, including purpose-built centres for science and mathematics, art, drama, music and sports.

Our tailored approach means that pupils benefit from extensive one-to-one time with their tutor and also with subject teachers each week, providing the academic and pastoral support they need to achieve their full potential.

Outside the core IB curriculum there is a fulfilling academic enrichment programme, as well as a range of over 100 extra-curricular activities on offer and all our pupils, whether they are studying the IB or A levels, are encouraged to pursue a wide range of interests.

As a full-time boarding school, weekends are an integral part of life at Bryanston, with many of the school's facilities open and the chance to take part in a range of sports fixtures, outdoor activities and rehearsals. There is a particular focus for the whole school on some weekends and more specialised activities on others. It makes all weekends busy but there is also time for pupils to relax.

Our website includes further information on the IB Diploma at Bryanston including details of the range of subjects on offer. In September 2019, we began teaching the IB Career-related Programme. It offers the same as the IB Diploma in terms of breadth of subjects studied, but has additional vocational qualifications. You can also attend one of our Information Afternoons, held in the autumn before you would be due to join us, to meet members of staff and get a feel for what Bryanston is like.

Entrance procedures for our IB courses require candidates to sit both an English and a maths test, have an interview with the Headmaster and meet Heads of Departments. Candidates unable to attend our Test and Interview Day can sit their papers at a suitable venue overseas and have a Skype interview with the Headmaster.

Successful candidates are invited to an induction week in June to explore their chosen subjects before confirming their academic programme. This gives candidates the chance to familiarise themselves with the school, make friends and get to know their tutor. It means that when starting sixth form in the following September each pupil is already a member of the Bryanston family.

Charterhouse

(Founded 1611)

Headmaster
Dr Alex Peterken

DP coordinator
Mr Peter Price

Status Private

Boarding/day Boarding

Gender Coeducational

Language of instruction
English

Authorised IB programmes
DP

Number of pupils enrolled
810

Fees
Day Boarding £11,210 per term
Boarding £13,565 per term

Address
Godalming
Surrey
GU7 2DX | UK

TEL +44 (0)1483 291501
FAX +44 (0)1483 291507

Email
admissions@charterhouse.org.uk

Website
www.charterhouse.org.uk

Motto: *Deo Dante Dedi*

Founded in 1611, Charterhouse is one of the UK's leading independent boarding schools, providing a first class education for boys and girls aged 13 to 18.

Building on the success of its mixed Sixth Form, the School is moving to full coeducation from the age of 13, and will welcome the first girls into Year 9 in September 2021.

Campus

The School is set within an inspiring 250-acre campus, conveniently located close to London and within 50 minutes of Heathrow and Gatwick airports.

With 17 grass sports pitches, 3 full-sized Astroturf pitches, an athletics stadium, a sports centre, 24 tennis courts and a 9-hole golf course, not to mention beautiful lawns and gardens, the campus is one of the best, if not the best, in the country. Combined with a 235-seat theatre and separate music performance and art display spaces, the School's setting encourages pupils to contribute, and provides a safe community in which to explore and grow.

Academic

Charterhouse's curriculum is all about choice and challenge for the individual. Of course it is firmly rooted in its hallmark academic rigour, intellectual curiosity and independent learning, though it is the breadth of options available to each pupil at every stage of their education that make it stand out from the rest. The curriculum has recently seen the introduction of an innovative course in Informatics (Computational Sciences) for all its youngest pupils, and once through their GCSEs, pupils benefit from the dual offer available in the Sixth Form: A Levels and Pre U courses with extended projects, a wonderful range of academic electives (Psychology, History of Art, *ab initio* languages and Business Entrepreneurship are all on the cards this year) or the breadth of the highly regarded IB Diploma Programme. The university destinations of leavers reflect both their abilities and the quality of the education provided at the School: Oxbridge, Ivy League, top Russell group and Bocconi all feature in abundance this year.

Co-curricular Activities

With more than 80 different sports and activities, including music, drama and other creative opportunities, everyone is encouraged to develop existing interests to exciting levels or take up new ones. A great many clubs and societies are pupil-led, offering real leadership opportunities and few limits to what can be pursued. Outdoor education, including a thriving DofE programme and a growing community and partnerships agenda, foster teamwork, service and leadership.

Boarding

Charterhouse is one of the very few schools now that is almost 100% boarding, with daily life for all pupils revolving around the Houses. The Housemasters/Housemistresses and their families live in the Houses and are supported by resident Matrons, Assistant Housemasters and a team of tutors. Each tutor has a small number of pupils with whom he or she meets at least once a week to provide the help and encouragement that enables every pupil to make the most of

life at the School. They take an active interest in their tutees, attending concerts, plays and sporting events in which they participate.

Admissions

Around 75 girls and 30 boys join the Sixth Form each year. Admission is by competitive examination and interview. Boys and girls should submit an application form by October of the year before entry, and will be assessed at Charterhouse in early November. Offers of places are made on 1 December. For further information please contact the Admissions Department: admissions@charterhouse.org.uk

Beau Soleil

Collège Alpin International

(Founded 1910)

Headmaster Stuart White

DP coordinator Helen Taylor-Cevey

Status Private

Boarding/day Boarding

Gender Coeducational

Language of instruction English, French

Authorised IB programmes DP

Age Range 11 – 18

Address
Route Du Village 1
Villars-sur-Ollon
1884 | SWITZERLAND

TEL +41 24 496 2626

Email
info@beausoleil.ch

Website
www.beausoleil.ch

At Beau Soleil, we believe it's what you do that counts: Our educational philosophy encourages students to become responsible and ambitious world citizens through the challenging and inspirational range of activities offered each day both inside and outside of the classroom setting.

Founded in 1910, we welcome students from more than 55 different nationalities, a melting pot of cultures that supports the IB philosophy of internationalism and global mindset. With educational pathways in both English and French,at IB level, our students are able to pursue their studies in either language or a combination of the two.

Outstanding academic results are ensured by our passionate teaching staff, who inspire and support students to achieve to their highest potential. With a teacher to student ratio of 1 to 4 we are able to offer a personalised approach to learning and a diverse range of educational experiences. Our dedicated college counsellor and mentoring programme supports our graduates to enter many of the world's leading universities.

Exciting experiences both inside and outside of the classroom – from extended curriculum days, to educational trips across the world, full-school challenges and our winter ski programme – help our students to develop a greater understanding and appreciation of the world around them and to develop skills including team work, collaboration and resilience.

The spectacular school campus, located in a beautiful and safe alpine location, gives access to an enviable lifestyle. Blending tradition with modernity, the campus offers facilities of the highest quality and inspiring views across the Swiss Alps.

A full boarding school with a capacity of 260 students, our boarders experience the ideal balance of warmth, care and discipline, encouraging in them a sense of independence. Our home from home boarding philosophy promotes the creation of lifelong friendships based on a common set of values: responsibility, respect, ambition and determination.

COLLÈGE
CHAMPITTET
FONDÉ EN 1903

(Founded 1903)

Head of School
Philippe de Korodi

DP coordinator
Keith Sykes

Status Private

Boarding/day Mixed

Gender Coeducational

Language of instruction
English, French

Authorised IB programmes
DP

Age Range 3 – 18

Number of pupils enrolled
800

Fees
Day: CHF10,300 – CHF33,200
Boarding: CHF66,900 – CHF90,200

Address
Chemin de Champittet 1
1009 Pully | SWITZERLAND

TEL +41 21 721 0505

Email
admissions@champittet.ch

Website
www.champittet.ch

Collège Champittet is a world-renowned Swiss School with a long tradition of being "open to the world".

Founded in 1903 the school is embedded in the cultural and academic fabric of the city of Lausanne. The school is not only part of the local community but has a real sense of community itself. Students are nurtured in a caring and supportive environment by a full range of highly qualified and experienced pastoral and academic staff.

The ethos of Champittet is perfectly matched to the ethos of the International Baccalaureate.

The IB's core aims are to promote internationalism and peace along with a broad and challenging academic curriculum. Champittet has a long and rich Swiss pedagogical tradition based on an ambition to link to the world. The IB at Collège Champittet has the trademark Swiss quality with a global mindset.

Champittet has one of the most amazing campus locations in the world, on the shores of Lake Geneva. Students can even choose to live at school and enjoy the camaraderie and activities that come with it.

Collège Champittet is part of the global Nord Anglia Education group. This provides our students with amazing opportunities in music thanks to the partnership with Juilliard and in science projects with the Massachusetts Institute of Technology (MIT). They can also take part in sports tournaments against students from all over the world and engage in Humanitarian missions in Africa and Asia.

Students also have access to the online Global Campus. This amazing resource allows students from across the Nord Anglia group from Shanghai, to Chicago, via Dubai – to collaborate on projects and competitions all year round. Competitions include debates, photography and arts and collaboration can be centred around subjects, courses and expeditions. Collège Champittet is a truly international place to study with students from all over the world.

Multilingualism is embedded through the school and with that the advantages it brings our students for their academic and cultural development.

Our Pre-IB and IB classes are kept small and as a result we can offer our students individual attention and care not afforded by large classes. Knowing our students thoroughly as individuals is essential for us to help provide the specific support our students need to succeed. That support includes a dedicated Dean, experienced tutors and homeroom teachers. We understand the need for a holistic approach for our young people to succeed.

Coming to Champittet is more than just starting a school – it is joining a community.

Here at Collège Champittet we believe that being traditional is a strength. Values such as politeness, respect and understanding of others are central to the development of the whole child that has been the hallmark of a Champittet education through the years.

(Founded 1960)

Director General
Mrs Pauline Nord

DP coordinator
Jana Krainova Samuda

CP coordinator
Julie Hutchins

Status Private

Boarding/day Mixed

Gender Coeducational

Language of instruction
English, French

Authorised IB programmes
DP, CP

Age Range 2 – 18

Fees
Day: CHF22,700 – CHF35,900
Boarding: CHF79,200 – CHF92,500

Address
74, route de Sauverny
1290 Versoix
Geneva | **SWITZERLAND**

TEL +41 22 775 56 56
FAX +41 22 775 55 59

Email
admissions@cdl.ch

Website
www.cdl.ch

We are an international college preparatory school located in Geneva, Switzerland. Our boarding and day school programmes offer individual growth and academic excellence to students from Pre-K through to Grade 12. Collège Du Léman belongs to the Nord Anglia Family of schools, a worldwide group of elite college preparatory schools that offer students the highest standards in education and unique, international learning opportunities.

Our campus is an 8-hectare landscaped campus nestled between the Jura mountains and Lac Léman on the outskirts of the city of Geneva. It offers comfortable residential facilities and recreational areas, providing students with a wide range of sport and leisure activities. In addition to our commitment to excellence in education, our philosophy also includes stimulating enthusiasm for lifelong learning and intellectual growth.

Students benefit from our multicultural learning environment. By nurturing a sense of social responsibility and respect for others, they are well-prepared to become respected world citizens. The knowledge students gain must be applicable across cultures and be supported by qualifications recognised worldwide. Each student's individuality as well as his or her integration into society is highly valued.

We have offered the Diploma Programme (DP) since 2005 and the Careers Programme (CP) since 2016. The DP is very successful and attracts around half of our graduates every year. Our broad choice of subjects allows students to focus on their strengths and fulfil their interests. This, combined with a strong pastoral programme and the professionalism and dedication of our teachers, contribute to consistently excellent exam results.

Our thorough university advising programme enables students to enroll in the universities of their choice all around the world. Our IBDP graduates come from over 100 countries worldwide.

For the IBCP we offer two career-related streams: Hospitality and Sustainability Management. Each course has been developed in partnership with the Les Roches School of Hotel Management in Bluches and the Sustainable Management School in Gland. Students will, in addition, study a minimum of 3 IB subjects.

Collège Du Léman-Made for success, Made for you!

(Founded 1613)

Head of School
Mr N J Whittle

DP coordinator
Kirstin Smith

CP coordinator
Kirstin Smith

Status State

Boarding/day Mixed

Gender Coeducational

Language of instruction
English

Authorised IB programmes
DP, CP

Age Range 11 – 18

Number of pupils enrolled
1000

Fees
Boarding: £12,160 – £13,550

Address
Milnthorpe
Cumbria
LA7 7DD | UK

TEL +44 (0)15395 65165
FAX +44 (0)15395 65175

Email
enquiries@dallamschool.co.uk

Website
www.dallamschool.co.uk

Located on the southern fringes of the English Lake District, Dallam School has been an IB World School since 2007 and our students consistently achieve results that are above the world average.

At the heart of this success is the fact that Dallam provides a learning environment where our students develop the skills and mind-sets that enable them to progress in life with confidence and a passion for learning. That is why so many students not only move on to some of the most prestigious universities, including Oxbridge, but go on to excel in whatever they choose to do.

Dallam offers the IB as well as the more traditional UK A Levels. Beyond the classroom our students develop as young people by taking advantage of our extensive enrichment opportunities. The Duke of Edinburgh Award Scheme is extremely popular as are the Community Sports Award programmes. Music and theatre provide strong extra-curricular opportunities. Students can also take advantage of our excellent sporting facilities and many participate in competitive sports.

Underpinning this, we are proud of our student-centred approach that ensures that all students feel valued and cared for.

Not only is Dallam in a beautiful setting, part-way between the historic city of Lancaster and the market town of Kendal, our community is easily reached from major airports and cities such as Manchester and Liverpool. There is also a direct train from London to Lancaster that takes a little over two and a half hours.

As a co-educational school with state boarding, we are a learning community of local and international students and we embrace the internationalism of the IB programmes. Dallam Boarding provides a caring and secure home to many of our international students. A dedicated team of boarding staff provide for the pastoral needs of our boarders and has helped to create an environment in which young people are valued and their individual needs catered for.

Ecole Des Roches

(Founded 1899)

Head of School
Mr David Johnson

DP coordinator
Mrs Fatima Dif

Status Private

Boarding/day Mixed

Gender Coeducational

Language of instruction
English, French

Authorised IB programmes
DP

Age Range 6 – 18 years

Number of pupils enrolled
320

Address
295 avenue Edmond Demolins
27130 Verneuil d'Avre et d'Iton
FRANCE

TEL +33 (0) 232 6040 00

Email
ecoledesroches@
ecoledesroches.com

Website
www.ecoledesroches.com

Founded in 1899, École des Roches is an international coeducational day and boarding school located on a spacious wooded campus in the heart of the beautiful Normandy countryside. We welcome students aged 6 years to 18 years from 52 nationalities to our Primary, Middle and High school.

École des Roches offers several programmes: French curriculum, International curriculum with the IB Diploma Programme, French as a Foreign Language short stays or full academic year, and also summer and winter intensive language courses.

International Baccalaureate Diploma Programme

In response to the needs of its increasingly international community, École des Roches has been an IB World School since 2016, offering the International Baccalaureate Diploma Programme in English.

In high school, the school offers a special programme of studies to prepare our students for the International Baccalaureate, with the goal of preparing them for the top universities around the world. We also advise our students in their career choices and accompany them in the university admissions process.

In Ecole des Roches, the IB Diploma Programme is characterised by:

- Its academic breadth, depth and rigour
- The respect in which it is held by universities worldwide
- The attention it gives to international awareness and the development of socially responsible citizens of the world

In addition to preparing the students for the IB Diploma, all of our students are encouraged to take advantage of the school context, heritage and resources to improve in their French language proficiency, whether that be at a beginner, intermediate or advanced level.

Boarding Life

Our Boarding School consists of 7 residences called Maisons, which are large historic Normandy houses. Boys and girls are divided by age range in these single-sex boarding houses. Foreign students are accommodated with French-speaking students in pleasant and recently renovated rooms. The educational focus of École des Roches from its origins has been to offer educational, psychological and emotional support to our students in order to promote their intellectual and personal development throughout their schooling achievement. Extracurricular activities range from horseback riding and golf to karting on the school's course located on campus.

Admissions

Students can apply to our school year-round based on availability. Students must submit two years' of school reports, a letter of recommendation as well as a letter of motivation. For further information about admissions or to schedule a tour of the school, please contact us at ecoledesroches@ecoledesroches.com.

Ecole Internationale Bilingue Le Cartésien (EIBC)

(Founded 1997)

Chef d'établissement
Steve Mbikayi Mabuluki

DP coordinator
Armand Ngolomingi Mudiandambu

Status Private

Boarding/day Day

Gender Coeducational

Language of instruction
French, English

Authorised IB programmes
DP

Age Range 3 – 19

Number of pupils enrolled
500

Address
34, 7ème Rue, Q. Industriel
Limete
Kinshasa | **DEMOCRATIC REPUBLIC OF THE CONGO**

TEL +243812621704

Email
stevembikayi@yahoo.fr

Website
www.lecartesien.cd

L'Ecole Internationale Bilingue Le Cartésien (EIBC) est une école du monde du baccalauréat international autorisée à dispenser le programme du diplôme et candidate au programme primaire. C'est une école de choix qui attire les familles locales et étrangères de Kinshasa qui sont à la recherche d'une éducation progressive dans un environnement scolaire mixte, non confessionnel et non racial.

Le Cartésien est membre de l'International Schools association ''ISA'' ainsi que la Société des Ecoles du monde du Baccalauréat International du Québec et de la francophonie ''SEBIQ''.

Le Cartésien est une école qui prône une éducation holistique et sur mesure pour les enfants voulant avoir un profil exceptionnel dans leur vie. C'est un milieu de brassage culturel où se côtoient et se tolèrent, dans un environnement ouvert et inclusif, les enfants de plusieurs nationalités.

Notre philosophie est la Formation de l'esprit et du corps des véritables citoyens du monde : altruistes, tolérants, dotés d'un bagage intellectuel solide; multiculturels, respectueux de l'autre et capables de contribuer à l'évolution de notre monde.

Cette philosophie prône la problématisation des leçons qui permet à l'élève de construire son savoir (constructivisme et recherche personnelle) : Nous mettons à la disposition des élèves des questions ouvertes favorisant les débats en vue d'atteindre l'appropriation et appréhension des notions envisagées dans divers contextes tant locaux qu'internationaux. Cela se fait soit individuellement soit en groupe. Nous prenons également en compte les spécificités de chaque élève en vue d'une mise à niveau obligatoire. En sus, nous intégrons les réalités mondiales, continentales et régionales (en rapport avec les pays de la CEAC, de la SADC, du CIRGIL) ainsi que celles qui se rapportent à la RDC et ses provinces, de manière particulière. Ces réalités peuvent concerner la politique des échanges culturels. La journée de cultures autochtones permet à la communauté scolaire de réfléchir sur les situations ayant trait aux problèmes locaux, culturels, économiques, politiques, …

Enfin, nous procédons aux évaluations diagnostiques, formatives et sommatives pour atteindre les objectifs spécifiques d'apprentissage. Dans ces approches nous démontrons l'importance de chaque élément en vue d'ouvrir les élèves à toutes ces entités en favorisant la connaissance sur les autres ; ce qui permet de former des citoyens du monde.

École Jeannine Manuel - Lille

(Founded 1992)

Head of School
Constance Devaux

DP coordinator
Nicola French

Status Non-Profit Private

Boarding/day Mixed

Gender Coeducational

Language of instruction
French, English

Authorised IB programmes
DP

Age Range 3 – 18 years

Number of pupils enrolled
970

Fees
Day: €5,301
Boarding: €14,145 – €21,465IB
Classes €18,500

Address
418 bis rue Albert Bailly
Marcq-en-Baroeul
59700 | FRANCE

TEL +33 3 20 65 90 50

FAX +33 3 20 98 06 41

Email
admissions-lille@ejm.net

Website
www.ecolejeanninemanuel.org

École Jeannine Manuel Lille is a non-profit nursery-12 coeducational school founded in 1992. As the sister school of École Jeannine Manuel Paris, they have the same educational project and the same mission: promote international understanding through bilingual (French/English) education. An associated UNESCO school, École Jeannine Manuel Lille is the only non-denominational independent school in Nord-Pas-de-Calais, with almost 1000 pupils representing 50 nationalities and every major cultural tradition. The school's academic excellence matches its diversity: École Jeannine Manuel Lille achieves excellent performances, both at the French Baccalaureate and the International Baccalaureate. The school is accredited by the French Ministry of Education, the International Baccalaureate Organization (IBO), the Council of International Schools (CIS) and the New England Association of Schools and Colleges (NEASC).

The school campus extends over 3,5 hectares and includes a boarding house, a restaurant, two football fields, a multi-sport room, and high standard sports facilities and equipment. The boarding house welcomes 120 pupils from 6th to 12th grades.

Each year, École Jeannine Manuel Lille welcomes non-French speaking students. Over the years École Jeannine Manuel has developed a program to suit the needs of these students, for whom the emotional challenge of relocation is often as great than its academic challenge. Thanks to their French teachers and their methods, the students will be fluent in French in a few months.

The lower and middle school follow the French national curriculum with several exceptions: English is taught every day and, in middle school, experimental sciences, history and geography are taught in English. The curriculum is enriched at all levels, not only with a more advanced English language and literature curriculum, but also, for example, with Chinese language instruction (compulsory in grades 3-4-5), an integrated science programme in lower school, and independent research projects in middle school.

In upper school, tenth graders follow the French national curriculum, albeit taught 50% in French and 50% in English. In 11th grade, pupils choose between the French track (international option of the French baccalaureate (OIB)) and the International Baccalaureate Diploma Programme (IBDP). Approximately 25% of our pupils opt for the IBDP. (Please note that, since the IBDP does not receive any government subsidies, its tuition is three times the French track tuition.) In 12th grade, students receive the High School Diploma.

Admission

Although admission is competitive, every effort is made to reserve space for international applicants, including children of families who expect to remain in France for a limited period of time and wish to combine a cultural immersion in French education with the ability to re-enter their own school systems and excel.

(Founded 1954)

Principal
Jérôme Giovendo

DP coordinator
Sabine Hurley

Status Non-Profit Private

Boarding/day Day

Gender Coeducational

Language of instruction
English, French

Authorised IB programmes
DP

Age Range 4 – 18 years

Number of pupils enrolled
2400

Fees
Day: €6,417 – €6,765IB Classes
€21,390

Address
70 rue du Théâtre
Paris
75015 | FRANCE

TEL +33 1 44 37 00 80
FAX +33 1 45 79 06 66

Email
admissions@ejm.net

Website
www.ecolejeanninemanuel.org

École Jeannine Manuel is a non-profit pre-K-12 coeducational school founded in 1954 with the mission to promote international understanding through bilingual (French/English) education. An associated UNESCO school, École Jeannine Manuel welcomes pupils representing 80 nationalities and every major cultural tradition. The school's academic excellence matches its diversity: École Jeannine Manuel is regularly ranked among the top five French high schools (state and independent) for its overall academic performance (ranked first for seven consecutive years). The school is accredited by the French Ministry of Education, the International Baccalaureate Organization (IBO), the Council of International Schools (CIS) and the New England Association of Schools and Colleges (NEASC).

Each year, the school welcomes more than 100 new non-French speaking pupils. These students, key to the cultural diversity of the school, are enrolled in an adaptation programme where they receive intensive and immersive French tuition tailored to their individual level.

The lower and middle school follow the French national curriculum with several exceptions: English is taught every day and, in middle school, experimental sciences, history and geography are taught in English. The curriculum is enriched at all levels, not only with a more advanced English language and literature curriculum, but also, for example, with Chinese language instruction (compulsory in grades 3-4-5), an integrated science programme in lower school, and independent research projects in middle school.

In upper school, tenth graders follow the French national curriculum, albeit taught 50% in French and 50% in English. In 11th grade, pupils choose between the French track (international option of the French baccalaureate (OIB)) and the International Baccalaureate Diploma Programme (DP). Approximately 25% of our pupils opt for the DP. (Please note that, since the DP does not receive any government subsidies, its tuition is three times the French track tuition.) In 12th grade, students receive the High School Diploma.

Over the past three years, approximately 20% of our graduating class have gone to US colleges or universities, 48% chose the UK or Canada, 37% entered the French higher education system, and the balance pursued their education all over the world.

Admission

Although admission is competitive and applications typically exceed available spaces by a ratio of 7:1, every effort is made to reserve space for international applicants, including children of families who expect to remain in France for a limited period of time and wish to combine a cultural immersion in French education with the ability to re-enter their own school systems and excel.

INTERNATIONAL
SCHOOL EST.1906

(Founded 1906)

General Director
Mr. Nicolas Catsicas

DP coordinator
Mr. David Mills

Status Private

Boarding/day Mixed

Gender Coeducational

Language of instruction
French, English

Authorised IB programmes
DP

Age Range 3 – 18

Number of pupils enrolled
600

Fees
Day: CHF12,200 – CHF25,400
Weekly Boarding: CHF51,700 – CHF59,800
Boarding: CHF64,600 – CHF72,700

Address
Chemin de Rovéréaz 20
CP 161
1000 Lausanne 12 |
SWITZERLAND

TEL +41 21 654 65 00
FAX +41 21 654 65 05

Email
info@ensr.ch

Website
www.ensr.ch
www.ensrswiss.cn

Ecole Nouvelle de la Suisse Romande (ENSR) / International Boarding School of Lausanne (IBSL) Quality of Education since 1906

We offer

- Complete schooling from Kindergarten, including a Montessori section, to Senior school in bilingual French-English or in English
- Swiss Maturity in French
- International Baccalaureate Diploma programme in French, English or bilingual French-English
- All Cambridge, Goethe-Institut and Cervantes examinations
- Boarding facilities
- Camps (Ski, Easter, Summer, Windsurf, Fall)
- Holidays: day care for children aged from 3 to 7 years old

Languages

The main language can be either French or English, the other is introduced at the age of 3 years old in order to be very quickly assimilated.

German is introduced in year 4 (9 y.o.). Introduction classes to Spanish, Italian and Latin are proposed in the Middle School (10-14 y.o.). Other languages are offered in High School (14-19 y.o.).

French or English for beginners are provided for new students, beginners and those requiring further support.

Summer Camp

Our summer camp takes place from July to mid-August for children aged from 9 to 18 years old.

Mornings, 9 am to 12 pm: French and English classes (elementary, intermediate and intensive).

Students are placed according to their language level in classes of 4 to 7 students.

Afternoons and weekends: sports, leisure, cultural activities and trips.

Multisports formula (only sports, no language classes).

Boarding School

Boarding facilities are offered for students as from Middle school, year 5 (10 years of age).

Our boarding school provides a friendly and warm atmosphere offering security, care and support.

Boarding is offered for either 5 or 7 days per week.

Ecole Oasis Internationale

(Founded 1994)

Principal
Mrs. Esmat Lamei

PYP coordinator
Mrs. Imane Radwan

MYP coordinator
Mr. Omar El Sarky

DP coordinator
Fatma Hussein

CP coordinator
Fatma Hussein

Status Private

Boarding/day Day

Gender Coeducational

Language of instruction
French

Authorised IB programmes
PYP, MYP, DP, CP

Age Range 3 – 18

Number of pupils enrolled
1340

Address
Zahraa El Maadi
Quarter no 3 and no 7 Part A & B
Cairo | **EGYPT**

TEL +20 2 2516 2608
FAX +20 2 2754 5280

Email
admission@oasisdemaadi.com
oasis.edu@oasisdemaadi.com

Website
www.oasisdemaadi.com

Being the first private trilingual school in Egypt and the first one allowed to offer the four programs of the International Baccalaureate in French, Oasis International School makes it a point to always put forward a quality education enabling students to thrive whilst developing their natural curiosity and open-mindedness.

Throughout our thirty years of educational service, we have achieved a high success rate having witnessed the graduation of thirteen generations of classes and made their way to universities. A great number of our students have travelled abroad to study in the most prestigious universities in countries like The United States of America, The United Kingdom, Canada and many others.

Oasis closely blends teaching pedagogy with technology. Thereby, the school implements advanced aspects of technology, such as the IPad One to One program in order to facilitate meaningful constructivist learning. Our job as educators is to be innovative with our teaching methods to make learning an enjoyable experience. The project has indeed supported student engagement and motivation through creative activities on campus, community service projects, and through Adventure Learning. In this context, students have the opportunity to participate in national as well as in international trips in which they learn to put into practice their theoretical knowledge. Under the headline and values of community service projects, patronage of a public school which the entire school community participates in.

Our school mission has also improved teacher productivity while facilitating communication between both parties, thanks to the application of differential instruction and positive discipline.

Last but not least, the school attributes its success mostly to the yearly extracurricular and academic activities that are being offered. A high percentage of its students participate every year in activities such as the Model United Nations, The Francophonie Forum and the Model Arab League in Egypt and abroad. In all of these activities, the IB Learner Profile that has been implemented over the years has made students better communicators and has helped them with their presentation and their negotiation skills. Emphasis is on both international mindedness and self-esteem. The future is looking good now that even some of our alumni have decided to join our staff after finishing their university studies.

Eerde International Boarding School Netherlands

(Founded 1934)

Director CEO
Niki Holterman

IGCSE principal
Ydo Jousma

DP coordinator
Aaron Lane

Status Private

Boarding/day Mixed

Gender Coeducational

Language of instruction
English

Authorised IB programmes
DP

Age Range 4 – 18

Number of pupils enrolled 70

Fees
Primary €7,500
Middle School Day €19,100
High School IGCSE and IB Day €22,300
Boarding: €28,300 (excl. academic fee)

Address
Kasteellaan 1
Ommen
PJ 7731 | NETHERLANDS

TEL +31 529 451452
FAX +31 529 456377

Email
admission@eerdeibs.nl

Website
www.eerde.nl

"Where students become family"
Eerde International Boarding School is situated at a historical estate with an abundance of green lands surrounding it, assuring a clean and healthy living environment. Our campus knows several buildings of which one is a castle dating from the year MDCCXV (1715). Moreover, located in a country famous for its innovative trade mentality, water management and quality of life, The Netherlands is the perfect gateway for pupils to experience the best Europe has to offer.

Eerde provides a holistic learning environment in which students are guided to develop their full potential. We do so by inspiring academic excellence, stimulating inquiring minds and developing our students as active members in their community. Furthermore, we promote a healthy and balanced lifestyle that is a combination of physical exercise, fresh and nutritious meals and social-emotional wellbeing. At Eerde, students will gain experience and confidence to become compassionate and capable global citizens.

Small classes, excellent staff/pupil ratios and the international environment provide opportunities to succeed at international examinations; allowing access to university and further education worldwide. Our enthusiastic team of international educators provide students with the tools and guidance to learn and grow. Mentors closely monitor the progress of each pupil – both in academic achievements and personal development. Our academic programmes are designed to empower students to innovate and be creative in their own ways.

In boarding we stimulate boarders to develop a sense of responsibility and care for one another. Boarders (age 12 and above) share a double room and are looked after by boarding parents, who are dedicated to creating a happy and safe home. Boarders can join a variety of activities offered during weekends. All members of our boarding community treat each other with respect, honesty and tolerance.

Head of School
Dr. Paul Ellis

DP coordinator
Dona Jones

Status Private

Boarding/day Boarding

Gender Coeducational

Language of instruction
English

Authorised IB programmes
DP

Age Range 16 – 19

Number of pupils enrolled
188

Fees
IB Diploma £42,000 (£14,000 per term)

Address
Pullens Lane
Headington
Oxfordshire
OX3 0DT | UK

TEL +41 (0) 43 430 4095

Email
iaeurope@ef.com

Website
www.ef.com/academy

EF Academy International Boarding Schools prepares students for a global future with an exceptional high school education in the US or UK. At EF Academy, we believe in every student's ability to succeed. We empower them to do so through our renowned curricula, as well as quality one-on-one relationships with teachers and mentors alike. With a student body made up of 75 different nationalities, multilingualism and intercultural exchange are built into every course and our students live the IB ethos every single day.

The School

This IB World School is situated in the city of Oxford, renowned for its scholastic tradition and rich cultural and architectural heritage. EF Academy students join Oxford's vibrant academic community, which attracts leading scholars from around the world. 10 minutes from the city center, the campus has spacious classrooms, modern science labs and inviting lounges. Students also benefit from access to the library and sports center of nearby Oxford Brookes University. Students live in on-campus residences with their classmates and house parents. House parents look after the students and ensure that they are safe and comfortable when they are not in class.

Academics

Education at EF Academy Oxford is highly individualized. Students follow the IB Diploma Programme and benefit from an enrichment program that includes visits to Oxford University lectures and laboratories. Our students are supported by faculty members who offer guidance, giving students the ultimate pre-university experience.

University Placements

EF Academy Oxford graduates have gone on to attend universities such as the University of Oxford, London School of Economics, Imperial College London, the University of St. Andrews and Durham University. All of our students receive acceptance to university degree programs, many for highly competitive courses such as economics, engineering or medicine.

Dedicated university advisors work together with students to help them prepare the best applications possible. Our advisors also support students who are interested in applying to universities in the US or in their home country.

Student Life

Students at EF Academy Oxford have access to a wide range of co-curricular activities. From subject-specific academic groups and competitions to sports and arts, there is an option for every student. The school's activities coordinator also arranges excursions for students on the weekends so they have the opportunity to experience the culture in and around Oxford and other parts of the UK.

(Founded 1941)

Head of School Benjamin Hunter

Head of International Studies Program Margaret Peyrard

MYP coordinator Christine Collie

DP coordinator Wayne Hodgkinson

Status Private

Boarding/day Mixed

Gender Coeducational

Language of instruction English, French

Authorised IB programmes MYP, DP

Age Range 3 – 18

Number of pupils enrolled 1320

Fees €18,250 – €38,700

Address
46 Avenue Eglé
78600 Maisons-Laffitte | FRANCE

TEL +33 1 39 62 81 75

Email admissions@ermitage.fr

Website www.ermitage.fr

Ermitage International School of France is a bilingual K-12 school located in the historic town of Maisons-Laffitte, just 20km west of Paris. With a student body of approximately 1300 students, representing over 50 nationalities, Ermitage offers student-centered learning, with a focus on internationalism, leadership and service. Weekday and full-time boarding is available in traditional French residences.

- International Studies Program (IBMYP & IBDP)
  185 students enrolled, offering English instruction, with French lessons from a beginner to native-level.
- French Primaire, Collège & Lycée (French bac, OIB)
  1135 students enrolled, instructed in French.
- IBPYP Candidate School (offered as of Fall 2020)

Middle Years Programme (MYP) 1-5

The Middle Years Programme provides a broad and balanced range of subjects allowing students to discover and develop their interests. The MYP encourages students to be active learners, asking challenging questions, as well as developing a strong sense of identity, cultural understanding and communication skills. The MYP curriculum is inquiry-directed and students take appropriate risks while exploring themes in and outside of the classroom.

During the MYP, our team of experienced teachers accompany and guide students on their journey to becoming IB Learners. Emphasis is placed on individual growth and encouraging students to reflect upon their classroom projects and co-curricular initiatives. Teachers facilitate students' learning and help prepare them for the rigorous demands of the IB Diploma Programme.

IB Diploma 1-2

Following the MYP, students enter the IBDP prepared and motivated after gaining experience with character-based projects and developing their critical thinking skills in a supportive learning environment.

Within the dynamic IB environment, students are encouraged to think critically and become independent learners, coming prepared to class, presenting the material and being coached by their teachers. Assignments are demanding, but by graduation the calibre of research, writing and project management skills will be exceptional. The balance between academic work and co-curricular activities allows students to tailor the programme according to their interests and develop an impressive university profile in the process.

Round Square

As a Global Member of the Round Square organization, Ermitage is connected to like-minded schools, offering a variety of service-learning trips, global exchanges and leadership conferences.

Students also discover their interests outside of the classroom through a daily co-curricular program with the opportunity to initiate projects, participate in leadership experiences, sports and more while connecting with local and global communities.

What sets us apart

- Student-centered approach with a balance of academics and character-developing projects
- Opportunities for student leadership via well-rounded co-curricular and CAS programs
- Teachers are approachable and serve as coaches, guiding students individually
- Students learn in engaging ways both inside and outside of the classroom
- Learning environment is interactive and collaborative, located in a lovely family-friendly suburb of Paris close to historic sites and nature
- In 2017, the national daily newspaper, Le Figaro, placed L'Ermitage second in the national rankings for the best performing high schools in France.

Eyüboğlu Schools

(Founded 1985)

Head of School
Ms Aysegül Erbil

PYP coordinator
Mevce Selek

MYP coordinator
Gülsah Cekic

DP coordinator
Oguz Günenc

Status Private

Boarding/day Day

Gender Coeducational

Language of instruction
Turkish, English

Authorised IB programmes
PYP, MYP, DP

Age Range 3 – 18

Number of pupils enrolled
3009

Fees
TL36,000 – TL57,500

Address
Esenevler Mah
Dr Rüstem Eyüboglu sok 3,
Ümraniye
Istanbul
34762 | TURKEY

TEL +90 216 522 12 12
FAX +90 216 335 71 98

Email
eyuboglu@eyuboglu.k12.tr

Website
www.eyuboglu.k12.tr

Eyüboğlu Educational Institutions are a group of private, coeducational schools founded in 1985. Eyüboglu Educational Institutions (EEI) is comprised of six kindergartens, three elementary schools, 3 middle, 1 high school, and a science and technology high school that offers a bilingual education to students from aged 3 to 18. All Eyüboglu schools are accredited or re-accredited by CIS. School philosophy is based on academic excellence, internationalism, intercultural and social awareness. Eyüboğlu schools were the first Turkish institutions to achieve authorization to offer all three IB programmes: Diploma, Middle Years and Primary Years Programme. With this unique feature, the schools' internationally recognized high standards of academic excellence enables Eyüboğlu graduates to further their studies in the finest universities, both locally in the US, Canada, UK and other prestigious universities around the world.

In addition to a heavy focus on IB qualifications, there is a strong EAL program in all sections, leading our students to UCLES and TOEFL English proficiency examinations. Starting from grade 5, German and Spanish are taught as a second foreign language. Elective subjects offer more intensive and specialized study in the fields of social sciences, sciences, arts, music, technology and astronomy. Individualized instruction is part of the curriculum. There is a wide variety of extracurricular activities in art, music, humanities, technology and drama. Besides traditional sports activities, archery, golf, horse riding, fencing, swimming, folk dancing, and modern dance are also offered.

Teachers have an average of ten years of teaching experience, and 43% of the subject teachers hold postgraduate degrees. The average tenure at the school is seven years.

Facilities on the main campus include an arts and sports complex with a swimming pool, various art studios and sports areas for handball, volleyball, athletics, basketball, golf, archery, ballet and folk-dancing. There is a theatre hall (seating 500), a full-sized gymnasium, four smaller multi-purpose PE halls, activity rooms, four art and ceramic studios, 2 libraries with over 113,000 volumes, tennis, basketball and football courts, and a general playing field. There are 11 science laboratories. The two observatories are equipped with powerful telescopes, which enable the school and wider community to make astronomical observations.

Admission to Eyüboğlu is offered on the basis of a school administered interview up to grade 3 and a written examination and interview for grade 3 upwards. Entrance to the middle and high school is in accordance with Turkish Ministry of Education regulations.

GEMS Modern Academy – Dubai

(Founded 1986)

Principal
Mrs. Nargish Khambatta

DP coordinator
Dr. Sunipa Guha Neogi

Status Private

Boarding/day Mixed

Gender Co-educational

Language of instruction
English

Authorised IB programmes
DP

Age Range 16 – 18

Number of pupils enrolled
160

Fees
AED6,835 per month

Address
PO Box 53663
Nad al Sheeba 3,4
Dubai | **UNITED ARAB EMIRATES**

TEL +971 4 326 3339
FAX +971 4 326 3402

Email
info_mhs@gemsedu.com

Website
www.gemsmodernacademy-dubai.com

In keeping with the vision of GEMS Education the founder and chairman, Mr. Sunny Varkey, GEMS Modern Academy (GMA) assures every student a world-class education that is wholesome and exciting. Spread over 120,000 square meters, this state-of-the-art institution is located in the heart of Dubai and has been making its mark on the local and global education scene for the last 33 years. The school is recognized and accredited by Ministry of Education, Dubai, UAE, the Council for Indian School Certificate Examinations (ICSE – New Delhi, India) and the International Baccalaureate.

'Modern' as it is fondly called, lives up to its name as it strives ceaselessly to nurture 21st-century learners who will become active, sensitive and responsible world citizens. Our educational philosophy aims at making students independent and lifelong learners who will contribute positively to society. The faculty and management work passionately to keep the balance between modern educational demands and the wholesome traditional values that the institution embodies.

In addition to being rated as an 'Outstanding' school for eight consecutive years by the Knowledge and Human Development Authority of Dubai, the school has also been awarded the coveted Hamdan Award for Distinguished Academic Excellence and School Administration. The highly qualified and committed faculty ensures that all pupils at Modern strive to reach their goals and prepares them to take their place in the world. Modern's alumni receive admission to Ivy League and other world renowned universities and the school boasts of a 100% placement record.

Modern offers the IBDP to students of grades 11 and 12, with twenty-three individual subject options available. We are very pleased with the achievements of our four graduating batches since 2016. May 2019 batch achieved average of 34.7 points with 100% diploma pass rate, with the topper securing a perfect score of 45 points. This balance between strong academic performance and fantastic experiential outcomes from areas such as CAS is a hallmark of our growing Diploma Programme.

Modern also has a unique advantage that sets it apart from other IB schools – our bespoke "Bridge Programme". This consists of 13 modules designed and delivered by our teachers prior to students entering the Diploma Programme. The Bridge helps students develop a clear idea of the philosophy behind the Diploma Programme and the skills needed to be successful in it. This is accomplished through modules such as "Critical Thinking", "Global Citizenship", "Academic Honesty" and "Investigative Science" which are directly linked to key IB themes like the learner profile, approaches to teaching and learning, international-mindedness, and CAS. By proactively engaging students in these interactive modules, we aim to ensure that they hit the ground running in the Diploma Programme and aspire to be lifelong learners afterward.

German International School Beirut

(Founded 1954)

President of the Board
Omar Salloum

DP coordinator
Petra Machlab

Status Private

Boarding/day Day

Gender Coeducational

Language of instruction
English

Authorised IB programmes
DP

Age Range 3 – 18

Number of pupils enrolled
1200

Fees
Day: US$7,000 (€6,145)

Address
PO Box 11-3888
Bliss Street, Ras Beirut
Beirut | **LEBANON**

TEL +961 1 740523/+961 5 803787
FAX +961 1 740523/+961 5 803787

Email
admissions@dsb.edu.lb

Website
www.dsb.edu.lb

Our mission is to create lifelong learners who possess the competencies, confidence, and knowledge to meet the challenges that face them. Living in a diverse society and globalized world, we work on graduating students who are contributing members of society, tolerant of others and empowered to shape their own future.

The German International School Beirut maintains its progress through constant improvement in both structural and curricular aspects, having the students at the top of its pyramid of priority. Our motto is "Inspire-Educate-Support".

Inspire

One of our main goals has always been to inspire our students to follow their passion. We support our students to decide what course their life will take at such an early stage, and so to aid their decision we try and expose them to as many activities and experiences as possible. From our balanced and eclectic subject offerings to our wide range of CAS projects and experiences, we want our students to have the most fulfilling educational process possible. As such, we've made full use of technology in order to turn our classrooms into informational ecosystems that allow students to freely exchange ideas and take advantage of interactive media to truly immerse themselves in their work. While the written word is the cornerstone of education, we also want our students to learn with sights and sounds, and their state-of-the-art PC's they have the world at their fingertips. Beyond that, we strongly believe in going green, and our technology initiatives have helped us work towards a totally green campus. We hope that our efforts to promote environmental awareness can really inspire our students to help make the world a better place.

Educate: Curricular Aspects

Our school offers a variety of academic programs. Aside from the IB Diploma Programme, our school also offers the Lebanese National Programme as well as the official German Language Diploma (DSD I, II). Each curriculum strives to impart students with the necessary skills and knowledge they need to excel in academics. Our teaching methods emphasize collaborative learning and critical thinking, and we have developed a highly skilled student body as a result. We also want our students to have a truly international education and as such we offer a variety of language courses in English, German, Arabic, French, and Spanish.

Support: School Community and atmosphere

Inspiring people is all about making them believe they can do something, and we want our students to truly believe in themselves. Our school fosters a diverse, supportive environment that encourages students to be both expressive and patient. Missteps and false starts are part of every process, and our students need to be given the freedom to grow freely and safely. Overall, we want to give our students the setting in which they can reach their fullest academic, emotional, physical, and spiritual potential.

Global Paradigm International School

Member of El Rabwa Network

Principal
Sanaa Shoukri

DP coordinator
Omnia Mostafa

Status Private

Boarding/day Day

Gender Coeducational

Language of instruction
English

Authorised IB programmes
DP

Address
First Settlement
Block K1, Sector 8
New Cairo
16834 | EGYPT

TEL +20 222 461 809/10/12
FAX +20 222 461 816

Email
info@gpschool-eg.com

Website
www.gpschool-eg.com

Global Paradigm International School is committed to preparing distinguished students from Pre-K to G12 to excel in a future of their choice. In Global Paradigm International School the love and lure for learning is nurtured and fostered in a way where the individual acquires confidence and competence. In an enriched diverse community of students, teachers and parents, we at GPIS value every individual as an independent thinker and decision maker.

Global Paradigm International School is a private international school owned by El Rabwa Company for Integrated Educational Services. The school follows the Common Core Learning Standards and Framework as well as the IB Diploma Curriculum. It is accredited by both the North Central Association Commission on Accreditation and School Improvement (NCA CASI) under the auspices of Cognia, and the Middle States Association Commissions on Elementary and Secondary Schools (MSA-CESS). GPIS has been an IB World School since March 2015 and offers the Diploma Programme for 18 subjects at both the standard and high level.

The school occupies an area of about 8300 M2, housing 44 spacious classrooms providing the latest technology in teaching methods with smart boards operating in all classrooms. There are staff rooms, administrative offices, 3 Science Labs, 2 Computer labs, 2 music rooms, 3 art rooms, a 200-seat auditorium, a library, a cafeteria, a picnic area, a multi-purpose court, a, 2 soccer fields, A basketball field, multi-purpose field, a gymnasium, 3 playgrounds and a swimming pool. Playgrounds, sport court surfaces and outdoor areas are covered with artificial shock-absorbent turf.

At GPIS we encourage respecting differences of others yet treasuring one's own traditions and values in order to present a responsible, self-content, and an assertive global citizen. The IB Learner Profile, CAS, International-mindedness and Approaches to Teaching and Learning are the lynchpins of learning at GPIS.

(Founded 1994)

Founding Chairman
Amr Ahmed Mokhtar

PYP coordinator
Francoise Bencteux

MYP coordinator
May Waly

DP coordinator
Mona Khalil

Status Private

Boarding/day Day

Gender Coeducational

Language of instruction
French, English, Arabic

Authorised IB programmes
PYP, MYP, DP

Age Range 3 – 18

Number of pupils enrolled
1103

Fees
Day: E£94,500 – E£157,500

GPIS Giza
405, Geziret Mohamed Road
Giza | EGYPT

GPIS Zayed
2nd Neighborhood – 5th district,
Sheikh Zayed, Giza | EGYPT

TEL +20 2 01002226053/50/54

Email
info@greenlandschool.org

Website
gpis-egypt.org

Green Land – Pré Vert International Schools (GPIS-Egypt) is a member of Green Land Educational Foundation (GEF-Egypt). Since 2005, GPIS has been the only IB world school in Egypt authorized to offer all three IB programmes (IBPYP – IBMYP – IBDP) in two languages beside Arabic (French and English languages).

GPIS is the only school in Egypt that holds four quality assurance certificates ISO 9002:1994 since 1997 until the latest update BS EN ISO 9001:2015 from the British Standard Institution BSI – UK.

GPIS has been granted several awards from the International Gold Star for Quality from BID in Spain in 2002, followed by the Robert Blackburn Award by the IBO in 2007 for best Community and Services project in IBAEM. GPIS also was shortlisted out of 200 applications for the International School Awards 2019 (International Impact Award).

GPIS students' results in their bilingual IB Diploma are higher than the world average in all subjects. Starting from GPIS first promotion in session 2007, 14% of students' results were among the top 5% IB diploma students' results worldwide, which put them in the top 200 students; ending with session 2019, GPIS students' pass rate of full IB bilingual diploma was 100% with an average 8% higher than world average, where 92% of the students scored 6-7/7 in Group 2 subjects and more than 70% of the students scored A & B in their Extended Essay.

GEF-Egypt initiated a pilot project with the Egyptian Ministry of Education and the IBO in 2014 to apply the three IB programmes in Arabic in two governmental schools (Egyptian International Schools – EIS). One of the schools was established in 2014, authorized for two programmes IBPYP, IBMYP and a candidate school for DP to become the first governmental school in Africa authorized for the three IB programmes. The second school was inaugurated in October 2018.

(Founded 2007)

Principal Dr. Allan Weston

Head of Secondary
Peter Fremaux

Head of Primary
Andrew Mitchell

PYP coordinator Jill Shadbolt

MYP coordinator Chris Cooke

DP coordinator Sarah Atienza

CP coordinator Mike Worth

Status Private

Boarding/day Day

Gender Coeducational

Language of instruction
English

Authorised IB programmes
PYP, MYP, DP, CP

Age Range 3 – 18

Number of pupils enrolled 1183

Fees
Pre-K: AED31,750
KG 1: AED36,750
KG 2: AED38,750
Grade 1 to 6: AED49,732
Grade 7 to 10: AED62,440
Grade 11 and 12: AED76,315

Address
Dubai Investments Park
Dubai | **UNITED ARAB EMIRATES**

TEL +971 (0)4 885 6600

Email admissions@gischool.ae

Website www.gischool.ae

Greenfield International School (GIS), a member of the highly regarded Taaleem group, opened its doors in 2007, and since then has promoted and inspired the limitless potential of young minds of diverse backgrounds. We are fully authorised as an International Baccalaureate Continuum World School and offer the IB Curriculum from Pre-Kindergarten through to Grade 12. We were also one of the first schools in the Middle East that successfully piloted the IB's Career-related Programme and each year our number of graduates from this programme grow. With our students coming from over 80 different countries, we are a truly international school, rich with cultural diversity. The spirit of internationalism is reflected in the philosophy of the International Baccalaureate (IB) Curriculum, as well as extracurricular activities (ECA) we offer our students. This approach enriches our students' minds, their skills and talents through collaborative approaches to learning. Our holistic education allows students to not only achieve excellent academic results but also to thrive outside the classrooms by developing their talents and communication skills through extracurricular activities. As committed IB practitioners, our team are experienced international educators and the driving force behind the school's academic and pastoral success. Our classrooms are vibrant student-centred environments where inquiry-based approaches are balanced with direct teaching. Our teachers actively strive to encourage children's natural curiosity and love of learning. They take great care to support each child's social and emotional growth. We also know how important it is to build strong parent-teacher relationships as we recognise what a pivotal role the teacher plays in the child's life. As a result, we encourage parents to be active participants in school life and we welcome you to be part of our many family events and class activities. As a mark of quality assurance, GIS is fully accredited by two of the world's most highly regarded accreditation bodies; the Council of International Schools (CIS) based in Europe and the New England Association of Schools and Colleges (NEASC), based in the USA. Along with the IB authorisation, the CIS and NEASC accreditation offer a guarantee of quality knowing that your school meets or exceeds international standards.

(Founded 1555)

Headmaster
Mr Douglas Robb MA, MEd

DP coordinator
Mr Darren Latchford

Status Private

Boarding/day Mixed

Gender Co-educational

Language of instruction
English

Authorised IB programmes
DP

Age Range 2 – 18

Number of pupils enrolled
500

Fees
Day: £24,140
Boarding: £36,030

Address
Cromer Road
Holt
Norfolk
NR25 6EA | UK

TEL 01263 714 614

Email
admissions@greshams.com

Website
www.greshams.com

Established in 1555, Gresham's is a vibrant, co-educational day and boarding school for children aged 2 to 18 set in 200 acres of beautiful countryside just four miles from the stunning north Norfolk coast in the East of England. The city of Norwich is within easy reach and pupils can travel from Norwich Airport to their international destination via Schiphol Airport in Amsterdam.

Gresham's is a small school where every child's strength and talents, whatever they may be, are recognised and nurtured. In 2016, we were awarded an 'Excellent' rating in all nine categories by the Independent Schools Inspectorate which is testament to our progressive academic curriculum, high quality teaching and excellent pastoral care.

We provide a broad yet rigorous curriculum combined with an extensive range of sporting and cultural opportunities. In Year 11 (16 years), students sit IGCSE and GCSE exams and in Year 12 students have the option to choose between the IB Diploma Programme or A levels. From Sixth Form pupils progress to UK and overseas universities.

Seven boarding houses provide a welcoming, home-from-home environment where all year groups support each other. Pupils joining the school immediately become part of a unique community where they will become immersed in a fulfilling and hugely varied school life, supported by our dedicated and caring team of house staff.

Our excellent facilities enable pupils to make the most of their interests and hobbies. Sir James Dyson, Founder of Dyson and Gresham's alumnus, has donated £19 million for a new centre for Science, Technology, Engineering, Arts and Mathematics (STEAM) education. The Dyson Building will be located at the heart of Gresham's School and will be completed by September 2021.

Gresham's has a tradition of producing outstanding achievers in a wide variety of fields. Old Greshamians include the poet W H Auden, hovercraft inventor Sir Christopher Cockerell, as well as more recently Oscar winning actress Olivia Colman, film director Stephen Frears and international rugby players Tom and Ben Youngs.

Groupe Scolaire la Résidence

(Founded 1982)

Heads
Mrs. Nawal and Kenza Hefiri & Mr. Nasser Hefiri

MYP coordinator
Mrs. Fatima Nassimi

Status Private

Boarding/day Day

Gender Coeducational

Language of instruction
French

Authorised IB programmes
MYP

Age Range 2 – 20

Number of pupils enrolled
3611

Address
87-89 Avenue 2 mars
Casablanca | MOROCCO

TEL +212 522 809050/51
FAX +212 22809052

Email
gsr@gsr.ac.ma

Website
www.gsr.ac.ma

Depuis sa création en 1982, le Groupe Scolaire la Résidence (GSR) place ses apprenants au centre de ses préoccupations pour former des citoyens aptes à s'adapter tant au monde qui les entoure qu'à l'échelle internationale. Conformément à sa volonté d'innover dans ses pratiques pédagogiques, l'équipe du GSR a trouvé dans les programmes (notamment le PP et le PEI) de l'IB, en 2000, cet épanouissement professionnel et personnel tant recherché, tout en respectant les exigences nationales Françaises et Marocaines. En effet, leader dans son domaine, le GSR a toujours souhaité offrir:

- Une formation d'excellence à ses apprenants, basée sur un continuum pédagogique et éducatif de la Petite Section aux classes préparatoires aux grandes écoles de commerce et d'ingénierie, quelle que soit la filière choisie (Française ou Bilingue), leur permettant de s'ouvrir à d'autres modes de réflexions et d'autres cultures tout en préservant leur identité nationale et leur inculquant des valeurs citoyennes capitales et universelles telles que l'humilité, le partage et la tolérance;
- Un accompagnement personnalisé à ses apprenants tout au long de leur parcours afin qu'ils définissent leur projet de vie en cohérence avec leurs valeurs, leurs ambitions et leurs compétences;
- un parcours riche humainement et professionnellement à ses équipes mixtes et expertes, les amenant ainsi à réfléchir régulièrement sur leurs pratiques et les faire évoluer selon les exigences mondiales.

Depuis ces cinq dernières années, le GSR a également revu toute sa politique afin de s'inscrire dans une démarche de qualité sur tous les plans pour assurer à ses apprenants des espaces adaptés à leurs besoins spécifiques et garantissant ainsi leur épanouissement global. A ce titre, des établissements ont refait peau neuve, d'autres ont vu le jour dans des zones géographiquement attractives sur Casablanca dont trois sont certifiés Haute Qualité Environnementale (HQE). Le dernier ouvert à Casa-Anfa en septembre 2018 a reçu le prix international du GREEN SOLUTIONS AWARDS 2018 et se veut un modèle innovant d'école pilote au Maroc ; un espace ouvert sur son environnement, à la fois lieu et objet d'apprentissage.

Le GSR, en tant qu'école citoyenne, partage, dans le cadre d'un partenariat avec l'Office Chérifienne de Phosphates (OCP) depuis 2011 avec une présence dans six villes nationales, son expertise afin de permettre aux enfants du personnel de ce groupe leader au Maroc, de bénéficier de la formation d'excellence dont seul le GSR a la recette.

Gymnasium am Münsterplatz

Erziehungsdepartement des Kantons Basel-Stadt

Gymnasium am Münsterplatz

Head of School
Dr. Eugen Krieger

DP coordinator
Dr. Manuel Pombo

Status State

Boarding/day Day

Gender Coeducational

Language of instruction
German, English

Authorised IB programmes
DP

Address
Münsterplatz 15
4051 Basel | SWITZERLAND

TEL +41 61 267 88 70
FAX +41 61 267 88 72

Email
gymnasium.muensterplatz@bs.ch

Website
www.gmbasel.ch

The Gymnasium am Münsterplatz, the second oldest school in Switzerland, is situated in the heart of Basel on Roman foundations opposite the cathedral. It enjoys considerable prestige in the city and commands a worldwide net of alumni whose generous donations go to support numerous extra-curricular activities in our school. The historical buildings are equipped with state-of-the-art equipment specially designed so that students can focus entirely on their studies in a dynamic modern atmosphere. Throughout the successive reforms in the educational sector over the last years, reflecting the social dynamics of our city, the school has changed considerably both within and without. Our recently installed Learning Centre allows pupils to carry out independent research under constant coaching provided by teachers and senior students. The integration of foreign-language-speaking pupils into Swiss society through the public school system is another of our major concerns.

The main objective of our Learning Support Centre is to provide individual didactic counselling, subject-specific backup courses, as well as various integrative measures for pupils with diverse educational biographies. It also aims to furnish individual, accompaniment and supervision for highly-talented pupils.

Apart from the modern foreign languages, French, English and Spanish, we also offer a choice of main elective subjects including; Latin, Greek, Spanish, English, and the combination Philosophy, Pedagogics, and Psychology. Of course, our Mathematics and Natural Science departments together with our Arts and Sports departments also furnish their necessary contribution to the education of our students.

The School has a rich and varied extra-curricular life. Every year, each of our 4th classes (11th grade) prepares and performs a drama project under the guidance of professional directors. We also have an annual Winter or Spring Ball. We have both a top-quality jazz band and a choir. Almost every year, one of our delegated teams to the National Session of the European Youth Parliament has been selected to represent Switzerland at the European Youth Parliament. We invite politicians and diplomats on a regular basis to discuss world affairs in our classrooms.

Apart from successfully preparing our students for third level education, the Gymnasium am Münsterplatz, in keeping with its humanistic tradition, places great importance on the development of individual personalities. We aim to address and promote our pupils as whole persons in their psychological, spiritual and physical integrity.

Outside our regular school programme, and our local interdisciplinary weeks, we also offer numerous activities away from Basel, such as study trips linked to the main elective subjects (Spain, Greece, Rome, UK, Vienna), annual skicamps, and concentrated study-weeks elsewhere in Switzerland.

As the first public school in Basel to be accredited in 2011, the GM has been offering the IB Diploma Programme as an ideal complement to the state gymnasium syllabus. Thanks to the great popularity of the IB Curriculum, our IB scores continue to improve every year and are well above world average, giving our students easier access to the world's leading universities.

(Founded 1862)

The Master
Mr Martin Collier MA BA PGCE

DP coordinator
Kate Brazier

Status Private

Boarding/day Mixed

Gender Co-educational

Language of instruction
English

Authorised IB programmes
DP

Age Range 11 – 18

Number of pupils enrolled
876

Fees
Day: £5,904 – £8,882 per term
Boarding: £7,643 – £12,048 per term

Address
Haileybury
Hertford
Hertfordshire
SG13 7NU | UK

TEL +44 (0)1992 706200

Email
admissions@haileybury.com

Website
www.haileybury.com

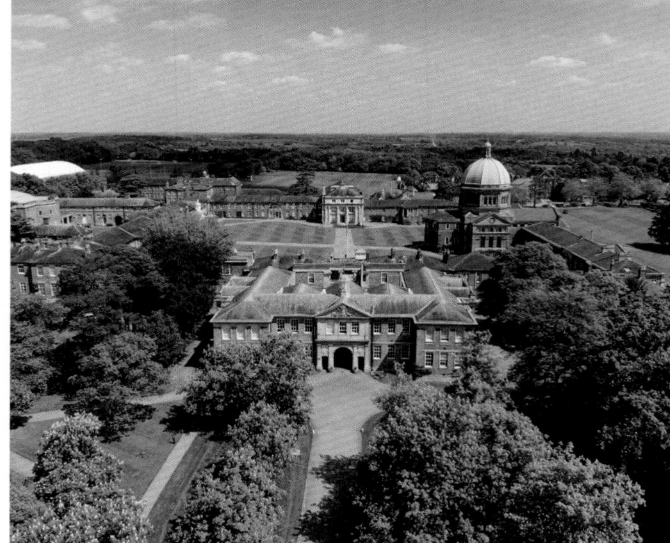

Founded in 1862, Haileybury is one of the UK's top independent co-educational boarding and day schools offering a well-rounded education to 11-18 year olds. The school is a short 20 miles north of London, nestled in over 500 acres of woodland, playing fields and superb facilities.

Academic

A key part of the school's philosophy is about empowering each child to follow their passion and build their self-confidence. Pupils are encouraged to be independent, creative and intellectually ambitious. The school offers a dedicated Lower School for Years 7 and 8, a wide range of GCSE and (I)GCSEs and the choice of the International Baccalaureate (IB) Diploma or A Level Course in Sixth Form. Haileybury is ranked Top 10 in The Times league table for co-ed independent schools which offer the IB.

Co-curricular

Haileybury offers an enormous range of co-curricular opportunities; pupils can choose from over 130 options. There is also a wide array of clubs and societies, broad enough to cater for the most eclectic individuals. From trekking in the Himalayas to debating global issues at its Model United Nations programme, to performing at the latest music or drama production. The school is among the Top 3 for 'Best for extra-curricular activities' according to the Good Schools Guide (2018).

Sport is central to Haileybury life and the school has an outstanding reputation for sport. The school is regularly selected as one of the top 100 secondary schools in the UK for its cricket provision by The Cricketer's Good School Guide.

Boarding

The Independent School's Inspectorate describes the quality of boarding at Haileybury as excellent. The houses lie at the heart of a Haileybury education and have done so for over 150 years. They are vibrant, happy, productive and homely communities where lifelong bonds are formed. The school believes that a caring environment is crucial to happiness and fulfilment. For those who board, Haileybury is like a home-from-home, warm and friendly where each and every child is supported to develop their confidence and to help them find their identity, embracing failings as much as successes in their personal journey of discovery.

HAYAH International Academy حياة

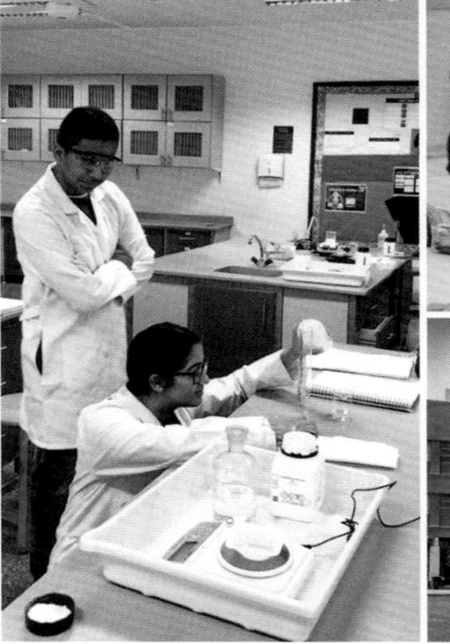

(Founded 2003)

Head of School
Abeya Fathy

PYP coordinator
Shymaa Elkotb

DP coordinator
Omneya Hamdy

Status Private

Boarding/day Day

Gender Coeducational

Language of instruction
English

Authorised IB programmes
PYP, DP

Number of pupils enrolled
1315

Fees
$10,242 *

Address
South of Police Academy
5th District
New Cairo | EGYPT

TEL +202 25373000/3333

Email
admission@hayahacademy.com

Website
www.hayahacademy.com

Hayah International Academy is committed to create and maintain an environment that fosters and enriches the personal and academic growth of each student. Hayah empowers students to live with purpose, honor their cultural identity, respect diversity, and serve humanity by positively impacting local and global communities.

Hayah International Academy is a distinguished entity founded on the belief that every child is creative, special, and capable of achieving outstanding results if provided with the proper support. Hayah provides a wide selection of educational programs and extracurricular activities aiming to generate well rounded students and promoting social, academic and physical development.

The school campus is located on a land lot of 55,000 square meters with separate buildings for Early Childhood, Elementary and Middle / High school, all equipped to support various learning opportunities.

Our IB teachers are characterized by their educational excellence. They undergo on-going development to maintain their professional experience.

IB Diploma subjects offered at Hayah:
English Literature HL/SL – English Language and Literature HL/SL – English B HL – Arabic Language and Literature HL/SL – Arabic B HL – Arabic *Ab-initio* SL – French B HL/SL – French *Ab-initio* SL – Economics HL/SL – History HL – Business and Management HL/SL – Psychology HL/SL – Information Technology in Global Society ITGS HL/SL – Chemistry HL/SL – Physics HL/SL – Biology HL/SL – Environmental Systems and Societies SL – Mathematics analysis & approaches HL/SL – Mathematics applications & interpretation SL – Visual Arts HL/SL – Film HL/SL – Global Politics HL/SL.

Class of 2019 students received outstanding results with a 100 % pass rate and an average IB Diploma score of 34.15. A total of 90% of students scored above 30 points, 52% scored 35 and above and 13% of students scored 40 and above with 43 as the highest score.

Class of 2019 students have joined many top level universities around the world in countries such as: United States, Canada, Egypt, Europe, UK, UAE, Netherlands, Spain, Belgium and Australia.

***Fees are collected in EGP equivalent**

(Founded 1915)

Headmistress
Mrs Caroline Jordan MA(Oxon)

DP coordinator
Mr James Stephenson

Status Private

Boarding/day Mixed

Gender Female

Language of instruction
English

Authorised IB programmes
DP

Fees
Day: £6,090 – £6,635 per term
Boarding: £8,282 – £13,395 per term
Prep £3,205 – £4,880 per term

Address
London Road
Oxford
Oxfordshire
OX3 7TD | UK

TEL +44 (0)1865 759100
FAX +44 (0)1865 760268

Email
admissions@headington.org

Website
www.headington.org

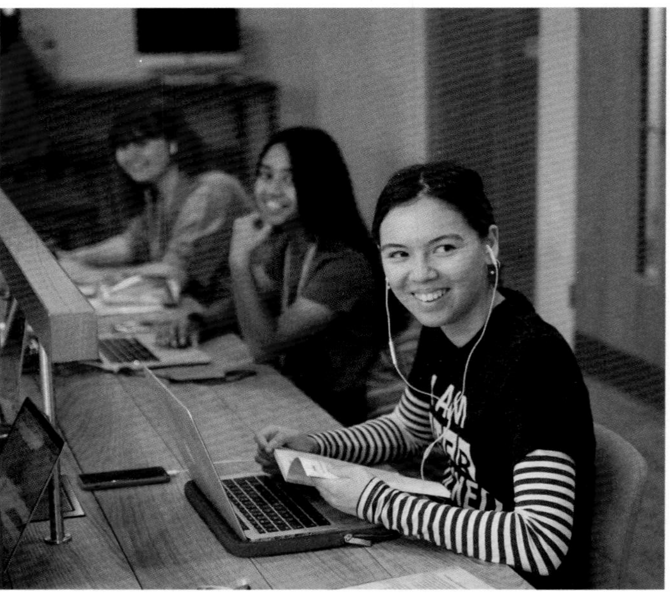

Headington School is a leading day and boarding school for girls aged three to 18, set in 23 acres just a mile from Oxford city centre. A major refurbishment and extension of the Sixth Form Centre was completed in 2019. Other facilities include an award-winning library, complete with 'sonic chairs' where girls can listen to music or lectures without disturbing their neighbours and interactive tables for group working, a state-of-the-art Music School, a purpose-built 240-seat Theatre, light and airy Art School and spacious Dance and Fitness Centre, which features a fully-equipped gym, training rooms and a large dance studio. Work started in 2019 on a new Creativity and Innovation Centre, due to open in 2021.

Results

A top 10 IB UK school, Headington's results regularly place it among the top schools in the country, with girls going on to study at top universities around the world. Headington offers an extremely broad curriculum with a choice of 30 subjects across A Level and IB in the Sixth Form. A growing number of girls opt for IB each year with great results. The average points score, out of a perfect 45, is consistently above 38. Nearly a third of our girls scored 40 points or more in 2018 with three candidates scoring an impressive 44 points.

Oxford

With inspirational Oxford on its doorstep, Headington girls benefit from the city's fantastic museums, art galleries, theatres, restaurants and cafes. The Dreaming Spires of Oxford have inspired countless famous writers while 27 British Prime Ministers, at least 30 international leaders, 50 Nobel Prize winners and 120 Olympic medal winners boast an Oxford education. Today girls can take advantage of a host of academic events such as thought-provoking and challenging talks, lectures and workshops both in school and in the historic colleges, meeting and learning from experts in their field.

Beyond the classroom

Headington also offers an excellent extra-curricular programme, with more than 150 clubs and activities to choose from. In the Sixth Form girls are given leadership responsibilities and gain experience doing everything from running clubs to leading expeditions. There are currently over 45 different nationalities represented throughout the School, reflecting Oxford's culturally and ethnically diverse make-up.

An education at Headington prepares girls for every aspect of life. Headington girls are intellectually curious, emotionally confident, kind and considerate to each other and to adults.

(Founded 1980)

Joint Acting Principals
Sarah Pearson &
Alasdair Mackenzie

MYP coordinator
Michelle Butler

DP coordinator
Bradley Snell

Status State

Boarding/day Mixed

Gender Coeducational

Language of instruction
English

Authorised IB programmes
MYP, DP

Age Range 11 – 18

Number of pupils enrolled
850

Fees
£13,833 – £17,340

Address
Dunmow Road
Bishops Stortford
Hertfordshire
CM23 5HX | UK

TEL 01279 658451
FAX 01279 755918

Email
admissions@hockerill.com

Website
www.hockerill.com

Hockerill Anglo-European College has offered the International Baccalaureate Diploma programme since 1998 and is one of the largest UK centres with on average 125 students per year sitting the IB Diploma examinations. The College also offers the Middle Years Programme.

The College's results are significantly above global averages and each year students gain admission to leading universities around the world. In 2019, 74% of its students' UK destinations were to prestigious Russell Group universities. Popular destinations include University College London, Imperial College London, London School of Economics, King's College London, Queen Mary University of London and the Universities of Oxford, Cambridge, Durham, Exeter, Glasgow, Nottingham, Manchester, Bristol, Leeds, Bath, Birmingham, Newcastle, Southampton, Sheffield, St Andrews and York, plus several top overseas institutions. Courses of university study include: Economics, History, Natural Sciences, Neuroscience, Medicine, Law, Modern Languages, Business, Architecture, Design, PPE, Engineering, Biomedical Sciences, Veterinary Science, Psychology, Social Sciences, Anthropology, International Relations and Politics amongst many others.

Hockerill prides itself on the manner in which IB principles inform teaching and learning across all stages of the College.

Hockerill offer both day and boarding places with the main intake years being at age 11 and age 16. It provides high quality boarding provision, comparable with many leading Independent Schools despite being half the cost. Each student at Hockerill is known and every student benefits from an outstanding pastoral system. Students are inspired, motivated and challenged as well as being provided with the best possible preparation for their future.

The College has been praised for its strong extra-curricular provision which includes: Sports (Rugby, Hockey, Football, Basketball, Netball, Equestrian, Cricket and Athletics); Music Ensembles, Bands and Choirs; Debating and Model United Nations, Amnesty and Interact Charity Fundraising.

The trips and exchanges programme starts from Year 7 right through to Year 13 and encompasses such destinations as Uganda, India, Japan, China, South Africa, Spain, France, Croatia, Belgium, Germany, Italy and Canada.

Hockerill was listed as the top UK comprehensive school in the Sunday Times 2018 Schools Guide.

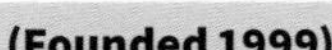

(Founded 1999)

Head of School
Gavin Budd

PYP coordinator
Rhona Sehested-Larsen

DP coordinator
Winell Gous

Status Private

Boarding/day Day

Gender Coeducational

Language of instruction
English

Authorised IB programmes
PYP, DP

Age Range 2.5 – 18

Number of pupils enrolled
400

Fees
Day: R42,000 – R126,218

Address
61 Main Road
Hout Bay
Cape Town
7806 | SOUTH AFRICA

TEL +27 21 791 7900
FAX +27 21 791 7950

Email
hbis@iesmail.com

Website
www.houtbayinternational.co.za

Introduction

Hout Bay International School is more than a school – it is a community of diverse individuals and families, a centre for academic excellence, for some a home away from home and yet more importantly a family for all those that are part of it. Few schools can boast that they belong to two international organisations spanning across almost every continent of the globe. The first being International Education Systems (IES), a family of international schools committed to quality educational experiences for all who attend and, second, the International Baccalaureate Organisation (IBO), renowned for its high quality and rigorous academic programme.

Our School is as diverse as the location in which it finds itself, our commitment to highlighting social injustice, the celebration of differences and the fostering of international mindedness goes beyond the classroom. Students are encouraged to 'think outside the box', 'have a voice' and engage on pertinent topics daily. From the Primary Years Programme (PYP) through to the Diploma Programme (DP), students, staff and parents are part of a learning community that seeks to encourage awareness of the wider world. They have a sense of their own role as global citizens, who respect and value diversity, who have an understanding of how the world works and who take responsibility for their actions.

We are proudly South African, embodying an international mindset, where the spirit of 'ubuntu' – the idea that humanity is bound together and expressed by caring for each other – can be seen and felt. The teachers genuinely care for their students and love practicing their craft. The students genuinely love learning and are encouraged to become life-long learners.

Facilities

Our campus is cradled between beautiful mountains on three sides with the sparkling Atlantic Ocean on the other; and houses the following facilities: 35 Classrooms (each equipped with Wi-Fi and Data Projectors). Two Fully Equipped Science/Biology Laboratories, Robotics Lab, Black Box Drama Studio, Visual Art Studio, Design Studio, School Library, 2 Music Rooms, Creative Arts Outdoor Courtyard, Courtyards equipped with climbing walls and Sand pits, Canteen for daily lunches and snacks, Junior Hall, Stop and Drop / Pick Up Facilities, 2 Netball / Tennis Courts, 3 Cricket Nets, 2 Multi-purpose playing fields, Bio-Diversity Sanctuary, Sustainable Vegetable Garden. In 2019 our campus was enhanced with the completion of our brand new Early Years and Junior Primary building which also houses our newest addition, our Nursery Class.

Extra-Curricular Programme

Our students enjoy an extensive Extra-Curricular programme exposing them to various sports, creative arts, dance, martial arts, community service activities, all contributing to their 'Whole Child' educational experience and embracing the concept of CAS.

Admissions

We accept students year round, in all grade levels except the Diploma Programme which requires a two year commitment from the student. Application forms and previous school reports are required for entry.

Ibn Khuldoon National School

(Founded 1983)

President
Dr Kamal Abdel-Nour D.Ed

DP coordinator
Roula Barghout

Status Private

Boarding/day Day

Gender Coeducational

Language of instruction
English, Arabic

Authorised IB programmes
DP

Age Range 4 – 18

Number of pupils enrolled
1650

Address
Building 161, Road 4111
Area 841, P.O. Box 20511
Isa Town | **BAHRAIN**

TEL +973 17780661
FAX +973 17689028

Email
r.barghout@ikns.edu.bh

Website
www.ikns.edu.bh/

Ibn Khuldoon National School (IKNS) is a non-profit self supporting coeducational institution that is dedicated to providing high quality education for local and expatriate students. The school offers a bilingual programme of study for students from Kindergarten to Grade 12. IKNS students can communicate in both Arabic and English with ease and lucidity from an early stage of their lives.

A diverse faculty, whether teaching in Arabic or English, provide a rich and supportive learning environment for students. The faculty is supported by a dedicated team of administrative and support staff.

At the top level of the school's governance stand the board of trustees, board of directors and specialist committees. Their members volunteer their expertise, time and effort to ensure that the school is always heading in a forward direction.

IKNS opened its doors to students in 1983. The first group of students walked up the graduation stage in 1992. Since then, the institution has graduated more than 2000 young men and women, with a current student population of 1,650.

IKNS has been affiliated with the International Baccalaureate (IB) since 1990, as an IB Diploma Programme provider. The first group of students sat for the IB Diploma examinations in 1992. Since then, the IB Diploma has been a popular choice for motivated students at IKNS.

IKNS is also a PYP and MYP candidate school since 2017 and 2018 respectively.

In addition to the IB Diploma, IKNS offers an American high school diploma. A large number of high school diploma students opt to study one or more DP courses. IKNS students go on to complete their tertiary education in different parts of the world including UK, USA, Canada and Arab countries, many gaining admission to prestigious institutions.

The school received its full accreditation from the Middle States Association of Colleges and Schools (MSA) in 1994, and it continues to be in good standing with the association. The Accredited status of the school affirms that it provides the level of quality in its educational programmes, services, activities and resources expected by its stakeholders. IKNS continues to be rated as an "Outstanding School" by the Education and Training Quality Authority (BQA).

Head of School
Ryan Kelsall

DP coordinator
Johanna Sale

CP coordinator
Leanne Gibbons

Status State

Boarding/day Day/Homestay

Gender Coeducational

Language of instruction
English

Authorised IB programmes
DP, CP

Age Range 11 – 19

Number of pupils enrolled
1311

Address
New Road
Impington
Cambridge
Cambridgeshire
CB24 9LX | UK

TEL 01223 200400

Email
sixthform@ivc.tmet.org.uk

Website
www.impington.cambs.sch.uk

An IB World School education: broad, balanced and international

Offering a broad and balanced sixth form education, yet with opportunity for specialization, the International Baccalaureate Diploma Programme (IB DP) has been taught at Impington International College since 1991, making us the most experienced IB educators in Cambridge. One of the pioneer state IB World Schools in the UK, Impington is a truly international environment and is proud to combine academic excellence with enrichment and educational opportunities unrivalled in the state sector. The International Baccalaureate Diploma Programme, recognised by the British Higher Education Statistical Agency (HESA 2011) as superb preparation for university, combines depth of specialist knowledge balanced by breadth of understanding across a range of disciplines and encourages the development of students fit for both university and for an interdisciplinary, globalised future.

Impington International College is an Ofsted 'outstanding' sixth form and a flagship provider for not only the IB DP but also the IB Careers Programme, the ground-breaking combination of vocational and academic courses designed to give students the best of both worlds; the specialism of the BTEC courses coupled with the range and breadth of the IB courses. The first school in the world to have a student gain an offer from Cambridge University for the Careers Programme; Impington International College celebrates a high level of Russell group university placements every year.

In 2019 Impington students once again celebrated their success with pass and individual point scores well in excess of the international and national averages, before heading to universities including Oxbridge, Bristol, Durham, the University of Bologna, the University of Warsaw as well as further afield to the USA to study at Brown, Colombia and Colorado State Universities.

Renowned for the Performing Arts, Impington BTEC students outdid themselves again in 2019 in the number of distinctions and distinction stars attained, a pattern followed in Creative and Digital Media. Specialist pathways available in Sports Scholarships, offered in football and netball, allow students to focus on their specific talent while keeping their academic qualifications going as well as training and playing at a professional level.

Impington International College is genuinely international. Students join us from the local area of Cambridge, wider regions of the UK and from approximately 15 other countries. Such a rich mix of cultural perspectives enables our students to develop a sense of their own national and international identity and take their place in the global forum.

INSTITUT FLORIMONT

(Founded 1905)

Director General
Mr. Sean Power

DP coordinator
Noha Benani

Status Private

Boarding/day Day

Gender Coeducational

Language of instruction
English, French

Authorised IB programmes
DP

Age Range 3 – 18

Number of pupils enrolled
1490

Fees
Day: CHF15,800 – CHF26,300

Address
37 Avenue du Petit-Lancy
Petit-Lancy
1213 | SWITZERLAND

TEL +41 2287 90000

FAX +41 2279 20918

Email
admissions@florimont.ch

Website
www.florimont.ch

Institut Florimont is a co-educational day school offering children from 3 to 18 years of age a complete education from kindergarten to the three diplomas that will open the doors to higher education. As well as encouraging academic excellence, Florimont fosters the traditional values and beliefs that are important for life.

Since 1905, Florimont has been preparing students for the French Baccalaureate and, as of 1942, for the Swiss Maturité. Since September 2014 our range of final examinations includes the bilingual (French-English) International Baccalaureate. Therefore, Florimont offers children more opportunities and more choices, allowing them easier access to the world's best universities.

All sections of our school work together to ensure the continuity and coherence of the programme of study. Clear procedures are in place to ensure that new students joining us from other private or public schools are successfully integrated.

Close communication with parents, additional lessons and one-to-one tutoring are just some of the ways that Florimont supports students during their studies.

Our student body is made up of more than fifty nationalities making Florimont a rich multicultural and multilingual learning environment. The importance we attach to this is reflected in our language learning programme. In addition to English, emphasis is placed on German, Switzerland's predominant language, as well as on Chinese, Spanish and Italian. Other languages such as Russian and Arabic are individually tutored or taught to small groups. Bilingual classes in French and English are offered from the primary and throughout the school.

Priority is given to partnerships and exchanges with leading schools worldwide, as well as to many activities that can add value to a university application, such as the CAS programme.

Philosophy lessons are initiated in the primary years in preparation for a better appreciation of Theory of Knowledge in the IB Diploma Programme.

Our students are encouraged to be entrepreneurial, bold, adaptable and creative because we know that these qualities will not only strengthen their university applications but also prepare them to face the challenges of working life.

Find more information on www.florimont.ch

Institut Moderne Du Liban

(Founded 1959)

Head of School
Mr. Maroun Khalifé

MYP coordinator
Grace Renno

Status Private

Boarding/day Day

Gender Coeducational

Language of instruction
French

Authorised IB programmes
MYP

Age Range 3 – 18

Number of pupils enrolled
380

Address
Rue 51 n.19 Metn nord
Fanar, Région Jaber
90593 | LEBANON

TEL +961 1680160/1/2

Email
administration@instmod.edu.lb

Website
www.instmod.edu.lb

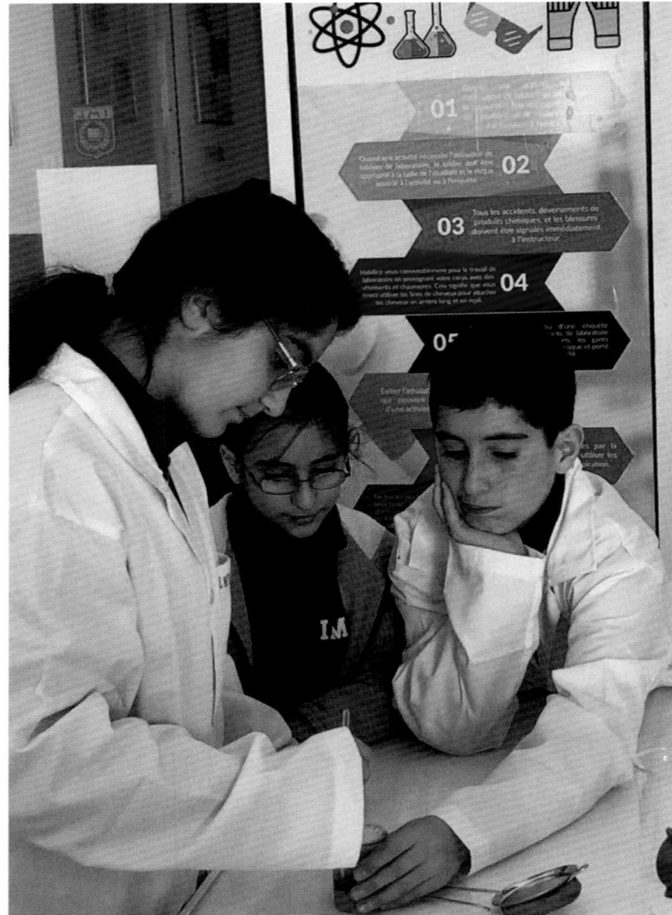

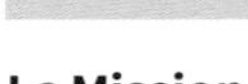

La Mission

Engagé dans une mission de service pédagogique et scolaire, l'Institut Moderne du Liban est un établissement scolaire ouvert à la participation des citoyens, des familles, et de la société civile. Il revêt un caractère mixte, conduit en partenariat avec plusieurs organismes éducatifs internationaux (AEFE, UNESCO, IB organisation) dont il en tire enrichissement et avantage. L'IML gagne en dynamisme et en légitimité par son engagement à promouvoir l'enseignement français.

Cette ouverture internationale, volontaire et naturelle aux différents besoins des apprenants met l'IML en situation d'évolution constante ce qui lui permet de leur donner une souplesse suffisante et adaptée pour un enseignement riche et ciblé.

Cet approfondissement constant dans le monde de l'éducation et de la pédagogie le place aussi au centre de la concurrence et du défi pour s'adapter aux différentes méthodologies vers un meilleur encadrement de tout élève (en difficulté scolaire ou à la recherche de l'excellence et de la réussite tant sur la plan personnel que sur le plan académique)

De cette visée se crée la motivation de l'établissement et le souci de traduire les quatre piliers de l'éducation pour le XXIe siècle, pratiques exemplaires pour une éducation de qualité:

- Apprendre à connaître
- Apprendre à faire
- Apprendre à être
- Apprendre à vivre ensemble

Depuis sa fondation, l'IML s'est engagé à promouvoir une éducation de qualité à la recherche de la paix, de la liberté, de la justice et du développement humain afin de répondre l'évolution du monde éducation et d'honorer les principales valeurs de sa création *le modernisme et l'acceptation de l'autre dans toutes ses dimensions*.

Les programmes

Etant un établissement d'enseignement français à l'étranger, homologué-partenaire, l'IML respecte les principes définis de dispenser un enseignement conforme non seulement aux programmes français mais également aux objectifs pédagogiques et aux règles d'organisation applicables en France, tout en prenant en compte le contexte local du pays et les valeurs internationales qui promeut la sensibilisation aux contextes mondiaux définis à l'international.

Dans ce contexte, la communauté éducative œuvre pour l'implémentation des programmes enseignés à l'établissement d'où la prise en charge des élèves tout au long de leur cursus, ainsi que leur encadrement dans l'élaboration de leur projet personnel de formation et d'insertion sociale et professionnelle, Cette approche personnalisée ne se limite pas uniquement aux apprenants mais s'étend aux parents pour les impliquer dans un choix plus approprié aux compétences et aux attentes de l'apprenant.

Le projet Educatif

Les principes généraux qui sont à la base du projet éducatif de l'Institut Moderne du Liban, sont conçus comme une structure éducative et pédagogique, dans l'idéal de la modernité, et dans une formule heureuse que le fondateur feu Père Michel Khalifé a puisée, il y a plus de soixante ans, dans l'œuvre du philosophe allemand Friedrich Nietzsche, une formule qui n`est pas sans évoquer une des dimensions de cette modernité: *Le gai savoir*.

La gaieté du connaître qui renforce le plaisir de vivre.

La passion du connaître c'est Connaître pour vivre plus et vivre mieux.

Le projet passionnant qui interprète le Savoir tel un projet passionnant et ambitieux grâce auquel l'homme se branche au réel et se l'approprie en se faisant ou en se re-faisant.

L'Ouverture et la disponibilité qui font du Connaître est une entreprise continuelle où l'on ne connaît jamais assez.

La priorité à la vie qui présente Le Savoir au service de la vie.

Director
Alexander Biner

DP coordinator
Dr Anne Faassen

Status Private

Boarding/day Mixed

Gender Coeducational

Language of instruction
English, German

Authorised IB programmes
DP

Age Range 6 – 18

Number of pupils enrolled
300

Address
Schönfels 5
6300 Zug | SWITZERLAND

TEL +41 41 729 11 99

Email
admissions@montana-zug.ch

Website
www.montana-zug.ch

Institut Montana was founded in 1926 by Dr Max Husmann. His humanist vision continues to guide us to help every student find their own individual path and thrive.

Learning, Personal Growth, Community

Our combination of small class sizes and individual support fosters a family atmosphere that builds up enthusiasm for learning and motivation to excel. Our international school community is highly diverse yet also promotes typically Swiss values, such as a strong work ethic, respect for each other and dedication to achieving excellence.

We are a fully accredited Swiss international boarding school. Since 1987 we have been an official IB World School.

A central location in a natural setting

Our 60 acres campus, at an altitude of 950m, offers seclusion and contact with nature while benefitting from its proximity to Switzerland's major cities and the rich opportunities they offer (15 minutes by public transport from the city of Zug, 55 minutes from Zurich airport).

The Pursuit of Excellence

Students have the opportunity to choose the academic path that suits their interests and aspirations. We offer (grades 1-12) the best of Swiss and international educational programmes, carefully structured to ensure the highest standards of teaching and learning. Bilingual Elementary and Secondary School, pre-IGCSE and IGCSE programmes (7-10), IB Diploma Programme (11-12), Swiss High School (9-12).

Home at School

Life at Montana is unique: we breathe mountain air, drink our own spring water and eat fresh food that accommodates all dietary restrictions. Our daily routine promotes self-responsibility while maintaining a well-balanced, active lifestyle.

Our campus is equipped with everything a modern teenager needs to live and learn comfortably. The location encourages outdoor activity throughout the seasons.

Empowering Students

We want our students to grow into confident adults who will make the most of their life. Our extracurricular activities encourage them to pursue their passion, whether that is athletic, intellectual or cultural. Our students participate in athletic competitions, Model United Nations conferences, entrepreneurship programmes, theatre productions and more.

A Student Council actively influences all aspects of school life with the school's full support. Our students are global citizens supporting charity projects within Switzerland and around the world.

Montana for Life

We are a vibrant community with strong connections that continue across years as across continents. From scientists to politicians and film directors, our alumni are a diverse group of passionate people who share the same background and values.

(Founded 1960)

Head of School
Mary-Lyn Campbell

Secondary Principal
James Penstone

Primary Principal
Julian Edwards

PYP coordinator
Claire Febrey

MYP coordinator
Graham Gardner

DP coordinator
Ann Lautrette

Status Private

Boarding/day Day

Gender Coeducational

Language of instruction
English

Authorised IB programmes
PYP, MYP, DP

Age Range 3 – 18

Number of pupils enrolled
840

Address
Strubenacher 3
8126 Zumikon | **SWITZERLAND**

TEL +41 44 919 8300
FAX +41 44 919 8353

Email
contact@icsz.ch

Website
www.icsz.ch

School Description

The Inter-Community School Zurich (ICS) is the longest-established international school in the Zurich area. A private co-educational day school, established in 1960, we provide a world-class international education for students aged 3 to 18.

Our language of instruction, in a multilingual context, is English. Our 'English as an Additional language' (EAL) programme supports students with limited English. All students learn German, the language of our host country.

Students undertake the full IB Diploma. As well as offering the full IB Diploma to all students, ICS champions excellence in Sports and Arts and offers students a broad range of exciting extra – curricular opportunities alongside the academic IB programme.

Learning Beyond the Classroom

ICS believes that learning beyond the classroom, as well as within, adds value to a rigorous educational experience. We offer collaborative and innovative extra-curricular activities to inspire and engage students.

Service Learning, both locally and internationally, is a key component of the ICS curriculum. Students are constantly encouraged to look beyond themselves. As a Round Square member school, ICS offers students opportunities to join Round Square Service initiatives.

Zurich, Switzerland

With vast natural and cultural resources, Switzerland is a perfect environment for "learning through doing". By deliberately structuring authentic learning experiences outside the classroom, we foster students' holistic development. Field trips are an integral part of learning at ICS, giving students the chance to apply their learning, broaden their horizons and develop leadership and independence.

Admissions

As an international school, we welcome students of all nationalities; we currently have students from 48 countries here.

We welcome applications from prospective students throughout the year. Please contact us at contact@icsz.ch if you have any questions or if you would like to arrange a visit.

Location

We are conveniently located on a single campus, situated near the Zurich city centre and easily accessed by public transportation. We also offer a school bus service.

International Bilingual School of Provence

(Founded 1984)

General Director
Jean-Marc Gobbi

DP coordinator
Trevor Alan Tricker

Status Private

Boarding/day Mixed

Gender Coeducational

Language of instruction
English, French

Authorised IB programmes
DP

Age Range 2 – 18

Number of pupils enrolled
700

Fees
Day: €10,000 – €15,000
Boarding: €21,550 – €30,000

Address
500 Route de Bouc-Bel-Air
Domaine des Pins, Luynes
Aix en Provence
13080 | FRANCE

TEL +33 (0)4 4224 0340
FAX +33 (0)4 4224 0981

Email
info@ibsofprovence.com

Website
www.ibsofprovence.com/

The International Bilingual School of Provence, an independent coeducational school located near Aix-en-Provence in the south of France, owes its international character to the diversity of its student population. The school, established since 1984, has an annual enrolment of 800 students from more than 75 different countries in its day and boarding sections. In addition to the French students who make up 50% of the student population, IBS welcomes pupils from the five continents desiring to pursue their education in English, French or both.

A particularity of the school is that the international section is not dominated by any one nationality and new students are made to feel at home immediately. Committed to French-English bilingualism, the school offers both the International Baccalaureate Diploma Programme and the French Baccalaureate. The school also offers seven first languages to ensure that the student maintains his/her own language skills.

Philosophy

Small classrooms, qualified teachers, modern facilities in a tranquil, calm environment help ensure the success of each student. IBS of Provence recently invested in a new 7000m2 state-of-the-art campus which includes a sports complex, four new tennis courts (2 hard surface, 2 synthetic clay), football field, indoor gymnasium, 400+ seat auditorium for theatre performances and international conferences as well as a three-level academic building with fully equipped laboratories, art rooms, library, multi-media room and rooftop terrace.

The school also has a boarding section with over 150 students residing in one of the five boarding houses which offer a home-like atmosphere in a beautiful Provençal setting. Involvement in various extracurricular activities is expected and enhances the development of each individual's character within the spirit of the school. Politeness, respect and consideration for others are important values at IBS. Students leave IBS, the majority for 1st choice university placements, as caring, responsible young citizens.

Summer school

During the spring and summer holidays, IBS offers intensive French as a Foreign Language and English immersion programmes. Over 400 students from all over the world join IBS every summer to develop their language skills while discovering the beauty of the Provence region. For more information about our summer program or group visits, please contact Ms. Lisanne Harms, Spring/Summer Camp Coordinator, by email at lharms@ibsofprovence.com.

Admissions

We accept applications for admission to our school year-round based on availability. There is no formal entrance exam but students must submit two years' of school reports, a letter of recommendation from a teacher/Head of School as well as a letter of motivation. For more information about admissions or to schedule a tour of the school, please contact Ms Wendy Heinicken at admissions@ibsofprovence.com.

(Founded 1979)	**Gender** Coeducational
Director Bradley Roberts	**Language of instruction** English
Senior School Principal Timothy Walsh	**Authorised IB programmes** PYP, MYP, DP
Middle School Principal Tico Oms	**Age Range** 3 – 19 years
Junior School Principal George Dolesch	**Number of pupils enrolled** 1371
PYP coordinator Lyneth Magsalin	**Address** Fleischbachstrasse 2, 4153 Reinach | SWITZERLAND
MYP coordinator Siân Thomas	**TEL** +41 61 715 33 33
DP coordinator Sean Coffey	**FAX** +41 61 715 33 15
Status Private	**Email** info@isbasel.ch
Boarding/day Day	**Website** www.isbasel.ch

Mission:

"We all want to learn more;
We all do it in different ways;
We all have fun learning;
We all help."
– ISB Student

ISB is a private, not-for-profit, co-educational day school established in 1979. Our students and teachers come from all corners of the world, creating a diverse community. We live our Mission every day in every area of the school, as it reminds us to appreciate our learning differences, help each other out, and in our quest for excellence, find a way to make it fun and engaging. Here at ISB, we firmly believe that true education neither ends nor begins in the classroom alone. As our students explore the world beyond the classroom, our well-qualified teachers and staff instill a skill set that will help them remain lifelong learners, no matter where they live and what they do in the world. That is why our Mission begins with the simple phrase, "We all want to learn more." We live in a rapidly changing world, thus, education must lead that change. Investing in professional development at all levels to stay at the forefront of educational trends is our priority to prepare our students to embrace challenge and shape a better world.

Campuses

The campuses of ISB, located on the outskirts of the city of Basel on the edge of the Swiss countryside, provide students with world-class learning opportunities. An efficient public transport system and convenient pedestrian and bicycle paths ensure easy access to ISB campuses. Age-appropriate and supportive learning environments encourage students' potential and nurture their talents at all stages of intellectual, physical and emotional development, providing them with the means to grow and thrive.

Inclusion

One of the guiding statements in our Mission is "We all do it in different ways." ISB understands that all children learn differently and possess individual strengths and areas for growth. ISB embraces diversity, not only in race or culture, but in the learning profiles of our students. ISB serves learners by aligning student needs with appropriate resources and support by qualified and experienced teachers and staff.

Academic Results

In 2018, 100 students took the IB Diploma exams and achieved an overall average of 34 points, four points above the world average. 50% of students achieved 35 points or more, and 6 students gained 40 points or more. ISB graduates have successfully transferred to top universities around the world.

(Founded 2009)

Head of School
Penny Garner

PYP coordinator
Rachel Bestow

MYP coordinator
Anne Vollmer

Status Private

Boarding/day Day

Gender Coeducational

Language of instruction
English

Authorised IB programmes
PYP, MYP

Age Range 2 1/2 – 16 years

Number of pupils enrolled 90

Address
Via Don Orione, 1
Botticino
25082 Brescia | **ITALY**

TEL +39 030 2191182

Email
info@isbrescia.com

Website
www.isbrescia.com

Teaching and learning at International School Brescia is about preparing our students in a global community to have the skills, the knowledge and the capacity to problem solve that will enable them to meet the challenges of the future. With a strong emphasis on developing the IB Learner Profile*, and by learning through inquiry, action and reflection our students acquire in-depth knowledge and become deep thinkers.

ISB is a co-educational private day school located in the small town of Botticino, in the province of Brescia, Italy. Founded in 2009 we are an authorised World School for the Primary Years Programme and the Middle Years Programme and we are a candidate school for the Diploma Programme.

Our school vision for the future is to become an IB Continuum School offering our students the best possible international education in a supportive and inclusive, caring environment. Principled IB learners are honest and fair and take responsibility for their own learning and actions and our students are guided to act with integrity.

Our open-minded and respectful culture encourages the whole school community to contribute to the teaching and learning in school and this collaboration and involvement makes our school a very welcoming and special place to learn.

Our student body is made up of around 15 nationalities and we cultivate a truly international outlook whilst fostering knowledge and experience of our host country, Italy. English is our language of instruction, and we provide support for those students joining us, who have limited knowledge, to be communicators.

In addition to delivering the IB subjects, our balanced curriculum provides many opportunities for extra-curricular experiences such as workshops, field trips, sporting exchanges and international travel. We enable our students to be risk-takers and support out of school interests and achievements.

As ISB grows and develops we continue to reflect on our practices and to participate in the wider IB world community to produce a positive impact on student learning outcomes.

**IB Learner Profile – International Baccalaureate Organisation 2006*

International School of Bergamo

Heads of School
Mrs. Guia Ghidoli & Mrs. Chiara Traversi

Head of Primary
Roisin Cosgrove

PYP coordinator
Helen Bird

MYP coordinator
Roberta Sana

Status Private

Boarding/day Day

Gender Coeducational

Language of instruction
English, Italian

Authorised IB programmes
PYP, MYP

Age Range 2 – 15

Number of pupils enrolled
275

Address
Via Gleno 54
24125 Bergamo | ITALY

TEL +39 035 213776

Email
info@isbergamo.com

Website
www.isbergamo.com

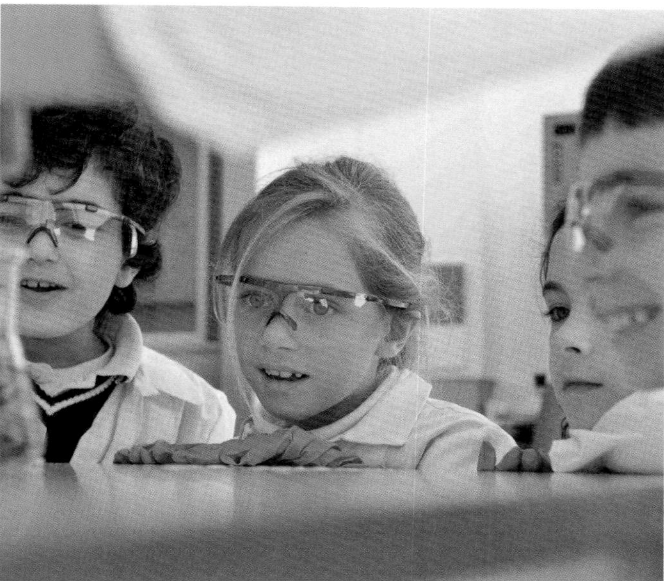

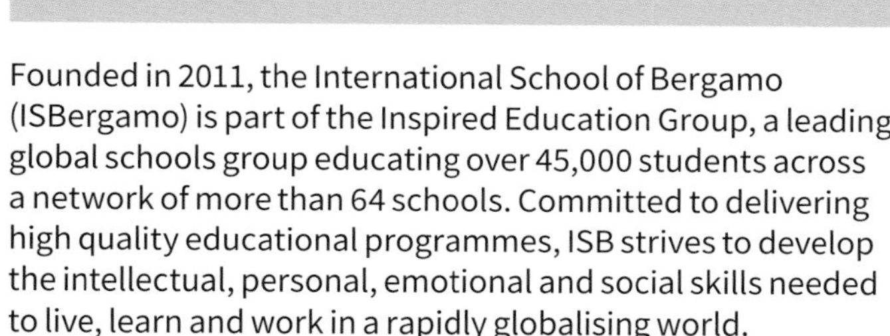

Founded in 2011, the International School of Bergamo (ISBergamo) is part of the Inspired Education Group, a leading global schools group educating over 45,000 students across a network of more than 64 schools. Committed to delivering high quality educational programmes, ISB strives to develop the intellectual, personal, emotional and social skills needed to live, learn and work in a rapidly globalising world.

The school offers the IB (International Baccalaureate) Primary Years and Middle Years Programmes and, at present, caters for children born in 2005 or after. Every year, the school opens subsequent classes, with the aim of providing a full international curriculum up to Grade 13.

Joining ISBergamo offers a fantastic opportunity to enter a safe and nurturing environment, where the Italian culture is valued alongside the recognition and appreciation of a multicultural collective diversity. Technology plays an important role in the school and is embedded in the school curriculum through a blended approach where we feel it adds value to teaching and learning.

The school is located in a modern building in the Eastern part of Bergamo, in a green and quiet environment. The area is rich in sporting facilities, including a modern football pitch located just next to the school as well as rugby fields and an athletics track at the end of the road.

Students can benefit from a totally refurbished building with new, specialised facilities, including a dedicated Early Years area, an Art & Design Lab, a school library, and an outdoor multipurpose sports facility, as well as a cafeteria and playgrounds.

Recent additions to the facility include a Secondary School wing with a specialised Science Laboratory, a Music, Drama & Dance studio, an Innovation Lab, and a newly expanded indoor gym.

Thanks to an efficient bus service, the school covers the city of Bergamo as well as a large number of the surrounding communities.

(Founded 1961)

Director
Denise Coates

Principal
Scott Jackson

PYP coordinator
Dominic Thomas

MYP coordinator
Kirsty DeWilde

DP coordinator
Brette Book

Status Private

Boarding/day Day

Gender Coeducational

Language of instruction
English

Authorised IB programmes
PYP, MYP, DP

Age Range 3 – 19

Number of pupils enrolled
300

Fees
CHF12,800 – CHF34,900

Address
Allmendingenweg 9
3073 Gümligen
Bern | **SWITZERLAND**

TEL +41 (0)31 959 10 00
FAX +41 (0)31 959 10 01

Email
admissions@isberne.ch

Website
www.isberne.ch

The International School of Berne (ISBerne) serves Berne's expatriate community, principally the multinational corporate and diplomatic communities. The school is a multicultural community of 340 students, representing over 40 countries, located in the village of Muri-Gümligen, just 15 minutes from Berne, the capital city of Switzerland.

ISBerne is proud to be an IB World School, offering all three core IB Programmes. Additionally, ISBerne is accredited by the Council of International Schools (CIS) and the New England Association of Schools and Colleges (NEASC) and as such, offers a fully accredited US High School diploma, in addition to the IB Diploma. ISBerne also offers this US High School Diploma to successful graduates of its affiliate distance learning programme, ISBerne Online.

Admission to ISBerne is based upon two criteria; the potential of the applicant to benefit from the educational services provided and the capacity of the school to meet the educational needs of the applicant. ISBerne welcomes applications from students who have demonstrated academic and social skills, a sound character, reliability and an eagerness to learn. These traits, combined with an ISBerne education, will prepare students for the future, teach them cultural appreciation and enable them to work with others. Graduates from ISBerne are regularly accepted to top university around the world.

The ISBerne curriculum reflects a carefully considered balance between guided inquiry and the acquisition of essential skills. Students benefit from small class sizes, a highly qualified faculty, and numerous language programmes and are active in the local community through various field trips, sporting events and other experiences such as Outdoor Education Week and the Ski Fridays Programme. The curriculum is supported by an expansive extra-curricular After School Activities Programme as well as competitive sports teams which compete against teams across Switzerland in the Swiss Group of International Schools (SGIS) circuit.

To support our curriculum, and the future technology of learning, ISBerne has a new state-of-the-art campus under construction, slated for completion in December of 2016. This new campus will not only allow for continued growth in enrollment but will also better support current conduits of learning, such as our online electives, and the advancements in the technology that will accompany future generations.

As an IB World School, ISBerne takes its commitment to internationalism very seriously. The diversity of cultures that make up the school community requires an appreciation, acceptance and respect of oneself and others. ISBerne prides itself on developing positive and enriching relationships between teachers, students and parents. Through choices made, daily operations and the philosophy embraced, the school places the child at the center of all it does.

International School of Bologna

Head of School
Mr. Fabio Corvaglia

PYP coordinator
Ms. Rachel Burgess

MYP coordinator
Ms. Helen Exler

DP coordinator
Ms. Nazanin Nikanjam

Status Private

Boarding/day Day

Gender Coeducational

Language of instruction
English

Authorised IB programmes
PYP, MYP, DP

Age Range 3 – 18

Number of pupils enrolled
270

Fees
€8,000 – €17,000

Address
Via della Libertà 2
40123 Bologna | **ITALY**

TEL +39 051 6449954
FAX +39 051 3390424

Email
info@isbologna.com

Website
www.isbologna.com

The International School of Bologna was founded in 2004. The enrollment is currently 270 students. This enrollment size ensures that each student can receive individual attention and differentiated instruction, recognizing that not all students learn at the same pace: a key feature of the planning in an ISB classroom.

ISB offers an Early Years to university preparation educational programme in the medium of the English language that provides an education that develops international mindedness based on cultural understanding, our common humanity, human diversity, and shared values.

The curriculum is designed in conjunction with the International Baccalaureate (IB) and draws on the growing educational research worldwide informing effective teaching and learning. ISB incorporates the three IB programmes: the Primary Years Programme (PYP) for students from 3 years old to 10 years old; the Middle Years Programme (MYP) for students from 11 years old to 16 years old, and the Diploma Programme for 17 and 18 years old students. Successful completion of the Diploma is an outstanding preparation for university and research has shown that Diploma students report being excellently prepared for their studies and tend to find greater choice in their university admissions. The Diploma is accepted as an entrance qualification to university in many countries around the world, including Italy.

The IB curriculum offered by ISB has its own unique character which is influenced by the particular context of Bologna which itself has a rich educational heritage. The school is staffed by qualified and experienced teachers drawn from around the world. This international mix of faculty itself provides outstanding opportunities to draw on the best practices of national systems, including Italy. Apart from being part of the network of IB schools which spans the world, the quality of the programmes is further assured by an accreditation process through the Council of International Schools (CIS). Through this combination of the local and global we are preparing students not just to cope with a changing world, but to lead the change.

Lastly, ISB earned the distinction of being the first Google Referenced school in Italy in October 2019.

(Founded 1996)

Director
Mr. Sinan Kosak

DP coordinator
Mr. Yusuf Suha Orhan

Status Private

Boarding/day Day

Gender Coeducational

Language of instruction
English

Authorised IB programmes
DP

Age Range 2 – 18

Number of pupils enrolled
710

Address
1R Gara Catelu Str., Sector 3
Bucharest 032991 | **ROMANIA**

TEL +40 21 3069530

Email
admissions@isb.ro

Website
www.isb.ro

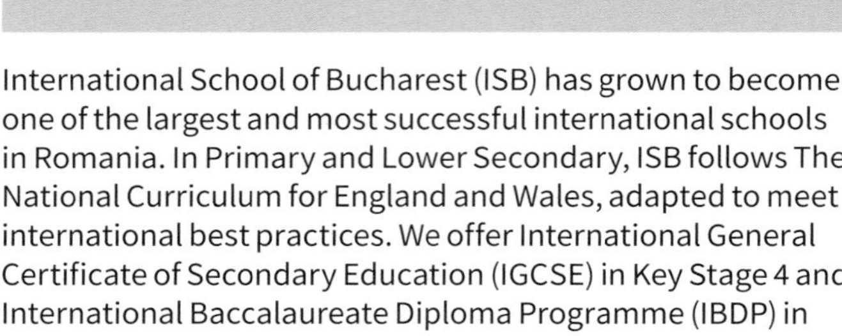

International School of Bucharest (ISB) has grown to become one of the largest and most successful international schools in Romania. In Primary and Lower Secondary, ISB follows The National Curriculum for England and Wales, adapted to meet international best practices. We offer International General Certificate of Secondary Education (IGCSE) in Key Stage 4 and International Baccalaureate Diploma Programme (IBDP) in the Sixth Form.

The curriculum offers students from age of 2 to 18 a broad-based, challenging and reflective education with an international perspective.

Our Mission is to provide each student with a broad, balanced education in a safe and supportive environment.

We promote an enjoyment of learning, creativity and excellence whilst working in close harmony with our diverse community.

We enable students to reach their full potential and develop skills to become independent, respectful and caring adults who will be successful and contribute to global society.

We offer a wide variety of DP courses, all taught by specialist teachers, making use of an extensive range of facilities and up to date educational technology.

Our Sixth Form has a significant rate of acceptance from the top universities in the UK – Russell Group, the USA and the Netherlands.

We expect our Sixth Form students to apply the core values of ISB in their future careers as independent and well-rounded individuals. IB DP enables them to discover their skills and interests; and encourage them to push their limits.

We take pride in our students' achievements, and teachers are committed to helping each individual succeed. This is at the heart of our community.

"One of the main benefits of the IB is that it is geared to prepare you for university. It also encourages more mature discussions with teachers, getting feedback and asking questions, allowing students to become more engaged and proactive about improving their work." **Oana I, ISB alumna**

Head of School
Ms. Emanuela Ferloni

PYP coordinator
Jane Marie Whittle

MYP coordinator
Karen Lockett

DP coordinator
Nicole Pearce

Status Private

Boarding/day Day

Gender Coeducational

Language of instruction
English, Italian

Authorised IB programmes
PYP, MYP, DP

Age Range 2 – 18

Number of pupils enrolled
340

Address
Via Adda 25
22073 Fino Mornasco (CO) | ITALY

TEL +39 031 572289

Email
info@iscomo.com

Website
www.iscomo.com

Founded in 2002, the International School of Como (IS Como) has grown to stand for excellence and has contributed to the expansion of international education in Northern Italy, as one of the almost 5,000 International Baccalaureate (IB) schools located worldwide. Today, IS Como welcomes over 340 students from 2 to 18 years old of 47 nationalities and an international staff of more than 60 qualified teachers and assistants.

IS Como is committed to providing children with the best educational experience possible. IS Como offers the IB (International Baccalaureate) Primary Years, Middle Years and Diploma Programmes and aspires to create a community where learning is the central driving factor of a journey in which our students become ethical thinkers, creative problem-solvers, community-minded and individuals of action on the world stage.

Our state-of-the-art campus was designed and built specifically for our students and provides for every aspect of a vibrant, innovative and rigorous education. Over 10,000 square metres of internal and external spaces house our extremely large classrooms, a Robotics lab, two Art Studios, indoor gym and outdoor multipurpose sports facility, cafeteria and playgrounds. Recent additions to the facility include a Secondary School wing, 3 fully equipped Science Laboratories, a Drama Studio, and Primary and Secondary School Libraries, newly expanded and renovated.

With our efficient bus service we can cover a large number of the surrounding communities, and beyond, including: Como, Cantù/Carimate Lecco, Varese, and Lugano (Switzerland).

At ISC we are driven by our Mission Statement which is "IS Como is a student-centered community of internationally-minded learners. We offer a balanced and challenging curriculum, in a safe and nurturing environment, where we respect and value the Italian culture and our collective diversity. We empower all students to be active, reflective and responsible lifelong learners who can achieve their full potential and contribute to an ever-changing world."

International School of Havana

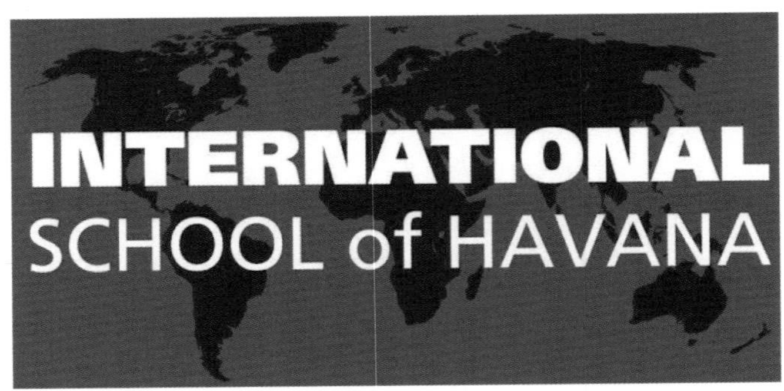

(Founded 1965)

Director
Mr. Michael Lees

DP coordinator
Osmery Martínez

Status Private

Boarding/day Day

Gender Coeducational

Language of instruction
English

Authorised IB programmes
DP

Age Range 2½ – 17 years

Number of pupils enrolled
330

Fees
US$14,385 (Additional fees paid only once upon registration)

Address
Calle 22 No 115 e/1ra y 3ra Avenida
Miramar, Playa
La Habana
11300 | CUBA

TEL +53 7214 0773

Email
office@ish.co.cu

Website
www.ishav.org

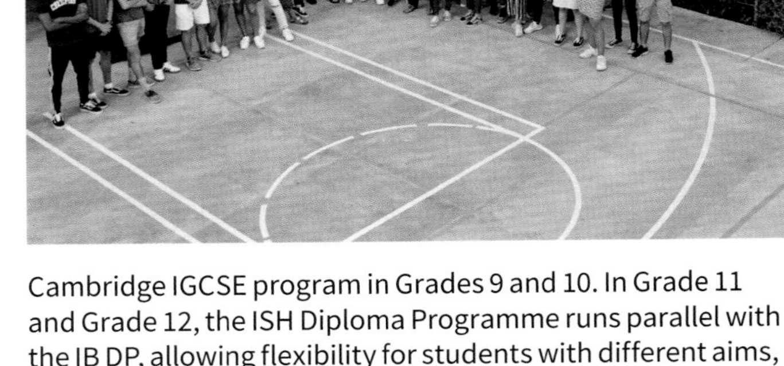

Founded in 1965, the International School of Havana, Cuba has been Cuba's leading international school for over 50 years. It provides a warm, nurturing environment for around 330 students from Early Years to Grade 12. The student body is made up of the children of diplomatic and expatriate business families and with over 50 different nationalities, we are hugely proud of our cultural diversity and at ISH, our mission of Learning to Make a Difference impacts everything we do.

The teaching body at ISH is comprised of almost 70 expatriate and Cuban teachers, working together to bring a variety of different backgrounds, skills and methods to the classroom. Our school's curriculum is adapted to serve a dynamic international student body with diverse needs. In the Lower School, students follow the International Primary Curriculum; in the Secondary School, students prepare for CIE Checkpoint examinations in Grade 8, and then follow the Cambridge IGCSE program in Grades 9 and 10. In Grade 11 and Grade 12, the ISH Diploma Programme runs parallel with the IB DP, allowing flexibility for students with different aims, abilities and educational experiences.

Graduates from ISH attend universities around the globe. In the past five years, we have sent students to a wide range of prestigious universities from McGill University in Canada, to New York University in the United States, to University College London in the UK, to Sciences Po in France and Erasmus University in the Netherlands. We encourage our students to aim high and provide pathways that will open as many doors as possible for them.

ISH is split over two campuses, one hosting our Early Years to Grade 8 students and the other a beautiful and recently-opened High School. Enrolment is open throughout the year and we always welcome enquiries and visits from prospective families.

International School of Herzen University

Headteacher
Lilia B. Lapteva

MYP coordinator
Irina Tomashpolskaia

Status Private

Boarding/day Day

Gender Coeducational

Language of instruction
English

Authorised IB programmes
MYP

Age Range 6 – 18

Number of pupils enrolled
115

Address
Vosstania str., 8 "B"
St. Petersburg | **RUSSIAN FEDERATION**

TEL +7 812 275 7684

Email
school@interschool.ru

Website
www.interschool.ru

St. Petersburg – the cultural capital of Russia!
Our school is located in the heart of downtown St. Petersburg, the cultural capital of Russia that is home to over 200 museums, 100 theatres, and several world-renowned universities. Founded in 1993 as the first private school in the city, we use the city with its rich history and cultural life as an extension of our classrooms. And we boast a historic tie with Herzen University, arguable Russia's finest pedagogical institute of higher learning from where much of our staff studied.

Our Tailor-Made Approach to Education
From our founding 25 years ago until the present day we have always been about our students. We love to share that our staff to student ratio is 1:2. Meaning we can meet students and families wherever they are in their educational journey. From the moment families enter our school we work with the student, with their parents, and with our teaching staff to ensure that they get the education they need to succeed in an increasingly internationalized world of tomorrow that values critical thinking skills over the learning of content. We develop a flexible individual educational pathway that allows for learning in a class setting (never more than 10 students in a group), one-one-one with a subject teacher and even independent study.

Languages
We proudly employ over 20 highly qualified language teachers that allow us to offer standard and advanced language classes in English, Russian, German, Spanish and French.

Our World School Journey
Our school gained authorization as an IB MYP school in September 2017. In Fall 2019 we successfully hosted an IB verification team and our school is on its way to be the only school in the city to offer the IB Diploma Programme. But our journey as a world school began much earlier. Besides our approach to education, our director always wanted our school to be different from other schools in our city in three main ways: (1) a focus on constant innovation in educational practices, (2) an internationally-minded environment, and (3) a holistic approach to the development of our students.

When we found IB – we instantly knew it was the right fit for us. Even though we are newly authorized as an IB World School, we are proud that most of its principles, if not the system, have been integral to our community since our founding. And this is proved by our first set of MYP e-assessment results, which were particularly impressive in Mathematics and in English Language and Literature. With our strong focus on hiring the best and helping them integrate educational best practice in the classroom – we are confident that our Diploma Programme students will soar.

All Are Welcome
Although many of our students are local, we also boast diverse demography with students from Korea, China, the USA and all over Europe. Due to our small size, we gladly welcome all students, whether they plan to stay in Russia for a semester or a lifetime. And with IB transitioning to another school is that much easier.

International School of London

(Founded 1972)

Principal Mr Richard Parker

Primary Principal Ms Kathryn Firebrace

Secondary Principal Mr Paul Rose

PYP coordinator Ms Iliana Gutierrez

MYP coordinator Ms Hyun Jung Owen

DP coordinator Paul Morris

Status Private

Boarding/day Day

Gender Coeducational

Language of instruction English & Mother-tongue

Authorised IB programmes PYP, MYP, DP

Age Range 3 – 18 years

Number of pupils enrolled 500

Fees Day: £19,000 – £26,300

Address 139 Gunnersbury Avenue
London
W3 8LG | UK

TEL +44 (0)20 8992 5823

Email mail@isllondon.org

Website www.isllondon.org

The International School of London (ISL) is an International Baccalaureate (IB) World School with embedded mother tongue language programmes and over 40 years' experience of delivering education excellence for ages 3-18. Our school has earned a global reputation as a leading International Baccalaureate (IB) school and is widely recognised as one of the UK's best and most experienced international schools.

We offer an exceptional world of learning for every student. Starting with a genuinely warm welcome to our multi-cultural environment from our award winning transitions team, we work with each child to devise an individual learning programme tailored to their unique needs and goals. Our strong focus on student wellbeing, in a supportive environment, is complemented in the classroom by dynamic teaching practises. It's this all-round approach that we believe leads to the academic and personal success that characterises ISL pupils.

We are a culturally diverse community. Students' cultural and linguistic identities are valued and nurtured through our international curriculum and mother tongue programme. Our school develops the attitudes, skills and understanding needed for active and responsible contributions to both local and global communities.

ISL has high academic standards, offering three IB programmes: the Primary Years, Middle Years and Diploma Programmes. These three align to the unique developmental needs of students from age three through to pre-university.

We are committed to intercultural and high-quality education taking learning beyond the walls of the classroom. We provide many opportunities in sports, service learning, and the arts which challenge our students to grow and develop. Our location in the city of London provides fantastic opportunities for innovative projects. The breadth and depth of our programmes ensure that our graduates are prepared for life at leading universities worldwide.

ISL has a family atmosphere, and we give a voice to all members of our community, with active parent groups and a committed student government. Students at ISL develop a keen sense of inter-cultural understanding which is something of great value in our globalised world. ISL actively celebrates this diversity throughout the year from class activities to whole school events.

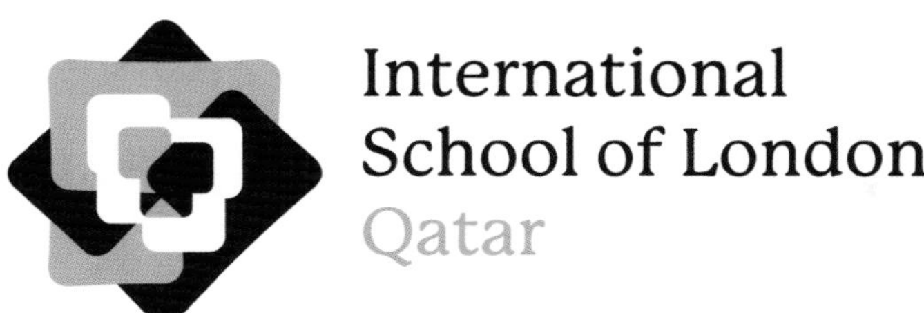

(Founded 2008)

Head of School
David Monk

PYP coordinator
James Kendall

MYP coordinator
Helen Jeffery

DP coordinator
Anna Burkett

Status Private

Boarding/day Day

Gender Coeducational

Language of instruction
English

Authorised IB programmes
PYP, MYP, DP

Age Range 3 – 18 years

Number of pupils enrolled
1150

Fees
QR53,005 – QR75,655

Address
PO Box 18511
North Duhail
Doha | QATAR

TEL +974 4433 8600
FAX +974 4499 5208

Email
mail@islqatar.org

Website
www.islqatar.org

Founded in 2008, The International School of London (ISL) Qatar is an International Baccalaureate (IB) World School, authorized to offer the IB Primary Years, Middle Years and Diploma Programmes.

ISL Qatar has developed a strong presence both locally and internationally as a pioneering educational institution, that is continually exploring the process of learning and considering what constitutes effective learning. ISL Qatar has an outstanding reputation for high academic standards, prestigious International Baccalaureate (IB) programmes.

ISL Qatar is part of the International School of London Group, which has a tradition of over 40 years of outstanding educational achievement in the UK. The IB curriculum fulfils the School's vision of combining intellectual rigour and high academic standards with a strong emphasis on the ideals of international mindedness and responsible global citizenship.

ISL Qatar's unique and pioneering Mother Tongue programme is a particular highlight of the school, as we are the only school in Qatar to offer Mother Tongue Programmes in over ten languages and constantly adding more. Students' cultural and linguistic identities are valued and nurtured through the Mother Tongue programmes. This added bi-lingual focus maintains home culture and language as well as improves the overall academic performance.

ISL Qatar is a culturally diverse community which fosters a passion and enthusiasm for learning through outstanding educational practice from ages 3-18 from over 70 countries. The school's international staff represent 40 different nationalities. ISL Qatar develops the attitudes, skills and understanding needed for active and responsible contributions to both local and global communities.

Headmaster
Mr. Stephen Rogers

PYP coordinator
Sara Lomas

MYP coordinator
Giuseppe Redaelli

DP coordinator
Tony Burtenshaw

Status Private

Boarding/day Mixed

Gender Coeducational

Language of instruction
English, Italian

Authorised IB programmes
PYP, MYP, DP

Age Range 2 – 18 (Boarding 14-18 years)

Number of pupils enrolled
940

Address
Via I Maggio, 20
20021 Baranzate (MI) | **ITALY**

TEL +39 02 872581

Email
admissions@ism-ac.it

Website
www.
internationalschoolofmilan.it

Welcome to the International School of Milan. Although we are the longest established international school here in the city, at our school you will find the strongest academic standards supported by the most progressive educational thinking that has served the international and Italian communities in Milan for over 60 years. We are confident that our ethos, focused on achievement and underpinned by opportunity for all, will enable your children to develop their confidence and be ready to embrace the challenges of the future.

The IB curriculum (which runs throughout all years) is a truly international one and is a perfect fit for the needs of all our students. Our PYP, MYP and IB Diploma programmes thoroughly prepare our students for further study all around the world, including at some of the world's leading universities. Our results are significantly above world averages with achievement in the Diploma for example at a particularly high level.

Our international, dedicated and skilled teaching body works well with our students in order to make them the success we know they can be. Their desire to challenge young minds is shaped by a growth mindset, ensuring that the focus is on every student achieving beyond what a school might 'normally expect'. In short, we believe your son or daughter can achieve more and be happier with us here at IS Milan.

We opened our brand new boarding house in September 2018 and can accommodate up to approximately 50 students. With the care and attention given by our staff, boarding at IS Milan provides a truly transformative international educational experience for 14 to 18-year-olds.

The International School of Milan is proud of its position in the city as the premier international IB school in terms of its curriculum and outlook and is renowned for its high educational standards and caring learning environment. We are also an international community with over 50 nationalities and a student body that is proud to belong to our school community and enthusiastic about the learning they take part in. We are certain that you will see the International School of Milan as a place where learning is genuinely celebrated and where each of our students are valued and challenged to succeed from the age of 2 up to 18.

Head of School
Mrs. Caroline Troughton

PYP coordinator
Jacky Payne

MYP coordinator
Anna Chiara Forti

DP coordinator
Caroline Searle

Status Private

Boarding/day Day

Gender Coeducational

Language of instruction
English

Authorised IB programmes
PYP, MYP, DP

Age Range 2 – 18

Number of pupils enrolled
250

Address
Piazza Montessori, 1/A
41051 Montale Rangone (MO) |
ITALY

TEL +39 059 530649

Email
office@internationalschoolofmodena.it

Website
www.internationalschoolofmodena.it

Welcome to the International School of Modena. Inaugurated in 1998 as a joint venture with Tetra Pak, whose global research and development unit is located in Modena, ISM is now a proud member of Inspired which is the fastest growing premium international schools' group operating on 5 continents and educating over 45,000 students globally. Our modern, purpose-built campus, surrounded by green open spaces, is located 12km outside of the city of Modena.

We are a truly international school representing approximately 30 different nationalities and offering the full continuum of International Baccalaureate (IB) education, with the Primary Years Programme (PYP) for children ages 3-11, Middle Years Programme (MYP) for ages 11-16 and the Diploma Programme (DP) for 16-18 years. ISM is one of only a handful of schools in Italy currently authorised to offer this programme which will thoroughly prepare your child for study all around the world, including at some of the world's leading universities.

In September 2019 the school opened its first class for 2-year olds, further extending our innovative Early Years department which features beautiful spaces and play structures specially designed to support the delivery of the IB PYP and Reggio-Inspired Early Years Curriculum.

The curriculum at ISM is carefully designed to reflect the ethos of the school and of the International Baccalaureate with a commitment to inquiry-based learning, encouraging every student to ask questions, to think for themselves and develop the skills to become confident, independent learners who will grow up to be balanced, caring and principled citizens. Our dedicated, international teaching body ensures that students achieve highly at the school. We believe in challenging young minds, ensuring that our focus is on every student achieving beyond expectations both inside and outside of the curriculum. Over the last three years, we have achieved an average of 35 in the IBDP with a top score of 45.

The International School of Modena is a small, friendly school, with just over 250 students at present but it is growing fast due to its popularity with both expat and local families. We are proud to be a premium international school offering high quality education in a caring environment with happy, contented students. We are certain that you will see that ISM is a place that celebrates learning and values each and every student, offering them a challenging, enjoyable education aimed at developing a range of skills required for future success.

International School of Monza

(Founded 1984)

Head of School
Mr. Iain Sachev

PYP coordinator
Becky Taylor

MYP coordinator
Gaelle D'Inca

DP coordinator
Joe Cope

Status Private

Boarding/day Day

Gender Coeducational

Language of instruction
English, Italian

Authorised IB programmes
PYP, MYP, DP

Age Range 2 – 18

Number of pupils enrolled
270

Address
Via Solferino 23
20900 Monza (MB) | **ITALY**

TEL +39 039 9357701

Email
ismmonza@ism-ac.it

Website
www.
internationalschoolofmonza.it

At ISMonza, a full International Baccalaureate (IB) continuum school authorised to offer the Primary Years Programme (PYP), Middle Years Programme (MYP) and Diploma Programme (DP), we endeavour to deliver the International Baccalaureate programmes in the purist of forms, with the school's core values and the IB's Learner Profile embodied in everything that we do. Both the school and the group to which it belongs, have an established record of success in the IB, from age 2 all the way through to admission to the world's leading universities at age 18.

Perhaps most of note is the sense of collaboration that exists amongst all members of the school community. This is most evident in the way in which our highly qualified mother-tongue teachers and inquisitive students work towards a common goal of academic success which is seamlessly balanced with an inherent commitment to active global citizenship at every level. Although all classrooms are fitted with smart TVs and students bring tablets or laptops to school, we use technology in a blended approach where we feel it adds value to teaching and learning and not merely to replace traditional methods (yes, we do use books and, yes, we do talk to one another).

All this takes place in our city-centre campus – a stylish and colourful factory conversion – which has been specifically designed to foster collaborative approaches to teaching and learning. Our science laboratories are fitted with state-of-the-art equipment and we also boast carefully designed on-site spaces which support the delivery of our Reggio-Inspired Early Years Curriculum, three beautiful libraries, as well as studios for visual arts, drama and music, supported by a brand new sports complex. That said, living in such a culturally rich part of the world, we take many opportunities to knock down our classroom walls and learn from opportunities in the local and not-so-local area.

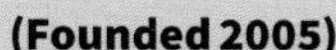

(Founded 2005)

Head of School
Stuart Rich

PYP coordinator
Michelle Rich

DP coordinator
Jacques Marais

Status Private

Boarding/day Day

Gender Coeducational

Language of instruction
English

Authorised IB programmes
PYP, DP

Age Range 4 – 19

Number of pupils enrolled
160

Fees
Day: €14,000 – €16,700

Address
Maximilianstr 43
67433 Neustadt an der Weinstrasse | **GERMANY**

TEL +49 6321 8900 960

Email
info@is-neustadt.de

Website
www.is-neustadt.de

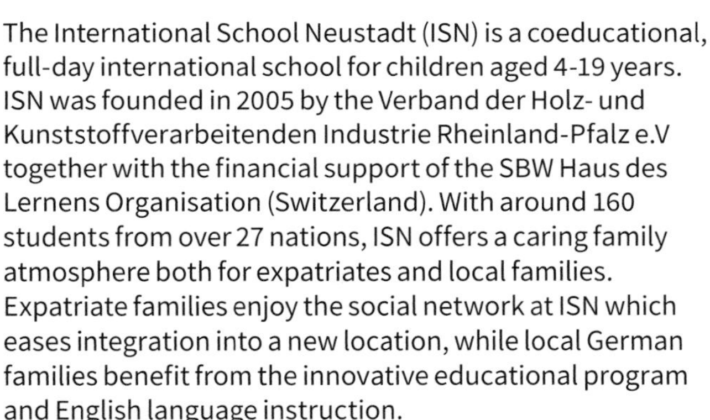

The International School Neustadt (ISN) is a coeducational, full-day international school for children aged 4-19 years. ISN was founded in 2005 by the Verband der Holz- und Kunststoffverarbeitenden Industrie Rheinland-Pfalz e.V together with the financial support of the SBW Haus des Lernens Organisation (Switzerland). With around 160 students from over 27 nations, ISN offers a caring family atmosphere both for expatriates and local families. Expatriate families enjoy the social network at ISN which eases integration into a new location, while local German families benefit from the innovative educational program and English language instruction.

As an IB World School, ISN was accredited in 2009 by the International Baccalaureate (IB) to offer both the Primary Years Programme for students between 4 and 12 years of age, and the IB Diploma Programme for students aged 16 and above. ISN is also an accredited examination center for Cambridge International Examinations and offers the full range of English examinations and IGCSE (International General Certificate of Secondary Education).

The school, which is located in several adjacent vineyard villas, offers a full day program from 8am until 5pm. While the main language of instruction is English, German classes are also taught daily to all students from beginner to native-speaker level. French is offered from year 7. Before and after school supervision is available each day, at no extra cost, to students from kindergarten up to grade 6. ISN also provides a wide range of after-school activities including music, drama, art and sports.

ISN is recognized by the state of Rhineland-Palatinate as an accredited supplementary school ('anerkannte Ergaenzungsschule'). The operators of the school, SBW Haus des Lernens in Switzerland have over 30 years schooling experience and 15 schools in Switzerland and Germany. In recent years the SBW has dedicated its expertise to the development of its International Schools which strive towards the implementation of the globally recognized IB PYP, IGCSE and IB Diploma qualifications.

For more information please contact the Admissions Office: info@is-neustadt.de

International School of Siena

Principal
Ms. Lianne Knibb

PYP coordinator
Isaac Driver

MYP coordinator
Letizia Rosati

DP coordinator
Lucio Pessia

Status Private

Boarding/day Day

Gender Coeducational

Language of instruction
English, Italian

Authorised IB programmes
PYP, MYP, DP

Age Range 3 – 18

Number of pupils enrolled
180

Address
Via del Petriccio e Belriguardo, 49/1
53100 Siena | **ITALY**

TEL +39 0577 328103

Email
office@internationalschoolofsiena.it

Website
www.internationalschoolofsiena.it

The International School of Siena opened in 2010 and has developed and grown considerably during the subsequent years. We are the only IB through school in Tuscany, fully authorised for the Primary Years Programme (PYP), Middle Years Programme (MYP) and Diploma Programme (DP).

Learning at IS Siena is exciting and engaging, as students strive for excellence in a climate that is caring and responsive to individual needs and goals. Our global vision is coordinated by an outstanding team of educational leaders and implemented by our highly skilled and dedicated professional staff.

We have recently relocated to our stunning new school building where we enjoy a spacious, light, modern teaching spaces with a spacious indoor gym, Drama/Dance studio, 2 Libraries, Music and Art rooms and Science laboratories fitted out to the highest standards. Our Early Years spaces are specially designed to complement the Reggio Inspired teaching approach. Our Inspired approach to PYP Early Years also draws inspiration from the Reggio Approach.

Learning at the International School of Siena is an international experience with students from around 25 nationalities. This leads to a perception of the world that merges understanding of our global context with the development of skills and attitudes that young people require to participate fully in the world of tomorrow, both as national and global citizens.

At the same time, we deeply appreciate the diversity of mother tongue languages in our school community and aim to utilise our diversity as well as supporting each student to appreciate our host country of Italy and become fully bilingual in English and Italian. We are so fortunate to be located in a beautiful area of Tuscany where we have access to a variety of cultural and educational resources in our local area which we strive to incorporate into the experience of the students, making connections between the classroom and the world around us.

We are a welcoming school community in which parents, students and staff work together to provide a stimulating programme, which engages each child in a concept-driven and inquiry-based environment.

International School of Ticino SA

Head of School
Mr. Andrew Ackers

PYP coordinator
Katarzyna Krohn

Status Private

Boarding/day Day

Gender Coeducational

Language of instruction
English, Italian

Authorised IB programmes
PYP

Age Range 3 – 14

Number of pupils enrolled
130

Address
Via Ponteggia, 23
Cadempino
6814 Lugano | **SWITZERLAND**

TEL +41 919710344

Email
frontoffice@isticino.com

Website
www.isticino.com

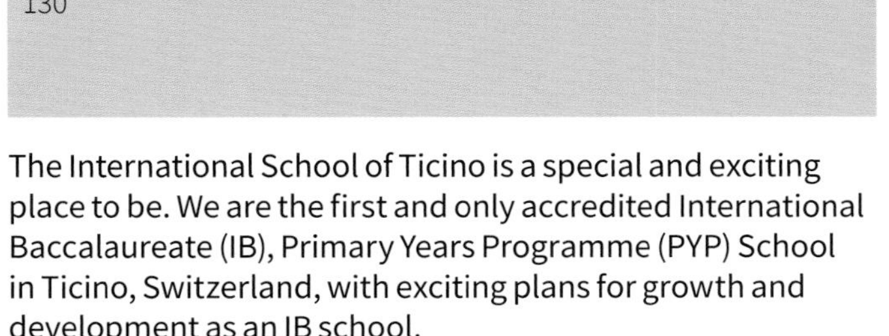

The International School of Ticino is a special and exciting place to be. We are the first and only accredited International Baccalaureate (IB), Primary Years Programme (PYP) School in Ticino, Switzerland, with exciting plans for growth and development as an IB school.

Here at the International School of Ticino we place the student at the centre of all we do to facilitate them to become lifelong learners. We achieve this through our school culture, which is rooted in the IB Mission statement, which states: The International Baccalaureate aims to develop inquiring, knowledgeable and caring young people who help to create a better and more peaceful world through intercultural understanding and respect.

The school opened as a kindergarten in 2014, as a feeder school to the International School Como in Italy, which had been in operation since 2002. The school was established to offer the local and international residents of Ticino an IB education. As of 2017 the International school of Ticino became independent and with IS Como joined the education group Inspired, who educate over 45000 students in 64 schools worldwide.

This grounding and combination with a leading education group has laid the foundations for the special community of learning which we see today in our new campus. The school now accommodates students from Kindergarten, 3 years old, to 14, offering the IB PYP and MYP programme. The design and build of the new campus have drawn upon our foundations, the IB mission and the vision of the school; Inspiring the extraordinary.

We accommodate our students in a facilitated student-centred learning environment, where we equip the child to develop in the international sector or in line with Ticino requirements. The opening of our new campus has enabled the International school of Ticino to open middle school with high school to follow in 2020, becoming a candidate school for the IB Middle Years Programme (MYP) and the Diploma Programme (DP) in 2019. This will enable your child to study at our school from the age of 3-18.

The International School of Ticino is a special and exciting place to be and we look forward to welcoming you to our community for a school visit, trial day and enrolment.

(Founded 2006)

Headmaster
Mr. Simon Hatton-Burke

PYP coordinator
Rebeca Albarrán Corroto

MYP coordinator
Pilar Molina

DP coordinator
Philip Brotherton

Status Private

Boarding/day Mixed

Gender Coeducational

Language of instruction
English, Spanish

Authorised IB programmes
PYP, MYP, DP

Number of pupils enrolled
560

Address
Juan de Vergara, 1
Urbanización La Legua
45005 Toledo, Castilla-La Mancha | **SPAIN**

TEL +34 925 280 363

Email
infotoledo@colegiosanpatricio.es

Website
colegiosanpatriciotoledo.com/en

International School San Patricio Toledo – Boarding School, offers the complete range of the International Baccalaureate study plan. From 3 to 17 years. PYP (Primary Years Programme) MYP (Middle Years Programme) and DP (Diploma Programme) bilingual or English only.

International School San Patricio Toledo also offers its students the chance to obtain the official certificates issued by the University of Cambridge and Trinity College of London. Also the DELE (Diploma of Spanish as a foreign language) of the Cervantes Institute.

The programs encourage students to take an active attitude towards lifelong learning in order to achieve their personal and academic goals.

Location:
It is located in an exclusive residential area of Toledo (1 hour from Madrid by car and 30 min by train). It covers an area of 30,000 square meters, with different spaces, where students develop different activities.

The boarding school is within the school grounds, which facilitates the use of the premises at all times without the need for transfers or departures from the campus. This ensures that students live in a fully-equipped campus with maximum security and control.

Furthermore, International School San Patricio Toledo Boarding School offers a complete educational experience for students between 12 and 17 years of age, allowing them to develop the communication and social skills essential for their later life and which form part of the educational objectives of the school model.

Foreign languages:
English, German, French, Chinese

Accommodation:
First class facilities.

Rooms are designed to allow groups to be formed according to the personal characteristics and diversity of the students. We can therefore accommodate 2, 3, or 4 students per room on both male and female floors.

Weekends:
We take great pride in our programmed weekend activities that make this educational experience, one of the best ways to discover a culture and deepen the three pillars of our educational model: Autonomy, Communication and Relationships.

(Founded 1980)

Principal
Júlia Ladeira Santos

PYP coordinator
Jenie Noite

MYP coordinator
Jane Gordon

Status Private

Boarding/day Day

Gender Coeducational

Language of instruction
English

Authorised IB programmes
PYP, MYP

Age Range 3 – 16

Number of pupils enrolled
150

Fees
€4,230 – €7,265

Address
Caminho Dos Saltos 6
9050-219 Funchal
Madeira | PORTUGAL

TEL +351 291 773218

Email
office@madeira.sharingschool.org

Website
www.sharingschool.org

The International Sharing School is a highly respected school on the lovely island of Madeira, Portugal. The school offers the PYP and the MYP programmes, teaching students aged 3 to 16, currently representing 23 different nationalities and with teachers from 8 different countries, in an international, multilingual and multicultural environment.

With 38 years of experience of international education, the International Sharing School recently decided to embrace the challenge of IB education , receiving full authorisation one year ago for both PYP and MYP, thus becoming the only IB World School in Madeira for both phases.

We are dedicated to achieving enjoyment and excellence in education for all.

As we continue to follow our ethos statement – “The passion of learning, the pride of teaching” – the International Sharing School aims to provide an excellent and continuous international educational experience, in order to develop enquiring knowledgeable and caring young people who help create a better and more peaceful world through intercultural understanding and respect.

The International Sharing School offers a curriculum focused on personal and professional development, preparing students for an increasingly global, competitive, multicultural and multilingual world.

Students begin their school learning at 3 years of age in a bilingual environment, with educators who are English and/or Portuguese native speakers, so that by the age of 6 they enter PYP 1 with a sound foundation of bilingualism. The language of instruction throughout the school is English but in respect to the host nation and, as the “heart” language for most of our students, there is a daily lesson of Portuguese for all students. In addition, the academic curriculum includes the teaching of German, Spanish, French, Mandarin and Russian. Students, therefore, are able to move to upper secondary and university education, having had the opportunity to learn, with a great degree of fluency, at least 5 of the 7 languages we offer.

We are very proud of our learning-journey and the traditions we have created. We are innovative and always strive to reflect the best of current practices and adapt to the demands of an ever-changing world.

Choosing a school is one of the most important decisions and has high significance as a long-term family investment. We offer a happy, enthusiastic and effective learning environment, combined with the expectation of challenging work experiences and high standards.

We encourage each and every student to fulfil their potential both academically and as a person in readiness for them to take their place successfully in the world of today and for the future.

ISTEK Baris Schools

Head of School
Füsun Sirmaci

PYP coordinator
Ceni Alpanda

Status Private

Boarding/day Day

Gender Coeducational

Language of instruction
Turkish, English

Authorised IB programmes
PYP

Age Range 3 – 11

Number of pupils enrolled
550

Fees
TL31,100 (pre-school) – TL43,900 (primary school)

Address
Bagdat Cad. No: 238/1
Ciftehavuzlar – Kadiköy
Istanbul
34730 | TURKEY

TEL +90 216 360 12 18
FAX +90 216 385 25 16

Email
baris.ilkokul@istek.k12.tr

Website
www.istek.k12.tr

The ISTEK Schools is comprised of several K-12 campuses. As an educational organization and a community that believes in life-long learning, the Foundation is committed to constant innovation and by providing scholarships the Foundation strives for equal opportunity education. Working in national and international contexts, aiming to make positive contributions to both the country and the world's future, and giving priority to scientific inquiry defines ISTEK as a foundation apart.

ISTEK Baris Schools' student body is mainly composed of Turkish students. About 5% come from bilingual/bicultural backgrounds. The Turkish National Curriculum is implemented under the PYP framework.

The school library is very active and has a central role in the lives of the school community. The classrooms that are equipped with modern technology, the field trips organized during the year and access to various databases develop students' research skills and lead them to become active inquirers.

With open mindedness as a goal, open communication is promoted by all the members of the school community. The Student Council is very active and participates in code of conduct related management decisions, regarding the suggestions and wishes of the students. Students are always encouraged to express their opinions and respect others' views. Their opinions are valued and they are provided with many opportunities to take action.

Learning together and learning from one another through cooperative learning and our reflective-thinking-oriented assessment system, support ongoing development of the students and play a pivotal role in leading them to become autonomous learners.

ISTEK Baris Schools as a community is committed to life long learning and responsible action that will help to create a better and more peaceful world.

Admission to ISTEK Baris Schools is offered on the basis of a school administered evaluation and according to the regulations of Turkish Ministry of Education.

ISTEK Kemal Atatürk Schools (Kindergarten & Primary School)

Head of Primary School
Esra Türken

Head of Pre-School
Nihan Keles

PYP coordinator
Mine Özge Topaloglu

Status Private

Boarding/day Day

Gender Coeducational

Language of instruction
Turkish

Authorised IB programmes
PYP

Age Range 3 – 10

Address
Tarabya Bayiri Cad. No: 60
Tarabya/Sariyer
Istanbul
34457 | TURKEY

TEL +90 212 262 7575
FAX +90 212 262 7958

Email
kemalataturk@istek.k12.tr

Website
www.istek.k12.tr

Situated on the European side of Istanbul overlooking the Bosphorus, lies Istek Kemal Atatürk Schools, which educates students from pre-school to high school. Apart from the Preschool and Primary School National Education Curriculum, PYP was added with IB authorization in 2013.

Since 1985 Istek Kemal Atatürk Schools offers a safe environment with open and closed sport centers, a semi-olympic swimming pool, well equipped laboratories, and libraries rich in resources and modern educational technologies. One can also find a spacious dining area, art rooms, a bicycle training zone, and a 7400m garden!

We believe that every child is gifted in a unique way. We aim to discover those gifts by offering different programmes such as; chess, musical instruments, visual arts, swimming, gym, modern dance, drama and brain teasers.

Throughout the year we assess our students in order to provide the best support for those whose needs differ from their peers. Our educational program is continuously developing out of consideration for our children's age, level of development, needs and any international developments. The curriculum is enhanced by making changes that allows students to perform at their top cognitive capacity. We support them in reaching this capacity by activating their curiosity, asking them to research, explore and solve problems. The IB Baccalaureate PYP Primary Years Programme helps students to experience learning and the process of knowledge. Taking into account each students individual differences, we have tutorials for students who need extra support. We believe that students should care about the issues facing their communities and environment, and it's our responsibility to create a community of well rounded, knowledgeable, internationally minded, and caring students.

English is taught intensively at our school. Our students are evaluated by internationally recognized tests such as Cambridge, Trinity, and GESE every year. From fourth grade on, we teach French and German intensively in an effort to broaden our students horizons and to show them that they are citizens of the world.

We aim to create experiences that will make our students well rounded, organized, mature and socially responsible. We open new clubs in areas where we see students show interest, in addition to the arts and sports lessons that they normally attend. Students are selected to take part in after school clubs aimed at advancing their knowledge of science, and their abilities in arts and sports. These students go on to represent our school in national and international competitions.

Jubilee School

School Principal
Suha Jouaneh

DP coordinator
Yara Kajo

Status Private

Boarding/day Mixed

Gender Coeducational

Language of instruction
English

Authorised IB programmes
DP

Address
P.O.Box: 830578
Amman
11183 | JORDAN

TEL +962 6 5238216
FAX +962 6 5234231

Email
jubilee@jubilee.edu.jo

Website
www.jubilee.edu.jo

The Jubilee School. The Jubilee School (JS), founded in 1993, is an independent, non-governmental, not-for-profit, residential, co-educational secondary school for the duration of four years (grades 9-12), that promotes academic excellence and provides a unique opportunity for outstanding students to reach their highest potential.
Mission. Contribute to the development of future leaders committed to serving their country and capable of addressing global challenges by advancing national and regional educational standards through the development of innovative curricula and quality programs.
Educational Program. The Jubilee School provides a comprehensive educational program that includes both compulsory and elective courses. The compulsory courses are mandated by Jordan's Ministry of Education (MOE), the British International General Certificate of Secondary Education (IGCSE), and The International Baccalaureate. Concurrently, the students study nine out of over 40 elective courses. Additionally, a prerequisite for graduation is the successful completion of a Graduation Project and 120 hours of community service.

In addition to the Academic Program, the school focuses on the interpersonal development which is a variety of scheduled classes and training workshops that allow students to be critical thinkers capable of effective communication and innovation in a new economy that prizes individual excellence.
Extra-Curricular Program. The School is distinguished by its activities. All students are exposed to a variety of experiences on both national and international levels. They are offered opportunities to meet and converse on current issues and future challenges with politicians, academicians, economists and social leaders. They are also encouraged to design and implement research studies and surveys, as well as to take part in student-exchange programs, competitions, workshops and seminars, computer networking, camping and voluntary work in Jordan and abroad.
The Students. The JS brings together approximately 500 students from various socio-economic backgrounds and geographic regions in Jordan, majority of whom come from families with limited financial sources, and from areas and social environments that lack adequate educational and life counseling resources required to nourish their unique intellectual capabilities. Their diversity is a living model in pluralism, tolerance and democracy.

Each year, around 150 students from public and private schools are selected to join the Jubilee School. JS employs rigorous multiple-criteria admission system based on exceptional students' academic performance and demonstration of leadership potential.

(Founded 2010)

Principal
Richard Drew

PYP coordinator
Amiee Clark

MYP coordinator
David Bauzà-Capart

DP coordinator
Michelle Andrews

CP coordinator
Lisa Postlethwaite

Status Private

Boarding/day Day

Gender Coeducational

Language of instruction
English

Authorised IB programmes
PYP, MYP, DP, CP

Age Range 3 – 18

Number of pupils enrolled
803

Fees
Pre-K to KG2: AED39,750–48,500
Grade 1 to 5: AED52,500–62,500
Grade 6 to 10: AED72,970
Grade 11 and 12: AED84,197

Address
53 B Street, off Al Wasl Road
Jumeira 1
Dubai | UNITED ARAB EMIRATES

TEL +971 (0)4 344 6931

Email admissions@jbschool.ae

Website www.jbschool.ae

Campus

Founded in 2010, Jumeira Baccalaureate School (JBS) is part of Taaleem, the UAE's second largest school provider.

The JBS campus sits on approximately eight acres of prime land in the heart of Dubai, with outstanding learning, sporting and performing arts facilities; including a FIFA sized grass field, swimming pool and separate infant pool, two large gymnasiums, designated music and visual arts rooms, primary and secondary library and shared play areas for younger students.

Vision and Mission

Our vision is to prepare all of our students for the innovation age by igniting their passions, purpose and curiosity through challenge and high expectations. Our students will be responsible, confident, and independent learners who are respectful; they embrace and celebrate diversity and have awareness of the environment. They strive to reach excellence whilst maintaining happiness and wellbeing.

Our mission is:

- To embrace and respect diversity
- To foster the wellbeing of all members of our community
- To create a culture in which learning can flourish
- To engage with high levels of challenge, enabling academic and personal success
- To support cognitive and social skill development using innovative, research-based practice to enhance learning for all
- To support the development of emotional intelligence, guided by the elements of the IB learner profile
- To promote environmental awareness, sustainability and entrepreneurship

Extended Learning and Inclusion

At JBS, we aim to provide exceptional opportunities for each of our students in a supporting and challenging environment.

We welcome all students to JBS. This could include students with special educational or learning needs, students with English as an additional Language (EAL), and those who are Gifted or Talented. Our dedicated Inclusion team works on a graduated response to identify and remove barriers to learning.

We pride ourselves on high academic standards, however we are more than this. Truly excellent education is about developing a passion for life-long learning and a capability for independent thinking.

KENT COLLEGE
CANTERBURY

(Founded 1885)

Executive Head
Dr David Lamper

Senior School Head
Mr Phil Wise

Junior School Head
Mr Andy Carter

DP coordinator
Mr Graham Letley

Status Private

Boarding/day Mixed

Gender Coeducational

Language of instruction
English

Authorised IB programmes
DP

Age Range 0 – 18 years
(Boarding from 8)

Number of pupils enrolled
785

Fees
Day: £16,794 – £18,864
Boarding: £26,244 – £35,628

Address
Whitstable Road
Canterbury
Kent
CT2 9DT | UK

TEL +44 (0)1227 763 231

Email
admissions@kentcollege.co.uk

Website
www.kentcollege.com

Kent College Facilities
Kent College sits on the outskirts of the historic city of Canterbury on an 80 acre campus. As well as boasting 26 acres of sports fields, the school has a working farm where students can join the Farm Club or receive riding lessons. This year will also see the completion of the Great Hall, a 600 seat state-of-the-art auditorium for the performing arts.

Curriculum
Kent College offers a full range of IB subjects for study over the two years of the Diploma. We also offer a very popular pre IB course in Year 11, this allows students to get a taste of their IB options. Our IB results are consistently very high with students achieving an average points score of 37 for the last 3 years, placing the school in the top 10 Independent IB schools in the UK. The ISI Inspection in February 2015 compared our results as "exceptional in comparison to worldwide averages".

Many of our students gain the bilingual diploma as they are able to study literature courses in their first language alongside the main programme. All our Diploma candidates gained places at their first choice universities including Oxbridge, top London Universities alongside other European Universities.

We are very flexible when it comes to constructing the timetables for Diploma candidates and encourage applicants to identify courses and subjects they wish to study even if we do not offer them as we are able to bespoke most options. Kent College offers outstanding levels of teaching and support for the IB Diploma with additional classes and tutoring available as standard to ensure the very best outcomes for individuals. Class sizes are small – generally between 8 -14. The school also offers A Level, GCSE and IGCSE.

Extra Curricular
The academic life of the IB student is complemented with a rich and diverse extracurricular programme. There are large numbers of clubs and societies for every interest and new ones established each year to meet the changing desires of our students. National representation in sport is common with equally high standards in music and drama, there is simply something for everyone at Kent College.

Pastoral Care
The pastoral system in the school is highly valued and central to our ethos as a Methodist school, the family atmosphere and supportive environment in the boarding and day school community means that well rounded global citizens leave the school on graduation from the IB. The majority of students are British but the school's students represent over 40 different nationalities. The school operates a strong pastoral network from House Parents to Tutors and Heads of Year that ensures all students receive the wrap around care that they need to flourish academically and to grow into confident young adults.

King Abdulaziz School

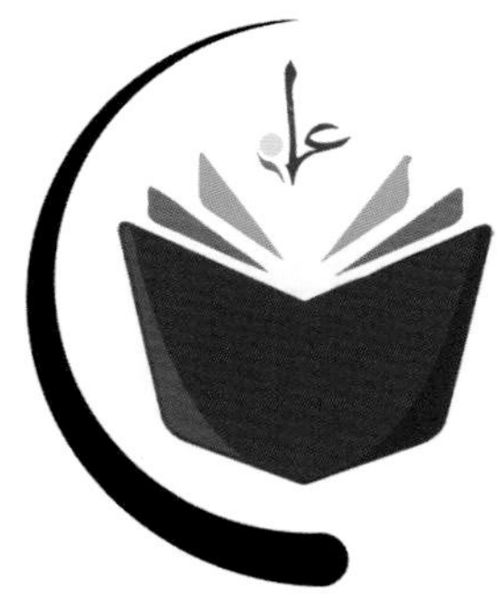

(Founded 2013)

Principal
Mr Abdennaceur Saadaoui

PYP coordinator
Raheela Akram

Status Private

Boarding/day Day

Gender Male

Language of instruction
English

Authorised IB programmes
PYP

Number of pupils enrolled
165

Fees
Day: SR32,000

Address
Ali Ibn Abi Taleb Road
P.O. Box 43111
Medina
41561 | SAUDI ARABIA

TEL +966 503 454 420 / +966 553 039 300

Email
asaadaoui@kaism.org
rakram@kaism.org

Website
www.kaism.org

School Background
King Abdulaziz School Medina, established in 2013, is an accredited IB school that offers the Primary Years Programme and is a candidate school for the IB Middle Years Programme.

Our Mission Statement
King Abdulaziz School strives to cultivate international educational experiences that prepare active and lifelong learners. KAS aims at providing stimulating academic programmes supported by rigorous assessment implemented through an inquiry based, caring learning environment.

Learners are equipped with the skills they require to reach their full potential and become responsible global citizens.

KAS prepares students to be open to other perspectives, values and traditions whilst recognizing their own identity and taking pride in their cultural heritage.

Curriculum and Activities
King Abdulaziz School's academic enrichment initiatives are embedded in local and global programmes mapped to the UN's sustainability goals, peace and tolerance, celebrations of cultural and international events, e-learning, arts, sports and student leadership programmes to create a basis for interactive experiential learning.

The School Faculty
The teaching staff comprises of more than 30 educators who are professionally trained by the IB through continuous professional development. Many of our staff members are native English speakers and have vast experience in teaching in international schools.

The Facilities
KAS strives to provide a wide array of facilities for both students and teachers in order to implement the IB programmes effectively. The facilities include a purpose-built campus, libraries, computer and science laboratories, an art room and an auditorium.

KAS inspires the individual potential of all students to enable them to become principled, proficient, inquiring, and caring lifelong learners.

(Founded 1553)

Head
Mrs Joanna Wright

DP coordinator
Zeba Clarke

Status Private

Boarding/day Mixed

Gender Coeducational

Language of instruction
English

Authorised IB programmes
DP

Age Range 11 – 18

Number of pupils enrolled
400

Fees
Day: £15,975 – £21,285
Weekly Boarding: £31,125 – £32,325
Boarding: £32,775 – £34,050

Address
Godalming
Surrey
GU8 5SG | UK

TEL +44 (0)1428 686700

Email
admissions@kesw.org

Website
www.kesw.org

King Edward's Witley, a co-educational independent British boarding and day school for pupils aged 11-18, is situated in stunning 100-acre grounds in a designated Area of Outstanding Natural Beauty in Surrey. The School benefits from a convenient location with excellent road and rail links between London, the South Coast and Heathrow and Gatwick international airports.

Founded in 1553, King Edward's enjoys established links with the City. The School embraces its heritage and traditions with a modern outlook consistent with a world-class centre of excellence, with a commitment to the pastoral and education needs of the children it serves.

King Edward's is one of the UK's top 25 co-educational day and boarding schools offering the International Baccalaureate Diploma Programme (IBDP), opening university opportunities in the UK and globally. In 2019 every student passed the IB, with an average score of 34.7 points, well outstripping the worldwide average for IB students of 30 points out of a possible 45. 56% of individual subject grades were 7 or 6 – the equivalent to A Level A* and A, an outstanding achievement.

The School offers a Pre-Sixth one-year programme for overseas students as a stepping stone to the IB. Pre-Sixth gives students, aged 15-16, a taste of boarding life, an opportunity to improve their spoken and written English and enjoy cultural trips around the UK. For Pre-Sixth students looking to continue into King Edward's Sixth Form or return to education in their home country, they are able to take GCSE examinations in a range of subjects.

Living in houses alongside students aged 11 – 18, our Pre-Sixth and Sixth Form students are fully integrated with their peers and build deep friendships. There are currently 400 boarding and day pupils from over 40 countries. 70% are English native speakers.

Academic and sporting facilities are extensive affording a broad curriculum and co-curricular programme. There are over 50 Clubs & Societies including many sporting opportunities; much music-making with over twenty ensembles and choirs; an array of art and DT workshops; extended drama and theatre experiences, trips and much more from the cerebral chess and debating to the challenging Duke of Edinburgh to the more the mindful bee keeping and yoga.

KING WILLIAM'S COLLEGE

(Founded 1833)

Principal
Mr Joss Buchanan

DP coordinator
Alasdair Ulyett

Status Private

Boarding/day Mixed

Gender Coeducational

Language of instruction
English

Authorised IB programmes
DP

Age Range 11 – 18

Number of pupils enrolled
375

Fees
Day: £18,250 – £23,250
Boarding: £29,250 – £34,250

Address
Castletown
Isle of Man
IM9 1TP | UK

TEL +44 (0)1624 820110

Email
admissions@kwc.im

Website
www.kwc.im

We are a relatively small school, under 400 students. Approximately 20% of students board, with half of the boarders living on the Island and the rest from a wide variety of countries around the world. We are non-selective, but through the dedication of our staff, the structure of support for each individual and the work ethic of our students, we achieve excellent results. Our students go to top universities in the UK, Europe and the USA.

The Isle of Man is a beautiful environment in which to live. It is a safe haven with a very low crime rate, giving students the freedom to explore and take advantage of the fresh air, open countryside and beaches, away from the hustle and bustle and pollution of a busy city. The Island is easy to get to with air links from the major airports in the UK.

We are one of a few schools where every student in the Sixth Form studies for the International Baccalaureate Diploma. The IB philosophy – particularly its emphasis on skills and its focus on internationalism – is central to our approach and we are one of the largest and most experienced IB schools in the British Isles.

Our pupils follow a broad curriculum of sporting activities, competing in the major sports against UK and Island schools. Every three years, the senior rugby and hockey teams embark on a world sports tour during the summer months. We have our own Golf Academy and rock climbing and sailing are also on offer, along with a wide variety of other extra-curricular activities.

Drama and Music thrive and pupils are given the opportunity to perform at many events and productions. There are workshops throughout the year and students are also encouraged to participate in competitions.

'An Island Education for a Global Future'

(Founded 2010)

Headteacher
Mr David Collins

CP coordinator
Mrs Jane Elliott

Status State

Boarding/day Day

Gender Coeducational

Language of instruction
English

Authorised IB programmes
CP

Age Range 11 – 18

Number of pupils enrolled
1379

Address
Bradbourne Vale Road
Sevenoaks
Kent
TN13 3LE | UK

TEL 01732 454608

Email
enquiries@knoleacademy.org

Website
www.knoleacademy.org

Knole Academy is an all-ability academy situated in the beautiful and desirable area of Sevenoaks in Kent. Close to London and with excellent connections to Europe, it enjoys the benefits of both, with cultural and educational excursions to the capital, the continent and beyond.

At the core of Knole is aspiration and high expectations for every child, regardless of background or ability. As a result, the taught curriculum is both broad and balanced, ensuring all pupils are engaged and enthused. All pupils receive high quality teaching that is equally as ambitious for the grammar stream as it is for the wider student body. In order for every child to achieve his or her potential the learning environment generated is calm, safe and inclusive.

Knole pupils benefit from state of the art facilities that offer a vast range of co and extra-curricular opportunities. The academy's Expressive Arts status drives the many school performances, concerts, productions, dance shows and exhibitions; in sport, the facilities and staff provide an unrivalled range of activities and the school has large cohorts of successful Duke of Edinburgh participants as well as an expanding Combined Cadet Force, one of the few in a state school.

The sixth form is excellent, providing pupils with the opportunity to study academic IB diplomas and career related studies through the IBCP. All pupils undertake the National Citizen Service in year 12 as part of the service learning element of the core programme. IBCP students undertake to learn Italian as their language development, having already had the opportunity to study French and Spanish to GCSE level.

The academy is justly proud that the outcome of such a well-structured curriculum and the diverse opportunities outside the classroom is global citizens who are:

- Knowledgeable
- Nurturing
- Open minded
- Locally and globally focussed
- Excellence driven.

KNIGHTSBRIDGE
SCHOOLS
INTERNATIONAL

Head of School
Robert Ingham

Head of Boarding
Robert Ingham

PYP coordinator
Marija Djukic

MYP coordinator
Kevin Osborne

DP coordinator
Jacqueline Cussen

Status Private

Boarding/day Mixed

Gender Coeducational

Language of instruction
English

Authorised IB programmes
PYP, MYP, DP

Age Range 3 – 18

Number of pupils enrolled
113

Fees
Day: €7,440 – €17,220
Boarding: €13,750

Address
Seljanovo bb
Porto Montenegro
Tivat | MONTENEGRO

TEL +382 32 672 655

Email
info@ksi-montenegro.com

Website
www.ksi-montenegro.com

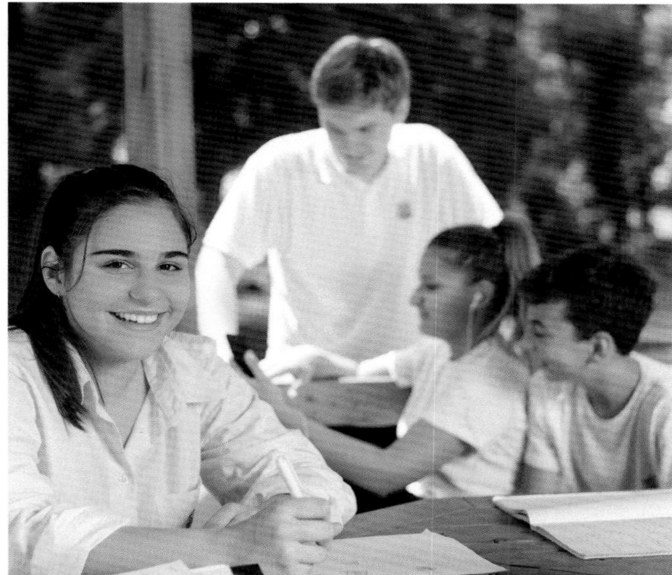

Knightsbridge Schools International Montenegro is an IB World School authorised to offer the Primary Years Programme, Middle Years and the Diploma Programme. School is also fully licensed by the Montenegrin Ministry of Education, and a member of Council of International Schools (CIS). KSI Montenegro is a member of an international network of schools – KSI, based in London.

Located in the tranquil surroundings of Boka Bay, within the luxury superyacht marina and nautical village Porto Montenegro, KSI offers students a challenging and rewarding educational experience. Students benefit from our stimulating surroundings which promote our healthy body, healthy mind philosophy.

Boarding at KSI is a great addition to the school and a new aspect of education in our community. It opened in September 2013 offering a British model of pastoral support with an international ethos. It is available to students aged 11-18. KSI Montenegro strives to create an environment of comfort, safety and fun for boarders.

While KSI Montenegro has a diverse student body with children from about 18 different countries, the teachers are mainly coming from English speaking regions.

KSI Montenegro provides a holistic, balanced and varied curriculum that addresses the needs of all learners and supports the development of learning strategies that prepare them for each stage of their education. All students are encouraged to take initiative and develop personal responsibility, and are expected to actively participate in developing a friendly, welcoming and culturally understanding environment. This adds to the holistic experience of boarding and allows students to develop as a community of empowered and engaged global citizens.

KSI Montenegro aims to develop the knowledge, skills and values of learners through active inquiry, participation and reflection, so that they may become collaborative and compassionate global citizens who are committed to making a positive difference.

The main language of instruction in the school is English, but the school is developing multilingualism through its language programmes by currently offering the host country language, as well as French and German lessons.

At KSI, we believe that learning is year-round. During the summer months KSI offers exciting summer camp, which includes a variety of outdoor activities such as sailing, rowing, swimming etc. Winter months bring great possibility to enjoy hiking and sightseeing. There is also an expanding after school activities programme that makes school life much more interesting.

(Founded 2006)

Head of School
Barbara Manke-Boesten

DP coordinator
Dr. Stefan Wester

Status Private

Boarding/day Day

Gender Coeducational

Language of instruction
English, German

Authorised IB programmes
DP

Age Range 6 – 19

Number of pupils enrolled
1000

Fees
Annual €4,800

Address
Ramskamp 64B
Elmshorn
25337 | GERMANY

TEL +49 4121 261040

Email
info@leibniz-privatschule.de

Website
www.leibniz-privatschule.de

School
Leibniz Privatschule (LPS) is a coeducational German and English-language day school. LPS provides education from kindergarten, primary school, to secondary school. In our German-language program students can graduate with the German school leaving certificates of middle school and Abitur. As an International Baccalaureate (IB) World School, LPS is serving the internationally-minded community of the metropolitan region Hamburg. We teach the IB Diploma Programme, an ambitious two-year program in English language leading to an internationally acknowledged university entrance degree. Our primary school follows the language-immersion method where children are embedded in an English-language environment. LPS was founded in 2006 by educators and teachers. The modern school campus is located in Elmshorn, a town with 500 inhabitants 35 km northwest of Hamburg. A second campus was founded in 2008 and is now residing at a newly build site in Kaltenkirchen, 35 km north of Hamburg.

Mission
We seek to deliver not only education but to help young people to develop strong personalities and to be prepared for life. It is our aim to enable them to flourish in their chosen fields, for example in academic, cultural and sporting pursuits. We encourage intercultural understanding while paying respect to cultural and national identities.

Community
Students attending LPS comprise a variety of nations. While most students have a German background a growing number of students are non-German totaling 40 different nationalities. Our teachers reflect this internationality. Some have worked and lived abroad before teaching at LPS. A substantial part of our teachers have non-German mother tongue.

Why to choose us?
Learning structure: In all classes standardized instructional method are applied. It is based on latest neuroscientific and educational knowledge.

Reliable from 7.30 am to 5 pm: Our school provides all-day activities. Five to seven 45 minute lessons, lunch, afternoon training sessions, and clubs in sports, music, handcrafts and other activities.

No class cancellations: We do not cancel classes. There is always a substitution if the teacher gets ill. Therefore, no student has to leave school early.

We care: If there are problems of any kind, the teachers are there for you. They spend the entire working day at their office in school and are contactable via phone or email.

Daily sports classes: Physical activity is crucial for children: it prevents health problems, and supports cognitive capacities. LPS is the only school in Germany offering daily physical education for children in primary and secondary school.

Leighton Park School

LEIGHTON PARK

FOUNDED 1890

(Founded 1890)

Head
Mr Matthew L S Judd BA, PGCE

DP coordinator
Mrs Helen Taylor

Status Private

Boarding/day Mixed

Gender Coeducational

Language of instruction
English

Authorised IB programmes
DP

Age Range 11 – 18

Number of pupils enrolled
495

Fees
Day: £22,860
Weekly Boarding: £31,080
Boarding: £37,170

Address
Shinfield Road
Reading
Berkshire
RG2 7ED | UK

TEL 0118 987 9600

Email
admissions@leightonpark.com

Website
www.leightonpark.com

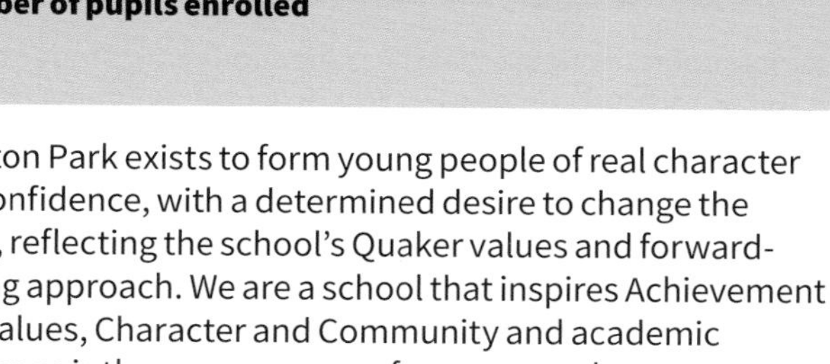

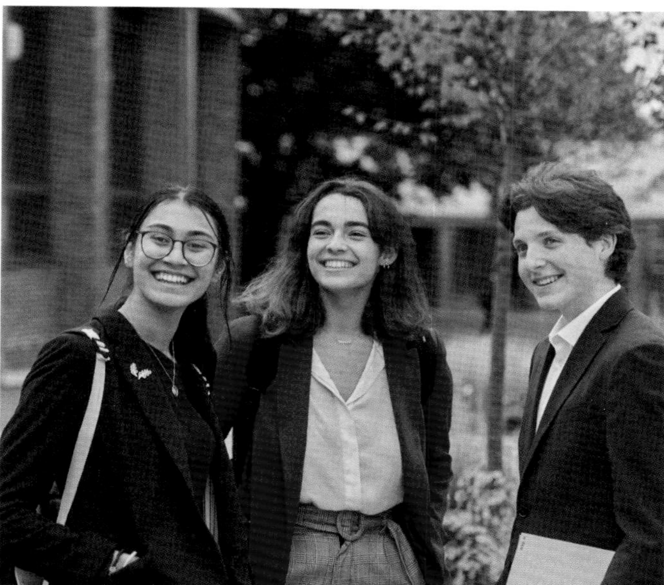

Leighton Park exists to form young people of real character and confidence, with a determined desire to change the world, reflecting the school's Quaker values and forward-looking approach. We are a school that inspires Achievement with Values, Character and Community and academic excellence is the consequence of our approach.

Our vibrant learning community empowers each student to achieve excellent outcomes, through supporting their choices, nurturing individuality and encouraging talent in whatever direction it may lie. Ours is an education for succeeding in life, as well as in academic assessments. Set in 65 acres of beautiful parkland, our students have an enriching environment in which to learn, reflect and grow.

The success of our approach is demonstrated by UK Government 16-18 league tables, which place the school in the top 3% in England for the academic progress made by our Sixth Form students.

Leighton Park is particularly known for STEAM (Science, Technology, Engineering, Arts and Maths), with a particular emphasis on creative problem solving and interdisciplinary approaches. Music is another particular strength of the School with a brand new Music and Media Centre providing students with exceptional facilities, including a Yamaha Live Lounge recording studio. Our Music department is accredited as a Flagship Music Education Partner, the only school in Europe to hold this status.

With Quaker values held strongly at the centre of all that we do, our emphasis is on our students loving their learning, encouraging them to try a huge range of new experiences and developing their greatest talents. You will be struck on visiting us by the warmth of relationships that characterise the school, the wealth of opportunities for development of body and mind, and the sense of calm and space in which that development takes place.

Lincoln
Community School
Learn, Lead, Connect

(Founded 1968)

Head of School
Sheena Nabholz

PYP coordinator
Natalie Wilhelm

MYP coordinator
Lisa Thompson

DP coordinator
Luke MacBride

Status Private/Not For Profit

Boarding/day Day

Gender Coeducational

Language of instruction
English

Authorised IB programmes
PYP, MYP, DP

Age Range 4 – 18

Number of pupils enrolled
680

Fees
US$14,788 – US$25,761

Address
#126/21 Reindolf Road
Abelemkpe, Accra | **GHANA**

TEL +233 302 21 8100

Email
headofschool@lincoln.edu.gh

Website www.lincoln.edu.gh

In 1968, six American families joined together to create Lincoln Community School. Some 50 years later, Lincoln Community School is an International Baccalaureate World School offering IB curriculum through the lens of U.S. curricular standards and is recognized as a leading international school in Africa. LCS is accredited by the Middle States Association of Colleges and Schools in the USA, and authorized to offer the International Baccalaureate Primary Years, Middle Years, and Diploma Programmes (PYP, MYP, DP). LCS is also a member of the Council of International Schools, the Association of International Schools in Africa (AISA) and part of the West Africa International Schools Activities League (WAISAL).

In keeping with our ethos as an American-style international school, LCS offers a rich extracurricular program that embraces appreciation for and participation in the arts, personal fitness and a healthy, well-balanced lifestyle. LCS students frequently stay beyond the regular school day to enjoy our after-school activity programs, programs that not only bring us together, but make sure that we keep "community" in the middle of Lincoln School. Lincoln Community School serves students from pre-kindergarten (4 years old by September 1 for the start of that year) through grade 12.

As an international school in an increasingly cosmopolitan Accra, our students and faculty come from countries around the globe. With a student population of 680 for the 2019-2020 school year, LCS boasts some 60 different nationalities among its community. 28% of the students are U.S. citizens, constituting the largest national group of students at LCS. Our faculty is also intentionally diverse to ensure that the demographic of our teachers is a reflection of our student body.

The school has stimulating co-curricular programs that include a wide range of sports, art, and service activities. With a caring, respectful, multicultural environment, the school is committed to instilling in each student a desire to learn, to take appropriate risks, and to accept challenges. The school community is committed to developing students who are resilient and adaptable, equipped with the knowledge and skills and disposition to continue their education and become personally fulfilled, interdependent, socially responsible adults. Due to the curriculum, the faculty and the community atmosphere on campus, students attending LCS are able to transition quickly and smoothly when entering our community or leaving for their next school.

The school is located on a 6.5 acre site in a residential area of Accra. School facilities are air conditioned with 81 classrooms including 4 art rooms, 3 science labs, 3 music rooms, 2 visual and performing arts stages, elementary, middle school, and high school libraries, an early childhood center, counseling offices and office space for administration. Sports facilities include a multipurpose hall, playing field, a semi-Olympic swimming pool, 2 multipurpose courts, and dressing room facilities. Playground space includes grassy playing areas, 2 sandy areas with recreational apparatus and open access to one of the multipurpose court spaces. Food services are provided by a local catering company. A new four storey elementary school, soon to be completed, reflects state of the art learning space design including 2 STEM labs. The building exhibits environmentally friendly features and energy efficient technology.

LWIS Keserwan-Adma International School

Adma International School

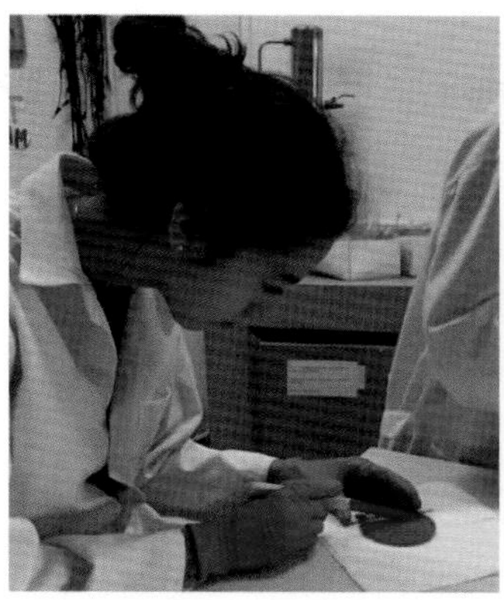

(Founded 1997)

Head of School
Dr. Nabil Husni

DP coordinator
Jacques El Khoury

Status Private

Boarding/day Day

Gender Coeducational

Language of instruction
English

Authorised IB programmes
DP

Age Range 3 – 18

Number of pupils enrolled
400

Fees
Day: $3,350 – $8,200

Address
Mar Nohra
Fatqa, Keserwan | **LEBANON**

TEL +961 9 740 226

Email
info@lwis-ais.edu.lb

Website
www.lwis-ais.edu.lb

Vision

LWIS-AiS, home of Peace Education, will set the pace for holistic learner-centered education.

Mission

LWIS-AiS promotes life-long learning through Peace Education, professional development, and facilitated classrooms that utilize differentiation, inquiry, cooperative learning, and interactive technology.

We endorse a partnership where students, parents, staff, and community members work together in a safe and nurturing environment to develop higher order thinking, academic excellence, ethical behavior, and personal growth. We honor the gift and support the need of every child. We also empower learners to become active and innovative contributors to an ever diverse international and multicultural society.

Values

LWIS-AiS ensures that the actions of all learners are guided by its PACER values:

Perseverence
Agility
Clarity
Empathy
Respect
Facilities

LWIS-AiS is located in Fatka, Lebanon. It overlooks the beautiful bay of Jounieh in what is an entirely green landscaped and residential neighborhood. The school features well-equipped classrooms with technology for both main stream and individualized learning students, internet connectivity, music and art rooms, indoor and outdoor playgrounds, as well as a library, science and computer labs, and a dance and drama area. The school consists of two campuses. The Upper Campus encompasses Grades 5 to 12 while the Lower Campus hosts Kindergarten through Grade 4.

Programs

LWIS-AiS has been accredited by NEASC since 2009. It offers the American High School Diploma in addition to the National Program. Furthermore, it became an authorized International Baccalaureate World School for the Diploma Programme in May 2019.

Teachers

LWIS-AiS teachers are highly qualified, experienced teachers. The IB DP teachers have received IB authorized training.

Students

The School's diverse student body is one of its special assets. The approximate number of students is 400 representing over 46 nationalities.

We invite you to join our journey and discover how we measure success one happy learner at a time.

Lycée Franco-Britannique Ecole Internationale

(Founded 1989)

Head of School
Milijana Jovic

Administrator
Anna Milasin

PYP, MYP & DP coordinator
Nathaniel Akue Mackaya

Status Private

Boarding/day Day

Gender Coeducational

Language of instruction
French, English

Authorised IB programmes
PYP, MYP, DP

Age Range 3 – 18

Number of pupils enrolled
200

Address
Batterie IV
B.P. 159
Libreville | **GABON**

TEL +241 01 73 71 17
+241 01 73 43 49
+241 07 70 25 65
FAX +241 01 73 43 49

Email
jovicefb@yahoo.com
ecolefrancobritannique@yahoo.fr

Website
www.efblbv.org

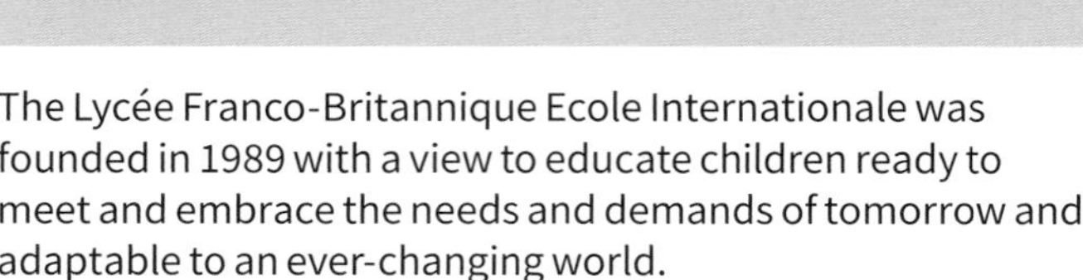

The Lycée Franco-Britannique Ecole Internationale was founded in 1989 with a view to educate children ready to meet and embrace the needs and demands of tomorrow and adaptable to an ever-changing world.

Our School was the first in Gabon to become a candidate school for the IB programmes as well as authorized to dispense the PYP and the MYP (both 2015). Pupils have the possibility to sit the Brevet des Collèges General (French exam) at the end of Middle School alongside the MYP Certificate.

At present, we are also authorized to offer the DP to ensure the continuum.

The core of our program is taught in French with a particular emphasis on foreign languages which occupy a key position within our School and are taught daily: English is offered from the age of 3 and Spanish from age 7 onwards. However this is not to the detriment of other subjects which all hold an equal importance within our taught curriculum.

Moreover, a plethora of nationalities are represented within our School. This multi-national spectrum nurtures a spirit of tolerance and respect for the values, beliefs and culture of every single pupil whilst encouraging cultural diversity and international awareness. Our philosophy has for aim to develop responsible and solidary citizens through the various activities undertaken during the Service and Action Programme.

Class size doesn't exceed 16 pupils per class which enables a personalised follow-up. In the afternoons, supervised study is offered to pupils with learning difficulties or to those with higher capabilities to deepen their knowledge. Students have the opportunity to partake in various extra-curricular activities (creative writing, film club, debating …) as well as swimming, athletics and team sports.

Throughout our 30 years of education, we take pride in seeing our pupils travel abroad to study in Europe and America. We believe that by offering a holistic education, which hones the abilities of each pupil so that they can fulfil their individual potential, we can reach our objective which is to endow them with the required skills to become active citizens of the world, driven by their will to change it for the better.

Lycée International de Londres Winston Churchill

Head of School
Mireille Rabaté

DP coordinator
Maaike Kaandorp

Status Private, Independent

Boarding/day Day

Gender Coeducational

Language of instruction
English, French

Authorised IB programmes
DP

Age Range 3 – 18

Address
54 Forty Lane
London
HA9 9LY | UK

TEL +44 (0)203 824 4900

Email
admissions@lyceeinternational.london

Website
www.lyceeinternational.london

Located on a beautiful 5-acre campus, Lycée International de Londres Winston Churchill aims to develop students from age 3 to 18 into forward-thinking, principled and joyful citizens of the world and take on the challenges of the future.

"Through a rigorous, bilingual programme and innovative methods, we educate pupils to become responsible, creative and principled global citizens. We teach them to think critically and act ethically, to form and express their own opinions and respect those of others, to define their own life goals and to make sense of and embrace change."

Our students learn to ask questions and think critically, to form and express their opinions with confidence. They thrive in a bilingual and international environment, underpinned by excellence and a dynamic flow of pedagogical innovation.

It is our firm belief that learning can take multiple forms, and therefore be enhanced by the variety of approaches as well as the responsible use of technology. Our teachers think creatively and use a vast array of methods inspired by the latest research to help each student discover his or her own learning style, talents and potential.

We also believe that each student deserves the best possible education according to his or her needs, with the goal of achieving excellence in both intellectual and social endeavours. Learning should be a fulfilling, joyful experience and a school should foster curiosity, creative thinking and openness. Our school encourages individual and collective initiatives that enable our children to think positively about themselves and to recognise and value their own talents and those of others.

We encourage teamwork and foster a sense of community and solidarity within and outside the school, from positive collaboration and healthy competition in the classroom to volunteering and community involvement both locally and globally. We welcome students, families and employees from all backgrounds and cultures. We respect and celebrate their identity, lifestyles, preferences and individual differences and we expect every member of our community, children and adults, to do the same.

Integrity, creativity, courage, awareness and respect are the core values we encourage them to develop, with the aim, ultimately, that they become active and principled global citizens. Furthermore, we believe that honesty is of paramount importance in character building. We encourage our students to own their mistakes and learn from them, to embrace change and to welcome the inevitable challenges in our lives.

A member of the prestigious Council of International Schools as well as of the Independent Schools Association and AEFE, Lycée International de Londres Winston Churchill has been rated 'Outstanding' by Ofsted for its Sixth Form Provision and for Wellbeing and Personal Development.

(Founded 1865)

Headmaster
Keith Metcalfe MA (Cantab)

DP coordinator
Stephen Holroyd

Status Private, Independent

Boarding/day Mixed

Gender Coeducational

Language of instruction
English

Authorised IB programmes
DP

Age Range 13 – 18

Number of pupils enrolled
640

Fees
Day: £8,807 per term
Boarding: £13,185 – £13,646 per term

Address
College Road
Malvern
Worcestershire
WR14 3DF | UK

TEL +44 (0)1684 581613

Email
admissions@malverncollege.org.uk

Website
www.malverncollege.org.uk

Malvern College is forward-looking and ambitious in its aspirations for the future. As one of the first schools to run the International Baccalaureate in the UK, the school celebrated 25 years of running the IB alongside A levels in 2017.

Academic results are excellent and, through an extensive co-curriculum, pupils can develop the necessary skills and personal qualities required for life beyond school. Emphasis on nurturing the individual is balanced by an understanding of the responsibility each has to play in the lives of others. We encourage resilience in our pupils and a life-long love of learning that will sustain them throughout their lives and periods of change.

We are ideally located in the inspirational setting of the Malvern Hills and near to the town of Great Malvern where we are close to major transport links, motorways and rail, and to Birmingham Airport.

At Malvern College, we are proud of our innovative spirit, superb and developing facilities, and outstanding teaching staff that enable pupils to flourish, all of which make this is the very best environment in which to benefit from transformational learning.

The IB at Malvern

The IB Diploma Programme is taught at Malvern in a school with all the benefits of full boarding life and in a context of global awareness. We offer pupils a real choice of subjects so that they are able to shape their future. Our 'Malvern Qualities' are clearly linked to the IB Learner Profile with the IB ethos firmly embedded in school life. The IB's holistic philosophy of education clearly matches our own approach to the development of the individual.

The IB Diploma at Malvern focuses on opening minds and developing a pupil's curiosity. Our outstanding candidates have gone on to achieve academic excellence at top universities all over the world, and are involved in exciting projects worldwide in careers that seek to make a difference.

Boarding at Malvern

Malvern is a full boarding school – 77% of our pupils board and weekends are busy. We seek to prepare those who study at Malvern for a world that is constantly changing. Our House system engenders a sense of community and collective purpose. Pupils eat in their Houses creating the family feel for which Malvern is well-known.

Admissions

Each year, around forty new pupils enter the Sixth Form to join one of our eleven boarding houses. Registrations are requested 18 months in advance of the proposed term of entry. Please contact our Admissions team for details: admissions@malverncollege.org.uk Tel:+44 (0) 1684 581613

Headmaster
Mr. Wayne Maher

DP coordinator
Jessica Swann

Status Private

Boarding/day Day

Gender Coeducational

Language of instruction
English

Authorised IB programmes
DP

Age Range 2.6 – 18

Number of pupils enrolled
800

Fees
Day: EGP130,000 – EGP240,000

Address
B2-B3 South Ring Road
Investment Zone Kattameya
Cairo | **EGYPT**

TEL +202 26144400

Email
info@malverncollege.edu.eg

Website
malverncollege.edu.eg

Malvern College Egypt initially opened in August 2016 with just over 300 pupils, and today we are proud to have 780 pupils ranging from pre-Nursery to Year 12. After a successful application with the International Baccalaureate Organisation (IBO) in 2016, we now offer the IB Diploma Programme, the International General Certificate of Secondary Education (IGCSE), and A-Levels. Furthermore, as a renowned British international school, we are a member of the British Schools of the Middle East (BSME).

Malvern College Egypt is a part of the family of Malvern international schools across the globe, including our mother school Malvern College UK, Malvern College Chengdu, Malvern College Hong Kong, and Malvern College QingDao, each adhering to high academic standards. We work closely with Malvern College UK, who regularly provide quality assurance visits in order to strengthen rapport and share educational expertise. Albeit a young school, we are fortunate to have over 150 years of experience in education from Malvern College UK.

At the College, English is the primary language of instruction and our language of inclusion. We follow an enhanced form of the English National Curriculum, enabled through our excellent teaching staff, all of whom hold UK or International teaching qualifications, and the vast majority are British nationals. Alongside this, we have outstanding teachers of Arabic, social studies and religion classes, maintaining the importance of Egyptian culture in our education. The College has outstanding facilities where a wide and variant co-curricular activities take place. We provide an inquiry-based, pupil-centred method of education for our pupils, focusing on their character development as well as academic achievement, ultimately striving to produce kind, open-minded, self-aware, motivated, and passionate individuals eager and able to contribute in our society.

Mar Qardakh School

(Founded 2011)

Head of School
Sally Boya

PYP coordinator
Rasha Mansour

MYP coordinator
Martin Niqola

DP coordinator
Carolen Kossa

Status Private

Boarding/day Day

Gender Coeducational

Language of instruction
English

Authorised IB programmes
PYP, MYP, DP

Age Range 4 – 17 years

Address
Mar Qardakh Street
P.O. Box 34
Erbil
1065 | IRAQ

TEL +964 750 144 5031

Email
info@marqardakh.com

Website
www.marqardakh.com

Mar Qardakh school inauguration anniversary

On the eleventh of November 2011, Mar Qardakh international school was opened to the public. The students and staff celebrate the anniversary every year. The celebration starts as the students come out of their classes with their teacher and stand in the center of the hub. The coordinators and head of the school then give a speech to the students. The students proceed to sing the school's anthem and pray. Later they head back to their classes and complete the rest of the day.

Why MQS?

Mar Qardakh School strives to perpetuate a great and ancient heritage. Iraq is often thought of as the Cradle of Civilization, the land where some of the first and greatest ancient civilizations of Mesopotamia – Sumer, Babylon, and Assyria – began. The beginning of multiple languages, the beginning of writing and the beginning of education have often been associated with this region. Today, Mar Qardakh School is building upon this ancient heritage and carrying it forward by providing a comprehensive, rigorous education, centered on the holistic development of the entire person, in order to invest in the well-being of each individual and of the community as a whole. Mar Qardakh is also the only school in Iraq offering PYP, MYP and DP levels.

Mission

Our mission is to empower students for life in the 21st century by providing them with a holistic and international education, encompassing academic, social, spiritual and personal development, and an awareness of the world around them.

Our values

Mar Qardakh school offers an environment for students to develop their critical thinking skills, their sense of responsibility and their openness to international diversity. Furthermore, Mar Qardakh school prepares students to become virtuous leaders; who can shape a peaceful society and a peaceful future.

Our students

Being one of the first IB schools in the country, MQS trains students and prepares them to overcome the challenges and difficulties they face. The newly established system in the region helps students to become better leaders who can face future challenges with confidence, self-discipline, and determination.

Pastoral Care

The pastoral care system at Mar Qardakh School is regarded as one of the school's several strengths. Its highly effective network of relationships between the students and staff offers unique but complementary levels of care. Active committees organize the lively calendar of events to celebrate the richness of culture diversity and ensure all our students fulfill their potential and feel secure.

(Founded 1946)

Head of School
Ms. Sarah Gallagher

DP coordinator
Orla Ni Riordain

Status Private

Boarding/day Day

Gender Coeducational

Language of instruction
English

Authorised IB programmes
DP

Age Range 2 – 18

Number of pupils enrolled
810

Fees
€11,400 – €22,600

Address
Via di Villa Lauchli, 180
00191 Rome | **ITALY**

TEL +39 06 3629 1012
FAX +39 06 3629 1099

Email
admissions@marymountrome.com

Website
www.marymountrome.com

Marymount International School Rome is a private, Catholic, co-educational day school. The oldest international school in Italy, we are located on a 40-acre campus of protected parkland just 20 minutes north of the city center. An English-language Early Childhood through 12th Grade School, our standards-based international curriculum is complemented by a wide range of extracurricular activities. These include visits to Rome's famous attractions, to national and international sites. After school activities include Varsity athletics, S.T.E.A.M. classes in our FabLab building, classes in journalism, theatre, choir/band, Model United Nations, and photography. Marymount graduates obtain an accredited American High School Diploma and the majority of our students work towards the full IB Diploma with around 15% opting for individual IB course certificates.

Marymount has been an IB World School for over 30 years. The Diploma Programme (DP) has become an integral component of Marymount's academic program. School-wide curriculum alignment prepares students with the academic rigor necessary to fully engage with the Diploma. We offer over 30 subjects at this level, including 9 languages.

Marymount consistently obtains well above world average results. In 2019, for example, 95% of the School's DP candidates obtained the Diploma and the School's average score was 34 points (with one student scoring an outstanding 45). Marymount is a culturally and responsibly inclusive School, with an open admissions policy, and is therefore particularly proud of its students' results. The internationalism of the program is reflected in that 52% of the students achieve the Bilingual Diploma.

The School's IB students go on to study in many of the world's top universities and colleges; in the UK this includes Cambridge, University College London, London School of Economics, Imperial College London, and King's College London, and Yale, New York University, Boston College, Johns Hopkins, and UC Berkeley in North America, in addition to Bocconi, IE and more.

The Marymount Learner Profile and the School's Mission and Vision are built on principles of internationalism, intercultural understanding, and global mindedness. Our students take part in an array of local and international service-learning projects.

Classroom activities focus on conceptual understanding, authentic learning, and skills development. The School also has an ever-growing commitment to technology and Artificial Intelligence learning. All Marymount students work with personal Apple devices and the School is equipped with the latest technology, art and science labs, including a Forest School.

Marymount welcomes students from over 75 different nationalities and of all faiths to participate in its vibrant community life, providing an inclusive environment in which each student is valued and nurtured to become tomorrow's leaders.

Marymount London

Headmistress
Mrs Margaret Frazier

MYP coordinator
Nicholas Marcou

DP coordinator
Nicholas Marcou

Status Private

Boarding/day Mixed

Gender Female

Language of instruction
English

Authorised IB programmes
MYP, DP

Number of pupils enrolled
274

Fees
Day: £24,985
Weekly Boarding: £40,515
Boarding: £42,305

Address
George Road
Kingston upon Thames
Surrey
KT2 7PE | UK

TEL +44 (0)20 8949 0571
FAX +44 (0)20 8336 2485

Email
admissions@
marymountlondon.com

Website
www.marymountlondon.com

Marymount London is an independent school for girls, nurturing the limitless potential of curious, motivated students (ages 11 to 18) of diverse faiths and backgrounds. Founded in 1955 through the charism of the Religious of the Sacred Heart of Mary (RSHM), we proudly stand as the first all-girls school in the United Kingdom to adopt the International Baccalaureate curriculum (IB MYP and Diploma), where girls are inspired to learn in a creative, collaborative, interdisciplinary, and exploratory environment.

Just 20 minutes from London, Marymount is located on a seven acre idyllic garden campus which offers outstanding facilities, including a sports hall, tennis courts, dance studio and modern dining hall. The School's challenging academic program is based on the International Baccalaureate curricula:

- The Middle Years Programme (MYP), offered in Grades 6 to 10, focuses on an integrated STEAM (Science, Technology, Engineering, Arts, Mathematics) approach, with an additional emphasis on language acquisition.
- The International Baccalaureate Diploma Programme (DP) for Grades 11 and 12 builds on the strong foundation of the MYP, leading to independent research opportunities and exceptional university placement within the UK and around the world.
- Our results are outstanding: 100% pass rate and an average of 37 points.

Marymount's holistic approach to learning delivers a well-rounded education that encourages critical thinking, intercultural understanding, and participation in a wide array of interesting extracurricular offerings. Transport services from London and the surrounding areas as well as boarding options (weekly, full, and flexi) are available.

Admissions Process

Marymount offers year-round rolling admission. The admissions section of the website, featuring an online application portal, provides all of the information necessary to get started. Applicant families are encouraged to learn more about the School's strong tradition of excellence by exploring the website, making contact by phone/email, and scheduling a campus/Skype visit.

Modern Montessori School

(Founded 1985)

Principal
Randa Hasan

PYP coordinator
Noor Elkhub

MYP coordinator
Abeer Al Azzeh

DP coordinator
Hoor Hawamdeh

Status Private

Boarding/day Day

Gender Coeducational

Language of instruction
English, Arabic

Authorised IB programmes
PYP, MYP, DP

Age Range 3 – 18

Number of pupils enrolled
1808

Address
PO Box 1941
Khilda
Amman
11821 | JORDAN

TEL +9626 5535190
FAX +9626 5535831

Email
mms@montessori.edu.jo

Website
www.montessori.edu.jo

The Modern Montessori School (MMS) aims to provide a rich and stimulating environment where children can develop to their full potential. Understanding and appreciating the differences that make every student unique, each child is valued as an independent thinker and encouraged to make choices on his or her own.

Our system of personalised education encourages every student to develop his or her own talent, to respect the differences in others, and to be a respectable member of a community, thus achieving the finest possible holistic education. This aims to instil a pride in accomplishments, providing the students with the confidence needed to use their abilities to the fullest and enabling them to define and achieve success in college, career and, above all, in life.

To this end, the IB Diploma Programme at MMS is designed largely to cater for the needs of individuals, rather than for the collective needs of a group; our subject menu is varied and enjoys a degree of flexibility, which in turn allows students to choose the subjects that appeal to their different learning preferences and future university courses.

Furthermore, MMS has devised an extracurricular, three-level award scheme, which has the IB CAS perched atop its golden level. The Amin Hasan Award (AHA) provides students from grade 6-10 with the ability to participate in enjoyable yet beneficial and thought-provoking activities. This non-academic aspect of their education is extremely valuable in the overall development of the whole child, as it fosters a sense of compassion, teamwork, and mutual respect among students, in addition to promoting the principles of model citizenship and the importance of solidarity and togetherness among people, irrespective of their ethnic, religious, or gender differences. One of the many AHA activities was having students work together to meet the challenge of scaling Jordan's highest peak.

At MMS, we also believe in the inherent ability of each student to achieve distinction. This is why our LEAD Department (inclusive assessment) works hand-in-hand with administrators, programme coordinators, and teachers to cater for students who have special learning needs, through the application of an inclusion programme.

We also believe that cooperation between home and school is required to ensure the personal and intellectual development of each student. Consequently, we have designed an e-school portal where both parents and students are kept up-to-date with everything they need from report cards and academic calendars to forums and e-learning material.

As a PYP/MYP accredited school, the MMS prepares students through a devised preparation programme and curricula that will ultimately expose students to the IB continuum of international education.

The Modern Montessori School is accredited by the International Centre for Montessori Education (ICME), Cambridge and Edexcel International Examinations' syndicates and is an authorised IB World School.

(Founded 1992)

Chairman of the Board
Mr. Bassam Malhas

School Director
Dr. Hana Al-Nasser Malhas

School Principal
Hana Hamdan

PYP coordinator
Reema Kassem (Primary)
Reem Samara (KG)

MYP coordinator
Ruba Daibes (Grades 9 & 10)
Niveen Salem (Grades 7 & 8)

DP coordinator Fadia Khoury

Status Private

Boarding/day Day

Gender Coeducational

Language of instruction
Arabic, English

Authorised IB programmes
PYP, MYP, DP

Age Range 3 – 18 years

Number of pupils enrolled
1551

Address
PO Box 1412, Amman
11118 | JORDAN

TEL +962 79 9577771
FAX +962 6 5411143

Email
administration@mashrek.edu.jo

Website www.mashrek.edu.jo

Mashrek International School is a private bilingual coeducational school founded in 1992, governed by a team of educators and professionals, located in Western Amman with a spectacular view and picturesque landscape.

Our Vision: Being an influential educational institution that empowers passionate future leaders who positively impact the world.

Our Mission: We strive for excellence in education through providing personalized learning that incorporates innovative instructional strategies and actively engages the school community in learners' experiences that are applied within diverse environments while taking pride in our own culture and preserving it.

Our Values: IRESPECT

The acronym IRESPECT was developed to outline the eight values:

Integrity: We are honest, truthful and transparent. We practice our beliefs.

Resilience: We are adaptable, flexible and quickly overcome challenges.

Equity: We are fair and impartial to all.

Selflessness: We are unselfish and concerned about others' needs.

Passion: We are enthusiastic and eager about everything we do.

Excellence: We are outstanding in what we do. Quality is at the essence of our being.

Compassion: We treat all with the utmost gentleness, kindness and empathy.

Team Spirit: We cooperate, coordinate and interrelate.

Our Motto: "Maximizing Each Student's Potential"

Academic Programme: Mashrek International School has been an IB World School since 2005 offering the IBPYP, IBMYP and IBDP.

Accreditations:

In February 2018, Mashrek International School was awarded the CIS Accreditation. This was based on evidence of excellent and effective alignment with the standards for CIS accreditation. This accreditation supports the school's mission in maintaining high international standards of education.

In May 2019, the school was accredited as an Athlete Friendly Education Center (AFEC) by the World Academy of Sport. This will support the school in assisting athletes throughout their sports journey. Mashrek is a member of Educational Collaborative for International Schools (ECIS) – an organization that provides professional learning, quality assurance, school services, research, advocacy as well as grants and awards for the benefit of its members.

Learning Principles:

Learning should be:

- Driven by authentic application; therefore, learners should be aware of the purpose of learning.
- Framed in terms of core concepts, skills and transferable ideas; therefore, it should be contextualized.
- Deepened through classification, reasoning, analysis, evaluation, synthesis and metacognition; therefore,

learners should be engaged in problem solving, creative, critical and reflective thinking.
- Enable learners to use and transfer their knowledge to innovative situations and find solutions to problems.
- Stimulate learners' prior knowledge to construct meaning as they learn.
- Provide opportunities for learners to develop their cognitive, social, emotional, intellectual and spiritual well-being.
- Driven by the school's mission, vision and values.
- Dynamic and should involve learners in developing core concepts and processes.
- Focused on understanding goals, producing quality work and meeting high expectations; therefore, learners require regular, timely and constructive feedback.
- Inquiry-based, conceptually driven and research-based.
- Differentiated to address learners' various learning styles, prior knowledge, interests and different abilities in order to provide students with equal opportunities to learn.
- Learning and language are intertwined (all teachers are language teachers).

The School's Definition of Internationalism/ Interculturalism:
"The ability of students to be proud of their cultural identity, respect others despite cultural differences, call for justice and integrity, interact with local, national and global issues, show empathy and care for the planet they live on."

Leadership Practices and International Mindedness:
Mashrek aims to transform students into leaders who recognize their common humanity and help to create a better and more peaceful world.

Mashrek students are exposed to a variety of experiences in which they practice community service and communicate with local and international distinguished organizations and individuals. They learn how to investigate, plan, take actions, find solutions and reflect.

Mashrek students develop their emotional, physical and social skills through participation in sports, music, drama and visual arts. They participate in national and International events, musical productions, art exhibitions, plays and conferences which allow for meaningful involvement and ownership.

Student well-being is the school's priority. An Advisor-Advisee Programme was designed to ensure that every student is recognized, cared for and guided. This programme is supported by a comprehensive counselling system.

Staff Professional Development Approach:
Professional development needs for teachers are aligned with the school's appraisal system and teachers' professional growth. The School's PD Programme offers specialized in-school training for teachers on research-based practices in education. They also participate in international workshops organized by accredited organizations.

Teachers within the school have the opportunity to undergo internal and external training and professional development on a regular basis that qualifies them to become IB workshop leaders and examiners through the IB Organization.

Partnership with Parents:
Parents are key participants within the school community. We reach out for their ideas and involve them in our strategic plan and future goals in order to achieve a shared vision. This is achieved by the Parent Partnership and Communication Department, the Parent Ambassadors Programme and the Parent Consultation Committee.

Moscow Economic School

(Founded 1993)

Head of School
Nataliya Kadzhaya

PYP coordinator
Larisa Zaitseva

MYP coordinator
Antonina Andrianova (Gaydash)

DP coordinator
Valeriya Rotershteyn

Status Private

Boarding/day Day

Gender Coeducational

Language of instruction
Russian, English

Authorised IB programmes
PYP, MYP, DP

Age Range 3 – 16

Number of pupils enrolled
620

Fees
Day: US$17,500

Address
1-A, Zaitsevo Village
Odintsovo Region
Moscow Oblast
143020 | RUSSIAN FEDERATION

Presnya Campus
29 Zamorenova Street, Moscow
123022 | RUSSIAN FEDERATION

TEL +7 495 780 5230
FAX +7 495 780 5235

Email mes@mes.ru

Website www.mes.ru

Moscow Economic School was registered on February 1, 1993, as a non-government educational institution.

MES is a secondary school with grades ranging from 1st through 11th. It also has a kindergarten and a pre-school department. The admission age ranges from 3 to 5 years.

There are two campuses. “Presnya” Campus is located in the center of Moscow. Odintsovo Branch is in the countryside, outside Moscow.

MES is a bilingual school with the languages of instruction being Russian and English. Other foreign languages include German, Spanish, French, Italian and Chinese, are introduced in the second grade.

Moscow Economic School is a member of the Council of International Schools (CIS), the European Council of International Schools (ECIS) and the Association for Advancement of International Education (AAIE).

Since 1996 the school has been following the International Baccalaureate programmes for primary (PYP), middle (MYP) and high (DP) schools (grades 1-11).

Since 2001 the school has been providing research opportunities for the Russian Academy of Education and for Moscow State Pedagogical University.

In 2013 the Council of International Schools (CIS) reaccredited MES.

Extra-curricular activities (art studios, clubs, etc.) are available. MES students actively take part in the “Moscow Giraffes” sport school and the children’s “Camerton” school of music.

Principal of Kindergarten & Primary School
Ms. Evrim Duyum

Vice Principal of Kindergarten & Primary School
Ms. Elçin Kizilkaya

PYP coordinator
Ms. Nagihan Uca

Status Private

Boarding/day Day

Gender Coeducational

Language of instruction
Turkish

Authorised IB programmes
PYP

Age Range 4 – 18

Number of pupils enrolled
900

Address
Maden District Bakır Street
No: 2A, 2B, 2C Sarıyer
Istanbul
34450 | TURKEY

TEL +90 212 342 43 33
FAX +90 212 342 43 36

Email
info@evyapokullari.k12.tr

Website
www.evyapokullari.k12.tr

Mürüvvet Evyap Schools were founded in 2008 in the name of the late sister of the philanthropic shareholders of Evyap Holding Company, dating back to 1927.

The campus is located in Sarıyer which is one of the most prestigous districts on the European side of Istanbul. It is close to the Bosphorus Strait and the Belgrad Forest. It is located in the heart of nature, easy to reach and is in a safe and green neighbourhood, far away from the city noise.

Our school community enjoys a 20,000m2 campus, 6000m2 garden including social activity areas, 90 indoor classrooms and 2 outdoor learning areas. There are a total of 130 qualified and experienced teachers. Currently we serve 900 students from diverse linguistic and social-cultural backgrounds.

Mürüvvet Evyap Schools are home to state of the art 21st century education learning spaces and environments which include Science and Computer Laboratories, Visual Arts, Music and Drama Studios. The campus additionally has indoor/outdoor sports fields, richly resourced libraries and a modern conference hall with facilities.

Mürüvvet Evyap Schools develop individuals who internalize universal values, communicate in Turkish and at least one additional foreign language effectively, are able to reflect through self-inquiry and think scientifically and analytically, care about their immediate environment and nature at large, are respectful of other cultural values and norms, display life-long learning skills, participate in art, sports and social service activities and are inspired to be leaders and role models for the society under the guidance of Ataturk's principles and reforms.

Mürüvvet Evyap Schools, an authorized IB World School since 2015, implement the Turkish National Curriculum from kindergarten up to 12th grade, within the framework of IBPYP in kindergarten and primary school.

Our school community embraces the significance of social solidarity, and implements various social responsibility projects throughout the year, providing opportunities for cooperation among individuals. Our students earn awards and certifications in science, art, sports and cultural studies through national and international recognised organizations such as INEPO, IYIPO, SEPTO, MOSTRATEC, TUBITAK, DI, ISBO, ATAST Festivals, Junior FLL, FLL and Picasso Art Contests.

MySchool Principal
Samia Moosa Al Balushi

MySchool owner
Nabil Abdullah Al Raisi

PYP coordinator
Emna Beji

Status Private

Boarding/day Day

Gender Coeducational

Language of instruction
English, Arabic

Authorised IB programmes
PYP

Age Range 3 – 17

Number of pupils enrolled
315

Address
Al Hail South, Al Seeb, Al Huda Street
Way # 2933, Building # 3344
Muscat | **OMAN**

TEL +968 24555171

Email
info@myschool.edu.om

Website
www.myschool.edu.om

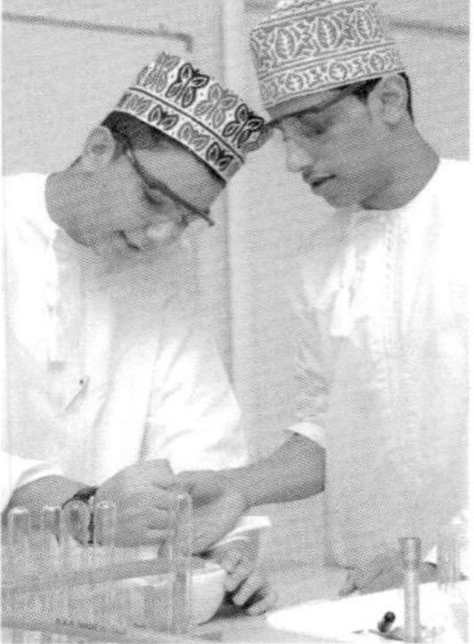

MySchool was founded in 2012, led by an experienced Omani leadership and is adopting the Primary Years, and Middle Years IB programmes.

Fundamental to our teaching and learning approach is the recognition that children are natural inquirers who will develop socially, physically and academically in different times and at different speeds, as we believe that education is a process, not a race.

To cope with the international approaches to education, meet the IB requirements and respond to the learners' needs, MySchool has adopted the inquiry-based & concept-based approaches to teaching and learning which we think allow for students to develop as critical thinkers, and problem solvers. Students are able to own their learning, inquire into, investigate, take decisions, transfer and apply what they are learning in school to real life.

Developing international mindedness among the school community has always been an integral element of MySchool philosophy. Indeed, we focus on the global concepts that allow students to think deeply. We encourage investigation, research, collaboration and communication as key elements of the teaching and learning practices. As a result, students are motivated to think independently and critically to take the responsibility of their own learning and to raise a sense of awareness towards the human condition through their personal experiences and those of the others in their national and international communities.

At MySchool, we pay close attention to students' language needs and abilities to ensure they are able to reach their full potential and to cope with national and international challenges.

Students learn through a bilingual program that offers English as the language of instruction and Arabic as their mother tongue to maintain their cultural identity in addition to French as a third language and the chinese as a fourth.

Like the IB, we think that when students learn an additional language, other than their mother tongue, they will develop a broader understanding of other cultures as well as accept the others with all their differences.

The implementation of the IB programs helped us to develop the concept of leadership and the creation of young leaders who are able to easily deal with the global issues and changes in a positive and contributing way.

We also believe that the uniqueness of the IB learner profile contributes in developing students as citizens who respect all the people with their different nationalities, customs and beliefs in a global peaceful world.

NORD ANGLIA
INTERNATIONAL SCHOOL
DUBLIN

DP coordinator
Joanna Cooper

Status Private

Boarding/day Day

Gender Coeducational

Language of instruction
English

Authorised IB programmes
DP

Age Range 3 – 18

Address
South County Business Park
Leopardstown
Dublin 18 | **IRELAND**

TEL +353 1 5442323

Email
admissions@naisdublin.com

Website
www.naisdublin.com

Nord Anglia International School Dublin (NAIS Dublin) is a member of Nord Anglia Education's global family of premium schools in Europe, South East Asia, North America and the Middle East and is Ireland's newest IB World School. NAIS Dublin is the only school in Ireland to unite an international curriculum with world-class learning opportunities and global experiences that enable students to achieve more than they ever thought possible. Nord Anglia International School Dublin is fully accredited to deliver the IB Diploma Programme (DP) from age 16 to 18 and is a candidate school* for the Primary Years Programme (PYP) from age 3 to 11 and the Middle Years Programme (MYP) from age 11 to 16. These programmes teach students to think critically and independently, to inquire with care and logic, and to become confident and resilient. We have developed our curriculum in conjunction with the Massachusetts Institute of Technology and The Juilliard School of Performing Arts in New York. True learning and innovation happens at the intersection of disciplines, so your child will be encouraged to tackle problems by calling on knowledge from several subjects. As a truly international school, our students collaborate and learn with over 64,000 of their peers in 29 countries every day through our Global Campus: whether that be physically in school, virtually online, or by travelling worldwide to other schools to participate in sporting events in the USA, cultural exchanges with China, adventure activities in Switzerland and philanthropic outreach experiences in Tanzania. Our state-of-the-art campus has been designed for the future of learning and is centred around a custom designed building in Leopardstown, South County Dublin. Our facilities include a custom-built sports centre, dance studio, design and technology studios, performing arts spaces, auditorium, libraries and a parent café. Parents choose a Nord Anglia Education because we offer academic, social and personal success for every student. Through opportunities to learn from the best, experiences beyond the ordinary, and the encouragement to achieve more than they ever thought possible, we help our students succeed anywhere through our unique global educational offer. We do this by investing in our people, our schools, and above all, our students. At Nord Anglia International School Dublin, your child will grow as a confident global citizen in an engaging environment, which will ensure that he or she will love learning for life.

*Only schools authorized by the International Baccalaureate can offer any of its four academic programmes: the Primary Years Programme (PYP), the Middle Years Programme (MYP), the Diploma Programme or the Career-related Programme (CP). Candidate status gives no guarantee that authorization will be granted.

(Founded 1850)

Headmistress
Mrs Sarah Clark

DP coordinator
Mr Henry Linscott

Status Private

Boarding/day Day

Gender Female

Language of instruction
English

Authorised IB programmes
DP

Number of pupils enrolled
1080

Fees
Day: £5,641 – £6,676 per term

Address
Canons
Canons Drive
Edgware
Middlesex
HA8 7RJ | UK

TEL +44 (0)20 8952 0912
FAX +44 (0)20 8951 1391

Email
office@nlcs.org.uk

Website
www.nlcs.org.uk

North London Collegiate School is internationally recognised as an outstanding school which provides an exceptional education. One of the oldest day schools for girls in England, we have maintained our position as an established force at the forefront of women's education, and our girls consistently excel in every area. Our students leave us not just with outstanding qualifications, but also as articulate and independent young women who possess the confidence, intellectual curiosity, and passion for learning and understanding that will endure for life.

Whilst ensuring academic excellence, equal attention is given to supporting the development of the whole person, inspiring confidence, individuality and self-esteem. Consequently, the school is a positive and energetic community where girls are encouraged to take advantage of the opportunities open to them, with around 36 productions, 40 societies and 30 foreign trips offered each year.

International Outlook

NLCS has a highly international perspective that is unique amongst London day schools. We feel it is vital to prepare our students to become global citizens, by providing opportunities for them to be outward-looking, internationally minded and well informed about the world beyond school. Our growing family of sister schools in South Korea and Dubai, with more branches planned for the future, benefits pupils and staff through exchange opportunities and internships. The IB Diploma resonates with the values of NLCS, and its international dimension affords students the opportunity to be part of a programme which is offered in, and recognised by, almost every country in the world.

Academic Excellence

We have offered the IB programme since 2004, and have had a consistent record of success. Our students consistently achieve an average Diploma score in excess of 40 points. We had another superb set of IB results in 2019 with an average point score of 41, and three students gaining the maximum score of 45 points, something usually only achieved by around 150 students out of 160,000 candidates across the globe, placing us once more among the best IB schools in the world.

Looking to the future

Our IB students have received offers from a range of impressive institutions including Oxford, Cambridge, Harvard, Yale, Georgetown, Stanford and Princeton, as well as other leading universities such as Bristol, Edinburgh and the London colleges and medical schools.

The IB Diploma programme offered at NLCS ensures that students enjoy an exciting and academically stimulating Sixth Form experience, providing them with an excellent preparation for life at university and in the wider world beyond.

(Founded 1584)

Headmaster
Mr Henry Price MA (Oxon)

Director of IB
Simone Lorenz-Weir

DP coordinator
Vic Russell

Status Private

Boarding/day Mixed

Gender Coeducational

Language of instruction
English

Authorised IB programmes
DP

Age Range 10 – 18

Number of pupils enrolled
1044

Fees
Day: £17,250 – £21,360
Boarding: £26,115 – £35,010
Flexi Boarding (2-5 nights)
£20,550 – £33,255

Address
Chapel Close
Oakham
Rutland
LE15 6DT | UK

TEL 01572 758500

Email
admissions@oakham.rutland.sch.uk

Website
www.oakham.rutland.sch.uk

Oakham School has always been at the forefront of educational developments, having successfully offered the IB Diploma for nearly 20 years. We are well known and loved for being a friendly and unpretentious co-educational boarding and day school with over 500 boarders.

Our educational ethos reflects the IB's vision to nurture intellectually ambitious thinkers, giving them the ability to learn effectively and independently at school and beyond. Our IB Diploma results far exceed the global average and our teachers are leading practitioners.

Whilst we are proud of our 400-year heritage, we continue to look to the future and our focus now, as we introduce the IB MYP to our pupils in Forms 1-3, is on equipping our students with the knowledge, aptitudes and skills to thrive in the world of 2030 and beyond.

Students benefit from the School's location close to Rutland Water, in the heart of safe, rural England. The beautifully green campus is just a few minutes' walk from Oakham's historic town centre, whilst Oakham's excellent road and rail links mean that London, Birmingham and Cambridge are all within easy reach.

At Oakham, learning is never just confined to the four walls of a classroom. Hundreds of students take part in the Arts – there are five major drama productions every year, we teach over 500 individual music lessons each week, and our award-winning Art & Design Department is a hive of creative activity. Oakham also has a national reputation for Sport, offering 30 different sports to students of all levels – from enthusiasts to elite athletes. Activities are also an integral part of life beyond the classroom, with students able to choose from over 130 activities to take part in each week, to discover and develop their interests and talents, and provide service to others. In addition to Duke of Edinburgh, CCF, and Voluntary Action, options range from dance to robotics, e-textiles to sailing – there is something for everyone!

Oakham is an exceptionally caring and vibrant boarding community. Our unique House structure ensures we nurture all aspects of our pupils' well-being during every stage of their Oakham journey. Expertly trained staff support our students, helping them to become resilient and responsible within a home-from-home environment.

Our students leave Oakham as well rounded and confident young adults, who are effective and independent learners, well equipped with the skills and habits of mind to succeed in tomorrow's world.

Oeiras International School

(Founded 2010)

Principal
Steve Lewis

Head of Pastoral Care
Amanda Murphy

Head of Curriculum
Francisco Vargas

MYP coordinator
Carol Pratt

DP coordinator
Jan Van Hees

CP coordinator
Ramona Dietrich

Status Private

Boarding/day Day

Gender Coeducational

Language of instruction
English

Authorised IB programmes
MYP, DP, CP

Age Range 6 – 18

Number of pupils enrolled
420

Fees
Day: €10,000 – €19,800

Address
Quinta Nossa Senhora da Conceicao
Rua Antero de Quental no 7
Barcarena
2730-013 | PORTUGAL

TEL +351 211935330

Email
info@oeirasinternationalschool.com

Website
www.oeirasinternationalschool.com

OIS – Oeiras International School, offers the International Baccalaureate (IB) MYP, DP and CP. In addition we are a PYP candidate school.

Why OIS?

- We invest in our students. OIS is a non-profit school: all generated earnings are re-invested in the school for the benefit of the children.
- We have individual care and attention to each child – average class sizes do not exceed 18 students, so as to facilitate multi-level teaching and to focus on individual learning styles.
- We have created a supportive, caring environment in which students take responsibility for their own learning process.
- Its beautiful campus and facilities, sports fields, woods and vegetable gardens promote a healthy and challenging environment.
- OIS only hires experienced teachers with degrees and teaching credentials from their home countries.

This non-profit school was founded with a commitment to academic excellence and intellectual rigour. Our intention is to maintain the sense of community and freedom amongst the students and teachers under the IB learner profile umbrella.

For students this means that the school has an innovative and creative character, provides an environment of openness and mutual respect, and develops the individual talents of each and every student. Extracurricular activities focus on creativity and community service. A huge variety of sports and activities is provided, as well as it is meant that every student learns his/her mother tongue as a language and literature subject.

At OIS happy students are taught by committed and contented teachers.

Qatar Academy Al Khor

الخور Al Khor
أكاديمية قطر Qatar Academy
عضو في مؤسسة قطر
Member of Qatar Foundation

Director
Ms Aisha M. Al Megbali

PYP coordinator
Ms Nadia Hussain

MYP coordinator
Mr Martin McCurrach

DP coordinator
Mr David Leadbetter

Status Private

Boarding/day Day

Gender Coeducational

Language of instruction
Arabic, English

Authorised IB programmes
PYP, MYP, DP

Age Range 3 – 18 years

Number of pupils enrolled
1190

Fees
Day: QR40,000 – QR75,000

Address
P.O.Box: 60774
Mowasalat Street
Al Khor | QATAR

TEL +974 44546775

Email
qaksenior@qak.edu.qa
qakprimary@qak.edu.qa

Website
www.qak.edu.qa

Qatar Academy Al Khor (QAK) was established in 2008 to serve students who live in Al Khor and the different areas in the north of Qatar, extending our groundbreaking curriculum to a broader community. As a full IB World School that predominantly educates native Qatari students and long-time residents, QAK is especially dedicated to developing local human capital. QAK seamlessly blends its world-class international curriculum with Qatar's heritage and culture. In part, this is achieved by enabling students to thrive in a truly bilingual environment that develops rich language skills in English and Arabic concurrently, since the student base is predominantly Qatari.

QAK strives to empower students to be open-minded, inquiring and knowledgeable life-long learners who are able to adapt to an ever-changing world through intercultural understanding and respect.

At QAK, we envision our future leaders as courageous problem-solvers who will make a positive difference in the world.

Our mission at QAK is to create a safe yet dynamic learning environment that inspires innovation. QAK empowers learners to think critically as compassionate and principled global citizens grounded in Arab values while celebrating Qatari National heritage and culture.

(Founded 2011)

Director
Ms Bedriyah Itani

PYP coordinator
Ms Samira Jurdak

MYP coordinator
Ms Jaime Fontenot

Status Private

Boarding/day Day

Gender Coeducational

Language of instruction
Arabic, English

Authorised IB programmes
PYP, MYP

Age Range 3 – 17 years

Number of pupils enrolled
1102

Fees
Day: QR40,000 – QR60,000

Address
P.O. Box: 2589
Al Farazdaq Street, street No.: 1034, Zone: 90
Doha | QATAR

TEL +974 44547418

Email
qataracademyal-wakra@qf.org.qa

Website
www.qaw.edu.qa

Qatar Academy Al Wakra (QAW) was established to serve the needs of the rapidly growing Al Wakra coastal community and surrounding areas in the south of Qatar. It serves over 1100 students from preschool to Grade 10 and is continuing to expand by one grade level each year. Through an educational model that enables learning in two languages, encourages innovation, and develops a strong code of ethics, QAW has been nurturing students to become leaders in their communities. The talented faculty at QAW go above and beyond to cultivate the spirit of discovery and creativity in students' learning experiences.

QAW teachers and administrators are highly collaborative, energetic, and supportive team players who are passionate about working with children and making a difference. The school moved into its new, state-of-the-art, purpose-built campus in September 2018. Facilities include sports and recreational areas, swimming pools, a 450-seat theater with music and art studios, and well-equipped science, technology, engineering, art, mechanics, and food technology laboratories.

(Founded 1996)

Director
Mr Stephen Meek

Primary School Principal
Ms Marie Green

Senior School Principal
Mr Steven Thomson

PYP coordinator
Ms Sana Alavi

MYP coordinator
Ms Roma Bhargava

DP coordinator
Ms Zeina Jawad

Status Private

Boarding/day Day

Gender Coeducational

Language of instruction
Arabic, English

Authorised IB programmes
PYP, MYP, DP

Age Range 3 – 18 years

Address
P.O. Box: 1129
Luqta Street
Doha | QATAR

TEL +974 44542000

Email
qataracademy@qf.org.qa

Website
www.qataracademy.edu.qa

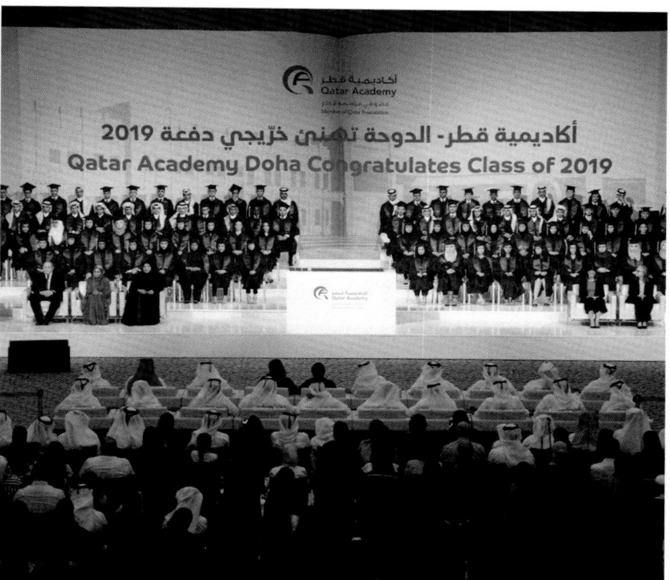

Vision: Empowering students to achieve academic excellence and be responsible citizens

Qatar Academy Doha (QAD) is one of the Middle East's premier educational institutions; a leading private, non-profit international school established as the first learning organization in Qatar Foundation's landmark Education City. Founded in 1996, it marked an important step for a country on the cusp of transforming itself from a gas- and oil-producing economy to a knowledge-based society.

QAD was the first school in Qatar authorized to offer all three IB Programmes.

Over 1,800 students representing different nationalities experience an extensive academic and co-curricular program grounded in traditional values and steeped in the best practices in education.

Inquiry-based learning starts at the Primary School. Students, parents and faculty are encouraged to challenge themselves and their thinking through the framework of the PYP, and Units of Inquiry based on the IB transdisciplinary themes provide students with structure and direction in their learning. This learning environment extends beyond the classroom to involve the wider community, supporting real-world connections.

The MYP and DP are offered in the Senior School, with the Middle School serving to address the specific needs of the pre-adolescent age group from Grades 6-8.

QAD's strength lies in its comprehensive DP curriculum, and its rigorous and effective university preparation program.

Access to many community and service, athletic and academic after-school activities challenge students beyond the curriculum, and student e-portfolios and student-led conference structure ensure that focus is consistently on learning and growing, while acquiring the grades, necessary for success in the DP and beyond.

QAD teachers are recruited from a variety of academic and cultural settings. Through encouragement and a caring, innovative and creative approach to instruction, our faculty ensure that our students achieve their fullest potential in a learning environment designed to promote cultural understanding and respect.

Qatar Academy Msheireb

Director
Ms Belinda Holland

PYP coordinator
Ms Jennifer Magierowicz & Mr Raed Al Khoshman

Status Private

Boarding/day Day

Gender Coeducational

Language of instruction
Arabic, English

Authorised IB programmes
PYP

Age Range 3 – 10 years

Number of pupils enrolled
402

Fees
Day: QR44,180 – QR53,058

Address
Msheireb Downtown Doha
QATAR

TEL +974 44542116

Email
qamsheireb@qf.org.qa

Website
www.qam.qa

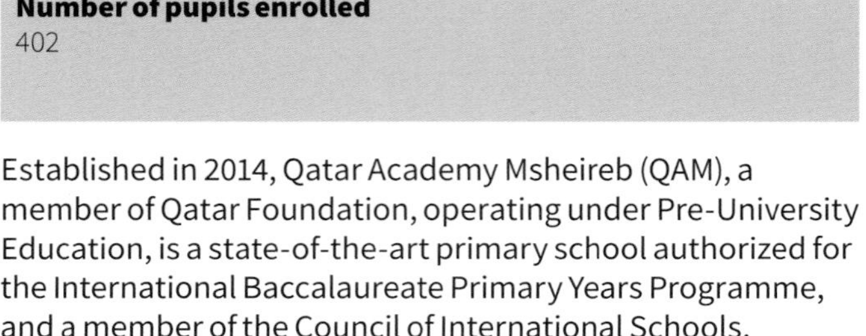

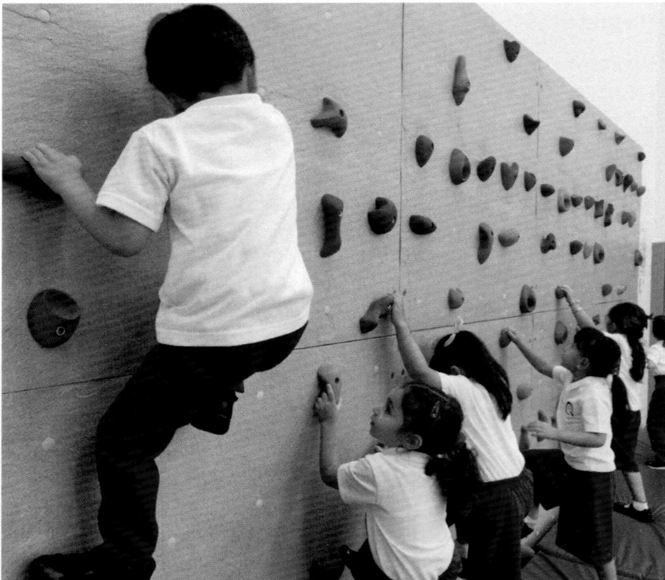

Established in 2014, Qatar Academy Msheireb (QAM), a member of Qatar Foundation, operating under Pre-University Education, is a state-of-the-art primary school authorized for the International Baccalaureate Primary Years Programme, and a member of the Council of International Schools.

QAM's mission is to create an effective learning environment to develop internationally minded and empathetic lifelong learners through a dual-language program emphasizing inquiry-based practices.

At QAM everything has a purpose, and learning is relevant to the 'real world' within a dual-language curriculum that is structured to be rigorous, stimulating and challenging. The Program of Inquiry centers around 'big ideas' and provides students with opportunities of learning about issues that have local, national and global significance, and hence nurtures an understanding of human commonalities. The transdisciplinary nature of the themes ensures that learning transcends the confines of traditional subject areas, and facilitates student connections between life in school, life at home and life in the world.

QAM offers an inclusive education where students evolve as individuals who are self-motivated, creative and can think, question and reason logically, i.e. individuals who are independent, confident and capable of making decisions.

All students are encouraged to be curious about what they are learning, and differentiation allows them to demonstrate what they have learned by using a variety of mediums or tools at different levels that are appropriate to individual needs.

Director
Ms Kim Green

PYP coordinator
Mr Barry Grogan

MYP coordinator
Ms Alison Bainbridge

DP coordinator
Mr Gary Craggs

Status Private

Boarding/day Day

Gender Coeducational

Language of instruction
English

Authorised IB programmes
PYP, MYP, DP

Age Range 3 – 18 years

Number of pupils enrolled
580

Fees
Day: QR40,280 – QR74,556

Address
P.O. Box: 34077
Doha | QATAR

TEL +974 44542322

Email
qasidra@qf.org.qa

Website
www.qasidra.com.qa

Qatar Academy Sidra (QAS) is a rapidly growing school, currently serving over 580 students who represent approximately 40 nationalities. QAS was initially established to serve the needs of Qatar Foundation (QF) and Sidra Medicine employee families, and has since expanded to cater to the growing demand for QF schools.

QAS is a dynamic, kind and responsive learning community that challenges learners of today to inspire them to be the change-makers of tomorrow. QAS believes there is a leader in everyone, hence they empower learners with strong skills and a sense of self for a life filled with opportunity and meaning to ensure their graduates are compassionate responsible citizens who achieve their full academic and personal potential.

As an inclusive and multilingual community, QAS is committed to creating opportunities for every child so that every individual is personally and academically empowered with 'roots to grow and wings to fly'. The school values of respect, integrity and unity lead to a culture of kindness. This culture enables QAS to create a nurturing environment for each child's wellbeing, passion, and talents.

The school is currently located in the lively Education City campus and is scheduled to have a new, purpose-built facility ready by 2021.

QSI International School of Bratislava

(Founded 1994)

Head of School Mr. Daniel Blaho

DP coordinator Mr. Jeff Varney

Status Private

Boarding/day Day

Gender Coeducational

Language of instruction English

Authorised IB programmes DP

Age Range 3 – 19

Number of pupils enrolled 303

Address
Záhradnicka 1006/2
Samorin 93101 | **SLOVAKIA**

TEL +421 903 704 436

Email
bratislava@qsi.org

Website
bratislava.qsi.org

QSI International School of Bratislava (QSIB) is a private, nonprofit institution that opened in September of 1994. It offers a rigorous, high-quality American international education in the English language for children ages 3-18. The warm and welcoming community that is QSIB makes it an ideal setting for children to grow in ability with the finest faculty and educational opportunities in Bratislava. Students in the secondary earn stellar results in our International Baccalaureate (IB) and Advanced Placement (AP) Programs.

After 24 years in one location, QSI International School of Bratislava opened two new campuses. The school campuses are pleasantly situated in the quaint village of Samorin (less than 20km from the outskirts of Bratislava) with expansive natural green spaces. The brand new state-of-the-art Elementary facility (opened in January 2018) is a large 2-story complex, which has 35 classrooms, a library (over 10,000 titles), a computer laboratory, a gymnasium, an atrium, several outdoor playgrounds, a full-court outdoor basketball court, an artificial grass mini pitch for soccer, a parent work space and several offices. The new (August 2019) Middle and Secondary School Campus at the X-bionic Sphere Resort [www.x-bionicsphere.com/domov] provides the upper school students and teachers with 30 additional classrooms, offices, laboratories, and libraries. There is also immediate access to the partner facility's indoor and outdoor swimming pools, a fitness facility, dance/exercise rooms, track & field, three full soccer pitches, multipurpose playgrounds and a movie cinema. QSI International School of Bratislava (QSIB) provides full security for its students, teachers, staff and visitors with guards, an advanced key card system and an elaborate security camera network. Free Shuttle Buses to/from the campus are available from different locations in and around Bratislava.

QSIB offers the IB Diploma Programme to students ages 16-19, during the final two years (Secondary III & IV). The QSI courses offered in Secondary I & II prepare students to take IB courses. Students may elect to enroll in the IB Diploma Programme as full diploma candidates or as course candidates. Enrollment of students is done through one-to-one counseling with the Director of Instruction and the IB Coordinator. Prerequisite skills are required for the program, but specific prerequisite courses are not typically required. QSIB students enjoy a high success rate of 94% passing the rigorous diploma programme with an average score of 31.9 over the last 10 years. Subjects offered:

Group 1:
- English A Language & Literature
- Slovak A Literature
- Self-taught Language A SL-only

Group 2:
- German *ab initio* SL-only
- German B
- French **ab initio** SL-only
- French B
- Spanish *ab initio* SL-only
- Spanish B

Group 3:
- Psychology
- Economics
- History

Group 4:
- Biology
- Physics
- Chemistry

Group 5:
- Mathematics: Application & Interpretations
- Mathematics: Analysis & Approaches

Group 6:
- Visual Arts

QSI Kyiv International School

(Founded 1982)

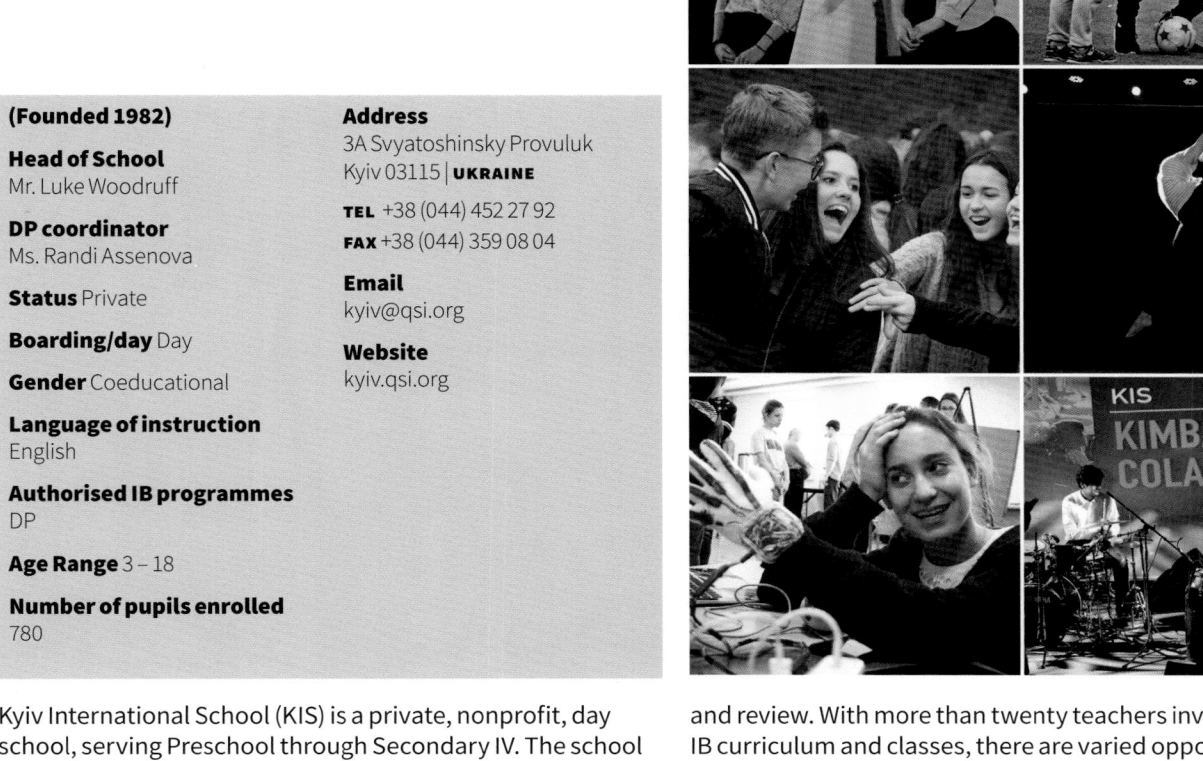

Head of School
Mr. Luke Woodruff

DP coordinator
Ms. Randi Assenova

Status Private

Boarding/day Day

Gender Coeducational

Language of instruction
English

Authorised IB programmes
DP

Age Range 3 – 18

Number of pupils enrolled
780

Address
3A Svyatoshinsky Provuluk
Kyiv 03115 | **UKRAINE**

TEL +38 (044) 452 27 92
FAX +38 (044) 359 08 04

Email
kyiv@qsi.org

Website
kyiv.qsi.org

Kyiv International School (KIS) is a private, nonprofit, day school, serving Preschool through Secondary IV. The school was founded in 1992 to provide a quality education in English for the children of expatriates living in Kyiv. Parents of the students are primarily employed by large corporations and governments. Kyiv International School is a member of Quality Schools International, a consortium of non-profit college-preparatory international schools with American-style curriculum. QSI has 37 schools in 31 countries.

The world headquarters of QSI is in Ljubljana, Slovenia.

Mastery Learning Philosophy: Kyiv International School believes in personalized instruction within a positive learning environment leading to mastery of clearly defined objectives. The educational philosophy emphasizes cooperative and collaborative learning, reflection, innovation, and higher-order and critical thinking. Mastery learning prepares our students for the higher level thinking, reflection, and self-motivation that is so fundamental for students engaged in the IB Diploma Programme.

International Baccalaureate Diploma Programme: Kyiv International School has offered the International Baccalaureate Diploma Programme since 2004 and the program continues to grow and evolve through reflection and review. With more than twenty teachers involved in the IB curriculum and classes, there are varied opportunities for students enrolled in the program. Students are encouraged to enroll in the full Programme, but also have the opportunity to enroll in classes for IB certificates.

IB Language Courses: KIS is proud to offer German, French, Spanish, Russian, and Ukrainian which students can study as either first or second languages. We also encourage students to enroll in school-supported self-study of their native language. Students have recently received bilingual diplomas in Russian, French, Ukrainian, German, Italian, and Korean.

Facilities and location: KIS is located just 10 km from the city center. The park-like campus includes 95 classrooms (including fully equipped science laboratories to support Group 4 subjects), a learning center, 2 sensory rooms, 3 art rooms, 3 music rooms, a recording studio, 3 computer laboratories, 2 indoor gymnasiums, an indoor pool, a fitness center, a climbing wall, a cafeteria, a snack café, 2 playgrounds, a purpose built track, an artificial turf soccer field, an artificial turf soccer mini pitch, an outdoor basketball court, an outdoor fitness area, other outdoor spaces, and a brand new auditorium with a seating capacity of 350.

Raha International School

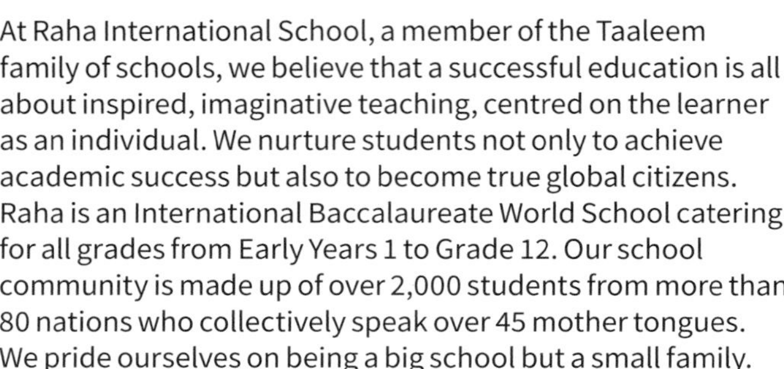

(Founded 2006)

Executive Principal
Iain Colledge

PYP coordinator
Vanessa Keenan

MYP coordinator
Vaughan Kitson

DP coordinator
Andrew Tomlinson

Status Private

Boarding/day Day

Gender Coeducational

Language of instruction
English

Authorised IB programmes
PYP, MYP, DP

Age Range 4 – 18

Number of pupils enrolled
2200

Fees
EY1: AED39,330
EY2: AED41,300
G1-G6: AED54,100
G7-G12: AED61,900

Address
Al Raha Gardens
Khalifa City 'A'
Abu Dhabi | **UNITED ARAB EMIRATES**

TEL +971 (0)2 556 1567

Email
admissions@ris.ae

Website
www.ris.ae

At Raha International School, a member of the Taaleem family of schools, we believe that a successful education is all about inspired, imaginative teaching, centred on the learner as an individual. We nurture students not only to achieve academic success but also to become true global citizens. Raha is an International Baccalaureate World School catering for all grades from Early Years 1 to Grade 12. Our school community is made up of over 2,000 students from more than 80 nations who collectively speak over 45 mother tongues. We pride ourselves on being a big school but a small family.

Situated on 14 acres of beautifully landscaped property in a bustling residential suburb, our campus boasts an abundance of open spaces and play areas. We support our students and rigorous curriculum with state-of-the-art facilities that include; libraries, a purpose-built arts centre and auditorium, sports and training facilities, wellness areas, parent and visitors' café and more.

Raha was the first school in Abu Dhabi to achieve accreditation in the full IB curriculum. The IB is internationally acclaimed and respected for its relevance in today's multicultural and increasingly global society. We are also the only K-12 school in Abu Dhabi to receive the highest rating of 'Outstanding' from the Abu Dhabi Department of Education and Knowledge for a second time, an amazing achievement for our staff and students.

Our programmes feature an inquiry approach that aligns student interest with what they learn, thereby enriching their natural curiosity and promoting a love of learning. Our team of internationally-experienced, skilled and passionate teachers model the attributes of the IB Learner Profile and encourage students to "respect themselves, others and the world around them". A strong sense of common purpose pervades our learning community. We believe that trust and strong parental participation are an integral part of a quality education and we see parents as our partners in their children's learning journey.

Raha International School will be opening a second campus in September 2020, starting in its first year with an Early Years School and expanding to all grades in subsequent years. The Khalifa City Campus is being built to satisfy the exceptionally high demand for places at Raha, and the ever-increasing popularity of the International Baccalaureate curriculum. The new campus will cater for up to 3,000 K-12 students. It will be located in Khalifa City, near to the current Raha Gardens Campus.

Rome International School

(Founded 1988)

Headteacher & Elementary School Principal
Mr Graham Thompson

Principal, Middle & High School
Mr Anthony Allard

PYP coordinator
Mrs Maïa Lawand

DP coordinator
Mrs Laela El Sheikh

Status Private

Boarding/day Day

Gender Coeducational

Language of instruction
English

Authorised IB programmes
PYP, DP

Age Range 2 – 18

Number of pupils enrolled
500

Fees
Day: €10,800 – €21,650

Address
Via Guglielmo Pecori Giraldi n.137
00135 Rome | **ITALY**

TEL +39 06 8448 2651
FAX +39 06 8448 2653

Email
info@romeinternationalschool.it

Website
www.romeinternationalschool.it

For over thirty years, Rome International School (RIS) has meant knowledge, opportunity and discovery both personal and intellectual.

Our mission is to provide a nurturing environment, in which children of all nationalities and faiths can explore and respect their own and each other's cultural and religious heritage. We aspire to equip our students with the skills needed to become life-long learners, so that every child is able to realise their unique gifts and talents and achieve their full potential.

We are the only school in Rome authorized to offer both the IB PYP and the IB DP programmes. We are also an accredited centre for the IGCSE, as validated by Cambridge Assessment for the first two years of High School, thereby ensuring the quality and consistency of a true international education and a passport to the world's best universities.

Our highly specialised and experienced international staff, who represent 19 different nations, are committed to our students' education and are there to support, inspire and motivate students. We are a non-denominational school and welcome students from all cultural backgrounds.

The school offers a broad variety of extra-curricular activities where students can develop and promote the attributes of the IB Learner Profile.

Students from Year 3 have the opportunity to study either Arabic or Chinese within the curriculum, taught by mother-tongue teachers. French, Chinese and Spanish language courses are also available as extra-curricular options in the Elementary School allowing students the possibility to continue these courses in the Middle and High School.

Creativity, physical health and well-being is important for all of our students. Middle and High School students have lessons in Art, Music, Drama and P.E. is taught in all years.

Information Communication Technology is embedded in everyday learning. Students across the school have access to banks of laptops and iPads and the school. A thriving Italian department is present in the school and the didactic activities of our Italian subject teachers are carefully coordinated across the school.

Our school building and campus are specifically designed for 21st century education. Nestled in almost four hectares of natural parkland, our students benefit from ample outdoor play and learning spaces and state-of-the-art facilities. The school is part of the Eco Schools network and proudly flies the Eco School flag.

RIS is a proud member of the Globeducate network (formerly known as NACE Schools), one of the leading education networks in Europe. This brings many new opportunities for our community. RIS students and teachers benefit from exchange of best practices and a range of annual art, sports and inter-cultural events with other schools across the Globeducate network.

With a student intake of 50 different nationalities, Rome International School is the ideal context for a rewarding and progressive educational experience.

EXPANDING HORIZONS

(Founded 1844)

Head
Mr Jeremy Quartermain

PYP coordinator
Julia Clapp

DP coordinator
Bethan Jones

Status Private

Boarding/day Mixed

Gender Coeducational

Language of instruction
English

Authorised IB programmes
PYP, DP

Age Range 2 – 18

Number of pupils enrolled
665

Fees
Day: £2,815 – £4,580 per term
Boarding: £4,850 – £13,070 per term

Address
Broadway
Fleetwood
Lancashire
FY7 8JW | UK

TEL +44 (0)1253 774201

Email
admissions@rossall.org.uk

Website
www.rossall.org.uk

Rossall has been described as a 'warm, inclusive and remarkably happy place to be'.

Set on an historic 160-acre campus, Rossall is one of the country's leading independent co-education boarding and day schools, where boys and girls aged 2-18 are nurtured in a safe, secure and supportive environment.

The School currently provides one of the broadest curriculum programmes available in the UK independent school market.

The senior school continues to follow the British National Curriculum culminating with GCSE/iGCSE examinations at the end of Year 11. In the Sixth Form, students then have the choice to study either A Levels or the globally recognised IB Diploma Programme.

Small class sizes and a rigorous tutor system ensures academic excellence with 95% of Rossall students entering higher education at universities around the world.

Rossall's enviable on-campus facilities include 150 acres of outdoor grassed sports pitches, floodlit all-weather surfaces, a brand new £4 million sports centre, heated indoor swimming pool, Fives courts, shooting range and multi-use-games-area. In 2016, Rossall opened its Golf Academy, boasting an indoor golf studio, equipped with the latest video analysis equipment and GC2 launch monitor/simulator, as well as an indoor putting lab and swing room. Rossall also has its very own football academy, in partnership with League 1 football club, Fleetwood Town.

The School is also home to the Lawrence House Astronomy and Space Science Centre, the only centre of its kind in Britain, specialising in astronomy education.

A huge range of extracurricular activities are offered to all pupils throughout the school. Aside from a large number of successful sports teams, students can join everything from the world famous Chapel Choir to the oldest Combined Cadet Force in the country. The diverse range of clubs at Rossall ensures that there is something for everybody.

This year, the School has developed its own petting zoo, Graeme's Garden, named after a former student. It houses two giant continental rabbits, Penelope and Bluebell, as well as two pygmy goats, Hercules and Romeo. Students are able to help out with the zoo and also visit the animals in their free time.

Admitting boarders as young as seven years old, Rossall's 'family structure' provides the framework for its exceptional standards of pastoral care. With major investments recently ploughed into its 8 boarding houses, each house is a well-equipped and comfortable home, which are in the process of being sensitively modernised to the highest of standards.

Rossall School is a registered charity (No. 526685) that exists to provide education for children.

(Founded 1988)

Principal
Ms Monicá Gilbert-Sáez

Deputy Principal
Ms Lani du Plessis

DP coordinator
Ms Miranda de Vries

Status State

Boarding/day Day

Gender Coeducational

Language of instruction
English

Authorised IB programmes
DP

Age Range 12 – 18

Number of pupils enrolled
380

Fees
Day: €8,000 (excluding extra curricular activities and trips)

Junior Campus
Bentincklaan 294
3039 KK Rotterdam |
NETHERLANDS

Senior Campus
Schimmelpenninckstraat 23,
3039KS, Rotterdam |
NETHERLANDS

TEL +31 (0)10 890 77 44

Email
admissions.riss@wolfert.nl

Website
riss.wolfert.nl

Our Vision

Educating for self-awareness, curiosity and integrity in a changing world.

Our Mission

Our mission is for every student to enjoy their youth.
We do this by providing innovative approaches to learning, by encouraging achievement, by fostering international mindedness with local and global engagement, by modelling ethical behaviour and by acting respectfully and with honesty.

Our Core Values

- Respect
- Responsibility
- Relationships
- Courage

RISS holds a unique position both within The Netherlands and Rotterdam's Wolfert school group. We are a state subsidised semi-private school and a provider of excellent international education, as recognised by our recent CIS/NEASC and IB re-accreditation and re-evaluation visits.

RISS serves the growing need Rotterdam has for quality education serving foreign nationals and returning Dutch citizens, one that is not based on exclusivity or privilege.

While many schools claim to be international simply because of the curriculum they offer or the students they serve, RISS offers a genuine and comprehensive coalition of international teachers drawn from across the globe. What unites us is the RISS school culture and our common belief in an inclusive, culturally-diverse, student-centred, enquiry-driven and concept-based education that not only prepares young people for university and life beyond school, but also ensures that they simply love their time being young.

RISS offers a caring community, dedicated to the broad development of all students yet small enough to ensure that all our young people are known and supported as individuals. This is something backed up by our newly revamped pastoral programme led by our tutors. English is our language of instruction and students are also encouraged to study their own language and sit their own language exams. And, of course, Dutch is offered at all levels.

Our recent reaccreditation by both CIS and NEASC underlines that we deliver the highest quality international education and we offer external examinations both with Cambridge Assessment (IGCSE) and the International Baccalaureate Organisation (IBDP). Our students are well placed to enter the many top higher education institutions in The Netherlands and worldwide. We foster a culture of a love for and enjoyment of learning and a joy in achievement. This is inspired by high expectations from our leadership team and all our staff with everyone collaborating to promote collaboration, tolerance, diversity, belonging and a sense of service.

Ryde School with Upper Chine

RYDE SCHOOL
WITH UPPER CHINE

(Founded 1921)

Headmaster
Mr M. A. Waldron MA (Cantab)

DP coordinator
Kerry Gallop

CP coordinator
David Shapland

Status Private, Independent

Boarding/day Mixed

Gender Coeducational

Language of instruction
English

Authorised IB programmes
DP, CP

Age Range 2.5 – 18

Number of pupils enrolled
744

Fees
Day: £7,935 – £13,740
Weekly Boarding: £27,030
Boarding: £30,300

Address
Queen's Road
Ryde
Isle of Wight
PO33 3BE | UK

TEL 01983 617970

Email
admissions@rydeschool.net

Website
www.rydeschool.org.uk

The school has an excellent record of academic achievement throughout all age groups and was the first independent school in the UK to offer the IB Career-related Programme alongside the IB Diploma Programme and our A Level Plus Programme, through which pupils study for A Levels but also take advantage of the IB courses on offer and add them as enrichment options. We also offer a one year GCSE and Pre-Sixth Form course providing excellent preparation for entry into the Sixth Form.

Pupils leave to go on to study at Oxbridge, medical schools, other Russell Group Universities and Art, Music and Drama colleges. Pupils succeed academically and are well-mannered, characterful, happy and independent; a result of Ryde School's dynamic yet welcoming environment.

Our pupils benefit from an extensive range of excellent resources and extra-curricular activities. Sailing is on the curriculum in both the Junior and Senior Schools and has a strong focus throughout the School. In addition to the extensive academic, creative arts and sporting programmes, the location of our school enables us to offer a full extra-curricular programme including fencing, riding and water sports.

Situated in a beautiful, safe and idyllic island setting just off the South Coast of England, Ryde School with Upper Chine (known locally as Ryde School) is a thriving, prosperous independent day and boarding school for boys and girls aged 2.5 to 18, providing exceptional educational opportunities in a nurturing environment – helping them to be resourceful and resilient in the face of challenge and change.

Just ten minutes by Hovercraft from the mainland, the School and both Junior and Senior boarding houses benefit from being near high-speed sea, rail and air links to regional, European and international destinations and the School is minutes from Cowes, the home of international sailing.

Constantly investing in the future of our pupils, we have recently updated the science labs and libraries, the Sixth Form Centre and added a new Sixth Form boarding house offering flexi, weekly and full boarding options, with another boarding house opening in January 2020, helping pupils to learn to adapt to more independent living and study. The aims of Ryde School as embedded in the School motto, 'Ut Prosim', have always been focused on service to others, and our pupils are encouraged towards self-knowledge, good governance, academic excellence and leadership in order to contribute positively within their chosen fields.

(Founded 1975)

Principal
Richard Tangye OBE

PYP coordinator
Fiona Kemp

MYP coordinator
Simon Downing

DP coordinator
Carla Morais

Status Private

Boarding/day Day

Gender Coeducational

Language of instruction
English

Authorised IB programmes
PYP, MYP, DP

Age Range 3 – 18

Number of pupils enrolled
800

Fees
Day: €9,700 – €18,000

Address
Rua Maria Brown
Outeiro de Polima
2785-816 S Domingos de Rana |
PORTUGAL

TEL +351 21 444 0434
FAX +351 21 444 3072

Email
school@dominics-int.org

Website
www.dominics-int.org

St. Dominic's International School, Portugal, is a highly respected and well-known international school. It is the only school in Portugal authorised to offer three of the International Baccalaureate Programmes: Primary (PYP), Middle (MYP), and the Diploma, and is celebrating its 23rd year as an IB World School.

Our commitment to the IB and its programmes is at the core of SDIS' educational philosophy of 'Nurturing and Educating International Minds'. The IB programmes encourage students to question perceived truths and beliefs and reflect on their place in, and contribution to, the society in which they live.

The principle of inquiry based learning ensures that students develop into independent learners, equipped to embrace both the challenges and opportunities they will face throughout their lives. Situated 15 kilometers from central Lisbon, in the district of Cascais, St. Dominic's is a private, non-selective, coeducational day school serving students aged 3 to 18 years in the international community, through the medium of English. We currently have 58 nationalities amongst our student population, making us a truly international school.

The school is housed in three one-storey buildings. In addition to 48 classrooms, it has a self-contained nursery and kindergarten for our youngest students, two gym halls, three art rooms, two libraries, five science and technology laboratories, two music rooms and a drama studio. Our ICT facilities include both dedicated ICT suites as well as portable devices. We have an excellent reputation for sport, and have facilities for football, basketball and volleyball on site; a wide range of other sports are played using outside facilities.

The junior school offers: English, Portuguese, mathematics, social studies, information technology, art, music, PE and social education through the curriculum of the PYP from nursery to grade 5. In the senior school, students in grades 6 to 10 study the MYP, and in grades 11 and 12 we prepare students for the full diploma or for diploma courses. Our students go on to study at prestigious universities and colleges around the World.

Classes begin in early September and run to the end of June with breaks for Christmas and Easter and shorter mid-term breaks. The teaching day is from 8:30am to 3:30pm, with a wide range of extra-curricular and co-curricular activities offered after school to support the holistic development of our students.

School of Young Politicians – 1306

Head of School
Elena Sporysheva

PYP coordinator
Azat Mazkenov

MYP coordinator
Karina Salway

DP coordinator
Sholpan Mussina

Status State

Boarding/day Day

Gender Coeducational

Language of instruction
English, Russian

Authorised IB programmes
PYP, MYP, DP

Address
Michurinskiy avenue 15
blocks 2,3,4
119192 Moscow | **RUSSIAN FEDERATION**

TEL +7 495 932 99 58

FAX +7 495 932 99 58

Email
1306@edu.mos.ru

Website
gymg1306.mskobr.ru

The School of Young Politicians (SYP) is a Russian state school located in the Western administrative district of Moscow. It is currently one of the first state schools in Eastern Europe to realise the IB continuum programme alongside the national curriculum. The students have a rare opportunity to receive two Diplomas, both the IB and Russian state.

A great emphasis is placed on selecting the teaching staff: all of our teachers are university graduates with international qualifications from Russia as well as other countries from around the world (currently the UK, USA, Australia, India and France). The school offers them ongoing professional training both in Russia and abroad.

The student body, aged between 3-17, is comprised of children from 44 nationalities. This fact provides for a very international environment that ensures cultural diversity and an ethos of tolerance as well as an open-mindedness beneficial to the educational process.

The school sees its mission as raising holistic life-long learners who care about the world around them. Therefore we offer a wide range of subjects and rigorous assessment as well as a huge variety of extra-curriculum activities such as choir, ballroom dancing, sport dancing, drama classes in English and Russian, robototechnics as well as many others. The school also offers many unique activities as monthly meetings with distinguished people who have achieved public recognition in various fields of life – writers, musicians, philosophers, sportsman, entrepreneurs etc. In addition, the school runs a Club of Young Politicians, where active politicians are invited to speak, discuss and debate burning issues from the world of politics, economics and international relationships.

We don't only pay attention to theoretical knowledge but also put emphasis on transferring this knowledge into real-life situations and making its application practical. To realise this, the school is well equipped with libraries, science laboratories, a botanic garden, both indoor and outdoor sport stadiums and other sporting facilities, dance halls, choreography classrooms as well as a fully-equipped theatre and cinema halls. Each classroom is equipped with interactive white boards and projectors.

Specifically in the arts field the school hosts an annual international arts festival that encourages and promotes theatre, dance and choral singing. A top panel of judges and professionally offered workshops and masterclasses offer students both a competitive and supportive experience that culminates in public performances in a prestigious Moscow theatre.

The school plays a vital role in the life of the community. Children initiate and realise various projects addressing the needs of disadvantaged children, war veterans, victims of domestic abuse and others in need. As volunteers they support the work of several charity organisations, initiate fund-raising activities and other socially important campaigns.

During its seventeen years the school has been nominated for numerous awards and prizes. A recent special independent survey published in Tatler magazine called our school "unique". It offers a happy, productive environment for children to learn.

(Founded 1999)

Principal
Luis Carlos Jiménez Gámez

PYP coordinator
Elnara Israfilova

MYP coordinator
Sebastián Fuentes Valenzuela

DP coordinator
Estefania Sánchez

Status Private

Boarding/day Day

Gender Coeducational

Language of instruction
English, Spanish

Authorised IB programmes
PYP, MYP, DP

Age Range 4 months – 18 years

Number of pupils enrolled
670

Address
C/ Barlovento 141
Urb. Almerimar, El Ejido
04711 Almería, Andalusia | SPAIN

TEL +34 950 49 72 73

Email
sek-alboran@sek.es

Website
alboran.sek.es

Located on the seashore and adjacent to the Punta Entinas Natural Park, in Almería, SEK International School Alborán is regarded as a high quality international school in Andalusia. It is the only school in Almeria that offers three IB International Baccalaureate Programmes, from 3 to 18 years of age (Primary Years Programme Middle Years Programme – MYP and the Diploma Programme, either bilingually in English and Spanish or fully in English). These programmes are coordinated closely with the Spanish education system.

For the SEK Education Group, to which SEK-Alborán belongs, physical fitness and respecting one's health are an essential element of the learning process. SEK-Alborán has extensive recreational areas, and 28,000m2 of outdoor spaces, as well as extensive sports facilities and a heated indoor pool. Its classrooms are equipped with cutting-edge technology (makerspace, video recording and editing spaces, radio, 3D printer, robotic tables, TED ED Club). It is considered a model of educational innovation in Andalusia.

Social and emotional learning programmes are of particular importance in students' curricula to foster the social and personal awareness. In the Intelligent Classroom, each student progresses according to their potential, working in teams and having individual efforts rewarded. Teachers and tutors are afforded an open space for dialogue with students and parents both in-person and online. Students can take advantage of the Flipped Classroom to work on content and tackle issues from a broad perspective, solving doubts with their teachers, and learning by doing.

SEK-Alborán offers a bilingual Spanish-English education that is incorporated progressively over all educational stages (50% of the subjects are taught in English). The school is the only Cambridge English School in Almeria, and in addition to preparing official Cambridge exams, students also prepare Goethe Institut (German) and Alliance Française exams.

Principal
Jacobo Olmedo

PYP coordinator
Sara Bouzada Sanmartin

MYP coordinator
Mónica Azpilicueta Amorín

DP coordinator
Yolanda Cenamor Montero

Status Private

Boarding/day Day

Gender Coeducational

Language of instruction
English, Spanish

Authorised IB programmes
PYP, MYP, DP

Age Range 4 months – 18 years

Number of pupils enrolled
670

Address
Rúa Illa de Arousa 4
Boavista. A Caeira, Poio
36005 Pontevedra, Galicia |
SPAIN

TEL +34 98 687 22 77

Email
sek-atlantico@sek.es

Website
atlantico.sek.es

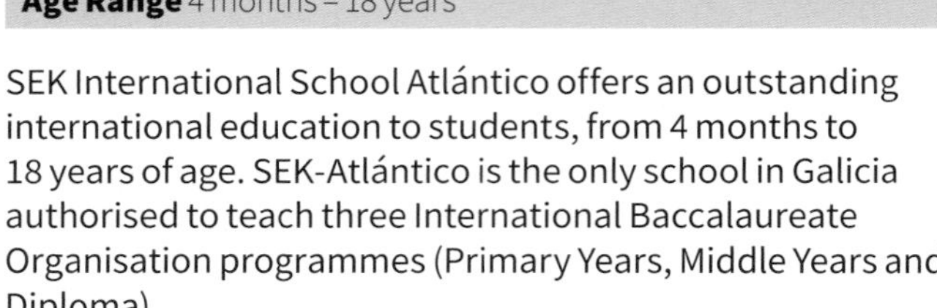

SEK International School Atlántico offers an outstanding international education to students, from 4 months to 18 years of age. SEK-Atlántico is the only school in Galicia authorised to teach three International Baccalaureate Organisation programmes (Primary Years, Middle Years and Diploma).

SEK International Schools are committed to offering each student a learning experience focused on personal development and learning, preparing them for success in later life. Situated close to Pontevedra and Vigo, between the sea and the mountains, SEK-Atlántico boasts modern well-designed school spaces and buildings.

Students are afforded a bilingual education and learn to live with other cultures from an early age. The school places great importance on students' oral and written expression, fostering fluency in different languages. Considered a leader in educational innovation in Galicia, SEK-Atlántico offers learning in Galician, Spanish, English and French from year 3 of Primary.

The SEK education model allows students to play a leading role in their education. They explore and discover for themselves, and build and organise their own knowledge and skills, with expert support from teachers.

SEK-Atlántico students learn in facilities designed for their physical, social and creative development. They include: makerspaces, a psychomotor skills classroom for younger students, laboratories, music and art rooms, a library, language classrooms, a learning lab and large indoor and outdoor sports and recreational areas.

Technological spaces are integrated in the day to day lessons of the school and are designed to contribute fully to student learning. Devices have portability and compatibility enabling them to be used in any space.

From the second year of Primary to Baccalaureate, SEK-Atlántico students prepare for Cambridge University Examinations. In the Middle Years Programme and in Baccalaureate, students can also opt to take the Alliance Française Diplôme d'etude de langue française.

(Founded 1995)

Principal
Roberto Prata

PYP coordinator
Concepció Muntada

MYP coordinator
Carmen Fernández

DP coordinator
Adrià Van Waart

Status Private

Boarding/day Mixed

Gender Coeducational

Language of instruction
English, Spanish, Catalan

Authorised IB programmes
PYP, MYP, DP

Age Range 4 months – 18 years

Number of pupils enrolled
840

Address
Av. del Tremolencs, 24
La Garriga
08530 Barcelona, Catalonia |
SPAIN

TEL +34 93 871 84 48

Email
sek-catalunya@sek.es

Website
catalunya.sek.es

SEK International School Catalunya is located in a quiet and safe residential area spanning 100,000 m², including a large expanse of Mediterranean forest. The school is in La Garriga, a picturesque town just 30 minutes from the centre of Barcelona, one of the most cosmopolitan cities in Europe.

SEK-Catalunya boasts modern facilities and innovative learning spaces and teaches the three International Baccalaureate Programmes. The Middle Years Programme is offered in Spanish and English and the Diploma Programme is offered entirely in English or in both languages. We lead international rankings thanks to our excellent results in IB Diploma exams.

SEK-Catalunya is accredited by the New England Association of Schools and Colleges (NEASC), which is a process of external globally recognised quality assurance.

The school offers its Secondary School and Baccalaureate students the opportunity to take part in the prestigious Duke of Edinburgh's International Award. An all-round personal development scheme focused on the development and training of skills such as: leadership, autonomy, problem solving and teamwork.

We also offer international boarding, catering for students from Spain and abroad in modern, comfortable and functional facilities, designed for residents to live together, grow as individuals and develop their personal identity thanks to a multicultural environment and a rich offer of complementary activities.

SEK International School Ciudalcampo

(Founded 1977)

Principal
Maricruz Lagar

PYP coordinator
Marisa Iglesias Lorenzo

MYP coordinator
James Shaw

DP coordinator
Daniella Spoones

Status Private

Boarding/day Day

Gender Coeducational

Language of instruction
English, Spanish

Authorised IB programmes
PYP, MYP, DP

Age Range 4 months – 18 years

Number of pupils enrolled
1420

Address
Urb. Ciudalcampo, Paseo de las Perdices, 2
San Sebastián de los Reyes
28707 Madrid | **SPAIN**

TEL +34 91 659 63 03

Email
sek-ciudalcampo@sek.es

Website
ciudalcampo.sek.es

SEK International Schools are committed to offering each student a learning experience focused on personal perfection, preparing for success in later life. SEK Schools are bilingual and pioneers in offering International Baccalaureate programmes, boasting an educational model that has made a tradition of innovation, placing them among the best schools in Spain since their foundation in 1892. SEK International School Ciudalcampo offers the IB Primary Years Programme, the IB Middle Years Programme, the IB Diploma Programme (in English and Spanish, or fully in English), and the Spanish Bachillerato LOMCE.

SEK-Ciudalcampo offers an innovative educational model based on early stimulation, immersion in English and the development of talent and creativity in a digital environment that favours the development of emotional intelligence.

SEK Ciudalcampo boasts over 20,000m2 of grounds and buildings and a large outdoor sports complex that exceeds 10,000m^2.

Through an active learning approach, SEK-Ciudalcampo turns the classrooms into a flexible learning place for all students. The student becomes an active agent, building learning for themselves. The Design Thinking methodology helps students to develop skills such as cooperation, creativity and innovation.

The Team Le@rning space allows students to experiment and improve their social skills and develops their curiosity and critical thinking. Under the motto Learning by Doing, our Makerspace is a pioneering 'ideas' lab in Spain. In this space resources and knowledge are shared, with over 300m2 devoted to innovation, creativity and student talent.

SEK-Ciudalcampo is accredited by the New England Association of Schools and Colleges (NEASC), and is the first Spanish school to be recognised as a global member of Round Square.

Principal
Mónica Prieto Peris

MYP coordinator
Gareth Finn

DP coordinator
Gareth Finn

Status Private

Boarding/day Mixed

Gender Coeducational

Language of instruction
English

Authorised IB programmes
MYP, DP

Age Range 12 – 19 years

Address
Belvedere Hall
Windgates
Bray, Co. Wicklow | **IRELAND**

TEL +35 31 287 41 75

Email
sek-dublin@sek.es

Website
dublin.sek.es

SEK International School Dublin is located in a stunning natural setting, where the landscape of the Irish countryside meets the Atlantic coast, between the cities of Bray and Greystones. The latter was named one of the best cities in the world to live as a family, and is only 30 km from Dublin. SEK-Dublin combines architectural tradition with cutting-edge technology, spanning over 250,000 m² of grounds and boasting extensive green areas where our students can enjoy a diverse range of sports and outdoor activities, while enhancing their academic development.

SEK-Dublin is the first and only school in Ireland authorised by the International Baccalaureate Organisation to teach the Middle Years Programme (12-15 years) and the Diploma Programme (16-19 years), taught fully in English with optional languages, including German, French and Spanish.

SEK-Dublin opened its doors in 1981. The success of the school is based on several factors including: a multicultural team of highly trained teachers; the effective use of learning technologies; an individualised programme to cover the educational needs of each student; small class sizes; and an outstanding programme guaranteed by SEK schools' standards of excellence. Aware that education does not only take place in the classroom, we offer residential options with carefully selected local host families or in our on-campus high quality residential facilities, and diverse extracurricular and cultural activities. These aspects combine to nurture the holistic personal and academic development of our students. This all-round education serves them well for their future, enabling them to become mature and independent individuals, and providing them with lasting memories of their experiences at school.

SEK International School El Castillo

(Founded 1972)

Head of School
Eloísa López

PYP coordinator
Melanie McGeever

MYP coordinator
Elvira Chiquero

DP coordinator
Fátima González

Status Private

Boarding/day Mixed

Gender Coeducational

Language of instruction
English, Spanish

Authorised IB programmes
PYP, MYP, DP

Age Range 4 months – 18 years

Number of pupils enrolled
1210

Address
Urb. Villafranca del Castillo,
Castillo de Manzanares, s/n
Villanueva de la Cañada
28692 Madrid | **SPAIN**

TEL +34 91 815 08 92

Email
sek-castillo@sek.es

Website
elcastillo.sek.es

SEK International School El Castillo offers an innovative educational model based on early learning stimulus, talent development, creativity and emotional intelligence. We cater for students from over 40 different nationalities, living and learning in an environment of multicultural understanding, in a stunning natural setting in the north of Madrid.

The school has been authorised as an International Baccalaureate (IB) World School for over 40 years. We offer the IB Primary Years, Middle Years and Diploma programmes fully in English, or through an English-Spanish bilingual syllabus, with outstanding recent examination results We boast first-rate sports facilities and offer international boarders an incomparable environment for the development of individualised, personal growth and personalised pastoral care, provided by specialised school staff, in a safe and secure environment.

In addition, as a sign of our commitment to talent development, we offer a high-performance sports programme, the SEK International Sports Academy, that allows athletes to combine their academic studies with the highest levels of sports training. Students on this programme can reside in the boarding house, allowing them to combine their academic enrichment with high performance sports programmes. We also offer to students between 14 and 18 years, the opportunity to take part in the prestigious Duke of Edinburgh International Award.

SEK-El Castillo is accredited by the New England Association of Schools and Colleges (NEASC), which is a process of external globally recognised quality assurance.

(Founded 2009)

Head of School
Verónica Sánchez

PYP coordinator
Nikki Merval

MYP coordinator
Maria del Carmen Palma

DP coordinator
Andrew Jenkinson

Status Private

Boarding/day Day

Gender Coeducational

Language of instruction
Arabic, English, Spanish

Authorised IB programmes
PYP, MYP, DP

Age Range 3 – 18 years

Address
Onaiza 65
Doha | QATAR

TEL +974 4012 7633

Email
info@sek.qa

Website
www.sek.qa

SEK International School Qatar was founded in 2009 within the framework of the Outstanding Schools Programme of the Ministry of Education of Qatar. The school today caters for students from over 50 nationalities, with teachers from over 25 different countries. The school is an innovative coeducational, international and multilingual school in Qatar, with a cutting-edge learning campus located in the sophisticated West Bay district of Doha. English is the language of instruction, and the school also offers Spanish and Arabic courses for all students.

SEK-Qatar teaches the International Baccalaureate Organisation (IB) programmes, from pre-school to grade 12, which combines a rigorous curriculum with a methodology that fosters the development of skills and understanding.

Since its foundation in 1892, the SEK Group has launched over a hundred pioneering initiatives introducing innovations such as the classrooms without walls, makerspaces, the SEKMUN Model United Nations and the International Baccalaureate Organisation programmes.

SEK-Qatar has a unique educational model. We are committed to offering quality education that promotes individualisation, places emphasis on learning rather than teaching, and fosters activity and effort, freedom, interaction and teamwork and transformational learning. Technology, sports, artistic and social activities also play a major role in the SEK educational model. The ultimate goal is for students to acquire skills, knowledge and understanding to become active citizens, committed and determined to build a better world.

SEK International School Santa Isabel

Principal
Javier Presol

PYP coordinator
William Ivey

Status Private

Boarding/day Day

Gender Coeducational

Language of instruction
English, Spanish

Authorised IB programmes
PYP

Age Range 3 – 12 years

Number of pupils enrolled
450

Address
Calle San Ildefonso, 18
28012 Madrid | SPAIN

TEL +34 91 527 90 94

Email
sek-santaisabel@sek.es

Website
santaisabel.sek.es

SEK International School Santa Isabel is one of nine schools comprising SEK International Schools. Located in the centre of Madrid, SEK-Santa Isabel is the only school in the area authorised to offer the International Baccalaureate Primary Years Programme (PYP).

Set in a district full of history and culture, the school has flexible and innovative environments that allow collaboration and teamwork between students and teachers, and is equipped with all the resources necessary for learning.

SEK-Santa Isabel teaches Early Childhood and Primary Education. The school is bilingual, with 65% of the learning and teaching in English. The teaching staff is native-English speaking or bilingual, with extensive experience and training in English-speaking countries.

In addition, the school also prepares its students to take external language examinations. The school has a spacious gym on the school grounds, as well as outdoor areas for sports such as swimming, tennis and padel tennis, football and basketball.

SEK-Santa Isabel students are part of a Virtual Learning Community 2.0, equipped with the necessary resources and devices for connected learning available on different platforms and devices (e.g. iPads, digital whiteboards, laptops, notebooks, Wi-Fi or Live@edu spaces).

At SEK-Santa Isabel, students learn the diverse skills necessary for the third millennium, through values education, developing emotional and multiple intelligences, nurturing mindfulness, honing public speaking and debate skills, and becoming technologically accomplished through practice in makerspaces. One of our major objectives is to discover and nurture the talents of our students, through our Stellar Programme for high-achieving students, with the aim of enriching their personal development.

Sevenoaks School

(Founded 1432)

Acting Head (to August 2020)
Miss Theresa Homewood BSc MA

Head (from September 2020)
Mr Jesse Elzinga BA MSt

DP coordinator
Nigel Haworth

Status Private

Boarding/day Mixed

Gender Coeducational

Language of instruction
English

Authorised IB programmes
DP

Age Range 11 – 18

Number of pupils enrolled
1165

Fees
Day: £24,291 – £27,585
Boarding: £38,790 – £42,084

Address
High Street
Sevenoaks
Kent
TN13 1HU | UK

TEL +44 (0)1732 455133
FAX +44 (0)1732 456143

Email
regist@sevenoaksschool.org

Website
www.sevenoaksschool.org

Sevenoaks is one of the leading schools in the UK, providing an outstanding modern education. All 450+ students in the sixth form study the IB Diploma Programme, which the school has taught since 1978. The leafy 100-acre campus is in the Kent countryside, just half an hour from Central London and Gatwick Airport. International students make up around 20 per cent of the student body and the school provides pupils with a balanced and intellectually stimulating education while promoting global understanding. Pastoral care is consistently excellent, enabling friendships between all members of a peer group to flourish. Sevenoaks was The Sunday Times Independent Secondary School of the Year 2018.

Curriculum

A wide range of subjects is offered at GCSE, IGCSE and the school's own Sevenoaks School Certificate. In the sixth form all pupils study the IB Diploma Programme. Academic results are outstanding. In 2019, 15 students gained 45 points in the IB, and the average score was 39.4 points (around ten points above the world average). Virtually every student goes on to one of the world's best universities, with around 80 per cent taking places at leading UK universities, and up to 20 per cent accepting places at top US, Canadian, European and international universities.

A wide range of sport is offered, and pupils achieve honours in cross country, rugby, football, hockey, netball, cricket, athletics, sailing, shooting, swimming and tennis. There is a strong emphasis on music, drama and art, with chamber music a particular strength. The school is proud of its strong tradition of community service and DofE Award participation.

Facilities

Facilities are first class. Recent developments include a striking, state-of-the-art boarding house, an award-winning performing arts centre, a Science & Technology Centre uniting the four core fields of science, and an innovative Sixth Form centre. There are seven boarding houses, including five single-sex houses (13-18), and two sixth form houses (16-18). Accommodation ranges from a charming Queen Anne house to a modern building with contemporary social spaces and en-suite study bedrooms.

Entrance

Year 7 (11+): entrance examination, school reference and interview.

Year 9 (13+): pre-assessment, entrance examination or Common Entrance or scholarship examination, plus school reference and interview.

Sixth form (16+): entrance examination, personal statement and interview.

Up to 50 scholarships are awarded annually at 11, 13 and 16, for academic excellence, music, sport, art and drama, and means-tested bursaries are available.

Sevenoaks School is a registered charity for purposes of education. Charity No. 1101358.

(Founded 1699)

Headmaster
Iain Kilpatrick BA MEd FRSA

DP coordinator
Graham Hartley

Status Private

Boarding/day Mixed

Gender Coeducational

Language of instruction
English

Authorised IB programmes
DP

Age Range 3 – 18

Number of pupils enrolled
609

Fees
Day: £2,720 – £6,080 per term
Boarding: £9,180 – £11,230 per term

Address
Oakridge Lane
Winscombe
Somerset
BS25 1PD | UK

TEL 01934 843102

Email
info@sidcot.org.uk

Website
www.sidcot.org.uk

Sidcot School is a lively and popular co-ed boarding and day school where students work hard and achieve excellent results. We encourage individuality, creativity, and challenge our students to think with greater depth to reach a better understanding of themselves and the world they live in. It is these characteristics which make the IB Diploma such a good fit for the School.

Boarding at Sidcot

Sidcot has a well-established international community with around 30 different nationalities. Every effort is made to integrate the day students with the boarding students so everyone benefits from the rich mixture of cultures and backgrounds. Within the boarding houses, international diversity is celebrated and shared. Sidcot is a Quaker school and welcomes students of all faiths and none.

Convenient rural location

The School is close to Bristol and Bath and only two hours from London. Bristol International Airport is 20 minutes away by car. In this setting, students can enjoy the best of both rural and city life: a peaceful environment in which to concentrate on their studies, and access to the cities for educational opportunities and weekend activities.

Academic success

We set out to provide a creative and stretching education that inspires children to want to learn. We help students develop the self-motivation that will enable them to take responsibility for their own learning. It is no surprise that these personal qualities go together with academic excellence. In 2019 the school achieved an IB Mean Score of 31.9 with one student achieving a world class maximum score of 45 out of 45.

Outstanding facilities

As well as 160 acres of organic farmland, Sidcot has superb sporting grounds, a 25-metre indoor swimming pool, all-weather pitch, and an Equestrian Centre. Our Arts Centre bridges traditional genres with modern technology and includes studios for painting, sculpture and ceramics, textiles, photography, a digital media suite, a dedicated performance hall, practice rooms, recording studio and music technology suite and drama studio. We also have some more unusual facilities – for example, an allotment where students get involved in growing produce for the kitchens, a yurt village, beehives to learn about beekeeping and even a well-equipped Observatory enabling students to explore the night sky.

Caring relationships

Quakers place a high value on equality – at Sidcot this is evident in the open and friendly relationships between staff and students, and between students of all ages and cultures. It's often remarked on that our students are extremely supportive of each other, making newcomers – students, teachers and visitors – quickly feel at home.

Special characteristics

- Outstanding reputation in sciences, maths and creative arts
- Centre for Peace and Global Studies
- Equestrian boarding school
- Year 11 Pathway – one-year GCSE course – integrated to give a truly UK boarding school experience

Member of inspired

(Founded 1978)

Head of School
Mr. James Kearney

PYP coordinator
Andrea Bennett

MYP coordinator
Belén González

DP coordinator
Hélène Caillet

Status Private

Boarding/day Mixed

Gender Coeducational

Language of instruction
English

Authorised IB programmes
PYP, MYP, DP

Age Range 3 – 18

Number of pupils enrolled
1040

Fees
Please see our website

Address
Avda La Reserva SN
11310 Sotogrande, Cádiz,
Andalusia | **SPAIN**

TEL +34 956 795 902

Email
info@sis.gl

Website
www.sis.ac

Sotogrande International School (SIS) is a day and boarding school, that follows the IB programme from 3-18 years. Home to a passionate learning community who inspire and encourage learning and intercultural understanding, promoting education as a force for good in the world.

Academic results are consistently excellent, with both MYP and Diploma students achieving well above world average scores year after year. As a result of the impressive average point score of 34.2 in 2019, 90% of students went on to be placed at their first choice of university.

With more than 1000 children from 50 countries, SIS is more than just a school, it's a place where individuals flourish. Throughout the IB programmes, internationally qualified teachers provide a challenging, nurturing and academically-rigorous education. Specialist programmes in golf, tennis and music provide opportunities for talented students to excel.

As an Apple Distinguished School, the use of technology is creatively embedded into the curriculum for all students from the age of 3, while the F1 in Schools programme and the Hyperbaric Challenge provide an exciting way for students to learn Science, Technology, Engineering and Maths (STEM) related subjects. Students are encouraged to think independently and critically, developing their unique interests, gifts and talents benefiting from opportunities to be the best they can be.

Sotogrande International Boarding House is a warm vibrant community, where the staff are dedicated to caring for, and getting the best out of each individual. The academic support received by students is reflected in IB Diploma exam results where, over the past two years, the top-performing students have both been boarders, one achieving the maximum IB score of 45 points.

Students are encouraged to take part in every aspect of boarding life helping them to grow into happy, motivated and morally committed citizens of the world.

Southlands International School

(Founded 1988)

Principal
Mr Deryck Wilson

DP coordinator
Mr Paul Johnson

Status Private

Boarding/day Day

Gender Coeducational

Language of instruction
English

Authorised IB programmes
DP

Age Range 3 – 18

Number of pupils enrolled
400

Fees
€6,950 – €18,000

Address
Via Teleclide 40
Casal Palocco
00124 Rome | ITALY

TEL +39 06 5053932

Email
info@southlands.it

Website
www.southlands.it

Founded in 1976, Southlands International School is one of the oldest and only truly international school in the south of Rome. We offer six key programmes for students between the ages of 3 and 18 years old. The school is non-denominational and welcomes pupils from all cultures and backgrounds. Children from over thirty-five countries attend the school.

Having the best teachers is the key to our students' progress and success. All of our teachers are mother-tongue English speakers and hold teaching qualifications as well as academic credentials. Southlands is an International Baccalaureate World School authorised to offer the IB Diploma Programme (IBDP) in the senior school.

The whole school is fully aligned with the IB ethos. This philosophy and methodology extends far beyond examination success and its basic principle is to support the development of lifelong learners and global leaders in a caring and supportive capacity.

With our international student community in mind, the completion of the IB Diploma Programme is often the best pathway for students wishing to continue their international education.

In order to be truly successful in the IBDP programme students need to follow a rigorous pre-IB syllabus. This is achieved by undertaking other established and successful education programmes.

At Southlands, we start this process in our Foundation Stage (Nursery and Reception) where we follow the Early Years Foundation programme of England. Children then follow the National Curriculum for England from Year 1 (5 years old) until Year 9 (13 years old).

Our aim is for our students to be confident, caring, resilient, inquisitive young adults with a desire to learn and achieve the best they can, in all they do. Very effective teaching and exceptionally positive attitudes amongst pupils are instrumental in ensuring that pupils make excellent progress both academically and personally.

We offer them an abundance of opportunities to enrich their learning, including regular visitors to the school and trips to local places of interest. We also offer opportunities for residential activities from Year 6 to Year 12.

Our school is set in five acres of parkland, which include gardens, orchards, playgrounds and sports fields. This space allows students to enjoy the outdoor classroom and learn about the environment, insects, flowers and birds. We even have a friendly school rabbit who wanders freely around the grounds!

The values of the IB Learner Profile are apparent throughout the whole school. Students are encouraged to become curious and independent learners through participating actively in carefully graded practical and exciting learning experiences. In this way they experience success, achieve self-confidence and become motivated individuals.

Southlands International School is a proud member of the Globeducate network. Formerly known as NACE Schools, Globeducate is one of the leading education networks in Europe. This brings many new opportunities for our community. Our students and teachers benefit from exchange of best practices and a range of annual art, sports and inter-cultural events with other schools across the Globeducate network.

ST CLARE'S OXFORD

(Founded 1953)

Principal
Mr Andrew Rattue

Vice Principal Academic
Alastair Summers

Vice Principal Pastoral
Elena Hesse

DP coordinator
Darrel Ross

Status Private

Boarding/day Mixed

Gender Coeducational

Language of instruction
English

Authorised IB programmes
DP

Age Range 14 – 18

Number of pupils enrolled
271

Fees
Day: £19,878
Boarding: £41,375

Address
139 Banbury Road
Oxford
Oxfordshire
OX2 7AL | UK

TEL +44 (0)1865 552031

Email
admissions@stclares.ac.uk

Website
www.stclares.ac.uk

St Clare's Oxford is an independent, co-educational, day and boarding college located in elegant north Oxford and has been offering the International Baccalaureate Diploma for over 40 years, longer than any other school or college in England. It is also an IB World School. The college has a worldwide reputation for expertise in providing the IB Diploma and embraces internationalism and academic excellence as its core values.

Students from over 45 countries study at St Clare's, including a significant number of British students. The atmosphere is informal and friendly, with an equal emphasis on hard work and developing personal responsibility and mutual respect between staff and students.

St Clare's has an especially wide range of subjects on offer at higher and standard level and, in addition, can teach literature face-to-face in over 25 different languages, something that is not available in any other school in the UK. In recent years, 19 of our students have gained the maximum 45 points and obtained places at top ranking universities worldwide.

The college also offers a one year Pre-IB course which includes English and Maths GCSEs, a two year Middle School Programme including 5 GCSEs and a three week IB Introduction Course in the summer to prepare for the start of the diploma in September.

Students live in college houses close to the central campus, under the care of residential staff. St Clare's also welcomes students from the local area as day students.

There is an extensive programme of social, cultural and sporting activities and students are encouraged to take full advantage of the opportunities that Oxford provides.

St Clare's is most definitely different to any other college in Oxfordshire and rightly so. We have a different approach to studying, living and developing the students as young adults, creating knowledgeable, open-minded and inquiring minds.

St Edward's College
Malta

(Founded 1929)

Headmaster
Mr Nollaig Mac an Bhaird

DP coordinator
Mr Jolen Galea

Status Private

Boarding/day Mixed

Gender Coeducational

Language of instruction
English

Authorised IB programmes
DP

Age Range 2 – 4 & 16–18

Fees
Day: €1,836 – €6,729
Boarding: €16,200 – €22,500

Address
Triq San Dwardu
Birgu (Vittoriosa)
BRG 9039 | MALTA

TEL +356 2788 1199

Email
admissions@stedwards.edu.mt

Website
www.stedwards.edu.mt

If you are looking for a top Sixth Form offering the IB Diploma programme, then look no further – St Edward's College in Birgu, Cottonera is only a few minutes from Malta's Capital, Valletta. St Edward's was established in 1929, basing itself on British Public School ideals, to fill the void left in the Maltese education system by the departure of the English Jesuits.

The College site originally served as a Military Hospital and has extensive grounds between the bastion walls and the old hospital buildings, which serve as ideal recreational areas. St Edward's College was authorised to offer the International Baccalaureate (IB) Diploma Programme (DP) commencing September 2009 and following successful years, applications for boarders and day students have been increasing.

Between the age of 16 and 18 we offer the 2-year International IB Diploma programme which is recognised by both local and international universities. The IB was designed to meet the needs of these students to ensure that they can effortlessly integrate into different International Schools when the need arises.

After carefully looking at the options available to Maltese students we reached a conclusion that the IB Diploma would also be their best option.

The International Baccalaureate® (IB) aims to do more than other curricula by developing inquiring, knowledgeable and caring young people who are motivated to succeed.

The College is an English speaking school so all the lessons are in conducted in English.

St Edward's offers a unique opportunity for parents seeking a boarding school also. We have five-day and seven-day options. Our boarding facilities are split over two floors where single and double rooms are available.

- The school operates on British boarding school principles with high academic standards
- The location and environment are superb with year round sunshine on a Mediterranean island
- Malta is within 3 hours of any European capital city by air
- The IB Diploma is recognised by all top universities
- Our fees offer some of the best value of any European boarding schools

Come and join our students on the IB Diploma Programme!

ST. EDWARD'S
OXFORD

(Founded 1863)

Warden
Stephen Jones

DP coordinator
Anna Fielding

Status Private

Boarding/day Mixed

Gender Coeducational

Language of instruction
English

Authorised IB programmes
DP

Age Range 13 – 18

Number of pupils enrolled
700

Fees
Day: £10,530 per term
Boarding: £13,160 per term

Address
Woodstock Road
Oxford
Oxfordshire
OX2 7NN | UK

TEL +44 (0)1865 319200
FAX +44 (0)1865 319202

Email
registrar@stedwardsoxford.org

Website
www.stedwardsoxford.org

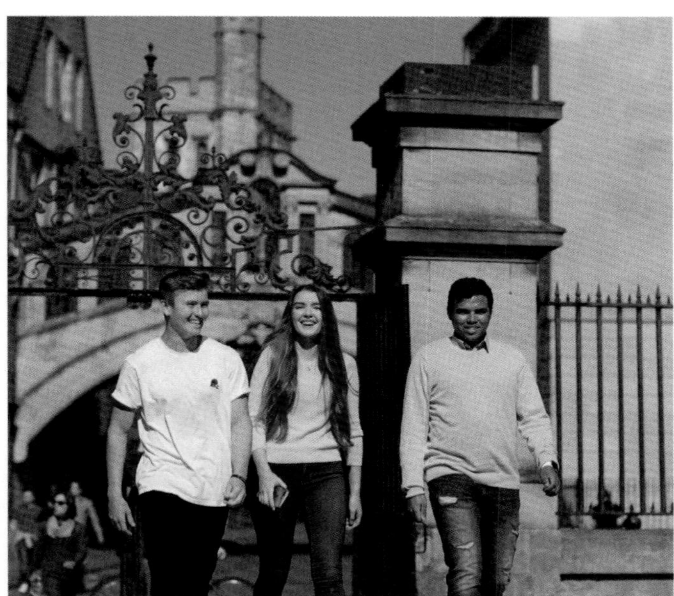

St Edward's

The number of pupils choosing to study the IB at St Edward's has increased significantly in recent years. We now have an excellent balance in the Sixth Form between the IB and A Level, with candidates for both qualifications achieving equal levels of success. IB candidates at St Edward's are part of a friendly, engaged academic community where there are countless opportunities to try out new things and get involved. The School sits on a vast 100-acre estate, complete with riverside boat house, pitches, courts, sports complex and arts centre – yet is only a 5-minute bus ride away from the centre of one of the most famous university cities in the world.

Oxford

Being so close to all the amenities and attractions of Oxford is of enormous benefit to our pupils. The city's rich architectural history and the University's global reputation for scholarship are an intoxicating combination. Venues such as the Ashmolean Museum, the Oxford Playhouse, The Museum of Modern Art and Blenheim Palace offer important learning opportunities – but also welcome distraction from the busy school day. In Oxford, pupils can attend talks and lectures by notable speakers at countless venues across the city. Pupils enjoy being part of this international cultural and intellectual community.

Sixth Form Achievements

Over the past four years, IB candidates achieved an average point score of 35. In 2019, 87% of all Higher Level grades were Levels 7-5. Each year, a number of pupils are awarded places at Oxford and Cambridge whilst the majority (around 85%) go on to top universities in Britain and overseas. Pupils are increasingly interested in studying outside the UK and we have considerable experience in this area. In recent years, pupils have gone on to study at US and Canadian universities including Dartmouth, UCLA, McGill, Northeastern and NYU's Tisch School of the Arts. Pupils have also been successful in their applications to universities in Hong Kong, Japan, Ireland and elsewhere in Europe.

Pastoral Care

The pastoral care system at St Edward's has long been regarded as one of the school's great strengths. Underpinned by a highly effective network of relationships, the system offers distinct but interwoven levels of care. An active Overseas Pupils' Committee organises a lively calendar of events to celebrate our rich cultural diversity and to ensure that our international pupils find their niche and feel at home.

The School and the Admissions Process

St Edward's has around 700 pupils, 85% of whom board. The boy/girl split is 60%/40%. The Sixth Form has around 285 pupils, some 25% of whom are from overseas (15% overseas across the school). Entry to the Sixth Form is competitive with around 4 applicants per place. Academic Scholarships are available at 13+ and 16+ entry, as well as further awards in Music, Sport, Art, Drama and Dance.

Find out more about school life on Teddies TV via the website.

(Founded 1958)

Principal
David Tongue

DP coordinator
Helen Andrew

Status Private

Boarding/day Day

Gender Coeducational

Language of instruction
English

Authorised IB programmes
DP

Age Range 3 – 18

Number of pupils enrolled
895

Fees
€10,700 – €20,750

Address
Via Cassia, km 16
La Storta
00123 Rome | ITALY

TEL +39 06 3086001

Email
admissions@stgeorge.school.it

Website
www.stgeorge.school.it

St George's British International School was founded in 1958, in order to provide an outstanding British education to Rome's international and expatriate families. Today, St George's is one of the leading UK-curriculum schools in continental Europe, and educates boys and girls from ages 3 to 18.

Academic Excellence

St George's is a non-selective school that gives priority admission to international families. Emphasis throughout the curriculum is on developing academic excellence in every child, and results are consistently outstanding: in 2019 the average IB Diploma score was 34.5 points. Nearly all St George's graduates go on to attend leading universities, primarily in the UK, USA, Canada and Australia. Recent destinations have included Cambridge, Oxford, UCL, Imperial, London School of Economics, MIT, Stanford and University of California, Berkley.

Truly International

A total of 87 nationalities are represented amongst the diverse student cohort. Approximately 30% of pupils hold Italian passports and 25% hold British passports. Other nationalities with large representation include American, Chinese, Indian, German, Spanish, Dutch and Russian. New pupils are welcomed throughout the year, subject to availability.

Expansive Facilities

The school's main campus is a leafy and spacious 14-acre site in the North of Rome, housing both Junior and Senior sections. Facilities include seven fully-equipped science labs, a drama studio, specialist teaching rooms for music, art and design technology, two multi-purpose 4G AstroTurf pitches, tartan running track, tennis, basketball and volleyball courts. A second campus is located in close proximity to the Vatican in the heart of the City, serving Junior School pupils from ages 3 to 11.

Beyond the Classroom

Pupils at St George's are always encouraged to try new activities. Music is a lively department with a full orchestra, jazz band, percussion group and a range of choirs. Drama is popular, with various productions running throughout the year. Sports teams include football, rugby, hockey, volleyball, basketball and tennis. Other clubs include MUN, Environmental Awareness and Zambian Orphans Appeal, a charity established by the school.

St Leonards

St Andrews, Fife

(Founded 1877)

Head of School
Dr Michael Carslaw

PYP coordinator
Kathryn McGregor (Acting)

MYP coordinator
Kathryn McGregor

DP coordinator
Ben Seymour

Status Private Independent

Boarding/day Mixed

Gender Coeducational

Language of instruction
English

Authorised IB programmes
PYP, MYP, DP

Age Range 5 – 18

Number of pupils enrolled
540

Fees
Day: £9,552 – £15,474
Boarding: £24,651 – £37,452

Address
St Andrews
Fife
KY16 9QJ | UK

TEL 01334 472126

FAX 01334 476152

Email
contact@stleonards-fife.org

Website
www.stleonards-fife.org

St Leonards is an independent, coeducational boarding and day school in the heart of St Andrews. Less than an hour from Edinburgh Airport, this special Scottish coastal town is renowned as the home of golf and Scotland's first university.

St Leonards is a progressive yet traditional British boarding school with the benefit of an international outlook and was named Scotland's Independent School of the Year 2019 by The Sunday Times Schools Guide. It welcomes pupils from around 30 nationalities, with boarding from age 10.

Boarding houses are stylish, comfortable, with a 'home-from-home' warmth, having recently undergone a £4m programme of refurbishment, the latest stage of which was completed in 2019. Many bedrooms have inspiring sea views beyond the school playing fields. Classes are small and a lively academic ethos encourages pupils to explore ideas and develop their thinking, enabling them to form ways of learning that last for life.

Curriculum

Pupils are welcomed from schools across Scotland, the UK and internationally. Children also move up from St Leonards Junior School, which received accreditation in 2018 to teach the PYP curriculum, and progress through the MYP to IGCSE and GCSE exams in Years 10 and 11. Everyone in Sixth Form studies the IB Diploma Programme, so each student follows a curriculum tailored to his or her individual requirements. In addition, a BTEC in Business or Sport combined with IB courses is offered as a more vocational curriculum choice for students in the Sixth Form.

St Leonards leads the way with its IB provision in Scotland; it is the first school in Scotland to be accredited for the all-through PYP, MYP and DP approach to learning, and has excellent links with universities. The school recently held an IB conference, attended by Scotland's universities' admissions staff, and hosts annual higher education fairs featuring UK and international institutions.

In 2019, 76% of St Leonards leavers achieved the equivalent of A*/A/B at A Level, going on to top UK and global universities. The average points score was 33 – an excellent outcome in an all-IB Sixth Form that welcomes students with a range of academic abilities.

A leading five-tier Golf Programme is offered, as well as activities including music, drama, art, outdoor pursuits, horse riding and team and individual sports. The school fosters an imaginative choice of projects for the CAS component of the IB, as well as for the MYP Community Project. Recent examples include teaching languages to younger children, tree-planting, singing at community events and a sunrise swim in the North Sea for charity.

Entry requirements

Tests and interviews are held throughout the year. Entry into the IB Diploma Programme is by CAT4 assessment, along with school reports and interview. A Pre-IB programme is offered, usually for one year before a student starts Sixth Form.

St. George's International School, Switzerland

(Founded 1927)

Head of School
Mrs Jenny Aviss

DP coordinator
Dr David Brooke

Status Private

Boarding/day Mixed

Gender Coeducational

Language of instruction
English

Authorised IB programmes
DP

Age Range 1.5 – 18

Number of pupils enrolled
400

Fees
Please enquire

Address
Chemin de St. Georges 19
CH-1815 Clarens/Montreux |
SWITZERLAND

TEL +41 21 964 3411
FAX +41 21 964 4932

Email
admissions@stgeorges.ch

Website
www.stgeorges.ch

Founded in 1927, St. George's International School combines its well-structured, traditional ethos with academic excellence in an international environment. Enjoying a safe location, our whole school community fosters mutual respect and understanding whilst cultivating individual talents and potential.

As stated in our motto, 'Levavi Oculos', St. George's International School encourages students to lift their eyes and recognise positive qualities within themselves and others and to nurture a caring and dynamic attitude in today's demanding world.

The school's Learning Principles closely relate to the IB learner profile and students are challenged to become more curious, thoughtful, resilient, reflective, collaborative and balanced.

The school provides a 'Home away from Home' to approximately 80 boarders and over 300 day students from 60 different nationalities. Nestled between the Alps and Lake Geneva, the school includes tennis courts, football field, sports hall, play parks and opened landscaped grounds. During winter students ski and in the summer they make use of the lake, surrounding countryside and local sports facilities.

The curriculum contains the following subject groups:

Groups 1 & 2: Languages
Students usually select from English and French. Spanish, German, Chinese, Russian and other languages as part of the mother tongue Literature self-taught programme are also possible.

Group 3: Individuals and Societies
- Economics
- Geography
- History
- Environmental Systems and Societies
- Business Management

Group 4: Experimental Sciences
- Biology
- Chemistry
- Physics
- Sports, Exercise and Health Science
- Computer Science
- Envrionmental Systems and Societies

Group 5: Mathematics
St. George's offers Mathematics in higher and standard levels.
- Applications and Interpretations
- Analysis and Approaches

Group 6: The Arts (or elective subject)
Students can follow courses in either Visual Arts, Music, Dance or Theatre Studies.

Alternatively students may follow a second subject chosen from Groups 2, 3 or 4.

St. Louis School

CARPE MAGNIFICENTIAM

Executive Principal High School
Mr. Gerry Rafferty

Principal Colonna School
Mrs. Kathleen Slocombe

Principal Caviglia School
Mrs. Jennifer Devine

DP coordinator
Hatty Rafferty

Status Private

Boarding/day Mixed

Gender Coeducational

Language of instruction
English, Italian

Authorised IB programmes
DP

Age Range 2 – 18 (14-18 boarding)

Number of pupils enrolled
1500

Address
Via E. Caviglia, 1
20139 Milan | ITALY

St. Louis Colonna
Via Marco Antonio Colonna, 24,
20149 Milan | ITALY

St. Louis High School
Via Olmetto, 6, 20123 Milan | ITALY

TEL +39 02 55231235

Email
info@stlouisschool.com

Website
www.stlouisschool.com

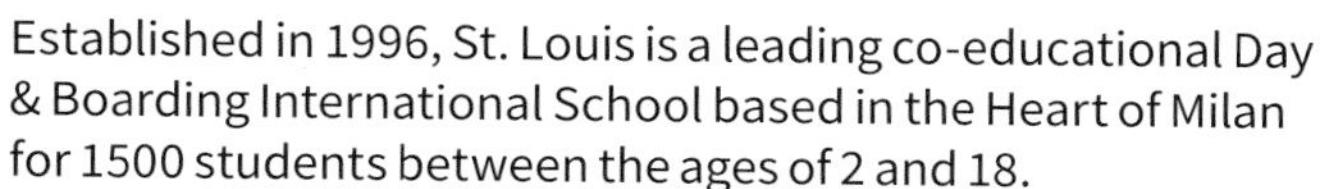

Established in 1996, St. Louis is a leading co-educational Day & Boarding International School based in the Heart of Milan for 1500 students between the ages of 2 and 18.

Located across three sites, the south-east premises comprise of an Infant, Primary and Middle School, and the High School is located in a prime position, a stone throw from the Duomo. The Day & Boarding School, located in the Corso Sempione/Portello area, offers school opportunities for 2-14 year olds as well as full time boarding places for 14-18 year olds.

The St. Louis School's academic programme is rigorous and challenging. The Infant School programme is based on the British Early Years Foundation Stage (EYFS) Curriculum.

Primary and Middle School follow the British National Curriculum with an option for students 6 years and upwards to also follow the Italian curriculum.

The High School, which provides boarding facilities, comprises of IGCSE examinations for Years 10-11 and the International Baccalaureate Diploma (IB) for Years 12-13 with over 100 students each year studying this unique course.

The approach reinforces the importance of creative and critical thinking, with the school developing independent learners well equipped to succeed in the IB and beyond. St. Louis achieves outstanding academic results with the IB diploma results the highest average in Europe five years running (36.2 average).

The school opened its new High School in the centre of Milan (Palazzo Archinto) in September 2019. A magnificent historic building located in via Olmetto, will accommodate all senior school students from Years 10-13. Designed by architect Francesco Maria Richini in the 17th century and situated in the centre of Milan, the Palazzo provides the perfect learning environment for students of this age, blending state-of-the art educational facilities within historic surroundings.

St. Stephen's School

(Founded 1964)

Head of School
Eric Mayer

DP coordinator
Nadia El-Taha

Status Private

Boarding/day Mixed

Gender Coeducational

Language of instruction
English

Authorised IB programmes
DP

Age Range 14 – 19

Number of pupils enrolled
299

Fees
Day: €25,145
Boarding: €39,095

Address
Via Aventina 3
00153 Rome | ITALY

TEL +39 06 575 0605

Email ststephens@sssrome.it

Website www.sssrome.it

Why Choose St. Stephen's
St. Stephen's provides a demanding academic program taking full advantage of its location in the historic center of Rome. We offer a rigorous college preparatory curriculum, which is balanced by a diverse co-curricular program that fulfills the requirements for the full International Baccalaureate Diploma Programme and a US high school diploma.

The First IB School in Italy
In 1975, St. Stephen's was the first school in Italy to offer the International Baccalaureate Programme to students in grades 11 and 12. As a leading IB World School, our graduates have consistently ranked in the top percentile of IB exams, including perfect scores of 42 and the highest IB scores in the history of the School in recent years. Our average IB score is 35.

Building Futures Since 1964
St. Stephen's offers specialized career and university counseling services that aid students in the college or university search process, as well as potential academic and career choices. Our international student body applies to multiple education systems and matriculates to universities throughout the world whose admissions requirements vary widely.

A Focus on Internationalism and Global Citizenship
Our internationally-minded community aims to foster a keen sense of global citizenship in our students, who hail from more than fifty nations. We value the American roots of the School; we embrace Rome as our location, in both its historical and contemporary dimensions; and we are global in our outlook, both in terms of our active interest in histories, cultures, languages and belief systems from around the world, and in our awareness of the global impact of our actions. We welcome students, faculty, and staff from all backgrounds and believe that every one of us contributes in equal measure to the evolving cultural fusion that makes St. Stephen's special.

Rome Is Our Classroom
Our English language high school is surrounded by Western Civilization's most significant historic monuments, such as the Colosseum, the Roman Forum, and Circus Maximus – all within minutes of our campus. Teachers use the Eternal City as their classroom, and students gain first-hand knowledge of history, art, archaeology, classics, and cultural heritage. We provide a world-class education in an intellectually challenging environment that transforms young minds and prepares them to excel in high school and in their future endeavors.

World-Class Professionals Comprise Our Faculty
St. Stephen's employs award-winning authors, playwrights, researchers, archaeologists, art historians, accomplished musicians, scientists, and professionals in many sectors who have distinguished themselves in their respective fields. The real-life experience of our faculty enables them to share a high level of expertise with students. Ninety percent of our faculty have advanced degrees, and twenty percent have earned a PhD.

A Commitment to Discovering Rome and the World
A program unique to St. Stephen's is our dynamic faculty-led trips and experiential service-learning program. Trips take students to regions throughout Italy every fall, and to destinations throughout Europe and the Mediterranean Basin every spring. Paired with summer service-learning experiences in Rwanda, Senegal, and Sri Lanka, students

benefit by gaining new insights and develop a global mindset balanced with compassion and consideration for others.

Signature Programs

Through the St. Stephen's Lyceum, students benefit from enriched classics courses and collaborations with prestigious institutions. Students may elect to take Classical Greek & Roman Studies in the IB Diploma Programme. Our classical studies courses build on the past and unite with the world of technology and globalization.

iLabs

Students enhance their technology skills in the iLab as they learn to design, program, build, and compete in robotics using EV3 Lego Mindstorm or Tetrix Java-based robots. Artists use Wacom tablets to design in 2D and digitally cut and assemble various products and models. Students explore 3D design via Google Sketchup, AutoDesk's Fusion 360 or Inventor programs, as well as Unity, widely used for creating animations and augmented and virtual reality. Students can learn to create and program a myriad of problem-solving devices using Arduino, and a variety of drones, photographic and video equipment, and small robots such as Sphero are available to explore and program. Students can explore virtual reality experiences and learn to make their own Virtual and Augmented Reality applications, and with Cozmo programmable robots, IBM Watson they construct chatbots and learn about creating and using Artificial Intelligence.

Molecular Genetics

St. Stephen's offers science students an advanced molecular genetics program. Developed in partnership with the European Molecular Biology Labs, Europe's flagship laboratory for Life Sciences, this collaboration allows students to develop inquiry-based lab skills and participate in university-level research with state-of-the-art equipment so they may expand and deepen their scientific literacy and competencies.

Five Core Values Anchor Our Community

A strong commitment to our core values of care, integrity, scholarship, independence, and creativity defines us and provides an essential foundation for building character. Students feel supported and free to achieve their personal best.

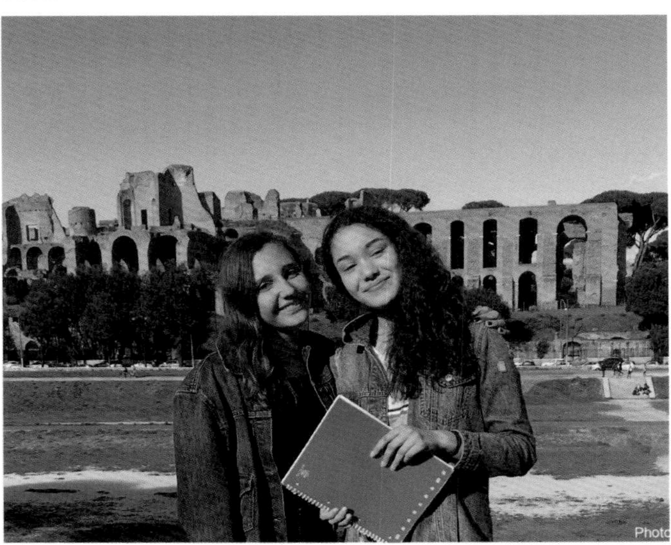

stephen perse

foundation

(Founded 1881)

Head of Sixth Form
Mr Spencer Pinkus

DP coordinator
Jacqueline Paris

Status Private

Boarding/day Mixed

Gender Coeducational

Language of instruction
English

Authorised IB programmes
DP

Age Range 16 – 18

Number of pupils enrolled
210

Fees
Day: £5,830
Boarding: £12,670

Address
Shaftesbury Road
Cambridge
Cambridgeshire
CB2 8AA | UK

TEL +44 (0)1223 454762

Email
admissions@stephenperse.com

Website
www.stephenperse.com/ib

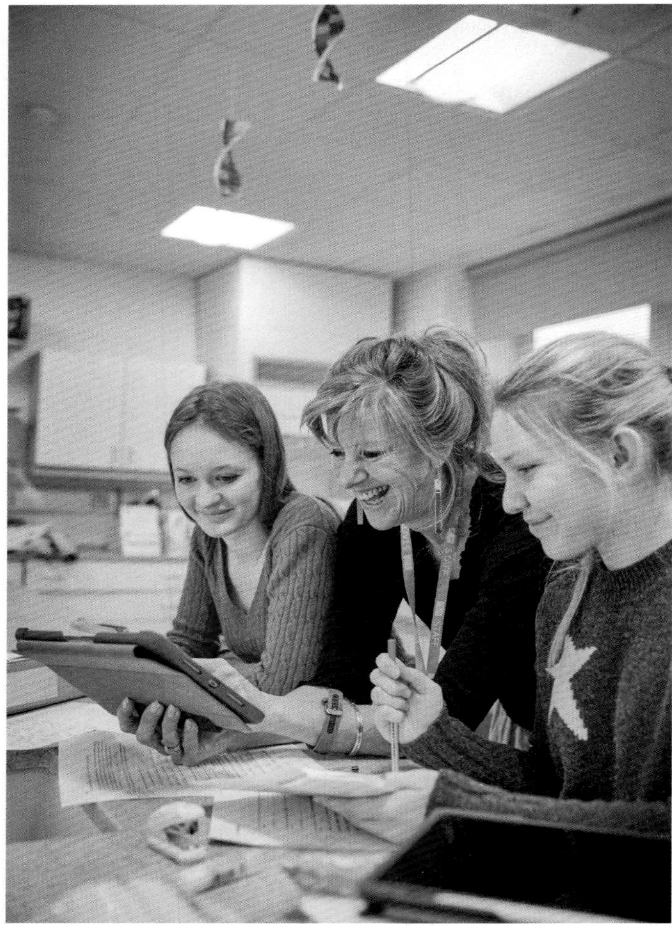

Stephen Perse Sixth Form offers students the chance to succeed; to succeed in key exams, in university applications, in making the right career choice, but most of all to gain the building blocks to succeed in life.

At Stephen Perse students achieve exceptional results and go on to top universities to study a wide range of subjects, but education is more than good grades. It is about learning to think critically and independently, developing logic and strength of character as well as skills in communication and collaboration. These educational goals and personal competencies are core to the International Baccalaureate (IB) programme and at the heart of all the schools in the Stephen Perse Foundation. Stephen Perse advocates that social values and educational achievement are intertwined. As an International Baccalaureate World School, Stephen Perse aims to develop young people to have a global outlook by exposure to a world of opportunity and to encourage personal and social responsibility.

Choosing to follow the IB programme as an alternative to A Levels is popular at Stephen Perse Sixth Form and students repeatedly achieve excellent results, with an average score of over 40 points. Since becoming an IB World School in 2007, Stephen Perse has twice been awarded International Baccalaureate School of the Year by the Sunday Times. As the IB Diploma is highly prized globally as a gold standard for university entry, candidates from the Stephen Perse Sixth Form have secured places across the full range of disciplines in the UK and several students have taken their IB qualification overseas to study in the USA, Canada and Europe.

A co-ed campus with dynamic spaces and immersive digital engagement

Education at Stephen Perse Sixth Form takes place in a co-ed college campus where every student is known and supported and where no uniform is standard. This inspirational setting includes university style one-to-one tutorials and small group supervisions. Immersive digital engagement is provided alongside the provision of dynamic spaces to encourage learning and curiosity.

University preparation through specialist advice and guidance

University preparation is exemplary at Stephen Perse with wide-ranging specialist advice across the arts, humanities, sciences and medicine with guidance about courses and future careers. Navigating the process for both UK and overseas applications is provided by a specialist team with in-depth knowledge and guidance expertise. This means students are well-prepared for the early applications required by Oxbridge, for different requirements overseas as well as UK's UCAS. The resulting success each year is testament to the approach; students are accepted on courses in medicine, law, arts, natural sciences and humanities at Cambridge, Oxford, LSE, UCL and many other Russell Group universities.

Academic achievement is supported by extensive sport, music, art and drama

Extensive sport, music, drama, art, creative and

extracurricular opportunities support and enhance academic rigour and achievement. Students gain the skills, breadth of knowledge and practical experience to become the changemakers of their future world. Being involved in clubs and societies provide experiences that universities and employers value. The opportunities available are diverse and designed to suit all interests, from the Duke of Edinburgh's Award to Beginners' Chinese, from Model United Nations to TED Ed Club, from journalism to community outreach, from drama to music, from basketball to fencing and from yoga to rowing and football. The campus is close to the centre of Cambridge so access to leaders in science, arts and humanities through talks and visiting lecturers is part of the Stephen Perse breadth of education and stimulation.

Community, wellbeing and social life on campus

The Sixth Form is more than just a place to study. There is a genuine sense of community which starts each year with a special event at Cambridge University's Girton College when all the students across the two years gather for a celebration and a unique chance to experience a legendary college formal dinner. New friends soon become established and the relaxed but supportive atmosphere from staff and teachers ensures that at all stages of the two years of study students' well-being is paramount. The emphasis at Stephen Perse is on the individual and there is time to support every student for the best outcomes.

Boarding is an option too

For increasing numbers of students from either the UK or abroad, the opportunity to board for the Sixth Form is very appealing. Living and studying in Cambridge, one of the most stimulating and academic cities in the UK, is available at the Stephen Perse Sixth Form. Students live in the heart of the city just a short walk or cycle away from teaching buildings and the library. There's space to study and time to make the most of all that Cambridge offers to students. This really is a perfect stepping-stone to future university life.

Stiftsschule Engelberg

Abbey School Since 1120

(Founded 1120)

Rektor
Andri Tuor OSB

DP coordinator
Hansueli Flückiger

Status Private

Boarding/day Mixed

Gender Coeducational

Language of instruction
German, English

Authorised IB programmes
DP

Age Range 12 – 19

Number of pupils enrolled
120

Fees
Boarding: CHF40,000 – CHF43,500
Weekend CHF5,500

Address
Benediktinerkloster 5
Engelberg
6390 | SWITZERLAND

TEL +41 41 639 61 00

Email
info@stiftsschule-engelberg.ch

Website
www.stiftsschule-engelberg.ch

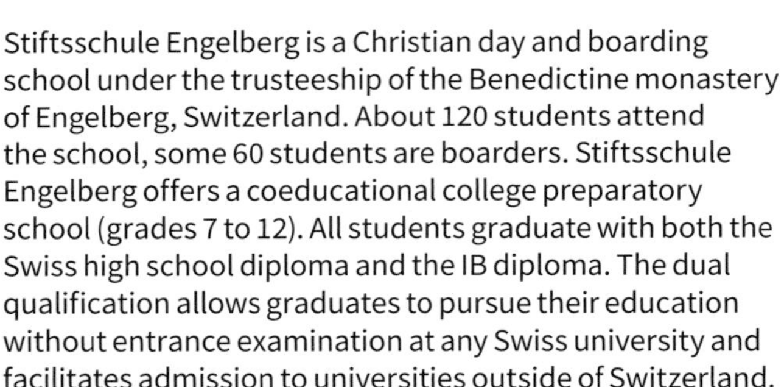

Stiftsschule Engelberg is a Christian day and boarding school under the trusteeship of the Benedictine monastery of Engelberg, Switzerland. About 120 students attend the school, some 60 students are boarders. Stiftsschule Engelberg offers a coeducational college preparatory school (grades 7 to 12). All students graduate with both the Swiss high school diploma and the IB diploma. The dual qualification allows graduates to pursue their education without entrance examination at any Swiss university and facilitates admission to universities outside of Switzerland.

Engelberg is situated in Central Switzerland, near Lucerne. The town is a renowned mountain resort. Our students take advantage of the local facilities to participate in a variety of sports.

Stiftsschule Engelberg follows the Swiss curricula for bilingual college preparatory schools: All teaching from grade 7 to 9 is done in German, from grade 10 geography, biology and mathematics are taught in English. In grade 11 and 12 the teaching of these subjects follows IB curricula. Three languages, that is German, French and English, complete the number of the six IB subjects. Additional subjects are taught to meet the requirements of the Swiss high school diploma („Matura“). The dual qualification program provides a broad academic education to ensure that graduates are fully prepared to pursue their education at university in any subject of their choice, be it in Switzerland or abroad.

Besides mandatory education in sports, music and the arts our students have the opportunity to do a variety of sports, play musical instruments, join an orchestra and choir, or take part in plays.

Due to the bilingual character of the program applicants must have prior knowledge of German and must be willing to acquire proficiency in German during their stay at Stiftsschule Engelberg. Knowledge of English is expected to be appropriate to the grade applicants wish to enter. Applications are accepted throughout the year. Admission usually takes place at the beginning of the academic year in mid-August. For more information please contact the secretary’s office at +41 41 639 61 00 or info@stiftsschule-engelberg.ch.

LOUISENLUND

LERNEN LEISTEN LEBEN

(Founded 1949)

Head of School
Dr Peter Rösner

DP coordinator
Damien Vassallo

Status Private

Boarding/day Mixed

Gender Coeducational

Language of instruction
English

Authorised IB programmes
DP

Number of pupils enrolled
440

Fees
€3,665

Address
Louisenlund 9
Güby 24357 | **GERMANY**

TEL +49 (0)4354 999 0
FAX +49 (0)4354 999 171

Email
admission@louisenlund.de

Website
www.louisenlund.de/en

Preserving values, taking responsibility, shaping the future – Louisenlund, the only IB boarding school in Northern Germany, impresses with its beautiful surroundings, a thoroughly international character and education of the highest quality. Located on the Schlei, the school is committed to forming open-minded and responsible citizens.

Louisenlund seeks to develop personalities and promote talents. Practical, proactive and experiential learning enables students to actively acquire and develop knowledge and to achieve their individual educational objectives. Louisenlund's students are expected to become the principle players in their learning process and to be accountable for their own academic process. Nevertheless, each student is accompanied by a faculty mentor, who acts as an academic advisor and helps students maximize their potential. Committed to the IB Learner Profile, Louisenlund not only aims for the best possible academic achievement amongst our young learners; the sense of community, companionship and consideration for others, as well as the readiness to take on responsibility are of particular importance.

Since its founding in 1949, Stiftung Louisenlund stands for a top-class education, with high standards for academic achievement and character development. We offer the possibility to choose between the German Abitur and the International Baccalaureate (IB) Diploma, two widely recognized qualifications. 440 pupils, including 66 from abroad, currently attend the half-day primary school and the full-day 'Gymnasium' (German secondary school) or the IB Diploma Programme. Nearly 325 students are residents of our boarding community, which impresses with its relaxed and familial atmosphere. Because of the large number of Anglophone teachers, various native speakers teach their own language (English, Spanish and Chinese) and our membership in the esteemed Round Square network, Louisenlund enjoys a good reputation worldwide.

Another important feature is the exceptionally good relationship between students and staff, deriving from the small learning groups. Particular talents and weaknesses can be specifically fostered.

Besides the educational possibilities and the broad range of extracurricular activities, life at Louisenlund is a time to remember for other reasons: local and international projects, linguistic and cultural diversity on the campus, lifelong friendships and the exceptional team spirit of our community.

(Founded 1593)

Headmaster
Mr John Browne BA LLB MBA

DP coordinator
Mrs Deborah Kirkby BSc

CP coordinator
Emily Ashe

Status Private

Boarding/day Mixed

Gender Coeducational

Language of instruction
English

Authorised IB programmes
DP, CP

Age Range 13 – 18

Number of pupils enrolled
760

Fees
Day: £22,550
Weekly Boarding: £30,750
Boarding: £35,850

Address
Stonyhurst
Clitheroe
Lancashire
BB7 9PZ | UK

TEL 01254 827073
FAX 01254 827131

Email
admissions@stonyhurst.ac.uk

Website
www.stonyhurst.ac.uk

Stonyhurst is the UK's leading co-educational Catholic boarding and day school for 3-18 year olds. Inspired by the beautiful Stonyhurst estate and the heritage of the world's oldest continuous Jesuit school, our students pursue academic excellence alongside spiritual and emotional growth and learn to embody their school motto: "Quant je puis", meaning "all that I can", in every activity. The IB mission reflects Stonyhurst's Jesuit mission and identity, in that both organisations seek to develop the whole person – intellectually, physically and emotionally.

Students come from the UK and around the world to experience an IB education at Stonyhurst. We offer an extremely full and enriching educational experience and our students flourish in a safe, happy, ordered environment and vibrant, close-knit community. Thoughtful, age-appropriate pastoral care encourages all students, whether day, weekly boarders or full boarders, to become increasingly self-reliant and considerate global citizens.

Since its introduction in 2013, we have found our IB offering has grown rapidly in popularity at Stonyhurst, and our year 12 IB intake now comprises around a quarter of total admissions into our sixth form. Our academic results for the IB Diploma bear testimony to the hard work and dedication of both highly qualified staff and motivated students. Our 2019 average points score in the Diploma was 35.6, with 67% of students achieving over 35+ points. Our IB students consistently perform above the world average and have gone onto prestigious universities in the UK and beyond, in a wide variety of challenging subjects, such as law, economics, medicine and engineering.

We also offer the IB Career-Related Programme with a sport or business career related pathway. With exceptional sports facilities, pupils who take on the IBCP sport related option can expect to study in one of the best environments in the country. This includes a brand new state of the art gym, an exciting outdoor pursuits programme, as well as the recent installation of LTA standard indoor tennis courts. Our global alumni network, as well as strong links with the local business community, can provide unique opportunities for our IBCP business students. Of course, these experiences are available for all students at Stonyhurst, and our students benefit from a huge range of co-curricular options, with over 100 clubs and societies running through the week.

An IB education at Stonyhurst provides an exceptional foundation for any young person, and we look forward to being a part of your future.

Tas Private Elementary School

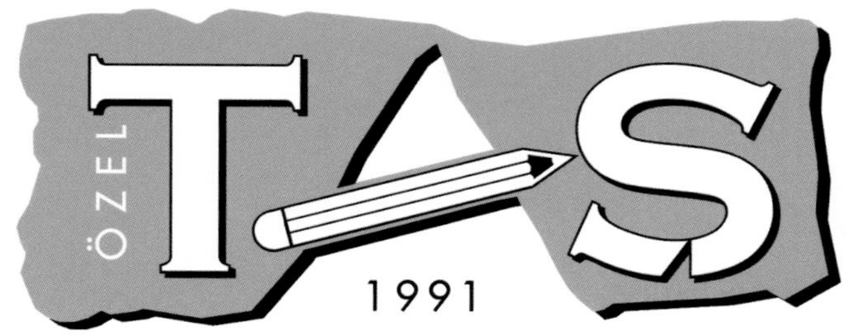

(Founded 1991)

Head of School
Mr. Ali Akdogan PhD

PYP coordinator
Sena Bataklar

Status Private

Boarding/day Day

Gender Coeducational

Language of instruction
Turkish, English

Authorised IB programmes
PYP

Address
Cevizlik Mah. Hallaç Hüseyin
Sk. No:11, Bakirköy
34142 | TURKEY

TEL +90 (212) 543 6000
FAX +90 (212) 570 6187

Email
aliakdogan@taskolej.k12.tr

Website
www.taskolej.k12.tr

'Family is the cornerstone of our school.'
We believe that there is no such thing as an unsuccessful student. Our programme is based on this philosophy. We endeavour to develop not only the confidence and skills of our children, but to help them realize their maximum potential through balanced personal and interpersonal development. The positive environment is reinforced by the limited presence of externally imposed discipline – students are not punished, and bells are not rung. We focus on facilitating the knowledge, as well as the behaviour, attitudes and skills that will help our children become successful adults, whatever challenges they choose to undertake in the future.

We are committed to the responsibility and privilege of educating and nurturing inquirers and critical thinkers. Our goal is to become internationally recognised for our active participation in enriching the qualities of our countries' human resource, and thereby improving the world we live in, and the cultural patrimony of future generations.

Towards this end we energetically pursue a course of study that holds the essential elements of the PYP (Action, Attitudes, Concepts, Knowledge and Skills) at its heart, and not only for our students. We embrace the continuing education of our parents as well by offering them a range of studies, and symposiums designed to stimulate and continue their personal development. We regularly reach out to our alumni and encourage them to maintain contact as role models and examples. Throughout the year our students participate in charity and fundraising events to support communities both locally and nationally.

The TAS School family; our parents, teachers, students, and support staff look forward to the challenges of the future. We embrace the diversity of our community and plan for our successes carefully and consciously.

THE AMERICAN SCHOOL IN SWITZERLAND

(Founded 1956)

Head of School
Christopher Nikoloff

DP coordinator
Howard Stickley

Status Private

Boarding/day Mixed

Gender Coeducational

Language of instruction
English

Authorised IB programmes
DP

Age Range 3 – 19

Number of pupils enrolled
715

Address
Via Collina d'Oro 15
6926 Montagnola-Lugano |
SWITZERLAND

TEL +41 91 960 5151
FAX +41 91 993 2979

Email
admissions@tasis.ch

Website
www.tasis.ch

Founded by M. Crist Fleming in 1956, TASIS is a day and boarding international school committed to creating global citizens through education, travel, and service.

The oldest American boarding school in Europe, TASIS welcomes 710 students from 60 nations in grades Pre-Kindergarten (beginning at age three) through Postgraduate. Approximately 250 students between ages 12–19 reside on campus.

High School students can choose from individual Advanced Placement courses or pursue the International Baccalaureate (IB) Diploma, helping them receive offers from more than 400 universities in 20 different nations over the past five years. The School offers an extensive Fine Arts program that includes courses in Drama, Music, and the Visual Arts, enabling aspiring artists of any ilk to find their creative voice and nurture their talent.

Accredited by the European Council of International Schools (ECIS) and the New England Association of Schools and Colleges (NEASC), TASIS is proud to employ gifted, passionate educators who encourage intellectual curiosity. Nearly 80 percent of the High School faculty hold advanced degrees.

The campus includes more than 25 buildings dating from the 17th century Villa De Nobili to the state-of-the-art Campo Science Center. Perched on a hillside in sunny southern Switzerland with commanding views of snow-capped mountains, palm trees, and Lake Lugano, the School's enviable location makes possible an impressive Academic Travel program that brings students face-to-face with the rich cultural heritage of Europe and the spectacular natural beauty of the Alps and beyond.

The School's pioneering Global Service Program transforms lives by providing every High School student with a unique opportunity to connect across borders – whether geographic, economic, or social – through comprehensive experiences that build empathy and encourage personal responsibility. The Program awakens students to humanitarian needs, inspires them to build enduring relationships, and leads them toward a life of active service and committed service.

TASIS encourages physical fitness and healthy lifestyles. Varsity sports teams compete throughout Switzerland and Europe, and a variety of other fitness activities are offered to cater to all interests. Each year also brings many opportunities to ski and explore the breathtaking Alps. Students leave TASIS with a heightened appreciation for the outdoors and an understanding of what it takes to succeed in challenging environments.

Each summer, hundreds of students aged 4 1/2–18 journey to Lugano for the TASIS Summer Programs, which feature intensive academic courses, an unparalleled performing arts program, thrilling outdoor adventures, advanced sports training, and exciting cultural excursions around Europe.

The Abbey
Connected to each other. Connected to the World.

(Founded 1887)

Head
Mrs Rachel S E Dent

DP coordinator
Julie Mackie

Status Private

Boarding/day Day

Gender Female

Language of instruction
English

Authorised IB programmes
DP

Number of pupils enrolled
1059

Fees
Day: £17,640

Address
Kendrick Road
Reading
Berkshire
RG1 5DZ | UK

TEL 0118 987 2256
FAX 0118 987 1478

Email
schooloffice@theabbey.co.uk

Website
www.theabbey.co.uk

Where learning goes beyond.
Described as 'much more than a school', The Abbey is a place where academic excellence becomes a natural process of growth and curiosity at every stage of the journey, from the age of 3 to 18. We are a school that celebrates success in all its forms, and every girl is encouraged to explore her own unique strengths and discover her passions through a vast choice of opportunities – both inside and outside the classroom.

As an International Baccalaureate school, our internationally-minded ethos means that we collaborate across divides and strive to provide a real-world education that prepares students to step out into an uncertain world with confidence, empathy, and at ease with those from all cultures. Our pioneering methods put the 'why' back at the heart of learning and our holistic approach places equal emphasis on academic achievement, intellectual agility and emotional wellbeing.

The results of this more organic, relaxed approach to learning, speak for themselves. The Abbey is consistently one of the top performing schools academically – not only in the UK, but globally. In 2019 half of our students studying the IB scored 40 points or more, out of a maximum 45 points. The average of 39 points (against a global average of 29 points), places The Abbey within the very top tier of IB schools in the world.

The Abbey's town centre location places us at the heart of a vibrant community, whilst our extensive coach network helps provide accessibility from locations across Oxfordshire and Berkshire for both Junior and Senior girls. A range of scholarships are available, as well as financial assistance offered through means-tested bursaries.

Above all, The Abbey is passionate about creating a learning experience that is joyful and meaningful. Our self-regulating culture helps us all to look after each other, and our inspiring teachers are dedicated to fostering a special relationship with each and every individual.

The Academy International School

(Founded 1985)

Headteacher
Clare Mooney

DP coordinator
Caroline Foster

Status Private

Boarding/day Day

Gender Coeducational

Language of instruction
English

Authorised IB programmes
DP

Age Range 2 – 19

Fees
Diploma Programme €10,630

Address
Camí de Son Ametler Vell, 250
07141 Marratxí, Balearic Islands
| **SPAIN**

Carrer d'Antoni Furió, 2
Ses Cases Noves, Pont d'Inca
07141 Marratxí, Balearic Islands
| **SPAIN**

TEL +34 971 605008
FAX +34 971 226158

Email
info@theacademyschool.com

Website
www.theacademyschool.com

The Academy International School, established in 1985, has long been recognised as a centre of excellent academic achievement, where the whole school community shares the joy of learning. We are also proud to be the first International British School to bring the International Baccalaureate Diploma Programme to Mallorca.

In a beautiful setting in the Mallorcan countryside students enquire, discover, analyse and evaluate. They are creative, innovative and proud to be part of this school community. The Academy teaching team accompanies the students on a wonderful learning journey from our Nursery classrooms all the way through to IBDP.

Academy students are encouraged, supported and challenged. They are offered a broad and balanced curriculum, delivered by motivated and creative teachers, to ensure that learning is effective and promotes a lifelong passion for education. The Academy International School prepares students to compete in a rapidly changing international marketplace where academic content is important, but is no longer enough.

In today's evolving global society, inquiry, critical thinking, and international mindedness are essential skill sets that students must have to determine their success as a leader and in the workforce. The Academy International School offers students multiple ways to develop and demonstrate what they know and understand. Students complete collaborative projects, oral presentations, essay writing, inquiry-based experiments, and take part in discussion and debate that mirror what they will experience in the challenging fields they hope to enter after university.

The Academy students see how our school connects with the world at large through community projects and activities locally, nationally and internationally.

Our goal is to help students achieve their dreams.

The Aga Khan Academy, Nairobi

(Founded 1970)

Head of Senior School Mr Christian Schmelz

Head of Junior School Mrs Rani Karim

Head of Nursery School Ms Waseema Khawaja

PYP coordinator Ms. Nadia Janmohamed

MYP coordinator Ms. Julliet Kithinji

DP coordinator Mr. William Wanyonyi

Status Private

Boarding/day Day

Gender Coeducational

Language of instruction English

Authorised IB programmes PYP, MYP, DP

Age Range 3 – 19

Address
1st Parklands Avenue,
off Limuru Road
PO Box 44424-00100
Nairobi | KENYA

TEL Junior: +254 0733 758 510,
Senior: +254 736 380 101
Nursery: +254 717 5744 89

Email infos@akesk.org
infoj@akesk.org
info.aknsn@akesk.org

Website www.agakhanschools.org/kenya/akan

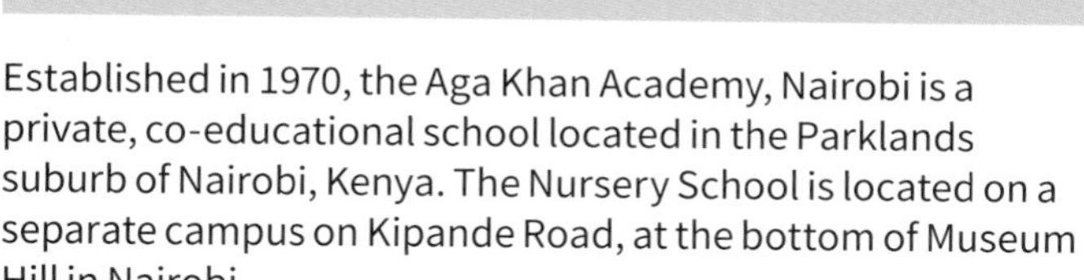

Established in 1970, the Aga Khan Academy, Nairobi is a private, co-educational school located in the Parklands suburb of Nairobi, Kenya. The Nursery School is located on a separate campus on Kipande Road, at the bottom of Museum Hill in Nairobi.

Together, our schools have an enrolment of over 1,000 students and are authorised to offer the International Baccalaureate Primary Years Programme, Middle Years Programme and Diploma Programme.

School Overview

The Aga Khan Academy is one of few schools in Kenya offering International Baccalaureate Programmes, and is one of the two schools in Kenya authorized to offer the IB continuum – the Primary Years Programme (PYP), the Middle Years Programme (MYP) and the Diploma Programme (DP).

The Aga Khan Academy, in keeping with the IB philosophy, 'touches hearts as well as minds'. Our students not only learn to be knowledgeable, open-minded thinkers, inquirers, principled, risk takers, well-balanced, and caring but also to be leaders and stewards.

Mission statement

Enable many generations of students to acquire both the knowledge and the essential spiritual wisdom needed to balance that knowledge and enable their lives to attain the highest fulfilment.

Exam Results

The Aga Khan Academy provides an outstanding academic education and enables students to fulfil their potential. Although the Nursery School does not have a grading system, it typically holds an annual graduation and exhibition celebrating the completion of the Early Years PYP. The Junior School has obtained above global average results in the International Student Assessment by ACER.

Relevant Curriculum

The IB curriculum enables students to learn using a transdisciplinary and an interdisciplinary approach and to develop critical thinking, creativity and international-mindedness – identified by leading educators globally as some of the necessary skills for the 21st Century learning.

Admission

Admission is based primarily on merit determined by a wide range of criteria, including academic strengths and overall potential.

Our curriculum combines academic excellence with athletics and visual performing arts programmes.

Examinations offered

MYP eAssessment, IB Diploma Programme (IB DP)

Facilities

ICT resource centres, film studio, music rooms, art rooms, science labs, well-resourced libraries, pools, wireless connectivity and data projectors in classrooms.

The American International School Vienna

(Founded 1959)

Director
Steve Razidlo

DP coordinator
Beth Dagitses

Status Private

Boarding/day Day

Gender Coeducational

Language of instruction
English

Authorised IB programmes
DP

Age Range 4 – 18

Number of pupils enrolled
800

Fees
Pre-Kindergarten €11,603
Kindergarten-Grade 5 €18,118
Grades 6-8 €20,104
Grades 9-10 €20,910
Grades 11-12 €21,220

Address
Salmannsdorfer Strasse 47
A-1190 Vienna | **AUSTRIA**

TEL +43 1 40132

Email
info@ais.at

Website
www.ais.at

Set within the rich cultural context of Austria, The American International School Vienna is one of the top international schools in the country. Founded in 1959 and currently celebrating our 60th Anniversary, AIS Vienna today serves around 800 students, representing more than 60 countries, from Pre-Kindergarten through Grade 12 (International Baccalaureate (IB) or American diploma). AIS' core values – nurture, include, challenge and respect – ensure that students develop intellectually and interculturally while internalizing the commitment and leadership necessary in today's globally-minded world.

AIS Vienna provides comprehensive opportunities for learners from around the world. Our students succeed academically, as well as in athletics, music, and visual arts. A variety of activities, including class trips to mountain ranges and service-oriented community projects, allow students to practice commitment, leadership, and meaningful self-reflection. We maintain a broad set of offerings to help us serve our students and be true to our mission.

The tightly knit school community allows students to develop personal relationships with both highly qualified teachers and their peers. We maintain a culture of high expectations and close connection to the pulse of international education. Investments in the quality and skill of our staff are on-going, and recent enhancements to our facilities and technology resources are assuring our role as a vital partner and a leader in our city and region.

AIS Vienna recently celebrated its 40th anniversary as an IB World School. The distinction coincided with the 50th anniversary of the IB. Since its inception at AIS, the program has shown impressive growth. In 1977, its first year of the IB program, AIS had 10 IB Diploma candidates. Currently, we have over 55 IB Diploma candidates. Perhaps most striking is the massive growth in the percentage of AIS seniors graduating with an IB Diploma: 18% in 1977 compared to a projected 80% in 2019-20.

We welcome all to our community of learners; we work every day to assure learners understand the connections between learning and living. We make decisions based on the understanding that we are not only guiding children towards learning but building experiences and memories that will serve to inform futures not yet imagined. Our goal is to help each of our students define success in a nurturing environment that supports excellence. Ultimately, we prepare our students for the next step in their lives after AIS Vienna.

(Founded 1969)

Principal Melanie Warnes MA

Co-Heads of Senior Section Sue Munday & James Willis

DP coordinator James Willis

Status Private

Boarding/day Day

Gender Coeducational

Language of instruction English, French (bilingual programme for ages 4-14 years)

Authorised IB programmes DP

Age Range 1 – 18

Number of pupils enrolled 1350

Fees Day: €28,400 – €36,325

Address
Pater Dupierreuxlaan 1
3080 Tervuren | **BELGIUM**

TEL +32 (0)2 766 04 30
FAX +32 (0)2 767 80 70

Email admissions@britishschool.be

Website www.britishschool.be

The school was founded in 1969 and officially opened in 1970. It has a beautiful site of ten hectares, surrounded by woodlands and lakes in Tervuren (20 minutes drive from central Brussels). The school is a coeducational non-selective day school for children aged 1-18, with over 1,350 on roll. There is an Early Childhood Centre for children aged 1-3. 30% of the students are British with approximately 70 other nationalities represented.

Students follow a British-based curriculum up to age 16 – (I)GCSE. This is adapted to our European context and international cohort and is followed by the choice of three internationally recognised pre-university examination courses from age 16-18: English GCE A Level, The International Baccalaureate (IB) Diploma Programme (French/Dutch options) and BTEC Business, Hospitality, Sport and Applied Science. French and Dutch are taught from an early age and there is a bilingual French/English programme for students aged 4-14 years. German or Spanish are additionally available from age 11. There is an Additional Educational Needs (AEN) department and extensive support provided with an English as an Additional Language (EAL) department. A specialist international careers team provides guidance and support to Post-16 students.

The school has excellent facilities including a state-of-the-art design & technology workshop, food technology rooms, networked IT suites, drama studios, nine science laboratories, four art studios and cafeteria. BSB is the only international school in Belgium to have its own 25m indoor swimming pool.

Arts, music and drama thrive and a wide range of performances are held regularly in the 240-seat theatre. The music department has a music technology suite, full-scale recording studio and a rehearsal studio.

Our academic results are amongst the highest of any international school in Europe and well above the worldwide average. In 2019 results at Post-16 for A Level, BTEC and the IB Diploma were fabulous, translating into brilliant university places worldwide on a wide variety of competitive and exciting courses.

At A Level, our results were excellent despite the move to the new, more challenging linear A Level system. BSB students achieved a splendid 99% pass rate, with an impressive 31% of grades at A*/A (26.2% national average 2018) and an excellent 62% at grade A*-B.

Our IB Diploma students again produced some outstanding results. All our IB students sat the IB Diploma and achieved a marvellous 35 point average (IB 2018* world average of 29.8 points). A remarkable 70% of our students obtained 34 points or higher compared to just 39% of students worldwide; 44% scored an impressive 37 points or higher which is double the worldwide figure.

This year our results in the BTEC courses continue to be outstanding, with over half of the grades achieved at Distinction* level and our students once more gaining a 100% pass rate through this course.

BSB does not select students by ability. For many, English is not the native language. This makes success even more tremendous. The programmes are led by a highly committed and well-qualified team of teachers and our academic, university and pastoral support is organised throughout the two years to help individual students to be the best they can be and aim high.

The British School of Milan (Sir James Henderson)

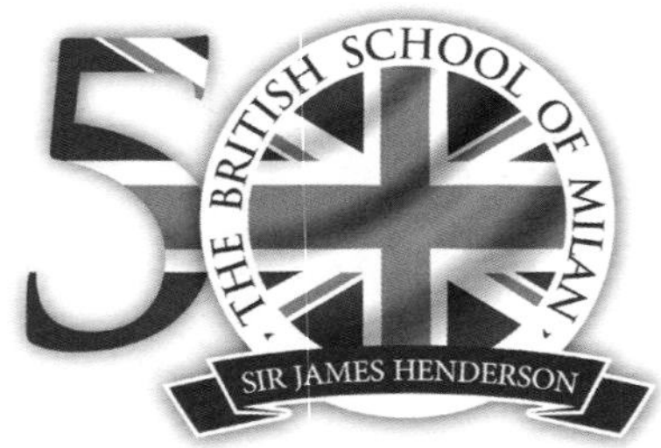

(Founded 1969)

Principal
Dr Chris Greenhalgh

DP coordinator
Mr Antony Pinchin

Status Private, Not-For-Profit

Boarding/day Day

Gender Coeducational

Language of instruction
English

Authorised IB programmes
DP

Age Range 3 – 18

Number of pupils enrolled
730

Fees
€12,420 – €19,580

Address
Via Carlo Alberto Pisani Dossi, 16
20134 Milan | ITALY

TEL +39 02 210941

Email
info@bsm.school

Website
www.britishschoolmilan.com

The British School of Milan (Sir James Henderson) has been educating students in Milan since 1969. This year marks not only its 50th anniversary but also the 10th anniversary of its IB Diploma programme. The school is not-for-profit and the only Milanese school inspected by the UK's Independent Schools Inspectorate (ISI). It achieved the highest rating of 'Excellent' on a full inspection.

The BSM provides a high quality balanced and academic British education to age 16 with IGCSE examinations in Year 11 and then the IB Diploma in the Sixth Form. With over 40 nationalities represented, the school offers a rich international and educational experience.

Academic results are excellent and students progress to top universities around the globe. In the last few years they have gained places in both arts and sciences at Oxford, LSE, Imperial, University College London, The University of Edinburgh, Trinity College Dublin, Università Bocconi, University of British Colombia, Sciences Po and many other leading universities.

There is a strong emphasis on the co-curricular with over 100 activities on offer. The school is particularly proud of its outstanding music, art and drama departments. In addition, the school acts as the Italian centre for the UK-based ABRSM, the exam board of the Royal Schools of Music. The school is very proud of its strong tradition of community service, with a scholarship and bursary fund recently inaugurated and its involvement in the International Duke of Edinburgh's Award Scheme.

The BSM is situated just outside the centre of Milan, close to the metro and on several bus routes. Linate airport and the popular Milano 2 residences are just minutes from the school.

Admission applications are accepted throughout the year.

The English School of Kyrenia

Head of School
Hector MacDonald

DP coordinator
Ms Zelis Omer

Status Private

Boarding/day Mixed

Gender Coeducational

Language of instruction
English

Authorised IB programmes
DP

Age Range 2 – 18

Number of pupils enrolled
990

Fees
Day: £4,700 – £7,560
Boarding: £17,000

Address
Bilim Sokak
Bellapais
Kyrenia, North Cyprus | **CYPRUS**

TEL +90 392 444 0375
FAX +90 392 815 7140

Email
info@englishschoolkyrenia.org

Website
www.englishschoolkyrenia.org

The English School of Kyrenia (ESK) is a purpose-built modern IB World School offering exciting opportunities for academic excellence and personal development for boys and girls aged 2 to 18. An enviable and spacious learning environment, the campus is set in the inspiring surroundings of the Kyrenia foothills, overlooking the Mediterranean to the front and the Kyrenia mountains to the rear.

The Little Learners building is a welcoming, calming and nurturing environment for our Pre-Nursery students. Designed with soft, earth inspired tones, students thrive in the fundamental stage of their development along with support from our professional and qualified teachers. Our Nursery – Year 2 students are located in the eco-friendly Early Years building. The unique building aims to generate its own electricity requirements and seeks to provide all ESK students with a living example of green sustainability.

For the current 2019-2020 academic year, ESK has 990 students drawn from both international and local backgrounds. In September 2015, ESK opened a modern boarding house on campus, and welcomed its first intake of boarders. Boarders reap the benefits of a world-class education with A-level and IB course offerings, and fees in the region of 50% less than a traditional Boarding School in the UK.

The sections of the school are Little Learners (Pre-Nursery), Early Years (Nursery – Year2), Primary (Year 1 – Year 6), and Secondary (Year 7 – Year 13).

All classes are taught in English, with an addition of Turkish as a second language, and an option of Mandarin, Russian, French, or Spanish. The Early Years follow the UK's EYFS (Updated) curriculum and the Primary School follows the Cambridge International Primary Programme (CIPP).

In the Secondary School the widely respected IGCSE, A-Level and International Baccalaureate (IB) Diploma Programme give students the opportunity to develop an international perspective and attend the world's top universities. Over 88% of graduates attend University in the UK, and 10% in the EU or North America. Graduates have attended prestigious universities such as The University of Cambridge, UCL, LSE, Parson's School of Design and Charles University, to name a few.

Today's students are tomorrow's leaders and decision makers: we afford every opportunity for our boys and girls to reach their personal and academic potential whilst nurturing their curiosity and encouraging individuality and creative thought.

IBDP Subjects available:

Group 1: English Language & Literature, Russian Language & Literature, Turkish Literature

Group 2: English B, Spanish *ab initio*

Group 3: Geography, History, Business and Management

Group 4: Biology, Chemistry, Physics

Group 5: Mathematics HL, Mathematics SL, Mathematics Studies

Group 6: Visual Arts, Music, Theatre Arts or one other subject taken from groups 3-4 above.

The Godolphin and Latymer School

(Founded 1905)

Head Mistress
Dr Frances Ramsey

DP coordinator
Audrey Dubois

Status Private, Independent

Boarding/day Day

Gender Female

Language of instruction
English

Authorised IB programmes
DP

Number of pupils enrolled
800

Fees
Day: £23,085

Address
Iffley Road
Hammersmith
London
W6 0PG | UK

TEL +44 (0)20 8741 1936
FAX +44 (0)20 8735 9520

Email
office@godolphinandlatymer.com

Website
www.godolphinandlatymer.com

The Godolphin and Latymer School is an independent day school for girls aged between 11 and 18; it is located in Hammersmith, West London, and is easily accessible by public transport from the surrounding areas. Means-tested bursaries are available at 11+ and 16+ entry covering up to 100% of fees. The school offers an exciting range of facilities including the Rudland Music School, with its own recording studio, and a drama and performance space in the recently opened Bishop Centre. A state of the art Sports and Fitness Centre opened in September 2015, providing a sports hall, climbing wall, dance studio and fitness suite. Tennis/netball courts and an Astroturf hockey pitch are also on-site.

We are a school with a strong pastoral ethos, where academic excellence is encouraged in a caring environment and where each individual girl is able to develop her interests and her talents in all areas. We aim to provide choice and challenge for each pupil with the IB Diploma Programme or traditional A levels being offered as part of the sixth form curriculum. The school has an excellent academic record and when girls leave us at 18, to take up their places at leading universities in this country and overseas, they are confident, articulate and independent.

Girls are proud of their school and value its unique character. They enjoy a wide range of extracurricular activities and appreciate the many opportunities to take responsibility within the school community and contribute to its future development. Girls have the chance to enjoy an exciting range of visits during their time at the school, recent examples being to Iceland, Italy, Washington and a ski trip to Vermont. Sixth form girls are able to participate in European work experience in Versailles or Berlin, giving them an opportunity to gain an insight into possible future careers as well as practising their language skills. The school aims to develop students who will become the leading citizens of the future; girls who are capable of thinking for themselves and who can demonstrate a critical awareness of the wider world, having a sense of their own worth whilst being appreciative of others.

The International School of Monaco

(Founded 1994)

Director
Stuart Burns MA (Cantab)

DP coordinator
Hannah Gettel

Status Private

Boarding/day Day

Gender Coeducational

Language of instruction
English, French

Authorised IB programmes
DP

Age Range 3 – 18

Number of pupils enrolled
670

Fees
Day €10,800 – €27,300

Address
10-12 Quai Antoine Premier
Monte Carlo
98000 | MONACO

TEL +377 9325 6820
FAX +377 9325 6830

Email
admissions@ismonaco.com

Website
ismonaco.org

Founded in 1994, the International School of Monaco is an independent, co-educational, not for profit day school, beautifully situated on the port Hercule in Monaco. ISM is presently the only fully accredited international private school in the Principality of Monaco and today is well established catering for 670 pupils aged from 3-18, drawn from over fifty countries.

The school's mission:

We will work with you and your child to do everything we can to ensure that she/he becomes an academically successful, internationally minded, caring person, and a motivated learner able to communicate effectively using two or more languages, and well prepared for the challenges of an ever-changing world.

The school's values emphasize integrity, caring, respect and learning, with clearly defined principles and expectations of its students.

ISM offers a distinctive bilingual education in English and French (Classes Kindergarten to 6) and from Year 7, the Secondary School offers a broad and balanced programme, taught in English, leading to Cambridge IGCSE and the IB Diploma qualifications. Languages are an important part of the programme with Spanish, Italian, Russian and German, in addition to French, on offer. Highly qualified teachers and support staff are recruited from around the world.

There is an extensive programme of enrichment including sports, Model United Nations, an annual Arts Festival , the Duke of Edinburgh International Award plus ABRSM and LAMDA music and drama qualifications. The school's unique location on the Cote d'Azur enables access to world class museums and places of interest. There are field trips to France, Italy, Spain, Germany and Iceland, and a service trip to Vietnam for first year IB students. Excursions to the Big Bang Science Fair in the UK and CERN in Geneva support the school's comprehensive science programme.

Outreach is an important element of school life: through giving projects, environmental associations and supporting charities from Monaco and France to Africa and Vietnam.

Pastoral care is a major priority for the school; an extensive PHSE programme is delivered by teachers who receive regular training in child protection and welfare, and a full time Head of Wellbeing is supported by a wellbeing team including a school counsellor. Regular workshops are offered to parents.

ISM students are well-rounded, academically successful young people who are admitted to top universities in Europe, the UK and North America. Our graduates are already pursuing exciting careers in many diverse fields.

The International School of The Hague

(Founded 1983)

Secondary Principal Richard Matthews

Primary Principal Juliette van Eerdewijk

MYP coordinator Maria Lamminaho

DP coordinator Camelia Constantinescu

CP coordinator Alma Trumic

Status State/Semi Private

Boarding/day Day

Gender Coeducational

Language of instruction English

Authorised IB programmes MYP, DP, CP

Age Range 4 – 18

Number of pupils enrolled 1500

Fees Day: €8,000 – €10,000

Address
Wijndaelerduin 1
The Hague
2554 BX | NETHERLANDS

TEL +31 70 328 1450
FAX +31 70 328 2049

Email admissions@ishthehague.nl

Website www.ishthehague.nl

We encourage students to pursue personal excellence by being curious, connected, and compassionate lifelong learners. Our vision is to shape a better future for all: inspiring students to become compassionate and proactive global citizens.

The International School of The Hague (ISH), with over 90 nationalities within the International City of Justice and Peace is well placed to provide a dynamic learning environment that is conducive to intercultural learning and global citizenship.

We offer a high quality international education, fostering academic success as well as encouraging sporting and creative abilities in a community based on honesty, fairness, open-mindedness and tolerance.

Our Primary School is the first in the world to have achieved accreditation at 'Mastering' Level from the International Primary Curriculum (IPC). Years 7-11 offer the International Baccalaureate Middle Years Programme (IB MYP), and Years 12-13 offer the International Baccalaureate Diploma Programme (IBDP) and Career-related Programme (IBCP).

As a part of a Dutch school foundation, ISH benefits from the rich learning opportunities our host country offers. Dutch is taught to all students in the MYP to assist them in integrating in the Netherlands.

The IBMYP provides the framework for the broad range of subjects that are offered in Years 7-11. Learning across the MYP eight subject groups is integrated through Approaches to Teaching and Learning, particularly focussing on concepts and inquiry, and through the global contexts. All students participate in our Service as Action Programme.

The IBDP aims to continue the education of critical and empathetic global citizens in six selected subjects and the mandatory components of Creativity, Activity and Service (CAS), Theory of Knowledge (TOK), and the Extended Essay, which prepares students for writing at university level.

The IBCP provides an opportunity for students who wish to focus their pre-university studies in Business. This rigorous and demanding programme provides an excellent route to university. Students study the BTEC Business course, plus a set of highly-relevant core IB activities that include Personal and Professional Skills, Service Learning, a Reflective Project and Language Development, as well as two IBDP diploma courses in subjects of their choosing.

Supporting our international community is key in all aspects of the school. Our EAL, Home Languages, Learning Support, and Wellbeing departments play important roles in meeting the individual needs of our students.

Director
Michelle Remington

Secondary Principal
David Tigchelaar

Elementary Principal
Jeff Woodcock

PYP coordinator
Jon Davidson

MYP coordinator
Peter Powell

DP coordinator
Susan Rhodes

Status Private

Boarding/day Day

Gender Coeducational

Language of instruction
English

Authorised IB programmes
PYP, MYP, DP

Address
Safaa Gardens School, Office 1132
4700 KAUST
Thuwal
23955-6900 | SAUDI ARABIA

TEL +966 12 808 6803

Email
schools@kaust.edu.sa

Website
tks.kaust.edu.sa

The KAUST School (TKS) proudly serves a thriving multi-cultural University community, with an enrollment of approximately 1,500 students from more than 60 nations. As an International Baccalaureate World School authorized in three programs: Primary Years, Middle Years and the Diploma Programme, we share a common philosophy and a commitment to high quality, challenging international education for children from K1 through to Grade 12. TKS is accredited by the Council of International Schools (CIS) and the New England Association of Schools and Colleges (NEASC).

Our Resources

The school is uniquely located within the university campus of King Abdullah University of Science and Technology (KAUST), a destination of choice for world-class scientific and technological graduate education and research, north of Jeddah on the shores of the Red Sea.

The School is purpose built with a design that supports a balanced curriculum. The Gardens Campus which houses the Elementary and Secondary School, has technology equipped classrooms, science laboratories, a design and technology hub, two library media centers, two indoor gymnasiums, two performance theatres, outdoor basketball and tennis courts, an outdoor swimming pool and soccer pitch. The Kindergarten Campus is filled with natural light, color and materials that stimulate learning. The buildings include activity rooms, two libraries and several specialized rooms for Art, Music, Arabic and Islamic studies.

The School offers a state-of-the-art technology environment that incorporates a broad spectrum of educational solutions while maintaining a 1:1 Apple computing environment.

Our People

Our students are the children of KAUST academic and professional staff, TKS staff, graduate students and University partners.

TKS Staff consists of over 330 teachers, specialist support staff and administrators from across the globe, with over 70% having advanced degrees and the majority with previous international school experience.

The school maintains classroom ratios of one teacher to 15 students in early childhood; to 18 students in Elementary; and to 22 students in Secondary.

Our IB Diploma Curriculum

TKS offers a co-educational IB academic program in English. Targeted support is provided for students with instructional needs, including intensive English language support, as required. Both Arabic and French are offered as a first language to native speakers and as a second language to non-native speakers in Secondary. In Kindergarten and Elementary only Arabic language is offered.

Co-curricular Activities

With the benefit of being located on a university campus and enclosed community, TKS utilizes all university and community facilities enriching the co-curricular programs.

The Sultan's School

(Founded 1977)

Principal
Dr Glenn Canterford

Head of Secondary
Paul Toomer

DP coordinator
Charles Hearsum

Status Private

Boarding/day Mixed

Gender Coeducational

Language of instruction
Arabic, English

Authorised IB programmes
DP

Age Range 4 – 18

Number of pupils enrolled
1119

Fees
OMR2,690 – OMR5,416

Address
PO Box 665
Seeb
121 | OMAN

TEL +968 24536 777
FAX +968 24536 997

Email
principal@sultansschool.org

Website
www.sultansschool.org

...opening minds for life!
The Sultan's School was established in 1977 under the guidance of His Majesty Sultan Qaboos Bin Said with the vision of providing a world class, holistic education that incorporated the best of Islamic and Omani culture and values within an international context. To enable this vision to become a reality His Majesty gave the school a campus that was, and continues to be, the envy of many educational establishments. Located in Seeb, a suburb of Muscat, the school sits on 500,000 square metres (approx 220 acres) and is blessed with excellent academic and sporting facilities, that continue to be improved as the school develops. Future initiatives will include, but are not restricted to, additional staff housing, new boarding facilities, a specialised IB centre, a new multimedia centre/library and an expansion of the sporting facilities.

Sultan's School students learn in both Arabic and English. The majority of them join the school at the age of four and then follow a rigorous bilingual programme based on an abridged English National Curriculum, as well as the Omani National Curriculum for Arabic, Islamic and Social Studies. This is continued in middle school which leads into Cambridge IGCSE courses in Years 10 and 11 and the International Baccalaureate (IB) Diploma in Years 12 and 13.

Within the IB programme, students are given extensive careers guidance to assist them in planning for their future. The school boasts a full time university counsellor who, in conjunction with the IBDP Coordinator, provides student support in the selection of IB subjects to match academic abilities and personal interests with potential and future aspirations. In addition to internal guidance, The Sultan's School often hosts prestigious international universities, who offer additional advice to the students through careers fairs, workshops and presentations. Our graduates attend many of the world's leading universities, studying subjects as diverse as medicine, geology, computer science, law, engineering and psychology. A large number of our graduates attend university on full scholarships that have been awarded by the Omani Ministry of Higher Education.

The Sultan's School also offers all of its students numerous opportunities to engage in community service and afterschool activities through the extensive ECA and CAS programmes. Each week, they can choose from a host of clubs and activities that range from drama to sailing, from eco club to working at the local children's hospital and from golf to working with disabled students. The school also has a well-deserved reputation for its sporting prowess and has won numerous local and international tournaments in a variety of sports, including swimming and football. A number of our students have gained further recognition by representing Oman in international competitions.

Our students are also given the chance to broaden their experiences and horizons by participating in numerous international trips. Most recently, the school has organised trips to the UAE, Spain, Italy, Switzerland and England to engage in activities that range from IB revision courses to

cultural trips. The school also organises three ski trips each year for primary and secondary students.

Although the majority of our students are Omani, the faculty represent a wide variety of cultural and academic backgrounds. Our teachers are drawn from all over the world including Morocco, Tunisia, Syria, the UK, Belgium, New Zealand, USA, and South Africa. A number of our staff hold advanced degrees and are IB workshop leaders.

The original intention of the school was to educate the future leaders of Oman. We can now proudly say with confidence, that we have been extremely successful in our aim. Today our alumni include many of the country's leading political and business figures, including the Minister of Education; and proudly, in a testament to the success of our school, many of them now choose The Sultan's School for their own children's education.

The Royal High School, Bath GDST

(Founded 1865)

Head
Mrs Kate Reynolds

DP coordinator
Ms Jude Taylor

Status Private

Boarding/day Mixed

Gender Female

Language of instruction
English

Authorised IB programmes
DP

Age Range 3 – 18

Number of pupils enrolled
640

Fees (per term)
Day: £3,432 – £4,865
Weekly Boarding: £7,961 – £9,674
Boarding: £8,906 – £10,762

Address
Lansdown Road
Bath
Bath & North-East Somerset
BA1 5SZ | UK

TEL +44 (0)1225 313877

Email
admissions@rhsb.gdst.net

Website
www.royalhighbath.gdst.net

Royal High School Bath (RHS) is a leading independent day and boarding school. Part of the GDST family, RHS provides outstanding, contemporary, education for girls aged 3-18.

Academic

Committed to high academic standards, RHS offers a choice of A level or IB with a wide range of subjects delivered by specialist teachers. Staff are highly qualified and engage and inspire their students - with 14 years' experience of the Diploma Programme, the school's results are excellent, and consistently above the global average. In 2018 RHS was awarded Best Small Cohort Independent IB School. Students go on to study at prestigious universities in the UK and oversees, including Oxford, Cambridge, Imperial and UCL.

Global perspective beyond the Classroom

Students value the international-mindedness of the IB and enjoy a school exchange to Sweden. This gives experience of other young people from very different backgrounds and nationalities. Students choose from a wide range of CAS options including an expedition to Cambodia where they teach in a partner school. Model United Nations enables students to refine skills including public speaking, critical thinking and leadership.

Orientation

The school's expertise means the induction of students is quick and effective. A residential orientation experience helps students gain an understanding of the programme ahead, and provides the space to plan their final years at school.

Boarding

Gloucester House is the Sixth Form boarding house and girls quickly settle into a caring and supportive community. House staff value students as individuals and the pastoral care and wellbeing of each girl is paramount.

Location

Situated in Bath, RHS has good transport links. Just 15 minutes from M4 motorway and with easy access to London, Bristol, Cardiff and Birmingham. Mainline rail links to London Paddington. Airports in Bristol, Southampton, Heathrow and Gatwick are easy to access and a shuttle to west London for weekly boarders can be arranged as required.

(Founded 2005)

Principal Chris Bromham

Head of Secondary Scott Moore

Head of Primary Pali Nahal

Head of Early Years Jodie Eardley

PYP coordinator Lee Higginbottom

MYP coordinator Hebatallah Gaber

DP coordinator Sheugnet Carter

CP coordinator Sarah Wakeling

Status Private

Boarding/day Day

Gender Coeducational

Language of instruction English

Authorised IB programmes PYP, MYP, DP, CP

Age Range 3 – 17

Number of pupils enrolled 1343

Fees
Pre-KG: AED40,500
KG 1 to 2: AED46,500 – AED48,500
Grade 1 to 5: AED57,500
Grade 6 to 10: AED67,500
Grade 11 & 12: AED72,500

Address
Corner of Algeria Road & Tripoli Street, Mirdif
PO Box 78181
Dubai | UNITED ARAB EMIRATES

TEL +971 (0)4 2515001

Email
admissions@uptownschool.ae

Website
www.uptownschool.ae

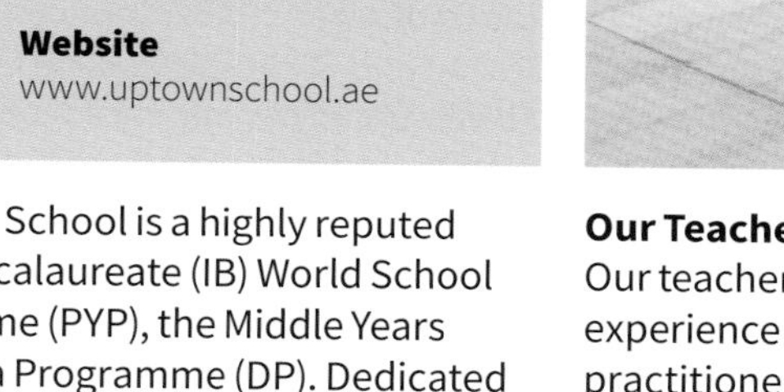

A member of Taaleem, Uptown School is a highly reputed and certified International Baccalaureate (IB) World School for the Primary Years Programme (PYP), the Middle Years Programme (MYP) and Diploma Programme (DP). Dedicated to nurturing the development in all aspects of education and personal growth. Our mission is to encourage curiosity and enthusiasm, creativity and independence, and compassion and communication through an exciting, rich and engaging learning experience.

Vision and Mission
A school for the whole of our international community, that delivers a World class education and achieves excellent student outcomes, by all measures, for all our students, in line with UAE National Agenda. Our Missions is to use education to make the world a better place to be, at the individual, community and global level.

KHDA Rating: "Very Good" with "Outstanding" features.

Our Facilities
Our facilities are spread over 14 acres of landscaped grounds and were designed to ensure that our students have the best environment to support their learning and development including a 25-metre swimming pool, a multi-purpose Sports Field, DT studios and more.

Our Teachers
Our teachers are highly qualified educators with vast experience in IB and education. All our teachers are trained IB practitioners, with many being IB workshop trainers and IB site visitors.

Student body: Co-educational, ages 3 to 17 years, over 85 different nationalities.

Extra-Curricular Activities
Our students have access to over 145 afterschool activities that fall under sports, arts, academic interests, and various enrichment programmes. Examples include: Model United Nations, TEDx Youth, Choir, Dance, Football, Gymnastics, Rugby, World Scholars Debate, Chess Club, French DELF, Emirates Literature Club, Uptown Record Label and more.

UTS also offers a broad range of educational visits and excursions, which are a vital part of supporting our students' unit of inquiries.

Uptown School (UTS) is part of Taaleem, the United Arab Emirates' second largest school provider for early years, primary and secondary schools founded in 2004.

(Founded 1982)

Head of College
William Turner

DP coordinator
Soraya Fathi

Status Private

Boarding/day Boarding

Gender Coeducational

Language of instruction
English

Authorised IB programmes
DP

Age Range 16 – 19

Number of pupils enrolled
187

Fees
Two-year Fee €46,000
(scholarships available)

Address
Frazione Duino, 29
34011 Duino TS | ITALY

TEL +39 040 3739111

Email
uwcad@uwcad.it

Website
www.uwcad.it

Introduction

UWC Adriatic is set in the picturesque village of Duino, near Trieste, in north-eastern Italy which was heavily influenced by political and ethnic divisions during World War I and the Second World War. By entering this arena of ethnic and historical complexity, UWC Adriatic has embraced an educational role of highly-charged political meaning and stepped into a world of extraordinary cultural diversity.

Inside the Classroom

Within the International Baccalaureate Diploma Programme curriculum, in addition to standard courses, the College offers Arabic, Slovene, Serbian, Croatian and Bosnian, World Arts and Cultures, Environmental Systems, and Art. Additionally, all students are expected to take Italian as a subject, although this does not have to be an IBDP exam subject.

Outside the Classroom

UWC Adriatic places a special emphasis on the "service" component of its Creativity, Activity, Services (CAS) program, with music playing a major role thanks to the presence of the ICMA – International Community Music Academy. Being physically integrated into the life of the local community, the College has long-standing collaborative relations with many associations that lead volunteering activities in a wide range of areas. Social services activities include work with Italian and Slovene speaking children through art, providing study support to immigrant primary school pupils, refugee work, offering companionship to the elderly and performing musical concerts in hospitals and retirement homes. Creative activities include chess, creative writing, current affairs study group, debate club, photography, robotics and theatre. UWC Adriatic also capitalizes its seaside village setting on Trieste's karst highlands and in the vicinity of the Alps to offer its students a range of related outdoor activities, such as sailing, kayaking, climbing, hiking and cross-country skiing.

Campus and Facilities

The college has student residences scattered all over the village of Duino. Rooms vary in size and may be single, double, triple or quadruple. Each residence is unique and this is reflected by the distribution of students/rooming and facilities. Every residence is manned by one or more residence tutors. A fully equipped music centre is available, as well as sports facilities shared with other local associations, which fosters socialising with the local youth and population.

Admissions

Students can apply through their UWC national committee or through the UWC Global Selection Programme.

(Founded 1962)

Head of College
Mr Peter T. Howe

DP coordinator
Gabor Vincze

Status Private

Boarding/day Boarding

Gender Coeducational

Language of instruction
English

Authorised IB programmes
DP

Age Range 16 – 19

Number of pupils enrolled
350

Fees
Two-year fee £66,000
(scholarships available)

Address
St Donat's Castle
St Donat's
Llantwit Major
Vale of Glamorgan
CF61 1WF | UK

TEL +44 (0)1446 799000

Email
principal@atlanticcollege.org

Website
www.atlanticcollege.org

Founded in 1962, UWC Atlantic is the flagship college of the inspirational UWC global education movement, comprising 18 schools and colleges worldwide. The UWC mission is to make education a force to unite people, nations and cultures for peace and a sustainable future. The College is the co-creator of the International Baccalaureate Diploma Programme, and is now re-engineering the IBDP through its Changemaker Curriculum, to meet 21st century challenges.

Our Founding Principles:

- To be innovators in education
- To provide opportunity to deserving students from around the world to access this education irrespective of their ability to pay
- For this education to take place in a unique and exceptional setting where the entire campus is the classroom

Based in 12th Century St Donat's Castle in Wales – a 122 acre site with its own seafront, woodland and farm – boarders aged 16 to 19 from over 90 nationalities are selected to study the IBDP every year based on personal motivation and potential. The deliberate diversity of the student body is achieved by attracting students from vastly differing political, religious, ethnic and socio-economic backgrounds. Selection is through 160 National Committees. Prospective students can apply to a National Committee in their country of residence or citizenship. 65% of students selected this way receive full or partial scholarship funding for their education. The alternative route is through the fee-paying UWC Global Selection Programme.

"I am proud to help develop changemakers who embody the UWC spirit. Students bring us their hopes, fears, sense of adventure, courage and idealism, their critical minds and their enthusiasm. The unique experience that is lived at a UWC hangs on our shared humanity, the trust that we have in each other, our willingness to celebrate each other's unique talents, and the support that we provide to each other every day as we extend the limits of our comfort zones. Such a community is something truly special and is what makes attending a UWC college so life affirming and life changing."

Peter T. Howe, Principal, UWC Atlantic

(Founded 2009)

Head of College
Lodewijk van Oord

MYP coordinator
Louis Odendaal

DP coordinator
Maurice Tonnaer & Jack Borthwick

Status State

Boarding/day Mixed

Gender Coeducational

Language of instruction
English

Authorised IB programmes
MYP, DP

Age Range 4 – 18

Number of pupils enrolled
900

Fees
Two-year fee: €68,000
(scholarships available)

Address
Discusworp 65
Maastricht
6225 XP | NETHERLANDS

TEL +31 432 410 410

Email
admissions@uwcmaastricht.nl

Website
www.uwcmaastricht.nl

Introduction

In addition to the highly recognized International Baccalaureate curriculum, UWC Maastricht is a multicultural school that hosts students from more than 100 different nationalities. The school operates within the Dutch public educational system and is subsidized by the Dutch government. It is formed to serve both the needs of the Maastricht international community and the students chosen by UWC national committees all over the world.

Inside the Classroom

At age 4, children can start their education at UWC Maastricht. The Primary Curriculum (until 11 year) is composed of a variety of subjects, at various levels of English language proficiency. After primary school UWC Maastricht offers the IB-Middle Years Programme (11-16 year-olds) in which students are encouraged to become critical and reflective thinkers. For 16-18 year-olds, UWCM applies the IB Diploma Programme Curriculum. Alongside the IB standard courses, the school offers Dutch, Spanish, German, Italian, Arabic, World Arts and Cultures, Global Politics, Visual Arts, Film and Music.

Outside the Classroom

UWC Maastricht has designed a social impact programme including action-oriented courses, social entrepreneurship and community service projects. The students develop the skills and attitudes needed to be active participants in society, to identify problems and injustices wherever they exist. They design a local Project Week providing service to the Maastricht community, they organise and lead conferences and they learn to engage critically with the world around them. Because the students come from all over the world and from many different backgrounds, there are always unique insights and always interesting discussions going on.

Campus and Facilities

UWCM campus is located in a very green and leafy part of Maastricht, close to the city centre. The site is surrounded by sports fields, a nature reserve and modern housing. Students live on residences across three buildings consisting of three floors, each comprised of six rooms. Every room hosts four students, of different nationalities, so it is a lively setting. Each floor has a common room, study room, laundry room and kitchenette and is supported by a Residence Mentor who lives in an apartment adjacent to the floors.

Admission

Day student applications for Primary and Secondary must meet the requirements of the Dutch Law on International Education. Residential IB Diploma Programme students are recruited through UWC's National Committee system (NC) or through the UWC Global Selection Programme.

(Founded 1995)

Acting Head of College
Jo Loiterton

DP coordinator
Natasha Lambert

Status Private

Boarding/day Boarding

Gender Coeducational

Language of instruction
English

Authorised IB programmes
DP

Age Range 16 – 19

Number of pupils enrolled
200

Fees
Two-year fee NOK600,000 (scholarships available)

Address
Hauglandsvegen 304
6968 Flekke, Sogn og Fjordane |
NORWAY

TEL +47 5773 7000

Email
info@uwcrcn.no

Website
uwcrcn.no

Introduction
UWC Red Cross Nordic College has three pillars: Nordic, Humanitarian and Environmental. All Nordic countries contribute to the funding of the College, enabling the College to undertake a selection entirely based on merit and potential, creating a learning environment where diversity is truly experienced as a value for all.

Inside the Classroom
UWC Red Cross Nordic offers the International Baccalaureate Diploma Programme (IBDP). Alongside standard courses, students can take Danish, Norwegian, Swedish, Global Politics and Theater Arts. Additionally, all students take a Red Cross Diploma, and first year students attend weekly sessions in the Life Skills program, exploring and developing their familiarity with topics relating to the Nordic, Humanitarian and Environmental pillars of the College. Distinctive of UWC Red Cross is the The Survivors of Conflict Program, which enables young people with disabilities coming from conflict zones to attend UWC RCN. The aim is that the participants will return to act as resourceful and active society members in their home countries. This is assisted by the Foundation Year Program, a necessary prerequisite for including students from a marginalised background and is offered to students who arrive with a disrupted educational background and limited competence in English. UWC RCN also runs a preparatory Summer Course in advance of the academic year to give new students with limited English exposure lessons in the language, provide them with a supportive network and introduce them to life at UWC.

Outside the Classroom
The college places a strong emphasis on community service with a wide range of cultural and outdoor activities (e.g. Ski Week, Cultural Days, crafts and other activities at Haugland Rehabilitation Centre). The College has its own centre for visitors, which receive camp school children in spring and autumn. This is a central part of the College Service program. The beautiful fjord landscape provides an excellent setting for activities in the water and on the mountains.

Campus and Facilities
The College has 5 student residences, each housing 40 students. The rooms are furnished in traditional Norwegian style and each has its own bathroom facilities. There is good access to the swimming pool at the Haugland Centre as well as a weight training room and a gym.

Admissions
Students can apply through their UWC national committee or through the UWC Global Selection Programme. There is a special selection process for the Survivors of Conflict Program.

VIII Prywatne Akademickie Liceum Ogólnokształcące

(Founded 1993)

Founder, Director & Principal
Prof. Jerzy Waligóra

DP coordinator
Ewa Dudek

Status Private

Boarding/day Day

Gender Coeducational

Language of instruction
English

Authorised IB programmes
DP

Age Range 6 – 18

Number of pupils enrolled
830

Fees
Day: €2,700 – €5,500

Address
ul Karmelicka 45
31-128 Krakow | **POLAND**

TEL +48 12 632 93 13

Email
dyrektor@pack.edu.pl

Website
www.pack.edu.pl

PACK belongs to the group of most rapidly developing non-public schools in Krakow imparting holistic education to the students for over a period of 25 years.

The first school to open within the branches of Prywatne Akademickie Centrum Ksztalcenia (PACK) was VIII Prywatne Akademickie Liceum Ogólnokształcące, instituted in the year 1993. Afterwards, all the sister schools such as Friderick Chopin Private Academic Middle School (1999), Academos Private Primary School (2008), International Baccalaureate World School 006265 (2012), World Around Intercultural Middle School (2015), and World Around Intercultural Primary School (2015) began operating.

The vision of the Founder Director Principal Professor Jerzy Waligóra, is to ensure thorough intellectual and emotional growth. PACK aims toward academic excellence in order to educate and enable the youth leaders to be men and women of character who pursue their individual passions with the help of internationally recognized and innovative academic, and co-curricular programme. Thereby, becoming valued representatives of their local, national, and international communities.

For several years the school has taken the leading place in the All-Polish Secondary Schools League Tables compiled and published by "Perspektywy", "Rzeczpospolita" and "Gazeta Wyborcza". It has been ranked among the first five schools between the years 2015 to current year 2019 in the Malopolska region.

The academic programme benefits because of the teaching staff of the school, who are also academicians at Krakow universities, thus guaranteeing high standards of scholastic support.

The school offers the National Polish Curriculum for students of the primary and senior section. The International Baccalaureate Diploma Programme welcomes students from diverse nationalities.

Learning from life is an integral part of the curriculum. The school provides international, educational and cultural opportunities through community service projects, exchange programmes and international engagements. Each year students participate in the Exchange Programme with India, Nepal, the USA, Norway and Germany. They also collobrate and participate in International Summits, International Model United Nations Symposium and International Competetive Events. The School has also been accredited as UNESCO Associated School. The students participate in various global projects promoting peace and international understanding.

PACK's model of educational excellence and co-scholastic engagement enables and encourages its students to learn and discover and be mindful citizens of this millenium.

(Founded 2008)

Head of School
Marcella Margaria Bodo

DP coordinator
Deborah Gutowitz

Status Private

Boarding/day Day

Gender Coeducational

Language of instruction
English

Authorised IB programmes
DP

Age Range 5 – 19

Fees
Nursery School €5,100
Cambridge Primary €6,400
Cambridge Lower Secondary €7,500
Cambridge IGCSE €7,500
IBDP €11,000

Address
Via delle Rosine 14
10123 Turin | ITALY

TEL +39 011 889870

Email
infovis@vittoriaweb.it

Website
www.vittoriaweb.it

Founded in 1975 as one of the first linguistic high schools in Italy, the Vittoria International School Torino offers bilingual education for children and young adults starting from elementary school and continuing through to the IB diploma. Located in the heart of Turin's city center, the school ensures a modern and innovative learning environment for students of all ages and nationalities.

Since the very beginning, we have leveraged the best of tradition and innovation both in the choice of educational pathways and teaching methods. Fully certified by the Italian Ministry of Education, the school offers bilingual primary and secondary programs in addition to traditional Italian and international, English-language high school programs.

We have been an authorized IB World School since 2008. We offer the IBDP grades 11 and 12. The Italian Government recognizes our DP as equivalent to the Italian Maturità Linguistico or Scientifico, depending on the track chosen by each candidate.

We have been a Cambridge Upper Secondary School IGCSE (grades 9 and 10) since 2010. We have welcomed students at all phases of their education beginning in the Primary years and Lower Secondary since September 2018.

Our curriculum is constantly growing and adapting to the individual needs of our students. The final scores and completion rates of our students are consistently above the international average. We provide professional, personalized career and university guidance, and many of our students go on to study at world-class universities around the globe. Our students are supported in their pursuit of excellence in extracurricular activities, and many have been rewarded nationally and internationally in sports and the arts.

A low student-teacher classroom ratio allows for individual attention as part of a socially and academically rich formative experience. Our door is always open to parents and students who have ideas to propose or concerns to express, and we use a centralized, password-protected system to keep parents and students updated on all school activities.

Our teachers are all university graduates; IB and Cambridge trained. They are passionate about their subjects and dedicated to their students.

A vibrant discussion of global issues begins in our classrooms and extends into CAS projects. Students experience world issues as they play out in our local community and abroad. We have an ongoing relationship important international organizations located in Turin.

(Founded 1707)

Headmaster
Mr Mark Mortimer MBA BA

DP coordinator
Dr Mark Martin BSc, PGCE, PhD

CP coordinator
Dr Mark Martin

Status Private

Boarding/day Mixed

Gender Coeducational

Language of instruction
English

Authorised IB programmes
DP, CP

Age Range 3 – 18

Number of pupils enrolled
530

Fees
Day: £5,110 per term
Boarding: £10,880 per term

Address
Church Street
Warminster
Wiltshire
BA12 8PJ | UK

TEL +44 (0)1985 210100
FAX +44 (0)1985 210154

Email
admissions@warminsterschool.org.uk

Website
www.warminsterschool.org.uk

Warminster is a coeducational school of 550 students aged 3 to 18, located in the South-west of England. Founded in 1707, the school is a member of HMC and has been an authorized IB World School since December 2005.

Warminster School prides itself on its ability to combine a strong academic record and excellent facilities with a warm, friendly family ethos. A comprehensive pastoral care programme, centred around the role of the tutor, provides appropriate levels of support at all times.

Warminster School's students have consistently achieved excellent results, averaging 34 points in 2016, an average of 31 and a 100% pass rate in 2017, and an average of 30 in 2018. 95% of our students go on to study at leading universities around the world, including Oxford and Cambridge, where the IB Diploma is particularly well received. Several individual candidates have secured exceptional IB results; the highest candidate points scored to date is an outstanding 44 points out of 45.

Warminster School welcomes students from over twenty-eight different countries into a community that celebrates its own diversity and encourages service to local, national and global societies. With a talented and enthusiastic staff and a diverse range of subjects and activities on offer, pupils are able to develop their potential to the full. The wide range of co-curricular activities include music, drama, a comprehensive range of sports and opportunities to go on challenging international visits.

Experienced resident house staff provide a supportive environment for boarding students in comfortable, well equipped boarding houses. Recreational activities and trips are arranged each weekend. For medical care there is a school nursing sister on duty every day.

Subjects offered vary according to student demand but typically include: English A and B, German A, 'self-taught languages', French B, Spanish B, Spanish *Ab Initio*, History, Geography, Economics, Biology, Physics, Chemistry, Maths, Maths Studies and Art. In addition to offering the Diploma Programme, from September 2017 Warminster School has offered the IB Career-Related Programme, combining Diploma Programme subjects with vocational qualifications (OCR Cambridge Technicals at level 3) in Business, Art and Design and Sport.

(Founded 1963)

Head of College
Stephen Lowry

DP coordinator
Elizabeth Cummergen

Status Private

Boarding/day Mixed

Gender Coeducational

Language of instruction
English

Authorised IB programmes
DP

Age Range 11 – 20

Number of pupils enrolled
600

Fees
Two-year fee €38,000
(scholarships available)

Address
Waterford Park
Mbabane H100 | SWAZILAND

TEL +268 24220867

Email
principal@waterford.sz

Website
www.waterford.sz

Introduction

Waterford Kamhlaba UWC of Southern Africa was founded in 1963 as a response to the separate and unequal educational systems in South Africa. When His Majesty King Sobhuza II visited the school, he gave it the name "Kamhlaba", which meant both "of the world" and also that we are "of the earth" and without distinctions such as race. Differently to all the other schools, the academic year at runs from January to November.

Inside the Classroom

Waterford offers the Waterford curriculum in the junior school, the University of Cambridge International General Certificate of Secondary Education (IGCSE) program in the middle school and the International Baccalaureate Diploma Programme in the senior school. For the IBDP, alongside standard courses SiSwati, French, Spanish, Anthropology, Psychology, Business Management, Music, Theatre are offered.

Outside the Classroom

As the only UWC school in Africa, Waterford is an ambassador of UWC's mission on the continent and having educated a large group of African changemakers since its inception. With the School having been the first multiracial school in Southern Africa; founded as a direct response to its system of apartheid, its history of embracing and celebrating diversity from across Africa and beyond is something deeply ingrained into Waterford Kamhlaba's nature and continues to be at the core of its values today. The School, through community service, has strong relations with local organizations such as the refugee camp and neighborhood care points (children welfare centres). A commitment to community service has been recognized as an essential part of the school's policy, organisation and life. A regular commitment to a service project is required of IBDP and Form 5 students, and projects usually vary from involvement at the local hospital to work for the disabled. UWC WK offers a wide variety of sporting- and recreational activities run by both staff and students (e.g. kayaking, art clubs, etc.).

Campus and Facilities

Ekukhuleni residence accommodates up to 80 Form 1, 2 and 3 students. Esiveni accommodates up to 110 Form 4 and 5 students. Emhlabeni and Elangeni accommodate, respectively, up to 130 and 68 IBDP students, in either single rooms or shared rooms; consisting of separate wings for males and females. Each day there is one male and one female residence tutor on duty in each residence.

Admissions

Students can apply through their UWC national committee or through the UWC Global Selection Programme.

Wellington College

WELLINGTON COLLEGE

(Founded 1853)

Master
Mr James Dahl

Director of IB
Mr Richard Atherton

DP coordinator
Richard Atherton

Status Private

Boarding/day Mixed

Gender Coeducational

Language of instruction
English

Authorised IB programmes
DP

Age Range 13 – 18

Number of pupils enrolled
1060

Fees
Day: £30,375 – £34,890
Boarding: £41,580

Address
Duke's Ride
Crowthorne
Berkshire
RG45 7PU | UK

TEL +44 (0)1344 444000

Email
admissions@wellingtoncollege.org.uk

Website
www.wellingtoncollege.org.uk

Wellington College is a vibrant, inspiring and challenging all-round coeducational boarding and day school set in 400 acres of parkland, 40 minutes from Heathrow. At present there are 635 boys and 425 girls, of whom 210 are day pupils.

The College seeks to provide a transformative experience by focusing on its key values of Kindness, Courage, Respect, Integrity and Responsibility, values which allow the pupils to develop a unique identity inspired by intellectual curiosity, true independence, a generous and far-reaching inclusivity and a determination to be properly and unselfishly individual. Its international reputation in sports, arts, service, wellbeing and leadership, and its genuine commitment to an education that extends far beyond the classroom ensures that students leave school equipped for the challenges and opportunities of tomorrow's world.

Currently 190 pupils take the IB Diploma in the Sixth Form. 65% are from England and the rest are from 50 different countries, which sets us apart from competitors who tend to have smaller programmes attracting only international pupils. In 2019 we had 95 Diploma students who obtained an average of 40.2 points, with 62% scoring 40 or more and nine students achieving the perfect score of 45. 15 of the 95 went on to Oxbridge or Ivy League. Indeed, over 100 Wellingtonians have been offered places at Oxford or Cambridge over the past four years and on average 25 pupils move on to US universities each year, many to Ivy League institutions. The high academic expectations we have for our pupils are expressed through encouragement and support – nearly 40% of teachers have Masters or Doctorates and all are specialists.

Wellington College introduced the International Baccalaureate Diploma Programme in 2007. Its philosophy – of combining academic rigour with breadth and depth – is very much in sympathy with our own. We offer a wide range of subjects, at all levels, and we believe our support for the IB Core – the extended essay, theory of knowledge, and creativity, activity, service – is truly world class, combining as it does academic expertise with outstanding opportunities and resources. This is a school that actively promotes excellence without compromising the ideals embedded within the IB's learner profile.

Subjects offered in the IB Diploma Programme are all at both HL and SL unless stated:

Group 1: English literature, German literature, German language and literature, English literature and performance SL.

Group 2 Modern B (HL, SL and ab initio): German, Spanish, French, Mandarin.

Group 2 Modern B (HL and SL): Italian, Russian.

Group 2 Classical: Greek, Latin.

Group 3: business and management, economics, history, philosophy, psychology, geography, global politics, environmental systems and societies SL, art history SL.

Group 4: biology, chemistry, computer science, design technology, physics, sports, exercise and health science, environmental systems and societies SL, astronomy SL.

Group 5: analysis and approaches, applications and interpretation.

Group 6: music, visual arts, theatre arts.

(Founded 2007)

Head of School
Kathleen Battah

PYP coordinator
Ola Itani Zein

MYP coordinator
Tala Al Massarweh

DP coordinator
Kathleen Saleh

Status Private

Boarding/day Day

Gender Coeducational

Language of instruction
English

Authorised IB programmes
PYP, MYP, DP

Age Range 3 – 19

Number of pupils enrolled
923

Address
Al Mathaf, Main Street
Near National Museum, PO Box 116-2134
Beirut | **LEBANON**

City Centre Campus (CCC)
Lamma Street, Ain El Roumaneh Area, PO Box 116-2134, Beirut | **LEBANON**

TEL +961 1 423 444
FAX +961 1 423 444 Ext: 106

Email info@wellspring.edu.lb

Website www.wellspring.edu.lb

Wellspring Learning Community is the first IB Continuum World School in Lebanon and it is the realization of a belief that children of Lebanon deserve to study in a high quality learning environment that opens up space for developing their talents and intellectual potential, as well as their capacity for caring about the world around them. Wellspring is a non-sectarian community with no political affiliations. Depending on availability, enrolment is open throughout the year. We welcome inquiries and visits from interested families.

Authorization/Accreditations
Wellspring is authorized for the IB Diploma, Middle Years Programme, and Primary Years Programme, Council of International Schools (CIS), New England Association of Schools and Colleges (NEASC).

Vision and Mission
Wellspring is an inquiry-based learning environment where students are given every opportunity to realize their social, emotional and academic capacities. Teachers, students and parents work collaboratively in an atmosphere of mutual respect and trust by sharing a positive learning environment that builds on an ongoing process of self-assessment, evidence-based decision making, and continual improvement. Our students will become confident, resourceful, creative, caring, responsible and thinking citizens, prepared to use their education to contribute in meaningful ways to improve society; locally and internationally.

Teachers
Our 195 faculty members are highly qualified and experienced teachers; many are native English speakers. In addition to being IB trained, some teachers hold additional positions within the IBO such as workshop leader and workshop evaluator and examiner.

Students
Wellspring has a large international population, with 59 countries represented across our two campuses, in addition to our local students who come from diverse backgrounds within Lebanon.

Facilities
We are proud to offer two campuses in the vibrant heart of Beirut. Both environments are attractive, technologically advanced, and continuously upgraded to keep pace with the demands of the educational program. Facilities include music and art rooms, science labs, computer labs, cafeteria (CCC), libraries, play areas and sports spaces.

(Founded 1863)

Head of School
Ian Lavender

DP coordinator
Lynn Moses

CP coordinator
Lynn Moses

Status Private

Boarding/day Mixed

Gender Coeducational

Language of instruction
English

Authorised IB programmes
DP, CP

Age Range 3 – 18

Number of pupils enrolled
350

Fees
Day: £18,300
Weekly Boarding: £31,050
Boarding: £32,280

Address
Patterdale Road
Windermere
Cumbria
LA23 1NW | UK

TEL 015394 46164

FAX 015394 88414

Email
admissions@windermereschool.co.uk

Website
www.windermereschool.co.uk

Windermere School is stunningly situated in a UNESCO World Heritage Site: England's Lake District National Park. The rugged beauty of the landscape not only makes for an inspiring educational setting but enables students to make use of what surrounds them.

Windermere School is not academically selective and we aim to help each student find the pathway most suitable for their ambitions. We believe that it is essential that students have access to high quality careers advice and are given the opportunity to explore an extensive range of career options. We are committed to finding what is right for each student, whether it be the DP or Career-related programme.

Over the past few years, leavers have gone onto a variety of universities, including Oxford, Cambridge, Imperial College and Durham.

We are a Round Square School and this blends perfectly with the IB philosophy and the two intersect with Service at their cores and we support many Service initiatives. Each year a group of students travel to South Africa to support the Thussanang Service project. We also support worldwide humanitarian appeals and, locally, provide support in residential care homes and with conservation projects.

There is a vast array of academic and extra-curricular opportunities available to students: School musical, sports and adventurous expeditions. The School boasts its very own RYA accredited watersports centre and in 2018 it was the first school in the UK to become a British Youth Sailing Recognised Centre for its race training.

The Sixth Form boarding house is designed to promote the successful transition between School and Higher Education. It is laid out in apartments with twin and single bedrooms, a bathroom, common room and kitchen. There is also a large communal space for socialising and numerous socials events are held throughout the year.

XXI Century Integration International Secondary School

(Founded 1996)

Head of School
Svetlana Kulichenko

PYP coordinator
Kristina Moavad

MYP coordinator
Leonid Tevlin

DP coordinator
Nigiar Mekhtieva

Status Private

Boarding/day Day

Gender Coeducational

Language of instruction
English

Authorised IB programmes
PYP, MYP, DP

Age Range 5 – 18

Number of pupils enrolled
180

Fees
€11,000 – €24,000

Address
16 Marshala Katukova St.
Building 3
Moscow
123592 | RUSSIAN FEDERATION

TEL +7 495 750 3102

FAX +7 495 750 0197

Email
school@integration21.ru

Website
www.integration21.ru

The XXI Century Integration School is an independent day school for girls and boys from Kindergarten to Grade 11. The school has a proud tradition of excellence in education, sports and cultural pursuits.

XXI Century Integration is comprised of a kindergarten for five and six-year olds, based on ideas such as respect, trust, compassion, rights and responsibilities; a primary school with an emphasis on numeracy and literacy and a senior school, where students choose from the National Programme, or the IB Diploma Programme. The school campus is located to the North-West of Moscow in Strogino, one of the green districts of the capital. The facilities are modern, well-equipped and easily accessible by public transport. XXI Century Integration is an internationally minded school that encourages cultural exchange and welcomes students from all over the world.

XXI Century Integration has an inclusive school policy and all students are welcome. We offer the IB Primary Years Programme, the IB Middle Years Programme and the IB Diploma Programme and/or the National Programme.

The IB Diploma Programme subjects on offer are Russian, Croatian, English, French, Italian, German, Chinese, Spanish, Business management, History, Environmental Systems and Societies, Biology, Chemistry, Physics, Computer Science, Mathematics, Visual Arts and Music.

XXI Century Integration's academic results are outstanding: 51% of the 2015-2018 IB Diploma students achieved a score of 38-42. The school balances excellent academic results with a range of exciting co-curricular activities including sports, arts, music, drama and community service.

The most important attributes of school life are the school's five core values of relationships, courage, creative reflection, intellectual enquiry and engagement in life. It's values are aligned with the IB philosophy of developing inquiring, knowledgeable and caring people who create a better world through intercultural understanding. Students learn in an environment that nurtures important life skills, thus ensuring that students leave XXI Century Integration as well-rounded, self-reliant and confident individuals.

We participate in the IB Schools to Schools Projects in Russia and abroad. In August XXI Century Integration runs a summer school in a beautiful area of Croatia where students take part in fun activities that prepare them for future studies within all the IB Programmes.

XXI Century Integration also holds a signed agreement with the City University of Hong Kong (City U) to provide scholarship opportunities for highly talented students at our school, thereby allowing our students to pursue full-time undergraduate education at City U.

Yago School

yago school

(Founded 2010)

Chairman & Headmaster
Ramón Resa

DP coordinator
Blanca Domínguez

Status Private

Boarding/day Day

Gender Coeducational

Language of instruction
English, Spanish

Authorised IB programmes
DP

Age Range 0 – 18

Number of pupils enrolled
750

Address
Avda. Antonio Mairena, 54
41950 Castilleja de la Cuesta,
Seville, Andalusia | **SPAIN**

TEL +34 955 51 1234

Email
admissions@yagoschool.com

Website
www.yagoschool.com

At Yago School, we are completely transforming the educational-learning system in the South of Spain so that our students from 0 to 18 years can successfully confront many of the educational challenges of the 21st century, by offering the Diploma Programme of International Baccalaureate, together with the Spanish educational system and by using the English and Spanish languages as a communicative instrument inside and outside the classroom, with Chinese and French as part of its dynamic curriculum. Our unique curriculum is also accredited by WASC (Western Association of Schools and Colleges).

Over a decade in the educational field, we have grown to represent more than 20 nationalities. The Yago team strives to inspire, nurture and empower every student to achieve their personal best and become enquiring, knowledgeable, lifelong learners who create a better world through intercultural understanding and respect.

Our purpose is for students to develop their abilities and potential to the maximum, to build knowledge through projects, broaden their interests and their own experience using integrative, innovative and cooperative methodologies in traditional and technological environments so that they can adapt to universities and successfully integrate into companies all over the world.

Yago School's principles have been built on five educational pillars: traditional values, bilingualism, sports, music and new technologies. Five bases that, combined with demanding academic training, provide our students with an extremely solid foundation promoting success in both their personal and professional lives. The use of technology is embedded in the curriculum for all students from the age of four. Music is performed at a wide range of events and students are prepared for examinations in theory, piano and singing with the Associated Board of the Royal Schools of Music. The outstanding sporting facilities, including sports pitches and a sports hall, provide many opportunities for students to compete in team and individual events.

The avant-garde architecture of its facilities, along with its privileged location in the "Aljarafe", just 15 minutes from the international airport and the high-speed AVE train station, all enhance the multitude of diverse and personalised opportunities and complementary experiences Yago School offers.

Admission: Admissions are open throughout the academic year, subject to availability. Every effort is made to reserve a space for international applicants. We currently arrange homestays for international students and, beginning in September 2021, we will offer a student residence for boarding which is under construction.

Directory of schools in the Africa, Europe and Middle East region

Key to symbols

- CP
- Diploma
- MYP
- PYP
- Fee Paying School
- Boys' School
- Girls' School
- Coeducational School
- Boarding School
- Day School

ALBANIA

Albanian College Tirana
Rruga Dritan Hoxha 1, Tirana 1000
DP Coordinator Jill Vincent
MYP Coordinator Rachel Damon
PYP Coordinator Victoria Swank
Languages English
T: +355 44 513 471
W: www.actirana.edu.al

World Academy of Tirana
Rruga e Rezervave, Lunder, Tirane
DP Coordinator Peter Thompson
MYP Coordinator Ervin Dauti
PYP Coordinator Shikha Ahuja
Languages English
T: +355 69 6056 123
W: www.wat.al

ANGOLA

Luanda International School
Via S6, Bairro de Talatona, Município de Belas, Luanda
DP Coordinator Rene Bradford
MYP Coordinator Dave Chilton
PYP Coordinator Alison Francis
Languages English
T: +244 222 460752
W: www.lisluanda.com

ARMENIA

Quantum College
Bagratuniats 23/2, Shengavit, Yerevan 0046
DP Coordinator Robert Vardanyan
Languages English
T: +37410 422217
W: www.quantum.am

Shirakatsy Lyceum International Scientific-Educational Complex
35 Artem Mikoyan, 15 Mushegh Galshoyan, Yerevan 0079
DP Coordinator Anna Stepanyan
MYP Coordinator Mane Gevorgyan
PYP Coordinator Marina Sahakyan
Languages English, Armenian
T: +374 10 680 102
W: www.shirakatsy.am

UWC Dilijan
7 Getapnya Street, Dilijan 3903
DP Coordinator Marta Inga Bobiatynska
Languages English
T: +44 (0)1446 799000
W: www.uwcdilijan.org

AUSTRIA

AMADEUS INTERNATIONAL SCHOOL VIENNA
Bastiengasse 36-38, 1180 Vienna
DP Coordinator Melanie Pages
MYP Coordinator Amanda Cornish
PYP Coordinator Kevin Osborne
Languages English
T: +43 1 470 30 37 00
E: admissions@amadeus-vienna.com
W: www.amadeus-vienna.com

See full details on page 70

BG/BRG Klosterneuburg
Buchberggasse 31, Klosterneuburg 3400
DP Coordinator Siegfrid Opelka
Languages English
T: +43 2243 32155
W: www.bgklosterneuburg.ac.at

Campus Wien West
Seuttergasse 29, Wien 1130
DP Coordinator Jutta Zopf-Klasek
Languages English
T: +43 680 5577 573
W: www.campus-wien-west.at

Danube International School Vienna
Josef-Gall Gasse 2, 1020 Vienna
DP Coordinator Chloe Pollack
MYP Coordinator Maura Lichtscheidl-Fegerl
PYP Coordinator Bridie Anderson
Languages English
T: +43 1 7203110
W: www.danubeschool.com

GIBS Graz International Bilingual School
Georgigasse 85, 8020 Graz
DP Coordinator Ursula Schatz
Languages English
T: +43 316 771050
W: www.gibs.at

International Christian School of Vienna
Panethgasse 6a, (right by Wagramer Strasse), Vienna A-1220
DP Coordinator Adesola Adebesin
Languages English
T: +43 1 25122 0
W: www.icsv.at

International Highschool Herzogberg
Herzogbergstraße 230, Perchtoldsdorf 2380
DP Coordinator Veronika Weiss
Languages English, German
T: +43 6991 7750 055
W: www.am-herzogberg.com

International School Carinthia
Rosentaler Straße 15, 9220 Velden Am Worthersee
PYP Coordinator Scott French
Languages English, German
T: +43 4274 52471 10
W: www.isc.ac.at

International School Innsbruck
Angerzellgasse 14, Innsbruck A-6020
DP Coordinator Rosmarie Knoflach
Languages English
T: +43 512 58 70 64
W: agi.tsn.at

International School Kufstein Tirol
Andreas-Hofer-Straße 7, Kufstein 6330
DP Coordinator Louise Canham
Languages English
T: +43 5372 21990
W: www.isk-tirol.at

Linz International School Auhof (LISA)
Aubrunnerweg 4, 4040 Linz
DP Coordinator Oliver Kim
Languages English
T: +43 732 245867- 23
W: www.europagym.at/lisa

Lower Austrian International School
Bimbo Binder-Promenade 7, St. Pölten 3100
DP Coordinator Michael Hofbauer
Languages English
T: +43 2742 73453
W: www.borglsp-stpoelten.ac.at

St. Gilgen International School
Ischlerstrasse 13, 5340 St. Gilgen
DP Coordinator John Patton
Languages English
T: +43 62 272 0259
W: www.stgis.at

THE AMERICAN INTERNATIONAL SCHOOL VIENNA
Salmannsdorfer Strasse 47, A-1190 Vienna
DP Coordinator Beth Dagitses
Languages English
T: +43 1 40132
E: info@ais.at
W: www.ais.at

See full details on page 218

Vienna International School
Strasse der Menschenrechte 1, 1220 Vienna
DP Coordinator William Johnson
MYP Coordinator Joseph O'Rourke
PYP Coordinator Lea Pedlow
Languages English
T: +43 1 203 5595
W: www.vis.ac.at

AZERBAIJAN

Dunya School
9 Ajami Nakhchivani street, Baku AZ1130
DP Coordinator Rana Hasanova
PYP Coordinator Leila Mammadova
Languages English
T: +994 12 563 59 40/47/48
W: dunyaschool.az

Educational Complex No. 132-134
Istiglaliyyat 33A, Baku, Absheron AZ1001
DP Coordinator Francis Wilfrid Mang-Benza dit Manthota
Languages Azerbaijani
T: +994 (0)12 492 27 32
W: www.132-134.com

European Azerbaijan School
7 Basti Bagirova, Yasamal District, Baku City
DP Coordinator Francesco Banchini
PYP Coordinator Kamilla Orujova
Languages English
T: +994 12 539 89 35/36/37/38
W: www.eas.az

Idrak Lyceum
2 Samad Vurghun, Sumqayit 5001
DP Coordinator Nuriya Allahverdiyeva
Languages English
T: +994 18 655 59 73
W: idrak.edu.az

School-Lyceum N6
2 Sh Alakparova Str, Baku 1001
DP Coordinator Deepa Boodhoo
MYP Coordinator Deepa Boodhoo
PYP Coordinator Deepa Boodhoo
Languages English
T: +99 412 492 2221
W: www.mekteb.az

The International School of Azerbaijan, Baku
Yeni Yasamal, Stonepay, Royal Park, Baku AZ1070
DP Coordinator Gareth Hubbuck
MYP Coordinator Marie Favret
PYP Coordinator Karen Noble
Languages English
T: +994 12 404 01 12
W: www.tisa.az

XXI Century International Education and Innovation Center
30 Inshaatchilar Avenue, Baku 1065
DP Coordinator Nigar Ismayilova
Languages English
T: +994 12 510 0205
W: www.21century.edu.az

BAHRAIN

Abdul Rahman Kanoo International School
P.O. Box 2512, Manama
DP Coordinator Mrs. Sana Sharif
Languages English, Arabic
T: +973 1787 5055
W: www.kanooschool.edu.bh

Al Rawabi School
Bldg 689, Road 3514, Block 435, Jeblat Hibshi, P.o.Box 18575, Manama, Jeblat Hibshi 435, 00973
DP Coordinator Fatema Radhi
Languages English
T: +973 17 595 252
W: alrawabi.edu.bh

AMA International School – Bahrain
PO Box 18041, Building 208, Road 408, Block 704, Salmabad
DP Coordinator Yodgor Yakubov
Languages English
T: +973 1759 8440
W: www.amais.edu.bh

Arabian Pearl Gulf (APG) School
PO Box 26299, Adliya, Manama
DP Coordinator John Labor
Languages English
T: +973 17 403 666
W: www.apgschool.com

Bahrain Bayan School
Building No. 230, Road 4112, Block 841, Isa Town
DP Coordinator Brita Nash
Languages English
T: +973 7712 2244
W: www.bayanschool.edu.bh

Bahrain School
PO Box 934, Manama
DP Coordinator Constance McAninch
Languages English
T: +973 17727 828
W: www.dodea.edu/BahrainEHS

IBN KHULDOON NATIONAL SCHOOL
Building 161, Road 4111, Area 841, P.O. Box 20511, Isa Town
DP Coordinator Roula Barghout
Languages English, Arabic
T: +973 17780661
E: r.barghout@ikns.edu.bh
W: www.ikns.edu.bh/
See full details on page 115

Modern Knowledge Schools
PO Box 15826, Bldg 515, Manama
DP Coordinator Bindu Nair
Languages English
T: +973 17727838
W: www.mks.edu.bh

Naseem International School
PO Box 28503, Riffa
CP Coordinator Kathy Dancer
DP Coordinator Fuad Prins
MYP Coordinator Ali AlShehab
PYP Coordinator Karlien Theron
Languages English, Arabic
T: +973 17 782 000
W: www.nisbah.com

Riffa Views International School
PO Box 3050, Manama 934
DP Coordinator James Bushmiller
Languages English
T: +973 1656 5000
W: www.rvis.edu.bh

Shaikha Hessa Girls' School
PO Box 37799, Riffa
DP Coordinator Maudhulika Jain
Languages English
T: +973 17 756 111
W: www.shgs.edu.bh

St Christopher's School
PO Box 32052, Isa Town
DP Coordinator Emma Thomas
Languages English
T: +973 1760 5000
W: www.st-chris.net

BELGIUM

Antwerp International School
Veltwijcklaan 180, B-2180 Ekeren, Antwerp
DP Coordinator Thierry Torres
MYP Coordinator Karin Hartog-Kroeze
PYP Coordinator Wayne Quenneville
Languages English
T: +32 (0)3 543 93 00
W: www.ais-antwerp.be

Bogaerts International School
555 Rue Engeland, Brussels 1180
DP Coordinator Colin Sinclair
MYP Coordinator Mark Trilling
PYP Coordinator Danielle Robertson
Languages English, French
T: +32 2 230 03 39
W: www.bischool.com

D Y Patil International School, Belgium
Kontichsesteenweg 40, 2630 Aartselaar
DP Coordinator Pauline Kimman
Languages English
T: +32 3 271 0943
W: www.dypisbelgium.be

Ecole Internationale Montgomery – Brussels
Rue du Duc 133, Bruxelles 1200
DP Coordinator Danielle Franzen Daoudy
Languages French, English
T: +32 2 733 63 23
W: www.ecole-montgomery.be
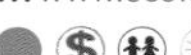

International Montessori School
Kleinenbergstraat 97-99, 1932 St. Stevens-Woluwe
DP Coordinator Carolina Massie
MYP Coordinator Stéphanie Cnudde
Languages English, French
T: +32 2 767 63 60 / +32 2 721 21 11
W: www.international-montessori.org

Scandinavian School of Brussels
Square d'Argenteuil 5, Waterloo 1410
DP Coordinator Marianne Hafvenström
Languages English
T: +32 2 357 06 70
W: www.ssb.be

St. John's International School
146 Drève Richelle, Waterloo 1410
DP Coordinator James Prowse
MYP Coordinator Simon Vanderkelen
PYP Coordinator Kathy Anderson
Languages English
T: +32 2 352 0610
W: www.stjohns.be

THE BRITISH SCHOOL OF BRUSSELS (BSB)
Pater Dupierreuxlaan 1, 3080 Tervuren
DP Coordinator James Willis
Languages English, French (bilingual Programme For Ages 4-14 Years)
T: +32 (0)2 766 04 30
E: admissions@britishschool.be
W: www.britishschool.be
See full details on page 219

The International School of Brussels (ISB)
Kattenberg 19, Brussels 1170
CP Coordinator Stephanie Lacher
DP Coordinator Julie Deegan
Languages English
T: +32 2 661 4211
W: www.isb.be

BOSNIA & HERZEGOVINA

Druga Gimnazija Sarajevo
Sutjeska 1, Sarajevo 71000
DP Coordinator Dolores Neimarlija
MYP Coordinator Iris Čapelj
Languages English
T: +387 33667438
W: www.2gimnazija.edu.ba

Gimnazija Banja Luka
Zmaj Jovina 13, Banja Luka
DP Coordinator Dijana Jujic
Languages English
T: +387 51 213 259/283/249
W: www.gimnazijabl.rs.ba

UWC Mostar
Spanski trg 1, Mostar 88000
DP Coordinator Selma Sarancic
Languages English
T: +387 36 320 601
W: www.uwcmostar.ba

BOTSWANA

Northside Primary School
PO Box 897, Plot 2786, Tshekedi Crescent Ext 9, Gaborone
PYP Coordinator Joanna Poweska Laverick
Languages English
T: +267 395 2440
W: www.northsideschool.net

Westwood International School
Plot 22978, Mmankgwedi Road, P.O. Box 2446, Gaborone
DP Coordinator Mrs Karuna Datta-Bhatnagar
MYP Coordinator Anandhi Lakshminarayan
PYP Coordinator Nidhi Bhatnagar
Languages English
T: +267 3906 736
W: www.westwood.ac.bw

BULGARIA

American College Arcus
16 Dragoman Str., Veliko Turnovo
DP Coordinator Kameliya Antonova
Languages English
T: +359 62 619959
W: www.ac-arcus.com

American College of Sofia
P.O. Box 873, Sofia 1000
DP Coordinator Zornitsa Semkova
Languages English
T: +359 2 434 10 08
W: www.acs.bg

Anglo American School of Sofia
1 Siyanie St., Sofia 1137
DP Coordinator Kalina Belivanova
Languages English
T: +359 2 923 88 10
W: www.aas-sofia.org

British International School Classic
7 Lady Strangford Street, Plovdiv 4000
DP Coordinator Teodora Ivanovska
Languages English, Bulgarian
T: +359 886 902 295
W: www.classicschool.org

British School of Sofia
Lozenets, quarter;, 1. Ekaterina Nencheva str, Sofia 1700
DP Coordinator Naomi van Wyngaarden
Languages English, Bulgarian
T: +359 886 510 510
W: www.britishschoolbg.com

International School UWEKIND
136 Voivodina Mogila Street, Knyajevo, Sofia 1619
DP Coordinator Desislava Ilieva-Popova
MYP Coordinator Aglika Damaskova
Languages English
T: +359 2 8572000
W: www.uwekind.com

Meridian 22 Private High School
Mladost 2 bl.227, Sofia 1799
DP Coordinator Yoana Kalapish
Languages English
T: +359 2 8876 423; +359 2 8840 238
W: www.meridian22-edu.com

Zlatarski International School
49 Kliment Ohridski Boulevard, BG-Sofia 1756
DP Coordinator Raya Pancheva
Languages English
T: +359 2 876 67 67
W: www.zlatarskischool.org

BURKINA FASO

Enko Ouaga International School
BP1756, 09 Ouaga, Ouagadougou
DP Coordinator Fabrice Aguibou
Languages French, English
T: +226 67 82 90 01
W: enkoeducation.com/ouaga

CAMEROON

Academic School of Excellence
BP 4323, Yaoundé
DP Coordinator Jean-Victor Yogo
Languages English, French
T: +237 222 20 03 23
W: www.academicschool-ofexcellence.com

American School of Yaounde
BP 7475, Yaounde
DP Coordinator Wendy Welander
MYP Coordinator Bruce Doig
PYP Coordinator Ella Mona Persson
Languages English
T: +237 2223 0421
W: www.asoy.org

Enko Bonanjo International School
Rue 1.171, no. 414, in front of Camwater, Bonanjo, Douala
DP Coordinator Atumo Gerald ManiH Khurde
Languages English, French
T: +237 6 93 06 82 98
W: www.enkoeducation.com/bonanjo

Enko La Gaiete International School
P.O. Box 784728, Nouvelle Route Bastos (échangeur simplifié), Yaoundé 14853
DP Coordinator Veronica Agogho
Languages English
T: +237 698 15 61 76
W: www.enkoeducation.com/lagaiete

COTE D'IVOIRE

Enko John Wesley International School
P.O. 08 BP 840, Abidjan
DP Coordinator Jimmy Goua
Languages English
T: +225 87 24 24 16
W: www.enkoeducation.com/johnwesley

Enko Riviera International School
Riviera Golf, Carrefour M'Pouto, Sol Beni, next to the Embassy of Lebanon, Abidjan
MYP Coordinator Régis Assemian
Languages English, French
T: +225 22 54 10 98
W: enkoeducation.com/riviera

International Community School of Abidjan
Boulevard Arsene Usher Assouan, Riviera III, Abidjan
DP Coordinator Fatoumata Amany
Languages English
T: +225 22 47 11 52
W: www.icsabidjan.org

CROATIA

American International School of Zagreb
Vorcarska 106, Zagreb 10000
DP Coordinator Sarah Hawkins
Languages English
T: +385 1 4680 133
W: www.aisz.hr

Matija Gubec International School
Davorina Bazjanca 2, Zagreb 10000
MYP Coordinator Linda Zelic
PYP Coordinator Zilha Redzebasic
Languages English
T: +385 1364 9133
W: www.os-mgubec.hr

Prva Gimnazija Vara din
Petra Preradovica 14, HR-42000 Vara din
DP Coordinator Ksenija Kipke
Languages English
T: +385 42 302 123
W: www.gimnazija-varazdin.skole.hr

XV. Gimnazija
Jordanovac 8, Zagreb 10000
DP Coordinator Ljiljana Crnkovic
MYP Coordinator Darija Kos
Languages English
T: +385 1 230 2255
W: www.mioc.hr/wp

CUBA

INTERNATIONAL SCHOOL OF HAVANA
Calle 22 No 115 e/1ra y 3ra Avenida, Miramar, Playa, La Habana 11300
DP Coordinator Osmery Martínez
Languages English
T: +53 7214 0773
E: office@ish.co.cu
W: www.ishav.org

See full details on page 130

CYPRUS

American International School in Cyprus
PO Box 23847, 11 Kassos Str, Nicosia 1686
DP Coordinator Kika Coles
Languages English
T: +357 22 316345
W: www.aisc.ac.cy

PASCAL Private English School – Larnaka
2, Polytechniou Street, Larnaka, 7103 Aradippou
DP Coordinator Despina Lioliou
Languages English
T: +357 22509300
W: www.pascal.ac.cy

PASCAL Private English School – Lefkosia
177, Kopegchagis Street, Lefkosia, 2306 Lakatamia
DP Coordinator Ariana Milutinovic
Languages English
T: +357 22509000
W: www.pascal.ac.cy

THE ENGLISH SCHOOL OF KYRENIA
Bilim Sokak, Bellapais, Kyrenia, North Cyprus
DP Coordinator Ms Zelis Omer
Languages English
T: +90 392 444 0375
E: info@englishschoolkyrenia.org
W: www.englishschoolkyrenia.org

See full details on page 221

CZECH REPUBLIC

1st International School of Ostrava
Gregorova 2582/3, Ostrava 702 00
DP Coordinator Philip Corkill
MYP Coordinator Jiri Svoboda
PYP Coordinator Tjasa Buh
Languages English
T: +420 599 442 085
W: www.is-ostrava.cz

Carlsbad International School
Slovenska 477/5, Karlovy Vary 36001
DP Coordinator Ryan Jordan
Languages English
T: +420 353 227 387
W: www.carlsbadschool.cz

Gymnasium Evolution
Jizni Mesto, Tererova 2135 / 17, Prague 4 149 00
DP Coordinator Tomas Vavra
Languages English, Czech
T: +420 267 914 553
W: www.gevo.cz

Czech Republic

Gymnázium Duhovka
Ortenovo námestí 34, Hole ovice, 170 00 Praha 7
DP Coordinator Keith Berry
Languages English, Czech
T: +420 241 404 217
W: www.duhovkagymnazium.cz

International School of Brno
Cejkovicka 10, Brno-Vinohrady 628 00
DP Coordinator Barbara Albrechtova
Languages English
T: +420 544 233 629
W: www.isob.cz

International School of Prague
Nebusicka 700, Prague 6 164 00
DP Coordinator Karen Ercolino
Languages English
T: +420 2 2038 4111
W: www.isp.cz

Open Gate - Boarding School
Babice 5, Rícany 251 01
DP Coordinator Rupert Marks
Languages English
T: +420 724 730 512
W: www.opengate.cz

Park Lane International School - Prague 1
Vald tejnská 151/6a, Praha – Malá Strana 118 01
DP Coordinator Jan Cihák
Languages Czech, English
T: +420 257 316 182
W: www.parklane-is.com

PORG International School - Ostrava
Rostislavova 7, Ostrava – Vítkovice 703 00
DP Coordinator Iain Benzie
Languages English
T: +420 597 071 020
W: www.porg.cz

PORG International School - Prague
Pod Krcskym lesem 1300/25, Praha 4 – Krc 142 00
DP Coordinator Jason Kucker
Languages English
T: +420 244 403 650
W: www.porg.cz

Prague British International School
Brunelova 960/12, 142 00 Praha 4
DP Coordinator David Lawlor
Languages English
T: +420 272 181 911
W: www.eisp.cz

Riverside School, Prague
Roztocka 9/43, Sedlec, 160 00 Praha 6
DP Coordinator Peter Celosse
Languages English
T: +420 2 24315336
W: www.riversideschool.cz

Soukromé osmileté gymnázium DINO-HIGH SCHOOL, s.r.o.
Bellova 352, Praha 10 10900
DP Coordinator Stephan Starkweather
Languages Czech, English
T: +420 240 200 082
W: www.dinoskola.cz

The English College in Prague
Sokolovska 320, 190 00 Prague 9
DP Coordinator Stephen Hudson
Languages English
T: +420 2 8389 3113
W: www.englishcollege.cz

The Prague British School - Kamyk Site
K Lesu 558/2, Praha 4 142 00
CP Coordinator Alexander Klaiss
DP Coordinator David Lawlor
Languages English
T: +420 226 096 200
W: www.pbschool.cz/kamyk-site

Democratic Republic of the Congo

ECOLE INTERNATIONALE BILINGUE LE CARTÉSIEN (EIBC)
34, 7ème Rue, Q. Industriel, Limete, Kinshasa
DP Coordinator Armand Ngolomingi Mudiandambu
Languages French, English
T: +243812621704
E: stevembikayi@yahoo.fr
W: www.lecartesien.cd
See full details on page 93

The American School of Kinshasa
Rte de Matadi, Ngaliema Kinshasa II, Kinshasha
DP Coordinator Garrett Austin
Languages English
T: +243 818846619
W: www.tasok.net

Denmark

Aarhus Academy for Global Education
Dalgas Avenue 12, 8000 Aarhus
MYP Coordinator Kathryn Templeman
PYP Coordinator Megan Behnke
Languages English
T: +45 20 30 20 79
W: www.aarhusacademy.dk

Birkerød Gymnasium, HF, IB & Boarding School
Søndervangen 56, Birkerød 3460
DP Coordinator Christina Rye Tarp
Languages English
T: +45 45 16 82 20
W: www.birke-gym.dk

Copenhagen International School
Levantkaj 4-14, Nordhavn DK-2150
DP Coordinator Mary Donnellan
MYP Coordinator Tammy Debets
PYP Coordinator Rachel Curle
Languages English
T: +45 39463300
W: www.cis.dk

Esbjerg Gymnasium & HF
Spangsbjerg Møllevej 310, Esbjerg 6705
DP Coordinator Marianne Helms
Languages English
T: +45 75 14 13 00
W: www.e-gym.dk

Esbjerg International School
Guldager Skolevej 4, 6710 Esbjerg
PYP Coordinator Grant Davis
Languages English, Danish
T: +45 7610 5399
W: www.esbjerginternationalschool.dk

EUC Syd
Hilmar Finsens Gade 8, Soenderborg 6400
DP Coordinator Mikkel Simonsen
Languages English
T: +45 7412 4242
W: www.eucsyd.dk

Grenaa Gymnasium
N. P. Josiassens vej 21, DK-8500 Grenaa
DP Coordinator Eike Strandsby
Languages English
T: +45 87 58 40 50
W: www.grenaa-gym.dk

Hasseris Gymnasium
Hasserisvej 300, DK-9000 Aalborg
DP Coordinator Karin Mølgaard Skals
Languages English
T: +45 96 32 71 10
W: www.hasseris-gym.dk

Herlufsholm Skole
Herlufsholm Allé 170, Naestved 4700
DP Coordinator Natascha Philip
Languages English
T: +45 55 75 35 00
W: www.herlufsholm.dk

Ikast-Brande Gymnasium
Bøgildvej 2, Ikast-Brande 7400
DP Coordinator Gitte Pilley
Languages English
T: +45 9715 3611
W: www.ikast-gym.dk

International School of Billund
Skolevej 24, Billund 7190
MYP Coordinator Tue Rabenhoej
PYP Coordinator Karen Serritslev
Languages English
T: +45 2632 7800
W: www.isbillund.com

International School of Hellerup
Rygårds Allé 131, Hellerup 2900
DP Coordinator Evis Qeska
MYP Coordinator Abenaa Uttenthal
PYP Coordinator Joanna Okolowicz
Languages English
T: +45 70 20 63 68
W: www.ish.dk

Kolding Gymnasium, HF-Kursus
Skovvangen 10, Kolding DK 6000
DP Coordinator Mel Malone
Languages English
T: +45 7633 9600
W: www.kolding-gym.dk/

Langkaer STX/HF/IB World School
Kileparken 25, Tilst 8381
DP Coordinator Rikke Hupfeld
Languages English
T: +45 86242011
W: www.langkaer.dk

Nörre Gymnasium
Mörkhöjvej 78, 2700 Brönshöj
DP Coordinator Jutta Rüdiger
Languages English
T: +45 44 94 27 22
W: www.norreg.dk

Nyborg Gymnasium
Skolebakken 13, Nyborg 5800
DP Coordinator Ulrik Nørum
Languages English
T: +45 6531 0217

Stenhus Gymnasium
Stenhusvej 20, Holbæk 4300
DP Coordinator Paul Bjergfelt
Languages English
T: +45 59 43 64 65
W: www.stenhus-gym.dk

Struer Statsgymnasium
Jyllandsgade 2, Struer 7600
DP Coordinator Morten Rødgaard Jensen
Languages English
T: +45 9785 4300
W: www.struer-gym.dk

Viborg Katedralskole
Gl Skivevej 2, Viborg 8800
DP Coordinator Mads Henriksen
Languages English
T: +45 86620655
W: www.viborgkatedralskole.dk

EGYPT

American International School in Egypt – West Campus
Sheikh Zayed City, Entrance 2, Greens Compound, Giza 12588
DP Coordinator Mark Harrington
Languages English
T: +20 2 3854 0600
W: www.aiswest.com

American International School in Egypt, Main Campus
PO Box 8090, Masaken, Nasr City, Cairo 11371
DP Coordinator Malak Issa
Languages English
T: +20 2 2618 8400
W: www.aisegypt.com

Bedayia International School
1st Urban Distrcit, El Banafseg Zone, New Cairo 11865
DP Coordinator Rania Aly
Languages English
W: www.bedayia.com

Cairo American College
PO Box 39, Maadi, Cairo 11431
DP Coordinator Niall Williams
Languages English
T: +20 2 2755 5555
W: www.cacegypt.org

Cairo English School
PO Box 8020, Masaken Nasr City, New Cairo 11371
DP Coordinator Heba Serry
Languages English
T: +20 22 249 0200
W: www.cesegypt.com

Deutsche Schule Beverly Hills Kairo
Beverly Hills Compound, Sheikh Zayed 2
DP Coordinator Shahira Yehia
Languages English
T: +20 238 570 510 +11
W: www.bhs-egypt.com

Deutsche Schule Hurghada
Post Box 99, Hurghada, Red Sea
DP Coordinator Michaela Jocham
Languages English
T: +20 100 4612747
W: deutsche-schule-hurghada.de

Dr Nermien Ismail Language School NIS
Tagamoa El-Awaal, End of Zakor Hussein, Cairo
DP Coordinator Soha Salem
Languages English
T: +20 114 5599992
W: www.nis-egypt.com

ECOLE OASIS INTERNATIONALE
Zahraa El Maadi, Quarter no 3 and no 7 Part A & B, Cairo
CP Coordinator Fatma Hussein
DP Coordinator Fatma Hussein
MYP Coordinator Mr. Omar El Sarky
PYP Coordinator Mrs. Imane Radwan
Languages French
T: +20 2 2516 2608
E: admission@oasisdemaadi.com; oasis.edu@oasisdemaadi.com
W: www.oasisdemaadi.com
See full details on page 97

Egyptian International School
13 district, Giza, Zayed
MYP Coordinator Eman Hussein
PYP Coordinator Hala Seif
Languages English
T: +20 1128695389
W: www.eis-zayed.com

Elite International School
Airport Road off Ring Road, behind Nozha Airport, Abees 10th, Alexandria
PYP Coordinator Alia Mostafa
Languages English
T: +20 109 330 7078
W: onlineelite.net

GLOBAL PARADIGM INTERNATIONAL SCHOOL
First Settlement, Block K1, Sector 8, New Cairo 16834
DP Coordinator Omnia Mostafa
Languages English
T: +20 222 461 809/10/12
E: info@gpschool-eg.com
W: www.gpschool-eg.com
See full details on page 104

GREEN LAND – PRÉ VERT INTERNATIONAL SCHOOLS – GPIS-EGYPT
405, Geziret Mohamed Road, Giza
DP Coordinator Mona Khalil
MYP Coordinator May Waly
PYP Coordinator Francoise Bencteux
Languages French, English, Arabic
T: +20 2 01002226053/50/54
E: info@greenlandschool.org
W: gpis-egypt.org
See full details on page 105

HAYAH INTERNATIONAL ACADEMY
South of Police Academy, 5th District, New Cairo
DP Coordinator Omneya Hamdy
PYP Coordinator Shymaa Elkotb
Languages English
T: +202 25373000/3333
E: admission@hayahacademy.com
W: www.hayahacademy.com
See full details on page 111

International New Future School (Neue Deutsche Schule Alexandria)
El Prince Street, off Moustafa Kamel Street, Mandara Kebly, Alexandria
DP Coordinator Fatma Soliman
Languages English
T: +203 958 64 81
W: www.future-schools.com/DSA/English/index.aspx

International School of Elite Education
Road 90- Behind El Masraweya Compound, Cairo 11835
DP Coordinator Shaimaa AbdelHafez
Languages English
T: :+20 111 114 3225
W: www.eliteeducation-eg.com

Leaders International College
21 El Narges Service Area, 5th Settlement, New Cairo
DP Coordinator Menna Shawky
MYP Coordinator Menna Shawky
PYP Coordinator Debbie Cunnea
Languages English
T: +20 127 292 4777
W: www.leadersintcollege.com

MALVERN COLLEGE EGYPT
B2-B3 South Ring Road, Investment Zone Kattameya, Cairo
DP Coordinator Jessica Swann
Languages English
T: +202 26144400
E: info@malverncollege.edu.eg
W: malverncollege.edu.eg
See full details on page 159

Manaret Heliopolis International School
Hazem Salah Street, Ext. Mostafa El Nahas, Nasr City, Cairo 11351
PYP Coordinator Beata Kroczek
Languages English
T: +20 127 06 04 011
W: www.manaretheliopolis.net

Modern English School Cairo
South of Police Academy, PO Box 5 New Cairo, New Cairo 11835
DP Coordinator Suzie Sheehan
Languages English
T: +202 2618 9600
W: www.mescairo.com

Narmer American College
20 El-Narguis Service Area, New Cairo City, Cairo 11477
DP Coordinator Salma Omar
Languages English
T: +202 29201200
W: www.nacegypt.com

Nefertari International School
Km 22 Cairo-Ismailia Desert Road, Nefertari Street, Cairo 11341
DP Coordinator Marwa Hosny
Languages English, Arabic
T: +20 1026604040
W: www.niscl.com

New Cairo British International School
Road 17, 1st Zone, 3rd Settlement, 5th District, New Cairo City, Cairo
DP Coordinator Paul Highdale
PYP Coordinator Christina Seeley
Languages English
T: +20 2 2565 7115
W: www.ncbis.co.uk

New Vision International Schools
S1-14 Beverly Hills, Sheikh Zayed, Giza 12588
DP Coordinator Yasmine Hamoda
MYP Coordinator Randa Gamal
PYP Coordinator Yasmine Hamoda
Languages Arabic, English
T: +202 3857 1220
W: nviseg.com

Egypt

Nile International College
New Cairo, Fifth Settlement, 5th District, (S5-1), Beside Qeba Mosque, Cairo 1121
PYP Coordinator Nouran Elghandour
Languages English
T: +20 2 010 6883 6751
W: www.nic-edu.net

Notion International School
Metwaly el Sharawy street (Lebeny), Maryotyah, Giza
MYP Coordinator Ms Iman Ragab
PYP Coordinator Yomna El Ashram
Languages English
T: +20 1120004926
W: www.notion-edu.com

Rahn Schulen Kairo
Extension of Hassan Ma'moun Str., Zaher Buildings, Nasr City, Cairo ET-11371
DP Coordinator Aliaa Saloum
Languages German
T: +20 10 27933321
W: www.rahn-schulen-kairo.org

The British International School, Cairo
PO Box 137, Gezira, Cairo
DP Coordinator Richard Young
Languages English
T: +202 3827 0444
W: www.bisc.edu.eg

The Egyptian International School in El Marag
Mogawra 2, Bloc G, Elmarag City, Maadi, Cairo 11435
MYP Coordinator Mohamed Said
PYP Coordinator Mohamed Said
Languages English
T: +20 229700217
W: m-eis.com

ERITREA

Asmara International Community School
PO Box 4941, 117-19 Street, #6, Asmara
DP Coordinator Kate Britton
Languages English
T: +291 1 161705
W: www.aicsasmara.com

ESTONIA

Audentes School
Tondi str 84, Tallinn 11316
DP Coordinator Anneliis Kõiv
Languages English
T: +372 699 6591
W: www.audentes.ee

International School of Estonia
Juhkentali 18, Tallinn 10132
DP Coordinator Ritu Dubey
MYP Coordinator Kadri Tomson
PYP Coordinator Terje Äkke
Languages English
T: +372 666 4380
W: www.ise.edu.ee

Miina Härma Gümnaasium
Tõnissoni 3, Tartu 50409
DP Coordinator Kirstin Karis
MYP Coordinator Sigrid Butlers
PYP Coordinator Triinu Pihus
Languages English, Estonian
T: +372 736 1920
W: www.mhg.tartu.ee

Tallinn English College
10 Estonia Avenue, Tallinn 101 48
DP Coordinator Liisa Kukk
MYP Coordinator Liis Prikk
PYP Coordinator Marja Popov
Languages English
T: +372 6 46 13 06
W: www.tik.edu.ee

Tartu International School
J. Liivi 2d, Tartu 50409
PYP Coordinator Liis Tahiste
Languages English
T: +372 742 4241
W: www.istartu.ee

ETHIOPIA

German Embassy School Addis Ababa
PO Box 1372, Addis Abeba
DP Coordinator Christoph Abt
Languages English
T: +251 11 553 4465
W: www.ds-addis.de

International Community School of Addis Ababa
Mauritania Road, Old Airport, Addis Ababa
DP Coordinator Heidi Zickefoose
PYP Coordinator Kacey Molloy
Languages English
T: +251 11 317 1544
W: www.icsaddis.edu.et

Sandford International School
PO Box 30056 MA, Addis Ababa
DP Coordinator Colin Beet
Languages English
T: +251 111 233726
W: www.sandfordschool.org

FINLAND

Espoo International School
PL 3222, 02070 Espoo, Uusimaa
MYP Coordinator Darrell Germo
Languages English
T: +358 50 343 2460
W: www.espoo.fi/espoointernationalschool

Etelä-Tapiolan lukio
PL 3234, 02070 Espoo, Uusimaa
DP Coordinator David Crawford
Languages English
T: +358 9 816 39101
W: www.etela-tapiola.fi

Helsingin Suomalainen Yhteiskoulu
Isonnevantie 8, 00320 Helsinki, Uusimaa
DP Coordinator Minna Ankkuri
Languages English
T: +358 9 4774 1814
W: www.syk.fi

Imatran Yhteislukio upper-secondary school
Koulukatu 5, 55120 Imatra, South Karelia
DP Coordinator Marketta Kolehmainen
Languages English
T: +358 5 6815 820
W: www.imatranyhteislukio.fi

International School of Helsinki
Selkämerenkatu 11, 00180 Helsinki, Uusimaa
DP Coordinator Mark Kilmer
MYP Coordinator Minna Tammivuori-Piraux
PYP Coordinator Sharyn Skrtic
Languages English
T: +358 9 686 6160
W: www.ishelsinki.fi

Joensuun Lyseon Lukio
Koskikatu 8, 80100 Joensuu, North Karelia
DP Coordinator Adam Lerch
Languages English
T: +358 13 267 7111
W: www.lyseo.jns.fi

Jyväskylän Lyseon Lukio
Yliopistonkatu 13, 40100 Jyväskylä, Central Finland
DP Coordinator Riikka Lahtonen
Languages English
T: +358 403414690

Kannaksen lukio
Kannaksenkatu 20, 15140 Lahti, Päijänne Tavastia
DP Coordinator Sami Sorvali
Languages English
T: +358 3 8144220
W: www.kannaksenlukio.fi

Kuopion Lyseon Lukio
Puijonkatu 18, 70110 Kuopio, North Savo
DP Coordinator Suvi Tirkkonen
Languages English
T: +358 17 184 563
W: www.koulut.kuopio.fi/lyseo/

Lyseonpuiston Lukio
IB section, Ruokasenkatu 18, 96100 Rovaniemi, Lapland
DP Coordinator Timo Lakkala
Languages English
T: +358 16 322 2540
W: www.lyska.net

Mattlidens Gymnasium
PB 3340, 02070 Esbo, Uusimaa
DP Coordinator Anna Martikainen
Languages English
T: +358 9 816 43050
W: www.mattliden.fi/gym

Oulu International School
Kasarmintie 4, 90130 Oulu, North Ostrobothnia
MYP Coordinator Marja Peedo
PYP Coordinator Heidi Tuomela
Languages English
T: +358 50 371 6977
W: ouka.fi/oulu/oulu-international-school/etusivu

Oulun Lyseon Lukio
Kajaaninkatu 3, 90100 Oulu, North Ostrobothnia
DP Coordinator Heli-Maarit Miihkinen
Languages English
T: +358 44 703 9451
W: www.lyseo.edu.ouka.fi

Oulun seudun ammattiopisto
Kiviharjuntie 6, 90220 Oulu, North Ostrobothnia
CP Coordinator Eeva Vehmas
Languages English, Finnish
W: www.osao.fi

Ressu Comprehensive School
PO BOX 3107, Kaupunki, 00099 Helsinki, Uusimaa
MYP Coordinator Petra Grönros
PYP Coordinator Anne Marin-Nuutinen
Languages English, Finnish
T: +358 9 310 82102
W: www.ressuy.edu.hel.fi

Ressun Lukio
PO Box 3809, 00099 Helsinki, Uusimaa
DP Coordinator Tiina Nurmi
Languages English
T: +358 9 604 849
W: www.ressunlukio.fi

Tampereen Lyseon lukio
F E Sillanpään Katu 7, 33230 Tampere, Pirkanmaa
DP Coordinator Tuija Laurila
Languages English
T: +358 40 801 6717
W: lukiot.tampere.fi/lyseo

Tikkurilan Lukio
Valkoisenlahteentie 53, 01370 Vantaa, Uusimaa
DP Coordinator Maarit Berg
Languages English
T: +358 9 8392 5119
W: www.edu.vantaa.fi/tilu

Turun Normaalikoulu
Annikanpolku 9, 20610 Turku, Southwest Finland
DP Coordinator Marianna Vanhatalo
Languages English
T: +358 (0)29 450 1000
W: sites.utu.fi/tnk

Valkeakoski Tietotie Upper Secondary School
Tietotie 3, 37630 Valkeakoski, Pirkanmaa
DP Coordinator Tomi Pakalen
Languages English
T: +358 40 335 6255
W: www.valkeakoski.fi

Vasa Ovningsskola
Kirkkopuistikko 11-13, 65100 Vaasa, Ostrobothnia
DP Coordinator Ann-Christin Häggblom
Languages English
T: +358 (0)6 324 7115
W: oldwww.abo.fi/vos/

FRANCE

American School of Paris
41 rue Pasteur, 92216 Saint-Cloud
DP Coordinator Alyssa Pierce
Languages English
T: +33 1 41 12 82 82
W: www.asparis.org

Collège-Lycée Saint François-Xavier
3 rue Thiers, Vannes 56000
DP Coordinator Chantal Thomas
Languages English, French
T: +33 (0)2 97 47 12 80
W: www.saint-francois-xavier.com

EBICA
245 Route les Lucioles, 06560 Valbonne
DP Coordinator Katia Abboud
PYP Coordinator Jayne Pirson
Languages English, French
T: +33 (0)4 93 64 32 84
W: www.ebicaschool.com

ECOLE DES ROCHES
295 avenue Edmond Demolins, 27130 Verneuil d'Avre et d'Iton
DP Coordinator Mrs Fatima Dif
Languages English, French
T: +33 (0) 232 6040 00
E: ecoledesroches@ecoledesroches.com
W: www.ecoledesroches.com
See full details on page 92

ÉCOLE JEANNINE MANUEL – LILLE
418 bis rue Albert Bailly, Marcq-en-Baroeul 59700
DP Coordinator Nicola French
Languages French, English
T: +33 3 20 65 90 50
E: admissions-lille@ejm.net
W: www.ecolejeanninemanuel.org
See full details on page 94

ÉCOLE JEANNINE MANUEL – PARIS
70 rue du Théâtre, Paris 75015
DP Coordinator Sabine Hurley
Languages English, French
T: +33 1 44 37 00 80
E: admissions@ejm.net
W: www.ecolejeanninemanuel.org
See full details on page 95

Ecole Privée Bilingue Internationale
Domaine de massane, Baillargues 34670
DP Coordinator Alexandra David
Languages English, French
T: +33 4677 07844
W: www.lycee-prive-international-montpellier.fr

EIB Victor Hugo School
23 rue de Cronstadt, Paris 75015
DP Coordinator Ioannis Iliopoulos
Languages English
T: +33 (0)1 5656 6070
W: www.eab.fr/ecoles/presentation_internationalschool_victorhugo.cfm

ERMITAGE INTERNATIONAL SCHOOL OF FRANCE
46 Avenue Eglé, 78600 Maisons-Laffitte
DP Coordinator Wayne Hodgkinson
MYP Coordinator Christine Collie
Languages English, French
T: +33 1 39 62 81 75
E: admissions@ermitage.fr
W: www.ermitage.fr
See full details on page 100

INTERNATIONAL BILINGUAL SCHOOL OF PROVENCE
500 Route de Bouc-Bel-Air, Domaine des Pins, Luynes, Aix en Provence 13080
DP Coordinator Trevor Alan Tricker
Languages English, French
T: +33 (0)4 4224 0340
E: info@ibsofprovence.com
W: www.ibsofprovence.com/
See full details on page 122

International School of Lyon
80 Chemin du Grand Roule, 69110 Sainte Foy Lès Lyon
DP Coordinator Mark Ingrey
PYP Coordinator Alison Pattinson
Languages English
T: +33 (0) 478 866 190
W: www.islyon.org

International School of Nice
15 Ave Claude Debussy, 06200 Nice
DP Coordinator Nalinka Kalder
PYP Coordinator Clare Moor
Languages English, French
T: +33 4 93 21 04 00
W: www.isn-nice.com

International School of Paris
6 rue Beethoven, Paris 75016
DP Coordinator Philip Anderson
MYP Coordinator Lucy Whitfield
PYP Coordinator Daniel Barker
Languages English
T: +33 1 4224 0954
W: www.isparis.edu

International School of Toulouse
2 Allee De L'Herbaudiere, Route de Pibrac, Colomiers 31770
DP Coordinator Gareth Hunt
PYP Coordinator Laura Maxwell
Languages English
T: +33 562 74 26 74
W: www.intst.eu

Le Gymnase Jean Sturm/ Lucie Berger
8, place des Etudiants, Alsace, Strasbourg 67000
DP Coordinator Janel Hooven-Boulogne
Languages English
T: +33 (0)3 88 15 77 10
W: www.jsturm.fr

Notre Dame International High School
106, Grande-Rue, 78480 Verneuil-sur-Seine
DP Coordinator Emilie Champeix
Languages English, French
T: +33 9 70 40 79 22
W: www.ndihs.com

Ombrosa, Lycée Multilingue de Lyon
95 Quai Clemenceau, Caluire 69300
DP Coordinator Sylvie Henderson
Languages English, French
T: +33 4 78 23 22 63
W: www.ombrosa.com

Sainte Victoire International School
Domaine Sainte Victoire, Fuveau 13710
DP Coordinator Brad Edwards
Languages English, French
T: +33 4 42 26 51 96
W: www.svis.fr

GABON

LYCÉE FRANCO-BRITANNIQUE ECOLE INTERNATIONALE
Batterie IV, B.P. 159, Libreville
DP Coordinator Nathaniel Akue Mackaya
MYP Coordinator Nathaniel Akue Mackaya
PYP Coordinator Nathaniel Akue Mackaya
Languages French, English
T: +241 01 73 71 17
E: jovicefb@yahoo.com
W: efblbv.org/ecole-franco-britannique-lbv.php
See full details on page 156

The International School of Gabon Ruban Vert
Batterie IV, Libreville 2144
DP Coordinator Shruthi Satheesh
PYP Coordinator Eunah Njoroge
Languages English
T: +241 04 84 33 80/+241 01 44 26 70
W: www.ecolerubanvert.com

GEORGIA

European School

#2 I. Skhirtladze Str., Tbilisi 0177
DP Coordinator Ramaz Sartania
MYP Coordinator Linda Tsitskishvili
PYP Coordinator Dinara Rysmagambetova
Languages English
T: +995 32 239 59 64
W: europeanschool.ge/en/

New School, International School of Georgia

35 Tskneti Highway, 0179 Bagebi, Tbilisi
DP Coordinator Kety Tsurtsumia
MYP Coordinator Tamuna Dzidziguri
PYP Coordinator Nino Tsinaridze
Languages English, Georgian
T: +995 32 223 1728
W: www.newschoolgeorgia.com

GERMANY

ACCADIS INTERNATIONAL SCHOOL BAD HOMBURG

Norsk-Data-Strasse 5, 61352 Bad Homburg
DP Coordinator Prof. Dr. Christoph Kexel
Languages English, German
T: +49 6172 9841 41
E: info@accadis-isb.com
W: www.accadis-isb.com

See full details on page 63

Aloisiuskolleg

Elisabethstraße 18, 53177 Bonn
DP Coordinator Uta Schäpers
Languages English, German
T: +49 228 82003 (101)
W: www.aloisiuskolleg.de

Bavarian International School e.V. – City Campus

Leopoldstrasse 208, D-80804 Munich
PYP Coordinator Nicola Moloney
Languages English
T: +49 (0)89 89655 (512)
W: www.bis-school.com

Bavarian International School e.V. – Haimhausen Campus

Hauptstrasse 1, D-85778 Haimhausen
CP Coordinator Sophie Kropman
DP Coordinator Loay Malek
MYP Coordinator Erin Foley
PYP Coordinator Annette Austin
Languages English
T: +49 (0)8133 917 (100)
W: www.bis-school.com

Berlin Brandenburg International School

Schopfheimer Allee 10, 14532 Kleinmachnow
CP Coordinator Julia Peters
DP Coordinator Karin Schnoor
MYP Coordinator Daniel Stiles
PYP Coordinator Lisa Roy
Languages English
T: +49 (0)33203 8036 0
W: www.bbis.de

Berlin British School

Dickensweg 17-19, Berlin 14055
DP Coordinator Gemma Ritchie
PYP Coordinator Joanne Wolff
Languages English
T: +49 (0)30 35109 180
W: www.berlinbritishschool.de

Berlin Cosmopolitan School

Rückerstr 9, Berlin 10119
DP Coordinator Fatima Camara
PYP Coordinator Orlando Pola-Rivera
Languages English
T: +49 30 688 33 23 0
W: www.cosmopolitanschool.de

Berlin International School

Lentzeallee 8/14, Berlin 14195
DP Coordinator Emma Jean Moffatt
PYP Coordinator Angeline Aow
Languages English
T: +49 (0) 30 8200 7790
W: www.berlin-international-school.de

Berlin Metropolitan School

Linienstraße 122, 10115 Berlin
DP Coordinator Dorian Rosso
PYP Coordinator Suzanne Tomlinson
Languages English, German
T: +49 30 8872 7390
W: www.metropolitanschool.com

Bertolt-Brecht-Gymnasium Dresden

Lortzingstraße 01, Dresden 01307
DP Coordinator Laura Protextor
Languages English
T: +49 351 449040
W: www.bebe-dresden.de

Berufskolleg am Wasserturm

Herzogstrasse 4, Northrhine Westphalia, Bocholt 46399
DP Coordinator Ellen Baumann
Languages English
T: +49 2871 2724300
W: www.bkamwasserturm.de

Bonn International School e.V.

Martin-Luther-King Str 14, Bonn 53175
DP Coordinator Peter Owen
MYP Coordinator Cijith Jacob
PYP Coordinator Casey Ranson
Languages English
T: +49 228 30854 0
W: www.bonn-is.de

Dresden International School e.V

Annenstr 9, 01067 Dresden
DP Coordinator Hadi Bou Hassan
MYP Coordinator Flora Mather
PYP Coordinator Maria Tran
Languages English
T: +49 351 440070
W: www.dresden-is.de

Evangelisch Stiftisches Gymnasium Gütersloh

Feldstraße 13, Gütersloh NRW 33330
DP Coordinator Marcus Kühle
Languages English
T: +49 5241 98050
W: www.esg-guetersloh.de

Felix-Klein-Gymnasium

Böttingerstr 17, 37073 Göttingen
DP Coordinator Silke Neumann
Languages English
T: +49 551 400 2909
W: www.fkg-goettingen.de

Franconian International School

Marie Curie-Strasse 2, 91052, Erlangen
DP Coordinator Chandra Mcgowan
MYP Coordinator Chandra McGowan
Languages English
T: +49 9131 940390
W: www.the-fis.de

Frankfurt International School

An der Waldlust 15, Oberursel 61440
CP Coordinator Ashley van der Meer
DP Coordinator Ashley van der Meer
PYP Coordinator Gioia Morasch
Languages English
T: +49 6171 2024 0
W: www.fis.edu

Frankfurt International School (Wiesbaden Campus)

Rudolf-Dietz-Strasse 14, Wiesbaden-Naurod 65207
PYP Coordinator Jason Bentley
Languages English, German
T: +49 6127 99400
W: www.fis.edu

Freiherr-vom-Stein-Gymnasium Hamm

Karl-Koßmann-Straße 2, 59071 Hamm
DP Coordinator Christian Flick
Languages English
T: +49 2381 91496 0
W: www.ham.nw.schule.de

Friedrich-Ebert-Gymnasium

Ollenhauerstrasse 5, Bonn 53113
DP Coordinator Gabriele Josten
Languages English
T: +49 228 777520
W: www.feg-bonn.de

Friedrich-Schiller-Gymnasium Marbach

Schulstrasse 34, D-71672 Marbach am Neckar
DP Coordinator Andrea Saffert
Languages English, German
T: +49 (0)7144 8458-0
W: www.fsg-marbach.de

Goethe-Gymnasium

Friedrich-Ebert-Anlage 22-24, Frankfurt 60325
DP Coordinator Hans-Dieter Bunger
Languages English
T: +49 69 2123 3525
W: www.gg-ffm.de

Goetheschule Essen

Ruschenstrasse 1, Essen 45133
DP Coordinator Michael Franke
Languages English
T: +49 201 841170
W: www.goetheschule-essen.de

Gymnasium Birkenfeld

Brechkaul 12, 55765 Birkenfeld
DP Coordinator Dagmar Orlian
Languages English, German
T: +49 (0)6782 99940
W: www.gymnasium-birkenfeld-nahe.de

Gymnasium im Stift Neuzelle

Stiftsplatz 7, 15898 Neuzelle
DP Coordinator Daniel Lauris
Languages English, German
T: +49 341 3939 2810
W: rahn.education/en/freies-gymnasium-im-stift-neuzelle-.html

Gymnasium Paulinum

Am Stadtgraben 30, Münster 48143
DP Coordinator Kirsten Brinkmann
Languages English
T: +49 251 510500-0
W: www.muenster.org/paulinum

Gymnasium Schloss Neuhaus
Im Schlosspark, Paderborn D-33104
DP Coordinator Gabriele Kipp
Languages English
T: +49 5254 992200
W: www.gymnasium-schloss-neuhaus.de

Hansa-Gymnasium, Hamburg-Bergedorf
Hermann-Distel-Straße 25, Hamburg 21029
DP Coordinator Vivien Dudek
Languages English
T: +49 (0)40 724 18 60
W: www.hansa-gymnasium.de

Heidelberg International School
Wieblinger Weg 7, 68782 Heidelberg
DP Coordinator Kevin Whitmore
MYP Coordinator Sarah Al-Benna
PYP Coordinator Erica Mingay
Languages English
T: +49 6221 75 90 600
W: www.hischool.de

Heidelberg Private School Centre (Heidelberger Privatschulcentrum)
Kurfürsten-Anlage 64-68, Heidelberg D-69115
DP Coordinator Elke Heinicke
Languages English
T: +49 (0)6221 7050 4038
W: www.hpc-schulen.de

Helene-Lange-Gymnasium
Bogenstr 32, Hamburg 20144
DP Coordinator Maike Fruehling
Languages English
T: +49 40 428 9810
W: www.hlg-hamburg.de

Helmholtz-Gymnasium Bonn
Helmholtzstr. 18, Bonn 53225
DP Coordinator Brigitte Lauth
Languages English
T: +49 228 777250
W: www.helmholtz-bonn.de

Herderschule Gießen, Gymnasium der Universitätsstadt Gießen
Kropbacher Weg 45, Gießen 35398
DP Coordinator Corinna Schwarz
Languages English
T: +49 641 306 2559
W: www.herderschule-giessen.de

Hermann-Böse-Gymnasium
Hermann-Böse-Straße 1-9, Bremen 28209
DP Coordinator Till Stollmann
Languages English
T: +49 421 361 6272
W: www.hbg.schule.bremen.de

IBSM – International Bilingual School Munich
Lerchenauerstraße 197, 80935 München
PYP Coordinator Susanne Green
Languages English
T: +49 89 540426627
W: school.theikc.com

International Kids Campus
Lerchenaurstrße 197, München 80935
PYP Coordinator Susanne Green
Languages English, German
T: +49 174 193 6722
W: www.internationalkidscampus.com

International School Augsburg (ISA)
Wernher-von-Braun-Str. 1a, 86368 Gersthofen
DP Coordinator Riccardo Italiano
PYP Coordinator Katharina Baumgartner
Languages English
T: +49 821 45 55 60 0
W: www.isa-augsburg.com

International School Braunschweig-Wolfsburg
Helmstedter Straße 37, Braunschweig 38126
DP Coordinator Naresh Seetharam
Languages English
T: +49 531 889210 0
W: www.cjd-braunschweig.de

International School Campus
Eggerstedter Weg 19, 25421 Pinneberg
DP Coordinator Lalita Ramakrishna
Languages English, German
T: +49 (0)41 01 80 503 00
W: www.isceducation.de

International School Hannover Region
Bruchmeisterallee 6, Hannover 30169
DP Coordinator Naomi Resmer
MYP Coordinator Jacob Eagle
PYP Coordinator Ashley Eames
Languages English
T: +49 511 270 416 50
W: www.is-hr.de

International School Mainfranken e.V.
Kalifornienstr. 1, Schweinfurt 97424
DP Coordinator Joe Caruso
PYP Coordinator Niko Lewman
Languages English
T: 0049 9721 53861-80
W: www.the-ism.de

International School of Bremen
Badgasteiner Str 11, D-28359 Bremen
DP Coordinator Kim Walton
Languages English
T: +49 421 5157790
W: www.isbremen.de

International School of Düsseldorf e.V.
Niederrheinstrasse 336-323, Düsseldorf 40489
DP Coordinator Clinton Olson
MYP Coordinator Laura Maly-Schmidt
PYP Coordinator Chris Coker
Languages English
T: +49 211 (0) 9406 712
W: www.isdedu.de

International School of Hamburg
Hemmingstedter Weg 130, 22609 Hamburg
CP Coordinator Claire Butler-Walker
DP Coordinator James Edward Dalton
MYP Coordinator Kathryn Freeburn
Languages English
T: +49 (0)40 8000 500
W: www.ishamburg.org

INTERNATIONAL SCHOOL OF NEUSTADT
Maximilianstr 43, 67433 Neustadt an der Weinstrasse
DP Coordinator Jacques Marais
PYP Coordinator Michelle Rich
Languages English
T: +49 6321 8900 960
E: info@is-neustadt.de
W: www.is-neustadt.de

See full details on page 137

International School of Stuttgart
Sigmaringer Str 257, Stuttgart 70597
DP Coordinator Tom Penny
MYP Coordinator Vedran Kapetanovic
PYP Coordinator Alex Whitaker
Languages English
T: +49 711 769 6000
W: www.issev.de

International School of Ulm/Neu Ulm
Schwabenstraße 25, D-89231 Neu-Ulm
DP Coordinator Richard Tomes
PYP Coordinator David Benson
Languages English
T: +49 731 379 353-0
W: www.is-ulm.de

International School Ruhr
Moltkeplatz 1 + 61, D-45138 Essen
DP Coordinator Genevieve Chavaria
PYP Coordinator Ms. Yuniarti Santosa and Ms. Jessee Range
Languages English
T: +49 (0)201 479 104 09
W: www.is-ruhr.de

International School Stuttgart, Sindelfingen Campus
Hallenserstr. 2, Sindelfingen 71065
MYP Coordinator Rebecca Jones-Buerk
Languages English, German
T: +49 (0)7031 6859780
W: www.international-school-stuttgart.de

Internationale Friedensschule Koln
Neue Sandkaul 29, Köln 50859
DP Coordinator Edward Parker
PYP Coordinator Leonie Julien
Languages English, German
T: +49 221 310 6340
W: www.if-koeln.de

Internationales Gymnasium Geithain
Friedrich-Fröbel-Straße 1, Geithain 04643
DP Coordinator Marco Dietz
Languages German
T: +49 34341 46012
W: internationales-gymnasium-geithain.de

Internationales Gymnasium Reinsdorf
Mittlerer Schulweg 13, Reinsdorf 08141
DP Coordinator Marco Dietz
Languages English, Spanish
T: +49 376 3408 2300
W: www.saxony-international-school.de

ISF International School Frankfurt Rhein-Main
Strasse zur Internationalen Schule 33, 65931 Frankfurt am Main
DP Coordinator Dirk Lehmann
Languages English
T: +49 69 954319-710
W: www.isf.sabis.net

ISR International School on the Rhine – NRW
Konrad-Adenauer-Ring 2, 41464 Neuss
DP Coordinator Emil Cete
Languages English
T: +49 2131 40388-0, -11
W: www.isr-school.de

Leibniz Gymnasium Dortmund
Kreuzstrasse 163, Dortmund 44137
DP Coordinator Martin Tiaden
Languages English
T: +49 231 912 3660
W: www.leibniz-gym.de

LEIBNIZ PRIVATSCHULE ELMSHORN
Ramskamp 64B, Elmshorn 25337
DP Coordinator Dr. Stefan Wester
Languages English, German
T: +49 4121 261040
E: info@leibniz-privatschule.de
W: www.leibniz-privatschule.de
See full details on page 152

Leipzig International School
Könneritzstr. 47, 04229 Leipzig
DP Coordinator Rebecca Hillyer
Languages English
T: +49 341 39377 500
W: www.lis.school

Leonardo Da Vinci Campus
Zu den Luchbergen 13, Brandenburg, Nauen 14641
DP Coordinator Anne Pritzlaff
Languages English, Spanish
T: +49 3321 74 878 20
W: www.ldvc.de

Lessing-Gymnasium
Heerstr 7, 51143 Köln
DP Coordinator Silke Flüßhöh
Languages English
T: +49 2203 99201 66
W: www.lessing-gymnasium.eu

Metropolitan School Frankfurt
Eschborner Landstrasse 134-142, 60489 Frankfurt
DP Coordinator Katell Dodd
PYP Coordinator Brooke Antcliff
Languages English
T: +49 69 96 86 405-0
W: www.m-school.de

Munich International School e.V.
Schloss Buchhof, Percha, Starnberg 82319
DP Coordinator John McMurtry
MYP Coordinator Angela Brassington
PYP Coordinator Vicki Shaver
Languages English
T: +49 8151 366 0
W: www.mis-munich.de

Nelson Mandela State International School Berlin
Pfalzburgerstr 30, Berlin 10717
DP Coordinator Charles Spiller
Languages English
T: +49 (0)30 902928 01
W: www.nelson-mandela-school.net

Nymphenburger Schulen
Sadelerstraße 10, München 80638
DP Coordinator Susanna Seibert
Languages English
T: +49 89 159 120
W: www.nymphenburger-schulen.de

Phorms Campus Munich
Maria-Theresia-Straße 35, Munich 81675
DP Coordinator Marc Nevin
Languages English
T: +49 89 324 9337 00
W: www.muenchen.phorms.de

Sächsisches Landesgymnasium Sankt Afra zu Meißen
Freiheit 13, Meißen 01662
DP Coordinator Fabian Habsch
Languages German, English
T: +49 3521 456 0
W: www.sankt-afra.de

Schillerschule Hannover
Ebellstrasse 15, Hannover 30625
DP Coordinator Bernd Flügge
Languages English
T: +49 511 16848777
W: www.schillerschule-hannover.de

Schule Schloss Salem
Schlossbezirk 1, 88682 Salem
DP Coordinator Constanze Schummer
Languages English, German
T: +49 7553 919 352
W: www.schule-schloss-salem.de

SIS Swiss International School Berlin
Heerstraße 465, (school entrance at Reimerweg 11), Berlin 13593
DP Coordinator Carol Clonan
Languages English
T: +49 30 36 43 98 20
W: www.swissinternationalschool.de/standorte/berlin

SIS Swiss International School Friedrichshafen
Fallenbrunnen 1, Friedrichshafen 88045
DP Coordinator Marie Bertschinger
Languages English
T: +49 7541 954 37 0
W: www.swissinternationalschool.de/standorte/friedrichshafen

SIS Swiss International School Ingolstadt
Stinnesstraße 1, Ingolstadt 85057
DP Coordinator Veronika Hinkofer
Languages English, German
T: +49 841 981 446 0
W: www.swissinternationalschool.de/standorte/ingolstadt

SIS Swiss International School Regensburg
Erzbischof-Buchberger-Allee 23, Regensburg 93051
DP Coordinator Christine Scheid
Languages English, German
T: +49 941 9925 930 0
W: www.swissinternationalschool.de/standorte/regensburg

SIS Swiss International School Stuttgart-Fellbach
Schmidener Weg 7/1, Stuttgart-Fellbach 70736
DP Coordinator Genea Pittman-Zupic
Languages English, German
T: +49 711 469 194 10
W: www.swissinternationalschool.de/standorte/stuttgart-fellbach

St Leonhard Gymnasium
Jesuitenstr. 9, Aachen 52062
DP Coordinator Sonja Rustemeyer
Languages English
T: +49 (0) 241 41 31 98 0
W: www.leoac.de

St. George's School Cologne
Husarenstraße 20, Cologne 50997
CP Coordinator Shirley Briggs
DP Coordinator Russell Johnston
Languages English
T: +49 2233 808 870
W: www.stgeorgesschool.com

St. George's School Duisburg-Düsseldorf
Am Neuen Angerbach 90, Duisburg 47259
CP Coordinator Vincent Keat
DP Coordinator Vincent Keat
Languages English
T: +49 203 456 860
W: www.stgeorgesschool.de/en/duisburg-dusseldorf

St. George's School Munich
Heidemannstraße 182, Munich 80939
CP Coordinator Matthew Jones
DP Coordinator Patrick Heuff
Languages English, German
T: +49 89 7246 9330
W: www.stgeorgesschool.com

State International School Seeheim-Jugenheim
Schuldorf Bergstraße, Kooperative Gesamtschule, Sandstraße, Seeheim-Jugenheim 64342
DP Coordinator Wolfgang Scheuerpflug
Languages English, German
T: +49 6257 9703 0
W: www.schuldorf.de

STIFTUNG LOUISENLUND
Louisenlund 9, Güby 24357
DP Coordinator Damien Vassallo
Languages English
T: +49 (0)4354 999 0
E: admission@louisenlund.de
W: www.louisenlund.de/en
See full details on page 211

Strothoff International School Rhein-Main Campus Dreieich
Frankfurter Strasse 160-166, Dreieich 63303
DP Coordinator Laura Hartel
MYP Coordinator Jeremy Prichard
PYP Coordinator Wayne Quenneville
Languages English
T: +49 6103 8022 500
W: www.strothoff-international-school.de

Theodor-Heuss-Gymnasium
Freyastr 10, Ludwigshafen 67059
DP Coordinator Heike Maass
Languages English
T: +45 621 504 431 710
W: www.thg-lu.de

Thuringia International School – Weimar
Belvederer Allee 40, Weimar 99425
DP Coordinator Wayne Andrew Symes
MYP Coordinator Joseph Hamkari
PYP Coordinator Kimberly Aguirre
Languages English
T: +49 (0)3643 776904
W: www.this-weimar.com

UWC Robert Bosch College
Kartäuserstrasse 119, Freiburg 79104
DP Coordinator Christian Bock
Languages English
T: +49 761 708 395 00
W: www.uwcrobertboschcollege.de

Werner-Heisenberg-Gymnasium
Werner-Heisenberg-Str 1, Leverkusen 51381
DP Coordinator Carmen Mercé Alvaro
Languages English
T: +49 2171 70670
W: www.whg-gp.de

GHANA

AL-RAYAN INTERNATIONAL SCHOOL
Boundry Road, East Legon, Accra
DP Coordinator Dorinda Tham
MYP Coordinator Barbara Bilgre
PYP Coordinator Sandeepa Chavan
Languages English, French
T: +233 (0)541 897254
E: communication@aris.edu.gh
W: www.aris.edu.gh
See full details on page 69

Association International School
6 Patrice Lumumba Road, Airport Residential Area, Accra
DP Coordinator Kukua Frempong
Languages English
T: +233 0302 777735
W: www.associationinternationalschool.org

LINCOLN COMMUNITY SCHOOL
#126/21 Reindolf Road, Abelemkpe, Accra
DP Coordinator Luke MacBride
MYP Coordinator Lisa Thompson
PYP Coordinator Natalie Wilhelm
Languages English
T: +233 302 21 8100
E: headofschool@lincoln.edu.gh
W: www.lincoln.edu.gh
See full details on page 154

Morgan International Community School
PO Box SW 63, Gomoa-Manso, Swedru
DP Coordinator Anthony Abaidoo
Languages English
T: +233 205 560 199
W: www.mics.edu.gh

SOS-Hermann Gmeiner International College
Private Mail Bag, Community 6, Tema
DP Coordinator Julian Kitching
Languages English
T: +233 303 202907
W: www.soshgic.edu.gh

Tema International School
PO Box CO 864, Tema International Close, Tema
DP Coordinator David Spooner
MYP Coordinator Yvonne Tagoe
Languages English
T: +233 24 9637 762; +233 30 3305134
W: www.tis.edu.gh

GREECE

AMERICAN COMMUNITY SCHOOLS OF ATHENS
129 Aghias Paraskevis Str., Halandri, 152 34 Athens
DP Coordinator Dr Andreas Tsokos
Languages English
T: +30 210 639 3200
E: acs@acs.gr
W: www.acs.gr
See full details on page 71

ANATOLIA HIGH SCHOOL
PO Box 21021, 60 John Kennedy Avenue, 555 35 Pylea
DP Coordinator Anna Billi Petmeza
MYP Coordinator Elisavet Exidaveloni
Languages English (IBDP), Greek (MYP)
T: +30 2310 398 200
E: info@anatolia.edu.gr
W: www.anatolia.edu.gr/highschool
See full details on page 75

Campion School Athens
PO Box 674 84, Pallini 153 02
DP Coordinator Kate Varey
Languages English
T: +30 210 607 1700
W: www.campion.edu.gr

Costeas-Geitonas School
Pallini – Attikis, Athens 15351
DP Coordinator Venia Papaspyrou
MYP Coordinator Jenny Matsota
PYP Coordinator Pandora Sifnioti
Languages English
T: +30 210 6030 411
W: www.cgs.gr

Doukas School SA
151 Mesogion Street, 15125 Paradissos, Marousi, Athens 15125
DP Coordinator Nikolaos Sympouras
Languages English
T: +30 210 618 6000
W: www.doukas.gr

European Interactive School (DES)
Barakos Hill, Ribas 19400
PYP Coordinator Theodoros Belefas
Languages English, Greek
T: +30 210 8974143
W: dimotiko.deschool.eu

Geitonas School
International Baccalaureate Diploma Programme, PO Box 74128, Sternizes, Koropi, Attiki 166 02
DP Coordinator Vasileios Xyrafas
Languages English
T: +30 210 9656200-10
W: www.geitonas-school.gr

HAEF, Athens College
15 Stephanou Delta Street, Attiki, Athens 154 52
MYP Coordinator Tania Gaitani
Languages English, Greek
W: www.haef.gr

HAEF, Psychico College
Psychico College, PO Box 65005, Psychiko, Athens 15410
DP Coordinator Sophia Arditzoglou
Languages English
T: +30 210 6798208
W: www.haef.gr

International School of Athens
PO Box 51051, Kifissia, Athens 14510
DP Coordinator Kalliope Pateras
MYP Coordinator Constantina Venieris
PYP Coordinator Louise Kalokairinou
Languages English
T: +30 210 6233 888
W: www.isa.edu.gr

International School of Piraeus
66-70 Praxitelous street, Piraeus 18532
PYP Coordinator Antonia Daponti
Languages English
T: +30 210 417 5580
W: www.isp.edu.gr

Ionios School
PO Box 13622, Filothei 15202
DP Coordinator Antigoni Nounou
Languages English
T: +30 210 6857130
W: www.ionios.gr

Lampiri Schools
Metamorphosis 155 and Ilissou, Moschato, Athens
DP Coordinator Neveen Zaki Shenouda
Languages English
T: +30 210 9480530
W: www.lampiri-schools.gr

Moraitis School
A Papanastasiou & Ag Dimitriou, Paleo Psychico, Athens 15452
DP Coordinator George Kartalis
Languages English
T: +30 210 679 5000
W: www.moraitis.edu.gr

Pierce – The American College of Greece
6 Gravias Street, Aghia Paraskevi, Athens 153 42
DP Coordinator Emmanuel Vrontakis
Languages English
T: +30 210 600 9800
W: www.pierce.gr

Pinewood – American International School of Thessaloniki, Greece
14th km Thessalonikis – N. Moudanion, P.O. Box 60606, Thermi – Thessaloniki GR-57001
DP Coordinator Dimitrios Terzidis
Languages English
T: +30 2310 301 221
W: www.pinewood.gr

Platon School
Eleytheriou Venizelou Street, Glyka Nera, Attika 15354
DP Coordinator Miltiadis-Spyridon Kitsos
MYP Coordinator Maria Tsangari
PYP Coordinator Stelios Stilianidis
Languages English, German, Greek
T: +30 210 6611 793
W: www.platon.gr

St Catherine's British School
Leoforos Venizelou 77, Lykovrissi, Athens 141 23
DP Coordinator Anne Veronica Peters
Languages English
T: +30 210 2829 750
W: www.stcatherines.gr

HUNGARY

American International School of Budapest
Nagykovácsi út 12, Nagykovácsi 2094
DP Coordinator Arpita Tyagi
Languages English
T: +36 26 556 000
W: www.aisb.hu

BME International Secondary School
Egry Jozsef utca 3-11, Budapest 1111
DP Coordinator Gordon Maclean
Languages English
T: +36 12094983
W: www.bmegimnazium.hu

Karinthy Frigyes Gimnázium
Thököly utca 7, Budapest 1183
DP Coordinator Attila Salamon
Languages English
T: +36 1 291 2072
W: www.karinthy.hu

Korösi Csoma Sándor Két Tanítási Nyelvu Baptista Gimnázium
Szentendrei út 83, Budapest 1033
DP Coordinator Anikó Hörmann
Languages English
T: +36 1 250 17 44
W: korosi.hu

SEK Budapest International School
Hüvösvölgyi út 131, Budapest 1021
DP Coordinator Ivana Cvetkovic
Languages English
T: +36 1 394 2968
W: budapest.iesedu.com

The British International School
Kiscelli Köz 17, Budapest 1037
DP Coordinator Ashley Phillipson
Languages English
T: +36 1 200 9971
W: www.bisb.hu

Tóth Árpád Gimnázium
Szombathi István utca 12., Debrecen 4024
DP Coordinator Ibolya Kovácsné Ilyés
Languages English
T: +36 52 411 225
W: www.tagdebr.sulinet.hu

ICELAND

Menntaskolinn vid Hamrahlid
Hamrahlí 10, Reykjavik 105
DP Coordinator Soffía Sveinsdottir
Languages English
T: +354 595 5200
W: www.mh.is

IRAN

German Embassy School Tehran (DBST)
Shariati, under the Sadr Bridge, Shahid Keshani St. (Mahale Darbdowom), Tehran
PYP Coordinator Mandana Rashidi
Languages English
T: +98 21 22 60 49 02
W: www.dbst.ir

Mehr-e-Taban International School
Ghasrodasht st, corner of Shahed st, Shiraz, Fars
DP Coordinator Seyedeh Mina Hosseini
MYP Coordinator Seyedeh Mina Hosseini
PYP Coordinator Mina Hosseini
Languages English
T: +98 713 6359983
W: www.mehrschool.com

Shahid Mahdavi Educational Complex
Kouh-Daman, Mina, Zanbagh, Ejazi, Zafaranie St., Tehran 19888-7536
DP Coordinator Nasrin Barootchi
PYP Coordinator Mahboobeh Hajizadeh
Languages English, Persian
T: +98 21 22435550 (EXT:190)
W: www.mahdavischool.org

Soodeh Educational Complex
End of Arabshahi Avenue, Ashrafi Isfahani Highway, Tehran 1461988511
MYP Coordinator Atefeh Khanjari
Languages English
T: +98 21 44 24 97 03
W: www.soodeh.com/?lang=en-US

Tehran International School
East Sarv Street, Kadj Sq Saadat Abad, Tehran 19816
DP Coordinator Nasrin Barootchi
Languages English
T: +98 21 2236 69757 / +98 21 2208 02401
W: www.tisschool.com

IRAQ

Da Vinci World School
Amed Street, Malta QR, Duhok, Kurdistan Region
DP Coordinator Brian Beck
MYP Coordinator Mahsa Sadraei
PYP Coordinator Rewan Hussien
Languages English
T: +964 750 757 4333
W: davinciworldschool.com

Deutsche Schule Erbil
Postfach 67, Post Office Newroz, 100-Meter-Street, Erbil, Kurdistan
DP Coordinator Parthena Papadopoulou
Languages German
T: +964 770 3016 560
W: www.ds-e.org

Global United School
Iraq-Baghdad-Palestine Street, Residential Quarter 510-lane 16-building 20, Baghdad
PYP Coordinator Bassam Omar
Languages English
T: +964 782 714 9199
W: www.globalunitedschool.com

International College University School (ICUS) Baghdad
Zayouna, Baghdad
PYP Coordinator Yasmin S. Asaf
Languages English
T: +964 7828867431
W: icusbaghdad-ib.com

International Maarif Schools Erbil
P.O. Box No. 43/0383, Mardin District, 120m Street, Opposite to Toreq Village, Erbil
PYP Coordinator Ursula Hatchard (Davies)
Languages Arabic, English, Kurdish, Turkish
T: +964 (66) 264 49 17/18
W: www.iderbilcollege.org

MAR QARDAKH SCHOOL
Mar Qardakh Street, P.O. Box 34, Erbil 1065
DP Coordinator Carolen Kossa
MYP Coordinator Martin Niqola
PYP Coordinator Rasha Mansour
Languages English
T: +964 750 144 5031
E: info@marqardakh.com
W: www.marqardakh.com

See full details on page 160

IRELAND

International School of Dublin
Barclay Court, Temple Road, Blackrock, Dublin
PYP Coordinator Nana Isa
Languages English, Spanish
T: +353 1 668 9255
W: www.internationalschooldublin.ie

NORD ANGLIA INTERNATIONAL SCHOOL DUBLIN
South County Business Park, Leopardstown, Dublin 18
DP Coordinator Joanna Cooper
Languages English
T: +353 1 5442323
E: admissions@naisdublin.com
W: www.naisdublin.com

See full details on page 169

SEK INTERNATIONAL SCHOOL DUBLIN
Belvedere Hall, Windgates, Bray, Co. Wicklow
DP Coordinator Gareth Finn
MYP Coordinator Gareth Finn
Languages English
T: +35 31 287 41 75
E: sek-dublin@sek.es
W: dublin.sek.es

See full details on page 191

St Andrew's College
Booterstown Avenue, Blackrock, County Dublin
DP Coordinator William Hehir
Languages English
T: +353 1 288 2785
W: www.st-andrews.ie

Villiers School
North Circular Road, Limerick
DP Coordinator Shane Hanna
Languages English
T: +353 61 451447
W: villiers-school.com

ISRAEL

Anglican International School Jerusalem
PO Box 191, 82 Rechov Haneviim, Jerusalem 91001
DP Coordinator Robin Press
MYP Coordinator Meira Yan
Languages English
T: +972 2 567 7200
W: www.aisj.co.il

Eastern Mediterranean International School
Hakfar Hayarok school, Ramat Hasharon 4870000
DP Coordinator Helen Lucas
Languages English
T: +972 3 6730232
W: www.em-is.org

Givat Haviva International School
D.N. Menashe 37850
DP Coordinator Yuval Dvir
Languages English
T: +972542102636
W: www.gh-is.org

ITALY

Ambrit International School
Via F Tajani 50, 00149 Rome
MYP Coordinator Susan Kammerer
PYP Coordinator Kathryn Ramsay
Languages English
T: +39 06 5595 305/301
W: www.ambrit-rome.com

American Overseas School of Rome
Via Cassia 811, 00189 Rome
DP Coordinator Belinda Fiochi
Languages English
T: +39 06 334 381
W: www.aosr.org

American School of Milan
Via K. Marx, 14, 20090 Noverasco di Opera (MI)
DP Coordinator Valeria Meroni
Languages English
T: +39 02 5300 0015
W: www.asmilan.org

Bilingual European School
Via Val Cismon 9, 20162 Milan
PYP Coordinator Aaron Downey
Languages English, Italian
T: +39 02 6611 7449
W: www.beschool.eu

Canadian School of Milan
Via M. Gioia 42, 20124 Milano
DP Coordinator Elena Cipullo
Languages English
T: +39 02 67074775
W: www.canadianschool.it

CEI International School Palermo
Centro Educativo Ignaziano, Via Piersanti Mattarella, 38/42, 90141 Palermo
PYP Coordinator Vicky Tarolla
Languages English
T: +39 0917 216111 EXT 3
W: www.isp.istitutocei.it

Collegio San Carlo
Corso Magenta, 71, 20123 Milan
DP Coordinator Anne Hallihan
Languages English
T: +39 02 43 06 31
W: www.collegiosancarlo.it

Deledda International School
Corso Mentana 27, 16128 Genoa
DP Coordinator Elizabeth Coykendall Rice
MYP Coordinator Chiara Colucci
Languages English
T: +39 010 5536268
W: www.genoaschool.eu

Gentium Schola Opitergium – International School of Talents
Viale Brandolini 6, 31046 Oderzo
DP Coordinator Kim Philot
Languages English
T: +39 0422 1883580
W: www.gsoschool.com

H-International School
Via Milano 1, 31048 Olmi di San Biagio di Callalta
MYP Coordinator Alba Manso
PYP Coordinator Rebecca Goswell
Languages English, Italian
T: +39 0422 794061
W: h-internationalschool.com

INTERNATIONAL SCHOOL BRESCIA
Via Don Orione, 1, Botticino, 25082 Brescia
MYP Coordinator Anne Vollmer
PYP Coordinator Rachel Bestow
Languages English
T: +39 030 2191182
E: info@isbrescia.com
W: www.isbrescia.com
See full details on page 124

INTERNATIONAL SCHOOL OF BERGAMO
Via Gleno 54, 24125 Bergamo
MYP Coordinator Roberta Sana
PYP Coordinator Helen Bird
Languages English, Italian
T: +39 035 213776
E: info@isbergamo.com
W: www.isbergamo.com
See full details on page 125

INTERNATIONAL SCHOOL OF BOLOGNA
Via della Libertà 2, 40123 Bologna
DP Coordinator Ms. Nazanin Nikanjam
MYP Coordinator Ms. Helen Exler
PYP Coordinator Ms. Rachel Burgess
Languages English
T: +39 051 6449954
E: info@isbologna.com
W: www.isbologna.com
See full details on page 127

INTERNATIONAL SCHOOL OF COMO
Via Adda 25, 22073 Fino Mornasco (CO)
DP Coordinator Nicole Pearce
MYP Coordinator Karen Lockett
PYP Coordinator Jane Marie Whittle
Languages English, Italian
T: +39 031 572289
E: info@iscomo.com
W: www.iscomo.com
See full details on page 129

International School of Florence
Via del Carota 23/25, Bagno a Ripoli, 50012 Florence
DP Coordinator Jason Blackstone
PYP Coordinator Nicky Shamash
Languages English, Italian
T: +39 055 6461 007
W: www.isfitaly.org

INTERNATIONAL SCHOOL OF MILAN
Via I Maggio, 20, 20021 Baranzate (MI)
DP Coordinator Tony Burtenshaw
MYP Coordinator Giuseppe Redaelli
PYP Coordinator Sara Lomas
Languages English, Italian
T: +39 02 872581
E: admissions@ism-ac.it
W: www.internationalschoolofmilan.it
See full details on page 134

INTERNATIONAL SCHOOL OF MODENA
Piazza Montessori, 1/A, 41051 Montale Rangone (MO)
DP Coordinator Caroline Searle
MYP Coordinator Anna Chiara Forti
PYP Coordinator Jacky Payne
Languages English
T: +39 059 530649
E: office@internationalschoolofmodena.it
W: www.internationalschoolofmodena.it
See full details on page 135

INTERNATIONAL SCHOOL OF MONZA
Via Solferino 23, 20900 Monza (MB)
DP Coordinator Joe Cope
MYP Coordinator Gaelle D'Inca
PYP Coordinator Becky Taylor
Languages English, Italian
T: +39 039 9357701
E: ismmonza@ism-ac.it
W: www.internationalschoolofmonza.it
See full details on page 136

INTERNATIONAL SCHOOL OF SIENA
Via del Petriccio e Belriguardo, 49/1, 53100 Siena
DP Coordinator Lucio Pessia
MYP Coordinator Letizia Rosati
PYP Coordinator Isaac Driver
Languages English, Italian
T: +39 0577 328103
E: office@internationalschoolofsiena.it
W: www.internationalschoolofsiena.it
See full details on page 138

International School of Turin
Strada Pecetto 34, 10023 Chieri, Turin
DP Coordinator Lorenzo Borgotallo
MYP Coordinator Kirsty Wilkinson
PYP Coordinator Farhana Bari
Languages English
T: +39 011 645 967
W: www.isturin.it

International School of Verona
Aleardo Aleardi, Via Segantini 20, 37138 Verona
DP Coordinator Erik Johnstone
Languages English
T: +39 04557 8200
W: www.aleardi.it

Lonati Anglo American School
Via Bormioli 60, 25135 Brescia
PYP Coordinator Melania Ferrari
Languages English
T: +39 03 02 35 73 60
W: www.laaslonati.org

MARYMOUNT INTERNATIONAL SCHOOL ROME
Via di Villa Lauchli, 180, 00191 Rome
DP Coordinator Orla Ni Riordain
Languages English
T: +39 06 3629 1012
E: admissions@marymountrome.com
W: www.marymountrome.com
See full details on page 161

O.M.C. – Collegio Vescovile Pio X
Borgo Cavour 40, 31100 Treviso
DP Coordinator Claudia Placidi
Languages English
T: +39 0422 411725
W: www.fondazionecollegiopiox.org

ROME INTERNATIONAL SCHOOL
Via Guglielmo Pecori Giraldi n.137, 00135 Rome
DP Coordinator Mrs Laela El Sheikh
PYP Coordinator Mrs Maïa Lawand
Languages English
T: +39 06 8448 2651
E: info@romeinternationalschool.it
W: www.romeinternationalschool.it
See full details on page 181

SOUTHLANDS INTERNATIONAL SCHOOL
Via Teleclide 40, Casal Palocco, 00124 Rome
DP Coordinator Mr Paul Johnson
Languages English
T: +39 06 5053932
E: info@southlands.it
W: www.southlands.it
See full details on page 198

ST GEORGE'S BRITISH INTERNATIONAL SCHOOL, ROME
Via Cassia, km 16, La Storta, 00123 Rome
DP Coordinator Helen Andrew
Languages English
T: +39 06 3086001
E: admissions@stgeorge.school.it
W: www.stgeorge.school.it
See full details on page 202

IB AFRICA | EUROPE | MIDDLE EAST

ST. LOUIS SCHOOL
Via E. Caviglia, 1, 20139 Milan
DP Coordinator Hatty Rafferty
Languages English, Italian
T: +39 02 55231235
E: info@stlouisschool.com
W: www.stlouisschool.com
See full details on page 205

ST. STEPHEN'S SCHOOL
Via Aventina 3, 00153 Rome
DP Coordinator Nadia El-Taha
Languages English
T: +39 06 575 0605
E: ststephens@sssrome.it
W: www.sssrome.it
See full details on page 206

THE BRITISH SCHOOL OF MILAN (SIR JAMES HENDERSON)
Via Carlo Alberto Pisani Dossi, 16, 20134 Milan
DP Coordinator Mr Antony Pinchin
Languages English
T: +39 02 210941
E: info@bsm.school
W: www.britishschoolmilan.com
See full details on page 220

The English International School of Padua
Via Forcellini 168, 35128 Padova
DP Coordinator Debra Mackenzie
Languages English
T: +39 049 80 22 503
W: www.eisp.it

The International School in Genoa
Via Romana Della Castagna 11A, 16148 Genova
DP Coordinator Mrs. Elizabeth Rosser Boiardi
Languages English
T: +39 010 386528
W: www.isgenoa.it

UWC ADRIATIC
Frazione Duino, 29, 34011 Duino TS
DP Coordinator Soraya Fathi
Languages English
T: +39 040 3739111
E: uwcad@uwcad.it
W: www.uwcad.it
See full details on page 230

VITTORIA INTERNATIONAL SCHOOL
Via delle Rosine 14, 10123 Turin
DP Coordinator Deborah Gutowitz
Languages English
T: +39 011 889870
E: infovis@vittoriaweb.it
W: www.vittoriaweb.it
See full details on page 235

Westminster International School
Piazza G. Toniolo, 4, 56125 Pisa
PYP Coordinator Wendy Fish
Languages English
T: +39 050 28466
W: www.westminsterinternationalschool.org

World International School of Torino
Via Traves 28, 10151 Torino
MYP Coordinator Ivan Martinez
PYP Coordinator Magdalena Matysow
Languages English
T: +39 (0)11 197 2111
W: worldinternationalschool.com

JORDAN

Amman Academy
PO Box 840, Khalda 11821
DP Coordinator Suha Abdelbaqi
MYP Coordinator Tania Masarwa
PYP Coordinator Sara Al Shami
Languages English
T: +962 6 535 4118
W: www.ammanacademy.edu.jo

AMMAN BACCALAUREATE SCHOOL
Al Hijaz Street, Dabouq, PO Box 441 Sweileh 11910, Amman
CP Coordinator Ms Gill Deesi
DP Coordinator Ms Jwan Kolaghassi
MYP Coordinator Ms Dina Katafago
PYP Coordinator Ms Noura Dissy
Languages English, Arabic
T: +962 6 5411191
E: info@abs.edu.jo
W: www.abs.edu.jo
See full details on page 74

Amman Baptist School
P.O.Box 17033, Alrabieh – Abdallah Bin Rawaha St. 300 m off Mecca str+, Amman 11195
DP Coordinator Linda Kakish
Languages English, Arabic
T: +962 6 551 6907
W: www.baptist.edu.jo

Amman National School
PO Box 140565, Amman 11814
DP Coordinator Diana Dahleh
Languages English
T: +962 654 11067/8
W: www.ans.edu.jo

Aqaba International School
PO Box 529, 77110 Aqaba
DP Coordinator Violet Bawab
Languages English, Arabic
T: +962 3 203 9933
W: www.aqabainternationalschool.com

ASAMIAH INTERNATIONAL SCHOOL
Khalda, Taqi al-Din al-Subki, Amman
DP Coordinator Ms. Yasmine Haddadin
PYP Coordinator Ms. Nour Maroun
Languages English, Arabic
T: +962 6 5335 301
E: info@ais.edu.jo
W: www.ais.edu.jo
See full details on page 77

British International Academy (BIA)
P.O.Box 829, Amman 11831
DP Coordinator Maram Theep
PYP Coordinator Huda Abu jiab
Languages English, Arabic
T: +962 6 5508200
W: www.bia.edu.jo

Cambridge High School
Al Rabia, Abdel Kareem Al Dabbas Street, PO Box 851771, Amman 11185
DP Coordinator Kathleen Awwad
MYP Coordinator Shireen Bakri
Languages English
T: +962 6 5512556
W: www.cambridge.edu.jo

Collège De La Salle – Frères
P.O.Box 926126, Ar-Razi St., Jabal Al-Hussien, Amman 11110
DP Coordinator Hani Tayyem
Languages English, Arabic
T: +962 6 5666428
W: www.lasallejordan.org

English Talents School
P.O.Box 18082, Amman 11195
DP Coordinator Norah Attari
MYP Coordinator Nasreen Alshawwa
Languages English
T: +962 65370201
W: www.englishtalentsschool.edu.jo

IBN Rushd National Academy
PO Box 940397, Amman 11194
DP Coordinator Fouad Majdalawi
MYP Coordinator Fouad Majdalawi
PYP Coordinator Ferdows Khatib
Languages English, Arabic
T: +962 6 5377601
W: www.ibnrushd.edu.jo

Islamic Educational College – Al Jubeiha
P.O Box 373, Amman 11941
DP Coordinator Lina Subeh
Languages English, Arabic
T: +962 6516 0121
W: www.islamic-ec.edu.jo

JUBILEE SCHOOL
P.O.Box: 830578, Amman 11183
DP Coordinator Yara Kajo
Languages English
T: +962 6 5238216
E: jubilee@jubilee.edu.jo
W: www.jubilee.edu.jo
See full details on page 144

MASHREK INTERNATIONAL SCHOOL
PO Box 1412, Amman 11118
DP Coordinator Fadia Khoury
MYP Coordinator Ruba Daibes (Grades 9 & 10) Niveen Salem (Grades 7 & 8)
PYP Coordinator Reema Kassem (Primary) Reem Samara (KG)
Languages Arabic, English
T: +962 79 9577771
E: administration@mashrek.edu.jo
W: www.mashrek.edu.jo
See full details on page 164

MODERN MONTESSORI SCHOOL
PO Box 1941, Khilda, Amman 11821
DP Coordinator Hoor Hawamdeh
MYP Coordinator Abeer Al Azzeh
PYP Coordinator Noor Elkhub
Languages English, Arabic
T: +9626 5535190
E: mms@montessori.edu.jo
W: www.montessori.edu.jo
See full details on page 163

National Orthodox School
P.O.Box: 941502, Amman 11194
DP Coordinator Alas Haddad
Languages Arabic, English
T: +962 6 5674418
W: www.oes.org.jo

The Ahliyyah School for Girls
PO Box 2035, Jabal Amman, Amman 11181
CP Coordinator Eva Haddad
DP Coordinator Lana Zakarian
MYP Coordinator Abeer Sweiss
PYP Coordinator Rana Amarin
Languages English
T: +962 6 4649861
W: www.asg.edu.jo

The International Academy – Amman
PO Box 144255, King Hussein Parks, Sa'eed Khair Street, Amman 11814
DP Coordinator Antony Nesling
MYP Coordinator Hala Asaad
Languages English
T: +962 6550 2055
W: www.iaa.edu.jo

The Little Academy
PO Box 143771, Amman 11844
PYP Coordinator Rula Daher
Languages English
T: +962 65858282
W: www.tlacademy.edu.jo

KAZAKHSTAN

Haileybury Astana
Panfilov Street, Bldg. 4, Nur-Sultan 010000
DP Coordinator Paul Rowe
Languages English
T: +7 (7172) 55 98 55 (122)
W: www.haileybury.kz

International College of Continuous Education Astana
2 Molodezhny Microdistrict, Astana 0100000 473000
MYP Coordinator Yelena Shebalina
PYP Coordinator Yelena Shebalina
Languages Russian, English
T: +7 7172 224590
W: www.mkno.kz

International College of Continuous Education, Almaty
69A Zheltoksan Street, Almaty 480004
MYP Coordinator Aizhan Sanagul
PYP Coordinator Aizhan Sanagul
Languages English, Russian
T: +7 3272 399736
W: www.icce-kazakhstan.kz

International School of Almaty
40b Satpayev Street, Almaty 050057
MYP Coordinator Roza Bazarbayeva
PYP Coordinator Inna Klimenko
Languages Russian, English
T: +7 727 2744808 / +7 727 2748189
W: www.isoa.kz

International School of Astana
Turkistan street, 32/1, Akmolinskaya oblast, Astana 010000
MYP Coordinator Gulnaz Sailybayeva
PYP Coordinator Maira Kunanbayeva
Languages English, Russian
T: +7 7172 916177
W: isa.nis.edu.kz

Kazakhstan International School
102a Utegen Batyra, 050062 Almaty
MYP Coordinator Oxana Akimova
PYP Coordinator Nina Babintseva
Languages English, Kazakh, Russian
T: +7 727 395 33 54
W: www.kisnet.org

Miras International School, Almaty
190 Al-Farabi Avenue, Almaty
DP Coordinator Anna Mashura
MYP Coordinator Samat Ongarbayev
PYP Coordinator Ainagul Mussakulova
Languages English, Kazakh, Russian
T: +7 727 227 6942
W: www.miras.kz

Miras International School, Astana
30 Ablai Khan Avenue, Astana 010009
DP Coordinator Anatoliy Kuznetsov
MYP Coordinator Vishal Ganguli
PYP Coordinator Rachel Wayne
Languages English, Russian, Kazakh
T: +7 7172 369867
W: www.miras-astana.kz

Nazarbayev Intellectual School of Astana
35, Street 31, (crossing of Kabanbai Batyr and Turan Avenues), Astana 010000
DP Coordinator Azamat Mergenbayev
MYP Coordinator Magripa Altaibekova
Languages English, Kazakh, Russian
T: +7 8 7172 558033
W: www.nisa.edu.kz

KENYA

Aga Khan Academy Mombasa
PO Box 80100-90066, Mbuyuni Road, Kizingo, Mombasa
DP Coordinator Shouquot Hussain
MYP Coordinator Esther Nondi
PYP Coordinator Khona Bhattacharjee
Languages English, Swahili
T: +254 (0)735 931 144
W: www.agakhanacademies.org/mombasa

Braeburn Garden Estate School
PO Box 16944, 00620 Mobil Plaza, Nairobi
CP Coordinator Mercy Gichuhi
DP Coordinator Andrew Sjoberg
Languages English
T: +254 720 667 622
W: www.gardenestate.braeburn.com

International School of Kenya
End of Peponi Road/Kirawa Road, PO Box 14103, Nairobi 00800
DP Coordinator Linda Henderson
Languages English
T: +254 20 209 1308/9
W: www.isk.ac.ke

Naisula School
P O Box 41, Nairobi-Namanga Road, 01100 Kajiado
DP Coordinator Maureen Mukanzi
Languages English, Swahili
T: +254 712245702
W: www.naisulaschool.ac.ke

St Mary's School
PO Box 40580, Rhapta Road, Nairobi 00100
DP Coordinator Jackline Akinyi Otula
Languages English
T: +254 20 4444 569
W: www.stmarys.ac.ke

THE AGA KHAN ACADEMY, NAIROBI
1st Avenue Parklands, PO Box 44424-00100, Nairobi
DP Coordinator Mr. William Wanyonyi
MYP Coordinator Ms. Julliet Kithinji
PYP Coordinator Ms. Nadia Janmohamed
Languages English
T: JUNIOR: +254 0733 758 510, SENIOR: +254 736 380 101
E: infos@akesk.org; infoj@akesk.org
W: www.agakhanschools.org/kenya/akan
See full details on page 217

The Aga Khan Nursery School, Nairobi
PO Box 14998, Nairobi 00800
PYP Coordinator Benter Bolo
Languages English
T: +254 020 374 2114
W: www.agakhanschools.org/kenya/akan

KUWAIT

American Creativity Academy
PO Box 1740, Hawalli 32018
DP Coordinator Shaheed Carter
Languages English
T: +965 2267 3333
W: www.aca.edu.kw

AMERICAN INTERNATIONAL SCHOOL OF KUWAIT
PO Box 3267, Salmiya 22033
DP Coordinator Amel Limam
MYP Coordinator Teri Kwiatkowski
PYP Coordinator Emma Wheatley
Languages English
T: +965 1 843 247
E: superintendent@ais-kuwait.org
W: www.ais-kuwait.org
See full details on page 72

Kuwait Bilingual School
PO Box 3125, Al Jahra City 01033
MYP Coordinator Fares Obaid
PYP Coordinator Dan Stratford
Languages English
T: +965 2458 1118; +965 1877 881
W: www.kuwaitbilingualschool.com

KYRGYZSTAN

ESCA Bishkek International School
67a Bronirovannaya Street, Chui Oblast, Bishkek 720044
DP Coordinator Makiko Inaba
MYP Coordinator Timothy Johnson
PYP Coordinator Krisha Gandhi
Languages English
T: +996 312 21 44 06
W: www.esca.kg

Oxford International School
Mira Avenue 153/1, Bishkek
DP Coordinator Poonam Shokeen
Languages English, Russian
T: +996 700 55 11 55
W: www.oxford.kg

LATVIA

Exupery International School
Jauna iela 8, Pinki, Babites pagasts LV-2107
PYP Coordinator Mark Stephen Wragg
Languages English, French
T: +371 26 62 23 33
W: exupery.lv

International School of Latvia
Meistaru 2, Pinki, Babites pag., Babites nov. LV-2107
DP Coordinator Jessica Krueger
MYP Coordinator Joseph Szalay
PYP Coordinator Erika Olson
Languages English
T: +371 6775 5146
W: www.isl.edu.lv

International School of Riga
Zvejnieku iela 12, Riga 1048
PYP Coordinator Ginta Karklina
Languages English
T: +371 6762 4622
W: www.isriga.lv

Riga State Gymnasium No. 2
Kr. Valdemara str. 1, Riga 1010
DP Coordinator Inga Treimane
MYP Coordinator Ingrida Breidaka
Languages English
T: +371 67181225
W: www.r2vsk.edu.lv

Riga State Gymnasium No.1
Raina bulv 8, Riga 1050
DP Coordinator Liga Reitere
Languages Latvian (national Curriculum), English (ib Dp)
T: +371 67 228 607
W: www.r1g.edu.lv

LEBANON

Al-Hayat International School
Aramoun
PYP Coordinator Sherin Khudari
Languages English
T: +961 5 806 306
W: www.his.edu.lb

American Community School at Beirut
PO Box 8129, Riad Solh, Beirut 11072260
DP Coordinator Nada Chatila
Languages English
T: +961 1 374 370
W: www.acs.edu.lb

Antonine International School
PO Box 55035, Ajaltoun, Dekwaneh
DP Coordinator Georgia Hachem Najem
Languages English
T: +961 9 230969
W: www.ais.edu.lb

Brummana High School
PO Box 36, Brummana BT
DP Coordinator George Rizkallah
Languages English
T: +961 4 960 430
W: www.bhs.edu.lb

Eastwood College – Kafarshima
P.O. Box 46, Kafarshima
DP Coordinator Majida Harakeh
Languages English, Arabic
T: +961 5 431525
W: www.eastwoodcollege.com

Eastwood International School
Sami Solh St, Mansourieh El Metn
DP Coordinator Cendrella El Kettaneh
PYP Coordinator Dana Dimassi
Languages English
T: +961 4 409307
W: eastwoodschools.com

GERMAN INTERNATIONAL SCHOOL BEIRUT
PO Box 11-3888, Bliss Street, Ras Beirut, Beirut
DP Coordinator Petra Machlab
Languages English
T: +961 1 740523
E: admissions@dsb.edu.lb
W: www.dsb.edu.lb
See full details on page 103

Greenfield College
Al Mourouj Street – Bir Hassan, Beirut
DP Coordinator Nibal Hamdan
Languages English
T: +961 1 834 838
W: www.greenfieldcollege.com

INSTITUT MODERNE DU LIBAN
Rue 51 n.19 Metn nord, Fanar, Région Jaber 90593
MYP Coordinator Grace Renno
Languages French
T: +961 1680160/1/2
E: administration@instmod.edu.lb
W: www.instmod.edu.lb
See full details on page 118

International College Beirut
P.O. Box 113-5373 Hamra, Bliss Street, Beirut
DP Coordinator Rasha Daouk
PYP Coordinator Souad Mounla
Languages Arabic, English, French
T: +961 1 362 500
W: www.ic.edu.lb

International College, Ain Aar
Bliss Street, PO Box 113-5373, Beirut
PYP Coordinator Lina Melki
Languages Arabic, English, French
T: +96 149 28468
W: www.ic.edu.lb

LWIS KESERWAN-ADMA INTERNATIONAL SCHOOL
Mar Nohra, Fatqa, Keserwan
DP Coordinator Jacques El Khoury
Languages English
T: +961 9 740 226
E: info@lwis-ais.edu.lb
W: www.lwis-ais.edu.lb
See full details on page 155

LWIS-City International School
Hussein Beyhum Street, Zkak El-Blat, Down Town, Beirut
DP Coordinator Fuad El Haddad
Languages English, Arabic
T: +961 (1) 369 500
W: lwis-cis.edu.lb/lwis-international-school

Makassed Houssam Eddine Hariri High School
PO Box 67, Saida
DP Coordinator Mona Majzoub
PYP Coordinator Farah Darazi
Languages Arabic, English, French
T: +961 7 739898
W: www.mak-hhhs.edu.lb

Rafic Hariri High School – Saida
P.O.Box 384, Saidon
PYP Coordinator Samar Darazi
Languages English
T: +961 7 723 551
W: www.rhhs.edu.lb

Sagesse High School
Aïn Saadeh, Metn
DP Coordinator Lady Maalouf
Languages English
T: +961 1 872 145
W: www.sagessehs.edu.lb

WELLSPRING LEARNING COMMUNITY
Al Mathaf, Main Street, Near National Museum, PO Box 116-2134, Beirut
DP Coordinator Kathleen Saleh
MYP Coordinator Tala Al Massarweh
PYP Coordinator Ola Itani Zein
Languages English
T: +961 1 423 444
E: info@wellspring.edu.lb
W: www.wellspring.edu.lb
See full details on page 239

LESOTHO

Machabeng College, International School of Lesotho
PO Box 1570, Maseru 100
DP Coordinator Motselisi Ismail
Languages English
T: +266 2231 3224
W: www.machcoll.co.ls

LITHUANIA

Kaunas Jesuit High School
Rotuses a. 9 4428
DP Coordinator Au rine erepkiene
Languages English
T: +370 37423098
W: www.kjg.lt

Siauliai Didzdvaris gymnasium
Vilniaus g 188, Siauliai 76299
DP Coordinator Rima Tamosiuniene
Languages English
T: +370 41 431 424
W: www.dg.su.lt

Taurągės Versmės Gimnazija
J. Tumo-Vai ganto g. 10, Tauragė LT-72261
DP Coordinator Ingrida Vaiciene
Languages English
T: +370 446 61922
W: www.versme.org

The American International School of Vilnius
Subaciaus 41, Vilnius 11350
DP Coordinator Sofia Segedy
Languages English
T: +370 5 212 1031
W: www.aisv.lt

Vilnius International School
Turniskiu Str 21, Rusu Str 3, Vilnius 01125
MYP Coordinator Deirdre Jennings
PYP Coordinator Kate Benson
Languages English
T: +370 5 276 1564
W: www.vischool.lt

Vilnius Lyceum
Sirvintu 82, Vilnius LT-08216
DP Coordinator Vilija Balciunaitė
Languages English
T: +370 5 2775836
W: www.licejus.lt

LUXEMBOURG

Athénée de Luxembourg
24 Bd Pierre Dupong, L-1430, Luxembourg
DP Coordinator Joanne Goebbels
Languages English
T: +352 26 04 60
W: www.al.lu

Fräi-Ëffentlech Waldorfschoul Lëtzebuerg
45 rue de l'Avenir, Luxembourg 1147
DP Coordinator Michael Schulz
Languages French
T: +352 466932
W: www.waldorf.lu

International School of Luxembourg
36 Boulevard Pierre Dupong, 1430 Luxembourg
DP Coordinator Robert Sinclair
Languages English
T: +352 26 04 40
W: www.islux.lu

Lycée technique du Centre

106 avenue Pasteur, Luxembourg L-2309
DP Coordinator Mariette Kauthen
Languages French
T: +352 47 38 11 1
W: www.ltc.lu

MACEDONIA

IPS Macedonia

st. Dragisha Mishovic building 2, Detska gradinka Orce Nikolov, 1000 Skopje
PYP Coordinator Donche Risteska
Languages English
T: +389 (0)2 3073 700
W: ips.mk

Josip Broz Tito – High School

Dimitrije Cupovski bb, 1000 Skopje
DP Coordinator Gordiana Gjorgova
Languages English
T: +389 2 3214 314
W: josipbroztito.edu.mk

NOVA International Schools

Praska 27, 1000 Skopje
DP Coordinator Eda Starova Tahir
Languages English
T: +389 2 3061 907
W: www.nova.edu.mk

OU Braka Miladinovci

Ul. Vladimir Komarov No.5, 1000 Skopje
PYP Coordinator Nikola Odjakov
Languages Macedonian
T: +389 (02) 2 460 479
W: oubrakamiladinovci-aerodrom.edu.mk

MADAGASCAR

The American School of Antananarivo

Lot II J 161 A, Ambodivoanjo, Ivandry, Antanarivo
DP Coordinator Richard Reilly
PYP Coordinator Michael Rourke
Languages English
T: +261 20 22 420 39
W: www.asamadagascar.org

MALAWI

Bishop Mackenzie International School

PO Box 102, Lilongwe
DP Coordinator Steven Robson
MYP Coordinator Kathryn Leaper
PYP Coordinator Alexandra Francesconi
Languages English
T: +265 1 756 631
W: bmis.mw

MALI

Enko Bamako International School

Quartier du Fleuve, rue 310, porte 510, Ancien CompuMali, En face de l'industrie Boissons et G+, Bamako
DP Coordinator Louise d'Aragon
Languages English, French
T: +223 63 21 24 26
W: www.enkoeducation.com/bamako

MALTA

ST EDWARD'S COLLEGE, MALTA

Triq San Dwardu, Birgu (Vittoriosa) BRG 9039
DP Coordinator Mr Jolen Galea
Languages English
T: +356 2788 1199
E: admissions@stedwards.edu.mt
W: www.stedwards.edu.mt

See full details on page 200

Verdala International School

Fort Pembroke, Pembroke PBK 1641
DP Coordinator Liliana Gomez
Languages English
T: +356 21375133
W: www.verdala.org

MAURITIUS

Clavis International Primary School

Montagne Ory, Moka
PYP Coordinator Nadine Koenig
Languages English
T: +230 433 4439/4337708
W: www.clavis.mu

International Preparatory School

Village Labourdonnais, Mapou 31803
PYP Coordinator Heidi Ashton
Languages English, French
T: +230 266 1973
W: www.ips.intnet.mu

Le Bocage International School (Progos)

Mount Ory, Moka 80803
CP Coordinator Namrata Gujadhur
DP Coordinator Marie-Claire Luchmun
MYP Coordinator Asha Joypaul
Languages English
T: +230 433 9900
W: www.lebocage.net

Northfields International High School

Labourdonnais Village, Mapou
DP Coordinator Rosemary Abbott
Languages English
T: +230 266 9448/9
W: www.northfieldsonline.com

MONACO

THE INTERNATIONAL SCHOOL OF MONACO

10-12 Quai Antoine Premier, Monte Carlo 98000
DP Coordinator Hannah Gettel
Languages English, French
T: +377 9325 6820
E: admissions@ismonaco.com
W: ismonaco.org

See full details on page 223

MONTENEGRO

KSI MONTENEGRO

Seljanovo bb, Porto Montenegro, Tivat
DP Coordinator Jacqueline Cussen
MYP Coordinator Kevin Osborne
PYP Coordinator Marija Djukic
Languages English
T: +382 32 672 655
E: info@ksi-montenegro.com
W: www.ksi-montenegro.com

See full details on page 151

MOROCCO

Casablanca American School

Route de la Mecque, Lotissement Ougoug, Quartier Californie, Casablanca 20150
DP Coordinator Alina Zamfirescu
Languages English
T: +212 522 79 39 39
W: www.cas.ac.ma

Écoles Al Madina, Site Ain Sebaa

Km 9, route de Rabat, Hay Chabab, Ain sébâa, Casablanca 20250
MYP Coordinator Zhor Lerhmame
Languages French, Arabic
T: +212 0522 75 69 69
W: www.almadina.ma

Écoles Al Madina, Site Californie

Lotissement Bellevue 2, Rue 3 Californie, Casablanca
MYP Coordinator Kamar Guennoun
Languages French, Arabic
T: +212 522 5050 9 7/8/9
W: www.almadina.ma

Écoles Al Madina, Site Polo

52 Bd Nador, Casablanca 20420
MYP Coordinator Zhor Lerhmame
Languages French, Arabic
T: +21 20 22 210 505
W: www.almadina.ma

GDGSR – Khouribga

Bld 2 Mars, Khouribga
MYP Coordinator Salah Toufani
Languages Arabic, French
T: +212 (0)6 00 03 40 11
W: www.gdgsr.ma/site/khouribga

GDGSR – Youssoufia

Rue Allal Ben Abdellah, Youssoufia
MYP Coordinator Habiba Maanaoui
Languages Arabic, French
T: +212 (0)6 00 03 77 53
W: www.gdgsr.ma/site/youssoufia

George Washington Academy

Km 5.6 Rte d'Azemour, Dar Bouazza, Casablanca 20220
DP Coordinator Mason Grine
Languages English, French, Arabic
T: +212 522 953 000
W: www.gwa.ac.ma

Groupe scolaire Alkaraouiyine

350 Boulevard Sebta, Lotisement Anfa, Mohammedia 28000
MYP Coordinator Hanane Sbit
Languages Arabic, French
T: +212 23 30 13 57
W: www.alkaraouiyine.ma

GROUPE SCOLAIRE LA RÉSIDENCE

87-89 Avenue 2 mars, Casablanca
MYP Coordinator Mrs. Fatima Nassimi
Languages French
T: +212 522 809050/51
E: gsr@gsr.ac.ma
W: www.gsr.ac.ma

See full details on page 108

Institut Scolaire les Palmiers

76 Rue Abdelhamid Bnou Badis, Casablanca Ain sebâa 20250
MYP Coordinator Mohamed Marouane
PYP Coordinator Fatima Maroua
Languages Arabic, English, French
T: +212 522343757
W: www.institutscolairelespalmiers.com

Morocco

Institution El Yakada
Lotissement Koutoubia, Route de Kenitra, Salé 11160
MYP Coordinator Mokhtar Saufi
Languages English
T: +212 (0)5 37 84 48 44
W: www.elyakada.com

International School of Morocco
3 Impasse Jules Gros, Quartier Oasis, Casablanca 20150
PYP Coordinator Meredith Achlim
Languages English
T: +212 0 552 993 987
W: www.ism-c.ma

Newton International School
Rue Ibn Khafaja, Anfa, Mohammedia 208000
DP Coordinator Mohamed Hatti
MYP Coordinator Khalid Mouroudy
Languages French
T: +212 5 23 31 65 52
W: www.nischool.org

Rabat American School
c/o US Embassy, BP 120 Rabat
DP Coordinator Fabienne Gerard
Languages English
T: +212 537 671 476
W: www.ras.ma

MOZAMBIQUE

Aga Khan Academy Maputo
Av. Zimbabwe, 212 Matola, Maputo
PYP Coordinator Maike Silver
Languages English, Portuguese
T: +258 21 720963
W: www.agakhanacademies.org/maputo

American International School of Mozambique
Caixa Postal 2026, Maputo
DP Coordinator Gabriel Di Mauro
MYP Coordinator Michael BondClegg
PYP Coordinator Taryn BondClegg
Languages English
T: +258 21 49 1994
W: www.aism-moz.com

Enko Riverside International School
Rua José Macamo 175, Polana, Maputo
DP Coordinator Lois Katsidzira(Kandwe)
Languages English
T: +258 845 40 91 51
W: www.enkoeducation.com/maputo

NAMIBIA

Windhoek International School
P/Bag 16007, Scheppmann Street, Pioneerspark, Windhoek
DP Coordinator Padmini Nadar-Japal
PYP Coordinator Avril van Zyl
Languages English
T: +264 61 241 783
W: www.wis.edu.na

NETHERLANDS

AMERICAN SCHOOL OF THE HAGUE
Rijksstraatweg 200, 2241BX Wassenaar
DP Coordinator Victor Ferreira
Languages English
T: +31 70 512 1060
E: admissions@ash.nl
W: www.ash.nl

See full details on page 73

Amsterdam International Community School
Prinses Irenestraat 59, 1077 WV Amsterdam
DP Coordinator Stavros Melachroinos
MYP Coordinator Elizabeth Ann Young
Languages English
T: +31 20 577 1240
W: www.aics.espritscholen.nl

DENISE- De Nieuwe Internationale School Esprit
Pieter de Hoochstraat 78, 1071 EJ Amsterdam
DP Coordinator Marlise Achterbergh
Languages English
T: +31 (0)20 480 2700
W: denise.espritscholen.nl

EERDE INTERNATIONAL BOARDING SCHOOL NETHERLANDS
Kasteellaan 1, Ommen PJ 7731
DP Coordinator Aaron Lane
Languages English
T: +31 529 451452
E: admission@eerdeibs.nl
W: www.eerde.nl

See full details on page 98

Gifted Minds International School
c/o Corporate Office, Landtong 18, Amstelveen 1186 GP
PYP Coordinator Ramesh Mahalingam
Languages English
T: 0031 23 888 8874
W: www.giftedmindsinternationalschool.com/gifted-minds-international-school/

International School Almere
Heliumweg 61, Almere Poort 1362 JA
DP Coordinator Simona Ghizdareanu
MYP Coordinator Sabrina Stremke
Languages English
T: +31 36 7600750
W: www.internationalschoolalmere.nl

International School Breda
Mozartlaan 27, Breda 4837 EH
DP Coordinator Mark Sherlock
MYP Coordinator Jean Atkinson
Languages English
T: +31 76 5601350
W: www.isbreda.nl

International School Delft
Jaffalaan 9, 2628BX Delft
PYP Coordinator Marianne Mink
Languages English
T: +31 1528 50038
W: www.isdelft.com

International School Eindhoven
Oirschotsedijk 14b, 5651GC Eindhoven
DP Coordinator David Bailly
MYP Coordinator Laura Malone
Languages English, Dutch
T: +31 (0)40 251 9437
W: www.isecampus.nl

International School Hilversum 'Alberdingk Thijm'
Emmastraat 56, Hilversum 1213 AL
DP Coordinator Nicola Isaac
MYP Coordinator Rachel Gorman
PYP Coordinator Anniek Bruijnzeels
Languages English
T: + 31 35 6729931
W: www.ishilversum.nl

International School of Amsterdam
PO Box 920, Sportlaan 45, Amstelveen 1180 AX
DP Coordinator Matt Lynch
MYP Coordinator Paul Griffiths
PYP Coordinator Lisa Verkerk
Languages English
T: +31 20 347 1111
W: www.isa.nl

International School The Rijnlands Lyceum Oegstgeest
Apollolaan 1, Oegstgeest BA 2341
DP Coordinator Jonathan Symmons
MYP Coordinator Annelies Lynn Brabant
Languages English
T: +31 71 5193 555
W: www.isrlo.nl

International School Twente
Tiemeister 20, Enschede 7541 WG
DP Coordinator Anke Kolkman
Languages English
T: +31 (0)53 482 11 00
W: www.istwente.org

International School Utrecht
Van Bijnkershoeklaan 8, Utrecht 3527 XL
DP Coordinator Geertje Van Hal
MYP Coordinator Liam Moody
PYP Coordinator Eryn Wiseman
Languages English
T: +31 30 870 04 00
W: www.isutrecht.nl

IPS Hilversum
Rembrandtlaan 30, Hilversum BH 1213
PYP Coordinator Stephanie Noda
Languages English
T: +31 35 6216 053
W: www.ipsviolen.nl

Laar & Berg
Langsakker 4, Laren (NH) 1251 GB
MYP Coordinator Eva Goossens
Languages English
T: +31 3553 95422
W: www.laarenberg.nl

Maartenscollege & International School Groningen
Hemmenlaan 2, 9751 NS Haren
DP Coordinator Joke Jansma
MYP Coordinator Simone Hartholt
Languages English
T: +31 50 537 52 00
W: maartenscollege.nl

Nord Anglia International School Rotterdam
Verhulstlaan 21, Rotterdam 3055WJ
DP Coordinator Eva Tarrasón Dualde
Languages English
T: +31 10 422 5351
W: www.aisr.nl

Rivers International School Arnhem
Groningensingel 1245, Arnhem 6835 HZ
DP Coordinator Monique Vergoossen-Ottevanger
MYP Coordinator Micha Oosterhoff
Languages English
T: +31 26 3202840
W: www.arnheminternationalschool.nl

ROTTERDAM INTERNATIONAL SECONDARY SCHOOL
Bentinckl aan 294, 3039 KK Rotterdam
DP Coordinator Ms Miranda de Vries
Languages English
T: +31 (0)10 890 77 44
E: admissions.riss@wolfert.nl
W: riss.wolfert.nl
See full details on page 183

The British School in The Netherlands
Vrouw Avenweg 640, Den Haag 2493 WZ
CP Coordinator Michelle Cooke
DP Coordinator Michelle Cooke
Languages English
T: +31 (0)70 315 4077
W: www.britishschool.nl

THE INTERNATIONAL SCHOOL OF THE HAGUE
Wijndaelerduin 1, The Hague 2554 BX
CP Coordinator Alma Trumic
DP Coordinator Camelia Constantinescu
MYP Coordinator Maria Lamminaho
Languages English
T: +31 70 328 1450
E: admissions@ishthehague.nl
W: www.ishthehague.nl
See full details on page 224

UWC MAASTRICHT
Discusworp 65, Maastricht 6225 XP
DP Coordinator Maurice Tonnaer & Jack Borthwick
MYP Coordinator Louis Odendaal
Languages English
T: +31 432 410 410
E: admissions@uwcmaastricht.nl
W: www.uwcmaastricht.nl
See full details on page 232

NIGER

Lycée Enoch Olinga
B.P. 366, Quartier Daresalam (face marché Daresalam), Niamey 8001
DP Coordinator Fumundjibo Kahila
Languages French
T: +227 94 54 60 75
W: www.lycee-enoch-olinga.org

NIGERIA

American International School of Lagos
Behind 1004 Federal Estates, Lagos
DP Coordinator Scott Williams
Languages English
T: +234 11 77 64 535
W: www.aislagos.org

British Nigerian Academy
Drive 6, Prince and Princess, Duboyi District, P.M.B 5285, Wuse, Abuja
DP Coordinator Dawn Savage
Languages English
T: +234 8144084741
W: www.bna.edu.ng

Greensprings School, Lagos
P.O. Box 4801K Ikeja Headquarters, Ikeja, 32 Olatunde Ayoola Avenue, Anthony, Lagos
DP Coordinator Isaac Obashe
Languages English
T: +234 8776874
W: www.greenspringsschool.com

Ibadan International School
24 Jibowu Crescent, Iyaganku, Ibadan
PYP Coordinator Helen Chatburn-Ojehomon
Languages English
T: +234 2 291 8483
W: www.ibadaninternationalschool.com

NORWAY

Aalesund International School
Borgundvegen 418, 6015 Aalesund, Møre og Romsdal
PYP Coordinator Kristen Carulli
Languages English
T: +47 908 69 948
W: www.aais.no

Arendal International School
Julius Smiths vei 40, 4817 His, Aust-Agder
MYP Coordinator Marius Larsen Strand
PYP Coordinator Will Warren
Languages English
T: +47 37 055 100
W: www.aischool.no

Arendal Videregående Skole
Postboks 325, 4803 Arendal, Aust-Agder
DP Coordinator Haldor Berge
Languages English
T: +47 37 00 02 00
W: www.arendal.vgs.no

Ås videregående skole
Postboks 10, 1430 Ås, Akershus
DP Coordinator Graham Ryan
Languages English
T: +47 64 97 57 00
W: www.aas.vgs.no

Asker International School
Johan Drengsruds Vei 60, 1383 Asker, Akershus
MYP Coordinator Brent Jane
PYP Coordinator Andrew Johns
Languages English
T: +47 9089 0609
W: www.askeris.no

Bergen Cathedral School
Postboks 414 Marken, Kong Oscarsgate 36, 5832 Bergen, Hordaland
DP Coordinator Gillian Boniface
Languages English
T: +47 55 33 82 00
W: www.hordaland.no/bergenkatedralskole

Bjørnholt Skole
Slimeveien 17, 1277 Oslo
DP Coordinator Eirik Hardersen
Languages English
T: +47 23 46 35 00
W: bjornholt.osloskolen.no

Blindern Videregående Skole
Sognsveien 80, 0855 Oslo
DP Coordinator Emmanuelle Bjerkem
MYP Coordinator Margaret Puntervold
Languages English, Norwegian
T: +47 90 80 80 59
W: blindern.vgs.no

British International School of Stavanger
Gauselbakken 107, Gausel, 4032 Stavanger, Rogaland
CP Coordinator Victoria Reed
DP Coordinator Victoria Reed
MYP Coordinator Inger Torkelsen
PYP Coordinator Susanne Fischer
Languages English
T: +47 519 50 250
W: www.biss.no

Children's International School Fredrikstad
Torsnesveien 5-7, 1630 Gamle Fredrikstad, Østfold
MYP Coordinator Kylie Curteis
PYP Coordinator Alison Kronstad
Languages English
T: +47 69 00 25 00
W: cisschools.no/fredrikstad

Children's International School Moss
Moss Verk 1, 1534 Moss, Østfold
MYP Coordinator Pamela Castberg
PYP Coordinator Shauna Ross
Languages English
T: +47 400 01 128
W: www.cismoss.no

Elverum videregående skole
Postboks 246, 2402 Elverum, Hedmark
DP Coordinator Mikael Sjöholm
Languages English
T: +47 6243 1500
W: www.elverum.vgs.no

Fagerhaug International School
Post Office Box 4, 7510 Skatval, Trøndelag
PYP Coordinator Cherise Kristoffersen
Languages English
T: +47 74 84 07 70
W: fagerhaugoppvekst.no/en/international-school

Frederik II videregående skole
PB 523, Merkurveien 2, 1612 Fredrikstad, Østfold
DP Coordinator Lise Ringstad
Languages English
T: +47 69 36 64 00
W: www.frederikii.vgs.no

Gjøvik videregående skole
PO Box 534, 2803 Gjøvik, Oppland
DP Coordinator Molly Williams Thoresen
Languages English
T: +47 61149400
W: www.gjovik.vgs.no

Gjøvikregionen International School
Studieveien 17, 2815 Gjøvik, Oppland
MYP Coordinator Paul Venter
PYP Coordinator Heidi Brenner
Languages English, Norwegian
T: +47 240 76 141
W: www.gjovikis.no
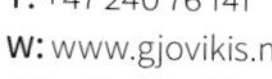

Haugesund International School
Halandvegen 175, 4260 Torvastad, Karmøy, Rogaland
MYP Coordinator Daniel Krolack
PYP Coordinator Ryan Moore
Languages English, Norwegian
T: +47 40670871
W: www.hischool.no
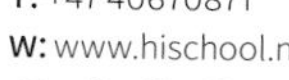

International School of Bergen
Sandslihaugen 30, 5254 Bergen, Hordaland
MYP Coordinator Peter Ledger
PYP Coordinator Zachary Gagnon
Languages English
T: +47 55 30 63 30
W: www.isob.no

Norway

International School of Stavanger
Treskeveien 3, 4043 Hafrsfjord, Rogaland
DP Coordinator Lynn Park
Languages English
T: +47 51 55 43 00
W: www.isstavanger.no

International School Telemark
Hovet Ring 7, 3931 Porsgrunn, Telemark
MYP Coordinator Julie Strøm
PYP Coordinator Tjandra Purnama
Languages English
T: +47 35291400
W: www.istelemark.no

Kirkenes Videregående Skole
Postboks 44, 9916 Hesseng, Finnmark
DP Coordinator Juha Törmikoski
Languages English
T: +47 78 96 18 00
W: www.kirkenes.vgs.no

Kongsberg International School
Dyrmyrgata 39-41, 3611 Kongsberg, Buskerud
MYP Coordinator Hilde Bakken
PYP Coordinator Sofie Jørstad
Languages English
T: +47 32 29 93 80
W: www.kischool.org

Kongsberg videregående skole
Postboks 424, 3604 Kongsberg, Buskerud
DP Coordinator Kelvin Peters
Languages English
T: +47 3286 7600
W: www.kongsberg.vgs.no

Kristiansand International School
Kongsgård alle 20, 4631 Kristiansand, Vest-Agder
MYP Coordinator Susan Heiseldal
PYP Coordinator Tabitha Ford
Languages English
T: +47 95826601
W: www.kisschool.no

Kristiansand Katedralskole Gimle
Postboks 1010, Lundsiden, 4687 Kristiansand, Vest-Agder
DP Coordinator Vibeke Lauritsen
Languages English
T: +47 38 70 50 00
W: www.kkg.vgs.no

Lillestrom Videregaende Skole
Postboks 333, Henrik Wergelands gt. 1, 2001 Lillestrom, Akershus
DP Coordinator Line Skaugset
Languages Norwegian, English
T: +47 63 89 06 00
W: www.lillestrom.vgs.no

Manglerud skole
Plogveien 22, 0681 Oslo
PYP Coordinator Liv Halvorsen
Languages English
T: +47 22 75 73 10
W: manglerud.osloskolen.no

Nesbru Videregående Skole
Halvard Torgersensvei 8, Postbox 38, 1378 Nesbru, Akershus
DP Coordinator Helen Elizabeth Laney-Mortensen
Languages English
T: +47 66 854 408
W: www.nesbru.vgs.no

Norlights International School
Skådalsveien 33, 0781 Oslo
MYP Coordinator Kamil Koc
PYP Coordinator Sakhi Kochar
Languages English
T: +47 40 07 35 50
W: nlis.noredu.no

Oslo International School
PO Box 53, 1318 Bekkestua, Akershus
DP Coordinator Helen Piene
Languages English
T: +47 67 8182 90
W: www.oslointernationalschool.no

Porsgrunn videregående skole
Kjølnes ring 58, 3918 Porsgrunn, Telemark
DP Coordinator Margrethe Hauff
Languages English
T: +47 35 91 75 06
W: www.porsgrunn.vgs.no

Sandefjord Videregående Skole
Postboks 2006, 3202 Sandefjord, Vestfold
DP Coordinator Siân Stickler
Languages English
T: +47 33 488 690
W: www.svgs.vfk.no

Senja Vidaregåande Skole
Skoleveien 55, 9300 Finnsnes, Troms
DP Coordinator Vivian Jakobsen
Languages English
T: +47 77 85 08 00
W: www.finnfjordbotn.vgs.no

Skagerak International School
Framnesveien 7, 3222 Sandefjord, Vestfold
DP Coordinator Niklas Winander
MYP Coordinator Katheryn Tester
PYP Coordinator Andrea Helgesen
Languages English
T: +47 33456500
W: www.skagerak.org

Spjelkavik videregående skole
Langhaugen 22, 6011 Alesund, Møre og Romsdal
DP Coordinator Camilla Moritz-Olsen
Languages English
T: +47 70178230
W: www.spjelkavik.vgs.no

St Olav Videregaende Skole
Jens Zetlitzgt. 33, 4008 Stavanger, Rogaland
DP Coordinator Fiona Andvik
Languages English
T: +47 51 84 99 00
W: www.st-olav.vgs.no

Tromsø International School
4 Breiviklia, 9019 Tromsø, Troms
MYP Coordinator Rosie Hydar
PYP Coordinator Susanne Hebnes
Languages English
T: +47 99200780
W: www.trint.org

Trondheim International School
Festningsgata 2, 7014 Trondheim, Trøndelag
MYP Coordinator Virginia Neilsen
PYP Coordinator Hope Steen
Languages English, Norweigan
T: +47 7351 4800
W: www.this.no

Trondheim Katedralskole
Munkegaten 8, 7013 Trondheim, Trøndelag
DP Coordinator Elin Øksnes
Languages English
T: +47 73 19 55 00
W: www.trondheim-katedral.vgs.no

UWC RED CROSS NORDIC
Hauglandsvegen 304, 6968 Flekke, Sogn og Fjordane
DP Coordinator Natasha Lambert
Languages English
T: +47 5773 7000
E: info@uwcrcn.no
W: uwcrcn.no
See full details on page 233

Vardafjell Videregående Skole
Spannaveien 25, 5532 Haugesund, Rogaland
DP Coordinator Hanne Christine Gilje Birkeland
Languages English
T: +47 5270 9910
W: www.vardafjell.vgs.no

OMAN

ABA - An IB World School
PO Box 372, Medinat Al Sultan Qaboos, Post Code 115, Muscat 115
DP Coordinator Guy Essex
MYP Coordinator Megel Barker
PYP Coordinator Wayne Derrick
Languages English
T: +968 24955800
W: www.abaoman.edu.om

Al Batinah International School
PO Box 193, Postal Code 321, Sohar
DP Coordinator Jonathan Adams
PYP Coordinator Cheryl Isles
Languages English
T: +968 26850001
W: www.abisoman.com

Al Sahwa Schools
PO Box 644, PC 116, Mina-Al-Fahal, Muscat
PYP Coordinator Sandi Stone
Languages English, Arabic
T: + 968 2460 7620 / 7621 / 2469 3887

MYSCHOOL OMAN
Al Hail South, Al Seeb, Al Huda Street, Way # 2933, Building # 3344, Muscat
PYP Coordinator Emna Beji
Languages English, Arabic
T: +968 24555171
E: info@myschool.edu.om
W: www.myschool.edu.om
See full details on page 168

OURPLANET International School Muscat
Al-Inshirah Street, Building No. 205, Plot No. 95, Block No. 221, Muscat, 111
PYP Coordinator Ana Castro
Languages English
T: +968 2200 5642
W: www.ourplanet-muscat.com

THE SULTAN'S SCHOOL
PO Box 665, Seeb 121
DP Coordinator Charles Hearsum
Languages Arabic, English
T: +968 24536 777
E: principal@sultansschool.org
W: www.sultansschool.org
See full details on page 226

PALESTINE

Ramallah Friends School (Lower School)
Ramallah
PYP Coordinator Sandy Ziadeh
Languages English
T: +970 2 295 6240
W: www.rfs.edu.ps

Ramallah Friends School (Upper School)
P.O Box 66, Ramallah
DP Coordinator Luai Awwad
MYP Coordinator Mohammad Suleiman
Languages English
T: +970 2 295 2286
W: www.rfs.edu.ps

POLAND

2 Spoleczne Liceum Ogolnoksztalcace STO im. Pawla Jasienicy (2SLO)
ul. Nowowiejska 5, Warsaw 00-643
DP Coordinator Tomasz Mazur
Languages English
T: +48 22 825 11 99
W: www.2slo.pl

33 Liceum im M Kopernika
ul Bema 76, Warsaw 01-225
DP Coordinator Agnieszka White
MYP Coordinator Iwona Berse
Languages English
T: +48 22 632 75 70

American School of Warsaw
Bielawa, ul Warszawska 202, Konstancin-Jeziorna 05-520
DP Coordinator Patricia Deo
MYP Coordinator Elizabeth Swanson
PYP Coordinator Miranda Rose
Languages English
T: +48 22 702 8500
W: www.aswarsaw.org

British International School of Cracow
ul.Smolensk 25, Kraków 31-108
DP Coordinator Patrick Lagendijk
Languages English
T: +48 1229 264 78
W: www.bisc.krakow.pl

Gimnazjum Dwujezyczne Nr 26
Grochowa 13, Wroclaw 53523
MYP Coordinator Katarzyna Druzycka
Languages Polish, English
T: +48 71 798 6913
W: www.lo5.wroc.pl

I Liceum Ogolnoksztalcace Dwujezyczne im. E. Dembowskiego w Gliwicach
ul Zimnej Wody 8, Gliwice 44-100
DP Coordinator Anita Kwiatkowska
MYP Coordinator Joanna Korek
Languages English
T: +48 32 2314732
W: www.zso10.gliwice.pl

I Liceum Ogólnoksztalcace im St Staszica w Lublinie
Al Raclawickie 26, Lublin 20043
DP Coordinator Monika Trznadel
Languages English
T: +48 81 441 1460
W: www.1lo.lublin.pl

I Liceum Ogólnoksztalcace im. A. Mickiewicza w Olsztynie
Mickiewicza 6, Olsztyn 10-551
DP Coordinator Lukasz Jakubowski
Languages English, Polish
T: +48 (89) 527 5353
W: lo1.olsztyn.pl/mm

II Liceum Ogólnoksztalcace im Mieszka I
ul Henryka Poboznego 2, Szczecin 70507
DP Coordinator Artur Strozynski
Languages English
T: +48 91 433 61 17
W: www.lo2.szczecin.pl

II Liceum Ogólnoksztalcace im Mikolaja Kopernika w Lesznie
Ul Boleslawa Prusa 33, Leszno 64-100
DP Coordinator Jolanta Perczak
Languages English
T: +486 5526 8485
W: www.IILO.leszno.eu

II Liceum Ogólnoksztalcace im Stefana Batorego
ul Mysliwiecka 6, Warsawa 00459
DP Coordinator Joanna Szczesniak
Languages English
T: +48 22 628 2101
W: www.batory.edu.pl

II Liceum Ogólnoksztalcace im. Romualda Traugutta w Czestochowie
Gmina Miasto Czestochowa, ul.Slaska 11/13, Czestochowa 42-217
DP Coordinator Tomasz Muskala
Languages English, Polish
T: +48 343612568
W: www.traugutt.net

II Liceum Ogólnoksztalcace im. Tadeusza Kosciuszki
ul. Szkolna 5, Kalisz 62800
DP Coordinator Alina Rzepiak
Languages English
T: +48 6276 76657
W: www.2lo.kalisz.pl

II Liceum Ogólnoksztalcace in Bialystok
ul. Narewska 11, Bialystok 15840
DP Coordinator Emilia Makarska
Languages English
T: +48 85 6511416
W: zso2bialystok.pl

II LO im Gen Zamoyskiej i H Modrzejewskiej
Matejki 8/10, Poznan 60760
DP Coordinator Edyta Sobczak
Languages English
T: +48 61 866 2892
W: www.2lo.poznan.pl

III Liceum Ogolnoksztalcace im A. Mickiewicza w Katowicach
ul. Mickiewicza 11, Katowice 40-092
DP Coordinator Beata Zygadlewicz-Kocus
Languages English
T: +48 32 258 93 05
W: www.mickiewicz.katowice.pl

III Liceum Ogolnoksztalcace, Gdynia
Legionów 27, Gdynia 81-405
DP Coordinator Zofia Krakowiak-Michlewicz
MYP Coordinator Marta Smalara-Lewandowska
Languages English, Polish
T: +48 58 622 1833
W: www.lo3.gdynia.pl

International American School
Ul Dembego 18, Warszawa 02-796
DP Coordinator Kenneth McBride
Languages English
T: +48 22 649 1442
W: www.ias.edu.pl

International European School Warsaw
ul. Wiertnicza 140, Warsaw 02-952
DP Coordinator Malcolm Bannerman
Languages English
T: +48 22 842 44 48
W: ies.waw.pl/en

International High School of Wroclaw
ul. Raclawicka 101, 53-149 Wroclaw
MYP Coordinator Dorota Zielazna
Languages English
T: +48 71 782 26 26
W: www.highschool.fem.org.pl

International Primary School
52 Drukarska St, Wroclaw 53-312
PYP Coordinator Magdalena Blum
Languages English
T: +48 503 188 843
W: www.ipschool.pl

International School of EKOLA
Ul Zielinskiego 56, Wroclaw 53534
DP Coordinator Adriana Kurowska-Mitas
Languages English
T: +48 71 3614 370
W: www.ekola.edu.pl

International School of Gdansk
ul. Sucha 29, Gdansk 80 531
PYP Coordinator Malgorzata Kilian
Languages English, Polish
T: +48 58 342 31 00
W: www.isg.gfo.pl

International School of Krakow
ul Sw Floriana 57, Lusina, 30-698 Krakow
DP Coordinator Lou Panetta
Languages English
T: +48 12 270 1409
W: www.iskonline.org

International School of Poznan
Ul Taczanowskiego 18, Poznan 60-147
DP Coordinator Iwona Richter
PYP Coordinator Malgorzata Pyda
Languages English
T: +48 61 646 37 60
W: www.isop.pl

IS of Bydgoszcz
Ul. Galczynskiego 23, Bydgoszcz 85-322
DP Coordinator Malgorzata Kozielewicz
MYP Coordinator Marta Dereszynska
PYP Coordinator Anna Smigielska
Languages English
T: +48 523 411 424
W: www.isob.ukw.edu.pl

POLAND

IV Liceum Ogolnokształcace im.Emilii Szczanieckiej
ul Pomorska 16, Lódz 91-416
DP Coordinator Malgorzata Kudra
Languages English
T: +48 42 6336293
W: www.4liceum.pl

Jam Saheba Digvijay Sinhji
Ul Raszyńska 22, Warszawa 02 026
DP Coordinator Brian Williamson
Languages English
T: +48 22 822 25 15
W: www.bednarska.edu.pl

Kolegium Europejskie
ul. Metalowców 6, Kraków 31-537
DP Coordinator Edyta Zajac
Languages English
T: +48 12 632 46 29
W: www.ke.edu.pl

Meridian International High School
ul. Gladka 31, Warsaw 02-172
DP Coordinator Magorzata Byca
Languages English
T: +48 510 161 597
W: www.meridian.edu.pl

Monnet International School
ul. Abramowskiego 4, Warsaw 02-659
DP Coordinator Joanna Majorek
MYP Coordinator Angelika Maj
PYP Coordinator Aneta Borkowska
Languages English
T: +48 22 852 31 10
W: www.maturamiedzynarodowa.pl

Open Future International School
ul. Kwiecista 25, 30-389 Kraków
PYP Coordinator Anna Boguń
Languages English, Polish
T: +48 123 524 525
W: www.openfuture.edu.pl

Paderewski Private Grammar School
ul Symfoniczna 1, Lublin 20-853
DP Coordinator Agnieszka Bojczuk
MYP Coordinator Magdalena Krzeminska
PYP Coordinator Katarzyna Kijek-Kubejko
Languages English
T: +48 81 740-75-43
W: www.paderewski.lublin.pl

Private Primary School 97
Abramowskiego Street 4, Warsaw 02-659
PYP Coordinator Agnieszka Koterwas
Languages English
T: +48 22 853 36 60
W: www.leonardo.edu.pl

Prywatne Liceum Ogolnokształcace im.M.Wankowicza
ul. Witosa 18, Katowice 40-832
DP Coordinator Justyna Proksza
Languages English
T: +48 32 254 9194
W: wankowicz.edu.pl

Szczecin International School
ul Starzynskiego 3-4, Szczecin 70506
DP Coordinator Diane Howlett
Languages English
T: +48 91 4240 300
W: www.sis.info.pl

Szczecinska Szkola Witruwianska SVS
Wojska Polskiego, 164, Szczecin 71-335
PYP Coordinator Marta Zaborowska
Languages English, Polish
T: +48 512 868 176
W: svs.edu.pl

The British School Warsaw
ul. Limanowskiego 15, 02-943 Warsaw
DP Coordinator Jacek Latkowski
Languages English
T: +48 22 842 32 81
W: www.thebritishschool.pl

The Canadian School of Warsaw
Kanadyjska Szkola Podstawowa, Ul. Belska 7, Warszawa 02-638
PYP Coordinator Christine Mamo
Languages English
T: +48 22 646 92 89
W: www.canadian-school.pl

The Nazareth Middle and High School in Warsaw
ul. Czerniakowska 137, Warszawa 00-720
DP Coordinator Marcin Jurkowski
Languages English, Polish
T: +48 22 841 3854/+48 601 644 102
W: www.nazaretanki.edu.pl

V Liceum Ogolnokształcace in Gem
Jakuba Jasinskiego, ul Grochowa 13, Warsaw 53 523
DP Coordinator Barbara Czuszkiewicz
Languages English
T: +48 71 361 92 66
W: lo5.wroc.pl

VI Liceum Ogólnokształcace im J Slowackiego w Kielcach
ul Gagarina 5, Kielce 25031
DP Coordinator Edyta Roman
Languages English
T: +48 41 361 55 56
W: slowacki.kielce.eu

VIII PRYWATNE AKADEMICKIE LICEUM OGÓLNOKSZTALCACE
ul Karmelicka 45, 31-128 Krakow
DP Coordinator Ewa Dudek
Languages English
T: +48 12 632 93 13
E: dyrektor@pack.edu.pl
W: www.pack.edu.pl
See full details on page 234

Wroclaw International School
Foundation of International Education, ul. Raclawicka 101, 53-149 Wroclaw
MYP Coordinator Jill Bieniek
PYP Coordinator Maria Kachmar
Languages English
T: +48 71 782 26 24
W: www.wis.fem.org.pl

XXXV Liceum Ogólnokształcace z Oddzialami Dwujezycznymi im. Boleslawa Prusa
Zwyciezców 7/9, Warsaw 03-936
DP Coordinator Katarzyna Krajewska
Languages English, Polish
T: +48 22 617 74 13
W: www.prus.edu.pl

Zespól Szkól nr 1 im. Ignacego Paderewskiego in Walbrzych
ul. Paderewskiego 17, Walbrzych, Dolnoslaskie 58301
DP Coordinator Beata Urbaniak
MYP Coordinator Beata Urbaniak
Languages English, Polish
T: +48 74 842 36 83
W: www.1lo.walbrzych.pl

Zespól Szkól nr 6 w Plocku
4 3-go Maja Street, Plock, Mazowieckie 09402
DP Coordinator Marcin Jaroszewski
Languages English
T: +48 24 364 59 20
W: www.jagiellonka.plock.pl

Zespol Szkol Numer 4 – IX Liceum Ogólnokształcace
Ul Zofii Nalkowskiej 9, Bydgoszcz 86866
DP Coordinator Monika Obrebska
Languages English
T: +48 52 3610 885
W: www.lo9gim17.pl

Zespól Szkól Ogólnokształcacych im. Pawla z Tarsu
ul Poezji 19, Warsaw 04-994
DP Coordinator Agnieszka Dziwota
Languages English
T: +48 22 789 14 02
W: www.kulszkola.pl

Zespól Szkól Ogólnokształcacych No 2 in Tarnow
ul Mickiewicza 16, Tarnów 33100
DP Coordinator Maria Trojanowska
Languages English
T: +48 14 655 88 95
W: www.ii-lo.tarnow.pl

ZSO No.13 Gdansk
ul Topolowa 7, Gdansk 80255
DP Coordinator Alina Spychala
Languages English
T: +48 5834 10671
W: www.lo3.gdansk.ids.pl

PORTUGAL

Carlucci American International School of Lisbon
Rua Antonio dos Reis, 95, Linhó, Sintra 2710-301
DP Coordinator Ana Almeida
Languages English
T: +351 21 923 9800
W: www.caislisbon.org

Colégio Mira Rio
Estrada de Telheiras, no. 113, Lisbon 1600-768
DP Coordinator Isabel Pinto
Languages English, Portuguese
T: +351 21 303 0480
W: www.colegiomirario.pt

Colegio Planalto
Rua Armindo Rodrigues, 28, Lisbon 1600-414
DP Coordinator Antonio Leitao
Languages English
T: +351 21 754 15 30 / 29
W: www.colegioplanalto.pt

Escola da A.P.E.L.
Caminho dos Saltos, nº 6, Funchal 9050-219
DP Coordinator Graça Valerio
Languages English
T: +351 2917 40470
W: www.escola-apel.com

INTERNATIONAL SHARING SCHOOL
Caminho Dos Saltos 6, 9050-219 Funchal, Madeira
MYP Coordinator Jane Gordon
PYP Coordinator Jenie Noite
Languages English
T: +351 291 773218
E: office@madeira.sharingschool.org
W: www.sharingschool.org
See full details on page 141

OEIRAS INTERNATIONAL SCHOOL
Quinta Nossa Senhora da Conceicao, Rua Antero de Quental no 7, Barcarena 2730-013
CP Coordinator Ramona Dietrich
DP Coordinator Jan Van Hees
MYP Coordinator Carol Pratt
Languages English
T: +351 211935330
E: info@oeirasinternationalschool.com
W: www.oeirasinternationalschool.com
See full details on page 172

Oporto British School
Rua da Cerca 338, Foz do Douro, Porto 4150-201
DP Coordinator John Simpson
Languages English
T: +351 22 616 6660
W: www.obs.edu.pt

SAINT DOMINIC'S INTERNATIONAL SCHOOL, PORTUGAL
Rua Maria Brown, Outeiro de Polima, 2785-816 S Domingos de Rana
DP Coordinator Carla Morais
MYP Coordinator Simon Downing
PYP Coordinator Fiona Kemp
Languages English
T: +351 21 444 0434
E: school@dominics-int.org
W: www.dominics-int.org
See full details on page 185

St Julian's School
Secondary School, Quinta Nova, Carcavelos Codex 2776-601
DP Coordinator Noelle Lobato
Languages English
T: +351 21 4585300
W: www.stjulians.com

St. Peter's International School
Quinta dos Barreleiros CCI 3952, Volta da Pedra – 2950-201, Palmela
DP Coordinator Telma Fresta
Languages English, Portuguese
T: +351 21 233 6990
W: st-peters-school.com

QATAR

ACS Doha International School
PO Box 200568, Al Oyoun Street, Al Gharrafa, Doha
DP Coordinator Oliver Lemuel Chua
MYP Coordinator Holly Fairbrother
PYP Coordinator Barbara Carolissen
Languages English
T: +974 4000 9797
W: www.acs-schools.com

Al Bayan Educational Complex for Girls
PO Box 23533, Doha
DP Coordinator Shaheen Khadri
Languages English
T: +974 44591791
W: albayansec.education.qa

Al Wakra Independent Secondary School
PO Box 80150, Al Wakrah
DP Coordinator Ghassan N. Badwan
Languages English
T: +974 464 3739
W: wissb.edupage.org

American School of Doha
PO Box 22090, Doha
DP Coordinator Katrina Charles
Languages English
T: +974 4459 1500
W: www.asd.edu.qa

Arab International Academy
Al Sadd Area, Sports Roundabout, Doha 15810
DP Coordinator Nael Hamamra
MYP Coordinator Abdullah Azzam Khan
PYP Coordinator Rasha Hammoud
Languages Arabic, English
T: +974 40414999
W: www.aia.qa

Compass International School Doha, Madinat Khalifa
P.O. Box 22463, Al Baihaqi Street, Building 34, Zone 32, Street 926, Madinat Khalifa
DP Coordinator Justin Hughes
Languages English, French
T: +974 4034 9888
W: www.nordangliaeducation.com/our-schools/doha/madinat-khalifa

Deutsche Internationale Schule Doha
Ibn Seena School Street No. 30, Doha
DP Coordinator Furuzan Cuhadar
Languages English, German
T: +974 4451 6836
W: www.ds-doha.de

Doha British School
PO Box 6142, Doha
DP Coordinator Nicholas Taylor
Languages English
T: +974 4019 8000
W: www.dohabritishschool.com

INTERNATIONAL SCHOOL OF LONDON (ISL) QATAR
PO Box 18511, North Duhail, Doha
DP Coordinator Anna Burkett
MYP Coordinator Helen Jeffery
PYP Coordinator James Kendall
Languages English
T: +974 4433 8600
E: mail@islqatar.org
W: www.islqatar.org
See full details on page 133

QATAR ACADEMY AL KHOR
P.O.Box: 60774, Mowasalat Street, Al Khor
DP Coordinator Mr David Leadbetter
MYP Coordinator Mr Martin McCurrach
PYP Coordinator Ms Nadia Hussain
Languages Arabic, English
T: +974 44546775
E: qaksenior@qak.edu.qa
W: www.qak.edu.qa
See full details on page 173

QATAR ACADEMY AL WAKRA
P.O. Box: 2589, Al Farazdaq Street, street No.: 1034, Zone: 90, Doha
MYP Coordinator Ms Jaime Fontenot
PYP Coordinator Ms Samira Jurdak
Languages Arabic, English
T: +974 44547418
E: qataracademyal-wakra@qf.org.qa
W: www.qaw.edu.qa
See full details on page 174

QATAR ACADEMY DOHA
P.O. Box: 1129, Luqta Street, Doha
DP Coordinator Ms Zeina Jawad
MYP Coordinator Ms Roma Bhargava
PYP Coordinator Ms Sana Alavi
Languages Arabic, English
T: +974 44542000
E: qataracademy@qf.org.qa
W: www.qataracademy.edu.qa
See full details on page 175

QATAR ACADEMY MSHEIREB
Msheireb Downtown Doha
PYP Coordinator Ms Jennifer Magierowicz & Mr Raed Al Khoshman
Languages Arabic, English
T: +974 44542116
E: qamsheireb@qf.org.qa
W: www.qam.qa
See full details on page 176

QATAR ACADEMY SIDRA
P.O. Box: 34077, Doha
DP Coordinator Mr Gary Craggs
MYP Coordinator Ms Alison Bainbridge
PYP Coordinator Mr Barry Grogan
Languages English
T: +974 44542322
E: qasidra@qf.org.qa
W: www.qasidra.com.qa
See full details on page 177

SEK INTERNATIONAL SCHOOL QATAR
Onaiza 65, Doha
DP Coordinator Andrew Jenkinson
MYP Coordinator Maria del Carmen Palma
PYP Coordinator Nikki Merval
Languages Arabic, English, Spanish
T: +974 4012 7633
E: info@sek.qa
W: www.sek.qa
See full details on page 193

Swiss International School Qatar
Al Hashimaya Street, Al Luqta, Doha
DP Coordinator Nancy Le Nezet
MYP Coordinator Lana Kulas
PYP Coordinator Anne Bradley
Languages English
T: +974 40363131
W: www.sisq.qa

The Gulf English School
PO Box 2440, Doha
DP Coordinator Hannah Cashel
Languages English
T: +974 4457 8777
W: www.gulfenglishschool.com

ROMANIA

American International School of Bucharest
Sos Pipera-Tunari 196, Voluntari, Jud Ilfov, 077190 Bucharest
DP Coordinator David White
MYP Coordinator Andrew Pontius
PYP Coordinator Courtney Hughes
Languages English
T: +40 (21) 204 4300
W: www.aisb.ro

Bucharest - Beirut International School
Sos.Vergului, nr.14, District 2, 022448 Bucharest
DP Coordinator Roxana Salajanu
Languages English
T: +40 (0)744 309 199
W: bbischool.ro

INTERNATIONAL SCHOOL OF BUCHAREST
1R Gara Catelu Str., Sector 3, Bucharest 032991
DP Coordinator Mr. Yusuf Suha Orhan
Languages English
T: +40 21 3069530
E: admissions@isb.ro
W: www.isb.ro

See full details on page 128

Liceul Teoretic Scoala Europeana Bucuresti
33 Baiculesti st., 013913 Bucharest
DP Coordinator Ana-Maria Obezaru
Languages English
T: +40 21 3117 770
W: www.scoalaeuropeana.ro

Little London International Academy
Strada Erou Iancu Nicolae 65, Pipera, 077190 Voluntari, Ilfov
PYP Coordinator Costea Iuliana
Languages English
T: +40 721 689 762
W: www.lliacademy.ro

Mark Twain International School
25 Erou Iancu Nicolae Street, Baneasa, 077190 Bucharest
DP Coordinator Melania Ilinca
MYP Coordinator Floriana Florea
PYP Coordinator Orlandina Bulie
Languages English, Romanian
T: +40 730 800 933
W: www.marktwainschool.ro

RUSSIAN FEDERATION

Alabuga International School
Nord Drive, Building 1, Yelabuga, Tatarstan 423600
PYP Coordinator Ksenia Mikhedekina
Languages English, Russian
T: +7 855 575 3405
W: alabugais.ru

Colegio Rosalía de Castro No. 1558
Chukotsky Proyezd, 6, c/ Lenskaya 6, 28/1, 24, 19a, Moscow 129327
MYP Coordinator Irina Terekhova
Languages English
T: +7 495 472 47 30
W: colegio1558.ru

European Gymnasium
Sokolnichesky Val., d.28, Sokolniki, Moscow 107113
DP Coordinator Tagir Zainullin
MYP Coordinator Elena Kraevskaya
PYP Coordinator Maria Bogantseva
Languages English
T: +7 985 795 4273
W: www.eurogym.ru

Far Eastern Centre of Continuing Education (International Linguistic School)
44 Partizanskiy Av., Vladivostok 690990
DP Coordinator Natalia Tischenko
Languages English
T: +7 423 240 42 84
W: www.mlsh.ru

Gosudarstvennaya Stolichnaya Gymnasiya
94 Altyf'evskoye Shosse, Moscow 127349
PYP Coordinator Alla Zavidey
Languages English
T: +7 495 707 07 62
W: www.gsgschool.ru

INTERNATIONAL SCHOOL OF HERZEN UNIVERSITY
Vosstania str., 8 "B", St. Petersburg
MYP Coordinator Irina Tomashpolskaia
Languages English
T: +7 812 275 7684
E: school@interschool.ru
W: www.interschool.ru

See full details on page 131

International School of Kazan
5 Mavlyutova St., Kazan
MYP Coordinator Chris Clover
PYP Coordinator Olivia Hall
Languages English, Russian
T: +7 843 204 12 82
W: www.iskazan.com

International School of Samara
ul. Kyibysheva, Building 32, Samara 443099
DP Coordinator Léo MOROT
PYP Coordinator Svetlana Tsareva
Languages English, French, Russian
T: +7 846 332 2880

Kaluga International School
Parkovaya Str. Building 1, Voskresenskoe 249815
PYP Coordinator Gary Herbison
Languages English
T: +7 3538 5179 7514
W: www.kischool.ru

Khoroshevskaya Shkola
45 Marshala Tukhachevskogo St., appt. 2, Moscow 123154
DP Coordinator Andrey Nozdrevatykh
Languages English, Russian
T: +7 (499) 401 02 71
W: horoshkola.ru/en

Kogalym Secondary School No. 8
11 Yantarnaya Street, Khanty-Mansiisk Autonomous Area, Yugra, Kogalym, Tyumen Region 628481
DP Coordinator Eskaeva Svetlana Ivanovna
Languages English
T: +7 34 66 72 71 13
W: www.school8-kogalym.narod.ru

Letovo School
35 Valovaya str., Moscow
DP Coordinator Kwok Wai Chiang
Languages English, Russian
T: +7 8 800 100 51 15
W: letovo.ru/en/home

Linguistic School No. 1531
Godovikov Street 4, Moscow RU-129085
MYP Coordinator Svetlana Ushakova
Languages English
T: +7 495 287 25 71
W: gym1531sv.mskobr.ru

Lyceum 10 of Perm
22 Tehnicheskaya Street, Perm 614070
DP Coordinator Mikhail Novoselov
PYP Coordinator Elena Timofeeva
Languages English
T: +7 342 2819780
W: www.hselyceum.perm.ru

MAOU Gymnasium "Vector" Zelenogradsk
ul. Turgenev, 5-B, Kaliningrad Region, Zelenogradsk 238326
PYP Coordinator Valeria Lorich
Languages Russian
T: +7 401 503 1171
W: www.school2zel.ru

Medical Technical Lyceum
Polevaya str 74, Samara 443002
DP Coordinator Natalia Kabanova
Languages English
T: +7 846 237 0343

MOSCOW ECONOMIC SCHOOL, ODINTSOVO BRANCH
1-A, Zaitsevo Village, Odintsovo Region, Moscow Oblast 143020
DP Coordinator Valeriya Rotershteyn
MYP Coordinator Antonina Andrianova (Gaydash)
PYP Coordinator Larisa Zaitseva
Languages Russian, English
T: +7 495 780 5230
E: mes@mes.ru
W: www.mes.ru

See full details on page 166

Moscow Economic School, Presnya Campus
29 Zamorenova Street, Moscow 123022
DP Coordinator Alexander Galiguzov
MYP Coordinator Irina Nikitina
PYP Coordinator Tatyana Filatova
Languages English, Russian
T: +7 499 255 55 66
W: www.mes.ru

Moscow Gymnasium No. 1409
7, Khodynski blvd, Moscow 125252
MYP Coordinator Ada Kozaeva
Languages Russian
T: +7 499 740 5213

Moscow Gymnasium No. 1530
Egerskaya str., 4, Moscow 107014
MYP Coordinator Alexandra Isaeva
Languages English
T: +7 495 603 09 62
W: gym1530.mskobr.ru

Moscow School No. 1231
Spasopeskovsky lane 6, building 7, Moscow 119002
PYP Coordinator Elena Alexandrova
Languages English
T: +7 499 241 43 81
W: sch1231.mskobr.ru

Moscow School No. 1296
Keramicheskiy proezd, Bld.55/3, Moscow 127591
PYP Coordinator Irina Rafalskaya
Languages English
T: +7 499 900 0852
W: cos1296.mskobr.ru

Moscow School No. 1329
Nikulinskaya street, 10, Moscow 119602
DP Coordinator Irina Gorkunova
Languages English
T: +7 495 651 33 97
W: sch1329.mskobr.ru

Moscow School No. 1527
17/5 Andropov prospect, Moscow 115407
MYP Coordinator Olga Shevchenko
Languages English
T: +7 49961 87005

Moscow School No. 1811
bul. Izmaylovsky, 52, Moscow 105077
PYP Coordinator Ekaterina Prokosheva
Languages English, Russian
T: +7 495 465 14 49
W: 1811.mskobr.ru

Moscow School No. 45
8 Grimau Str, Moscow 117036
DP Coordinator Marianna Rovneyko
MYP Coordinator Sofya Dobroshevskaya
PYP Coordinator Darya Romm
Languages English
T: +7 499 126 33 82
W: www.ms45.edu.ru

Moscow State Budget School No. 1583
25, Smolnaya, Moscow 125493
MYP Coordinator Svetlana Dvoryantseva
Languages English
T: +7 499 458 02 57

Moscow State Lyceum No. 1575
6, Usievicha Street, Moscow 125319
MYP Coordinator Oksana Solosina
Languages English
T: +7499 151 89 24
W: lyc1575s.mskobr.ru

Moscow State Secondary General School No. 2086
5, Universitetsky prospect, Moscow 119296
PYP Coordinator Tatiana Serebrova
Languages English
T: +7 910 450 11 70
W: the26.ru

MSE Lyceum & Grammar School Complex
Zelenodolskaya stree, 32 block 6, Moscow 109457
MYP Coordinator Liudmila Vladimirovna Gavrilova
Languages English
T: +7 4991 720605
W: gymuv1599.mskobr.ru

Municipal Autonomous Educational Institute Multitype Lyceum 20
4, Novosondetski Avenue, Ulyanovsk 432072
MYP Coordinator Evgeniia Gennadievna Shulga
Languages English
T: +7 842 220 4550
W: education.simcat.ru/school20

President School
OK Sosny, P/O Uspenskoye, Odintsovski r-n, Moscow Region 1 43030
DP Coordinator Natalia Vlasova
Languages English
T: +7 495 955 0000
W: school-president.ru

Private Lomonosov School Nizhny Novgorod
Gogol Street, 62, Nizhny Novgorod 603109
DP Coordinator Daria Barteneva
MYP Coordinator Dmitry Klochkov
PYP Coordinator Inna Klochkova
Languages Russian
T: +7 831 430 08 63
W: www.chastnayashkola.ru

Pushkin School No. 9 Perm
ul. Komsomolsky Prospect, 45, Perm 614039
MYP Coordinator Mariia Okulova
PYP Coordinator Karina Alenina
Languages English
T: +7 342 212 80 71
W: www.school9.perm.ru

SBGEI of the Moscow City 'School No. 1411'
Severny boulevard, 1a, Moscow 127566
PYP Coordinator Alexandra Shumilova
Languages English, Russian
T: + 7 (499) 204 43 11

School 1557 named after P. Kapitsa
Korp 529, Zelenograd, Moscow 124482
MYP Coordinator Ekaterina Nikonorova
Languages English, Russian
T: +7 4997360846
W: lyczg1557.mskobr.ru

School No. 1434 "Ramenki"
Ramenki St., Moscow 119607
DP Coordinator Natalia Kazankina
Languages English
T: +7 495 932 0000
W: sch1434.mskobr.ru

School No. 1560
7 Mnevniki street, building 5, Moscow 123308
MYP Coordinator Ekaterina Ilina
Languages English
T: +7 499 946 4196
W: 1560.mskobr.ru

School No. 1589, Moscow
Initsiativnaya street, house 1, Moscow 121357
DP Coordinator Elena Yurchenko
PYP Coordinator Ksenia Karnatskaya
Languages English, Russian
T: +7 495 4442571
W: lycc1589.mskobr.ru

School No. 185 of the City of Moscow
Mikhalkovskaya Street, 3, Moscow 125008
PYP Coordinator Fatima Dokshukina
Languages English
W: sch185s.mskobr.ru/#

SCHOOL OF YOUNG POLITICIANS - 1306
Michurinskiy avenue 15, blocks 2,3,4, 119192 Moscow
DP Coordinator Sholpan Mussina
MYP Coordinator Karina Salway
PYP Coordinator Azat Mazkenov
Languages English, Russian
T: +7 495 932 99 58
E: 1306@edu.mos.ru
W: gymg1306.mskobr.ru
See full details on page 186

Specialized English Language School No. 7
7450 Lunacharskiy Street, Perm 614000
DP Coordinator Natalya Sukhanova
PYP Coordinator Tatiana Zakirova
Languages English
T: +7 342 2360580
W: www.sc7.perm.ru

State Budget Educational Institution No. 1252 after Cervantes
Dubosekovskaya str.3, Moscow 125080
MYP Coordinator Liudmila Novikova
Languages English
T: +7 49915 80222

State Classical School No. 1272
17, 1st Kozhukhovsky pr., Moscow 115280
PYP Coordinator Maria Andreichenko
Languages English
T: +7 495 710 36 39
W: sch1272.mskobr.ru

The Anglo-American School of Moscow
1 Beregovaya Street, Moscow 125367
DP Coordinator Sean Sonderman
PYP Coordinator Maureen Sackmaster Carpenter
Languages English
T: +7 (495) 231 44 88
W: www.aas.ru

The British International School, Moscow
Novoyasenevsky prospekt 19/5, Moscow 117593
DP Coordinator Claire Powis
Languages English
T: +7 495 426 0311; +7 495 987 4486
W: www.bismoscow.com

The International Gymnasium of the Skolkovo Innovation Center
Skolkovo Innovation Center, Zvorykin Street 7, Moscow 143026
DP Coordinator Raisa Baragyan
MYP Coordinator Elena Andreeva
PYP Coordinator Elena Ovakimyan
Languages English
T: +7 (495) 956 00 33
W: sk.ru/city/gymnasium

The Romanov School
3, Bolshoi Kondratievsky side-street, New Arbat street, 22, app. 118, Moscow 123056
DP Coordinator Svetlana Grunvald
Languages English
T: +7 916 115 61 50
W: 1240.ru

XXI CENTURY INTEGRATION INTERNATIONAL SECONDARY SCHOOL
16 Marshala Katukova St., Building 3, Moscow 123592
DP Coordinator Nigiar Mekhtieva
MYP Coordinator Leonid Tevlin
PYP Coordinator Kristina Moavad
Languages English
T: +7 495 750 3102
E: school@integration21.ru
W: www.integration21.ru
See full details on page 241

RWANDA

Green Hills Academy
PO Box 6419, Nyarutarama, Kigali
DP Coordinator Mathias Ndinya
Languages English
T: +250 735 832 348
W: www.greenhillsacademy.rw

SAUDI ARABIA

Advanced Learning Schools
PO Box 221985, Riyadh 11311
DP Coordinator Tania Maana
MYP Coordinator Sherina Mohammed
PYP Coordinator Haya Abdulrahim
Languages English
T: +966 1 207 0926
W: www.alsschools.com

AL FARIS INTERNATIONAL SCHOOL
Tawaan Area, Imam Saud Road, Khan Younes Street, Riyadh 9483
DP Coordinator Mrs. Farah Kiblawi
MYP Coordinator Mrs. Salwa Ghandour
PYP Coordinator Mrs. Rasha Ghraizi
Languages English
T: +966 011 454 9358
E: info@alfarisschools.com
W: www.alfarisschool.com
See full details on page 67

AL HUSSAN INTERNATIONAL SCHOOL KHOBAR
PO Box 297, Dammam 31411
DP Coordinator Maria Faisal
Languages English
T: +966 13 858 7566
E: ahisk@alhussan.edu.sa
W: international.alhussan.edu.sa
See full details on page 68

American International School – Riyadh
PO Box 990, Riyadh 11421
DP Coordinator Liam Trimm
Languages English
T: +966 11 491 4270
W: www.aisr.org

Deutsche Internationale Schule Jeddah
P.O. Box 7510, Jeddah 21472
DP Coordinator Tonia Whewell
Languages English
T: +966 12 691 3584
W: www.disj.de

Dhahran Ahliyya Schools
P.O.Box 39333, Dhahran 31942
PYP Coordinator Rola Abu-Sager
Languages English, Arabic
T: +966 138919222
W: www.das.sch.sa

Dhahran High School
PO Box 31677, Al-Khobar 31952
DP Coordinator Emily Bearns
Languages English
T: +966 13 330 0555
W: dhs.isg.edu.sa

International Programs School
P.O. Box 691, Dhahran Airport 31932
DP Coordinator Ciara Johnson
PYP Coordinator Siham Dabouk
Languages English
T: +966 13 857 5603
W: www.ipsksa.com

International Schools Group (ISG) Jubail
PO Box 10059, Jubail 31961
DP Coordinator Thomas McLean
Languages English
T: +966 13 341 7550
W: www.isg-jubail.org

Jeddah Knowledge International School
Al Salamah District, Mohammed Mosaud St. (Behind Iceland), PO Box 7180, 21462 Jeddah
DP Coordinator Natasha Awada
MYP Coordinator Amal Alotaibi
PYP Coordinator Amal Sinno
Languages English, Arabic
T: +966 2 691 7367
W: www.jks.edu.sa

KING ABDULAZIZ SCHOOL
Ali Ibn Abi Taleb Road, P.O. Box 43111, Medina 41561
PYP Coordinator Raheela Akram
Languages English
T: +966 503 454 420 / +966 553 039 300
E: asaadaoui@kaism.org / rakram@kaism.org
W: www.kaism.org
See full details on page 147

King Faisal Pre-School
PO Box 94558, Riyadh 11614
PYP Coordinator Randa Dahshe
Languages Arabic, English
T: +966 1 482 0802
W: www.kfs.sch.sa

King Faisal School
PO Box 94558, Riyadh 11614
DP Coordinator Khaled Qattawi
MYP Coordinator Mohammed Bahzat
PYP Coordinator Kalwant Rana
Languages English, Arabic
T: +966 1 482 0802
W: www.kfs.sch.sa

Les Écoles Internationales Al-Kawthar
PO Box 52280, Jeddah 21563
PYP Coordinator Mrs. Hanene Karouch
Languages French
T: +966506561717; +966506359280
W: www.alkawthar.edu.sa

Qurtubah Private Schools
Prince Sultan Street, North-West Al-Tareekh Square, Jeddah 21581
PYP Coordinator Ikrami Farraj
Languages Arabic
T: +966 551757472
W: qps.edu.sa

Rand International School
P.O.box 9712, Dammam 31423
PYP Coordinator May Ismail Issa
Languages Arabic, English
T: +966 13 8504488
W: www.randschools.com

The British International School of Jeddah
PO Box 6453, Jeddah 21442
DP Coordinator Dean El-Hoss
Languages English
T: +966 1 2 699 0019
W: www.bisj.com

THE KAUST SCHOOL
Safaa Gardens School, Office 1132, 4700 KAUST, Thuwal 23955-6900
DP Coordinator Susan Rhodes
MYP Coordinator Peter Powell
PYP Coordinator Jon Davidson
Languages English
T: +966 12 808 6803
E: schools@kaust.edu.sa
W: tks.kaust.edu.sa
See full details on page 225

Yusr International School (YIS)
King Abdulaziz Rd, Opp Redsea Mall, An Nahdah, Jeddah 23614
PYP Coordinator Ahmed Abdelrazzaq
Languages English, Arabic
T: +966 12 699 4640
W: www.yusrschool.com

SENEGAL

Enko Dakar International School
Cité Keur Gorgui, Mermoz-Sacré-Cœur, Dakar
DP Coordinator Jean Croteau
Languages English, French
T: +221 33 821 30 64
W: enkoeducation.com/dakar

Enko Waca International School
BP 24340, Ouakam, Dakar
DP Coordinator Alanna Ross
Languages French
T: +221 33 820 49 29
W: enkoeducation.com/waca

International School of Dakar
BP 5136 Fann, Dakar
DP Coordinator Paul Lennon
Languages English
T: +221 33 860 2332
W: www.isdakar.org

Le Collège Bilingue de Dakar
Sacré Coeur 3, Cité Keur Gorgui No.53, Dakar 00221
DP Coordinator Souleymane DIAW
Languages English, French
T: +221 33 860 60 10
W: lecollegebilingue-dakar.net

SERBIA

Crnjanski High School
Djordja Ognjanovica 2, Belgrade 11030
DP Coordinator Gordana Medakovic
Languages English
T: +381 11 23 98 388
W: www.crnjanski.edu.rs

Gymnasium Jovan Jovanovic Zmaj
Zlatne grede 4, Novi Sad, Vojvodina
DP Coordinator Aleksandra Strahinic
Languages English, French
T: +381 21 529 977
W: jjzmaj.edu.rs/pocetna

International School of Belgrade
Temisvarska 19, Belgrade 11040
DP Coordinator Branka Sreckovic-Minic
MYP Coordinator Branka Sreckovic-Minic
PYP Coordinator Barbara Netzel
Languages English
T: +381 11 206 9999
W: www.isb.rs

Ruder Bo kovic
Kneza Vi eslava 17, Belgrade 11000
DP Coordinator Aleksandra Ivanovski
MYP Coordinator Ivana Golac
PYP Coordinator Katarina Milosevic
Languages English
T: + 381 11 35 407 86
W: www.boskovic.edu.rs

SLOVAKIA

English International School of Bratislava
Kalinciakova 12, Bratislava 83101
DP Coordinator Bronislava Dvorecka
MYP Coordinator Robert Thorn
Languages English
T: +421 907 462 297
W: www.eisbratislava.com

QSI INTERNATIONAL SCHOOL OF BRATISLAVA
Záhradnicka 1006/2, Samorin 93101
DP Coordinator Mr. Jeff Varney
Languages English
T: +421 903 704 436
E: bratislava@qsi.org
W: bratislava.qsi.org
See full details on page 178

Spojená skola Novohradská
Novohradská 3, Bratislava 821 09
DP Coordinator Matej Gonda
MYP Coordinator Gabriela Markusová
PYP Coordinator Veronika Darwell
Languages English
T: +421 25 557 6396
W: www.gjh.sk

The British International School, Bratislava
J. Vala tana Dolinského 1 (Pekníkova 6), Bratislava 841 02
DP Coordinator Karina Rodegra
Languages English
T: +421 2 6930 7081
W: www.bis.sk

SLOVENIA

Danila Kumar Primary School
Godezeva 11, Ljubljana 1000
MYP Coordinator Lidija Janes
PYP Coordinator Kristina Fürst
Languages English
T: +386 01 5636 834
W: www.gimb.org

Gimnasija Kranj
Koroka Cesta 13, 4000 Kranj
DP Coordinator Nata a Kne
Languages English
T: +386 4 281 17 10
W: www.gimkr.si

Gimnazija Bezigrad
Periceva 4, Ljubljana 1000
DP Coordinator Irena Cesnik
MYP Coordinator Katja Kvas
Languages English
T: +386 1 3000 400
W: www.gimb.org

II gimnazija Maribor
Trg Milosa Zidanska 1, 2000 Maribor
DP Coordinator Polona Vehovar
Languages English
T: +386 33 04 434
W: www.druga.si

SOUTH AFRICA

American International School of Johannesburg
Midrand, Johannesburg
DP Coordinator Penny Keet
Languages English
T: +27 11 464 1505
W: www.aisj-jhb.com

HOUT BAY INTERNATIONAL SCHOOL
61 Main Road, Hout Bay, Cape Town 7806
DP Coordinator Winell Gous
PYP Coordinator Rhona Sehested-Larsen
Languages English
T: +27 21 791 7900
E: hbis@iesmail.com
W: www.houtbayinternational.co.za
See full details on page 114

Redhill School
20 Summit Road, Morningside, Sandton, Johannesburg 2057
DP Coordinator Michele Marnitz
Languages English
T: +27 11 783 4707
W: www.redhill.co.za

SPAIN

Agora International School Barcelona
c. Puig de Mira, 15-21, Sant Esteve Sesrovires, 08635 Barcelona, Catalonia
DP Coordinator Adoracio Sillero
Languages English, Spanish
T: +34 93 779 89 28
W: colegioagorabarcelona.es

Agora International School Madrid
C/ Duero 35 Urb El Bosque, 28670 Madrid
DP Coordinator Iris Oliva
Languages English, Spanish
T: +34 91 616 71 25
W: www.colegioagoramadrid.es

Agora Portals International School
Carretera vella d'Andratx, s/n, Portals Nous, 078181 Mallorca, Balearic Islands
DP Coordinator Rocio Baquero
Languages English, Spanish
T: +34 971684042
W: www.nace.edu.es/portals

Agora Sant Cugat International School
C / Ferrer y Guardia s / n, Sant Cugat del Vallés, 08174 Barcelona, Catalonia
DP Coordinator Montse Martí Linares
PYP Coordinator Mireia Cuxart
Languages English, Spanish
T: +34 93 590 26 00
W: www.nace.edu.es/SantCugat

Aloha College
Urbanización el Angel, 29660 Marbella, Málaga, Andalusia
DP Coordinator Elaine Brigid Mc Girl
Languages English, Spanish
T: +34 95 281 41 33
W: www.aloha-college.com

American School of Barcelona
Calle Balmes 7, Esplugues de Llobregat, 08950 Barcelona, Catalonia
DP Coordinator Charmaine Monds
Languages English
T: +34 93 371 4016
W: www.asbarcelona.com

American School of Bilbao
Soparda Bidea 10, 48640 Berango, Biscay, Basque Country
DP Coordinator Mariana Curti
PYP Coordinator Rafael Trinidad
Languages English
T: +34 94 668 0860
W: www.asob.es

American School of Madrid
Apartado 80, 28080 Madrid
DP Coordinator Martina Bree
Languages English
T: +34 91 740 19 00
W: www.asmadrid.org

American School of Valencia
Urbanización Los Monasterios, Apartado de Correos 9, 46530 Puzol, Valencia
DP Coordinator Josep Vicent Frechina
Languages English, Spanish, Valencia
T: +34 96 140 5412
W: www.asvalencia.org

Angel de la Guarda
Calle Andalucía 17-20, 03016 Alicante, Valencia
DP Coordinator Rosario Pérez Escoto
Languages English, Spanish
T: +34 9652 61899
W: www.angeldelaguarda.eu

Aquinas American School
Calle Transversal Cuatro, 4, Urbanización Monte Alina, Pozuelo de Alarcon, 28223 Madrid
DP Coordinator Ana Curbera
Languages English
T: +34 91 352 31 20
W: www.aquinas-american-school.es

Aula Escola Europea
Avinguda Mare de, Déu de Lorda, 34-36, 08034 Barcelona, Catalonia
DP Coordinator Maria Muñoz
Languages Spanish
T: +34 93 203 03 54
W: www.aula-ee.com

Bell-lloc Del Pla
Carrer de Can Pau Birol, 2, 17005 Girona, Catalonia
DP Coordinator Manel Juny Pastells
Languages Spanish
T: +34 972 232 111
W: www.bell-lloc.org/ca

BENJAMIN FRANKLIN INTERNATIONAL SCHOOL
Martorell i Pena 9, 08017 Barcelona, Catalonia
DP Coordinator Laura Blair
Languages English
T: +34 93 434 2380
E: info@bfischool.org
W: www.bfischool.org
See full details on page 79

BRAINS INTERNATIONAL SCHOOL, LA MORALEJA
Calle Salvia, N° 48, 28109 Alcobendas, Madrid
DP Coordinator Michael Harvey
Languages English
T: +34 91 650 43 00
E: michael@colegiobrains.com
W: www.colegiobrains.com
See full details on page 82

Centre Cultural I Esportiu Xaloc
Can Tries, 4-6, L'Hospitalet de Llobregat, 08902 Barcelona, Catalonia
DP Coordinator Martin Curiel
Languages Spanish
T: +34 93 335 1600
W: www.xaloc.org

Centro de Estudios Ibn Gabirol Colegio Estrella Toledano
Paseo de Alcobendas 7 (La Moraleja), 28109 Alcobendas, Madrid
DP Coordinator Julio Fernando Zapata
Languages English
T: +34 916 50 12 29
W: www.colegiogabiroltoledano.com

Centro Educativo Agave
Camino de la Gloria no 17, 04230 Huercal de Almería, Almería, Andalusia
DP Coordinator Isabel Maria Fenoy Gázquez
Languages English
T: +34 9503 01026
W: www.colegioagave.com

Col·legi Sant Miquel dels Sants
Jaume I, 11, 08500 Vic, Barcelona, Catalonia
DP Coordinator Vanesa Ferrreres Vergés
Languages Catalan, Spanish
T: +34 93 886 12 44
W: www.santmiqueldelssants.cat

Colegio Alameda de Osuna
Paseo de la Alameda de Osuna, 60, 28042 Madrid
DP Coordinator Arantza Carrillo Alonso
Languages English, Spanish
T: +34 91 742 70 11
W: www.colegio-alameda.com

Colegio Alauda
Cerillo 6, 14014 Córdoba, Andalusia
DP Coordinator Laura Paños Díaz
Languages English
T: +34 957 40 55 07
W: www.colegioalauda.org

Colegio Alegra
Calle de Sorolla 4, 28222 Majadahonda, Madrid
DP Coordinator Militza Hernandez
MYP Coordinator Beatriz Duro Aneiros
Languages English, Spanish
T: +34 916 39 79 03
W: www.alegrabritishschool.com

Colegio Antamira
C/ Los Cuadros, 2, Miramadrid, 28860 Paracuellos de Jarama, Madrid
DP Coordinator Pedro Pablo Sacristán Sanz
Languages English, Spanish
T: +34 91 667 27 07
W: www.colegioantamira.com

Colegio Arcangel Rafael
Calle Maqueda no. 4, 28024 Madrid
DP Coordinator Maria de Fatima Casablanca
Languages English, Spanish
T: +34 91 711 93 00
W: www.colegio-arcangel.com

Colegio Arenas Atlántico
Paseo San Patricio, No 20, 35413 Trasmontaña, Las Palmas, Canary Islands
DP Coordinator David Arbelo Llorente
MYP Coordinator Encarnación Lorenzo de Armas
Languages Spanish
T: +34 928 629 140
W: www.colegioarenas.es

Colegio Arenas Internacional
Avenida del Mar 37, Lanzarote, 35509 Costa Teguise, Las Palmas, Canary Islands
DP Coordinator Jose Antonio Paz Botana
MYP Coordinator Brian Foster
PYP Coordinator Estela Medina
Languages Spanish
T: +34 928 590 835
W: www.colegioarenas.es

Colegio Arenas Sur
Las Margaritas s/n, 35290 San Agustín, Las Palmas, Canary Islands
DP Coordinator Patricia Bergström
Languages Spanish
T: +34 928 765 934
W: www.colegioarenassur.com

Colegio Atalaya
Calle Pico Alcazaba 24-28, Urbanización El Marqués, 29680 Estepona, Málaga
DP Coordinator Iraia Manterola Berrueta
Languages English, Spanish
T: +34 952 003 171
W: www.colegioatalaya.es

Colegio Base
Calle del Camino Ancho, 10, 28109 Alcobendas, Madrid
DP Coordinator Victor Acosta Ferreras
Languages Spanish
T: +34 9165 00313
W: www.colegiobase.com

Colegio Cervantes
Avda. de la Fuensanta, 37, 14010 Córdoba, Andalusia
DP Coordinator Manuel Porras García
Languages English
T: +34 957 255150
W: www.maristascordoba.com

Colegio CEU San Pablo Montepríncipe
Avda. Montepríncipe, s/n, 28668 Boadilla del Monte, Madrid
DP Coordinator José Manuel Ruiz Vila
Languages English
T: +34 91 352 05 23
W: www.colegioceumonteprincipe.es

Colegio CEU San Pablo Sanchinarro
Niceto Alcalá Zamora, 43, 28050 Madrid
DP Coordinator Ruth Jiménez Balboa
Languages English
T: +34 91 392 34 40/41
W: www.colegioceusanchinarro.es

Colegio CEU San Pablo Valencia
Edificio Seminario Metropolitano, 46113 Moncada, Valencia
DP Coordinator Angel Luis Peris Suay
PYP Coordinator Francisco Haro Canet
Languages Spanish
T: +34 961 36 90 14
W: www.colegioceuvalencia.es

Colegio de San Francisco de Paula
C/ Santa Angela de la Cruz, 11, 41003 Seville, Andalusia
DP Coordinator German Delgado
MYP Coordinator Rocío Moreno Borrego
PYP Coordinator Macarena Vázquez de Cruces
Languages Spanish, English
T: +34 95 422 4382
W: www.sfpaula.com

Colegio El Valle Alicante
Avda. Condomina 65, 03540 Alicante, Valencia
DP Coordinator Nuria Espinosa Juan
MYP Coordinator Hannah Harding
PYP Coordinator Alberto Fernández de Aguilar
Languages English, Spanish
T: +34 965 155 619
W: www.colegioelvalle.com

Colegio El Valle II – Sanchinarro
Calle Ana De Austria, 60, 28050 Madrid
DP Coordinator Nuria Alvarez Herranz
Languages Spanish
T: +34 91 7188426
W: www.colegioelvalle.com

Colegio Heidelberg
Apartado de Correos 248, Barranco Seco 15, 35090 Las Palmas de Gran Canaria, Las Palmas, Can+
DP Coordinator Juan Antonio Domínguez Silva
MYP Coordinator José Luis Moreno Roque
Languages Spanish
T: +34 928 350 462
W: www.colegioheidelberg.com

Colegio HH. Maristas Sagrado Corazón Alicante
Calle de la Isla de Corfú, 5, 03005 Alicante, Valencia
DP Coordinator Fernando Fuentes Guzmán
Languages Spanish
T: +34 965 130 941
W: www.maristasalicante.com

Colegio Internacional Ausias March
Urbanización Residencial Tancat de l'Alter s/n, 46220 Picassent, Valencia
DP Coordinator María Pérez Galván
Languages Spanish
T: +34 96 123 05 66
W: www.ausiasmarch.com

Colegio Internacional de Levante
Río Jalón 25 Urbanización Calicanto, 46370 Valencia
DP Coordinator Alejandra Mezquida Ferragut
Languages Spanish
T: +34 961980650
W: www.colintlev.net

Colegio Internacional Meres
Carretera Meres, s/n, 33199 Meres, Asturias
DP Coordinator Maria Crespo Iglesias
MYP Coordinator Cristina Cuadrado Martínez
PYP Coordinator Carmen González Aller
Languages Spanish
T: +34 985 792 427
W: www.colegiomeres.com

Colegio Internacional SEK Eirís
C Castaño de Eiris, 1, 15009 A Coruña, Galicia
DP Coordinator Ana González
Languages English, Spanish
T: +34 981 28 44 00
W: www.eiris.edu.es

Colegio Internacional Torrequebrada
C/ Ronda del Golf Este, 7-11, Urbanización Torrequebrada, 29639 Benalmádena, Málaga, Andalusia
DP Coordinator Guillermo Chaves
PYP Coordinator Iciar Garcia
Languages English, Spanish
T: +34 952 57 60 65
W: www.colegiotorrequebrada.com

Colegio Liceo Europeo
C/ Camino Sur 10, 28100 Alcobendas, Madrid
CP Coordinator Esther Arama Ibáñez
DP Coordinator Esther Arama Ibáñez
MYP Coordinator Esther Arama Ibáñez
PYP Coordinator Fatima Rodriguez Vicens
Languages English, Spanish
T: +34 91 650 00 00
W: www.liceo-europeo.es

Colegio Logos
Urbanización Molino de la Hoz c/, Sacre 2, 28232 Las Rozas de Madrid, Madrid
DP Coordinator Héctor Martínez
Languages English
T: +34 91 630 34 94
W: www.colegiologos.com

Colegio Manuel Peleteiro
Monte Redondo – Castiñeiriño, 15702 Santiago de Compostela, A Coruña, Galicia
DP Coordinator Rafael Gómez Montero
Languages Spanish
T: +34 98 1591475
W: www.peleteiro.com

Colegio Mater Salvatoris
Calle Valdesquí no. 4, 28023 Madrid
DP Coordinator Almudena Alonso
Languages Spanish
T: +34 91 307 1243
W: matersalvatoris.org

Colegio Mirabal
Calle Monte Almenara, s/n, 28660 Madrid
DP Coordinator Kristof Heylen
Languages Spanish
T: +34 916 331 711
W: www.colegiomirabal.com

Colegio Montserrat
Av Vallvidrera, 68, 08017 Barcelona, Catalonia
DP Coordinator Juan Antonio Fernández-Arévalo
Languages English, Spanish
T: +34 932 038 800
W: www.cmontserrat.org

Colegio Nuestra Señora del Recuerdo
Plaza Duque de Pastrana 5, 28036 Madrid
DP Coordinator Belén Esteban
Languages English
T: +34 91 3022640
W: www.recuerdo.net

Colegio Obradoiro
Rua Obradoiro 49, 15190 A Coruña, Galicia
DP Coordinator Pedro-Jesus Rubal Garcia
MYP Coordinator Consuelo Gajino Cousillas
PYP Coordinator Jorge Muiños Guereca
Languages English, Spanish
T: +34 981 281 888
W: www.colegioobradoiro.es

Colegio Retamar
Madrid España, c/ Pajares 22, 28223 Madrid
DP Coordinator Juan Navalpotro
Languages Spanish
T: +34 91 714 10 22
W: www.retamar.com

Colegio San Cristóbal
Calle San Jorge del Maestrazgo, 2, 12003 Castellón de la Plana, Castellón, Valencia
DP Coordinator Ana Belen Baldayo
Languages English
T: +34 964 228 758
W: sancristobalsl.com

Colegio San Fernando
Avenida San Agustín, s/n, 33400 Avilés, Asturias
DP Coordinator Paula Claros Suárez
Languages Spanish
T: +34 985 565 745
W: www.sanfer.es

Colegio San Ignacio Jesuitas
Avenida Richard Grandío, S/N, 33193 Oviedo, Asturias
DP Coordinator Arnau Pla Novoa
Languages Spanish
T: +34 985 233 300
W: www.s-ignacio.com

Colegio San Jorge
Soc. Coop. Enseñanza la Alcayna. CIF: F30410328, Avda. Picos de Europa s/n, 30507 Molina de Segura, Murcia
DP Coordinator Maria Esther Pérez Esquerdo
Languages English, Spanish
T: +34 968 430 711
W: colegiosanjorge.es

Colegio San José Estepona
Avd. Litoral 22, 29680 Estepona, Málaga, Andalusia
DP Coordinator Miguel Angel Salazar Troya
Languages Spanish
T: +34 952 800 148
W: www.colegiosanjose.net

Colegio San Patricio
Calle Jazmin 148, El Soto de la Moraleja, 28109 Alcobendas, Madrid
DP Coordinator Borja Díaz
Languages Spanish
T: +34 916 50 06 02
W: www.colegiosanpatricio.es

Colegio Virgen de Europa
Valle de Santa Ana 1, Las Lomas, 28669 Madrid
DP Coordinator Mary Larrosa
Languages Spanish
T: +34 91 633 0155
W: www.colegiovirgendeeuropa.com

Colegios Ramón Y Cajal
C/ Arturo Soria, 206, 28043 Madrid
PYP Coordinator Laura Pérez
Languages English
T: +34 91 413 56 31
W: www.colegiosramonycajal.es

Complejo Educativo Mas Camarena
C/ 1 Urbanización, Mas Camarena, 46117 Bétera, Valencia
DP Coordinator Louise Grint
Languages Spanish
T: +34 961687535
W: www.colegios-sigloxxi.com

Cooperativa de Enseñanza San Cernin
Avda. Baranain 3, 31007 Pamplona, Navarre
DP Coordinator Arantxa Hernández
Languages English
T: +34 948176288
W: www.sancernin.es

El Plantío International School of Valencia
Calle 233 No36 Urb El Plantío, La Cañada, 46182 Paterna, Valencia
DP Coordinator Alicia Ocón Crespo
Languages English, Spanish
T: +34 96 132 14 10
W: plantiointernational.com

Escola Andorrana de batxillerat
C/ Tossalet i Vinyals, 45, AD500 La Margineda, Andorra la Vella
DP Coordinator Carles Vallverdú Berges
Languages Spanish, Catalan, Valencian
T: +376 723030
W: adbatx.educand.ad

Escola Internacional del Camp
Salvador Espiriu s/n, 43840 Salou, Tarragona, Catalonia
DP Coordinator Astrid de la Torre Lüderitz
Languages English, Spanish
T: +34 977325620
W: www.escolainternacional.org

Escola Voramar
Passeig de García Fària, 08005 Barcelona, Catalonia
DP Coordinator Mirela Domitrovic
Languages English, Spanish
T: +34 932 251 324
W: www.voramon.cat

Eurocolegio Casvi
Avenida de Castilla, 27, Villaviciosa de Odón, 28670 Madrid
DP Coordinator Jose Vicente Belizón Collado
MYP Coordinator Félix David Vozmediano León
PYP Coordinator Pablo Martín Sánchez
Languages Spanish
T: +34 91 616 22 18
W: www.casvi.es

Spain

Eurocolegio Casvi Boadilla
C/ Miguel Ángel Cantero Oliva, 13, Boadilla del Monte, Madrid
PYP Coordinator Álvaro Feijoo Pérez
Languages Spanish
T: +34 91 632 96 53
W: www.casviboadilla.es

Fundacion Privada Oak House School
Sant Pere Claver 12-18, 08017 Barcelona, Catalonia
DP Coordinator Elaine Sibley
Languages English
T: +34 932 524 020
W: www.oakhouseschool.com

Gredos San Diego (GSD) Buitrago
Avda. de Madrid 16, 28730 Buitrago del Lozoya, Madrid
DP Coordinator Luis Bartolomé Herrero
Languages Spanish
T: +34 91 868 02 00
W: www.gsdeducacion.com

Gredos San Diego (GSD) Las Rozas
C/ Clara Campoamor, 1, 28232 Las Rozas, Madrid
DP Coordinator Encarnación López Mateo
Languages English
T: +34 91 640 89 23
W: www.gsdeducacion.com

GRESOL International-American School
Ctra. Sabadell a Matadepera, (BV-1248) km. 6, 08227 Terrassa, Barcelona, Catalonia
DP Coordinator Vanessa Fernandez del Viso
Languages English, Spanish
T: +34 937 870 158
W: www.gresolschool.com

Hamelin-Laie International School
Ronda 8 de Marc 178-180, 08390 Montgat, Barcelona, Catalonia
DP Coordinator Thom Gibbs
Languages English, Spanish
T: +34 93 5556717
W: www.hamelininternacionallaie.com

I.E.S. Alfonso X 'el Sabio'
Avda D Juan de Borbón 3, 30007 Murcia
DP Coordinator María Dolores Romero Carbonell
Languages Spanish
T: +34 968 232 040
W: www.iesalfonsox.com

I.E.S. Juan de la Cierva y Codorníu
C/San Antonio, 84, 30850 Totana, Murcia
DP Coordinator Vicente Sanz Duart
Languages Spanish
T: +34 968 42 19 19
W: www.murciaeduca.es/iesjuandelacierva/sitio

I.E.S. Maestro Matías Bravo
Avenida Mar Egeo S/N, Valdemoro, 28341 Madrid
DP Coordinator Anastasio Calvo de Miguel
Languages Spanish
T: +34 91 801 8044
W: www.educa.madrid.org/web/ies.maestromatiasbravo.valdemoro

IES Bachiller Sabuco
Albacete, Avenida de España 9, 02002 Albacete, Castilla-La Mancha
DP Coordinator María del Mar Buendía Navarro
Languages Spanish
T: +34 967 229 540
W: www.sabuco.com

IES Cardenal López de Mendoza
Plaza Luis Martin Santos s/n, 09002 Burgos, Castile & León
DP Coordinator Antonio Becerro
Languages Spanish
T: +34 947 257701
W: ieslopezdemendoza.centros.educa.jcyl.es

IES Carlos III de Toledo
Avenida de Francia 5, 45005 Toledo, Castilla-La Mancha
DP Coordinator Ángel Castelló Pola
Languages Spanish
T: +34 925 212 967

IES Castilla
Calle Alonso Velázquez s/n, 42003 Soria, Castile & León
DP Coordinator Ángel Martínez Moreno
Languages English
T: +34 975 221 283

IES Jorge Manrique
Avda. Republica Argentina s/n, 34002 Palencia, Castile & León
DP Coordinator Miguel Angel Arconada Melero
Languages Spanish
T: +34 979 720 384
W: www.iesjorgemanrique.com

IES Jorge Santayana
Calle Santo Tomás 6, 05003 Ávila, Castile & León
DP Coordinator Ana Rodríguez Pérez
Languages Spanish
T: +34 920 35 21 35
W: iesjorgesantayana.centros.educa.jcyl.es

IES Lucas Mallada
C/Torre Mendoza No 2, 22005 Huesca, Aragon
DP Coordinator Laura Domingo Capella
Languages Spanish
T: +34 974 244 834
W: www.ieslucasmallada.com

IES Manacor
c/ Camí de Ses Tapareres, 32, 07500 Manacor, Balearic Islands
DP Coordinator Pilar Caldentey Gomila
Languages Spanish, Catalan, Valencian
T: +34 971 551 489
W: www.iesmanacor.cat

IES Marqués de Santillana
Avda España, 2, Torrelavega, 39300 Cantabria
DP Coordinator José Manuel Piñeiro Moratinos
Languages Spanish
T: +34 942 88 16 00
W: www.iesmarquesdesantillana.com

IES Martinez Montanes
C/Fernández de Ribera no. 17, 41005 Seville, Andalusia
DP Coordinator Jorge Mejías López
Languages Spanish
T: +34 955 623 877
W: iesmartinezmontañes.es

IES Mateo Sagasta
Glorieta del Doctor Zubia s/n, 26003 Logroño, La Rioja
DP Coordinator Gloria Bernad Pérez
Languages Spanish
T: +34 941 256 500
W: iessagasta.edurioja.org

IES Navarro Villoslada
Arcadio Mª Larraona, 3, 31008 Pamplona, Navarre
DP Coordinator Gabriel María Rubio Navarro
Languages Spanish
T: +34 848 431 150
W: www.iesnavarrovilloslada.com

IES Pere Boïl
C/Ceramista Alfons Blat 20, 46940 Manises, Valencia
DP Coordinator Nieves Fernández Feijoo
Languages Spanish
T: +34 961 20 62 25
W: www.pereboil.com

IES Príncipe Felipe
Calle de Finisterre No. 60, 28029 Madrid
DP Coordinator Rebeca González Barreiro
Languages Spanish
T: +34 913 14 63 12
W: iespf2014.villatic.org

IES Ramiro de Maeztu
C/ Serrano 127, 28006 Madrid
DP Coordinator José Miguel Moreno Sánchez
Languages Spanish
T: +34 91 561 7842
W: www.educa.madrid.org/web/ies.ramirodemaeztu.madrid

IES Real Instituto de Jovellanos
Avenida de la Constitucion s/n, 33071 Gijon, Asturias
DP Coordinator Juan Francisco Antona Blázquez
Languages Spanish
T: +34 985 38 77 03
W: www.iesjovellanos.com

IES Rosa Chacel
Calle Huertas 68, Colmenar Viejo, 28770 Madrid
DP Coordinator Marco A. García Ollero
Languages Spanish
T: +34 91 846 48 01
W: ies.rosachacel.colmenarviejo.educa.madrid.org

IES Rosalia De Castro
San Clemente 3, Santiago de Compostela, 15705 A Coruña, Galicia
DP Coordinator Arantxa Fuentes
Languages Spanish
T: +34 981 569 650
W: www.iesrosalia.net

IES Santa Clara
c/ Santa Clara 13, 39001 Santander, Cantabria
DP Coordinator María Jesús Temprano Marañón
Languages Spanish
T: +34 942 216 550

Institut d'Educació Secundària Josep Lladonosa
Pla?a Maria Rúbies S/N, 25005 Lleida, Catalonia
DP Coordinator Jacint Llauradó
Languages Spanish
T: +34 97 3239531
W: www.insjoseplladonosa.cat

Institut D'Educacio Secundaria Son Pacs
Carretera de Soller 13, 07120 Palma De Mallorca, Balearic Islands
DP Coordinator Antonia Vidal Nicolau
Languages Catalan, Spanish, English
T: +34 97 1292050
W: www.iessonpacs.cat

Institut Gabriel Ferrater i Soler
Carretera de Montblanc 5-9, 43206 Reus, Tarragona, Catalonia
DP Coordinator David Moyano Cervelló
Languages English
T: +34 977342010
W: institutgabrielferrater.wordpress.com

Institut Jaume Vicens Vives
Isabel la Católica, 17, 17004 Girona, Catalonia
DP Coordinator Farners Brugués
Languages Catalan, Spanish
T: +34 972 200 130
W: ins-jvicensvives.xtec.cat

Institut Moisès Broggi
Calle Sant Quintí 32-50, 08041 Barcelona, Catalonia
DP Coordinator Anna Diaz Albors
Languages Spanish
T: +34 93 436 89 03
W: www.institutbroggi.org

Instituto de Educación Secundaria do Castro
C/Posada Curros 1, 36203 Vigo, Pontevedra, Galicia
DP Coordinator Isabel Flores Seijas
Languages Spanish
T: +34 986422974
W: centros.edu.xunta.es/iesdocastro

Instituto de Educación Secundaria Lancia
c. Egido Quintín, s/n, 24006 León, Castile & León
DP Coordinator Julio Fernandez Alcalde
Languages Spanish
T: +34 987259800
W: ieslancia.centros.educa.jcyl.es

International College Spain
C/Vereda Norte, 3, La Moraleja, 28109 Alcobendas, Madrid
DP Coordinator Jeroen Kuipers
MYP Coordinator Jennifer Barnett
PYP Coordinator Rosemary Cabedo
Languages English
T: +34 91 650 2398
W: www.icsmadrid.org

International School of Barcelona
Passeig Isaac Albeniz s/n, Vallpineda, 08870 Sitges, Barcelona, Catalonia
DP Coordinator Maria Kovac
Languages English
T: +34 93 894 20 40
W: educa4all.com

INTERNATIONAL SCHOOL SAN PATRICIO TOLEDO
Juan de Vergara, 1, Urbanización La Legua, 45005 Toledo, Castilla-La Mancha
DP Coordinator Philip Brotherton
MYP Coordinator Pilar Molina
PYP Coordinator Rebeca Albarrán Corroto
Languages English, Spanish
T: +34 925 280 363
E: infotoledo@colegiosanpatricio.es
W: colegiosanpatriciotoledo.com/en
See full details on page 140

Irabia-Izaga Colegio
Calle Cintruénigo, 31015 Pamplona, Navarre
DP Coordinator Daniel Doyle
Languages English, Spanish
T: +34 948 12 62 22
W: www.irabia-izaga.org

La Salle Bonanova
Passeig de la Bonanova, 8, 08022 Barcelona, Catalonia
DP Coordinator Joan Ferretjans i Marco
Languages English
T: +34 93 254 09 50
W: www.bonanova.lasalle.cat

Laude El Altillo School
C/ Santiago de Chile, s/n, 11407 Jerez de la Frontera, Cádiz, Andalusia
DP Coordinator María Teresa Martos Martos
Languages English, Spanish, French
T: +34 956 302 400
W: www.laudealtillo.com

Laude Newton College
Camino Viejo de Elche-Alicante Km, 3, Alicante, Valencia
DP Coordinator Jorge Sevilla Esclapez
MYP Coordinator Antonio Soriano
Languages Spanish, English
T: +34 96 545 14 28
W: www.laudenewtoncollege.com

Les Alzines
La Creu de Palau 2, 17003 Girona, Catalonia
DP Coordinator Roser Jorba Campo
Languages Spanish
T: +34 972 212162
W: www.institucio.org/lesalzines

Lestonnac L'Ensenyança
Carrer Arc de Sant Llorenç, 2, 43003 Tarragona, Catalonia
DP Coordinator Carmen García Valiente
Languages English
T: +34 977 23 25 19
W: lestonnac-tarragona.net

Liceo Sorolla c
Avda. Bularas 4, 28224 Pozuelo de Alarcón, Madrid
DP Coordinator José Manuel de los Ríos Beca
Languages English
T: +34 91 715 04 99
W: www.colegioliceosorolla.es

Lledo International School
Camino Caminàs, 175, Castellón de la Plana, 12003 Castellón, Valencia
DP Coordinator Ester Escrig de Casas
Languages Spanish
T: +34 964723170
W: www.nace.edu.es/lledo

Lycée Français de Gavà Bon Soleil
Camí de la Pava, no. 15, Gavà, 08850 Barcelona, Catalonia
DP Coordinator Victor Solà
Languages English, French
T: +34 93 633 13 58
W: www.bonsoleil.es

Princess Margaret School
Passeig de la Fond d'en Fargas 15-17, 8032 Barcelona, Catalonia
PYP Coordinator Marta García
Languages English, Spanish
T: +34 934 290 313
W: www.princessmargaret.org

Salesians Sant Àngel (Salesians de Sarriá)
Rafael Batlle nº 7, 08017 Barcelona, Catalonia
DP Coordinator Carlos Escriche Marco
Languages Spanish
T: +34 932031100
W: sarria.salesians.cat

SEK INTERNATIONAL SCHOOL ALBORÁN
C/ Barlovento 141, Urb. Almerimar, El Ejido, 04711 Almería, Andalusia
DP Coordinator Estefania Sánchez
MYP Coordinator Sebastián Fuentes Valenzuela
PYP Coordinator Elnara Israfilova
Languages English, Spanish
T: +34 950 49 72 73
E: sek-alboran@sek.es
W: alboran.sek.es
See full details on page 187

SEK INTERNATIONAL SCHOOL ATLÁNTICO
Rúa Illa de Arousa 4, Boavista. A Caeira, Poio, 36005 Pontevedra, Galicia
DP Coordinator Yolanda Cenamor Montero
MYP Coordinator Mónica Azpilicueta Amorín
PYP Coordinator Sara Bouzada Sanmartin
Languages English, Spanish
T: +34 98 687 22 77
E: sek-atlantico@sek.es
W: atlantico.sek.es
See full details on page 188

SEK INTERNATIONAL SCHOOL CATALUNYA
Av. del Tremolencs, 24, La Garriga, 08530 Barcelona, Catalonia
DP Coordinator Adrià Van Waart
MYP Coordinator Carmen Fernández
PYP Coordinator Concepció Muntada
Languages English, Spanish, Catalan
T: +34 93 871 84 48
E: sek-catalunya@sek.es
W: catalunya.sek.es
See full details on page 189

SEK INTERNATIONAL SCHOOL CIUDALCAMPO
Urb. Ciudalcampo, Paseo de las Perdices, 2, San Sebastián de los Reyes, 28707 Madrid
DP Coordinator Daniella Spoones
MYP Coordinator James Shaw
PYP Coordinator Marisa Iglesias Lorenzo
Languages English, Spanish
T: +34 91 659 63 03
E: sek-ciudalcampo@sek.es
W: ciudalcampo.sek.es
See full details on page 190

SEK INTERNATIONAL SCHOOL EL CASTILLO
Urb. Villafranca del Castillo, Castillo de Manzanares, s/n, Villanueva de la Cañada, 28692 Madrid
DP Coordinator Fátima González
MYP Coordinator Elvira Chiquero
PYP Coordinator Melanie McGeever
Languages English, Spanish
T: +34 91 815 08 92
E: sek-castillo@sek.es
W: elcastillo.sek.es
See full details on page 192

SEK INTERNATIONAL SCHOOL SANTA ISABEL
Calle San Ildefonso, 18, 28012 Madrid
PYP Coordinator William Ivey
Languages English, Spanish
T: +34 91 527 90 94
E: sek-santaisabel@sek.es
W: santaisabel.sek.es
See full details on page 194

SOTOGRANDE INTERNATIONAL SCHOOL
Avda La Reserva SN, 11310 Sotogrande, Cádiz, Andalusia
DP Coordinator Hélène Caillet
MYP Coordinator Belén González
PYP Coordinator Andrea Bennett
Languages English
T: +34 956 795 902
E: info@sis.gl
W: www.sis.ac
See full details on page 197

St George, Madrid
Calle Padres Dominicos 1, 28050 Madrid
DP Coordinator Louise Clement
Languages English, Spanish
T: +34 916 508 440
W: stgeorgeinternational.es/madrid

St Peter's School Barcelona
C/Eduard Toldrà, 18, 08034 Barcelona, Catalonia
DP Coordinator Xavier Salvado
Languages English, Spanish
T: +34 93 204 36 12
W: www.stpeters.es

Swans International Secondary School
C/Lago de los Cisnes, s/n, Urb. Sierra Blanca, 29602 Marbella, Málaga, Andalusia
DP Coordinator Jose Prieto
Languages English
T: +34 952 902 755
W: www.swansschoolinternational.es

THE ACADEMY INTERNATIONAL SCHOOL
Camí de Son Ametler Vell, 250, 07141 Marratxí, Balearic Islands
DP Coordinator Caroline Foster
Languages English
T: +34 971 605008
E: info@theacademyschool.com
W: www.theacademyschool.com
See full details on page 216

YAGO SCHOOL
Avda. Antonio Mairena, 54, 41950 Castilleja de la Cuesta, Seville, Andalusia
DP Coordinator Blanca Domínguez
Languages English, Spanish
T: +34 955 51 1234
E: admissions@yagoschool.com
W: www.yagoschool.com
See full details on page 242

SUDAN

Confluence International School of Khartoum
Building No.5, Gamhouria Avenue, Khartoum 11111
MYP Coordinator Ikhlas Ahmed
PYP Coordinator Shaimaa Suleiman
Languages English, Arabic
T: +249 960099970
W: www.confluencesudan.org

Khartoum International Community School
PO Box 1840, Khartoum
DP Coordinator Linda Round
PYP Coordinator Darwin Balog-ang
Languages English
T: +249 183 215 000
W: www.kics.sd

SWAZILAND

WATERFORD KAMHLABA UWC OF SOUTHERN AFRICA
Waterford Park, Mbabane H100
DP Coordinator Elizabeth Cummergen
Languages English
T: +268 24220867
E: principal@waterford.sz
W: www.waterford.sz
See full details on page 237

SWEDEN

Aranäsgymnasiet
Gymnasiegatan 44, 434 42 Kungsbacka, Halland
DP Coordinator Ruth Walton
Languages English
T: +46 300 83 40 00
W: www.aranasgymnasiet.kungsbacka.se

Åva Gymnasium
Box 1450, 183 14 Täby, Stockholm
DP Coordinator Jo-Anne Ahlmen
Languages English
T: +46 (0) 855 55 8000
W: www.taby.se/ava

Bladins International School of Malmö
Box 20093, Själlandstorget 1, 200 74 Malmö, Skåne
DP Coordinator Daniel Nordin Baker
MYP Coordinator Daniel Baker
PYP Coordinator Anisa Throup
Languages English
T: +46 40 987970
W: bism.bladins.se

British International School of Stockholm
Östrka Valhallavagen 17, 182 68 Djursholm, Stockholm
DP Coordinator Melanie Stell
Languages English
T: +46 8 755 2375
W: www.bisstockholm.se

Carlforsska gymnasiet
Sångargatan 1, 722 19 Västerås, Västmanland
CP Coordinator Annelize Deuchar
DP Coordinator Tony Nicolas
Languages English
T: +4621390703
W: www.vasteras.se/carlforsska

Europaskolan in Södermalm
Gotlandsgatan 43, 116 65 Stockholm
MYP Coordinator Julian Bethell
PYP Coordinator Emelie Pettersson
Languages English, Swedish
T: +46 8 335054
W: www.europaskolan.nu

Europaskolan in Vasastan
Luntmakargatan 101, 113 51 Stockholm
MYP Coordinator Tobias Löfgren
PYP Coordinator Maria Angelidou
Languages Swedish
T: +46 8 335095
W: www.europaskolan.nu

Haganässkolan
Box 501, 343 23 Älmhult, Kronoberg
DP Coordinator Krista Baker
Languages English
T: +46 476 552 22
W: haganasgymnasiet.se/haganasskolan

Hvitfeldtska Gymnasiet
Rektorsgatan 2, 411 33 Göteborg, Västra Götaland
DP Coordinator James Du Priest
Languages English
T: +46 31 36 70 608
W: goteborg.se/hvitfeldtska

International High School of the Gothenburg Region
Molinsgatan 6, 411 33 Göteborg, Västra Götaland
DP Coordinator Lee Brown
Languages English
T: +46 31 708 92 00
W: www.ihgr.se

International School of Helsingborg
Östra Vallgatan 9, 254 37 Helsingborg, Skåne
DP Coordinator Daniel Blair
MYP Coordinator Pernilla Rankin
PYP Coordinator Magdalena Simons
Languages English
T: +46 42 105 705
W: www.helsingborg.se/internationalschool

International School of Lund – Katedralskolan
Nygatan 21, 222 29 Lund, Skåne
MYP Coordinator Darrell Piper
PYP Coordinator Alison Kruckow
Languages English
T: +46 463 571 24

International School of the Gothenburg Region (ISGR)
Molinsgatan 6, 411 33 Göteborg, Västra Götaland
MYP Coordinator Alexei Gafan
PYP Coordinator Ellen Trelles
Languages English
T: +46 31 708 92 00
W: www.isgr.se

International School of the Stockholm Region
Bohusgatan 24-26, 116 67 Stockholm
DP Coordinator Martin Davidsson
MYP Coordinator Christiane Candella
PYP Coordinator Jenny Arvidsson
Languages English
T: +46 8 508 426 50
W: internationalschoolofthestockholmregion.stockholm.se

Internationella Engelska Gymnasiet
Allhelgonagatan 4, 118 58 Stockholm
DP Coordinator Nikki Sang
Languages English
T: +46 8 562 28 700
W: www.engelskagymnasiet.se

IT-Gymnasiet i Skövde
Kylarvägen 1, 541 34 Skövde, Västra Götaland
DP Coordinator Ruth Morrisson Svensson
Languages English
T: +46 500 41 69 90
W: www.it-gymnasiet.se

Katedralskolan in Linköping
Platensgatan 20, 582 20 Linköping, Östergötland
DP Coordinator Jonathan Lowrey
Languages English
T: +46 132 07549
W: www.linkoping.se/katedral

Katedralskolan in Lund
St Södergatan 22, 222 23 Lund, Skåne
DP Coordinator Katarina Flennmark
Languages English
T: +46 4635 76 09
W: www.katte.se

Katedralskolan in Uppsala
Skolgatan 2, 753 12 Uppsala
DP Coordinator Maria Elevant Grönberg
Languages English
T: +46 18 568100
W: www.katedral.se

Katedralskolan, Skara
Brunsbogatan 1, 532 88 Skara, Västra Götaland
DP Coordinator Annemarie Matsson
Languages English
T: +46 511 326 00
W: www.katedralskolan.nu

Lund International School
Warholmsväg 3, 224 65 Lund, Skåne
MYP Coordinator Lesley Pitman-Lundqvist
PYP Coordinator Lesley Pitman-Lundqvist
Languages English
T: +46737087926
W: www.lundinternationalschool.com

Malmö Borgarskola
Box 17029, 200 10 Malmö, Skåne
CP Coordinator Andreas Lejon
DP Coordinator Magnus Andersson
Languages English
T: +46 4034 1000
W: www.malmoborgarskola.se

Malmö International School
Packhusgatan 2, 205 80 Malmö, Skåne
MYP Coordinator Patrick Kelly
PYP Coordinator Kristina Pettersson
Languages English, Spanish, German
T: +46 (0)733 23 70 37

Per Brahegymnasiet
Residensgatan, 553 16 Jönköping
DP Coordinator Allyson Neuberg
Languages English
T: +46 36 105 472
W: www.pb.edu.jonkoping.se

Rudbecksgymnasiet
Box 31160, 701 35 Örebro
DP Coordinator Anne-Sophie Skalin
Languages English
T: +46 19 21 65 69
W: www.ru.orebro.se

Sannarpsgymnasiet
Frennarpsvägen 1, 302 44 Halmstad, Halland
DP Coordinator Lotta Hydén
Languages English
T: +46 3513 7675
W: www.sannarpsgymnasiet.halmstad.se

Sigtunaskolan Humanistiska Läroverket
Box 508, 193 28 Sigtunase, Stockholm
DP Coordinator Kerry Browning
MYP Coordinator Eva Fellin
Languages English, Swedish
T: +46 8 592 571 00
W: www.sshl.se

Söderportgymnasiet
Västra Boulevarden 53, 291 31 Kristianstad, Skåne
DP Coordinator Charlotte Mechura
Languages English
T: +46 4413 6049
W: www.buf.kristianstad.se/soderport

St Eskils Gymnasium
Smedjegatan 3-5, 631 86 Eskilstuna, Södermanland
DP Coordinator Trevor Ayton
Languages English
T: +46 16 710 10 00
W: www.eskilstuna.se

Stockholm International School
Johannesgatan 18, 111 38 Stockholm
DP Coordinator Jarno Ampuja
MYP Coordinator Bradley Lister
Languages English
T: +46 (0)8 412 40 00
W: www.intsch.se

Sven Eriksonsgymnasiet
Sven Eriksonplatsen, 501 80 Borås, Västra Götaland
DP Coordinator Martin Idehall
Languages English
T: +46 33 35 80 48
W: boras.se/svenerikson

Täljegymnasiet
Erik Dahlbergs väg 1-3, 152 40 Södertälje, Stockholm
DP Coordinator Rose-Marie Fallgren
Languages English
T: +46 8 52301336
W: www.sodertalje.se

Teleborg Centrum Skola
Smedsvängen 72, 352 54 Växjö, Kronoberg
MYP Coordinator Shane Lewis
Languages English
T: +46 470 419 34
W: vaxjo.se/teleborgcentrum

The International School of Älmhult
Skolgatan 1, 343 23 Älmhult, Kronoberg
MYP Coordinator Jessie Aaron
PYP Coordinator Harpreet Mehta
Languages English
T: +46 476 55188
W: www.almhult.se/english

Torsbergsgymnasiet
Läroverksgatan 36, 821 33 Bollnäs, Gävleborg
DP Coordinator Margaretta Eriksson
Languages English
T: + 46 278 254 91
W: www.torsbergsgymnasiet.se

Växjö Katedralskola
Samuel Ödmans Väg 1, 352 39 Växjö, Kronoberg
DP Coordinator Gilles Kennedy
Languages English
T: +46 470 41736
W: www.katedralskolan.se

SWITZERLAND

AIGLON COLLEGE
Avenue Centrale 61, 1885 Chesières-Villars
DP Coordinator Mr. Esmond Tweedie
Languages English
T: +41 (0)24 496 6177
E: admissions@aiglon.ch
W: www.aiglon.ch

See full details on page 65

COLLÈGE ALPIN BEAU SOLEIL
Route Du Village 1, Villars-sur-Ollon 1884
DP Coordinator Helen Taylor-Cevey
Languages English, French
T: +41 24 496 2626
E: info@beausoleil.ch
W: www.beausoleil.ch

See full details on page 88

COLLÈGE CHAMPITTET, PULLY
Chemin de Champittet 1, 1009 Pully
DP Coordinator Keith Sykes
Languages English, French
T: +41 21 721 0505
E: admissions@champittet.ch
W: www.champittet.ch

See full details on page 89

COLLÈGE DU LÉMAN
74, route de Sauverny, 1290 Versoix, Geneva
CP Coordinator Julie Hutchins
DP Coordinator Jana Krainova Samuda
Languages English, French
T: +41 22 775 56 56
E: admissions@cdl.ch
W: www.cdl.ch

See full details on page 90

Ecole des Arches
Chemin de Mornex 2-4, PO Box 566, Lausanne, Vaud 1001
DP Coordinator Didier Curty
Languages French
T: +41 21 311 09 69
W: www.ecoledesarches.ch

ECOLE NOUVELLE DE LA SUISSE ROMANDE – CHAILLY
Chemin de Rovéréaz 20, CP 161, 1000 Lausanne 12
DP Coordinator Mr. David Mills
Languages French, English
T: +41 21 654 65 00
E: info@ensr.ch
W: www.ensr.ch

See full details on page 96

GYMNASIUM AM MÜNSTERPLATZ
Münsterplatz 15, 4051 Basel
DP Coordinator Dr. Manuel Pombo
Languages German, English
T: +41 61 267 88 70
E: gymnasium.muensterplatz@bs.ch
W: www.gmbasel.ch

See full details on page 109

Gymnasium Bäumlihof
Zu den drei Linden 80, Basel 4058
DP Coordinator Isla Ward
Languages German
T: +41 61 606 33 11
W: www.gbbasel.ch

Haut-Lac International Bilingual School
Ch. de Pangires 26, St-Légier-la Chiésaz CH-1806
DP Coordinator David Newsam
MYP Coordinator David Bauzá
Languages English, French
T: +41 (0)21 555 50 00
W: www.haut-lac.ch

Institut auf dem Rosenberg
Hohenweg 60, Ch-9000 St Gallen
DP Coordinator Carmen Dare
Languages English, German
T: +41 71 277 77 77
W: www.instrosenberg.ch

INSTITUT FLORIMONT
37 Avenue du Petit-Lancy, Petit-Lancy 1213
DP Coordinator Noha Benani
Languages English, French
T: +41 2287 90000
E: admissions@florimont.ch
W: www.florimont.ch
See full details on page 117

Institut International de Lancy
24, avenue Eugène-Lance, Grand-Lancy CH-1212
DP Coordinator Tania McMahon
Languages English, French
T: +41 22 794 2620
W: www.iil.ch

Institut Le Rosey
Château du Rosey, 1180 Rolle
DP Coordinator Craig Foreman
Languages English, French
T: +41 21 822 5500
W: www.rosey.ch

INSTITUT MONTANA
Schönfels 5, 6300 Zug
DP Coordinator Dr Anne Faassen
Languages English, German
T: +41 41 729 11 99
E: admissions@montana-zug.ch
W: www.montana-zug.ch
See full details on page 120

INTER-COMMUNITY SCHOOL ZURICH
Strubenacher 3, 8126 Zumikon
DP Coordinator Ann Lautrette
MYP Coordinator Graham Gardner
PYP Coordinator Claire Febrey
Languages English
T: +41 44 919 8300
E: contact@icsz.ch
W: www.icsz.ch
See full details on page 121

INTERNATIONAL SCHOOL BASEL
Fleischbachstrasse 2, 4153 Reinach
DP Coordinator Sean Coffey
MYP Coordinator Siân Thomas
PYP Coordinator Lyneth Magsalin
Languages English
T: +41 61 715 33 33
E: info@isbasel.ch
W: www.isbasel.ch
See full details on page 123

INTERNATIONAL SCHOOL OF BERNE
Allmendingenweg 9, 3073 Gümligen, Bern
DP Coordinator Brette Book
MYP Coordinator Kirsty DeWilde
PYP Coordinator Dominic Thomas
Languages English
T: +41 (0)31 959 10 00
E: admissions@isberne.ch
W: www.isberne.ch
See full details on page 126

International School of Central Switzerland
Lorzenparkstrasse 8, Cham 6330
DP Coordinator Kamran Baig
PYP Coordinator Kamran Baig
Languages English
T: +41 41 781 44 44
W: www.isocs.ch

International School of Geneva (Campus des Nations)
11 route des Morillons, CH-1218 Grand Saconnex
CP Coordinator Alexandra Juniper
DP Coordinator Alexandra Juniper
MYP Coordinator Robin Smith
PYP Coordinator Nikki Ross
Languages English, French
T: +41 22 770 4700
W: www.ecolint.ch/campus/campus-des-nations

International School of Geneva (La Châtaigneraie Campus)
2, chemin de la Ferme, 1297 Founey
DP Coordinator Julian Jefferys
PYP Coordinator Mrs Carine Lagacé
Languages English
T: +41 22 960 9111
W: www.ecolint.ch/campus/la-chataigneraie

International School of Geneva (La Grande Boissière Campus)
62, route de Chêne, 1208 Geneva
DP Coordinator Conan de Wilde
Languages English, French
T: +41 22 787 2400
W: www.ecolint.ch/campus/la-grande-boissiere

International School of Lausanne
Chemin de la Grangette 2, 1052 Le Mont-sur-Lausanne
DP Coordinator Oliver Alexander
MYP Coordinator Darryl Anderson
PYP Coordinator Erin Threlfall
Languages English
T: +41 21 560 02 02
W: www.isl.ch

International School of Rheinfelden
Zürcherstrasse 9, Drei Könige, Rheinfelden CH-4310
PYP Coordinator Bryan Murray
Languages German
T: +41 61 831 06 06
W: www.isrh.ch

International School of Schaffhausen
Mühlentalstrasse 280, Schaffhausen CH-8200
DP Coordinator Ashley Thorpe
MYP Coordinator Ebru Guever
PYP Coordinator Sara Goacher
Languages English
T: +41 52 624 1707
W: www.issh.ch

INTERNATIONAL SCHOOL OF TICINO SA
Via Ponteggia, 23, Cadempino, 6814 Lugano
PYP Coordinator Katarzyna Krohn
Languages English, Italian
T: +41 919710344
E: frontoffice@isticino.com
W: www.isticino.com
See full details on page 139

International School of Zug & Luzern, Riverside Campus
Rothustrasse 4b, 6331 Hünnenberg
CP Coordinator Robert Sugden
DP Coordinator Zoe Badcock
MYP Coordinator Maria le Guen
Languages English
T: +41 41 768 2950
W: www.iszl.ch

International School of Zug & Luzern, Zug Campus
Walterswil, 6340 Baar
PYP Coordinator Sarah Osborne
Languages English
T: +41 41 768 29 00
W: www.iszl.ch

International School Rheintal
Aeulistrasse 10, Buchs 9470
DP Coordinator Steve Bavaro
MYP Coordinator Oliver Beck
PYP Coordinator Nilde Pais
Languages English
T: +41 81 750 6300
W: www.isr.ch

International School Zurich North
Industriestrasse 50, Wallisellen CH-8304
PYP Coordinator Rebecca Nolan
Languages English
T: +41 44 830 7000
W: www.iszn.ch

Kantonsschule am Burggraben St. Gallen
Burggraben 21, St. Gallen 9000
DP Coordinator Peter Litscher
Languages English, German
T: +41 712281414
W: ksbg.ch

Kantonsschule Wettingen
Klosterstrasse 11, Wettingen 5430
DP Coordinator Heinz Anklin
Languages English
T: +41 (0)56 437 24 00
W: www.kanti-wettingen.ch

KV Zürich Die Wirtschaftsschule
Limmatstrasse 310, Zürich 8031
DP Coordinator Sara Bucher
Languages English, German
T: +41 44 444 66 00
W: www.kvz-schule.ch

La Côte International School
Chemin de Clamogne 8, 1170 Aubonne
DP Coordinator Andrew Mcloughlin
MYP Coordinator Emily Hardwicke
Languages English
T: +41 (0)22 823 26 26
W: www.international-school.org

Le Régent Crans-Montana College
Rue du Zier 4, CH-3963 Crans-Montana
DP Coordinator Jennifer Cogbill
Languages English, French
T: +41 (0)27 480 3201
W: www.leregentcollege.com

Lemania College Lausanne
Chemin de Préville 3, CP 550, 1001 Lausanne
DP Coordinator Giovanna Crisante
Languages English, French
T: +41 21 320 15 01
W: www.lemania.ch

Lémania International School Altdorf
St. Josefsweg 15, 6460 Altdorf
DP Coordinator Sébastien Morard
Languages English
T: +41 41 874 0000
W: lisa.swiss

Leysin American School in Switzerland
3 Chemin de la Source, Leysin 1854
DP Coordinator Ronan Lynch
Languages English
T: +41 24 493 4888
W: www.las.ch

Literargymnasium Rämibühl
Rämistrasse 56, Zürich 8001
DP Coordinator Annette Haueter
Languages English
T: +41 1 265 62 11
W: www.lgr.ch

Lyceum Alpinum Zuoz
Aguêl 185, CH-7524 Zuoz
CP Coordinator Erna Romeril
DP Coordinator Marie-Louise Brown
Languages English
T: +41 81 851 30 00
W: www.lyceum-alpinum.ch

Mutuelle d'études secondaires
7bis boulevard Carl-Vogt, Genève 1205
DP Coordinator Nathalie Rapaille
Languages French
T: + 41 (0)22 741 00 01
W: www.ecolemes.ch

Neue Kantonsschule Aarau
Schanzmättelistrasse 32, Aarau 5000
DP Coordinator Francisca Ruiz
Languages English
T: +41 62 837 94 55
W: www.nksa.ch

Obersee Bilingual School
Eichenstrasse 4C, 8808 Pfaeffikon
DP Coordinator Louise Hoyne-Butler
Languages English, German
T: +41 55 511 38 00
W: www.oberseebilingualschool.ch

Realgymnasium Rämibühl
Rämistrasse 56, Zürich 8001
DP Coordinator Philipp Wettstein
Languages English
T: +41 44 265 63 12
W: www.rgzh.ch

Rudolf Steiner Schule Oberaargau
Ringstrasse 30, 4900 Langenthal
DP Coordinator Philip Pflugbeil
Languages English, German
T: +41 (0)62 922 69 05
W: www.rsso.ch

SIS Swiss International School Basel
Erlenstrasse 15, Basel CH-4058
DP Coordinator Grayson McCready
Languages English
T: +41 61 683 71 40
W: www.swissinternationalschool.ch/schulorte/basel

SIS Swiss International School Zürich
Seidenstrasse 2, Wallisellen CH-8304
DP Coordinator Christoph Neuenstein
Languages English
T: +41 44 388 99 44
W: www.swissinternationalschool.ch/schulorte/zuerich

ST. GEORGE'S INTERNATIONAL SCHOOL, SWITZERLAND
Chemin de St. Georges 19, CH-1815 Clarens/Montreux
DP Coordinator Dr David Brooke
Languages English
T: +41 21 964 3411
E: admissions@stgeorges.ch
W: www.stgeorges.ch
See full details on page 204

STIFTSSCHULE ENGELBERG
Benediktinerkloster 5, Engelberg 6390
DP Coordinator Hansueli Flückiger
Languages German, English
T: +41 41 639 61 00
E: info@stiftsschule-engelberg.ch
W: www.stiftsschule-engelberg.ch
See full details on page 210

TASIS THE AMERICAN SCHOOL IN SWITZERLAND
Via Collina d'Oro 15, 6926 Montagnola-Lugano
DP Coordinator Howard Stickley
Languages English
T: +41 91 960 5151
E: admissions@tasis.ch
W: www.tasis.ch
See full details on page 214

Zurich International School
Steinacherstr 140, 8820 Wädenswil
DP Coordinator Joseph Amato
Languages English
T: +41 58 750 2500
W: www.zis.ch

TANZANIA

Dar es Salaam International Academy
PO Box 23282, Dar es Salaam
DP Coordinator Linet Edison
MYP Coordinator Susan Ngoye
PYP Coordinator Saviona Furtado
Languages English
T: +255 22 2600 202
W: www.diatz.cc

International School of Tanganyika Ltd
United Nations Road, PO Box 2651, Dar es Salaam
DP Coordinator Jason Crook
MYP Coordinator Dharma Sears
PYP Coordinator Michael Mansell
Languages English
T: +255 22 2151817
W: www.istafrica.com

Iringa International School
PO Box 912, Lumumba Street, Gangilonga, Iringa
PYP Coordinator Kristeen Chachage
Languages English
T: +255 26 2702018
W: iis.ac.tz

The Aga Khan Mzizima Secondary School
P.O. Box 21563, Fire Road, Upanga, Dar es Salaam
DP Coordinator Daniel Swai
PYP Coordinator Blandina Duwe
Languages English
T: +255 22 215 1253
W: www.agakhanschools.org/tanzania/akmss

UWC East Africa, Arusha Campus
PO Box 2691, Arusha
DP Coordinator Reed Anderson
MYP Coordinator Florence Larpent
PYP Coordinator Amanda Bowen
Languages English
T: +255 27 250 5029
W: www.uwcea.org

UWC East Africa, Moshi Campus
PO Box 733, Lema Road, Moshi
DP Coordinator Margaret Brunt
MYP Coordinator David Oloo
PYP Coordinator Catherine Saha
Languages English
T: +255 762 326 385
W: www.uwcea.org

TOGO

Arc-en-Ciel International School
Nyekonakpoe, Lomé BP: 2985
DP Coordinator Taid Rahimi
MYP Coordinator Taid Rahimi
PYP Coordinator Taid Rahimi
Languages French, English
T: +228 2222 0329
W: www.arc-en-ciel.org

The British School of Lomé
Residence du Benin, Lomé 20050
DP Coordinator Philip Smith
Languages English
T: +228 2226 46 06
W: www.bsl.tg

TUNISIA

American Cooperative School of Tunis
ACST BP150, Cite Taieb M' Hiri, Laouina 2045
DP Coordinator Lucie Lecocq Otsing
Languages English
T: +216 71 760 905
W: www.acst.net

École Canadienne de Tunis
Rue des Minéraux Charguia 1, Tunis 2035
MYP Coordinator Imen Ben aissa
PYP Coordinator Meriem Cammoun
Languages French
T: +216 71 206 035
W: www.ec-tunis.com

TURKEY

Adapazari Enka Schools
Camyolu Mah, Adapazari Sakarya 54100
MYP Coordinator Asli Sanli Mutlu
PYP Coordinator Zühal Ergül
Languages English
T: +90 264 323 37 74
W: www.enka.k12.tr

Aka School
Radyum Sok No 21 Basin Sitesi, Bahcelievler, Istanbul
DP Coordinator Besime Erbilen
Languages English
T: +90 2125572772
W: www.akakoleji.k12.tr

ALKEV Schools
Alkent 2000 Mah. Mehmet Yesilgül Cd. No: 7, Büyükcekmece, Istanbul
DP Coordinator Seda Cakir
Languages English, German
T: +90 212 886 88 40
W: www.alkev.k12.tr

American Collegiate Institute
Inonu Caddesi, No 476, Goztepe, Izmir 35290
DP Coordinator Mine Erim
Languages English
T: +90 232 285 3401
W: www.aci.k12.tr

Ankara Türk Telekom Sosyal Bilimler Lisesi
Mutlukent Mah. 1919, Sokak NO1 Ümitköy, Çankaya, Ankara 06810
DP Coordinator Zeliha Gökben Kardeş
Languages English
T: +90 312 236 63 77
W: asbl.meb.k12.tr

AREL Schools (Kindergarten/Primary/ Middle/High)
Merkez Mah, Selahattin Pinar Sok, No:3 Yenibosna – Bahcelievler, Istanbul 34197
MYP Coordinator Burcu Geçici
PYP Coordinator Umut Brezina
Languages English, Turkish
T: +90 212 550 4930
W: www.arel.k12.tr

Beykoz Doga Campus
Adres:Fener Yolu Cad. No:6 Dereseki, Akbaba, Beykoz, Istanbul
PYP Coordinator Keziban Kose
Languages English
T: +90 (216) 320 52 00
W: www.dogaokullari.com/eng/schools/beykoz-doga-campus

Bilkent Erzurum Laboratory School
Prof. Dr. Ihsan Dogramaci Bulvari, Çat Yolu/Palandöken, Erzurum 25070
DP Coordinator Dincer Akis
Languages English
T: +90 442 342 6171
W: www.obel.bilkent.edu.tr

Bilkent Laboratory & International School
East Campus, Ankara 06800
DP Coordinator Feray Ozdemir Gur
PYP Coordinator Ayten Korkmaz
Languages English, Turkish
T: +90 312 2905361
W: www.blisankara.org

Bodrum Private Marmara College
Ortakent Mahallesi, Cumhuriyet Caddesi No: 2A-1, Ortakent Yahsi Beldesi, Bodrum, Mugla 48420
DP Coordinator Berrin Yurdakul
Languages English
T: +90 2523 586113
W: www.mek.k12.tr

Bodrum Private Marmara Primary School
Bodrum Özel Marmara Koleji, Bitez Mahallesi, Zeytinli caddesi No 60/A, Mugla, Bodrum 48470
PYP Coordinator Gul Pasali Yagci
Languages English
T: +90 252 3191010
W: www.mek.k12.tr

British International School – Istanbul
Etiler Mahallesi Cengiz Topel Sokak Tugcular Caddesi, No:27 Etiler, Istanbul MASLAK
DP Coordinator Seef Eddeen Marsden
Languages English
T: +90 212 257 51 36
W: www.bis.k12.tr

Cakir Schools
Orhaneli Yolu, Egitimciler Cd 15, Nilufer, Bursa
DP Coordinator Sencer Donmez
MYP Coordinator Bahar Cakir
PYP Coordinator Naile Cigdem Durukan
Languages English, Turkish
T: +90 224 451 9330
W: www.cakir.k12.tr

Çanakkale Özel ilkokulu
Izmir Yolu 12.Km Güzelyali, Çanakkale 17100
PYP Coordinator Pinar Usta
Languages English, Turkish
T: +90 286 232 86 86
W: www.canakkalekoleji.com

Deutsche Schule Izmir
Kuscular Cad. No 82, Kuscular Köyü, Urla/Izmir 35430
DP Coordinator Filiz Ünal
Languages English
T: +90 (0)232 234 7507
W: www.ds-izmir.com

Edirne Beykent Schools
Ayse Kadin Tren Gari Yani, Edirne 22100
DP Coordinator Onder Gurkaynak
MYP Coordinator Onder Gurkaynak
PYP Coordinator Secil Sen
Languages English
T: +90 506 301 7073
W: www.beykent.k12.tr

Enka Schools
Sadi Gülçelik Spor Sitesi, Istinye, Istanbul 34460
DP Coordinator Natalie Parker
MYP Coordinator Teni Karaman
PYP Coordinator Zeyneb Sengezer
Languages English, Turkish
T: +90 212 705 65 00
W: www.enkaokullari.k12.tr

Ernst-Reuter-Schule
Tunus Cad 56, 06680 Kavaklidere-Ankara
DP Coordinator Suna Ahmad
Languages English
T: +90 312 426 63 82
W: www.ers-ankara.com

Eyüboglu Atasehir Primary School
2 Cadde 59 Ada Manolya 4, Bloklari yani No 6, Atasehir, Istanbul 34758
PYP Coordinator Firuze Vanlioglu
Languages Turkish, English
T: +90 216 522 12 22
W: www.eyuboglu.com

Eyüboglu Kemerburgaz Middle School
Mithatpasa Mah. Pirinccikoy Yolu, Istanbul 34075
MYP Coordinator Arzu Onat Konusmaz
Languages English, Turkish
T: +90 216 522 12 72
W: www.eyuboglu.com

Eyüboglu Kemerburgaz Preschool & Primary School
Mithatpasa Mah. Pirinccikoy Yolu, Istanbul 34075
PYP Coordinator Meliz Katlav
Languages English
T: +90 216 522 12 72
W: www.eyuboglu.com

EYÜBOGLU SCHOOLS
Esenevler Mah, Dr Rüstem Eyüboglu sok 3, Ümraniye, Istanbul 34762
DP Coordinator Oguz Günenc
MYP Coordinator Gülsah Cekic
PYP Coordinator Mevce Selek
Languages Turkish, English
T: +90 216 522 12 12
E: eyuboglu@eyuboglu.k12.tr
W: www.eyuboglu.k12.tr

See full details on page 101

Ezgililer Private Primary School
Kusculu Mah. 1728 Sok. No:6, Ilkadim, Samsun
PYP Coordinator Müge Öztürk
Languages English
T: +90 362 233 2122
W: ezgililer.k12.tr

FMV Ayazaga Isik High School
Buyukdere Cad. No. 106 Maslak, Sariyer, Istanbul 34460
DP Coordinator Jenny Chavush
Languages English
T: +90 0212 286 1130
W: www.fmv.edu.tr

FMV Erenköy Isik High School
Sinan Ercan Cad. No: 17, Kazasker Erenköy, Istanbul 34736
DP Coordinator Sinem Özgöz
Languages English
T: +90 216 355 22 07
W: www.fmv.edu.tr

Gazi University Foundation Private High School
Ali Suavi Street, Eti Quarter No 15, Maltepe, Ankara 06570
DP Coordinator Arzu Aksoy
Languages English
T: +90 312 232 28 12
W: www.kolej.gazi.edu.tr

GKV Cemil Alevli College
Guvenevler Mahallesi, Hoca Ahmet Yesevi Caddesi, No. 2, Sehitkamil, Gaziantep 27060
DP Coordinator Ozlem Kara
Languages English
T: +90 342 321 01 00
W: www.gkv.k12.tr

Gökkusagi Koleji – Bahçelievler
Eski Londra Asfalti No: 15 Haznedar, Bahçelievler, Istanbul
DP Coordinator Murat Kotan
Languages English, Turkish
T: +90 212 644 59 00
W: www.gokkusagi.k12.tr

Gökkusagi Koleji – Bahçesehir
Orhan Gazi Mah, 1654 sk. No: 40, Esenyurt, Istanbul
PYP Coordinator Pinar Calis
Languages English, Turkish
T: +90 212 672 84 26
W: www.gokkusagi.k12.tr

Gökkusagi Koleji – Ümraniye
Inkilap Mh. Alemdag Cd. Üntel Sk. No:30, Ümraniye, Istanbul
PYP Coordinator Lale Tugba Oral
Languages English
T: +90 216 634 60 60
W: www.gokkusagi.k12.tr

IDV Özel Bilkent High School
IDV Özel Bilkent Ilkokulu, Ortaokulu ve Lisesi Universiteler Mah 1600, Cad. No. 6, Dogu Kampus, Ankara 06800
DP Coordinator Andrew Miller
Languages English, Turkish
T: +90 312 290 8939
W: www.obl.bilkent.edu.tr

IDV Özel Bilkent Middle School
IDV Özel Bilkent Ilkokulu, Ortaokulu ve Lisesi, Universiteler Mah 1600, Cad. No. 6, Dogu Kampus, Ankara 06800
MYP Coordinator Servet Altan
PYP Coordinator Gülsen Çiçek Keskinsoy
Languages Turkish, English
T: +90 312 2905440
W: www.obi.bilkent.edu.tr

IELEV Private High School
Ensar Cad. No:4/3 Nisantepe Mah. B Blok, Çekmeköy, Istanbul 34794
DP Coordinator Mrs. Rüya Dogan
Languages English, German, Turkish
T: +90 216 30430 92
W: www.ielev.k12.tr/tr/lise

Irmak School
Cemil Topuzlu Caddesi No:100, Caddebostan P.K. 34728, Kadiköy, Istanbul
PYP Coordinator Tuba Yoleri
Languages Turkish, English
T: +90 216 411 3923/4/5
W: www.irmak.k12.tr

Isikkent Egitim Kampusu
6240/5 Sokak No. 3, Karacaoglan Mah, Yesilova, Izmir 35070
DP Coordinator Lyudmyla Boysan
MYP Coordinator Lyudmyla Boysan
PYP Coordinator Evrim Yalcin Onder
Languages Turkish, English
T: +90 232 462 71 00
W: www.isikkent.k12.tr

Istanbul Beykent Schools
Gurpinar E-5 Yol Ayrimi, Beykent Büyükçekmece, Istanbul 34500
DP Coordinator Fatma Gunal
MYP Coordinator Fatma Gunal
PYP Coordinator Fatma Gunal
Languages English
T: +90 212 872 6432
W: www.beykent.k12.tr

Istanbul International Community School
Karaagac Koyu Mahallesi, Kahraman Caddesi, 27/1, 34500 Buyukcekmece, Istanbul
DP Coordinator Omer Kipmen
MYP Coordinator Heath Fontes
PYP Coordinator Monika Hoge
Languages English
T: +90 212 857 8264
W: www.iics.k12.tr

Istanbul Prof. Dr Mümtaz Turhan Sosyal Bilimler Lisesi
Fevzi Çakmak Cad. Fatih Mah., No:2 Yenibosna, Bahçelievler, Istanbul
DP Coordinator Selin Sethi
Languages English
T: +902 1255 16146
W: www.isbl.k12.tr

ISTEK BARIS SCHOOLS
Bagdat Cad. No: 238/1, Ciftehavuzlar – Kadiköy, Istanbul 34730
PYP Coordinator Ceni Alpanda
Languages Turkish, English
T: +90 216 360 12 18
E: baris.ilkokul@istek.k12.tr
W: www.istek.k12.tr
See full details on page 142

ISTEK KEMAL ATATÜRK SCHOOLS (KINDERGARTEN & PRIMARY SCHOOL)
Tarabya Bayiri Cad. No: 60, Tarabya/ Sariyer, Istanbul 34457
PYP Coordinator Mine Özge Topaloglu
Languages Turkish
T: +90 212 262 7575
E: kemalataturk@istek.k12.tr
W: www.istek.k12.tr
See full details on page 143

ISTEK Private Acibadem Schools
Ibrahimaga Mahallesi, Bag Sokak Acibadem, Kadiköy, Acibadem-Istanbul 34178
DP Coordinator Gonca Tasar
Languages English
T: +90 324 613 5148
W: www.istek.org.tr

ISTEK Private Atanur Oguz Schools
Balmumcu Mah. Gazi Umurpasa Sk., No:26 Balmumcu, Istanbul 34349
PYP Coordinator Filiz Gunay
Languages English
T: +90 (0)212 211 34 60
W: www.istek.k12.tr/atanur-oguz-kampusu

ISTEK Private Bilge Kagan Schools
Florya Asfalti Senlikkoy Mah. No: 2 Florya, Bakirkoy, Istanbul 34153
PYP Coordinator Süheyla Batmaca
Languages English
T: +90 212 663 2971
W: www.istek.k12.tr/bilge-kagan-kampusu

ITU Gelistirme Vakfi Özel Ekrem Elginkan Lisesi
ITU Ayazaga Kampusu, Maslak, Istanbul 34469
DP Coordinator Gülizar Didem Özeser
Languages English
T: +90 212 367 1300
W: www.itugvo.k12.tr/web/default.asp

Jale Tezer Educational Institutions
Bagcilar Mahallesi Açin Caddesi No:7, Ankara
DP Coordinator Nükte Engin
Languages English, Turkish
T: +90 (312) 447 49 49
W: www.jaletezer.k12.tr

Kartal Anadolu Imam Hatip Lisesi
Esentepe Mah. Pamuk Sk. No 3, Kartal, Istanbul 34870
DP Coordinator Vedat Genç
Languages English
T: +90 (0)216 387 15 44
W: kartalaihl.meb.k12.tr

Kültür2000 College
Karaagaç Mah.,, Sirtköy Bulvari No: 2, Büyükçekmece, Istanbul 34500
DP Coordinator Angela Lucca
MYP Coordinator Fatih Guler
Languages English, Turkish
T: +90 212 850 8181
W: www.kultur.k12.tr

Marmara Education Group
Marmara Egitim Köyü, Basibüyük, Maltepe, Istanbul 34857
DP Coordinator Guzide Pinar Cirpanli
PYP Coordinator Tugba Tufan Altiok
Languages Turkish, English
T: +90 216 626 10 00
W: www.mek.k12.tr

MEF International School
Ulus Mah. Öztopuz Cad., Leylak Sok. 34340, Ulus/Besiktas, Istanbul
DP Coordinator Alina Zamfirescu
PYP Coordinator Evelyn Galan
Languages English
T: +90 (212) 287 6900 EXT 1340
W: www.mefis.k12.tr

MEF Schools of Turkey
Amberlidere Mevkii -Dereboyu, Cad-Ortakoy, OrtaKöy, Istanbul 34340
DP Coordinator Lauren Fajobi
Languages English
T: +90 212 2876900/237
W: www.mef.k12.tr

MURUVVET EVYAP SCHOOLS
Maden District Bakir Street, No: 2A, 2B, 2C Sariyer, Istanbul 34450
PYP Coordinator Ms. Nagihan Uca
Languages Turkish
T: +90 212 342 43 33
E: info@evyapokullari.k12.tr
W: www.evyapokullari.k12.tr
See full details on page 167

Nesibe Aydin Okullari
Haymana Yolu 5. Km, Karsiyaka Mahallesi 577, Sokak No:1, Gölbasi, Ankara 06830
DP Coordinator Muhammed Fatih Özdemir
Languages English
T: +90 312 498 2525
W: www.nesibeaydin.k12.tr

NUN Okullari
Elmali Mahallesi, Beykoz Elmali Yolu Sokak No:5/1 Beykoz, Istanbul
DP Coordinator Tugba Firat
MYP Coordinator Ahmet Uzuncinar
Languages English, Turkish
T: +90 (0)216 686 1 686
W: www.nunokullari.com

NUN Primary School
Elmali Mahallesi, Beykoz Elmali Yolu Sokak No:5/1 Beykoz, Istanbul 34676
PYP Coordinator Sule Ozcan
Languages English
T: +90 216 686 1 686
W: ozelnunilkokulu.com

Ozel Acarkent Doga Anadolu Lisesi
Acarkent Mah, 3 Kisim 3 Cadde, T25 Villa 34820, Kavacik, Istanbul
DP Coordinator Mihrican Satis
Languages English
T: +90 216 4853580
W: www.dogakoleji.com

Özel Ari Anadolu Lisesi
Ögretmenler cad. No: 16/ C 100., Yil Çukurambar, Çankaya, Ankara 06530
DP Coordinator Bülent Inal
Languages English
T: +90 312 286 8585
W: www.ariokullari.k12.tr

Özel Egeberk Anaokulu
Özlüce Mah. Hazal Sk. No:3 Nilüfer, Bursa 16010
PYP Coordinator Irem Güngör
Languages English
T: +90 533 593 9290
W: www.egeberkanaokulu.com

Özel Kocaeli Bahçesehir Anadolu Lisesi
Fatih Mah, Demokrasi Cad No.8 B.K.3, Köseköy, Kartepe 41135
DP Coordinator Orçun Barış
Languages English
T: +90 262 373 69 69
W: kocaelianadolulisesi.bahcesehir.k12.tr/en/

Özel Minecan Okullari (Private Minecan Schools)
Karsli mah 82064 sok. No12-14, Adana 010101
PYP Coordinator Aysin Gün
Languages English, Turkish
T: +90 322 2333045
W: minecan.com.tr

Private ALEV Schools
Kadirova Cad. 52/3, Ömerli Mah. Cekmeköy, Istanbul 34797
DP Coordinator Burcu Isik Keser
Languages Turkish, German, English
T: +90 216 435 83 50
W: www.alev.k12.tr

Private Sahin Schools
Prof. Dr. Sabahattin Zaim Bulvari Karaman Yolu 4., Km, Karakamis Mah., Adapazari, Sakarya 54100
PYP Coordinator Gail Onurlay
T: +90 264 777 1700
W: www.sahinokullari.com

SEV American College
Nisantepe Mah. Kerem Sok. 76, Cad. No:5-9 Çekmeköy, Istanbul
DP Coordinator Rachel Litwak
Languages English
T: +90 216 625 27 22
W: sevkoleji.k12.tr

Tarsus American School
Cengiz Topel Caddesi, Caminur Mahallesi No 66, Tarsus, Mersin 33440
DP Coordinator Ibrahim Sapmazli
Languages English
T: +90 324 241 81 81
W: www.tac.k12.tr

TAS PRIVATE ELEMENTARY SCHOOL
Cevizlik Mah. Hallaç Hüseyin, Sk. No:11, Bakirköy 34142
PYP Coordinator Sena Bataklar
Languages Turkish, English
T: +90 (212) 543 6000
E: aliakdogan@taskolej.k12.tr
W: www.taskolej.k12.tr
See full details on page 213

TED Ankara College Foundation High School
Golbasi Taspinar Koyu Yumrubel, Mevkii No:310, Ankara 06830
DP Coordinator Serenay Tarhan Guler
Languages English
T: +90 (312) 5869000
W: www.tedankara.k12.tr

TED Bursa College
21 Yüzyil Cad Mürsel, Köyü Mevkii, Bademli, Bursa
DP Coordinator Nuray Bayulgen
Languages English
T: +90 224 549 2100
W: www.tedbursa.k12.tr

Terakki Foundation Schools
Ebulula Mardin Cad. Öztürk Sok, No:2 34335, Levent, Istanbul
DP Coordinator Haluk Kocak
PYP Coordinator Hulya Salt Aygun
Languages Turkish
T: +90 212 351 0060
W: www.terakki.org.tr

Terakki Foundation Sisli Terakki High School in Tepeören
Tepeören Mah., Medeniyet Blv. no. 55L, Tuzla-Istanbul 34959
DP Coordinator Yasar Kurun
Languages English, Turkish
T: +90 (216) 709 18 77
W: www.terakki.org.tr/high-school/campuses/high-school—tepeoren

Terakki Tepeoren Kindergarten and Primary School
Tepeören Mah. Medeniyet Bul., No:55L, Bogazici Kurumlar V.D. 839 005 1455, Istanbul 34959
PYP Coordinator Ebru Karakas Duzyol
Languages English, Turkish
T: +90 (216) 709 18 77
W: anadoluyakasi.terakki.org.tr

Tev Inanc Turkes High School For Gifted Students
Muallimkoy Mevkii, PK 125, Gebze, Kocaeli 41490
DP Coordinator Joshua Lisi
Languages English
T: +90 262 679 3636
W: www.tevitol.k12.tr

The Koç School
Tepeören Mahallesi, Eski Ankara Asfalti Caddesi No: 60, 34941 Istanbul
DP Coordinator Richard Fower
Languages Turkish, English
T: +90 216 585 6200
W: www.kocschool.k12.tr

Üsküdar American Academy
Vakif Sk., No: 1 Baglarbasi, Uskudar, Istanbul 33664
DP Coordinator David Simon Cousens
Languages English
T: +90 216 333 1100
W: www.uaa.k12.tr

Vefa High School
Kalenderhane Mah. Dede Efendi Cad., No. 5 Sehzadebasi, Fatih, Istanbul 34134
DP Coordinator Evrim Gulec Akova
Languages English, Turkish
T: +90 212 527 38 72
W: vefalisesi.meb.k12.tr

YUCE Schools
Ozel YUCE Okullari, Zuhtu Tigrel Caddesi, Ismet Eker Sokak No 5, Oran-Ankara 06450
DP Coordinator Senol İsleyen
MYP Coordinator Ahu Unsal Batum
PYP Coordinator Sila Derici
Languages English, Turkish
T: +90 312 490 02 02
W: www.yuce.k12.tr

Zafer Koleji
Eskisehir Yolu, Baglica Kavsagi, No: 461 Cayyolu, Ankara 06790
DP Coordinator Önder Sit
Languages English
T: +90 312 444 5512
W: zaferkoleji.com.tr

UGANDA

ACORNS INTERNATIONAL SCHOOL (AIS)
Plot 328, Kisota Road, (Along) Northern Bypass, Kisaasi Roundabout, Kampala
PYP Coordinator Evans Kimani
Languages English
T: +256 393 202 665
E: admin@ais.ac.ug
W: www.ais.ac.ug
See full details on page 64

Aga Khan High School, Kampala
PO Box 6837, Kampala
DP Coordinator Alexander Kakungulu
Languages English
T: +256 414 308 245
W: www.agakhanschools.org

International School of Uganda
Plot 272/3 Lubowa Estate, Lubowa, Kampala
DP Coordinator Andres Bradshaw
MYP Coordinator Lucy Allsopp
PYP Coordinator Ryan Hopkins Wilcox
Languages English
T: +256 757 754808
W: www.isu.ac.ug

Kampala International School Uganda (KISU)
P.O.Box 34249, Bukoto, Kampala
DP Coordinator Matthew Holborow
Languages English
T: +256 752 711 882; +256 752 711 909
W: www.kisu.com

UK

ACS Cobham International School
Heywood, Portsmouth Road, Cobham, Surrey KT11 1BL
DP Coordinator Henrietta Knight
Languages English
T: +44 (0) 1932 867251
W: www.acs-schools.com

ACS Egham International School
Woodlee, London Road, Egham, Surrey TW20 0HS
CP Coordinator Kristi Sedlacek
DP Coordinator Anne-Marie Robb
MYP Coordinator Marie MacPhee
PYP Coordinator Anya Dalais
Languages English
T: +44 (0) 1784 430 800
W: www.acs-schools.com

ACS Hillingdon International School
Hillingdon Court, 108 Vine Lane, Hillingdon, Uxbridge, Middlesex UB10 0BE
DP Coordinator Dougal Fergusson
Languages English
T: +44 (0) 1895 259 771
W: www.acs-schools.com

ANGLO EUROPEAN SCHOOL
Willow Green, Ingatestone, Essex CM4 0DJ
CP Coordinator Mr Ben Knights
DP Coordinator Mr Stuart Newton
Languages English
T: 01277 354018
E: admissions@aesessex.co.uk
W: www.aesessex.co.uk
See full details on page 76

Ardingly College
College Road, Ardingly, Haywards Heath, West Sussex RH17 6SQ
DP Coordinator Helen Stuart
Languages English
T: +44 (0)1444 893320
W: www.ardingly.com

ASHCROFT TECHNOLOGY ACADEMY
100 West Hill, London SW15 2UT
DP Coordinator Joseph Anson
Languages English
T: +44 (0)208 877 0357
E: joseph.anson@ashcroftacademy.org.uk
W: www.atacademy.org.uk
See full details on page 78

Aylesford School – Sports College
Teapot Lane, Aylesford, Kent ME20 7JU
CP Coordinator Ayaz Iqbal
Languages English
T: +44 (0)1622 717341
W: www.aylesford.kent.sch.uk

Bedford Girls' School
Cardington Road, Bedford, Bedfordshire MK42 0BX
DP Coordinator Jennifer Walters
Languages English
T: 01234 361900
W: www.bedfordgirlsschool.co.uk

Bedford School
De Parys Avenue, Bedford, Bedfordshire MK40 2TU
DP Coordinator Mr Adrian Finch MA
Languages English
T: +44 (0)1234 362216
W: www.bedfordschool.org.uk

Bexley Grammar School
Danson Lane, Welling, Kent DA16 2BL
DP Coordinator Tina Leffen
Languages English
T: +44 (0)2083 048538
W: www.bexleygs.co.uk

BOX HILL SCHOOL
London Road, Mickleham, Dorking, Surrey RH5 6EA
DP Coordinator Julian Baker
Languages English
T: 01372 373382
E: registrar@BoxHillSchool.com
W: www.boxhillschool.com
See full details on page 80

BRADFIELD COLLEGE
Bradfield, Berkshire RG7 6AU
DP Coordinator Kirstie Parker
Languages English
T: 0118 964 4516
E: admissions@bradfieldcollege.org.uk
W: www.bradfieldcollege.org.uk
See full details on page 81

BRENTWOOD SCHOOL
Middleton Hall Lane, Brentwood, Essex CM15 8EE
DP Coordinator Mr Rob Higgins
Languages English
T: 01277 243243
E: headmaster@brentwood.essex.sch.uk
W: www.brentwoodschool.co.uk
See full details on page 83

Bridgwater & Taunton College
Bath Road, Bridgwater, Somerset TA6 4PZ
DP Coordinator Rebecca Miller
Languages English
T: 01278 455464
W: www.bridgwater.ac.uk

Bristol Grammar School
University Road, Bristol BS8 1SR
DP Coordinator Ben Schober
Languages English
T: 0117 973 6006
W: www.bristolgrammarschool.co.uk

Broadgreen International School
Queens Drive, Liverpool, Merseyside L13 5UQ
CP Coordinator Claire McKendrick
DP Coordinator Claire McKendrick
Languages English
T: 0151 228 6800
W: www.broadgreeninternationalschool.com/

BROMSGROVE SCHOOL
Worcester Road, Bromsgrove, Worcestershire B61 7DU
DP Coordinator Michael Thompson
Languages English
T: +44 (0)1527 579679
E: admissions@bromsgrove-school.co.uk
W: www.bromsgrove-school.co.uk
See full details on page 84

BRYANSTON SCHOOL
Blandford Forum, Dorset DT11 0PX
CP Coordinator Rose Ings
DP Coordinator Jo Strange
Languages English
T: 01258 484633
E: admissions@bryanston.co.uk
W: www.bryanston.co.uk/ib
See full details on page 85

Buckswood School
Broomham Hall, Rye Road, Guestling, Hastings, East Sussex TN35 4LT
DP Coordinator Carol Richards
Languages English
T: 01424 813 813
W: www.buckswood.co.uk

CATS Canterbury
68 New Dover Road, Canterbury, Kent CT1 3LQ
DP Coordinator Jemma Jones
Languages English
T: +44 (0)1227866540
W: www.catseducation.com

CHARTERHOUSE
Godalming, Surrey GU7 2DX
DP Coordinator Mr Peter Price
Languages English
T: +44 (0)1483 291501
E: admissions@charterhouse.org.uk
W: www.charterhouse.org.uk
See full details on page 86

Cheltenham Ladies' College
Bayshill Road, Cheltenham, Gloucestershire GL50 3EP
DP Coordinator Becky Revell
Languages English
T: +44 (0)1242 520691
W: www.cheltladiescollege.org

Chester International School
Queen's Park Campus, Queen's Park Road, Handbridge, Chester, Cheshire CH4 7AE
CP Coordinator Katrina Brown
DP Coordinator Katrina Brown
Languages English
T: 01244 683935
W: www.christletoninternationalstudio.co.uk

Christ's Hospital
Horsham, West Sussex RH13 0LJ
DP Coordinator Martin Stephens
Languages English
T: 01403 211293
W: www.christs-hospital.org.uk

Coopers School
Hawkewood Lane, Chislehurst, Kent BR7 5PS
CP Coordinator Fran Lane
Languages English
T: +44 (0)20 8467 3263
W: coopersschool.com

DALLAM SCHOOL
Milnthorpe, Cumbria LA7 7DD
CP Coordinator Kirstin Smith
DP Coordinator Kirstin Smith
Languages English
T: +44 (0)15395 65165
E: enquiries@dallamschool.co.uk
W: www.dallamschool.co.uk
See full details on page 91

Dane Court Grammar School
Broadstairs Road, Broadstairs, Kent CT10 2RT
CP Coordinator Melissa Linton
DP Coordinator Annie Hale
Languages English
T: +44 1843 864941
W: www.danecourt.kent.sch.uk

Dartford Grammar School
West Hill, Dartford, Kent DA1 2HW
DP Coordinator Michaela Kingham
MYP Coordinator Michaela Kingham
Languages English
T: 01322 223039
W: www.dartfordgrammarschool.org.uk

Deutsche Schule London
Douglas House, Petersham Road, Richmond, Surrey TW10 7AH
DP Coordinator Edna Howard
Languages German, English
T: +44 20 8940 8776
W: www.dslondon.org.uk

Dover Christ Church Academy
Melbourne Avenue, Whitfield, Kent CT16 2EG
CP Coordinator Victoria Wallis
Languages English
T: +44 (0)1304 820126
W: www.dccacademy.org.uk

Dwight School London
6 Friern Barnet Lane, London N11 3LX
DP Coordinator William Bowry
MYP Coordinator Karine Villatte
PYP Coordinator Jenna Brooks
Languages English
T: +44 (0)20 8920 0637
W: www.dwightlondon.org

UK

École Jeannine Manuel – London
43-45 Bedford Square, London WC1B 3DN
DP Coordinator Jeanne Gonnet
Languages English, French
T: 020 3829 5970
W: www.ecolejeanninemanuel.org.uk

EF ACADEMY OXFORD
Pullens Lane, Headington, Oxfordshire OX3 0DT
DP Coordinator Dona Jones
Languages English
T: +41 (0) 43 430 4095
E: iaeurope@ef.com
W: www.ef.com/academy
See full details on page 99

EF Academy Torbay
Castle Road, Torquay, Devon TQ1 3BG
DP Coordinator Mr. Andrew Thain
Languages English
T: +41 (0) 43 430 4095
W: www.ef.com/academy

Ellesmere College
Ellesmere, Shropshire SY12 9AB
DP Coordinator Dr Ian Tompkins
Languages English
T: 01691 622321
W: www.ellesmere.com

Eltham Hill School
Eltham Hill School, London SE9 5EE
CP Coordinator Rebecca Crean
Languages English
T: +44 (0)208 859 2843
W: elthamhill.com

Exeter College
Hele Road, Exeter, Devon EX4 4JS
DP Coordinator Jan England
Languages English
T: 01392 400500
W: www.exe-coll.ac.uk

Felsted School
Felsted, Great Dunmow, Essex CM6 3LL
DP Coordinator Karen Woodhouse
Languages English
T: 01371 822605
W: www.felsted.org

Fettes College
Carrington Road, Edinburgh EH4 1QX
DP Coordinator Mark Henry
Languages English
T: +44 (0)131 332 2281
W: www.fettes.com

Folkestone Academy
Academy Lane, Folkestone, Kent CT19 5FP
CP Coordinator Jenni van Deelen
Languages English
T: +44 (0)1303 842400
W: www.folkestoneacademy.com

George Green's School
100 Manchester Road, Isle of Dogs, London E14 3DW
CP Coordinator Hilde Lewis
DP Coordinator Lucy Cientanni
Languages English
T: +44 (0)207 987 6032
W: www.georgegreens.com

GRESHAM'S SENIOR SCHOOL
Cromer Road, Holt, Norfolk NR25 6EA
DP Coordinator Mr Darren Latchford
Languages English
T: 01263 714 614
E: admissions@greshams.com
W: www.greshams.com
See full details on page 107

Guernsey Grammar School and Sixth Form Centre
Les Varendes, St Andrews, Guernsey GY8 6TD
DP Coordinator Paul Montague
Languages English
T: +44 (0)1481 256571
W: web.grammar.sch.gg

HAILEYBURY
Haileybury, Hertford, Hertfordshire SG13 7NU
DP Coordinator Kate Brazier
Languages English
T: +44 (0)1992 706200
E: admissions@haileybury.com
W: www.haileybury.com
See full details on page 110

Halcyon London International School
33 Seymour Place, London W1H 5AU
DP Coordinator Jo Cooper
MYP Coordinator Lori Fritz
Languages English
T: +44 (0)20 7258 1169
W: halcyonschool.com

Hartsdown Academy
George V Ave, Margate, Kent CT9 5RE
CP Coordinator Jessica Gipson
Languages English
T: +44 (0)1843 227957
W: www.hartsdown.org

Hautlieu School
Wellington Road, St Saviour, Jersey JE2 7TH
CP Coordinator Mandy Campbell
DP Coordinator Mandy Campbell
Languages English
T: +44 1534 736 242
W: www.hautlieu.net

HEADINGTON SCHOOL
London Road, Oxford, Oxfordshire OX3 7TD
DP Coordinator Mr James Stephenson
Languages English
T: +44 (0)1865 759100
E: admissions@headington.org
W: www.headington.org
See full details on page 112

HOCKERILL ANGLO-EUROPEAN COLLEGE
Dunmow Road, Bishops Stortford, Hertfordshire CM23 5HX
DP Coordinator Bradley Snell
MYP Coordinator Michelle Butler
Languages English
T: 01279 658451
E: admissions@hockerill.com
W: www.hockerill.com
See full details on page 113

Homewood School & Sixth Form Centre
Ashford Road, Tenterden, Kent TN30 6LT
CP Coordinator Kate Farrell
Languages English
T: 01580 764222
W: www.homewood-school.co.uk

Hugh Christie Technology College
White Cottage Road, Tonbridge, Kent TN10 4PU
CP Coordinator Matt Goss
Languages English
T: 01732 353544
W: www.hughchristie.kent.sch.uk

IMPINGTON INTERNATIONAL COLLEGE
New Road, Impington, Cambridge, Cambridgeshire CB24 9LX
CP Coordinator Leanne Gibbons
DP Coordinator Johanna Sale
Languages English
T: 01223 200400
E: sixthform@ivc.tmet.org.uk
W: www.impington.cambs.sch.uk
See full details on page 116

International Community School
7B Wyndham Place, London NW1 4PT
DP Coordinator Alexandra Moreno Hemming
MYP Coordinator Svetlana Klyuyeva
PYP Coordinator Meghan Kemp
Languages English
T: +44 (0) 20 7298 8817
W: www.icschool.co.uk

INTERNATIONAL SCHOOL OF LONDON (ISL)
139 Gunnersbury Avenue, London W3 8LG
DP Coordinator Paul Morris
MYP Coordinator Ms Hyun Jung Owen
PYP Coordinator Ms Iliana Gutierrez
Languages English & Mother-tongue
T: +44 (0)20 8992 5823
E: mail@isllondon.org
W: www.isllondon.org
See full details on page 132

KENT COLLEGE, CANTERBURY
Whitstable Road, Canterbury, Kent CT2 9DT
DP Coordinator Mr Graham Letley
Languages English
T: +44 (0)1227 763 231
E: admissions@kentcollege.co.uk
W: www.kentcollege.com
See full details on page 146

King Edward's School
Edgbaston Park Road, Birmingham, West Midlands B15 2UA
DP Coordinator Natalie Lockhart-Mann
Languages English
T: 0121 472 1672
W: www.kes.org.uk

KING EDWARD'S WITLEY
Godalming, Surrey GU8 5SG
DP Coordinator Zeba Clarke
Languages English
T: +44 (0)1428 686700
E: admissions@kesw.org
W: www.kesw.org
See full details on page 148

King Ethelbert School
Can ter bury Road, Birch ing ton, Kent CT7 9BL
CP Coordinator Jocelyn Rebera
Languages English
T: 01843 831999
W: www.kingethelbert.com

King Fahad Academy
Bromyard Avenue, Acton, London W3 7HD
DP Coordinator Mohammed Baba
MYP Coordinator James Nevin
PYP Coordinator Hania Farwati
Languages English
T: 020 8743 0131
W: www.thekfa.org.uk/wp/

KING WILLIAM'S COLLEGE
Castletown, Isle of Man IM9 1TP
DP Coordinator Alasdair Ulyett
Languages English
T: +44 (0)1624 820110
E: admissions@kwc.im
W: www.kwc.im

See full details on page 149

King's College School
Southside, Wimbledon Common, London SW19 4TT
DP Coordinator Mark Allen
Languages English
T: 020 8255 5300
W: www.kcs.org.uk

KNOLE ACADEMY
Bradbourne Vale Road, Sevenoaks, Kent TN13 3LE
CP Coordinator Mrs Jane Elliott
Languages English
T: 01732 454608
E: enquiries@knoleacademy.org
W: www.knoleacademy.org

See full details on page 150

LaSWAP Sixth Form Consortium
Highgate Road, London NW5 1RL
CP Coordinator Ella Schlesinger
Languages English
T: +44 (0)20 7692 4157
W: laswap.camden.sch.uk

LEIGHTON PARK SCHOOL
Shinfield Road, Reading, Berkshire RG2 7ED
DP Coordinator Mrs Helen Taylor
Languages English
T: 0118 987 9600
E: admissions@leightonpark.com
W: www.leightonpark.com

See full details on page 153

LYCÉE INTERNATIONAL DE LONDRES WINSTON CHURCHILL
54 Forty Lane, London HA9 9LY
DP Coordinator Maaike Kaandorp
Languages English, French
T: +44 (0)203 824 4900
E: admissions@lyceeinternational.london
W: www.lyceeinternational.london

See full details on page 157

MALVERN COLLEGE
College Road, Malvern, Worcestershire WR14 3DF
DP Coordinator Stephen Holroyd
Languages English
T: +44 (0)1684 581613
E: admissions@malverncollege.org.uk
W: www.malverncollege.org.uk

See full details on page 158

MARYMOUNT LONDON
George Road, Kingston upon Thames, Surrey KT2 7PE
DP Coordinator Nicholas Marcou
MYP Coordinator Nicholas Marcou
Languages English
T: +44 (0)20 8949 0571
E: admissions@marymountlondon.com
W: www.marymountlondon.com

See full details on page 162

NORTH LONDON COLLEGIATE SCHOOL
Canons, Canons Drive, Edgware, Middlesex HA8 7RJ
DP Coordinator Mr Henry Linscott
Languages English
T: +44 (0)20 8952 0912
E: office@nlcs.org.uk
W: www.nlcs.org.uk

See full details on page 170

Northfleet School for Girls
Hall Road, Northfleet, Kent DA11 8AQ
CP Coordinator Jo Dowden
Languages English
T: +44 (0)1474 831 020
W: www.nsfg.org.uk

Northfleet Technology College
Colyer Road, Northfleet, Kent DA11 8BG
CP Coordinator Emma Campbell
Languages English
T: 01474 533802
W: ntc.kent.sch.uk

OAKHAM SCHOOL
Chapel Close, Oakham, Rutland LE15 6DT
DP Coordinator Vic Russell
Languages English
T: 01572 758500
E: admissions@oakham.rutland.sch.uk
W: www.oakham.rutland.sch.uk

See full details on page 171

Parkside Sixth
Parkside, Cambridge, Cambridgeshire CB1 1EH
CP Coordinator Lucy White
DP Coordinator Hannah Holt
Languages English
T: +44 (0)1223 712600
W: www.parksidesixth.org.uk

Plymouth College of Art
Tavistock Place, Plymouth, Devon PL4 8AT
CP Coordinator Timothy Dickinson
Languages English
T: +44 (0)1752 203434
W: www.plymouthart.ac.uk

ROSSALL SCHOOL
Broadway, Fleetwood, Lancashire FY7 8JW
DP Coordinator Bethan Jones
PYP Coordinator Julia Clapp
Languages English
T: +44 (0)1253 774201
E: admissions@rossall.org.uk
W: www.rossall.org.uk

See full details on page 182

RYDE SCHOOL WITH UPPER CHINE
Queen's Road, Ryde, Isle of Wight PO33 3BE
CP Coordinator David Shapland
DP Coordinator Kerry Gallop
Languages English
T: 01983 617970
E: admissions@rydeschool.net
W: www.rydeschool.org.uk

See full details on page 184

Scarborough College
Filey Road, Scarborough, North Yorkshire YO11 3BA
DP Coordinator James Fraser
Languages English
T: +44 (0)1723 360620
W: www.scarboroughcollege.co.uk

SEVENOAKS SCHOOL
High Street, Sevenoaks, Kent TN13 1HU
DP Coordinator Nigel Haworth
Languages English
T: +44 (0)1732 455133
E: regist@sevenoaksschool.org
W: www.sevenoaksschool.org

See full details on page 195

Sherborne Girls
Bradford Road, Sherborne, Dorset DT9 3QN
DP Coordinator David Banks
Languages English
T: +44 (0)1935 818224
W: www.sherborne.com

SIDCOT SCHOOL
Oakridge Lane, Winscombe, Somerset BS25 1PD
DP Coordinator Graham Hartley
Languages English
T: 01934 843102
E: info@sidcot.org.uk
W: www.sidcot.org.uk

See full details on page 196

Southbank International School – Hampstead
16 Netherhall Gardens, London NW3 5TH
PYP Coordinator Flora Winter
Languages English
T: 020 7243 3803
W: www.southbank.org

Southbank International School – Kensington
36-38 Kensington Park Road, London W11 3BU
PYP Coordinator Charlotte Gregson
Languages English
T: +44 (0)20 7243 3803
W: www.southbank.org

Southbank International School – Westminster
63-65 Portland Place, London W1B 1QR
DP Coordinator Amal Hirani
MYP Coordinator Carole Lewthwaite
Languages English
T: 020 7243 3803
W: www.southbank.org

St Benedict's Catholic High School
Kinwarton Road, Alcester, Warwickshire B49 6PX
DP Coordinator Donna Munford
Languages English
T: +44 (0)1789 762888
W: www.st-benedicts.org

ST CLARE'S, OXFORD
139 Banbury Road, Oxford, Oxfordshire OX2 7AL
DP Coordinator Darrel Ross
Languages English
T: +44 (0)1865 552031
E: admissions@stclares.ac.uk
W: www.stclares.ac.uk

See full details on page 199

ST EDWARD'S, OXFORD
Woodstock Road, Oxford, Oxfordshire OX2 7NN
DP Coordinator Anna Fielding
Languages English
T: +44 (0)1865 319200
E: registrar@stedwardsoxford.org
W: www.stedwardsoxford.org

See full details on page 201

St John's International School
Broadway, Sidmouth, Devon EX10 8RG
PYP Coordinator Luke Towe
Languages English
T: 01395 513984
W: www.stjohnsdevon.co.uk

ST LEONARDS SCHOOL
St Andrews, Fife KY16 9QJ
DP Coordinator Ben Seymour
MYP Coordinator Kathryn McGregor
PYP Coordinator Kathryn McGregor (Acting)
Languages English
T: 01334 472126
E: contact@stleonards-fife.org
W: www.stleonards-fife.org
See full details on page 203

St Simon Stock Catholic School
Oakwood Park, Maidstone, Kent ME16 0JP
CP Coordinator Andrew Williams
Languages English
T: 01622 754551
W: www.ssscs.co.uk

STEPHEN PERSE SIXTH FORM
Shaftesbury Road, Cambridge, Cambridgeshire CB2 8AA
DP Coordinator Jacqueline Paris
Languages English
T: +44 (0)1223 454762
E: admissions@stephenperse.com
W: www.stephenperse.com/ib
See full details on page 208

STONYHURST COLLEGE
Stonyhurst, Clitheroe, Lancashire BB7 9PZ
CP Coordinator Emily Ashe
DP Coordinator Mrs Deborah Kirkby BSc
Languages English
T: 01254 827073
E: admissions@stonyhurst.ac.uk
W: www.stonyhurst.ac.uk
See full details on page 212

Strood Academy
Carnation Road, Strood, Kent ME2 2SX
CP Coordinator Christopher Simmons
Languages English
T: 01634 717121
W: stroodacademy.org.uk

TASIS The American School in England
Coldharbour Lane, Thorpe, Surrey TW20 8TE
DP Coordinator Stephanie Feo-Hughes
Languages English
T: +44 (0)1932 582316
W: www.tasisengland.org

Taunton School
Staplegrove Road, Taunton, Somerset TA2 6AD
DP Coordinator Adrian Roberts
Languages English
T: +44 (0)1823 703703
W: www.tauntonschool.co.uk

Thamesview School
Thong Lane, Gravesend, Kent DA12 4LF
CP Coordinator Elizabeth Terry
Languages English
T: +44 (0)1474 566 552
W: www.thamesviewsch.co.uk

THE ABBEY SCHOOL
Kendrick Road, Reading, Berkshire RG1 5DZ
DP Coordinator Julie Mackie
Languages English
T: 0118 987 2256
E: schooloffice@theabbey.co.uk
W: www.theabbey.co.uk
See full details on page 215

The Abbey School, Faversham
London Road, Faversham, Kent ME13 8RZ
CP Coordinator Nicci Jones
Languages English
T: +44 (0)1795 532633
W: www.abbeyschoolfaversham.co.uk

The Beaconsfield School
Wattleton Road, Beaconsfield, Buckinghamshire HP9 1SJ
CP Coordinator Fiona Palmer Garrett
Languages English
T: 01494 673450
W: www.beaconsfield.bucks.sch.uk

The Bridge AP Academy
Finlay Street, Fulham, London SW6 6HB
DP Coordinator Olga Williamson
Languages English
T: +44 (0)207 610 8340
W: www.tbap.org.uk/bridge

The Chalfonts Independent Grammar School
19 London Road, High Wycombe, Buckinghamshire HP11 1BJ
DP Coordinator Pawel Hladki
MYP Coordinator Alex Iredale
Languages English
T: +44 (0)1494 875502
W: www.thechalfontsgrammar.co.uk

The Ebbsfleet Academy
Southfleet Road, Ebbsfleet Garden City, Kent DA10 0BZ
CP Coordinator Jonathan Field
Languages English
T: +44 (0)1322 623100
W: www.theebbsfleetacademy.kent.sch.uk

THE GODOLPHIN AND LATYMER SCHOOL
Iffley Road, Hammersmith, London W6 0PG
DP Coordinator Audrey Dubois
Languages English
T: +44 (0)20 8741 1936
E: office@godolphinandlatymer.com
W: www.godolphinandlatymer.com
See full details on page 222

The Halley Academy
Corelli Road, Blackheath, London SE3 8EP
CP Coordinator Will Burrows
Languages English
T: +44 (0)20 8516 7977
W: www.thehalleyacademy.org.uk

The Holmesdale School
Malling Road, Snodland, Kent ME6 5HS
CP Coordinator Lee Downey
Languages English
T: 01634 240416
W: holmesdale.kent.sch.uk

The International School of Aberdeen
Pitfodels House, North Deeside Road, Pitfodels, Cults, Aberdeen AB15 9PN
DP Coordinator Jennifer Purpura
Languages English
T: 01224 730300
W: www.isa.aberdeen.sch.uk

The Leigh Academy
Green Street, Green Road, Dartford, Kent DA1 1QE
CP Coordinator Lee Forcella-Burton
Languages English
T: +44(0)1322 620400
W: www.theleighacademy.org.uk

The Leigh UTC
The Bridge Development, Brunel Way, Dartford, Kent DA1 5TF
CP Coordinator Sophie Dickinson
Languages English
T: +44 (0)1322 626 600
W: www.theleighutc.org.uk

The Lenham School
Ham Lane, Lenham, Kent ME17 2LL
CP Coordinator Anna Burden
Languages English
T: 01622 858267
W: www.thelenham.viat.org.uk

The Malling School
Beech Road, East Malling, West Malling, Kent ME19 6DH
CP Coordinator Kelly Chimanga
Languages English
T: +44 (0)1732 840995
W: www.themallingschool.kent.sch.uk

The Portsmouth Grammar School
High Street, Portsmouth, Hampshire PO1 2LN
DP Coordinator Simon Taylor
Languages English
T: +44 (0)23 9236 0036
W: www.pgs.org.uk

The Red Maids' Senior School
Westbury Road, Westbury-on-Trym, Bristol BS9 3AW
DP Coordinator Peter Brealey
Languages English
T: +44 (0)117 962 2641
W: www.redmaids.co.uk

The Rochester Grammar School
Maidstone Road, Rochester, Kent ME1 3BY
DP Coordinator Lisette Sturt
Languages English
T: +44 (0)1634 843049
W: www.rochestergrammar.medway.sch.uk

The Royal Harbour Academy
Newlands Lane, Ramsgate, Kent CT12 6RH
CP Coordinator Linda Regan
Languages English
T: 01843 572500
W: www.rha.kent.sch.uk

THE ROYAL HIGH SCHOOL, BATH GDST
Lansdown Road, Bath, Bath & North-East Somerset BA1 5SZ
DP Coordinator Ms Jude Taylor
Languages English
T: +44 (0)1225 313877
E: admissions@rhsb.gdst.net
W: www.royalhighbath.gdst.net
See full details on page 228

The Sixth Form College, Colchester
North Hill, Colchester, Essex CO1 1SN
DP Coordinator Karen Burns
Languages English
T: 01206 500778
W: www.colchsfc.ac.uk

The Skinners' Kent Academy
Blackhurst Lane, Tunbridge Wells, Kent TN2 4PY
CP Coordinator Helena Read
MYP Coordinator Katherine McCreadie
Languages English
T: +44 (0)1892 534377
W: www.twhs.kent.sch.uk

The Whitstable School
Bellevue Road, Whitstable, Kent CT5 1PX
CP Coordinator Luci Brown
Languages English
T: 01227 931300
W: www.thewhitstableschool.org.uk

Tonbridge Grammar School
Deakin Leas, Tonbridge, Kent TN9 2JR
DP Coordinator Darryl Barker
MYP Coordinator Caroline Ghali
Languages English
T: +44 (0)1732 365125
W: www.tgs.kent.sch.uk

Torquay Boys' Grammar School
Shiphay Manor Drive, Torquay, Devon TQ2 7EL
DP Coordinator James Hunt
Languages English
T: +44 1803 615 501
W: www.tbgs.co.uk

Towers School and Sixth Form Centre
Faversham Road, Ashford, Kent TN24 9ALE
CP Coordinator Victoria Reed
Languages English
T: +44 (0)1233 634171
W: www.towers.kent.sch.uk

Truro and Penwith College
College Road, Truro, Cornwall TR1 3XX
DP Coordinator Caroline Keech
Languages English
T: +44 (0) 1872 267000
W: www.truro-penwith.ac.uk

UWC ATLANTIC
St Donat's Castle, St Donat's, Llantwit Major, Vale of Glamorgan CF61 1WF
DP Coordinator Gabor Vincze
Languages English
T: +44 (0)1446 799000
E: principal@atlanticcollege.org
W: www.atlanticcollege.org
See full details on page 231

Varndean College
Surrenden Road, Brighton, East Sussex BN1 6WQ
DP Coordinator Lee Finlay-Gray
Languages English
T: 01273 508011
W: www.varndean.ac.uk

WARMINSTER SCHOOL
Church Street, Warminster, Wiltshire BA12 8PJ
CP Coordinator Dr Mark Martin
DP Coordinator Dr Mark Martin BSc, PGCE, PhD
Languages English
T: +44 (0)1985 210100
E: admissions@warminsterschool.org.uk
W: www.warminsterschool.org.uk
See full details on page 236

WELLINGTON COLLEGE
Duke's Ride, Crowthorne, Berkshire RG45 7PU
DP Coordinator Richard Atherton
Languages English
T: +44 (0)1344 444000
E: admissions@wellingtoncollege.org.uk
W: www.wellingtoncollege.org.uk
See full details on page 238

Westbourne School
Hickman Road, Penarth, Glamorgan CF64 2AJ
DP Coordinator Lisa Phillips
Languages English
T: 029 2070 5705
W: www.westbourneschool.com

Westminster Academy
The Naim Dangoor Centre, 255 Harrow Road, London W2 5EZ
CP Coordinator Holly Youlden
DP Coordinator Stephen Butler
Languages English
T: +44 (0)20 7121 0600
W: www.westminsteracademy.biz

Whitgift School
Haling Park, South Croydon, Surrey CR2 6YT
DP Coordinator Andrew Marlow
Languages English
T: +44 20 8633 9935
W: www.whitgift.co.uk

Wilmington Academy
Common Lane, Wilmington, Dartford, Kent DA2 7DR
CP Coordinator Kathleen Sanders
Languages English
T: +44 (0)1322 272111
W: wilmingtonacademy.org.uk

WINDERMERE SCHOOL
Patterdale Road, Windermere, Cumbria LA23 1NW
CP Coordinator Lynn Moses
DP Coordinator Lynn Moses
Languages English
T: 015394 46164
E: admissions@windermereschool.co.uk
W: www.windermereschool.co.uk
See full details on page 240

Worth School
Paddockhurst Road, Turners Hill, Crawley, West Sussex RH10 4SD
DP Coordinator Naomi Williams
Languages English
T: +44 (0)1342 710200
W: www.worthschool.co.uk

Wotton House International School
Wotton House, Horton Road, Gloucester, Gloucestershire GL1 3PR
MYP Coordinator Daniel Sturdy
Languages English
T: +44 (0)1452 764248
W: www.wottonhouseschool.co.uk

Wrotham School
Borough Green Rd, Sevenoaks, Kent TN15 7RD
CP Coordinator Samantha Williams
Languages English
T: +44 (0)1732 884207
W: www.wrothamschool.com

UKRAINE

Pechersk School International Kyiv
7a Victora Zabily, Kyiv 03039
DP Coordinator David Freeman
MYP Coordinator Paul Horkan
PYP Coordinator Glen Nicholson
Languages English
T: +380 44 377 5292
W: www.psi.kiev.ua

QSI KYIV INTERNATIONAL SCHOOL
3A Svyatoshinsky Provuluk, Kyiv 03115
DP Coordinator Ms. Randi Assenova
Languages English
T: +38 (044) 452 27 92
E: kyiv@qsi.org
W: kyiv.qsi.org
See full details on page 179

The British International School Ukraine (Nivki Primary Campus)
36a Scherbakivskogo Str., Kyiv 03190
PYP Coordinator Brianne Eddy-Lee
Languages English
T: +38 (044) 239 21 21
W: britishschool.ua

The British International School Ukraine (Pechersk Campus)
1 Dragomirova Street, Kiev 01103
DP Coordinator Paul Hodgson
PYP Coordinator Neil Johnstone
Languages English
T: +38 (044) 596 18 28
W: britishschool.ua

UNITED ARAB EMIRATES

Abu Dhabi International (Pvt) School
Karamah Street, PO Box 25898, Abu Dhabi
DP Coordinator Issam Kobrsi
Languages English
T: +971 2 443 4433
W: aisschools.com

AJMAN ACADEMY
Sheikh Ammar Road, Mowaihat 2, Ajman
PYP Coordinator Rachel Poulton
Languages English
T: +971 6 731 4444
E: school@ajmanacademy.com
W: www.ajmanacademy.com
See full details on page 66

Al Adab Iranian Private School for Boys
Behind Al Bustan Center, Al Nahda 1, Qusais, Dubai
DP Coordinator Naghmeh Dadpanah
Languages English
T: +971 42633405
W: www.adabschool.org

Al Bateen Academy
PO Box 128484, Abu Dhabi
DP Coordinator Peter Atkins
Languages English
T: +971 2 813 2000
W: www.albateenacademy.sch.ae

Al Najah Private School
PO Box 284, Abu Dhabi
DP Coordinator Ahmed Al Zuhairi
Languages English
T: +971 2 553 0935
W: alnajahschool.com

American Community School, Abu Dhabi
PO Box 42114, Abu Dhabi
DP Coordinator Jonathan Diaz
Languages English
T: +971 2 681 5115
W: www.acs.sch.ae/acs

American International School in Abu Dhabi
PO Box 5992, Abu Dhabi
DP Coordinator Victoria Johnson
PYP Coordinator Elizabeth Younk
Languages English
T: +971 2 4444 333
W: www.aisa.sch.ae

Australian International School
PO Box 43364, Sharjah
DP Coordinator Paul Lange
Languages English
T: +971 6 558 9967
W: www.ais.ae

Australian School of Abu Dhabi
Khalifa City B, PO Box 36044, Abu Dhabi
DP Coordinator Mahmoud Dabet
MYP Coordinator Amal Elgamal
PYP Coordinator Ayan Abdullahi
Languages English
T: +971 2 5866980
W: www.aia.vic.edu.au

Collegiate American School
50, Al Maydar street, Umm Suqeim 2, P.O. Box: 121306, Dubai
CP Coordinator Karen Nyborg
DP Coordinator Karen Nyborg
Languages English
T: +971 4 427 1400
W: www.casdubai.com

Dar Al Marefa Private School
P.O.Box: 112602, Dubai 112602
DP Coordinator Inas Al Derbashi
MYP Coordinator Adam Fitzgerald
PYP Coordinator Llinos Roberts
Languages English
T: +971 42885782
W: www.daralmarefa.ae

Deira International School
PO Box 79043, Dubai
CP Coordinator Brian Cleary
DP Coordinator Brian Cleary
Languages English
T: +9714 2325552
W: www.disdubai.ae

Dubai American Academy
PO Box 32762, Al Barsha, Dubai
DP Coordinator Katie Sheffield
Languages English
T: +971 4 347 9222
W: www.gemsaa-dubai.com

Dubai International Academy
First Al Khail Street, Emirates Hills, P.O. Box: 118111, Dubai
CP Coordinator Robert Bunyan
DP Coordinator Pam Parasram
MYP Coordinator Sean Kelly
PYP Coordinator Emma Cottingham
Languages English, Arabic
T: +971 4 368 4111
W: www.diadubai.com

Dunecrest American School
P.O. Box 624265, Wadi Al Safa 3 (next to Al Barari), Dubai
DP Coordinator Eric Barrett
Languages English
T: +971 4 508 7444
W: www.dunecrest.ae

Emirates International School – Jumeirah
PO Box 6446, Dubai
CP Coordinator Aiden Maher
DP Coordinator Nausheen Arif
MYP Coordinator Adele Teasel
PYP Coordinator Scott Kirkland
Languages English
T: +971 4 3489804
W: www.eischools.ae

Emirates International School – Meadows
PO Box 120118, Dubai
DP Coordinator Eleanor Nolan
MYP Coordinator Sarah Robson
PYP Coordinator Natalie Bridges
Languages Arabic, English
T: +971 4 362 9009
W: www.eischools.ae

Emirates National School – Abu Dhabi City Campus
P.O. Box 44759, Abu Dhabi
DP Coordinator Lauren Brown
MYP Coordinator Alan Georges
PYP Coordinator Misaal Gill
Languages English, Arabic
T: +971 2 642 5993
W: www.ens.sch.ae

Emirates National School – Al Ain City Campus
PO Box 69392, Al Ain
DP Coordinator Rania Hab Alrumman
MYP Coordinator Benjamin Smith
PYP Coordinator Dinaulu Neilako
Languages English, Arabic
T: +971 3 761 6888
W: www.ens.sch.ae

Emirates National School – Mohammed Bin Zayed Campus
PO Box 44321, Mussafah, Abu Dhabi
DP Coordinator Eric Healy
MYP Coordinator Vanda Gammoh
PYP Coordinator Christina Girouard
Languages Arabic, English
T: +971 2 559 00 00
W: www.ens.sch.ae

Emirates National School – Ras Al Khaimah Campus
Ras Al-Khaimah
PYP Coordinator Ugo Aimakhu
Languages English
T: +971 7 203 3333
W: www.ens.sch.ae

Emirates National School – Sharjah Campus
Al Rahmaniya, Sharjah
PYP Coordinator Jillane Strickland
Languages English
T: +971 6 599 0999
W: www.ens.sch.ae

GEMS American Academy – Abu Dhabi
PO Box 145161, Abu Dhabi
DP Coordinator Monica Martin
PYP Coordinator Tiffany Pulci
Languages English
T: +971 2 557 4880
W: www.gemsaa-abudhabi.com

GEMS International School – Al Khail
Al Khail Road, Dubai
DP Coordinator Ruairi Cunningham
MYP Coordinator Juan Angel Mendoza
PYP Coordinator Mark Krabousanos
Languages English
T: +971 4 339 6200
W: www.gemsinternationalschool-alkhail.com

GEMS MODERN ACADEMY – DUBAI
PO Box 53663, Nad al Sheeba 3,4, Dubai
DP Coordinator Dr. Sunipa Guha Neogi
Languages English
T: +971 4 326 3339
E: info_mhs@gemsedu.com
W: www.gemsmodernacademy-dubai.com

See full details on page 102

GEMS Wellington Academy – Silicon Oasis
Dubai Silicon Oasis, Dubai
CP Coordinator Christopher Pownall
DP Coordinator Robert Hugh Tremayne Gauntlett
Languages English
T: +971 4 342 4040
W: www.gemswellingtonacademy-dso.com

GEMS Wellington International School
PO Box 37486, Al Sufouh 1, Sheikh Zayed Road, Dubai
CP Coordinator Emma Ashton
DP Coordinator Fleur Baikie
Languages English
T: +971 (4) 348 4999
W: www.wellingtoninternationalschool.com

GEMS World Academy – Abu Dhabi
Fatima Bint Mubarak Street, PO Box 110273, Abu Dhabi
PYP Coordinator Catherine Erpen
Languages English
T: +971 2 641 6333
W: www.gemsworldacademy-abudhabi.com

GEMS World Academy – Dubai
Al Khail Road, Al Barsha South, Dubai
CP Coordinator Brian Hull
DP Coordinator Rania Hussein
MYP Coordinator Jon Howarth
PYP Coordinator Peter Bonner
Languages English
T: +971 4 373 6373
W: www.gemsworldacademy-dubai.com

German International School Sharjah
German School Sharjah, PO Box 1465, Sharjah
DP Coordinator Katharina Cordes
Languages English
T: +971 6 5676014
W: www.dssharjah.org

GREENFIELD INTERNATIONAL SCHOOL
Dubai Investments Park, Dubai
CP Coordinator Mike Worth
DP Coordinator Sarah Atienza
MYP Coordinator Chris Cooke
PYP Coordinator Jill Shadbolt
Languages English
T: +971 (0)4 885 6600
E: admissions@gischool.ae
W: www.gischool.ae

See full details on page 106

International Concept for Education (ICE Dubai)
Al meydan Rd, Nad al Sheba1, Near Meydan Hotel, Meydan, Dubai
PYP Coordinator Timothy Bullock
Languages English, French
T: +971 4 3377818
W: icedubai.org

JUMEIRA BACCALAUREATE SCHOOL
53 B Street, off Al Wasl Road, Jumeira 1, Dubai
CP Coordinator Lisa Postlethwaite
DP Coordinator Michelle Andrews
MYP Coordinator David Bauzà-Capart
PYP Coordinator Amiee Clark
Languages English
T: +971 (0)4 344 6931
E: admissions@jbschool.ae
W: www.jbschool.ae
See full details on page 145

Jumeirah English Speaking School (JESS), Arabian Ranches
Main entrance of Arabian Ranches community, PO Box 24942, Dubai
DP Coordinator Kosta Lekanides
Languages English
T: +971 4 3619019
W: www.jess.sch.ae

Nord Anglia International School, Dubai
off Hessa Street, Dubai
DP Coordinator Lee Banfield
Languages English, French
T: +971 (0)4 2199 999
W: www.nasdubai.ae

North London Collegiate School Dubai
Nad Al Sheba, Mohammed Bin Rashid Al Maktoum City, Dubai
DP Coordinator Sara Noemi Gonzalez Saavedra
MYP Coordinator Stephanie Duarte
PYP Coordinator Catherine Schmidt
Languages Arabic, English
T: +971 (0)4319 0888
W: www.nlcsdubai.ae

Raffles World Academy
Al Marcup Street, Umm Suqeim 3, P.O. Box 122900, Dubai
CP Coordinator Cathal O'Mahony
DP Coordinator Anissa Pereira
MYP Coordinator Stephen Pinto
PYP Coordinator Yolanda Maccallum
Languages English
T: +971 4 4271351/2
W: www.rwadubai.com

RAHA INTERNATIONAL SCHOOL
Al Raha Gardens, Khalifa City 'A', Abu Dhabi
DP Coordinator Andrew Tomlinson
MYP Coordinator Vaughan Kitson
PYP Coordinator Vanessa Keenan
Languages English
T: +971 (0)2 556 1567
E: admissions@ris.ae
W: www.ris.ae
See full details on page 180

Ras Al Khaimah Academy
PO Box 975, Ras Al Khiamah
DP Coordinator George Heusner
PYP Coordinator Jason Barton
Languages English
T: +971 7 236 2441
W: www.rakaonline.org

Repton School, Dubai
PO Box 300331, Nad Al Sheba 3, Dubai
CP Coordinator Aimon Sabawi
DP Coordinator Jennifer Horan
Languages English
T: +971 4 426 9300
W: www.reptondubai.org

Sunmarke School
District 5 (Behind Limitless Building on Al Khail Road), Jumeirah Village Triangle, Dubai
CP Coordinator Claire Young
DP Coordinator Claire Young
Languages English
T: +971 4 423 8900
W: www.sunmarkedubai.com

Swiss International Scientific School of Dubai
Dubai Healthcare City, Phase 2, Al Jaddaf, PO Box 505002, Dubai
DP Coordinator Urs Jungo
MYP Coordinator Martin Keon
PYP Coordinator Shona Tait
Languages English
T: +971 4 375 0600
W: sisd.ae

The British International School, Abu Dhabi
PO Box 60968, Abu Dhabi
DP Coordinator Mrs. Victoria Collinson
Languages English
T: +971 2 510 0176
W: www.bisabudhabi.com

Towheed Iranian School for Boys
Al Qouz 1, Sheikh Zayed Rd, Dubai
DP Coordinator Afsaneh Moayedzadeh
Languages English
T: +971 4 3389953
W: www.bi-st.com

Universal American School, Dubai
PO Box 79133, Al Rashidiya, Dubai
DP Coordinator Tracey Cummins
PYP Coordinator Sabrina Sambola
Languages English, Arabic
T: +971 4 232 5222
W: www.uasdubai.ae

UPTOWN SCHOOL
Corner of Algeria Road & Tripoli Street, Mirdif, PO Box 78181, Dubai
CP Coordinator Sarah Wakeling
DP Coordinator Sheugnet Carter
MYP Coordinator Hebatallah Gaber
PYP Coordinator Lee Higginbottom
Languages English
T: +971 (0)4 2515001
E: admissions@uptownschool.ae
W: www.uptownschool.ae
See full details on page 229

Victoria International School of Sharjah
PO Box 68600, Al Mamzar, Sharjah
DP Coordinator Sara Santrampurwala
Languages English
T: +971 6 577 1999
W: www.viss.ae/victoria-international-school

UZBEKISTAN

Tashkent International School
38 Sarikulskaya Street, Tashkent 100005
DP Coordinator Jeffrey Mortelette
MYP Coordinator Sharna Tobin
PYP Coordinator Robyn Ibrahim
Languages English
T: +998 71 291 9670
W: www.tashschool.org

ZAMBIA

American International School of Lusaka
PO Box 320176, Lusaka
DP Coordinator Monica Murphy
MYP Coordinator Ingrid Turner
PYP Coordinator Christine Kelly
Languages English
T: +260 211 260509
W: www.aislusaka.org

International School of Lusaka
PO Box 50121, Ridgeway, Lusaka
DP Coordinator Nathalie Vignard
PYP Coordinator Grace Kambeu
Languages English
T: +260 211 252291
W: islzambia.org

ZIMBABWE

Harare International School
66 Pendennis Road, Mount Pleasant, Harare
DP Coordinator Richard Hawkins
MYP Coordinator Michael Schuetze
PYP Coordinator Mrs Philippa Farrelly
Languages English
T: +263 4 870 514
W: www.harare-international-school.com

IB
ASIA-PACIFIC

IB Asia-Pacific

Some facts about this region

In the Asia-Pacific region, we support over 950 schools offering more than 1,430 programmes in 29 countries and territories. The largest concentration of IB World Schools in Asia-Pacific can be found in Australia with 193 schools, Greater China with over 230 schools and India where there are over 160 IB World Schools offering one or more IB programmes.

You will find the IB World Schools in:

Australia	Guam	Lao People's Democratic Republic	New Caledonia	Solomon Islands
Bangladesh	Hong Kong	Macao	New Zealand	Sri Lanka
Brunei Darussalam	India	Malaysia	Pakistan	Taiwan
Cambodia	Indonesia	Mongolia	Papua New Guinea	Thailand
China	Japan	Myanmar	Philippines	Timor-Leste
Fiji	Republic of Korea	Nepal	Singapore	Vietnam

IB Asia-Pacific Global Centre, Singapore

Our IB Global Centre, Singapore provides ongoing support to Candidate and authorized IB World Schools across the globe in implementation of IB programmes. The IB Global Centre, Singapore is responsible for functions including the supporting schools interested in becoming IB World Schools and schools in candidacy working towards authorization. Regular, ongoing and rigorous evaluations of authorized IB World Schools are part of our commitment to keeping high quality, consistent academic standards around the world. We also organize teacher professional development workshops for schools in the Asia Pacific and develop greater recognition of IB programmes by directly working with universities and governments.

Commitment to serve the diverse needs of our schools

We continue to enhance our services and support to schools as two dedicated teams, Authorization and IB World Schools (IBWS), focusing on the specific needs of Candidate and Authorized IB World Schools respectively. In addition to our ongoing strategic initiative working with the Ministry of Culture, Sports, Education, Science and Technology (MEXT) in Japan to expand access to DP subjects and examinations in Japanese, we have recently signed a memorandum of cooperation with Jeju and Daegu Offices of Education in South Korea to offer a select group of DP subjects in Korean.

The IB Educator Network (IBEN)

The IB Educator Network (IBEN) in Asia-Pacific is made up of IB practitioners fulfilling the roles of workshop leaders, field representatives, school visitors, consultants, readers and lead educators; and is part of the wider Global IBEN community. Through the contributions of the IBEN educators (IBEs), we can provide support and training to promote high-quality experiences in classrooms and schools.

Thank you to all IB Educators, Heads of Schools and their staff from the IBEN Team for your continued interest and support of the educator network and your collaborative contributions to the wider IB community. Look out for our 2020 recruitment/development opportunities in MyIB. We look forward to identifying and providing development opportunities to new educators to meet our identified growth areas, and ongoing support to those network members currently carrying out roles for us.

We also look forward to working with you all in 2020 and hope to see many of you at the Global Conference in Hong Kong in March. Thank you to all IBEs who have submitted proposals to lead a break-out session at the conference.

Professional development in the Asia-Pacific region

In Asia Pacific, schools have a choice between attending one of our regional events or run an on demand in-school workshop at a time and location of their choosing.

Regional workshops are scheduled 3 or 4-day events containing a list of workshops that educators can join. These events encapsulate the IB Learner Profile and International Mindedness by bringing educators together from a range of schools and countries to share ideas and learn in a collaborative environment. Most of our events are also hosted by IB World Schools so educators will get to experience different learning environments as they progress through the IB.

We rely on our IB World Schools to host regional events to support our peer to peer learning philosophy. If you are a school interested in hosting IB regional workshops, please reach out to us via www.ibo.org/globalassets/events/ap/host-a-workshop-ap-en.pdf.

Visit www.ibo.org/pd for our full professional development workshop schedules and catalogue.

On demand in-school workshops provide professional development to meet the needs of educators in your own school or local network. This is a good option if you want to upskill many teachers at the same time as the overall cost of providing PD is lower and you can run workshops at a time that suits your school calendar.

You can apply for an on demand in-school workshop via www.ibo.org/en/about-the-ib/the-ib-by-region/ib-asia-pacific/pd-asia/#in-school.

We work closely with regional networks of IB Programme Coordinators and schools to deliver high quality PD. Please get in contact with us if you would like to discuss your school's PD needs.

University recognition

We have more than 2,000 published recognition policies from universities around the world, including 500 policies in Asia-Pacific. In the past five years, student university destinations within the Asia-Pacific region includes (in order of preference): Australia, Hong Kong, India and Singapore. These include foreign students going to these countries as well as students remaining in their home country. In Hong Kong, for example, which has a high diversity of student nationalities and university destinations, the most popular choices are Hong Kong, United Kingdom, Canada, the US and Australia.

In Australia, the Group of Eight (Go8) universities and all major tertiary institutions recognize that the IB Diploma is a comprehensive and challenging programme.

In India, we have a long-standing partnership with the Association of Indian Universities (AIU). Through our work with the AIU, the IB Diploma has been recognized as an entry qualification to all universities in India since 1983, and this was renewed in 2012 with the additional recognition of the MYP and the DP Course where students attempting the IB Diploma with a score of 24 points along with 3 higher level

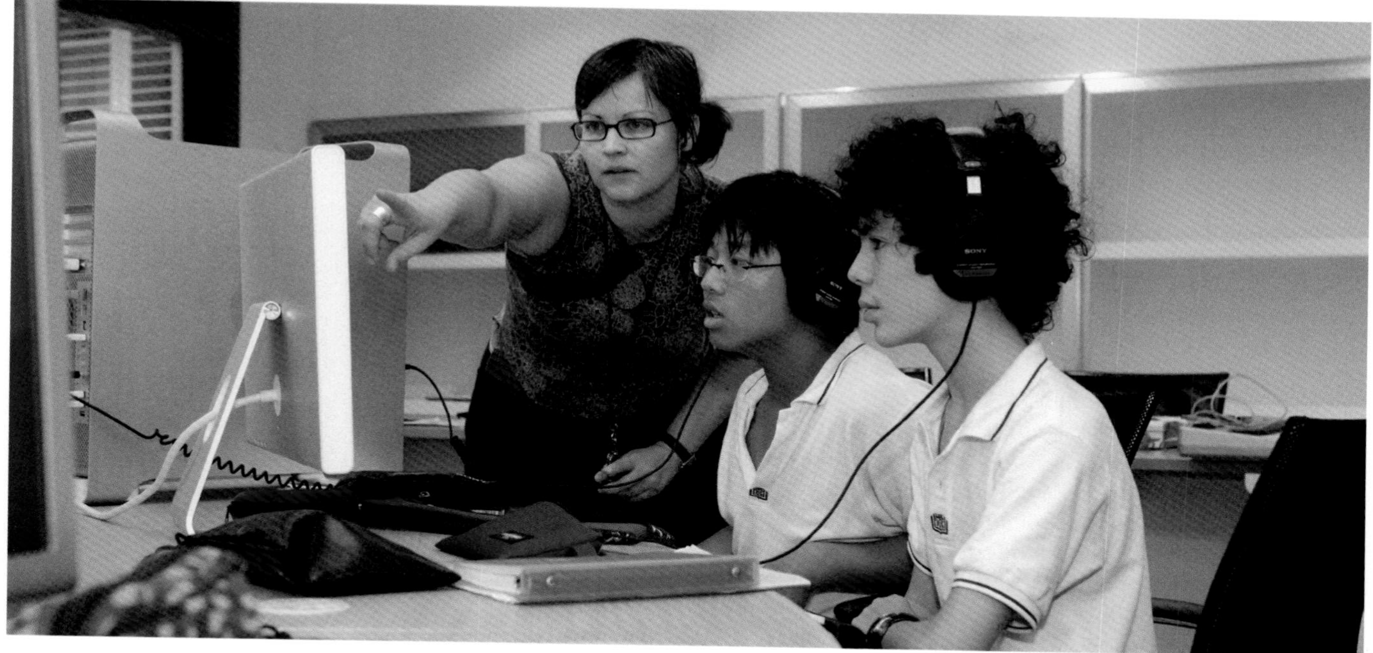

and 3 standard level subjects are granted equivalency to the local board's Year 12 qualification.

The Malaysian Qualifications Authority (MQA) has granted the IB Diploma as having equivalency to STPM or Malaysia's Grade 12 qualification while the MYP Certificate is equivalent to the country's SPM or Grade 10 qualification.

The IB in the Asia-Pacific is continuously collaborating with Japan's Ministry of Education, Culture, Sports, Science, and Technology (MEXT) in implementing the Dual Language Diploma Programme in Japanese.

Associations of IB World Schools in the Asia-Pacific

Associations of IB World Schools are independent organizations established under the Guidelines of Associations of the IB. The members are commonly IB Candidate and IB World Schools. Groupings in the Associations are based on geographically relevant communities to support IB World Schools as well as schools new to the IB in the region. Most associations charge a fee to schools belonging to their group.

Associations, who are independent of the IB, support member schools through advocacy and by:

- providing current information on the local and regional context, e.g. what is happening in education, changes affecting the schools in their Association, feedback, advisory capacity, a platform for collaboration and IB research.
- disseminating updates and seeking advice from the IB about core IB services such as professional development (PD), school services, government and university recognition.
- providing professional development in association with the IB, when a separate agreement is in place.

There are currently five Associations of IB World Schools in the Asia-Pacific region:

- IB Schools Australasia (IBSA)
- IB Association of Japan (IBAJ)
- IB Association of World Schools for South Korea Resource Centre Society
- The Association of Chinese and Mongolian International Baccalaureate Schools (ACMIBS)
- The Association of International Schools of India (TAISI)

IB research

Key findings from research on the impact of IB programmes in the Asia-Pacific region:

- A study across five countries (one of which was China) explored student, teacher and parent **experiences with the PYP exhibition**—the in-depth, culminating project of the PYP. Study participants found the exhibition to be a pivotal experience that helped students to develop critical thinking skills, international-mindedness and learner profile attributes. Additionally, parents valued the exhibition for fostering "real world" skills, such as evaluating information and reflectiveness (Medwell et al 2017).
- Researchers examined **student performance** in 14 state and private schools in **New Zealand** as well as **curriculum alignment** between the PYP and the New Zealand Curriculum (NZC). Analysis of a national standardized test indicated that achievement in the PYP schools generally exceeded achievement in non-IB schools with similar student populations. The study also found that the PYP and NZC are largely compatible, although there were a few points of difference, specifically the emphasis on international-mindedness, inquiry and action in the PYP (Kushner et al 2016).
- A study in **Australia** examined perspectives of teachers, coordinators and school principals on the **benefits of the MYP for learning and teaching**.

Educators in this study believed that the MYP is a high-quality learning framework that provides genuine benefits for learning and teaching. All participants valued the philosophy and principles embedded in the MYP. The study indicated that the MYP has great potential to improve the relevance and authenticity of schooling for adolescents in Australia, while providing rigour and holistic development.

- In **China, Hong Kong, India, Indonesia and Japan**, researchers compared the **DP outcomes** achieved by students who completed their middle years studies in the MYP, a state or national curriculum, or another international programme. Former MYP students performed significantly better than non-MYP students in the total DP points earned, as well as in subject exams in language and literature, language acquisition, individuals and societies and mathematics. The MYP students also reported using higher-order thinking skills, such as critical thinking and analytical skills, more frequently than the non-MYP students (ACER 2015).
- At two leading universities in **East Asia** and one in **Australia**, researchers examined **post-secondary outcomes** and **critical thinking skills** of DP and non-DP alumni. While there was no significant difference in grade point average (GPA) between the two groups, in general, DP alumni reported higher capacities for a variety of critical thinking skills compared to their non-IB peers. DP graduates were particularly confident in their capacity for cultural sensitivity, global-mindedness, critical thinking, leadership, and time management (Lee et al 2017).
- Researchers investigated the impact of **creativity, activity, service** (CAS) by exploring the perceptions of those involved in the programme, past and present. Coordinators, students and alumni surveyed from **across the world** (including in the Asia-Pacific region) believed that CAS helps students to become better at "taking on new challenges", "learning to persevere" and "developing better interpersonal skills" (Hayden et al 2017).
- Researchers in a **global** study conducted a curricular comparison of four DP **mathematics courses** along with five mathematics qualifications from around the world (Alberta Diploma, Advanced Placement, GCE A levels, **Singapore-Cambridge GCE A Levels and Gāokǎo**). Of the curriculums investigated in this study, the DP offered the greatest number of mathematical course options for students with different needs. Additionally, based on the criteria used in this analysis, the IB's further mathematics HL was determined to be the most cognitively demanding course of the curriculums examined, followed by A level Further Mathematics and Singapore H3 Mathematics respectively (Alcántara 2016 and UK NARIC 2016).
- A study in **Japan** investigated the implementation of the **dual language (Japanese and English) DP** in Japanese secondary schools. Taken as a whole, the study highlighted the need for more practical help in addition to general advice from the Japanese Ministry of Education, Culture, Sports, Science and Technology (MEXT) and the IB as well as greater flexibility with regard to determining curricular equivalency. An additional finding was that Japanese DP students reported higher ratings than non-DP students for being internationally-minded and had higher expectations of acquiring problem-solving and leadership skills while at high school (Yamamoto et al 2016).

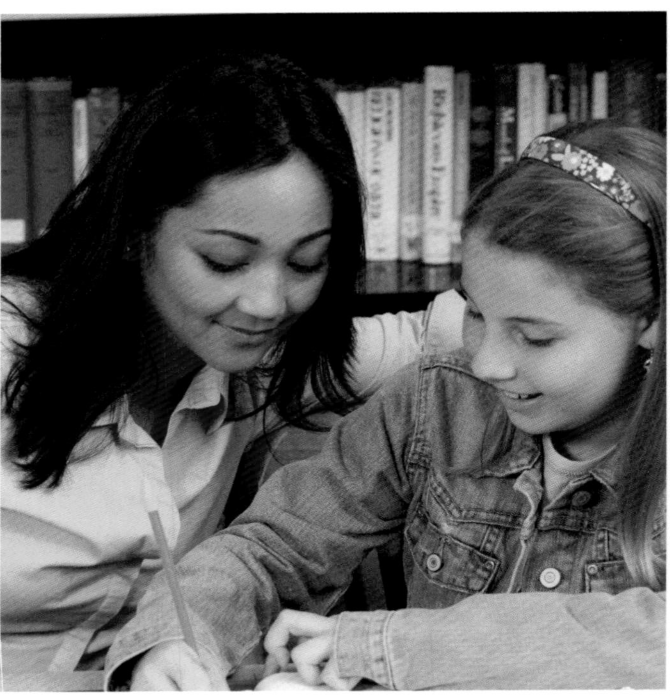

The IB alumni network (Asia-Pacific)

The IB Alumni Network is a resource for IB graduates around the world. The network links graduates from IB World Schools in 156 countries to support their future studies and careers. By connecting with the IB, former students have the opportunity to participate in research, support development efforts and speak at our events. These graduates are also supporting educators and parents in understanding the impact of an IB education from a student's perspective. To see how graduates are supporting IB programmes, visit ibo.org/programme-stories and connect with us at ibo.org/alumni.

Contact

IB Asia-Pacific
600 North Bridge Road #21-01 Parkview Square
Singapore 188778, Republic of Singapore

Main: +65 6579 5000
Web: www.ibo.org/ib-ap

IB ASIA-PACIFIC

(Founded 2011)

Heads of School
David Cao, Bob Darwish

DP coordinator
Navnita Karmakar

Status Private

Boarding/day Boarding

Gender Coeducational

Language of instruction
English, Mandarin

Authorised IB programmes
DP

Age Range 12 – 19

Address
14 Guang Sheng Road
Nansha District
Guangzhou City, Guangdong
511458 | CHINA

TEL +86 20 8618 3999/3666
FAX +86 20 8619 4107

Email
bdarwish@aicib.org

Website
aicib.org

Alcanta International College is a unique school with high ambitions. We put students at the center of their own international education with the goal of developing global citizens prepared for a world of options when they leave our campus. Established in 2011, AIC has been inspired by the IB philosophy. We push students to inquire, to be open-minded as they live among a diverse student body, to care for one another, and to maintain balance in their own lives.

AIC is an IB World School located in the Nansha District of Guangzhou city, China, priding itself on its ability to inspire tomorrow's leaders via its unique learning environment. The school runs the IB Diploma for senior students, a qualification that's recognized by universities worldwide. This is in addition to its unique 4-year Pre-Diploma program that blends the school's needs with ideas borrowed from a diverse international curriculum.

While following the IB Diploma, AIC also places special emphasis on Chinese language and culture, and international mindedness helping students embrace global citizenship. Students here enjoy small class sizes and an intimate learning environment, helping them identify their unique strengths and areas for growth.

Through rigorous academic and robust CAS programs, AIC encourages its students to explore universal issues, and in so doing promotes their understanding of themselves and the world around them, in addition to building their linguistic, analytical, creative and communicative skills.

With some 22 nationalities represented on-campus, AIC opens the door to a powerful international education experience. The school embraces active experiential learning; as a testament to its prowess, 82 percent of their students last year were accepted into top 50 QS ranked universities.

AIC offers scholarships to exceptional students who demonstrate high potential and abilities, as well as leadership skills. Fifteen international students can obtain 100 percent funding for the academic year, renewable for the remaining duration of the student's enrollment at AIC, subject to an annual review.

Aoba-Japan International School

Head of School
Mr Ken Sell

PYP coordinator
Harukako Ikeura

MYP coordinator
Lisa de Pierres

DP coordinator
Glenn Connelly

Status Private

Boarding/day Day

Gender Coeducational

Language of instruction
English

Authorised IB programmes
PYP, MYP, DP

Age Range 2 – 18

Number of pupils enrolled
520

Address
7-5-1 Hikarigaoka
Nerima-ku
Tokyo, Kanto
179-0072 | JAPAN

TEL +81 3 4578 8832
FAX +81 3 5997 0091

Email
hikarigaoka@aobajapan.jp

Website
www.japaninternationalschool.com

Welcome
Our team is waiting to welcome you at our school either online or in person.

Mission Statement
A spirit of community shapes the A-JIS experience. We are dedicated to developing global-minded, compassionate, collaborative learners inspired to learn, take risks, and lead change in the world.

Vision
A-JIS will continue to be a leading international school. We provide our young people with a vigorous international education conducive to learning. Learners' needs and perspectives are supported and respected and their unique qualities valued and nurtured. Through a continued emphasis on educational excellence and innovation, each individual learner is provided with relevant resources and opportunities that will enable them to secure the best of what the future holds for them.

Our Philosophy
We believe that our young people are enabled to reach their full potential as international citizens who are dedicated to learning and who are inspired to succeed in an ever-changing world.

Our 5 core Values
At A-JIS we value the concepts of:
- Global Leadership
- Entrepreneurship and Innovation
- Effective Communication
- Wise Risk Taking
- Effective Problem Solving

Our Learning Environment
The school is a welcoming, inclusive and engaging place for learning. We proudly follow the IB curriculum in the PYP, MYP and DP. Owned by BBT (Business Breakthrough University – Japan's largest online university), our recent focus has been on investing in our people and providing contemporary learning environments for our learners. Apart from our renovated playing fields, all our classrooms are equipped with interactive technologies providing connections to the world.

Our Learning Aims
Embracing the IB philosophies and practices, our school aims to support our learners to become global leaders capable of making positive changes in the world. We aim to have all our learners achieve their personal goals by connecting learning, and their development as learners, through constructive and proactive membership within the communities they live in – school, local, home and global. Our learners are encouraged to follow their passions and interests and build the critical and discerning capacities needed to make wise decisions. We have dramatically increased the choices our learners have within school and for when they leave us, be it into university, business, creative industries, or the social sectors in our society.

Location
A-JIS is a caring K-12 learning community set in the peaceful

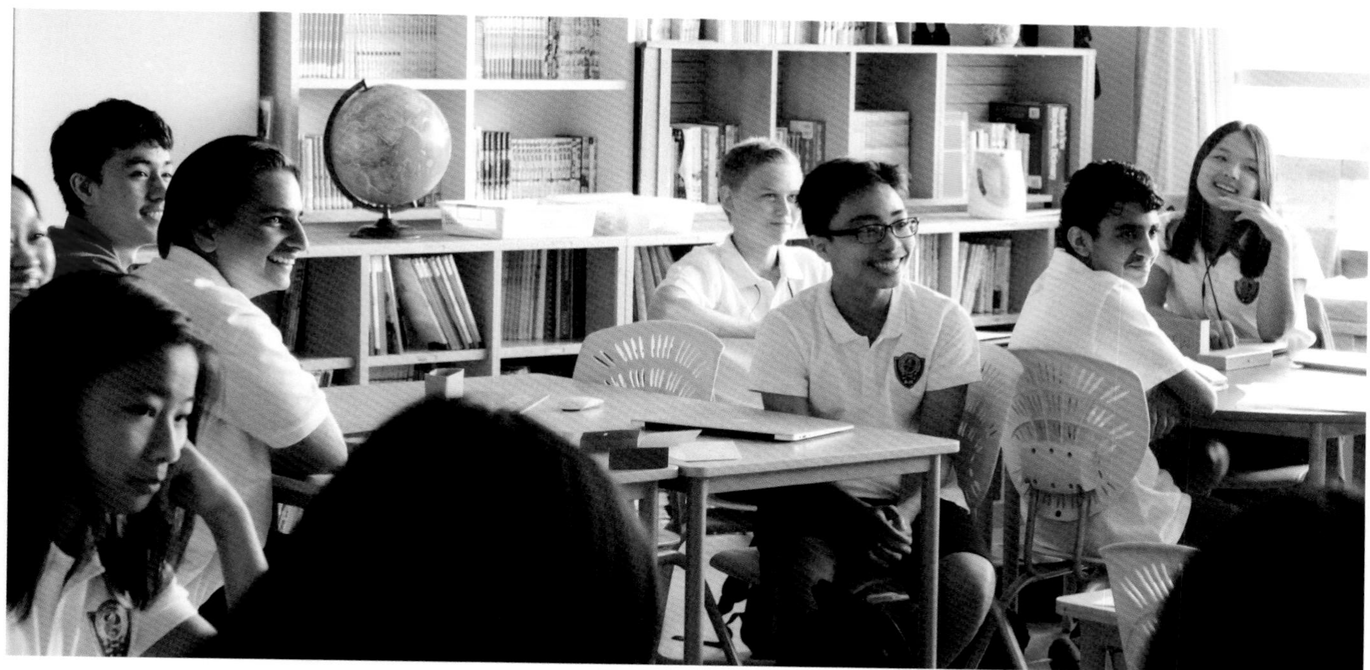

and leafy north-western suburb of Tokyo. It is easily accessible by the Tokyo metro train system and a short 10-minute walk from Hikarigaoka station, which is 25 minutes from downtown Tokyo. The school has a long tradition of being a welcoming and inclusive place of learning and that tradition is being continued under the new ownership of Business Breakthrough University. The partnership between BBT and A-JIS has already produced benefits for our learners and teachers alike. With a focus on investing in our people and learning environments we are driven to provide our young people with a wealth of opportunities to learn, develop as learners and use what they learn to good effect.

Support Program

We provide extensive support for both English as an Additional Language and Learning Support. Our expert teacher teams and faculty have university-level EAL course qualifications. We also have opportunities for sports, swimming, after-school clubs, and summer school. We look forward to connecting with you soon.

American School of Bombay

(Founded 1981)

Head of School
Craig Alan Johnson

PYP coordinator Fay Martin

DP coordinator Tamara Pfantz

Status Private

Boarding/day Day

Gender Coeducational

Language of instruction
English

Authorised IB programmes
PYP, DP

Age Range 3 – 18

Number of pupils enrolled
733

Fees
Day: US$15,250 – US$34,020

Secondary School
SF 2, G-Block
Bandra Kurla Complex
Road, Bandra East, Mumbai,
Maharashtra **400051 | INDIA**

Elementary School
Commercial 2, Tower 4
Kohinoor City, Kirol Road, Off
LBS Marg, Kurla (W), Mumbai
400 070 | INDIA

Early Childhood Campus – Powai Learning Village
701, Hiranandani Knowledge
Park, Technology Street, Powai,
Mumbai | **INDIA**

TEL SS: +91 22 6772 7272
ES: +91 22 6131 3600
ECC: +91 22 6131 3600

Email inquiry@asbindia.org

Website www.asbindia.org

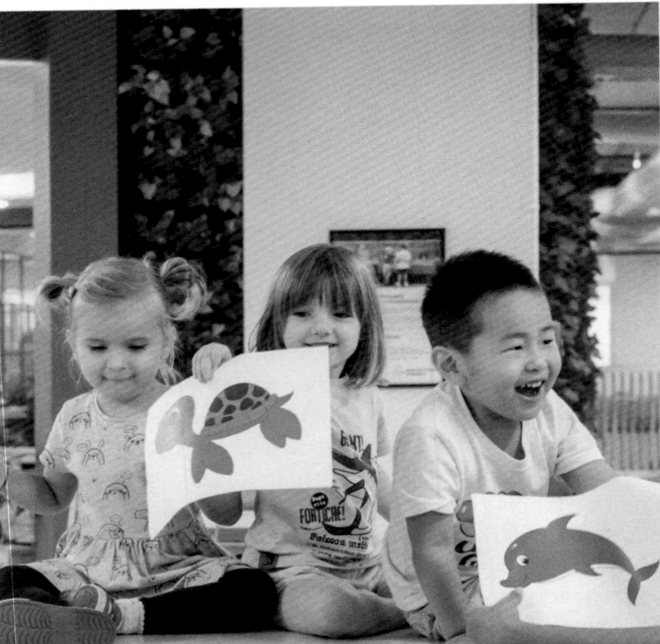

The American School of Bombay (ASB) is an independent, coeducational day school in Mumbai, India. The school offers a U.S.-style educational program from Prekindergarten through grade 12 for 700+ students representing over 50 nationalities.

In 1981, a group of international parents started the American School of Bombay with just 12 students in a room at the American Consulate. In August 2012, ASB evolved from a single campus school to a dual campus school, and in August 2019, it became a three-campus school: early childhood campus (Powai Learning Village), elementary campus, and secondary campus. Located in the central suburbs of the city, the three campuses offer 220,000 square feet of custom-designed instructional spaces for delivering unique and individualized programs to the students.

The school's structure, curriculum methods, and pedagogy integrate an American approach to education with the International Baccalaureate Program. IB courses of study in Prekindergarten-grade 5 and grades 11-12 include Primary Years Programme in the elementary school, Pre-IB Programme in grades 9-10, and the Diploma Program in grades 11-12. The middle school, comprising grades 6-8, offers students a full program to prepare them for high school.

ASB also offers several extended learning opportunities after school and during school holidays. ASB is a member of the South Asia Inter-School Association and the American Schools in India Activities Conference and provides students the opportunity to compete in sports and collaborate in arts with other international schools. Students also participate in Model United Nations, International Schools Theatre Association, and international choral and instrumental concerts. Besides, all middle and high school students participate in a Week Without Walls/Yatra programs that are directly linked with the curriculum and reflect the concept of learning beyond the classroom. Students are encouraged to be aware of their personal, social, and civic responsibility towards themselves and others – this is emphasized through our well-established Community and Social Responsibility (CSR) and Creativity, Activity, Service (CAS) programs.

ASB's endeavor to provide optimum indoor air quality for students is an ongoing process that utilizes knowledge, research, and best practices from around the world. Purifying air by three-stage HEPA filtration, monitoring with real-time air-quality sensors, enclosing the play areas and recreational spaces, and having more than 50,000 live indoor plants, including green walls, are some of the initiatives that ensure the best possible indoor air quality.

Our rigorous program is about developing critical thinking skills while acquiring academically relevant content knowledge. At the American School of Bombay, we recognize each child's unique abilities and develop their individual skills to become compassionate citizens who understand that their choices can make an impact on the world.

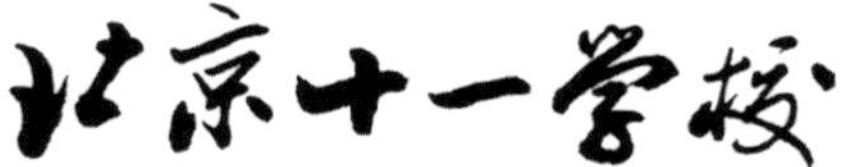

(Founded 1952)

Superintendent
Li Xigui

Principal
Tian Jun

Vice Principal & Director of the International Department
Wu Fengqin

IB Director & DP coordinator
Jhony Arias Vivas

Status State

Boarding/day Mixed

Gender Coeducational

Language of instruction
English

Authorised IB programmes
DP

Number of pupils enrolled
5000

Address
No. 66 Yuquan Road
Haidan District
Beijing
100039 | CHINA

TEL +86 (10) 88625495
FAX +86 (10) 88628424

Email
bettywufq@163.com

Website
www.bndsedu.com

Background

Beijing National Day School (BNDS) is a public, co-educational day school founded in 1952, providing superior education for China's high achieving youth. Through collaborative inquiry and holistic approaches to teaching, BNDS is a unique community that supports student success in an inclusive and academically challenging environment. Faculty and staff at BNDS join together to inspire and prepare future global leaders, providing opportunities for cross-cultural exchange and adapting instruction to meet the needs of 21st-Century learners. As an internationally accredited school offering the prestigious International Baccalaureate Diploma Programme, BNDS graduates are consistently admitted to the best universities in the United States, Canada and the UK.

Facilities and Curriculum

BNDS is located 12-kilometres directly west of Tiananmen Square in the multicultural city of Beijing. The school's vibrant, modern, and technologically integrated facilities reflect its goal of providing students with the best learning environment. The campus is extensive (over 156,000 square metres), boasting numerous classroom buildings, arts centres, libraries, gymnasiums, science centers, and sports fields. The school-wide campus intranet connects more than 1,100 computers, and 116 classrooms are equipped with interactive whiteboards, printers, and multi-media resources connected to the internet. Additionally, the science and technology building has modern labs for mathematics, physics, chemistry, and biology.

BNDS offers four different curricula: Chinese National Curriculum, A Level, AP, and IB Diploma Programme. Additionally, BNDS offers students a wide range of extra-/co-curricular activities including advertising, animation, automobile design, debate, economics, environmental studies, equestrian, fashion design, fencing, foreign languages, skiing, and student government.

Moreover, 30 field-research courses, 280 clubs and organizations are part of the daily life of IB Diploma students at BNDS.

Faculty

BNDS teachers and administrators are highly experienced and qualified professionals who are committed to the learning and development of each student. BNDS has more than 460 educators most of whom hold advanced degrees in their respective fields from prestigious universities in China and abroad. The school's international department has 79 international teachers, counselors, and administrators of 12 different nationalities from North America, South America, Europe, Asia, and Australia.

(Founded 2012)

Principal
Dr. Cinde Lock

PYP coordinator
Mrs. Virginia Sutton

MYP coordinator
Ms. Paula Swartz

DP coordinator
Mr. Nick Daniel

Status Private

Boarding/day Mixed

Gender Female

Language of instruction
English

Authorised IB programmes
PYP, MYP, DP

Address
234 Global edu-ro, Daejeong-eup
Seogwipo-si
Jeju-do
63644 | REPUBLIC OF KOREA

TEL +82 64 902 5000
FAX +82 64 902 5481

Email
admissions@branksome.asia

Website
www.branksome.asia

Branksome Hall Asia is the sister school of Branksome Hall, a 116-year-old independent girls' school in Canada, consistently ranked as one of the world's best boarding schools. Founded in 2012, we are an IB World School that offers the academically rigorous and challenging Diploma Programme, Middle Years Programme and the Primary Years Programme.

At Branksome Hall Asia, girls take center stage as they learn and grow. We nurture the development of global perspectives and leadership through service, which benefits all students as they discover their "Remarkable" and their place as leaders locally, nationally and globally. Our distinctive educational journey actively pursues our mission, "To challenge and inspire girls each day to love learning and to shape a better world." This educational journey promises to support each student to discover within themselves a strong voice, to take risks and step outside their comfort zones, and the power to lead lives of curiosity, empowerment, service to others, and personal fulfillment.

Dedicated to providing exemplary educational programs, our students grow as globally minded learners and leaders prepared for the challenges and opportunities they will meet in a rapidly changing interdependent world. They grow as architects, athletes, debaters, doctors, engineers, historians, lawyers, mathematicians, musicians, researchers, scientists, writers and much more, and often at the same time.

From JK Prep to Grade 12, our students share their learning and living in a state-of-the-art world-class facility that embodies and encourages our value for intellectual inquiry, collaboration, effective communication, and strength of character. Branksome Hall Asia vibrates with students' energy and warmth.

The exceptional Branksome Hall Asia faculty fuels this energy. Experts in their field and dedicated to professional growth, their commitment to the highest levels of learning, to ensure each student discovers her unique "Remarkable," is central to our success.

Branksome Hall Asia has an International Merit Scholarship program for non-Korean students to provide deserving future female leaders the chance to benefit from our IB World School program. Scholarships are given in recognition of a student's academic success, leadership commitments, co-curricular involvement, and other talents and achievements. More information is available through the school website.

British International School, Hanoi

BRITISH INTERNATIONAL SCHOOL HANOI
A NORD ANGLIA EDUCATION SCHOOL

(Founded 2012)

Head of School
Ms Sue Hill

DP coordinator
Mr Adrian Duckett

Status Private

Boarding/day Day

Gender Coeducational

Language of instruction
English

Authorised IB programmes
DP

Age Range 2 – 18

Number of pupils enrolled
1100

Fees
Day: US$11,000 – US$31,000

Address
Hoa Lan Road, Vinhomes
Riverside
Long Bien District
Hanoi
100000 | VIETNAM

TEL +84 24 3946 0435
FAX +84 24 3946 0438

Email
bishanoi@bishanoi.com

Website
www.bishanoi.com

As a member of Nord Anglia Education – the world's leading premium schools' organization with 66 schools located across 29 countries, the British International School Hanoi (BIS Hanoi) is a selective, independent and co-educational day school, providing a British-style education for an international student body aged between 2 and 18 years old in Vietnam's vibrant capital city.

BIS Hanoi is a state-of-the-art, purpose-built school whose campus boasts exceptional facilities including a dedicated Early Years Centre, a large library, a theatre, an auditorium, a 25-meter indoor swimming pool, a sports hall, and artificial turf playing fields. The school also has specialist suites for STEAM, Science, Computing, Art, Music, Drama and Dance.

Students at BIS Hanoi follow the English National Curriculum from the Early Years Foundation Stage through Key Stage 3, supplemented by IPC – the International Primary Curriculum. The IGCSE qualification is available to students in Key Stage 4 through Cambridge Assessment International Education.

The school became an IB World School in January 2016 and began offering the IB Diploma Programme from August 2016. School-wide curriculum alignment builds toward Key Stage 5 where a rigorous academic program is supplemented by a wide variety of available CAS experiences. In the academic year 2018-19, BIS Hanoi achieved an impressive average of 33.4 points, up from 32.3 points the previous year and significantly ahead of the global average of approximately 29.6 points this year. 20 percent of BIS Hanoi's IB students obtained 40 points and above. These results enabled students to apply to and be accepted by some of the best universities in the US, Canada, UK and beyond.

Students at BIS Hanoi can participate in the globally renowned Duke of Edinburgh's International Award, the world's leading youth achievement award. In the summer of 2017, four DP candidates at BIS Hanoi became the first in Vietnam to complete the Gold Award, with an expedition in the highlands of South Korea.

In 2015, BIS Hanoi was granted membership of FOBISIA – the Federation of British International Schools in Asia, while in 2017 the school became a fully accredited member of CIS – the Council of International Schools as well as ACS WASC – the Western Association of Schools and Colleges.

At BIS Hanoi, we are a caring community that enables children to realise their academic and personal potential in a dynamic and challenging learning environment, which values enquiry, perseverance and reflection. Our students act with integrity and treat one another with respect, learning together as responsible global citizens.

(Founded 2010)

Principal
Ms. Anvita Gupta

Chairman & Founder
Dr. Suresh Reddy

PYP coordinator
Shivani Nagar

DP coordinator
Gourab Das Sharma

Status Private

Boarding/day Mixed

Gender Coeducational

Language of instruction
English

Authorised IB programmes
PYP, DP

Age Range 3 – 17

Number of pupils enrolled
600

Address
Begur – Koppa Road, Hullahalli
Off Bannerghatta Road, Near
Electronic City
Bengaluru, Karnataka
560105 | INDIA

TEL +91 77 6029 9992

Email
admissions@candorschool.com

Website
candorschool.edu.in

Candor International School is a Day cum Residential School, housed in a sprawling green campus of 30 acres in South Bangalore, founded by Dr. Suresh Reddy.

We offer International Baccalaureate Primary Years Programme, Diploma Programme and the Cambridge Program (IGCSE) from the University of Cambridge, AS & A Levels.

The education offered at Candor is dynamic and progressive, run by a team of dedicated and trained teachers. Our students are passionate, committed and involved in building the school culture. Candor has had good university placements with our students around the world.

Age appropriate community service is part and parcel of the school programme. Candor aims to sensitize students to local and global needs and contribute towards creating a better world. The Candor community has a genuine interest in CAS activities and runs programs to make a difference.

At Candor, Music, Dance, Drama and Visual Arts are taught as an integral part of the curriculum, as Candor believes that the performing arts adds to the emotional and creative dimension of learning.

Sports and Physical Education programme of the school ensures that all sports as well as track and field events are taught and learnt in relation to physiology, anatomy and nutrition in an enjoyable and interesting way.

The school also integrates Pre-SAT and SAT preparations for high school students through a College Advisory Service and an experienced in-house college counsellor who interacts with both students and parents.

Awards & Accolades:

- Ranked No.1 School in India for Academic Reputation, by Education Today (2019)
- First certified “Green School” in India
- Forbes Great Indian Schools (2018-19)
- Eco School Project of the year 2019
- Ranked among India’s top 5 International Day Cum Boarding Schools

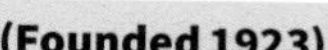

(Founded 1923)

Head of School
Mr Jonathan Walter BA, Dip Ed, MA (School Leadership)

DP coordinator
Frederique Petithory

Status Private

Boarding/day Day

Gender Coeducational

Language of instruction
English

Authorised IB programmes
DP

Age Range 3 – 18

Number of pupils enrolled
2526

Fees
Day (Local) $21,352 – $33,052
Day (International) $38,154 – $39,232

Address
349 Barkers Road
Kew
VIC 3101 | AUSTRALIA

TEL +61 3 9816 1222

Email
admissions@carey.com.au

Website
www.carey.com.au

Founded in 1923, Carey Baptist Grammar School is a Christian independent coeducational school offering 3-year-old Early Learning to Year 12. Carey is situated close to the Central Business District of Melbourne, within easy distance of public transport.

As one of Australia's leading schools, Carey maintains an even gender balance, fostering the development of confidence, communication skills and self-esteem in all students. Students participate in community service; study different cultures, religions and beliefs; learn the importance of human rights; and are encouraged to respect and appreciate the world beyond their own experience.

Carey works in partnership with families to develop wise, independent, motivated young people who are inspired and equipped to create positive change. The Senior School offers both IB and VCE and fosters a dynamic and stimulating environment. Our students achieve university entrance scores that place Carey amongst the top schools in Victoria.

Recruiting and developing highly professional teaching and support staff is one of our greatest priorities. Carey is known for being innovative, progressive and leading the way in best practice teaching and learning, supporting strong academic results and personal development for each student. Carey's philosophy of student-centred learning requires students to be active, responsible participants in their own learning, with the teacher working as a mentor, facilitator and guide.

To support the learning program, Carey is committed to providing inspiring buildings and resources. In 2016, Carey officially opened the new Centre for Learning and Innovation, developed on principles of contemporary education and the latest pedagogical thinking and understanding. At the heart of the building is the Information Resource Centre which, in addition to housing our extensive catalogue, offers a variety of spaces that cater for the different needs of our students. On the top of this building sits the United Nations Room which reflects Carey's diversity, inclusivity and commitment to social justice, thus preparing our students for the rapidly changing local, national and international communities in which they live, work and serve.

Carey students are curious, aspirational and engaged global citizens. We build on their individual qualities to develop young people who flourish and can lead and serve with courage, compassion and intelligence.

We welcome the cultural diversity that international students bring to our community.

For more information about our programs and purpose-built facilities, visit www.carey.com.au or call our Admissions Manager on +61 3 9816 1242, or email admissions@carey.com.au

Head of School
Frederick T. "Ted" Hill

PYP coordinator
Pamela Castillo (Lower Primary) & Mei-Lyn Freeman (Upper Primary)

Director of Teacher & Learning
Barbara Wrightson

DP coordinator
Benedict Hung

CP coordinator
Jason Reagin

Status Private

Boarding/day Day

Gender Coeducational

Language of instruction
English

Authorised IB programmes
PYP, MYP, DP, CP

Age Range 4 – 18

Number of pupils enrolled
1300

Address
45, Art center-daero 97 beon-gil
Yeonsu-gu, Incheon
22002 | REPUBLIC OF KOREA

TEL +82 32 250 5000

Email
songdo-admissions@chadwickschool.org

Website
www.chadwickinternational.org

Chadwick International is a PreK- G12 international school fully equipped with the state-of-the-art facility built in the Songdo International Business District, Incheon, Republic of Korea.

Chadwick International is the sister campus of Chadwick School, a K-12 school in the greater South Bay area of Los Angeles, which was founded by Margaret Lee Chadwick in 1935. The two campuses share the same mission that Chadwick Schools develop global citizens with keen minds, exemplary character, self-knowledge, and the ability to lead.

Chadwick International is an authorized four programme International Baccalaureate (IB) world school, offering PYP, MYP, DP and CP. Chadwick International emphasizes experiential and inquiry-based learning both in and outside the classroom including Outdoor Education and Service Learning programs. The Outdoor Education allows students to develop conflict-resolution abilities and leadership skills through various outdoor experiences. Meanwhile, Service Learning program teaches students how to interact with both their local and international communities and problem solve on a deeper level. These fundamental programs assist students in transferring valuable lessons learned in the classroom and develop them as contributing members and leaders of tomorrow.

Physical Education plays an integral part of the Chadwick curriculum as it focuses on the promotion of good personal health and a holistic lifestyle for our students. Its activity-based program emphasizes the skill development that improves the fitness and well-being of the individual student as well as healthy and safe lifestyles.

Chadwick International has rich and diverse Visual and Performing Arts programs. In these classes, students develop their knowledge, skills, creativity and ability to respond to artistic ideas. Also, students are exposed to a variety of theatrical mediums to express themselves and heighten their awareness of themselves in relation to the people and culture around them.

Chadwick International helps to achieve its educational mission through recruiting and supporting highly experienced, dedicated, and diverse faculty members from around the world. With the support of the faculty, Chadwick International is capable of a low teacher to student ratio of 1:8.

Chadwick International's superior educational facilities include an aquatic center with scuba diving capabilities, two gymnasiums, two performing arts indoor theaters, a television studio that allows production up to eight channels, a working garden, purpose-built science laboratories and three design/maker spaces. These facilities permit the students to cultivate their intellectual, artistic and physical abilities based on Chadwick International's experience-based curriculum.

Chadwick International is accredited by Western Association of Schools and Colleges (WASC) and Council of International Schools (CIS).

Delia Memorial School (Glee Path)

(Founded 1972)

Principal
Dr. Chan Kui Pui

DP coordinator
Mr. Paolo Yap

Status State

Boarding/day Day

Gender Coeducational

Language of instruction
Cantonese, English, Mandarin

Authorised IB programmes
DP

Age Range 12 – 18

Number of pupils enrolled
695

Fees
Secondary 4-6 HKDSE: HK$3,000 (US$385)
IBDP Y1 and Y2: HK$25,000 (US$3,200)

Address
1-3 Glee Path, Mei Foo Sun Chuen
Kowloon
Hong Kong, SAR | **HONG KONG, CHINA**

TEL +852 2741 5239
FAX +852 2745 2250

Email
gp@deliagroup.edu.hk

Website
www.deliagp.edu.hk

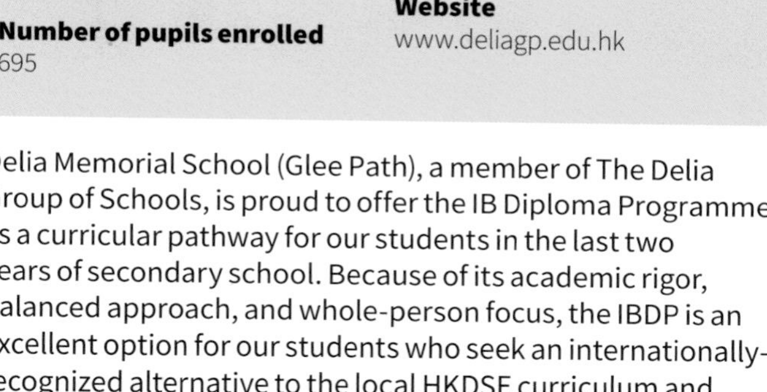

Delia Memorial School (Glee Path), a member of The Delia Group of Schools, is proud to offer the IB Diploma Programme as a curricular pathway for our students in the last two years of secondary school. Because of its academic rigor, balanced approach, and whole-person focus, the IBDP is an excellent option for our students who seek an internationally-recognized alternative to the local HKDSE curriculum and a thorough preparation for the demands of university education in Hong Kong and abroad.

As a school that celebrates our students' diverse backgrounds and multicultural identities, Glee Path is especially a committed believer in the IB mission. Our students, hailing mostly from South and Southeast Asia and studying side-by-side with local and overseas Chinese, interact harmoniously with each other in a vibrant, English-speaking learning environment that promotes tolerance, empathy, and understanding.

To put into practice our educational belief in equity and equality, Glee Path makes the IBDP available to our students regardless of their financial circumstances. As such, our school offers the lowest tuition fees of any IB World School in Hong Kong, with full need-based scholarships also available to those who qualify. Even learning resources such as laptops, iPads, and course companions, can be covered by financial aid as do our extracurricular activities and overseas study tours to places like Australia, Canada, Greece, and Nepal. These measures ensure that our students benefit not only from the equitable access to the IBDP but also from being fully included in the learning opportunities enjoyed by the Glee Path community.

As the only IB World School in Hong Kong's Mei Foo neighborhood, our school is easily accessible by public transportation options. So, why not drop by and pay us a visit? We would love to welcome you to Glee Path, where the journey towards excellence begins.

DOVER COURT
INTERNATIONAL SCHOOL
SINGAPORE

A NORD ANGLIA EDUCATION SCHOOL

(Founded 1972)

Head of School
Mr. Christopher Short

DP coordinator
Mr. Dominic O'Shea

Status Private

Boarding/day Day

Gender Coeducational

Language of instruction
English

Authorised IB programmes
DP

Age Range 3 – 18

Number of pupils enrolled
1650

Fees
S$21,810 – S$33,855

Address
301 Dover Road
Singapore
139644 | SINGAPORE

TEL +65 6775 7664
FAX +65 6777 4165

Email
admissions@dovercourt.edu.sg

Website
www.dovercourt.edu.sg

Founded in 1972, Dover Court International School is an established British international school in Singapore. Our school, all on one site, is set on a spacious, green 12 acre campus, situated in the heart of Singapore. We welcome students from 3 to 18 years old, from Nursery to Year 13, with our student body comprising of over 60 nationalities. The students in Years 9 to 11 students work towards their iGCSEs and our Sixth Form students, Years 12 and 13, complete the IB Diploma Programme.

We are passionate about how children learn and are committed to ensuring that the aspirations and potential of every student are fostered and nurtured. DCIS offers a broad, balanced and differentiated programme operating within the framework of the National English Curriculum followed by the IB Diploma Programme. At DCIS, academic success is as important as all-round development. All students respect, support and interact with people from different cultures and become socially and intellectually confident.

Dover Court International School is committed to providing a high quality, challenging, international education at all levels and this shaped our decision to offer the International Baccalaureate Diploma Programme. Having launched the IBDP in August 2017 our first cohort of students graduated in May 2019. The 2019 Graduates achieved an average IBDP score of 32.5 points with our highest point score being 41. Our Graduates are now attending universities in Singapore, UK, New Zealand and Canada.

As part of Nord Anglia Education we benefit from the unparalleled opportunities gained from being part of a larger network and we can draw on the experiences from other NAE schools. With over 60 schools worldwide, with the majority having offered the IBDP for many years, Nord Anglia Education provide us with the support needed.

(Founded 1961)

Principal
Howard Gee

DP coordinator
Declan Sharp

Status Private

Boarding/day Day

Gender Coeducational

Language of instruction
English, German

Authorised IB programmes
DP

Age Range 3 – 18

Number of pupils enrolled
210

Fees
INR30,000 – INR120,000 per month

Address
25 Dadi Seth Road
Babulnath Temple
Mumbai, Maharashtra
400007 | INDIA

TEL +91 (22) 23 673883

Email
admissions@dsbindia.com

Website
www.dsbindia.com

South Mumbai location
DSB International School is a boutique international school located in South Mumbai. We are a modern school with a rich history. Founded in 1961, the first international school in Mumbai, the school was originally established to cater to the German expatriate community. It has since grown to incorporate a diverse range of local and international students representing 40 different countries.

German Heritage
We are proud of our German heritage, which lays the foundation for inter-cultural learning and international mindedness to embrace the true philosophy of an international education. Mumbai is a dynamic, cosmopolitan, multi-cultural metropolis. We are uniquely placed to provide learning experiences that draw upon the local context and the wider global community.

English and German curricula
DSB International School is part of a large network of German Schools Abroad (ZfA), present in 30 countries. We offer duel International and German curricula. Our International Primary and Lower Secondary sections (Kindergarten to grade 8) follow an International Curriculum based on English National Curriculum, whilst the German Section (KGto 8) follows an approved version of the Curriculum of Thüringen. Students in grade 9 and 10 study the International General Certificate of Secondary Education (IGCSE) while our most senior students (grade 11 & 12) study the International Baccalaureate Diploma Programme (IBDP). We will soon be offering the German IB where, as part of the IBDP, students can study a science and/or a humanities subject in German and achieve a bilingual degree.

Best teacher-student ratio
Growing Learning Minds is the school vision and we pride ourselves on providing quality education for all students to achieve academically and develop holistically into informed, principled, global citizens. We aim to equip our students with the necessary skills for success at university and beyond. DSB International School has the best teacher-student ratio in Mumbai with classes ranging from 1:1 to 1:13. This enables us to maximise our support structures for every student to ensure successful, meaningful learning. Our two campus' have state-of-the art facilities including a rooftop football pitch, a Design & Technology studio, modern science labs, a music room, a visual art studio and a 3-D printing studio.

New Euro-campus 2020
The senior school campus will be moving to the brand-new 'Euro-campus' in 2020, which we will share with the French school. This will provide even better facilities, including a swimming pool plus great opportunities for collaboration.

DSB International School is a warm and friendly school community that is unparalleled in Mumbai or India.

DULWICH COLLEGE

| SINGAPORE |

(August 2014)

Headmaster
Mr. Nick Magnus

Head of Senior School
Dr. Jeff Aitken

DP coordinator
Mr. Alan Perkins

Status Private

Boarding/day Day

Gender Coeducational

Language of instruction
English

Authorised IB programmes
DP

Age Range 2 – 18 years

Number of pupils enrolled
2467

Fees
Day: S$30,060 – S$46,840

Address
71 Bukit Batok West Avenue 8
Singapore
658966 | SINGAPORE

TEL +65 6890 1003

Email
admissions@
dulwich-singapore.edu.sg

Website
singapore.dulwich.org

Heritage and Tradition

Dulwich College (Singapore) is an international school with a British independent school ethos and values, which draws upon 400 years of excellence and tradition from Dulwich College in London. Our traditions form part of our culture and are firmly embedded in all that we do. Additionally, our collaborations across the network of schools in Asia and London stimulate innovation and encourage an international outlook, which we believe fully prepares students for their futures. The result is a community where academic ability is nourished, creativity is valued, diversity is celebrated, and inspiration is paramount.

Our students go to some of the best universities and colleges in the world and we are proud of our individualised university counselling service and the network of schools which support this.

What is the Dulwich College (Singapore) IB Diploma Programme Difference?

- Embedded enrichment and leadership for all students
- Passionate, highly experienced IB Diploma Programme teachers who put students first
- Three-year (I)GCSE programme which ensures enriched activities and a focus on skills which enable students to be fully prepared for the IB Diploma Programme
- Part of a network of schools that truly supports students in terms of opportunities and shared knowledge
- Holistic programme where the arts and sport are a valued and integral part of each student's education
- Small cohort and class sizes which focus on student wellbeing
- Academically rigorous but holistic at the centre
- Personalised IB Diploma Programme application process
- Individualised university application process supported by the Dulwich College International network
- An IB Diploma Programme which focuses on feedback and metacognition, so students can independently plan and improve their own learning
- State-of-the-art facilities for IB students to collaborate, study independently and flourish, including a purpose built IB common room and quiet study areas
- A personalised pathway for every single student

ELCHK Lutheran Academy

Principal
Andy FUNG Wa-chau

PYP coordinator
Neil Johnstone

DP coordinator
John Law

Status Private

Boarding/day Day

Gender Coeducational

Language of instruction
English, Cantonese, Mandarin

Authorised IB programmes
PYP, DP

Age Range 6 – 18

Number of pupils enrolled
1108

Fees
IBPYP HK$52,080 – HK$74,060
IBDP HK$90,130

Address
25 Lam Hau Tsuen Road
Yuen Long, New Territories
Hong Kong | **HONG KONG, CHINA**

TEL +852 8208 2092
FAX +852 2443 1400

Email
info@luac.edu.hk

Website
www.luac.edu.hk

ELCHK Lutheran Academy (LA) is a through-train school with its primary and secondary sections at the same location. We gained authorization to offer the Diploma Programme (DP) in September 2014 and the Primary Years Programme (PYP) in 2018, and we are a candidate school for the Middle Years Programme (MYP).

We offer a wide range of subjects for all the programmes. DP subjects comprise the 6 subject groups: Languages (Chinese, English, and French), Sciences (Physics, Chemistry, and Biology), Individuals and Societies (Economics, Business & Management, and History), and The Arts (Visual Arts and Music). MYP subjects encompass the 8 subject groups such as Languages (Chinese, English), Arts (Visual Arts, Drama, Music), and Design and so on.

The PYP, as the foundation of the curriculum, initiates students to develop ideas contributing to international mindedness. Embracing the Unit of Inquiry (UOI), students are encouraged to question and refine their understanding of individual wellbeing, learning communities, and the world from different perspectives.

Away from the hustle and bustle of city life in Hong Kong, we are dedicated to make a difference in students' lives. Creating a warm and friendly campus, students are nurtured to explore their potentials and develop their talents through diverse experiences.

By offering holistic and balanced Christian education, the professional teaching team with teachers from different cultural backgrounds is committed in nurturing students to strive for excellence and to become global leaders of tomorrow. To maximize the learning opportunities and provide adequate care to individual needs, LA adopts small-class teaching that our overall teacher-student ratio is around 1:8.

We encourage students to explore concepts in manifolds of forms to ensure their whole-person development. Students are exposed to learning from varieties of activities, including field trips, Co-curricular and Extra-Curricular activities. During the EOTC (Education Outside the Classroom) week, students visit places of diversified cultures around the world to experience the learning outside the classroom and broaden their horizons. After the tour, they showcase to share what they have acquired to their classmates, parents and teachers.

To support programme implementation, Information and Communication Technology (ICT) has been well integrated into education to equip students with ICT skills. With the "Apple One-to-One Program", each secondary student is equipped with a laptop for daily learning. Together with the whole school Wi-Fi coverage, the ICT-infused inquiry-based learning has been effectively and efficiently facilitated.

With the enthusiastic support from the LA community, the school is growing from strength to strength to provide high quality education for the future rising generation.

(Founded 2002)

Principal
Ms Frances Hurley

PYP coordinator
Ms Frances Hurley

Status ESF Educational Services Limited Kindergarten / Non-Profit

Boarding/day Day

Gender Coeducational

Language of instruction
English, Mandarin

Authorised IB programmes
PYP

Age Range 3 – 5

Number of pupils enrolled
190

Fees for 2018/19
English Stream HK$80,000
Bilingual Stream HK$93,000

Address
Mang Kung Uk Village
Clearwater Bay Road
Hong Kong SAR | **HONG KONG, CHINA**

TEL +852 27195712
FAX +852 27196690

Email
kinder@abacus.edu.hk

Website
www.abacus.edu.hk

ESF Abacus International Kindergarten's programme is for children aged 2 years 9 months to 5 years of age. Children attend for three hours per day, five days per week. The average class size is 22 children and classes are structured into K1 & K2 groups.

Abacus is authorised to deliver the IBO Primary Years Programme, providing an inquiry-based and highly interactive programme. Children learn through play experiences and are encouraged to discover, experiment and reflect on their learning. Our aim at Abacus is to encourage children to become confident and independent learners. We teach children to respect themselves, others and the world around them and to work hard to reach their full academic potential.

Abacus offers two streams in both K1 and K2: English and Bilingual.

English
The programme is conducted in English with Chinese as a specialist language, taught by a Chinese teacher who undertakes specialist sessions, introducing Chinese vocabulary and Chinese customs and festivals and reinforces the classroom teacher's planning and activities in Chinese.

Bilingual
The bilingual programme is jointly planned and delivered by two teachers, one English and the other Chinese. Children receive instruction in both languages and all areas of the curriculum are delivered in both languages with the exception of English and Chinese Languages. There are differentiated sessions for all children in English Language and Chinese Language, meeting the language needs of each child.

(Founded 1967)

Principal
Ms Brenda Cook

PYP coordinator
Mr Andy Thompson

Status English Schools Foundation School/Non-Profit

Boarding/day Day

Gender Coeducational

Language of instruction
English

Authorised IB programmes
PYP

Age Range 5 – 11

Number of pupils enrolled
540

Fees for 2019/20
Years 1 to 4 HK$115,800
Years 5 to 6 HK$98,500
Non-refundable capital levy: HK$38,000 for each new Year 1 student

Address
23 Ede Road
Kowloon Tong
Hong Kong SAR | HONG KONG, CHINA

TEL +852 2336 5221
FAX +852 2338 7895

Email
bhs@bhs.edu.hk

Website
www.beaconhill.edu.hk

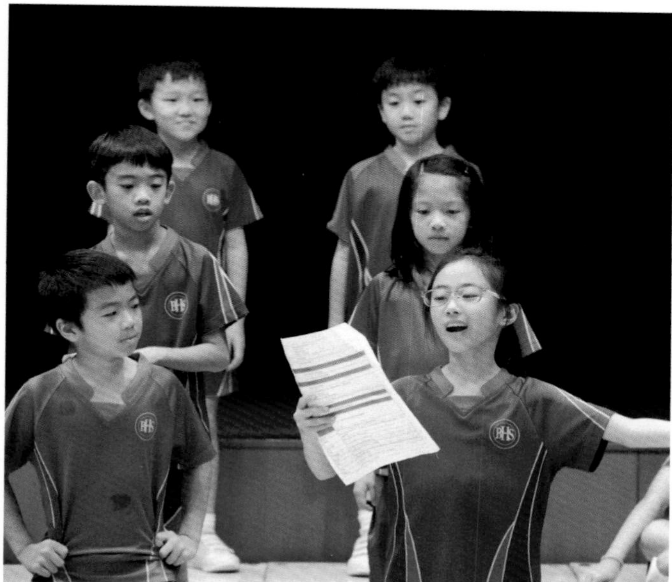

Our Vision
To be a happy, diverse and inclusive community where everybody has confidence to aspire to be the best they can be, now and in the future.

Our Mission

- We create a safe, caring and supportive environment enabling purposeful challenge through a dynamic and rigorous curriculum
- We inspire and develop creativity and academic potential
- We encourage global and social responsibility
- We foster independence in thought and action

Beacon Hill School is part of the English Schools Foundation (ESF), the largest provider of English-medium international education in Hong Kong.

Beacon Hill School was founded in 1967 and moved to its present location in 1968. It occupies a well-equipped seven storey building and has classroom space to accommodate a three form entry. There are a number of special purpose rooms that are state of the art; these include a fully equipped drama studio, music rooms, learning technologies room, art room and library.

Beacon Hill School staff is made up of dedicated professionals providing an all-round education of the very highest quality academically, creatively and socially ensuring that each child has the opportunity to reach their potential.

The students come to us from many countries and this international mix adds a great deal to the atmosphere and the richness of the school experience. An active Parent Teacher Association and School Council support our school ensuring the school achieves its aims.

Beacon Hill School is an International Baccalaureate (IB) World School authorised to implement the Primary Years Programme (PYP). We have single-subject teachers for learning technology, PE, music and Mandarin. We encourage the development of creativity amongst our students and place a strong emphasis on the arts. Our students also experience cutting-edge technology learning, such as virtual reality art creation, 3D printing or coding. We are well-resourced with 1:1 Chrome books for students in Years 3 to 6. We have a strong focus on language, both in the Mandarin and English literacy provision. We are an inclusive school with 21 students with more moderate special educational needs. These students are catered for within the mainstream classes with additional learning support teachers and educational assistants. We offer a range of programmes to depending on the needs of the students, such as a Perceptual Motor Programme, Social Thinking, Friends for Life, B2 – Social/Emotional tracking system, Fine Motor and individualised sensory programmes. Our SEN provision is world leading.

(Founded 1980)

Principal
Ms Sandra Webster

PYP coordinator
Ms Amanda Bremner

Status English Schools Foundation School/Non-Profit

Boarding/day Day

Gender Coeducational

Language of instruction
English

Authorised IB programmes
PYP

Age Range 5 – 11

Number of pupils enrolled
720

Fees for 2019/20
Years 1 to 4 HK$115,800
Years 5 to 6 HK$98,500
Non-refundable capital levy: HK$38,000 for each new Year 1 student

Address
43C Stubbs Road
Hong Kong SAR | **HONG KONG, CHINA**

TEL +852 2574 8249
FAX +852 2834 7880

Email
enquiries@bradbury.edu.hk

Website
www.bradbury.edu.hk

Bradbury School offers a caring environment, providing children with an all round education of the very highest quality. The calibre of all of our staff and the positive, encouraging approach in our classrooms produce outstanding results. We encourage our children to become independent thinkers who care about the world around them, through an active sustainability approach; and who develop the skills to become learners and leaders. We place a high importance on partnership with parents and see this as a cornerstone to how we operate on a daily basis. Our Parent Teacher Association is active and hardworking, contributing much to the life of our school. We are governed by a knowledgeable School Council.

Bradbury School is an IB World School, and is a member of The Association of China and Mongolia International Schools Association (ACAMIS). We use the Primary Years Programme (PYP) as the basis of our instruction and to underpin our beliefs as expressed in our school mission statement – to inspire learners, inquire together and to enhance our world. At the same time, we place a high value on our students becoming numerate and literate in a 21st century learning environment, embracing an extended concept of these areas that new technologies offer us. Chinese is taught to all students, with levels of instruction adjusted according to ability.

Our school has excellent resources, offering a number of specialist subjects in dedicated spaces. We have a state of the art library, which is seen as the hub of inquiry throughout the school. In addition, we have a full gymnasium, school hall, music room, including soundproof studios, netball courts, a variety of large adventure playgrounds installed across various levels, undercover play areas, a large free form sandpit and art studio. Bradbury has an extensive sports programme and offers amongst others, rugby, netball, cricket, soccer, swimming, basketball and running, as well as other activities such as judo and kick boxing. The school makes provision for 21 children with moderate learning difficulties through a Learning Support Programme and we believe in a full inclusion approach for all of our students.

(Founded 1992)

Principal
Mr Chris Hamilton

PYP coordinator
Ms Wendy Egan

Status English Schools Foundation School/Non-Profit

Boarding/day Day

Gender Coeducational

Language of instruction
English

Authorised IB programmes
PYP

Age Range 5 – 11

Number of pupils enrolled
720

Fees for 2019/20
Years 1 to 4 HK$115,800
Years 5 to 6 HK$98,500
Non-refundable capital levy: HK$38,000 for each new Year 1 student

Address
DD229, Lot 235, Clearwater Bay Road
New Territories
Hong Kong SAR | **HONG KONG, CHINA**

TEL +852 2358 3221
FAX +852 2358 3246

Email
info@cwbs.edu.hk

Website
www.cwbs.edu.hk

Clearwater Bay School is an IB World School serving the Sai Kung, Clearwater Bay and Tseung Kwan O communities in the Eastern New Territories of Hong Kong. We are accredited by both the Council of International Schools and the International Baccalaureate Organization and offer a world class international primary education to students in years 1-6. There is strong demand for admissions and the school is currently at capacity with 720 students enrolled.

Our school values create a safe, welcoming learning environment that fosters care, respect and intercultural understanding. We value and celebrate the rich cultural diversity of students and families who come from more than 35 different nationalities and cultural backgrounds. Through the IB Primary Years Programme, we offer an engaging, challenging inquiry programme that develops students' creativity, confidence and willingness to achieve their personal best. High standards of academic achievement combined with a strong emphasis on the arts, physical education and sport provides students with a comprehensive, well rounded curriculum. Specialist Chinese, physical education, music and library programs are also taught. An extensive co-curricular programme provides opportunities for students to participate in a range of arts, sport and special interest activities.

We cater to the individual learning needs of students through a developmentally appropriate curriculum that is differentiated to extend students needing further challenge and to support students who experience difficulties. Specialist learning support, English as an additional language and counseling services are available.

We have skilled and passionate staff and an active parent community who work collaboratively to create a learning community that strives to provide every student with the best possible education.

(Founded 2007)

Principal
Mr James Smith

PYP coordinator
Ms Kate Agars

MYP coordinator
Ms Annette Garnett

DP coordinator
Mr Brian McCann

CP coordinator
Ms Emma Neuprez

Status A Private Independent School Of The English Schools Foundation

Boarding/day Day

Gender Coeducational

Language of instruction
English

Authorised IB programmes
PYP, MYP, DP, CP

Age Range 5 – 18

Number of pupils enrolled
1400

Fees for 2019/20
Years 1 to 6 HK$129,700
Years 7 to 11 HK$173,500
Years 12 to 13 HK$175,400
Non-refundable Building Levy: HK$7,530 per student per year

Address
38 Siena Avenue
Discovery Bay, Lantau Island
Hong Kong SAR | **HONG KONG, CHINA**

TEL +852 3969 1000
FAX +852 2987 8115

Email office@dc.edu.hk

Website www.discovery.edu.hk

Grow. Discover. Dream. This vision statement, created by the College community when the school was founded in 2007, recognizes Discovery College's belief that students are to be independent, critical and creative thinkers, equipped with the skills, attitudes and values to contribute positively in this complex world in which we live. At Discovery College we believe that powerful learning and teaching occurs under a shared spirit of respect, which dignifies and prizes our diversity of experiences and perspectives, reaches into our traditions as well as into the future, excites a passion for ongoing inquiry and strives to help all learners reach for enduring excellence.

Discovery College was established by the English Schools Foundation to serve the needs of the local and expatriate communities in Hong Kong. It is a full Years 1 to 13 school offering the PYP, MYP, Diploma and Career-related programmes. Partial and full scholarships are available for exceptional secondary students.

The College strongly supports all subject areas with a robust academic curriculum, including the performing and creative arts, design and ICT. Technology is embedded across the curriculum, supported by a number of digital literacy staff and a 1:1 laptop programme from Year 6 onwards. Apple Asia provides a dedicated Mac Service Centre and technician on site.

The teaching staff represent more than 20 nationalities and are chosen from amongst the world's best. The student population comprises more than 45 nationalities and almost as many mother tongues.

The College uses English as the medium for teaching and learning. There is also a strong emphasis on the acquisition of Chinese (Putonghua) as a second language. The College focuses on international-mindedness throughout the community.

The College's facilities are second to none, with an award-winning design that incorporates an exceptional performing arts centre, gymnasium spaces, 25m rooftop heated swimming pool, library, science labs and design technology rooms.

(Founded 1959)

Principal
Mr Chris Briggs

PYP coordinator
Mr David Buckley

Status English Schools Foundation School/Non-Profit

Boarding/day Day

Gender Coeducational

Language of instruction
English

Authorised IB programmes
PYP

Age Range 5 – 11

Number of pupils enrolled
360

Fees for 2019/20
Years 1 to 4 HK$115,800
Years 5 to 6 HK$98,500
Non-refundable capital levy: HK$38,000 for each new Year 1 student

Address
7 Hornsey Road
Mid Levels
Hong Kong SAR | **HONG KONG, CHINA**

TEL +852 2522 1919
FAX +852 2521 7838

Email
enquiry@glenealy.edu.hk

Website
www.glenealy.edu.hk

Glenealy is a community-based school. We are proud of the positive relationships that we build with students, their families and the wider community. Being a 2-form entry ESF primary school of 360 students, we are able to offer a personalised, inclusive and flexible approach to meeting the needs of our learners.

At Glenealy, highly skilled teachers ensure an education that is transformational. We develop caring and curious global citizens who make a positive difference. We provide meaningful and relevant experiences where learners develop skills, knowledge, understanding and attitudes for success in life. Our safe, nurturing environment values learners' voice and choice, fostering positive relationships in which learners flourish.

At Glenealy our mission statement is to empower learners to flourish and make a positive difference. Our vision for every student is to be the best that they can be. At Glenealy we support and challenge students to ensure continual academic progress, personal growth and high standards.

As an International Baccalaureate (IB) World School we offer a significant, engaging and high quality international education for our students. Using the IB Primary Years Programme (PYP) as a framework, students learn through an inquiry approach where they are encouraged to explore concepts and ideas that are meaningful and relevant to their lives, now and in the future. Our modern, flexible learning spaces are integral to the learning process.

We help our students become confident, caring, curious, independent and resilient learners who are empowered to achieve their best in all aspects of life. The multitude of experiences offered through the arts, sport, the outdoors, learning Chinese language and culture, partaking in environmental action groups and opportunities for students to take on leadership roles within the school, offers the students many opportunities to find and follow their passions and interests.

When you join Glenealy, you don't just join a school, you join a community of likeminded people who work in collaboration with the school so that every child can be the best that they can be.

(Founded 1999)

Acting Head of School
Ms Audrey Tang

PYP coordinator
Ms Brenda Yuen

Status ESF Educational Services Limited Kindergarten/ Non-Profit

Boarding/day Day

Gender Coeducational

Language of instruction
English

Authorised IB programmes
PYP

Age Range 3 – 5

Number of pupils enrolled
354

Fees for 2019/20
HK$77,000

Address
43B Stubbs Road
Hong Kong SAR | **HONG KONG, CHINA**

TEL +852 2540 0066
FAX +852 2517 0923

Email
kinder@hillside.edu.hk

Website
www.hillside.edu.hk

ESF Hillside International Kindergarten has eight classes, four in K1 and four in K2. Children start K1 in the year in which they are three years old. Children attend the kindergarten on a part time basis, five morning or five afternoon sessions per week, with sessions being three hours long. The school community is diverse with children and staff coming from a variety of ethnic groups, and we are able to draw on this culture richness to enhance teaching and learning.

In January 2014 we were authorised as an IB World School, delivering the Primary Years Programme. Through their inquiry into four of the six PYP transdisciplinary themes each year, the children in both K1 and K2 develop knowledge and understanding, as well as skills and attitudes that they can use in Kindergarten and take with them into their future learning.

At ESF Hillside International Kindergarten, play is the primary mode of learning and the learning environment is set up to promote inquiry through a broad range of play opportunities that promote creativity, critical thinking, and communication. At Hillside the students develop their sense of self, and further develop the skills necessary to nurture positive friendships with other children. They become more aware of their place in the wider-world. Staff work with children on adult-initiated inquiries and to support those that are child-initiated.

The attributes of the learner profile have a significant place within our school and are acknowledged in the actions and achievements of both our children and staff.

(Founded 1967)

Principal
Mr Stephen Loggie

DP coordinator
Mr Matt Rappel

CP coordinator
Mr Roger Wilkinson

Status English Schools Foundation School/Non-Profit

Boarding/day Day

Gender Coeducational

Language of instruction
English

Authorised IB programmes
DP, CP

Age Range 11 – 18

Number of pupils enrolled
1200

Fees for 2019/20
Years 7 to 11 HK$133,800
Years 12 to 13 HK$140,700
A one-off non-refundable capital levy of HK$26,000 is required for each new Year 7 student – and will be reduced on a sliding scale for students who join in later years.

Address
20 Borrett Road
Hong Kong SAR | **HONG KONG, CHINA**

TEL +852 2524 7135
FAX +852 2840 1673

Email
school@online.island.edu.hk

Website
www.island.edu.hk

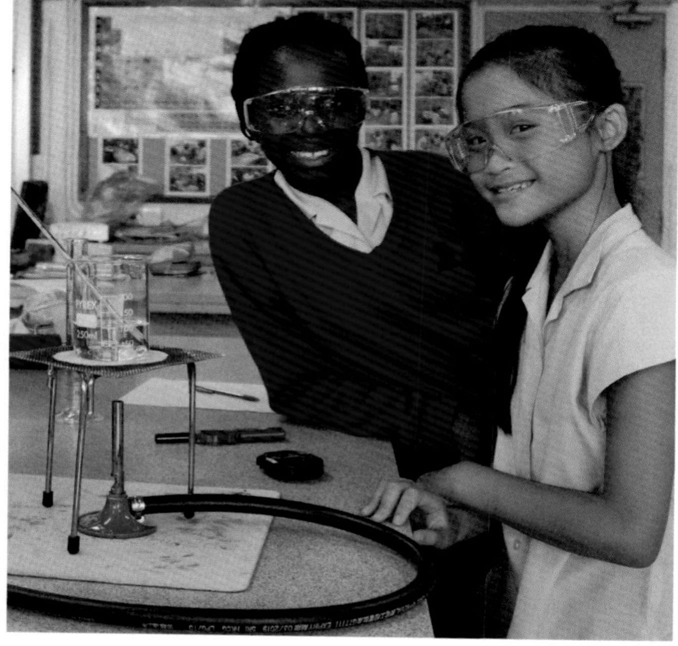

At Island School we do something different. Our focus is on igniting a passion for learning in every student. Teaching students facts and figures is no longer enough for them to succeed once they enter higher education and the workforce. We encourage students to problem solve, question and think creatively with new concepts and ideas. Students are encouraged to become resourceful, adaptable and confident learners.

Island School students come from all over the world and central to our international heritage is the celebration and understanding of each other's' cultures.

Students learn to care for each other, for the environment and for other people through our rich co-curricular programme and the family atmosphere of the House system.

Our academic record is excellent with students going on to the foremost universities and colleges in the world. You will find details of the curriculum and qualifications on offer on our website. In the senior years students can choose to study IB Diploma, IB Careers and BTEC courses. Island School prepares students for these qualifications with a broad based middle school curriculum including IGCSEs and a wide range of exciting options in our unique Futures curriculum. Our aim is to help students develop a passion for learning in a range of areas, whether it be Law or Robotics and Coding or Music producing.

Currently Island School is going through a period of redevelopment. The building at Borrett Road which was Island School's home for 50 years is now being redeveloped, during this time the Island School community is using two temporary campuses in Sha Tin.

Temporary campuses in 2019/20:
Island School Sha Tin Wai (Years 7, 8, 12, 13):
Pok Hong Estate, Area 5A, Sha Tin, New Territories, Hong Kong
Island School Tai Wai (Years 9, 10, 11):
Sun Chui Estate, Sha Tin, New Territories, Hong Kong

(Founded 1961)

Principal
Mr John Brewster

PYP coordinator
Ms Yoon-Ah Lee

Status English Schools Foundation School/Non-Profit

Boarding/day Day

Gender Coeducational

Language of instruction
English

Authorised IB programmes
PYP

Age Range 5 – 11

Number of pupils enrolled
900

Fees for 2019/20
Years 1 to 4 HK$115,800
Years 5 to 6 HK$98,500
Non-refundable capital levy: HK$38,000 for each new Year 1 student

Address
19 Sha Wan Drive
Pokfulam
Hong Kong SAR | HONG KONG, CHINA

TEL +852 2855 0711
FAX +852 2817 7471

Email
admissions@kennedy.edu.hk

Website
www.kennedy.edu.hk

Kennedy School was established in 1961. The school occupies a pleasant location on the west of Hong Kong Island, and benefits from the use of the swimming and sporting facilities of The University of Hong Kong's Stanley Ho Centre, which is adjacent to the school. Music, performing arts and physical education are strengths of the school. A strong interest in environmental and ecological issues is also a feature of the school.

We offer a high-quality, modern, liberal education based on the IBO PYP with links to the English National Curriculum and adapted to meet the needs of children living in Asia.

The school boasts a rich mix of nationalities and cultures among its 900 students, and had received Council of International Schools (CIS) Accreditation status in May 2010 and had a five-year review in November 2015 by CIS. It received IB authorisation in December 2011 and was recently evaluated in November 2015.

Occupying a pleasant location overlooking the South China Sea, the school has regular use of the adjacent Stanley Ho Sports Centre. All children receive regular swimming lessons in terms one and three. The school provides daily Mandarin lessons for all students and also offers a very rich and varied extra-curricular programme.

(Founded 1902)

Principal
Mr Mark Blackshaw

MYP coordinator
Mr Duncan Shiel

DP coordinator
Mr Chris Wightman

Status English Schools Foundation School/Non-Profit

Boarding/day Day

Gender Coeducational

Language of instruction
English

Authorised IB programmes
MYP, DP

Age Range 11 – 18

Number of pupils enrolled
1800

Fees for 2019/20
Years 7 to 11 HK$133,800
Years 12 to 13 HK$140,700
A one-off non-refundable capital levy of HK$26,000 is required for each new Year 7 student – and will be reduced on a sliding scale for students who join in later years.

Address
2 Tin Kwong Road
Homantin, Kowloon
Hong Kong SAR | HONG KONG, CHINA

TEL +852 2711 3029
FAX +852 2760 7116

Email office@kgv.edu.hk

Website www.kgv.edu.hk

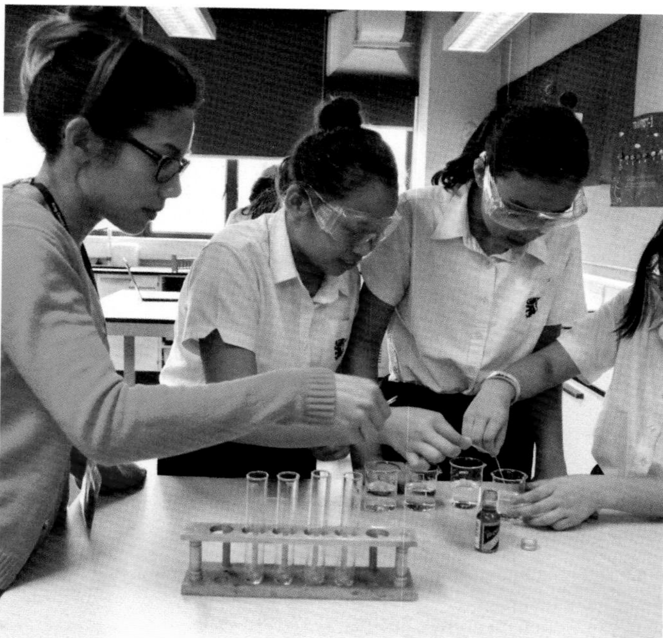

At King George V School, our purpose is based on our belief that every student can 'be their own remarkable…' as they achieve, improve and learn. Our vision is to create a 'school for one'. A place where each and every person engages in remarkable learning to achieve at high levels and be the best they can be.

Our school is also about continual improvement. As an agile school, we collaborate and innovate to make a difference in the communities we serve and lead. KGV School is part of the English Schools Foundation (ESF), the largest provider of English-medium international education in Hong Kong.

KGV School reflects the goals of ESF where the comprehensive programme of extra-curricular activities brings out the best in every student through a personalised approach to learning and by inspiring curious minds. Our strategic intent is to be the key driver of best practice in teaching and learning. Our model of education is on the cutting-edge of global innovation producing excellent outcomes for our students.

King George V School originated as the Kowloon British School in 1902, moving to its present site in 1936. The present name dates from 1948. Today it serves students from Kowloon and the New Territories. It occupies a large site of over ten acres and has its own AstroTurf sports field and outdoor swimming pool. There are two new buildings completed in 2013 (Performing Arts and a Science Block) on the school site and an extensive Learning Resource Centre (LRC).

The school is well known for its commitment to developing all aspects of student life and it has a fine tradition in sport, music, drama, dance, community service, charity work and environmental sustainability. Our school has a very strong House system, which is run and inspired by our students and provides a wide range of learning opportunities and activities.

Our school is implementing the IB Middle Years Programme (MYP) in Years 7 to 9, after which the school delivers the IGCSE in Years 10 and 11. Students then progress to study either the IB Diploma Programme or the more vocationally oriented BTEC applied learning programme.

The school motto is Honestas Ante Honores: Honesty before Glory. Our alumni are passionate and connected to our school. We have a proud history and even more excited about our future as we strive to provide opportunities for each and every student to 'be their own remarkable…'

(Founded 1902)

Principal
Mr Neill O'Reilly

PYP coordinator
Ms Dawn Doucette

Status English Schools Foundation School/Non-Profit

Boarding/day Day

Gender Coeducational

Language of instruction
English

Authorised IB programmes
PYP

Age Range 5 – 11

Number of pupils enrolled
900

Fees for 2019/20
Years 1 to 4 HK$115,800
Years 5 to 6 HK$98,500
Non-refundable capital levy: HK$38,000 for each new Year 1 student

Address
20 Perth Street
Homantin, Kowloon
Hong Kong SAR | **HONG KONG, CHINA**

TEL +852 3765 8700
FAX +852 3765 8701

Email
office@kjs.edu.hk

Website
www.kjs.edu.hk

KJS is a five-form entry school with 900 students. Our learning environments are designed to support our learners and help ignite their passions. Within our year group areas and dedicated Chinese area, the shared spaces ensure opportunities for true collaboration between students and teachers. Learning is further supported by access to a very spacious, light and airy library which houses a wide variety of books and resources. The dance studio, music suite, specialist creative arts area and multi-media room support students to express themselves in a wide variety of ways. Our gymnasium and diverse outdoor spaces, including an outdoor classroom designed by students, are used for a wide variety of sports and recreation. The sustainable action by students of designing learning spaces at KJS includes further development of outdoor garden spaces ("Secret Gardens") to enhance student wellbeing. Our large hall and stage with professional light and sound, ensures our whole school community can enjoy a wide range of celebratory events.

The school's Vision of 'Success for Every Child' permeates all levels of the school. Success at KJS is defined as **A**chieving, having **A**gency (the capacity to act intentionally, having voice, choice and ownership of learning), showing **R**espect (for self, others and the environment), taking advantage of **O**pportunities and having positive **W**ellbeing, we call these the **AAROW**s of Success at KJS!

Teachers and support staff take time to know their students, personalising learning goals to stretch learners and ensuring students are active participants in their learning process. Our Learning Enhancement Team provides excellent support for students with additional needs.

KJS works within the PYP framework which allows the school to incorporate the best educational practice from around the world and places a great deal of emphasis on developing international mindedness; positive learner attitudes; inquiry learning; creative, critical and collaborative thinking and learning through meaningful experiences. Our students enjoy stimulating learning within their homerooms together with opportunity to learn with specialist teachers in music, dance, the arts, physical education and Chinese. Students have an immense opportunity to pursue their passions through in class inquiries, specialist classes and the extensive co-curricular activities offered during the day, after school and in the weekends. Our students benefit from the ongoing working relationships that we have with King George V High School, our main feeder school, and Jockey Club Sarah Roe School. The close proximity of these schools ensures students have opportunities for support or extension whilst ensuring a smooth transition to the next phase of their education.

We warmly welcome visitors who would like to get a first hand experience of our school, KJS.

PEAK SCHOOL

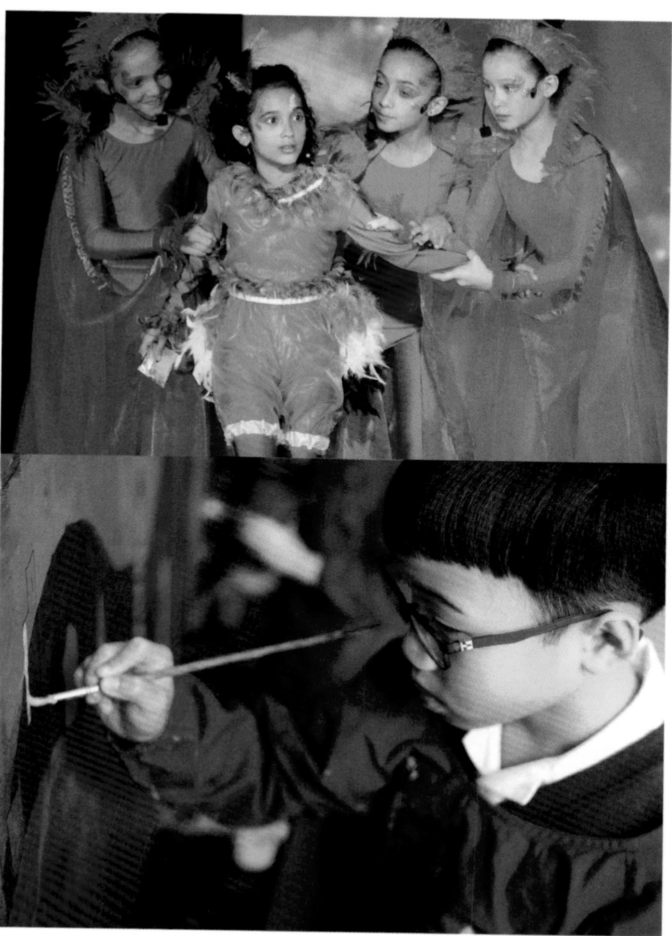

(Founded 1911)

Principal
Mr Bill Garnett

PYP coordinator
Ms Chrissy Etchells-Bailey

Status English Schools Foundation School/Non-Profit

Boarding/day Day

Gender Coeducational

Language of instruction
English

Authorised IB programmes
PYP

Age Range 4 – 11

Number of pupils enrolled
360

Fees for 2019/20
Years 1 to 4 HK$115,800
Years 5 to 6 HK$98,500
Non-refundable capital levy: HK$38,000 for each new Year 1 student

Address
20 Plunkett's Road
The Peak
Hong Kong SAR | HONG KONG, CHINA

TEL +852 2849 7211
FAX +852 2849 7151

Email
office@ps.edu.hk

Website
www.ps.edu.hk

Peak School opened in 1911 and grew rapidly to serve the needs of the community in the area. It moved into its current buildings in 1954. The school has 360 places mainly serving the Peak area of Hong Kong. The school prides itself on being a community school that respects and appreciates the contributions of everyone involved.

Peak School offers the PYP which is based on an inquiry approach to learning. We live by and up to all the attributes and attitudes of the Learner Profile to develop students who are open minded, knowledgeable, confident, caring and internationally minded.

Peak School is an extremely well resourced school and has a team of highly committed and skillful staff. The school makes provision for children with moderate learning difficulties with support from our Learner Enhancement Team. Boasting a large playing field, the envy of schools across Hong Kong, the school is fortunate to be able to have all children playing together at both snack and lunch breaks. This helps enhance the 'family atmosphere' which we proudly foster.

(Founded 1926)

Principal
Ms Mina Dunstan

PYP coordinator
Miss Ceri Hill

Status English Schools Foundation School/Non-Profit

Boarding/day Day

Gender Coeducational

Language of instruction
English

Authorised IB programmes
PYP

Age Range 5 – 11

Number of pupils enrolled
720

Fees for 2019/20
Years 1 to 4 HK$115,800
Years 5 to 6 HK$98,500
Non-refundable capital levy: HK$38,000 for each new Year 1 student

Address
6 Hau Yuen Path, Braemar Hill
North Point
Hong Kong SAR | **HONG KONG, CHINA**

TEL +852 2566 4242
FAX +852 2887 9849

Email
office@qbs.edu.hk

Website
www.qbs.edu.hk

Quarry Bay School opened over 80 years ago and was relocated to new, purpose-built premises at Braemar Hill, on the north eastern side of Hong Kong Island in 1985. In recent years, our school premises have benefitted from being refurbished and redesigned. This has resulted in the creation of an outstanding environment for teaching and learning. The school aims to encourage a love of learning by providing learning experiences both inside and outside the classroom that help to develop confident, enthusiastic and successful learners who are able to inquire about the world. We have 40 different nationalities represented in our school contributing to a rich and diverse learning environment. Quarry Bay School is an inclusive school where all students are included as part of the school community. We feel that all children have talents which can be developed and that all children can succeed. Our school provides equality of opportunity irrespective of race, gender, religion or disability for all children. We encourage our students be active learners who work collaboratively and support one another.

Quarry Bay School prides itself on its high quality relationships; students and adults work collaboratively and support each other enabling all to reach their full potential. Children with a range of learning needs are effectively supported by the school's Individual Needs team. The school makes provision for children with moderate learning difficulties through the support of a specialist Learning Support teacher.

Quarry Bay School uses the International Baccalaureate's Primary Years Programme (PYP) as its curriculum framework. This transdisciplinary, concept-driven approach allows us to meet the challenges of educating in the 21st century by constructing a personalised programme that is engaging, relevant, challenging and significant for our diverse school population. Making use of collaborative planning in the development of teaching and learning engagements, teachers model lifelong learning and the attributes of the IB Learner Profile to the school community. Quarry Bay School completed a successful PYP Evaluation in October 2013 and in 2019 will undertake their five year review.

(Founded 2006)

Principal
Dr Harry Brown

PYP coordinator
Mr Jason Doucette

MYP coordinator
Ms Brandy Stern

DP coordinator
Ms Jess Davey-Peel

CP coordinator
Ms Wilma Shen

Status A Private Independent School Of The English Schools Foundation

Boarding/day Day

Gender Coeducational

Language of instruction
English

Authorised IB programmes
PYP, MYP, DP, CP

Age Range 5 – 18

Number of pupils enrolled
2100

Fees for 2019/20
Years 1 to 6 HK$124,000
Years 7 to 11 HK$166,000
Years 12 to 13 HK$167,900
Building Levy: HK$50,000 for each new Year 1 student

Address
5 Hang Ming Street
Ma On Shan, New Territories
Hong Kong SAR | **HONG KONG, CHINA**

TEL +852 3556 3556
FAX +852 3556 3446

Email info@rchk.edu.hk

Website www.rchk.edu.hk

Renaissance College Hong Kong (RCHK) is a world-class coeducational independent school and an IB World School. It was the first school in Asia to offer all four of the IB programmes: PYP, MYP, DP and CP. Located in the heart of Hong Kong's New Territories, the college was established in 2006 by the English School Foundation (ESF) to serve the needs of the local and expatriate communities in Hong Kong.

Students are educated from Year 1 to Year 13 on one site, guided and encouraged by a team of experienced international educators. Our student body comprises 40 nationalities, with 20 languages represented. English is the medium of instruction, with Mandarin taught at every level.

The Renaissance College Scholarship Programme provides pathways for motivated and talented secondary students, who strive for academic excellence and are empowered to take progressive action in their lives.

Apple Asia described Renaissance College as a leading school in the region. Technology is integrated college-wide throughout the curriculum.

Creativity, activity, service (CAS) is integral to college life. Students participate in a myriad of artistic, musical, sporting and service activities conducted on-site and off-campus.

Renaissance College encourages young people to be curious and caring global citizens. Our aim is to prepare well-educated young people to lead future generations, to seek and create an environment of intercultural understanding and respect for others.

The purpose-built campus provides the context for students to excel. State-of-the-art facilities include the Performing Arts Centre, ICT Centre, Black Box theatre, 25-metre indoor swimming pool, music rooms, library, science laboratories, gymnasiums, climbing wall, outdoor basketball courts, an outdoor sports field and cafeterias.

(Founded 1982)

Principal
Ms Carol Larkin

DP coordinator
Ms Kellie Fagan

CP coordinator
Mr Luke Smetherham

Status English Schools Foundation School/Non-Profit

Boarding/day Day

Gender Coeducational

Language of instruction
English

Authorised IB programmes
DP, CP

Age Range 11 – 18

Number of pupils enrolled
1200

Fees for 2019/20
Years 7 to 11 HK$133,800
Years 12 to 13 HK$140,700
A one-off non-refundable capital levy of HK$26,000 is required for each new Year 7 student – and will be reduced on a sliding scale for students who join in later years.

Address
3 Lai Wo Lane
Fo Tan, Sha Tin, New Territories
Hong Kong SAR | **HONG KONG, CHINA**

TEL +852 2699 1811
FAX +852 2695 0592

Email
info@shatincollege.edu.hk

Website
www.shatincollege.edu.hk

Sha Tin College opened in September 1982 to meet the increasing demand for places from families in northern Kowloon and the New Territories. The school provides 1,200 places and has over 30 nationalities represented within the student body. Sha Tin College is committed to providing the best possible teaching and learning experiences for every individual through the medium of English. The education provided leads to a variety of internationally recognised examinations, granting students access to higher education and career opportunities worldwide.

Unique to Sha Tin College is a culture where we take responsibility for fulfilling our own potential and that of others for the good of humanity at all levels. Ample opportunities exist to challenge students to become mature, open-minded, caring, responsible and committed individuals with a passion for learning, creativity, sports and a sense of compassion.

With commanding views over the Sha Tin countryside, the College boasts a swimming pool and multipurpose sports hall, music rooms, drama studios, design and technology workshops, science labs and a food technology centre, Senior School Centre, climbing walls, and a Counselling and Well-being Centre.

As part of quality assurance, Sha Tin College embraces review and accreditation processes with the IB five-year review; ESF internal review and ESF stakeholder surveys. These processes assist the school in its strategic developmental planning.

(Founded 1988)

Principal
Ms Rehana Shanks

PYP coordinator
Ms Trudy Mcmillin

Status English Schools Foundation School/Non-Profit

Boarding/day Day

Gender Coeducational

Language of instruction
English

Authorised IB programmes
PYP

Age Range 5 – 11

Number of pupils enrolled
900

Fees for 2019/20
Years 1 to 4 HK115,800
Years 5 to 6 HK98,500
Non-refundable capital levy: HK$38,000 for each new Year 1 student

Address
3A Lai Wo Lane
Fo Tan, Sha Tin, New Territories
Hong Kong SAR | **HONG KONG, CHINA**

TEL +852 2692 2721
FAX +852 2602 5572

Email
info@sjs.esf.edu.hk

Website
www.sjs.edu.hk

Sha Tin Junior School is part of the English Schools Foundation (ESF). ESF is the largest provider of English medium international education in Hong Kong. Our vision is for every student to be the best that they can be. Our mission is to inspire creativity and nurture global citizens and leaders of the future. We do this by creating joyful learning environments, led by a community of exceptional teachers who bring out the best in every child through a personalised approach to learning and by inspiring curious minds.

The school opened in 1988 and provides an English-medium education for the children of families who reside in the New Territories of Hong Kong. We share a safe, secure and well-resourced site with our partner secondary school, Sha Tin College.

A recent school refurbishment programme has ensured the provision of new facilities and the upgrade of existing learning spaces for our 900 students. Facilities include well-resourced Learning and Access Centres, a gymnasium, a performing arts studio, a Learning Technologies Suite and a DARC (Design, Arts, Recording and Cooking) Room. Shared facilities (with Sha Tin College) include an indoor swimming pool and a sports hall.

Our School Vision – 'Learning for Life' – is underpinned by four core values. In order to aspire towards a life of learning, we encourage our students to focus on:

- Wellbeing
- Inclusivity
- Flexible minds and
- Making a difference.

We offer a balanced programme ensuring learners have the opportunity to develop academically, mentally, socially and physically. Our programme is guided by the philosophy of Positive Education and is inquiry based in outlook. Individual needs are catered for through an inclusive approach, implementing a range of teaching and learning approaches.

All stakeholders are encouraged to develop resilience, use a growth mindset and a 'can do' attitude. We empower learners to take meaningful action and realise the impact each and every one of us can have in reaching the 2030 Global Goals.

Sha Tin Junior School is fully authorised to offer PYP. Re-evaluation took place in 2018.

(Founded 1977)

Principal
Mr Tom Vignoles

MYP coordinator
Mr Shaine Bushell

DP coordinator
Ms Kelly Diaz

CP coordinator
Mr Gwillym Cornes

Status English Schools Foundation School/Non-Profit

Boarding/day Day

Gender Coeducational

Language of instruction
English

Authorised IB programmes
MYP, DP, CP

Age Range 11 – 18

Number of pupils enrolled
1440

Fees for 2019/20
Years 7 to 11 HK$133,800
Years 12 to 13 HK$140,700
Non-refundable capital levy: HK$26,000 for each new Year 7 student

Address
50 Nam Fung Road
Hong Kong SAR | **HONG KONG, CHINA**

TEL +852 2555 9313

FAX +852 2553 8811

Email
sis@sis.edu.hk

Website
www.sis.edu.hk

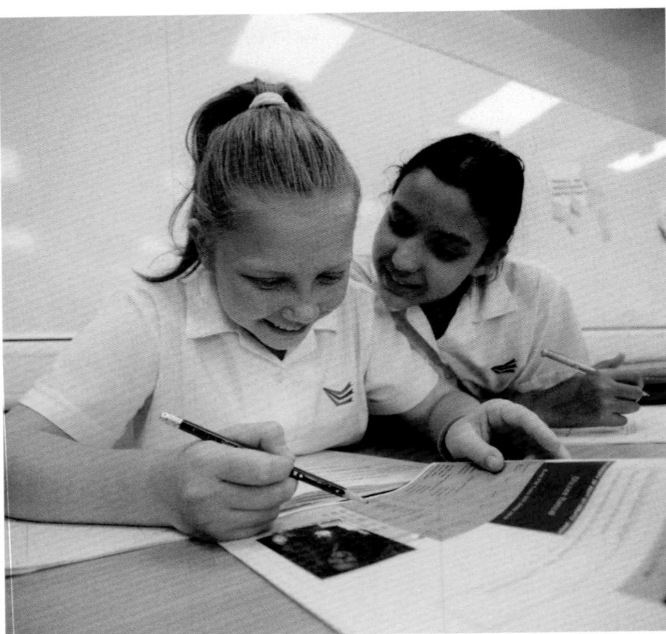

South Island School is a dynamic, innovative and forward looking school located in a green setting on the south side of Hong Kong Island. It caters for 1,440 students from around 40 different nations. The school prides itself on a strong values-based philosophy, an international outlook, a personalised curriculum and very high academic standards. There is a focus on the development of students' personal qualities, fostering a skill set which is creative and contemporary and which develops community responsibility under the banner 'Making a Difference'. The school is inclusive and makes excellent provision for students with a range of individual needs.

The school is authorised by the IBO to offer the MYP (Years 1-3), the IBDP, and the IBCP.

(Founded 1999)

Acting Head of School
Ms Suzannah Large

PYP coordinator
Ms Suzannah Large

Status ESF Educational Services Limited Kindergarten / Non-Profit

Boarding/day Day

Gender Coeducational

Language of instruction
English

Authorised IB programmes
PYP

Age Range 3 – 5

Number of pupils enrolled
352

Fees for 2019/20
HK$84,200

Address
Maritime Square, 33 Tsing King Road
Tsing Yi, New Territories
Hong Kong SAR | **HONG KONG, CHINA**

TEL +852 2436 3355
FAX +852 2436 3105

Email
kinder@tyk.edu.hk

Website
www.tyk.edu.hk

ESF Tsing Yi International Kindergarten has eight classes, four in K1 and four in K2. Children start K1 in the year in which they are three years old. Children attend the kindergarten on a part time basis, five morning or five afternoon sessions per week, with sessions being three hours long. The school community is diverse with children coming from 15 ethnic groups. The cultural richness within the school enhances the learning.

In July 2013 we were authorised as an IB World School, delivering the Primary Years Programme. Through their inquiry into four of the six PYP transdisciplinary themes each year, the children in both K1 and K2 develop knowledge and understanding, as well as skills and attitudes that they can use in kindergarten and take with them into their future learning.

At Tsing Yi, play is the primary mode of learning and the learning environment is set up to promote inquiry through a broad range of play opportunities that promote creativity, critical thinking, and communication. At Tsing Yi the students develop their sense of self, and further develop the skills necessary to nurture positive friendships with other children. They become more aware of their place in the wider-world. Staff work with children on adult-initiated inquiries and to support those that are child-initiated.

The attributes of the learner profile have a significant place within our school and are acknowledged in the actions and achievements of both our children and staff.

(Founded 2016)

Principal
Ms Allison Banbury

PYP coordinator
Ms Cathy Boon

Status ESF Educational Services Limited Kindergarten / Non-Profit

Boarding/day Day

Gender Coeducational

Language of instruction
English

Authorised IB programmes
PYP

Age Range 3 – 5

Number of pupils enrolled
352

Fees for 2019/20
HK$86,400

Address
1/F, Commercial Accommodation, The Visionary
1 Ying Hong Street, Tung Chung,
Lantau, New Territories
Hong Kong SAR | **HONG KONG, CHINA**

TEL +852 3742 3500

Email
kinder@tc.esf.org.hk

Website
www.tck.edu.hk

The custom designed school for 3 to 5 year olds in Tung Chung opened in 2016. It is structured into morning and afternoon 3 hour sessions for both K1 and K2. The space is functional, adaptable and well-resourced to meet the dynamic needs of the three to five year olds who inhabit it. The spaces are not only carefully and intentionally planned, but are also places of beauty that support learning, stimulate imaginations, nurture children, families and staff – and truly inspire the wonderful memories of childhood. Both indoor and outdoor spaces, materials, technology and equipment intrigue, invite, and stimulate students to move, dance, role play, create art, develop language skills and investigate scientific principles.

The school reflects our aspiration for each of our children to flourish. Our goal is to nourish each child, individually, and meet their changing social and emotional needs every day. We strive to provide children with strong foundational skills for future academic success and also to equip them to participate as flexible, creative thinkers and engaged citizens in an increasingly complex and interdependent world.

(Founded 1991)

Principal
Mr Chris Sammons

DP coordinator
Mrs Helen Devine Costa

CP coordinator
Ms Emily Clarke

Status English Schools Foundation School/Non-Profit

Boarding/day Day

Gender Coeducational

Language of instruction
English

Authorised IB programmes
DP, CP

Age Range 11 – 18

Number of pupils enrolled
1220

Fees for 2019/20
Years 7 to 11 HK$133,800
Years 12 to 13 HK$140,700
A one-off non-refundable capital levy of HK$26,000 is required for each new Year 7 student – and will be reduced on a sliding scale for students who join in later years.

Address
250 Victoria Road
Pokfulam
Hong Kong SAR | HONG KONG, CHINA

TEL +852 2819 1962
FAX +852 2816 7257

Email
wis@wis.edu.hk

Website
www.wis.edu.hk

The West Island School motto "Strength from Diversity" reflects that the school caters for students from over 40 nationalities in a modern building overlooking the University of Hong Kong and the vibrant shipping lanes of the South China Sea. The school has a strong focus on the value of international mindedness and the importance of community. It has a reputation for academic excellence balanced with compassion and service beyond the classroom. The vast majority of students graduate to a range of international universities with 90% achieving their first choice. In 2019, the average score of the IB diploma was 35 with 19% achieving 40 or more.

Students are encouraged to become "responsible global citizens" as part of the mission of the school. Training for leadership roles within the school and beyond is a strength which the school believes heralds access to better choices beyond Year 13. Over 120 activities are offered termly and one week annually focuses exclusively on CAS projects within Asia. The school has a unique one to one tutoring model where students meet individually with their tutor to consider academic progress and commitment to CAS.

Facilities

The school has purpose built specialist rooms in all subjects and in particular: specialist science laboratories, a modern library, performance space for drama and dance, two gymnasiums, state of the art design technology workshops incorporating a graphics studio, textiles and food, three art studios, 7 music studios and 2 music classrooms both with raised performance platforms, outdoor courts for a range of sports, a 25 metre swimming pool and a large auditorium. The proximity to Hong Kong university playing fields provides further sport facilities. WIS is a one to one laptop school with digital literacy as part of the curriculum.

Curriculum

WIS is an authorised IB Diploma school offering DP for 300 students at Post 16. Since 2018, WIS offers the IB Careers-related Programme. IGCSEs and some BTEC courses are offered for Pre 16 students.

West Island School is a candidate school for the MYP. As an IB World School, we share a common philosophy – a commitment to high-quality, challenging, international education – that we believe is important for our students.

(Founded 2009)

Principal
Mr Chris Coyle

PYP coordinator
Ms Helen Thomson

Status ESF Educational Services Limited Kindergarten / Non-Profit

Boarding/day Day

Gender Coeducational

Language of instruction
English

Authorised IB programmes
PYP

Age Range 3 – 5

Number of pupils enrolled
343

Fees for 2019/20
HK$85,500

Address
599 Sai Sha Road
Ma On Shan, Sha Tin
Hong Kong SAR | **HONG KONG, CHINA**

TEL +852 2435 5291
FAX +852 2435 6322

Email
kinder@wksk.edu.hk

Website
www.wksk.edu.hk

ESF Wu Kai Sha International Kindergarten is located in Ma On Shan and opened in August 2009. We cater for children aged 3-5 years old and follow the International Baccalaureate Primary Years Programme (PYP). The school was authorised as an IB World School in July 2013.

In partnership with families we aim to develop confident, creative, knowledgeable children who respect all others and participate actively within the school community. Our inquiry based curriculum encourages children to explore relevant concepts and ideas through child-centred play and exploration, real-life experiences and focused learning and teaching activities, allowing them to develop a range of understandings, knowledge and skills in all areas of the curriculum.

We have a wonderful team of highly qualified and experienced teaching staff who are both nurturing and knowledgeable about early childhood education. Children work closely with their class teacher and EAs to develop a range of skills, knowledge and understanding. A range of groupings are used to enable all children to learn effectively. Learning is planned to cater for the needs of all children and is differentiated for individual children's skill levels.

We strive to provide an engaging and enriching environment that stimulates children's curiosity and supports independent learning. The school has large, bright spaces for learning and play and children spend their time in classrooms, shared areas and in the indoor and outdoor play areas. All classrooms have an excellent range of resources which includes a wealth of technology resources. We also have a dedicated, well stocked library from which children and families can borrow a range of books, story sacks and other resources.

Principal
Dr. Vincent Chian

PYP coordinator
Ms. Elaine Lam

MYP coordinator
Dr. Evan Hui See Chin

DP coordinator
Ms. Andi Elisa

Status Private

Boarding/day Mixed

Gender Coeducational

Language of instruction
English, Mandarin

Authorised IB programmes
PYP, MYP, DP

Age Range 3 – 19 years

Number of pupils enrolled
3000

Fees (per semester)
PYP RM14,000 (US$3,370)
MYP RM27,000 (US$6499)
DP RM30,000 (US$7,221)

Address
Lot 4178, Jalan 1/27D, Section 6
Wangsa Maju
Kuala Lumpur
53300 | MALAYSIA

TEL +60 3 4142 0888
FAX +60 3 4149 0222

Email
enquiries@fairview.edu.my

Website
www.fairview.edu.my

Ever Onwards

Fairview is a network of 5 International Baccalaureate world schools and one candidate school in Scotland. The 5 IB World Schools are located in strategic cities across Malaysia namely in Kuala Lumpur, Penang, Johor, Subang Jaya and Ipoh. Our mission is to serve the local and international community with the best in education in line with the IB philosophy of education for a better world. As the largest provider of IB programmes, Fairview stands tall in delivering the IB programmes exclusively in line with our steadfast commitment to the IB philosophy.

Fairview Students

- **Academically outstanding** – Fairview's IB Diploma Programme consistently achieves outstanding results with a class average of 36 points for the past four years, placing the school among the top 27% IBDP schools in the world.
- **International minded and globally responsible** – Learners go on international expeditions twice a year, learning about different cultures and developing a deep understanding that others may also be right.
- **Centered with Great Values** – Learning at Fairview is interwoven with many opportunities to develop an understanding of the Learner Profile attributes, built naturally into the curriculum. The value of being principled are taught seamlessly in the same class, allowing our students to link classroom experiences to real world ethical challenges.
- **Balanced** – Our unique music programme ensures that every Fairview student has the opportunity to learn an orchestral instrument, learning musical theory within the IB programmes. Fairview is working towards becoming an all Steinway school. Having invested on the pianos, the school has also has an in built concert hall known as Dominus, showcasing the best in arts.
- **Creative and Inquiring** – A first of its kind, all Fairview students take a trip annually to our very own purpose built Fairview EduResort at Port Dickson. Twice a year students take their learning outdoors by going on education field trips to the United Kingdom, Australia, China and a host of other countries. This education journey is adventurous, exciting, and helps students develop an incredible sence of inquiry and creativity.
- **Proficiency in Language B** – English is the lingua franca of the school, supported with Mandarian, Bahasa Malaysia and Spanish language programmes.

Garden International School (Rayong Campus)

(Founded 1994)

Principal
Mrs Dinah Hawtree BA (Hons), PGCE, NPQH

DP coordinator
Lauren Hucknall

Status Private

Boarding/day Mixed

Gender Coeducational

Language of instruction
English

Authorised IB programmes
DP

Age Range 3 – 18 years

Number of pupils enrolled
475

Fees
Day THB542,800 (US$17,900)

Address
188/24 Moo 4, Pala-Ban Chang Road
Tambol Pala, Ban Chang
Rayong
21130 | THAILAND

TEL +66 3803 0808

Email
ibcoord@gardenrayong.com

Website
www.gardenrayong.com

Garden International School (GIS) is the most experienced IB school on Thailand's Eastern Seaboard. For nearly 25 years, GIS has provided a world-class IB education to students.

GIS is based in a safe, secure, semi-rural environment, around two hours' drive from Bangkok. The area includes a recently-developed airport, excellent transportation links, and a large expat community.

Quality Education

The school has an excellent track record. In 2016, 2017 and 2018 we enjoyed a 100 per cent pass rate for the IB Diploma and our points' average of 35 was far higher than the global average. In recent years, GIS students have gone on to study at world-famous institutions such as UCLA and Berklee College of Music in the US and the University of Cambridge and University College London in the UK.

Our IB numbers continue to grow, but we are still able to offer a low teacher-student ratio. These small class sizes mean teachers can offer extensive support and help to students. Our teachers are highly experienced, with many years of IB experience.

Pastoral Care

As well as support in classes, GIS has a strong pastoral element which offers significant extra guidance. This includes a University Counsellor, trips to university exhibitions and workshops. The workshops help students know how to apply to universities, give advice about living independently and also show students how to write a CV and personal statement. We also offer boarding.

Outstanding Facilities

Students at GIS have access to excellent, state-of-the-art facilities. These include fully-equipped laboratories, ICT suites, high-quality musical sound rooms and 3D and laser printers for our well-equipped DT classrooms. Our sports' facilities include two swimming pools, a football pitch and basketball courts.

Leadership Roles

Our student leadership programme offers IB students the chance to take on significant leadership roles within school. This experience is also useful and influential when applying to universities. In addition, we operate a popular Model United Nations (MUN) club and have strong after-school sports and community programmes.

As the only school in the region with full accreditation from the Council of International Schools (CIS), we have the experience and quality to offer outstanding opportunities for IB students.

(Founded 1971)

Headteacher
Mr Christof Martin

PYP coordinator
Joram Hutchins

MYP coordinator
Isabel Martin

DP coordinator
Joanna Fitts

Status Private

Boarding/day Day

Gender Coeducational

Language of instruction
English

Authorised IB programmes
PYP, MYP, DP

Age Range 18 months – 18 years

Number of pupils enrolled
1750

Fees
Day: S$35,000

Address
2 Dairy Farm Lane
Singapore
677621 | SINGAPORE

TEL +65 6461 0881

Email
admissions@gess.sg

Website
www.gess.sg

With almost 15 years of experience in offering the IB Curriculum starting from the Primary Years Programme (PYP), through Middle Years Programme (MYP) and concluding with the Diploma Programme (DP), GESS has long established itself as a top IB world school in Singapore. The school produces exemplary IB scores that are always above the world average and the students get the chance to study in esteemed universities around the world.

More than that, GESS aligns itself closely with the IB mission and invests its efforts in developing students who become better citizens through education. From encouraging students to serve the local Singaporean community through programmes such as the Junior Neighbourhood Ambassadors programme and enabling students to learn beyond the classroom through research expedition trips to places like South Africa, the school builds a necessary connection between knowledge and the world.

The school, which has students of over 65 nationalities, also encourages its diverse students to maintain a strong cultural identity through varied initiatives such as the German, Dutch and Danish Mother Tongue Language Programmes running from Primary School to High School and the Language Enrichment Programme that provides immersive avenues for students to practice their home languages and learn more about their own cultures. Celebrations such as International Language Day, International Summer Party, Chinese New Year and more create opportunities for students to reflect on, understand and express their cultural identities.

While primarily non-selective, the school also creates multiple avenues for students with stronger academic inclinations to grow: GESS is the first ever school outside Europe to have the prestigious Junior Engineer Academy that allows students to learn real life application of engineering together with industry partners like BOSCH, Pepperl & Fuchs and XentiQ.

At GESS, every child is encouraged to push boundaries, work towards their aspirations, big and small, and become strong characters with a dedication to serving their communities.

Promising Futures

School Director
David Brazeau

PYP coordinator
Shailja Datt

MYP coordinator
K Rajarao

DP coordinator
Rajeev Pargaien

Status Private

Boarding/day Mixed

Gender Coeducational

Language of instruction
English

Authorised IB programmes
PYP, MYP, DP

Address
A-12, Sector 132
Noida, Uttar Pradesh
201304 | INDIA

TEL +91 9711000560/625/626

Email
principal.dpigcse
@genesisgs.edu.in

Website
www.genesisglobalschool.edu.in

Situated in Noida, a satellite city of Delhi, Genesis Global School is part of the National Capital Region (Delhi NCR). The School is spread over a 30-acre campus, with efficient connectivity via an Expressway. It is an hour's drive from Indira Gandhi International Airport, Delhi and around 25 minutes' drive from cosmopolitan South Delhi.

Genesis Global School celebrated its 10th anniversary this year and has become a hub of national and international educational excellence, where every child is important and accepted for who they are. At GGS we ensure that our students have exposure to the best in current global practices, provide them with a truly holistic environment where modern facilities and high-quality teaching and learning practices allow our school ideals to be developed.

Our school ideals depicted in the School logo – the hexagon are: International mindedness, Educational Excellence, Integrity and Persistence, Resilience, Stewardship and Compassion and Care. These six pillars underpin our mission statement making them the guiding light of our practices.

Our Mission Statement is: "GGS graduates will be responsible global citizens empowered to contribute to society in various capacities by providing them the freedom to be, to act, to impress and to dream. GGS incorporates an inquiry–based curriculum and extensive co-curricular experiences, acknowledging the role of community voice and student agency."

A GGS education allows students to achieve their potential and take their place in the world. We continuously strive to reflect and improve our curriculum to meet the needs of all learners in an ever-changing world both inside and outside the classroom.

As an IB World School, Cambridge accredited centre and a member of the Council of International Schools (CIS) GGS is also part of a community working collaboratively to shape international education. We are committed to incorporating international and intercultural perspectives into our programmes so that students can move forward with the attitudes, knowledge and understanding that will provide them with a solid base wherever their studies or work may take them.

Junior School
The Junior School comprises of Grades Pre-Nursery to 5 and follows the IB Primary Years Curriculum (PYP). The PYP is an interdisciplinary curriculum where no subject is taught in isolation. Project based and experiential learning opportunities allow our students to be encouraged, and enable them to become independent critical thinkers who can take increasing responsibility for their learning. Our student to teacher ratio is 13:1 which enables every child to have the support they need. Students' progress is regularly assessed both formally and informally by staff to ensure every child reaches their potential.

Middle School
The Middle School (grades 6, 7, 8) follow the MYP framework integrated with the Cambridge curriculum. The skill-based, concept-based and context driven curriculum of the middle

school enables our learners to be part of the teaching and learning process. The inquiry-based teaching approach ensures every child's voice is heard and every learner gets the best support to reach their highest potential.

Our curriculum is planned to consider student differences and is accessible to all. We give students the opportunity to find the area they are strongest in and to grow in it.

The teaching and learning approaches ensure that the learners explore and understand WHAT they are learning, HOW they are learning things and most importantly, WHY they are learning. The focus is not only on teaching academics but having students use their knowledge and skills in different known and unknown situations. By applying these skills they become lifelong learners, develop learner attributes such as being knowledgeable inquirers, who are caring and open minded, who value everything and everyone, who are ready to be global citizens and successful leaders.

Senior School

The Senior School has two phases: IGCSE with grades 9 and 10 and IB DP with grades 11 and 12. In the senior school students are given the opportunity to specialise and explore subjects of their interest. Though academic rigour increases, students are still taught with a great focus on the development of their skills through an inquiry-based approach to teaching and learning. Complimenting the individualised teaching, our senior students also have the extensive guidance of the Support Department which is a combination of student counselling services, learning needs support and university counselling. This ensures that the students are provided with everything they need for a well-balanced life and studies to be successful learners both at and beyond their time at GGS.

Scholars in Residence

Our boarding houses are equipped with modern facilities providing "a home away from home". The School has separate air-conditioned residences for boys and girls, where they are given personal attention and care by experienced, professional House Parents.

Genesis Global School endeavours to nurture resilient, holistic, empathetic & lifelong learners in a multi-cultural environment, for a sustainable future.

Glendale International School

Head of School
Ms Shoma Goswami

PYP coordinator
Ms Neerja M.

Status Private

Boarding/day Day

Gender Coeducational

Language of instruction
English

Authorised IB programmes
PYP

Age Range 1.5 – 11 years

Number of pupils enrolled
250

Address
Plot A, Road No. 20
HMDA Layout, Tellapur
Hyderabad, Telangana
502032 | INDIA

TEL +91 90 3000 1128

Email
gipinfo@glendale.edu.in

Website
www.glendale.edu.in/glendale-international-school/ib-pyp-tellapur

"Willingness to be puzzled is a valuable trait to cultivate, from childhood to advanced inquiry" – Noam Chomsky.

About:

Since our inception in 2003, Glendale Education's twin focus is on building character and competence, and our approach of implementing the best of global pedagogies, has made us a name to reckon with. Founded and managed by educationists with decades of experience in educational reform and student development we are creating vibrant learning environments that develop students who possess the skills, competencies and empathetic perspective necessary to succeed in the 21st century.

Curriculum

We here at Glendale International School-PYP thrive on inquiry and learning. Glendale Group of schools have been pioneers in creating intelligent and child centric pedagogy. This pedagogy is a culmination of years of research, learning and collaboration. Hence, Multiple intelligences are a huge part of our PYP curriculum and differentiation within the homeroom is a norm. The 7 Habits of Highly Effective People and The Leader in me are part of the six themes of PYP learning. Brain Compatible learning is understood, practiced and modelled in our school.

On a regular day in school you will see the children busy having fun. Art, Music, PE, Craft, Pottery, Drama, Dance, Library all contribute to the academics and children come back enthused about various aspects of their learning. Our inquiry units are devised in such a way that collaboration and communication become necessities and learning spirals horizontally and vertically. Our Objective is too provide enriching, empowering and exploratory experiences for the harmonious growth of the children's mind and body. Nurturing creativity through exposure to culture and arts and inculcate a scientific temperament and a spirit of inquiry with critical thinking skills fosters an attitude of "lifelong learning" and forges real life connections with curriculum. We endeavor to create an atmosphere of mutual respect, synergy and open mindedness, so that children understand that they are not just part of a family or country but of a global community.

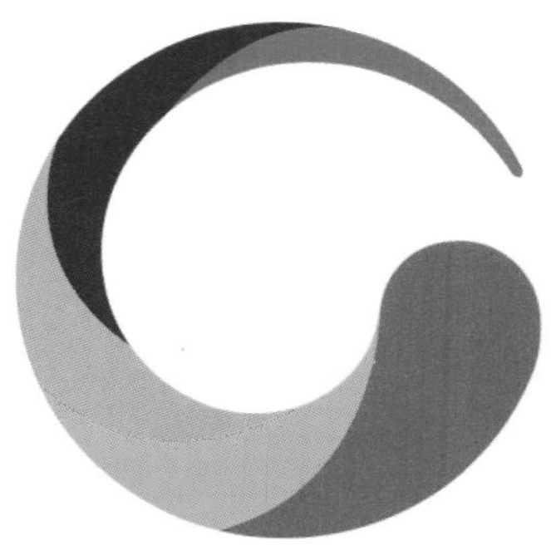

Global Indian International School

(Founded 2002)

Chairman and Co-Founder Atul Temurnikar

Principal Melissa Maria

Academic Supervisor Deepika Sodhi

DP coordinator Deepa Chandrasekaran

Status Private

Boarding/day Day

Gender Coeducational

Language of instruction English

Authorised IB programmes DP

Age Range 2½– 18

Number of pupils enrolled 2700

Address
27, Punggol Field Walk
828649 | SINGAPORE

TEL +65 69147000

FAX +65 67228350

Email principal.pg@globalindianschool.org

Website sg.globalindianschool.org

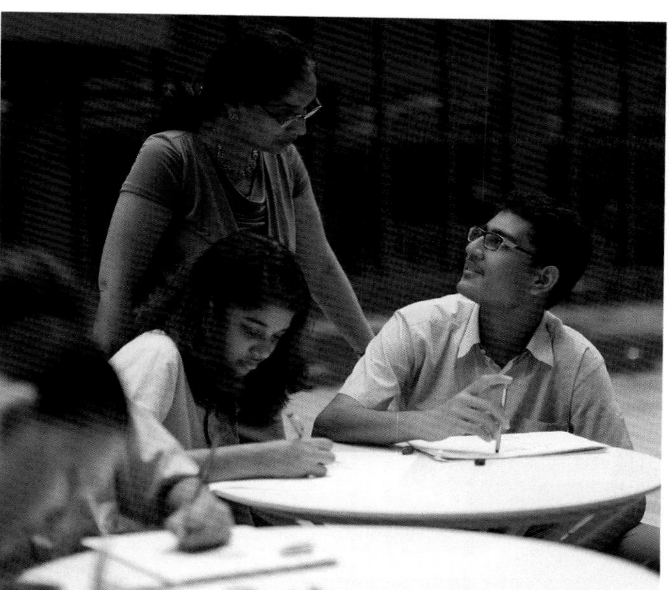

Global Indian International School (GIIS), operated by the Global Schools Foundation, is a frontrunner in international school education from Nursery to Grade 12, in Asia. The foundation proudly manages a blossoming network of 21 campuses across 7 countries with a vision of becoming the global role model for teaching and learning through its award-winning holistic framework of 9 GEMS.

GIIS has two campuses in Singapore – East Coast Campus from Nursery to Grade 7 and SMART Campus, Punggol, from Nursery to Grade 12.

Our flagship campus, GIIS SMART Campus with a capacity of 3.5 K students is a school of the future. The campus offers cutting-edge facilities like digital classrooms, video conferencing, collaborative learning spaces, data analytics in sports and more than 40 skill-based studios, all of which add up to create an environment for students to effectively explore a world of ideas.

The school offers complete international curricula – IB Primary Years Programme (IB PYP), Cambridge Lower Secondary Programme, IGCSE and IB Diploma Programme (IB DP). Students begin their educational journey with a strong foundational framework like IB PYP, that sparks curiosity and makes them inquiry-driven. In middle-year grades, the Cambridge curriculum offers them analytical skills and a stronghold over diverse subjects, thus preparing them for the challenges of IBDP in Grades 11 and 12.

The IB DP at GIIS is a much sought after course with high achieving students, trained and qualified teachers and NextGen facilities at the SMART Campus. In the last 13 years, GIIS has produced 14 IB World Toppers (45/45 points) and 24 near-perfect scorers (44/45 points).

Close to 250 students graduate every year from the school. The school's unique performance-measuring metrics, called 7S, tracks and monitors each student's academic progress thus enabling teachers to roll-out a systematic improvement plan.

Our graduates are sought after and enter prestigious universities across the world including the University of Cambridge, University of Oxford, University of California, Cornell University, New York University, National University of Singapore, Nanyang Technological University, etc.

An amalgamation of great factors like complete international curricula, excellent teachers, futuristic infrastructure and holistic pedagogy contribute towards making our students well-rounded individuals and global leaders of the 21st-century.

Good Shepherd International School

(Founded 1977)

Founder & Principal
Dr. P.C. Thomas

DP coordinator
Suresh Thangarajan

Status Private

Boarding/day Boarding

Gender Coeducational

Language of instruction
English

Authorised IB programmes
DP

Age Range 8 – 17

Number of pupils enrolled
1000

Address
Good Shepherd Knowledge Village
M Palada PO
Ootacamund, Tamil Nadu
643 004 | INDIA

TEL +91 423 2550371
FAX +91 423 2550386

Email
info@gsis.ac.in

Website
www.gsis.ac.in

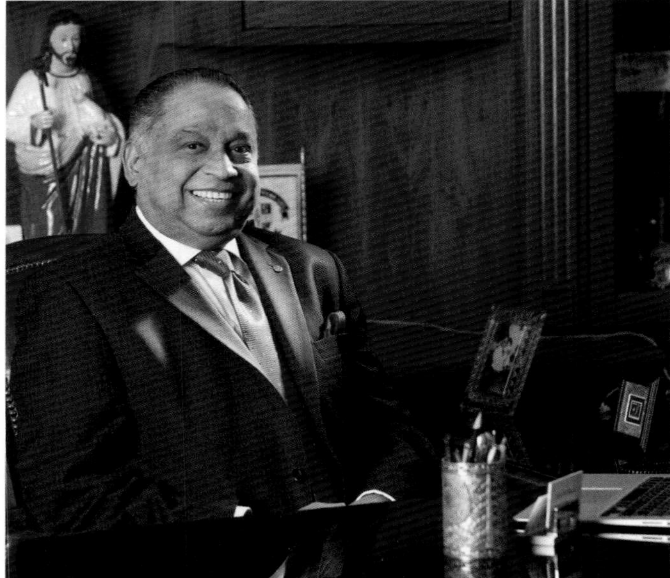

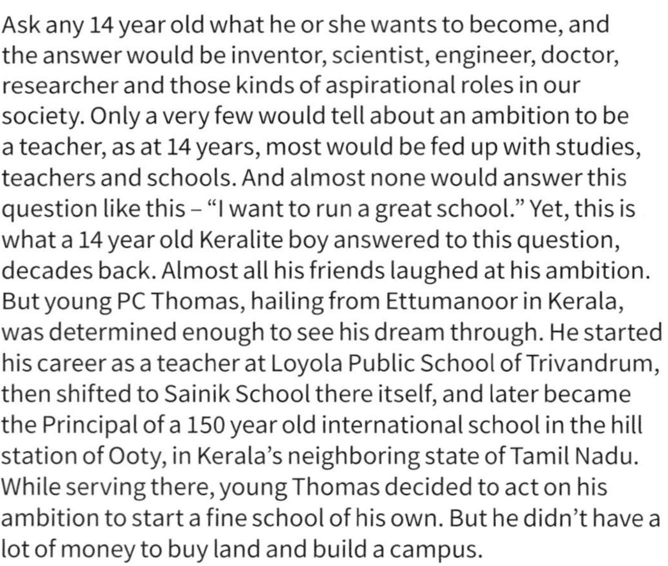

Ask any 14 year old what he or she wants to become, and the answer would be inventor, scientist, engineer, doctor, researcher and those kinds of aspirational roles in our society. Only a very few would tell about an ambition to be a teacher, as at 14 years, most would be fed up with studies, teachers and schools. And almost none would answer this question like this – "I want to run a great school." Yet, this is what a 14 year old Keralite boy answered to this question, decades back. Almost all his friends laughed at his ambition. But young PC Thomas, hailing from Ettumanoor in Kerala, was determined enough to see his dream through. He started his career as a teacher at Loyola Public School of Trivandrum, then shifted to Sainik School there itself, and later became the Principal of a 150 year old international school in the hill station of Ooty, in Kerala's neighboring state of Tamil Nadu. While serving there, young Thomas decided to act on his ambition to start a fine school of his own. But he didn't have a lot of money to buy land and build a campus.

One day in those days he came across an advertisement by the erstwhile King of Baroda to sell off the famous Baroda Palace at Ooty. Thomas had no hope of getting the property as many buyers was there to buy the prestigious property at sky high prices. Yet, he met the Maharajah and conveyed to him his need for a ready campus and building to create a noble institution in education. Much to his surprise, the King agreed and conveyed to all other bidders his decision to hand over the land and palace to PC Thomas at a much lesser rate than the prevailing market rate. Today, this is known as the Baroda Palace Campus of the Good Shepherd International School. 42 long years have passed since then.

GSIS has grown from strength to strength, branching out from the original ICSE syllabus to the more international IGCSE and IB curricula. A fully residential school with no day scholars for ensuring perfect discipline, the integrated nature of GSIS would stun anyone as the campus is fully self-sufficient with its own organic farm for sourcing unpolluted vegetables for students, a cattle farm of 450 cows for the milk needed by students and a poultry farm with 50,000 birds for the eggs and meat! GSIS is also renowned for having the most extensive sporting facilities including equestrian with 30 thoroughbred horses, polo ground, golf course, swimming pools, grounds for all popular outdoor sports including a cricket ground, which is the highest cricket ground, not just in India, but in the whole world!

Now, under the visionary guidance of Dr. PC Thomas, GSIS is expanding its bigger Palada campus with an additional 4 lakh sq ft of construction for housing new world-class cubicle based hostels and a new Indoor Sports Complex where all students can play simultaneously! Dr. Thomas is a visionary edupreneur who dreams and executes larger than – life visions like how he sends 50 of his students each year to NASA for their renowned Space Camp program. Yet, Dr. Thomas is particular that his students have their feet planted firmly in the ground realities of India, and inspires them to do a lot of charitable and relief works for the afflicted and the downtrodden segments of the society. A firm disciplinarian,

Thomas has brushed aside all temptations to diversify the Good Shepherd brand to start international schools in India's metro cities or to admit day scholars or to get into related fields like higher education. Unlike most of his peers, he is a firm believer of quality over quantity.

Says, Dr. Thomas, "My professional ambition was to build just one fine school in all respects, not to be the largest or fastest growing school chain. Schools are not saloons or parlours to be replicated fast." He derives his satisfaction from the fact that some of the finest surgeons, engineers and entrepreneurs in USA, India and elsewhere are GSIS alumni. GSIS was the first School in India to install a state-of the-Art 3d printer, which is even now rare in India's Leading engineering Colleges and a Design Technology Lab which give its students a head start in designing, innovating and inventing. With such initiatives it is no wonder that over 35 renowned universities from across the world come to GSIS every year to invite students to their institutions for higher studies. Dr. Thomas next aim is to make GSIS the very best in Asia and one of the Top-10 schools in the world. His wife Elsamma Thomas has been a pillar of strength for him and the school and has been in charge of the renowned Good Shepherd Finishing School for long.

(Founded 2011)

Head of School
Ms. Chen Qingnian

DP coordinator
Mr. Yu Yue

Status Private

Boarding/day Mixed

Gender Coeducational

Language of instruction
English

Authorised IB programmes
DP

Age Range 2 – 18

Number of pupils enrolled
300

Fees
Day: RMB115,000 – RMB180,000

Address
Minxing Road, New District
Daliang
Shunde, Guangdong
528300 | CHINA

TEL +86 0757 22325121

Email
admin.dsi@desheng-school.com

Website
www.desheng-school.com

Guangdong Shunde Desheng School has an illustrious history of achievements and has consistently ranked as the top school in Shunde, China based on its sterling academic results and students' performance.

In 2011, the school, under the visionary leadership of its Chairman, Mr. Chen Ji Ye, started the International Education Division to prepare students for an overseas education. The division is now known as Desheng School (International), in short DSI.

DSI was accredited by the Cambridge Assessment International Education (CAIE) in 2014 to offer the Cambridge IGCSE. In 2015, the school was accredited by the International Baccalaureate Organisation to offer the International Baccalaureate Diploma Programme (IBDP).

DSI is proud to have:

• **Student-Centric Education Philosophy**

SCHOOL VISION

A global centre of excellence that promotes holistic education.

OUR MISSION

To nurture independent life-long learners who strive for excellence and serve with compassion.

SCHOOL CORE VALUES

R.I.S.E. – Respect. Integrity. Self-Discipline. Excellence.

DESIRED STUDENTS OUTCOMES

Scholars, Leaders, Global Citizens.

International Standard Learning Environment

DSI is located in a newly built complex with state-of-the-art facilities. The environment is ideal for students to fully engage in academic and non-academic activities, with its multi-media library, Artificial Intelligence laboratory, range of sports facilities and some other facilities which meet the needs of both teachers and students.

• **Professional Educators**

In DSI, outstanding teaching staff, including experienced IB trained teachers, are integral to the implementation of the curriculum. The Pedagogical Team and the Student Development Team work together to ensure the overall wellbeing of students. The school is proud to have Dr. Hon Chiew Weng, former principal of Hwa Chong Institution, Singapore, as Education Director, to enrich its management team.

• **Holistic Education**

DSI offers a wide range of subject options to cater to various needs of students in line with the requirements of Cambridge IGCSE and IBDP.

From 2017 to 2019, three batches of students have graduated from DSI. 80% of the IBDP students have enrolled in top 50 universities in the world, including Oxford University, Imperial College London, University College London; New York University, University of California (various campuses); University of Toronto; The Australian National University, University of Melbourne; Nanyang Technological University, etcetera.

The school also has a number of programmes to prepare them for the changing dynamics of the world. This comprises

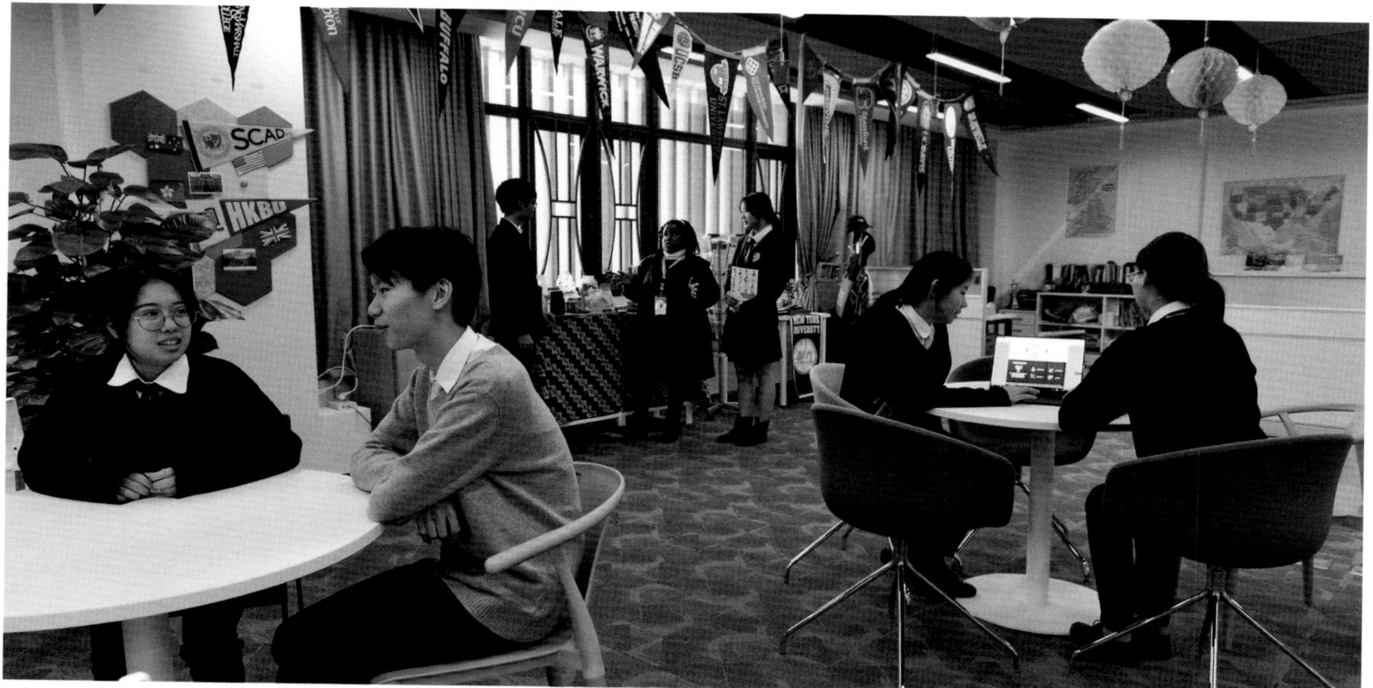

Champions of Innovation, focusing on Artificial Intelligence, Cyber Safety, 3D Printing, etcetera. In the 1st International Artificial Intelligence Fair held in Beijing, Desheng School AI Challenge Team was awarded the Qomolangma Prize (The First Prize) for their project "Research on Nursing Home Caring System Based on Deep Learning". This marked a milestone in DSI's history of developing students' innovative potential.

DSI also puts emphasis on students' language development and critical thinking. In addition to compulsory Super Curriculum subjects like Philosophy of Disciplines, Research Skills, we provide a rich variety of Co-Curricular Activities. Students gain national and international exposure through platforms such as the Model United Nation conferences, Future Problem Solving Programmes, as well as Experiential Programmes (Local/Overseas/University).

The House system contributes to a dynamic culture on campus and imparts a sense of camaraderie and excellence among DSI students.

With strong emphasis on both academic and student-centric activities, the school is well prepared to nurture its students to become Scholars, Leaders, and Global Citizens.

- **Admission**

For application enquiries, kindly contact the school directly.

Greenwood High International School

Head of School
Mr. Aloysius D'Mello

DP coordinator
Nishanth Nagavar

Status Private

Boarding/day Mixed

Gender Coeducational

Language of instruction
English

Authorised IB programmes
DP

Age Range 6 – 19 years

Address
No.8-14, Chickkawadayara Pura
Near Heggondahalli, Gunjur
Post, Varthur via
Bengaluru, Karnataka
560087 | INDIA

TEL +91 80 22010500
FAX +91 80 27822200

Email
admissions.intl@greenwoodhigh.edu.in

Website
www.greenwoodhigh.edu.in

Greenwood High students pride themselves in being able to not only balance academics, sports and co-curricular activities, but excel in them. Greenwood High IB results far outshine the world average; this year (2019) two students achieved a perfect score of 45 in IBDP, in IGCSE results 78% students received a distinction and 20.2% students secured a merit. The school has produced India toppers in both IGCSE and ICSE. And yet, these very same industrious students immerse themselves in theatre and with support from their theatre, art and music teachers, and their talents blossomed into a musical 'Annie' that was compared to professional theatre productions. To encourage them further, the school has held various workshops including one from the prestigious Globe Education.

The school is an open art gallery, for its hallways and open spaces display artwork by the promising young artists. In sports too, the students are champions, for they have won various Basketball, Soccer and Badminton championships. The students are very socially aware, and the Model United Nations debates and forums begin from middle school itself, so that they grow into international minded global citizens.

Greenwood High students are extremely involved in social projects and have contributed to various causes. Our student designs include a six wheeled hand cart with steering, gears and brakes to help street vendors maneuver their hand carts over uneven, hilly terrains, and this has won her the President's Award. Another student had developed a cell phone app 'Corner Shop' "aiming to give small time vendors a platform to boost their sales." One student developed an App for the blind to help them in purchasing groceries and was hailed by IBM while another launched an online debate forum at global level, which was funded by Google and Microsoft. One student has been awarded the Diana Legacy Award for setting up science laboratories in schools for the underprivileged.

The CAS students volunteer in hospitals, paint government run schools for the underprivileged, create breast cancer awareness, clean streets and recycle waste. They raise funds for education and health in rural areas. The CAS students also worked on a social project in Prague.

The students of Greenwood High aim high and reach higher. This year IBDP students has received acceptances in over 200 universities around the world, for many have been accepted in Ivy League colleges, with scholarships to a total of 7.1 million USD. Greenwood High already has students in the University of Pennsylvania, Columbia University, Cornell University, Brown University, Johns Hopkins, Georgia Tech, UCLA, Berkeley, Duke, Imperial College London, to name a few. Indeed, they all take the school motto 'Rooted in Knowledge' very seriously, and while spreading out their wings to soar high, remain rooted deeply in knowledge.

High School Affiliated to Shanghai Jiao Tong University

Head of School
Dr. Xu Xiangdong

DP coordinator
Mr. Charles Pflanz

Status State

Boarding/day Mixed

Gender Coeducational

Language of instruction
English, Chinese

Authorised IB programmes
DP

Age Range 15 – 18

Address
No 42 Yin Gao Road
Bao Shan District
Shanghai
200439 | CHINA

TEL +86 21 65910979
FAX +86 21 65912370

Email
jdfzib@jdfzib.org

Website
www.jdfz.cn

The High School Affiliated to Shanghai Jiao Tong University (known as JDFZ in Chinese Abbreviation) is one of Shanghai's most renowned and competitive public high schools, situated in Shanghai's northern suburbs. In 2014 the school marked its 60th anniversary.

The school established its International Curriculum Center in 2011 and gained IB authorization for the Diploma Programme in 2012, saw its first cohort of 65 DP graduates in 2014. In the year of 2020, there are 350 students in total, ranging in age from 15-19. The students come from in and around Shanghai, with some from provinces across China. The vast majority of students are boarders. Students undergo a foundation year of IGCSE before moving into the DP in years two and three. The graduates from IBDP have earned outstanding offers of admissions from top universities, largely in the United States, Canada, and the UK, such as Chicago, Duke, Johns Hopkins, Northwestern, Cornell, Dartmouth, Toronto, McGill, Oxford and Cambridge.

The centre has had excellent results in its short history as an IB World School, with each year graduates finishing above IB world averages in nearly every subject offered. This success comes from both the hard work of the students, and the passion of the teaching staff. Staff are dedicated, enthusiastic, and professional, hailing from both China and abroad. English is the medium of instruction in all lessons other than Group 1.

One of the core elements of the school's ethos is the balance between love for one's mother country and the growth of an international outlook. This thread is woven into all subjects. The IB Learner Profile is also very much a living part of the school, with regular discussions, events, and activities making it relevant. HSASJTU also strives to utilize IB concepts to promote the educational reform of the national curriculum.

Hangzhou Greentown Yuhua School

Head of School
Zha Pinyang

MYP coordinator
Liu Xiaohong

Status Private

Boarding/day Mixed

Gender Coeducational

Language of instruction
Chinese, English

Authorised IB programmes
MYP

Address
No. 532 Wenyi West Road
Hangzhou, Zhejiang
310012 | CHINA

TEL +86 571 88477561

Email
greentownedu@163.com

Website
www.hzlcyhcz.cn

Hangzhou Greentown Yuhua School is a fully licensed, private school located at 532 Wenyi West Road, Hangzhou, China. Our mission is to cultivate global citizens with integrity, a rational spirit, cultural literacy and a strong sense of duty; to advocate for professionalism and a healthy lifestyle. We encourage our students to have global literacy, enable them to respect different cultures and beliefs and integrate into multicultural world. The Education Philosophy at Greentown Yuhua provides the students both academic and self-development educational streams, allowing for full cognitive and social development, meeting the requirements and needs of each individual student. Moreover, campus Life at Greentown Yuhua is devoted to improving the quality of student's life on campus. Activities include various student societies and clubs, such as tae kwon do, piano, painting, studios and foreign language courses. The school motto is "Being Benovelent and Tolerant while seeking the Truth". We are dedicated in providing a well-rounded educational experience for our students; both as individuals and as a collective.

Since its foundation in 1992, Greentown Yuhua School has been striving to achieve educational excellence by providing an all-round quality education that will serve the needs for the future development of local community. In previous years, the school was awarded "The National Outstanding Private School" by the Ministry of Education. Since 2000, Zhejiang Greentown Real Estate Group (a national Top 2 real estate company in year 2010) has invested more than 1 billion yuan RMB in the school. And the school now takes up an area of 16.867 hectares, with the construction area about 70,000 square meters. The school is a modern institution with a beautifully landscaped environment and first-class facilities.

We provide Middle Years Programme for students from year 7 to year 9. In this program we are committed to cultivating learners to be inquirers, knowledgeable, thinkers, communicators, principled, open-minded, caring, risk-takers, balanced and reflective. In order to help students achieve these attributes, the school provides English language acquisition, Chinese language and literature, individuals and societies, mathematics, design, drama, music, and visual arts, science, physical and health education. We encourage our students to become active, compassionate and lifelong learners who understand that other people, with their differences, can also be valuable. We participate in the construction of international courses based on the domestic compulsory curriculum to help students adapt to overseas study.

We have a faculty of 280 and 2400 students. All the teachers have the recognized qualifications and are conscientious in their work. They are dedicated to the well-being of each student and have a vacation to provide for the welfare, mentoring of individual students within the harmonious environment of their classes. We also have a beautiful campus, modern teaching facilities, technology and resources. The school has high-standard on-campus rooms for boarding students, along with spacious classrooms,

specialized laboratories, a library, lecture halls, auditorium, gymnasium, etc. We have a fully computerized management and monitoring system.

As the only world-wide affiliated boarding school in mainland China, a quality-oriented educationally advanced school in China, a grade-A model school in Zhejiang province, and one of "The most beautiful schools" in Hangzhou, nothing can stop us from constantly improving in warmth, safety, and dignity; both on campus and globally.

(Founded 2014)

Head of School Anne Fowles

PYP coordinator Aga Chojnacka

MYP coordinator Darryl Harding

DP coordinator Magnus Drechsler

CP coordinator Magnus Drechsler

Status Private

Boarding/day Day

Gender Coeducational

Language of instruction English

Authorised IB programmes PYP, MYP, DP, CP

Age Range 3 – 19

Address
Jalan Sierramas Utama
Sungai Buloh
Kuala Lumpur, Selangor
47000 | MALAYSIA

TEL +60 3 6145 4688

FAX +60 3 6145 4600

Email
enquiries@igbis.edu.my

Website
www.igbis.edu.my

IGB International School (IGBIS) is a vibrant Early Years to Grade 12 International Baccalaureate (IB) World School in Kuala Lumpur, Malaysia. The School has an Elementary School (ages 2-10), and a Secondary School (ages 11-19) serving more than 500 students.

In a diverse and inclusive learning community, students receive a challenging IB education which empowers them as caring global citizens to contribute to a flourishing Malaysia and a sustainable and peaceful global society.

Our team of internationally experienced IB educators are trained to deliver an innovative international education that inspires our students to be lifelong learners who aim to make a positive impact on the world. Our teachers and administrators are recruited worldwide for their expertise, commitment and international experience.

IGBIS is the only IB continuum school in Malaysia authorised for all four IB programmes: the Primary Years Programme, the Middle Years Programme, the Diploma Programme and the Career-related Programme. IB continuum schools share a common philosophy – a commitment to a high quality, stimulating international education for all students from Early Years to Grade 12, that IGBIS believes is important for its students.

The school offers two career-related streams through the CP, where students can study either accountancy through the Institute of Chartered Accountants in England and Wales (ICAEW), or undertake college-level art and design subjects through the Savannah College of Art and Design (SCAD).

Graduating students have consistently achieved outstanding results, scoring well above the world average on the IB Diploma, and achieving acceptances to prestigious universities including University of Cambridge, Imperial College London, University College London, Cornell, NUS Singapore and University of Edinburgh.

Through the curriculum, co-curriculum and after-school programmes, IGBIS offers a focus on sports, the visual and performing arts, languages, outdoor education and community service. This focus complements the school's commitment to providing students with a 21st Century learning environment by incorporating the latest information technology into classrooms, including an established digital platform, a one-to-one laptop programme in the secondary school, the latest touch-enabled devices throughout the whole school.

The 10-acre campus is located only 12 kilometres from central Kuala Lumpur, Malaysia. The outstanding facilities that provide students opportunities to explore their talents and interests, include a 50-metre Olympic-size swimming pool and a 25-metre learn-to-swim pool, an 8-lane 400-metre running track surrounding a FIFA-standard artificial turf football pitch, five visual arts studios and a multi-media art studio, purpose-built music and drama rooms, and a 520-seat state-of-the-art theatre.

The school is a member of the Association of International Malaysian Schools (AIMS), the East Asia Council of Schools (EARCOS) and is accredited with both the Council of International Schools (CIS) and the New England Association of Schools and Colleges (NEASC).

(Founded 1951)

Head of School
Dr. Andrew Davies

DP coordinator
Justyna McMilan

Status Private

Boarding/day Day

Gender Coeducational

Language of instruction
English

Authorised IB programmes
DP

Age Range 3 – 18

Number of pupils enrolled
1686

Fees
US$16,528 – US$30,034

Address
39/7 Soi Nichada Thani
Samakee Road, Pakkret
Nonthaburi
11120 | THAILAND

TEL +66 2 963 5800
FAX +66 2 583 5432

Email
admissions@isb.ac.th

Website
www.isb.ac.th

International School Bangkok (ISB), widely recognized as one of the world's leading international schools, was the first to be established in Thailand. Opened on the grounds of the U.S. Embassy in 1951, ISB has proudly provided a high-quality international education to students from over a hundred nationalities and is the pioneer International Baccalaureate school in Thailand.

ISB is a learning-focused, US-accredited, IB authorized, independent Pre-K to Grade 12 school offering a challenging international curriculum to a multicultural and multilingual student body of over 1,700 students from 60 different nationalities. Learning at ISB is informed by leading educational research and global best practice, incorporated into North American and International Baccalaureate Diploma frameworks.

ISB has long valued its globally-minded, inclusive and vibrant community and its strong culture of care. ISB is committed to encouraging students to follow their passions in academics, the arts, athletics, and many other areas both in and out of school. ISB maintains a constant focus on quality with respect to learning, faculty, leadership, professional development, and facilities.

ISB graduates attend colleges and universities around the world. ISB takes great pride in the accomplishments of thousands of alumni who are enriching our local and global communities.

Located in the safe and beautiful community of Nichada Thani, ISB's 15-hectare campus houses world-leading facilities purpose built to align with the multitude of subjects and activities on offer for students. These include state-of-the-art performance venues and studios, international standard sports facilities, fully-equipped science and design labs, innovative libraries and learning spaces, and cutting-edge technology integrated across the school.

Through outstanding teaching and learning, ISB inspires students to achieve their academic and personal potential; be passionate, reflective learners; become caring, global citizens, and lead active, healthy, balanced lives. ISB's vision is *to enrich communities through the intellectual, humanitarian and creative thoughts and actions of our learners*.

International School Brunei

Everyone Excels

(Founded 1964)

Executive Principal
Mrs. Laura Thomas

DP coordinator
Mrs. Jane Snell

Status Private/Not For Profit

Boarding/day Mixed

Gender Coeducational

Language of instruction
English

Authorised IB programmes
DP

Age Range 3 – 18 years

Number of pupils enrolled
1100

Fees
Day: S$17,340
Boarding: S$16,500 (5 days) – S$21,500 (7 days)

Address
Jalan Utama Salambigar
Kampong Sungai Hanching
Berakas 'B' BC2115 | **BRUNEI DARUSSALAM**

TEL +673 233 0608
FAX +673 233 7446

Email
admissionmgr@ac.isb.edu.bn
PreUniDept@ac.isb.edu.bn

Website
www.isb.edu.bn

International School Brunei (ISB) is a vibrant, friendly and internationally diverse school situated in a bespoke, eco-accredited campus nestled in rainforest in the heart of Borneo. Brunei and the ASEAN region offers an incredible range of extra-curricular and CAS opportunities. Through social action, community support and environmental projects our students develop into global citizens, ready to take on the world.

Modern teaching areas, excellent facilities, wonderful outdoor spaces and a family-oriented boarding facility help our committed and highly qualified staff to provide students with a warm and supportive environment where students of all abilities and backgrounds are inspired and challenged to achieve – in the classroom, on the sports field, in the creative and performing arts and across the wider community.

Proud to be an inclusive school, at ISB *Everyone Excels*. We value a broad-based, holistic curriculum driven by our school mission "Inspiring Minds, Shaping Values, Building Futures". We offer a wide range of subjects, designing customised packages where applicable, so that every student is celebrated as an individual. Excellent support from our Higher Education advisor means students achieve offers from top universities around the world and access a myriad of career pathways.

To enhance the IBDP core and embrace the IB Learner Profile attributes, our annual student-led Borneo Global Issues Conference (BGIC) is a highlight of the year. Run as a Model United Nations Conference, BGIC is a student led initiative welcoming more than 350 students from over 20 schools, offering students the opportunity to form local and regional links; interact with global experts and to develop awareness of different perspectives on issues affecting the local and global communities.

The unique combination of opportunity, challenge and care provided by ISB ensures that our students leave secure in the knowledge they are prepared for the challenges of university life and beyond.

International School Ho Chi Minh City (ISHCMC)

Head of School
Mr Adrian Watts

PYP coordinator
Nancy Snyder & Tania Mansfield

MYP coordinator
Simon Scoones

DP coordinator
Teresa Foard

Status Private

Boarding/day Day

Gender Coeducational

Language of instruction
English

Authorised IB programmes
PYP, MYP, DP

Age Range 2 – 18

Address
28 Vo Truong Toan St, An Phu
District 2
Ho Chi Minh City | **VIETNAM**

Secondary Campus
1 Xuan Thuy Street, Thao Dien, District 2, Ho Chi Minh City | **VIETNAM**

TEL +84 28 3898 9100

Email
admissions@ishcmc.edu.vn

Website
www.ishcmc.com

International School Ho Chi Minh City (ISHCMC) is the most established international school in Ho Chi Minh City. Students are taught through a progressive educational model set in modern learning environments. Educators are experienced and trained to facilitate the International Baccalaureate (IB) programmes, specializing in inquiry-led teaching. This, paired with international-standard safeguarding policies ensures that all children are safe and supported to reach their potential. ISHCMC students enjoy coming to school and inquire beyond knowledge taught in the classroom and develop life-long skills.

ISHCMC is proudly the first fully accredited IB World School in Ho Chi Minh City offering three IB Programmes (Primary Years Programme, Middle Years Programme and the IB Diploma) for all students.

Founded in 1993, ISHCMC has more than 1,450 students aged 2 to 18 years old representing over 55 nationalities. ISHCMC creates a Culture of Achievement where students are energized, engaged and empowered to become active participants in their communities. ISHCMC is inclusive and all students can pursue the full IB Diploma Programme. This is supported by ISHCMC now offering more secondary subject options than any other school in Ho Chi Minh City.

The Primary campus boasts world-class facilities such as an indoor gymnasium, a large 4.0 artificial grass field and numerous covered and uncovered hard surface play and sports areas. There are also facilities to help our students to become well-rounded, balanced individuals with a passion for learning in all its diverse forms such as information technology lab, a makerspace and an exclusive area for art.

In 2018, ISHCMC opened a new state-of-the-art Secondary campus for students 11 to 18 years old. The facility features Vietnam's first Innovation Centre for collaborative learning between students and the corporate sector, a 350-seat professional theater, Multi-purpose room, outdoor courts, rooftop sports field, and a 25 meter – 8 lanes competitive swimming pool.

International School of Islamabad

Superintendent
Ms Rose Puffer

Secondary Principal
Timothy Musgrove

Elementary Principal
Liz Abbasi

PYP coordinator
Mary Frances Penton

DP coordinator
Dora Flores

Status Private

Boarding/day Day

Gender Coeducational

Language of instruction
English

Authorised IB programmes
PYP, DP

Age Range 2 – 19

Number of pupils enrolled
280

Address
Sector H-9/1, Johar Road
P.O. Box 1124
Islamabad
44000 | PAKISTAN

TEL +92 51 443 4950
FAX +92 51 444 0193

Email
school@isoi.edu.pk;
registrar@isoi.edu.pk

Website
www.isoi.edu.pk

The International School of Islamabad (ISOI) is a private, coeducational, college-preparatory day school. ISOI offers an inquiry-based curriculum to students of thirty-two nationalities. The school operates on the semester system and is accredited by Middle States Association of Colleges and Schools. ISOI is an IB World School, offering the International Baccalaureate Diploma (IBDP) in grades 11/12. ISOI is also an IB PYP school. ISOI was founded in 1965. The campus is located on 23+ acres on the outskirts of Islamabad, Pakistan. The campus includes Elementary School, Middle School and High School quads, a gym, an auditorium, an open-air theater, an IB art gallery, a physical education center, tennis courts, a climbing wall, a running track, playing fields, a swimming pool, two library media centers and three technology centers. Students are admitted on the basis of previous academic records, standardized test scores, a writing sample and verification of the need for an international, English curriculum.

The school year runs from August to early June and is divided into two semesters. The first semester runs from August to December and the second semester runs from January to June. The school follows a two week, rotating block schedule.

Vision

The International School of Islamabad inspires open collaboration to create a student-centered, inquiry-based learning environment that cultivates enthusiastic and globally-minded individuals.

Mission

The International School of Islamabad ensures that each student strives for academic success, develops intellectual curiosity, and becomes a responsible global citizen.

International School of Nanshan Shenzhen

Head of School
David Swanson

DP Principal
Brian Kelley

MYP Principal
Chris Irvin

Upper PYP Principal
Ashley Simpson

Lower PYP Principal
Thomas Tucker

PYP coordinator
Blessy Monica & Jennifer Nicklas

MYP coordinator
Ernie Boyd

DP coordinator TBD

Status Private

Boarding/day Day

Gender Coeducational

Language of instruction
English

Authorised IB programmes
PYP, MYP, DP

Age Range 3 – 19

Fees
US$26,900 – US$32,000

Address
11 Longyuan Road
Taoyuan Sub-District, Nanshan District
Shenzhen
518052 | CHINA

TEL +86 755 2666 1000

Email admissions@isnsz.com

Website www.isnsz.com

Founded in 2002, through the foresight and partnership among the Government of Canada, the Province of New Brunswick, and Dr. Francis Pang, the International School of Nanshan Shenzhen (ISNS) is a leading IB World School providing quality education to students from age 3 to grade 12.

Unique to ISNS is our globally-relevant curriculum. ISNS is accredited by the Department of Education, New Brunswick Canada and is the first continuum IB World School in Shenzhen, China. ISNS is fully authorized across three programmes: Primary Years Programme (PYP), Middle Years Programme (MYP) and Diploma Programme (DP).

At ISNS, students have the opportunity to graduate with a New Brunswick diploma and an IB diploma. The School's education philosophy caters to developing globally responsible and compassionate citizens of the world by encouraging students to become active and inquiring life-long learners within an intercultural community.

The IB programme is renowned for its intentional design, rigorous academics and high standards. ISNS provides students with the tools to achieve excellence in academics, personal growth and success beyond the classroom.

Representing over 30+ different nationalities, the ISNS family values cultural diversity, fostering international-mindedness and independent thinking. ISNS encourages students to share their different perspectives and experiences while providing them with the opportunity to learn through a variety of cultural exchanges both locally and abroad.

ISNS strives to engage students with innovative technology as a vehicle for learning and ensure that our students are well prepared for a future that will be deeply immersed in technology. We explore new ideas and approaches to learning to meet the needs of all children and the demands of our ever-changing global environment.

With a state-of-the-art campus, ISNS is a place where students can learn in a nurturing and safe environment. A full outdoor track and field, playground, indoor gymnasium, and courts for basketball, volleyball and badminton provides a variety of spaces for Athletics, PE and Extracurricular programs. Indoor classrooms and laboratories are equipped with the latest technology for innovative lessons. Our library, music, media, art and dance rooms are fully equipped to add a creative and enriching dimension to each student's learning experience.

ISNS cultivates the whole child, fostering student growth in all areas so that they are inspired to pursue their own dreams as global leaders while taking with them a love of learning.

International School of Western Australia

(Founded 2005)

Principal
Maria Coate

PYP coordinator
Fleur Churton

MYP coordinator
Janice Murray

DP coordinator
Mini Balachandran

Status Private

Boarding/day Day

Gender Coeducational

Language of instruction
English

Authorised IB programmes
PYP, MYP, DP

Age Range 4 – 18

Number of pupils enrolled
350

Fees
Fees: Please see our website

Address
22 Kalinda Drive
City Beach
WA 6015 | AUSTRALIA

TEL +61 8 9285 1144
FAX +61 8 9285 1188

Email
info@iswa.wa.edu.au

Website
www.iswa.wa.edu.au

The International School of Western Australia (ISWA) is fast becoming a school of choice for both international and local Perth families looking for progressive education in a co-educational, non-denominational, boutique school environment. They support the growth and achievement of children from families who desire a unique boutique education that is characterized by an experience of excellence and student voice within an internationally-minded, open-minded and culturally-minded 21st century learning environment.

Topics are studied with both a local and global perspective. ISWA offers the outstanding International Baccalaureate program in all year levels, from K-12. The IB approach to learning is: inquiry-based; concept-based and transdisciplinary. The emphasis is on curiosity, creativity, critical thinking and community service, and on creating well-rounded, independent, engaged individuals.

Amongst the strengths of ISWA's academic approach is the ability to nurture students from a wide variety of backgrounds, with a wide range of learning styles, in a safe, encouraging learning environment. ISWA takes pride in their academic rigor and strong academic results, which are achieved in a relaxed, friendly atmosphere. As part of their transdisciplinary approach, a key focus is developing students as well-rounded individuals. There is an emphasis on language learning, with students spending the same amount of time studying a second language as they do their other core subjects. With so much extra time spent on immersion-based language learning, ISWA students graduate with real second language skills, a valuable asset that they will use throughout their lives.

As IB educators, ISWA understands that examinations do not always accurately measure the true abilities of children. ISWA's progressive system of assessment helps all children maximize their potential. This belief is echoed in ISWA's scholarships program. While strong academic performance is imperative for scholarship recipients, ISWA scholarship students must also be well-rounded. That is why ISWA never asks prospective scholarship recipients to sit an exam, which only ever measure a student's performance in a specific circumstance on one day. Instead, ISWA scholarships are evaluated on ePortfolios, past academic transcripts, examples of leadership and community service, and face-to-face interviews. This helps ISWA award scholarships to students who will thrive in this unique school.

ISWA offers further education academic pathways that are unique in Perth. ISWA is the only school in Western Australia that enables senior school students the choice between studying for the International Baccalaureate Diploma, or the U.S. College Board Advanced Placement courses, whilst also delivering the requirements of the Western Australian curriculum. Successful completion of these rigorous academic pathways opens up the opportunity of university study at prestigious and specialist higher education institutions across the globe.

The ISWA school community plays a particularly

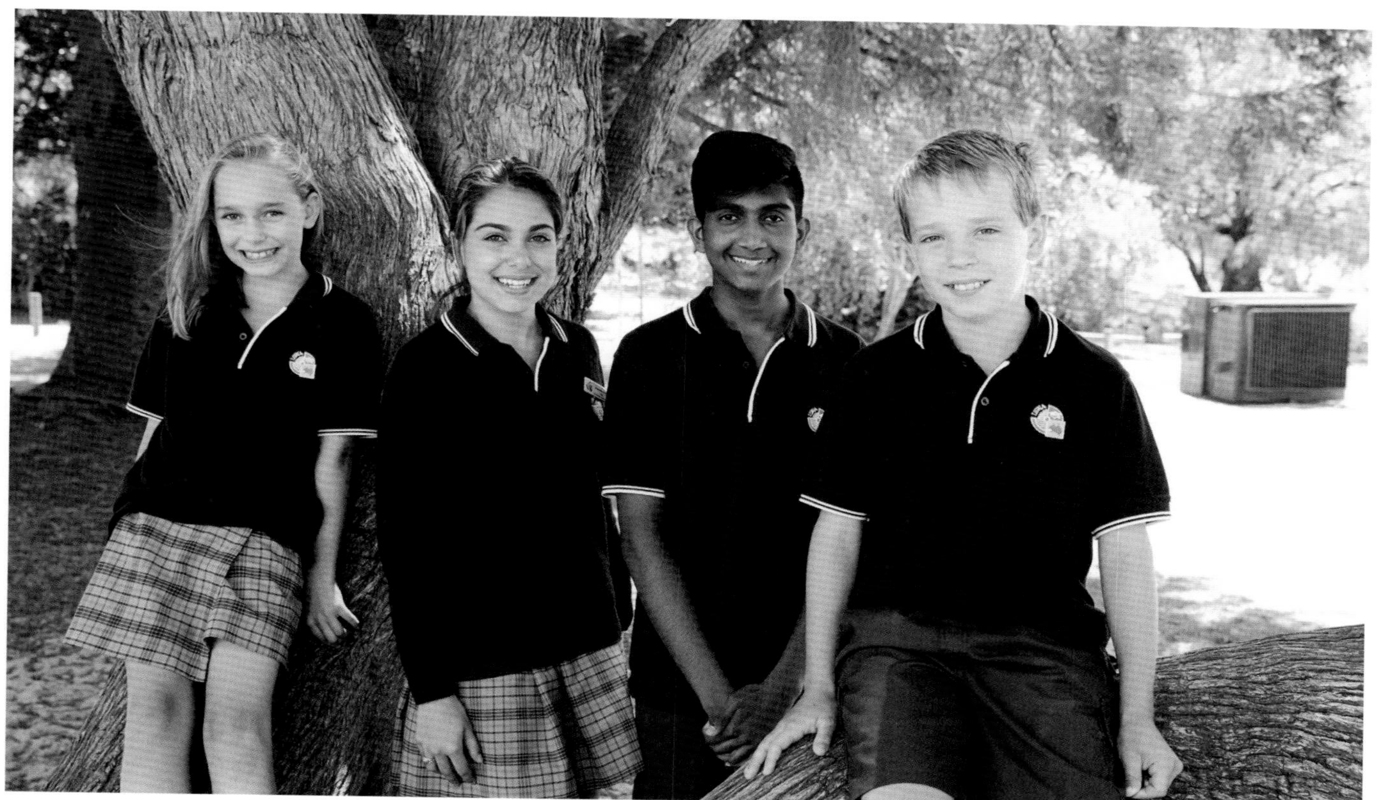

important role in the lives of students and their families. An inclusive, welcoming school community and active Parent Association have numerous strategies in place to ensure newcomers are welcomed and settle quickly and happily into their new Perth lifestyle. This welcome is not exclusive to ISWA's international families. Due to the egalitarian, open-minded and progressive nature of the school community, local students who did not fit into their mainstream Perth school structure find their place at ISWA; often for the first time ever in a school environment, they find they belong. The family atmosphere of our campus is enhanced by our co-educational K-12 campus, where vertical age interactions are facilitated and encouraged. The connectedness between primary, middle and secondary school, between staff and pupils, and school and parents is at the core of ISWA's holistic approach to education. Due to these unique benefits, ISWA has a growing community of local Western Australian families at the school. These families enjoy the world-class education that ISWA offers. Local families are also able to take advantage of significant reductions in school fees. ISWA is a wonderful community made up of caring, highly qualified and experienced teachers, supportive parents and very happy students.

Founder & Chairperson
Pinky Dalal

Managing Director
Kunal Dalal

DP coordinator
Sergio J. Chiri (Parel)
Ana Dominguez (Oshiwara)

Status Private

Boarding/day Day

Gender Coeducational

Language of instruction
English

Authorised IB programmes
DP

Age Range 3 – 18

Parel Campus
Yogi Mansion, CTS No. 244, Dr Vinay Walimbe Road
Off Dr S.S. Rao Marg, Parel East
Mumbai, Maharashtra
400012 | INDIA

Oshiwara Campus
Survey No. 41, CTS No. 1, Off Andheri Link Road, Behind Tarapore Towers, Mhada Colony, Oshiwara, Andheri West,
Mumbai, Maharashtra
400058 | INDIA

TEL +91 22 24114626

Email
enquiry@jbcnschool.edu.in

Website
www.jbcnschool.edu.in

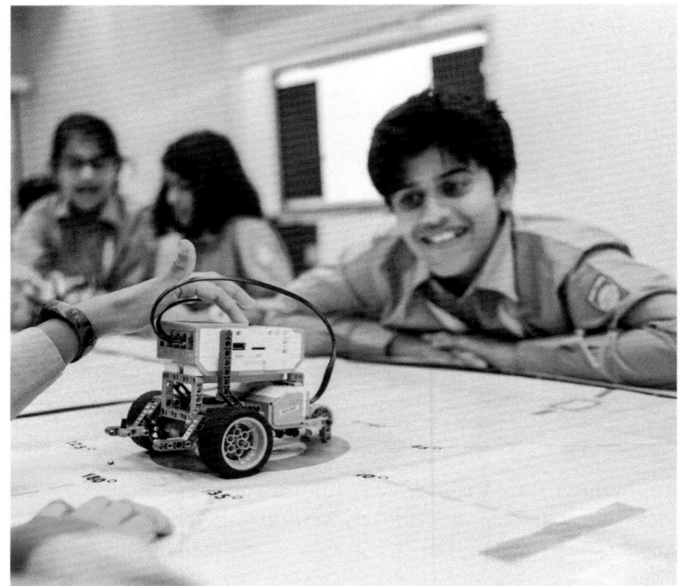

JBCN International School, Mumbai

JBCN International School is a co-ed school located in Mumbai, India offering a progressive education programme for learners from Kindergarten to Grade XII. Founded in 2009, JBCN now operates across 4 campuses in Mumbai. With over 4,000 learners and 450 faculty members across the campuses, JBCN International School's uniqueness shows itself through its innovative pedagogy, adoption of sustainable practices and developing future ready skills through a dynamic curriculum delivered in the classroom each day.

The JBCN Philosophy: Why Educate, When You Can EduCreate

The EduCreative experience at JBCN International School comprises a gamut of challenging engagements and programmes, which along with a programme of academic excellence, facilitate the development of the "Mind-Body-Soul" of each learner.

International Baccalaureate Programme at JBCN

The JBCN schools at Parel and Oshiwara are affiliated with the IB Diploma Programme and are PYP candidate schools. In addition to providing a well designed curriculum through a variety of teaching-learning methodologies, learning at JBCN International Schools is further fortified through:

Global Affiliations: Learners engage with students, faculty and guest speakers from across the world. An Entrepreneurship Programme by Columbia Business School through Venture for all and certified courses in Design Thinking, Data Analytics, Persuasive Communication, Mindfulness, Robotics, Leadership etc add to the holistic development of JBCN learners.

iPROPEL: This unique programme comprises multiple skill-based programmes. Broadly classified as performing arts, research and reasoning, outreach, physical fitness, experiential learning and leadership skills, every component of the programme is age-appropriate and further augments the curriculum.

Events and Initiatives: Events such as intra-school MUN, theatre carnival, JBCN Radio, InsiprUs, the Innovators' Convention and more, bring to the fore the skills the learners have acquired.

InspirUs is a multi day event spanning a host of activities classified under four broad quadrants: Artistic, Athletic, Cerebral and Expressive, that aims to provide one of the largest ever platforms for the learners to showcase their passion and talents.

Innovators Convention celebrates the spirit of innovation and opens new arenas for the learners to explore, experiment and design solutions for real life problems/needs.

Through a range of CAS activities such as fund raising, providing amenities and building homes in rural areas etc, learners bring about quantifiable changes in the world.

Career Counselling: An in-house Career Counselling Unit guides learners through subject, course and campus selection. They organize planned visits to universities in India and abroad, as well as opportunities for exchange programmes.

These are just few of the highlights of the IB programme at JBCN International School.

John Wollaston Anglican Community School

(Founded 1989)

Principal
Ms Anne Ford

PYP coordinator
Mrs Fiona Currey

Status Private, Independent

Boarding/day Day

Gender Coeducational

Language of instruction
English

Authorised IB programmes
PYP

Age Range 3 – 18

Number of pupils enrolled
900

Fees
Please see website

Address
Centre Road
Camillo
WA 6111 | AUSTRALIA

TEL +61 (08) 9495 8100

Email
mail@jwacs.wa.edu.au

Website
www.jwacs.wa.edu.au

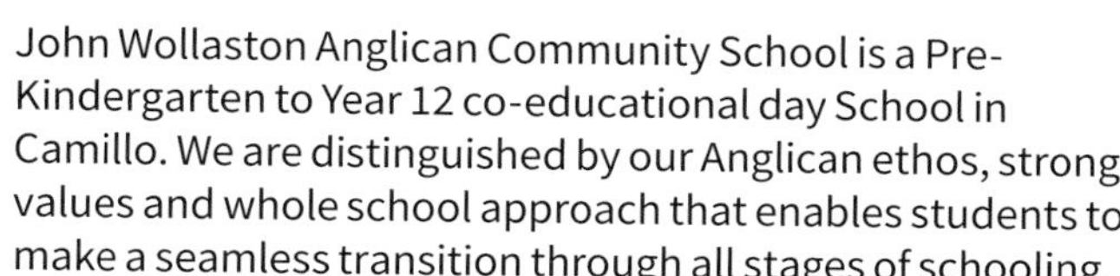

John Wollaston Anglican Community School is a Pre-Kindergarten to Year 12 co-educational day School in Camillo. We are distinguished by our Anglican ethos, strong values and whole school approach that enables students to make a seamless transition through all stages of schooling.

We are a World School of the International Baccalaureate Primary Years Programme with a strong academic and pastoral reputation.

Our established *'Bright Future Positive Education Model'* forms the framework of the pastoral approach at John Wollaston. We believe character development is as important as academic progress. Our pastoral strategies are designed to embed social and emotional learning across all age groups. Wellbeing at John Wollaston is comprised of six elements that underpin the School's *'Bright Futures'* concept of flourishing; positive emotions, engagement, relationships, purpose, health and achievement.

At John Wollaston we develop the whole person through Service Learning and Encounter experiences which facilitate character development and personal growth.

The School has differentiated programs for the gifted and those who require learning support and there are many co-curricular clubs and activities which encompass sport, artistic and cultural pursuits.

The IB Primary Years Programme culminates with the Year 6 PYP Exhibition in which students interrogate a central idea to showcase the depth and breadth of their learning.

In the Secondary School students are exposed to Harvard Graduate School of Education's Project Zero, Cultures of Thinking. Cultures of Thinking focus on the development of both the individual and the group as effective learners and thinkers able to engage with and adapt to a changing world.

Secondary students have the choice to follow an ATAR or Vocational Education and Training pathway. Students undertaking an ATAR pathway are offered a full complement of subjects. The Vocational Education and Training pathway offers Certificate courses and workplace learning experiences to prepare for the real world beyond school.

John Wollaston graduates leave with a strong foundation for life, valuing personal best and possessing integrity and compassion. A bright future awaits.

(Founded 1997)

Principal
Nicholas Sheehan BSc. Geography, PGCE

DP coordinator
Dr Colin Dickinson

Status Private

Boarding/day Mixed

Gender Coeducational

Language of instruction
English

Authorised IB programmes
DP

Age Range 2 – 18 years (Boarding from 11)

Number of pupils enrolled
1663

Fees
Day: B$18,108 – B$26,952
Weekly Boarding: B$17,688 – B$23,500
Boarding: B$23,688 – B$29,500

Address
Jalan Universiti
Kampong Tungku
Bandar Seri Begawan
BE2119 | BRUNEI DARUSSALAM

TEL +673 241 1000

FAX +673 241 1010

Email enrol@jis.edu.bn

Website www.jerudonginternationalschool.com

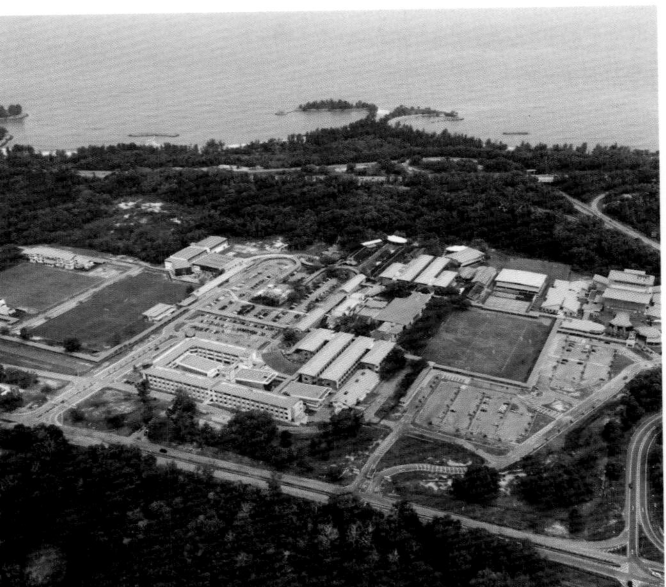

In January 2019, Jerudong International School, an IB World School, became the first international school in the world to achieve the highest rating in all 9 areas inspected by the British Schools Overseas (BSO) inspectorate. These are:

- Quality of Education provided
- Spiritual, moral, social and cultural development of pupils
- Welfare, health and safety of pupils
- Suitability of proprietor and staff
- Premises and accommodation
- Provision of information to parents, carers and others
- Manner in which complaints are handled
- Quality of leadership in and management of schools
- Minimum standards for boarding

When parents and students first visit our lovely school, they always say "We knew it would be special but we weren't expecting this" Why not come and see for yourself?

Founded in 1997, we are located in South East Asia, in the small, country of Brunei, on the island of Borneo. A direct flight from major regional hubs including Beijing, Shanghai, Singapore, Bangkok, Jakarta, Kuala Lumpur, it is easy to access, making it an ideal school of choice for parents seeking an outstanding school in a safe, secure environment.

JIS is an IB World School; a British School Overseas (BSO), an international HMC School and recognised by the prestigious Good Schools Guide. A leading member of the Federation of British Schools in Asia (FOBISIA), Council of British International Schools (COBIS).

The school is a thriving community with 1663 students from 55 countries (40% Bruneian), 3-18 years in age. 196 Boarders form a close community in bespoke accommodation, on campus. The School aims are: Communication, Engagement, Integration, Leadership, Resilience and Thinking. Students are encouraged to Challenge Yourself, Respect Others and Inspire Change.

The IB Diploma Programme at JIS

The 95 IBDP Students study in small classes (5-15 students) with up to 21 subjects on offer across the six IB Group areas. Theory of Knowledge (TOK) is taught in lectures, small group discussions and supplemented by lunchtime lectures from outside speakers, staff and students. The IBDP programme at JIS is a student centred programme designed to enable students to be actively engaged in academic subjects but also thoroughly grounded in world events so they can really make a difference.

Outstanding IB Diploma Results

In 2019, JIS IB students' average score was 36. World Average IB Score was 29.8; 94% of JIS students exceeded the world average. The highest score achieved was 44 points (going to University of Cambridge, UK). 36% of JIS IB Diploma students achieved 40 points or more. These results are consistent and build upon the results of the past 8 years.

University Destinations

A specialist team of Higher Education advisors guide and prepare students for ACTs, SATS, IELTS and University applications. 2019 graduate destinations include UK – Cambridge, Imperial College, King's College, Durham University. USA – Brown University.

CANADA – University of Toronto, University of British Columbia. AUSTRALIA – Melbourne. IB Diploma students also received a number of Scholarships.

Teaching Staff

JIS has almost 200 highly qualified teachers primarily from the UK but also a small number from Australia, New Zealand, South Africa. Our language teachers are native language speakers from China, France and Brunei. The IBDP is staffed by experienced academic teachers.

Pastoral Care

All students and teachers in the School are members of a House (a community of about 70 students) which plays a vital role in establishing and maintaining a strong school spirit and enabling leadership opportunities. The 16 Houses in Senior School, named after birds in Borneo, provide leadership, mentoring and teamwork opportunities. Weekly House sports competitions and other House Events including House Debates, House Music, JIS has Talent and Spelling Bees in addition to House social events are highlights.

The Campus

The 120 acre single campus is 'Outstanding'. The purpose-built, fully WiFi and ICT networked school facility is located near the coast – a 15 minute drive from the airport. Students can use the Arts Centre (725 seat theatre, dance studio, black box theatre and rehearsal rooms), 27 science laboratories, extensive music faculty, art, design and technology and textile studios, libraries and traditional classrooms as well as the 2 swimming pools (50m and 25m), 3 large air-conditioned Sports Halls, outdoor netball/basketball and tennis courts and 3 soccer/rugby pitches. A well-equipped medical centre is on site to take care of students. An award winning Outdoor Discovery Centre – an eco-forestry initiative on tropical heathland on the campus is regularly used for activities and also as an Outdoor Classroom learning space.

Boarding facilities

The recently inspected and accredited 'outstanding' Boarding facilities for students age 11 years + are purpose designed and built for the community of boarders. 196 girls and boys presently enjoy separate Boarding Houses cared for by experienced staff. The Boarding Housemaster or Housemistresses are all teachers in the School. Boarders can also use the school facilities. A programme of weekend activities is arranged for the boarders to fully embrace the wonderful environment of Brunei. A special partnership exists between the boarding staff and a student's family with mutual trust at the heart of the relationship between home and school.

Co-curricular Programme

Creativity, Activity and Service (CAS) builds on an extensive co-curricular programme with over 300 activities including a mature International Award programme, Model United Nations (MUN), ECO JIS, Diving, Sports and Performing Arts programmes. Students are involved in projects locally; also Malaysia, Cambodia, Vietnam and China.

Head of School
Mr Shane Hogan

Acting DP coordinator
Megan Armstrong

Status Private

Boarding/day Mixed

Gender Female

Language of instruction
English

Authorised IB programmes
DP

Number of pupils enrolled
1000

Address
794 New South Head Road
Rose Bay
Sydney
NSW 2029 | AUSTRALIA

TEL +612 93886777

Email
enrolments@
kambala.nsw.edu.au

Website
www.kambala.nsw.edu.au

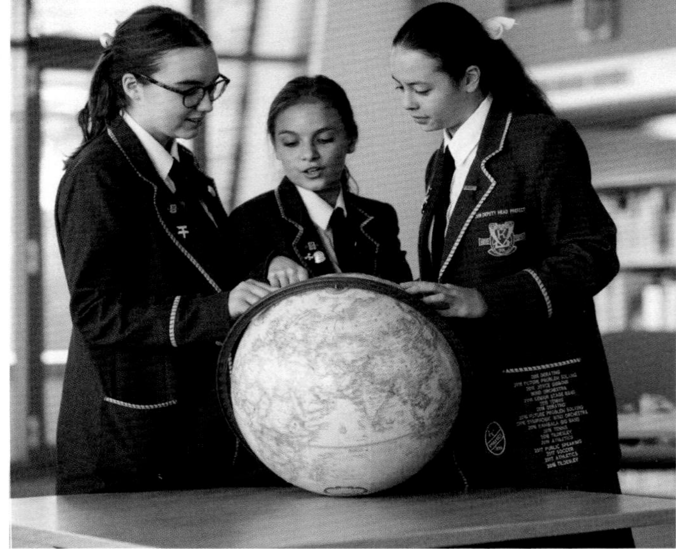

Authorised as an International Baccalaureate World School since 2010, Kambala is the first independent girls' school in Sydney's Eastern Suburbs to offer the IB. The Kambala girl, her care and academic development is at the heart of the School's Strategic Vision. With academic curiosity and a compassionate constitution, she is both self-aware and prepared to make a difference in the world. Kambala believes in raising women equipped to embrace and achieve their personal successes. This vision complements the aim of the IB Diploma Programme: to develop students who flourish physically, intellectually, emotionally and ethically.

Kambala's reputation as a leader of girls' education, enhanced by the exceptional results of its IB students, is a testament to the expertise of the staff and to the students' academic engagement and commitment. Kambala's academic success is complemented by its broad cultural extra curricular program and focus on charity that facilitates IB students' participation in the 'creativity, activity and service' components of the IB Diploma Programme. Kambala's large lawns and courtyard areas, grassy oval and tennis courts, are situated against the panoramic backdrop of iconic Sydney Harbour. Other facilities include flexible learning spaces, an indoor swimming pool and specialist learning areas for Music, Visual Arts, Science and various technological subjects.

Kambala's onsite boarding houses provide a nurturing and supportive communal family environment for 90 girls. Years 7 to 9 boarders occupy the beautiful heritage-listed Tivoli House, while Years 10 to 12 boarders enjoy the greater privacy, independence and social privileges of purpose-built Fernbank building. To assist boarders to structure their time in a positive way and to develop and maintain productive study habits, Kambala employs in-house tutors to work with girls on homework each evening. Technology enables parents who are not based in Sydney to have greater personal involvement with their daughter's learning, including three-way Skype sessions with the student and her teachers. The shared experience of boarding creates a strong network of friends and a feeling of community that lasts for life.

For further information contact Mrs Tracy Mulligan, Director of Enrolments, at +61 02 9388 6844 or email enrolments@kambala.nsw.edu.au.

Kardinia International College

Principal
Mrs Catherine Lockhart

PYP coordinator
Geoff Geddes

DP coordinator
Dianne Vella

Status Private

Boarding/day Day

Gender Coeducational

Language of instruction
English

Authorised IB programmes
PYP, DP

Age Range 3 – 18

Address
29-31 Kardinia Drive
Bell Post Hill
Geelong
VIC 3215 | AUSTRALIA

TEL +61 3 5278 9999
FAX +61 3 5278 9529

Email
kardinia@kardinia.vic.edu.au

Website
www.kardinia.vic.edu.au

For more than 20 years, Kardinia International College has focused on the ideal of international understanding. The College was established as a symbol of hope for the world by being a place of quality and exceptional personal development, where people from every corner of the earth feel welcome and at home.

One of our aims is educating our students to a profound sense of internationalism. Graduates of Kardinia, live in a global village. An understanding and deep respect of all other cultures is an essential characteristic of leaders and productive citizens of the 21st Century.

The College is independent, coeducational and non-denominational, providing a caring environment for 1900 day and international students from Kindergarten-Year 12.

As an IB World school, we offer the Primary Years Programme (PYP) in Kindergarten-6, a vertical curriculum based on the guidelines of the Victorian Curriculum and Assessment Authority to students in Years 7-10 and both the International Baccalaureate Diploma Programme (IB) and the Victorian Certificate of Education (VCE) in Years 11 and 12.

In the Senior School, the vertical curriculum offers advantages, as students' progress at a rate appropriate to their ability. Able students can fast track subjects, while other students can allow extra time for consolidation. Some students complete the IB Diploma or VCE in five years, most in six. An extensive range of VCE and IB subjects are available.

The Senior School curriculum is further strengthened by our International Immersion Programs. Our Year 9 students can join our positive, life changing eight-week Chiang Mai program in Thailand. Students can also visit our sister schools; Gotemba Nishi High in Japan, Saint Alyre in France and Discovery College in Hong Kong.

Our world class facilities include; Katsumata Centre – our 1500 seat theatre and gymnasium, Goodfellow Aquatic Centre, a 25-metre indoor pool and cafe, School of Performing Arts, Learning Commons, Six ovals, six tennis courts, a 1560 seat outdoor Amphitheatre and much more. Our main, 22-hectare campus is in Geelong, our Year 5, 11-hectare farm campus in Lovely Banks and our 2.5-hectare campus in Chiang Mai, Thailand.

The emphasis at every year level at Kardinia International College is on academic rigour and we are renowned for the outstanding results our students achieve in Year 12 examinations every year. Integral to our success is that we encourage and expect positive student attitudes, understanding and actions towards each other, our community and the wider global environment.

(Founded 1998)

Head of School
Paul Johnson

PYP coordinator
Kirsten Durward

MYP coordinator
Alison Ya-Wen Yang

DP coordinator
Daniel Trump

Status Private

Boarding/day Day

Gender Coeducational

Language of instruction
English

Authorised IB programmes
PYP, MYP, DP

Age Range 3 – 18

Number of pupils enrolled
800

Fees
Baht363,000 – Baht765,000

Address
999/123-124 Pracha Utit Road
Samsennok, Huay Kwang
Bangkok
10310 | THAILAND

TEL +66 (0)2 2743444
FAX +66 (0)2 2743452

Email
admissions@kis.ac.th

Website
www.kis.ac.th

KIS's vision is Inspiring Individuals!
The community of KIS International School in Bangkok aims to inspire students to challenge themselves to become better people, who in turn become inspiring individuals who help make the world become a better place.

The school was founded in 1998 as one of the first full IB Schools in Thailand, offering the PYP, the MYP and the DP.

As a mid-sized school with around 800 students from 55 different countries, the atmosphere at KIS is one of the school's great strengths. Students and parents quickly feel at home and develop a sense of pride in their school. KIS's excellent teacher to student ratios mean there is individual attention for each student and openness to creative and progressive ideas.

Students at KIS have a positive attitude to learning, as they are encouraged and nurtured by a group of vibrant, highly qualified, IB trained, supportive and, above all, exceptional educators. The school supports the learning of many languages, with between 10-20 different languages taught at KIS at any time.

The programmes are well-balanced and not only engage our students with a world perspective in the humanities, languages, mathematics, the arts, technology and the sciences, but there is also a strong focus on contributing to the community. The wide range of extracurricular activities further allows students to develop their interests and skills outside of the classroom. Activities include arts and crafts, technology and robotics, games, dance, competitive sports, non-competitive sports, leadership programmes, Model United Nations, and entrepreneurial activities.

Academic results are strong. KIS MYP students have top level results on the MYP Personal Project. KIS DP students have consistent high Diploma pass rates and high average scores, which have paved the way for KIS graduates to enter top universities around the world.

The green, spacious campus with excellent facilities is situated in a gated and guarded housing estate, near the city centre, providing a fine learning environment away from the noise and pollution while being easily accessible from both central Bangkok and the suburbs.

We invite you to visit KIS and discover the Knowledge, Inspiration and Spirit!

Kororoit Creek Primary School

Head of School
Bethany Riseley

PYP coordinator
Sarah Afiouni

Status State

Boarding/day Day

Gender Coeducational

Language of instruction
English

Authorised IB programmes
PYP

Age Range 3 – 12

Number of pupils enrolled
1600

Address
130 Tenterfield Drive
Burnside Heights
VIC 3023 | AUSTRALIA

TEL +61 3 8358 0600
FAX +61 3 8358 0699

Email
kororoit.creek.ps@edumail.vic.gov.au

Website
www.kororoitcreekps.vic.edu.au

Kororoit Creek Primary School is a fully authorized PYP school, catering for 3-12-year olds. The school is in Public-Private Partnership, maintained and operated through a connection of government and private sector companies. Established in a high growth area, the school has grown from 260 students in 2011 to over 1600 in 2020. We pride ourselves on being a true representation of our community, with over 50 languages and cultural backgrounds.

The school implements the PYP framework underpinned by the Victorian Curriculum, a transdisciplinary curriculum outlining the key outcomes and expectations of the Victorian Government. The curriculum supports us to unpack the Essential Elements using explicit Scope and Sequence documents, ensuring all students are working within their Zone of Proximal Development.

Being a PYP school, we have a major focus on documented curriculum, assessment and shared pedagogical approaches. We also have a major emphasis on evidence-based school improvement strategies. These strategies include the moderation of common student assessment tasks, data collection and analysis as well as evaluation of student learning growth over time. Timely and effective feedback to its community of learners underpins every student's personal learning goals. Teacher professional practice activities are rigorous and differentiated.

With a whole school approach to health, wellbeing, inclusion and engagement, KCPS supports strong community values that underpin its safe and orderly learning environment. These contribute directly to the school's positive standing and high reputation within the immediate and broader area.

Kodaikanal International School

(Founded 1901)

Principal
Corleigh Robert Stixrud

PYP coordinator
Pearlin Joseph

MYP coordinator
Graham Lambert

DP coordinator
Kurian Alex

Status Private

Boarding/day Mixed

Gender Coeducational

Language of instruction
English

Authorised IB programmes
PYP, MYP, DP

Age Range 3 – 18

Number of pupils enrolled
457

Fees
K-8: US$19,900
Grades 9-10: US$21,000
Grades 11-12: US$21,800

Address
PO Box 25
Seven Roads Junction
Kodaikanal, Tamil Nadu
624101 | INDIA

TEL +91 4542 247500

Email
principal@kis.in

Website
www.kis.in

Education with a global perspective
Kodaikanal International School (KIS) is an autonomous, international, residential school located in South India offering education for Grades K-12. With a rich heritage spanning over a century since its establishment in 1901, KIS has been serving young people from diverse cultures and backgrounds to become leaders the world needs. We do this through a rigorous and broad college-oriented IB curriculum that emphasizes deep learning and critical thinking and celebrates the arts, music, sports, social justice, and environmental awareness.

Key milestones include a number of 'firsts' – from when we became the first IB school, first international school in India (and the third in Asia) by adopting the International Baccalaureate Diploma Programme in 1976, at the time among only nine other schools worldwide; to when we became the first school in India to have its own separate campus for camping and outdoor activities in 1994. At the heart of the programs is a balanced approach catering to the student's passions, strengths and academic requirements.

International community living
The school's student community consists of over 450 children, representing around 25 countries. Our greatest strength lies in our learning as a community – living together in an assortment of cultures, distinct faiths and varied experiences spanning the globe. We provide a wide range of opportunities to our students to be citizens of the world – from student exchange programs to providing a platform to practice and exercise their leadership capabilities in our local community through our social and environmental programs. Our students also participate in a variety of national and international experiences such as the Model United Nations, other multidisciplinary exchanges, conferences and competitions.

Qualified for life
As the first school in India and the second in Asia to offer the IB Diploma, KIS has an outstanding 40+ year track record of consistently scoring above the world average. Students can earn the IB Diploma by passing at least six examinations in prescribed subject areas: three must be at a Higher Level and three at a Standard Level. IB examination papers are set and marked externally by members of the IB and experts around the world.

The evaluation of the IB includes a mini thesis and a recorded presentation of the topic. The school also provides a bilingual option of undertaking the IB Diploma that allows for international students to pursue and complete the diploma at KIS. Apart from core subjects, students are encouraged to complete courses in Religious Education, Sports & Health, Fine and Practical Arts, Computer Education and Community Service.

Beyond the classroom
With a range of extensive student exchange programs the school provides the opportunity to be citizens of the world. The programs develop students academically and nurtures them into resilient and culturally competent personalities,

enabling them to contribute positively in the communities they are established in. Critical thinking, ethical decision making and emotionally intelligent human beings are hallmarks of a KIS graduate.

Extracurricular programs have been designed for students to contribute positively to the local community and sustaining the natural environment. Initiatives are aimed at blending the classroom teaching program with a variety of community-oriented activities providing students with abundant opportunities for enriching personal growth, enhanced civic awareness and a progressive global outlook in line with the KIS vision and mission.

Our unique location and the natural beauty of Kodaikanal, a hill station nestled in the Palani Hills at 7000 feet above sea level, provides our students with an unparalleled experience of the environment and extraordinary adventures with nature. Hiking and Camping has been a staple feature of the KIS education since 1991 and provides students the opportunity to explore the natural beauty of the Western Ghats. The school's 100-acre off-campus camping property, gives students an opportunity to raft, canoe, swim, explore archery, zipline, and enjoy the different climbing facilities.

Musical excellence is a hallmark of the KIS education and our alumni include a host of distinguished composers and professional musicians. In addition to the regular curricular music offerings, KIS offers IB Music to IB Diploma students and annually presents students for Royal Schools of Music

(RSM), London examinations in Music, Practical and Theory which are held on campus.

With infrastructure to support up to 8 different sports, KIS provides an opportunity for learning the fundamentals, rules and strategies for the sport of choice. The sports curriculum provides a broad understanding for individuals through physical activities with a strong emphasis on the relationship between the physical, intellectual and emotional well-being.

(Founded 1978)

Headmaster
Mr Mark Wilson

PYP coordinator
Mr Rob Hutton

MYP coordinator
Mr John Osborne

DP coordinator
Mrs Debbie Dwyer

Status Private

Boarding/day Day (with accommodation options)

Gender Co-educational

Language of instruction
English

Authorised IB programmes
PYP, MYP, DP

Age Range 6 months – 18 years

Number of pupils enrolled
1650

Address
360 Albany Highway
Albany, Auckland 0752
NEW ZEALAND

TEL +64 9 415 9566

Email
admissions@kristin.school.nz

Website
www.kristin.school.nz

Kristin School is an independent, modern, co-educational International Baccalaureate (IB) World School located in Albany, Auckland with approximately 1650 students aged from six months to 18 years old. Established in 1978, Kristin is non-denominational and welcomes students from all cultures and backgrounds.

All learning environments share the same 50-acre, park-like campus: Little Doves Early Learning Centre, Kristin Kindergarten, Kristin Junior School (for 5-10 year olds), Kristin Middle School (for 10-15 year olds) and Kristin Senior School (for 15-18 year olds).

Kristin was the first IB World School in New Zealand offering the IB Diploma Programme since 1986, and the first school to offer the IB Primary Years Programme, IB Middle Years Programme and IB Diploma Programme catering for students from Year 0-13.

Our small class sizes are critical in providing personalised learning opportunities, and a balanced education at Kristin goes beyond providing a positive school culture. We ensure students are taught skills that will enhance their wellbeing, help them cope with life's challenges, strengthen their relationships with others and enable them to pursue a happy, healthy and prosperous life.

In summary, Kristin offers a:

- Modern, multicultural, co-educational, non-denominational environment with traditional values
- Proud record of high academic results and scholarships being awarded locally and internationally
- Team of quality teachers and support staff under the leadership of an inspiring and innovative Executive Principal
- Focus on student well-being and developing future-ready citizens
- Choice between national NCEA or IB Diploma Programme curriculum options for senior students
- Nationally acclaimed performing arts programme
- Vast range of community service and leadership opportunities
- 29 different popular and niche sporting codes
- Experiential Learning through a wide array of trips and exchanges
- 50-acre, park-like campus and extensive facilities
- Dedicated bus service travelling 20 routes across Auckland

For all admission enquiries, please visit kristin.school.nz or call our Admissions Manager on +64 9415 9566 ext 2324. We look forward to sharing more information with you to help show why Kristin School is the right choice for your child.

LÉMAN CHENGDU
INTERNATIONAL SCHOOL
A NORD ANGLIA EDUCATION SCHOOL

Principal
Tom Ferguson

DP coordinator
James Sutcliffe

Status Private

Boarding/day Day

Gender Coeducational

Language of instruction
English

Authorised IB programmes
DP

Age Range 3 – 18 years

Number of pupils enrolled
500

Fees
Day: RMB124,000 – RMB237,000

Address
No.1080 Da'an Road,
Zheng Xing County
Tianfu New Area
Chengdu, Sichuan
610218 | CHINA

TEL +86 28 6703 8650
FAX +86 28 6703 8630

Email
admissions@lis-chengdu.com

Website
www.lis-chengdu.com

Léman International School Chengdu (LIS) opened in the fall of 2009. Our school serves the pre-kindergarten to children of expatriate families from age 3 to 18 years in a Pre-kindergarten to Grade 12 program. Our purpose built campus occupies 50 acres (20 hectares) in the Tianfu New Area of Chengdu and has capacity for approximately 1,000 students.

Léman International School is part of the Nord Anglia Education (NAE) group which is the world's leading premium school organization with 66 international schools, boarding schools and private schools around the world. LIS students benefit from the Juilliard Performing Arts Programme and the STEAM programme which are the collaborations between NAE, Juilliard School and MIT. They may also work with over 64,000 NAE students through in school, online and worldwide opportunities with Global Campus.

Léman boasts world class facilities on an extensive campus. These include fully equipped modern classrooms, science laboratories, an art studio, music studio, I.T. rooms, gymnasium, 25 meter indoor swimming pool and large outdoor sports facilities.

Our student body represents more than 30 nationalities and the school provides an international curriculum with the commitment to support students return to their home country. The Primary School curriculum is based on the International Primary Curriculum (IPC), currently provided in 1,000 schools in 65 countries. The grade 6 to 10 utilizes the IB Middle Years Programme (MYP). LIS is an IB World School and offers the IB Diploma Programme for students in Grade 11 and 12.

LIS is committed to the provision of an exceptional education for all of its students. To that end, all teachers are fully qualified, experienced and most have worked in other international schools. The school is fully accredited by the Council of International Schools (CIS) and the New England Association of Schools and Colleges (NEASC).

Visit our website www.lis-chengdu.com and the Nord Anglia Education website www.nordangliaeducation.com for more information.

(Founded 2005)

Senior Principal
Dr. Bhavanishankar Subramanian MA, MS, MSc, M.Phil, PhD, PGDT, Dip. Russian, CAE

DP coordinator
Murali J

Status Private

Boarding/day Mixed

Gender Coeducational

Language of instruction
English

Authorised IB programmes
DP

Age Range 3 – 18

Number of pupils enrolled
4252

Fees
Day: INR360,000
Boarding: INR175,000

Address
79, Omega School Road
(Pallavaram Road)
Kolapakkam, Kovur Post
Chennai, Tamil Nadu
600128 | INDIA

TEL +91 44 66241127

Email
info@omegaschools.org

Website
www.omegaschools.org

Lalaji Memorial Omega International School Chennai, set in a serene and green 22 acre campus, provides a unique environment for both day-scholars and boarders. We are one of the few schools in Chennai to offer a wide range of national and international curricula, all in one campus.

- Cambridge Assessment International Education (CAIE)
- International Baccalaureate Diploma Programme (IBDP)
- Central Board of Secondary Education (CBSE)
- National Institute of Open Schooling (NIOS)

Omega's Value Based Spiritual Education and Life Skills Activities programs are, together, the foundation on which the children's education is built. The school places a lot of emphasis on Humanities and Arts and Crafts. The school actively promotes many sports and games and offers coaching programs in quite a few of them; athletics, football, basketball, badminton and cricket, for example. Our students regularly participate at the District and State level tournaments and have been to the Nationals in both girls and boys soccer. A few of our boys are now playing at the junior level of ISL with the Delhi Dynamos and Chennaiyin FC. We also own two Football Clubs and a first division Cricket Club at the District level that give our students vital exposure to play sports at the league level.

Innovators & Communicators

- Students are encouraged to showcase their innate thinking and creative abilities. The research and analyses undertaken for their Extended Essays is a true testimony of their commitment to make a difference. Under the able guidance of trained facilitators, students brought about quality essays such as, "Imperial Fears and Scientific Superstitions – Does Dracula reflect Victorian ambiguities?" and "Exploring the Mathematics behind the approximations of multi-layer perceptron", among others.
- Students have initiated and now manage, specialized clubs including Robotics & Astronomy, Debate Club, TED Ed Club among others.
- Omega encourages students to take up volunteering initiatives that could pave the way for deeper and out-of-the-box thinking. It is commendable to highlight that a particular student, through her initiatives with Blue Cross, was able to present a phenomenal study on depression and the unique relationship between human beings and animals.

Balanced and Principled

- To understand the local environment around the school, students have adopted an adjoining canal. Through their various initiatives, the once derelict canal is now becoming a sustainable ecosystem with many indigenous species of flora and fauna.
- Most recently, the students have initiated an apiary program and have placed ten bee hives along the banks of this canal to encourage pollination. This project is part of the school's initiative with UN Academic Impact.
- Students have undertaken a Youth Exchange Program in collaboration with a delegation from Sri Lanka to Singapore and Malaysia to promote Peace & Partnerships

beyond Boundaries.

- Students regularly participate in national and international events and competitions; most recently in The World Scholar's Cup. One of our students finished as the 15th Best Debater and our entourage has qualified for the Tournament of Champions at Yale University.

Resources

- The IBDP team comprises of well trained and dedicated facilitators, who ably guide each student through the demanding requirements of the program. We regularly engage with subject matter experts to further enhance the students' knowledge and awareness. Our Facilitators periodically attend IB Qualified Professional Development training programs.
- Our library is stocked with around 32,000 books, apart from a collection of audio and e-books and numerous IB authorized journals. Students have access to our museum exhibits and our pictorial biodiversity record of over 2000 different reptiles, insects, amphibians and birds. We are one of the first schools in the region to set up a Government initiated Incubation Centre – the Atal Tinkering Lab. Our STEAM subject labs on campus include tools like Vernier Labquest, Phase contrast Microscopes and a 3D Printer.
- We have one of the largest faculties in Fine Arts, Performing Arts & Visual Arts.

Careers Education and University Guidance

- Through the school's Career Counselling team and an online career guidance platform, students are able to identify their aspirations and are guided suitably to realize them. Students have access to tools that facilitate academic writing and enhanced research skills, and are encouraged to build and work on their portfolio from Grade IX.
- Students get to interact directly with University representatives from all over the world. These initiatives, combined with their excellent performance, have seen our students go to prestigious Universities such as Imperial College London, University of Cambridge, Brown University, University of Texas at Austin, University of California, Berkley, KU Leuwen University, Belgium, to name a few.
- Omega has collaborated with some of the best Universities to enable student research projects,

immersion programs and partnership programs that form an integral part of a student's life while at school.

Creativity, Activity & Service

Omega students are actively engaged in a variety of social integration programs:

- Our school has the unique distinction of being the only institution from India to participate in the UN Student Leadership Conferences on Development for the last seven years, and have also been endowed with the responsibility of identifying topics of global significance for the conference.
- Students organize and manage "Kalanjali" – an annual event to showcase India's rich heritage in the Performing Arts. This event, comprising of an annual workshop and concert, usually held at a premium location in the city, is completely managed by students, and gives them event management skills beyond anything that they would normally receive at any school.
- Students operate the school's paper recycling plant, to convert waste paper generated on campus into modern office stationery & souvenirs.
- Students identify avenues and events within the campus to undertake projects for videography and photography.
- To enhance peer learning experiences, students of the IBDP program assist primary students in their foreign language classes.

Recognitions and awards

Omega has been recognized by the British Council with the "International School Award" since 2016.

We have the distinction of being recognized as one of the 'Future 50 International & Residential Schools Shaping Success' out of 600 schools surveyed in India by Future 50 – a Fortune India magazine initiative.

We are one of only 45 schools to be recognized as a "Great Place to Study" by Global League Institute for 2019-20, based on a Student Satisfaction Survey.

(Founded 1969)

Principal
Sebastien Mathey

DP coordinator
Cybele Gonzalez

Status Private

Boarding/day Day

Gender Coeducational

Language of instruction
French, English

Authorised IB programmes
DP

Age Range 3 – 18

Number of pupils enrolled
851

Fees
Day: AUS$8,502 – AUS$29,343

Address
758 Anzac Parade
Maroubra
NSW 2035 | AUSTRALIA

TEL +61 2 9344 8692

FAX +61 2 9349 2626

Email
ib@condorcet.com.au

Website
www.condorcet.com.au

Lycée Condorcet – the International French School of Sydney is situated in Sydney, Australia and offers a bilingual (French and English) immersion program from Prep-school to Year 12 (ages 3 to 18).

The school is approved and regulated by French authorities and is accredited to prepare students for the Diplôme National du Brevet and the French Baccalauréat. The school belongs to the network of the AEFE (Agency for French Teaching Abroad) and is the French exam centre for the whole of Australia.

Lycée Condorcet also offers the International Baccalaureate Diploma Programme which is taught in English. It is registered with the New South Wales government as a specialist school and it also belongs to the Association of Independent Schools (AIS).

Underpinning these registrations is a multiplicity of administrative and legal obligations with the French and Australian Governments and the International Baccalaureate Organisation. They are the foundation of the partnership which allows us to offer our children a bilingual and bicultural education – to experience and appreciate another culture and way of 'seeing our world'.

The International Baccalaureate Diploma Programme is offered at the school as an alternative to the French Baccalaureate for students who wish to pursue their senior studies in the English language.

Students with a background in French graduate with a Bilingual Diploma which confirms proficiency in both languages. However, the ability to speak French is not a pre-requisite for enrolment as all levels of the French language are catered for – from beginners to advanced.

Importantly, although situated in Australia, the school operates on the northern hemisphere calendar so that the school year begins in August and final IB diploma examinations are held in May.

The school population is comprised of students from over 20 different nationalities and every effort is made to integrate non francophone students by providing French as a Foreign Language classes.

Through the promotion of French and Australian cultures, we aim to develop inquiring, knowledgeable and caring young people while working to promote international and intercultural understanding and respect.

Mentone Girls' Grammar School

(Founded 1899)

Head of School
Natalie Charles

PYP coordinator
Donnah Ciempka

Status Private

Boarding/day Day

Gender Female

Language of instruction
English

Authorised IB programmes
PYP

Number of pupils enrolled
800

Fees
Day: AUS$13,000 – AUS$29,845

Address
11 Mentone Parade
Mentone
VIC 3194 | AUSTRALIA

TEL +61 3 9581 1200
FAX +61 3 9581 1291

Email
info@mentonegirls.vic.edu.au

Website
www.mentonegirls.vic.edu.au

Mentone Girls' Grammar is one of the finest schools for girls in Melbourne, Australia, consistently ranked among the best schools in the State of Victoria. We have been providing a premium education for girls from Kindergarten to Year 12 since 1899; accepting students of all talents and abilities, faiths and cultures.

We understand how girls think, learn and interact. Our contemporary curriculum is specifically designed to engage girls at each age and stage in order to support their growth as happy, independent, confident and capable individuals. Our beautiful beachfront single campus has inspired our **WAVES** priorities – key principles which guide the way we meet the particular learning needs of girls by contributing to their **Wellbeing, Achievement**, positive **Values, Enterprising** nature and **Success**. These priorities contribute to the unique culture and success of our School, as well as our personalised approach to learning.

As the first school in the world to receive the prestigious Council of International Schools International Certificate, and as an IB World School, we are often benchmarked against some of the best schools in the world. Our rich curriculum challenges and inspires our students to learn, lead and live with an international focus.

In the Junior School, at the heart of the Primary Years Programme (PYP) philosophy is a commitment to developing inquiring, knowledgeable and caring young people who help to create a better and more peaceful world through intercultural understanding and respect. Every aspect of the curriculum is designed to engage students with these key concepts. We also have strong programs in STEAM (Science, Technology, Engineering, Arts & Mathematics), enterprise and financial literacy and align these initiatives within our Programme of Inquiry, delivered through an inquiry mode of instruction.

In the Senior School, we provide four languages (French, German, Chinese & Japanese), as well as Arts/Humanities offerings that form a significant component of our global learning program ranging from Accounting and Economics to Business Management, Geography, History, Digital Technologies, Global Politics and Legal Studies.

As an IB School, we receive professional development in exceptional IB practice and work hard to implement teaching and learning practices that deliver an outstanding educational experience for our students.

We aim to give our students an international education, one which will empower them to, as global citizens, meet the challenges of their times. Mentone Girls' Grammar is filled with staff and students who have passion, dedication and perseverance. We have high expectations and take great pride and joy in exceeding them.

MERCEDES COLLEGE

(Founded 1954)

Principal
Mr Andrew Balkwill

PYP coordinator
Mr Simon Munn

MYP coordinator
Mr Stuart Wuttke

DP coordinator
Mr Marc Whitehead

Status Private

Boarding/day Day

Gender Coeducational

Language of instruction
English

Authorised IB programmes
PYP, MYP, DP

Age Range 5 – 18

Fees
Day: AUS$8,950 – AUS$14,475

Address
540 Fullarton Road
Springfield
SA 5062 | AUSTRALIA

TEL +61 8 8372 3200
FAX +61 8 8379 9540

Email
mercedes@mercedes.catholic.edu.au

Website
www.mercedes.catholic.edu.au

Mercedes College understands the importance of nurturing and inspiring students to become lifelong learners to meet the demands of the 21st century.

The co-educational Catholic school incorporates the globally renowned International Baccalaureate (IB) framework with the Australian curriculum to provide students with a world class education.

Set in a single location at the base of the Adelaide Foothills, and as one of few South Australian schools to offer the IB from Reception to Year 12, Mercedes presents a wealth of opportunities to nurture and challenge students, and enables continuity of learning at the same campus across their entire schooling.

"In such a rapidly evolving world, there is no way to be sure what today's young people will face in their future academic, employment and spiritual journeys, but we can provide them with the skills to meet the challenges and adapt to whatever lies ahead," said Principal Andrew Balkwill.

The College is proud of its history of academic excellence and is also committed to supporting students beyond the classroom. A range of pastoral care programmes are designed to help develop the whole person and enable students to flourish.

Mercedes College is a learning community in the Mercy tradition, committed to being people who are responsible, compassionate and loyal, show integrity and mutual respect, and have a strong sense of justice.

"It is one thing to declare good intentions and another to live them each day," said Principal Andrew Balkwill. "We invite you to visit our school and experience the sense of welcome and belonging that is a fundamental part of our culture."

For information about enrolment opportunities please visit www.mercedes.catholic.edu.au.

MLC

(Founded 1882)

Principal
Ms Diana Vernon

Registrar
Ms Sam Rimmer

DP coordinator
Rebecca Bunnett

Status Private

Boarding/day Mixed

Gender Female

Language of instruction
English

Authorised IB programmes
DP

Fees
Day: AU$19,800 – AU$33,180
Boarding: AU$30,141
International Full Fee Student (Prep – Year 9) AU$43,020
International Full Fee Student (Year 10 – Year 12) AU$46,530

Address
207 Barkers Road
Kew
VIC 3101 | AUSTRALIA

TEL +61 3 9274 6316
FAX +61 3 9819 5143

Email
admissions@mlc.vic.edu.au

Website
www.mlc.vic.edu.au

MLC in Melbourne, Australia is a leading independent girls' school, internationally recognised for its extensive curriculum choice, cutting-edge approach to education, authentic learning experiences and outstanding academic results. As an open-entry, non-selective day and boarding school, we are a welcoming, diverse community offering a broad, holistic education that prepares world-ready women for their lives beyond school.

MLC has a proud 138 year history of educational innovation and academic excellence. With an interdisciplinary approach to learning with a strong focus on STEAM (Science, Technology, Engineering, Art and Design, and Mathematics), we are committed to developing the next generation of skilled, technologically capable and creative problem solvers.

MLC offers opportunity and choice with a broad choice of electives to explore in the younger year levels. Over 60 subjects are offered across VCE, VCE VET and IB (International Baccalaureate) pathways in Years 11 and 12. All of our subjects are offered on campus, with learning support and extension programs designed to help our students be their best. Within our diverse learning environment, there are multiple opportunities for students to form friendships across the College.

MLC's unique programs include our two external Outdoor Education campuses, MLC Banksia (Years 5-8) and MLC Marshmead (Year 9), and over 50 Australian and international tours each year.

MLC's state-of-the-art learning environment provides students with world-class opportunities for achievement, exploration and personal development. From the advanced science centre and renovated Library, state-of-the-art Physical Education Centre, commercial training restaurant and professional TV studio and video editing suites, MLC's facilities are exceptional, especially our new world-class Year 7-8 Nicholas Learning Centre that opened in 2019.

Our over-arching goal is to nurture and develop each MLC student so that she leaves school with the skills, knowledge and values necessary to be a world-ready woman.

(Founded 1886)

Principal
Lisa Moloney

DP coordinator
Anne Layman

Status Private

Boarding/day Day

Gender Female

Language of instruction
English

Authorised IB programmes
DP

Number of pupils enrolled
1240

Fees
AU$18,052 – AU$31,584

Address
Rowley Street
Burwood
Sydney
NSW 2134 | AUSTRALIA

TEL +61 2 9747 1266
FAX +61 2 9745 3254

Email
enrol@mlcsyd.nsw.edu.au

Website
www.mlcsyd.nsw.edu.au

MLC School is an independent, non-selective Uniting Church school for girls from Pre-Kindergarten to Year 12 in the Inner West of Sydney. From Pre-Kindergarten through to their time as Senior School students, MLC School girls dare to be more.

Led by a highly professional staff under the guidance of Principal, Lisa Moloney, girls are challenged and encouraged to question traditional perceptions and roles of women and are instilled with the skills and confidence to take their place in an ever-changing society.

MLC School prepares girls for a life of learning by motivating them to pursue excellence, demonstrate integrity, celebrate diversity, embrace world citizenship and live with humility. A wide selection of subject choices, as well as an extensive co-curricular program aims to empower girls to be self-reliant and play an active role in their futures.

The new Senior Centre, opened in 2019, takes classroom practice to a new level and is reflective of modern workplaces. The aim is to equip girls with the skills to be successful in a collaborative, team environment and to be comfortable in open-planned, flexible spaces designed for impromptu group work sessions.

Year 7 to Year 10 are pivotal years at MLC School where girls experience Immersive Learning journeys that broaden each year. From a Week in Shakespeare's World to exploring Sydney, outback Broken Hill and then travelling abroad to Chiang Mai Thailand, MLC School girls experience learning in many different environments.

Academically, each girl takes responsibility for her own path in the final years, and this is a crucial stage in her journey towards becoming an independent, fearless and empowered young woman. Girls can choose between the Higher School Certificate (HSC) or the International Baccalaureate (IB) Diploma Programme, with nearly 40 per cent of students choosing to study the IB.

Visit the campus, meet the girls and professional teaching staff and experience the benefits of joining the MLC School community.

(Founded 1992)

Head of School
Mr Brett Penny

PYP coordinator
Bryony Maxted-Miller

MYP coordinator
Jacqueline Arce

DP coordinator
Paul Cooper

Status Private

Boarding/day Day

Gender Coeducational

Language of instruction
English

Authorised IB programmes
PYP, MYP, DP

Age Range 3 – 18

Number of pupils enrolled
1650

Fees
THB533,700 – THB961,400

Address
36 Sukhumvit Soi 15
Wattana
Bangkok
10110 | THAILAND

TEL +66 2 017 5888
FAX +66 2 253 3800

Email
admissions@nist.ac.th

Website
www.nist.ac.th

As the first and only full, not-for-profit IB World School in Bangkok, NIST International School offers a world-class education to students from the early years to high school levels. Established in 1992 with the guidance and support of the United Nations, the school now welcomes over 1,600 students representing more than 60 nationalities. NIST is governed by the parent-elected NIST International School Foundation and was the first school in Thailand to receive triple accreditation through the Council of International Schools (CIS), New England Association of Schools and Colleges (NEASC) and Office for National Education Standards and Quality Assessment (ONESQA).

Recognized worldwide for its progressive approach and international scope, the IB framework provides students with critical 21st century skills that align to the demands of the modern workplace. Through the IB and its own unique programmes, NIST aims to inspire, empower and enrich lives. The academic structure encourages students to explore, take risks and make connections across disciplines. Student-driven service learning plays a central role, as they learn to understand and empathize with others, and take an active role in solving local, national and global issues. NIST also partners with other top schools around the globe to offer the Global Citizen Diploma, an optional qualification that allows graduates to showcase strengths in leadership, service and community engagement.

In addition to its rigorous academics, NIST offers an expansive World Languages Programme and over 300 extra-curricular activity options. As one of the founding members of the Southeast Asia Student Activity Conference (SEASAC), the NIST Falcons compete against their peers from other top schools in Southeast Asia, as well as students around the globe. NIST has also committed itself to excellence and innovation in the use of technology. Students benefit from personal MacBook Air computers, iPads, a completely wireless campus, SMART Boards, the FrontRow classroom amplification system, and LCD-equipped classrooms.

NIST represents the future of learning through its stellar academic achievements and expansive resources. More importantly, the school has been successful in fostering reflective, principled learners with a passion for making a difference in the lives of others. With its graduates attending the best universities around the globe and going on to become community leaders, NIST has become recognized as one of the world's leading international schools.

Newington College

(Founded 1863)

Headmaster
Mr Michael Parker

PYP coordinator
Mrs Sue Gough

DP coordinator
Ms Cheryl Priest

Status Private

Boarding/day Mixed

Gender Male

Language of instruction
English

Authorised IB programmes
PYP, DP

Number of pupils enrolled
2080

Fees
Boarding: AUS$27,297 (inc GST)Tuition: AUS$18,594 – AUS$33,984

Address
200 Stanmore Road
Stanmore
NSW 2048 | AUSTRALIA

TEL +61 2 9568 9333
FAX +61 2 9568 9521

Email
admissions@newington.nsw.edu.au

Website
www.newington.nsw.edu.au

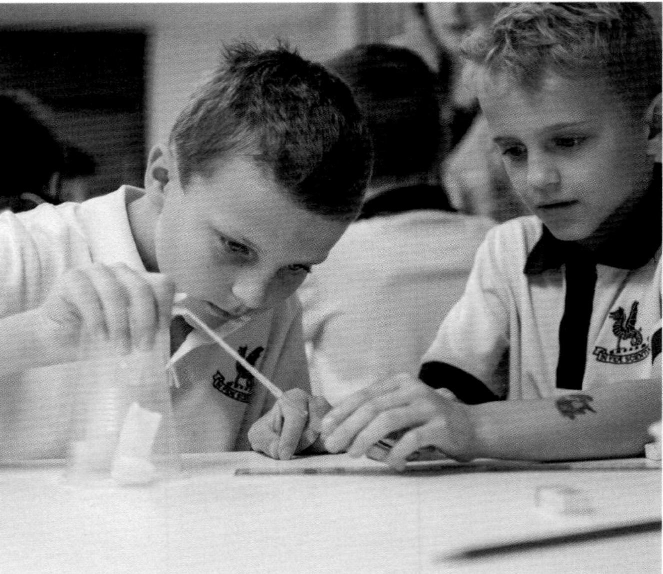

In the hub of Sydney, Australia
Newington College is an International Baccalaureate World School in inner Sydney. It includes a PYP satellite prep school and a boarding house for secondary school students that attracts boys from greater Sydney, regional areas and the Asia Pacific.

Its location in the heart of an expanding international city gives boys of all ages the opportunity to access a range of learning and cultural resources. Surrounded by universities, theatres, libraries and museums, Newington College regularly engages with experts from nearby centres of learning.

The College has 25 acres of gardens and playing fields that create an oasis of learning within a busy city. Newington is only 10 minutes from Sydney International Airport and Central Station and five minutes from the University of Sydney.

A liberal tradition of innovation
Newington College was founded in 1863 with a liberal policy of inclusion that declared the College 'open to the sons of all'. Newington's fathers realised the need for a quality educational establishment to develop boys of promise into men of substance.

Newington's approach, with its focus on critical and creative thinking, makes the College a remarkable place to educate your son.

A diverse and inclusive community
Newington is committed to providing a holistic education for boys.

Newington families value the broad perspectives and liberal outlook of the College community. They embrace the opportunity for their sons to experience the International Baccalaureate's belief that others can be different – and also be right. Every day, boys at Newington are encouraged to approach their education with rigour and a mind open to diverse views and perspectives.

Newington College strives to create young men of integrity who are courageous, open-minded, creative and curious; whose views are formed through truly critical thinking and who value both independence and teamwork.

Academic Rigour in Learning and Teaching
In the primary years, Lindfield Preparatory School offers the Primary Years Programme. Newington's senior school is the only Greater Public School in Sydney that offers a choice between the state-wide Higher School Certificate examination and the IB Diploma Programme. The IB Diploma at Newington is a popular option for many boys and the results achieved by the College are outstanding.

Newington is committed to providing an internationally respected education with access to the best teachers, facilities and opportunities. Students at Newington are encouraged to develop a broad understanding of the world and to immerse themselves in their own particular areas of interest and passion.

The College is equipped with the latest technology infrastructure and subject specific, industry level facilities including a modern technology centre, 200-seat drama theatre, light-filled library, lecture theatre and super-labs.

Well-being and character

At Newington, teachers share their passion for their area of expertise and build strong relationships with their students. They tailor their teaching to suit the learning styles of each student.

The College is committed to ensuring that every person feels respected and valued in the school community. The boys admire their teachers and coaches for their genuine interest in each student's well-being, passions, goals and setbacks.

Spirituality, Values and Ethics

As a Uniting Church school, Christian values are a strong part of the way that the College has built its community. This includes welcoming students and families of all faiths and cultural backgrounds.

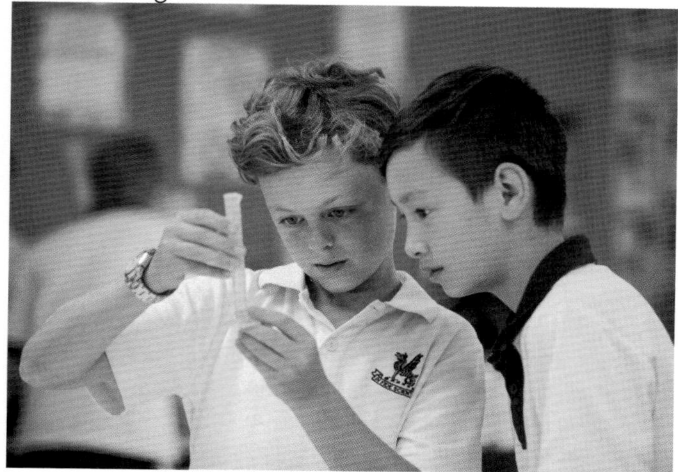

The boys are expected to build a sense of social responsibility and justice and are encouraged to test out their ideas and to seize every opportunity available to them.

Co-curricular Engagement

Newington College is committed to providing all boys with the chance to experiment and thrive through participating in a varied range of co-curricular activities. These opportunities are a large part of what distinguishes a school such as Newington College. Boys combine academic life with a number of sports, arts, outdoor education and hands-on learning activities. They are supported and encouraged in the journey to discovering their own unique passions and interests.

Community in Partnership

An exceptional sense of community is part of the Newington culture, which emphasises service to others and the development of strong and lasting relationships. This involves not only teachers and students but parents, families and Old Boys. The College strives for every member of the Newington community to feel welcome, connected and appreciated.

Results

The IB cohort for 2018 was made up of 39 boys, including one who achieved a perfect score of 45/45 (the equivalent to an ATAR of 99.95). Twenty per cent of Newington's IB students achieved an IB score over 42, the equivalent of an ATAR of 99.4. Newington's IB graduates achieved a mean score of 37.2, well above the global average of 29.8, and two were offered positions at one of the world's most prestigious seats of learning, Oxford University.

(Founded 2007)

Principal
Judy Cooper

PYP coordinator
Paul Rimmer

DP coordinator
Melanie Brown

Status Private

Boarding/day Day

Gender Coeducational

Language of instruction
English

Authorised IB programmes
PYP, DP

Age Range 3 – 18 years

Number of pupils enrolled
900

Fees
Day: S$30,900 – S$40,338

Address
1 Alunied Walk
Singapore
387293 | SINGAPORE

TEL +65 6536 6566

Email
enquiry@nexus.edu.sg

Website
www.nexus.edu.sg

About Nexus

At Nexus, we believe in doing things differently. We think that if we inspire our staff to be innovative and creative we can push the boundaries of education to create truly engaging learning environments for children. This philosophy is echoed by every teacher, in every class and in every extra-curricular activity.

Being an Apple Distinguished School, we understand the importance of using technology in a meaningful way to extend and redefine learning. By combining Apple devices with expert teachers and first class, flexible learning spaces, we capitalise on the opportunities digital technologies provide to promote inquiry-based learning, collaboration and a personalised education for all our learners.

Primary Years Programme

Primary School is from Nursery to Year 6, ages 3 to 11 years. The Primary School is both the longest period of a child's education and the time when the most connections and discoveries take place.

Our Primary School provides a rich and dynamic, forward-looking learning environment. Our children build strong foundations in reading, writing, numerical skills and scientific understandings. In addition, we teach our learners to develop the skills and approaches to learning that are essential in this rapidly changing world.

Areas of learning are Language Arts, Social Studies, Mathematics, Science and Technology, Arts, and Personal, Social and Physical Education. All our learners have the opportunity to learn in a second language. French or Chinese is taught through intensive and immersive daily language tuition from specialist teachers.

Diploma Programme

Our IB Diploma programme offers a wide range of subject choices, small tutor classes, and excellent career and university guidance. Children have the opportunity to prepare for the demands of their IB Diploma with opportunities such as the Duke of Edinburgh and Learner Leadership Programmes. Children are inspired to take meaningful action, following their passions with an innovative spirit before taking up places at Universities across the world.

Innovative Learning Spaces

We have had the unbelievable opportunity to build our dream school based on innovative and flexible learning spaces that enhance a child's learning experience. Because teaching is not confined to four walls, we use a wide range of spaces to engage children in their learning including our double storey treehouse. We have included exhibition spaces for children to present their work and design and technology rooms to integrate STEAM into lessons throughout the school.

In Business and Economics, a boardroom enables children to engage in real life lessons. Furthermore our Science department has an open concept classroom that can accommodate 80 learners at once, allowing a whole year group to create experiments and analyse large data sets.

Bringing together so many learners encourages them to collaborate in exciting and stimulating environments.

(Founded 2002)

Principal
Lesley-Ann Wallace

DP coordinator
Bevan Graham

Status Private

Boarding/day Day

Gender Coeducational

Language of instruction
English

Authorised IB programmes
DP

Age Range 2 – 18

Fees
RMB115,003 – RMB321,497

Address
2888 Junmin Road
Pudong New District
Shanghai
201315 | CHINA

TEL +86 (0)21 5812 7455

Email
admissions@naispudong.com

Website
naispudong.com

Established in 2002, Nord Anglia International School Shanghai, Pudong (NAIS Pudong) is an excellent international school focusing on high achievement for every child and success across all subject areas. The school offers the very best of the British education system in China for children aged 2 to 18 years.

NAIS Pudong provides students with a highly academic environment, and a warm, welcoming and diverse international community. Its rigorous, contemporary and globally focused curriculum challenges and excites children from their early years through to the International Baccalaureate Diploma Programme (IBDP).

To complement classroom teaching, NAIS Pudong offers a broad co-curricular programme that encourages students to take risks, nurture their passions and serve others. Globally respected curricula are enhanced by innovative collaborations with world leading organisations such as The Juilliard School, Massachusetts Institute of Technology (MIT) and UNICEF to ensure that every student develops the skills and mindset needed to thrive in an ever-changing world. Its Global Campus connects the Nord Anglia Education family of 61 schools, giving NAIS Pudong students access to a variety of exceptional learning opportunities worldwide.

NAIS Pudong wholeheartedly embraces the educational philosophy and pedagogical principles that underpin all IB programmes. This approach has resulted in the establishment of an optimal learning environment whereby its students are able to achieve above average academic outcomes.

At NAIS Pudong, we nurture every student to achieve academic success, enabling entry into the world's leading universities.

You want your child to excel, so do we.

(Founded 2014)

Principal
Mr Brian Cooklin

DP coordinator
Karen Simpson

Status Private

Boarding/day Day

Gender Coeducational

Language of instruction
English

Authorised IB programmes
DP

Age Range 3 – 18

Fees
Pre-school HK$81,000 – HK$163,000
Primary HK$163,000
Secondary HK$182,000

Address
11 On Tin Street
Lam Tin
Kowloon | **HONG KONG, CHINA**

TEL +852 3958 1428

Email
admissions@nais.hk

Website
www.nais.hk

Nord Anglia International School (NAIS) is part of Nord Anglia Education's (NAE) global family of international schools. A through-train school known for its warm and friendly global community, made up of over 40 nationalities, NAIS nurtures every child to develop a love of learning, enabling them to achieve more than they ever thought possible.

NAE's Global Campus helps students explore the world, learn new skills and set their sights higher, developing a truly international perspective through outstanding online, in-school and worldwide experiences.

NAIS educates children for the future, enhancing its curricula through collaborations with the world's best organisations including MIT and Juilliard. Through opportunities to learn from the best, experiences beyond the ordinary, and the encouragement to achieve more than what they thought possible, NAIS helps students succeed anywhere through a unique global educational offer. NAIS follows the frameworks of EYFS, IGCSE and IBDP. With a focus on individualised learning, the school's rigorous curricula ensure that students have a creative and challenging learning experience. Students across the NAE family produce final year results well above the world average with one in three students admitted into the world's top 100 universities each year.

(Founded 2011)

Principal
Ms Lynne Oldfield

DP coordinator
Ms Justine Oliver

Status Private

Boarding/day Mixed

Gender Coeducational

Language of instruction
English

Authorised IB programmes
DP

Age Range 4 – 18

Number of pupils enrolled
1300

Fees
Day: US$34,236
Boarding: US$13,250

Address
33, Global edu-ro 145beon-gil
Daejeong-eup
Seogwipo-si, Jeju-do
63644 | REPUBLIC OF KOREA

TEL +82 64 793 8000

Email
info@nlcsjeju.kr

Website
www.nlcsjeju.co.kr

North London Collegiate School Jeju, is internationally recognised as a school which provides an exceptional education. Our students consistently excel in every area. They leave us with outstanding qualifications, but also become articulate and independent young people who possess the confidence, intellectual curiosity, and passion for learning and understanding that will endure for life.

In tandem with our mission to develop academic excellence, we are also dedicated to supporting the development of the whole person. Our programme is designed to inspire confidence, individuality and develop self-esteem. Modelled on our mother school in London, we are a positive and energetic community where both boarders and day students are encouraged to take advantage of the exceptional range of opportunities open to them; academic, sporting and cultural.

International Outlook

NLCS students are internationally minded and well informed about the world beyond school. The IB Diploma resonates with the values of NLCS, and its international dimension affords students the opportunity to be part of a programme which is recognised throughout the world.

Academic Excellence

We have offered the IB programme since 2011 and have had a consistent record of success. All 123 students in the class of 2019 passed the IB Diploma, with 42 achieving 40 points or higher, including a maximum 45, and an average score of 37 overall with 65% scoring 7/6.

Looking to the future

Last year our IB students received offers from a range of impressive institutions including Oxford, Cambridge, Yale, Columbia, Stanford, McGill, Princeton, Melbourne, Keio, Hong Kong and Seoul National Universities.

The IB Diploma programme offered at NLCS Jeju ensures that students enjoy an exciting and academically stimulating Sixth Form experience, providing them with an excellent preparation for life at university and in the wider world beyond.

NPS International School

(Founded 2008)

Head of School
Dr Matthew Sullivan B.A., D.Phil. (Oxford)

DP coordinator
Sushmita Chatterjee

Status Private

Boarding/day Day

Gender Coeducational

Language of instruction
English

Authorised IB programmes
DP

Age Range 3 – 18

Number of pupils enrolled
1750

Fees
Day: S$15,000 – S$30,000

Address
10-12 Chai Chee Lane
Singapore
469021 | SINGAPORE

TEL +65 62942400
FAX +65 64482089

Email
headofschool@npsis.edu.sg

Website
www.npsinternational.edu.sg

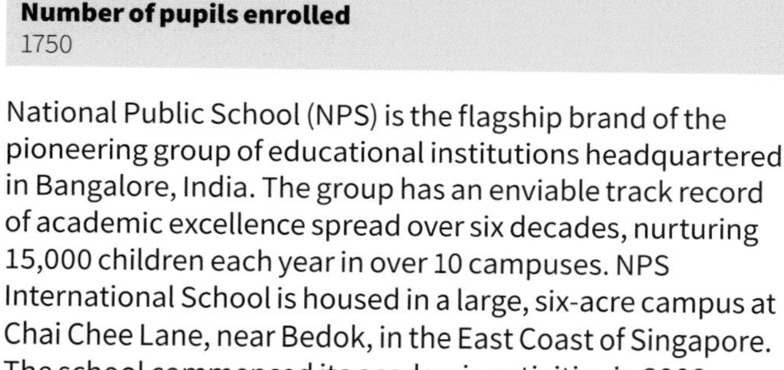

National Public School (NPS) is the flagship brand of the pioneering group of educational institutions headquartered in Bangalore, India. The group has an enviable track record of academic excellence spread over six decades, nurturing 15,000 children each year in over 10 campuses. NPS International School is housed in a large, six-acre campus at Chai Chee Lane, near Bedok, in the East Coast of Singapore. The school commenced its academic activities in 2008.

NPS International School, a day school, welcomes students to its child-centred environment, offering Montessori, Nursery, Kindergarten and Grades I to XII and the IB and CBSE programmes for grades XI and XII.

The key difference between NPS and many other groups of schools is that its founding member leaders are practising teachers with vast experience in a wide range of educational contexts.

That richness of experience brings a maturity of systems and vision which has also been confirmed through the four-year Edutrust award, and, more importantly, has been recognised, valued and praised by parents.

Vision

Inspiring young minds and empowering them to have a positive impact on the world.

Mission

- Providing a child-centred, holistic and value-based learning experience.
- Encouraging creativity, innovation, confidence and critical thinking in a safe and nurturing environment.
- Fostering leadership, empathy and engagement in humanitarian and environmental service.

Principal
Mr Mark Robertson

MYP coordinator
Haydn Flanagan

Status Private

Boarding/day Day

Gender Coeducational

Language of instruction
English

Authorised IB programmes
MYP

Age Range 2 – 18

Number of pupils enrolled
904

Fees
Prep – Year 12 AUS$8,002 – AUS$10,539

Address
77-81 Willesden Road
Oakleigh
VIC 3166 | AUSTRALIA

TEL +61 3 9569 6128
FAX +61 3 9568 6558

Email
admissions@oakleighgrammar.vic.edu.au

Website
www.oakleighgrammar.vic.edu.au

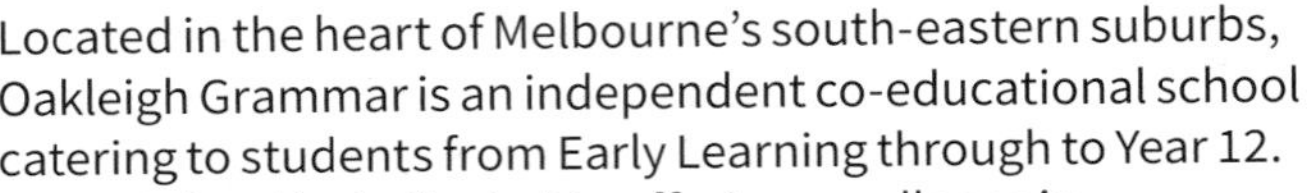

Located in the heart of Melbourne's south-eastern suburbs, Oakleigh Grammar is an independent co-educational school catering to students from Early Learning through to Year 12.

Our School is dedicated to offering excellence in education, while catering to each of our student's individual learning needs. At Oakleigh Grammar, we ensure that every child is known personally, and we place the utmost importance on student welfare and safety. The school is a multicultural environment, embracing over 50 nationalities, all underpinned by our Christian values, where diversity is celebrated and inclusion is encouraged.

We constantly strive for the best learning environments for our students, with the School offering a wide array of programs, to not only excel educational success, but to ensure our students understand the importance of community, and are open to a global perspective in how they learn. These qualities develop through programs such as: camps, sporting opportunities, embracing the Reggio Emilia Philosophy in the Early Learning Centre and The Leader In me Program in our Junior School, as well as other co-curricular enrichment programs.

Added to our wide array of programs, Oakleigh Grammar prides itself on offering the International Baccalaureate Middle Years Programme, which encourages Year 6 to 10 students to become creative, critical and reflective thinkers, while fostering the development of skills for communication, intercultural understanding and global engagement. The program fundamentally assists with the progression of our students, with qualities that are essential for learning and life in the 21st century.

At Oakleigh Grammar our students are not just a number or a learning outcome, but an integral part of the fabric of our School and wider Community. We pride ourselves on seeing the development and progression of our students throughout their educational lives, helping inspire their passion to exceed in the outside world.

Headteacher
Michelle Dickinson

PYP coordinator
Erin Smith

DP coordinator
Iris Tay

Status Private

Boarding/day Day

Gender Coeducational

Language of instruction
English

Authorised IB programmes
PYP, DP

Age Range 3 – 18

Number of pupils enrolled
1235

Fees
Day: S$17,514 – S$20,136

Address
21 Jurong West Street 81
Singapore
649075 | SINGAPORE

TEL +65 69146700

Email
admissions@owis.org

Website
www.owis.org

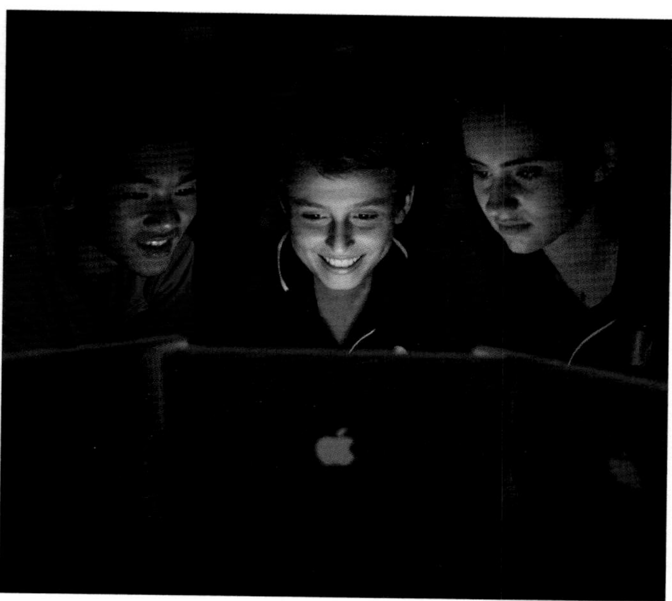

A World-Class Educational Framework, a Child-Centred Approach
One World International School offers a rigorous, developmentally-appropriate IB education at a thoughtfully-priced fee structure. The curriculum combines a personalised approach with international standards, focusing on nurturing the natural love of learning within every child. Research has repeatedly demonstrated that for children to thrive academically, they must be engaged and enthused about their learning. At OWIS, our carefully designed curriculum incorporates hands-on learning experiences within a supportive environment to prepare students to become the leaders of tomorrow.

A truly international learning environment
OWIS brings together students from over seventy nationalities with a diverse staff. Children have the opportunity to learn and discover in an international environment that prepares them for our global society. As part of our programme, we are committed to providing all students with opportunities to learn other languages with a particular focus on Mandarin across the whole school.

A holistic learning environment
Students at OWIS have access to a-well-respected curriculum that not only prepares them for the future in terms of academic excellence, but also emphasises the importance of holistic development. Children are nurtured inside and outside the classroom environment with rich and varied opportunities to learn sports, perform on stage and work with hands-on projects that excite their love of learning.

At OWIS, we understand the importance of personalised learning with each child being given individualised attention and feedback. Our classes therefore are capped at 24 students to maintain a small and inclusive environment ensuring that each child receives the attention they need to thrive academically, emotionally and socially. The deep relationships that our teachers develop with their students help to create a welcoming, safe environment for every child to succeed.

Access to the latest in technology and education
Society has rapidly become dominated by digital technology and students today need to be given appropriate opportunities to embrace these technologies. At OWIS, we believe that students should have access to this technology under the guidance of their teachers who carefully consider how and when to incorporate it into the teaching and learning. Our focus is to enhance every child's creativity, communication skills and technical skills.

The OWIS values of being "One with the World" provides a balanced, rigorous educational experience that nurtures lifelong learners and unique thinkers to be leaders.

深圳东方英文书院
Shenzhen Oriental English College

(Founded 1994)

Head of School
Mr Weiquan Shen

PYP coordinator
Jinlong Li (Joe)

DP coordinator
Kongjing Wang

Status Private

Boarding/day Boarding

Gender Coeducational

Language of instruction
Chinese, English

Authorised IB programmes
PYP, DP

Age Range 6 – 18

Fees
RMB60,000 – RMB130,000

Address
No 10 Xuezi Road
Education Town, Bao'an
Shenzhen, Guangdong
518128 | CHINA

TEL +86 755 2751 2624
FAX +86 755 2751 2866

Email
principal@oecis.cn

Website
www.szoec.com.cn

History and development
OEC International School (OECIS) is funded by Daming Group and is a division of Shenzhen Oriental English College founded in 1994. OECIS is a co-educational school with students enrolled from primary school to high school. Our school is a set of primary school, secondary school, Hong Kong and Taiwan schools and an IB International School in one of the fulltime, full-boarding private schools.

OECIS has been an authorized IB World School since 2004, delivering an IB structured curriculum for over 15 years. OEC covers an area of 150,000 square meters (about 37 acres). With 114 classrooms, 4600 students and staff, advanced facilities and the campus provides for collaborative spaces and areas for group and individual teaching and learning. Located in the Baoan Education District, only a five-minute drive from the Shenzhen International Airport, it is situated at the foot of the Phoenix Mountain and surrounded by picturesque natural scenery. Shenzhen City, also known as the first Special Economic Zone in China is easily accessible from Guangzhou and Hong Kong.

Curricula
A well-acclaimed international IB programme is offered to meet our students' diverse educational needs. In addition, we also offer intensive English training courses to help students prepare for both their English instruction in class and the various language requirements set by universities. The ratio of student-faculty is 6:1, which ensures each student receives enough attention and guidance. Our students have achieved remarkable results and continue to excel in all areas.

Classrooms
All classrooms have a comprehensive range of resources which includes a wealth of technology resources. Each classroom is equipped with interactive white boards and are used to present classes. We also have a dedicated, well stocked library from which children and families can borrow a range of books, story sacks and other resources.

Technology
By integrating technology and computers in the classroom students are learning faster and expressing themselves creatively more than ever before. With WeChat Work (School information system) students, parents and teachers enjoy an open classroom environment, bringing parents closer to the classroom. Empowering students through innovation in the classroom is the goal, here at OECIS!

(Founded 2001)

Head of School
Rachel Keys

PYP coordinator
Mary Ann Van De Weerd

MYP coordinator
Andrew Parlby

DP coordinator
Catherine Schlei

CP coordinator
Elisabeth Wojciuk

Status Private

Boarding/day Mixed

Gender Coeducational

Language of instruction
English

Authorised IB programmes
PYP, MYP, DP, CP

Age Range 3 – 19

Number of pupils enrolled
500

Fees
Day: THB343,460 – THB673,760
Boarding: THB398,340

Address
234 Moo 3, Huay Sai
Mae Rim, Chiang Mai
50180 | THAILAND

TEL +66 53 301 500

Email
admissions@ptis.ac.th

Website
www.ptis.ac.th

Prem Tinsulanonda International School is a leading co-educational boarding and day International Baccalaureate (IB) World School. Located on its lush 100-acre campus set in the foothills north of the ancient and historic city of Chiang Mai, Thailand, Prem is the first IB World School in South East Asia and the only one in Thailand to offer all four IB programmes: the Primary Years Programme (PYP), the Middle Years Programme (MYP), the IB Diploma Programme (IBDP), and the IB Career-related Programme (IBCP).

Since its inception in 2001, Prem Tinsulanonda International School has been dedicated to academic excellence. At Prem, students from all over the world receive a rigorous international education that provides them with the global competencies required for a future of increasing cross-cultural interdependence, rapid technological change and critical environmental challenges.

To complement their academic work, students also participate in Exploria, the after-school co-curricular activity programme available from Grade 1 to Grade 12. Exploria aims to expose students to many different possible activities which explore creative, physical, academic and service challenges.

As a four-programme International Baccalaureate boarding and day school, we offer every child an appropriate educational challenge, which is augmented by an innovative boarding curriculum. Prem boarding apartments offer flexible boarding options for students from Grade 3 – Grade 12. Our boarding residences provide a warm, homely atmosphere that fosters a sense of "family", on a beautiful, safe campus that fully supports the diverse needs of our students, and this is very important when our students come to us from so many different cultural backgrounds.

Prem graduates have gone on to study a variety of courses that include medicine, engineering, liberal arts, economics, business management, mathematics, the arts, environmental science, biochemistry and international relations. Prem alumni have been welcomed into leading universities around the world.

The most prestigious educational organisations and major educational agencies in the world have accredited Prem Tinsulanonda International School. Our thorough review process every five years ensures we continue to meet the exacting standards of international accreditation.

As of the end of 2017, the school has also officially joined a network of innovative schools in 50 countries in the Round Square organisation that share a passion for experiential learning built around six IDEALS of learning: Internationalism, Democracy, Environmentalism, Adventure, Leadership, and Service.

(Founded 2002)

Director
Dr. Clare McDermott

Secondary Director of Instruction
Mr. Robert G. Mullins

Elementary Director of Instruction
Ms. Hafida Becker

DP coordinator
Mr. David Becker

Status Private

Boarding/day Day

Gender Coeducational

Language of instruction
English

Authorised IB programmes
DP

Age Range 3 – 18

Number of pupils enrolled
350

Address
American Garden
188 South 3rd Ring Road
Chengdu, Sichuan
610041 | CHINA

TEL +86 28 8511 3853

Email
chengdu@qsi.org

Website
chengdu.qsi.org

Statement of Purpose
QSI International School of Chengdu promotes the success for every child through quality instruction and character development in a caring, challenging, multicultural environment.

Academic Program
QSI has a strong belief that all students can succeed. The learned outcomes needed at mastery level are clearly defined; students have more than one chance to be successful in demonstrating mastery.

In addition to academics, our Success Orientations are a vital part of the entire school experience. Personal habits, the ability to interact successfully with others, responsibility, trustworthiness, kindness, and other factors in this realm are as important as the knowledge one learns and the competencies one gains. The QSI Success Orientations complement the IB Learner Profile.

IB Program
The IB program at QSI Chengdu is our most rigorous college preparatory program. We take an inclusive approach with all students and do not restrict access to IB courses. We encourage students to challenge themselves and have a 100% pass rate on all IB exams.

Faculty & Staff
We are a family of leaders and learners at QSI Chengdu. Our faculty and staff come from across the world, which reflects our student diversity. Our staff come prepared with qualifications and training in best practices to ensure they have the skills to facilitate higher level learning and social-emotional development of all students.

Accreditation
QSI International School of Chengdu has been accredited by the Middle States Association since 2008.

(Founded 2001)

Head of School
Mr. Scott D'Alterio

DP coordinator
Mr. Zackary Varvel

Status Private

Boarding/day Day

Gender Coeducational

Language of instruction
English

Authorised IB programmes
DP

Age Range 2 – 18

Number of pupils enrolled
1400

Address
5th Floor, Bitao Building,
8 Taizi Road
Shekou
Shenzhen, Guangdong
518069 | CHINA

TEL +86 755 2667 6031
FAX +86 755 2667 6030

Email
shenzhen@qsi.org

Website
shenzhen.qsi.org

Success for All at QSI International School of Shekou!
QSI International School of Shekou (Shenzhen) is a non-profit institution that has operated in Shenzhen since 2001 as one of the only true international schools in Shenzhen, serving children of foreign families ages 2-18.

The city's largest international school with the longest-standing International Baccalaureate (IB) Diploma Programme authorization, QSI Shenzhen's four campuses offer an American-accredited education in the English Language (Middle States Association of Schools and Colleges, MSA). Prior to beginning the IB DP Programme, students also have the option of taking Advanced Placement (AP) courses.

Students can choose over 22 IB course options, meeting the interests of our students and their university aspirations.

In 2019, 58 graduating students of 18 nationalities received offers from over 100 universities in 9 different countries.

QSI Shenzhen is one of 37 schools in 31 countries on 5 continents operated by Quality Schools International (QSI).

QSI Shenzhen follows a mastery learning pedagogy that nurtures and challenges the whole student by offering choice, rigor, performance-based learning, and time as a resource. Mastery learning pairs well with the IB Diploma Programme to challenge students to authentically learn, explore, and be challenged in accordance with the IB Learner Profile.

QSI educates the whole child by offering a variety of activities ranging from sports to music, visual and graphic arts, and opportunities to learn programming and robotics, plus film & podcast/vlogging production. Other options include Model United Nations (MUN), World Scholar's Cup, Experiential Learning Week, and the opportunity for membership in several honor societies.

Our licensed teaching staff of over 200 teachers is largely North American. Our IB DP teachers are IB trained and collaborate with the QSI-wide network of IB teachers who are experienced in pairing the QSI mastery-learning approach with the IB Diploma Programme.

Queensland Academy
for Science Mathematics
and Technology

(Founded 2007)

Principal
Ms Kathryn Kayrooz

DP coordinator
Mr Meng-Yin Leong

Status State

Boarding/day Day

Gender Coeducational

Language of instruction
English

Authorised IB programmes
DP

Age Range 12 – 18

Number of pupils enrolled
852

Fees
DP AUS$2,291.45 + Resource Fees

Address
78 Bywong Street
Toowong
QLD 4066 | AUSTRALIA

TEL +61 7 3377 9333
FAX +61 7 3377 9300

Email
admin@qasmt.eq.edu.au

Website
qasmt.eq.edu.au

The Queensland Academy for Science Mathematics and Technology (QASMT) allows high achieving students to develop skills through leading edge curriculum and links with the University of Queensland and other leading universities. QASMT offers an enriched program to enhance development of students with an interest and ability in the related fields of Science, Mathematics and Technology.

Students achieve outstanding academic results with a proven record in attaining offers to some of the most prestigious universities throughout the world. In 2018, Queensland Academy for Science Mathematics and Technology was the top performing school in Queensland. More details can be found at www.bettereducation.com.. 40.3% of our graduating cohort received a rank of 99 (OP1 equivalent) – the highest rank attainable, with 29% of students achieving an IB score of 40+ and one student receiving the top IB score of 45.

Underpinning our academic success is an outstanding pastoral care system supporting every student and helping each one to feel a vital part of the QASMT 'family'. Student welfare is implemented through a Mentor Program ensuring all students achieve their potential. We believe in the importance of guiding students to become responsible and caring individuals, who are sensitive, open-minded and respectful of all cultures. QASMT aims to develop tomorrow's leaders; individuals who will be internationally minded citizens.

We provide a valuable transition from senior school to university for highly capable students from Years 7 to 12 (International student intakes Years 10-12 only). Teachers and students enjoy flexible learning spaces that support innovative teaching practice and embed elements of personalised learning. Spaces are designed to reflect the type of learning that takes place. Students and teachers work collaboratively and respectfully together.

We develop students' abilities to research, investigate and reflect on local and global matters. The relationship of the students and teachers is based on intellectual challenge and interdependent inquiry.

Students who graduate from QASMT enjoy careers in new science fields such as Biotechnology and Nanotechnology, as well as established fields like Health Sciences, Engineering, Chemical Sciences, Robotics, Neuroscience, ICT and The Arts.

Our facilities are world standard. The addition of a new STEM Precinct and Languages Precinct opening for the commencement of 2020 provides further dynamic use and enhancement of our learning environments. Students enjoy the benefits of working in wireless learning spaces with computer network access from all work and recreation areas. In addition we have virtual classrooms; an observatory; extensive recreational and sporting facilities, including a gymnasium, full size volleyball and basketball courts, tennis courts and sports ovals. A central HUB of the school is our new and stylish Student Precinct, providing innovative learning and maker spaces, quiet individual study spaces and learning areas with up to date e-resources. Students also enjoy the contemporary university style lecture theatre and large auditorium, plus well – equipped music and art rooms.

QASMT is located at 78 Bywong Street, Toowong, Brisbane; a convenient 10 minute drive from Brisbane CBD with excellent access to both train and bus public transport.

(Founded 1925)

Principal
Ms Elizabeth Stone

DP coordinator
Sarah Thompson

Status Private

Boarding/day Day

Gender Female

Language of instruction
English

Authorised IB programmes
DP

Number of pupils enrolled
900

Address
Locked bag 1
Mosman
NSW 2088 | AUSTRALIA

TEL +61 2 89687777
FAX +61 2 89687778

Email
q@queenwood.nsw.edu.au

Website
www.queenwood.nsw.edu.au

A rigorous academic curriculum within a balanced program of activities has been the hallmark of a Queenwood education for over 90 years. Within a strong learning community, we create space for our girls to engage with big ideas and connect with a diverse range of people and communities. At Queenwood, our commitment is to a liberal education – an education which, at its core, develops rigorous thinking and the practice of inquiry.

Our Programs

We are an independent Kindergarten to Year 12 non-selective day school for girls that provides a well-balanced curriculum catering to individual differences. We seek to develop in our students the knowledge, skills and habits which will be the foundation for a lifelong awakening to the complexity of the world. As girls move through the school there are increasing opportunities and expectations for independence. Our curriculum, pastoral care structures and extra-curricular programs create a safe but challenging framework within which girls learn to manage their work, their time, their relationships and responsibilities – skills which are essential to a happy and productive life.

International Baccalaureate

We offer dual IB and HSC pathways for Year 11 and 12 students, and each girl has the opportunity to choose the pattern of study which bests suits her individual interests and preference. Our IB results demonstrate the commitment to academic rigour offered at Queenwood, with 56% of students completing our last IB Program placing in the Top 5% of the state with their overall mark. This has enabled our alumnae to attend Universities within Australia, as well as in the United Kingdom and the United States of America, such as Oxford, Cambridge, Harvard and Brown Universities. Our commitment to the life of the mind reaches far beyond the examination syllabus, and we recognise the school years as an essential grounding in developing an intelligent and sensitive awareness of the world.

Our Values

Truth, Courage and Service underpin a Queenwood education. Growing in wisdom with a strong sense of identity and self-knowledge aid students in seeking a deep understanding of the truths of the world. That sense of purpose, the willingness to engage with challenge and the desire to make a contribution remain at the heart of Queenwood's mission. By thinking and acting independently, our girls are keen to courageously engage with contemporary social and political issues, thereby deepening their knowledge of themselves and gaining deeper and more nuanced perspectives on the world. We encourage our students at every level to contribute in thought, word and deed: responding to the vulnerable and marginalised with respect and compassion; speaking out with courage; and taking action in their service.

Principal
Patrick Gale

DP coordinator
Melanie Waugh

Status State

Boarding/day Day

Gender Coeducational

Language of instruction
English

Authorised IB programmes
DP

Address
564 East Coast Road
Mairangi Bay
Auckland 0753 | **NEW ZEALAND**

TEL +64 9 477 0150

Email
info@rangitoto.school.nz

Website
www.rangitoto.school.nz

This world-class institution is the largest school in New Zealand with over 3000 students, and is perhaps the most internationally acclaimed New Zealand school. Rangitoto's success is the result of expert teaching in a wide range of academic subjects and extensive extra-curricular opportunities including music, dance, drama and over 40 different sports. The facilities, passionate staff and culture of excellence inspire students to become the best they can be.

Rangitoto has a focus on diversity and has around 50 different nationalities in the school. Our IB students have been accepted into some of the world's best universities, including Cambridge and Oxford in the UK, and Princeton in the USA.

Rangitoto College is located on the beautiful, safe North Shore of Auckland, New Zealand. The school is close to beaches, parks, shops and cinemas, and is about 25 minutes from downtown.

Rangitoto College has some of the best facilities in the Southern Hemisphere including: modern classrooms, a library and information centre featuring senior study and reading rooms, computer access for all students, an auditorium, an Olympic standard all weather hockey turf, three gymnasiums and a weights room, an all-weather athletics track, five sports fields. A purpose built Science block with laboratories for Physics, Chemistry, Biology and Electronics. An English block featuring television and film studios and drama rooms, a music block with practice and performance space. A new dance studio with sprung floor, and a large modern swimming pool and sports institute on the school boundary.

Rangitoto College has been hosting international students for over 15 years and we have developed excellent systems to help students adapt to life in a new country. First language support is available for Korean, Chinese and Spanish speaking students.

A dedicated team of non-teaching and teaching staff, the IB Diploma co-ordinator and a Deputy Principal takes care of our IB students, meeting with them regularly to check they are doing well academically and personally.

(Founded 1884)

Principal
Mr Stephen Webber

DP coordinator
Darren Taylor

Status Private

Boarding/day Day

Gender Coeducational

Language of instruction
English

Authorised IB programmes
DP

Age Range 3 – 19

Address
272 Military Road
Cremorne
NSW 2090 | AUSTRALIA

TEL +61 2 9908 6479

Email
dtaylor@redlands.nsw.edu.au
registrar@redlands.nsw.edu.au

Website
www.redlands.nsw.edu.au

Redlands is a leading Australian independent school that offers a contemporary real world education, fostering academic excellence and confidence for life.

We have offered the International Baccalaureate Diploma Programme for Years 11-12 since 1988, longer than any other school in New South Wales. The 30-year association with the IB has helped the school build its reputation as a leading provider of a well-rounded global education.

Redlands provides an extensive range of opportunities – academic, sports, creative, outdoor education, service – for students to learn, to achieve and to develop their unique skills and talents.

The rich and balanced education program is aimed at developing well-rounded, confident and compassionate young adults who are prepared for life after school, ready to meet challenges and embrace opportunities and change in the 21st century.

Our students work together within an inclusive, real world, coeducational environment, complemented by a comprehensive leadership and service programme, to develop the knowledge, capability and confidence to let their light shine – at school and beyond.

At Redlands students receive an outstanding academic education as a result of the school's individual approach, committed teachers and world-class learning programmes and resources.

In embarking on the IB Diploma Programme at Redlands, students will commit themselves to:

- a two-year journey of discovery and self-awareness;
- an experience that will be ultimately both rewarding and empowering; and
- an outcome that will enable a smooth transition between school and university.

As a non-selective school, students who come from over 30 different countries have the opportunity to study for the IB Diploma Programme if they so wish. Careful guidance is undertaken in considering course structure and styles of learning to assist students in making the right choice for them. Each year approximately 50% of Redlands students select the IB.

Redlands IB Results

- In recent years, ten Redlands students have achieved the perfect IB score – 45/45, putting them in the top 0.2% of IB Diploma Programme students worldwide.
- In 2018, 47% of candidates achieved an IB score of 37+, equating to an ATAR of 95 and above.
- From 2011 to 2018, 12% of candidates were awarded rare bilingual diplomas – in French, German, Italian, Chinese, Japanese, Korean, Dutch, Danish, Swedish and Spanish.

At Redlands, all components of the IB Diploma Programme are delivered by a strong team of IB teachers, including moderators in their subject areas, IB trained workshop leaders and experienced teachers.

For more information about Redlands please contact the Registrar or visit our website: www.redlands.nsw.edu.au.

(Founded 1994)

School Principal
Ms. Sarah Osborne-James

DP coordinator
Sara Morrow

Status Private

Boarding/day Mixed

Gender Coeducational

Language of instruction
English

Authorised IB programmes
DP

Age Range 2 – 18 years

Number of pupils enrolled
1000

Fees
US$10,600 – US$22,860

Address
33/3 Moo 1, Pong
Banglamung
Chonburi
20150 | THAILAND

TEL +66 (0)93 135 7736

Email
admissions@
regents-pattaya.co.th

Website
www.nordangliaeducation.com/
our-schools/pattaya

About Our School

Regents International School Pattaya is like no other school in Thailand. As part of the global family of 66 premium Nord Anglia schools located around the world, we provide unique learning opportunities far beyond the ordinary. We are an exciting, vibrant and inclusive school which has something to offer to every child and every family in our dynamic and diverse community.

We have just over 1000 students aged from 2 to 18, spread evenly across our Early Primary, Primary and Secondary schools, including around 70 boarding students. As both a day and boarding school we encourage our students to be ambitious in their learning and believe there is no limit to what your child can achieve. We are the most successful school on the Eastern Seaboard with a long-established reputation over the past 25 years. Our students are successful because our approach encourages children to think for themselves, how to question, how to learn – skills that will last them for a lifetime.

Regents is the leading school on the Eastern Seaboard for good reason. We have joined forces with the world famous Juilliard School of Performing Arts in New York, and we also collaborate with the prestigious Massachusetts Institute of Technology (MIT). As well as being part of the Nord Anglia family of schools, who provide an outstanding education to over 64,000 students around the world, we are also proud to be a Round Square school, offering unique opportunities for our students to take part in many exciting global projects.

Boarding

We provide a safe, friendly and active boarding community with the emphasis on continued learning. We provide opportunities to collaborate, study independently, have fun, be active and have a sense of adventure. Our boarders develop into confident, independent, resilient and caring individuals who will make the world a better place. The outstanding range of learning opportunities and new environments to discover in Thailand and in South East Asia, make the boarding experience here so much richer and better value-for-money when compared with boarding schools in the UK, Western Europe and North America.

We Invite You to Experience It For Yourself

Choosing the right community and learning environment for your child is a major decision. We hope you agree that Regents is not only a fabulous school but also the right school for you and we look forward to welcoming you into our family.

Ritsumeikan Uji Junior and Senior High School

(Founded 1994)

Head of School
Charles Fox

DP coordinator
Marcelo Schwarz

Status Private

Boarding/day Mixed

Gender Coeducational

Language of instruction
English, Japanese (IBDP in English)

Authorised IB programmes
DP

Age Range 12 – 17

Number of pupils enrolled
1520

Fees
¥1,600,000

Address
33-1 Hachikenyadani
Hirono-cho
Uji, Kyoto, Kansai
611-0031 | JAPAN

TEL +81 774 41 3000
FAX +81 774 41 3555

Email
ib-info@ujc.ritsumei.ac.jp

Website
www.ujc.ritsumei.ac.jp/ujc_e/

About
Ritsumeikan Uji Junior and Senior High School is located in Uji City, a beautiful and historic site with easy access to Kyoto and Osaka. The school is mixed boarding and day, coeducational, and offers an integrated six-year curriculum. Ritsumeikan Uji High School was established in 1994 as an affiliated school of Ritsumeikan University, one of the largest and most prestigious universities in Japan. The school was rebuilt in its current location in 2002 and established a junior high school in 2003.

IPS
The IPS (International Preparatory Stream) is a junior high school programme, specially designed for young Japanese returnees and non-Japanese expatriates to experience an authentic Japanese education, while engaging in a rigorous core of internationally-oriented academic subjects. Those core subjects are taught in English by IB-trained teaching staff, and accredited by the Ministry of Education towards the Japanese junior high school certificate. On completion, students have the knowledge, skills, and moral grounding to matriculate successfully into our IB Diploma Programme, or any other top-level educational courses of study in the world.

IBDP
Authorized as an IB World School in 2009, Ritsumeikan Uji was the first Japanese (non-international) school in the Kansai region to offer the Diploma Programme. Since then, we have honed our course to provide all the academic rigour, moral development, and future-oriented learning of the English IBDP in an approach that recognises the unique needs of students in Japan. Our course structure guarantees students the chance to not only finish high school with an English language or bilingual IB Diploma, but also the Japanese high school graduation certificate. Our programme prides itself on small class sizes, individualised care, and a supportive learning community, guided by a team of highly experienced and professional staff. With their bicultural abilities and top level educational backgrounds, our graduates have gone on to study at leading Japanese universities such as Tokyo, Kyoto, and Tohoku universities, as well as prestigious schools overseas including at Amherst College, the Australian National University, Brown University, Dartmouth University, Duke University, Imperial College London, the National University of Singapore, New York University Abu Dhabi, Toronto University, and many others.

Resources and Events
IPS and DP students at Ritsumeikan Uji have access to first-class resources, including four fully equipped science labs, a multilingual library, media labs, and an observatory. Our community calendar is full of whole-school and IB-specific events including Culture Week, Sports Day, Research Presentation Day, Astronomy Night, Talent Show, and our annual art festival. Our GCP (Global Challenge Program) also offers DP students regular chances each year to travel overseas, learn more about the world, make friends, and broaden their horizons.

Boarding
IBDP students are welcome to join our dormitory community with students from around the world. The dormitory provides meals, wireless internet, is a short bus ride to campus and an easy walk to the city centre.

Royal Military College

Head of School
Mr. Razmi Bin Abdul Razak

DP coordinator
Lee Ling Low

Status State

Boarding/day Boarding

Gender Male

Language of instruction
English

Authorised IB programmes
DP

Number of pupils enrolled
500

Address
Kem Perdana Sungai Besi
Kuala Lumpur
57000 | MALAYSIA

TEL +60 3 89465402
FAX +60 3 89465453

Email
mtdibdp@rmc.edu.my

Royal Military College (RMC), also known as Maktab Tentera Diraja (MTD) was established on 3 July 1952. As inspired by the then Malaya High Commissioner, Field Marshall Tun Sir Gerald Templer, RMC aims to prepare young Malaysians to take their places as officers in the Malaysian Armed Forces, in the higher divisions of the public service and as leaders in the professional, commercial and industrial life of the country. Embracing the slogan "SERVE TO LEAD", it is also the mission of the school to provide a comprehensive smart learning environment to develop leaders with calibre, high integrity and noble personality to serve in the public and corporate sector.

Uniquely set in a multiracial context, students aged 16 to 19, are put through an active menu of training, combined with classes, games, extra-mural activities and prep work. These training and education inculcated self-discipline, self-reliance and self-confidence. Experience of living together in a multi-cultural and multi-religious society develops tolerance, empathy, trust, strong moral values and camaraderie. Dynamic and distinguished mentors and teachers impressed upon them the meaning of integrity, courage, loyalty and honour. Together, they have successfully produced a new generation of leaders and have achieved scholastic excellence with a relentless spirit of high-self-esteem to see through the tough to become the prominent. Graduates of the school have taken positions as ministers, secretary-generals, chiefs of Armed Forces, academicians, heads of non-governmental organizations, chief executive officers of companies, sportsman and international artist.

RMC receives authorization to become an IB World School on 3 July 2015 to implement the International Baccalaureate Diploma Programme (IBDP) and has its first cohort of DP students on 10 August 2015. To enable RMC to continue to produce leaders of tomorrow, we need to rededicate ourselves to the spirit of the founding charter. Having the IB Learner Profile in mind and empowered by the mission of the International Baccalaureate, RMC now aspires to develop principled, inquiring, knowledgeable and caring leaders who are life-long learners, to create a better and more peaceful world.

(Founded 1957)

Head of School
Daniel Smith

DP coordinator
Timothy Pettine

Status Private, Non-Profit

Boarding/day Mixed

Gender Coeducational

Language of instruction
English

Authorised IB programmes
DP

Age Range 2 – 18

Number of pupils enrolled
1200

Fees
US$13,140 – US$24,130

Address
6 Ramkhamhaeng 184
Minburi
Bangkok
10510 | THAILAND

TEL +66 (0)2 791 8900
FAX +66 (0)2 791 8901

Email
admissions@rism.ac.th

Website
www.rism.ac.th

RUAMRUDEE
INTERNATIONAL SCHOOL

Founded in 1957, Ruamrudee International School (RIS) was one of the first international schools in Asia to be accredited by the Western Association of Schools and Colleges. Today, RIS continues to deliver an outstanding academic program and is a model of excellence and innovation in global education. The school's core values embed service learning, character development, and global citizenship into our enriched American curriculum. Our teachers are creative, compassionate experts in their fields; 72% of our faculty hold master's degrees or higher.

An IB World School since 1998, RIS offers students a rigorous and extremely successful International Baccalaureate Diploma Programme. Our IB Diploma students scored an average of 35 for the past four years, far above world averages. After graduation, our students go on to attend the most prestigious universities in the world and can then be found working in all branches of medicine; as government leaders, diplomats, and researchers; in the entertainment and film industries, as professional athletes, and in the emerging fields of AI and design technologies.

Located just outside of Bangkok, the school's 29-acre clean-air campus is less than half an hour from Suvarnabhumi International Airport and is supported by a thriving local community. State-of-the-art facilities include 21st-century learning spaces, a culinary arts center, recording studio, industrial design studio, and a makerspace/robotics lab. Our middle and high school students who live on campus enjoy a contemporary boarding facility with a warm, familial feel.

At Ruamrudee International School, we nurture the minds, hearts, and hands of our students. From PreK 2 through grade 12, students benefit from small class sizes, relevant and innovative electives, modern languages, a vibrant performing and visual arts program, and one of the largest athletic programs of any international school in Southeast Asia. RIS offers a comprehensive extended day program with creative enrichment opportunities. Our Student Services department, led by school psychologists, ensures that our English Language Development and Learning Support programs meet the diverse needs of all our students. All RIS students are able to excel, both in and out of the classroom.

As it has been for over 60 years, our deeply ingrained culture of self-reflection and self-improvement has resulted in students who are creative, compassionate, critical thinkers. Their commitment to leading happy, healthy lives while helping others do the same is why RIS students continue to forge positive, lasting legacies for the world.

Head of School
Ms Snehal Pinto

PYP coordinator
Bhavi Furia

Status Private

Boarding/day Day

Gender Coeducational

Language of instruction
English

Authorised IB programmes
PYP

Address
Yamuna Nagar
Lokhandwala, Andheri (west)
Mumbai, Maharashtra
400058 | INDIA

TEL +91 22 2632 0203/05

Email
rgs.andheri@ryanglobal.org

Website
www.ryanglobalschools.com

Ryan Global School is a vibrant and dynamic coeducational day school providing global curriculum in order to develop young minds to be prepared for an international interface and be lifelong learners. The school has established reputation in academic excellence and the extra-curricular activities. In the recent C-fore survey by Education World Magazine, the school has been adjudged amongst the best International Schools in India. Child centric friendly atmosphere is achieved through a meaningful partnership with the stakeholders ie parents, well wishers, staff, faculty and our students.

Our Mission Statement:- Ryan Global School delivers high quality teaching and learning within a safe, energetic and intellectually-challenging environment. We encourage our students to be inquirers, reflective and collaborative thus preparing them as life long learners and ethical citizens within a democratic society and global community.

Facilities

Ryan Global School provides facilities appropriate for quality teaching and learning. Besides the current norm of providing facilities which is conducive for learning it specially offers a plethora of enriching school activities, trans-disciplinary in nature and aspire to go beyond the given requirements in enhancing the learning experience for its students.

Academic

Ryan Global believes in developing a dedicated team of staff and teachers who are professionally trained and equipped to channelize their energy towards innovative teaching practices and are encouraged regularly to participate in a variety of training workshops, seminars, conferences and team building exercises which play a vital role in upgrading the knowledge base and the latest trends in education.

As an authorized IB World School and also an authorized Leaning Centre for the Cambridge International Examinations (CIE), Ryan Global School offers:

- The IB PYP (IB Primary Years Programme)
- CIE – IGCSE and AS/A Levels

Beyond Academic

Ryan Global School is part of the Ryan International Group of Institutions which has a nationwide presence. With farsighted vision of its Chairman, Dr. A. F. Pinto and MD, Madam Grace Pinto, the group has pioneered significant national and international events in order to develop excellence in leadership. By going beyond the traditional academic practices, the group has made a lasting impact in the segment of education.

The Ryan Group has been the first in the country to host the International Children's Festival of Performing Arts (ICFPA) and Indian Model United Nations (INMUN). Ryan hosted the prestigious World Scholar's Cup with record breaking participation from the students which is now the largest ever regional round in the history of the World Scholar's Cup amongst 40 countries of the world. Cultural Exchange Programmes, NASA – USA educational Trip, Social Service Camp are regular fixtures on the school calendar. RYAN TV – a media initiative mentors students to create India's youngest breed of technicians, news anchors, cinematographers and so forth. In the field of sport, the school has collaborated with the best in the industry to bring world-class coaching to its children.

Sanjan Nagar
Public Education Trust
Higher Secondary School

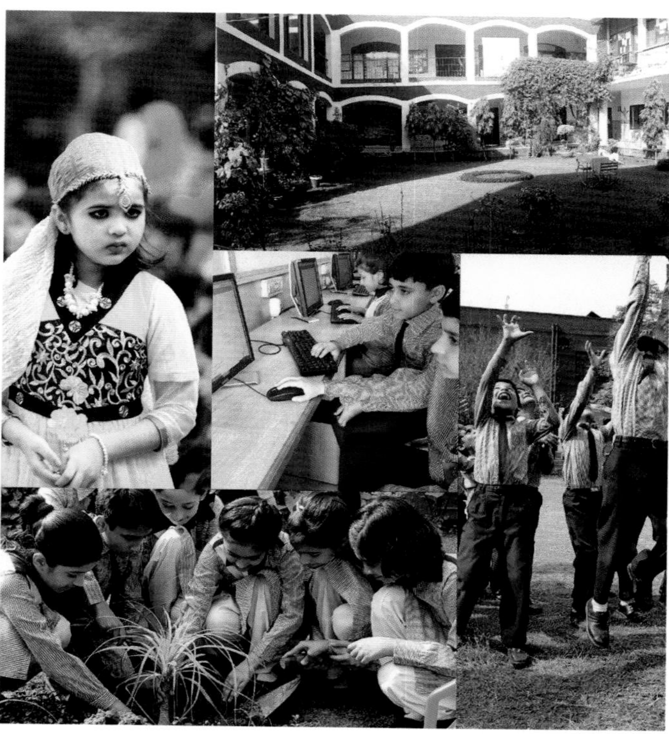

Principal of the School
Ms. Farzana Kausar

Section Head Misbah Rani

PYP coordinator Danial Ishaq

Status Private
(Not For Profit Trust School)

Boarding/day Day

Gender Coeducational

Language of instruction
English

Authorised IB programmes
PYP

Address
117 A, Anum Street
Glaxo Town, Ferozepur Road
Lahore, Punjab | PAKISTAN

TEL +92 42 35950676

Email
principalsnss@snpet.org

Website
www.snpet.org

Background: Sanjan Nagar is a journey of lifelong learning unlocking the potential of children/families from diverse and disadvantaged backgrounds. It is an evolving school for the future nurturing young learners through inquiry based liberal education in a global context bearing the motto 'Enabling our Future'.

'Sanjan Nagar' means 'people's voice'. 'Sanjan' is 'truth seeking' and 'Nagar' means abode for in depth inquiry. Inspired by the philosophy of Mr. Raza Kazim, the patron of the school, Pakistan's Renaissance man, the school was established in 1995 through philanthropy for low income communities. The Board and the Education Committee are active governance bodies providing close oversight for the IB PYP and recently embarked MYP.

School Vision: *"To enable children and youth to become caring, knowledgeable and creative citizens of tomorrow for the meaningful progress of our society through a holistic education experience."*

The School: The Sanjan Nagar School shifted to its current purpose built facility in 2003. A co-education facility since 2006, today the flagship campus is a single shift facility with 910 students enrolled from pre-school to grade XII, providing 15 years of rich experiential learning, respecting diversity.

It boasts of many alumni returning to school, as teachers and young leaders, an inspiration for the Sanjan Nagar chronicles.

IB Primary Years Programme: Sanjan Nagar is the only non-elite IB school in the country; it was the first school in Punjab province to be authorized for IB PYP. The school seeking authorization for the MYP and is in the consideration phase.

Student activities: The school's enrichment program is embedded in programs on peace, tolerance, language development, exploring literature, e-learning, youth leadership, arts and crafts, theatre /music, sports, field visits, hosting/participating in the children's literature festivals; students exchange programs in USA (IEARN-YES) and South Asia for experiential learning.

Facilities: Students Club spanned a three week program in Chess, Literature, Debates, Communication; Design; Citizenship; Science, Environment, and Guiding; teaching expression, experiential and collaborative learning. Sanjan Nagar provides rich facilities and atmosphere for cultural inquiry, exploration and exposure to multiple identities. The facilities include: a Custom Built School; well stocked Library, Computer and Science Labs; Auditorium; Theatre/Arts spaces, Sports/Play areas; kitchen garden; health/ referrals. The campus is an optimized space for its large & diverse student body and local community.

Sanjay Ghodawat International School

Head of School
Mrs. Sasmita Mohanty

Chairman
Mr. Sanjay D. Ghodawat

DP coordinator
Dhruv Prajapati

Status Private

Boarding/day Mixed

Gender Coeducational

Language of instruction
English

Authorised IB programmes
DP

Address
Gat No. 555
Kolhapur – Sangli Highway
Atigre, Maharashtra | **INDIA**

TEL +91 230 2689700

Email
principal@sgischool.in

Website
www.sgischool.in

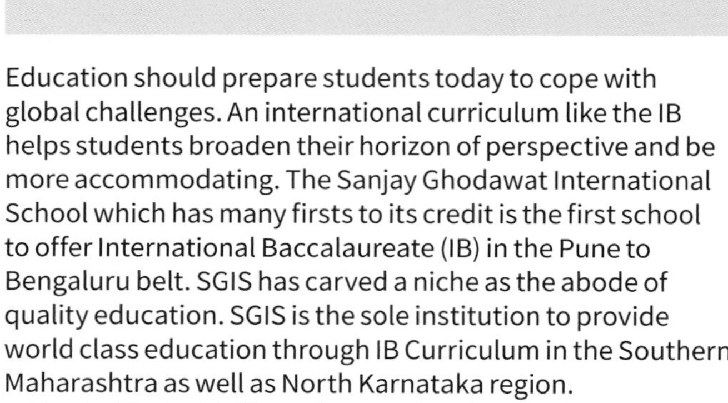

Education should prepare students today to cope with global challenges. An international curriculum like the IB helps students broaden their horizon of perspective and be more accommodating. The Sanjay Ghodawat International School which has many firsts to its credit is the first school to offer International Baccalaureate (IB) in the Pune to Bengaluru belt. SGIS has carved a niche as the abode of quality education. SGIS is the sole institution to provide world class education through IB Curriculum in the Southern Maharashtra as well as North Karnataka region.

Nestled in the idyllic and serene locale away from the hustle and bustle of city life, SGIS offers the ideal high seat of learning. The state of the art infrastructure complements the needs of the 21st century learner. The attributes of the IB learner profile are emphasized at SGIS to provide all round education which nurture young people to make changes in the country they live in. Our core values, leadership, discipline, academic excellence and global citizenship, illuminate our way, as we guide our students to become independent and productive humans.

We offer residential facilities with comfortable and cozy pastoral care. The hightech classrooms, top notch psychology and science laboratories, world class sports facilities make SGIS the perfect destination for global education. We offer variety of indoor and outdoor sports including horse riding, swimming, archery, rifle shooting, badminton, table tennis, lawn tennis etc. While Multi- Gym is the biggest attraction, the magnanimous stadium can host international sporting events like Cricket, Football, Volley Ball. SGIS takes utmost care about the health and wellness. The balanced nutritious food is the icing on the cake. All these facilities are provided at very affordable fees with the sole intention of extending global curriculum to the beloved students.

SCOTS COLLEGE

Learning. For Life

(Founded 1916)

Headmaster
Mr Graeme Yule

Senior School Principal
Mr Christian Zachariassen

Middle School Principal
Mr Matt Allen

Senior School Principal & PYP coordinator
Mr Mike Hansen

MYP coordinator
Ms Kate Bondett

DP coordinator
Mr Mike McKnight

Status Private

Boarding/day Mixed

Gender
Male (Yrs 1-10), Co-ed (Yrs 11-13)

Language of instruction
English

Authorised IB programmes
PYP, MYP, DP

Number of pupils enrolled
870

Address
PO Box 15064
Strathmore, Wellington
6243 | NEW ZEALAND

TEL +64 4 388 0850
FAX +64 4 388 2887

Email enrolments@scotscollege.school.nz

Website
www.scotscollege.school.nz

Scots College is an independent Presbyterian day and boarding school, Years 1-13, located in Wellington, New Zealand. Founded in 1916, Scots College has a proud history and reputation for providing a world-class education. The rigorous academic curriculum is supported by a diverse range of sporting, cultural, service and leadership opportunities, enabling each student to reach their potential in all aspects of their lives.

The College is comprised of three schools; Preparatory, Middle and Senior. It is an authorized IB World School and the IB programmes are an integral part of the school's ethos and curriculum design, developing students prepared to learn for life. The school House system provides another dimension to life at Scots with a Dean and Tutor overseeing the pastoral care of each student.

Prep School (Boys, Years 1-6)

Scots Prep School provides a safe and caring environment where boys can experience the joys and challenges of learning as they build strong foundations for their future years. The Prep School proudly delivers the IB Primary Years Programme (PYP).

Middle School (Boys, Years 7-10)

Scots Middle School provides the opportunity for young men to realise their potential in a supportive and positive learning environment. Students take specialist classes, specifically in science, arts, technology and languages, and are provided opportunities outside the classroom with weekly sporting programmes, service initiatives and an EOTC programme. The Middle School delivers the Middle Years Programme (MYP).

Senior School (Co-educational, Years 11-13)

Scots College's Senior School is unique in providing a dual pathway education in Years 12-13; where students can choose to study via either the IB Diploma Programme or New Zealand's National Certificate of Education Achievement system (NCEA), in which Scots College consistently achieves above a 90% university entrance pass rate. In his final year of schooling Scots College student Andrew Tang received the 2017 Top Scholars Award for the top national Scholarship NCEA results.

Located in Wellington

Wellington is the capital of New Zealand – a harbour city at the heart of government, the centre of business, home to international embassies and renowned for its vibrant city culture and cosmopolitan population of 180,000 centrally, and 450,000 within the region. The Scots College campus is located in the suburb of Strathmore, just ten minutes drive to the central city.

Boarding School

Scots College boarding provides accommodation and care for over 100 students in a supportive and family orientated environment. There are currently over 60 international students at Scots College and over 40 nationalities are represented within the school community.

Santa Sabina College

Principal
Paulina Skerman

PYP coordinator
Karen Campbell

DP coordinator
Julie Harris

Status Private

Boarding/day Day

Gender Coeducational P-4, Female 5-12

Language of instruction
English

Authorised IB programmes
PYP, DP

Number of pupils enrolled
1210

Fees
Day: AU$14,675 – AU$23,650

Address
90 The Boulevarde
Strathfield
Sydney
NSW 2135 | AUSTRALIA

TEL +61 2 9745 7000
FAX +61 2 9745 7001

Email
enrolment@ssc.nsw.edu.au

Website
www.ssc.nsw.edu.au

Welcome to Santa Sabina College. We are a Catholic Dominican P-12 school located in the diverse, multicultural Inner West of Sydney.

Established in 1894 by a group of Dominican Sisters, Santa Sabina College, a Catholic school in the Dominican tradition, educates students to achieve personal excellence, to act with justice and compassion, and to embrace the future with an optimistic global vision.

As a P-12 College we benefit from the continuity of approaches to learning from the early years to Year 12. Inquiry learning in a student-centred learning environment characterises each stage of the learning journey. Our early education centre, Mary Bailey House, embeds the principles of inquiry learning through the Reggio Emilia programme.

We are an IB World School for the Primary Years Programme (Years P-5) and the Diploma Programme (Years 11 and 12).

Our Middle Years (6-8) and Senior Years (9-12) at Santa Sabina College are similarly committed to inquiry at increasingly sophisticated levels. Our strategic intent is to grow a community of discerning scholars who are intellectually curious, creative and reflective.

The pastoral care of our students is integral to our approaches to teaching and learning.

The significant sporting and co-curricular life of the College ensure that education is holistic and inclusive of a wide variety of student interests and abilities. Music education P-12 is designed to maximise students' opportunities for authentic performances in a range of contexts.

The structures and processes we employ at different stages of a student's education share common principles that reflect our values of community, service, prayer and learning. We encourage students to make good choices, and support them when they don't. Our aim is always to work with students and families in a spirit of community. The emotional, social and spiritual growth of students is critical to their present and future lives. It cannot be an afterthought to academic achievement.

Learning is enabled through a rich variety of educational experiences. Students participate in retreats, outdoor education, curricular and co-curricular programmes at our Tallong campus in the Southern Highlands. In the secondary years, students are encouraged to participate in immersion experiences to Central Australia, Solomon Islands and to South Africa to deepen their understanding of global interconnectedness. These experiences are part of the fabric of life at Santa Sabina.

Our ex-student community is active, involved and committed to both the legacy and the future of the College. Our Dominican Sisters have a continuing presence on our campuses, and offer pastoral support to families, as well as to students.

We invite you join us in 'this place' that is so special to generations of families.

Scottish High International School

(Founded 2005)

Head of School
Ms Sudha Goyal

PYP coordinator
Ms Seema Bhati

DP coordinator
Ms Sudha Goyal

Status Private

Boarding/day Boarding

Gender Coeducational

Language of instruction
English

Authorised IB programmes
PYP, DP

Age Range 3½ – 17

Fees
On request

Address
G-Block, Sector 57
Sushant Lok-II
Gurugram, Haryana
122011 | INDIA

TEL +91 124 4112781-90

FAX +91 124 4112788

Email
schooldirector@scottishigh.com

Website
www.scottishigh.com

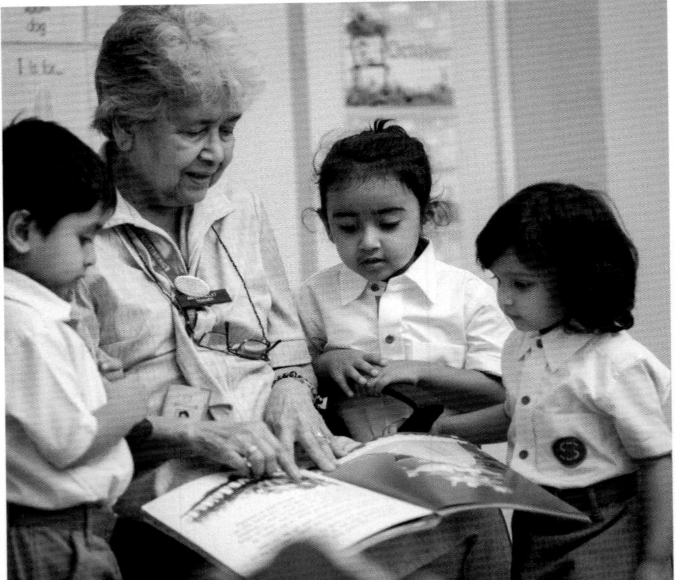

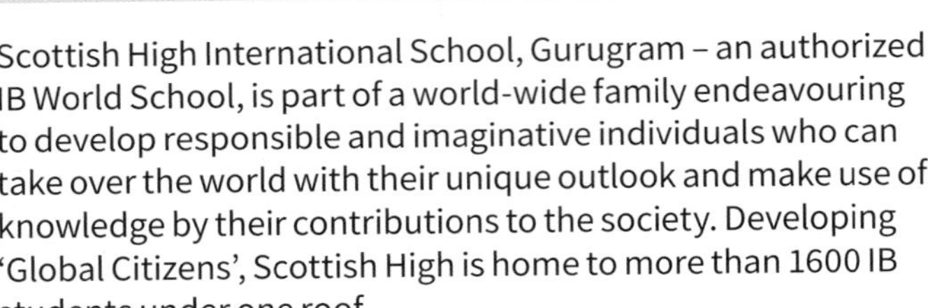

Scottish High International School, Gurugram – an authorized IB World School, is part of a world-wide family endeavouring to develop responsible and imaginative individuals who can take over the world with their unique outlook and make use of knowledge by their contributions to the society. Developing 'Global Citizens', Scottish High is home to more than 1600 IB students under one roof.

With EOMS ISO 21001:2018 Certification, for Educational Organisation Management System, Scottish High sustains and maintains its proud heritage of quality teaching & learning, occupational health & safety and safe environmental practices through the combined effort of the dedicated students, staff and parents. It is also the first school in India to be associated with this standard to maintain high-quality education.

Curriculum/Examinations offered

Scottish High International School offers:

- IB Primary Years Programme for Pre-Nursery to Grade V
- CAIE Secondary I and IGCSE for Grades VI to X
- IB Diploma Programme for Grades XI & XII
- The National Curriculum (ICSE) for Grades VI to X and ISC for Grades XI & XII

Apart from the academic curriculum, Scottish High:

- Has an authorized NCC(National Cadet Corps) wing for boys and girls
- Partners with The Global Education Leadership Foundation (TGELF), which trains young students to cultivate leadership qualities
- Is an authorized centre by CAIE to run the professional development qualifications for teachers
- Is a partner with TAISI, The Association of International Schools of India
- Is associated with Special Olympics, Bharat
- Collaborates with the Govt. of India for research in Autism
- Is an Institutional member of 'The British Council Library', 'The American Center Library', 'The Alliance Francaise De Delhi', 'DELNET' (Developing Library Network)

Facilities:

Structural

- 5 Acres Of Lush Green Campus
- Centrally Air-conditioned Campus with Full Power Back up (2000 KILOWATTS)
- Extended Day Boarding – 8:00 am to 4 pm
- Modern Medical Infirmary with Resident Doctor, Nurses & Dietician and Dental Centre
- 1000 Seating Dining Hall
- 1100 Seating Air-conditioned Auditorium
- CCTV Secured & Fully Wi-Fi enabled Campus
- Fleet of Air-Conditioned Buses with GPS & CCTV
- 100 seating Audio-Visual Rooms

Scholastic

- Hi-tech Science, IT, Maths, Home Science, Social Science & Language Labs
- State-of-the-Art 'Innovation Lab'
- Atal Stem Lab
- Well Stocked Libraries

- Classroom Libraries
- Resource Centre for Research and International Curriculum
- CLUBS- Zumba, Photography, Robotics, Bridge, Astronomy, Environment, Special Olympics, Formula 1, MUN etc.

Sports & Physical Education

- Archery/Gymnastics/Cricket /Soccer /Tennis
- Skating/Bridge/Horse Riding/Taekwondo
- Swimming (Half Olympic Size Swimming Pool)
- Golf (Indoor Golf Academy with Simulator)
- Badminton/Chess/Yoga/Judo
- Table Tennis/ Basketball

Admissions open for the next academic year around August/September of the previous year.

Sekolah Pelita Harapan

SPH

(Founded 1993)

Head of School
Matthew Brian Mann

PYP coordinator
Ratna Setyowati Putri

MYP coordinator
Daniel Admiraal

DP coordinator
Ezmieralda Kallista

Status Private

Boarding/day Day

Gender Coeducational

Language of instruction
English

Authorised IB programmes
PYP, MYP, DP

Age Range 1 – 18

Number of pupils enrolled
2145

Address
2500 Boulevard Palem Raya
Lippo Village
Tangerang, Banten
15810 | INDONESIA

TEL +62 21 546 0234

Email
sph-lv@sph.ac.id

Website
www.sph.edu

For over 26 years Pelita Harapan schools have offered high-quality Christian education in Indonesia. The schools' practices are aligned with their Vision: True Knowledge, Faith in Christ and Godly Character; and their Mission: Proclaiming the preeminence of Christ and engaging in the redemptive restoration of all things in Him through holistic education.

The Lippo Village campus was founded in 1993 by the Yayasan Pendidikan Pelita Harapan (YPPH), followed by Sentul City in 1994, Lippo Cikarang in 1995, Kemang Village in 2010 and Pluit Village in 2014. With total enrollments numbering 2,145 students from Early Childhood Education (age 1 year) to Grade 12 (age 18 years) across the 5 schools around Jakarta, SPH exists to prepare students to become tomorrow's Indonesian leaders and world citizens.

SPH schools are members of the Council of International Schools (CIS), and are accredited by the Western Association of Schools and Colleges (WASC) and the Association of Christian Schools International (ACSI). The curriculum is internationally recognized and accredited by the world-renowned International Baccalaureate Organization (IBO). At Kemang Village, Lippo Cikarang and Pluit Village, the curriculum includes Cambridge and International Baccalaureate Programs.

Our teachers are recruited from countries overseas, mainly from the USA, Canada, Australia, Philippines as well as Indonesian teachers. We challenge our students to succeed academically and to reach their full potential in cultural, artistic, and athletic arenas. Academic results continue to place our IB Diploma graduates scoring above the world average. Almost all our graduates pursue higher education in well-respected universities around the world.

Besides being academic, SPH has a proud history of excellence in the Performing Arts. Our students perform locally and internationally. We also offer purposeful physical activities to equip our students with the skills, knowledge, and attitudes necessary to enjoy a physically active and healthy lifestyle.

SPH has excellent facilities to support creative teaching and an effective learning environment. These include swimming pools, tennis courts, gymnasiums, athletic field, soccer fields, basketball courts, badminton courts, fitness center, computer and science laboratories, food technology & design technology workshops, music rooms, art rooms, multipurpose rooms, resource rooms, libraries, health centers, bookstores, canteens and playgrounds.

The Sentul City campus provides a boarding option for students in grades 7-12. A chaplain, residence supervisors, nurse, and tutors support the Pelita Harapan House community. The Residence Hall is surrounded by a green environment, clean air, and all the school's facilities; resident students are provided a comfortable and welcoming home away from home, where they can maximize their learning and develop life-long friendships.

The student composition at each school varies from location to location; families are primarily Indonesian but include over 15 nationalities. The language of instruction is

English. Mandarin and Bahasa Indonesia are also offered to students. School fee ranges from US$ 5,000 up to US$ 25,000/ year across campuses and grades. 90% of our graduates are accepted and choose to pursue university studies at many reputable universities around the world.

Find out more about us, our admissions counsellor will be happy to respond to any questions and to provide more detailed information. We invite you to experience our campus in person. Contact our admissions office for more information.

Sendai Ikuei Gakuen

Head of School
Takehiko Katoh

MYP coordinator
Kerry Winter

DP coordinator
Anthony Sweeney

Status Private

Boarding/day Mixed

Gender Coeducational

Language of instruction
English, Japanese

Authorised IB programmes
MYP, DP

Age Range 12 – 18 years

Number of pupils enrolled
3150

Fees
Day: ¥663,310

Address
2-4-1 Miyagino
Miyagino-ku
Sendai, Miyagi, Tohoku
983-0045 | JAPAN

TEL +81 22 256 4141

Email
t.sweeney@i-lion.org

Website
sendaiikuei-english.jp

Sendai Ikuei Gakuen High School is located in the coastal area of north-east Japan. 90-minutes from Tokyo by bullet train. Sendai is the capital city of Miyagi and a home to over 1 million people. It is a thriving metropolis boasting vibrant festivals, local specialty cuisine and a hub for the Arts.

Sendai Ikuei Gakuen offers the MYP and DP in a unique dual language environment. It is committed to equipping students with the knowledge and skills needed for the 21st century. Though it is impossible to predict what today's students will face in the 21st century, it is possible to give them the skills to succeed in an uncertain future. Through offering the IB programmes at Sendai Ikuei Gakuen, we aim to:

- Be sincere and confident global communicators.
- Be responsible in our learning.
- Be innovative in addressing local and international issues in our community.

There is a growing number of international students studying at Sendai Ikuei Gakuen from a variety of backgrounds including China, Korea, Indonesia, Thailand, Uganda, and Kazakhstan – many of whom aspire to enter Japanese universities. The IB programmes at Sendai Ikuei Gakuen provide these students with the opportunities to further their horizons in the future by strengthening both their English and Japanese language skills to an academic level. Students can board at the school dormitory close to the Tagajo campus.

Sendai Ikuei Gakuen IB students experience a unique bilingual (English and Japanese) education in an international environment. Opportunities to study abroad, participate in local field trips and cultural activities, interact in Japanese and English with teachers and students from a variety of countries, study in state-of-the art facilities, engage in school-based Model United Nations camps, and CAS workshops, while experiencing the uniqueness and richness of Japanese culture.

Senior High School at Sakado, University of Tsukuba

Headmaster
Prof. Kenji Tamura

DP coordinator
Regina Ver-Santos

Status State

Boarding/day Day

Gender Coeducational

Language of instruction
English, Japanese

Authorised IB programmes
DP

Age Range 15 – 18

Number of pupils enrolled
480 (10 IB students for each year level)

Fees
¥800,000

Address
1-24-1 Chiyoda
Sakado, Saitama
350-0214 | JAPAN

TEL +81 49 281 1541
FAX +81 49 283 8017

Website
www.sakado-s.tsukuba.ac.jp

Senior High School at Sakado, University of Tsukuba (UTSS) is Japan's first "Integrated Course" high school, actively promoting reforms in education and research. In line with the school's mission to provide diverse learning opportunities to students, UTSS is now an IB World School offering the dual-language Diploma Programme in Japanese and English.

UTSS is an affiliated Article One high school of the University of Tsukuba. The school campus is located at Sakado, Saitama, approximately an hour from the center of Tokyo, with access through the Tobu Tojo line.

Students in the IBDP course of UTSS complete a three-year programme, beginning Year 1 with pre-DP and foundational courses, followed by Years 2 and 3 covering the 6 groups in the IBDP. The high school currently offers the following subjects under the IBDP:

Subjects in Japanese
- Japanese A: Language and Literature (HL)
- History (HL)
- Biology (SL)
- Mathematics AI (SL)

Subjects in English
- English B (HL)
- Theatre (SL)

The core subjects, Creativity, Activity and Service (CAS), Extended Essay (EE) and Theory of Knowledge (TOK) are delivered and supervised in Japanese, however, students have the option to write their EE in English.

The dual-language program requires the students to work in the context of Japanese and English. The curriculum practices and develops reading, speaking, listening and writing skills in both languages, with emphasis on the use of higher order thinking skills. Students use Japanese and English as a means to understand and express critical and analytical ideas, thus, they are expected to have a solid grasp of both languages.

Even before becoming an IB World School, UTSS has consistently exercised experiential learning through fieldwork, school camps, research, clubs, volunteer work and international student exchange. These activities provide diverse platforms to enrich their learning experiences, and complement the core subjects of the IBDP.

The teachers and staff of UTSS recognize that each student is an individual with unique capabilities and intelligences. The curriculum is designed to encourage and support students in choosing career paths where they will thrive. UTSS graduates are empowered to meet the challenges of a changing world – both local and international.

Seoul Foreign School

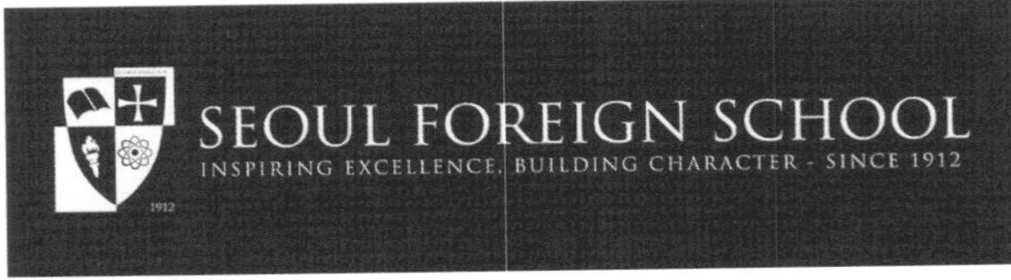

(Founded 1912)

Head of School
Mr. Colm Flanagan

Elementary School Principal
Damian Prest

Middle School Principal
Justin Smith

High School Principal
Jeffrey Holcomb

British School Principal
Andrew Freeman

PYP coordinator
Katherine Baird

MYP coordinator Adrian Gan

DP coordinator Piotr Kocyk

Status Private, Non-Profit

Boarding/day Day

Gender Coeducational

Language of instruction
English

Authorised IB programmes
PYP, MYP, DP

Age Range 2 – 18

Number of pupils enrolled
1450

Address
39 Yeonhui-ro 22-gil
Seodaemun-gu
Seoul 03723 | **REPUBLIC OF KOREA**

TEL +82 2 330 3100
FAX +82 2 330 1857

Email
admissions@seoulforeign.org

Website
www.seoulforeign.org

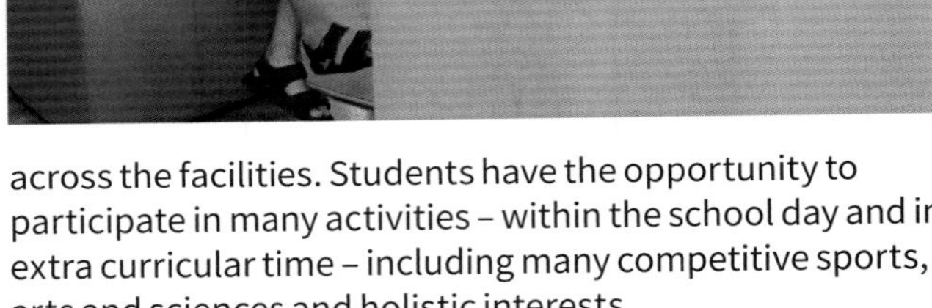

'International in Every way'
Seoul Foreign School is Seoul's longest established International school and was one of the first 10 international schools in the world. Founded in 1912 it offers a community of excellence coming together to educate children at all ages and all stages. We combine heritage with a passion for learning and are dedicated to the service of all.

The school has a current population of over 1400 students. Coming from over 50 countries and many diverse backgrounds our students have an opportunity to learn and understand about many cultures. We aim to build on this and offer a global perspective on all aspects of education.

Our four individual schools – Elementary, Middle, High and British – are situated together on a world class campus in central Seoul offering easy access from all popular residential areas. Physical, spiritual and academic needs are served across the facilities. Students have the opportunity to participate in many activities – within the school day and in extra curricular time – including many competitive sports, arts and sciences and holistic interests.

Teaching comprises a Pre- K to Grade 12 learning environment. The PYP and MYP are offered along with the English National Curriculum and both lead seamlessly into the IB Diploma Programme to prepare students for university and beyond. Our teachers are rigorously selected and their passion, inspiration and academic excellence ensure our students go on to attend prestigious colleges and schools and succeed in all walks of life.

We are a Christian school for all. Our students enjoy an education surrounded by our rich heritage in preparation for a future as global contributors.

(Founded 1996)

Director of Schools
Daniel Eschtruth

PYP coordinator
Janette Haggith

MYP coordinator
Maree Comerford

DP coordinator
Scott Simmons

Status Private

Boarding/day Day

Gender Coeducational

Language of instruction
English

Authorised IB programmes
PYP, MYP, DP

Age Range 2 – 18

Number of pupils enrolled
1800

Fees
Day: RMB117,500 – RMB270,000

Hongqiao Campus
1161 Hongqiao Road, Shanghai
200051 | CHINA

TEL +86 21 6261 4338
FAX +86 21 6261 4639

Hongqiao ECE Campus
2212 Hongqiao Road, Shanghai
200336 | CHINA

TEL +86 21 6295 1222

Pudong Campus
198 Hengqiao Road, Zhoupu, Pudong, Shanghai
201315 | CHINA

TEL +86 21 5812 9888

Email
admissions@scis-china.org

Website
www.scis-china.org

Established in 1996 as one of Shanghai's first international schools, Shanghai Community International School (SCIS) is a non-profit educational day school, governed by a self-perpetuating board of directors and overseen by the International Schools Foundation.

With over twenty years of rich tradition, SCIS offers a truly unique international experience. The SCIS community is unparalleled, consisting of a diverse mix of outstanding teachers, students, and parents representing over sixty nationalities and thirty-five languages, across six continents. SCIS leverages this unique community to provide a personalized approach to holistic education, ensuring all students have the opportunity to be successful.

SCIS is one of the first international schools in Shanghai to become fully authorized as an International Baccalaureate (IB) Continuum World School, a world class academic program aimed at rigorous critical thinking and global citizenship. This accreditation extends across all SCIS Campuses, including Hongqiao and Pudong, providing a seamless program for students aged 2-18, and comprised of the Primary Years Programme (PYP), Middle Years Programme (MYP), and Diploma Programme (DP).

Primary Years Programme (PYP) prepares students to become active, caring, lifelong learners who demonstrate respect for themselves and others and have the capacity to participate in the world around them. It focuses on the development of the whole child as an inquirer, both within and beyond the classroom. (Age 2-10)

Middle Years Programme (MYP) is a challenging framework that encourages students to make practical connections between their studies and the real world. The MYP is a five-year programme, which can be implemented in a partnership between schools. Students who complete the MYP are well-prepared to undertake the IB Diploma Programme (DP). (Age 11-15)

Diploma Programme (DP) is designed as an academically challenging and balanced program of education with final examinations that prepares students for success at university and life beyond. (Age 16-17)

Shanghai High School

(Founded 1865)

Head of School
Feng Zhigang

DP coordinator
Jiang Hao

Status State

Boarding/day Day

Gender Coeducational

Language of instruction
English

Authorised IB programmes
DP

Number of pupils enrolled
3923

Address
400 Shangzhong Road
Xuhui
Shanghai
200231 | CHINA

TEL +86 21 64765516

FAX +86 21 64533318

Email
admission@shsid.org

Website
www.shsid.org

The School

Established in 1865, Shanghai High School has an overall size of 340MU (223,617 square meters) and is historically one of the most well-known schools in China and around the world.

Shanghai High School International Division (SHSID) was founded on June 1, 1993. SHSID has two campuses and has enrolled about 3000 students from over 60 different countries.

In 1995, SHSID became an IB World School. SHSID has been authorized by the College Board to administer AP, SAT and PSAT exams and is also an authorized TOEFL, ACT and A-level exam center.

Highly Selective Curriculum

SHSID offers its students two different curricula: the US-based program and the IB Diploma Programme. In grades 11 and 12, the IB Diploma Programme is available and the Advanced Placement courses are offered to students from Grade 10 to Grade 12 as college preparation programs. There are 29 IB courses and 20 AP courses for students to choose from.

Approximately 600 compulsory and optional courses are offered for students in grades 1 through 12. A total of 5 different levels, including Standard, Standard Plus, and Honors, are available to meet the varying academic requirements of individual students.

SHSID's high school curriculum encourages a distinct focus on math, physics, chemistry, biology, and environmental science education. A strong foundation in science supports students' future advancement into higher education. In the humanities and arts, many students have been admitted to top liberal arts colleges, as well as various prominent arts and music academies. The curriculum at SHSID aims to fully develop and cultivate the personalities and talents of all students.

Digital Learning Environment

SHSID strives to create and maintain a modern and digitalized learning environment for students. The campus network, the school information system, the Desktop Cloud, digital libraries, and media centers provide students with opportunities to pursue learning and self-management online.

SHSID offers 30 world-class laboratories, including the Foundation Laboratory of Laser and Fiber Optics, the Modern Analytical Chemistry Laboratory, the Laboratory of Biochemistry and Molecular Biology, the Financial Investments Research Laboratory, and the Information Security Laboratory. At SHSID, these facilities offer students an excellent environment to pursue independent inquiry and research, while also encouraging them to identify and pursue their individual interests and aspirations for continued development.

SHSID also actively explores methods of applying digital tools toward education. New technology, such as the Cloud, Internet of Things, and modern tablets are introduced to stimulate individualized learning in a fully digitalized environment.

Green Campus and Excellent Facilities

Located in the south-west of Shanghai, SHSID has the largest school campus in the city. We devote over 50% of our site to green space containing seasonal flowers and over 10,000 trees. This beautiful location provides students with a pleasant environment that nurtures creativity.

SHSID owns a 400-meter standard rubberized running track, a FIFA-size soccer field, seven indoor and outdoor tennis courts, an Olympic-sized indoor swimming pool, an outdoor swimming pool, a multi-purpose gymnasium, an indoor table-tennis and badminton center, as well as several other facilities. With these numerous and varying amenities, students are able to enhance their physical development and sporting abilities in an easy and accessible manner.

SHSID also provides students with excellent art, music, and media facilities. The Digital Media Center, the Arts Center, and the Music and Performance Center are equipped with advanced devices and a wide array of musical instruments for students to improve their talents, skills, and artistic potential.

Excellent Faculty

SHSID maintains a top quality, diverse teaching staff by recruiting from China, the United States, Canada, and Great Britain. Over 45% of faculty members are expatriates, and the majority of our Chinese teachers have attended various educational programs abroad.

All of our educators have excellent educational backgrounds and extensive teaching experience. More than 65% of the teachers have completed post-graduate education, and over 50% of the teachers are professors, associate professors or senior teachers at SHSID.

SHSID enhances professional development by providing teachers with the chance to expand their teaching experience with opportunities to participate in seminars and training courses both at home and abroad.

Academic Achievement

IB Exam Results:

2017: Pass rate 100%, Average score 42
2018: Pass rate 100%, Average score 42
2019: Pass rate 100%, Average score 42

The AP program at SHSID produces outstanding results with an average score of approximately 4.6 (out of 5) on more than 700 exams.

SHSID graduates have been highly recognized by colleges worldwide, including Harvard University, Yale University, Princeton University, Stanford University, MIT, University of Chicago, Duke University, Brown University, University of Pennsylvania, Dartmouth College, University of California-Berkeley, etc in the U.S.; University of Oxford, University of Cambridge, Imperial College London, London School of Economics and Political Science, etc. in the U.K.; University of Toronto, McGill University, University of British Columbia, etc. in Canada; Tokyo University, Kyoto University, etc. in Japan; Seoul National University, Korea University, Yonsei University, etc. in South Korea; National University of Singapore, Nanyang Technological University, etc in Singapore; Peking University, Tsinghua University, University of Hong Kong, etc. in China. Talented graduates were even admitted into famous art or music schools, such as Rhode Island School of Design and Berklee College of Music. SHSID actively guides and supports every student towards realizing their own dreams. The high school college counseling office designs a series of personal growth programs to help students discover who they are and get into their best fit colleges.

Extracurricular Activities

SHSID offers a variety of extracurricular activities in many different areas, including studio arts, performing arts, gymnastics, science and technology, debate, drama, and news and media. All of these activities enable students to discover their personal interests and develop essential skills for the 21stCentury, including communication skills, collaboration skills, and leadership abilities.

SHSID encourages students to demonstrate their abilities, strengths and confidence in all manners of competition, both inside and outside of the school. Students have received numerous honors, such as, Best Delegation at the Harvard MUN (China), the top 10 of Envirothon North America, First Prize of Brainbee China, Bronze Medal of International Genetically Engineered Machine Competition, Champion of National Economic Challenge 2018 (China Round), and a wide range of sporting championships in events held with other international and local schools.

There are approximately one hundred clubs organized and managed by students at SHSID, covering a diverse and wide breadth of areas. Various clubs are devoted to charities and community service. These student clubs at SHSID support more than ten charity organizations and hundreds of people every year throughout the community and abroad.

Shanghai United International School, Hongqiao-Gubei Campus

上海協和双語学校
SHANGHAI UNITED INTERNATIONAL SCHOOL

(Founded 2003)

Principal
Mr David Walsh

PYP coordinator
Apple Zhang

DP coordinator
Derek Lee

Status Private

Boarding/day Day

Gender Coeducational

Language of instruction
English

Authorised IB programmes
PYP, DP

Number of pupils enrolled
1985

Gubei Campus
248 Hong Song Road (E), Gubei
Minhang District
Shanghai
201103 | CHINA

TEL +8621 51753030
FAX +8621 51753010

Hongqiao Campus
999 Hong Quan Road
Minhang District
Shanghai
201103 | CHINA

TEL +8621 34310090
FAX +8621 34316027

Email
annie.yan@suis.com.cn

Website
www.suis.com.cn

Shanghai United International School was founded in 2003 and was authorized as an IB World School in 2010.

Situated in Shanghai it caters for more than 1980 students on two campus,Hongqiao and Gubei. Hongqiao Campus offers IB PYP, Gubei Secondary Campus offers Key Stage 3, IGCSE and IBDP.

Students are drawn from more than 40 nationalities, represented across the schools. Close links with nearby Chinese primary and secondary schools allow for rich academic and cultural exchanges leading to the enhancement of the school's signature 'East meets West' characteristic.

At the end of Grade 5, students are bilingual, proficient in both Chinese and English and able to comfortably access the curriculum of their secondary school. Some students use three languages with ease.

Augmenting the academic work of the school is a wide-ranging programme of extracurricular activities catering for the cerebral, the athletic, the artistic and the social aspects of life – hugely supported and enjoyed by the students. The aim of the school is to produce students who are prepared to live life to the full and to contribute to making the world a better place for all.

School facilities include an extensive games field, a 400 seat auditorium, an indoor heated swimming pool, a very large gymnasium and a cultural centre for the benefit of the students (and community at weekends). The range of laboratories and specialist teaching rooms necessary to support the IB programmes are also available.

Staff are recruited from many countries, with the USA, Canada, the UK and Australia being particularly well represented. This staff teaches alongside highly qualified and talented local Chinese teachers to provide a practical cross-cultural pedagogical framework in which students thrive. A comprehensive programme of staff professional development, both locally and internationally, is in place to enhance IB skills and to develop further the expertise of all staff.

Living in Shanghai at the beginning of the 21st century is an extraordinary opportunity for students to be part of a rapidly developing social and economic milieux, with all the benefits and opportunities this possesses. Shanghai United International School is ideally positioned to work with students to maximize their learning in preparation for being truly global citizens.

Introducing Tomorrow's Innovators, Today

(Founded 1988)

Head of School
Greg Smith

DP coordinator
Craig Ortner

Status Private

Boarding/day Day

Gender Coeducational

Language of instruction
English

Authorised IB programmes
DP

Age Range 2 – 18

Number of pupils enrolled
1040

Address
Jingshan Villas, Nanhai Boulevard
Shekou, Nanshan
Shenzhen | **CHINA**

TEL +86 755 2669 3669
FAX +86 755 2667 4099

Email
admissions@sis.org.cn

Website
www.sis-shekou.org

Shekou International School (SIS) is a two-campus, private, co-educational, not-for-profit school located in Shenzhen, China. For over 30 years, SIS has long been at the forefront of international education for expatriate children in the region. SIS is an IB World School offering the Primary Years Programme (PYP) and the IB Diploma Programme (IBDP), and is fully accredited by the Western Association of Schools and Colleges (WASC). We are a member of the East Asian Council of Overseas Schools (EARCOS), the Association for the Advancement of International Education (AAIE), and a founding member of All-China and Mongolia International School (ACAMIS) organization.

SIS currently enrolls over 1000 international students from Nursery through Grade 12 (ages 2-18). Our student body represents more than 41 different countries, including the US, Canada, South Korea, Hong Kong, India, France, and Germany. We currently employ over 250 world-class licensed faculty and staff members hailing from 17 different countries. Our faculty and staff are masters of their craft, inspiring our students to become lifelong learners.

SIS provides a well-balanced, rigorous education that challenges students across all disciplines. At SIS, we use the best global practices in our curriculum. Our curriculum and programs develop students' knowledge, self-awareness, and self-confidence, allowing them to become the best representatives of the school as they enter universities and achieve success in a wide array of contexts. The language of instruction is English for all classes except for proficiency level Mandarin and French courses.

Service-learning is an essential part of the educational experience at SIS. Engaging students in community service projects is a way of encouraging our students to be principled, caring, and open-minded. Learning outside the classroom and helping others promotes empathy and understanding that supports students' ability to impact global and local communities.

Our co-curricular program engages students in opportunities to develop and extend themselves outside the classroom. Students are encouraged to participate in a wide variety of sporting events, after school activities, clubs, and service. We believe these play an essential role in the broader holistic program offered by our school.

A partnership between educators, parents, and students, all working together to create a caring, supportive, and engaged community is the foundation of life here at SIS. Together, we provide a vibrant learning environment that extends beyond the classroom. Our Parent Support Association (PSA) are an integral part of our community that enhances and promotes school spirit.

At SIS, our Mission is to provide a rigorous education in a caring community and inspires our students to become principled, innovative contributors in a transforming world.

Shiv Nadar School Gurugram

SHIV NADAR SCHOOL

Education for Life

Principal
Ms. Monica Sagar

DP coordinator
Sriparna Chakrabarti

Status Private

Boarding/day Day

Gender Coeducational

Language of instruction
English

Authorised IB programmes
DP

Fees
Annual: £6,755
(IRup6,40,000)

Address
DLF City, Phase -1 Block -E
Pahari Road
Gurugram, Haryana | **INDIA**

TEL +91 124 4549200

Email
admissions.gurgaon@sns.edu.in

Website
shivnadarschool.edu.in/gurgaon

Shiv Nadar School is an initiative of the Shiv Nadar Foundation and made its foray into urban K12 private education in 2012 to deliver educational excellence and nurture ethical, respectful, happy and purposeful citizens of society. At Shiv Nadar School, the term "school" has a different meaning. The school for us is a Sensitive(S) and Child-centric(C) environment fostering Critical enquiry, which is like a 'Home(H)' away from home and where the children develop a love for Life-long learning(L) through Observation(O) and experience, to become Outstanding(O) human beings. Our motto is Education for Life for students who are agents of change, who are strong and resilient yet flexible in the changing fortunes of time.

The School is progressive in its approach, follows an experiential pedagogy and integrates technology into its educational practices giving considerable curricular emphasis on IT, Sports and Arts. Learning at our schools is never linear; instead, students are immersed in the multidimensional and the experiential. They are encouraged towards value-led pursuits so that they comprehend their role in the larger context of community and the world. We integrate an experiential pedagogy and extensive use of technology into our educational practices. Our faculty is challenged and empowered to engage students in processes that help them develop initiative, risk-taking, self-esteem, self-discipline, cooperation, and the self-motivation necessary to be successful human beings. They learn how to think, not what to think – and we believe that's the best way to be prepared for life in the 21st century.

Our core values of integrity and loyalty, commitment to excellence, openness and transparency, life-long learning, respect and compassion and a sense of responsibility and purpose, define everything that we do. We offer IBDP to grades XI & XII as a choice; & CBSE from grades Nursery-Grade XII and look forward to offering IGCSE to grades IX & X as a choice.

Singapore International School, Mumbai

Singapore International School, Mumbai

Ready for the world. Ready for the future.®

An IB World School

A BOARDING SCHOOL WITH A DIFFERENCE

Principal Mr Riad Rojoa

PYP coordinator Abhimanyu DasGupta

DP coordinator Absolom Museve

Status Private

Boarding/day Mixed

Gender Coeducational

Language of instruction English

Authorised IB programmes PYP, DP

Age Range 4 – 18

Number of pupils enrolled 501

Address
On National Highway No. 8,
Post Mira Road, Dahisar
Mumbai, Maharashtra
401104 | INDIA

TEL +91 222 828 5200

Email admin@sisindia.net

Website www.sisindia.net

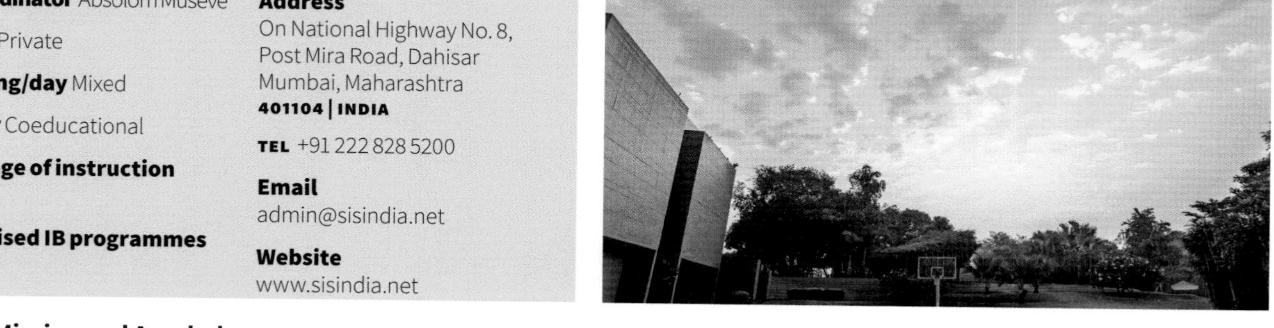

Vision, Mission and Accolades

Singapore International School (SIS) has been established in 2007, with a vision of creating an international, all-encompassing Boarding School environment in Mumbai. Comprising of a lush 8 acre campus with ultra-modern infrastructure; SIS mission is to impart Holistic learning.

Signature Boarding School

SIS is an exclusive term, monthly, weekly and day boarding school in Mumbai. Exclusively 500 students are admitted to ensure them receiving close care. The boarding environment at SIS is encompassing of evening prep activities fostering independence. A 'home away from home' where the student is nurtured, away from distractions.

Holistic Education – All Rounded development

'Carpe Diem' implying one to 'seize the day' is engraved in the SIS Logo & remains the ethos of how SIS functions. Each student is encouraged to achieve academic excellence along with a culture of learning & exploring artistic interests ranging from music, dancing, film-making or visual arts.

Currriculum

SIS adheres to an International Baccalaureate (IB) Diploma Programme for Grades 11 and 12, the Cambridge Checkpoint and the IGCSE for Grades 6-10, Singaporean curriculum combined with the IB Primary years programme for Grades KG-1, a Reggio Emilia inspired program for the Kindergarten. To ensure expert guidance we have an inclusion department with trained counsellors providing aid to students with special education needs.

Why SIS

- Small Batches make a big difference. Learning becomes an educational exchange with Individual attention.
- Close to 40 teachers with 20+ years of excellence & close to 60 post-graduated teachers impart knowledge.
- The residential staff provides academic assistance, a daily facility ensuring that no doubt remains unanswered.
- Student Exchange Programs provide life skills resulting from experiencing varied cultures & places.

Placements

SISites have obtained excellent university placements, year on year. The class of 2019 has secured acceptance from more than 550 Universities. The scholarship offered for the class of 2019 collectively amounts to net $ 2.7 million, spread over 4 years – record high at SIS! This is a result of our individualised college counselling service and the network of supporting schools.

Our students have been awarded substantial scholarships & offered the Honor & Dean's scholar program at prestigious international universities.

SIS Alumni is placed at the most world-renowned universities, namely: Brown University, Columbia University, Cornell University, Yale University, Princeton University, UCB – University of California-Berkley, University of California – Los Angeles, Johns Hopkins University, Georgia Institute of Technology, New York University, London School of Economics, King's College London, Mc Gill University, University of British Columbia, Hong Kong University of Science & Technology, Hong Kong and Singapore Management.

Amenities & Facilities

- Floodlit football & cricket ground
- Tennis & Basketball courts
- Music department – amongst best in city
- Film department with latest equipment + Amphitheatre
- SIS offers film & music as IGCSE and IB Diploma subjects.
- Distinguished personalities in business, politics & film-making are invited as guest speakers to inspire young minds at SIS!

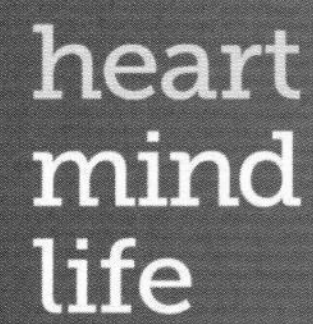

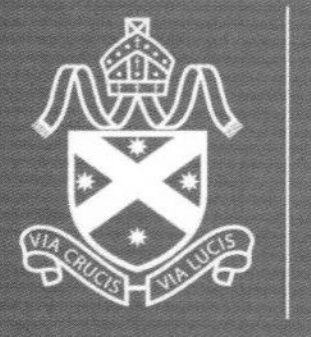

ST ANDREW'S CATHEDRAL SCHOOL
FOUNDED 1885

(Founded 1885)

Head of School
Dr John Collier

MYP coordinator
Kathleen Layhe

DP coordinator
Sharon Munro

Status Private

Boarding/day Day

Gender Coeducational

Language of instruction
English

Authorised IB programmes
MYP, DP

Age Range 5 – 18

Number of pupils enrolled
1300

Fees
Day: AUS$19,465 – AUS$33,270

Address
Sydney Square
Sydney
NSW 2000 | AUSTRALIA

TEL +61 2 9286 9500

FAX +61 2 9286 9550

Email
enrolments@sacs.nsw.edu.au

Website
www.sacs.nsw.edu.au

St Andrew's Cathedral School (SACS) is a dynamic, independent school located in the centre of Sydney's CBD. With modern facilities and innovative learning environments, our urban location presents innumerable opportunities for students to engage beyond the classroom; at city museums, concert halls, theatres, national institutions and galleries.

Our central city location enables students to travel with their parents to work, or easily reach the school by train, car or bus.

Our Academic Programme

SACS caters for all learners, encouraging each to develop a lifelong love of learning. The overwhelming majority of students pursue university education following graduation – with increasing numbers going overseas to study.

SACS offers two credentials for the final years of school (Years 11 – 12): the Higher School Certificate (HSC) from the NSW Board of Studies, Teaching and Educational Standards, and the International Baccalaureate Diploma Programme (DP). Typically, around 70 per cent of our Diploma receive ATAR (Australian Tertiary Admissions Rank) conversion scores above 90, that is, in the top 10 per cent of the state of New South Wales. As a fully comprehensive school, St Andrew's differentiates teaching practices to accommodate students with a broad range of interests and abilities. Our performance in public Australian examinations suggests an atmosphere of highly accomplished learning and teaching.

At SACS, every student is nurtured, encouraged and valued. A growing number of international students enrol every year and a diverse community of students are drawn from all over Sydney and beyond.

Special Programmes

Our comprehensive student wellbeing programs encourage a passion for learning and a culture of participation across sport, music, Outdoor Education and the performing arts. There are more than 20 music and drama ensembles at the school, along with an impressive variety of sporting opportunities and a comprehensive Outdoor Education programme, based at the school's rural Southern Highlands property. Each year, the school offers a number of international tours, providing educational opportunities in sport, community service, music, drama, languages, history, science or art.

For further information, contact us by telephone on +61 2 9286 9579 or +61 2 9286 9664 or email the Enrolments Department at enrolments@sacs.nsw.edu.au

(Founded 1997)

Head of School
Mr. Paul Schofield

DP coordinator
Mr. William Taylor

Status Private

Boarding/day Day

Gender Coeducational

Language of instruction
English

Authorised IB programmes
DP

Age Range 2 – 18

Number of pupils enrolled
2000

Fees
Day: THB331,000 – THB702,000

Address
1020 Sukhumvit Road
Phra Khanong, Khlong Toei
Bangkok
10110 | THAILAND

High School
1020 Sukhumvit Road, Phra Khanong, Khlong Toei, Bangkok
10110 | THAILAND

TEL +662 056 9555

Email
officehs@standrews.ac.th

Website
www.standrews.ac.th

St Andrews International School Bangkok was founded in 1997 on an attractive, conveniently located site, with excellent facilities and good access to local transportation. Today we are a school of more than 2,000 students representing some 50 nationalities ranging from Nursery (2 years) to Year 13 (18 years). In August 2017 we opened an additional campus at a nearby prime city centre location which delivers state of the art purpose-built learning facilities to our High School.

Our school provides a high quality, professional, well-resourced learning environment where each child's talents and abilities are recognised and nurtured, and their needs supported. Our teachers are professional and caring, selected for their awareness of the needs of a broad range of children who may come from different social, cultural, religious and educational backgrounds. They are capable educators who take care with their preparation of the curriculum, use a variety of strategies for its delivery and pay close attention to the progression of each individual.

We are an inclusive school that welcomes students of all abilities. To ensure that all our children have an equality of opportunity, we have a professional Learning Support Department. This team works with class teachers to identify and support children in their learning across the school, whether they need extra help with their studies or have been identified as gifted and talented.

The curriculum draws on the best UK practices, adapted to reflect the international context of the school. Students take IGCSE examinations at the end of Year 11 and then follow the Senior Studies Programme in Years 12 and 13. Our school offers the International Baccalaureate Diploma Programme, alongside an alternative school-based curriculum, both of which lead to graduation and provide the opportunity to apply to prestigious universities all around the world. As part of Nord Anglia Education, the world's leading premium schools organisation, we collaborate with the preeminent performing arts conservatory, The Juilliard School, and one of the world's leading universities, the Massachusetts Institute of Technology (MIT), to bring truly inspiring learning experiences to all of our students.

With high quality teaching, excellent facilities and small class sizes, St Andrews International School Bangkok offers students the opportunity to fulfil their academic potential in a stimulating, caring and nurturing environment. We are fully accredited by CfBT Education Trust and Thailand's Office for National Education Standards and Quality Assessment (ONESQA), the first school in Thailand to receive this joint accreditation award.

(Founded 1996)

Head of School
Mr. Andrew Harrison

PYP coordinator
Faye Wood

DP coordinator
Andrew Emery

Status Private, International

Boarding/day Day

Gender Coeducational

Language of instruction
English

Authorised IB programmes
PYP, DP

Age Range 2 – 18

Number of pupils enrolled
450

Fees
Day: THB340,470 – THB680,940

Address
Moo 7, Ban Chang-Makham Koo Road
Ban Chang
Rayong
21130 | THAILAND

TEL +66 38 030611

Email
admissionsgv@standrews-schools.com

Website
www.standrewsgreenvalley.com

About Us

We are an outstanding school situated on the Eastern Seaboard for our global family of 2 – 18 year old children. We pride ourselves on offering a balanced education whilst achieving some of the highest academic results in Thailand. We are also the 1st and only school on the Eastern Seaboard to have been awarded 'GOLD' status twice from the Education Development Trust (EDT) and achieved outstanding in all areas. Nestling in spacious and beautiful surroundings of Green Valley, our campus is home to a community of around 450 students from over 35 nationalities, all of whom enjoy close, personalised attention from highly qualified teachers which is key to their success.

Curriculum

In Primary, we provide a stimulating, child-centred learning environment where students follow the framework of the IB Primary Years Programme (PYP) integrated with the principles of the English National Curriculum to provide the best of international learning. Teachers facilitate opportunities for hands-on learning and exploration through the inquiry process, setting high expectations and opportunities to work independently. In Secondary, students complete IGCSEs in Year 10 and 11 and we follow the International Baccalaureate Diploma Programme (IB DP) in Years 12 and 13. We have found the IB DP challenges the students and provides an excellent preparation for top university courses around the world.

Over the past 10 years our IB Diploma students have achieved some exceptional results, with an average score for the past 5 years of 35 points and some students each year achieving 40+ points. One student recently achieved 45 points out of a possible maximum of 45 points (one of only 147 in the world).

Maintaining balance is key

At Green Valley we also emphasise the importance of our students being balanced as well as high achievers. Students are actively encouraged to develop themselves in all areas including sports, drama and music, being active in the wider community and pursuing their passions. The CAS (Creativity, Activity and Service) component of the IB complements this perfectly and allows the students to develop in these areas.

Part of the Cognita Group of Schools

We are proud to be a Cognita school and as such we are part of a wider community of over 70 schools who believe in 'an inspiring world of education' and we can liaise with colleagues across the world to support student liaison and interaction internationally.

(Founded 1997)

Headmaster
Dr. John Moore

PYP coordinator
Ms. Carole Parker

DP coordinator
Ms. Sarah McNish

Status Private, International

Boarding/day Day

Gender Coeducational

Language of instruction
English

Authorised IB programmes
PYP, DP

Age Range 2 – 18

Number of pupils enrolled
500

Fees
THB192,945 – THB586,400

Address
7 Sukhumvit 107 Road
Bangna
Bangkok
10260 | THAILAND

TEL +66 (0)2393 3883

Email
sukhumvit@
standrews-schools.com

Website
www.standrewssukhumvit.com

About us

St. Andrews International School Sukhumvit 107 (S107) is an international school for 2-18 year olds, focused on meeting your child's individual needs and offering a broad and balanced curriculum blending the best of the British curriculum, the International Baccalaureate and IGCSEs. The school is a spacious, well-resourced and attractive campus located just steps away from Bearing BTS Station. We believe in personalised learning in a caring environment where our young people are free to have fun and be themselves, building leadership skills, resilience and grit.

The IB Diploma Programme

The IB programme at S107 has developed over 5 years to the extent that our boutique style and size means that we can offer nearly every IB subject depending on student aptitudes and tastes. In the last few years we have introduced Theatre, Film and Spanish in response to student demand and next year we are offering Philosophy, Global Politics, Environmental systems and societies as a result of student requests. Our flexibility is based on a belief that if students study what they love they will make maximum progress and enjoy their learning to the fullest.

Our small class sizes and personalised learning programmes help us to closely support all our students and the last 4 years have seen results improve year on year with 2018 seeing the highest IB score at the school (42). This is a significant achievement for an inclusive school and we support all our students to achieve beyond their expectations academically and in their wider learning.

The S107 experience also supports students to engage with their own community and the community outside of school. As well as running student and school community clubs and events, our students use the CAS programme to work with a huge range of community organisations in educational, social and environmental settings. Our students have built water tanks in remote areas of northern Thailand, supported medical charities such as Operation Smile and worked closely with refugee organisations. We are proud to be a Cognita school and as such we are part of a wider global community of over 70 schools who believe in 'an inspiring world of education' and we can liaise with colleagues across the world to support student liaison and interaction internationally.

St. Andrews S107 IB experience is rich, varied, flexible and fun. Our ethos is to relentlessly support students in the belief that everyone succeeds at S107!

St Cuthbert's

(Founded 1915)

Principal
Justine Mahon

Deputy Principal
Fiona Cottam

DP coordinator
Buino Vink

Status Private

Boarding/day Mixed

Gender Female

Language of instruction
English

Authorised IB programmes
DP

Number of pupils enrolled
1420

Fees
Please refer to website

Address
122 Market Road
Epsom
Auckland
1051 | NEW ZEALAND

TEL +64 9 520 4159

Email
admissions@
stcuthberts.school.nz

Website
www.stcuthberts.school.nz

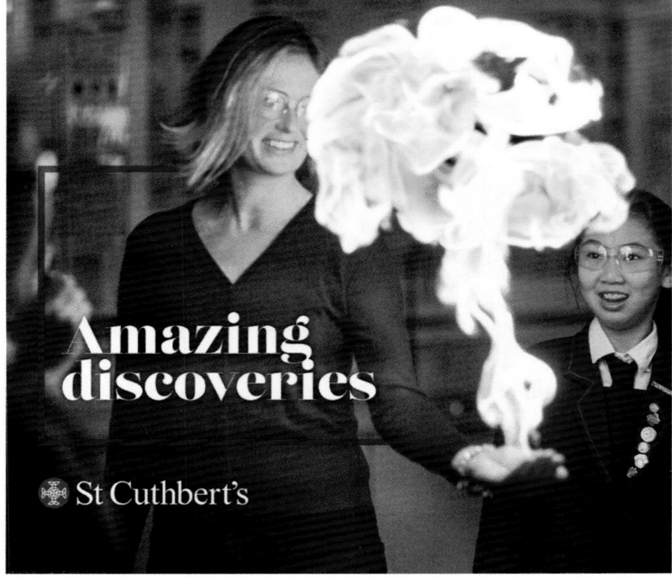

With over 100 years of experience in educating young women, St Cuthbert's is New Zealand's top academic school. With a dedicated Junior School (Years 1-6), Middle School (Years 7-8) and Senior School (Years 9-13), St Cuthbert's places an emphasis on embracing its founding heritage and traditions while ensuring that we impart skills that young women need for both tomorrow and into the future.

While our academic results are unrivalled, in choosing a school for your daughter it is important to also explore how we achieve these results while at the same time, growing every dimension of every girl.

Every girl is an individual, and we ensure that every girl has the support she needs to discover her unique talents, inside and outside the classroom. By identifying your daughter's strengths, she will be able to find her place, both in the St Cuthbert's community and in the wider world.

A reputation for excellence

At St Cuthbert's, excellence isn't just a grade – it's encouraging every girl to achieve her personal best. We recognise that every girl is a leader in some aspect of the school community. Whether she excels on the sports field or on the stage, in the classroom or in another unique way, we will ensure that your daughter is able to explore her strengths and talents in a supportive and inclusive environment.

St Cuthbert's students obtain exceptional academic results. With both National Certificates of Educational Achievement and International Baccalaureate (IB) qualifications on offer, no matter where your daughter's academic aspirations lie, our approach to teaching means that our students gain the tools to become adaptable, forward-thinking, life-long learners. With these essential life skills, our students go on to pursue a wide range of tertiary studies and careers, both domestically and overseas.

In 2017, over 50% of Year 13 St Cuthbert's IB students achieved a score of 40 or above. Three St Cuthbert's students received perfect scores of 45, making us the top performing school for IB in New Zealand. We have small IB classes enabling our teachers to establish good relationships with their students and tailor courses and options to them.

A Knowledge Rich School

As an independent school we have the freedom, resources, and teaching capacity that enables us to operate as a Knowledge Rich School. This approach is a key strategic focus at St Cuthbert's and is based on a strong conceptual framework and teaching staff with in-depth and specialist subject knowledge.

Our Knowledge Rich approach introduces our students to a way of learning that will stay with them for life. With a St Cuthbert's education, your daughter will acquire the digital, entrepreneurial, creative and analytical skills that are needed to future-proof her chosen career path.

Global Citizenship

St Cuthbert's is focused on growing our girls to be caring leaders and influencers who are true global citizens. As part of our responsibility to prepare girls for their future, an innovative and robust Global Citizenship framework is engrained across every aspect of school life.

ST MARGARET'S COLLEGE
JUNIOR, MIDDLE & SENIOR SCHOOL

Educating young women to live and lead

(Founded 1910)

Executive Principal
Mrs Diana Patchett

International Dean
Ms Chris Chambers

DP coordinator
Ms Beth Rowse

Status Private

Boarding/day Mixed

Gender Female

Language of instruction
English

Authorised IB programmes
DP

Number of pupils enrolled
830

Fees
International from NZ$48,554

Address
12 Winchester Street
Merivale
Christchurch
8014 | NEW ZEALAND

TEL +64 3 379 2000

Email
enrol@stmargarets.school.nz

Website
www.stmargarets.school.nz

St Margaret's College in Christchurch is one of New Zealand's leading girls' school with a proud history of academic, sporting and cultural excellence. An education at St Margaret's College is holistic, embracing the spiritual and emotional wellbeing of our girls as well as their academic growth and their development in sport and the arts. St Margaret's College is the only girls' school in New Zealand's South Island to offer the dual academic pathway of the International Baccalaureate Diploma as well as the National Certificate of Educational Achievement (NCEA).

As each girl journeys through St Margaret's College, either as a boarder or day girl, she is surrounded by people who care about her wellbeing and academic achievement. We know when a girl is happy, she is open to new learning and will embrace new challenges and experiences. At St Margaret's, when we talk about "happiness" we refer to a state of deep wellbeing and personal awareness – the state of wellbeing Maori call 'hauora'. We welcome and support every girl as a unique and precious individual and we work in partnership with her family to ensure she flourishes during her time with us.

St Margaret's College regularly leads New Zealand academically with the country's top NCEA results. International Baccalaureate results are equally impressive with 100% achieving their university goals including 10% achieving an impressive 40 or above, putting them amongst the top 3% of students in the world. The world average for the IB Diploma is 29.21 points. The St Margaret's College average is 35.0. In addition, 43 domestic and four international university scholarships were offered to the Class of 2018 from St Margaret's College.

In keeping with the school's holistic approach, St Margaret's College students realise outstanding sporting success at school, regional and national level, including seven girls selected to represent New Zealand at international level this year. They also excel in the arts with students achieving top national honours in speech and drama, representation in national dance, choirs and orchestras and a strong reputation in debating.

Students at St Margaret's College benefit from small class sizes in the most modern campus in Christchurch with its future-proofed learning, including our leading Centre for Innovation and STEM programmes. Our reputation attracts high quality teachers who are passionate about empowering future generations of young women. This vibrant new campus also embraces the 110-year history of St Margaret's College, with its traditional family values, creating the best of both worlds.

(Founded 1996)

Principal
Richard Bruford

PYP coordinator
Katriona Hoskins

MYP coordinator
Jesse Donnelly

DP coordinator
Laurence Mueller

Status Private

Boarding/day Day

Gender Coeducational

Language of instruction
English

Authorised IB programmes
PYP, MYP, DP

Age Range 2 – 18

Number of pupils enrolled
1150

Address
208 Zhong Nan Street
Suzhou Industrial Park
Jiangsu **215021 | CHINA**

TEL +86 512 6258 0388
FAX +86 512 6258 6388

Email
information@mail.ssis-suzhou.net

Website www.suzhousinternationalschool.com

SSIS is Suzhou's International School. We are a fully authorized IB World School as well as the oldest and largest international school in Suzhou, China. SSIS offers a challenging curriculum to cultivate global citizens and life-long learners. Everyday our 1150+ students (from 50 different nationalities) are challenged to actively participating in their education. This produces students that consistently perform well above world averages, and is why SSIS is one of the best schools in China.

Values and Mission

SSIS provides an excellent international education to the children of expatriate families. Our faculty and staff are committed to creating a learning environment that encourages and enables students to be self-motivated, lifelong learners. We educate students to become global citizens that value other cultures and are responsible, meaningful participants in the international community.

Curriculum and Activities

SSIS offers three IB programs; PYP, MYP and DP. A strong partnership between students, faculty and parents, enables us to maintain a rigorous and challenging education. We offer a wide range of academic, cultural and recreational programs ensuring we deliver the highest quality international education possible. Whether it is our visual arts program, showcased by a week-long celebration of the Arts; SSIS Book Week, celebrating global literacy or the much-anticipated International Family Day, there is something for everyone.

Accreditations and Affiliations

We are accredited by The New England Association of Schools and Colleges (NEASC), The Council of International Schools (CIS) and The National Center for School Curriculum and textbook Instruction (NCCT). Our students have the opportunity to compete against other peer schools in academics, arts and sports, through our memberships with ACAMIS, SISAC, EARCOS and CISSA. Go Dragons!

Faculty and Staff

The SSIS faculty and staff are at the heart of what makes our school outstanding. Comprised of over 170 dedicated professionals, the faculty come from over 20 countries, each bringing their own unique perspective on teaching and learning. Every faculty member is fully qualified and certified. Because we are serious about creating lifelong learners, over half hold advanced degrees in their respective subject areas.

Campus

SSIS is larger than life! Spread across a spacious campus, the building boasts integrated technology and air purification systems throughout all classrooms and common areas. Our Art and Performance facilities include 600-seat theater, black box theater, orchestra room, 3 dance studios, individual music practice spaces and individual art carrels. Our Recreational facilities include 2 outdoor and 3 indoor playgrounds, 2 gymnasiums, a new FIFA certified soccer pitch, new synthetic 400M running track, 25M swimming pool and tennis courts. The Science and Design facilities include fully equipped science labs, food technology labs and hard materials labs. Our Learning Technology Center includes 500+ ipads, charging stations, green room, podcast facilities and Lego robotics room. We are proud to be Suzhou's International School!

Taipei Kuei Shan School

Head of School
JaneDong Wu

PYP coordinator
Elizabeth Hu

MYP coordinator
Joe Woo

DP coordinator
Robert Chung

Status Private

Boarding/day Day

Gender Coeducational

Language of instruction
Chinese, English

Authorised IB programmes
PYP, MYP, DP

Age Range 4 – 12 years

Number of pupils enrolled
700

Address
200 Mingde Road
Taipei
11280 | TAIWAN

TEL +886 2 2821 2009
FAX +886 2 2820 5790

Email info@kss.tp.edu.tw

Website www.kshs.tp.edu.tw

Taipei Kuei Shan School is an International Baccalaureate World School offering three programmes – PYP, MYP, and DP. It is fully accredited by the Taipei City Government Department of Education and a member of the Association of Christian Schools International.

Kuei Shan was established in 1963 as a K-9 school, founded by Professor Hsiong Hui-Ying as a research project to improve Taiwan Education. Many decades ago, education in Taiwan was a "one-size-fits-all" approach. To allow a holistic development of learners, Professor Hsiong built Kuei Shan as a small school environment with smaller class size to promote active learning, both academically and socially. She practiced the use of unit teaching and theme-based learning to engage students in hands-on and collaborative learning activities. Upon the success of this long-term research, the school continues its commitment to educational research and excellence.

In 2015, the high school program was added, and Kuei Shan's first DP cohort graduated in 2017. As a small private school, we provide a lively campus community for more than 700 students from Pre-Kindergarten to Grade 12 by blending educational excellence and an international perspective with Christian values. About 80% of our student body are Taiwan nationals and 20% are from 10 other countries.

Our Mission

Taipei Kuei Shan School is a Christ-centered community where students have opportunities to know God, follow Him and strive to live uprightly in a way He would approve. Our mission is to educate the whole person and develop life-long learners who are equipped to become knowledgeable and critical thinkers, effective communicators, responsible and engaged world citizens, virtuous servant-leaders, and enthusiastic stewards to serve one another, their community, Taiwan, and the world.

Activities and Service

- The school supports students to participate in a Taiwan team sports program which includes basketball, volleyball, soccer, softball, swimming, track & field, and cross-country.
- Students have opportunities to participate in band, string ensemble, choir, worship band, and drama.
- Students have opportunities to conduct a wide range of outreach and community service for underprivileged children and people in need.
- Students participate in student government, scouts, model UN, and Global Issues Network.

Academic Achievement

Our three cohorts (2017-2019) earned diploma mean grade and average total points above worldwide average. Students are currently attending four-year universities in various regions – Asia, Australia, Canada, Europe, the U.K., and the U.S.

At Kuei Shan, we celebrate our distinctive place in PreK-12 education – where teaching, learning and faith guide the mind in understanding the complex diversity of God's creation and prepare the whole person for service and leadership.

Our students strive to be:
Scholars
Effective communicators
Reflective thinkers
Virtuous servant-leaders
Enthusiastic stewards

Tanglin Trust School, Singapore

(Founded 1925)

CEO
Mr Craig Considine

DP coordinator
Joseph Loader

Status Private

Boarding/day Day

Gender Coeducational

Language of instruction
English

Authorised IB programmes
DP

Age Range 3 – 18

Number of pupils enrolled
2824

Fees
Day: S$27,714 – S$45,828

Address
95 Portsdown Road
139299 | SINGAPORE

TEL +65 67780771

Email
admissions@tts.edu.sg

Website
www.tts.edu.sg

Established in 1925, Tanglin Trust School is the oldest British international school in South East Asia. Tanglin provides the English National Curriculum with an international perspective to children from 3 to 18 years in Singapore.

Tanglin is a vibrant co-educational school of 2,800 students representing over 50 nationalities and provides a unique learning environment for children from Nursery right through to Sixth Form. As a not-for-profit school, tuition fees are devoted to the provision of an outstanding education.

As the only school in Singapore to offer A Levels or the IB Diploma in Sixth Form, all of Tanglin's Sixth Formers study a programme that is tailored both to the subjects they are passionate about and to the style of learning that most suits them, ensuring they thrive and flourish.

Tanglin has an excellent academic reputation. Students' examination results consistently surpass Singapore and global averages, with around 95% of graduates typically receiving their first or second choice university, which are among the best in the world.

Tanglin is inspected every year within the British Schools Overseas (BSO) framework, recognised by Ofsted. All three schools have been awarded 'Outstanding', the highest possible grade in their latest inspections (2017, 2018 and 2019).

Drawing on professional and dynamic staff, Tanglin aims to nurture students to achieve their intellectual, spiritual, cultural, social and physical goals. We strive to make every individual feel valued, happy and successful. Responsibility, enthusiasm and participation are actively encouraged, and integrity is prized. Working together in a safe, caring yet stimulating environment, we set high expectations whilst offering strong support, resulting in a community of lifelong learners who can contribute with confidence to our world.

Tanglin encourages both broad participation and the achievement of excellence in the arts, sport, outdoor education and co-curricular activities.

Over 140 teams compete in 17 different sports each year, both in Singapore and the wider region. Exceptional sporting facilities enable students to participate in a wide range of competitive and non-competitive events. We look forward to the opening of our new world class facilities, which include a 50m pool, gymnastics centre, climbing wall, physiotherapy clinic and sport science centre.

Tanglin has a thriving and energetic Arts programme which plays an important part in school life. Students develop their skills in art, design, drama, music, and film-making, facilitating creative, social and intellectual development. Nearly 25% of students participate in a Music co-curricular activity. Throughout the year, there are many opportunities for students to participate in high-quality ensembles, recitals, performances and exhibitions.

Tanglin students are also encouraged to contribute actively to the local community, support service projects and participate in a wide variety of extra-curricular pursuits that stimulate and broaden student experience. These include 80 outdoor education trips, the International Duke of Edinburgh (DofE) Award, and the Creativity, Activity, Service (CAS) programme.

The Cathedral & John Connon School

(Founded 1860)

Headteacher
Mrs. Meera Isaacs

DP coordinator
Latha Balaji

Status Private

Boarding/day Day

Gender Coeducational

Language of instruction
English

Authorised IB programmes
DP

Age Range 3 – 18 years

Number of pupils enrolled
2072

Fees
International Curriculum
IRup864,000
National Curriculum
IRup185,000

Address
6 Purshottamdas Thakurdas Marg
Mumbai, Maharashtra
400001 | INDIA

TEL +91 22 2200 1282

Email
dean@cathedral-school.com

Website
www.cathedral-school.com

Enriched with spirit, legacy and character, the history of The Cathedral and John Connon School has been one of excellence and innovation. The School started the International Baccalaureate Diploma Programme (IBDP) in 2015 along with the IGCSE (2019-20), ICSE, ISC and Advanced Placement programmes.

Located in a beautiful stone edifice, which is also one of Mumbai's most prestigious heritage buildings, the IB programme has already made a wonderful start. While enjoying the freedom the IB programme extends, all stakeholders of the school also acknowledge the responsibility that comes with it.

That the school champions creativity and international mindedness is a known fact, which is exemplified by its Creativity, Activity, Service (CAS) component. Cultural activities such as debates and dramatics not only instil confidence and help hone communication skills, but also widen one's global outlook. And just as important, the pursuit of sportsmanship is encouraged through the wide variety of games offered, ranging from football and squash to gymnastics and swimming, all of which promote collaboration, cooperation and healthy competition.

Tolerance, compassion and inclusion form the warp and woof of this esteemed institution. Championing these values, along with the spirit of inquiry, are the various clubs such as Symposium (the School's Model United Nations Club), The Literary Club, The Makerspace and Innovations Club, The Nature Club, The Astronomy Club and The Music Club to name a few. In its quest to offer a truly global perspective, the school also caters to several international programmes such as the Harvard Model United Nations, USA; Sunburst Youth Camp, Singapore; EU Mind, The Netherlands; and London Science Youth Forum, U.K.

The school is equipped with an array of facilities that are regularly upgraded to keep pace with global demands. Fully air conditioned classrooms and laboratories, computerized and barcoded libraries and state of the art digitized interactive flat panels (IFP) for each classroom.

Above all, a team of highly dedicated and invested staff members aims to provide holistic development to the students. Interactive methods like team teaching are encouraged that optimise the teacher-student ratio, while adding a new dynamic to classroom interaction.

The IB programme will soon be shifted to a new location, not too far from the current hallowed hallways. This imminent development has fuelled a sense of excitement and expectation in the school community.

The Illawarra Grammar School

(Founded 1959)

Head of School
Mrs Judi Nealy

PYP coordinator
Mrs Karen Wallace

MYP coordinator
Mrs Sharon I'Ons

DP coordinator
Dr Meagan McKenzie

Status Private

Boarding/day Day

Gender Coeducational

Language of instruction
English

Authorised IB programmes
PYP, MYP, DP

Age Range 3 – 18

Number of pupils enrolled
900

Fees
See website

Address
10-12 Western Ave
Wollongong
NSW 2500 | AUSTRALIA

TEL +61 2 4220 0200
FAX +61 2 4220 0201

Email
info@tigs.nsw.edu.au

Website
www.tigs.nsw.edu.au

Stunning Coastal Location
The Illawarra Grammar School (TIGS) is an independent Anglican school located in Wollongong on the eastern coast of New South Wales, approximately 70km south of Sydney. Our campus is uniquely positioned between the mountains and the sea, with immaculate grounds decorated with purple Jacaranda trees. The atmosphere is warm and inclusive, reflected in the smiles, words and actions of students and staff.

Mission Statement
TIGS is committed to providing a caring and engaging environment where students thrive. Our mission statement is "the achievement of academic excellence in a caring environment that is founded on Christian belief and behaviour, so that students are equipped to act with wisdom, compassion and justice as faithful stewards of our world." The School has an inclusive enrolment policy and welcomes students from all faiths and denominations.

Academic Achievement
The outstanding academic performance of TIGS students is a testament to the expertise of our staff, the effort students put into their studies and the culture of learning that is embedded deeply into all that we do. TIGS has a close working relationship with the University of Wollongong with 70% of students on average being offered university placement prior to sitting their final exams.

TIGS is authorised to offer the Primary Years Programme, Middle Years Programme and Diploma Programme. As a result, there is a consistency and common philosophy to teaching and learning across the School, making the student experience both coherent and meaningful. TIGS students build their knowledge, skills and attitudes across their years of schooling to become enthusiastic and internationally minded lifelong learners.

Holistic approach to learning
Students at TIGS are encouraged to succeed across many fields of endeavour. They are challenged to become leaders of great character and resilience through a combination of academic, arts, sport, community service, outdoor and cultural experiences. TIGS offers a full range of experiences across the arts including music, dance, drama, visual arts, photo media and entertainment. Students also participate in a diverse range of activities from swimming and beach sports to bush walking, rock climbing and caving, taking advantage of our proximity to the coast and mountains. These experiences are built into our programmes in a structured manner resulting in valuable life lessons both within and beyond the classroom.

The International School Bangalore

(Founded 2000)

Principal
Dr Caroline Pascoe

DP coordinator
Mr Naveen Tom &
Mrs Sonia Mathew

Status Private

Boarding/day Mixed

Gender Coeducational

Language of instruction
English

Authorised IB programmes
DP

Age Range 3 – 18

Number of pupils enrolled
1100

Address
Whitefield-Sarjapur Road
Near Dommasandra Circle
Bengaluru, Karnataka
562125 | INDIA

TEL +91 80 22634900

Email
admission@tisb.ac.in

Website
tisb.org

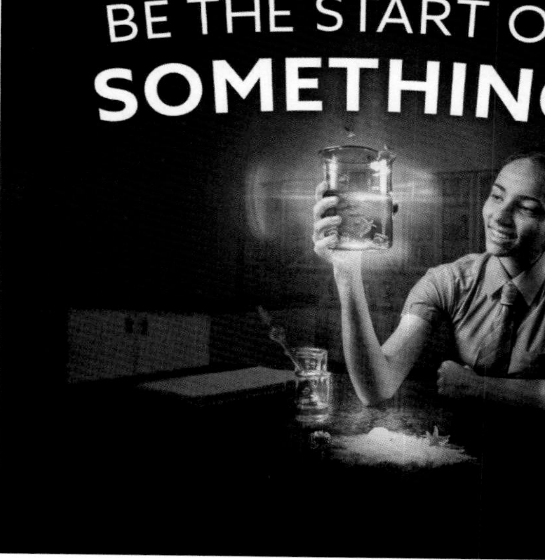

Overview

The International School Bangalore (TISB) was founded in 2000 and is one of India's most reputable, independent, selective, international boarding and day schools, set in 140 acres of stunning grounds on the outskirts of Bangalore, Asia's 'Silicon City' and India's 'Garden City'. Throughout its history the school has delivered consistently high academic standards in both IB and IGCSE. TISB is an authorized IB World School and is fully accredited by HMC, BSA, CIE and ISTA and offers a broad range of IB and IGCSE subject choices to its students.

The spirit of TISB is one of high energy and achievement and our students combine academic excellence and a deep love of learning with a wealth of co-curricular opportunities, to develop into exceptional individuals who believe that anything is possible. TISB students are encouraged to be independent in their learning and approach to life which is illustrated in their unique management and facilitation of 'Vivum', an annual two-day charitable event entirely overseen by Grade 12 students, and their success in academic and social-awareness activities such as 1M1B Future Leaders and the Model United Nations. In addition, students are encouraged and have the opportunity to be involved in numerous national and international sporting, theatrical and musical events and competitions.

The thriving boarding community at TISB is made up of three boarding houses, each one staffed by residential Houseparents. The boarding houses offer a home-from-home experience, with a balance of family life and academic support. Boarders are offered a variety of weekend activities ranging from sports matches, quiz nights and activity trips such as cycling, paintballing and archery to meals out and cinema trips.

TISB students are outward-looking, ambitious global thinking students who embrace opportunities and with the support of their teachers strive to be the best version of themselves.

It is our purpose to inspire and challenge every student to flourish and achieve their full potential, both now and in the future, and instill a passion for lifelong learning.

THE INTERNATIONAL SCHOOL OF KUALA LUMPUR

(Founded 1965)

Head of School
Mr Rami Madani MA, BSc

DP coordinator
Mr Michael Ortiz, MA, BA

Status Private

Boarding/day Day

Gender Coeducational

Language of instruction
English

Authorised IB programmes
DP

Age Range 3 – 18

Number of pupils enrolled
1750

Address
2, Lorong Kelab Polo Di Raja
55000 Kuala Lumpur | **MALAYSIA**

TEL +60 3 4813 5000

Email
admissions@iskl.edu.my

Website
www.iskl.edu.my

With a diverse student population of over 65 nationalities, ISKL nurtures and guides both expatriate and Malaysian students on their learning journey. Located on a 26-acre, state-of-the-art campus in the heart of Kuala Lumpur, ISKL offers a robust international curriculum which combines leading North American educational frameworks with global best practice. The curriculum delivers strong academic achievement and is complimented by a values-based educational philosophy which incorporates service learning and sustainability as integral components of school life.

ISKL is Malaysia's longest running IB World School and has been authorized to provide the International Baccalaureate Diploma Programme (IBDP) since 1989. With a 28-year Diploma pass rate of 96%, ISKL's results are consistently above regional and world averages. In 2019 22% of Diploma students scored 40 or more points, and 22% earned a Bilingual Diploma.

In addition to the IBDP, students have the option of combining individual IB, Advanced Placement and High School Diploma courses to create a customized program tailored to their abilities, interests, and aspirations. The flexibility of ISKL's academic program creates global opportunities; the 2019 graduating class received more than 450 acceptances from over 200 universities in 14 countries spanning four continents.

The IBDP is offered on a non-selective basis and every student is supported in maximizing their potential by expert international educators from all over the world including the US, Canada, UK, Europe, Australasia, and Asia. ISKL's language program supports students taking a bilingual IBDP with IB Language and Literature courses available in Chinese, English, French, Japanese, Korean, and Spanish.

ISKL is an inclusive school and is accredited internationally through the Council of International Schools, and in the United States through the Western Association of Schools and College.

The International School of Penang (Uplands)

(Founded 1955)

Principal
Mr Giles Mongare

PYP coordinator
Zita Joyce

DP coordinator
Geneva Robinson

Status Private

Boarding/day Mixed

Gender Coeducational

Language of instruction
English

Authorised IB programmes
PYP, DP

Age Range 4 – 18

Number of pupils enrolled
660

Fees
Day: RM33,400 – RM55,880
Boarding: RM47,790 – RM50,260

Address
Jalan Sungai Satu
Batu Feringgi
11100 Penang | **MALAYSIA**

TEL +604 8819 777
FAX +604 8819 778

Email
info@uplands.org

Website
www.uplands.org

The International School of Penang (Uplands) is a non-profit, co-educational Reception to Primary and Secondary School (Reception, Year 1 to Year 13) with boarding facilities, open to children aged 4 to 18 years old. It is one of the leading international schools in Malaysia, offering the IB PYP, IB Diploma and IGCSE qualifications.

Since being established in 1955 at the top of Penang Hill and now established in a modern campus in Batu Feringgi, Uplands has strived to embody a caring community; a school where both international and Malaysian students are happy to learn. Our motto: Respect for Self. Respect for Others.

Students receive a wealth of quality education from an international teaching faculty as well as a range of sporting and extracurricular activities cultivating teamwork, self-confidence and all-roundedness. Year upon year Uplands students have attained academic results that are consistently higher than global averages, with some achieving perfect scores in the IB Diploma pre-university course and receiving prestigious university scholarships.

Uplands is an IB World School, also recognised by the Malaysian Ministry of Education and permitted to admit both foreign and local students. Continuing its long history of excellence in education, Uplands received accreditation by The Council of International Schools (CIS), a global organisation committed to ensuring high-quality international education. Uplands is also accredited by The International Baccalaureate Organisation (IBO) and a member of:

- The Federation of British International Schools in Asia (FOBISIA);
- The Association of International Malaysian Schools (AIMS);
- The Boarding Schools' Association (BSA).

The School is approved to offer external examinations by The International Baccalaureate Organisation (IBO), Cambridge Assessment International Examinations (CIE) and Edexcel International Examinations. The School received an award from the Malaysian Ministry of Education in June 2003, recognising it as one of the leading international schools in the nation.

Languages offered at the school are English, Bahasa Malaysia, Mandarin, Japanese, Spanish, French and German. School facilities include air-conditioned classrooms, swimming pool, sports field, library, refectory, playground, basketball court, badminton court, IT resource centre, science laboratories, multi-purpose hall, audio/visual room, art rooms, music rooms, drama rooms, design technology workshops and modern boarding facilities. The campus is fully networked with wired and wireless access.

Student support services are also on deck including university guidance counsellors, learning support and school counsellors. Students are able to engage in a wide variety of extracurricular activities such as basketball, badminton, table tennis, football, fun softball, reading club, cooking club, bridge club, climbing club, French language club, athletics, chess, Chinese calligraphy, karate, taekwondo, gymnastics, yoga, Model United Nations and swimming among many others.

Tokyo Metropolitan Kokusai High School

Head of School
Tamako Yonemura

DP coordinator
Kazumasa Aoki

Status State

Boarding/day Day

Gender Coeducational

Language of instruction
English

Authorised IB programmes
DP

Age Range 15 – 18 years

Number of pupils enrolled
720

Fees
Annual Fees: ¥118,800
(US$1,130)

Address
2-19-59 Komaba
Meguro-ku
Tokyo, Kanto
153-0041 | JAPAN

TEL +81 3 3468 6811
FAX +81 3 3466 0080

Email
ibdp1@kokusai-h.metro.tokyo.jp

Website
www.kokusai-h.metro.tokyo.jp

Tokyo Metropolitan Kokusai High School is a coeducational public high school established in 1989 and maintained by the Tokyo Metropolitan Government. Located in a leafy suburb not far from the cosmopolitan west side of Tokyo. The school's motto is "Your Wings to the World" and its aim is to provide education to develop well-balanced students with an international mindedness.

In May 2015, Tokyo Metropolitan Kokusai High School was authorised as an International Baccalaureate World School offering the Diploma Programme, the first of which to be offered in a Japanese public high school.

Kokusai High School conducts the IBDP in English with the aim of cultivating internationally-minded students who will study overseas after graduation. The Kokusai IBDP strives to nurture future global leaders, and based on this philosophy, the ideal Kokusai IB students should demonstrate the following attributes.

A Kokusai High School IBDP student should:

1. Demonstrate a clear goal to enter the IBDP, a desire to contribute to a global society, and the willingness to gain entrance into universities overseas.
2. Approach learning with a self-starter mentality by showing a strong sense of inquiry and a willingness to use their own initiative, while having the courage to handle difficult challenges.
3. Exemplify a well-rounded character, being cooperative and considerate of others, and also have the willingness to positively accept and understand different perspectives and opinions.
4. Be motivated to broaden their viewpoints, and be able to maintain a healthy mental and physical mindset and actively participate in extracurricular activities.
5. Demonstrate strong academic performances across all subjects, and have a high level of English proficiency.

Kokusai High School offers entrance exams twice per year; April enrollment session (held in January) and September enrollment session (held in July). The April session is for students who will finish Year 9 school education by the end of March, and the September session is for those who will finish Year 9 school education between April and August. The maximum number of successful applicants is 25 per year. The ratio of Japanese students to International students for each enrollment session is announced by the Tokyo Metropolitan Board of Education. The assessment methods used in the entrance examinations are English Language Skills Test, Mathematics Academic Performance Test, Essay, Individual Interview, Group Discussion and Certificate of Academic Record.

Kokusai High School offers a three-year programme; Year 1 (Grade 10) is Foundation Year, Year 2 (Grade 11) and Year 3 (Grade 12) are IBDP. Students also graduate with a Japanese High School Diploma. Subjects we offer are listed below:

Studies in Language and Literature
Year 1: Comprehensive English, English for Academic Purposes, Integrated Japanese Language.
Year 2 and 3: IB Diploma English A SL and HL (Language and Literature); Japanese A SL and HL (Literature).

Language Acquisition
Year 1: Comprehensive English, English for Academic Purposes, Integrated Japanese Language.
Year 2 and 3: IB Diploma English B SL and HL; Japanese B SL and HL; Japanese *ab initio* (SL).

Individuals and Societies
Year 1: Japanese History B, World History B.
Year 2 and 3: IB Diploma History SL and HL, Economics HL, Geography HL.

Science
Year 1: Basic Physics, Basics Chemistry, Basic Biology.
Year 2 and 3: IB Diploma Physics SL and HL, Chemistry HL, Biology SL and HL.

Mathematics
Year 1: Mathematics I
Year 2 and 3: IB Diploma Mathematics: analysis and approaches SL and HL, IB Diploma Mathematics: applications and interpretation.

Other subjects
Year 1: Physical Education, Health, Inquiry-Based Learning, Fine Art 1, Homeroom Activity, Period for Integrated Study, Basic Home Economics.
Year 2 and 3: Physical Education, Health, Homeroom Activity, International Relations, Information Study by Scientific Approach, TOK, CAS.

Creativity Activity, Service (CAS)
Throughout their DP years, IB students explore their interests and personal development by participating in a wide range of CAS experiences such as sports, arts and music. Former IB students' passion led to many volunteer activities both locally and internationally, including in Tokyo, Hiroshima, Kenya, Senegal and Ghana. While doing these experiences for CAS, students also won various awards such as the 2018 and 2019 World Scholar's Cup, 2017 Interdisciplinary Workshop on Science and Patents (Rafael Kieboms Prize), and 2016 Eiga World Cup film festival.

Some universities where students have been accepted
UK: University College London, Imperial College London, University of Edinburgh, King's College London, University of Manchester, SOAS. USA: Princeton University, Purdue University, Illinois Institute of Technology, University of Illinois at Chicago, Lawrence University. Canada: University of Toronto, University of British Columbia, Dalhousie University. Australia: Australian National University, University of Melbourne, University of Sydney. Germany: Technical University of Munich, Jacobs University. Netherlands: Maastricht University, Radbound University. Hong Kong: University of Hong Kong, Hong Kong University of Science and Technology.

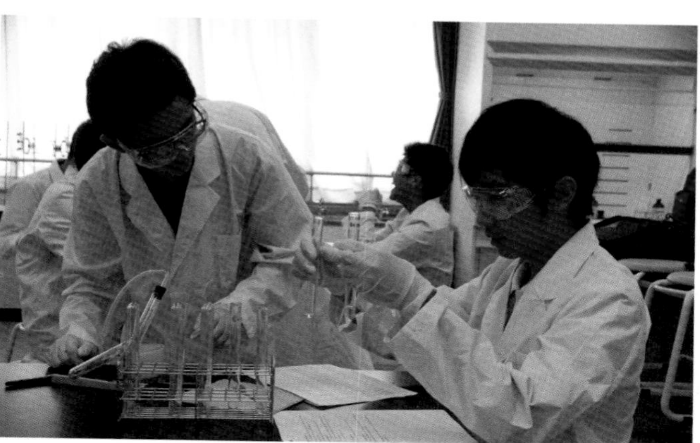

Trivandrum International School

Principal
Richard Hillebrand

PYP coordinator
Sanjay Prabhakaran

DP coordinator
Rachel Jacob

Status Private

Boarding/day Mixed

Gender Coeducational

Language of instruction
English

Authorised IB programmes
PYP, DP

Address
Edackcode
PO Korani
Trivandrum, Kerala
695104 | INDIA

TEL +91 471 2619051
FAX +91 471 2619510

Email
tis@trins.org

Website
www.trins.org

Nestled on a serene hilltop campus in the outskirts of Trivandrum, the capital city of Kerala, Trivandrum International School (TRINS) offers students the perfect blend of academic rigor, modern amenities and unspoilt, natural surroundings. A co-educational school with a lively combination of boarders, weekly boarders and day scholars, the school boasts of tastefully designed buildings with spacious class rooms, state-of-the-art science labs, sports fields, a swimming pool of international standards and separate hostel buildings for boys and girls.

There are more than 90 educators in the faculty and they all have advanced qualifications in their subjects. TRINS maintains a teacher-student ratio of 1:7 which allows for a very personalized approach with students. The school invests in the professional development of all faculty members through participation in local, regional and international training programs and workshops.

Trivandrum International School is the only authorised IB PYP (Primary Years Programme) school in Kerala. At the high school level, they also offer the IB DP (Diploma Programme) and share the IB mission to develop inquiring, knowledgeable and caring young people who help to create a better world by respecting and being open minded towards differences. A balance of curricular and extra curricular activities helps students to develop critical skills to face a rapidly evolving world.

The Middle Years offer an integrated curriculum which is again child-centred and interactive, but tailored to facilitate the smooth transition of students into either the IGCSE or ICSE curriculums in Grade 9.

TRINS continues to be among the best IB World Schools in India. Alongwith IGCSE and IB, the school also offers the ICSE qualification. Graduates from TRINS have gained admission to some of the best colleges in the world.

(Founded 2015)

Head of College
Pelham Philip Lindfield Roberts

DP coordinator
Arunananda Mukherjee

Status Private

Boarding/day Boarding

Gender Coeducational

Language of instruction
English

Authorised IB programmes
DP

Age Range 15 – 19

Number of pupils enrolled
580

Fees
Two-year fee ¥720,000
(scholarships available)

Address
No. 88 Kunchenghuxi Road
Changshu, Jiangsu
215500 | CHINA

TEL +86 512 5298 2602

Email
info.admissions@uwcchina.org

Website
www.uwcchina.org

Introduction
UWC Changshu China was founded in 2015 as the first UWC in the mainland of China on the initiative of Mark Jiapeng Wang and consists of Grades 10, 11 and 12. The college emphasizes its connection to its location and offers education focused on Chinese language and culture, youth leadership and environmental activism.

Inside the Classroom
UWC Changshu China offers the International Baccalaureate Diploma Programme curriculum, and a Foundation Programme for Grade 10 students. Within the IBDP curriculum, alongside standard courses, UWC Changshu offers foundation Chinese language programmes (for international students).

Outside the Classroom
UWC Changshu China emphasizes an immersive Chinese experience, providing rich Chinese cultural context to support teaching and learning through culture, language and literature lessons and the Creativity, Activity, Service (CAS) programme named Zhi Xing, meaning "learning by doing" as well as "putting knowledge into action". It enables the exploration of Chinese culture within the School and through interactions with the wider community. Many activities focus on building environmental stewardship.

Other activities, such as volunteering in local schools for kids of migrant workers stretch the boundaries of students' education and encourage youth leadership. In fact, many of the activities have student leaders, who use their knowledge to act as positive role models for their peers while also challenging themselves. Project weeks are an invaluable learning opportunity for students, allowing them to put UWC values into action. Students have the opportunity to interact with local communities and affect positive change.

Campus and Facilities
The 24-acre campus is built on an island on the northwest side of Kuncheng Lake. In architectural design, the campus is reminiscent of a southern Chinese waterside village, where connections between all parts are seamless and unobstructed. The campus is also comprised of several cutting-edge technologies to enhance its sustainability. Campus facilities include: a multi-function performing art space, STEM hub, a wellbeing centre, a design and innovation centre, a Chinese Programme Centre, residential houses for students and faculty; a dining hall and a library.

Admission
IBDP applicants apply through their UWC national committee or the UWC Global Selection Programme. Foundation Programme applicants need to contact the School directly.

(Founded 1997)

Head of College
Soraya Sayed Hassen

Deputy Head of College
Charlotte Blessing

DP coordinator
Ainhoa Orensanz

Status Private

Boarding/day Boarding

Gender Coeducational

Language of instruction
English

Authorised IB programmes
DP

Age Range 15 – 19

Number of pupils enrolled
240

Fees
Two-year fee $61,000
(scholarships available)

Address
Village Khubavali, PO Paud
Taluka Mulshi
Pune, Maharashtra
412108 | INDIA

TEL +91 97644 42751 54

Email
info@muwci.net

Website
uwcmahindracollege.org

Introduction

UWC Mahindra is a vibrant college with a rich tradition of curricular innovation and community engagement. Programs such as the IB's World Studies Extended Essay were conceived and piloted here. The College also runs a bridge program and the Akshara Foundation, both of which enhance the positive local impact of the College and provide students with numerous opportunities for project-based and service learning.

Inside the Classroom

UWC Mahindra College offers the International Baccalaureate Diploma Programme curriculum. Alongside standard courses, the College offers Art, Theatre, Film, Psychology, Global Politics. Additionally, students also benefit from the MUWCI Core – a specially designed curriculum for the College that encompasses the areas of Political Education, Social and Emotional Education, Host Studies and Ecological and Outdoor Education. UWC Mahindra also offers the Project Based Certificate to interested students, wherein they can utilize the second year to conceive and execute an impact-driven project.

Outside the Classroom

UWC Mahindra College offers an immense variety of co-curricular activities through its Creativity, Activity, Service program, referred to as "Triveni" program, which facilitates project-based learning. Students can choose from a rich diversity of Service Learning opportunities on and off campus spanning areas like menstrual health, organic farming, mental health and rural public education. Students are also active participants in decision-making processes that affect campus life, such as envisioning and executing resource management initiatives on campus. Students benefit from the cultural diversity of the surrounding valley and India at large and have immersive experiences in other parts of the country through Experiential Learning Weeks. MUWCI also conducts short programs which bring together students from around the world to learn about issues such as sustainability and globalization.

Campus and Facilities

Students live together in five residential clusters known as "wadas", each of which forms a more intimate community. The campus also offers many informal locations for gathering and hiking, and several areas are well known among students for their gorgeous vistas of the valley during sunset. Academic facilities include a science lab, a library, an art space overlooking the valley, specialized facilities for theatre and music practice and a large sporting ground along with a makerspace tinkering lab for STEAM projects.

Admissions

Students can apply through their UWC national committee or through the UWC Global Selection Programme.

(Founded 2008)

Head of College
Jason McBride

PYP coordinator
Jen Friske

MYP coordinator
Remke Langendonck

DP coordinator
Katharine Feather

Status Private, Non-Profit

Boarding/day Mixed

Gender Coeducational

Language of instruction
English

Authorised IB programmes
PYP, MYP, DP

Age Range 2 – 18

Number of pupils enrolled
470

Fees
Two-year fee THB2,720,000
(scholarships available)

Address
115/15 Moo 7 Thepkasattri Road
Thepkasattri, Thalang
Phuket
83110 | THAILAND

TEL +66 76 336 076

Email
Info@uwcthailand.ac.th

Website
uwcthailand.ac.th

Introduction

Encircled by rubber tree plantations and virgin rainforest, UWC Thailand sits nestled in the foothills of Phuket's green-capped mountains, away from the island's busy city centres. Its unique location is both symbolic and intentional; a physical reminder that in addition to academic rigour, the UWCT community values wellness and environmental stewardship.

Inside the Classroom

Within UWC Thailand's environment of authentic and targeted differentiation, emphasis is placed upon mental and emotional balance, as well as academic rigour. Students learn how to learn, analyse, think creatively and reach thoughtful conclusions, making it a demanding program that encourages students to the highest levels of academic achievement. The Nursery program is for students aged 2 – 3 years old. The Primary Years Programme is for students aged 3-11, and the Middle Years Programme is for students aged 11-16. To 16-19 year-olds, UWC Thailand offers the International Baccalaureate Diploma Programme.

Outside the Classroom

UWC Thailand offers a comprehensive activities program for students of all ages. The activities enable students to explore projects and passions in Service, Creativity, Sports, Social and Culture, and are run during lunchtimes, after school and on weekends (activities include mangrove restoration, dancing, international cooking, etc.). In addition, students embark upon expeditions with their classmates, which focus on adventurous training and push the boundaries of their experiences. The expeditions range from Grade 5 students spending 5 days camping and kayaking around the coast of Phuket to independently organised Project Weeks for the DP students. Some grade levels take trips to learn how to sail with their classmates, others work with a regional turtle sanctuary to help protect endangered species.

Campus and Facilities

UWC Thailand's campus is spacious and extensive hosting facilities for its Early Childhood, Lower Primary, Upper Primary and Secondary students. The boarding house is home to approximately 100 students from grades 8-12. The school is situated next door to Thanyapura, Asia's largest sports and wellness resort, and all community members have access to its excellent sports facilities.

Admission

Students for UWC Thailand's nursery, primary and middle schools apply to the school directly. The admissions process is based on UWC's mission and values. For Grade 11 admission, students can apply through their UWC national committee or through the UWC Global Selection Programme.

The School With A Difference

(Founded 6th January 1997)	**Gender** Coeducational
Founder President Robbin Ghosh	**Language of instruction** English
Vice President & Principal Saarada Ghosh	**Authorised IB programmes** PYP, MYP, DP
Director Sports Romen Ghosh	**Age Range** 6 weeks – 18 years
DP Head Bonila Sinha	**Number of pupils enrolled** 1113
MYP Head Jaya Kalsy	**Fees** Tuition Fee US$4,326 average
PYP Head Ira Ghosh	**Address** Kharadi, Pune, Maharashtra 411014 | INDIA
EYP Head Desiree Dhami	**TEL** +91 20-67116300/1/2
PYP coordinators Khushboo Sharma, Saakshi Suryavanshi (EYP)	**FAX** +91 20 67116341
MYP coordinator Vishwajeet Kumar	**Email** robbinghosh@victoriouskidsseducares.org
DP coordinator Jaya Kalsy	**Website** www.victoriouskidsseducares.org www.vkidss.org
Status Private	
Boarding/day Day	

"Every Child Matters"
Victorious Kidss Educares (VKE) is an IB World School in Pune (India) focused on guiding children to discover their secret power of brilliance from within, to allow them to become 'lifelong learners'. Our Motto is "Learning to Love to Learn". We believe if the child has not learnt, it is we who have not taught. We, as parents and educators, need to understand that our children are no longer the people, as we were in school. In today's world, we work with the philosophy, that 'Every Child Matters'.

PYP, MYP and DP Programmes - VKE is a complete IB World School offering a full spectrum of IB programmes. The learning journey at our school starts from the moment a mother conceives and goes on until the child is 19 years of age (IB Diploma). Our Children are being guided to become Successful Global Citizens and we prepare them to face the challenges of the future world.

Couple Vedanta with IB - Knowing "Who am I". Children are guided to that education by which, 'character is formed, the strength of mind is increased, and intellect is expanded, so that one can stand on their own feet' ~Swami Vivekananda. Intelligence plus character - that is the goal of our education.

Early Childhood Development – We practice this unique concept to tap the brain potential in the early years (6 weeks) and build the fundamentals of learning. VKE has professionally well trained and experienced teachers.

Not for Profit School - VKE takes great pride and special endeavour to make elite IB tuition fee affordable to all.

We teach, we touch lives and we make dreams come true.

Achievements:

- VKE has been commended for its philosophy and teaching techniques, by the IB Evaluation Team, since 2012, as a 'Model IB School for others to emulate'. All three programs (PYP, MYP & DP) have been successfully evaluated by IB with many commendations.
- VKE achieved 100% results for MYP and DP, with the highest score being 55/56 in MYP and 42/45 in DP.
- Our MYP has been successfully evaluated in September 2019 for the second time. As per the brilliant report we have received, IB has advised us to officially share and continue to drive excellence to join the educator network and influence changes for the betterment of students globally and present our concepts at a Global IB conference.

We offer:

- TED-Ed program and SAT training for MYP students
- Career Counselling, Placements and Internships

- Scholarships in top Universities for DP Students
- Courses on Vedic Mathematics, Robotics, Abacus and Design Technology
- Visual Art and Performing Art - we recently inaugurated 3D Digital Arts Lab and Pottery Studio
- Concentration Techniques - Pranayama, Yogic breathing exercises and Meditation
- Model UN Programme from Primary Years to ensure our students learn the art of communication and negotiation.

We believe that 'Every child has at birth, a greater potential of intelligence than Leonardo Da Vinci, Isaac Newton or Einstein ever used'. All children are born gifted, and every child's brain has infinite power. We all, as parents, as Teachers, as Guides are required to just let our children become aware, "Who they really are and be aware of the infinite potential within themselves"?

By providing the right ambience and giving freedom to explore and learn through inquiry, we nurture this power and create true leaders. With this consciousness, freedom of inquiry, understanding and concept - we discover, 'Success for Every Child'.

(Founded 1991)

Head of School
Elsa Donohue

PYP coordinator
Rose Golds

MYP coordinator
Mike McMillan

DP coordinator
Alistair Nelson

Status Private

Boarding/day Day

Gender Coeducational

Language of instruction
English

Authorised IB programmes
PYP, MYP, DP

Age Range 3 – 18 years

Number of pupils enrolled
500

Fees
Day: US$9,486 – US$22,542

Address
PO Box 3180
Ban Saphanthong Tai
Vientiane | **LAOS**

TEL +856 21 486001
FAX +856 21 486009

Email
contact@vislao.com
admissions@vislao.com

Website
www.vislao.com

The Vientiane International School (VIS) is an independent, non-profit IB World School offering the PYP, MYP and DP Programmes from Early Years through Grade 12. VIS is the only IB World School in Laos and the only school to be accredited by two international organizations – the Western Association of Schools and Colleges (WASC) and the Council of International Schools (CIS).

Our mission is to challenge, inspire and empower students to develop their unique potential in a changing world. Our vision is to lead the way toward a sustainable future. The campus facilities include two swimming pools, two soccer pitches, two basketball courts, ample playground spaces, a collaborative library, a Makerspace and a performing arts "BlackBox" Theater.

The VIS community is diverse. Students represent almost 50 nationalities and our faculty hail from over 25 nations. With a transient rate of about 20% per year, our curriculum ensures a successful transition for all students.

At VIS we value the arts, science, math and language acquisition and offer students various opportunities for expression and rigorous academic learning. Our Mother Tongue Programme supports the development and maintenance of 14 languages. In 2019, 75% of our IB Diploma graduates were awarded a bilingual diploma – well above the world average of 24%.

Our school has a strong ethos of service-learning and community service. We strive to develop empathy, cultural understanding and global awareness in students through meaningful interactions with the Lao community. As a member of the Mekong River International Schools Association (MRISA), we enable our students to take part in sporting and cultural exchanges with schools in neighboring countries.

Western International School of Shanghai (WISS)

Director
Dr. Greg Brunton

Secondary Principal
Myles D'Airelle

Primary Principal
Lisa Ellery

PYP coordinator
Judith Canning & Karin Tellis

MYP coordinator
Greg Cowan

DP coordinator
Edwige Singleton

CP coordinator
Stewart Paterson

Status Private

Boarding/day Day

Gender Coeducational

Language of instruction
English

Authorised IB programmes
PYP, MYP, DP, CP

Age Range 2½ – 17+ years

Address
555 Lianmin Road
Xujing Town, Qingpu
Shanghai
201702 | CHINA

TEL +86 21 6976 6388
FAX +86 21 6976 6833

Email
admissions@wiss.cn

Website
www.wiss.cn

The Western International School of Shanghai (WISS) has been educating and inspiring young people from around the world since 2006. WISS is the first and only full continuum IB World School in mainland China, authorized to offer the International Baccalaureate Primary Years Programme, Middle Years Programme, Diploma Programme, and the Career-related Programme. Continually striving for high standards of professional performance in international education WISS holds WASC Accreditation and was recently granted membership in the Council of International Schools (CIS), which is the first step towards obtaining CIS Accreditation.

Located on the western side of Shanghai, close to many popular housing compounds in the expatriate community, WISS has one of the largest international school campuses in Shanghai. The modern campus features open plan, bright classrooms equipped with ceiling air purification units, a well-resourced library, state of the art science and technology labs, spacious art studios, sleek film and music studios, and theatre spaces including a black box classroom and the innovative Orsini Theatre. Sports facilities include an impressive Astroturf football fields, basketball courts, a large gymnasium equipped with a rock-climbing wall, and two swimming pools.

Their robust after school activity program includes many distinguished programs and world-class academies such as the ISTA Performing Arts Academy, the Stoke City FC Football Academy, GAIL, the Duke of Edinburgh's International Award, and MUN. Additionally, Early Years and Primary students enjoy one afternoon per week of activities during the school day.

Representing over 50 different nationalities, WISS offers a truly international learning environment, while still fostering an appreciation and respect for our host country through well-developed Mandarin language and literature classes and by being actively engaged in the local community. WISS's warm and diverse community provides a unique environment for students to explore their passions, to develop holistically, and to succeed.

A *True* Education

(Founded 1866)

Principal
Mr Nicholas Evans

Status Private, Independent

Boarding/day Mixed

Gender Coeducational

Language of instruction
English

Authorised IB programmes
PYP, MYP, DP

Age Range 3 – 18

Number of pupils enrolled
3300

Fees
Years 7 & 8 AUS$38,680
Years 9–12 AUS$41,500

St Kilda Road
577 St Kilda Road
Melbourne
VIC 3004 | AUSTRALIA

Elsternwick
5 Gladstone Parade, Elsternwick
VIC 3185 | AUSTRALIA

Glen Waverley
620 High Street Road, Glen Waverley
VIC 3150 | AUSTRALIA

TEL +613 8102 6508

Email admissions@wesleycollege.edu.au

Website
www.wesleycollege.edu.au

Wesley College is a leading coeducational, open-entry International Baccalaureate World School. Established more than 150 years ago, the College has enriched the lives of thousands of students through its outstanding liberal, broad-based curriculum. International students from a range of cultures choose Wesley because of our strong tradition of academic excellence, outstanding curricular and cocurricular programs and state-of-the-art facilities.

Wesley has three metropolitan campuses in Melbourne:

- Elsternwick, 3-year-olds to Year 9
- Glen Waverley, 3-year-olds to Year 12
- St Kilda Road, 3-year-olds to Year 12

Boarding at Wesley

Wesley's dynamic new boarding facility, Learning in Residence, is purpose-built for Senior School students (Years 10–12), from metropolitan Melbourne, rural Australia and various international locations.

The modern Learning in Residence facility features twin-share rooms with en suites, a central courtyard and a 240 seat communal dining room. On the Glen Waverley Campus, adjacent to the Senior School, students have immediate access to sport, music and drama facilities. Students are supported with outstanding academic mentoring, pastoral care, and a range of extension and cocurricular opportunities to help them develop intellectually, emotionally, physically, socially and spiritually.

Enrolments are open for full-time or weekly boarding options.

Academic excellence

Wesley places the highest value on academic excellence, and encourages each student to aspire to achieve excellence in all areas of learning.

Wesley is one of the top International Baccalaureate (IB) schools in Australia, and one of the only schools in Victoria to offer the IB continuum from Primary through to Middle and Senior Schools.

Cocurricular learning

What sets Wesley apart are our unparalleled opportunities for students to explore their interests and talents across a variety of activities, from visual and performing arts, to sport, music, outdoor education and community service. With a choice of 19 sports, 23 bands, 21 chamber ensembles, 16 choirs, 10 orchestras, 7 musicals and 4 theatre performances, there's something for every student. Wesley students have won countless awards for their outstanding work – in debating, music, visual arts, drama and literary festivals.

Tertiary destinations

Our students graduate with much more than an ATAR score. Each student is encouraged to aspire to achieve excellence and personal best in all areas of endeavour. The majority of students are offered a place at either The University of Melbourne or Monash University. Many also choose to study at leading international universities including Oxford, Cambridge and Harvard, within such fields as medicine, law, commerce, politics, science and information technology.

Students applying to study at The University of Melbourne may receive preferential entry through the Melbourne Schools Partnership International, of which Wesley College is a member.

Wesley College alumni

Wesley has produced many outstanding alumni. The diversity of their achievements reflects the breadth of opportunities available at the College.

Below is a snapshot of some of our most prominent alumni:

- 2 former Australian Prime Ministers
- Internationally recognised award winners, including Nobel Prize, Kyoto Prize and Victoria Cross recipients
- Federal Government ministers, senators and representatives
- State Government ministers, legislative councillors and representatives
- Olympic and Commonwealth Games gold medallists, Test cricketers, Test netballers, AFL Brownlow Medallists and tennis professionals
- High Court, Supreme Court, Federal Court and Family Court Judges and Magistrates
- 13 Rhodes Scholars

At Wesley we believe a *True Education* realises the full potential of every girl and boy.

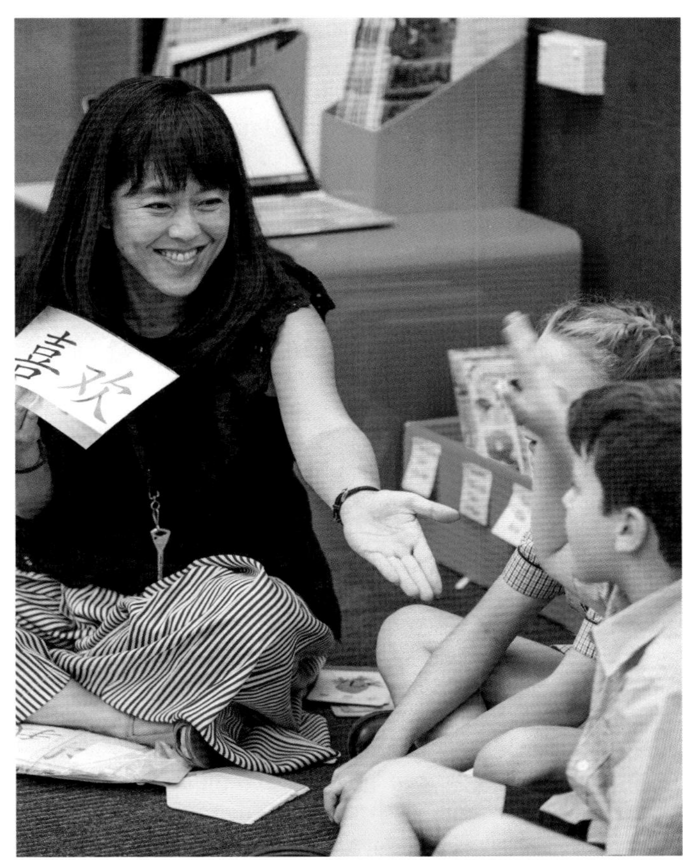

Woodcroft College

(Founded 1989)

Head of the College
Mrs Shannon Warren

PYP coordinator
Karen McCulloch

MYP coordinator
Elyse O'Malley

DP coordinator
Richard Pope

Status Private

Boarding/day Day

Gender Coeducational

Language of instruction
English

Authorised IB programmes
PYP, MYP, DP

Age Range 4 – 18

Number of pupils enrolled
1300

Fees
Day: AUS$6,500 – AUS$9,700

Address
Bains Road
Morphett Vale
SA 5162 | AUSTRALIA

TEL +61 8 8322 2333
FAX +61 8 8322 6656

Email
reception@woodcroft.sa.edu.au

Website
www.woodcroft.sa.edu.au

Woodcroft College is an independent coeducational Anglican school for students from Reception to Year 12.

As an International Baccalaureate (IB) World School, Woodcroft College offers the Primary Years Programme (PYP) in the Junior School, the Middle Years Programme (PYP) in the Middle School, and the Diploma (DP) in the Senior School. Senior School students may also choose the South Australian Certificate of Education (SACE) with its Vocational Education and Training (VET) pathway.

Woodcroft College is vibrant, innovative and inclusive. It seeks to provide students with an excellent, all-round education in a Christian environment. The curriculum is broad and relevant, aimed at meeting the students' intellectual, physical, social and emotional needs.

The school has a strong pastoral care focus, a broad extra-curricular program (involving outdoor education, sports, clubs, music and performing arts).

We also attract International students to study full time and for short term programs.

The Junior School (Reception to Year 5) provides young learners with the opportunity to learn and practise the essential social, emotional and problem solving skills they will need throughout their schooling. A major focus of our Junior school is to develop positive self-esteem, helping young children feel confident about who they are. We aim to encourage them in their ability to take on the challenges of new learning in a caring and nurturing environment.

Our Junior School is committed to laying a solid foundation to support all students in their learning throughout their educational journey from pre-school to Year 12.

The Middle School (Years 6 to 9) is committed to supporting young people through their adolescence. With a global perspective, we encourage them to discover, explore and engage in their learning. We cater for a wide range of learning needs and offer students broad academic experiences that will help them develop the knowledge, attitudes and skills they need for their Senior School years and beyond.

Our Middle School is committed to encouraging all students to achieve their personal best.

The Senior School (Years 10 to 12) is committed to nurturing the synergy between student, home and school. Effort, resilience, drive and grit are qualities developed by highly committed and encouraging staff. Students are encouraged to unlock their passions and interests, and pursue their individual strengths. Extensive subject selection and career counselling are offered to each of our students to ensure they are well aware of their options and post-school choices.

Our Senior School is committed to providing students with a holistic education, great opportunities, and a head start in life.

For further information, visit: www.woodcroft.sa.edu.au.

(Founded 2006)

Headteachers
Mr. Stephen O'Connor & Ms. Yvonne Ma

DP coordinator
Ms. Varsha Kumar

Status Private

Boarding/day Day

Gender Coeducational

Language of instruction
English

Authorised IB programmes
DP

Age Range 2 – 18 years

Number of pupils enrolled
331

Address
72 Tai Hang Shan Lu
Qingdao West Coast New Area
Huangdao, Shandong
266555 | CHINA

TEL +86 532 8699 5551
FAX +86 532 8687 0099

Email
enquiry@qd.ycef.com

Website
www.ycis-qd.com

Located in the West Coast New Area of Qingdao, Shandong province, Yew Chung International School of Qingdao has earned its reputation for excellence in international education with a commitment to global education.

The curriculum at YCIS Qingdao in ECE, Primary and Lower Secondary years is research based and unique to the Yew Chung foundation of schools, while students in Years 10-11 transition to the Cambridge IGCSE syllabi, which prepares them for the academically rigorous and internationally recognized IB Diploma Programme in Years 12-13. Our global citizens of over 15 nationalities immerse themselves in a truly multi-cultural and bilingual learning environment that wholly incorporates both Eastern and Western cultures.

YCIS Qingdao has a dedicated team of global educators working in partnership to provide a well-rounded, holistic learning experience for every subject and age group. Our education model provides opportunities in each classroom for students to hone skills in research, critical thinking, analysis, creativity, problem solving, and collaboration. The ultimate objective is to equip our students with the ability to succeed in an ever-changing globalised world throughout their adulthood.

At the root of YCIS's philosophy is the blend of Eastern and Western cultures. The real essence of a culture must not just be understood but truly valued. To this end, our Western and Chinese Co-Principals jointly lead the school. They represent the union of cultures by working closely alongside one another. In addition, our unique co-teaching model is implemented throughout Early Childhood and Primary year levels, to best support the development of bilingual and cross-cultural skills. Experiencing China field trips, moreover, take students beyond the classroom to gain hands-on cultural and historical experience as well as comprehensive knowledge about their host country.

Co-curricular activities are offered to inspire creativity and development of strong moral character. These include YCIS Seeds of Hope activities, communication and technology programmes, research and problem-solving clubs, sports and athletic competitions, applied arts exhibitions, music and drama performances, and much more.

At YCIS Qingdao, we offer students the possibilities to make a tangible and positive impact on the world. If you are moving to Qingdao, please don't hesitate to reach out to us – we would love to welcome you into our family!

Yew Chung International School of Shanghai

Co-Principals
Mr Don Collins (Puxi)
Mr Damien Hehir &
Ms Mary Yu (Pudong)

DP coordinator
Mr Jonathan Evans (Puxi)
Mr Matt Grady (Pudong)

Status Private

Boarding/day Day

Gender Coeducational

Language of instruction
English, Chinese (Mandarin)

Authorised IB programmes
DP

Age Range 2 – 18 years

Number of pupils enrolled
2500

Fees
Day: RMB146,900 – RMB317,400

Address
11 Shui Cheng Road
Puxi
Shanghai
200336 | CHINA

TEL +86 21 2226 7666
FAX +86 21 6242 7331

Email
enquiry@sh.ycef.com

Website
www.ycis-sh.com

Yew Chung International School of Shanghai (YCIS Shanghai) is one of the leading international schools in China. We are renowned for offering a progressive programme of international education.

Our five campuses are located in prime areas of both the Puxi and Pudong areas of Shanghai and collectively cater to Kindergarten, Primary, and Secondary students, aged 2 to 18. As a school for the children of international families, our students come from over 50 countries and regions and are educated by world-class teachers from more than 20 countries. Our international curriculum helps to develop individuals with multicultural perspectives.

Our unique multicultural and bilingual approach to education, which places a focus on both English and Chinese language learning, is recognised worldwide and helps distinguish our students in a globally competitive environment. YCIS students consistently achieve 'Top in China' and 'Top in the World' academic results, as well as outstanding extra-curricular successes.

YCIS Shanghai opened in 1993 as the first independent international school in the city officially recognised by and registered with the Chinese government. Our school was established to bring the educational philosophy, objectives, and pedagogy of Yew Chung to Shanghai's international families. For over a quarter of a century, YCIS Shanghai has grown rapidly and now has a student body of over 2,500 students.

YCIS Shanghai is a fully accredited school, recognised by the New England Association of Schools and Colleges (NEASC) and the Council of International Schools (CIS). Additionally, our Secondary School is authorised as an accredited Cambridge Assessment Examinations Centre for the International General Certificate of Secondary Education (IGCSE), and is an International Baccalaureate World School, offering the International Baccalaureate Diploma Programme (IBDP). We are proud to offer these world-class programmes as part of our international curriculum.

Notably, YCIS Shanghai is the only school in China to have received the Cambridge Award for Excellence in Education.

YCIS is at the forefront of implementing the 'Learning Communities' model, with the support of the award-winning architectural firm, Fielding Nair International (FNI), the global leader in educational facilities planning and architectural design. Our newest campus, Ronghua Campus, which opened in 2018, was purpose-built as a Learning Community school, and features FNI's innovative Learning Community configuration, with modifiable classrooms and multi-site teaching spaces, creating agile, learner-centred environments and fostering the enquiry-based learning environment for which YCIS Shanghai is known. We are integrating Learning Community spaces into the facilities at all four of our other YCIS Shanghai campuses.

Over the past several years, the Learning Community model has emerged as one of the most important trends in education worldwide. According to recent research from Harvard University, young learners benefit immensely from studying in Learning Communities as the environment helps connect students and enable their shared learning through collaborative inquiry, in which the students work together to learn and solve problems. This approach helps students to learn how to listen and work together while also gaining social confidence – one of the essential traits identified by educators as missing from more traditional teaching approaches. As a pioneer in realising and implementing the Learning Community model, we are proud to be equipped to continue leading the future of international education at YCIS Shanghai.

Forging a path for the future of international education means creating future leaders. To prepare our students for life after graduation, YCIS Shanghai has a dedicated team of expert University Guidance Counsellors who work with our students to help them to make the best individual choices when considering their options for further education and their careers beyond. As a result, in recent years, our students have been accepted to prestigious universities across the world, including: University of Cambridge, University of Oxford, London School of Economics, Stanford University, Brown University, New York University, University of Toronto, McGill University, University of British Columbia, Yale-NUS, National University of Singapore, Singapore Management University, University of Tokyo and University of Hong Kong.

With an abundance of learning opportunities inside and outside of the classroom, from kindergarten all the way through to Secondary, YCIS Shanghai enables its students to make the most of their time at school, in Shanghai, China, and the world far beyond. Growing up in the truly international environment that YCIS Shanghai offers – one where they're encouraged to think, challenge, learn, and develop into well-rounded individuals – our students feel empowered and ready for all of the challenges as they enter and enjoy their lives in a global society.

Directory of schools in the Asia-Pacific region

Key to symbols

- CP
- Diploma
- MYP
- PYP
- Fee Paying School
- Boys' School
- Girls' School
- Coeducational School
- Boarding School
- Day School

AUSTRALIA

Alamanda K-9 College
PO Box 6606, Point Cook VIC 3030
PYP Coordinator Carmen Sacco
Languages English
T: +61 3 8376 5200
W: alamandacollege.vic.edu.au

Albert Park College
83 Danks Street, Albert Park, Melbourne VIC 3206
DP Coordinator Kathryn Riosa
Languages English
T: +61 3 8695 9000
W: www.albertparkcollege.vic.edu.au

Anglican Church Grammar School
Oaklands Parade, East Brisbane QLD 4169
DP Coordinator Catherine Prosser
PYP Coordinator Scott Warfield
Languages English
T: +61 7 3896 2200
W: www.churchie.com.au

Annesley Junior School
28 Rose Terrace, Wayville SA 5034
PYP Coordinator Joanne Rossiter
Languages English
T: +61 8 8422 2288
W: www.annesley.sa.edu.au

Aspendale Gardens Primary School
96 Kearney Drive, Aspendale Gardens VIC 3195
PYP Coordinator Nadia Walker
Languages English
T: +61 (03) 9587 0877
W: www.agps.vic.edu.au

Aspendale Primary School
23 Laura Street, Aspendale, Melbourne VIC 3195
PYP Coordinator Sherri Jenkins
Languages English
T: +61 (0)3 9580 3255
W: www.aspendale.vic.edu.au

Auburn South Primary School
419 Tooronga Road, East Hawthorn, Melbourne VIC 3123
PYP Coordinator Benjamin Zonca
Languages English
T: +61 3 9882 2140
W: www.auburnsthps.vic.edu.au

Australian International Academy
653 Sydney Road, Coburg VIC 3058
DP Coordinator Berna Yusuf
MYP Coordinator Naima Keddar
PYP Coordinator Sonia Bilal
Languages English
T: +61 3 9354 0833
W: www.aia.vic.edu.au

Australian International Academy – Kellyville Campus
57-69 Samantha Riley Drive, Kellyville, Sydney NSW 2155
DP Coordinator Paul Apostolou
MYP Coordinator Lubna Sayed
PYP Coordinator Sara Shehata
Languages English
T: +61 02 8801 3100
W: kellyville.aia.nsw.edu.au

Australian International Academy – Sydney Campus
420 Liverpool Road, Strathfield, Sydney NSW 2135
DP Coordinator Simran Khan
MYP Coordinator Bedrieh Kheir
PYP Coordinator Oznur Aydemir
Languages English
T: +61 2 9642 0104
W: strathfield.aia.nsw.edu.au

Ballarat Grammar
201 Forest Street, Wendouree VIC 3355
PYP Coordinator Maria Cahir
Languages English
T: + 61 3 5338 0700
W: www.bgs.vic.edu.au

Balwyn North Primary School
Buchanan Avenue, Balwyn North VIC 3104
PYP Coordinator Nicole McLean
Languages English
T: +61 (0)3 9859 4258
W: balwynnorthps.vic.edu.au

Beaumaris North Primary School
Wood Street, Beaumaris, Melbourne VIC 3193
PYP Coordinator Debbie Murnane
Languages English
T: +61 3 9589 5449
W: www.beaumarisnorthps.vic.edu.au

Belair Primary School
45-83 Main Road, Belair SA 5052
PYP Coordinator Natalie Mayfield
Languages English
T: +61 8 8370 3733
W: www.belairps.sa.edu.au

Benowa State High School
PO Box 5733, Gold Coast Mail Centre, Benowa QLD 9726
DP Coordinator Adrian Hays
Languages English
T: +61 (07) 5582 7333
W: www.benowashs.eq.edu.au

Benton Junior College
261 Racecourse Road, Mornington VIC 3931
PYP Coordinator Jodie Brasher
Languages English
T: +61 3 5973 9100
W: www.benton.vic.edu.au

Berwick Primary School
37 Fairholme Boulevard, Berwick VIC 3806
PYP Coordinator Gillian Hartman
Languages English
T: +61 03 97071026
W: www.berwickprimary.vic.edu.au

Blackwood High School
4 Seymour Street, Eden Hills SA 5050
MYP Coordinator Lachlan McFarlane
Languages English
T: +61 8 8278 0900
W: www.bhs.sa.edu.au

Blackwood Primary School
4 Seymour Street, Eden Hills SA 5050
PYP Coordinator Amanda Gulliver
Languages English
T: +61 8 82785355
W: www.blackwoodps.sa.edu.au

Brighton Primary School
59 Wilson Street, Brighton, Melbourne VIC 3186
PYP Coordinator Joel Snowden
Languages English
T: +61 39592 0177
W: www.brighton.vic.edu.au

Brighton Secondary College
120 Marriage Road, Brighton East VIC 3187
DP Coordinator Rupert Hunt
Languages English
T: +61 3 9592 7488
W: brightonsc.vic.edu.au

Cairns State High School
PO Box 5643, Cairns QLD 4870
DP Coordinator Stefanie Biancotti
Languages English
T: +61 7 4050 3033
W: www.cairnsshs.eq.edu.au

Calamvale Community College
11 Hamish Street, Calamvale QLD 4116
DP Coordinator Melissa Ellis
PYP Coordinator Mark Smith
Languages English
T: +61 (0)7 3712 6333
W: calamvalecomcoll.eq.edu.au

Canberra Girls Grammar School
Melbourne Avenue, Deakin ACT 2600
DP Coordinator Sarah Trotter
PYP Coordinator Alex Galland
Languages English
T: +61 2 6202 6400
W: www.cggs.act.edu.au

Canberra Grammar School
40 Monaro Crescent, Red Hill, Canberra ACT 2603
DP Coordinator Adriaan van Wijk
PYP Coordinator Lucy Garven
Languages English
T: + 61 2 6260 9700
W: www.cgs.act.edu.au

CAREY BAPTIST GRAMMAR SCHOOL
349 Barkers Road, Kew VIC 3101
DP Coordinator Frederique Petithory
Languages English
T: +61 3 9816 1222
E: admissions@carey.com.au
W: www.carey.com.au
See full details on page 305

Caulfield Grammar School – Caulfield Campus
PO Box 610, 217 Glen Eira Road East, St Kilda VIC 3185
PYP Coordinator Jacinta Crimmins
Languages English
T: +61 3 9524 6300
W: www.caulfieldgs.vic.edu.au

Caulfield Grammar School – Wheelers Hill Campus
74-82 Jells Road, Wheelers Hill VIC 3150
PYP Coordinator Jonathan Twigg
Languages English
T: +61 3 8562 5300
W: www.caulfieldgs.vic.edu.au

Caulfield South Primary School
Bundeera Road, Caulfield South, Melbourne VIC 3162
PYP Coordinator Stacey Fallon
Languages English
T: +61 3957 83718
W: www.caulfieldsthps.vic.edu.au

Cleveland District State High School
Russell Street, Cleveland QLD 4163
DP Coordinator Karen Abraham
Languages English
T: +61 738 249 222
W: www.clevdistshs.eq.edu.au

Coatesville Primary School
21 Mackie Road, East Bentleigh VIC 3165
PYP Coordinator Matthew Cameron
Languages English
T: +61 03 9570 1652
W: www.coatesps.vic.gov.au

Concordia College
24 Winchester St, Highgate SA 5063
DP Coordinator Brendan Toohey
MYP Coordinator Emily Johnson
PYP Coordinator Rachel Muldoon
Languages English
T: +61 8 8272 0444
W: www.concordia.sa.edu.au

Cornish College
65 Riverend Rd, Bangholme VIC 3175
PYP Coordinator Pete Westwood
Languages English
T: +61 3 9781 9000
W: www.cornishcollege.vic.edu.au

Coromandel Valley Primary School
339 Main Road, Coromandel Valley SA 5051
MYP Coordinator Liz Pelling (Black)
PYP Coordinator Juli Bryan
Languages English
T: +61 8 8278 3693
W: www.coromandps.sa.edu.au

Cranbrook School
5 Victoria Road, Bellevue Hill NSW 2023
MYP Coordinator Nicholas Harleigh Hanrahan
PYP Coordinator Genet Erickson Adam
Languages English
T: +61 2 9327 9000
W: www.cranbrook.nsw.edu.au

Elonera Montessori School
21 Mount Ousley Road, Wollongong NSW 2519
DP Coordinator Carlos Hubbard
Languages English
T: +61 2 4225 1000
W: www.eloneramontessori.com.au

Encounter Lutheran College
64 Adelaide Road, Victor Harbor SA 5211
MYP Coordinator Adam Pfeiffer
PYP Coordinator Tori Weiss
Languages English
T: +61 8 8552 8880
W: www.encounter.sa.edu.au

Essendon North Primary School
112 Keilor Road, North Essendon VIC 3041
PYP Coordinator Alice Mckenzie
T: +61 (03) 9379 3979
W: www.enps.vic.edu.au

Fintona Girls' School
79 Balwyn Road, Balwyn VIC 3103
PYP Coordinator Nina Manning
Languages English
T: +61 3 9830 1388
W: www.fintona.vic.edu.au

Firbank Grammar Junior School – Brighton Campus
51 Outer Crescent, Brighton, Melbourne VIC 3186
PYP Coordinator Melanie Smith
Languages English
T: +61 3 9591 5141
W: www.firbank.vic.edu.au

Firbank Grammar Junior School – Sandringham Campus
45 Royal Avenue, Sandringham VIC 3191
PYP Coordinator Karen Chandler
Languages English
T: +61 3 9533 5711
W: www.firbank.vic.edu.au

Footscray Primary School
PO Box 6019, West Footscray VIC 3012
PYP Coordinator Stacey Richards
Languages English
T: +61 3 9687 1910
W: www.footscrayps.vic.edu.au

Forrest Primary School
Hobart Avenue, Forrest, Canberra ACT 2603
PYP Coordinator Kylie Dorsett
T: +61 2 6205 5644
W: www.forrestps.act.edu.au

Geelong Grammar School
50 Biddlecombe Avenue, Corio VIC 3214
DP Coordinator Steven Griffiths
PYP Coordinator Mario Gauci
Languages English
T: +61 3 5273 9200
W: www.ggs.vic.edu.au

German International School Sydney
33 Myoora Road, Terrey Hills NSW 2084
DP Coordinator Annie Thomson
Languages English, German
T: +61 (0) 2 94851900
W: www.giss.nsw.edu.au

Gilmore College for Girls
PO Box 2021, Footscray VIC 3011
MYP Coordinator Olga Mueller
Languages English
T: +61 3 9689 4788
W: www.gilmorecollegeforgirls.vic.edu.au

Glenroy West Primary School
P.O. Box 547, York Street, Glenroy VIC 3046
PYP Coordinator Lisa Brandecker
Languages English
T: +61 (0)3 9306 8955
W: www.glenroywestps.vic.edu.au

Glenunga International High School
L'Estrange Street, Glenunga SA 5064
DP Coordinator Corin Bone
Languages English
T: +61 88 379 5629
W: www.gihs.sa.edu.au

Gold Creek School
74 Kelleway Avenue, Nicholls, Canberra ACT 2913
MYP Coordinator Ingrid Osborn
PYP Coordinator Cindy Condon
Languages English
T: +61 (02) 6205 2955
W: www.goldcreek.act.edu.au

Golden Grove Lutheran Primary School
Corner of Richardson Drive and Sunnybrook Drive, Wynn Vale SA 5127
PYP Coordinator Jayne Zadow
Languages English
T: +61 8 8282 6000
W: www.goldengrove.sa.edu.au

Good Shepherd Lutheran College – Howard Springs Campus
Corner of Whitewood Road & Kundook Place, Howard Springs NT 0835
MYP Coordinator Kathryn Cummins
PYP Coordinator Mrs Rebecca Fletcher
Languages English
T: +61 8 89830300
W: www.goodshepherd.nt.edu.au

Good Shepherd Lutheran College – St Andrew Leanyer Campus
95 Leanyer Drive, Leanyer NT 0812
PYP Coordinator Rebecca Fletcher
Languages English
T: +61 8 8983 0300
W: www.goodshepherd.nt.edu.au

Good Shepherd Lutheran School – Angaston
7 Neldner Avenue, Angaston SA 5353
PYP Coordinator Melissa Hooker
Languages English
T: +61 8 8564 2396
W: www.goodshepherd.sa.edu.au

Grace Christian College
20 Kinchington Road, Leneva, Mellboune VIC 3691
DP Coordinator Joel Robotham
Languages English
T: +61 02 6056 2299
W: gcc.vic.edu.au

Heany Park Primary School
Buckingham Drive, Rowville VIC 3178
PYP Coordinator Kym Ryan
Languages English
T: +61 (0)3 9764 5533
W: www.heanyparkps.vic.edu.au

Helena College
PO Box 52, Glenn Forrest WA 6071
MYP Coordinator Robert Simpson
Languages English
T: +61 89 298 9100
W: www.helenacollege.wa.edu.au

Highton Primary School
PO Box 6093, Highton VIC 3216
PYP Coordinator Tracy Thornton
Languages English
T: +61 3 5243 1494
W: www.hightonps.vic.edu.au

Hills Grammar
43 Kenthurst Road, Kenthurst NSW 2156
PYP Coordinator Samantha Cordwell
Languages English
T: +61 2 9654 2111
W: www.hillsgrammar.nsw.edu.au

Hills International College
105-111 Johanna Street, Jimboomba QLD 4280
PYP Coordinator Stuart Ablitt
Languages English
T: +61 7 5546 0667
W: www.hills.qld.edu.au

Holy Trinity Primary School
18-20 Theodore Street, Curtin ACT 2605
PYP Coordinator Ms Katie Smith
Languages English
T: +61 26281 4811
W: www.holytrinity.act.edu.au

Hunter Valley Grammar School
42 Norfolk Street, Ashtonfield NSW 2323
PYP Coordinator Madeleine Smith
Languages English
T: +61 2 4934 2444
W: www.hvgs.nsw.edu.au

Immanuel College
32 Morphett Road, Novar Gardens SA 5040
MYP Coordinator Jolanta Stephens
Languages English
T: +61 08 8294 3588
W: www.immanuel.sa.edu.au

Immanuel Gawler
11 Lyndoch Road, Gawler East SA 5118
PYP Coordinator Andrew Boesch
Languages English
T: +61 8 8522 5740
W: www.ilsg.sa.edu.au

Immanuel Primary School
Saratoga Drive, Novar Gardens SA 5040
PYP Coordinator Sarah Nash
Languages English
T: +61 8 8294 8422
W: www.immanuelps.sa.edu.au

Indooroopilly State High School
PO Box 61, Ward Street, Indooroopilly, Brisbane QLD 4068
DP Coordinator Peter Day
Languages English
T: +61 7 3327 8333
W: www.indooroshs.eq.edu.au

INTERNATIONAL SCHOOL OF WESTERN AUSTRALIA
22 Kalinda Drive, City Beach WA 6015
DP Coordinator Mini Balachandran
MYP Coordinator Janice Murray
PYP Coordinator Fleur Churton
Languages English
T: +61 8 9285 1144
E: info@iswa.wa.edu.au
W: www.iswa.wa.edu.au
See full details on page 354

Ivanhoe Grammar School
PO Box 91, The Ridgeway, Ivanhoe VIC 3079
DP Coordinator Sean Johnson
Languages English
T: +61 3 9490 3501
W: www.ivanhoe.com.au

John Paul College
John Paul Drive, Daisy Hill, Queensland QLD 4127
DP Coordinator Kate MacLeod
PYP Coordinator Lindsay McQuattie
Languages English
T: +61 7 3826 3333
W: www.johnpaulcollege.com.au

JOHN WOLLASTON ANGLICAN COMMUNITY SCHOOL
Centre Road, Camillo WA 6111
PYP Coordinator Mrs Fiona Currey
Languages English
T: +61 (08) 9495 8100
E: mail@jwacs.wa.edu.au
W: www.jwacs.wa.edu.au
See full details on page 357

KAMBALA
794 New South Head Road, Rose Bay, Sydney NSW 2029
DP Coordinator Megan Armstrong
Languages English
T: +612 93886777
E: enrolments@kambala.nsw.edu.au
W: www.kambala.nsw.edu.au
See full details on page 360

KARDINIA INTERNATIONAL COLLEGE
29-31 Kardinia Drive, Bell Post Hill, Geelong VIC 3215
DP Coordinator Dianne Vella
PYP Coordinator Geoff Geddes
Languages English
T: +61 3 5278 9999
E: kardinia@kardinia.vic.edu.au
W: www.kardinia.vic.edu.au
See full details on page 361

Kingston Heath Primary School
25 Farm Road, Cheltenham VIC 3192
PYP Coordinator Charlotte Birbeck
Languages English
T: +61 3 9584 5805
W: www.khps.vic.edu.au

Kingsville Primary School
58 Bishop Street, Yarraville VIC 3013
PYP Coordinator Peter Ritchie
Languages English
T: +61 03 9315 8569
W: www.kingsvilleps.vic.edu.au

Kingswood College
355 Station Street, Box Hill, Melbourne VIC 3128
PYP Coordinator Heather Westwood
Languages English
T: +61 3 9896 1700
W: www.kingswoodcollege.vic.edu.au

KOROROIT CREEK PRIMARY SCHOOL
130 Tenterfield Drive, Burnside Heights VIC 3023
PYP Coordinator Sarah Afiouni
Languages English
T: +61 3 8358 0600
E: kororoit.creek.ps@edumail.vic.gov.au
W: www.kororoitcreekps.vic.edu.au
See full details on page 363

Kunyung Primary School
50 Kunyung Road, Mt Eliza VIC 3930
PYP Coordinator Melanie Woodland
Languages English
T: +61 (3) 9787 6102
W: www.kunyung.vic.edu.au/

Lauriston Girls' School
38 Huntingtower Road, Armadale VIC 3143
DP Coordinator Eirwen Stevenson
Languages English
T: +61 3 9864 7555
W: www.lauriston.vic.edu.au

Le Fevre High School
90 Hart Street, Semaphore South, Adelaide SA 5019
MYP Coordinator Sarah Craddock
Languages English
T: +61 8 8449 7004
W: www.lefevrehs.sa.edu.au

Linden Park Primary School
14 Hay Road, Linden Park, Adelaide SA 5065
PYP Coordinator Nicole Scrivener
Languages English
T: +61 (0)8 8379 2171
W: www.lindenpkr7.sa.edu.au

Lloyd Street School
Lloyd Street, East Malvern VIC 3145
PYP Coordinator Roshni Amaria
Languages English
T: +61 3 9571 0261
W: www.lloydstps.vic.edu.au

LYCÉE CONDORCET - THE INTERNATIONAL FRENCH SCHOOL OF SYDNEY
758 Anzac Parade, Maroubra NSW 2035
DP Coordinator Cybele Gonzalez
Languages French, English
T: +61 2 9344 8692
E: ib@condorcet.com.au
W: www.condorcet.com.au
See full details on page 370

Macclesfield Primary School
405 Macclesfield Road, Macclesfield VIC 3782
PYP Coordinator Andrea Goodey
Languages English
T: +61 3 5968 4734
W: www.macclesfieldps.vic.edu.au

Mater Christi College
28 Bayview Road, Belgrave, Melbourne VIC 3160
MYP Coordinator Collette Bond
Languages English
T: +61 3 9754 6611
W: www.materchristi.edu.au

McKinnon Primary School
253 Tucker Road, Ormond VIC 3204
PYP Coordinator Chris Barker
Languages English
T: +61 3 9578 1851
W: mckinnon-primary.vic.edu.au

Melba Copland Secondary School
Copland Drive, Melba ACT 2615
DP Coordinator Gai Britt
MYP Coordinator Sally Harriden
Languages English
T: +61 2 6142 0333
W: www.mcss.act.edu.au

Melbourne Montessori School
741 Hawthorn Road, Brighton East VIC 3187
DP Coordinator Casper Buisman
Languages English
T: +61 (0)3 9131 5203
W: melbournemontessori.vic.edu.au

MENTONE GIRLS' GRAMMAR SCHOOL
11 Mentone Parade, Mentone VIC 3194
PYP Coordinator Donnah Ciempka
Languages English
T: +61 3 9581 1200
E: info@mentonegirls.vic.edu.au
W: www.mentonegirls.vic.edu.au
See full details on page 371

MERCEDES COLLEGE
540 Fullarton Road, Springfield SA 5062
DP Coordinator Mr Marc Whitehead
MYP Coordinator Mr Stuart Wuttke
PYP Coordinator Mr Simon Munn
Languages English
T: +61 8 8372 3200
E: mercedes@mercedes.catholic.edu.au
W: www.mercedes.catholic.edu.au
See full details on page 372

Merici College
Wise Street, Braddon ACT 2612
DP Coordinator Natalie Fairfax
Languages English
T: +61 (0)2 6243 4100
W: www.merici.act.edu.au

METHODIST LADIES' COLLEGE
207 Barkers Road, Kew VIC 3101
DP Coordinator Rebecca Bunnett
Languages English
T: +61 3 9274 6316
E: admissions@mlc.vic.edu.au
W: www.mlc.vic.edu.au
See full details on page 373

Miles Franklin Primary School
Alderman Street, Evatt, Canberra ACT 2617
PYP Coordinator Nicole Jaggers
Languages English
T: +61 2 6205 7533
W: www.mfps.act.edu.au

Milgate Primary School
96 Landscape Drive, East Doncaster, Melbourne VIC 3109
PYP Coordinator Sarah Brown
Languages English, Mandarin
T: +61 3 9842 7744
W: www.milgateps.vic.edu.au

MLC SCHOOL
Rowley Street, Burwood, Sydney NSW 2134
DP Coordinator Anne Layman
Languages English
T: +61 2 9747 1266
E: enrol@mlcsyd.nsw.edu.au
W: www.mlcsyd.nsw.edu.au
See full details on page 374

Monte Sant' Angelo Mercy College
PO Box 1064, 128 Miller Street, North Sydney NSW 2059
DP Coordinator Kim Vandervelde
MYP Coordinator Katie Hogg
Languages English
T: +61 2 9409 6200
W: www.monte.nsw.edu.au

Montessori International College
880-932 Maroochydore Road, Forest Glen QLD 4556
CP Coordinator Kellie Doulin
Languages English
T: +61 7 5442 3807
W: www.mic.qld.edu.au

Moreton Bay Boys' College
302 Manly Road, Manly West QLD 4179
MYP Coordinator Leigh Ann Cadzow-Andreas
PYP Coordinator Larissa Guy
Languages English
T: +61 07 3906 9444
W: www.mbbc.qld.edu.au

Moreton Bay College
450 Wondall Rd, Manly West QLD 4179
PYP Coordinator Nicole Bowers
Languages English
T: +61 7 3390 8555
W: www.mbc.qld.edu.au/home

Mornington Primary School
Vale Street, Mornington VIC 3931
PYP Coordinator Tahlia Anver
Languages English
T: +61 3 5975 2561
W: www.morningtonps.vic.edu.au

Mount Eliza North Primary School
Moseley Drive, PO Box 219, Mount Eliza VIC 3930
PYP Coordinator Melissa Wisniewski
Languages English
T: +61 3 9787 6611
W: www.menps.vic.edu.au

Mount Macedon Primary School
641 Mount Macedon Rd, Mount Macedon VIC 3441
PYP Coordinator Annette Weinberger
Languages English
T: +61 3 5426 1446

Mount Scopus Memorial College
245 Burwood Highway, Burwood VIC 3125
MYP Coordinator Matthew Dufty
PYP Coordinator Edna Sackson
Languages English, Hebrew
T: +61 3 9834 0000
W: www.scopus.vic.edu.au

Mount View Primary School
Shepherd Road, Glen Waverley VIC 3150
PYP Coordinator Nina Chen
Languages English
T: +61 3 9560 0471
W: www.mountviewps.vic.edu.au

Mountain Creek State High School
PO Box 827, Mooloolaba QLD 4557
DP Coordinator Jessi Hunt
Languages English
T: +61 7 5477 8555
W: mtncreekshs.eq.edu.au

Murrumbeena Primary School
Hobart Road, Murrumbeena VIC 3163
PYP Coordinator Angela Houghton
Languages English
T: +61 3 9568 1300
W: www.murrumbeenaps.vic.edu.au

Narrabundah College
Jerrabomberra Avenue, Kingston ACT 2604
DP Coordinator Christine Ward
Languages English
T: +61 26 205 6999
W: www.narrabundahc.act.edu.au

Navigator College
PO Box 3199, Port Lincoln SA 5606
MYP Coordinator Sarah Smith
PYP Coordinator Nola Kennedy Williams
Languages English
T: +61 8 86825099
W: www.navigator.sa.edu.au

NEWINGTON COLLEGE – LINDFIELD
26 Northcote Road, Lindfield, New South Wales NSW 2070
PYP Coordinator Sue Gough
Languages English
T: +61 2 9416 4280
W: www.newington.nsw.edu.au

NEWINGTON COLLEGE – STANMORE
200 Stanmore Road, Stanmore NSW 2048
DP Coordinator Ms Cheryl Priest
Languages English
T: +61 2 9568 9333
E: admissions@newington.nsw.edu.au
W: www.newington.nsw.edu.au
See full details on page 376

North Ainslie Primary School
122 Majura Avenue, Ainslie, Canberra ACT 2602
PYP Coordinator Rikkie Klootwijk
Languages English
T: +61 02 62056533
W: www.nthainslieps.act.edu.au

OAKLEIGH GRAMMAR
77-81 Willesden Road, Oakleigh VIC 3166
MYP Coordinator Haydn Flanagan
Languages English
T: +61 3 9569 6128
E: admissions@oakleighgrammar.vic.edu.au
W: www.oakleighgrammar.vic.edu.au
See full details on page 384

Our Lady of the Nativity
29 Fawkner Street, Aberfeldie VIC 3040
PYP Coordinator Catherine Simone
Languages English
T: +61 3 9337 4204
W: www.olnaberfeldie.catholic.edu.au

Our Saviour Lutheran School
28 Taylors Road West, Aberfoyle Park SA 5159
PYP Coordinator Amanda McDonald
Languages English
T: +61 8 8270 5488
W: osls.sa.edu.au

Pedare Christian College
2-30 Surrey Farm Drive, Golden Grove SA 5125
MYP Coordinator Hayley Mayer
Languages English
T: +61 8 8280 1700
W: www.pedarecc.sa.edu.au

Pembroke School
342 The Parade, Kensington Park SA 5068
DP Coordinator Gabi Walldorf-Davis
PYP Coordinator Belinda Reitstatter
Languages English
T: +61 8 8366 6200
W: www.pembroke.sa.edu.au

Penrith Anglican College
PO Box 636, Kingswood NSW 2747
DP Coordinator Philip McIntyre
Languages English
T: +61 247 36 8100
W: www.pac.nsw.edu.au

Plenty Valley Christian College
840 Yan Yean Road, Doreen VIC 3754
PYP Coordinator Jacqui Ellison
Languages English
T: +61 3 9717 7400
W: www.pvcc.vic.edu.au

Presbyterian Ladies' College – Perth
14 McNeil Street, Peppermint Grove, Perth WA 6011
DP Coordinator Rebecca Garbenis
PYP Coordinator Jennifer Rickwood, Paul O'Brien
Languages English
T: +61 8 9424 6444
W: www.plc.wa.edu.au

Presbyterian Ladies' College Melbourne
141 Burwood Highway, Burwood VIC 3125
DP Coordinator Peter Francis
Languages English
T: +61 3 9808 5811
W: www.plc.vic.edu.au

Preshil – The Margaret Lyttle Memorial School
395 Barkers Road, Kew, Melbourne VIC 3101
DP Coordinator Linda Kay
MYP Coordinator John Collins
PYP Coordinator Cressida Batterham-Wilson
Languages English
T: +613 9817 6135
W: www.preshil.vic.edu.au

Prince Alfred College
PO Box 571, Kent Town SA 5071
DP Coordinator Martin Luke McKinnon
PYP Coordinator Lisa Foster
Languages English
T: +61 8 8334 1200
W: www.pac.edu.au

Queensland Academies Creative Industries Campus
61-73 Musk Avenue, Kelvin Grove QLD 4059
CP Coordinator John Carozza
DP Coordinator Michael Zornig
Languages English
T: +61 7 3552 9333
W: qaci.eq.edu.au

Queensland Academies Health Sciences Campus
102 Edmund Rice Drive, Southport QLD 4215
DP Coordinator Alan Craig-Ward
Languages English
T: +61 7 5510 1100
W: qahs.eq.edu.au

QUEENSLAND ACADEMY FOR SCIENCE MATHEMATICS AND TECHNOLOGY (QASMT)
78 Bywong Street, Toowong QLD 4066
DP Coordinator Mr Meng-Yin Leong
Languages English
T: +61 7 3377 9333
E: admin@qasmt.eq.edu.au
W: qasmt.eq.edu.au
See full details on page 390

QUEENWOOD
Locked bag 1, Mosman NSW 2088
DP Coordinator Sarah Thompson
Languages English
T: +61 2 89687777
E: q@queenwood.nsw.edu.au
W: www.queenwood.nsw.edu.au
See full details on page 391

Radford College
College Street, Bruce, Canberra ACT 2617
DP Coordinator Lindy Braithwaite
PYP Coordinator Nick Martin
Languages English
T: +61 2 6162 5332
W: www.radford.act.edu.au

Ravenswood
Henry Street, Gordon NSW 2072
DP Coordinator Monique Connor
PYP Coordinator Anne Gruenewald
Languages English
T: +612 9498 9898
W: www.ravenswood.nsw.edu.au

Red Hill School
PO Box 22, Red Hill ACT 2603
PYP Coordinator Emma Campbell
Languages English
T: +61 2 6205 7144
W: www.redhillps.act.edu.au

Redeemer Lutheran School, Nuriootpa
Box 397, Nuriootpa SA 5355
PYP Coordinator Graham Buxton
Languages English
T: +61 885 621655
W: www.redeemer.sa.edu.au

REDLANDS
272 Military Road, Cremorne NSW 2090
DP Coordinator Darren Taylor
Languages English
T: +61 2 9908 6479
E: dtaylor@redlands.nsw.edu.au
registrar@redlands.nsw.edu.au
W: www.redlands.nsw.edu.au
See full details on page 393

Rivercrest Christian College
500 Soldiers Rd, Clyde North VIC 3978
PYP Coordinator Caryn Johnson
Languages English
T: +61 3 97039777
W: www.rivercrest.vic.edu.au

Rochedale State School
694 Rochedale Road, Rochedale, Brisbane QLD 4123
PYP Coordinator Paul Kelly
Languages English
T: +61 733408333
W: www.rochedalss.eq.edu.au

Roma Mitchell Secondary College
Briens Road, Gepps Cross SA 5094
MYP Coordinator Noel Hernes
Languages English
T: +61 (0)8 8161 4600
W: rmsc.sa.edu.au

Rose Park Primary School
54 Alexandra Avenue, Rose Park, Adelaide SA 5067
PYP Coordinator Jo Hurn
Languages English
T: +618 8331 7521
W: www.roseparkps.sa.edu.au

Roseville College
Locked Bag 34, 27 Bancroft Avenue, Roseville NSW 2069
PYP Coordinator Jane Sloane
Languages English
T: +61 2 9884 1100
W: www.roseville.nsw.edu.au

Sacred Heart College Geelong
Retreat Road, Newtown VIC 3220
MYP Coordinator Daina Honey
Languages English
T: +61 3 52214211
W: www.shcgeelong.catholic.edu.au

Santa Maria College
50 Separation Street, Northcote, Melbourne VIC 3070
MYP Coordinator Bradley Denny
Languages English
T: +61 3 9488 1600
W: www.santamaria.vic.edu.au

SANTA SABINA COLLEGE
90 The Boulevarde, Strathfield, Sydney NSW 2135
DP Coordinator Julie Harris
PYP Coordinator Karen Campbell
Languages English
T: +61 2 9745 7000
E: enrolment@ssc.nsw.edu.au
W: www.ssc.nsw.edu.au
See full details on page 402

Scotch College
76 Shenton Road, Swanbourne, Perth WA 6010
DP Coordinator Michael Scaife
MYP Coordinator Sophie Berry
PYP Coordinator Warwick Norman
Languages English
T: +61 8 9383 6800
W: www.scotch.wa.edu.au

Seabrook Primary School
83-105 Point Cook Road, Seabrook VIC 3028
PYP Coordinator Rima El Souki
Languages English
T: +61 3 9395 1758
W: www.seabrook.vic.edu.au

Seaford North Primary School
81 Hallifax Street, Seaford VIC 3198
PYP Coordinator Chloe Gannon
Languages English
T: +61 3 9786 5674
W: seaford-northps.vic.edu.au

Seymour College
546 Portrush Road, Glen Osmond, Adelaide SA 5064
DP Coordinator Natalie Paelchen
PYP Coordinator Vanessa Browning
Languages English
T: +61 8 8303 9000
W: seymour.sa.edu.au

Somerset College
Somerset Drive, Mudgeeraba QLD 4213
DP Coordinator Stephen Walther
MYP Coordinator Michele Sauer
PYP Coordinator Brenda Millican
Languages English
T: +61 (0)7 5559 7100
W: www.somerset.qld.edu.au

Sophia Mundi Steiner School
St. Mary's Abbotsford Convent, 1 St Heller's Street, Abbotsford, Melbourne VIC 3067
DP Coordinator Helen Ashley Falzarano Dufty
Languages English
T: +61 3 9419 9229
W: www.sophiamundi.vic.edu.au

Southern Christian College
150 Redwood Road, Kingston, Tasmania TAS 7050
DP Coordinator Veronica Schuth
MYP Coordinator Damon Adams
PYP Coordinator Melanie Curé
Languages English
T: +613 6229 5744
W: www.scc.tas.edu.au

ST ANDREW'S CATHEDRAL SCHOOL
Sydney Square, Sydney NSW 2000
DP Coordinator Sharon Munro
MYP Coordinator Kathleen Layhe
Languages English
T: +61 2 9286 9500
E: enrolments@sacs.nsw.edu.au
W: www.sacs.nsw.edu.au
See full details on page 418

St Andrews Lutheran College
PO Box 2142, Burleigh BC QLD 4220
PYP Coordinator Jacqueline Faulkner
Languages English
T: +61 7 5568 5900
W: www.standrewslutheran.qld.edu.au

St Andrew's School
22 Smith Street, Walkerville SA 5081
PYP Coordinator Heather Wood
Languages English
T: +61 8 81685537
W: www.standrews.sa.edu.au

St Brigid's College
200 Lesmurdie Road, Lesmurdie, Perth WA 6076
MYP Coordinator Janine Walsh
PYP Coordinator Janine Walsh
Languages English
T: +61 8 9290 4200
W: www.stbrigids.wa.edu.au

St Dominic's Priory College
139 Molesworth Street, North Adelaide SA 5006
MYP Coordinator Aurora Reid
Languages English
T: +61 8 8267 3818
W: www.stdominics.sa.edu.au

St John's Anglican College
College Avenue, Forest Lake QLD 4078
MYP Coordinator Kelly Allgood
PYP Coordinator Martin Brownlow
Languages English
T: +61 (0)7 3372 0111
W: stjohnsanglicancollege.com.au

St John's Lutheran School, Eudunda, Inc.
8 Ward Street, Eudunda SA 5374
PYP Coordinator Coralee Hambour
Languages English
T: +61 8 8581 1282
W: www.stjohns-eudunda.sa.edu.au

St Leonard's College
163 South Road, Brighton East, Melbourne VIC 3187
DP Coordinator Craig Rodgers
PYP Coordinator Chris Stickman
Languages English
T: +61 3 9909 9300
W: www.stleonards.vic.edu.au

St Margaret's School
27-47 Gloucester Avenue, Berwick, Melbourne VIC 3806
PYP Coordinator Melissa Graham
Languages English
T: +61 3 9703 8111
W: www.stmargarets.vic.edu.au

St Mary Star of the Sea College
15 Harbour St, Wollongong NSW 2500
MYP Coordinator Katrina Wall
Languages English
T: +61 (0)2 4228 6011
W: www.stmarys.nsw.edu.au

St Michael's Lutheran School
6 Balhannah Rd, Hahndorf SA 5250
PYP Coordinator Evie Stevens
Languages English
T: +61 8 8388 7228
W: www.stmichaels.sa.edu.au

St Paul's Grammar School
Locked Bag 8016, Penrith NSW 2751
DP Coordinator Antony Mayrhofer
MYP Coordinator Mary Robyn
PYP Coordinator Corinne Day
Languages English
T: +61 2 4777 4888
W: www.stpauls.nsw.edu.au

St Peter's Anglican Primary School
Howe Street, Campbelltown NSW 2560
PYP Coordinator Melinda Richardson
Languages English
T: +61 (2) 4627 2990
W: www.stpeters.nsw.edu.au

St Peter's College
Hackney Road, Hackney, Adelaide SA 5069
DP Coordinator Paul Hadfield
Languages English
T: +61 8 8404 0400
W: www.stpeters.sa.edu.au

St Peter's Girls' School
Stonyfell Road, Stonyfell SA 5066
DP Coordinator Carolyn Victoria Farr
PYP Coordinator Helen Smith
Languages English
T: +61 88 334 2200
W: www.stpetersgirls.sa.edu.au

St Peters Lutheran College
66 Harts Road, Indooroopilly QLD 4068
DP Coordinator Roslynne Midgley
PYP Coordinator Simone Mitchell
Languages English
T: +61 7 3377 6222
W: www.stpeters.qld.edu.au

St Peters Lutheran School
71 Cumming Street, Blackwood SA 5051
PYP Coordinator Bronwyn Wilson
Languages English
T: +61 8 8278 0800
W: www.stpeterslutheran.sa.edu.au

St Peter's Woodlands Grammar School
39 Partridge Street, Glenelg, Adelaide SA 5045
PYP Coordinator Amanda Kelly
Languages English
T: +61 (8) 8295 4317
W: www.spw.sa.edu.au

Stradbroke School
73 Koonga Avenue, Rostrevor SA 5073
MYP Coordinator Sarah Button
PYP Coordinator Sarah Button
Languages English
T: +61 8 8337 2861
W: www.stradsch.sa.edu.au

Tara Anglican School for Girls
Masons Drive, North Parramatta, Sydney NSW 2151
MYP Coordinator Daryl Hinton
PYP Coordinator Wendy Abernethy
Languages English
T: +61 2 9630 6655
W: www.tara.nsw.edu.au

Telopea Park School / Lycée Franco-Australien de Canberra
New South Wales Crescent, Barton ACT 2600
MYP Coordinator Michele McLoughlin
Languages English
T: +61 2 6142 3388
W: www.telopea.act.edu.au

The Armidale School
Locked Bag 3003, 87 Douglas Street, Armidale NSW 2350
PYP Coordinator Veronica Waters
Languages English
T: +61 2 6776 5800
W: www.as.edu.au

The Friends' School
PO Box 42, North Hobart TAS 7002
DP Coordinator Sarah Walker
PYP Coordinator Wendy Crow
Languages English
T: +61 3 6210 2200
W: www.friends.tas.edu.au

THE ILLAWARRA GRAMMAR SCHOOL
10-12 Western Ave, Wollongong NSW 2500
DP Coordinator Dr Meagan McKenzie
MYP Coordinator Mrs Sharon l'Ons
PYP Coordinator Mrs Karen Wallace
Languages English
T: +61 2 4220 0200
E: info@tigs.nsw.edu.au
W: www.tigs.nsw.edu.au
See full details on page 428

The Kilmore International School
40 White Street, Kilmore VIC 3764
DP Coordinator Deanna Krilis
Languages English
T: +61 3 5782 2211
W: www.kilmore.vic.edu.au

The King's School
PO Box 1, Parramatta NSW 2124
PYP Coordinator Sonia Weston
Languages English
T: +612 9683 8555
W: www.kings.edu.au

The Montessori School
PO Box 194, Landsdale WA 6065
DP Coordinator Katharina Stillitano
Languages English
T: +61 89 409 9151
W: www.themontessorischool.wa.edu.au

The Norwood Morialta High School
Morialta Road West, Rostrevor SA 5073
MYP Coordinator Leisa Westerhof
Languages English
T: +61 8 83650455
W: www.nmhs.sa.edu.au

The Riverina Anglican College
127 Farrer Road, Wagga Wagga NSW 2650
DP Coordinator Patricia Humble
Languages English
T: +61 (0)2 6933 1811
W: www.trac.nsw.edu.au

The Scots School Albury
393 Perry Street, Albury NSW 2640
PYP Coordinator Matthew Boundy
Languages English
T: +61 (0)2 6022 0000
W: www.scotsalbury.nsw.edu.au

Tintern Grammar
90 Alexandra Road, PO Box 26, Ringwood East VIC 3135
DP Coordinator Nola Joy Brotchie
Languages English
T: +61 3 9845 7777
W: www.tintern.vic.edu.au

Toorak College
PO Box 150, Mount Eliza VIC 3930
PYP Coordinator Naomi Linssen
Languages English
T: +61 3 9788 7200
W: www.toorakc.vic.edu.au

Townsville Grammar School
45 Paxton Street, North Ward QLD 4810
DP Coordinator Katie Watson
Languages English
T: +61 7 4722 4900
W: www.tgs.qld.edu.au

Treetops Montessori School
PO Box 59, Darlington WA 6076
CP Coordinator Sharon Crossman
DP Coordinator Sharon Crossman
Languages English
T: +61 8 9299 6725
W: www.treetops.wa.edu.au

Trinity Grammar School Preparatory School

115-125 The Boulevarde, Strathfield NSW 2135
PYP Coordinator Kirsti Hitz-Morton
Languages English
T: +61 2 8732 4600
W: www.trinity.nsw.edu.au

Trinity Grammar School, Kew

40 Charles Street, Kew VIC 3101
PYP Coordinator Jonathan Knight
Languages English
T: +61 3 9854 3600
W: www.trinity.vic.edu.au

Trinity Grammar School, Sydney

119 Prospect Road, Summer Hill NSW 2130
DP Coordinator Chris Barnes
PYP Coordinator Merilyn Ormes
Languages English
T: +61 2 9581 6000
W: www.trinity.nsw.edu.au

Trinity Lutheran College

PO Box 322, Ashmore City QLD 4214
PYP Coordinator Melissa O'Shea
Languages English
T: +61 7 5556 8200
W: www.tlc.qld.edu.au

Urquhart Park Primary School

49 Inkerman Street, Newington, Ballarat VIC 3350
PYP Coordinator Janet Hillgrove
Languages English, Japanese
T: +61 3 5330 5400
W: urquhartps.vic.edu.au

Waikerie Lutheran Primary School

16 McCutcheon Street, Waikerie SA 5330
PYP Coordinator Michelle Burns
Languages English
T: +61 8 8541 2344
W: www.wlps.sa.edu.au

Wales Street Primary School

Wales Street, Thornbury VIC 3071
PYP Coordinator Luisa Kalenjuk
Languages English
T: +61 (03) 9484 394
W: www.walesstps.vic.edu.au

Walford Anglican School for Girls

316 Unley Road, Hyde Park SA 5061
DP Coordinator Mayra Franco
MYP Coordinator Carly Brooks
PYP Coordinator Annabel Howard
Languages English
T: +61 8 8272 6555
W: www.walford.asn.au

Werribee Secondary College

PO Box 314, Werribee VIC 3030
DP Coordinator Angela Callea
Languages English
T: +61 3 9741 1822
W: www.werribeesc.vic.edu.au

WESLEY COLLEGE MELBOURNE – ELSTERNWICK CAMPUS

5 Gladstone Parade, Elsternwick VIC 3185
Languages English
T: +61 3 8102 6808
W: www.wesleycollege.net

WESLEY COLLEGE MELBOURNE – GLEN WAVERLEY CAMPUS

620 High Street Road, Glen Waverley VIC 3150
Languages English
T: +61 3 8102 6508
W: www.wesleycollege.net

WESLEY COLLEGE MELBOURNE – ST KILDA ROAD CAMPUS

577 St Kilda Road, Melbourne VIC 3004
Languages English
T: +613 8102 6508
E: admissions@wesleycollege.edu.au
W: www.wesleycollege.edu.au
See full details on page 442

WOODCROFT COLLEGE

Bains Road, Morphett Vale SA 5162
DP Coordinator Richard Pope
MYP Coordinator Elyse O'Malley
PYP Coordinator Karen McCulloch
Languages English
T: +61 8 8322 2333
E: reception@woodcroft.sa.edu.au
W: www.woodcroft.sa.edu.au
See full details on page 444

Xavier College, Kostka Hall Campus

47 South Road, Brighton, Melbourne VIC 3186
PYP Coordinator Kate Bird
Languages English
T: +61 3 9519 0600
W: www.xavier.vic.edu.au

BANGLADESH

American International School, Dhaka

PO Box 6106, Gulshan, Dhaka 1212
DP Coordinator Sabahat Jahan
PYP Coordinator Rebecca Carter-Blignaut
Languages English
T: (8802) 984-2452
W: www.aisdhaka.org

American Standard International School

Plot 20B, Road No. 79/82, Gulshan, Dhaka 1212
DP Coordinator Ahmed Anwar Hasan
Languages English

W: www.asisbd.com

Australian International School, Dhaka

Purbachal Express Hwy, Dhaka
DP Coordinator Ponny Chacko
PYP Coordinator Taslima Khatoon
Languages English
T: +88 (0)17 11567236
W: www.ausisdhaka.net

International School Dhaka (ISD)

Plot 80, Block E, Bashundhara R/A, (Opposite Apollo Hospitals Dhaka), Dhaka 1229
DP Coordinator John Drury
MYP Coordinator Nilanthi Das
PYP Coordinator Lynette (Lyn) Weke-Kyalo
Languages English
T: +88 02 8431101
W: www.isdbd.org

Pledge Harbor International School

Singer Dighi, Maona, Dhaka, Gazipur 1741
CP Coordinator Juned Rabbani
DP Coordinator Sujata Chowdhury
MYP Coordinator Juned Rabbani
PYP Coordinator Babita Sidhu
Languages English
T: +880 96144 33444
W: pledgeharbor.org

The Aga Khan School, Dhaka

House 37#, Road# 6, Sector #4, Uttara, Dhaka 1230
DP Coordinator Usha Kasana
PYP Coordinator Latifa Rahman
Languages English
T: +88 02 8914042, +88 02 8950029, +88 02 8920481/82
W: www.agakhanschools.org/bangladesh

BRUNEI DARUSSALAM

INTERNATIONAL SCHOOL BRUNEI

Jalan Utama Salambigar, Kampong Sungai Hanching, Berakas 'B' BC2115
DP Coordinator Mrs. Jane Snell
Languages English
T: +673 233 0608
E: admissionmgr@ac.isb.edu.bn
W: www.isb.edu.bn
See full details on page 350

JERUDONG INTERNATIONAL SCHOOL

Jalan Universiti, Kampong Tungku, Bandar Seri Begawan BE2119
DP Coordinator Dr Colin Dickinson
Languages English
T: +673 241 1000
E: enrol@jis.edu.bn
W: www.jerudonginternationalschool.com
See full details on page 358

CAMBODIA

Australian International School Phnom Penh

76 Angkor Boulevard, Sangkat Toul Sangke, Khan Russey Keo, Phnom Penh
PYP Coordinator Helen Takano
Languages English, Khmer
T: +855 (0)92 111 136
W: www.aispp.edu.kh

HOPE International School – Phnom Penh Campus

PO Box 2521, Phnom Penh 3 12000
DP Coordinator Michael Emery
Languages English
T: +855 12 550 522
W: www.hope.edu.kh

International School of Phnom Penh

PO Box 138, Phnom Penh
DP Coordinator Angelique Hiscox
MYP Coordinator Matthew Clouter
PYP Coordinator Rachel Garthe
Languages English
T: +855 23 213 103
W: www.ispp.edu.kh

Northbridge International School Cambodia

PO Box 2042, Phnom Penh 3
DP Coordinator Christopher Krnic
MYP Coordinator Gillian Presland
PYP Coordinator Bissy (Elizabeth) Groom
Languages English
T: +855 23 900 749
W: www.nisc.edu.kh

CHINA

ALCANTA INTERNATIONAL COLLEGE
14 Guang Sheng Road, Nansha District, Guangzhou City, Guangdong 511458
DP Coordinator Navnita Karmakar
Languages English, Mandarin
T: +86 20 8618 3999/3666
E: bdarwish@aicib.org
W: aicib.org
See full details on page 297

American International School of Guangzhou
No 3 Yan Yu Street South, Er Sha Island, Yuexiu District, Guangzhou 510105
DP Coordinator Anne Martin-Bauer
PYP Coordinator Lydia Van Berkhout
Languages English
T: +86 20 8735 3392/3393
W: www.aisgz.org

Baowei Kindergarten
No.4 Baiyun Road, Xicheng District, Beijing 100045
PYP Coordinator Vivi Fan Ruirui
Languages Chinese, English
T: +86 13716522908
W: www.kidspower.cn

Beanstalk International Bilingual School BIBS – Shunyi Campus
No. 15 Liyuan Jie, TianZhu County, Beijing, Shunyi District 100000
DP Coordinator Emil Jamrich
MYP Coordinator Terrence Linton
PYP Coordinator John Nairn
Languages English
T: +86 (10) 6456 0618
W: www.bibs.com.cn

Beanstalk International Bilingual School BIBS – Upper East Side Campus
No.6 North East 4th Ring Rd, Beijing, Chaoyang District 100016
PYP Coordinator Annie Chew
Languages English
T: +86 (10) 5130 7951
W: www.bibs.com.cn

Beijing BISS International School
No 17, Area 4, An Zhen Xi Li, Chaoyang District, Beijing 100029
DP Coordinator Esther Kim
MYP Coordinator Joshua Brown
PYP Coordinator Glen Pamment
Languages English
T: +86 10 64 433151
W: www.biss.com.cn

Beijing City International School
77 Baiziwan Nan Er Road, Chaoyang District, Beijing 100022
DP Coordinator David Nguyen
MYP Coordinator Tanya Farrol
PYP Coordinator Chantelle Parsons
Languages English
T: +86 10 8771 7171
W: www.bcis.cn

Beijing Haidian International School
No.368-2 Hanhe Road, Haidian District, Beijing 100195
DP Coordinator Finian Brown
Languages English
T: +86 10 8843 8003
W: www.bjhdis.com

Beijing Huijia Kindergarten, Beiou Campus
No.80 Maliandao Road, Xicheng District, Beijing 100085
PYP Coordinator Kelly Min Li
Languages Chinese, English
T: +86 10 63354580
W: www.hjkids.com

Beijing Huijia Kindergarten, Changhewan Campus
No.59 Gaoliangqiao Xiejie Road, Changhewan Community, Haidian District, Beijing 100044
PYP Coordinator Lina Tang
Languages Chinese, English
T: +86 10 82149978
W: www.hjkids.com

Beijing Huijia Kindergarten, Shijixin Campus
No. 3 Landianchang West Road, Haidian District, Beijing 100097
PYP Coordinator Gao Jinling
Languages Chinese, English
T: +86 10 88874145
W: www.hjkids.com

Beijing Huijia Kindergarten, Wanquan Campus
No. 35 Bagou South Road, Wanquan Xinxin Jiayuan Building 14, Haidian District, Beijing 100089
PYP Coordinator Shidan Xu
Languages Chinese
T: +86 (10) 82551751
W: www.hjkids.com

Beijing Huijia Kindergarten, Xibahe Dongli Campus
No.103 Xibahe Dongli, Chaoyang District, Beijing 100028
PYP Coordinator Melissa Peng
Languages Chinese
T: +86 (10) 64655212
W: www.hjkids.com

Beijing Huijia Private School
157 Changhuai Road, Changping District, Beijing 102200
DP Coordinator Yao Chen
MYP Coordinator Jingyu Li
PYP Coordinator Catherine Ma
Languages Chinese, English
T: +86 (10) 608 49399
W: www.huijia.edu.cn

Beijing International Bilingual Academy
Monet Garden, No 5 Yumin Road, Houshayu, Shunyi, Beijing 101300
DP Coordinator Matt Lawson
Languages English
T: +86 10 80410390
W: www.bibachina.org

BEIJING NATIONAL DAY SCHOOL
No. 66 Yuquan Road, Haidan District, Beijing 100039
DP Coordinator Jhony Arias Vivas
Languages English
T: +86 (10) 88625495
E: bettywufq@163.com
W: www.bndsedu.com
See full details on page 301

Beijing No 55 High School
12# Xin Zhong Jie Street, Dong Cheng District, Beijing 100027
DP Coordinator Ying Ying Wu
MYP Coordinator Tian Jieping
Languages English, Chinese
T: +86 10 64162247

Beijing No. 80 High School
WangjingBeiluJia 16, Chaoyang District, Beijing 100102
DP Coordinator Xiaojun Li
Languages English
T: +86 10 5804 7300

Beijing Royal Foreign Language School
No. 11, Wangfu Street, Changping District, Beijing 102209
MYP Coordinator David Mandell
Languages Chinese, English
T: +86 10 81 785 511
W: www.brs.edu.cn

Beijing Royal School
No. 11, Wangfu Street, Changping District, Beijing 102209
DP Coordinator Miao Zhang
Languages English, Chinese
T: +86 10 81 785 511
W: www.brs.edu.cn

Beijing World Youth Academy
18 Hua Jia Di Bei Li, Chao Yang District, Beijing 100102
DP Coordinator Richard Ambler
MYP Coordinator Juan Xia
Languages English
T: +86 10 6470 6336
W: www.ibwya.net

Boston International School
9 Jinghui West Road, New District, Wuxi, Jiangsu 214000
DP Coordinator Matthew Kirk
MYP Coordinator Robert Young
PYP Coordinator David Bremner
Languages English
T: +86 400 032 8000
W: www.bostonis.org

British School of Beijing, Shunyi
South Side, No. 9 An Hua Street, Shunyi District, Beijing 101318
DP Coordinator Sarah Donnelly
Languages English
T: +8610 8047 3558
W: www.bsbshunyi.com

Bubble Kingdom International Kindergarten
No. 431, Linjiang Avenue, Zhujiang New Town, Tianhe District, Guangzhou, Guangdong 510620
PYP Coordinator Bonnie Fung
Languages English, Chinese
T: +86 20 6622 2520
W: www.bkik-kingold.com

Canadian International School Kunshan
1799 Zuchongzhi Road, Kunshan, Jiangsu Province 215347
DP Coordinator Kristie Newton
Languages English
T: +86 400-828-0084
W: www.ciskunshan.org

Canadian International School of Beijing
38 Liangmaqiao Lu, Chaoyang District, Beijing 100125
DP Coordinator Anjali Tyagi
MYP Coordinator Jade Bennett
PYP Coordinator Joey Creelman
Languages English
T: +86 10 64657788
W: www.cisb.com.cn

Canadian International School of Beijing – Jianguomen DRC Campus

No.1 Xiushui Street, Chaoyang District, Beijing 100600
PYP Coordinator Penny Liu
Languages Chinese, English
T: +86 10 85315312
W: www.cisb.com.cn/drc

Canadian International School of Hefei

Fuxing Rd., High-Tech Zone, Hefei 230088
DP Coordinator Jennifer Thompson
MYP Coordinator Sean Miller
PYP Coordinator Kathryn Viljoen
Languages English
T: +86 551 6267 6776
W: www.cish.com.cn

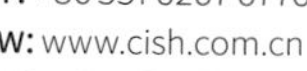

Canadian International School of Shenyang

No.301 Hui Shan Road, Hunnan District, Shenyang, Liaoning 110167
DP Coordinator Anna-Karin Berg
Languages English, Chinese
T: +86 24 66675379
W: www.cisshenyang.com.cn

Changchun American International School

2899 Dong Nan Hu Road, Changchun, Jilin Province 130033
DP Coordinator Santo Kurniawan
MYP Coordinator Flynn Boyle
PYP Coordinator Colin Attwood
Languages English
T: +86 431 8458 1234
W: www.caischina.org

Changjun High School International Department

No. 328 Chazishan Road, Yuelu District, Changsha, Hunan 410023
DP Coordinator Alan Delei Zhou
Languages Chinese, English
T: +86 (0)731 85287942
W: changjunap.xhd.cn

Changping Huijia Kindergarten of Beijing

Building No.25, Zone 1, Yunqu Garden, Huilongguan Cultural Community, Changping District, Beijing 102208
PYP Coordinator Wanni Zhao
Languages Chinese, English
T: +86 10 81715252
W: www.hjkids.com

Changsha Huijia Kindergarten, Jujiangyuan Campus

Jintai Road, Xiangjiangshijicheng Community, Kaifu District, Changsha, Hunan 410000
PYP Coordinator Kiki Xie
Languages English, Chinese
T: +86 (0)731 85798618
W: www.hjkids.com

Changsha Huijia Kindergarten, Yongjiangyuan Campus

Jiangwan Road, Kaifu District, Changsha, Hunan 415000
PYP Coordinator Xiaojuan Jin
Languages Chinese, English
T: +86 731 85185289
W: www.hjkids.com

Changsha WES Academy

8 Dongyi Road, Xingsha, Changsha National Economic & Technical Development Zone, Changsha, Hunan 410100
PYP Coordinator Michelle Naidoo
Languages English
T: +86 731 82758900
W: www.wes-cwa.org

Chengdu Meishi International School

1340 Middle Section of Tianfu Avenue, Chengdu, Sichuan 610042
DP Coordinator Lorry Luo
MYP Coordinator Lisa Lucas
PYP Coordinator Jian Zhang
Languages English, Chinese
T: +86 028 8533 0653
W: www.meishischool.com

Chengdu Shude High School

No.398, Bairihong West Road, Jinjiang District, Chengdu, Sichuan 610000
DP Coordinator Amy Jingyu Li
Languages English
T: +86 28 86119628/98
W: www.sdgj.com

Chenshan School

QiYunXiDaDao, XiuNing District, Huangshan, Anhui 245400
DP Coordinator Amee Loftis
Languages English, Chinese
T: +86 559 7511878
W: www.chenshanschool.com

Citic Lake Bilingual International School

Citic Lake Community, Lishui Town, Nanhai District, Foshan, Guangdong
DP Coordinator Snober Sohail
PYP Coordinator Shailani Borges
Languages English
T: +86 (0)757 81008639
W: www.cbis-gd.com

Country Garden Silver Beach School

Country Garden Silver Beach, Renshan Town, Huidong County, Huizhou, Guangdong Province 516347
DP Coordinator Miaomiao Song
PYP Coordinator Falin Zhang
Languages English, Chinese
T: +86 13929102096
W: sbs.gd.cn

Daystar Academy

No. 2, Shunbai Road, Chaoyang District, Beijing
MYP Coordinator William Tolley
PYP Coordinator Marissa Henkel
Languages English
T: +86 (0)10 64337366
W: daystarchina.cn

Dongguan Hanlin Experimental School

Chuangye Road No.5, Wanjiang District, Dongguan, Guangdong 523000
PYP Coordinator Ashley Yao Shujun
Languages Chinese
T: +86 769 22783301

Dulwich College Beijing

89 Capital Airport Road, Shunyi District, Beijing 101300 101300
DP Coordinator Kieran Burgess
Languages English
T: +86 10 6454 9011
W: beijing.dulwich.org

Dulwich College Shanghai Pudong

266 Lan An Road, Shanghai 201206
DP Coordinator Anthony Gillett
Languages English, Chinese
T: +8621 3896 1200
W: shanghai-pudong.dulwich.org

Dulwich College Suzhou

360 Gang Tian Road, Suzhou Industrial Park, Suzhou 215021
DP Coordinator Peter Roberts
Languages English
T: +86 (512) 6295 9500
W: suzhou.dulwich.org

ECNU Affiliated Bilingual

569 Anchi Road, Jiading District, Shanghai 201805
DP Coordinator Xuefeng Huang
Languages English
T: +86 400 920 6698
W: ecnuas.com

EtonHouse International School Times Residence, Chengdu

180 Zhiquan Section, East Avenue, Times Residence, Chengdu, Sichuan Province 610061
PYP Coordinator Grace Guo
Languages English
T: +86 28 8477 7977
W: chengdu.etonhouse.com.cn/timesresidence

EtonHouse International School, Nanjing

10 South Qing'ao Rd, Jianye District, Nanjing 210019
PYP Coordinator Erin Parnall
Languages English
T: +86 25 8669 6778
W: nanjing.etonhouse.com.cn

EtonHouse International School, Suzhou

102 Kefa Road, Suzhou Science & Technology Town, Suzhou, Jiangsu Province 215163
DP Coordinator Steven Hawkins
MYP Coordinator Murray Fowler
PYP Coordinator Natasha D'Costa
Languages English
T: +86 0512 6825 5666
W: suzhou.etonhouse.com.cn

EtonHouse International School, Wuxi

Regent International Garden, Junction of Taishan Road & Xixing Road, Wuxi New District, Jiangsu Province 214028
PYP Coordinator Juliana Sali
Languages English
T: +86 510 8522 5333
W: wuxi.etonhouse.com.cn

Fudan International School

No 324 Guoquan Road, Yangpu District, Shanghai 200433
DP Coordinator Moqian Zhang
Languages English
T: +86 (0) 21 65640560
W: www.fdis.net.cn

Fuzhou International Preschool @ 1 Park Avenue

1 Park Avenue, Jinju Road 826, Jinshan District, Fuzhou, Fujian 350000
PYP Coordinator Yu Jie Peng
Languages English, Chinese
T: +86 0591 83505222
W: www.srgedu.com/school/1/

Golden Apple International Preschool and Kindergarten
6 Chuangrui Street, Hi-tech District, Chengdu 610041
PYP Coordinator Yu Li
Languages English, Chinese
T: +86 28 8523 7403
W: www.61bb.com/

Golden Apple Tianfu International Preschool and Kindergarten
Shengxing East Rd.,Jiannan Street North, Hi-tech District, Chengdu, Sichuan Province 610041
PYP Coordinator Kun Dong
Languages English
T: +86 28 8517 1648

Guangdong Country Garden School
Beijiao Town, Shunde District, Foshan City, Guangdong Province
DP Coordinator Ms. Myra Wang
MYP Coordinator Zequn Deng
PYP Coordinator Josie Jiuhong Wang
Languages Chinese, English
T: +86 (0)757 2667 7888
W: bgy.gd.cn

GUANGDONG SHUNDE DESHENG SCHOOL
Minxing Road, New District, Daliang, Shunde, Guangdong 528300
DP Coordinator Mr. Yu Yue
Languages English
T: +86 0757 22325121
E: admin.dsi@desheng-school.com
W: www.desheng-school.com

See full details on page 342

Guangzhou Foreign Language School
No. 102, Fenghuang Avenue, Nansha District, Guangzhou, Guangdong 511455
DP Coordinator Gloria Ya Gao
Languages Chinese, English
T: +86 (0)20 22908716
W: chgzfls.com

Guangzhou International Primary School Baiyun ZWIE
998 Tonghe Rd. Baiyun District, Guangzhou City, Guangdong 510515
PYP Coordinator Hannah Palmer
Languages Chinese, English
T: +86 20 37243229
W: www.zwie.net

Guangzhou International Primary School Huangpu ZWIE
No. 188 Huangpu East Rd., Huangpu District, Guangzhou, Guangdong 510700
PYP Coordinator Qin Hu
Languages English, Chinese
T: +86 02082521726

Guangzhou Nanfang International School
No.1 Yu Cui Yuan North, Yinglong Road, Longdong, Tianhe District, Guangzhou
DP Coordinator Shwetangna Chakrabarty
MYP Coordinator Daniel Minton
PYP Coordinator Lucy Elliott
Languages English
T: +8620 87085090
W: www.gnischina.com

Guiyang Huaxi Country Garden International School
Country Garden Community, Mengguan Town, Huaxi District, Guiyang, Guizhou 550026
PYP Coordinator Huitao Yu
Languages English, Chinese
T: +86 (0)851 83651885

HANGZHOU GREENTOWN YUHUA SCHOOL
No. 532 Wenyi West Road, Hangzhou, Zhejiang 310012
MYP Coordinator Liu Xiaohong
Languages Chinese, English
T: +86 571 88477561
E: greentownedu@163.com
W: www.hzlcyhcz.cn

See full details on page 346

Hangzhou International School
78 Dongxin Street, Bin Jiang District, Hangzhou, Zhejiang 310053
DP Coordinator Jessamine Koenig
MYP Coordinator Patricia Long
PYP Coordinator Ben Milburn
Languages English
T: +86 571 8669 0045
W: www.his-china.org

Hangzhou Shanghai World Foreign Language School
167 Li Shui Road, Hangzhou, Zhejiang 310015
PYP Coordinator Frederic (Eric) Thiart
Languages English
T: +86 571 8998 1588

Hangzhou Victoria Kindergarten (Landscape Bay)
Hongyi Road, Xiaoshan District, Hangzhou, Zhejiang
PYP Coordinator Fay Nasrawi
Languages English, Chinese
T: +86 571 83515277
W: victoriachina.com

Hangzhou Wesley School (Gongshu)
269 Gongfa Road, Gongshu District, Hangzhou, Zhejiang 311231
PYP Coordinator Wen Zhang
Languages English, Chinese
T: +86 (0)571 88828880
W: www.wesleyschool.cn

Hefei Run'an Boarding School
292 Fanhua West Road, Economic & Technology Development Zone, Hefei, Anhui 230601
PYP Coordinator Ruilei Wang
Languages Chinese, English
T: +86 551 6982 1861
W: runanid.com

High School Affiliated To Nanjing Normal University
37 Chahaer Road, Jiangsu Province, Nanjing 210003
DP Coordinator Shujiang Zhang
Languages English
T: +86 25 8346 9000
W: www.nsfz.net

HIGH SCHOOL AFFILIATED TO SHANGHAI JIAO TONG UNIVERSITY
No 42 Yin Gao Road, Bao Shan District, Shanghai 200439
DP Coordinator Mr. Charles Pflanz
Languages English, Chinese
T: +86 21 65910979
E: jdfzib@jdfzib.org
W: www.jdfz.cn

See full details on page 345

High School Attached to Northeast Normal University
No 377 Boxue Road, Jingyue District, Changchun, Jilin 130117
DP Coordinator Mashome Ramotubei
Languages Chinese, English
T: +86 431 85608927

Hong Qiao International School
218 South Yi Li Road, Shanghai 201103
PYP Coordinator Anne E. Crylen
Languages English
T: +86 21 62682074
W: www.hqis.org

International School of Beijing-Shunyi
No 10 An Hua Street, Shunyi District, Beijing 101318
DP Coordinator Belinda McRoberts
Languages English
T: +86 10 8149 2345 EXT 1001
W: www.isb.bj.edu.cn

International School of Dongguan
#11 Jin Feng Nan Road, Dongguan, Guangdong Province 523000
DP Coordinator Alissa Gouw
Languages English
T: +86 769 2882 5882
W: www.i-s-d.org

INTERNATIONAL SCHOOL OF NANSHAN SHENZHEN
11 Longyuan Road, Taoyuan Sub-District, Nanshan District, Shenzhen 518052
DP Coordinator TBD
MYP Coordinator Ernie Boyd
PYP Coordinator Blessy Monica & Jennifer Nicklas
Languages English
T: +86 755 2666 1000
E: admissions@isnsz.com
W: www.isnsz.com

See full details on page 353

International School of Tianjin
Weishan Road, Shuanggang, Jinnan District, Tianjin 300350
DP Coordinator Darryl Davies
MYP Coordinator James Taylor
PYP Coordinator Katee Inghram
Languages English
T: +86 22 2859 2001
W: www.istianjin.org

ISA International School of Guangzhou
Block C2-2 Redtory, No.128 Siheng Road, Yuan Village, Tianhe District, Guangzhou 510655
MYP Coordinator Michael Urquhart
PYP Coordinator Rebecca Hawtin
Languages English
T: +86 (0)20 37039193
W: www.isagz.org

Jiaxiang International High School
No. 6, Chenhui North Road, Jinjiang District, Chengdu, Sichuan
DP Coordinator Tracy (Minjie) Wang
Languages English
T: +86 (0)28 69919908
W: www.cdjxihs.com

Jurong Country Garden School
No.2 Oiuzhi Road, Jurong Economic Development Zone, Zhengjiang City, Jiangsu Province 212400
DP Coordinator Xiaojia Gong
MYP Coordinator Huang Fangfang
PYP Coordinator Daisy Xiaomin Xu
Languages English
T: +86 511 8078 0326
W: www.jrbgy.net

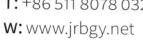

Kang Chiao International School (East China Campus)
No.500, Xihuan Rd., Huaqiao Economic Development Zone, Kunshan City, Jiangsu Province 215332
DP Coordinator Francis Abdurahman
MYP Coordinator Imogen A van der Bijl
Languages English, Chinese
T: +86 512 36869833
W: en.kcisec.com

Keystone Academy
11 Anfu Street, Houshayu, Hou Sha Yu Town, Shunyi District, Beijing 101318
DP Coordinator Rick Spadafora
MYP Coordinator Meredith Phinney
Languages English, Chinese
T: +86 10 8049 6008
W: www.keystoneacademy.cn

Kunming World Youth Academy
Building 2, No.3 High School Dianchixingcheng Campus, Chenggong District, Kunming, Yunnan 650500
DP Coordinator Kyle Gray
Languages English, Chinese
T: +86 871 6745 1511
W: www.kwya.top

LÉMAN INTERNATIONAL SCHOOL CHENGDU
No.1080 Da'an Road, Zheng Xing County, Tianfu New Area, Chengdu, Sichuan 610218
DP Coordinator James Sutcliffe
Languages English
T: +86 28 6703 8650
E: admissions@lis-chengdu.com
W: www.lis-chengdu.com
See full details on page 367

Manila Xiamen International School
No 735 Long Hu Shan Lu, Zeng Cuo An, Si Ming District, Xiamen 361005
DP Coordinator Eve Denise Coronel
Languages English
T: +86 592 2516373/5
W: www.mxis.org

Nanchang International School
1122 Phoenix Centre Road, Hong Gu Tan District, Nanchang, Jiangxi 330038
PYP Coordinator Kristina Potapova
Languages English
T: +86 791 83855352
W: www.wes-ncis.org

Nanjing Foreign Language School
No. 35-4 North Taiping Road, Nanjing City, Jiangsu Province 210018
DP Coordinator Walter Nagles
Languages English
T: +86 25 83282300
W: www.nfls.com.cn

Nanjing International School
No. 8 Xueheng Road, Nanjing 210023
DP Coordinator Ms. Katie Ham
MYP Coordinator Mrs. Ruth Clarke
PYP Coordinator Mr. Adam Dodge
Languages English
T: +86 25 85899111
W: www.nischina.org

New Oriental Stars Kindergarten
Room 506, 5th Floor, Building F, Phoenix Plaza, No. A5, Shuguangxili, Chaoyang District,Beijing 100028
PYP Coordinator Jana Zhou
Languages English
T: +86 4000 66 5030
W: www.babybrightfuture.cn

Ningbo Huamao International School
No 2 Yinxian dadao (Middle), Ningbo, Zhejiang Province 31519
DP Coordinator Shameek Gosh
MYP Coordinator Keola Johnson
PYP Coordinator Geoffrey Smith
Languages English, Chinese
T: +86 574 8821 1160
W: www.nbhis.com

Ningbo Huijia Kindergarten, Tingxiangyuan Campus
Tingxiangyuan of Century City, Hangzhouwan New District, Ningbo, Zhejiang 315336
PYP Coordinator Ying Wu
Languages English, Chinese
T: +86 (0)574 58975889
W: www.hjkids.com

Ningbo Xiaoshi High School
178 Baiyang Street, Ningbo 315012
DP Coordinator Peter Lenihan
Languages English
T: +86 574871 59613

Nord Anglia Chinese International School, Shanghai
1399 Jinhui Road, Minhang, Shanghai 201107
DP Coordinator Rebecca Curtin
Languages Chinese, English
T: +86 (021) 2403 8800
W: www.nordangliaeducation.com/our-schools/nacis/shanghai

NORD ANGLIA INTERNATIONAL SCHOOL SHANGHAI, PUDONG
2888 Junmin Road, Pudong New District, Shanghai 201315
DP Coordinator Bevan Graham
Languages English
T: +86 (0)21 5812 7455
E: admissions@naispudong.com
W: naispudong.com
See full details on page 380

Northeast Yucai School
No.41 Shiji Road, Hunnan New District, Shenyang, Liao Ning Province 110179
DP Coordinator Xun Sun
PYP Coordinator Daybreak Chen Tianliang
Languages Chinese
T: +86 24 23783945
W: www.neyc.cn

ORIENTAL ENGLISH COLLEGE, SHENZHEN
No 10 Xuezi Road, Education Town, Bao'an, Shenzhen, Guangdong 518128
DP Coordinator Kongjing Wang
PYP Coordinator Jinlong Li (Joe)
Languages Chinese, English
T: +86 755 2751 2624
E: principal@oecis.cn
W: www.szoec.com.cn
See full details on page 386

Oujing International Kindergarten
Beicun Road, Yiwu, Zhejiang Province 322000
PYP Coordinator Marli van Jaarsveld
Languages English
T: +86 159 5848 2980
W: www.oujinginternational.com

Overseas Chinese Academy Suzhou
208 Zhong Nan Street, Suzhou Industrial Park, Jiangsu 215021
DP Coordinator Donald Ah Pak
Languages Chinese, English
T: +86 (512) 65001600
W: www.ocasuzhou.net

Peking University Experimental School (Jiaxing)
No.2339, Huayuan Road, Jiaxing City, Zhejiang Province
DP Coordinator Han Li
Languages English, Chinese
T: +86 0573 8280 8280
W: www.pkujx.cn

Phoenix City International School
Xintang Town, Zengcheng City, Guangzhou 511340
MYP Coordinator Stuart Simpson
PYP Coordinator ShaoCheng Tan
Languages Chinese, English
T: +86 20 6228 6902
W: www.pcis.com.cn

Qingdao Academy
No 111 Huazhong Road, Gaoxin District, Qingdao, Shandong 266111
DP Coordinator Andie Tong Wang
Languages English, Chinese
T: +86 532 5875 3788
W: en.qdzx.net

Qingdao Amerasia International School
68 Shandongtou Lu, Qingdao 266061
DP Coordinator Glau Serralvo Kühn
MYP Coordinator Joshua Hatt
PYP Coordinator Kirsten Loza
Languages English
T: +86 532 8388 9900
W: qingdaoamerasia.org

QSI INTERNATIONAL SCHOOL OF CHENGDU
American Garden, 188 South 3rd Ring Road, Chengdu, Sichuan 610041
DP Coordinator Mr. David Becker
Languages English
T: +86 28 8511 3853
E: chengdu@qsi.org
W: chengdu.qsi.org
See full details on page 388

QSI INTERNATIONAL SCHOOL OF SHEKOU
5th Floor, Bitao Building, 8 Taizi Road, Shekou, Shenzhen, Guangdong 518069
DP Coordinator Mr. Zackary Varvel
Languages English
T: +86 755 2667 6031
E: shenzhen@qsi.org
W: shenzhen.qsi.org
See full details on page 389

School of the Nations
Rua de Minho, Taipa, Macau (SAR)
DP Coordinator William Leong
Languages English
T: +853 2870 1759
W: www.schoolofthenations.com

Shanghai American School (Pudong Campus)
Shanghai Links Executive Community, 1600 Lingbai Road, Sanjiagang, Pudong, Shanghai 201201
DP Coordinator Philip Hayes
Languages English
T: +86 21 6221 1445 (EXT:2000)
W: www.saschina.org/admission

Shanghai American School (Puxi Campus)
26 Jinfeng Road, Huacao Town, Minhang District, Shanghai 201107
DP Coordinator Toni Hewett
Languages English
T: +86 21 6221 1445
W: www.saschina.org

SHANGHAI COMMUNITY INTERNATIONAL SCHOOL – HONGQIAO CAMPUS
1161 Hongqiao Road, Shanghai 200051
DP Coordinator Scott Simmons
MYP Coordinator Maree Comerford
PYP Coordinator Janette Haggith
Languages English
T: +86 21 6261 4338
E: admissions@scis-china.org
W: www.scis-china.org
See full details on page 411

Shanghai Community International School – Pudong Campus
800 Xiuyan Road, Kangqiao, Pudong, Shanghai 201315
DP Coordinator Naomi Shanks
MYP Coordinator Frank Volpe
PYP Coordinator Ian Sylvester
Languages English
T: +86 21 5812 9888
W: www.scischina.org

Shanghai Foreign Language School
Zhong Shan Bei Yi Road No. 295, Shanghai 200083
DP Coordinator Jia Zhang
Languages English, Chinese
T: +86 (0)2165 423105
W: www.sfls.cn

SHANGHAI HIGH SCHOOL
400 Shangzhong Road, Xuhui, Shanghai 200231
DP Coordinator Jiang Hao
Languages English
T: +86 21 64765516
E: admission@shsid.org
W: www.shsid.org
See full details on page 412

Shanghai Jin Cai High School
2788 Mid-Yanggao Road, Pudong New Area, Shanghai 200135
DP Coordinator Angela Ying Zhang
MYP Coordinator Angela Ying Zhang
Languages Chinese, English
T: +86 21 6854 1158
W: www.jincai.sh.cn

Shanghai Liaoyuan Bilingual School
No. 150, Pingyang Road, Minhang District, Shanghai 201102
PYP Coordinator Yingying LI
Languages English, Chinese
T: +86 21 34225437
W: www.liaoyuanedu.org

Shanghai Pinghe School
261 Huang Yang Road, Pudong, Shanghai
DP Coordinator Jing Xu
Languages English
T: +86 21 5031 0791
W: www.shphschool.com

Shanghai Qibao Dwight High School
Physical Campus, 3233 Hongxin Road, Shanghai, Minhang District 201101
DP Coordinator Wendy Lin
Languages English
T: +86 21 6461 0367
W: www.qibaodwight.org

Shanghai Shangde Experimental School
No 1688 Xiu Yan Road, Pudong New District, Shanghai 201315
DP Coordinator Haitao Zhang
MYP Coordinator Honglin Xu
PYP Coordinator Hongxi Deng
Languages English
T: +86 21 6818 0001 OR +86 21 6818 0191
W: www.shangdejy.com

Shanghai Shixi High School
404 Yuyuan Rd, Jing'an District, Shanghai 200040
DP Coordinator Lily Hua Su
Languages English
T: +86 21 62521018
W: www.shixi.edu.sh.cn

Shanghai Singapore International School
301 Zhujian Road, Minhang District, Shanghai 201106
CP Coordinator Adam Crossley
DP Coordinator Adam Crossley
Languages English
T: +86 21 62219288
W: www.ssis.asia

SHANGHAI UNITED INTERNATIONAL SCHOOL, HONGQIAO-GUBEI CAMPUS
248 Hong Song Road (E), Gubei, Minhang District, Shanghai 201103
DP Coordinator Derek Lee
PYP Coordinator Apple Zhang
Languages English
T: +8621 51753030
E: annie.yan@suis.com.cn
W: www.suis.com.cn
See full details on page 414

Shanghai United International School, Wuxi
No. 8, Wenjing Road, Xishan District, Xidong New Town, Wuxi, Jiangsu Province 214104
DP Coordinator Rajashree Basu
Languages English
T: +86 510 8853 7700
W: wuxi.suis.com.cn

Shanghai Victoria Kindergarten (Gumei)
No. 300 Gu Mei Road, Xuhui, Shanghai
PYP Coordinator Simon Francis Marginson
Languages English
T: +86 (021) 6401 1084
W: gm.victoria.sh.cn

Shanghai Victoria Kindergarten (Pudong)
No. 38, Lane 39, Yin Xiao Road, Pudong, Shanghai
PYP Coordinator Selina Fang
Languages English
T: +86 (021) 5045 9084
W: pd.victoria.sh.cn

Shanghai Victoria Kindergarten (Xinzhuang)
No. 15, Lane 155, Bao Cheng Road, Xinzhuang, Shanghai
PYP Coordinator Emily Anne Cotey
Languages Chinese, English
T: +86 (021) 5415 2228
W: xz.victoria.sh.cn

Shanghai Victoria Kindergarten (Xuhui)
No. 1, Lane 71, Huating Road, Xuhui, Shanghai
PYP Coordinator Joel Rafferty
Languages Chinese, English
T: +86 (021) 5403 6901
W: xh.victoria.sh.cn

Shanghai Weiyu High School
No 1 Weiyu Road, Xuhui District, Shanghai 200231
DP Coordinator Gang Zhou
Languages English
T: +86 21 64966996 #8008
W: www.weiyu.sh.cn

Shanghai World Foreign Language Middle School
380 Pu Bei Road, Xu Hui District, Shanghai 200233
DP Coordinator Jiachun Chen
MYP Coordinator Ye Wang
Languages Chinese, English
T: +8621 6436 3556
W: www.wflms.cn

Shanghai World Foreign Language Primary School
No 380 Pubei Road, Xu Hui District, Shanghai 200233
PYP Coordinator Halina Werchiwski
Languages English, Chinese
T: +86 21 5419 2245
W: www.wflps.com

SHEKOU INTERNATIONAL SCHOOL
Jingshan Villas, Nanhai Boulevard, Shekou, Nanshan, Shenzhen
DP Coordinator Craig Ortner
Languages English
T: +86 755 2669 3669
E: admissions@sis.org.cn
W: www.sis-shekou.org
See full details on page 415

Shen Wai International School
29 Baishi 3rd Road, Nanshan District, Shenzhen 518053
DP Coordinator Ravi Mathapati
MYP Coordinator Ms. Amanda Shepherd
PYP Coordinator Ms. Natalie Campbell; Ms. Rene Ren
Languages English
T: +86 755 8654 1200
W: www.swis.cn

Shenzhen Senior High School
Chuntian Road, Futian District, Shenzhen, Guangdong 518040
DP Coordinator Daniel Sibo Ouyang
Languages English, Chinese
T: +86 755 8394 8654
W: www.cn-school.com

Shenzhen Shiyan Public School
No. 8 Yucai Rd, Shiyan Street, Baoan District, Shenzhen, Guangdong Province 518108
DP Coordinator Fangfang Kong
Languages English, Chinese
T: +86 0755 27766766
W: sygx.baoan.edu.cn

SNU-K International Department
Yidu Road Longchengyihao, Chengdu, Sichuan 610101
PYP Coordinator Joshua Groenewald
Languages Chinese, English
T: +86 18428393839

Suzhou Industrial Park Foreign Language School
No.89, Suzhou Industrial Park, Suzhou, Jiangsu Province 215021
DP Coordinator Joel Seow
Languages English
T: +86 512 62897710
W: www.sipfls.com

SUZHOU SINGAPORE INTERNATIONAL SCHOOL
208 Zhong Nan Street, Suzhou Industrial Park, Jiangsu 215021
DP Coordinator Laurence Mueller
MYP Coordinator Jesse Donnelly
PYP Coordinator Katriona Hoskins
Languages English
T: +86 512 6258 0388
E: information@mail.ssis-suzhou.net
W: www.suzhousinternationalschool.com
See full details on page 424

Suzhou Victoria Kindergarten
Bayside Garden, Phase 3, No.1 Linglong Street, Suzhou, Jiangsu Province 215027
PYP Coordinator Holly Radovanic
Languages Chinese, English
T: +86 512 8081 1610
W: www.victoriasuzhou.com

Taicang Walton Foreign Language School
No. 200 Middle Suzhou Road, Taicang, Jiangsu 215400
DP Coordinator Wendy Yi Fang Shui
Languages English, Chinese
T: +86 (0)512 33062226

The British International School Shanghai, Puxi
111 Jinguang Road, Huacao Town, Minhang District, Puxi, Shanghai 201107
DP Coordinator Thomas Housham
Languages English
T: +86 (0)21 62217542
W: www.bisspuxi.com

The Garden International School
Agile Cambridgeshire, Panyu District, Guangzhou, Guangdong 511400
PYP Coordinator Naida Kardas
Languages English
T: +86 (0)20 3482 3833
W: www.tgisgz.com

The High School Affiliated to Renmin University of China
No. 37 Zhongguancun Street, Haidian District, Beijing 100080
DP Coordinator Randall Crismond
Languages English
T: +86 10 62513962
W: www.rdfz.cn/en

The International School of Macao
Macau University of Science and Technology (Block K), Avenida Wai Long, Taipa, Macau
DP Coordinator Jody Hubert
Languages English
T: +853 2853 3700
W: www.tis.edu.mo

The International School of Rhodes
100 Xiangcheng Ave, Xiangcheng District, Suzhou, Jiangsu
DP Coordinator Cheng Rui Eric Liu
Languages English
T: +86 (0)512 65490211
W: tisr.chinabest.org

The Kindergarten of Hefei Run'an Boarding School
No. 268 Cui Wei Road, Economic and Technogical Development Zone, Hefei, Anhui 230601
PYP Coordinator Su Yang
Languages English
T: +86 (0)551 63821888
W: www.hfrayey.com

The MacDuffie School
No. 799, North Hui Feng Road, Fengxian Area, Shanghai 201403
DP Coordinator Hui Sun
Languages English
T: +86 21 400 600 2260
W: mingyuanschool.com

Tianjin Experimental High School
No 1 Pingshan Road, Hexi District, Tianjin 300074
DP Coordinator Lu Gan
MYP Coordinator Simon Zhang
Languages English, Chinese
T: +86 22 2335 4658
W: www.tjsyzx.cn

ULink College of Shanghai
No.559,Laiting South Road, Jiuting, Songjiang District, Shanghai 201615
DP Coordinator Miranda Lin
Languages English
T: +86 (0)21 67663819
W: en.ulink.cn/shanghai

Utahloy International School Guangzhou (UISG)
800 Sha Tai Bei Road, Bai Yun District, Guangzhou, Guangdong 510515
DP Coordinator Paul Johnson
MYP Coordinator Mauricio Joven Bonelo
PYP Coordinator Noah Beaumont
Languages English
T: +8620 8720 2019
W: www.utahloy.com

Utahloy International School Zengcheng (UISZ)
San Jiang Town, Zeng Cheng City, Guangdong 511325
DP Coordinator Martina Dirkje Catharina de Glopper
MYP Coordinator Gregory Peebles
PYP Coordinator Robin France
Languages English
T: +86 20 8291 3201
W: www.utahloy.com

UWC CHANGSHU CHINA
No. 88 Kunchenghuxi Road, Changshu, Jiangsu 215500
DP Coordinator Arunananda Mukherjee
Languages English
T: +86 512 5298 2602
E: info.admissions@uwcchina.org
W: www.uwcchina.org
See full details on page 435

Victoria Kindergarten Shenzhen (Arcadia Court)
No.1008, Haitian Road, Futian Central District, Shenzhen
PYP Coordinator Vicky Zou
Languages English
T: +86 755 83028229
W: www.victoria-sz.com

Victoria Kindergarten Shenzhen (Futian)
No. 19, Xinzhou Er Jie, Fuqiang Road, Futian Central District, Shenzhen
PYP Coordinator Jane Liu
Languages Chinese, English
T: +86 755 82961010
W: www.victoria-sz.com

Victoria Kindergarten Shenzhen (Le Parc)
No. 3011, Fuzhong 1st Rd., Futian Central District, Shenzhen
PYP Coordinator Millie Chen
Languages Chinese, English
T: +86 755 83282004
W: www.victoria-sz.com

Wellington College International Shanghai
No.1500 Yao Long Road, Pudong, Shanghai 200124
DP Coordinator Ewan McCallum
Languages English
T: +86 21 5185 3866
W: www.wellingtoncollege.cn/shanghai

Western Academy Of Beijing
PO Box 8547, 10 Lai Guang Ying Dong Lu, Chao Yang District, Beijing 100102
DP Coordinator Scott Lindner
MYP Coordinator Stephen Taylor
PYP Coordinator Jonathan Mueller
Languages English
T: +86 10 5986 5588
W: www.wab.edu

WESTERN INTERNATIONAL SCHOOL OF SHANGHAI (WISS)
555 Lianmin Road, Xujing Town, Qingpu, Shanghai 201702
CP Coordinator Stewart Paterson
DP Coordinator Edwige Singleton
MYP Coordinator Greg Cowan
PYP Coordinator Judith Canning & Karin Tellis
Languages English
T: +86 21 6976 6388
E: admissions@wiss.cn
W: www.wiss.cn
See full details on page 441

WHBC of Wuhan Foreign Languages School
7th Floor Administration Building, 48 Wan Song Yuan Road, Wuhan, Hubei Province 430022
DP Coordinator Daniel Hwang
Languages English
T: +86 027 8555 7389
W: www.whbc2000.com/english

Wuxi No 1 High School
98, Yun He Donglu, Wuxi, Jiangsu 214031
DP Coordinator Jeewaka Chaminda Marasinghe Pedige
Languages English, Chinese
T: +86 51082809787
W: www.wxyzedu.net

Xiamen International School
262 Xing Bei San Lu, Xinglin, Jimei District, Xiamen 361022
DP Coordinator Nick Potts
MYP Coordinator Tamara Studniski
PYP Coordinator Mary Collins
Languages English
T: +86 592 625 6581
W: www.xischina.com

Xi'an Hanova International School
188 Yudou Road, Yanta District, Xian, Shaanxi Province 710077
DP Coordinator Sharon Zhangyu Zhu
MYP Coordinator Sandy Trull
PYP Coordinator Trish Scott
Languages English
T: +86 29 88693780
W: www.his-xian.com

Xi'an Hi-Tech International School
1st Yishu Str., Hi-Tech Development Zone, Xi'an Shaanxi 710119
DP Coordinator Jaimala Quinlan
MYP Coordinator Arif Minhal
PYP Coordinator Maria Theresa Zialcita
Languages English
T: +86 29 8569 0529
W: www.xhisid.com

Yew Chung International School of Beijing
Honglingjin Park, 5 Houbalizhuang, Chaoyang District, Beijing 100025
DP Coordinator Prachi Gupta
Languages English
T: +86 10 8583 1836
W: www.ycis-bj.com

Yew Chung International School of Chongqing
No 2 Huxia Street, Yuan Yang Town, New Northern Zone, Chongqing 401122
DP Coordinator Will Vincent
Languages English, Chinese
T: +86 23 8879 1600
W: www.ycef.com

YEW CHUNG INTERNATIONAL SCHOOL OF QINGDAO
72 Tai Hang Shan Lu, Qingdao West Coast New Area, Huangdao, Shandong 266555
DP Coordinator Ms. Varsha Kumar
Languages English
T: +86 532 8699 5551
E: enquiry@qd.ycef.com
W: www.ycis-qd.com
See full details on page 445

Yew Chung International School of Shanghai – Century Park Campus
1433 Dong Xui Road, Pudong, Shanghai 200127
DP Coordinator Matthew Grady
Languages English
T: +86 21 2226 7666
W: www.ycis-sh.com

YEW CHUNG INTERNATIONAL SCHOOL OF SHANGHAI – HONGQIAO CAMPUS
11 Shui Cheng Road, Puxi, Shanghai 200336
DP Coordinator Mr Jonathan Evans (Puxi); Mr Matt Grady (Pudong)
Languages English, Chinese (mandarin)
T: +86 21 2226 7666
E: enquiry@sh.ycef.com
W: www.ycis-sh.com
See full details on page 446

YK Pao School
1800, Lane 900, North Sanxin Road, Songjiang District, Shanghai 201602
DP Coordinator Helen Lambie-Jones
Languages English
T: +86 21 61671999
W: www.ykpaoschool.cn

Zhangjiagang Foreign Language School
256 Ji Yang Dong Lu, Zhangjiagang City 215600
DP Coordinator Donna Pearl
Languages English
T: +86 512 5828 5972
W: www.zjgfls.com

Zhengzhou Middle School
2# Yinghua Street, Hi – Tech Development Zone, Zhengzhou, Henan 450001
MYP Coordinator Zhu Yulai
Languages Chinese
T: +86 371 67996825
W: www.zzms.com

Zhuhai International School
Qi ' Ao Island, Tang Jia Wan, Zhuhai, Guangdong 519080
DP Coordinator Michael Coffey
MYP Coordinator Hema Rai
PYP Coordinator Sharon Rose
Languages English, Chinese
T: +86 756 331 5580
W: www.zischina.com

EAST TIMOR

Dili International School
14 Rue Avenue de Portugal, Pantai Kelapa, Dili
MYP Coordinator Cheryl Stephens
PYP Coordinator Jordan Harries
Languages English
T: +670 77316065
W: www.distimor.org

FIJI

International School Nadi
Box 9686 Nadi Airport, Nadi
DP Coordinator Bethan Paterson
MYP Coordinator Shabha Begum
PYP Coordinator Kati Stice
Languages English
T: +679 6702 060
W: www.isn.school.fj

International School Suva
Lot 59, Siga Road, Laucala Beach Estate, Suva
DP Coordinator Yiyuan Chen
PYP Coordinator Rosi Uluiviti
Languages English
T: +679 339 3300
W: www.international.school.fj

GUAM

St John's School
911 Marine Drive, Tumon Bay 96913
DP Coordinator Ellen Petra
Languages English
T: +1 (671) 646 8080
W: www.stjohnsguam.com

HONG KONG, CHINA

Australian International School Hong Kong
3A Norfolk Road, Kowloon Tong, Hong Kong, SAR
DP Coordinator Chris McCorkell
Languages English
T: +852 2304 6078
W: www.aishk.edu.hk

Canadian International School of Hong Kong
36 Nam Long Shan Road, Aberdeen, Hong Kong, SAR
DP Coordinator Brian Hull
MYP Coordinator Julie Cook
PYP Coordinator Vivienne Wallace
Languages English
T: +852 2525 7088
W: www.cdnis.edu.hk

Carmel School
460 Shau Kei Wan Road, Shau Kei Wan, Hong Kong, SAR
DP Coordinator Nick Webber
MYP Coordinator Dan Bartholomew
PYP Coordinator Jeffrey-Dean Cain
Languages English
T: +852 3665 5388
W: www.carmel.edu.hk

Causeway Bay Victoria International Kindergarten
32 Hing Fat Street, Causeway Bay, Hong Kong, SAR
PYP Coordinator Shuk Ching Candy Au
Languages English, Chinese
T: +852 2578 9998
W: www.cbvictoria.edu.hk

Chinese International School
1 Hau Yuen Path, Braemar Hill, Hong Kong, SAR
DP Coordinator Janelle Codrington
MYP Coordinator Francis Murphy
Languages English, Mandarin
T: +852 2 510 7288
W: www.cis.edu.hk

Creative Primary School
2A Oxford Street, Kowloon Tong, Kowloon, Hong Kong, SAR
PYP Coordinator Bonnie Cheng Mei Wah
Languages Chinese, Englisg
T: +852 2336 0266
W: www.creativeprisch.edu.hk

Creative Secondary School
3 Pung Loi Road, Tseung Kwan O, Sai Kung, NT, Hong Kong, SAR
DP Coordinator Maria Cristina Guevara
MYP Coordinator Janice Lee
Languages English, Chinese
T: +852 2336 0233
W: www.css.edu.hk

DELIA MEMORIAL SCHOOL (GLEE PATH)
1-3 Glee Path, Mei Foo Sun Chuen, Kowloon, Hong Kong, SAR
DP Coordinator Mr. Paolo Yap
Languages Cantonese, English, Mandarin
T: +852 2741 5239
E: gp@deliagroup.edu.hk
W: www.deliagp.edu.hk
See full details on page 307

Diocesan Boys' School
131 Argyle Street, Mong Kok, Kowloon, Hong Kong, SAR
DP Coordinator Charles Kar Lun Wu
Languages English
T: +852 2711 5911
W: www.dbs.edu.hk

ELCHK LUTHERAN ACADEMY
25 Lam Hau Tsuen Road, Yuen Long, New Territories, Hong Kong
DP Coordinator John Law
PYP Coordinator Neil Johnstone
Languages English, Cantonese, Mandarin
T: +852 8208 2092
E: info@luac.edu.hk
W: www.luac.edu.hk
See full details on page 311

ESF ABACUS INTERNATIONAL KINDERGARTEN
Mang Kung Uk Village, Clearwater Bay Road, Hong Kong SAR
PYP Coordinator Ms Frances Hurley
Languages English, Mandarin
T: +852 27195712
E: kinder@abacus.edu.hk
W: www.abacus.edu.hk
See full details on page 312

ESF BEACON HILL SCHOOL
23 Ede Road, Kowloon Tong, Hong Kong SAR
PYP Coordinator Mr Andy Thompson
Languages English
T: +852 2336 5221
E: bhs@bhs.edu.hk
W: www.beaconhill.edu.hk
See full details on page 313

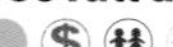

ESF BRADBURY SCHOOL
43C Stubbs Road, Hong Kong SAR
PYP Coordinator Ms Amanda Bremner
Languages English
T: +852 2574 8249
E: enquiries@bradbury.edu.hk
W: www.bradbury.edu.hk
See full details on page 314

ESF CLEARWATER BAY SCHOOL
DD229, Lot 235, Clearwater Bay Road, New Territories, Hong Kong SAR
PYP Coordinator Ms Wendy Egan
Languages English
T: +852 2358 3221
E: info@cwbs.edu.hk
W: www.cwbs.edu.hk
See full details on page 315

ESF DISCOVERY COLLEGE
38 Siena Avenue, Discovery Bay, Lantau Island, Hong Kong SAR
CP Coordinator Ms Emma Neuprez
DP Coordinator Mr Brian McCann
MYP Coordinator Ms Annette Garnett
PYP Coordinator Ms Kate Agars
Languages English
T: +852 3969 1000
E: office@dc.edu.hk
W: www.discovery.edu.hk
See full details on page 316

ESF GLENEALY SCHOOL
7 Hornsey Road, Mid Levels, Hong Kong SAR
PYP Coordinator Mr David Buckley
Languages English
T: +852 2522 1919
E: enquiry@glenealy.edu.hk
W: www.glenealy.edu.hk
See full details on page 317

ESF HILLSIDE INTERNATIONAL KINDERGARTEN
43B Stubbs Road, Hong Kong SAR
PYP Coordinator Ms Brenda Yuen
Languages English
T: +852 2540 0066
E: kinder@hillside.edu.hk
W: www.hillside.edu.hk
See full details on page 318

ESF ISLAND SCHOOL
20 Borrett Road, Hong Kong SAR
CP Coordinator Mr Roger Wilkinson
DP Coordinator Mr Matt Rappel
Languages English
T: +852 2524 7135
E: school@online.island.edu.hk
W: www.island.edu.hk
See full details on page 319

ESF KENNEDY SCHOOL
19 Sha Wan Drive, Pokfulam, Hong Kong SAR
PYP Coordinator Ms Yoon-Ah Lee
Languages English
T: +852 2855 0711
E: admissions@kennedy.edu.hk
W: www.kennedy.edu.hk
See full details on page 320

ESF KING GEORGE V SCHOOL
2 Tin Kwong Road, Homantin, Kowloon, Hong Kong SAR
DP Coordinator Mr Chris Wightman
MYP Coordinator Mr Duncan Shiel
Languages English
T: +852 2711 3029
E: office@kgv.edu.hk
W: www.kgv.edu.hk
See full details on page 321

ESF KOWLOON JUNIOR SCHOOL
20 Perth Street, Homantin, Kowloon, Hong Kong SAR
PYP Coordinator Ms Dawn Doucette
Languages English
T: +852 3765 8700
E: office@kjs.edu.hk
W: www.kjs.edu.hk
See full details on page 322

ESF PEAK SCHOOL
20 Plunkett's Road, The Peak, Hong Kong SAR
PYP Coordinator Ms Chrissy Etchells-Bailey
Languages English
T: +852 2849 7211
E: office@ps.edu.hk
W: www.ps.edu.hk
See full details on page 323

ESF QUARRY BAY SCHOOL
6 Hau Yuen Path, Braemar Hill, North Point, Hong Kong SAR
PYP Coordinator Miss Ceri Hill
Languages English
T: +852 2566 4242
E: office@qbs.edu.hk
W: www.qbs.edu.hk
See full details on page 324

ESF RENAISSANCE COLLEGE
5 Hang Ming Street, Ma On Shan, New Territories, Hong Kong SAR
CP Coordinator Ms Wilma Shen
DP Coordinator Ms Jess Davey-Peel
MYP Coordinator Ms Brandy Stern
PYP Coordinator Mr Jason Doucette
Languages English
T: +852 3556 3556
E: info@rchk.edu.hk
W: www.rchk.edu.hk
See full details on page 325

ESF SHA TIN COLLEGE
3 Lai Wo Lane, Fo Tan, Sha Tin, New Territories, Hong Kong SAR
CP Coordinator Mr Luke Smetherham
DP Coordinator Ms Kellie Fagan
Languages English
T: +852 2699 1811
E: info@shatincollege.edu.hk
W: www.shatincollege.edu.hk
See full details on page 326

ESF SHA TIN JUNIOR SCHOOL
3A Lai Wo Lane, Fo Tan, Sha Tin, New Territories, Hong Kong SAR
PYP Coordinator Ms Trudy Mcmillin
Languages English
T: +852 2692 2721
E: info@sjs.esf.edu.hk
W: www.sjs.edu.hk
See full details on page 327

ESF SOUTH ISLAND SCHOOL
50 Nam Fung Road, Hong Kong SAR
CP Coordinator Mr Gwillym Cornes
DP Coordinator Ms Kelly Diaz
MYP Coordinator Mr Shaine Bushell
Languages English
T: +852 2555 9313
E: sis@sis.edu.hk
W: www.sis.edu.hk
See full details on page 328

ESF TSING YI INTERNATIONAL KINDERGARTEN
Maritime Square, 33 Tsing King Road, Tsing Yi, New Territories, Hong Kong SAR
PYP Coordinator Ms Suzannah Large
Languages English
T: +852 2436 3355
E: kinder@tyk.edu.hk
W: www.tyk.edu.hk
See full details on page 329

ESF TUNG CHUNG INTERNATIONAL KINDERGARTEN
1/F, Commercial Accommodation, The Visionary, 1 Ying Hong Street, Tung Chung, Lantau, New Territories, Hong Kong SAR
PYP Coordinator Ms Cathy Boon
Languages English
T: +852 3742 3500
E: kinder@tc.esf.org.hk
W: www.tck.edu.hk
See full details on page 330

ESF WEST ISLAND SCHOOL
250 Victoria Road, Pokfulam, Hong Kong SAR
CP Coordinator Ms Emily Clarke
DP Coordinator Mrs Helen Devine Costa
Languages English
T: +852 2819 1962
E: wis@wis.edu.hk
W: www.wis.edu.hk
See full details on page 331

ESF WU KAI SHA INTERNATIONAL KINDERGARTEN
599 Sai Sha Road, Ma On Shan, Sha Tin, Hong Kong SAR
PYP Coordinator Ms Helen Thomson
Languages English
T: +852 2435 5291
E: kinder@wksk.edu.hk
W: www.wksk.edu.hk
See full details on page 332

French International School
165 Blue Pool Road, Happy Valley, Hong Kong, SAR
DP Coordinator Pauline Hall
Languages English
T: +852 25776217
W: www.fis.edu.hk

G. T. (Ellen Yeung) College
10, Ling Kong Street, Tiu Keng Leng, Tseung Kwan O, Hong Kong, SAR
DP Coordinator Vincent Tam
Languages English, Chinese
T: +852 2535 6867
W: www.gtcollege.edu.hk

Galilee International School
G/F & 1/F, Peace Garden, 2 Peace Avenue, Ho Man Tin, Kowloon, Hong Kong
PYP Coordinator Brenda Wong
Languages English
T: +852 2390 3000
W: gis.edu.hk

German Swiss International School
11 Guildford Road, The Peak, Hong Kong, SAR
DP Coordinator Zara Clayton
Languages English
T: +852 2849 6216
W: www.gsis.edu.hk

Hamilton Hill International Kindergarten
2/F Tang Kung Mansion, 31 Tai Koo Shing Road, Tai Koo, Hong Kong SAR
PYP Coordinator Alex Key
Languages English, Chinese
T: +852 2567 5454
W: www.hhik.edu.hk

Hong Kong, China

Han Academy
G/F – 2/F, 33-35 Wong Chuk Hang Road, Aberdeen, Hong Kong, SAR
DP Coordinator Vahagn Vardanyan
Languages English, Chinese
T: +852 3998 6300
W: www.hanacademy.edu.hk

Hong Kong Academy
33 Wai Man Road, Sai Kung, Hong Kong, SAR
DP Coordinator Jennifer Swinehart
MYP Coordinator Kristen Feren
PYP Coordinator Dean Johnson
Languages English
T: +852 2655 1111
W: www.hkacademy.edu.hk

International College Hong Kong
60 Sha Tau Kok Road, Shek Chung Au, Sha Tau Kok, New Territories, Hong Kong, SAR
DP Coordinator Flora Lai
Languages English
T: +852 2655 9018
W: www.ichk.edu.hk

International College Hong Kong – Hong Lok Yuen
20th Street, Hong Lok Yuen, Tai Po, New Territories, Hong Kong, SAR
PYP Coordinator Ho Mei Chau
Languages English
T: +852 26586935
W: www.ichk.edu.hk

Japanese International School
4663 Tai Po Road, Tai Po, New Territories, Hong Kong, SAR
PYP Coordinator Catherine Wan
Languages English
T: +852 2834 3531
W: www.jis.edu.hk

Kiangsu-Chekiang College, International Section
20 Braemar Hill Road, North Point, Hong Kong, SAR
DP Coordinator Calvin Tse
Languages English
T: +852 2570 1281
W: www.kcis.edu.hk

Kingston International Kindergarten
12-14 Cumberland Road, Kowloon Tong, Hong Kong, SAR
PYP Coordinator Michelle Chu
Languages English
T: +852 2337 9049
W: www.kingston.edu.hk

Kingston International School
113 Waterloo Road, Kowloon Tong, Hong Kong, SAR
PYP Coordinator Ms. Kellie Berry
Languages English, Putonghua
T: +852 2337 9031
W: www.kingston.edu.hk

Kornhill Victoria International Kindergarten
2/F., 18 Hong On Street, Kornhill, Hong Kong, SAR
PYP Coordinator Vincci Wong
Languages Chinese, English
T: +852 2885 1888
W: www.victoria.edu.hk

Logos Academy
1 Kan Hok Lane, Tseung Kwan, Hong Kong, SAR
DP Coordinator Patricia Yeung
Languages English
T: +852-23372123
W: www.logosacademy.edu.hk

NORD ANGLIA INTERNATIONAL SCHOOL, HONG KONG
11 On Tin Street, Lam Tin, Kowloon
DP Coordinator Karen Simpson
Languages English
T: +852 3958 1428
E: admissions@nais.hk
W: www.nais.hk
See full details on page 381

Parkview International Pre-school
Tower 18 Parkview, 88 Tai Tam Reservoir Road, Hong Kong, SAR
PYP Coordinator Laura Venezia
Languages English
T: +852 2812 6023
W: www.pips.edu.hk

Parkview International Pre-School (Kowloon)
Podium Level, Kowloon Station, 1 Austin Road West, Kowloon
PYP Coordinator Jonathan Cubitt
Languages English
T: +852 2812 6801
W: www.pips.edu.hk

Po Leung Kuk Choi Kai Yau School
6 Caldecott Road, Piper's Hill, Kowloon
DP Coordinator James Kuan
Languages English
T: +852 2148 2052
W: www.cky.edu.hk

Po Leung Kuk Ngan Po Ling College
26 Sung On Street, Tokwawan, Kowloon
DP Coordinator Mukunthan Anuradha
Languages English
T: +852 2462 3932
W: www.npl.edu.hk

Singapore International School (Hong Kong) – Secondary Section
2 Police School Road, Wong Chuk Hang, Hong Kong, SAR
DP Coordinator Alvin Soon
Languages English, Putonghua
T: +852 2919 6966
W: www.singapore.edu.hk

St. Paul's Co-educational College
33 MacDonnell Road, Central, Hong Kong, SAR
DP Coordinator Christopher Koay
Languages English
T: +852 2523 1187
W: www.spcc.edu.hk

St. Stephen's College
22 Tung Tau Wan Road, Stanley, Hong Kong
DP Coordinator Derek Barham
Languages English
T: +852 2813 0360
W: www.ssc.edu.hk

The Independent Schools Foundation Academy
1 Kong Sin Wan Road, Pokfulam, Hong Kong, SAR
DP Coordinator Kevin Hoye
MYP Coordinator Alan Johns
Languages English, Chinese
T: +852 2202 2000
W: www.isf.edu.hk

Think International School
117 Boundary Street, Kowloon Tong, Hong Kong, SAR
PYP Coordinator Niral Patel
Languages English
T: +852 2338 3949
W: www.think.edu.hk

UWC Li Po Chun
10 Lok Wo Sha Lane, Sai Sha Road, Ma On Shan, Sha Tin, Hong Kong, SAR
DP Coordinator Beta Chau
Languages English
T: +852 2640 0441
W: www.lpcuwc.edu.hk

Victoria (Belcher) International Kindergarten
Portion of Level 3 (Kindergarten Area), The Westwood, 8 Belchers Street, Hong Kong, SAR
PYP Coordinator Sharon Lui
Languages English, Chinese
T: +852 2542 7001
W: www.victoria.edu.hk

Victoria (Harbour Green) International Kindergarten
8 Sham Mong Road, G/F., Harbour Green, Kowloon, Hong Kong SAR
PYP Coordinator Kit Cheng
Languages English
T: +852 2885 1928
W: www.victoria.edu.hk

Victoria (Homantin) International Nursery
1/F., Carmel-on-the-Hill, 9 Carmel Village Street, Homantin, Kowloon, Hong Kong, SAR
PYP Coordinator Cheng Kar Wai Flora
Languages English
T: +852 2762 9130
W: www.victoria.edu.hk

Victoria (South Horizons) International Kindergarten
Podium Level 2, Phase 2, South Horizons, Ap Lei Chau, Hong Kong, SAR
PYP Coordinator Sau Kei Wendy Lam
Languages Cantonese, English, Mandarin
T: +852 2580 8633
W: www.victoria.edu.hk

Victoria Kindergarten
G/F., 2-8 Hong On Street, Kornhill, Hong Kong, SAR
PYP Coordinator Kathy SIU
Languages English
T: +852 2885 3331
W: www.victoria.edu.hk

Victoria Nursery
Ko Fung Court, Harbour Heights, 5 Fook Yum Road, North Point, Hong Kong, SAR
PYP Coordinator Claudia Wong Tsz Kwan
Languages Cantonese, English, Mandarin
T: +852 2571 7888
W: www.victoria.edu.hk

Victoria Shanghai Academy (VSA)
19 Shum Wan Road, Aberdeen, Hong Kong, SAR
DP Coordinator Doug Kane
MYP Coordinator Richard Greaves
PYP Coordinator Patricia Whatarau
Languages English, Putonghua
T: +852 3402 1000
W: www.vsa.edu.hk

Yew Chung International School of Hong Kong – Secondary Section
3 To Fuk Road, Kowloon, Hong Kong, SAR
DP Coordinator Alan Ramm
Languages English
T: +852 2338 7106
W: www.ycis-hk.com

INDIA

Aditya Birla World Academy
Vastushilp Annexe, Gamadia Colony, J D Road, Tardeo, Mumbai 400034
DP Coordinator Shalini John
Languages English
T: +91 22 2352 8400
W: www.adityabirlaworldacademy.com

Aga Khan Academy Hyderabad
Survey No 1/1 Hardware Park, Maheshwaram Mandal, Rangareddy District, Hyderabad, Telangana 501510
DP Coordinator Sudipta Roy
MYP Coordinator Meenakshi Joshi
PYP Coordinator Chloe Hill
Languages English
T: +91 40 66291313
W: www.agakhanacademies.org/hyderabad

Ahmedabad International School
Opp Rajpath Row Houses, Behind Kiran Motors, Judges Bungalow Road, Bodakdev, Ahmedabad 380015
DP Coordinator Deepti Shah
PYP Coordinator Jemily Kulkarni
Languages English
T: +91 79 2687 2459
W: www.aischool.net

Ajmera Global School
Yogi Nagar, Eksar Road, Borivali West, Mumbai 400092
PYP Coordinator Pushpalata Ajit
Languages English
T: +91 22 32401053
W: www.ajmeraglobalschool.com

Akal Academy Baru Sahib
Via Rajgarh, Teh. Pachhad, Distt. Sirmore, Himachal Pradesh 173101
PYP Coordinator P.D Mani
Languages English
T: +91 9816400538
W: www.akalacademybarusahib.com

Akshar Árbol International School – ECR Campus
Bethel Nagar, North 9th Street, Injambakkam, Chennai, Tamil Nadu 600115
PYP Coordinator Latha Muthukrishnan
Languages English
T: +91 94449 73275
W: www.akshararbol.edu.in

Akshar Árbol International School – West Mambalam
The Secondary Space (Grade 6 – 12), 16, Umapathy Street, West Mambalam, Chennai, Tamil Nadu 600033
DP Coordinator Nandini N
PYP Coordinator Prabha Dixit
Languages English
T: +91 44248 33275
W: www.akshararbol.edu.in

aLphabet School
178 St. Mary's Road, Alwarpet, Chennai, Tamil Nadu 600018
PYP Coordinator Minu Simon
Languages English
T: +91 44 4211 2025
W: www.alphabet.school

American Embassy School
Chandragupta Marg, Chanakyapuri, New Delhi, Delhi 110021
DP Coordinator Teresa Hjellming
Languages English
T: +91 11 2688 8854
W: aes.ac.in

American International School – Chennai
100 Feet Road, Taramani, Chennai 600113
DP Coordinator Michael Malone
Languages English
T: +91 44 2254 9000
W: www.aisch.org

AMERICAN SCHOOL OF BOMBAY
SF 2, G-Block, Bandra Kurla Complex Road, Bandra East, Mumbai, Maharashtra 400051
DP Coordinator Tamara Pfantz
PYP Coordinator Fay Martin
Languages English
T: SS: +91 22 6772 7272 ES: +91 22 6131 3600
E: inquiry@asbindia.org
W: www.asbindia.org

See full details on page 300

Amity Global School
Sector 46, Gurgaon, Harayana 122002
DP Coordinator Ved Prakash
PYP Coordinator Chandrei Choudhury
Languages English
T: +91 124 257 9770
W: www.amity.edu

Ascend International School
5 'F' Block, Opp. Govt. Colony, Bandra Kurla Complex (Bandra E), Mumbai 400051
MYP Coordinator Margaret Fitzpatrick
PYP Coordinator Varsha Agarwal Rodewald
Languages English
T: +91 22 7122 2000
W: www.ascendinternational.org

Bangalore International School
Geddalahalli, Hennur Bagalur Road, Kothanur Post, Bengaluru, Karnataka 560077
DP Coordinator Deepak Babu
Languages English
T: +91 80 2846 5060/2844 5852
W: www.bangaloreinternationalschool.org

BD Somani International School
625 GD Somani Marg, Cuffe Parade, Mumbai, Maharashtra 400005
DP Coordinator Shagun Sobti
Languages English
T: +91 22 2216 1355
W: www.bdsint.com

Bloomingdale International School
Municipal Employee Colony, Main Road, Vijayawada, Andhra Pradesh 520010
PYP Coordinator Boney Rao
Languages English
T: +91 7799787827
W: bloomingdale.edu.in

Bombay International School
Gilbert Building, 2nd Cross Lane, Babulnath, Mumbai, Maharashtra 400007
DP Coordinator Priya Aga
PYP Coordinator Nita Luthria Row
Languages English
T: +91 22 2364 8206
W: bis.edu.in

Bunts Sangha's S.M. Shetty International School & Jr. College
Hiranandani Gardens, Powai, Mumbai, Maharashtra 400076
DP Coordinator Snehal Bhortake
Languages English
T: +91 22 61327346
W: www.smshettyinstitute.org/bs-is-jc

Calcutta International School
724 Anandapur, E M Bypass, Kolkata, West Bengal 700107
DP Coordinator Samitava Mukherjee
Languages English
T: +91 33 2443 2054
W: www.calcuttais.edu.in

Caledonian International School
Near Power Gym, Saili Road, Pathankot, Punjab 145001
MYP Coordinator Sakshi Sehgal
Languages English
T: +91 98880 00189
W: www.caledonian.in

Calorx Olive International School
Besides Ahmedabad Dental College, Near Arjun Farm, Ranchodpura – Bhadaj Road, Ahmedabad, Gujarat 380058
DP Coordinator Ankur Upadhyay
MYP Coordinator Swini Bagga
PYP Coordinator Sujata Paul
Languages English, French, Hindi
T: +91 90 9993 3804
W: www.cois.edu.in

Cambridge International School
Choti Baradari, Phase II, Jalandhar 144001
DP Coordinator Rashmi Saini
PYP Coordinator Meenu Huria
Languages English
T: +91 181 462 3955
W: www.cambridgejalandhar.in

Canadian International School
Survey No 4 & 20, Manchenahalli, Yelahanka, Bengaluru, Karnataka 560064
DP Coordinator Ethan Salter
Languages English
T: +91 80 4249 4444
W: www.cisb.org.in

CANDOR INTERNATIONAL SCHOOL
Begur – Koppa Road, Hullahalli, Off Bannerghatta Road, Near Electronic City, Bengaluru, Karnataka 560105
DP Coordinator Gourab Das Sharma
PYP Coordinator Shivani Nagar
Languages English
T: +91 77 6029 9992
E: admissions@candorschool.com
W: candorschool.edu.in

See full details on page 304

Chennai Public School
TH Road, SH 50, Thirumazhisai, Chennai, Tamil Nadu 600124
DP Coordinator Jayu Ganesh
Languages English
T: +91 44 2654 4477
W: www.chennaipublicschool.com

Chinmaya International Residential School
Nallur Vayal Post, Siruvani Road, Coimbatore, Tamil Nadu 641114
DP Coordinator Ganesh Eswaran
Languages English
T: +91 422 261 3300/3303
W: www.cirschool.org

CHIREC International
1-55/12C, CHIREC Avenue, Kothaguda, Kondapur, Hyderabad, Telangana 500084
DP Coordinator Shirisha Kondury
Languages English
T: 91 40 44760999
W: www.chirec.ac.in

Choithram International
Choithram Hospital Campus, 5 Manik Bagh Road, Indore, Madhya Pradesh 452014
DP Coordinator Virginia D'Britto
MYP Coordinator Kamayani Sharma
PYP Coordinator Meenal Gavlani
Languages English
T: +91 731 2360345/6
W: www.choithraminternational.com

Christ Church School
Clare Road, Byculla, Mumbai, Maharashtra 400008
DP Coordinator Avila Luke
Languages English
T: +91 22 2309 9892
W: www.christchurchschoolmumbai.org

Christ Junior College
29 Hosur Road, Suddagunte Palya, Bengaluru, Karnataka 560029
DP Coordinator Sheela Chacko
Languages English
T: +91 80 40129292
W: www.christjuniorcollege.in

Christ Junior College – Residential
Mysore Road, Kanmanike, Kumbalgodu, Bengaluru, Karnataka 560074
DP Coordinator Nancy Mariyan
Languages English
T: + 91 80 28437915
W: www.cjcib.in

CP Goenka International School – Juhu
Plot No 44, Gulmohar Cross Road No 1, JVPD, Vile Parle (West), Mumbai, Maharashtra 400049
DP Coordinator Neha Pandit
Languages English
T: +91 22 61286900
W: www.cpgoenkajuhu.com

D Y Patil International College
DY Patil Knowledge City, Charholi(BK), Via. Lohegaon, Pune, Maharashtra 412105
DP Coordinator Suresh Wadhiya
Languages English
T: +91 20 30612700/752/753
W: www.dypispune.in

D Y Patil International School, Nerul
Dr D Y Patil Vidhyanagar, Sector 7, Nerul, Navi Mumbai, Maharashtra 400706
DP Coordinator Shan Liz Sanju
Languages English
T: +91 22 47700840
W: www.dypisnerul.in

D Y Patil International School, Worli
Opp MIG Colony A, Worli, Mumbai, Maharashtra 400025
DP Coordinator Huzefa Kagalwala
PYP Coordinator Sanjeevani Chindarkar
Languages English
T: +91 22 24371000
W: www.dypisworli.com

Delhi Public School Ghaziabad
Site #3, Industrial Area, Meerut Road, Ghaziabad, Uttar Pradesh 201002
DP Coordinator Gopalraj Rangaswamy
PYP Coordinator Sangeeta Mukherjee Roy
Languages English
T: +91 120 2712236
W: www.dpsghaziabad.com

Dhirubhai Ambani International School
Bandra-Kurla Complex, Bandra (East), Mumbai, Maharashtra 400098
DP Coordinator Soma Basu
Languages English
T: +91 22 40617000
W: www.da-is.org

Diamond Stone International School
Nallur Road, Madivallam Cross, Hosur, Tamil Nadu 635109
PYP Coordinator Sunila Radhesh
Languages English, Hindi, Tamil
T: +91 766 731 2999
W: www.dsischool.com

Don Bosco International School
Nathalal Parekh Marg, Matunga (E), Mumbai, Maharashtra 400019
DP Coordinator Aarti Malik
PYP Coordinator Gladys Gonsalves
Languages English
T: +91 22 2412 7474
W: dbis.in

DPS International, Gurgaon
HS-01, Block W, South City II, Gurgaon, Haryana 122001
DP Coordinator Jyotika Singh
MYP Coordinator Kanchan Misra
PYP Coordinator Arpita Saxena
Languages English
T: +91 8377000164
W: www.dpsiedge.edu.in

Dr Pillai Global Academy
Plot No 1, RSC 48, Gorai – II, Borivali (W), Mumbai, Maharashtra 400092
DP Coordinator Roshni Rajan
Languages English
T: +91 22 2868 4467/87
W: www.drpillaiglobalacademy.ac.in

Dr Pillai Global Academy, New Panvel
Sector-7, Khanda Colony, New Panvel, Navi Mumbai, Maharashtra 410206
DP Coordinator Mousumee Mishra
Languages English
T: +91 22 2748 1737
W: dpgapanvel.ac.in

DRS International School
Survey No. 523 Opp.Apparel Park, Gundla Pochampally, Medchal Mandal, Telangana, Hyderabad 500100
DP Coordinator Abha Hanspal
PYP Coordinator S. Ritika
Languages English, French, Spanish, Hindi
T: +91 40 237 92123/4/5
W: www.drsinternational.com

DSB INTERNATIONAL SCHOOL
25 Dadi Seth Road, Babulnath Temple, Mumbai, Maharashtra 400007
DP Coordinator Declan Sharp
Languages English, German
T: +91 (22) 23 673883
E: admissions@dsbindia.com
W: www.dsbindia.com
See full details on page 309

Eastern Public School
Ward 1, Abbas Nagar, Bhopal, Madhya Pradesh 462036
DP Coordinator Shehla Ali
PYP Coordinator Syeda Humera Riyaz
Languages English
T: +91 755 2805695
W: www.e-p-s.in

Ebenezer International School Bangalore
Singena Aghara, Via Huskur Road, Near APMC Fruit Yard, Electronic City Phase-I, Bengaluru, Karnataka 560099
DP Coordinator Abhinav Awasthi
PYP Coordinator Jyoti Andrew
Languages English
T: +91 80 67612222
W: www.eisbangalore.edu.in

Ecole Mondiale World School
Gulmohar Cross Road No. 9, J.V.P.D. Scheme, Juhu, Mumbai, Maharashtra 400049
DP Coordinator Ms. Vidya Bhaskar
MYP Coordinator Shamal Sarfare
PYP Coordinator Shilpa Dholakia
Languages English
T: +91 22 26237265/66
W: www.ecolemondiale.org

Edubridge International School
Wadilal A. Patel Marg, Grant Road (East), Mumbai, Maharashtra 400007
DP Coordinator Dixon Kibengo
MYP Coordinator Radha Trivady
PYP Coordinator Disha Kerkar
Languages English
T: +91 22 238 999 11
W: www.edubridgeschool.org

Excelsior American School
Sector 43 behind Dell Building, C-2 Block, Sushant Lok, Phase 1, Gurugram, Haryana 122001
DP Coordinator Deepakshi Verma
Languages English
T: +91 1 124 4049342
W: www.excelsioreducation.org

Fazlani L'Académie Globale
Shiv das Chapsi Marg, Opp. Wallace Flour Mills, Mazagaon, Mumbai, Maharashtra 400009
PYP Coordinator Mahera Goel
Languages English
T: +91 222 373 2730
W: www.flag.org.in

FirstSteps School
Opp. Blind Girls Hostel, Sector 26, Chandigarh, Punjab 160019
PYP Coordinator Rachanjit Kaur
T: +91 172 2793992
W: firststepsschool.org

Focus High School
Behind Salar Jung Museum, 22-8-321 Darushifa, Hyderabad, Telangana 500024
PYP Coordinator Sheherbanoo Fathi
Languages English
T: +91 40 2440 4060
W: www.focushighschool.org

Fountainhead School
Opp Ambetha Water Tank, Kunkni, Rander-Dandi Road, Surat, Gujarat 395005
DP Coordinator Bhargavi Bergi
MYP Coordinator Chinki Chhapia
PYP Coordinator Sanjana Amarnani
Languages English
T: +91 800 0130 031
W: www.fountainheadschools.org

G D Goenka World School
GD Goenka Education City, Sohna-Gurgaon Road, Sohna, Haryana 122103
DP Coordinator Dr Manisha Mehta
PYP Coordinator Poonam Singh
Languages English
T: +91 124 3315900
W: gdgws.gdgoenka.com

Garodia International Centre for Learning
153, Garodia Nagar, Ghatkopar East, Mumbai, Maharashtra 400077
DP Coordinator Elza Eldo Maliyil
Languages English
T: +91 22 25061133/3157
W: www.gicl.edu.in

Gateway International School
TOD Ashram, Jabakadal Street, Padur, Kazhipattur Post, Kelambakkam, Chennai, Tamil Nadu 603103
DP Coordinator V. P. Indra Elizabeth
MYP Coordinator Sangeetha Solomon
PYP Coordinator Susan Pramod
Languages English
T: + 91 860 811 7700
W: gatewayschools.edu.in

GENESIS GLOBAL SCHOOL
A-12, Sector 132, Noida Expressway, Uttar Pradesh 201304
DP Coordinator Rajeev Pargaien
MYP Coordinator K Rajarao
PYP Coordinator Shailja Datt
Languages English
T: +91 9711 000626
E: info@genesisgs.edu.in
W: www.genesisglobalschool.edu.in
See full details on page 336

GLENDALE INTERNATIONAL SCHOOL
Plot A, Road No. 20, HMDA Layout, Tellapur, Hyderabad, Telangana 502032
PYP Coordinator Ms Neerja M.
Languages English
T: +91 90 3000 1128
E: gipinfo@glendale.edu.in
W: www.glendale.edu.in/glendale-international-school/ib-pyp-tellapur
See full details on page 338

Goldcrest International
Sector 29, Plot No: 59, Near Rajiv Gandhi Park, Navi Mumbai, Maharashtra 400703
DP Coordinator Usha Karan Rana
Languages English
T: +91 22 2789 2261
W: www.goldcresthigh.com

GOOD SHEPHERD INTERNATIONAL SCHOOL
Good Shepherd Knowledge Village, M Palada PO, Ootacamund, Tamil Nadu 643 004
DP Coordinator Suresh Thangarajan
Languages English
T: +91 423 2550371
E: info@gsis.ac.in
W: www.gsis.ac.in
See full details on page 340

GREENWOOD HIGH INTERNATIONAL SCHOOL
No.8-14, Chickkawadayara Pura, Near Heggondahalli, Gunjur Post, Varthur via, Bengaluru, Karnataka 560087
DP Coordinator Nishanth Nagavar
Languages English
T: +91 80 22010500
E: admissions.intl@greenwoodhigh.edu.in
W: www.greenwoodhigh.edu.in
See full details on page 344

Heritage Xperiential Learning School, Gurgaon
Sector 62, Gurgaon, Haryana 122011
DP Coordinator Poonam Dahiya
Languages English
T: +91 124 2855124
W: www.ths.ac.in

HFS International Powai
Richmond Street, Hiranandani Gardens, Powai, Mumbai, Maharashtra 400076
DP Coordinator Jagruti Joshi
Languages English
T: +91 22 2576 3001
W: www.hfsinternationalpowai.com

Hill Spring International School
C Wing, NSS Educational Complex, MP Mill Compound, Tardeo, Mumbai, Maharashtra 400034
DP Coordinator Prashant Gohil
PYP Coordinator Nisha Vahi
Languages English
T: +91 22 2355 6201
W: www.nsseducation.org

HUS International School
5/63 Old Mahabalipuram Ro, Egattur Village, Padur PO, Kelambakkam, Chennai, Tamil Nadu 600130
DP Coordinator Shirin Bagchi
Languages English
T: +91 9500 118651
W: www.hus.edu.in

India International School
26/1, Sarjapur Road, Chikkabellandur, Bengaluru, Karnataka 560035
DP Coordinator Usha Murthy Shettigar
Languages English
T: +91 080 2843 9001
W: www.iis.edu.in

India International School
Kshipra Path, Opp VT Road, Mansarovar, Jaipur, Rajasthan 302020
DP Coordinator Mala Agnihotri
Languages English
T: +91 141 2786401
W: www.icfia.org

Indus International School (Bangalore)
Billapura Cross, Sarjapur, Bengaluru, Karnataka 562125
DP Coordinator Aparna Achanta
MYP Coordinator Saba Husain
PYP Coordinator Rachel Philip
Languages English
T: +91 80 2289 5900
W: www.indusschool.com

Indus International School, Hyderabad
Survey No 424 & 425, Kondakal Village, Near Mokila (M), Shankarpally, Hyderabad, Telangana 501203
DP Coordinator S R Radhakrishnan
MYP Coordinator Pinky Daniel
PYP Coordinator Sweta Jolly
Languages English
T: +91 8417 302100
W: www.indusschoolhyd.com

Indus International School, Pune
576 Bhukum, Near Manas Resort, Tal Mulshi, Pune, Maharashtra 411042
DP Coordinator Chitra Jeyakumar
MYP Coordinator Harsimran Kaur Kapany
PYP Coordinator Manju Suryanarayanan
Languages English
T: +91 80 2289 5900
W: www.indusschoolpune.com

International School Aamby
Aamby Valley City, Ambavene, Pune, Maharashtra 410401
DP Coordinator Snehal Joshi
Languages English
T: +91 20 3910 2500
W: www.internationalschoolaamby.com

International School of Hyderabad
c/o ICRISAT, Patancheru, Hyderabad, Telangana 502324
DP Coordinator Vandana Gupta
Languages English
T: +91 4030713865
W: www.ishyd.org

Jain International Residential School
Jakkasandra Post, Kanakpura Road, Ramanagara District, Bengaluru, Karnataka 562112
DP Coordinator Kalai Rajan. N
Languages English
T: +91 80 2757 7750
W: www.jirs.ac.in

Jamnabai Narsee International School
Narsee Monjee Bhavan, N.S. Road No.7, J.V.P.D Scheme, Vile Parle (West), Mumbai, Maharashtra 400049
DP Coordinator Mousumi Basu
MYP Coordinator Sonal Chabria
PYP Coordinator Purti Singh
Languages English
T: +91 (0)22 26187575/ 7676
W: www.jns.ac.in

Jayshree Periwal International School
Mahapura, SEZ Road, Ajmer Road, Jaipur, Rajasthan 302026
DP Coordinator Manisha Razdan
PYP Coordinator Juhi Trivedi
Languages English
T: +91 97827 44444/44445
W: www.jpischool.com

JBCN International School – Oshiwara
Survey No. 41, CTS No. 1, Off Andheri Link Road, Behind Tarapore Towers, Mhada Colony, Oshiwara, Andher+, Mumbai, Maharashtra 400058
DP Coordinator Ana Dominguez
Languages English
T: +91 22 ?26302441
W: www.jbcnschool.edu.in/oshiwara

JBCN INTERNATIONAL SCHOOL – PAREL
Yogi Mansion, CTS No. 244, Dr Vinay Walimbe Road, Off Dr S.S. Rao Marg, Parel East, Mumbai, Maharashtra 400012
DP Coordinator Sergio J. Chiri (Parel) Ana Dominguez (Oshiwara)
Languages English
T: +91 22 24114626
E: enquiry@jbcnschool.edu.in
W: www.jbcnschool.edu.in
See full details on page 356

JG International School
JG Campus of Excellence, JG Campus Road, Ahmedabad, Gujarat 380061
DP Coordinator Kavita Sharma
Languages English
T: +91 79 65411315
W: www.jgcampusindia.com

Johnson Grammar School ICSE&IBDP
Street No 3, Kakatiya Nagar, Habsiguda, Hyderabad, Andhra Pradesh 500007
DP Coordinator Bindu C G
Languages English
T: +91 40 27150555
W: www.johnsonib.com

KC High
12/4, Arunachalam Road, Kotturupuram, Chennai, Tamil Nadu 600085
DP Coordinator Charmaine Jesudoss
Languages English
T: +91 (44) 2447 3551
W: www.kchigh.com

KiiT International School
KiiT Campus 9, Patia, Bhubaneswar, Odisha 751024
DP Coordinator Anita George
Languages English
T: +91 99 3706 4660
W: www.kiitis.ac.in

KODAIKANAL INTERNATIONAL SCHOOL
PO Box 25, Seven Roads Junction, Kodaikanal, Tamil Nadu 624101
DP Coordinator Kurian Alex
MYP Coordinator Graham Lambert
PYP Coordinator Pearlin Joseph
Languages English
T: +91 4542 247500
E: principal@kis.in
W: www.kis.in
See full details on page 364

Kohinoor American School
Old Mumbai – Pune Highway, Near to The Dukes Retreat, Khandala, Maharashtra 410301
DP Coordinator Ms. Anuradha Paul
MYP Coordinator Ms. Monica Drego
Languages English
T: +91 9324323003
W: www.kohinooramericanschool.ac.in

LALAJI MEMORIAL OMEGA INTERNATIONAL SCHOOL
79, Omega School Road (Pallavaram Road), Kolapakkam, Kovur Post, Chennai, Tamil Nadu 600128
DP Coordinator Murali J
Languages English
T: +91 44 66241127
E: info@omegaschools.org
W: www.omegaschools.org
See full details on page 368

Lancers International School
DLF Phase V, Sector 53, Gurgaon, Haryana 122001
DP Coordinator Arpit Sharma
MYP Coordinator Aruna Muddana
PYP Coordinator Citlalli Martinez Garcia
Languages English
T: +91 124 4171900
W: www.lancersinternationalschool.in

Legacy School, Bangalore
6/1 A, 6/2 Byrathi Village, Bidarahalli Hobli, Off Hennur-Bagalur Main Road (New, International Airpo+, Bengaluru, Karnataka 560077
DP Coordinator Anthony Gonsalves
Languages English
T: +91 70222 92405
W: lsb.edu.in

M Ct M Chidambaram Chettyar International School
179, Luz Church Road, Mylapore, Chennai, Tamil Nadu 600004
DP Coordinator Sangita Varma
Languages English
T: +91 44 2467 0120
W: www.mctmib.org

Mahatma Gandhi International School
Sheth Motilal Hirabhai Bhavan, Opp. Induben Khakhrawala, Mithakali, Navrangpura, Ahmedabad, Gujarat 380006
CP Coordinator Meenakshi Ganeriwala
DP Coordinator Ravinder Kaur
MYP Coordinator Minoo Joshi
Languages English, Hindi
T: +91 79 2 646 3888
W: www.mgis.in

Mainadevi Bajaj International School
Plot No: 23-A, 24-28 Swami Vivekanand Road, Malad (West), Mumbai, Maharashtra 400064
DP Coordinator Husien Burhani
Languages English
T: +91 22 28733807
W: www.mbis.org.in

Manchester International School
SF 29/3A, Hudco Colony, Vellakinar, Coimbatore, Tamil Nadu 641029
PYP Coordinator Vishnu Carthica Guru Subbaian
Languages English
T: +91 422 655 5551
W: www.manchesters.in

Mercedes-Benz International School
P26, Rajeev Gandhi Infotech park, phase 1, Hinjewadi, Pune, Maharashtra 411057
DP Coordinator Tim Getter
MYP Coordinator Jose Campillo Campillo
PYP Coordinator Carla Swinehart
Languages English
T: +91 20 22934420
W: www.mbis.org

Meridian School For Boys and Girls
#8-2-541, Road No.7, Banjara Hills, Hyderabad, Telangana 500034
PYP Coordinator Sailaja Koduri
Languages English, Hindi
T: +91 40 2342 0562
W: meridianschool.in/banjarahills

Modern High School for Girls
78, Syed Amir Ali Avenue, Kolkata, West Bengal 700019
DP Coordinator Sheta Saha
Languages English
T: +913322875326
W: www.mhsforgirls.edu.in

Mody School
Mody Institute of Education & Research, Lakshmangarh, Rajasthan 332311
DP Coordinator Madhusudana Brahma
Languages English
T: +91 91 16637196
W: www.modyschool.ac.in

Mount Litera School International
GN Block, Behind Asian Heart Hospital, Near UTI Building, Bandra Kurla Complex, Bandra- East, Mumbai, Maharashtra 400051
DP Coordinator Suzanne Patel
MYP Coordinator Vishnu Sharma
PYP Coordinator Bushra Khan
Languages English
T: +91 22 6229 6000
W: www.mlsi.in

Mussoorie International School
Srinagar Estate, Polo Ground, Mussoorie, Uttarakhand 248179
DP Coordinator Meeta Sharma
Languages English
T: +91 135 2630250
W: www.misindia.net

Nahar International School
Nahar's Amrit Shakti, Chandivali Farm Road, Off Saki Vihar Road, Andheri East, Mumbai, Maharashtra 400072
DP Coordinator Resham Puri
Languages English, Hindi
T: +91 (0)22 2847 5511
W: www.nahar-is.org

Navrachana International School
Vasna Bhayali Road, Bhayali, Vadodara, Gujarat 391410
DP Coordinator Jyoti Nagar
MYP Coordinator Usha Singh
PYP Coordinator Viraaj Jhaveri
Languages English
T: +91 265 225 3851/2/3/4
W: www.navrachana.ac.in

Neerja Modi School
Shipra Path, Near Building Technology Park, Mansarovar, Jaipur, Rajasthan 302020
DP Coordinator Sarita Nathawat
Languages English
T: +91 141 2785 484
W: www.nmsindia.org

Neev Academy
No.16, Yemalur, Kempapura Main Road, Bengaluru, Karnataka 560037
DP Coordinator Colin Leslie Kelman
MYP Coordinator Gouri Kar
PYP Coordinator Soumya Anil Venkatram
Languages English
T: +91 080 88934740/1
W: www.neevacademy.org

NES International School Dombivli
Sankara Nagar, Kalyan-Shil Road Opp. DNS Bank, Sonarpada, Dombivli (E), Thane, Mumbai, Maharashtra 421203
PYP Coordinator Sonal Nichat
Languages English, Hindi
T: +91 84 22994436
W: www.nesisd.org

NES International School Mumbai
Malabar Hill Road, Vasant Garden, Mulund(W), Mumbai, Maharashtra 400082
DP Coordinator Ramaswamy Varadarajan
MYP Coordinator Cimmy Ajithkumar
PYP Coordinator Primrose Misquitta
Languages English
T: +91 22 25911478
W: www.nesinternational.org

IB ASIA-PACIFIC

Niraj International School
Kandlakoya, 5 km from Dhola-ri-Dhani, Hyderabad, Telangana 132133
PYP Coordinator Jayashree Arraguntla
Languages English
T: +91 84 18200476
W: www.nirajinternationalschool.com

Oakridge International School, Bachupally
Survey No 166/6, Bowrampet Village, Near Bachupally, Hyderabad, Telangana 500043
PYP Coordinator Ruchi Singh
Languages English
T: +91 720 764 8111
W: www.oakridge.in/bachupally

Oakridge International School, Bengaluru
Varthur Road, Near Dommassandra Circle, Sarjapur Hobli, Bengaluru, Karnataka 562125
DP Coordinator Saikrishna Pammi
MYP Coordinator Ruchira Banka
PYP Coordinator P. Sreeja Nair
Languages English
T: +91 0802 254 3600
W: www.oakridge.in/bengaluru
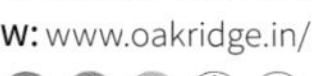

Oakridge International School, Gachibowli
Khajaguda, Nanakramguda Road, Cyberabad, Hyderabad, Telangana 500008
DP Coordinator Deepalatha Subramanian
MYP Coordinator Savitri Potluri
PYP Coordinator Vasundhara Achanta
Languages English
T: +91 0402 9800111
W: www.oakridge.in/gachibowli

Oakridge International School, Mohali
Next to Thunderzone Amusement Park, Mohali, Punjab 140307
PYP Coordinator Meera Chhabria
Languages English
T: +91 752 701 3370
W: www.oakridge.in/mohali

Oakridge International School, Visakhapatnam
NH 5 Road, Behind HP Petrol Bunk, Maharajpeta Junction, Tagarapuvalasa, Visakhapatnam, Andhra Pradesh 531162
DP Coordinator Molly Biju
Languages English
T: +91 773 081 6999
W: www.oakridge.in/contact

Oberoi International School
Oberoi Garden City, Off Western Express Highway, Goregaon (E), Mumbai, Maharashtra 400063
DP Coordinator Rucha Bhayani
MYP Coordinator Lucy Francis
PYP Coordinator Neha Minda
Languages English
T: +91 22 4236 3131
W: www.oberoi-is.org

Pathways School (Gurgaon NCR South)
Baliawas, Off Gurgaon Faridabad Road, Gurgaon, Haryana 122003
DP Coordinator Megha Oberoi
MYP Coordinator Varsha Sinha
PYP Coordinator Shefali Lakhina
Languages English
T: +91 124 487 2000
W: www.pathways.in/gurgaon

Pathways School Noida
Sector 100, Noida NCR East, New Delhi, Delhi 110062
DP Coordinator Samuel Osmond
MYP Coordinator Anshu Sharma
PYP Coordinator Vandana Parashar
Languages English
T: +91 11 2955 1090
W: www.pathways.in/noida

Pathways World School
Aravali Retreat, Off Gurgaon Sohna Road, Gurgaon, Haryana 122102
DP Coordinator Mona Sharma
MYP Coordinator Monika Bajaj
PYP Coordinator Monica Bhimwal
Languages English
T: +91 124 451 3000
W: www.pathways.in

Podar International School
Ramee Emerald Building, Near Shamrao Vithal Bank, S.V.Road, Khar (West), Mumbai, Maharashtra 400052
DP Coordinator Hema Rajan
PYP Coordinator Saachi Setpal
Languages English
T: +91 22 2648 7321
W: www.podarinternationalschool.com

Podar O.R.T International School, Worli
PODAR-ORT School Building, 68, Worli Hill Estate, Worli, Mumbai, Maharashtra 400018
PYP Coordinator Shreya Mahindra
Languages English
T: +91 7506112200
W: www.podareducation.org/school/worli

Rasbihari International School
Vrindavan, Nashik-Ozar Road, Nashik, Maharashtra 422003
PYP Coordinator Shilpa Ahire
Languages English
T: +91 253 230 4622
W: www.rasbihari.org

RBK International Academy
Opp. Indian Oil Nagar, Near Shankara Colony, Ghatkopar-Mankhurd Link Road, Mumbai, Maharashtra 400088
DP Coordinator Shuchi Shukla
MYP Coordinator Vidya Upadhyay
PYP Coordinator Dinaz Karbhari
Languages English
T: +91 7400091646/7/8/9
W: www.rbkia.org

Redbridge International Academy
#114, S Bingipura Village, Hulimangala Post, Begur-Koppa Road, Bangalore, Karnataka 560105
DP Coordinator Karen Kunder
Languages English
T: +91 9620863456
W: www.rbia.in

Rockwell International School
Sy No.160(p), Gandipet Main Rd, Kokapet, Hyderabad, Telangana 500075
DP Coordinator Shruti Sareen
Languages English
T: +91 9618662201
W: rockwellinternationalschool.com

Rungta International School
Near Nandan Van, Veer Savarkar Nagar, Raipur, Chhattisgarh 492099
DP Coordinator Iraban Haldar
MYP Coordinator Gagandeep Dhillon
PYP Coordinator Keathi Sharma
Languages English
T: +91 98261 45333
W: www.rungtainternational.org

RYAN GLOBAL SCHOOL
Yamuna Nagar, Lokhandwala, Andheri (west), Mumbai, Maharashtra 400058
PYP Coordinator Bhavi Furia
Languages English
T: +91 22 2632 0203/05
E: rgs.andheri@ryanglobal.org
W: www.ryanglobalschools.com
See full details on page 398

Sangam School of Excellence
N.H. 79, Atun, Bhilwara By Pass, Chittorgarh Highway, Bhilwara, Rajasthan 311001
DP Coordinator Soma Ghosh
Languages English
T: +91 1482 249 700
W: www.sangamschoolbhilwara.com

SANJAY GHODAWAT INTERNATIONAL SCHOOL
Gat No. 555, Kolhapur – Sangli Highway, Atigre, Maharashtra
DP Coordinator Dhruv Prajapati
Languages English
T: +91 230 2689700
E: principal@sgischool.in
W: www.sgischool.in
See full details on page 400

Sanskar School
117-121, Vishwamitra Marg, Hanuman Nagar Ext., Sirsi Road, Jaipur, Rajasthan 302012
DP Coordinator Manisha Chandra
PYP Coordinator Smita Benuskar
Languages English
T: +91 0141 2246189
W: www.sanskarjaipur.com

Sarala Birla Academy
Bannerghatta PO, Jigni Road, Bengaluru, Karnataka 560083
DP Coordinator Manoj Jaiswal
Languages English
T: +91 80 41348200/03
W: www.saralabirlaacademy.com

SCOTTISH HIGH INTERNATIONAL SCHOOL
G-Block, Sector 57, Sushant Lok-II, Gurugram, Haryana 122011
DP Coordinator Ms Sudha Goyal
PYP Coordinator Ms Seema Bhati
Languages English
T: +91 124 4112781-90
E: schooldirector@scottishigh.com
W: www.scottishigh.com
See full details on page 404

Seedling International Academy
Sector-4, Park Lane, Jawahar Nagar, Jaipur, Rajasthan 302004
DP Coordinator Shruti Kukar
Languages English
T: +91 141 2653377
W: www.seedlingschools.com

Sharanya Narayani International School
#232/1, Thoranahalli, Byranahalli post, Near Hoskote, Bengaluru, Karnataka 563130
DP Coordinator Sabita Sarma
PYP Coordinator Kapil Mehrotra
Languages English
T: +91 80 46629500
W: snis.edu.in

SHIV NADAR SCHOOL GURUGRAM
DLF City, Phase -1 Block -E, Pahari Road, Gurugram, Haryana
DP Coordinator Sriparna Chakrabarti
Languages English
T: +91 124 4549200
E: admissions.gurgaon@sns.edu.in
W: shivnadarschool.edu.in/gurgaon
See full details on page 416

Shiv Nadar School Noida
Plot No -SS -1, Expressway Sector 168, Noida, Uttar Pradesh 201305
DP Coordinator Jyotsna Gaur
Languages English
T: +91 8130200199
W: shivnadarschool.edu.in

Silver Oaks International School, Bangalore
Sy No:188/3 & 188/4, Sarjapur Road, Dommasandra village, Bengaluru, Karnataka 562125
MYP Coordinator Thota Nidhi
PYP Coordinator Rachana Kothapally
Languages English
T: +91 97394 75900
W: www.silveroaks.co.in/bangalore

Silver Oaks International School, Hyderabad
Miyapur-Dindigal Road, Bachupally, Hyderabad, Telangana 500090
PYP Coordinator Sangeeta Pratti
Languages English
T: +91 40 23047777
W: www.silveroaks.co.in/hyderabad

SINGAPORE INTERNATIONAL SCHOOL, MUMBAI
On National Highway No. 8, Post Mira Road, Dahisar, Mumbai, Maharashtra 401104
DP Coordinator Absolom Museve
PYP Coordinator Abhimanyu DasGupta
Languages English
T: +91 222 828 5200
E: admin@sisindia.net
W: www.sisindia.net
See full details on page 417

Smt. Sulochanadevi Singhania School
Pokharan Road No.1, J K Gram, Thane (West), Maharashtra 400606
DP Coordinator Deepti Vimal
Languages English
T: +91 22 4036 8410/1
W: www.singhaniaschool.org

Sreenidhi International School
Near Appa Junction, Moinabad, Hyderabad, Telangana 500075
DP Coordinator John Campbell
MYP Coordinator Tonderai Mutasa
PYP Coordinator Mary Vinodhini
Languages English
T: +91 9912244409
W: www.sis.edu.in

SRV International School
Marappan Thottam, 4/3 Gandhi Salai, Pattanam Road, Rasipuram, Namakkal, Tamil Nadu 637408
PYP Coordinator Asnaha Farheen
Languages English
W: www.srvisglobal.org

Step by Step School
Plot A 10, Sector 132 Taj Expressway, Noida, Uttar Pradesh 201303
DP Coordinator Urmi Debroy
Languages English
T: +91 0120 385 7300
W: www.sbs-school.org

Stonehill International School
259/333/334/335Tarahunise Village Jala Hobli, Bangalore North Taluk, Bengaluru, Karnataka 562157
DP Coordinator Manpreet Kaur
MYP Coordinator Jitendra Pandey
PYP Coordinator Anthony hamblin
Languages English
T: +91 80 4341 8300
W: www.stonehill.in

Strawberry Fields High School
Sector 26, Chandigarh, Punjab 160019
DP Coordinator Meenakshi Mehta
T: +91 172 279 5903/5904
W: www.strawberryfieldshighschool.com

Suncity School
Suncity Township, Sector 54, Gurgaon, Haryana 122002
DP Coordinator Vivek Mandal
Languages English
T: +91 (0)124 4845300 (EXT:302)
W: www.suncityschool.in

SVKM JV Parekh International School
CNM School Campus, Dadabhai Road, Off. S.V. Road, Vile Parle (West), Mumbai, Maharashtra 400056
DP Coordinator Shoma Bhattacharya
Languages English
T: +91 22 4233 3030
W: www.jvparekhintnl.ac.in

Symbiosis International School
Symbiosis Viman nagar Campus, Off. New AirPort road, Viman Nagar, Pune, Maharashtra 411014
DP Coordinator M. Madan Mohan
PYP Coordinator Nadia Patel
Languages English
T: +91 20 2655 7300
W: www.symbiosisinternationalschool.net

The British School
Dr Jose P Rizal Marg, Chanakyapuri, New Delhi, Delhi 110021
DP Coordinator Monisha Singh
Languages English
T: +91 11 4066 4166
W: www.british-school.org

THE CATHEDRAL & JOHN CONNON SCHOOL
6 Purshottamdas Thakurdas Marg, Mumbai, Maharashtra 400001
DP Coordinator Latha Balaji
Languages English
T: +91 22 2200 1282
E: dean@cathedral-school.com
W: www.cathedral-school.com
See full details on page 427

The Cathedral Vidya School, Lonavala
Village Shilatne, Taluk Maval, Post Office Karla, Pune, Lonavala, Maharashtra 410405
DP Coordinator Lucy Massey
Languages English
T: +91 2114 282693
W: cathedral-lonavala.org

The Doon School
Mall Road, Dehradun, Uttarakhand 248001
DP Coordinator Pankaj Joshi
Languages English
T: +91-135 2526 400
W: www.doonschool.com

The DPSG International (Delhi Public School Ghaziabad International)
P.O. Dasna, Hindon Nagar, Dasna, Kallu Garhi, Ghaziabad, Uttar Pradesh 201303
PYP Coordinator Malavika Yadav
Languages English
T: +91 858 795 1424
W: www.thedpsgint.in

The Galaxy School
SNK Main Building, University Road, Rajkot, Gujarat 360005
DP Coordinator Chirag Jhala
Languages English
T: +91 281 2588391/2588392
W: www.tges.org

The Gaudium School
Survey No. 148, Nanakramguda Village, Serilingampally, Nanakramguda, Hyderabad, Telangana 500008
DP Coordinator Vijeta Sinha
PYP Coordinator Kiran Singh
Languages English, Hindi
T: +91 73370 00200
W: www.thegaudium.com

The Heritage School, Kolkata
994 Maduraha, Chowbaga Road, Anandpur, PO East Kolkata Township, Kolkata, West Bengal 700107
DP Coordinator Amita Kaushik
Languages English
T: +91 33 2443 0448
W: www.theheritageschool.org

The Indian Public School (TIPS) Chennai
No.1 Nehru Nagar, 1st Main Road, Perungudi, Chennai, Tamil Nadu 600069
DP Coordinator Kavya Vishwanath
PYP Coordinator Agnes Joseph
Languages English
T: +91 44 7118 8011
W: www.tipsglobal.org/tips_chennai.php

The Indian Public School (TIPS) Coimbatore
193 Sathy Road, S.S.Kulam P.O., Coimbatore, Tamil Nadu 641107
DP Coordinator Ibson T. Arimbur
PYP Coordinator Sita Subramaniam
Languages English
T: +91 422 236 6666
W: www.tipsglobal.org/tips_coimbatore.php

The Indian Public School (TIPS) Erode
Chennimalai Road, Senapathipalayam, Goundachi palayam, Erode, Tamil Nadu 638112
PYP Coordinator Parasakthi Ayenan
Languages English
T: +91 424 6459999
W: www.tipsglobal.org/tips_erode.php

THE INTERNATIONAL SCHOOL BANGALORE
Whitefield-Sarjapur Road, Near Dommasandra Circle, Bengaluru, Karnataka 562125
DP Coordinator Mr Naveen Tom & Mrs Sonia Mathew
Languages English
T: +91 80 22634900
E: admission@tisb.ac.in
W: tisb.org
See full details on page 429

The Shri Ram School
Moulsari Avenue DLF Phase-3, Gurgaon, Haryana 122002
DP Coordinator Anjali Sharma
Languages English

W: www.tsrs.org

The Universal School
Plot No. 17, Near Lion's Garden, Tilak Road, Ghatkopar (E), Mumbai, Maharashtra 400077
DP Coordinator Lakshmi Thevar
Languages English, Hindi
T: +91 771 8888 999
W: ghatkopar.universalschool.edu.in

The White School International
HiLITE Knowledge Village, Parammal, Perumanna, Kozhikode, Kerala 673019
DP Coordinator Marline John Kurishingal
MYP Coordinator Manju Dominic
PYP Coordinator Radha Sunil
Languages English, Malayalam
T: +91 95260 777 78
W: www.thewhiteschool.in

Treamis
Hulimangala Post, near Electronics City, Bengaluru, Karnataka 560105
PYP Coordinator Uurmi Ghosh
Languages English, Kannada
T: +91 99723 99046
W: www.treamis.org

Trio World Academy
3/5 Kodigehalli Main Road, Sahakar Nagar, Bengaluru, Karnataka 560092
DP Coordinator Sajeena Joseph
PYP Coordinator Chitra R
Languages English
T: +91 80 40611222
W: trioworldschool.com

TRIVANDRUM INTERNATIONAL SCHOOL
Edackcode, PO Korani, Trivandrum, Kerala 695104
DP Coordinator Rachel Jacob
PYP Coordinator Sanjay Prabhakaran
Languages English
T: +91 471 2619051
E: tis@trins.org
W: www.trins.org
See full details on page 434

UWC MAHINDRA COLLEGE
Village Khubavali, PO Paud, Taluka Mulshi, Pune, Maharashtra 412108
DP Coordinator Ainhoa Orensanz
Languages English
T: +91 97644 42751 54
E: info@muwci.net
W: uwcmahindracollege.org
See full details on page 436

VICTORIOUS KIDSS EDUCARES
Survey No. 53, 54 & 58, Hissa No. 2/1A, Off. Shreeram Society, Nagar Road, Kharadi, Pune, Maharashtra 411014
DP Coordinator Jaya Kalsy
MYP Coordinator Vishwajeet Kumar
PYP Coordinator Khushboo Sharma
Languages English
T: +91 20-67116300/1/2
E: robbinghosh@victoriouskidsseducares.org
W: www.victoriouskidsseducares.org
See full details on page 438

Vidsan Charterhouse
Delhi NCR, Sector 93, Faridabad, Haryana 121002
DP Coordinator Balaji Thoppay
Languages English
T: +91 9999116900/01
W: vidsancharterhouse.com

Vidya Global School
Vidya Knowledge Park, Baghpat Road, Meerut, Uttar Pradesh 250002
PYP Coordinator Nalini Oberoi
Languages English
T: +91 121 2439188/89/92
W: vidyaglobalschool.com

Vidyatree Modern World College
Sector E, Aliganj, Lucknow, Uttar Pradesh 226024
PYP Coordinator Sumita Ghosh
Languages English, Hindi
T: +91 522 402 1406
W: www.themodern.in

Vishwashanti Gurukul
Rajbaug, off Pune-Solapur Highway, Loni, Pune, Maharashtra 412201
DP Coordinator Evelynn Sheen Singh
MYP Coordinator Rohit Jain
PYP Coordinator Prasuna Vemuri
Languages English
T: +91 20 39210000
W: www.mitgurukul.com

VIVA The School
Beside VVIT college campus, NAMBUR village, Pedakakani Mandal, Nambur, Guntur, Andhra Pradesh 522508
PYP Coordinator Madhavi Ayinada
Languages English, Telugu
W: www.viva.school

Wockhardt Global School
Dr Habil Khorakiwala Education and Health Foundation, E-1/NP-1, SEZ, Five Star Industrial Estate, MIDC, Shen+, Aurangabad, Maharashtra 431154
PYP Coordinator Hetal Ahivasi
Languages English
T: +91 240 6662888
W: wockhardtschools.com

Woodstock School
, Mussoorie, Uttarakhand 248179
DP Coordinator Mou Maiti
MYP Coordinator Robert Smith
Languages English
T: +91 135 263 9000
W: www.woodstock.ac.in

INDONESIA

ACG School Jakarta
Jl Warung Jati Barat, Taman Margasatwa, No 19 Ragunan, Jati Padang, Pasar Minggu, Jakarta Selatan, DKI 12510
DP Coordinator Dave Brundage
PYP Coordinator Wayne Martin
Languages English
T: +62 21 780 5636
W: jakarta.acgedu.com

ACS Jakarta
Jl Bantar Jati, Kelurahan Setu, Jakarta Timur, DKI 13880
DP Coordinator Annabella Ong
Languages English
T: +62 21 8459 7175
W: www.acsjakarta.sch.id

Al Jabr Islamic School
Jl Bango II No 38, Pondok Labu, Jakarta, DKI 12450
MYP Coordinator Tarra Abuchari
PYP Coordinator Diantari Wardriyana
Languages English
T: +62 21 75913675
W: www.aljabrschool.com

Australian Independent School (AIS) Indonesia
Jalan Imam Bonjol No.458a, Pemecutan, Denpasar Barat, Denpasar, Bali 80119
DP Coordinator Thomas Allan
Languages English
T: +62 361 845 20000
W: www.ais-indonesia.com

Australian Independent School, Jakarta – Pejaten Campus
Jl. Pejaten Barat No. 69, Pejaten Barat, Pasar Minggu, Jakarta Selatan, DKI 12510
DP Coordinator Inga Tamou
Languages English
T: +62 21 7884 8285
W: www.ais-indonesia.com

Bali Island School
Jalan Danau Buyan IV No. 15, Sanur, Denpasar, Bali 80228
DP Coordinator Matt Wood
MYP Coordinator Michele McLay
PYP Coordinator Craig Eldred
Languages English
T: +62 361 288 770
W: www.baliinternationalschool.com

Bandung Independent School
Jl. Surya Sumantri No. 61, Bandung, Jabar 40164
DP Coordinator Elizabeth Russell
PYP Coordinator Katherine Stone
Languages English
T: +62 22 201 4995
W: www.bisedu.or.id

Beacon Academy
Jalan Pegangsaan Dua. No 66, Kelapa Gading, Jakarta Utara, DKI 14250
DP Coordinator Suprio Bhowmick
Languages English
T: +62 21 460 3480
W: www.beaconacademy.net

Binus School Simprug
Jl Sultan Iskandar, Muda Kav G-8, Simprug, Jakarta Selatan, DKI 12220
DP Coordinator Erdolfo L Lardizabal
MYP Coordinator Jyoti Gupta
PYP Coordinator Richel Langit-Dursin
Languages English
T: +62 21 724 3663
W: www.binus-school.net

British School Jakarta
Bintaro Jaya Sector IX, Jl. Raya Jombang, Ciledug, Pondok Aren, Tangerang, Banten 15227
CP Coordinator Daniel Harbridge
DP Coordinator Jane Kilpatrick
Languages English
T: +62 21 745 1670
W: www.bis.or.id

BTB School (Sekolah Bina Tunas Bangsa)
Jl. Pluit Tumur Blok MM, Jakarta Utara, DKI 14450
DP Coordinator Christine Macaraig
Languages English
T: +62 21 30031300
W: www.btbschool.org

Canggu Community School
Jalan Subak Sari, Banjar Tegal Gundul, Canggu, Bali 80361
DP Coordinator Simon Baccanello
Languages English
T: +62 361 8446391
W: www.ccsbali.com

INDONESIA

Cita Hati Christian Senior School – East Campus

JL Kejawan Putih Barat 28-30, Pakuwon City, Surabaya, Jatim 60112
DP Coordinator Nettie Nettie
Languages English
T: +62 31 591 5773
W: www.bchati.sch.id

Cita Hati Christian Senior School – West Campus

Jl. Bukit Golf L2 No. 1, Citraland, Surabaya, Jatim 60211
DP Coordinator Marisi Sihombing
Languages English
T: +62 31 7404959
W: www.bchati.sch.id/citahati

Global Jaya School

Emerald Boulevard, Bintaro Jaya Sektor IX, Pondok Aren, Tangerang, Banten 15224
DP Coordinator Ram Pandey
MYP Coordinator Dannandyatti Priambodo
PYP Coordinator Anindya Hartono
Languages English
T: +62 21 745 7562
W: www.globaljaya.com

GMIS – Bali

Jl Tukad Yeh Penet No 8A Renon, Denpasar, Bali 80235
CP Coordinator Vijay Vardhan Singh
DP Coordinator Emil Macaraig
MYP Coordinator Meena Gaikwad
PYP Coordinator Sonia Ganguly
Languages English
T: +62 361 239744
W: www.gandhibali.org

GMIS Jakarta

Jalan Landas Pacu Timur, Kota Baru Bandar, Kemayoran, Jakarta Utara, DKI 14410
CP Coordinator Manish Semwal Kumar
DP Coordinator Rowena 'Winnie' Macaraig
MYP Coordinator Gurpreet Kaur Hanspal
PYP Coordinator Rachna Johar
Languages English
T: +62-21 65865667
W: www.gandhijkt.org

Jakarta Intercultural School

Jalan Terogong Raya No. 33, Cilandak, Jakarta Selatan, DKI 12430
DP Coordinator Darren Seath
Languages English
T: +62 21 769 2555
W: www.jisedu.or.id

Jakarta Multicultural School

Jl. Pisangan Raya No. 99 (Taman Wisata Situ Gintung), Cirendeu, Ciputat Timur, Banten 15419
DP Coordinator Corey Allison
PYP Coordinator Windriana Wibisono
Languages English
T: +62 21 744 4864
W: jms.sch.id

Medan Independent School

PO Box 1190, Jl Letjend Jamin Ginting Km10 / Jl Tali Air No 5, Medan, Sumut 20111
DP Coordinator Kenneth Kitchens
MYP Coordinator Gregory McGuire
PYP Coordinator Rachel Wayne
Languages English
T: +62 61 836 1816
W: www.mismedan.org

Mentari Intercultural School Bintaro

Jalan Perigi Baru No.7A, Tangerang, Pd. Aren, Tangerang Selatan, Banten 15228
DP Coordinator Alquin Alva
Languages English
T: +62 21 745 8418
W: mis.sch.id/w/mis-bintaro.html

Mentari Intercultural School Jakarta

Jl. H. Jian No.2, RT.4/RW.3, North Cipete, Kby. Baru, Jakarta Selatan, DKI 12150
DP Coordinator Joanna Via Teodoro
MYP Coordinator Matthew Roberge
PYP Coordinator Patricia Manning
Languages English
T: 21 727 94 870
W: mis.sch.id/w/mis-jakarta.html

Mt Zaagkam School

Tembagapura Raya Street No. 605, Tembagapura, Papua 99967
PYP Coordinator Raquel Acedo Rubio
Languages English
T: +62 901 408 767
W: www.mzs.sch.id

Sampoerna Academy, Jakarta Campus

L'Avenue Campus, Jln. Raya Pasar Minggu, Kav. 16 Pancoran, Jakarta 12780
DP Coordinator Devendar Singh Rawat
Languages English, Indonesian
T: +62 (0)21 5022 22 34
W: www.sampoernaacademy.sch.id

Sampoerna Academy, Medan Campus

Jln. Jamin Ginting, Kompleks Citra Garden, Medan
DP Coordinator Harish Kumar Gupta
Languages English, Indonesian
T: +62 (0)61 821 27 15
W: www.sampoernaacademy.sch.id/en/medan-campus

SDK BPK Penabur Banda

Jl Bahureksa No 26, Bandung, Jabar 40115
PYP Coordinator Dian Natalia
Languages English
T: +62 22 4210787
W: ib.penabur.sch.id

Sekolah Bogor Raya

Perumahan Danau Bogor Raya, Bogor, Jabar 16143
DP Coordinator Arning Rani Wulandari
PYP Coordinator Diana Karitas
Languages English
T: +62 251 837 8873
W: www.sekolahbogorraya.com

Sekolah Buin Batu

Jl Kayu Besi No 400, Townsite PTAMNT, Buin Batu, West Sumbawa, NTB
PYP Coordinator Arief Budiman
Languages English
T: +62372 635318 EXT:48443
W: www.sekolahbuinbatu.org

Sekolah Cikal Setu

Jl. Raya Setu No.3, Cipayung, Jakarta Timur, DKI 13880
DP Coordinator Stella Monica
MYP Coordinator Siti Fatimah
PYP Coordinator Marsaria Primadona
Languages English
T: +62 21 84998545
W: www.cikal.co.id

Sekolah Cikal Surabaya

Jl. Raya Lontar no. 103, Kel. Lontar kec. Sambikerep, Surabaya, Jatim 60216
PYP Coordinator Cholifah Yuniati
Languages English
T: +6231 752 7900
W: www.cikal.co.id

Sekolah Ciputra, Surabaya

Puri Widya Kencana, Citraland, Surabaya, Jatim 60213
DP Coordinator Simon Bradshaw
MYP Coordinator Neil Henderson
PYP Coordinator Diana Sumadianti
Languages English
T: +62 31 741 5018
W: www.sekolahciputra.sch.id

Sekolah Global Indo-Asia

Jalan Raya Batam Centre Kav SGIA, Batam Centre, Batam Island, Kepri
DP Coordinator Vijay Gupta
PYP Coordinator Marina Hastuti
Languages English
T: +62 778 467333
W: www.sgiaedu.org

Sekolah Madania

Telaga Kahuripan, Parung, Bogor, Jabar 16310
PYP Coordinator Gusva Havita
Languages English
T: +62 251 860 2777
W: www.madania.net

Sekolah Mutiara Harapan

Jl. pondok kacang raya no. 02, Pondok Aren, Bintaro, Tangerang, Banten
PYP Coordinator Ajeng Rucitra Nareswari
Languages English

W: mutiaraharapan.com/en

Sekolah Mutiara Nusantara

Jl. Sersan Bajuri – Setiabudi, Km 1.5, RT 3 RW 1, Bandung, Jabar 40559
DP Coordinator Sean Broussard
Languages English
T: +62 22 201 7773
W: www.mnis.sch.id

Sekolah Pelita Harapan, Kemang Village

Jl. Pangeran Antasari 36, Kemang Village, Jakarta Selatan, DKI 12150
DP Coordinator Chong Shim
Languages English
T: +62 21 290 56 789
W: kemangvillage.sph.edu

Sekolah Pelita Harapan, Lippo Cikarang

Jl. Dago Permai No.1 Komp. Dago Villas, Lippo Cikarang, Bekasi, Jabar 17550
DP Coordinator Sofia Sinaga
Languages English
T: +62 21 897 2786 87
W: lippocikarang.sph.edu

SEKOLAH PELITA HARAPAN, LIPPO VILLAGE

2500 Boulevard Palem Raya, Lippo Village, Tangerang, Banten 15810
DP Coordinator Ezmieralda Kallista
MYP Coordinator Daniel Admiraal
PYP Coordinator Ratna Setyowati Putri
Languages English
T: +62 21 546 0234
E: sph-lv@sph.ac.id
W: www.sph.edu

See full details on page 406

Sekolah Pelita Harapan, Sentul City
Jl. Babakan Madang, Sentul City, Bogor, Jabar 16810
DP Coordinator Elisabeth Pristiwi
MYP Coordinator Lisajanti Widjaja
PYP Coordinator Fany Oktavia
Languages English
T: +62 21 8796 0234
W: sentulcity.sph.edu
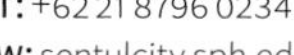

Sekolah Pilar Indonesia
Jl Dewa 9, Ciangsana, Kawasan Cibubur, Bogor, Jabar 16968
PYP Coordinator Rini Anggraini Effendi
Languages English
T: +62 21 84936222
W: www.sekolah-pilar-indonesia.sch.id

Sekolah Tunas Bangsa
Jalan Arteri Supadio, (Achmad Yani II) Km 2, Pontianak, Kalbar 78391
PYP Coordinator Ronald Sahat Tua Simbolon
Languages English
T: +62 561 725555
W: www.tunasbangsa.sch.id

Sekolah Victory Plus
Jl Kemang Pratama Raya, AN 2-3 Kemang Pratama, Bekasi, Jabar 17116
DP Coordinator Felix Foe Hakim
MYP Coordinator Agnes Budiastuti
PYP Coordinator Early Hapsari
Languages English
T: +62 21 8240 3878
W: www.sekolahvictoryplus-bks.sch.id

Sinarmas World Academy
Jl TM Pahlawan Seribu, CBD Lot XV, BSD City, Tangerang, Banten 15322
DP Coordinator Malcolm Drew
MYP Coordinator Christopher Hayden
Languages English
T: +62 21 5316 1400
W: www.swa-jkt.com

Singapore Intercultural School Bona Vista
Jl. Bona Vista Raya, Lebak Bulus, Jakarta Selatan, DKI 12440
DP Coordinator George Thomas
Languages English
T: +62 21 759 14414
W: www.sisschools.org/sisbv

Singapore School, Pantai Indah Kapuk
Jl. Mandara Indah 4, Pantai Indah Kapuk, Jakarta Utara, DKI 14460
DP Coordinator Callie Shyong
T: +62 21 588 3835
W: www.sis-pik.com

SIS Kelapa Gading
Jl. Pegangsaan Dua No.83, Kelapa Gading, Jakarta Utara, DKI 14250
DP Coordinator Alfredo Iii Garcia
Languages English
T: +62 21 460 8888
W: www.sis-kg.com

SIS Medan
Royal Sumatra Complex, Jl. Letjen Jamin Ginting Km. 8,5, Medan, Sumut
DP Coordinator Manish Shrivastava
Languages English
T: +62 61 836 2880
W: www.sis-medan.com

Stamford School, Bandung
Allegro Altura Complex, Jalan Citra Green, Dago, Bandung, Jabar 40142
DP Coordinator Jaya Gopalakrishnan
Languages English, Indonesian
T: +62 22 251 5255
W: stamford.sch.id

Stella Maris School
Sektor 8A, Vatican Cluster, Gading Serpong, Tangerang, Banten 15310
DP Coordinator Magda Dolly Ulaan
Languages English
T: +62 21 54 212 999
W: www.stellamaris.co.id

Surabaya Intercultural School
Citra Raya, Lakarsantri, Tromol Pos 2/SBDK, Surabaya, Jatim 60225
PYP Coordinator Tylene Desfosses
Languages English
T: +62 31 741 4300
W: sis.sch.id

The Intercultural School of Bogor
Jalan Papandayan No 7, Bogor, Jabar 16151
PYP Coordinator Nicolene Du Preez
Languages English
T: +62 251 8324 360
W: www.isbogor.org

Tunas Muda School Kedoya
Jl Angsana Raya D8/2, Taman Kedoya Baru, Jakarta Barat, DKI 11520
PYP Coordinator Meilianny Jap
Languages English
T: +62 21 581 8766
W: www.sekolahtunasmuda.com

Tunas Muda School Meruya
Jl. Meruya Utara No. 71, Kembangan, Jakarta Barat, DKI 11620
DP Coordinator Hendra Rusli
MYP Coordinator Arniel Defita
PYP Coordinator Maria Tiffany Thee
Languages English, Bahasa Indonesia
T: +62 (0)21 587 0329
W: www.tunasmuda.sch.id

Tzu Chi School, Pantai Indah Kapuk
Jl. Pantai Indah Kapuk Boulevard, Tzu Chi Centre, Kelurahan Kamal Muara, Kecamatan Penjaringan, Jakarta Utara, DKI 14470
DP Coordinator Kate Siaron
MYP Coordinator Patrick O Sullivan
Languages English
T: +62 21 5055 6668
W: tzuchi.sch.id

Yogyakarta Independent School
Jl. Tegal Mlati No. 1, Jombor Lor, Sinduadi, Mlati, Sleman, Yogyakarta, DIY 55284
DP Coordinator Elia Ekanindita
MYP Coordinator Kencana Candra
PYP Coordinator Karin Albers
Languages English
T: +62 822 4104 4242
W: www.yis-edu.org

YPJ School Kuala Kencana
Jalan Irian Jaya Barat No.1, Kuala Kencana, Timika, Papua 99910
PYP Coordinator Vini Quamilla
Languages English
W: ypj.sch.id

YPJ School Tembagapura
Jalan Raya Tembagapura No. 605, PO Box 14, Tembagapura, Papua 99910
PYP Coordinator Mary Bigwood
Languages Indonesian
W: ypj.sch.id

JAPAN

Abroad International School – Osaka
Being Yotsubashi Bldg 6F, 1-3-2 Kitahorie, Nishi-ku, Osaka, Kansai 550-0014
PYP Coordinator Ugur Yaldiz
Languages English
T: +81 (0)6 6535 0500
W: osaka.abroadschools.jp

AICJ Junior & Senior High School
2-33-16 Gion, Asaminami-ku, Hiroshima, Chugoku 731-0138
DP Coordinator Andrew Brown
Languages English
T: +81 82 832 5037
W: www.aicj.ed.jp

AIE International High School
1-48 Hama, Awaji, Hyogo, Kansai 656-2304
DP Coordinator Naoko Watanabe
Languages English
T: +81 799 74 0020
W: www.aie.ed.jp

Aoba-Japan Bilingual Preschool – Waseda Campus
1-14-8 Takadano-baba, Shinjuku-ku, Tokyo, Kanto 169-0075
PYP Coordinator Jenny Yan
Languages English, Japanese
T: +81 3 6385 2818
W: aoba-bilingual.jp/waseda

AOBA-JAPAN INTERNATIONAL SCHOOL
7-5-1 Hikarigaoka, Nerima-ku, Tokyo, Kanto 179-0072
DP Coordinator Glenn Connelly
MYP Coordinator Lisa de Pierres
PYP Coordinator Harukako Ikeura
Languages English
T: +81 3 4578 8832
E: hikarigaoka@aobajapan.jp
W: www.japaninternationalschool.com
See full details on page 298

Aoba-Japan International School JCQ Bilingual Preschool
Harumi Triton West 2f, 1-8-2 Harumi, Chuo-Ku, Tokyo, Kanto 104-0053
PYP Coordinator Haruko Isobe
Languages English, Japanese
T: +81 3 6228 1811
W: www.jcq.jp

Canadian Academy
4-1 Koyo-Cho Naka, Higashinada-ku, Kobe, Hyogo, Kansai 658-0032
DP Coordinator Greg River
MYP Coordinator Sarah Tudge
PYP Coordinator Trevor Rehel
Languages English
T: +81 78 857 0100
W: www.canacad.ac.jp

Canadian International School Tokyo
5-8-20 Kitashinagawa, Shinagawa-ku, Tokyo, Kanto 141-0001
PYP Coordinator Danna Bergantine
Languages English
T: +81 3 5793 1392
W: www.cisjapan.net

Chiyoda Jogakuen Senior High School
Chiyoda-ku, Tokyo, Kanto 102-0081
DP Coordinator Ryo Sakamoto
Languages English, Japanese
T: +81 3 3263 6551
W: www.chiyoda-j.ac.jp

Deutsche Schule Kobe International (DSKI)
3-2-8 Koyochonaka, Higashinada-ku, Kobe, Hyogo, Kansai 658-0032
PYP Coordinator Alex Inman
Languages English
T: +81 78 857 9777
W: www.dskobe.org

Doshisha International Academy Elementary School
7-31-1 Kizugawa-dai, Kizugawa, Kyoto, Kansai 619-0225
PYP Coordinator Tatsuhiko Aratani
Languages English
T: +81 774 71 0810
W: www.dia.doshisha.ac.jp/?page_id=5

Doshisha International School, Kyoto
7-31-1 Kizugawa-dai, Kizugawa, Kyoto, Kansai 619-0225
DP Coordinator Wendy Bigler
PYP Coordinator Sue Loafmann
Languages English
T: +81 774 71 0810
W: www.diskyoto.com

Eisugakkan School
980-1, Hikino-cho, Fukuyama, Hiroshima, Chugoku 721-8502
DP Coordinator Dennis Kelly
Languages English
T: +81 84 941 4115
W: www.eisu-ejs.ac.jp

Enishi International School
2-12-32 Kikui Nishi Ward, Nagoya, Aichi 451-0044
PYP Coordinator Mahmut Kaya
Languages English, Japanese
T: +81(0)52 581 0700
W: www.enishi.ac.jp

Fukuoka Daiichi High School
22-1 Tamagawa cho, Minami-ku, Fukuoka, Kyushu 815-0037
DP Coordinator Taiyo Rious
Languages English, Japanese
T: +81 9 2541 0165
W: f.f-parama.ed.jp

Fukuoka International School
3-18-50 Momochi, Sawara-ku, Fukuoka, Kyushu 814-0006
DP Coordinator Santiago Rey
PYP Coordinator Vincent Lehane
Languages English
T: +81 92 841 7601
W: www.fis.ed.jp

Gunma Kokusai Academy
1361-4 Uchigashima-cho, Ota, Gunma, Kanto 373-0813
DP Coordinator James Taylor
Languages English
T: +81 276 47 7711
W: www.gka.jp

Hiroshima International School
3-49-1 Kurakake, Asakita-Ku, Hiroshima, Chugoku 739-1743
DP Coordinator Annie Levasseur
MYP Coordinator Alexandra Omukova
PYP Coordinator Marisa Villarreal
Languages English
T: +81 82 843 4111
W: www.hiroshima-is.ac.jp

Horizon Japan International School
1-38-27 Higashi Terai, Tsurumi-ku, Yokohama, Kanagawa, Kanto 230-0077
DP Coordinator Gamze Abis
Languages English
T: +81 45 584 1945
W: www.horizon.ac.jp

Hosei University Kokusai High School
1-13-1 KIshiya, Tsurumi-ku, Yokohama, Kanagawa, Kanto 230-0078
DP Coordinator Andrew Gibbs
Languages English
T: +81 45 571 4482
W: hosei.ac.jp/general/jyoshi

India International School in Japan
1-20-20, Ojima, Koto-Ku -135-0004, Tokyo, Kanto 136-0072
DP Coordinator Suresh Bhakta Shrestha
Languages English
T: +81 03 3635 7850
W: www.iisjapan.com

International School of Nagano
1-2-2 Minami-Matsumoto, Matsumoto, Nagano, Chubu 390-0832
PYP Coordinator Taeko Ogasawara
Languages English
T: +81 26 387 5971
W: isnedu.org

K. International School Tokyo
1-5-15 Shirakawa, Koto-ku, Tokyo, Kanto 135-0021
DP Coordinator Hiro Komaki
MYP Coordinator Robert White
PYP Coordinator Oliver Sullivan
Languages English
T: +81 3 3642 9993
W: www.kist.ed.jp

Kaichi Nihonbashi Gakuen
7-6 Nihonbashi Bakurocho 2-chome, Chuo-ku, Tokyo, Kanto 103-8384
DP Coordinator Kenji Kondo
MYP Coordinator Jonathan Anzai
Languages English, Japanese
T: +81 3 3662 2507
W: www.kng.ed.jp

Kaichi-Nozomi Elementary School
3400 Tutudo Aza Suwa, Tsukubamirai, Ibaraki, Kanto 300-2435
PYP Coordinator Katsurou Kitamura
Languages English, Japanese
T: +81 0297 38 6000
W: www.kaichigakuen.ed.jp/nozomi

Kanagawa Prefectural Yokohama Senior High School of International Studies
1-731 Mutsukawa, Minami-ku, Yokohama, Kanagawa 232-0066
DP Coordinator Nobuho Ukita
Languages English, Japanese
T: +81 45 721 1434
W: yokohamakokusai-h.pen-kanagawa.ed.jp

Kansai International Academy
4-1-31 Shinzaike-Minamimachi, Nada-ku, Kobe, Hyogo, Kansai 657-0864
PYP Coordinator Yoko Morisaki
Languages English, Japanese
T: +81 78 882 6680
W: www.kis-g.jp

Katoh Gakuen Gyoshu Junior & Senior High School
1361-1 Nakamiyo Okanomiya, Numazu, Shizuoka, Chubu 410-0011
DP Coordinator Craig Sutton
MYP Coordinator Gay-Ann Bagotchay
Languages English, Japanese
T: +81 55 924 3322
W: www.katoh-net.ac.jp/gyoshuhs

Kids Tairiku Yokohama Nakagawa
1-19-23 Nakagawa, Tsuzuki-Ku, Yokohama, Kanagawa, Kanto 224-0001
PYP Coordinator Chikako Matsushima
Languages English, Japanese
T: +81 45 914 3770
W: www.kidstairiku.jp/school/nakagawa

Kofu Nishi High School
Shimoiida 4-1-1, Kofu, Yamanashi, Chubu 400-0064
DP Coordinator Yasuko Nozaki
Languages English, Japanese
T: +81 (0)55 228 5161
W: www.nishi.kai.ed.jp

Korea International School
2-13-35 Toyokawa, Ibaraki, Osaka, Kansai 567-0057
DP Coordinator Taeeun Kim
Languages English
T: +81 72 643 4200
W: www.kiskorea.ed.jp

Kyoto International School
252 Shinhigashidoin-cho, Sakyo-ku, Kyoto, Kansai 606-8355
PYP Coordinator Taylor Boyd
Languages English
T: +81 75 451 1022
W: www.kyotointernationalschool.org

Linden Hall High School
3-10-1 Futsukaichi-kita, Chikushino, Fukuoka, Kyushu 818-0056
DP Coordinator Fumiko Nelson
Languages English
T: +81 92 929 4558
W: www.lindenhall.ed.jp

Machida Kobato Kindergarten/ Gakkouhoujin Kanzou Gakuen
2904 Hon-Machida, Machida, Tokyo, Kanto 194-0032
PYP Coordinator Toshiko Ishikawa
Languages Japanese
T: +81 42 723 1494
W: www.m-kobato.ed.jp

Marist Brothers International School
1-2-1 Chimori-Cho, Suma-Ku, Kobe, Hyogo, Kansai 654-0072
DP Coordinator Brian Munro
Languages English
T: +81 78 732 6266
W: www.marist.ac.jp

Matsumoto Kokusai High School
3-6-25 Muraimachi minami, Matsumoto, Nagano, Chubu 399-0036
DP Coordinator Sjaak Mintjens
Languages English, Japanese
T: +81 263 88 0033
W: m-kokusai.ac.jp

Meikei High School
1-1 Inarimae, Tsukuba, Ibaraki, Kanto 305-8502
DP Coordinator Hideaki Matsuzaki
Languages English, Japanese
T: +81 29 851 6611
W: www.meikei.ac.jp

Miura Gakuen High School
3-80 Kinugasa-sakae, Yokosuka, Kanagawa 238-0031
DP Coordinator Kosaku Tanaka
Languages English, Japanese
T: +81 46 852 0284
W: miura.ed.jp

Mizuho School
3-2-25, Shakujiidai, Nerima-ku, Tokyo, Kanto 177-0045
PYP Coordinator Kiyohiko Motohashi
Languages English
T: +81 3 5372 1525
W: www.mizuho-edu.co.jp

Nagoya International Junior and Senior High School
1-16, Hiroji-Honmachi, Showa-Ku, Nagoya, Aichi, Chubu 466-0841
DP Coordinator Christopher Yap
Languages English
T: +81 52 858 2200
W: www.nihs.ed.jp

Nagoya International School
2686 Minamihara, Nakashidami, Moriyama-ku, Nagoya, Aichi, Chubu 463-0002
DP Coordinator Paul Moody
MYP Coordinator Marika Farrell
PYP Coordinator Holly Johnson
Languages English
T: +81 52 736 2025
W: www.nisjapan.net

Okayama University of Science High School
Daiomachi No. 1, Kita-ku, Okayama, Chugoku 700-0005
DP Coordinator Akemi Morioka
Languages English, Japanese
T: +81 (0)86 256 8511
W: okayama.ridaifu.net

Okinawa International School
143 Tamagusuku Fusato, Nanjo City, Okinawa, Kyushu 901-0611
MYP Coordinator Monina Liza Mendez
PYP Coordinator Sayuri Tatetsu
Languages English, Japanese
T: +81 (0)98 948 7711
W: www.ois-edu.com

Osaka International School
4-4-16 Onohara Nishi, Minoh, Osaka, Kansai 562-0032
DP Coordinator Stephen Frater
MYP Coordinator Kurt Mecklem
PYP Coordinator Ingela Summerton
Languages English
T: +81 72 727 5050
W: www.senri.ed.jp

Osaka Jogakuin Senior High School
2-26-54 Tamatsukuri, Chuo-ku, Osaka, Kansai 540-0004
DP Coordinator Nobumasa Kagimura
Languages English, Japanese
T: +81 6 6761 4113
W: www.osaka-jogakuin.ed.jp

Osaka YMCA International School
6-7-34 Nakatsu, Kita-ku, Osaka, Kansai 531-0071
PYP Coordinator Brendan O'Leary
Languages English
T: +81 6 6345 1661
W: www.oyis.org

RITSUMEIKAN UJI JUNIOR AND SENIOR HIGH SCHOOL
33-1 Hachikenyadani, Hirono-cho, Uji, Kyoto, Kansai 611-0031
DP Coordinator Marcelo Schwarz
Languages English, Japanese (ibdp In English)
T: +81 774 41 3000
E: ib-info@ujc.ritsumei.ac.jp
W: www.ujc.ritsumei.ac.jp/ujc_e/
See full details on page 395

Saint Maur International School
83 Yamate-cho, Naka-ku, Yokohama, Kanagawa, Kanto 231-8654
DP Coordinator Timothy Matsumoto
Languages English
T: +81 45 641 5751
W: www.stmaur.ac.jp

Sapporo Kaisei Secondary School
1-1 Kita 22 Higashi 21 Higashiku, Sapporo, Hokkaido 065-8558
DP Coordinator Satoshi Nishimura
MYP Coordinator Hiroshi Ohnishi
Languages English
T: +81 11 788 6987
W: www.kaisei-s.sapporo-c.ed.jp

Seisen International School
1-12-15 Yoga, Setagaya-ku, Tokyo, Kanto 158-0097
DP Coordinator James Hatch
PYP Coordinator Serrin Smyth
Languages English
T: +81 3 3704 2661
W: www.seisen.com

SENDAI IKUEI GAKUEN
2-4-1 Miyagino, Miyagino-ku, Sendai, Miyagi, Tohoku 983-0045
DP Coordinator Anthony Sweeney
MYP Coordinator Kerry Winter
Languages English, Japanese
T: +81 22 256 4141
E: t.sweeney@i-lion.org
W: sendaiikuei-english.jp
See full details on page 408

SENIOR HIGH SCHOOL AT SAKADO, UNIVERSITY OF TSUKUBA
1-24-1 Chiyoda, Sakado, Saitama, Kanto 350-0214
DP Coordinator Regina Ver-Santos
Languages English, Japanese
T: +81 49 281 1541
E:
W: www.sakado-s.tsukuba.ac.jp
See full details on page 409

Shiga Prefectural Torahime High School
2410 Miyabe-cho, Nagahama, Shiga, Kansai 529-0012
DP Coordinator Mariko Tomioka
Languages English, Japanese
T: +81 (0)749 73 3055
W: www.torahime-h.shiga-ec.ed.jp

Shinagawa International School
4-8-8 Higashishinagawa, Shinagawa, Tokyo, Kanto 140-0002
PYP Coordinator Hakan Abis
Languages English
T: +81 3 6433 1531
W: sistokyo.jp

Shogaku Gakuen Educational Foundation
747 Kokuba, Naha, Okinawa, Kyushu 902-0075
DP Coordinator Noriko Bousckri
Languages English
T: +81 98 832 1767
W: www.okisho.ed.jp/en

Shohei Junior and Senior High School
851 Shimono, Sugito, Saitama, Kanto 345-0044
MYP Coordinator Kohei Maeda
Languages English
T: +81 48 034 3381
W: www.shohei.sugito.saitama.jp/contents/jhs

Shukoh Middle School
Sendai Ikuei Gakuen, 241 Miyagino, Miyagino-ku, Sendai, Miyagi, Tohoku 985-0853
MYP Coordinator Kerry Winter
Languages English, Japanese
T: +81 22 256 4141
W: www.sendaiikuei.ed.jp/shukoh

St. Joseph's Primary School
11-1 HigashiTerao-Kitadai, Tsurumi-ku, Yokohama, Kanagawa, Kanto 230-0016
PYP Coordinator Mami Saito
Languages English, Japanese
T: +81 45 581 8808
W: www.st-joseph.ac.jp/primary

St. Mary's International School
1-6-19 Seta, Setagaya Ku, Tokyo, Kanto 158-8668
DP Coordinator Kimberly Fradale
Languages English
T: +81 3 3709 3411
W: www.smis.ac.jp

Summerhill International School
2-13-8 Moto-Azabu, Minato-ku, Tokyo, Kanto 106-0046
PYP Coordinator Anita Sutton
Languages English, Japanese
T: +81 3 3453 0811
W: www.summerhill.jp

Sunnyside International School
Iwai 4-10-25, Gifu, Chubu 501-3101
PYP Coordinator Mint Chau
Languages English, Japanese
T: +81 58 241 1000
W: www.sunnyside-international.jp

Tamagawa Academy K-12 & University
6-1-1 Tamagawa Gakuen, Machida, Tokyo, Kanto 194-8610
DP Coordinator Angela Rasmussen
MYP Coordinator Aidan Leach
Languages English
T: +81 42 739 8111
W: www.tamagawa.jp/en

Tohoku International School
7-101-1 Yakata, Izumi-ku, Sendai, Miyagi, Tohoku 981-3214
PYP Coordinator Hiroko Yoshida
Languages English
T: +81 22 348 2468
W: www.tisweb.net

Tokai Gakuen High School
2-901 Nakahira Tenpaku-ku, Nagoya, Aichi, Chubu 468-0014
DP Coordinator Trevor Wilson
Languages English, Japanese
T: +81 52 801 6222
W: tokaigakuen.ed.jp

Tokyo Gakugei University International Secondary School
5-22-1 Higashi-Oizumi, Nerima-ku, Tokyo, Kanto 178-0063
DP Coordinator Maki Komatsu
MYP Coordinator Shinichi Amemiya
Languages English, Japanese
T: +81 3 5905 1326
W: www.iss.oizumi.u-gakugei.ac.jp

Tokyo International School
3-4-22 Mita, Minato-Ku, Tokyo, Kanto 108-0073
MYP Coordinator Catherine Dick
PYP Coordinator Josef Kaufhold
Languages English
T: +81 3 5484 1160
W: www.tokyois.com

TOKYO METROPOLITAN KOKUSAI HIGH SCHOOL
2-19-59 Komaba, Meguro-ku, Tokyo, Kanto 153-0041
DP Coordinator Kazumasa Aoki
Languages English
T: +81 3 3468 6811
E: ibdp1@kokusai-h.metro.tokyo.jp
W: www.kokusai-h.metro.tokyo.jp

See full details on page 432

Tsukuba International School
Kamigo 7846-1, Tsukuba, Ibaraki, Kanto 300-2645
DP Coordinator Peter Congreve
MYP Coordinator Vincent Jan Africa
PYP Coordinator Ian Woollard
Languages English
T: +81 29 886 5447
W: www.tis.ac.jp

UPBEAT International School – Atsuta Campus
2-3-18, Hachiban, Atasuta, Nagoya, Aichi, Chubu
PYP Coordinator Astrid Manosalva
Languages English, Japanese
T: +81 (0)52 661 3155
W: www.upbeatjapan.com

UWC ISAK Japan
5827-136 Nagakura, Karuizawa-machi, Kitasaku-gun, Nagano, Chubu 389-0111
DP Coordinator Yaling Chien
Languages English
T: +81 26 746 8623
W: uwcisak.jp

Willowbrook International School
2-14-28 Moto-azabu, Minato-ku, Tokyo, Kanto 106-0046
PYP Coordinator Louise Boddy
Languages English
T: +81 3 3449 9030
W: www.willowbrookschool.com

Yamanashi Gakuin School
13-3-1, Sakaori, Kofu, Yamanashi, Chubu 400-0805
DP Coordinator Priw-Prae Litticharoenporn
PYP Coordinator Hidetoshi Horikawa
Languages English
T: +81 55 224 1200
W: www.ygk.ed.jp

Yokohama International School
258 Yamate-cho, Naka-ku, Yokohama, Kanagawa, Kanto 231-0862
DP Coordinator Mark Redlich
MYP Coordinator Rebekah Madrid
PYP Coordinator Shanel Catasti
Languages English
T: +81 45 622 0084
W: www.yis.ac.jp

LAOS

VIENTIANE INTERNATIONAL SCHOOL
PO Box 3180, Ban Saphanthong Tai, Vientiane
DP Coordinator Alistair Nelson
MYP Coordinator Mike McMillan
PYP Coordinator Rose Golds
Languages English
T: +856 21 486001
E: contact@vislao.com; admissions@vislao.com
W: www.vislao.com

See full details on page 440

MALAYSIA

Cempaka International School
No 19, Jalan Setiabakti 1, Damansara Heights, Kuala Lumpur
DP Coordinator Nik Zakiah Nik Kar
Languages English
T: +60 3 2094 0623
W: www.cempaka.edu.my

EtonHouse Malaysia International School
No. 9 Persiaran Stonor, Kuala Lumpur 50450
PYP Coordinator Eryn Sherman
Languages English
T: +60 3 2141 3301/02
W: etonhouse.edu.my

Excelsior International School
No. 8, Jalan Purnama, Bandar Seri Alam, Masai 81750
DP Coordinator Joe Demetro
Languages English
T: +60 7 888 999
W: www.eis.edu.my

FAIRVIEW INTERNATIONAL SCHOOL
Lot 4178, Jalan 1/27D, Section 6, Wangsa Maju, Kuala Lumpur 53300
DP Coordinator Ms. Andi Elisa
MYP Coordinator Dr. Evan Hui See Chin
PYP Coordinator Ms. Elaine Lam
Languages English, Mandarin
T: +60 3 4142 0888
E: enquiries@fairview.edu.my
W: www.fairview.edu.my

See full details on page 333

FAIRVIEW INTERNATIONAL SCHOOL IPOH
Hala Lapangan Suria Medan Lapangan, Suria, Ipoh, Perak 31350
PYP Coordinator Choon Pei Chin
Languages English
W: www.fairview.edu.my

FAIRVIEW INTERNATIONAL SCHOOL JOHOR
Kompleks Mutiara Johor Land, Jalan Bukit Mutiara, Bandar Dato' Onn, Johor Bahru 88100
MYP Coordinator Shaamini Devi Bala Krishnan
PYP Coordinator Ariel Schatenstein
Languages English
T: +60 7 358 5385
W: www.fairview.edu.my

FAIRVIEW INTERNATIONAL SCHOOL PENANG
Tingkat Bukit Jambul 1, Bayan Lepas, Penang 11900
MYP Coordinator Valerynne Yann Lyn Chang
PYP Coordinator Samantha Leong
Languages English
T: +60 4 640 6633
W: www.fairview.edu.my

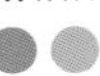

FAIRVIEW INTERNATIONAL SCHOOL SUBANG
2A, Jalan TP 2, Sime UEP Industrial Park, Subbing Jaya, Selangor 47600
MYP Coordinator Andrew Webber
PYP Coordinator Ranjana Manuel
Languages English
T: +60 3 8023 7777
W: www.fairview.edu.my

IGB INTERNATIONAL SCHOOL
Jalan Sierramas Utama, Sungai Buloh, Kuala Lumpur, Selangor 47000
CP Coordinator Magnus Drechsler
DP Coordinator Magnus Drechsler
MYP Coordinator Darryl Harding
PYP Coordinator Aga Chojnacka
Languages English
T: +60 3 6145 4688
E: enquiries@igbis.edu.my
W: www.igbis.edu.my

See full details on page 348

Kolej MARA Banting
Bukit Changgang, Banting, Selangor 42700
DP Coordinator Rozana Mohd Ikram
Languages English
T: +60 3 3149 1318
W: www.kmb.edu.my

Kolej MARA Seremban
Jalan Aminuddin Baki, Negeri Sembilan, Seremban 70100
DP Coordinator Rudi Hakimi Mohd Nasrumi
Languages English
T: +60 6 7622372/7622373
W: www.kmseremban.edu.my

Kolej Tunku Kurshiah
Kompleks Pendidikan Nilai, Bandar Enstek, Seremban, Negeri Sembilan 71760
DP Coordinator Hafitah Baharuddin
MYP Coordinator Ahmad Bidin
Languages English
T: +60 6 7979800
W: www.tkc.edu.my

Malay College Kuala Kangsar
Jalan Tun Abdul Razak, Kuala Kangsar 33000
DP Coordinator Norsafaliza Ibrahim
MYP Coordinator Azlinda Muda
Languages English
T: +60 5 7761400
W: www.mckk.edu.my

Marlborough College Malaysia
Jalan Marlborough, Nusajaya, Johor 79200
DP Coordinator Kenton Tomlinson
Languages English
T: +60 7 560 2200
W: www.marlboroughcollege.my

Mont'Kiara International School
22 Jalan Kiara, Mont'Kiara, Kuala Lumpur 50480
DP Coordinator Claudia Fidalgo
PYP Coordinator Dawn Brews
Languages English
T: +60 3 2093 8604
W: www.mkis.edu.my

MRSM Balik Pulau (Mara Junior Science College)
Jalan Pondok Upeh, Kampung Shee Tan, Balik Pulau, Pulau Pinang 11000
MYP Coordinator Norfairizam Nordin
Languages English
T: +60 4 8669499
W: bpulau.mrsm.edu.my

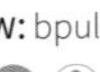

MRSM Tun Dr Ismail, Pontian

Jalan Benut Jelutong, Pontian, Johor 82100
MYP Coordinator Rosmurni Abdul Aziz
Languages English
T: +60 7 6933744
W: mrsmpontian.edu.my

MRSM Tun Mohammad Fuad Stephens Sandakan

Education Hub, Batu 10, Jalan Sungai Batang, Sandakan, Sabah 90000
MYP Coordinator Mohd Ali Mohd Yusof
Languages English
T: +60 8 9225609
W: tmfs.mrsm.edu.my/cms

Nexus International School Malaysia

No 1 Jalan Diplomatik 3/6, Presint 15, Putrajaya 62050
DP Coordinator Amanda O'Hara
Languages English
T: +60 3 8889 3868
W: www.nexus.edu.my

ROYAL MILITARY COLLEGE

Kem Perdana Sungai Besi, Kuala Lumpur 57000
DP Coordinator Lee Ling Low
Languages English
T: +60 3 89465402
E: mtdibdp@rmc.edu.my

See full details on page 396

Sekolah Menengah Kebangsaan Dato' Sheikh Ahmad

Jalan Besar Arau, Arau 02600
MYP Coordinator Shaharom Bakar
Languages English
T: +60 4 9861239
W: www.smkdsaperlis.edu.my

Sekolah Menengah Kebangsaan Sultanah Bahiyah

Lebuhraya Sultanah Bahiyah, Alor Star 05350
MYP Coordinator Noor Afiza Salleh
Languages English
T: +60 4 7331531
W: www.smksultanahbahiyah.edu.my

SMK Pantai, W.P Labuan

Jalan Pohon Batu, Labuan 87027
MYP Coordinator Edora Ellias
Languages English
T: +60 8 7410863
W: www.smkpantaiwpl.webs.com

SMK Putrajaya Presint 9(2)

Jalan P9A, Presint 9, Wilayah Persekutuan, Putrajaya 62250
MYP Coordinator Roslan Hassan
Languages English
T: +60 3 8881 1207
W: www.smkpp92.com

SMK Seri Tualang

28000 Temerloh, Pahang
MYP Coordinator Fazliyaton Isa
Languages English
T: +60 9 290 1061
W: www.smkseritualang.com

SMK Sungai Tapang

KM 13, Jalan Penrissen, Kuching 93250
MYP Coordinator Angela Yan Yan Bong
Languages English
T: +60 8 2612851
W: www.smksungaitapang.edu.my

SMKA Sheikh Abdul Malek

, Kuala Terengganu 20400
MYP Coordinator Huzzaimah Basir
Languages English
T: +60 96235155
W: www.shams.edu.my

SMS Tengku Muhammad Faris Petra

Taman Orkid, Kota Bharu, 16100 Pengkalan Chepa
MYP Coordinator Muhammad Daud
T: +60 9 773 8277
W: www.smstmfp.edu.my

Sri KDU International School

No. 3, Jalan Teknologi 2/1, Kota Damansara, Daerah Petaling, Selangor Darul Ehsan 47810
DP Coordinator Edward Baxter
Languages English
T: +60 3 6145 3888
W: www.srikdu.edu.my

St. Joseph's Institution International School Malaysia (Tropicana PJ Campus)

No. 1, Jalan PJU 3/13, Petaling Jaya, Kuala Lumpur, Selangor Darul Ehsan 47100
DP Coordinator Maureen Fitzgerald
Languages English
T: +603 8605 3605
W: www.sji-international.edu.my

Stella Maris Medan Damansara

7 Lorong Setiabistari, 2 Bukit Damansara, Kuala Lumpur, Wilayah Persekutuan 50490
DP Coordinator Madhu Singh
Languages English
T: +603 20830025
W: stellamaris.edu.my/home

Sunway International School, Bandar Sunway

No. 3, Jalan Universiti, Bandar Sunway, Selangor Darul Ehsan 47500
DP Coordinator Mark Milberg
T: +603 7491 8070
W: sis.sunway.edu.my

Sunway International School, Sunway Iskandar

Jalan Persiaran Medini 3, Sunway Iskandar, Johor 79250
DP Coordinator Birute Richardson
T: +60 7 533 8070
W: sis.sunway.edu.my

THE INTERNATIONAL SCHOOL OF KUALA LUMPUR (ISKL)

2, Lorong Kelab Polo Di Raja, 55000 Kuala Lumpur
DP Coordinator Mr Michael Ortiz, MA, BA
Languages English
T: +60 3 4813 5000
E: admissions@iskl.edu.my
W: www.iskl.edu.my

See full details on page 430

THE INTERNATIONAL SCHOOL OF PENANG (UPLANDS)

Jalan Sungai Satu, Batu Feringgi, 11100 Penang
DP Coordinator Geneva Robinson
PYP Coordinator Zita Joyce
Languages English
T: +604 8819 777
E: info@uplands.org
W: www.uplands.org

See full details on page 431

UCSI International School

1 Persiaran UCSI International School, Port Dickson, Negeri Sembalan 71010
DP Coordinator Anita Wijaya
MYP Coordinator Peter Vinoj
PYP Coordinator Jamie Kistler
Languages English
T: +60 6653 6888
W: www.uis.edu.my

MONGOLIA

International School of Ulaanbaatar

PO Box 36/10, Khan-Uul District 15th Horoo, 4 Seasons Garden, Ulaanbaatar-36 17032
DP Coordinator Torie Leinbach
MYP Coordinator Jonathan Armitage
PYP Coordinator David Hayden
Languages English
T: +976 70160010
W: www.isumongolia.edu.mn

Shine Ue School

UNESCO St 12, Sukhbaatar District, Ulaanbaatar 14220
DP Coordinator Khandjav Terbish
Languages English
T: +976 7012 8044
W: shineue.edu.mn

The English School of Mongolia

Bayanzurkh District, 1 Khoroo, Ulaanbaatar 13380
DP Coordinator Michael Depear
Languages English
T: +976 70 15 40 15
W: www.esm.edu.mn

MYANMAR

Bahan International Science Academy

No.25, Po Sein Road, Bahan Township, Yangon
DP Coordinator Veerle Hisken
Languages English
T: +95 1 548452
W: www.bfi-edu.com

The International School Yangon

20 Shwe Taungyar Street, Bahan Township, Yangon 11181
DP Coordinator Steven Powers
Languages English
T: +95 1 512793/94/95
W: www.isyedu.org

NEPAL

Genius School Lalitpur

Ringroad, Mahalaxmisthan, Lalitpur
PYP Coordinator Prakash Laxmi Joshi
Languages English
T: +977 1 5170746
W: www.geniusschool.edu.np

NEPAL

Premier International School
Khumaltar Height, Satdobato, Lalitpur
MYP Coordinator Pravina Thapa
PYP Coordinator Pravina Thapa
Languages English, Nepali
T: +977 1 552 8032
W: www.premier.edu.np

Ullens School
Khumaltar-5, Lalipur, Post Box Number 8975, EPC 1477, Kathmandu
DP Coordinator Raisa Pandey
Languages English
T: +977 1 5230824
W: www.ullens.edu.np

NEW ZEALAND

ACG Senior College
66 Lorne Street, Auckland 1141
DP Coordinator Alex Marshall
Languages English
T: +64 9 3074 474
W: www.acgedu.com/nz/senior

Ashburton Borough School
Winter St, Ashburton 7700
PYP Coordinator Dewdene Percy
T: +64 3 307 8529
W: ashborough.school.nz

Auckland International College
37 Heaphy Street, Blockhouse Bay, Auckland 0600
DP Coordinator Maureen Forsyth
Languages English
T: +64 9 309 4480
W: www.aic.ac.nz

Auckland Normal Intermediate School
Poronui Street, Mt Eden, Auckland 1024
PYP Coordinator Shane Devery
Languages English
T: +64 96 301109
W: ani.school.nz

Bay of Islands International Academy
935 Purerua Road, Kerikeri, Northland 0294
PYP Coordinator Jennifer Grant
Languages English
T: +64 9 407 9749
W: www.boi.ac.nz

Berkley Normal Middle School
26 Berkley Avenue, Hamilton, Waikato 3216
PYP Coordinator Beth Germaine
Languages English
T: +64 7856 6537
W: www.berkley.school.nz

Bucklands Beach Intermediate School
247 Bucklands Beach Road, Bucklands Beach, Auckland 2012
PYP Coordinator Ed Roper
Languages English
T: +64 9 534 2896
W: www.bbi.school.nz

Chilton Saint James School
PO Box 30090, Lower Hutt 5040
PYP Coordinator Michelle Hughes
Languages English
T: +64 4 566 4089
W: www.chilton.school.nz

Diocesan School for Girls
Clyde Street, Epsom, Auckland 1051
DP Coordinator Susan Marriott
PYP Coordinator Nicole Lewis
Languages English
T: +64 9 520 0221
W: www.diocesan.school.nz

Glendowie Primary School
217 Riddell Road, Glendowie, Auckland 1071
PYP Coordinator Christine Matos
Languages English
T: +64 9 575 7374
W: www.glendowieprimary.school.nz

Hingaia Peninsula School
171 Hingaia Road, Karaka, Auckland 2580
PYP Coordinator Jacqui Stenson
Languages English
T: +64 (0)9 299 3628
W: www.hingaiapeninsula.school.nz

John McGlashan College
2 Pilkington Street, Maori Hill, Dunedin 9010
DP Coordinator Brendan Porter
Languages English
T: +64 3 4676620
W: www.mcglashan.school.nz

KRISTIN SCHOOL
360 Albany Highway, Albany, Auckland 0752
DP Coordinator Mrs Debbie Dwyer
MYP Coordinator Mr John Osborne
PYP Coordinator Mr Rob Hutton
Languages English
T: +64 9 415 9566
E: admissions@kristin.school.nz
W: www.kristin.school.nz
See full details on page 366

Mt Pleasant Primary School
82 Major Hornbrook Road, Mt Pleasant, Christchurch 8081
PYP Coordinator Meagan Kelly
Languages English
T: +64 03 384 3994
W: www.mtpleasant.school.nz

Queen Margaret College
53 Hobson Street, PO Box 12274, Thorndon, Wellington 6011
DP Coordinator Holly Payne
MYP Coordinator Rahera Meinders
PYP Coordinator Jan Treeby
Languages English
T: +64 4 473 7160
W: www.qmc.school.nz

RANGITOTO COLLEGE
564 East Coast Road, Mairangi Bay, Auckland 0753
DP Coordinator Melanie Waugh
Languages English
T: +64 9 477 0150
E: info@rangitoto.school.nz
W: www.rangitoto.school.nz
See full details on page 392

Saint Kentigern Middle College and Senior College
130 Pakuranga Road, Pakuranga, Auckland 1021
DP Coordinator Philip Lee
Languages English
T: +64 9 577 0749
W: www.saintkentigern.com

SCOTS COLLEGE
PO Box 15064, Strathmore, Wellington 6243
DP Coordinator Mr Mike McKnight
MYP Coordinator Ms Kate Bondett
PYP Coordinator Mr Mike Hansen
Languages English
T: +64 4 388 0850
E: enrolments@scotscollege.school.nz
W: www.scotscollege.school.nz
See full details on page 401

Selwyn House School
PO Box 25049, 122 Merivale Lane, Christchurch 8014
PYP Coordinator Gregory Pearce
Languages English
T: +64 3 3557299
W: www.selwynhouse.school.nz

ST CUTHBERT'S COLLEGE
122 Market Road, Epsom, Auckland 1051
DP Coordinator Buino Vink
Languages English
T: +64 9 520 4159
E: admissions@stcuthberts.school.nz
W: www.stcuthberts.school.nz
See full details on page 422

ST MARGARET'S COLLEGE
12 Winchester Street, Merivale, Christchurch 8014
DP Coordinator Ms Beth Rowse
Languages English
T: +64 3 379 2000
E: enrol@stmargarets.school.nz
W: www.stmargarets.school.nz
See full details on page 423

St Mark's Church School
13 Dufferin Street, PO Box 7445, Wellington 6021
PYP Coordinator Angelee Jarrett
Languages English
T: +64 4 385 9489
W: www.st-marks.school.nz

St Peter's School, Cambridge
1716 Hamilton Road, Private Bag 884, Cambridge 3450
DP Coordinator Lee Hill
Languages English
T: +64 7 827 9899
W: www.stpeters.school.nz

Takapuna Grammar School
PO Box 33-1096, Takapuna, Auckland 0740
DP Coordinator Jack Chapman
Languages English
T: +64 94894167
W: www.takapuna.school.nz

Takapuna Normal Intermediate School
54B Taharoto Road, Takapuna, Auckland 1309
PYP Coordinator Alex Tiley
Languages English
T: +64 9 489 3940
W: www.tnis.school.nz

Te Hihi School
767 Linwood Rd, Karaka, Auckland
PYP Coordinator Kendall Crisp
Languages English
T: +64 9 292 7706
W: www.tehihi.school.nz

Waiheke Primary School
26 Seaview Road, Waiheke Island, Ostend 1971
PYP Coordinator Kate Ernst
Languages English
T: +64 9 372 2006
W: www.waiheke.school.nz

PAKISTAN

Angels International College
Faisal Town, Near Faisal Valley, West Canal Road, Faisalabad, Punjab 38000
DP Coordinator Khawaja Haris Abbas
MYP Coordinator Muhammad Imran Shahid
PYP Coordinator Sabahat Tatari
Languages English
T: +92 41 8850012
W: www.angelscollege.edu.pk

Beaconhouse College Campus Gulberg
3-C, Zafar Ali Road, Lahore 54000
DP Coordinator Asma Amanat
Languages English
T: +92 42 3588 6239
W: www.beaconhouse.edu.pk

Beaconhouse Newlands Islamabad
Hill View Road, Mohra Noor, Islamabad 44000
DP Coordinator Arham Kashif Sultan
PYP Coordinator Sabahat Bokhari
Languages English
T: +92 51 0000000
W: bni.beaconhouse.net

Beaconhouse Newlands Lahore
632/1 Street 10, Phase VI DHA, Lahore 54000
PYP Coordinator Lubaba Batool
Languages English
T: +92 (42) 111 111 020
W: www.beaconhousenewlands.net

Beaconhouse School System, Clifton Campus
Frere Town , 2/3 McNeil Road, Clifton, Karachi 75600
PYP Coordinator Tasneem Karbalai
Languages English
T: +92 21 35659190
W: www.beaconhouse.net/branch/clifton-campus-karachi

Beaconhouse School System, Defence Campus
207 A, Saba Avenue, Phase VIII, DHA, Karachi, Sindh 75500
DP Coordinator Nazia Adeel
Languages English
T: +92 2135847083 84
W: www.beaconhouse.net/branch/defence-campus-karachi

Beaconhouse School System, Margalla Campus
Pitras Bukhari Rd, H-8/4, Islamabad 44000
DP Coordinator Bushra Jamal
Languages English
T: +92 3345501113
W: ib.beaconhouse.net

Beaconhouse School System, PECHS Campus
35P/1, Block 6 Extension, PECHS, Karachi 75100
DP Coordinator Tooba Iqbal
Languages English
T: +92 21 34380045
W: www.beaconhouse.net/branch/beaconhouse-college-campus-pechs-bccp-karachi

Headstart School, Kuri Campus
Kuri Road, Off Park Rd, Near CDA/Park Enclave, Islamabad 44000
DP Coordinator Laraib Imdad
PYP Coordinator Nadine Murtaza
Languages English
T: +92 51 8435 473
W: www.headstart.edu.pk

Ilmesters Academy
B-31, PECHS, Block-6, Near Progressive Center, Karachi 75400
MYP Coordinator Ms. Khadija Bilkhawala
PYP Coordinator Ms. Neesha Feroz
Languages English
T: +92 21 34524423
W: www.ilmesters.edu.pk

INTERNATIONAL SCHOOL OF ISLAMABAD
Sector H-9/1, Johar Road, P.O. Box 1124, Islamabad 44000
DP Coordinator Dora Flores
PYP Coordinator Mary Frances Penton
Languages English
T: +92 51 443 4950
E: school@isoi.edu.pk; registrar@isoi.edu.pk
W: www.isoi.edu.pk
See full details on page 352

Lahore Grammar School Defence (Phase 1)
136 – E, Phase 1 Defence Housing Authority (DHA), Lahore Cantt, Punjab, Lahore 54810
PYP Coordinator Saima Asim
Languages English
T: +92 (42) 358 94306
W: lgsdefence.webflow.io

Lahore Grammar School Defence (Phase V)
#483/4, Block G, Education City, Phase V, Defence Housing Authority (DHA), Lahore Cantt, Lahore, Punjab 54810
PYP Coordinator Irma Ahsan
Languages English
T: +92 42 37176005/6/7
W: lgsdefence.edu.pk/phase-v

Lahore Grammar School International
32/3, Sector J, DHA Phase VIII, Lahore 54972
DP Coordinator Sania Rasool
MYP Coordinator Ali Jaffery
PYP Coordinator Fatima Khan
Languages English
T: +92 42 37175751
W: www.lgsinternational.edu.pk

Lahore Grammar School Islamabad
Plot # 86, Faiz Ahmad Faiz Road, Sector H-8/1, Islamabad 44000
PYP Coordinator Shagufta Hassan
Languages English
T: +92 51 4922092
W: www.lgsdefence.edu.pk

Learning Alliance
32/1 J block, DHA Phase VIII, Lahore 54000
DP Coordinator Amber Ahsan
MYP Coordinator Mehrunnisa Sammiullah
PYP Coordinator Maryam Haider
Languages English
T: +92 42 111 66 66 33
W: www.learningalliance.edu.pk

Roots International Schools Islamabad Pakistan
Campus # 66, Street 7, Wellington Campus H-8/4, Islamabad
DP Coordinator Syeda Sada Afaq
Languages English, Urdu, Chinese, German
T: +92 51 8439001-7
W: www.rootsinternational.edu.pk

Roots IVY International School – Chaklala Campus
Walayat Homes, Chakalala Scheme 3, Rawalpindi
PYP Coordinator Rubab Adnan
Languages English
T: +92 51 578 8380
W: www.rootsivyintschools.edu.pk

Roots Ivy International School – DHA Phase V Lahore
Plot #550/1, Sector G, DHA, Phase V (6,192.65 km), Lahore 54000
PYP Coordinator Manal Tahir
Languages English, Urdu
T: +92 302 6274309
W: www.rootsivyintschools.edu.pk

Roots IVY International School – Faisalabad Campus
Opposite Guttwala Park, Faisalabad
PYP Coordinator Noor Raza Cheema
Languages English
T: +92 321 8912555
W: www.rootsivyintschools.edu.pk

Roots IVY International School – Riverview Campus
Main GT Road, Rawalpindi
DP Coordinator Maimoona Malik
Languages English
T: +92 (0)51 4917302/3
W: www.rootsivyintschools.edu.pk

Roots Millennium Schools, Flagship Campus
No. 308, Street No. 3, Sector I-9/3, Islamabad 44000
DP Coordinator Shazia Afridi
Languages English
T: +92 51 8439981-6
W: millenniumschools.edu.pk/roots-college-international-flagship-campus

Roots Millennium Schools, One World Campus
Head Office, No.80, Street 1, Sector E-11/4, Islamabad 44000
MYP Coordinator Beenish Zahid
Languages English
T: +92 51 111 111 193
W: www.millenniumschools.edu.pk

SANJAN NAGAR PUBLIC EDUCATION TRUST HIGHER SECONDARY SCHOOL
117 A, Anum Street, Glaxo Town, Ferozepur Road, Lahore, Punjab
PYP Coordinator Danial Ishaq
Languages English
T: +92 42 35950676
E: principalsnss@snpet.org
W: www.snpet.org
See full details on page 399

Sheikh Zayed International Academy
Street 8, Sector H-8/4, Islamabad
DP Coordinator Amtul Qayyum
MYP Coordinator Sadia Tariq
PYP Coordinator Nadeyah Adnan
Languages English
T: +92 51 4939298
W: www.szia.ae

SICAS DHA Phase VI
310/2F DHA, Phase 6, Lahore, Punjab 54770
PYP Coordinator Hira Sheikh
Languages English
T: +92 4237338361-3
W: www.sicas.edu.pk

The City School, Capital Campus Islamabad
Pitras Bokhari Road, Sector H-8/1, Islamabad
DP Coordinator Farzana Khan
Languages English
T: +92 051 4939280
W: www.thecityschool.edu.pk

PAKISTAN

The International School (TIS)
Executive, 51-C Old Clifton, Near Mohatta Palace, Karachi 75600
DP Coordinator Nayma Hasan
MYP Coordinator Tahir Manto
PYP Coordinator Samrah Afghan
Languages English
T: +92 21 35835805-6
W: www.tis.edu.pk

The Learning Tree
F-8, Khayaban-e-Saadi, Block 5, Clifton, Karachi, Sindh 75600
PYP Coordinator Afshan Bandeali
Languages English
T: +92 213 587 0001
W: www.thelearningtree.edu.pk

TNS Beaconhouse
483/3 Sector G Phase 5 DHA, Lahore
DP Coordinator Rashid Khalid
MYP Coordinator Hina Chaudhry
Languages English
T: +92 42 111 867 867
W: www.tns.edu.pk

PAPUA NEW GUINEA

Port Moresby International School
PO Box 276, Boroko
DP Coordinator Ronan Moore
Languages English
T: +675 325 3166
W: www.pmis.iea.ac.pg

PHILIPPINES

Brent International School – Baguio
Brent Road, Baguio City 2600
DP Coordinator Celeste Coronado
Languages English
T: +63 74 442 2260
W: www.brentbaguio.edu.ph

Brent International School – Manila
Brentville Subdivision, Mamplasan, Biñan, Laguna 4024
DP Coordinator Maria Cristina Pozon
Languages English
T: +63 2 6001 0300/9
W: www.brent.edu.ph

Brent International School Subic
Building 6601 Binictican Drive, Subic Bay Freeport Zone, Zambales, Subic 2222
DP Coordinator Sheila Marie Griarte
Languages English
T: +63 47 252 6871/72
W: www.brentsubic.edu.ph

Cebu International School
PO Box 735, Pit-os, Talamban, Cebu City 6000
DP Coordinator Maria Socorro Laplana
PYP Coordinator Glenn Davies
Languages English
T: +63 32 401 1900/1/2/3
W: www.cis.edu.ph

Chinese International School Manila
Upper McKinley Road, McKinley Hill, Fort Bonifacio, Taguig City 1634
DP Coordinator Pierre Jasper Bacolod
Languages English
T: +63 (2) 815 2476
W: www.cismanila.org

Domuschola International School
Dormitory 1, Philsports Complex, Molave Street, Ugong, Pasig City
DP Coordinator Shalymar Evangelista
PYP Coordinator Ginalyn Delizo
Languages English, Filipino
T: +63 2 6359743
W: www.dis.edu.ph

German European School Manila
75 Swaziland Street, Better Living Subdivision, Paranaque City 1711
DP Coordinator Santanu Bhowmik
PYP Coordinator Viola Buck
Languages English
T: +63 2 776 1000
W: www.gesm.org

Immaculate Conception Academy
10 Grant St., Greenhills, San Juan, Metro Manila
DP Coordinator Paula Mae Mendoza
Languages English, Tagalog
T: +63 (02) 723 7041
W: www.icagh.edu.ph

International School Manila
University Parkway, Fort Bonifacio Global City, Taguig City 1634
DP Coordinator Michael Relf
Languages English
T: +63 2 840 8400
W: www.ismanila.org

Keys School Manila
951 Luna Mencias St., corner Araullo St., Mandaluyong City 1550
DP Coordinator Alfonso Mangubat
Languages English, Filipino
T: +63 27279357
W: www.ksm.ph

Learning Links Academy
Main Street, South Forbes Golf City, Silang, Cavite 4118
DP Coordinator Rizza Aquino
Languages English
T: +63 49 544 0818
W: www.learninglinks.edu.ph

Noblesse International School
Circumferential Roas, Friendship Highway, Barangay CutCut, Angeles City, Pampanga 2009
DP Coordinator Vladimir Sousek Medrano
Languages English
T: +63 (45) 459 9000
W: www.nis.com.ph

Saint Jude Catholic School
327 Ycaza Street, San Miguel, Manila 1005
DP Coordinator Genalyn Alfonso
Languages English
T: +63 (2) 735 6386
W: www.sjcs.edu.ph

Singapore School Cebu
Zuellig Avenue, North Reclamation Area, Mandaue City, Cebu 6014
DP Coordinator Jeanine Helmuth
Languages Chinese, English
T: +63 (32) 2365 772
W: www.singaporeschoolcebu.com

Singapore School Manila
Lots 1 & 40, Block 2 East Street, East District, Asena City, Paranaque
DP Coordinator Denise Villegas
Languages English
T: +63 2 966 9315
W: www.singaporeschoolmanila.com.ph

Southville International School & Colleges
1281 Tropical Avenue Corner, Luxembourg Street, BF Homes International, Las Pinas City 1740
DP Coordinator John Wraith
Languages English
T: +63 28 825 0766
W: www.southville.edu.ph

The Beacon Academy
Cecilia Araneta Parkway, Biñan, Laguna 4024
DP Coordinator Ma. Villafranca Nario
MYP Coordinator Maria Cecilia Francisco
Languages English
T: +632 425 1326
W: www.beaconacademy.ph

The Beacon School
PCPD Building, 2332 Chino Roces Avenue Extension, Taguig City 1630
MYP Coordinator Erica Gancayco
PYP Coordinator DJ Leonardia
Languages English
T: +632 840 5040 LOC 105
W: www.beaconschool.ph

The British School, Manila
36th Street, University Park, Bonifacio Global City, Taguig City, Makati, Metro Manila 1634
DP Coordinator Mathilde Mouquet
Languages English
T: +63 2 860 4800
W: www.britishschoolmanila.org

Victory Christian International School
339 Robinson Circle, Capt. Henry Javier Drive, Oranbo, Pasig City 1600
DP Coordinator Michael Mabag
Languages English
T: +63 28 671 8505
W: www.vcis.edu.ph

Xavier School
64 Xavier Street, Greenhills West, San Juan City, Metro Manila 1500
DP Coordinator Michael Ryan Bulosan
Languages English
T: +632 7230481
W: www.xs.edu.ph

REPUBLIC OF KOREA

BRANKSOME HALL ASIA
234 Global edu-ro, Daejeong-eup, Seogwipo-si, Jeju-do 63644
DP Coordinator Mr. Nick Daniel
MYP Coordinator Ms. Paula Swartz
PYP Coordinator Mrs. Virginia Sutton
Languages English
T: +82 64 902 5000
E: admissions@branksome.asia
W: www.branksome.asia

See full details on page 302

CHADWICK INTERNATIONAL
45, Art center-daero 97 beon-gil, Yeonsu-gu, Incheon 22002
CP Coordinator Jason Reagin
DP Coordinator Benedict Hung
MYP Coordinator Barbara Wrightson
PYP Coordinator Pamela Castillo (Lower Primary) & Mei-Lyn Freeman (Upper Primary)
Languages English
T: +82 32 250 5000
E: songdo-admissions@chadwickschool.org
W: www.chadwickinternational.org

See full details on page 306

Dulwich College Seoul
5-1 Banpo-2-dong, Seocho-Gu, Seoul 137-800
DP Coordinator Rebecca Gardner
Languages English
T: +82 2 3015 8500
W: www.dulwich-seoul.kr

Dwight School Seoul
21 World Cup Buk-ro 62-gil, Mapo-gu, Seoul 03919
DP Coordinator Andrew MacLachlan
MYP Coordinator Daniel Suarez
PYP Coordinator Laura Smith
Languages English
T: +82 2 6920 8600
W: www.dwight.or.kr

Gyeonggi Academy of Foreign Languages
30, Gosan-ro 105 Beon-gil, Uiwang-si, Gyeonggi-do 16075
DP Coordinator Ben Matthews
Languages English
T: +82 (0)31 361 0500
W: www.gafl.hs.kr

Gyeonggi Suwon International School
451 YeongTong-Ro, YeongTong-Gu, Suwon City, Gyeonggi-Do 16706
DP Coordinator Anthony Cartmel
MYP Coordinator Ronny Laroche
PYP Coordinator Lynda (Mei-Lyn) Freeman
Languages English
T: +82 31 695 2800
W: www.gsis.sc.kr

Gyeongnam International Foreign School
49-22, Jodong-gil, Sanam-myeon, Sacheon-si, Gyeongnam 52533
DP Coordinator Samuel Kuntz
Languages English
T: +82 (0)55 853 5125
W: www.gifs.or.kr

International School of Busan
50 Gijang-daero, Gijang-eup, Gijang-gun, Busan 46081
DP Coordinator Merriss Shenstone
MYP Coordinator Jennifer Montague
PYP Coordinator Michelle Roland
Languages English
T: +82 51 742 3332
W: www.bifskorea.org

Korea Foreign School
7-16, Nambusunhwan-ro 364-gil, Seocho-gu, Seoul 06739
MYP Coordinator Michael Donkin
PYP Coordinator Michael Donkin
Languages English
T: +82 2 571 2917/18
W: koreaforeign.org

Namsan International Kindergarten
8-6, Dasan-ro 8-gil,, Jung-Gu, Seoul 04597
PYP Coordinator Cathy Brown
Languages English
T: +82 2 2232 2451
W: www.nikseoul.org

NORTH LONDON COLLEGIATE SCHOOL JEJU
33, Global edu-ro 145beon-gil, Daejeong-eup, Seogwipo-si, Jeju-do 63644
DP Coordinator Ms Justine Oliver
Languages English
T: +82 64 793 8000
E: info@nlcsjeju.kr
W: www.nlcsjeju.co.kr
See full details on page 382

SEOUL FOREIGN SCHOOL
39 Yeonhui-ro 22-gil, Seodaemun-gu, Seoul 03723
DP Coordinator Piotr Kocyk
MYP Coordinator Adrian Gan
PYP Coordinator Katherine Baird
Languages English
T: +82 2 330 3100
E: admissions@seoulforeign.org
W: www.seoulforeign.org
See full details on page 410

Taejon Christian International School
77 Yongsan 2 Ro, Yuseong Gu, Daejeon 305-500
DP Coordinator Andy Hay
MYP Coordinator Jordan Williams
PYP Coordinator Jodi Deuth
Languages English
T: +82 42 620 9000
W: www.tcis.or.kr

SINGAPORE

ACS (International), Singapore
61 Jalan Hitam Manis, Singapore 278475
DP Coordinator Carol Ling
Languages English
T: +658 6472 1477
W: www.acsinternational.com.sg

Anglo-Chinese School (Independent)
121 Dover Road, Singapore 139650
DP Coordinator Siew Hwa Chock
Languages English
T: +65 6773 1633
W: www.acs.sch.edu.sg/acs_indep

Australian International School, Singapore
1 Lorong Chuan 556818
DP Coordinator Niamh Bowman
PYP Coordinator Kerryl Howarth
Languages English
T: +65 6653 7906
W: www.ais.com.sg

Canadian International School, Lakeside Campus
7 Jurong West Street 41, Singapore 659414
DP Coordinator Elsa Baptista
MYP Coordinator Victor De Melo
PYP Coordinator Simone Lieschke
Languages English
T: +65 6743 8088
W: www.cis.edu.sg

Canadian International School, Tanjong Katong Campus
371 Tanjong Katong Road, Singapore 437128
PYP Coordinator Patricia Pope
Languages English
T: +65 6345 1573
W: www.cis.edu.sg

Chatsworth International School – Bukit Timah Campus
72 Bukit Tinggi Road, Singapore 289760
DP Coordinator Harparsh Saxena
MYP Coordinator Phavana Silva
PYP Coordinator Tim Burch
Languages English
T: +65 6463 3201
W: www.chatsworth.com.sg

Chatsworth International School – Orchard Campus
37 Emerald Hill, Singapore 229313
PYP Coordinator Michael Jarvis Lucchesi
Languages English
T: +65 6737 5955
W: www.chatsworth.com.sg

DOVER COURT INTERNATIONAL SCHOOL SINGAPORE
301 Dover Road, Singapore 139644
DP Coordinator Mr. Dominic O'Shea
Languages English
T: +65 6775 7664
E: admissions@dovercourt.edu.sg
W: www.dovercourt.edu.sg
See full details on page 308

DULWICH COLLEGE (SINGAPORE)
71 Bukit Batok West Avenue 8, Singapore 658966
DP Coordinator Mr. Alan Perkins
Languages English
T: +65 6890 1003
E: admissions@dulwich-singapore.edu.sg
W: singapore.dulwich.org
See full details on page 310

EtonHouse International Pre-School, Mountbatten 718
718 Mountbatten Road, Singapore 437738
PYP Coordinator Rebecca Gough
Languages English
T: +65 6846 3322
W: www.etonhouse.com.sg/mountbatten-718

EtonHouse International Pre-School, Newton
39 Newton Road, Singapore 307966
PYP Coordinator Asmita Sharma
Languages English
T: +65 6352 3322
W: www.etonhouse.com.sg/newton

Etonhouse International Pre-School, Thomson
8 Thomson Lane, Singapore 297743
PYP Coordinator Mike Carrigan
Languages English, Mandarin
T: +65 6252 3322
W: www.etonhouse.com.sg/thomson

EtonHouse International School, Broadrick
51 Broadrick Road, Singapore 439501
PYP Coordinator Tina Cooper
Languages English
T: +65 6346 6922
W: www.ehis.edu.sg

GEMS World Academy (Singapore)
2 Yishun Street 42, Singapore 768039
CP Coordinator Michael Fletcher
DP Coordinator Michael Fletcher
MYP Coordinator Kylie Begg
PYP Coordinator Edna Lau & Paul Rimmer
Languages English
T: +65 6808 7300
W: www.gwa.edu.sg

GESS INTERNATIONAL SCHOOL
2 Dairy Farm Lane, Singapore 677621
DP Coordinator Joanna Fitts
MYP Coordinator Isabel Martin
PYP Coordinator Joram Hutchins
Languages English
T: +65 6461 0881
E: admissions@gess.sg
W: www.gess.sg
See full details on page 335

GLOBAL INDIAN INTERNATIONAL SCHOOL PTE LTD
27, Punggol Field Walk 828649
DP Coordinator Deepa Chandrasekaran
Languages English
T: +65 69147000
E: principal.pg@globalindianschool.org
W: sg.globalindianschool.org
See full details on page 339

Hillside World Academy
11 Hillside Drive 548926
DP Coordinator Xiaoxia Huang
MYP Coordinator Josephine Fong
PYP Coordinator Runzhen Zhai
Languages English, Chinese
T: +65 6254 0200
W: www.hwa.edu.sg

Hwa Chong International School
663 Bukit Timah Road, Singapore 269783
DP Coordinator Avril Teh
Languages English
T: +65 6464 7077
W: www.hcis.edu.sg

ISS International School
21 Preston Road 109355
DP Coordinator Christopher Garden
MYP Coordinator Christopher Hayward
PYP Coordinator Ariana Rehu
Languages English
T: +65 6475 4188
W: www.iss.edu.sg

Madrasah Aljunied Al-Islamiah
30 Victoria Lane, Singapore 198424
DP Coordinator Khalidah Abdullah
Languages English, Malay
T: +65 6391 5970/1
W: www.aljunied.edu.sg

NEXUS INTERNATIONAL SCHOOL (SINGAPORE)
1 Alunied Walk, Singapore 387293
DP Coordinator Melanie Brown
PYP Coordinator Paul Rimmer
Languages English
T: +65 6536 6566
E: enquiry@nexus.edu.sg
W: www.nexus.edu.sg
See full details on page 378

NPS INTERNATIONAL SCHOOL
10-12 Chai Chee Lane, Singapore 469021
DP Coordinator Sushmita Chatterjee
Languages English
T: +65 62942400
E: headofschool@npsis.edu.sg
W: www.npsinternational.edu.sg
See full details on page 383

Odyssey The Global Preschool – Fourth Avenue
20 Fourth Avenue 268669
PYP Coordinator Melise Wang
Languages English, Chinese
T: +65 6781 8800
W: www.theodyssey.sg

Odyssey The Global Preschool – Wilkinson
101 Wilkinson Road 436559
PYP Coordinator Alice Alagan
Languages English, Chinese
T: +65 6781 8800
W: www.theodyssey.sg

ONE WORLD INTERNATIONAL SCHOOL
21 Jurong West Street 81, Singapore 649075
DP Coordinator Iris Tay
PYP Coordinator Erin Smith
Languages English
T: +65 69146700
E: admissions@owis.org
W: www.owis.org
See full details on page 385

Overseas Family School
25F Paterson Road, Singapore 238515
DP Coordinator Phil Riordan
MYP Coordinator Nathalie Buckland-Brough
Languages English
T: +65 6 738 0211
W: www.ofs.edu.sg

School of the Arts, Singapore
1 Zubir Said Drive, Administration Office #05-01, Singapore 227968
CP Coordinator Soo Keong Koh
DP Coordinator Ronald Lim
Languages English
T: +65 63389663
W: www.sota.edu.sg

Singapore Sports School
1 Champions Way, Woodlands 737913
DP Coordinator Han Yong Lim
Languages English
T: +65 6766 0100
W: www.sportsschool.edu.sg

St Francis Methodist School
492 Upper Bukit Timah Road 678095
DP Coordinator Hung Yee Choo
Languages English
T: +65 6760 0889
W: www.sfms.edu.sg

St Joseph's Institution International
490 Thomson Road, Singapore 298191
DP Coordinator Guy Bromley
Languages English
T: +65 6353 9383
W: www.sji-international.com.sg

St. Joseph's Institution
21 Bishan Street 14, Singapore 579781
DP Coordinator Woh Un Tang
Languages English
T: +65 62500022
W: www.sji.edu.sg

Stamford American International School
1 Woodleigh Lane 357684
DP Coordinator Amit Khanna
MYP Coordinator Rhonda Weins & Natalie Martin
PYP Coordinator Perry Tkachuk & Pamela Chandler
Languages English
T: +65 6653 7907
W: www.sais.edu.sg

TANGLIN TRUST SCHOOL, SINGAPORE
95 Portsdown Road 139299
DP Coordinator Joseph Loader
Languages English
T: +65 67780771
E: admissions@tts.edu.sg
W: www.tts.edu.sg
See full details on page 426

The Little Skool-House International (By-the-Vista)
170 Ghim Moh Road, Ulu Pandan Community Club, #03-01, Singapore 279621
PYP Coordinator Nurazura Binte Mohamed Amran
Languages English
T: +65 6468 3725
W: www.littleskoolhouse.com

UWC South East Asia, Dover Campus
1207 Dover Road 139654
DP Coordinator Jensen Hjorth
Languages English
T: +65 6775 5344
W: www.uwcsea.edu.sg

UWC South East Asia, East Campus
1 Tampines Street 73 528704
DP Coordinator Gemma Elford Dawson
Languages English
T: +65 63055344
W: www.uwcsea.edu.sg

SOLOMON ISLANDS

Woodford International School
Prince Philip Highway, P.O. Box R44, Kukum, Honiara
PYP Coordinator Paola Osorio
Languages English
T: +677 30186
W: www.wis.edu.sb

SRI LANKA

The Overseas School of Colombo
PO Box 9, Pelawatte, Battaramulla 10120
DP Coordinator William Duncan
MYP Coordinator Clover Hicks
PYP Coordinator Samantha Wood
Languages English
T: +94 11 2784 920-2
W: www.osc.lk

TAIWAN

I-Shou International School
No 6, Sec 1, Xuecheng Rd., Dashu Dist., Kaohsiung City 84048
DP Coordinator Glen Johnston
MYP Coordinator Natasha Hale
PYP Coordinator Nicholas Staffa
Languages English, Chinese
T: +886 7 657 7115
W: www.iis.kh.edu.tw

Kang Chiao International School (Taipei Campus)
No. 800, Huacheng Road, Xindian District, New Taipei City 23153
DP Coordinator Steven Bates
MYP Coordinator Joseph Sun
Languages Chinese, English
T: +886 2 8665 2070
W: www.kcbs.ntpc.edu.tw/kcis/index.html

Kaohsiung American School
889 Cueihua Road, Zuoying District, Kaohsiung City 81354
DP Coordinator Debi Haines
MYP Coordinator Debi Haines
Languages English
T: +886 7 586 3300
W: www.kas.tw

Mingdao High School
497, Sec. 1, Zhongshan Rd., Wuri Dist., Taichung City 41401
DP Coordinator Alexandra Lopez
MYP Coordinator Feon Chau
Languages English
T: +886 4 23372101
W: mdhs-id.online

Taipei American School
800 Chung Shan North Road, Sec 6, Taipei
DP Coordinator Warren Emanuel
Languages English
T: +886 22 873 9900
W: www.tas.edu.tw

Taipei European School
Swire European Campus, 31 Jian Ye Road, Yang Ming Shan, Shihlin, Taipei 11193
DP Coordinator Hamish McMillan
Languages English
T: +886 2 8145 9007
W: www.taipeieuropeanschool.com

TAIPEI KUEI SHAN SCHOOL
200 Mingde Road, Taipei 11280
DP Coordinator Robert Chung
MYP Coordinator Joe Woo
PYP Coordinator Elizabeth Hu
Languages Chinese, English
T: +886 2 2821 2009
E: info@kss.tp.edu.tw
W: www.kshs.tp.edu.tw

See full details on page 425

Victoria Academy
1110 Jhen-Nan Rd., Douliu, Yun-Lin 640
DP Coordinator Nerissa Puntawe
Languages Chinese, English
T: +886 5 5378899 (EXT:22)
W: www.victoria.ylc.edu.tw

THAILAND

American Pacific International School
158/1 Moo 3, Hangdong-Samoeng Road, Banpong, Hangdong, Chiang Mai 50230
MYP Coordinator John Salgado
PYP Coordinator Erika Vargas
Languages English
T: +66 53 365 303/5
W: www.apis.ac.th

Ascot International School
80/82 Ramkhamhaeng Soi 118, Sapansung, Bangkok 10240
DP Coordinator Mark Allen
PYP Coordinator Karel Linden
Languages English
T: +66 2 373 4400
W: www.ascot.ac.th

Bangkok Patana School
643 La Salle Road, Sukhumvit 105, Bangkok 10260
DP Coordinator Andrew Roff
Languages English
T: +66 2 785 2200
W: www.patana.ac.th

British International School, Phuket
59 Moo 2, Thepkrasattri Road, T. Koh Kaew, A. Muang, Phuket 83000
DP Coordinator Jason Perkins
Languages English
T: +66 (0) 76 335 555
W: www.bisphuket.ac.th

Concordian International School
918 Moo 8, Bangna-Trad Highway Km 7, Bangkaew, Bangplee Samutprakarn 10540
DP Coordinator James Leung
MYP Coordinator Sally (Ya-Hsin) Wen
PYP Coordinator Nathalie Herve
Languages English
T: +66 2 706 9000
W: www.concordian.ac.th

GARDEN INTERNATIONAL SCHOOL (RAYONG CAMPUS)
188/24 Moo 4, Pala-Ban Chang Road, Tambol Pala, Ban Chang, Rayong 21130
DP Coordinator Lauren Hucknall
Languages English
T: +66 3803 0808
E: ibcoord@gardenrayong.com
W: www.gardenrayong.com

See full details on page 334

INTERNATIONAL SCHOOL BANGKOK
39/7 Soi Nichada Thani, Samakee Road, Pakkret, Nonthaburi 11120
DP Coordinator Justyna McMilan
Languages English
T: +66 2 963 5800
E: admissions@isb.ac.th
W: www.isb.ac.th

See full details on page 349

International School Eastern Seaboard
282 Moo 5 T. Bowin, SriRacha, Chonburi 20230
DP Coordinator Richard Kennedy
Languages English
T: +66 38 372 591
W: www.ise.ac.th

KIS INTERNATIONAL SCHOOL
999/123-124 Pracha Utit Road, Samsennok, Huay Kwang, Bangkok 10310
DP Coordinator Daniel Trump
MYP Coordinator Alison Ya-Wen Yang
PYP Coordinator Kirsten Durward
Languages English
T: +66 (0)2 2743444
E: admissions@kis.ac.th
W: www.kis.ac.th

See full details on page 362

Magic Years International School
22/122, Moo 3, Soi Prasoet Islam, Bang Talat, Pakkret, Nonthaburri 11120
PYP Coordinator Lynn Ware
Languages English
T: +66 2156 6222
W: www.magicyears.ac.th

NIST INTERNATIONAL SCHOOL
36 Sukhumvit Soi 15, Wattana, Bangkok 10110
DP Coordinator Paul Cooper
MYP Coordinator Jacqueline Arce
PYP Coordinator Bryony Maxted-Miller
Languages English
T: +66 2 017 5888
E: admissions@nist.ac.th
W: www.nist.ac.th

See full details on page 375

Pan-Asia International School
100 Moo 3, Charaemprakiat, Rama 9 St, Soi 67, Kwang Dokmai Prawet District, Bangkok 10250
DP Coordinator Sujith Kandathil
Languages English
T: +66 2 726 6273-4
W: www.pais.ac.th

PREM TINSULANONDA INTERNATIONAL SCHOOL
234 Moo 3, Huay Sai, Mae Rim, Chiang Mai 50180
CP Coordinator Elisabeth Wojciuk
DP Coordinator Catherine Schlei
MYP Coordinator Andrew Parlby
PYP Coordinator Mary Ann Van De Weerd
Languages English
T: +66 53 301 500
E: admissions@ptis.ac.th
W: www.ptis.ac.th

See full details on page 387

REGENTS INTERNATIONAL SCHOOL PATTAYA
33/3 Moo 1, Pong, Banglamung, Chonburi 20150
DP Coordinator Sara Morrow
Languages English
T: +66 (0)93 135 7736
E: admissions@regents-pattaya.co.th
W: www.nordangliaeducation.com/our-schools/pattaya

See full details on page 394

RUAMRUDEE INTERNATIONAL SCHOOL
6 Ramkhamhaeng 184, Minburi, Bangkok 10510
DP Coordinator Timothy Pettine
Languages English
T: +66 (0)2 791 8900
E: admissions@rism.ac.th
W: www.rism.ac.th

See full details on page 397

Satit Bilingual School of Rangsit University
52/347 Muang Ake, Phahonyothin Road., Lak Hok, Mueang, Pathum Thani 12000
PYP Coordinator Babita Seth
Languages English
T: +66 2 792 7500 4
W: bkk.sbs.ac.th

ST ANDREWS INTERNATIONAL SCHOOL BANGKOK
1020 Sukhumvit Road, Phra Khanong, Khlong Toei, Bangkok 10110
DP Coordinator Mr. William Taylor
Languages English
T: +662 056 9555
E: officehs@standrews.ac.th
W: www.standrews.ac.th

See full details on page 419

ST ANDREWS INTERNATIONAL SCHOOL, GREEN VALLEY CAMPUS

Moo 7, Ban Chang-Makham Koo Road, Ban Chang, Rayong 21130
DP Coordinator Andrew Emery
PYP Coordinator Faye Wood
Languages English
T: +66 38 030611
E: admissionsgv@standrews-schools.com
W: www.standrewsgreenvalley.com

See full details on page 420

ST ANDREWS INTERNATIONAL SCHOOL, SUKHUMVIT CAMPUS

7 Sukhumvit 107 Road, Bangna, Bangkok 10260
DP Coordinator Ms. Sarah McNish
PYP Coordinator Ms. Carole Parker
Languages English
T: +66 (0)2393 3883
E: sukhumvit@standrews-schools.com
W: www.standrewssukhumvit.com

See full details on page 421

The Regent's School, Bangkok

601/99 Pracha-Uthit Road, Wangthonglang, Bangkok 10310
DP Coordinator Darron Gray
Languages English
T: +66 (0)2 957 5777
W: www.regents.ac.th

Udon Thani International School (UDIS)

222/2 Moo. 2 Mittrapab Road, Tumbonkudsra, Aumpearmuang, Udon Thani 41000
PYP Coordinator Cynthia Thomas
Languages English
T: +66 (0)42 110 379
W: www.udoninternationalschool.com

UWC THAILAND INTERNATIONAL SCHOOL

115/15 Moo 7 Thepkasattri Road, Thepkasattri, Thalang, Phuket 83110
DP Coordinator Katharine Feather
MYP Coordinator Remke Langendonck
PYP Coordinator Jen Friske
Languages English
T: +66 76 336 076
E: Info@uwcthailand.ac.th
W: uwcthailand.ac.th

See full details on page 437

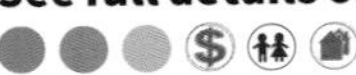

Wells International School – Bang Na Campus

10 Srinakarin Soi 62, Nong Bon, Prawet, Bangkok 10250
PYP Coordinator Bradford Moleon
Languages English, Thai
T: +66 02 746 6060 1
W: www.wells-school.com

Wells International School – On Nut Campus

2209 Sukhumvit Road, Bangchak, Prakanong, Bangkok 10260
DP Coordinator Katherine Caouette
Languages English
T: +66 097 920 8511
W: www.wells-school.com

VIETNAM

American International School of Vietnam

220 Nguyen Van Tao, Nha Be District, Ho Chi Minh City
DP Coordinator Elizabeth Tinnon
Languages English
T: +84 28378 00808
W: www.ais.edu.vn

Australian International School (AIS)

264 Mai Chi Tho, An Phu Ward, District 2, Ho Chi Minh City
DP Coordinator Mark Andrew Godfrey Beales
PYP Coordinator Mida Abdul
Languages English
T: +84 28 3742 4040
W: www.aisvietnam.com

BRITISH INTERNATIONAL SCHOOL, HANOI

Hoa Lan Road, Vinhomes Riverside, Long Bien District, Hanoi 100000
DP Coordinator Mr Adrian Duckett
Languages English
T: +84 24 3946 0435
E: bishanoi@bishanoi.com
W: www.bishanoi.com

See full details on page 303

British International School, Ho Chi Minh City

225 Nguyen Van Huong, Thao Dien Ward, District 2, Ho Chi Minh City
DP Coordinator Matthew Lambert
Languages English
T: +84 (0)28 3744 4551
W: www.bisvietnam.com

Canadian International School – Vietnam

No. 86, Road 23, Phu My Hung, Tan Phu Ward, District 7, Binh Chanh District, Ho Chi Minh City
DP Coordinator Andrew Lin
Languages English
T: +84 94 295 8557
W: www.cis.edu.vn

European International School HCMC

730 F-G-K Le Van Mien, Thao Dien, District 2, Ho Chi Minh City 70000
DP Coordinator Erin Tacey
MYP Coordinator Fleur Serriere
PYP Coordinator Michael Perry
Languages English
T: +8428 7300 7257
W: www.eishcmc.com

Hanoi International School

48 Lieu Giai Street, Ba Dinh District, Hanoi
DP Coordinator Heather Anne Neill
MYP Coordinator Sean Noga
PYP Coordinator Vani Veikoso
Languages English
T: +84 4 3832 8140
W: www.hisvietnam.com

INTERNATIONAL SCHOOL HO CHI MINH CITY (ISHCMC)

28 Vo Truong Toan St, An Phu, District 2, Ho Chi Minh City
DP Coordinator Teresa Foard
MYP Coordinator Simon Scoones
PYP Coordinator Nancy Snyder & Tania Mansfield
Languages English
T: +84 28 3898 9100
E: admissions@ishcmc.edu.vn
W: www.ishcmc.com

See full details on page 351

International School of Vietnam

No. 6-7 Nguyen Cong Thai Street, Dai Kim Urban area, Hoang Mai, Hanoi
DP Coordinator Colin Ralph Bradshaw Bastida
PYP Coordinator Boriana Stoyanova
Languages English
T: +84 (0)435 409 183
W: www.isvietnam.edu.vn

Renaissance International School Saigon

74 Nguyen Thi Thap Street, Binh Thuan Ward, District 7, Ho Chi Minh City
DP Coordinator Sarah Alexander
Languages English
T: +84 283 7733 171
W: www.renaissance.edu.vn

Saigon South International School

78 Nguyen Duc Canh, Tan Phong Ward, District 7, Ho Chi Minh City 70000
DP Coordinator Cassandra Armstrong
Languages English
T: +84 28 5413 0901
W: www.ssis.edu.vn

United Nations International School of Hanoi

G9 Ciputra, Tay Ho, Hanoi
DP Coordinator Elliott Cannell
MYP Coordinator Daniel Cooper
PYP Coordinator Joshua Smith
Languages English
T: +84 24 7300 4500
W: www.unishanoi.org

Western Australian Primary and High School

157 Ly Chinh Thang St., Ward 7, Dist. 3, Ho Chi Minh City
DP Coordinator Bao Tran
Languages English, Vietnamese
T: +84 (0)28 7109 5077
W: wass.edu.vn

IB
Americas

Americas

Some facts about this region

IB Americas includes IB World Schools in 33 countries and territories in Central, North and South America. IB World Schools in the Americas are state/public, private, independent, charter, international, parochial, and secular. They serve a broad and diverse range of students in urban, suburban and rural communities. As of November 2019, there were 6,840 IB programmes worldwide, more than half (3,589) of which are located in the Americas region.

The IB Educator Network (IBEN)

The IB Educator Network (IBEN) holds a critical position within the IB, by collaborating with IB educators from 164 countries who perform a variety of roles (e.g. workshop leader, consultant, school visit team leader, field representative, etc.) on behalf of the IB. With a peer-to-peer methodology, the IB Educator network allows the IB to make key achievements globally.

The IBEN department within the IB manages the network of educators, professionals who are highly experienced in IB pedagogy and leadership, by recruiting, training, and assigning them to events requested by other IB departments in support of school development (leading workshops, visiting and consulting schools, etc.). Research has shown that educators who belong to the IBEN have access to up-to-date resources prior to general launch of the documents, show greater commitment and engagement with the IB and their school, have greater opportunities to master core IB concepts, improve and practice andragogy and pedagogy, understand assessment strategies in depth and develop professional status.

The IB Educator Network is key in the development and growth of international mindedness and the IB mission.

IB AMERICAS

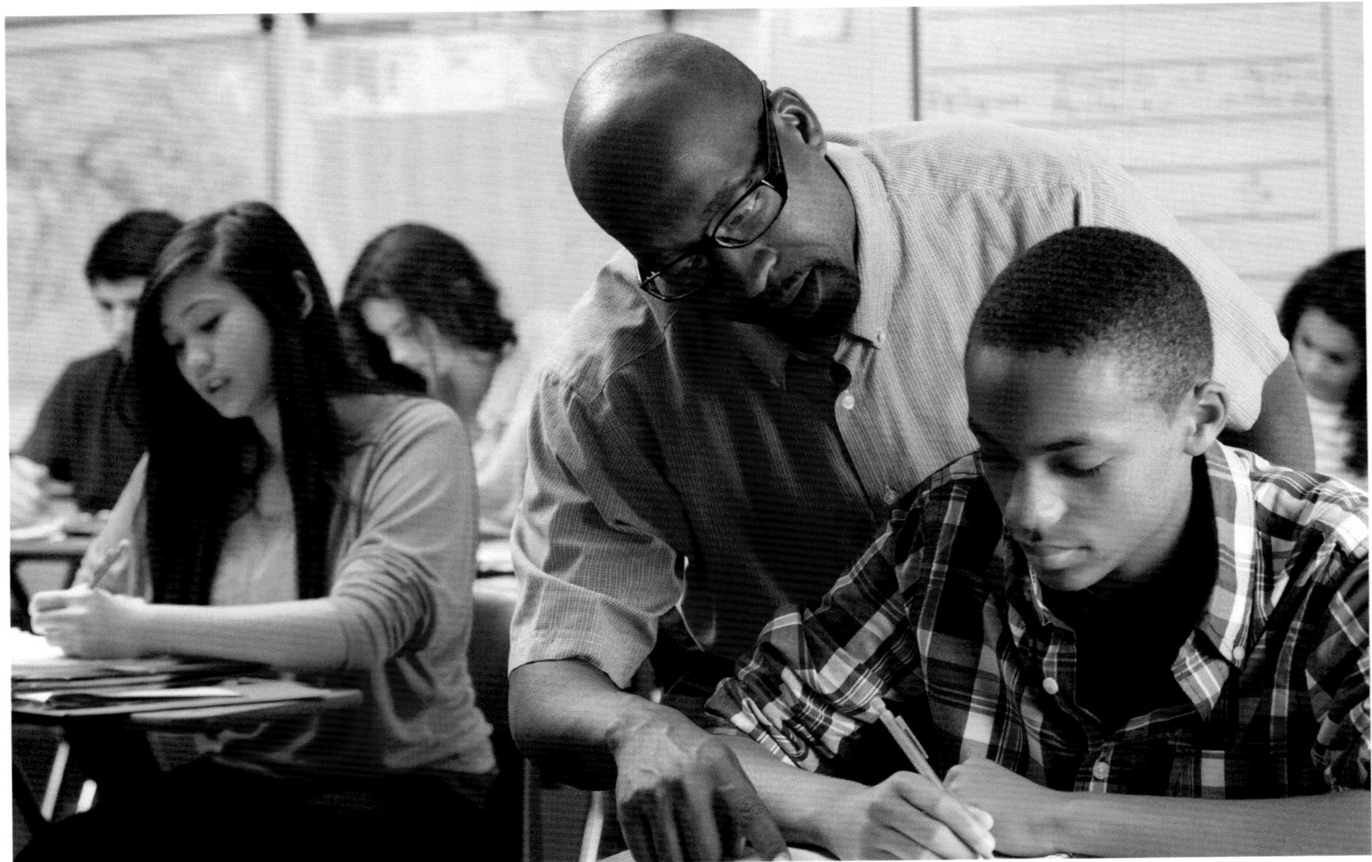

Professional development in the Americas region

In 2020, over 30,000 educators in the Americas region will attend IB professional development workshops, either in their schools or at one of our regional events. On-site workshops offer the opportunity to provide a variety of trainings to teachers from the same school, as an in-school workshop, or to teachers within a school community, as a district/cluster event.

The IB Leadership and IB Education workshop series will be offered throughout 2020 at our regional, in-school, and district/cluster events. IB Leadership workshops provide aspiring and experienced leaders with learning focused on leadership in an international context. IB Education workshops are appropriate for all educators at any point in their journey as lifelong learners. These workshops engage participants in provocative learning experiences around challenging ideas central to the IB's mission to make the world a better place through education.

University recognition

In the Americas region, more and more universities are deciding to accept IB credentials and recognize the rigor and depth of our programmes. In professional associations such as National Association of College Admission Counseling (NACAC), International Association of College Admission Counseling (Int'l ACAC), and many of their affiliates, the IB Diploma is regarded as the gold standard that combines high academic achievement with the reflection and personal growth that come from the Learner Profile.

Latin America

Private universities in Latin America have expressed great enthusiasm in partnering with the IB to recognize the competencies and personal qualities the DP and CP graduates possess. As such, several agreements have been signed and/or updated considering not only the full Diploma points, but also the core components. In the past year, IB has signed Memorandums of Understandings (MOUs) with universities in Argentina, Brazil, Peru, Mexico, and Colombia.

United States

In the US, most universities accept the IB Diploma as a school leaving credential and will grant advanced standing for IB courses as part of the Diploma Programme, as part of the Career-Related Programme, or through standard or higher individual courses. Over 1,000 universities have published recognition policies including all of the Ivy League institutions and most highly selective institutions.

There has been a growing trend in institutions using the full diploma to satisfy state/national testing requirements. As universities recognize the holistic nature of IB programmes, lobbying with state and government institution systems remain a high priority.

In the past year, close to 100 higher education institutions have worked with IB staff through webinars and in-person trainings to establish or improve their IB recognition policies to attract these top students.

Canada

All universities in Canada accept the IB Diploma as a school leaving credential and some of the top institutions award advanced standing for higher level courses. The two highest transcript receiving universities in the world are the University of Toronto and the University of British Columbia.

In the province of Quebec, students who complete the Middle Years Programme and complete the national requirements will obtain the Quebec Diploma of Secondary Studies which qualifies them for higher education studies.

Associations of IB World Schools in the Americas

Associations of IB World Schools are independent organizations established under the Guidelines of Associations of the IB. The members are commonly IB Candidate and IB World Schools. Groupings in the Associations are based on geographically relevant communities to support IB World Schools as well as schools new to the IB in the region.

Associations, who are independent of the IB, support member schools through advocacy and by:

- providing current information on the local and regional context, e.g. what is happening in education, changes affecting the schools in their association, feedback, advisory capacity, a platform for collaboration and IB research.
- disseminating updates and seeking advice from the IB about core IB services such as professional development (PD), school services, government and university recognition.
- providing professional development in association with the IB, when a separate agreement is in place.

The full listing of the current Associations of IB World Schools in the Americas region see in Appendix 4 'IB Associations Around the World', page 673.

IB research

Key findings from research in the IB Americas region:

1. Utilizing a mixed-methods case study, an investigation explored the perceptions of administrators, teachers and students within four PYP schools in **Colombia**. Student interviews identified teachers as the primary drivers of their positive learning experiences. In an accompanying survey, 89.3% of PYP students indicated that they enjoyed being a student at their school while over 90% reported that they were proud to be a student of their school (Lester and Lochmiller 2015).
2. Within a large school district in the **United States** (US), researchers investigated the impact of MYP participation on high school course enrollment and achievement. The findings indicated that former MYP students were 34% more likely than non-MYP students to take at least one DP or Advanced Placement (AP) exam in high school. Furthermore, MYP enrollment significantly increased the likelihood of earning at least one "college-ready" score[1] on a college preparatory exam (by 39%) (Wade and Wolanin 2015).

1 A "College-ready" score is defined in this study as a three or higher on an AP exam or a four or higher on a DP exam.

3. A study in **Costa Rica, Argentina (Buenos Aires) and Peru** explored the impacts of the DP on students and teachers in state schools. Students in all three countries reported highly positive views of the DP overall. In particular, students cited the programme as helpful in developing research, critical thinking and other key skills. Most teachers reported that the DP had reinvigorated their passion for teaching. In particular, teachers emphasized features of the DP such as curricular style, promotion of thinking skills, openness to learning, and feedback from IB examiners (Beech et al 2018).
4. In a large-scale quantitative study, researchers investigated the postsecondary outcomes of DP students in the US. Findings showed that, in 2013, 82.2% of all DP students enrolled in university immediately after high school. This compares favorably to the US national average for immediate enrollment of 66% (2013). DP students were also more likely to persist at university (continuing on to their second year) compared to students nationally (88.1% and 80% respectively in 2013). Lastly, in comparison to the 2011 national four-year graduation rate (41.1%), DP students had higher four-year graduation rates (56.3% in 2013) (Pilchen et al 2019).
5. IB Research conducted a study to examine the higher education pathways of all CP graduates in the US from 2013 to 2015. The study found that 81% of CP graduates enrolled in university sometime after secondary school, with 76% enrolling immediately. Additionally, 79% of students who enrolled in higher education chose four-year over two-year colleges, compared to 64% of students nationally. Regarding university persistence, 89% of CP graduates who enrolled in university came back for a second year (Mack et al 2017).

Conferences and events

Over 1,700 people attended the 2019 IB Global Conference in New Orleans, Louisiana, USA from 18-21 July. The 2020 IB Global Conference will be held in Toronto, Ontario, Canada from 23-26 July. The annual conference is an opportunity for members of the IB community to discuss best practices with colleagues, participate in engaging breakout sessions, and listen to stimulating keynote speakers who address some of the big questions facing the education community today.

The IB alumni network

The IB Alumni Network is a resource for IB graduates around the world. The network links graduates from IB World Schools in 153 countries to support their future studies and careers. By connecting with the IB, former students have the opportunity to participate in research, support development efforts and speak at our events. These graduates are also supporting educators and parents in understanding the impact of an IB education from a student's perspective. To see how graduates are supporting IB programmes, visit ibo.org/programme-stories and connect with us at ibo.org/alumni.

Contact

IB Global Centre Washington DC
7501 Wisconsin Avenue, Suite 200 West
Bethesda, Maryland, 20814 United States

Main: +1 301 202 3000
Web: www.ibo.org/en/iba

Baltimore International Academy

Principal
Ms. Elena Lokounia

PYP coordinator
Henriette Sindjui

MYP coordinator
Henriette Sindjui

Status State

Boarding/day Day

Gender Coeducational

Language of instruction
Spanish, Mandarin, Arabic, Russian, French

Authorised IB programmes
PYP, MYP

Age Range 5 – 14 years

Number of pupils enrolled
737

Address
4410 Frankford Avenue
Baltimore
MD 21206 | USA

TEL +1 410 426 3650
FAX +1 410 426 3656

Email
elokounia@bcps.k12.md.us

Website
www.baltimoreinternationalacademy.org

Mission
Baltimore International Academy is committed to providing a rigorous academic learning environment that challenges all students to achieve. Our immersion (Spanish, Chinese, Arabic, Russian, French) and International Baccalaureate Programmes provide a culturally and linguistically diverse education to help our students develop the knowledge, understanding, attitudes and skills necessary to participate responsibly in a changing world.

Who We Are
Baltimore International Academy (BIA) is a public charter school in an urban environment. We are located in Baltimore City, Maryland. We teach Kindergarten through Eighth Grades and have two signature programs, full Language Immersion and the International Baccalaureate. BIA offers a unique opportunity for Baltimore City children. Fluency in a second language will give them opportunities in their futures that their monolingual counterparts won't have. The international mindedness and critical thinking skills they gain by learning through the IB programmes are already setting them apart; their scores are higher than their City counterparts in the State's reading and math assessments. BIA's teachers are from numerous countries around the world, and our students enjoy a wide diversity of cultures and ethnicities as a result. This exposure gives them an open mindedness that is another advantage our students have over the majority of the City's other students who lack this exposure. The City is so pleased with BIA that they authorized the school to create a new, replication school, Baltimore International Academy West. This replication of BIA is located on the West side of Baltimore City. Baltimore City Public Schools wants to give more of their residents' children the advantages that current BIA students receive.

Academics
BIA follows the Maryland State Department of Education's curriculum, but with our full language immersion program, our students learn their core subjects (Science, Social Studies, Math, Target Language Arts) through one of five languages; Spanish, Chinese (Mandarin), Arabic, Russian or French. Our students are City residents and 98% come to us only speaking English. From the time these children walk into the school, their teachers only speak to them in their target language, never in English. Our students become fluent in speaking, understanding, reading and writing in their target languages. Beginning in the second grade, students receive one hour of English language arts daily to learn the mechanics of their native tongue.

BIA is also an International Baccalaureate (IB) World School for the Primary Years and Middle Years Programmes. As such, students learn through inquiry-based instruction, project-based assessments, and collaborative group work. They study in a way that increases their critical-thinking skills and prepares them well for high school, college, and a global marketplace. The school's environment, its Immersion and IB Programmes, are geared to our slogan, "International Education for Global Leadership."

Head of School
Nathalie Guyon

MYP coordinator
Ms. Aareena Dhillon

DP coordinator
Ms. Xiaoping Liu

Status Private

Boarding/day Day

Gender Coeducational

Language of instruction
English, French, Spanish, Chinese, Portuguese

Authorised IB programmes
MYP, DP

Age Range 6 weeks – 18

Address
5015 Auto Plex Drive
Baton Rouge
LA 70809 | USA

TEL +1 225 293 4338
FAX +1 225 293 4307

Email
info@brisla.com

Website
www.brintl.com

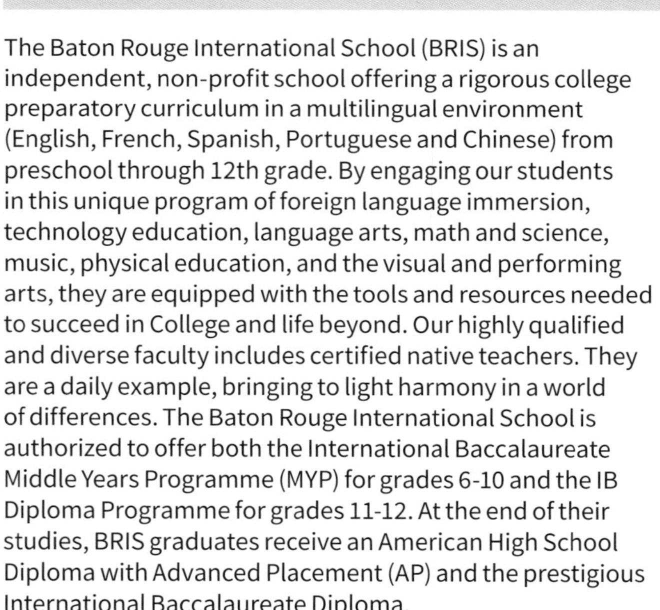

The Baton Rouge International School (BRIS) is an independent, non-profit school offering a rigorous college preparatory curriculum in a multilingual environment (English, French, Spanish, Portuguese and Chinese) from preschool through 12th grade. By engaging our students in this unique program of foreign language immersion, technology education, language arts, math and science, music, physical education, and the visual and performing arts, they are equipped with the tools and resources needed to succeed in College and life beyond. Our highly qualified and diverse faculty includes certified native teachers. They are a daily example, bringing to light harmony in a world of differences. The Baton Rouge International School is authorized to offer both the International Baccalaureate Middle Years Programme (MYP) for grades 6-10 and the IB Diploma Programme for grades 11-12. At the end of their studies, BRIS graduates receive an American High School Diploma with Advanced Placement (AP) and the prestigious International Baccalaureate Diploma.

Accreditation

The Baton Rouge International School is an IB World School authorized to offer the MYP and the DP. BRIS is also approved by the BESE and the Louisiana Department of Education/US Department of Education. In addition, BRIS is a full member of many professional/educational organizations in the United States and abroad.

Campus Facilities

The BRIS campus is located in Baton Rouge, Louisiana, USA. The modern facilities have been built on an 18 acre property in the heart of Baton Rouge. Its peaceful, green environment includes a lake visited by geese and falcons and plenty of space for playgrounds, fields for soccer and other sporting activities. The wooded site offers the tranquility needed for young minds to stay focused while enjoying campus life. BRIS recently started to implement its comprehensive campus master plan to design and build new buildings to serve as administrative, educational and recreational facilities for the future. The design, planning and buildings will reflect the innovative education that BRIS provides through contemporary and environmentally sustainable architecture.

Educating the global leaders of the future!

Head of School
Dr. Sandra B. Soto

Assistant Head of School
Kristen Pelekanakis

PYP coordinator
Christina Soriano

Status State

Boarding/day Day

Gender Coeducational

Language of instruction
English

Authorised IB programmes
PYP

Age Range 3 – 10 years

Address
443 St. Marks Ave.
Brooklyn
NY 11238 | USA

TEL +1 718 230 0851

Email brooklynartselementary@gmail.com

Website
www.brooklynartselementary.org

Brooklyn Arts and Science Elementary School: Mission & Vision

The mission of Brooklyn Arts and Science Elementary School (BASES) is to celebrate the unique complement of gifts and talents each learner possesses and to cultivate those strengths into powerful assets that serve the student and society. Through a rigorous, inquiry-based curriculum we equip our students to be fully active participants in local and global communities. Carefully designed learning experiences foster the development of personal attitudes that contribute to student success and academic achievement.

Our school values or *Compass Points* are embedded in everything we do:

North – Never miss an opportunity to lead
South – Safe and supportive environment
East – Ever striving for excellence
West – Wonder why and always question

As an International Baccalaureate World School, we are dedicated to the mission of creating a better, more peaceful world through intercultural understanding and with an intentional focus on social justice and equity. As our students learn to appreciate the contributions of others, they develop an awareness of their own value to the learning community as they discover, collaborate and reflect on projects that showcase their learning and development.

Brooklyn Arts and Science is proud to have been part of the New York City Department of Education's Diversity Pilot Program. We are committed to challenging our own biases and the systems that perpetuate inequitable outcomes for students of color.

In addition to the academic program, Brooklyn Arts offers a plethora of enrichment opportunities. The school offers music education to all classes and partners with the Noel Pointer Foundation for violin instruction. Students explore the visual arts in the school's studio and dance exploration in the dance studio. The school also offers fencing and chess. STEM is offered through a partnership with the BEAM Center.

(Founded 1983)

Head of School
Mr. Heath Sparrow M.A., M.Sc.

PYP coordinator
Maria Ines Mayaudon

DP coordinator
Ricardo Fumachi

Status Private

Boarding/day Day

Gender Coeducational

Language of instruction
English, Spanish

Authorised IB programmes
PYP, DP

Age Range 3 – 18 years

Fees
Kindergarten MEX$66,800
Elementary MEX$90,100
Middle School MEX$100,000
High School MEX$110,500

Address
Callejon del Jornongo #210
Colonia El Pedregal
Cabo San Lucas, B.C.S.
C.P. 23453 | MÉXICO

TEL +52 624 143 2100 (Ext:112)

Email
info@elcamino.edu.mx

Website
www.elcamino.edu.mx

Colegio El Camino is a Private K-12, non sectarian, nonprofit organization governed by a permanent board of governors made up by members of the three founding families and other invited members of the community.

Our mission at Camino is "to develop honorable, inquiring and caring life-long learners with intercultural understanding and respect for others who, through creativity and rigorous curriculum, become passionate leaders and participants in a global community."

El Camino has a current student population of 420 students. The majority of students are Mexican nationals but the school is represented by 23 nationalities that include Americans, Canadians, Australians, Israelis, Japanese, French, Swiss, Germans, Venezuelans, Brazilians, Peruvians and other Latin nationalities.

The increased diversity is a result of our international accreditation with both the Southern Association of Schools (SACS) AdvancED and the International Baccalaureate Organization.

We are 1 of 36 AdvancED accredited schools in Mexico demonstrating our commitment and adherence to the high standards of quality required by their organization based out of the United States.

We are honored to be 1 of the 116 IB World Schools in Mexico. We offer both the Diploma and Primary Years Programmes and are currently in the process of the feasibility study for the Middle Years Programme. We are registered with the Mexican Ministry of Education in all sections.

Camino is celebrating 36 years in offering the vanguard global education in Los Cabos to students from all nationalities, religions, cultures and socio economic standing. Our school provides students with a safe and caring learning environment supported by trained and certified staff from multiple nationalities.

In addition to our bilingual curriculum we offer many support services including certified and licensed psychologists, a mentoring program, career and college counseling, afternoon academic academies, afternoon sports program, the Camino Language Acquisition Support Program (CLASP), para-academic workshops and the IB Diploma CAS (Creativity, Activity, Service) program.

Colegio Hebreo Maguen David

CHMD

(Founded 1978)

Head of School
Dra. Lucila Minvielle

PYP coordinator
Graciela Silva Escobar

MYP coordinator
Naomi Rojas

DP coordinator
Susana Memun Zaga

Status Private

Boarding/day Day

Gender Coeducational

Language of instruction
Spanish, Hebrew, English

Authorised IB programmes
PYP, MYP, DP

Age Range 2 – 18 years

Number of pupils enrolled
1194

Address
Antiguo Camino a Tecamachalco #370
Lomas de Vista Hermosa
Mexico DF | **MÉXICO**

TEL +52 (55) 52 46 26 00

Email
chmd@chmd.edu.mx

Website
www.chmd.edu.mx

CHMD: A relevant educational model

At Colegio Hebreo Maguen David we are certain that it is possible to put together an educational project, which places the individual and the community at its core. For us, the school is a space in which creativity, experimentation and inquiry are promoted; it is an open space for collaborative learning, dialogue and innovation.

Hence, we have designed a school that enables the development of the talents of those who participate in this learning experience. That is why Maguen is a benchmark for educational innovation. In 2017 our school was recognized by Inter-American Development Bank as one of the 30 most innovative schools in Latin America. It was the first school in Latin America to have a Makerspace, a place inspired by the philosophy of learning by doing. After the transformation of our spaces into platforms that enhance interaction and collaborative learning, the design project of our school was awarded the bronze medal at the latest Design Awards in Milan. Additionally, nowadays we are renewing our Elementary School spaces in collaboration with renowned artist Rosan Bosch, known for her designs and perspectives on learning spaces for the future.

We also develop innovative academic programs as we strive to generate social and emotional conditions conducive to the well-being and growth of our entire school community. During the last year we put in motion the Year of Well-being because not only we focus in academic achievements but also in educating with values through a culture of well-being, working to create the conditions that provide a hopeful future for our students. Well-being CHMD was built by our own community as a shared frame reference of expectations of behavior which help us to live better.

Value, tradition and knowledge, represent our foundational beliefs and our commitment towards future endeavors. That is why, at CHMD we choose to take on the challenge of teaching to live as the biggest challenge of a relevant 21st century education.

Head of School
Arturo Camilo Williams Rivas

PYP coordinators
María del Pilar González Mata
Alejandra Silva Bringas

MYP coordinator
Erika Daniela Mendoza Pineda

DP coordinator
Laura Silva Rico

Status Private

Boarding/day Day

Gender Coeducational

Language of instruction
Spanish

Authorised IB programmes
PYP, MYP, DP

Mixcoac Campus
Empresa 8, Col Mixcoac, Alcaldía Benito Juárez México City
CP 03910 | MÉXICO

San Jerónimo Campus
Presa Reventada 53, Col. San Jerónimo Lídice, Alcaldía Magdalena Contreras
CP 10200 | MÉXICO

Ajusco Campus
Calle de la Felicidad S/N, Col San Miguel Ajusco, Alcaldía Tlalpan
| MÉXICO

TEL +52 55 1087 9797
FAX +52 55 1087 9797

Email
kblum@colegiowilliams.edu.mx

Website
www.colegiowilliams.edu.mx

Well-established and Innovative

At Colegio Williams being avant-garde has been a tradition for more than 100 years. The school was founded by the British pedagogue Camilo J. Williams. Since then, four generations of educators have developed a unique education philosophy, characterized by purposive and innovative approach.

Trendsetting

Colegio Williams was the first educational institution in México to include in its curricula sports, agro-livestock technology, and the most modern English learning methodologies and techniques.

At the Mixcoac Campus, there is a beautiful castle which up to 1917 belonged to José Ives Limantour Marquet, Minister of Treasury under President Pofirio Díaz. Both students and teachers find inspiration in the magical atmosphere of this 200- year old building.

Elevated Principles and Standards

- An education that re-signifies and strengthens the pride of being Mexican.
- An education that integrates mind and body, theory and practice, arts and science, voice and thought, project and reality.
- An education that is critical, objective, optimistic, that, by understanding the present, projects towards the future.
- An education that fosters research inquiry and for which individual growth and that of the community are promoted.
- An education that brings about values that are acquired by practising them.

Outdoor Activities and Facilities

Sports and contact with nature are essential to the development of Colegio Williams students, for which the school has top quality grounds, facilities, and instructors for a wide range of agro-livestock technology activities, which include breeding animals as well as growing vegetables, and sports activities such as swimming, scuba diving, horseback riding, soccer, Olympic gymnastics, cheerleading, dance, Tae-Kwon-do, tennis, volleyball, frontennis, and flag-football.

Computer facilities

Include 130 Mac Books in 4 Mac Shuttles to transport them to different classrooms plus 60 iMacs in computer labs.

Trips Abroad

Students are encouraged to participate in trips abroad that are organized by the school. The objectives are cultural and academic development, and the trips have included Canada, France, England, and the USA, to Iowa for scientific presentations and to New York for the National High School United Nations Model.

Founding Principal/Head of School
Dr Laurie B. Midgette

PYP coordinator
David Mercaldo, MEd

Status State

Boarding/day Day

Gender Coeducational

Language of instruction
English, Spanish

Authorised IB programmes
PYP

Age Range 5 – 10

Number of pupils enrolled
280

Address
1400 Linden Blvd
Brooklyn
NY 11212 | USA

TEL +1 718 683 3300

Email
caacs@caa-ny.org

Website
www.culturalartsacademy.org

Cultural Arts Academy Charter School's mission is to provide a college preparatory education, with exemplary cultural arts proficiency, to young leaders who will profoundly impact the human condition. CAACS opened as an NYCDOE authorized independent public charter school on August 30, 2010. Cultural Arts Academy Charter School is unique in that we have earned two global designations: on March 26, 2019 as a an authorized International Baccalaureate (IB) World School; and, in 2017 as the first charter school in New York State to receive the prestigious Franklin Covey Lighthouse School designation as an exemplary student leadership model. CAACS brings both initiatives together in one synergistic learning model. Our goal at Cultural Arts Academy Charter School is to fully prepare our students for college, career, and citizenship. Our students participate in the SIFMA Foundation's Invest It Forward initiative that connects financial professionals with our students in a classroom setting to deepen students' understanding of the capital markets and financial systems. The students have to develop a business, from conceiving the business plan all the way through to going public through an initial public offering (IPO). CAACS celebrates student voice and choice, particularly through our visual and performing arts, athletics, and our annual signature programs: tennis at the Billie Jean King Tennis Center, swimming at the Asphalt Green Facility, participation in the American Debate League, the National Elementary Honor Society, and extended learning experiences to museums and the like. Our international recognition allows us to deliver the best possible education for our scholars. In June 2020, we will graduate our 6th class in the 10-year history of the school. This achievement is evidenced not only by our school's consistent attendance rate of 95% and above every year, but also by the scholarship of our world-class scholars!

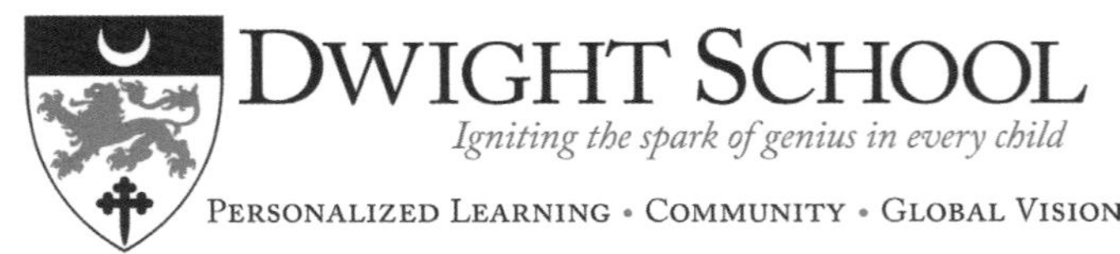

(Founded 1872)

Chancellor Stephen H. Spahn

Vice Chancellor Blake Spahn

Head of School Dianne Drew

PYP coordinator Brittany Dallal

MYP coordinator Shelby Levin

DP coordinator Liz Hutton

CP coordinator Jaya Bhavnani

Status Private

Boarding/day Day

Gender Coeducational

Language of instruction
English

Authorised IB programmes
PYP, MYP, DP, CP

Age Range 2 – 18

Number of pupils enrolled
957

Fees
Day: US$51,000

Address
291 Central Park West
New York
NY 10024 | USA

TEL +1 212 724 6360
FAX +1 212 724 2539

Email
admissions@dwight.edu

Website
www.dwight.edu

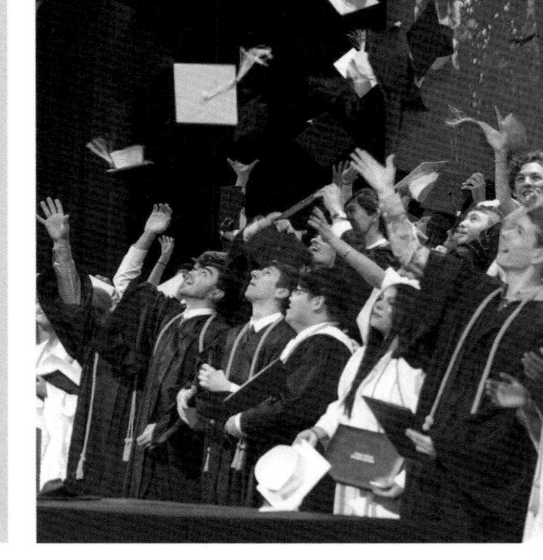

Dwight School is an internationally renowned college preparatory school with a rich, 148-year tradition of academic excellence and igniting the "spark of genius" in every child. Dwight's world-class education rests on three pillars: personalized learning, community, and global vision. The School's diverse faculty and student body represent over 40 countries, deepening the internationally minded, innovative learning environment.

A leader in global education, Dwight is the first school in the Americas to offer the comprehensive International Baccalaureate (IB) curriculum for students from preschool through grade 12. It was also the first school in New York City to offer the PYP. The rigorous IB is recognized as the "gold standard" in pre-university preparation. Through the IB, Dwight is educating students to become caring, open-minded and critical-thinking global leaders. Foreign language instruction is extensive and begins in preschool.

Through Spark Tank, Dwight's unique incubator designed to nurture innovation, entrepreneurship, and leadership skills beyond the classroom, K-12 students develop their own ideas for new businesses, non-profits, and products.

Dwight School in New York is the flagship campus of a global network, which includes schools in London, Seoul, Shanghai and Dubai. Dwight Global Online School – a campus in the cloud – extends a world-class Dwight education everywhere. Dwight Schools educate students around the world, who benefit from a wide range of exciting cross-campus academic, leadership, and creative collaborations.

Dwight School has a comprehensive college guidance program beginning early in grade 9. Graduates attend the finest colleges and universities in the world, including Harvard, Yale, Princeton, MIT, Stanford, Oxford, St. Andrew's and the University of Edinburgh, among many others. Upon graduation, they join an extensive global network of alumni leaders – all dedicated to making our world a better place.

Dwight is accredited by the Council of International Schools, the International Baccalaureate, the Middle States Association of Colleges and Secondary Schools, and the World Academy of Sport. Financial aid is granted on the basis of need.

Edgewood High School

Principal
Roni Maddox Ed.D

MYP coordinator
Manny Co

DP coordinator
Jennifer Zampiello

Status State

Boarding/day Day

Gender Coeducational

Language of instruction
English

Authorised IB programmes
MYP, DP

Age Range 14 – 18

Number of pupils enrolled
863

Address
1625 W Durness
West Covina
CA 91790 | USA

TEL +1 626 939 4600
FAX +1 626 939 4999

Email
jzampiello@wcusd.org

Website
edgewoodib.wcusd.org

Edgewood High School is a public high school located in the city of West Covina, 19 miles east of Los Angeles. Edgewood High School is an International Baccalaureate World School authorized to offer the Middle Years Programme and Diploma Programme and in the application process for the Career-related Programme. Edgewood is a school of choice serving a diverse population of 863 students. Edgewood recently reopened as a high school in 2010 with our first graduation class in May of 2014. We have been an IB World School since 2011 and we are accredited by the Western Association of Schools and Colleges through March 2021.

Edgewood offers a smaller learning community focused on preparing creative, inquiring, caring students prepared for college and career. This can be seen in our Mission Statement, *"Edgewood, an IB World School, is committed to building a globally aware community of lifelong learners who achieve high academic standards. Edgewood provides a diverse, challenging curriculum that is student-centered and develops inquisitive, knowledgeable, and empathetic students who actively engage in and contribute to their family, community, and the world around them."*

EHS offers a variety of courses to meet our diverse student needs. The curriculum includes: honors courses in 9th and 10th grade, both standard level and higher level IB courses, a world language program, a fine arts department offering visual arts, music, and drama, a health and physical education program, Career and Technical Education courses in Game Design and Video Production, and support services for special education and English learner students.

Students at EHS are provided personal and social development opportunities created by participation in extracurricular activities such as ASB, clubs, yearbook, dances, study trips, performances, cheer and athletics. Edgewood offers CIF sports in cross country, baseball, softball, tennis, basketball, volleyball, water polo, soccer, wrestling, track and swim.

Edgewood Middle School

Principal
Roni Maddox Ed.D

MYP coordinator
Manny Co

Status State

Boarding/day Day

Gender Coeducational

Language of instruction
English

Authorised IB programmes
MYP

Age Range 11 – 14

Number of pupils enrolled
582

Address
1625 W. Durness St.
West Covina
CA 91790 | USA

TEL +1 626 939 4600
FAX +1 626 939 4999

Email
mco@wcusd.net

Website
edgewoodib.wcusd.org

Edgewood, an IB World School, is committed to building a globally-aware community of lifelong learners who achieve high academic standards.

Edgewood provides a diverse, challenging curriculum that is student-centered and develops inquisitive, knowledgeable, and empathetic students who actively engage in and contribute to their family, community, and the world around them.

Edgewood Middle School is a public school located in the city of West Covina, 19 miles east of Los Angeles. Edgewood Middle School is an International Baccalaureate World School authorized to offer the IB Middle Years Programme. Edgewood is a school of choice serving a diverse population of 582 students in grades 6-8. Edgewood received the IB Middle Years Program authorization in December 2018. Edgewood provides a smaller learning community focused on preparing creative, inquiring, and caring students ready to make connections between subjects studied and the real world as well as develop critical and reflective thinking skills.

EMS offers a variety of courses to meet our diverse student needs. The curriculum includes: honors courses in 7th and 8th grade, a world language program offering both Mandarin and Spanish, a fine arts department offering visual arts, music, and drama, a health and physical education program, yearbook, and services for special education and English learner students. Edgewood Middle School offers outstanding student support through committed, compassionate teachers that provide multi-tiered systems of interventions and enrichment opportunities. Edgewood students are holistically taught in diverse learning environments that prepare students for a global workplace. Partnerships with community, local agencies, and organizations provide opportunities for students to participate in activities for service. Students at EMS are provided personal and social development opportunities created by participation in extracurricular activities such as ASB, clubs, dances, performances, cheer and athletics. Edgewood offers sports in track and field, flag football, softball, tennis, basketball, volleyball, and soccer.

Head of School
Dr. Vladimir D. Kuskovski

DP coordinator
Gabriela Deambrosio

Status Private

Boarding/day Mixed

Gender Coeducational

Language of instruction
English

Authorised IB programmes
DP

Age Range 14 – 19

Number of pupils enrolled
650

Fees
IB Diploma US$58,500
(US$19,500 per term)

Address
582 Columbus Avenue
Thornwood
NY 10594 | USA

TEL +1 914 495 6028

Email
iaadmissionsny@ef.com

Website
www.ef.edu/academy

EF Academy International Boarding Schools prepares students for a global future with an exceptional high school education in the US or UK. At EF Academy, we believe in every student's ability to succeed. We empower them to do so through our renowned curricula, as well as quality one-on-one relationships with teachers and mentors alike. Built into every course is an emphasis on multilingualism and intercultural exchange and our students live the IB ethos every single day.

The School

Our IB World School is located approximately 45 minutes from Manhattan. EF Academy's secure campus offers 100 acres of landscaped grounds, running trails and playing fields in the quiet suburban town of Thornwood. Our facilities include a premier science center, fully-equipped gym, auditorium, spacious classrooms and comfortable on-campus residences.

Academics

Instruction and guidance at EF Academy New York is highly personal. Students can follow the IGCSE program in their first two years of high school and the IB Diploma in the following two years. Alternatively, students can follow the US High School Diploma for all four years of high school. All students who successfully complete their high school studies with EF Academy New York are awarded a nationally recognized New York State High School Diploma.

University Placements

EF Academy New York graduates have been accepted to universities such as Harvard University, Yale University, Johns Hopkins University, New York University, several schools in the University of California network, as well as international universities ranked highly for the fields of art, business and engineering. Some of our artistically talented students have been accepted to Rhode Island School of Design and Parsons School of Design.

Support and Guidance

Each student at EF Academy New York is assigned a pathway manager who helps them select the right courses, supports them with school work and comforts them if they ever feel homesick. In addition to receiving one-on-one support from teachers, students also work together with university advisors who help them research and apply to the universities that best suit their goals and interests.

Student Life

We encourage students to participate in co-curricular activities, such as special-interest clubs, academic competitions, varsity sports and community service opportunities. Our school's activities coordinator also arranges teacher led excursions for students on the weekends so they have several opportunities to explore Manhattan by visiting all the museums, musicals, and sights for which the city is known.

Escola Americana do Rio de Janeiro – Gávea

(Founded 1937)

Headmaster
Mr Nigel J. Winnard EdD

Gávea Campus Principals
Nate Swenson (Lower) &
Jamie Robb (Upper)

Barra Campus Principals
Kirstin White (Lower) &
Tim Shirk (Upper)

DP coordinator
Flávia DiLuccio (Gávea Campus)
Scott Little (Barra Campus)

Status Private

Boarding/day Day

Gender Coeducational

Language of instruction
English

Authorised IB programmes
DP

Age Range 3 – 18

Number of pupils enrolled
1200

Gávea Campus
Estrada da Gávea 132
Gávea, Rio de Janeiro
RJ 22451-263 | BRAZIL

TEL +55 21 2125 9000

Email
admissions.gavea@earj.com.br

Barra Campus
Rua Colbert Coelho 155,
Barra da Tijuca, Rio de Janeiro
RJ 22793-313 | BRAZIL

TEL +55 21 3747 2000

Email
admissions.barra@earj.com.br

Website
www.earj.com.br

Escola Americana do Rio de Janeiro is one of Latin America's most respected international teaching institutions. Established in 1937, and an IB World School since 1982, EARJ is a non-profit school, providing an American international education to the expatriate and Brazilian communities of Rio de Janeiro that blends high quality academics with rich co-curricular opportunities.

EARJ occupies two campuses in differing parts of the city, each offering programs from Preschool through to the IB Diploma. EARJ is distinctive in that its 1,200 students can work towards graduating with three Diplomas concurrently: the IB Diploma, the US High School Diploma, and the Brazilian Diploma.

EARJ is proud to offer a holistic education that, through the philosophy and practices of the IB, inspires creativity, critical thinking, collaboration, communication, and the confidence to lead and excel in an ever-changing global community. The coming years will see EARJ extend its belief in and commitment to the IB programmes with the adoption of the PYP and MYP by 2024.

EARJ is a diverse international community of learners. Across our two campuses, our student body comprises 70% Brazillian and 30% International students, with our faculty demographic reflecting that same balance. The past three years have seen tremendous growth in our enrolment, with further growth expected in the coming years. Our community is spread far and wide, via our Panther Alumni network, who keeps us connected to our past as we work towards an even brighter future.

Each year EARJ graduates are accepted to the world's leading universities, and we pride ourselves on each student finding the institution that is best for them. Whilst a few graduates remain to study in Brazil, the vast majority head overseas to the USA, Canada and Europe for university.

The Escola American do Rio de Janeiro gladly accepts applications for entry in all grade levels throughout the year. For any further information please visit our website at www.earj.com.br or feel free to follow us on social media.

Head of School
Deivis Pothin

DP coordinator
Jason James

Status Private

Boarding/day Day

Gender Coeducational

Language of instruction
English, Portuguese

Authorised IB programmes
DP

Address
Rua Verbo Divino 993-A
Chacara Sto. Antonio
São Paulo
SP 04719-001 | BRAZIL

TEL +55 11 3512 2300

Website
www.pueridomus.com.br

Pueri Domus is proud to be a school that was born with the future in mind and the students at its heart. By using a learner-centred approach and active learning methodologies, Pueri Domus helps students to become leaders of their own learning. The school is recognized for its focus on using technology during the learning process. International recognition of this commitment came when Apple awarded the school the "Apple Distinguished Program", a worldwide program that acknowledges pioneering and outstanding initiatives which use technology to further transformative education. Bilingual education is education for the 21st century and technology is an essential pillar of any forward-looking education. Therefore, Coding and STEM are integral parts of the curriculum from Year 2 onwards.

Starting in the earliest years of Preschool, ethical values and social-emotional skills are part of the curriculum developed through practical structured activities within the ConViver Program. The objectives of this program are to foster students' self-knowledge and personal maturity, stimulate initiative and creativity, encourage leadership, and develop citizenship. As a Unesco Associated School, we also promote the students' commitment to Sustainable Development Goals by equipping them with social entrepreneurship skills and active participation in community service.

Pueri Domus's bilingual Portuguese-English program develops the students' language skills by ensuring real-life contexts to acquire, develop and consolidate Thinking Skills in both languages. English is taught not only in traditional Language Arts classes but through Logical Reasoning, Social Sciences and Natural Science classes, all of which are structured to enhance the understanding of information and concepts taught within our integrated bilingual curriculum. The holistic bilingual education offered at Pueri Domus expands students' opportunities to move on to university and college courses outside of Brazil. This culminates in the International Baccalaureate Diploma Programme on the Verbo Divino campus.

ESFERA Escola Internacional

(Founded 2004)

Head of School
Daisy Gava

PYP coordinator
Melissa Therriault Zaramella

MYP coordinator
Sandra Araujo

Status Private

Boarding/day Day

Gender Coeducational

Language of instruction
English, Portuguese

Authorised IB programmes
PYP, MYP

Age Range 2 – 14

Number of pupils enrolled
400

Address
Av Anchieta, 908 – Jardim Nova Europa
Sao José dos Campos
São Paulo
SP 12242-280 | BRAZIL

TEL +55 12 3322 1255
FAX +55 12 3322 1255

Email
secretaria@escolaesfera.com.br

Website
www.escolaesfera.com.br

São José dos Campos, Brazil, is a city known for its attractive surroundings and importance as a center of Science and Technology. Esfera Escola Internacional aims to contribute to the development of innovative citizens, who are able to interact in international contexts for the common good. Esfera offers an academically rigorous bilingual curriculum from Preschool to Middle School which is based on the Brazilian National Common Curricular Base and the IB standards. Esfera is also an UNESCO Associated School.

In Preschool, children are encouraged to develop their social skills and explore the world around them, through play-based learning, building new understandings and learning to communicate their ideas and feelings with respect. Relationships are at the heart of the Preschool program and multiple intelligences are valued, allowing for differentiated approaches to teaching and learning. Teachers recognize the full potential of each student, aiming to foster their talents through creativity and a joy for learning. In Elementary School, students engage in six transdisciplinary Units of Inquiry each year, exploring content and concepts, while developing essential skills and attitudes. Students become progressively more autonomous in their ability to think critically, work collaboratively, employ technology and propose solutions. Then, in the Year 5 Exhibition, they are able to demonstrate the breadth of their understanding, skills and values that they've acquired throughout the PYP.

In Middle School, students work with interdisciplinary units in an expansive curriculum that includes: Languages (Portuguese, English and Spanish), Mathematics, Science, Design, History, Geography, Art, Music and Physical Education. Students continue to develop their international mindedness and active pursuit of meaningful action through the international exchange programs and the Community Project in Year 8 and a personal research in Year 9. Throughout Middle School, the tutorship program allows students to become more aware of their learning process and how to develop strategies for thinking and relating to others as they change and grow.

Foxcroft Academy

Head of School
Mr Arnold Shorey

DP coordinator
Donna Newhouse

Status Private

Boarding/day Mixed

Gender Coeducational

Language of instruction
English

Authorised IB programmes
DP

Age Range 14 – 18

Number of pupils enrolled
420

Address
975 West Main Street
Dover-Foxcroft
ME 04426 | USA

TEL +1 207 564 8351

Email
admissions@foxcroftacademy.org

Website
www.foxcroftacademy.org

Foxcroft Academy, home of the Ponies, is an independent high school founded in 1823 on the principle that knowledge is power. Foxcroft Academy is committed to providing students from central Maine and beyond a rigorous college and career preparatory academic curriculum designed to produce informed and active global citizens. Foxcroft Academy will furnish all students with the underlying skills needed for post-secondary success while embracing its safe community and natural environment.

197 years since its founding, Foxcroft Academy exists as one of only nine remaining (from an original 122) private academies that serve the public trust as part of its mission. Today Foxcroft Academy is proud to have an enrollment of more than 400 day and boarding students from 16 Maine communities and over 20 different nations. Students at Foxcroft Academy can choose from more than 150 different course offerings, including college prep, AP, IB , and more. This extensive curriculum represents the core liberal arts requirements, college preparatory courses, advanced placement courses, vocational/technical courses, and an alternative education program. We offer over 20 interscholastic varsity sports and have dozens of clubs and organizations for students to work with and belong to. Learn more about Foxcroft Academy at www.foxcroftacademy.org. Together, we will ride on.

French-American School of New York

(Founded 1980)

Head of School
Mr. Francis Gianni

DP coordinator
Françoise Monier

Status Private

Boarding/day Day

Gender Coeducational

Language of instruction
English, French

Authorised IB programmes
DP

Age Range 3 – 18

Number of pupils enrolled
800

Fees
Tuition, per year US$26,640 – US$35,040

Address
320 East Boston Post Road
Mamaroneck
NY 10543 | USA

TEL +1 914 250 0000

Email
admissions@fasny.org

Website
www.fasny.org

The French-American School of New York (FASNY) is an international and bilingual independent coeducational day school providing an international education to approximately 800 students in Nursery through Grade 12. FASNY develops globally literate, multicultural lifelong learners through a unique program that integrates French, American and international curricula.

A unique location

FASNY is located in Westchester County, New York, 20 miles north of Manhattan (35 minutes from Grand Central Station by rail) and 9 miles south of Greenwich, Connecticut. Most families choose to enjoy the space and quiet that this peaceful yet active area has to offer. A number of large and medium sized companies are located here and the commute to Manhattan is very convenient. For families living in New York City, their older children easily come to school by rail.

Stellar academics

FASNY is the only school in the New York metropolitan area to be accredited by the International Baccalaureate Organisation and by the French Ministry of Education (AEFE). We are also accredited by the New York State Association of Independent Schools. Our students therefore enjoy the unique privilege of graduating with either the IBDP or the French Baccalaureate (with or without the International Option), and with a New York State High School Diploma.

The school offers a bilingual immersion program in Nursery through Kindergarten, bringing children of all cultural and linguistic backgrounds to academic fluency in French and English. In grades 1 through 8, students follow a rigorous bilingual program that combines official French and best-in-class American curricula, with classes taught in both languages. Students in grades 9 and 10 choose between the international program, taught in English, and the French-American program, taught bilingually or mainly in French. In grades 11 and 12, students choose between the International Diploma Programme track taught in English or bilingually, or the French Baccalaureate track taught in French or bilingually.

Each year FASNY sends students to top colleges and universities. Our acceptance list since the first graduating class in 2009 has included: Columbia, Harvard, MIT, Princeton, Stanford, and Yale in the United States, and Cambridge, Imperial College, LSE, Oxford, and UCL in the United Kingdom. Many students also choose to study in Canada, in France, and in other fine European institutions.

A vast array of co-curricular activities

Our strong Arts, Music and Athletics programs along with our many clubs ensure a well-rounded education and encourage leadership. Our strong Community Service program, our educational international trips, and a large choice of clubs all contribute to the development of balanced and caring individuals.

A diverse and welcoming community

Our community of teachers and students represents over 50 nationalities, and the fabric of our school is one of tolerance, acceptance, and appreciation of our diversity. We mix French and American school-life traditions, creating a warm and engaging experience for our students.

George School

(Founded 1893)

Head of School
Mr. Sam Houser

DP coordinator
Kim McGlynn

Status Private

Boarding/day Mixed

Gender Coeducational

Language of instruction
English

Authorised IB programmes
DP

Age Range 13 – 19

Address
1690 Newtown Langhorne Rd
Newtown
PA 18940-2414 | USA

TEL +1 215 579 6500

Email
admission@georgeschool.org

Website
www.georgeschool.org

Founded in 1893, George School is a Quaker, co-ed boarding and day school for students in grades 9 to 12 located in Newtown, PA. The school is close to major cities on a picturesque, expansive 240-acre campus of open lawns and beautiful woods. Students arrive from nearly fifty countries and more than twenty states.

George School is an experienced leader in education, offering the International Baccalaureate (IB) Diploma Programme for more than thirty years and boasting a diploma success rate of nearly 100 percent. In addition to the IB diploma, George School offers nearly 20 Advanced Placement (AP) courses.

Experiential learning across disciplines is a hallmark of a George School education. Students gain practical experience in subjects such as film, artificial intelligence, robotics, human geography, stagecraft, and more. Local and global service-learning opportunities are also an integral part of the curriculum and student life at George School. The chance to freely explore new passions, as well as dive deep into existing ones, makes for a journey of discovery and preparation for life beyond George School.

Understanding that knowledge and character go hand in hand is at the foundation of the George School community. Graduates enter the world confident and capable leaders rooted in self-awareness, self sufficiency, and the ability to listen deeply to others while letting their lives speak. They attend the most selective colleges and universities worldwide.

Greengates School

(Founded 1951)

General Director
Clarisa Desouches Ph.D.

Headmaster
Rupert Cox

Head of the Secondary School
Christopher Woodall

DP coordinator
David Grant

Status Private

Boarding/day Day

Gender Coeducational

Language of instruction
English

Authorised IB programmes
DP

Age Range 3 – 18

Number of pupils enrolled
1200

Fees
Please contact the school

Address
Av. Circunvalación Pte. 102
Balcones de San Mateo
Naucalpan, Edo. de México
C.P. 53200 | MÉXICO

TEL +52 55 5373 0088

Email
kuroda@greengates.edu.mx

Website
www.greengates.edu.mx

Greengates School, Mexico has been held in high esteem for close to 70 years. Its British style international education caters to 1200 students, aged 3-18. The student body is largely made up from the diplomatic and business communities of Mexico City.

International-mindedness and cultural diversity are seen daily through the participation of over 50 nationalities.

The mission statement of Greengates School holds as true as ever today as it did when it was written in 1951. We encourage our students to develop character, self-discipline, respect and reflection in a challenging learning environment which honours individual differences. At Greengates we act with integrity and seek to motivate our students to become socially responsible citizens while achieving academic excellence.

As a British international school English is the language of instruction, from the age of six all students also study Spanish. Support in both languages is given as required. Furthermore, French is taught in the Secondary School and can be taken at IGCSE and on the IB Diploma. Korean and Japanese are also available as options on the diploma.

Graduates from Greengates attend some of the most prestigious universities in the world. Of the 2019 cohort 16% are attending universities in the UK, acceptances to Greengates students were made by University College London, King's College London, Queen Mary University London, University of Edinburgh and many others. 13% of the year group are studying in Canada and another 13% in the USA with offers received from Brown University, University of California, Berkeley, Yale and many more. Our students also study at some of the very best universities in other regions such as Hosei and Waseda in Japan and Yonsei University in Korea, or across Europe. Greengates students received scholarship offers totalling over $0.75M USD.

The teaching body at Greengates is comprised of almost 140 teachers from a wide variety of backgrounds. Alongside the many British teachers, highly qualified and experienced educators come from across the world, with all regions represented. Teachers bring a variety of different skills and modern methods to the classroom and beyond. Approaches to teaching and learning are central to students' success.

The Primary School is a fully accredited International Early Years Curriculum (IEYC) and International Primary Curriculum (IPC) School with aspects of mastering in its practice. The Secondary School prepares students for the International General Certificate of Education (IGCSE). The IGCSE two-year course is studied prior to embarking on the IB Diploma Programme. The Secondary School has been authorised to offer the IB Diploma Programme since 1986. In each of the last three years the pass rate has been 98-100%, with overall points scores consistently well above the world average.

The Greengates campus covers are area of 20,000 square metres, with purpose-built facilities including two libraries, nine sciences laboratories, six computer media centres, four art studios, an auditorium, a large gymnasium, basketball courts, an indoor swimming pool, an organic learning garden used by all students, a cafeteria, an adventure playground designed by the famous architect Javier Senosiain and an all-weather field.

Enrolment is open throughout the year, depending on availability. We always welcome enquiries and visits from prospective families.

Instituto Anglo Británico

(Founded 1993)

IAB Campus La Fe Headmistress
Ms. Imelda Jiménez Rocha

IAB Campus Cumbres Headmistress
Ms. Julia Bautista Gutiérrez

IAB Campus La Fe PYP coordinator
Ms. Ana Laura Arellano Rodríguez

IAB Campus Cumbres PYP coordinator
Ms. Alejandra Tijerina Reyna

IAB Campus La Fe MYP coordinator
Ms. Elynn Vázquez Wong

IAB Campus Cumbres MYP coordinator
Ms. Esther Martha Keratry Cárdenas

Status Private

Boarding/day Day

Gender Coeducational

Language of instruction
English, Spanish

Authorised IB programmes
PYP, MYP

Age Range 1 – 15

Fees
Please see website

IAB Campus Le Fe
Av. Isidoro Sepúlveda #555
Col. La Encarnación
Apodaca, Nuevo León
C.P. 66633 | MÉXICO

TEL +52 8183 21 5000

Email contactus@iab.edu.mx

IAB Campus Cumbres
Paseo de los Leones 7001, Valle de Cumbres, García, Nuevo León, C.P. 66035 | MÉXICO

TEL +52 81 8526 2222

Email infocumbres@iab.edu.mx

Website www.iab.edu.mx

Instituto Anglo Británico Campus La Fe, and Campus Cumbres, belong to the Madison Group of Schools, which are located in different Mexican cities.

IAB Campus La Fe is located in a suburb of Monterrey, a modern and industrial city, known as one of the three most important cities in Mexico. Monterrey has at least four well-known universities with important international exchange programs and several smaller ones.

This school was founded in 1993 in order to offer our community an international school for their children (1 to 15 years old), with programs that help them develop critical skills necessary for the globalized world we live in. This year we proudly celebrate our 25th anniversary.

IAB Campus Cumbres is located to the west of Monterrey and was founded in 2015.

Our schools provide a holistic education to better prepare our students to thrive in a fast-changing and highly-connected world. They are committed to obtain the authorization and work under the curricular and training framework of the IB with the PYP and the MYP.

We welcome students from all religions and nationalities in order to encourage diversity and internationalism. We have had students from different countries such as Germany, Spain, India, Argentina, Korea, Japan and the United States.

The schools have programs that nurture its students' development: Young Leaders Explorers, Future Leaders, Model United Nations and Destination Imagination (DI).

One of the Madison Group of Schools' greatest strengths is an International Teachers Program that enhances our students' abilities to interact with foreign cultures and learn from them. We have had teachers from Canada, China, Colombia, Costa Rica, Croatia, Cuba, England, Ireland, Lebanon, Scotland, Poland, Venezuela, Egypt and the United States, teaching in our schools.

Our constructive learning environment allows students to be lifelong learners that are proficient in English and Spanish.

Students and graduates from our school are well-appreciated by the community and by the high schools they attend.

Our graduates (as well as current students) have already made a difference here in Mexico.

International Children's Academy

International
Children's Academy
of Beverly Hills

Inspire the Mind, Ignite the Soul

Head of School
Ian Mcfeat

PYP coordinator
Leyla Goldfinger

Status Private

Boarding/day Day

Gender Coeducational

Language of instruction
English

Authorised IB programmes
PYP

Address
1046 South Robertson Blvd
Los Angeles
CA 90035 | USA

TEL +1 310 657 6798

Email
info@icabh.org

Website
www.icabh.org

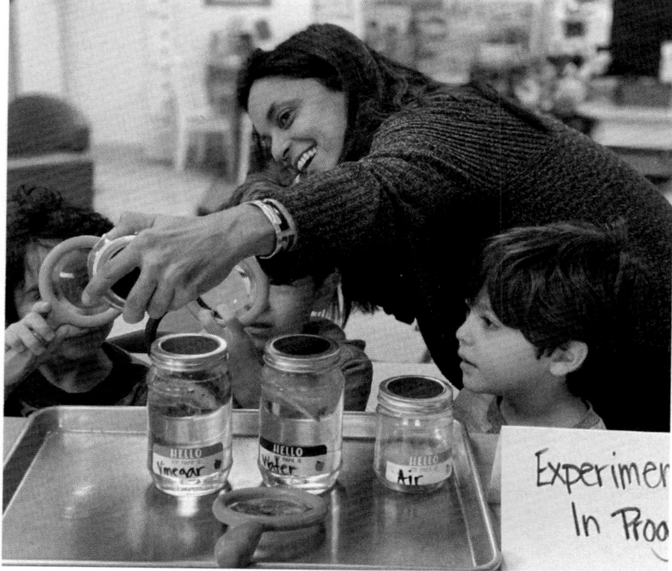

MISSION: Our mission is to develop caring and responsible global citizens striving to achieve their full potential through rigorous academic, social and spiritual programs in an inquiry based, inspiring environment that supports the growth of the whole child as a lifelong learner.

INTRODUCTION: The International Children's Academy welcomes families committed to a meaningful, intellectually rigorous, globally-centric education interwoven with spiritual values and tools for their young children from 2 years old through 6th grade. For students from 2 years through elementary.

PROGRAM: At ICA, students flourish in an environment where every child is known and valued. Our framework exceeds US Common Core requirements while preparing students with essential critical thinking and life skills. Student interests and passions are encouraged and built upon within all areas of our program including:

- STEM (science, technology, engineering and math) and environmental studies;
- reading, humanities, and language;
- performing and visual arts;
- athletics
- service and return to the community

Spiritual studies is foundational to our philosophy and woven into our entire course of study.

COMMITMENT: Small size classes and blended ages and grades allow students to work in multiple peer groups with common interests and at accelerated levels. While Primary Years IB accreditation is rare in Los Angeles, it is part of the recognition for our program that is academically comprehensive, spiritually centric, culturally diverse, and built on a global perspective.

FACULTY: ICA's exceptional group of teachers and staff are key to our success and growth. With impressive credentials including extensive Masters Degrees and certifications, and a passion for teaching and learning, they foster classroom environments where each student is known and valued for their personal strengths.

LOCATION: ICA is in the heart of Los Angeles, between downtown and the ocean, and UCLA and USC, within miles of multiple embassies and consulates, and a growing number of Fortune 1000 headquarters.

(Founded 1977)

Head of School
Bob Carignan

MYP coordinator
Hope Forgey

Status Private

Boarding/day Day

Gender Coeducational

Language of instruction
Chinese, English, French, Spanish

Authorised IB programmes
MYP

Age Range Preschool – 8th Grade

Number of pupils enrolled
730

Fees
Early Childhood Education (K1–K3) $17,750
Lower School (G1–G5) US$17,500
Middle School (G6–G8) US$19,500

Address
7701 E. 1st Pl, Unit C
Denver
CO 80230 | USA

TEL +1 303 340 3647
FAX +1 303 265 9529

Email
info@isdenver.org

Website
www.isdenver.org

The International School of Denver (ISDenver) is an inclusive, globally minded community that develops highly motivated and academically successful bilingual learners. ISDenver students are inter-culturally adept and make positive contributions in a complex world.

ISDenver is proud to be authorised to offer the three-year Middle Years Programme. Our preschool through 5th grade programs offer immersion in French, Chinese or Spanish to families who represent more than 50 nationalities. Our younger learners follow a rigorous, broad and balanced curriculum, based on the national standards and benchmarks from accrediting agencies of France, China and Spain, as well as Colorado State Standards. Our teachers are native speakers of the languages, and our specific approach to immersion education gives the learners an authentic bicultural as well as bilingual education. The development of their intercultural competencies provides a perfect foundation for their entry into the IB MYP in 6th grade.

Within the MYP structure, we continue to focus strongly on the development of bilingualism, while building international-mindedness. We capitalise on the students' broad knowledge base and help them apply their diverse approaches to learning to global contexts.

As a three-year MYP school, our culminating work is evidenced by both the Community Project and a service learning trip to Costa Rica. Our 8th grade students are well prepared to meet the challenges of high school: 100% of our graduates are admitted to their first or second choice high school, with 87% attending their first choice school – often a local IB World School.

International School of Los Angeles

(Founded 1978)

Head of School
Mr Michael Maniska

DP coordinator
John Lamphear

Status Private

Boarding/day Day

Gender Coeducational

Language of instruction
English, French

Authorised IB programmes
DP

Age Range 3 – 18

Number of pupils enrolled
1100

Fees
Day: $19,175 – $23,600

Address
1105 W. Riverside Drive
Burbank
CA 91506 | USA

TEL +1 626 695 5159
FAX +1 818 994 2816

Email
admissions@lilaschool.com

Website
www.internationalschool.la

The International School of Los Angeles is an independent, international, preschool through 12th grade school committed to bilingual education and academic excellence in a nurturing environment. Currently, all students study a common bilingual program from preschool through 8th grade, at which point they have a choice between the rigorous and well-balanced French baccalauréat (taught in French) and International Baccalaureate Diploma Programme (taught in English). Students entering the international track in the 9th grade are not required to demonstrate a proficiency level in French.

Possessing such a robust bilingual background, many of the School's IB students pursue the Diploma's bilingual option, demonstrating their proficiency by completing the requirements in both English and French at Literature level. The Washington Post consistently lists the International School of Los Angeles as one of the nation's most challenging private high schools.

With five Los Angeles-area campuses (Burbank, Los Feliz, Orange County, Pasadena, and West Valley), and over 1,000 students, the School holds triple accreditation from the French Ministry of Education, the Western Association of Schools and Colleges (WASC), and the International Baccalaureate (IB).

The International School of Los Angeles is committed to the values of respect, excellence, and diversity, and to preparing students of all backgrounds to excel in and contribute to a global world. Since 1978, the School has been instilling the love of learning in all its students through small classes and low student-to-teacher ratios. With over 60 nationalities and 39 spoken languages represented on the campuses, students study and live in a diverse global community every day.

Islands International School

Principal
Prof. Estela María Irrera de Pallaro

DP coordinator
Clotilde Alleva

Status Private

Boarding/day Day

Gender Coeducational

Language of instruction
Spanish, English, Italian, Portuguese

Authorised IB programmes
DP

Age Range 2 – 18

Address
Amenábar St. 1840.
Zip Code 1428
Buenos Aires | ARGENTINA

TEL +54 11 4787 2294
FAX +54 11 4786 9904

Email
info@intschools.org

Website
www.intschools.org/islands

Working together with Southern International School and Northern International School.

In 1981 Mrs. Estela María Irrera de Pallaro and her husband Andrés Pallaro founded a kindergarten in a lovely house situated in O'Higgins St. in Belgrano, which was later to become Islands International School. Some years later, as a result of hard work, clear objectives and true commitment, a primary school was opened in a spacious building situated in Virrey del Pino and Arcos St. In 1988, a secondary school was opened with a curriculum based on the latest, most prestigious syllabi in Argentina and the whole world. The new building situated in Amenábar St. offered our students appropriate facilities and modern equipment to meet the highest educational standards.

From the beginning, our aim has been to present our students with a demanding curriculum while emphasizing the values of hard work, effort and commitment. The outstanding achievements of our alumni both in college and later on in their jobs are irrefutable proof of our success.

In 1990 Islands embraced a new challenge by joining the International Baccalaureate Organization, a well known association of schools seeded in Geneva, Switzerland whose main objective is to foster the students' skills so that they can perform successfully in an increasingly demanding academic world and expanding job market. Furthermore, it is essential that our students should acquire full command of the languages taught at our school: Spanish, English and Italian.

By getting an IB diploma our students can also get the "Maturità Linguistica o Scientifica", which is a diploma issued by the Government of Italy at the end of secondary school and which grants students admission to European Universities.

Our school emphasizes the values of respect and hard work as the main tools, which will enable our students to achieve success. Islands International School provides students with quality education, which comprises the latest technological breakthroughs and the practice of human and social values.

La Scuola d'Italia
Guglielmo Marconi
www.lascuoladitalia.org

(Founded 1977)

Head of School
Dr. Maria Palandra

DP coordinator
Dr. Beatrice Paladini

Status Private

Boarding/day Day

Gender Coeducational

Language of instruction
English, Italian

Authorised IB programmes
DP

Age Range 2 – 18

Number of pupils enrolled
170

Fees
Preschool US$26,000
Elementary US$29,000
Middle & High School US$34,000

Address
12 East 96th Street
New York
NY 10021 | USA

Upper School
406 East 67th Street, New York
NY 10065 | USA

TEL +1 212 369 3290

Email
admissions@lascuoladitalia.org

Website
www.lascuoladitalia.org

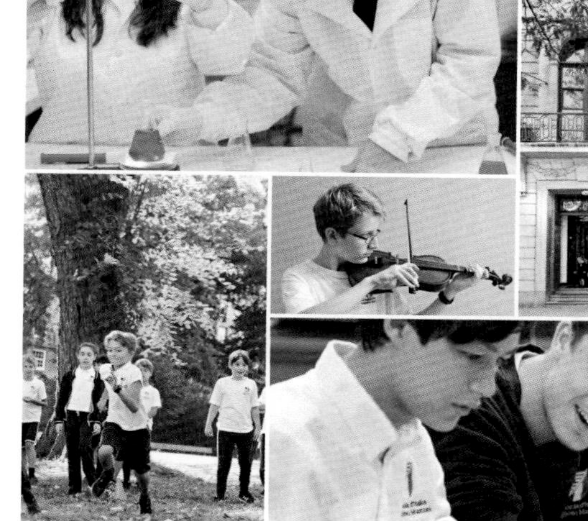

La Scuola d'Italia is a multicultural, multilingual institution located in the heart of Manhattan. At La Scuola, students pursue Italian and U.S. rigorous curricula simultaneously, supported by a nurturing international community comprised by people from all over the world who recognize the value of an internationally minded, multilingual and academically challenging education.

In addition to being recognized by the Italian Ministry of Education, La Scuola is chartered by the Regents of the University of the State of New York and accredited by the New York State Association of Independent Schools (NYSAIS). As a further confirmation of the quality of its educational offering, La Scuola was officially authorized to offer the International Baccalaureate Diploma Programme to its 11th and 12th grade students in May 2018.

As a result, La Scuola students enjoy the unique possibility of graduating with a high school diploma that is fully recognized by every university institution in Europe and the United States. Thanks to the International Baccalaureate Diploma Programme, our students now benefit from even greater opportunities to truly stand-out on the global stage.

La Scuola is committed to the harmonious integration of different disciplines, cultures, and languages into its carefully designed K-12 curriculum. An exceptionally dedicated and highly qualified faculty refines the curriculum regularly in a low teacher-student ratio environment.

La Scuola strives to prepare students for the academic, professional, social, cultural and ethical challenges deriving from a globalized world. The education we offer aims to:
a) develop in students the specific skills and knowledge required to excel in higher education and beyond within the domains of mathematics, science, modern and classical languages, history, philosophy, the arts and business management; b) foster in students a deeper understanding of their future role as thoughtful, respectful, caring and principled human beings in an ever expanding world community.

Head of School
Valentina Imbeni Ph.D.

Director of Admissions
Dunja Solari

IB coordinator
Douglas Lowney

Status Private, Non-Profit

Boarding/day Day

Gender Coeducational

Language of instruction
English, Italian and Spanish

Authorised IB programmes
PYP

Age Range 2 – 14

Number of pupils enrolled
300

Fees
Day: US$33,000

Early Childhood (PreK) Campus
728 20th Street
San Francisco
CA 94107 | USA

Elementary School Campus:
735 Fell Street, San Francisco
CA 94117 | USA

Middle School Campus:
3250 18th Street, San Francisco
CA 94110 | USA

TEL +1 415 551 0000
FAX +1 415 390 9006

Email admissions@lascuolasf.org

Website www.lascuolasf.org

Open to the World

The world has changed and it's time for education to catch up. That's why, every day, it's the students at La Scuola who ask the provocative questions... they lead – and embrace – their own ability to learn across languages, cultures and subject areas. Because when children are open to the world and protagonists in their own education, there's no limit to their ability to learn, find beauty in life, and discover extraordinary answers.

At La Scuola International School – the only Reggio Emilia inspired, International Baccalaureate-PYP and Italian language immersion school in the world – our mission is to inspire brave learners to shape the future.

We offer an inquiry based, immersive Italian language curriculum for Preschool-8th grade students. With Inquiry as the leading tool of our education, students foster critical and creative thinking skills, confidence, collaboration, and empathy.

La Scuola is also recognized as an Italian Accredited School abroad by the Ministry of Education in Italy. In our diverse and multicultural and multilingual school, students grow in a community that balances academic rigor with creativity and real-life tools like cultural awareness and global citizenship.

Nothing Without Joy!
Niente Senza Gioia!
¡Nada Sin Alegría!

(Founded 2005)

Head of School
Ms. Maria Castelluccio

DP coordinator
Ms. Lucy Alexander

Status Private

Boarding/day Mixed

Gender Coeducational

Language of instruction
English

Authorised IB programmes
DP

Age Range 16 months – 18 years

Number of pupils enrolled
900

Fees
16-24 Months US$7,000
2-4 Years US$28,000 – US$49,000
Kindergarten – Grade 12
US$55,200 – US$56,350
Boarding US$93,000

Address
41 Broad Street
New York
NY 10004 | USA

Upper School
1 Morris Street, New York
NY 10004 | USA

TEL +1 212 232 0266

Email admissions@lemanmanhattan.org

Website
www.lemanmanhattan.org

Located in Manhattan's most historic neighborhood, Léman Manhattan provides students with a rigorous academic program in the most dynamic, international education setting in the world. We are home to nearly 900 students ranging from 16 months old to grade 12, and New York City's only boarding program.

Léman Manhattan is an International Baccalaureate World School that sets high expectations for students from early childhood through 12th grade. Serving our local neighborhoods and a diverse international community, we prepare students with the knowledge, confidence and fluency they need to engage in a rapidly changing world.

Léman challenges students' intellect and inspires their creativity. We encourage them to think critically and work collaboratively. Celebrating each student's individuality, we foster the skills they need to grow in mind, body and spirit. Our unifying mission is to instill a positive outlook in each of our students and a certainty for all they can achieve in life.

Eighty percent of Léman faculty hold advanced degrees in their fields. Our commitment to instructional excellence leads to exceptional academic outcomes. Eighty percent of Léman graduates are accepted to top 50 ranked US universities, including highly selective colleges such as Brown, Columbia, Cornell, Dartmouth, Duke, Haverford, Johns Hopkins, New York University, Oberlin, Princeton, University of North Carolina Chapel Hill, University of Pennsylvania, University of Virginia, Wellesley, Wesleyan, Yale and many others.

As an integrated day and boarding community, the Léman student body represents more than 50 nationalities and is highly diverse. This allows for inquiry based learning in the IB philosophy and cultivates students who are open-minded, collaborative, principled, and balanced.

Léman Manhattan. Each student, future prepared.

Lincoln Park High School

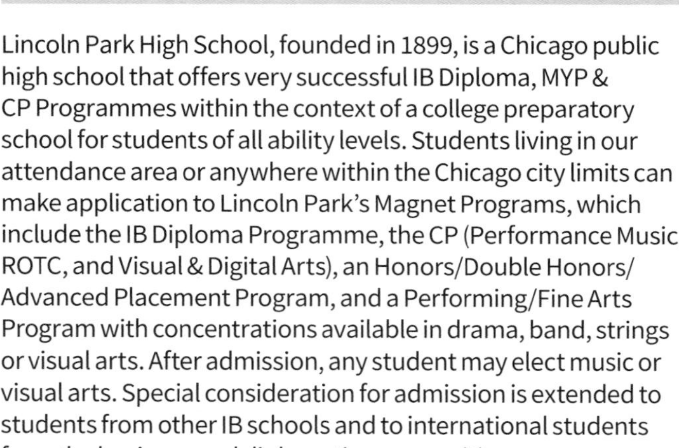

(Founded 1899)

Principal
John Thuet

MYP coordinator
Theresa McCormick

DP coordinator
Mary Enda Tookey

CP coordinator
Mary Enda Tookey

Status State

Boarding/day Day

Gender Coeducational

Language of instruction
English

Authorised IB programmes
MYP, DP, CP

Age Range 13 – 19

Number of pupils enrolled
2103

Address
2001 North Orchard Street
Chicago
IL 60614 | USA

TEL +1 773 534 8149
FAX +1 773 534 8214

Email
lpibprogram@aol.com

Website
www.lincolnparkhs.org

Lincoln Park High School, founded in 1899, is a Chicago public high school that offers very successful IB Diploma, MYP & CP Programmes within the context of a college preparatory school for students of all ability levels. Students living in our attendance area or anywhere within the Chicago city limits can make application to Lincoln Park's Magnet Programs, which include the IB Diploma Programme, the CP (Performance Music, ROTC, and Visual & Digital Arts), an Honors/Double Honors/ Advanced Placement Program, and a Performing/Fine Arts Program with concentrations available in drama, band, strings or visual arts. After admission, any student may elect music or visual arts. Special consideration for admission is extended to students from other IB schools and to international students from the business and diplomatic communities.

Fluent/bilingual French students can participate in a special program (EFAC) that can include preparation for DELF or the French Baccalaureate in addition to college prep, AP, and/or IB classes. All students with special needs are supported in their IB and college preparatory classes by a full special services program.

Newsweek magazine has ranked Lincoln Park as one of the top 100 high schools in the US and for the last six years US News & World Report awarded the school gold and silver medal rankings.

Its staff places high value on rigor, mutual respect and creativity, while encouraging students in both their academic and extracurricular activities to develop their talents and interests to the full. Personal excellence, a willingness to challenge oneself, inventiveness, and a can-do spirit are at the core of Lincoln Park's culture.

Students come from over 80 countries and speak more than 60 different languages at home. A significant number of students in the IB Diploma Programme were born in other countries, are first-generation in this country, or the children of internationals. Within this diverse context students acquire insight into others and the leadership skills needed in a global society.

A wide variety of extracurricular activities (50) and interscholastic sports opportunities (currently 26) are available for all students. IB students are active in sports, drama, music, art, school clubs, and local organizations. Many do community service beyond the CAS requirement and are active in their individual churches, synagogues, and mosques. In addition to their work in their classes, all Lincoln Park students participate in a number of academic competitions in writing, history, experimental science, literature, social issues, world languages, and the fine and performing arts; many have gone on to the national and international levels of these competitions. Every year, the boys' and girls' athletic teams win division and sectional championships. The music program regularly earns superior ratings in competitions and is currently ranked as the #2 music program in the state of Illinois.

Since 1984 approximately 82% of the IB students have gained the diploma on completion of the IB Diploma Programme. Lincoln Park enjoys an outstanding record of university acceptances both in the US and internationally.

(Founded 1909)

Headmaster
Mr. Christopher Shannon M.Ed, MA, BA

DP coordinator
Lisa Currie

Status Private

Boarding/day Day

Gender Coeducational

Language of instruction
English

Authorised IB programmes
DP

Age Range 5 – 17

Number of pupils enrolled
805

Fees
Day: CAD$18,695 – CAD$23,845

Address
4090, avenue Royal
Montréal QC
H4A 2M5 | CANADA

TEL +1 514 482 9916
FAX +1 514 482 0195

Email
admissions@lcc.ca

Website
www.lcc.ca

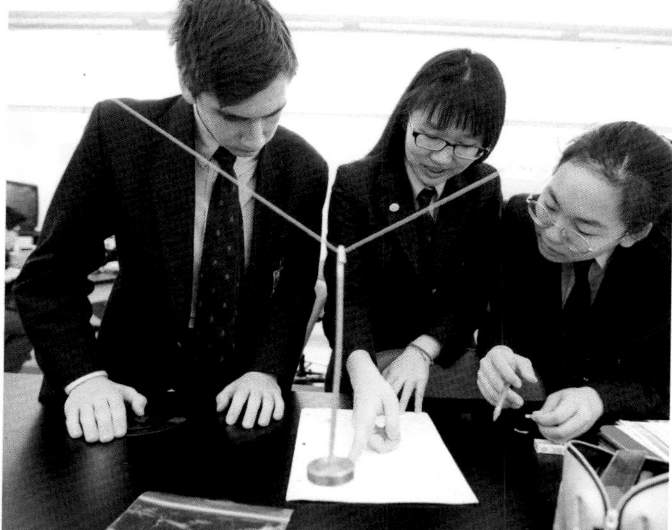

Founded in 1909, Lower Canada College (LCC) is a selective, independent, university-preparatory day school for girls and boys in kindergarten through grade 12. Montreal's leading global school, LCC has a rich history, an inspiring team of faculty, and a diverse and highly motivated student body. With a challenging academic programme and extensive co-curricular offerings that include athletics, arts, design, service, debating and leadership, our focus is on fully developing the mind, body, and heart of every student.

Located in in the heart of Montreal's Monkland Village, LCC's seven-acre campus includes two libraries, a dining room, four gymnasia and a fitness room, an indoor arena, two playing fields, a Fab Lab, and two auditoriums. The school also features band practice facilities, a black box theatre, and three art rooms.

The school enrolment is 805, with a student/ teacher ratio of 12:1. The student body is diverse, representing over 41 nationalities, with 23% of the students speaking a language other than English as their mother tongue. One hundred percent of graduates continue their education at college or university. Twenty-two percent of students in grades 7-12 receive a financial award.

In addition to being a recognized International Baccalaureate World School, LCC is sanctioned by the Quebec Ministry of Education (Ministère de l'Éducation, et de l'Enseignement supérieur), and is a member of the Canadian Accredited Independent Schools (CAIS), the Quebec Association of Independent Schools (QAIS), the National Association of Independent Schools (NAIS), Round Square, and the Duke of Edinburgh Awards Programme.

In March 2013, LCC became an authorized International Baccalaureate World School, offering the Diploma Programme (IBDP). Prior to becoming an IB World School, LCC was already offering a long-standing pre-university year option (corresponding to grade 12 in North America), with graduates going on to pursue their studies at top universities and colleges worldwide.

Lyceum Kennedy

French American School

(Founded 1964)

Head of School
Dr. Claude Bryant

DP coordinator
Dr. Vera Pohland

Status Private

Boarding/day Day

Gender Coeducational

Language of instruction
French, English

Authorised IB programmes
DP

Age Range 3 – 18

Number of pupils enrolled
300

Address
225 East 43rd Street
New York
NY 10017 | USA

TEL +1 212 681 1877
FAX +1 212 681 1922

Email
lkadmissions@lyceumkennedy.org

Website
www.lyceumkennedy.org

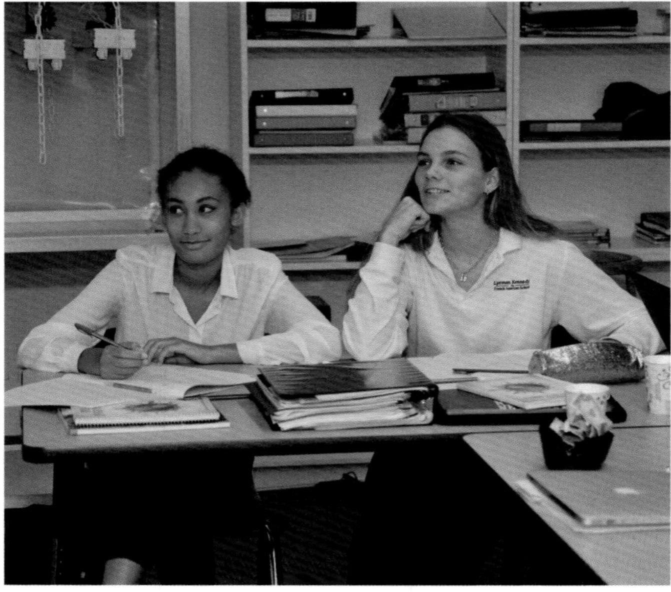

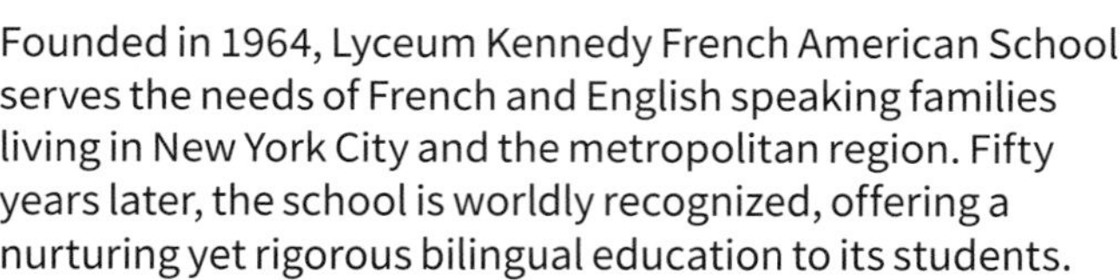

Founded in 1964, Lyceum Kennedy French American School serves the needs of French and English speaking families living in New York City and the metropolitan region. Fifty years later, the school is worldly recognized, offering a nurturing yet rigorous bilingual education to its students.

The school operates three campus locations – in the heart of Manhattan, just two blocks from Grand Central Terminal. The International Baccalaureate Diploma Programme (IBDP) is offered at the school's 815 Second Avenue campus location.

Currently, Lyceum Kennedy welcomes 300 students from more than 40 nationalities, ages 3 through 18 years old and provides a family-oriented school environment. Our teacher/student ratio in the upper school allows us to work with each student as an individual in order to instill a love of learning and to ensure academic success.

IBDP Mission

Lyceum Kennedy's mission is to provide its students with a unique bilingual and bicultural education based on the principles of self-expression and differentiated pedagogy. Committed to the IB Programme Lyceum Kennedy fulfills high educational standards through challenging programs of international education and rigorous assessment.

Core Values

At Lyceum Kennedy, we emphasize multiculturalism, bilingual education, transdisciplinary academic inquiry and critical thinking. We aim to develop inquiring, knowledgeable and caring people who help to create a better and more peaceful world through intercultural understanding and respect. The IB Programme encourages students to become active, compassionate and lifelong learners who understand that other people, with their differences, can also be right.

Curriculum and IB

In September 2014, Lyceum Kennedy became an authorized IB school for the Diploma Programme. We offer 11th and 12th graders a unique, bilingual French and English IB DP, with Spanish and German as additional foreign languages. This program is ideal for all students seeking an exceptional education that prepares them to become responsible citizens of the world and the leaders of tomorrow. In addition, students follow the New York State Board of Regents program.

Additional language support is provided to help students strengthen their second language so that they can participate in all English and French programs with native speakers. We also provide a wide range of after-school enrichment classes which allows students to fully develop further in their intellectual, creative and physical activities.

Madison Campus Monterrey

(Founded 1978)

Head of School
Lic. Esthela Diaz de May

PYP coordinator
Ricardo Domínguez Gámez

MYP coordinator
Perla Priscila Vargas Andrade

Status Private

Boarding/day Day

Gender Coeducational

Language of instruction
English, Spanish

Authorised IB programmes
PYP, MYP

Age Range 2 – 15

Number of pupils enrolled
550

Fees
PYP Programme US$4,900
MYP Programme US$5,800

Address
Marsella #3055
Col. Alta Vista
Monterrey, Nuevo León
C.P. 64840 | MÉXICO

TEL +52 81 8359 0627
FAX +52 81 8359 5166

Email contacto@colegiosmadison.edu.mx

Website
colegiosmadison.edu.mx/colegios-madison-monterrey.htm

Madison schools have been nurturing minds and creating successful learning experiences for the last 40 years in our community. We have been fulfilling internationally certified academic standards through collaborative work, positive attitudes and core values. These are highly regarded in our schools.

Madison Campus Monterrey was the first school founded in the Madison Group of Schools, which are located in different Mexican states: Nuevo León, Coahuila, Yucatán, and Chihuahua.

Monterrey is a modern and industrial city, known as one of the three most industrious and important cities in Mexico.

Monterrey has at least four well-known universities with important international exchange programs and several smaller ones.

Madison Campus Monterrey became bilingual in 1994. Since then, it has had a strong emphasis on the English language.

The school has programs that nurture its students' development:

- "Ruta de Independencia" School Trip: 5th-grade students spent five days travelling throughout different places in Mexico where the Independence Movement took place. This program enriches what they had learned in their classes, so they can live, themselves, a real learning experience.
- United Nations Model: Academic simulation of the United Nations that aims to educate participants about civics, effective communication, globalization, and multilateral diplomacy.
- Youth Leader Explorer exhibition: organized by one of the most important high schools in Mexico where students develop different scientific skills.
- French Immersion Program: a week program held in Quebec, Canada.
- International trips: Every year we offer a complete Educational Travel Program to reinforce our main objective, that is to educate citizens of the world.

In 1999 the school decided to become part of the IB and began working towards its authorization. The school achieved authorization to offer the International Baccalaureate Primary Years Programme (PYP) in 2003 and the International Baccalaureate Middle Years Programme (MYP) in 2007.

We have had students from Russia, Argentina, Venezuela, Canada, Nicaragua, Colombia, United States, Philippines, Lebanon, Poland, Switzerland, Germany, Spain, India, and Japan.

One of Madison Group of Schools' greatest strengths is an International Teachers Program that enhances our students' abilities to interact with foreign cultures and learn from them.

For the last fifteen years, we have had instructors from Canada, China, Costa Rica, Croatia, Cuba, England, Ireland, Lebanon, Scotland, Poland, and the United States, teaching at our schools. Students and graduates from our school are well appreciated by the community and by the high schools they attend. Our well-articulated, inquisitive, mature and responsible graduates and students have already made a difference here in Mexico.

Madison Campus Monterrey is a certified school by SEP, an active member of FEP as well as IBAMEX.

Madison International School

(Founded 2007)

Head of School
Sergio Reyes

PYP coordinator
Rolando De La Torre

MYP coordinator
Emerson García

Status Private

Boarding/day Day

Gender Coeducational

Language of instruction
English, Spanish

Authorised IB programmes
PYP, MYP

Age Range 1 – 15

Number of pupils enrolled
998

Fees
PYP US$8,000
MYP US$8,500

Address
Camino Real #100
Col. El Uro
Monterrey, Nuevo León
C.P. 64986 | MÉXICO

TEL +52 81 8218 7909
FAX +52 81 8218 7910

Email
admisiones@mis.edu.mx

Website
www.mis.edu.mx

We belong to the Madison Group of Schools, which has more than 35 years of educational experience.

On a national level, we have campuses in the cities of Torreón, Chihuahua and Mérida*. Locally, we have the Madison International School (MIS), Instituto Anglo Británico, and Madison Monterrey campuses.

Our particular campus opened its doors in 2007 in the south of Monterrey, in the El Uro area, and we offer Nursery, Kindergarten, Primary and Secondary levels of schooling.

MIS is located in Monterrey, an industrial and modern city in Northeastern Mexico. The city is anchor to the third-largest metropolitan area in Mexico. Its economic, cultural and social influence makes it one of Mexico's most developed cities with the highest per capita income in the nation.

MIS provides a first class education for students and gives children a head start in the modern world by taking their English skills to a higher level. Madison's superb bilingual program teaches children English beginning in their most formative years.

Madison International School uses the constructivist educational method and is also based on inquiry, reflexion, and active participation of our students.

As part of our international profile we encourage our students to participate in different programmes that nurture their development, such as:

- Destination Imagination: engage participants in project-based challenges that are designed to build confidence and develop extraordinary creativity, critical thinking, communication, and teamwork skills.
- Model United Nations: academic simulation of this international organization, which aims to educate participants about effective communication, globalization and multilateral diplomacy.

Madison International School proudly boasts some of the best student facilities in Monterrey such as computer and science labs, video and conference halls, library, cafeteria, music and art rooms, and substantial sports fields that are all staffed by teachers committed to creating a fun and interesting learning environment for the children. The school offers extracurricular classes ranging from guitar, piano, robotics, to sports teams. Madison's dedication to students' safety and wellbeing is the most important element, which is why we provide excellent security features that will give every parent and child peace of mind.

We encourage diversity and internationalism and therefore we welcome students, teachers and families from any religion, race, and nationality.

(Founded 2017)

Head of School
Rebekah Ghosh

PYP coordinator
Emily Seppa

MYP coordinator
Nikki Tanner

DP coordinator
Nikki Tanner

Status Private

Boarding/day Day

Gender Coeducational

Language of instruction
English

Authorised IB programmes
PYP, MYP, DP

Age Range 6 – 18

Number of pupils enrolled
150

Fees
Domestic Students: US$12,700 – US$19,250
International Students: US$24,450 – US$32,000

Address
6135 Old Washington Road
Elkridge
MD 21075 | USA

TEL +1 410 220 3792

Email info@marylandinternationalschool.org

Website www.marylandinternationalschool.org

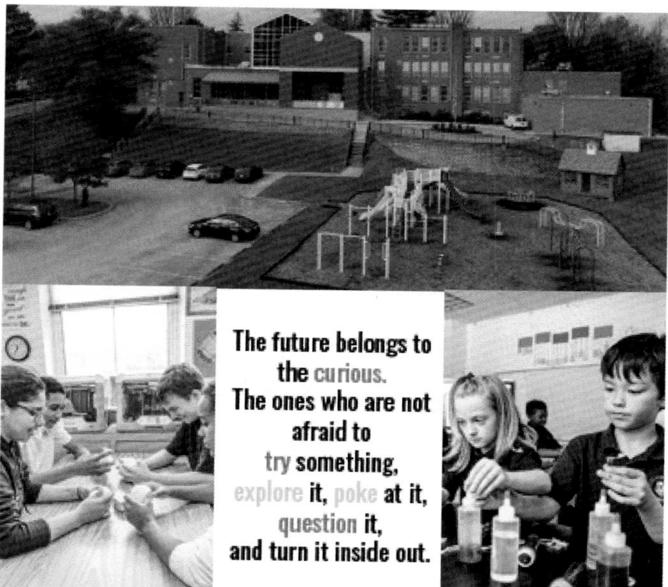

The future belongs to
the curious.
The ones who are not
afraid to
try something,
explore it, poke at it,
question it,
and turn it inside out.

About

Maryland International School (MDIS) is an independent, private school in Howard County, Maryland, conveniently located in the Baltimore-Washington metropolitan area. MDIS is the first school in the state of Maryland, and the second in the mid-Atlantic region, to offer three International Baccalaureate (IB) programmes: Primary Years Programme (PYP), Middle Years Programme (MYP), and Diploma Programme (DP).

Our beautiful 9 acre campus serves students from grades 1-12. Our mission and vision is to provide an academically rigorous and supportive college-preparatory education with an interdisciplinary and applied focus on the Science, Technology, Engineering, and Mathematics (STEM) disciplines in order to prepare students to become creative problem solvers, effective communicators, and tomorrow's leaders who think ethically, independently, and globally.

IB & STEM

Our curriculum integrates the International Baccalaureate curriculum with STEM specific programs and pathways. Our STEM-integrated curriculum was developed taking into account the principles of Universal Design for Learning (UDL), technology standards, disciplinary literacy standards, Next Generation Science Standards (NGSS), and transdisciplinary core content lessons. Our curriculum is designed to promote critical thinking, collaboration, and innovation in order to develop the academic, emotional and social skills that students will need to live and work in a globalized world. Our after school STEM programs include, but are not limited to: Robotics Club, Science Olympiad, FIRST Lego League, Coding Club, and a Drone Club.

Signature Programs

MDIS offers two signature programs: Global Studies Program and Global Ambassadors Program (GAP). We have designed a unique program of activities, experiences, and study abroad trips to help students thrive as leaders in a globalized world. Students gain intercultural skills and global perspectives through hands-on and experiential learning, language immersion, cross-cultural exchange, and collaborative service projects and service learning. Highlights of the Global Studies Program include the National Geographic GeoBee, Model UN, Harvard Model Congress, and IB School Exchange. The Global Ambassadors Program offers a signature experience for our upper school students in different locations around the world each year through our partnerships with WorldStrides, an accredited travel organization.

Admissions

Our admissions process operates on a rolling basis and so we welcome student applications year-round. When considering an applicant, we recognize that every child is unique. We evaluate a student's overall academic and developmental readiness and whether they will thrive in, and benefit from, the academic challenges of our curriculum. For additional information, please reach out by phone or email to learn more about the MDIS admission process.

(Founded 1926)

Principal
Tom Rinke

President
Ed Curtin

DP coordinator
Paul Cancilla

Status Private

Boarding/day Mixed

Gender Coeducational

Language of instruction
English

Authorised IB programmes
DP

Age Range 13 – 18

Number of pupils enrolled
510

Address
538 East Grandview Boulevard
Erie
PA 16504 | USA

TEL +1 814 824 2323
FAX +1 814 824 2116

Email
mditullio@mpslakers.com

Website
www.mpslakers.com

Mission
Mercyhurst Preparatory School (MPS) is a four year co-educational Catholic secondary school founded by the Sisters of Mercy to prepare students from all religious and ethnic backgrounds for a successful, productive, and compassionate life in an ever-changing and interdependent world. A Mercyhurst Prep education is based upon the teachings of Jesus Christ, the Mercy charism, and a modeling of Judeo Christian values. We strive for excellence in academic and co-curricular programs, promote service to our local and global communities, and foster the dedication and active support of the students, parents, faculty, staff, and alumni of the Mercyhurst community.

Community
Mercyhurst Prep is located on the beautiful shores of Lake Erie in the USA where students experience seasonal change and access to numerous outdoor activities in this safe community of 200,000. Erie, Pennsylvania has easy access to major US cities – Cleveland, Buffalo and Pittsburgh – as well as Toronto, Canada.

Curriculum
As a college preparatory school, the curriculum is rigorous. 98% of graduates matriculate to post-secondary institutions. The school offers a wide range of courses at the college prep, honors, and International Baccalaureate (IB) levels. Implemented in 1985, the International Baccalaureate program is geared towards knowledgeable and caring students who are motivated to succeed in a well-rounded interdisciplinary curriculum, which leads to IB certificates or the IB diploma.

Students take eight courses in each of the school's three terms. Our block schedule classes are ninety minutes long. We encourage every student to study at least one IB course.

STEAM (Science, Technology, Engineering, Arts and Math in the Classroom)
One-to-one iPad deployment provides a tremendous blending of cutting-edge classroom technology with best educational practice. MPS faculty receives extensive ongoing training in the use of iPads. Faculty and students are supported by a full-time technology expert and coach. iPad integration occurs across the curriculum.

Creative Arts
The school offers 49 courses in the performing and visual arts taught by a faculty of active award-winning artists. Students exhibit and perform year-round in the school's nationally recognized musical theater, dance and choral groups.

Collaboration with Mercyhurst University
Academically advanced students may begin college course work or pursue a subject in greater depth at Mercyhurst University. Some students may complete freshman year of college and senior year of high school simultaneously. The two schools are adjoined by a walkway, making each easily accessible to the other.

Athletics, Activities, and Clubs
A wide variety of extracurricular programs meets the interests of our students and helps them develop time

management skills, hone their ability to prioritize, assume responsibility for learning and social events, and compete in ventures that highlight their talents. Athletic teams include football, soccer, tennis, golf, volleyball, basketball, swimming, softball, cheerleading, baseball, rowing, cross country, track and dance team. MPS teams regularly win district, regional and state titles with a program philosophy that emphasizes dedication, teamwork, and good sportsmanship.

Boarding Opportunities

While 85% of the students are day students, the school also serves 75 international students from countries such as China, Vietnam, Taiwan, India, Brazil, Canada, Mexico, and Russia. A partnership with Pennsylvania International Academy (PIA) provides dormitory housing for international and American students who board full-time as well as weekdays. Visit piacademy.org for more information.

A small sampling of colleges attended by Mercyhurst Prep grads includes:

- Alfred University
- Boston College
- Columbia University
- Emerson College
- Georgetown University
- Harvard University
- Ithaca College
- Johns Hopkins University
- Rochester Institute of Technology
- Sarah Lawrence College
- University of Chicago
- University of Notre Dame

Faculty

60% of our faculty/administration hold postgraduate degrees. The student to faculty ratio is 11:1. Besides in-depth expertise in their specific fields, our faculty embody the Mercy charism, an attribute that makes them unique and exceedingly qualified to work with teens. Many teachers travel extensively during breaks and summer vacation, bringing an international mindset to instruction.

Admissions Policy

MPS admits students of any race, creed, color, or national origin without discrimination. When any student applies for admission, every effort is made to determine whether the school offers an educational program which will allow that student to develop intellectually, socially, spiritually, emotionally, and physically.

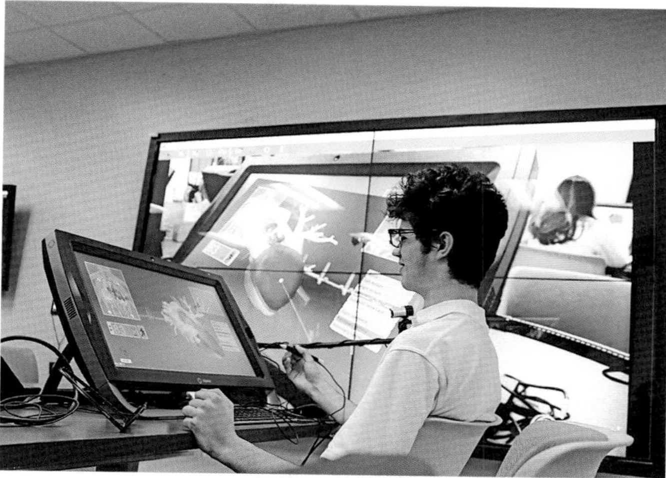

Recent Renovations:

Vorsheck Library and Research Center

Our newly transformed Library and Research Center enables our students to be miles ahead of the secondary standard in scholarly research and state-of-the-art technologies.

Hirt DREAM Labs

Design-Research-Engineering-Arts-Math

This innovative space facilitates creative endeavors with a combination of CADD (computer-aided design and drafting), 3-D design, and hands-on learning. We recently added "zSpace," an educational solution that creates the ultimate learning experience by combining Augmented Reality (AR) with Virtual Reality (VR). The DREAM Labs encourage technological experimentation, while supporting studies in English, graphics, robotics and self-directed learning across the curriculum.

Performing Arts Center (PAC)

Our newly renovated PAC boasts a cutting-edge flying system, acoustics, lighting, and climate control. These improvements will help prepare our students for the creative endeavors of a 21st century actor, dancer, vocalist, musician, lighting designer and technician.

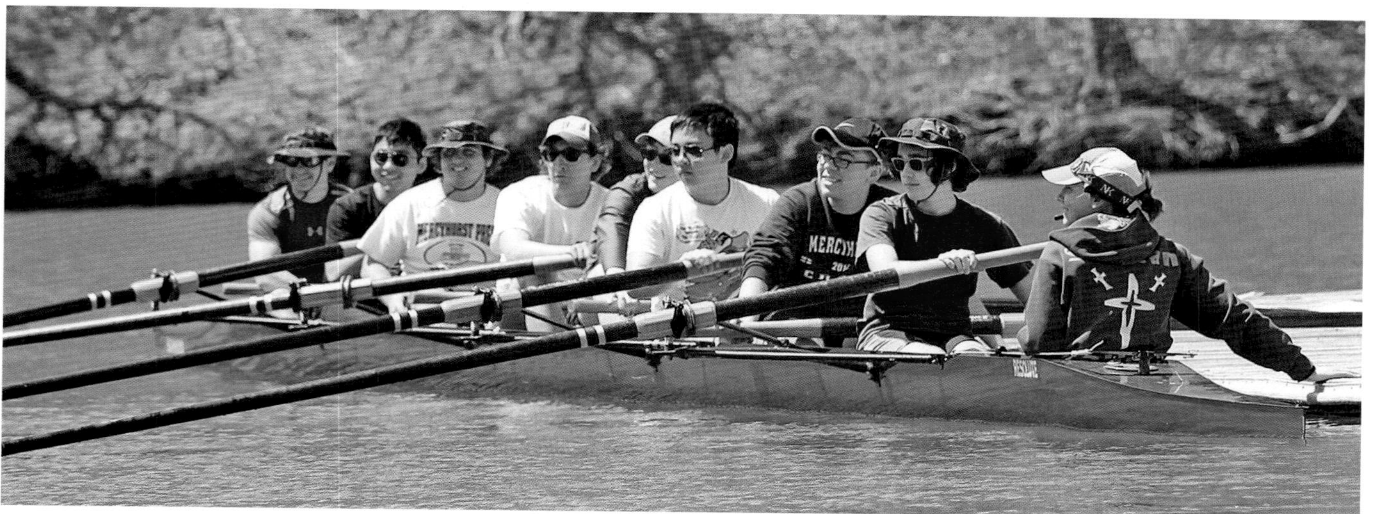

MEADOWRIDGE SCHOOL

(Founded 1985)

Head of School
Mr. Hugh Burke

Deputy Head of School
Mr. Scott Banack

PYP coordinator
Mrs. Heather Nicholson

MYP coordinator
Mr. Scott Rinn

DP coordinator
Ms. Kristal Bereza

Status Private

Boarding/day Day

Gender Coeducational

Language of instruction
English

Authorised IB programmes
PYP, MYP, DP

Age Range 4 – 18

Number of pupils enrolled
668

Fees
Domestic Fees C$22,500
International Fees C$32,500

Address
12224 240th Street
Maple Ridge BC
V4R 1N1 | CANADA

TEL +1 604 467 4444

Email admissions@meadowridge.bc.ca

Website
www.meadowridge.bc.ca

Meadowridge School exists as a point of departure for parents and students who are seeking more meaning from education; an unfettered education that has greater impact on the whole individual and more relevance to the realities of the world.

As an International Baccalaureate (IB) Continuum World School, we offer the academically-rigorous Primary Years Programme (PYP), Middle Years Programme (MYP) and Diploma Programme (DP) to students from Junior Kindergarten to Grade 12. This continuum of learning supports the growth and development of the whole child in a safe, supportive, and challenging environment. Through inquiry-based instruction, students learn to engage with challenging and complex questions effectively and creatively.

Our school, from classroom to natural woodland, is the setting for our program that challenges students to find out more about their own beliefs and society through striving for excellence in academics, arts, and service to the community.

Just 45 minutes east of Vancouver, British Columbia, Meadowridge is located in beautiful Maple Ridge on a unique, pastoral 27-acre campus complete with gardens, greenhouses, a discovery forest, and stream for students across the continuum to engage and explore.

Our 152,000 square foot facility includes state-of-the-art science labs, a theatre, a design lab, an international-sized soccer pitch, and a newly completed nine-classroom complex.

With our accreditation from the Council of International Schools (CIS) and the International Baccalaureate Organization, Meadowridge is committed to providing our students the highest quality of education and the knowledge to become engaged participants in the global community. Only two schools in Canada have this dual accreditation as both IB Continuum and CIS.

Through our outstanding teaching, programs and facilities, Meadowridge develops the confidence in students to not only meet the future, but also to create it.

To discover more about Meadowridge visit us online at meadowridge.bc.ca/discover.

Mott Hall Science and Technology Academy

Principal
Dr. Patrick Awosogba

Assistant Principals
Ms. Marcia Thomas &
Mr. Stany Leblanc

MYP coordinator
Ms. Yoshie Otomo

Status State

Boarding/day Day

Gender Coeducational

Language of instruction
English, Spanish

Authorised IB programmes
MYP

Age Range 11 – 14

Number of pupils enrolled
452

Address
250 East 164th Street
Bronx, New York
NY 10456 | USA

TEL +1 718 293 4017
FAX +1 718 293 7396

Email
MHSTAIB@motthallsta.org

Website
www.motthallsta.org

Mott Hall Science and Technology Academy is a rigorous math, science, and technology focused middle school. We offer families the opportunity for their children to meet the highest academic expectations and standards, to make smooth transitions to selective high schools, to compete successfully for admission to top public and private colleges and to succeed as a global citizen. Our school culture is characterized by a shared vision for academic excellence, the healthy personal growth of all students, and a commitment to our strong belief that all students can and will succeed in their endeavors.

At Mott Hall, students, faculty, and staff members have a shared vision of the individual's ability to achieve personal success each day as preparation to become active members of our global society. The journey our students embark on when they enter our doors is marked by continuous support and guidance academically, emotionally, and physically, to ensure the holistic development of our young people. Students enter a community that embraces them while challenging them.

Instruction in our school is rooted in collaboration and inquiry, which leads to deeper individual understanding of content and application of this content to real life. Our curriculum is driven by conceptual learning, uses hands on activities and is differentiated to meet the needs of our students. We aim to provide an equitable education that allows each student to discover and utilize their full potential, while finding joy in learning.

Along with strong support in our classrooms, we create a safe learning environment for our students, nurturing and supporting them as they grow. Students are equipped with tools to overcome obstacles they may face and to help them become understanding and respectful of different identities and cultures. To do so, we focus on our school's core values: respect, responsibility, honesty, integrity, compassion, generosity, and fairness, along with the International Baccalaureate learner profile traits. With these tools, our students become life long learners ready to actively participate in the world.

In 2014, our school became the first New York City public middle school to be certified as an International Baccalaureate Middle Years Programme. In addition, we have been a certified Advancement Via Individual Determination (AVID) model school since 2013. After over a decade of service to our students and families, we look forward to our continued growth as a community.

Mulgrave, The International School of Vancouver

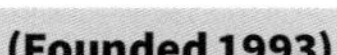

(Founded 1993)

Head of School
John Wray

PYP coordinators
Janet Hicks & Shanaz Ramji

MYP coordinator
Mike Olynyk

DP coordinator
Kathryn Clark

Status Private

Boarding/day Day

Gender Coeducational

Language of instruction
English

Authorised IB programmes
PYP, MYP, DP

Age Range 3 – 18

Number of pupils enrolled
1000

Fees
Day: CND$22,000

Address
2330 Cypress Bowl Lane
West Vancouver BC
V7S 3H9 | CANADA

TEL +1 604 922 3223

Email
admissions@mulgrave.com

Website
www.mulgrave.com

Mulgrave, The International School of Vancouver is a multicultural, coeducational International Baccalaureate World School (pre-school to Grade 12). Nestled on the slopes of Cypress Mountain, overlooking the Pacific Ocean and downtown Vancouver, our stunning campus provides students and faculty custom-built spaces where they can inspire each other as they are all inspired by the views. Our diverse community is united in its commitment to develop the interpersonal and intercultural skills, attitudes, and values that will allow our students to thrive and be happy no matter where in the world they find themselves. Our graduates go on to post-secondary institutions across the globe; this year, they have accepted offers spanning from UBC and McGill in Canada, to Stanford and NYU in the United States, and to Oxford and Cambridge in the UK.

Our Mission: Inspiring Excellence in Education and Life
Through the continuous pursuit of personal best, Mulgrave strives to equip lifelong learners to thrive in a culturally diverse and interdependent world. Our goal is for students to embrace, with passion and confidence, their responsibility to make a difference by serving their communities, both locally and in the world at large.

Our Culture: A warm, vibrant, supportive community
Developing growing independence in learning, service, and leadership is inherent to our school's ethos, as is a strong culture of caring and support. Mulgrave is highly valued for our positive community spirit, enriched by the diversity of families from more than 42 countries, and vibrant learning atmosphere.

Experienced teachers from around the world provide a comprehensive, appropriately challenging, and personalised IB curriculum to an equally ambitious and capable student body.

Our Strategic Plan:
Making Mulgrave Everything We Can Be
Our strategic plan endeavours to make a Mulgrave education even more personalised, enriched with 21st century skills, applied to authentic real world contexts, extended through the offering of an extensive array of varied co-curricular opportunities, and international. The school's commitment to athletics, service, outdoor education, arts, and leadership provide ample opportunity for students to find and develop their unique passions.

Accreditations
Mulgrave is proud to be an accredited member of the Council of International Schools (CIS), the Independent Schools Association of British Columbia (ISABC), and Canadian Accredited Independent Schools (CAIS), and is also authorised by the International Baccalaureate Organization as an IB Continuum School.

Navajo Preparatory School

(Founded 1991)

Head of School
Shawna Becenti

DP coordinator
Donna Fernandez

Status State

Boarding/day Mixed

Gender Coeducational

Language of instruction
English

Authorised IB programmes
DP

Age Range 13 – 18

Number of pupils enrolled
265

Fees
Day: US$1,000 (Native American) – US$3,000 (Non-Native American)

Address
1220 West Apache Street
Farmington
NM 87401 | USA

TEL +1 505 326 6571
FAX +1 505 564 8099

Email
sbecenti@navajoprep.com

Website
www.navajoprep.com

Navajo Preparatory School's mission reflects the integral values of the International Baccalaureate Programme:

- To develop inquisitive, compassionate life-long learners and leaders through a challenging curriculum of international education and assessment.
- To promote a strong foundation of Navajo Philosophy and holistic world view that fosters intercultural understanding and respect in a global society.
- The mission is reflected in the IB Learner Profile and the School's motto:

"Yideeskaago Naat'aanii – Leaders Now and Into the Future"

Navajo Preparatory School is the only authorized IB World School that serves primarily Native American students. We are a college-preparatory school for Native Americans and non-Native American students who desire to pursue higher education. Navajo Preparatory School recruits some of the best and brightest students of the Navajo Nation.

The school offers students a challenging, innovative curriculum. In harmony with the past, it steeps the youth in a deep appreciation of the Navajo language, culture, and history.

Forging ahead, students engage in STEM, writing and reading enjoyment and leadership development. Armed with this impressive, balanced education, students graduate with the skills to succeed in college and an understanding of the world around them. Over 95% of our graduates are accepted into college.

We employ the Navajo philosophy of learning Nitsáhákees (East-White) – Thinking, Nahat'á (South-Blue) – Planning, Iiná (West-Yellow) – Action, Sihasin (North-Black) – Reflection to guide our educational curriculum and Navajo Prep mindset.

Students participate in numerous Gifted & Talented programs, Student Senate, clubs, and interscholastic sports such as football, volleyball, basketball, baseball, softball, golf, cross country and track. Students also have opportunities for community service. Navajo Prep strides itself on a balanced student life to prepare them for international experiences.

New Hampton School

(Founded 1821)

Head of School
Joe Williams

DP coordinator
Jennifer McMahon

Status Private

Boarding/day Mixed

Gender Coeducational

Language of instruction
English

Authorised IB programmes
DP

Age Range 14 – 19

Number of pupils enrolled
340

Fees
Day: US$35,900
Boarding: US$62,500

Address
70 Main Street
New Hampton
NH 03256 | USA

TEL +1 603 677 3401
FAX +1 603 677 3481

Email
admission@newhampton.org

Website
www.newhampton.org

Lifelong Learners and Active Global Citizens
New Hampton School is an independent, coeducational, college preparatory school for boarding and day students, grades 9 through 12 and postgraduate. Nestled in the foothills of New Hampshire's White Mountains and in the heart of the beautiful Lakes Region, yet just 90 minutes from Boston, Massachusetts, the 350-acre campus features six contemporary classroom buildings. On-campus housing includes 13 dormitories, varying in size, each with resident dorm parents/family and complementary dorm life programming activities throughout the year.

Sharing the whole world
Our school's mission is to cultivate lifelong learners who will serve as active global citizens. Core values focused on respect and responsibility provide an essential foundation, while our inclusive community immerses students in an on-campus network of diverse cultures and a worldwide network of alumni, families, and travel opportunities. By allowing classroom conversations to represent more points of view, expertise from outside sources, and intellectual links to coursework, we ensure students are introduced to a full range of insights. Ours is a conscious curriculum, built on an interconnected understanding of the world.

The student body includes representation from 28 states and 30 different countries. Twenty-five percent of students are international. New Hampton routinely sends students to top colleges and universities including Dartmouth College, University of Michigan, Princeton University, Cornell University, Williams College, Syracuse University, UCLA, and University of Chicago.

Empowering Technology
New Hampton School features a 1:1 iPad Program and is considered a leader in technology integration. Our school is an Apple Distinguished School since 2012; this distinguishing recognition is only given to those schools embracing a vision of "continuous innovation." Students are assured of vital connectivity, file sharing, video conferencing, organizational tools, interactive course materials and tests, and all of the latest innovations via Apple.

Enlivened Learning
Our school is proud of programmatic variety including our strong athletic program, art offerings including Animation by the Walt Disney Family Museum, student leadership opportunities, clubs and activities. International Baccalaureate classes begin in eleventh grade and can be taken as part of the full Diploma Programme or as certificate courses. The IB philosophy pervades the curriculum, and ninth and tenth graders are prepared to embrace its challenges. Equally prominent is the school's commitment to the delivery of durable skills using relevant content with emphasis on experiential education, Habits of Mind, and career partnerships. The average class size is 11 and the breadth of academic offerings ranges from university rigor to support, from the IB Diploma Programme, honors courses, and independent study to tutorials and International Support classes that accommodate individual methods and pace of learning.

Weekend activities on and off campus include dances, dinner trips, shopping, hikes, concerts, day trips to Boston, and student-designed outings. The school's dining hall has been recognized for its outstanding cuisine.

Head of School
Mr. Roy Rongfeng Huang

Principal
Timothy Yawney

DP coordinator
Mr. Pavle Milutinovic

Status Private

Boarding/day Mixed

Gender Coeducational

Language of instruction
English

Authorised IB programmes
DP

Age Range 15 – 19

Number of pupils enrolled
250

Fees
IBDP CAD$35,000

Address
50 Featherstone Avenue
Markham ON
L3S 2H4 | CANADA

TEL +1 905 472 2002
FAX +1 905 472 2002

Email
royhuang@neworientalgroup.org

Website
noic.ca

NOIC Academy represents New Oriental Education & Technology Group China (New York Stock Exchange: EDU) in Ontario, Canada. New Oriental Education & Technology Group is the largest provider of private educational services in China. The company was listed on the New York Stock Exchange on September 7th, 2006, a first for a private education company in China. NOIC Academy is led by education experts and former leadership of International Baccalaureate Organization (IBO), Cambridge International Examinations and Eton College in the UK. The school's new Research and Development Centre will strive to be a top international innovation hub in Markham and a leading education centre in North America.

NOIC Academy, located in Toronto, is a private secondary school inspected by the Ontario Ministry of Education. The college currently has one boarding and two educational facilities. We provide university preparation courses to international students, as well as the opportunity to earn an Ontario Secondary School Diploma. We became an International Baccalaureate (IB) Diploma Programme school in March 2015 and the year of 2017 saw the first IB students graduate from NOIC Academy. The annual university enrolment rate of NOIC Academy is 100% and more than 80% of graduates are admitted by the University of Toronto and other top ranked universities. The College also provides international students with TOEFL, IELTS, SAT, and integrated English language instruction.

NOIC Academy students have competed in a variety of academic competitions. For instance, in the 2019 Euclid Mathematics Contest, the overall performance of NOIC Academy candidates ranked 21st among 1200 participating schools in Canada, 15th in the province of Ontario and 3rd in the district where the school is located. Also, we are one of the first schools in the world to develop and use an educational mobile application, iEdu, to facilitate the flow of information among students, parents, teachers, mentors, and the school administration.

The mission of NOIC Academy is to inspire students to improve their lives and expand their horizons through a lifelong commitment to learning, by empowering students to achieve their academic potential, to build self-confidence, and to develop a global vision which embraces cultural differences and promotes cultural exchanges. NOIC Academy is committed to educating a new generation of business and community leaders with international visions. At the same time, we strive to connect our education with rich Chinese history and tradition while fostering open-mindedness, creativity, and critical thinking in our students.

Head of School
Bruce Fawcett

DP coordinator
Tamara Wolpowitz

Status Private

Boarding/day Mixed

Gender Coeducational

Language of instruction
English

Authorised IB programmes
DP

Age Range 3 – 18

Address
7600 Lyons Road
Coconut Creek
FL 33073 | USA

TEL +1 954 247 0179
FAX +1 954 247 0012

Email
admissions@nbps.org

Website
www.nbps.org

Located in Sunny South Florida, North Broward Preparatory School is an extraordinary community of learners. Our teachers and leadership team think beyond traditional education to transform learning and provide an academically challenging environment including the International Baccalaureate Diploma Programme, often referred to as the gold standard of learning.

The International Baccalaureate Diploma Programme is a balanced program of education that prepares students for success at university and life beyond. It is designed to address the intellectual, social, emotional and physical wellbeing of students. At the heart of the IB program is a focus on developing students who are inquirers, thinkers, knowledgeable, communicators, principled, open-minded, caring, risk-takers, balanced and reflective.

As part of Nord Anglia Education, the world's leading educational organization, the student learning experience is enhanced through collaborations with Juilliard, MIT and UNICEF – giving our students the opportunity to experience a multi-disciplinary approach to STEAM and Performing Arts curriculum. Through Nord Anglia's UNICEF partnership and Global Campus, students participate in global expeditions, connect with 50,000 peers around the world and learn how they can be world changers.

At North Broward Preparatory School we believe in developing these qualities, not only in the students but also in our faculty members. Our teachers strive to support the personal needs of each student and create a customized learning environment that ensures their success. Our faculty members are committed to life-long learning and professional development and bring new and innovative ideas to the classroom, and nurture and encourage the passions and interests of each student.

Through our boarding and five-day residential programs, North Broward Preparatory School serves as a home away from home for over 300 students from 25 countries, including the U.S., that we welcome to our new International Village. Boarding students are surrounded by a nurturing environment with caring, dedicated professionals available 24-hours a day. Our Residential Life team ensures that students are given the resources they need to thrive both academically and socially. All of our students get the opportunity to be immersed in a multi-cultural community, become global citizens, celebrate their differences, cultivate a worldview and develop the confidence to impact their communities and the broader world around them.

We encourage you to schedule a tour to learn more about how we can customize the learning experience for your child, ignite their curiosity and ensure that your child loves coming to school. To schedule a tour, call 954-247-0179 or go to www.nbps.org/admissions.

NORTHERN INTERNATIONAL SCHOOL

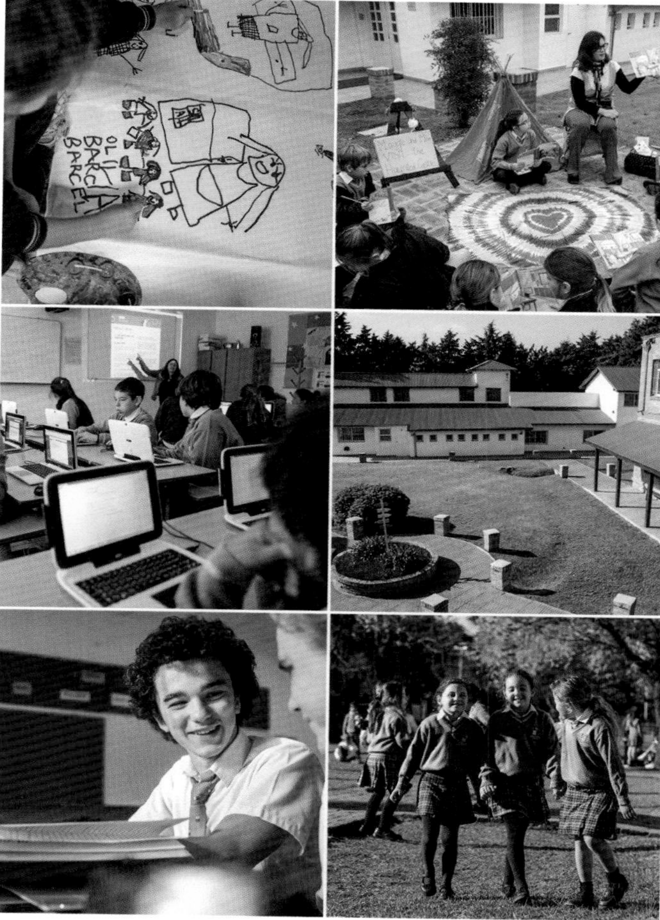

Principal
Prof. Estela María Irrera de Pallaro

DP coordinator
Marisa Zárate

Status Private

Boarding/day Day

Gender Coeducational

Language of instruction
Spanish, English, Italian, Portuguese

Authorised IB programmes
DP

Age Range 2 – 18

Address
Ruote 8 Km 61.5.
Zip Code 1633. Pilar
Buenos Aires | **ARGENTINA**

TEL +54 2322 49 1208
FAX +54 2322 49 1208

Email
info@intschools.org

Website
www.intschools.org/northern

Together with Islands International School and Southern International School.

Northern International School opened its doors in 1997 in a site of 8 hectares in Pilar.

Its founder, Prof. Estela María Irrera de Pallaro, has as an aim to offer a demanding educational quality for families looking for a better lifestyle for their children. With the benefits that contact with nature offers, Northern International School develops all its regular activities in a bright and cheerful environment.

The International Baccalaureate, of which we have been members since 1997, is key in this institution; that is why teachers and heads are trained regularly.

The school has all the facilities needed to comply with this modern and demanding programme: science and IT labs, a library for research, a multi-purpose hall as well as comfortable and bright classrooms.

Our three schools have fully equipped laboratories for the experimental sciences; they are an essential facility for classes in Physics, Chemistry and Biology. Our laboratory provisions are not only for demonstration classes but also for students to become personally acquainted with different research techniques and apply them in practice in experiments ranging from the simple to the more complex. Our students learn to handle laboratory materials safely and efficiently and make full use of them in different pieces of research.

At primary level, research projects include: photosynthesis, animal nutrition, the ill effects of tobacco, analysis of animal movements, electrical resistance, the structure of materials, magnetism, the human body, heat energy, ecosystems, soil, water, cells, life process in vegetables and diet in humans.

At secondary level, research projects include: coefficients of contact, genetics, physical and chemical properties of hydrocarbons, evolutionary theory, population growth, biodiversity, pollution of the environment, ecosystems, and health and human physiology.

Year after year, our students take part in different events and competitions, among these Physics and Biology Olympiads, science fairs organized by ESSARP (English Speaking Scholastic Association of the River Plate), local representative of the University of Cambridge, and Mathematics Olympiads organized by OMA (Argentine Mathematics Olympiads). In recent years the schools have taken part in the worldwide NASA projects and one of our schools has on three occasions won the regional competition and taken part in the world finals in Houston in the United States.

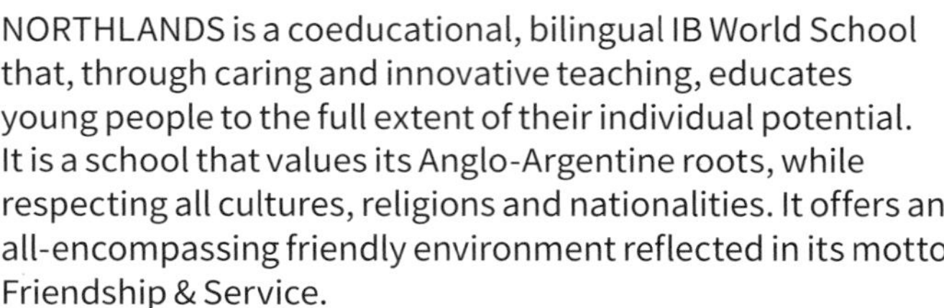

(Founded 1920)

Headmaster James Coulson MA

PYP coordinator Joanne Gillan & Natalia Torlaschi

DP coordinator Alicia Olea

Status Private

Boarding/day Day

Gender Coeducational

Language of instruction English, Spanish

Authorised IB programmes PYP, DP

Age Range 2 – 18

Number of pupils enrolled 1928

Olivos Site
Roma 1248, Olivos
Buenos Aires | **ARGENTINA**

TEL +54 11 4711 8400
FAX +54 11 4711 8401

Email admissionsolivos@northlands.edu.ar

Nordelta site
Av de los Colegios 680 Nordelta,
Provincia de Buenos Aires | **ARGENTINA**

TEL +54 11 4871 2668/9

Email admissionsnordelta@northlands.edu.ar

Website
www.northlands.edu.ar

NORTHLANDS is a coeducational, bilingual IB World School that, through caring and innovative teaching, educates young people to the full extent of their individual potential. It is a school that values its Anglo-Argentine roots, while respecting all cultures, religions and nationalities. It offers an all-encompassing friendly environment reflected in its motto: Friendship & Service.

We aim to strengthen our position as leaders in education and innovation by achieving outstanding international examination results, obtaining international credits, focusing on state-of-the-art technology, expanding our Education for Sustainable Development Projects, instilling a culture of healthy lifestyle choices, developing our campuses to meet the needs of our highly demanding programmes, and continuing to develop a closely knit community influenced by the diversity of our families.

Kindergarten Education

An all-embracing curriculum that works on physical, social, emotional, intellectual, ethic and aesthetic aspects through teaching and learning strategies focused on encouraging curiosity and the desire to know in children.

Primary Education

Our integral curriculum based on inquiry and research as the ideal vehicles for learning. We provide a caring and stimulating environment where children enjoy doing their work and develop positive academic and interpersonal attitudes, self-confidence and self-discipline.

Secondary Education

During this phase students develop critical thinking skills, creativity and autonomy. Individual talents and personal interests are nurtured so that students can make satisfactory career choices at the end of their school life.

Physical Education as an integral part of education

We understand that wellbeing is acquired through physical, mental and emotional balance and encourage our students to make healthy lifestyle choices.

Our students participate in interhouse, national and international inter-school events which promote team spirit and healthy competition.

Visual & Performing Arts

In Art classes at NORTHLANDS, we stimulate our students to find alternative and different ways in which to express themselves.

The initial learning process is based on games to learn and experiment different disciplines. As students mature, they have the opportunity to explore visual arts, music and drama through a variety of techniques, instruments and cultures.

D-Learning Model 1:1

We implement a1:1 model from Year 2 to Year 12. The aim is to improve the way they learn, making responsible use of 21 Century digital technologies.

Robotics Ed Tech Programme

Students have the opportunity to develop skills in construction, design, programming and start-up of robots, while learning logical processes.

Personal & Social Education Programme

This is a central part of the comprehensive education and through a well-defined programme, our students develop

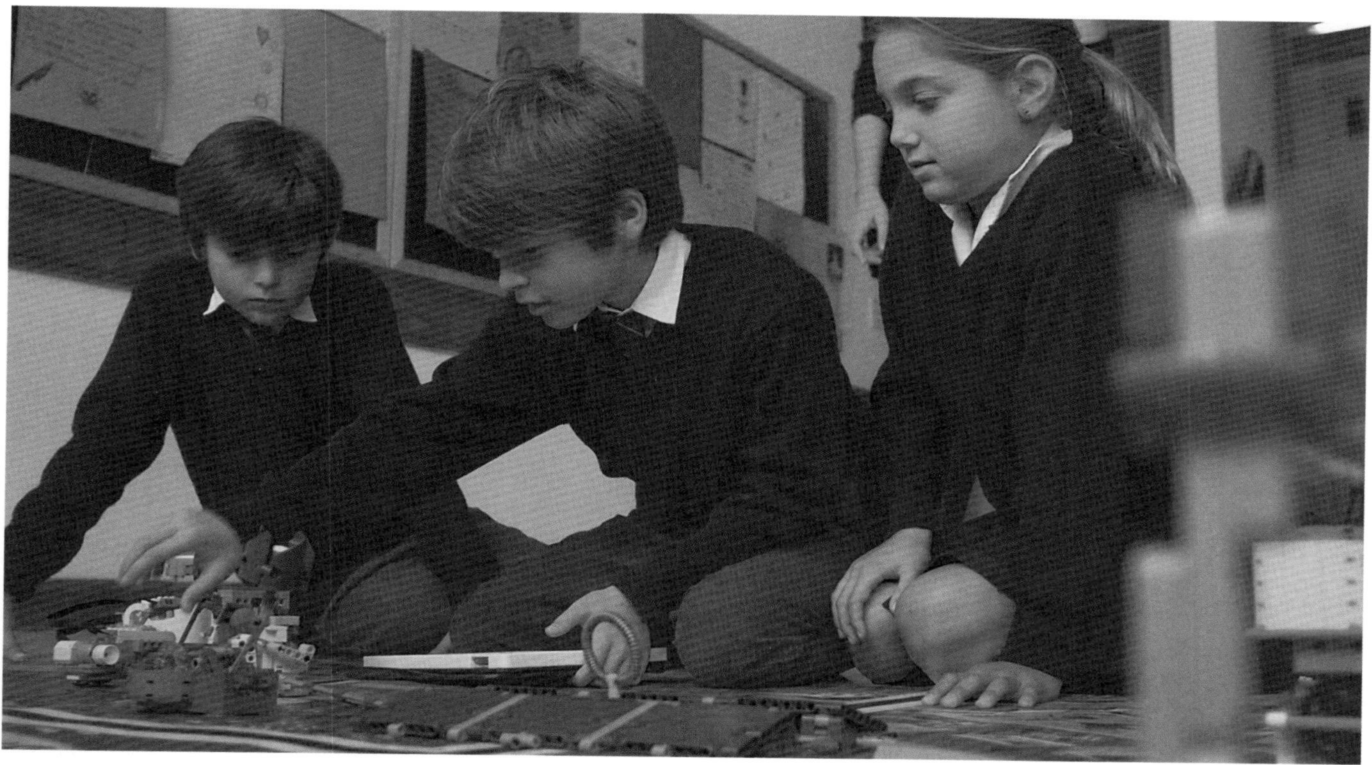

integrity based on high moral standards enabling them to freely choose what is right.

Spanish Immersion

We offer the teaching of Spanish language according to the needs of each student. Emphasis is placed on the child's ability to communicate and self-confidence.

Peer Friend Programme

Designed to accompany children when they join our School, and associate new students and their families with the NORTHLANDS community so that they can start the new School year with confidence and make their social integration a smooth process.

Global Citizenship

We appreciate the richness of diversity and promote international mindedness. Currently around 11% of our families coming from 18 countries in our Olivos site are international, and 19% coming from 28 countries in Nordelta.

(Founded 1853)

Head of School
Annemarie Lynch Kenneally

DP coordinator
Kate Carter

Status Private

Boarding/day Day

Gender Female

Language of instruction
English

Authorised IB programmes
DP

Number of pupils enrolled
435

Fees
Day: US$23,475

Address
1073 Main Street
Hingham
MA 02043-3996 | USA

TEL +1 781 749 5930
FAX +1 781 749 8366

Email
admissions@ndahingham.com

Website
www.ndahingham.com

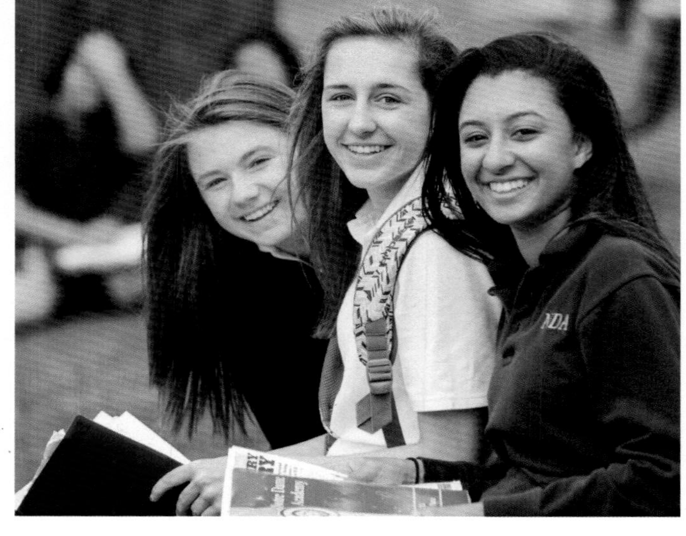

As the first all-girls school in Massachusetts, established in 1853, Notre Dame Academy continues to deliver a unique student experience. It has a rich heritage focused on the simple goal of developing young women of faith, character and scholarship through a dynamic college preparatory environment. The Sisters of Notre Dame de Namur aim to equip students with whatever is necessary for life which is evident today on the Hingham campus, home to over 435 students in grades 7-12. Students come from more than 30 communities and NDA welcomes students from China, Germany, Spain, Switzerland, and the United Kingdom.

Academics

The IB DP at NDA fosters risk-taking and nurtures curiosity. The IB Learner Profile is a powerful force for developing confident women. It requires students to embrace the world beyond their community and their borders, encouraging social responsibility on behalf of global justice, a key attribute of the school's mission.

Athletics

A community that stresses character above winning at any cost defines NDA athletics. It is a highly successful and regionally recognized program, a key part of over 80% of the student body's experience. A staff of over 50 coaches supervise interscholastic teams in 18 sports and 35 levels. NDA is proud of recent achievements including 33 state championships, multiple league and conference titles and Coach of the Year awards.

Co-Curricular

Student life at NDA extends beyond the classroom. NDA empowers students to become bold and thoughtful artists. In Visual Arts, students create work that challenges them to problem-solve. Music students showcase their talents to the entire school community through concerts and musicals. Thespians at NDA perform in three fully-staged productions.

Global Immersion

An integral part of the Notre Dame Academy experience is service to others. Students travel as far as Tanzania and Costa Rica or as near as Boston. The Academy believes that reflecting upon service is a life skill. Students are encouraged to examine their choices and decisions in the light of their faith and consider their influence on the global community. Faculty and staff believe it is their goal to help the young girls graduate as confident and compassionate women who are ready to impress the world.

For more information about Notre Dame Academy, please contact the Admissions Office at 1 (781) 749-5930 or admissions@ndahingham.com.

Notre Dame Academy is accredited by the New England Association of Schools and Colleges.

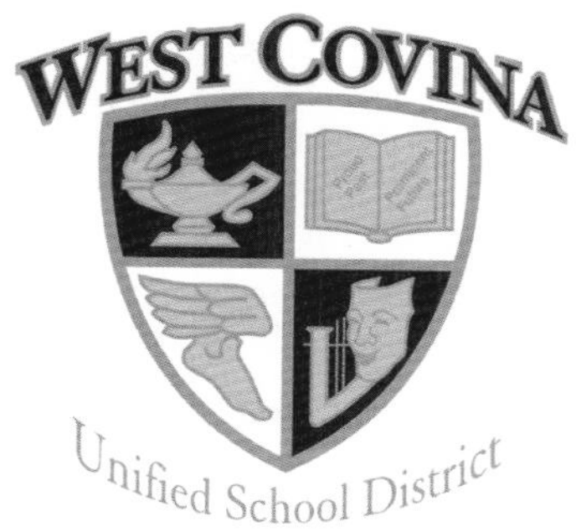

Principal
Ms. Janet Shirley

PYP coordinator
Ms. Jeanne Berrong

Status State

Boarding/day Day

Gender Coeducational

Language of instruction
English, Spanish

Authorised IB programmes
PYP

Age Range 4 – 11

Number of pupils enrolled
625

Address
1440 S. Orange Avenue
West Covina
CA 91790 | USA

TEL +1 626 939 4820
FAX +1 626 939 4825

Website
orangewood.wcusd.org

Reflecting Southern California's rich, multicultural heritage, Orangewood Elementary is a diverse TK-grade 5 learning community located in the San Gabriel Valley. Recognizing the power of the IB programmes, West Covina Unified School District established the International World Schools of West Covina, a TK-grade 12 continuum. In July 2017, Orangewood Elementary earned World School authorization, taking its place as the starting point for that continuum.

Students who read, write, think and communicate in two languages are best prepared for college, career, and the global economy. Dual immersion not only provides students with the advantage of bi-literacy, it cultivates cognitive flexibility and international mindedness. At Orangewood, families have the choice of enrolling their child in a Spanish or Mandarin dual immersion pathway. Students who continue their language studies in WCUSD will be eligible to earn the California Seal of Biliteracy with their high school diploma.

As part of Orangewood's commitment to providing a well-rounded curriculum, we incorporate technology and the arts. To enhance learning through 21st century skills, we introduce the use of 1:1 tech devices beginning with iPads in kindergarten and Chromebooks in grade 2. Coding and robotics are studied by all Orangewood students, serving as an early bridge to our district Career Technical Education pathway. Additionally, weekly dance lessons allow all students to explore, study and perform throughout elementary school.

Ultimately, the strength of Orangewood Elementary lies in our wholehearted approach to creating a principled, caring community that honors the uniqueness of each child. In 2019, Orangewood's commitment to kindness once again earned the distinction of being named a Capturing Kid's Hearts National Showcase School. The enthusiastic involvement of our families and the promotion of student action are evident in our grade level "IB Scholar Spotlights" and the numerous collaborative projects undertaken in our Learning Garden and the broader community.

Mission Statement:

"Orangewood Elementary is dedicated in developing globally-minded problem solvers. We enhance learning by inspiring students to inquire through transdisciplinary units, while empowering them to take action using the attributes of the Learner Profile."

Plantation Middle School

Head of School
Dr. Sherri N. Wilson

IB Assistant Head of School
Christine Clock

MYP coordinator
Pamela Van Horn

Status State

Boarding/day Day

Gender Coeducational

Language of instruction
English

Authorised IB programmes
MYP

Age Range 11 – 15 years

Number of pupils enrolled
688

Address
6600 West Sunrise Blvd
Plantation
FL 33313 | USA

TEL +1 754 322 4100
FAX +1 754 322 4185

Email
nicole.s.wilson@
browardschools.com

Website
browardschools.com/
plantationmid

Plantation Middle School is an International Baccalaureate Middle Years Programme magnet nestled in the heart of Plantation, located in the School district of Broward County, Florida. An accelerated honors program, their faculty and 688 students in sixth through eighth grade represent diverse nationalities. An internationally standardized course of study for highly motivated and academically talented students with higher-level thinking skills, integrated curriculum, thematic units, and intercultural awareness combine to provide a well-rounded education. This unique magnet challenges students to become self-directed learners and responsible world citizens. Their teachers develop inquiring, knowledgeable and caring young people who help to create a better and more peaceful world through intercultural understanding and respect. The program encourages students across the world to become active, compassionate and lifelong learners.

RIDLEY COLLEGE

SINCE 1889

(Founded 1889)	Fees
Headmaster Mr. J. Edward Kidd	Day: CAD$17,500 – CAD$33,950 Domestic Boarders: CAD$60,500 International Boarders: CAD$68,250
PYP coordinator Marcie Lewis	**Address**
MYP coordinator Paul O'Rourke	PO Box 3013 2 Ridley Road St Catharines ON L2R 7C3 | CANADA
DP coordinator Kathy Anderson	**TEL** +1 905 684 1889
Status Private	**FAX** +1 905 684 8875
Boarding/day Mixed	**Email** admissions@ridleycollege.com
Gender Coeducational	**Website** www.ridleycollege.com
Language of instruction English	
Authorised IB programmes PYP, MYP, DP	
Age Range 4 – 18	
Number of pupils enrolled 700	

As Canada's leader in positive education, Ridley College is focused on educating the whole child and providing them with the tools that will help them lead flourishing lives.

Founded in 1889, Ridley is a coeducational boarding and day school located on a beautiful 90-acre campus in St. Catharines, Ontario. An hour drive from Toronto and ten minutes from breathtaking Niagara Falls, the Ridley campus is easily accessible from both Toronto Pearson International Airport and Buffalo Niagara International Airport. Students range from JK through Grade 12 and come from 60 countries worldwide. With over 375 boarders, Ridley has the largest CAIS boarding programme in Ontario and is one of Canada's oldest and most prestigious boarding schools.

"World Prep" is what you find here: a forward-looking and rigorous programme that prepares students for a university education and a promising future. Ridley is one of only three International Baccalaureate (IB) continuum boarding schools in North America, offering the Primary Years Programme, Middle Years Programme, and Diploma Programme. In addition to the IB Programme, Ridley offers the Ontario Secondary School Diploma and a wide range of summer programmes, including our EAL credit course. Ridley graduates go on to study at some of the top colleges and universities in Canada, the United States and internationally, and are equipped with knowledge and skills for success.

Beyond academics, students experience a diverse co-curricular programme in the arts, athletics, leadership and, most importantly, community service. For over 129 years, Ridley College has held true to its motto, Terar Dum Prosim, or "May I be consumed in service." Opportunities abound for participation in Creativity, Activity, and Service activities year-round and for students to explore new interests, cultivate their passions, and be challenged to reach their potential.

One of the defining features of Ridley is the traditional House system, which integrates both boarding and day students into 10 boarding houses on campus, each with its own unique identity and sense of community. By incorporating our local day students into the boarding programme, Ridley provides students with a perfect balance of global cultures and a uniquely Canadian experience.

Santiago College

(Founded 1880)

Director
Ms Lorna Prado Scott

Academic Coordinator
Claudia Rose

PYP coordinator
Mónika Naranjo

MYP coordinator
Angel Girano

DP coordinator
Gustavo Paez

Status Private

Boarding/day Day

Gender Coeducational

Language of instruction
Spanish, English

Authorised IB programmes
PYP, MYP, DP

Age Range 3 yrs 9 mnths – 18

Number of pupils enrolled
1949

Address
Av. Camino Los Trapenses 4007
Lo Barnechea
Santiago | **CHILE**

TEL +56 2 27338800

Email
master@scollege.cl

Website
www.scollege.cl/index.php/es/

Santiago College is a bilingual, independent, co-educational day school, founded as a non-sectarian institution in 1880 with support from the US Methodist Church.

The educational programme at Santiago College meets the requirements of the Chilean Ministry of Education and is authorized to offer three of the IB Programmes: PYP, MYP and DP. Santiago College is accredited by CIS and NEASC.

Students normally enter Santiago College at PK level and stay until they graduate from 12th Grade. The students are mainly Chilean, but a considerable number of students come from other countries and priority admission is given to overseas applicants. Approximately 90% of the graduating class enters Chilean universities and the remainder pursues studies in the USA or Europe. The school operates a 180-day minimum calendar starting in early March and ending in mid-December. PK and kindergarten children have a half-day schedule. All other grades have a full school day beginning at 7:55am and ending at 3:35pm. The school campus of 11 hectares is located in Lo Barnechea, 30 minutes drive from the city centre. Facilities include a library of 40,000 volumes, 98 classrooms, AV rooms, an auditorium, gymnasium, swimming pool, playing fields, science and computing labs, music and art studios and one cafeteria. Students applying for admission to PK must be four years old by December 31st of the year prior to school entry. Santiago College accepts students without regard to gender, colour, creed, or ethnic, nationality or social origin. The selection process includes an interview with prospective students and their parents.

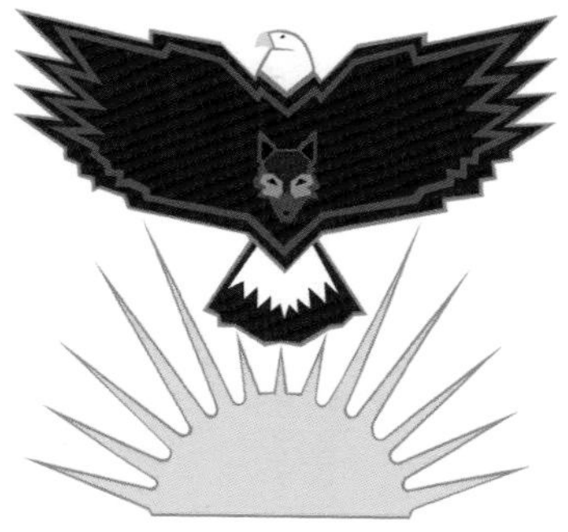

Head of School
Ms. Valerie Allen

PYP coordinator
Ms. Julie Shaw

Status Private

Boarding/day Day

Gender Coeducational

Language of instruction
English, nsyilxcen

Authorised IB programmes
PYP

Age Range 4 – 12

Number of pupils enrolled 96

Address
1156 SenPokChin Blvd
Oliver BC
VOH 1T8 | CANADA

TEL +1 250 498 2019
FAX +1 250 498 3096

Website
www.senpokchin.ca

Empowering indigenous identity to become a community of global thinkers

Set in the beautiful Okanagan Valley of British Columbia Canada, Senpaqcin School is a small independent, First Nations school on-reserve open to all. We provide quality education for children between the ages of 4 and 12 years old. Our School belongs to the Nk'mip people who are one of 7 Bands within the traditional lands of the Okanagan Nation. We are proud to be the first on-reserve authorized Primary Years IB World School in the North Americas. We believe that being part of IBO will help shift the stereotypes that exist within the country regarding First Nations education and that indigenous knowledge can be shared globally.

Our school is built on the foundation of indigenous knowledge (nsyilxcen) and the identity of the sqilxw people (Okanagan First Nations). Our mission is to explore our interconnectedness to the land locally and globally with a focus on stainability of the tmxwulxw (Earth). Our students participate in annual cultural experiences on the land. Through these hands-on learning experiences and the cultural captikwl stories, students compare the traditional beliefs and values of the Okanagan Nation and find similarities to other cultures around the world – past and present.

The Okanagan Valley is known for its agricultural land use. Our school is fortunate to have a 100 square metres of fenced garden space where the students are able to participate in a variety of learning experiences including planting, harvesting, and gathering of eggs for our lunch and breakfast programs. Students are able to have experiences that connect indigenous ways of knowing to current farming practices like planting using the 'Three Sisters' way of companion planting.

Our second language is the nsyilxcen (Okanagan) which is the traditional language of the people. Much of the culture is embedded within the language. Many of the elders believe that if the language dies, a large piece of the culture will die with it. We are at a critical tipping point for ensuring that this language is not lost for future generations.

Somersfield Academy

(Founded 1991)

Head of School
Mr. Carlos Symonds

MYP coordinators
Summer Wood
Brice Pursell

DP coordinator
Kate Ross

Status Private

Boarding/day Day

Gender Coeducational

Language of instruction
English

Authorised IB programmes
MYP, DP

Age Range 3 – 18

Number of pupils enrolled
511

Address
107 Middle Road
Devonshire
DV 06 | BERMUDA

TEL +1 441 236 9797

Email
admissions@somersfield.bm

Website
www.somersfield.bm

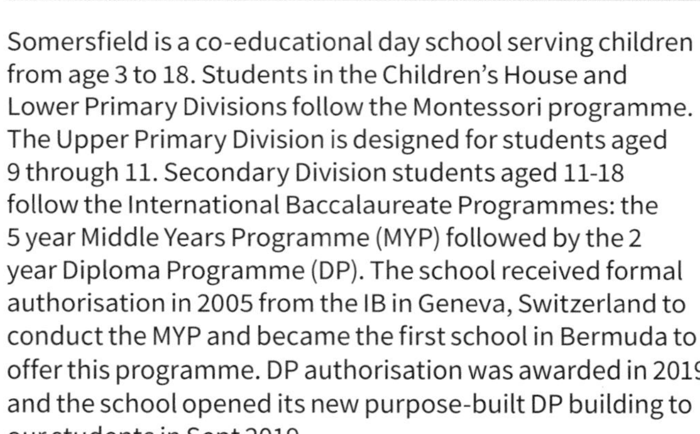

Somersfield is a co-educational day school serving children from age 3 to 18. Students in the Children's House and Lower Primary Divisions follow the Montessori programme. The Upper Primary Division is designed for students aged 9 through 11. Secondary Division students aged 11-18 follow the International Baccalaureate Programmes: the 5 year Middle Years Programme (MYP) followed by the 2 year Diploma Programme (DP). The school received formal authorisation in 2005 from the IB in Geneva, Switzerland to conduct the MYP and became the first school in Bermuda to offer this programme. DP authorisation was awarded in 2019 and the school opened its new purpose-built DP building to our students in Sept 2019.

The five-year MYP offers students a rigorous, comprehensive and well-rounded academic preparation for moving on to the final two years, (grades 11 and 12) with the internationally-regarded IB Diploma Programme.

College Preparation

The IB Diploma Programme is an academically challenging and balanced programme of education with rigorous coursework and final examinations that prepare students, aged 16-19, for success at university and in life beyond. The DP aims to encourage students to be knowledgeable, inquiring, caring, open-minded and to develop intercultural understanding and the attitude necessary to appreciate a range of viewpoints. In addition to their DP courses, students wishing to attend a US University are supported with SAT preparation classes in English and Math.

Mission

Somersfield Academy will provide a unique educational experience for all its students based firmly on the ideals of The Somersfield Promise, the explicit beliefs of the Core Values Statement and our commitment to Diversity.

Our Promise

To stimulate intellectual curiosity and accomplishment; to instill compassion and respect; and always to honour the daring dreams and hidden talents of the individual.

Our Core Values

We are a learning community
We practice peace
We inspire intellectual curiosity
We foster independence and responsibility
We embrace a sense of joy and wonder
We honour the strength and courage to stand for truth
We instill respect for self and others.

Vision

Our school aims to prepare students to be global citizens, independent, life-long learners and to acquire the problem-solving skills and knowledge necessary for educational success. Teachers encourage self-expression and creative thinking as well as respect for and understanding of different philosophies and cultures in accordance with the school's learner profile.

SOUTHERN
INTERNATIONAL
SCHOOL

Principal
Prof. Estela María Irrera de Pallaro

DP coordinator
Clotilde Alleva

Status Private

Boarding/day Day

Gender Coeducational

Language of instruction
Spanish, English, Italian, Portuguese

Authorised IB programmes
DP

Age Range 2 – 18

Address
Freeway Buenos Aires – La Plata Km 34.
Zip Code 1884. Hudson, Berazategui
Buenos Aires | **ARGENTINA**

TEL +54 11 4215 3636
FAX +54 11 4215 0707

Email
info@intschools.org

Website
www.intschools.org/southern

Working together with Islands International School and Northern International School.

A community committed to education

In 1999 Mrs. Estela María Irrera de Pallaro, backed up and encouraged by her experience in founding and developing a comprehensive educational project, creates a new school with the aim of improving the institution objectives in a place where families can not only find peace and privacy but also a space in contact with nature.

The school mission is to teach students to interact and adapt to a complex social environment in which they need numerous tools to be able to succeed, accompanied by a teaching staff permanently trained. For this purpose, with a history of more than three decades, the school provides a demanding education that not only abides by academic aspects but expects to educate upright people as well.

Southern International School develops the students' capacities through different activities so that they can interact with full independence and freedom in today's society.

International Baccalaureate Programme

International Schools want their students to complete their studies hand in hand with this organization. Born in Geneva, Switzerland, these programmes, which demand a strong commitment from teachers and heads, are worldwide recognized by their excellent quality.

To belong to or to be a member of this organization implies meeting certain requirements such as having fully equipped experimental sciences laboratories, where the students acquire and handle different research techniques in order to apply them in class in a practical manner, which will help them achieve a better understanding of all kinds of topics, easy or complex.

Southpointe
ACADEMY

(Founded 2000)

Head of School
Gordon MacIntyre

PYP coordinator
Jaya Van Praagh

MYP coordinator
Christine Yang

Status Private

Boarding/day Day

Gender Coeducational

Language of instruction
English

Authorised IB programmes
PYP, MYP

Fees
Kindergarten – Grade 12
CND$16,820 – CND$18,820
International CND$33,235

Address
1900 56th Street
Tsawwassen BC
V4L 2B1 | CANADA

TEL +1 604 948 8826
FAX +1 604 948 8853

Email
admissions@southpointe.ca

Website
www.southpointe.ca

To Learn, Lead, and Succeed

Southpointe Academy cultivates engaged, well-rounded citizens poised to thrive in their pursuit of post-secondary education and primed to achieve their full potential. Located in sunny Tsawwassen, 30 minutes from Vancouver, overlooking both farmland and the ocean, the School is a non-denominational institution offering a co-educational, university-preparatory program for students in Kindergarten to Grade 12.

We offer the International Baccalaureate (IB) Primary Years Programme (PYP) and the IB Middle Years Programme (MYP). The College Board's Advanced Placement (AP) Program, including the AP Capstone Diploma, is offered to students in Grades 10-12, preparing them for selective post-secondary institutions.

Our mission is to involve, instruct, and inspire our students to learn, lead and succeed. We aim to develop outstanding citizens who are intellectually engaged, intrinsically motivated, and globally responsible. Our balanced approach produces confident, well-rounded graduates, who are creative, independent thinkers and communicators. Our shared values of kindness, integrity, perseverance, respect and responsibility reflect our goal to be people of character and substance. The Southpointe student body represents a diverse community of learners that come from the greater Vancouver area and across the globe.

Our well qualified faculty, many of whom have taught internationally, continue to build a globally focused educational environment where students are inspired to learn for a lifetime. After graduating from Southpointe, our students are accepted to top universities in Canada, the United States and around the world. Southpointe students make meaningful connections locally and globally, learning additional languages in order to communicate more effectively. Emphasis is placed on teaching 21st century skills and engaging students in authentic inquiry into the world around them. At Southpointe, we encourage our students to actively involve themselves in all facets of school life: to cultivate their passions, to pursue their interests, and to build upon their strengths.

Southpointe offers a wide array of activities beyond the classroom to ensure a well-rounded experience for each of our students. A complement to our academic and physical education curriculum, our athletics programme develops character, leadership, and interpersonal skills through student participation in a wide variety of sports. As participants in an acclaimed arts programme, Southpointe students demonstrate creativity, dedication, and the ability to effectively collaborate with their peers. The school provides outlets for inventive thinking, allowing our students to push the bounds of their imagination.

St. Francis College

(Founded 2003)

College Principal
Mrs Shirley Hazell

Head of Early Years & Primary
Carolina Giannetto

Head of Secondary
Andrés Suárez

PYP coordinator Gisele Caselli

MYP coordinator
Fabrice Bidaury

DP coordinator
Sofie Muchardt Smith

Status Private

Boarding/day Day

Gender Coeducational

Language of instruction
English, Portuguese

Authorised IB programmes
PYP, MYP, DP

Age Range 2 – 18

Number of pupils enrolled
735

Fees
Day: US$21,000 – US$29,000

Address
Rua Joaquim Antunes 678
Pinheiros, São Paulo
SP 05415-001 | BRAZIL

TEL +55 11 3728 8050

Email office@stfrancis.com.br

Website www.stfrancis.com.br

Mission Statement

St. Francis College is an international school which strives for excellence providing a warm and friendly community committed to the IB Philosophy. We offer a challenging educational programme with rigorous assessment through inquiry-based instruction.

We empower pupils to be passionate lifelong learners, achieve academic and personal excellence and be committed to impact the world positively.

Curriculum

The international curriculum offered is taught in English. The formal curriculum is guided by the Brazilian and British National Curriculum and the IB Programmes. A broad approach of concept-based learning encompasses the humanities, arts, sciences, mathematics, and information technology. An important element in the curriculum are the Portuguese language subjects, which include Brazilian literature, Portuguese language as well as the history and geography of Brazil. The College provides pupils with academic challenge and key life skills in a flexible and transdisciplinary programme. Throughout the primary school we offer the IB PYP, in the secondary school we offer the IB MYP and the IB DP in the last two years. IGCSE exams are taken in the main subjects in MYP 5. Pupils will conclude their secondary education having also obtained their Brazilian studies diploma.

A wide range of physical activities and sports is offered to students as well as outstanding programmes in visual arts, drama and music, from Early Years throughout Secondary Years.

Once our students graduate from St. Francis they go on to both Brazilian and international universities and continue to excel academically, personally and professionally.

Extracurricular activities

Extracurricular activities offered include football, basketball, Volleyball, dance, skateboarding, martial arts, cooking, drama, music, arts.

Entry Requirements

Application to the college should be done through the Admissions Office at: admissions@stfrancis.com.br or +55 11 3728 8055/56.

Evaluations and interviews are held in October and March for acceptances during the next semester. Previous school reports, confidential references and IGCSE results (if applicable) are taken into account.

St. Paul's School

MANIBUS POTENTIA STUDIUM ANIMIS

(Founded 1926)

Head Teacher
Ms Louise Simpson

Registrar
Mrs Sandra Abatepaulo

DP coordinator
Ana Carolina Belmonte

Status Private

Boarding/day Day

Gender Coeducational

Language of instruction
English

Authorised IB programmes
DP

Age Range 3 – 18

Address
Rua Juquiá 166
Jardim Paulistano
São Paulo
SP 01440-903 | BRAZIL

TEL +55 11 3087 3399

Email
head@stpauls.br

Website
www.stpauls.br

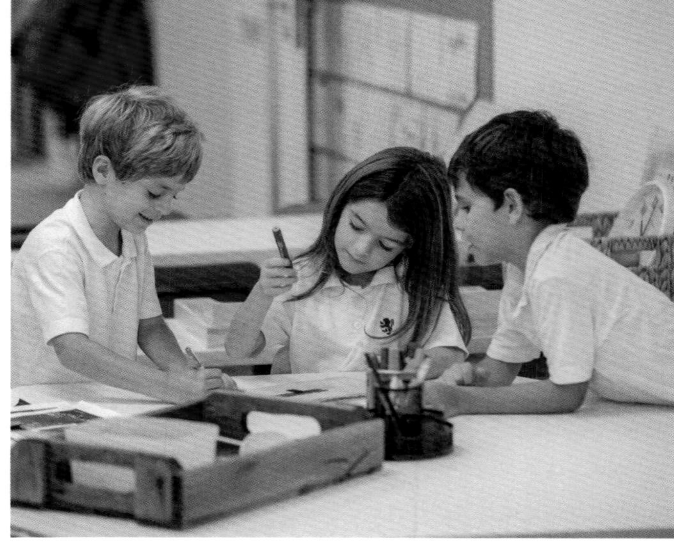

St. Paul's School was founded in 1926 and was the first British School in São Paulo. Fully coeducational, with approximately 1,000 pupils, aged from 3 to 18, it is a school with history and tradition, but which embraces innovation, contemporary values and technological developments. We offer a British curriculum, including the International Primary Curriculum (IPC) and courses up to IGCSE and the International Baccalaureate Diploma. At IB the following subjects are taught in the Sixth Form (and offered as standard and higher levels): English, Portuguese, Spanish, French, mathematics, mathematical studies, physics, chemistry, biology, Brazilian social studies, computer science, environmental systems and societies, geography, history, economics, business management, theatre, visual arts, and music.

The school prides itself on an excellent enrichment programme ranging from MUN to Duke of Edinburgh, from knitting classes to a robotics programme, from mathematical olympiads to outstanding drama and music. Field trips also form an integral part of the curriculum with every year group from the age of 8 years old going on residential visits throughout Brazil and beyond.

We prepare our pupils within a bilingual and bicultural Anglo-Brazilian community for a global future. We offer a broad and balanced but rigorous curriculum where the individual pupil is at the heart of the teaching and learning. It is our aim to discover the passion and talents of every pupil, and create the right environment to develop these. Pupils leave us confident, assured and well prepared for an exciting life, and a multitude of opportunities, often at top universities.

We are a world-class school; a member of HMC, COBIS and LAHC, and the first officially accredited British School Overseas in South America. We are proud of our local, national and international reputation and we constantly strive to improve the opportunities for our pupils and staff.

The school has undertaken an almost continuous programme of building works over the past 20 years as it has gradually grown; this includes extensive refurbishment and extension of the original school building, the creation of a sixth form centre and a multimillion dollar underground state of the art sports centre. We have been awarded as a Microsoft Showcase School and an Apple Distinguished School in recognition for our excellence in transforming and enhancing our physical and online learning environment to deliver more personalised education to our pupils.

S H
STRATFORD HALL
IB WORLD SCHOOL
2000
20
2020

(Founded 2000)

Head of School
Dean Croy

PYP coordinator
Amanda Lempriere

MYP coordinator
Mark Pulfer

DP coordinator
Stefania Iacchelli

Status Private

Boarding/day Day

Gender Coeducational

Language of instruction
English

Authorised IB programmes
PYP, MYP, DP

Age Range 5 – 18 years

Number of pupils enrolled
535

Fees
Annual Tuition: CAD$23,050

Address
3000 Commercial Drive
Vancouver BC
V5N 4E2 | CANADA

TEL +1 604 436 0608
FAX +1 604 436 0616

Email
info@stratfordhall.ca

Website
www.stratfordhall.ca

Stratford Hall is an independent, co-educational, nondenominational, university preparatory day school with a student population of 533 ranging from Kindergarten to Grade 12. Our location in a vibrant, urban setting in East Vancouver, British Columbia reflects our diverse community of students. Through the continuum of International Baccalaureate (IB) programmes, the Primary Years Programme (Kindergarten – Grade 5), Middle Years Programme (Grades 6 – 10) and Diploma Programme (Grades 11 & 12) the School provides a level of individual challenge and academic rigour beyond the norm. Equally important is our commitment to the IB Learner Profile as a guide fostering international-mindedness in students and adults alike.

At Stratford Hall, your child will be given the opportunity to learn and to thrive; to discover their unique strengths, and to explore the diverse opportunities our rapidly changing world offers. Under the care and guidance of Stratford Hall staff, they will grow and mature, while equipping themselves with intellectual tools, strength of character, and a global perspective.

Stratford Hall is a not-for-profit school operating under the authority of the Ministry of Education of British Columbia.

Our Mission
Stratford Hall educates students to the highest global standards through the programmes of the International Baccalaureate. Excellence and confidence are developed through a challenging academic curriculum with further emphasis on creativity, activity and service. We foster a strong pluralistic community built on integrity and respect.

Our Vision
Stratford Hall strives to be a global leader in the International Baccalaureate community. Our students will gain a deep understanding of the world around them, and they will act on their connections to the outside community. They will excel to the best of their abilities, and graduates will be equipped to achieve their chosen goals. This is accomplished by acquiring and retaining the best teachers, and by a commitment to a balanced and enriched curriculum. The success of Stratford Hall is deeply rooted in the establishment of a supportive, knowledgeable and committed community.

Stratford Hall is proud to be an accredited member of the Independent Schools Association of British Columbia (ISABC), Canadian Accredited Independent Schools (CAIS), National Association of Independent Schools (NAIS), and is authorized by the International Baccalaureate Organization as an IB Continuum School.

CANADA'S INTERNATIONAL SCHOOL | L'ÉCOLE INTERNATIONALE DU CANADA

(Founded 1962)

Head of School
Dr. Josep González

PYP coordinator
Zein Odeh

MYP coordinator
Leslie Miller

DP coordinator
Dr. Jennifer Elliott

Status Private

Boarding/day Day

Gender Coeducational

Language of instruction
French, English

Authorised IB programmes
PYP, MYP, DP

Age Range 2 – 18

Number of pupils enrolled
1470

Fees
Day: CAD$19,760 – CAD$33,970

Address
306 Lawrence Avenue East
Toronto ON
M4N 1T7 | CANADA

1293 Meredith Avenue,
Mississauga, ON
L5E 2E6

TEL +1 416 484 6533
FAX +1 416 488 3090

Email
admissions@tfs.ca

Website
www.tfs.ca

Bilingual and co-educational since 1962, TFS is renowned as Canada's leading bilingual International Baccalaureate (IB) school, providing an internationally focused education with high academic standards to 1,470 students. Teaching the curricula of France and Ontario through the framework established by the IB programs, we offer our students an education that is rich in academic excellence, diversity and opportunity.

Authorized to offer the PYP, MYP and IB Diploma, TFS is an IB World School and the only full continuum bilingual IB school in Canada.

We welcome boys and girls from age two to university entrance. No prior knowledge of French is required for entry up to and including Grade 7. Thanks to our Introductory Program, we successfully integrate students with no background in French. While 90% of TFS students have little or no knowledge of French when they enrol, they graduate fully bilingual with an international outlook that sets them on a path to a bright future.

TFS' mission is to develop multilingual, critical thinkers who celebrate difference, transcend borders and strive for the betterment of humankind.

Our educators come from around the world to teach at either our Toronto or West Campus in Mississauga, and provide a caring and supportive learning environment that encourages students of diverse backgrounds to become individuals who reflect, and citizens who act.

We demonstrate our commitment to the development of the whole child through stimulating academic and co-curricular programs that include recreational and competitive sports, music, visual and dramatic arts.

In addition to being authorized by the IB, TFS is accredited by the Ministry of Education of Ontario, the French Ministry of Education, and Canadian Accredited Independent Schools (CAIS). TFS is also a member of the Conference of Independent Schools of Ontario (CIS), the Council of International Schools, and Agence pour l'enseignement français à l'étranger (AEFE).

Please visit us at www.tfs.ca.

The Baldwin School of Puerto Rico

(Founded 1968)

Headmaster
Mr. James Nelligan

PYP coordinator
Mrs. Sarah Loinaz

MYP coordinator
Mrs. Cristina Castillo

DP coordinator
Mrs. Laura Maristany

Status Private

Boarding/day Day

Gender Coeducational

Language of instruction
English

Authorised IB programmes
PYP, MYP, DP

Age Range 3 – 18

Number of pupils enrolled
820

Fees
US$8,697 – US$13,527

Address
PO Box 1827
Bayamón 00960-1827 |
PUERTO RICO

TEL +1 787 720 2421
FAX +1 787 790 0619

Email
admission@baldwin-school.org

Website
www.baldwin-school.org

The Baldwin School of Puerto Rico, located in the greater San Juan metropolitan area, is the premier independent, PPK-12, college preparatory English language day school in Puerto Rico. It is the first school on the Caribbean island to offer the Primary, Middle and Diploma levels of the International Baccalaureate (IB) program. "Baldwin School has long been an exceptional institution, but IB pushes us further," says Headmaster James Nelligan. "It ensures that all children are challenged to become creative thinkers, problem solvers and effective communicators. We implemented IB to challenge the vagaries of traditional pedagogy while retaining its strengths, and to foster novel thinking and creative individual and intellectual endeavor."

At Baldwin School, technology is broadly integrated in the classroom. Students use a range of platforms, applications and web-based software; to research, organize and create content. A fully modern, wireless digital mainframe allows students to leverage the world's resources and conceive original content. Touchscreen technology supports literacy and numeracy across all grades. Interior and exterior laboratories combine hands-on and digital learning. "Technology is central to the world in which our students live, so we need to take advantage of it to reach them more fully, where their inclinations and needs intersect our learning expectations in an organic and meaningful way," says Mr. Nelligan.

Baldwin offers a beautiful and spacious twenty-three acre campus, which is also a Certified Wildlife Habitat. Its location means that students can take part in a range of outdoor activities. Spectacular facilities include a swimming pool, tennis courts, field house, outdoor courts, soccer field, and a rainforest biological field station. Indoor facilities include science and computer labs, a performing arts center, a recording studio, multiple art studios, a dance studio, and music rooms.

Baldwin's student body very much reflects Puerto Rico's diverse population. Students participate in dozens of co-curricular activities. Athletes compete at mini, youth, junior varsity, and varsity levels. Math, Science and Model United Nations teams also compete at the national level. Campus life includes opportunities to participate in many clubs and organizations, most of which serve the broader community through both service and donations. All of Baldwin's graduates go on to study at university, mostly abroad, including the United States' most prestigious colleges and universities.

Baldwin School is committed to the belief that every child can flourish if they are given the right combination of time, opportunity, and support.

Established 1926

(Founded 1926)

Principal
Gina C. Duarte-Romero M.Ed.

Assistant Principal
Ana V. Seoane

PYP coordinator
Isbel Salgueiro

Status Private

Boarding/day Day

Gender Coeducational

Language of instruction
English

Authorised IB programmes
PYP

Age Range 1 – 14

Number of pupils enrolled
200

Fees
US$9,800 – US$20,800

Address
1600 S. Red Road
Miami
FL 33155 | USA

TEL +1 305 266 4666
FAX +1 305 266 0299

Email
info@biltmoreschool.com

Website
www.biltmoreschool.com

Originally founded in Coral Gables in 1926, The Biltmore School is one of the oldest schools in Miami Dade County. Our school enjoys a tradition of educational excellence that has provided guidance to children for the past 90 years.

Our Principal, Gina Romero and our Biltmore Staff members are actively involved in the "Project Zero" research initiative, sponsored by Harvard University that promotes creative thinking, encourages children to be self-reliant, and empowers them to think "outside the box" through a challenging curriculum that incorporates instruction that maximizes the multiple intelligences, individual learning styles and modalities. Through participation in ongoing professional development workshops in partnership with Florida International University, our staff actively explores "Visible Thinking" strategies that promote the highest levels of abstract and critical thinking in children of all ages.

During the 2007-2008 school year our school was awarded accreditation by AISF (Association of Independent Schools of Florida), SACS (Southern Association of Colleges and Schools) and CASI (Council on Accreditation and School Improvement).

The Biltmore School has also been an IB World School since March 2012 and offers the IB Primary Years Programme and is currently a candidate school for the IB Middle Years Programme.

The Biltmore School believes that students are capable and knowledgeable agents of their learning. We feel that it is the responsibility of the educator to be both the partner and guide in the growth and development of the child. It is through much research and collaboration that our school has embraced and synthesized diverse educational views and practices to best benefit our students.

The Biltmore School offers a comprehensive program for students from age one through eighth grade.

THE BRITISH COLLEGE OF BRAZIL

A NORD ANGLIA EDUCATION SCHOOL

Principal
Mr. Duncan Rose

DP coordinator
Mr. Ben Holman

Status Private

Boarding/day Day

Gender Coeducational

Language of instruction
English

Authorised IB programmes
DP

Address
Rua Álvares de Azevedo, 50
Chácara Flora
São Paulo
SP 04671-040 | BRAZIL

TEL +55 11 5547 3030

Email
info@britishcollegebrazil.org

Website
www.britishcollegebrazil.org

The British College of Brazil (BCB), a Nord Anglia Education school, is São Paulo's school of choice for expatriate families looking to provide their children with an international education. We offer engaging learning environments to students in Early Years, Primary and Secondary in a warm and supportive atmosphere where they can thrive. Our schools and the one-of-a-kind opportunities we create inside and outside the classroom enrich learning, instill life-long memories and a deep sense of achievement. We welcome your family to become a valued member of our community.

At the British College of Brazil we teach the English National Curriculum adapted to an international environment, the IGCSE in Year 10 and 11 followed by the IB Diploma Programme. Throughout our core curricula and programs we help your child to develop a global mindset and nurture essential skills such as creativity, collaboration and resilience. We want every student to become lifelong learners, to try something new and, above all, to be ambitious.

We are part of the Nord Anglia Education family of 66 international schools, boarding schools and private schools located in 29 countries around the world. Together we are able to enrich your child's learning experience with opportunities beyond the ordinary. From online debates and challenges, to expeditions to the savannah of Tanzania or participating in our Performing Arts Festival in Miami, Nord Anglia's Global Campus connects our students around the world to learn together every day.

Additionally, our collaborations with world leading institutions such as The Julliard School, The Massachusetts Institute of Technology (MIT), and UNICEF enhance the curriculum and offer exceptional professional development for teachers. This approach results in high academic outcomes, and equips students with the skills that are essential to thrive in the 21st century.

We believe that there is no limit to what our students, our people, and our communities can achieve. We encourage your child to set their sights higher by fostering a global perspective together with our school's personalized approach to learning – helping every child to succeed, thrive and love learning.

The British School, Rio de Janeiro

A caring community, striving for excellence, where every individual matters.

(Founded 1924)

Directors
John Nixon MBE, Carlos Lima & Sonia Salgado

DP coordinator
Guy Smith & Leah Wilks

Status Private

Boarding/day Day

Gender Coeducational

Language of instruction
English

Authorised IB programmes
DP

Age Range 2 – 18

Number of pupils enrolled
2200

Fees
Day: R70,000

Address
Rua Real Grandeza 99
Botafogo, Rio de Janeiro
RJ 22281-030 | BRAZIL

TEL +55 21 2539 2717

Email edu@britishschool.g12.br

Website
www.britishschool.g12.br

Founded in 1924, we are a non-profit, independent and coeducational day school offering a complete and coherent curriculum for students of all nationalities from ages 2-18.

Our school aims to give students a broad, balanced and relevant educational experience. The educational philosophy and practice are primarily British in nature with international and Brazilian elements incorporated. Programmes of study are: Early Years Foundation Stage (EYFS) and International Primary Curriculum (IPC) for 2 to 11 year olds; Key Stage 3 (Middle Years) of the UK National Curriculum for 11 to 14 year olds; Cambridge IGCSE for 14 to 16 year olds; and the International Baccalaureate (IB) Diploma for 16 to 18 year olds. Over 80% of our students are Brazilian and the remainder are from over 30 different countries, with British and other European students being the biggest proportion. English is the main language of instruction with Portuguese, French and Spanish also being taught.

We are an IB World School accredited by the Council of International Schools (CIS). The director is a member of the Latin American Heads Conference (LAHC). There are 2200 students located on three sites. The Zona Sul Unit is split into two Sites: Botafogo Site (primary school) and Urca Site (secondary school). The Barra Unit caters for students from age 2 (Pre-Nursery) to age 18.

Classes are small and school environment is pleasant, well-resourced and stimulating, with a strong focus on health, safety and security. Performing arts, sports, Model United Nations, Duke of Edinburgh's Award Scheme and work experience provide a wide range of co-curricular opportunities. Experiences beyond the school include numerous local day visits and national or international residential trips for most year groups.

Our teachers are well-qualified (some 30% being recruited from overseas) and supported by a robust and effective programme of continuing professional development. The school continually invests in well-qualified staff and training, curriculum development, resources, technology and infrastructure.

Our school provides a caring and friendly, yet demanding, learning environment and makes every effort to ensure that each individual has the opportunity to develop their particular abilities and talents to the full. The emphasis on academic achievement is also balanced by our concern to meet our students' physical, emotional and social needs. We place a high value on good social behaviour and ethical standards, with respect for the individual and the environment.

We want our students to be happy in school and we hope that their school experience will be fondly and warmly remembered for life. We believe that this can be achieved through high expectations; clear guidelines and limits; constant encouragement; and addressing individual needs. We provide opportunities for our students to participate in a wide variety of co-curricular activities – social, sporting and cultural.

Extracurricular Activities

Football, capoeira, volleyball, basketball, ballet, artistic gymnastics, judo, choir, music (instruments and singing), cooking, drama and arts are available.

Facilities

Air-conditioned classrooms, interactive Whiteboards, computers, laptops, tablets, science and computer & technology & robotics labs, libraries, gymnasiums and open spaces for sports and games, playgrounds with a variety of toys, auditoriums for Drama classes, presentations and art exhibitions, sickbays (first-aid – nurses), and dining halls.

The Newman School

(Founded 1945)

Head of School
J Harry Lynch

DP coordinator
Andrew Nagy

Status Private

Boarding/day Day

Gender Coeducational

Language of instruction
English

Authorised IB programmes
DP

Age Range 11 – 18

Number of pupils enrolled
240

Fees
Day: US$36,500

Address
247 Marlborough Street
Boston
MA 02116 | USA

TEL +1 617 267 4530
FAX +1 617 267 7070

Email
admissions@
newmanboston.org

Website
www.newmanboston.org

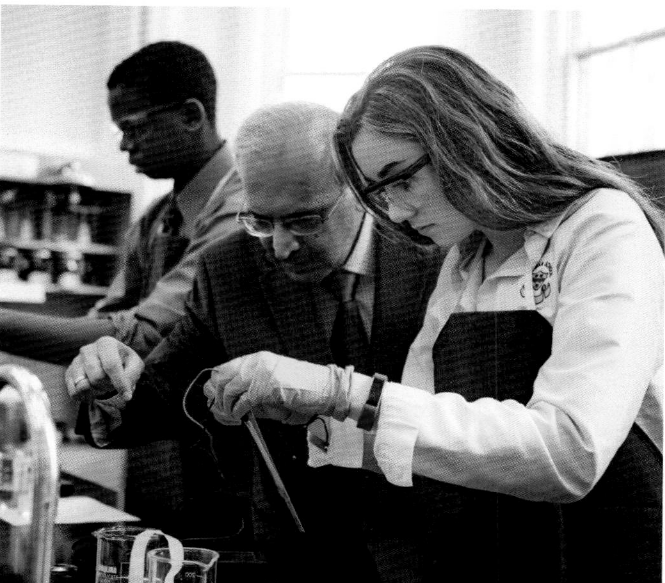

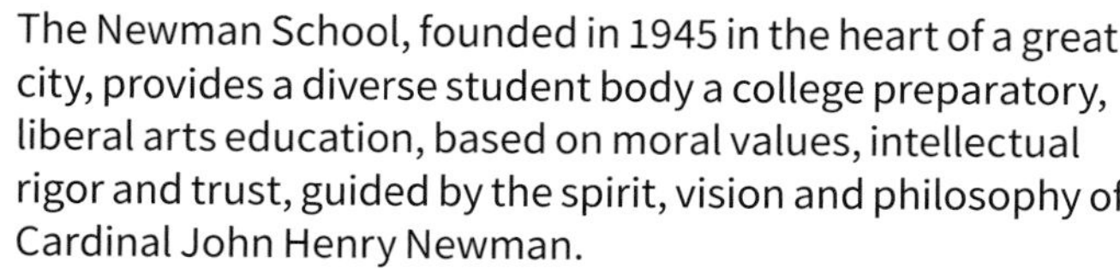

The Newman School, founded in 1945 in the heart of a great city, provides a diverse student body a college preparatory, liberal arts education, based on moral values, intellectual rigor and trust, guided by the spirit, vision and philosophy of Cardinal John Henry Newman.

Situated in Boston's Back Bay, The Newman School is within short walking distance of the Boston Public Library, Symphony Hall, the Boston Ballet, the Museum of Fine Arts, and the many colleges and universities – including Harvard, Boston College, Suffolk University, Boston University, and MIT – for which Boston is world-renowned. Of the 240 students (grades 7 through 12), international students comprise approximately one quarter of our student body. Homestays are arranged through an established network of experienced families known to the school. The school is approved to issue the I-20 required of students seeking approval for student visa status.

Authorized as an IB World School since 2009, Newman offers a broad selection of IB courses in order to meet students' interests. The school accepts transfer students interested in attending an IB school. All students work toward The Newman School diploma. Since we started our IB program we have had more than 125 students earn the International Baccalaureate Diploma. Recent college acceptances include: Babson, Barnard Boston University, Boston College, Brown, Cornell, Duke, Georgetown, Georgia TECH, McGill, MIT, New York University, University of Toronto, University of Virginia and Wellesley.

IB diploma candidates choose from the following IB courses: English A and B, SL Literature, Spanish B, French B, Latin B, History of the Americas, Economics, Business and Management, Environmental Systems, Biology, Chemistry, Physics, Computer Science, HL and SL Math, Math Studies, Visual Arts, Film.

Newman students participate in the following sports and extracurricular programs available at the school:

boys Crew and girls Crew (fall and spring), Sailing (fall and spring/coeducational), boys and girls Soccer (fall), Cross Country (fall/coeducational), boys and girls Basketball (winter), girls Volleyball (fall), Tennis (spring/coeducational), boys Lacrosse (spring), girls Softball (spring). Extracurricular, clubs and enrichment activities include: Model United Nations, Mock Trial, National Honor Society, Robotics, Engineering, NASA club, Chess, Musical Performance, Poetry, Junior Achievement, Film, Art, and a broad range of service opportunities.

Unidad Educativa Santana

(Founded 1985)

Headteacher
Pablo Crespo Andrade

DP coordinator
Xavier Tenorio Sánchez

Status Private

Boarding/day Day

Gender Coeducational

Language of instruction
Spanish

Authorised IB programmes
DP

Age Range 3 – 18

Number of pupils enrolled
800

Fees
Kindergarten $3,312
Elementary School $3,824
Baccalaureate $4,371

Address
Av. los Cerezos S/N y vía a Racar
Cuenca | **ECUADOR**

TEL +593 7 4121879

Email
comunicacion@santana.edu.ec

Website
www.santana.edu.ec

At Santana Educational School academic training is considered as an educational experience, that begins with students from the kindergarten to the third year of high school. Being a private lay school has allowed it to base its experience on its own educational philosophy, product of its growth since 1985, when it was founded.

Santana's orientation towards education is what makes it different, the awareness that its philosophy understands that success in life is determined by the inner potential of each person rather than by a specific knowledge. As a result of this recognition, Santana's structure supports the growth of individual qualities such as autonomy, responsibility and creativity, so that, from a self-critical and self-correcting practice, students can develop as autonomous and conscious human beings, with critical thinking capacity, problem-solving talent, social sensitivity and sense of responsibility.

In Santana, students and their teachers create their own curriculum, implement their rights and responsibilities as members of an active democracy. More importantly, they perform the difficult task of defining themselves.

Since April 2011 Santana has been authorized by the OBI to offer The Diploma Programme, in its last three years of high school. It is a rigorous educational program aimed at young people aged from 16 to 19 that is usually taught over a period of two years and culminates in examinations. It is an excellent preparation for university and adult life, it enjoys wide recognition among the world's leading universities. In short, this program encourages students to be active learners, to be compassionate, and to understand that others, with their differences, may also be right.

Both the IB's and Santana Educational Unit's goals are concerned with the development of intellectual, personal, emotional and social skills that students need to live, learn and work in an increasingly globalized world. Students immersed in this international program prepare themselves to face university studies in any region of the world and to integrate into adult life in a successful way.

(Founded 1932)

Principal
Mrs. Rita Canton

DP coordinator
Leslie Robbins

Status Private

Boarding/day Day

Gender Coeducational

Language of instruction
English

Authorised IB programmes
DP

Address
8100 McKnight Road
Pittsburgh
PA 15237 | USA

TEL +1 412 364 1616
FAX +1 412 367 5722

Email
admissions@
vincentianacademy.org

Website
www.vincentianacademy.org

Vincentian Academy, a Catholic high school in the spirit of the Sisters of Charity of Nazareth, inspires students to achieve academic success, nurture their faith, discover and develop their talents, and live the Christian values of respect and service.

An IB education at Vincentian Academy is unique because of its academic and personal rigor. We aim to develop well-rounded students, who respond to challenges with optimism and an open mind, are confident in their own identities, make ethical decisions, and are prepared to apply what they learn in real-world, complex and unpredictable situations.

As the only Catholic International Baccalaureate World High School in Southwestern Pennsylvania, we are proud that our program is highly regarded by colleges and universities throughout the world. We currently offer 21 IB courses in a variety of subjects, including, but not limited to:

- English Literature
- History
- Computer Science
- Math Studies
- Spanish
- French
- Biology
- Chemistry
- Economics
- Psychology
- Visual Arts
- Film
- Music

Although we are academically focused, the Academy encourages each student to also develop and pursue interests in arts, athletics, and other activities to ensure a balanced and fulfilling high school experience. We currently offer 16 varsity sports with a no-cut policy as well as more than 30 clubs and after school activities to engage our students' minds in different ways and foster teamwork and comradery amongst their classmates.

An IB education at Vincentian Academy provides an exceptional foundation and future for any young person. We are valued for preparing students to become leaders who use their gifts and talents to strengthen communities and bring hope and justice to people everywhere.

(Founded 1966)

Principal
Prof. María Elena Abreu

Academic Vice Principal
Prof. María Angélica Villota

MYP coordinator
Prof. Gianna De Sena

DP coordinator
Dr. José Ruggiero

Status Private

Boarding/day Day

Gender Coeducational

Language of instruction
Spanish, English

Authorised IB programmes
MYP, DP

Age Range 4 – 18 years

Number of pupils enrolled
520

Address
Calle C, Urb. Colinas de Valle Arriba
Caracas 1080 | **VENEZUELA**

TEL +58 212 9757077

Email
academiawashington@aw.edu.ve

Website
www.washington.academy

About us
Washington Academy is a private, bilingual (English/Spanish), K-12, co-ed school located in Caracas, Venezuela and registered in the Venezuelan School System, offering a science-oriented high school diploma. Founded in 1966 by American and Venezuelan educators, the school is non-profit and has an enrollment of Venezuelan children and other nationalities. Our classrooms are of maximum 20 students, and we have science laboratories, a library, two computer labs, two art rooms and outdoor sports facilities.

Curriculum and extracurricular activities
Washington Academy's curriculum follows the Venezuelan curriculum and an intensive English language curriculum. Each year, the students are required to demonstrate to the school community their learning through specific projects designed for each grade, such as Science Fair and Math Fair among others. Our school offers the IB MYP and DP and self-evaluates its performance through the Iowa Achievement Tests. Following the IB philosophy, we have recently included French and Japanese classes, clubs such as Debate & Persuasion, Logic & Math, Theater, Chess, and an Internship Program.

International minded education has always been present; our Washington Academy Model of United Nations started 15 years ago and more recently the International Mood Court and The Masters competition.

Mission
Promotes the integral education of students by emphasizing intellectual, personal, emotional, and social development through our educational model in conjunction with IB programs.

Our motto states: *"Washington Academy gives students the tools to cope with life."*

Vision & Values
Aims for excellence, "La excelencia hecha colegio", from a holistic standpoint, taking into consideration academic training, a conscientious practice of Washington Spirit, and support among our professional learning community.

Acts with integrity, honesty, responsibility, respect of the rights of others and awareness of their own; being an agent of social integration, promoting healthy mind and body, with a broad worldview and a vast cultural background.

Westlake Middle School

Principal
Anthony Mungioli

MYP coordinator
Dr. Susan Cowles-Dumitru

Status State

Boarding/day Day

Gender Coeducational

Language of instruction
English

Authorised IB programmes
MYP

Age Range 10 – 14

Number of pupils enrolled
438

Address
825 West Lake Drive
Thornwood
NY 10594 | USA

TEL +1 914 769 8540
FAX +1 914 769 8550

Email
amungioli@mtplcsd.org

Website
wms.mtplcsd.org

Westlake Middle School (WMS) is a public school located in the leafy suburbs of Westchester County in New York. The school is housed on a large green campus with ample outdoor athletic fields and indoor facilities. Served well by public transportation, it is approximately 45 minutes by train to the heart of New York City. The school offers The IB Middle Years Programme years 1-3, USA grades 6-8. At Westlake, all students engage in the full MYP Programme of eight subjects. Westlake Middle School is recognized as a middle school of excellence and is ranked by Niche as an 'A' school. WMS supports the whole child and our mission is to engage and develop independent, inquisitive, tenacious and open-minded students who think critically, perform innovatively and act ethically in our local and global community.

All students at Westlake have the opportunity to study the core subjects as well as the arts, design, physical education and health. Languages are offered in Spanish and Italian at all grade levels. WMS has a full inclusion program where students who require special education supports are given the necessary structures for them to thrive within the framework of the IB program. In MYP Year 3, students have the opportunity to take high school level classes in Algebra and Living Environment. The Community Project is the culminating experience for all year 3 students allowing them to connect to a personal passion or a community organization. They can grow themselves as caring, thoughtful human beings. Students also participate in advisory sessions where their social and emotional learning and well-being is supported. The school has full-time school counselors, a school psychologist and a school social worker to support students and families.

Extracurriculars are offered and open to all students. All Fours on Paws, Engineering Club, Environmental Club, Art Club, Student Council and Yearbook Club are just a few examples. Students also participate in national competitions such as Science Olympiad, Math League and the Robotics Competition Team, often bringing home medals of achievement. Competitive sports include track, lacrosse, football, cheerleading, baseball, volleyball, wrestling, soccer, swimming, diving and softball.

The community of Westlake Middle School is part of the Town of Mount Pleasant. There is a vibrant 'Westlake Wildcat' spirit surrounding the school and families move to our sought-after area for a safe and stable place to live and grow.

(Founded 2003)

Executive Director Dr. Mechelle Bryson

Primary Principal Rod Harding

Secondary Principal Stacy Stoyanoff

PYP coordinator Alison Schneider

MYP coordinator Terri Watson

DP coordinator Dr. James Owen

Status State Charter

Boarding/day Day

Gender Coeducational

Language of instruction English

Authorised IB programmes PYP, MYP, DP

Age Range 5 – 18 years

Number of pupils enrolled 878

Address
2600 J.T. Ottinger Road
Westlake
TX 76262 | USA

TEL +1 817 4905757
FAX +1 817 4905758

Email info@westlakeacademy.org

Website www.westlakeacademy.org

Who we are

Founded in 2003 with a mission to achieve academic excellence and develop life-long learners who become well-balanced, responsible global citizens, Westlake Academy is the first and only municipally-owned charter school in the State of Texas, USA. Celebrating 16 years of excellence, and having just graduated its tenth class, the Academy is nationally ranked and was awarded a top score (98%) for the second year in a row from the state education agency. These achievements are a direct reflection of the power of an IB World Education.

IB World School

Westlake Academy was the fifth public school in the US offering three IB programmes (PYP,MYP,DP) on a single campus. The IB curriculum and the school's smaller class sizes are enhanced by a breath-taking outdoor campus of innovatively designed stone-clad buildings clustered among 23 acres of verdant pastures and the crown of oak-adorned hills. Imagine how this helps create a premier, knowledge-based community that is truly unique.

College Preparation

Westlake Academy is an open enrollment college preparatory charter school, where great care and consideration is given to the mission and vision by the town leaders, citizens, and educational staff dedicated to academic excellence and personal achievement. The Town of Westlake is proud that results focus on high student achievement while offering IB for all, strong parent and community connections, financial stewardship and sustainability, student engagement in extracurricular activities and service, and effective educators and staff.

Mission

Westlake Academy is an IB World School whose mission is to provide students with an internationally minded education of the highest quality to become well-balanced and respectful life-long learners.

Vision

Westlake Academy inspires college bound students to achieve their highest individual potential in a nurturing environment that fosters the traits found in the IB learner profile.

Values

Maximizing Personal Development, Academic Excellence, Respect for Self and Others, Personal Responsibility, Compassion and Understanding, Global Citizenship.

International Mindedness

Providing an internationally minded education of the highest quality means students will become globally well-balanced. This is not an alternative to cultural and national identity, but an essential component of life in the 21st century. Successful interaction requires our students to clearly communicate, solve problems and create new possibilities in a global context, connecting individuals from around the world.

Extracurricular Activities

Westlake Academy believes student clubs, honor societies and after-school activities allow young citizens to further

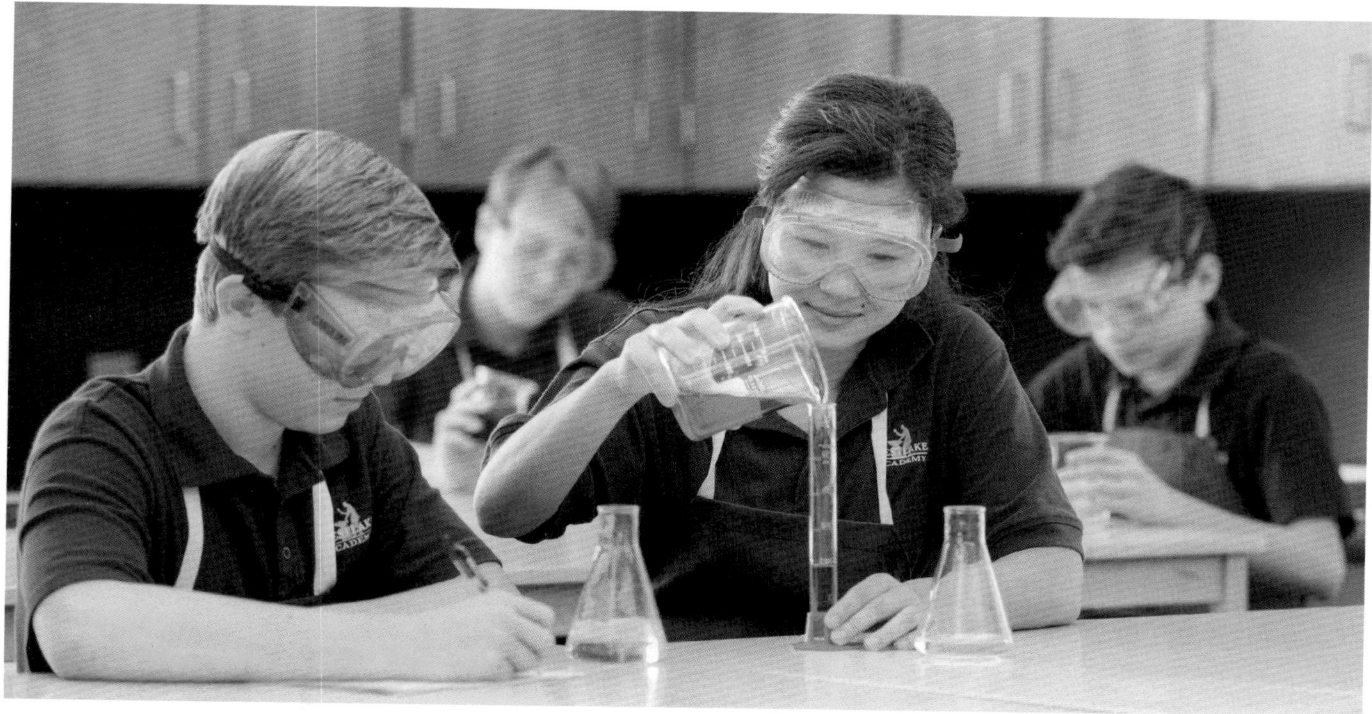

their academic foundation while developing essential interpersonal skills. After school clubs are student driven under the guidance of our faculty. IB learner profile traits are reinforced outside the classroom via athletics, music, art, foreign language, theatre, technology and specialty niches including math, coding, and science.

Global Citizenship and Collaboration

As internationally-minded educators, Westlake Academy creates authentic global collaboration experiences that prepare our students to meet the demands of the 21st century marketplace while encouraging them to think globally and act locally:

Costa Rica and Argentina: Student and teacher exchange programs offered with a school in Costa Rica and in Argentina.

International Student Leadership Symposium (ISLS): Students in grade 10 can apply to be a delegate at the ISLS with 8 other schools across the globe including Germany, China, Oman, South Africa to name a few. This year the symposium will be held in Brussels, Belgium.

Global Service: Extended service opportunities with Students Shoulder to Shoulder include destinations such as Tibet, Peru, Kenya and more.

Leadership: Our teachers and administration host the annual Westlake Academy International Mindedness Educator Symposium with 7 countries represented and over 50 participants.

Youth Ambassadors Program: We partner with neighboring cities Southlake and Fort Worth offering worldwide student travel opportunities.

Class Trips: Students are given experiential travel opportunities beginning in third grade.

Technology: Teachers and students engage in collaborative learning in a 1:1 iPad environment.

YingHua International School

YING HUA
INTERNATIONAL SCHOOL
English-Chinese Immersion School of Princeton
Excellence • Diversity • Integrity • Compassion

Head of School
Ms. Laura Desai

PYP coordinator
Ms. Wen-Lin Su

Status Private

Boarding/day Day

Gender Coeducational

Language of instruction
English, Chinese

Authorised IB programmes
PYP

Age Range 18 months – 13 years

Number of pupils enrolled
110

Fees
Day: US$8,000 – US$20,000

Address
25 Laurel Avenue
Kingston
NJ 08528-0088 | USA

TEL +1 609 375 8015

Email
admissions@yhis.org

Website
yhis.org

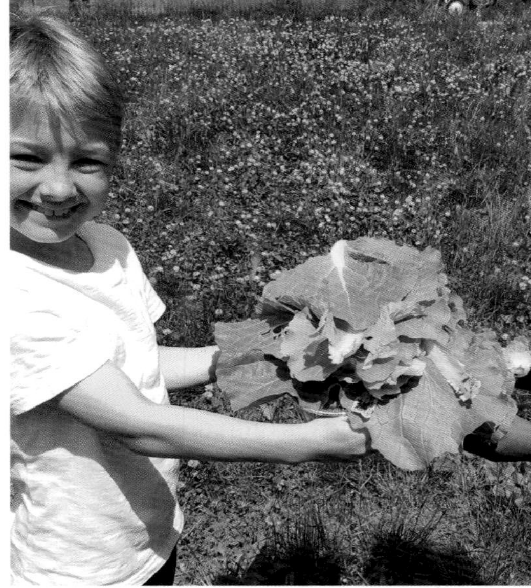

Nestled in the outskirts of Princeton, New Jersey, YingHua International School (YHIS) is the only not-for-profit, independent school in the greater Princeton area that offers English-Chinese dual language education with an internationally-focused, inquiry-based curriculum. YHIS is also the third school in the US that offers the IB Primary Years Programme with whole-school Chinese immersion.

YingHua International School (YHIS) was founded in 2007 with a mission to enable academic excellence and prepare students for compassionate, effective, and ethical global citizenship through English and Chinese language acquisition and instilling a passion for lifelong learning. A hidden gem in Central New Jersey, YHIS accomplishes its mission by combining total Chinese Immersion with IB inquiry-based learning.

Through this unique approach, YHIS enables ethnically diverse students from as young as 18 months old through 8th grade, to develop the skills and mindset needed to become leaders in an increasingly global world. Through exposure at an early age to a language-immersive environment combined with IB inquiry-based learning, YHIS students gain deeply rooted cognitive benefits that stay with them well into adulthood. At YHIS this approach is further characterized by small, nurturing, and inclusive classes led by passionate, dedicated teachers. The results are students who consistently outperform their suburban and private school peers on the local and national stage and in standardized testing. While many parents are initially drawn to YHIS for Chinese immersion, they often stay because of its ability to foster independence and self-reliance while instilling critical thinking skills and academic excellence in students.

Much of YHIS' success can be attributed to its core values of Excellence, Diversity, Integrity and Compassion. Excellence is striving for and being the best that we can be. It means high standards of teaching, learning, and all that we do. It includes well-rounded development in addition to intellectual curiosity and rigor. It requires teamwork, community service and leadership. Diversity is embracing difference and building on the best of all worlds. It embraces equity among cultures and peoples, and suggests respect for the natural world including its animal and plant inhabitants. Integrity is excellence of character and Compassion is caring for diverse others: both are essential for guiding how we relate to and treat one another and are a critical cornerstone for what YHIS stands for.

YHIS welcomes all into its warm and nurturing community!

Directory of schools in the Americas region

Key to symbols

- CP
- Diploma
- MYP
- PYP
- Fee Paying School
- Boys' School
- Girls' School
- Coeducational School
- Boarding School
- Day School

ANTIGUA

Island Academy International School

Oliver's Estate, PO Box W1884, St John's
DP Coordinator Karol Lyn Edwards
Languages English
T: +1 268 460 1094
W: www.islandacademy.com

ARGENTINA

Asociación Cultural Pestalozzi

R Freire 1882, C1428CYB Ciudad de Buenos Aires
DP Coordinator Mariel Santarelli
Languages Spanish
T: +54 11 4555 3688
W: www.pestalozzi.edu.ar

Asociación Escuelas Lincoln

Andres Ferreyra 4073, B1637 AOS La Lucila, Buenos Aires
DP Coordinator Alexandra Baines
Languages English
T: +54 11 4851 1700
W: www.lincoln.edu.ar

Austin Eco Bilingual School (Austin EBS) Argentina

Porto 463, Campana, Buenos Aires
DP Coordinator Jessica Gino
Languages Spanish, English
T: +54 3489 462203/4
W: www.austin-ebs.com.ar

Colegio Alemán de Temperley

Av. Fernández 27, Temperley 1834
DP Coordinator María Laura Galimberti
Languages English, Spanish
T: +54 114244 2832
W: www.temperleyschule.edu.ar

Colegio Carmen Arriola de Marin

Av del Libertador 17.115, San Isidro, Buenos Aires 1642
DP Coordinator Cristina Couceiro
Languages Spanish
T: +54 11 4743 0028
W: www.marin.edu.ar

Colegio De La Salle

Ayacucho 665, Buenos Aires 1025
DP Coordinator Laura Simonotto
Languages Spanish
T: +54 011 4374 0657/97
W: www.delasalle.esc.edu.ar

Colegio de Todos Los Santos

Thames 798, Villa Adelina, San Isidro, 1607 Buenos Aires
DP Coordinator Pedro Pablo Koller
Languages English, Spanish
T: +54 114 766 3878
W: www.tls.edu.ar

Colegio Franco Argentino

Lavalle 1067, Acassuso, San Isidro, Buenos Aires B1641ALU
DP Coordinator María Inés Martínez Asla
Languages Spanish
T: +54 11 4792 4628
W: www.cfam.edu.ar

Colegio Lincoln

Olleros 2283, Buenos Aires 1426
DP Coordinator Andrea García
Languages Spanish, English
T: +54 11 4778 1997
W: www.lincoln.esc.edu.ar

Colegio Mark Twain

José Roque Funes 1525, Córdoba 5009
DP Coordinator Pablo Esteban Cedro
Languages Spanish
T: +543 514 830 664
W: www.marktwaincba.com.ar

Colegio N°4 DE 9° 'Nicolás Avellaneda'

El Salvador 5228, Buenos Aires 1414
DP Coordinator Veronica Converti
Languages English
T: +54 11 47711103
W: www.colegioavellaneda.com.ar

Colegio N°9 DE N°12 – Justo José de Urquiza

Condarco 290, Buenos Aires 1406
DP Coordinator Fabiana Valiño
Languages Spanish
T: +54 11 46120327
W: www.urquizaflores.blogspot.com

Colegio Palermo Chico

Thames 2041/37, Buenos Aires 4892
DP Coordinator Nora Cavuto
Languages Spanish
T: +54 114 774 3975
W: www.colegiopalermochico.edu.ar

Colegio San Ignacio

Guardias Nacionales 1400, Río Cuarto (Cba.) X5806DWJ
DP Coordinator Horacio Toledo Carranza
Languages English, Spanish
T: +54 (358) 464 8484/0802
W: www.colegiosanignacio.edu.ar

Colegio San Marcos

Secundaria, Mariano Alegre 334, Monte Grande, Buenos Aires 1842
DP Coordinator Gustavo Junco
Languages Spanish
T: +54 114 296 4215
W: www.stmarks.com.ar

Colegio San Patricio

Moreno y Camino a las Higueritas, Yerba Buena, Tucumán 4107
DP Coordinator Mauro Juliano
Languages Spanish
T: +54 381 4250 708
W: www.sanpatriciotucuman.edu.ar

Colegio San Patricio de Luján

Provincia de Buenos Aires, Tucuman y Gaona sin / número, Luján, Buenos Aires 6700
DP Coordinator Maria Belen Mastellone
Languages Spanish
T: +54 2323 437998
W: www.sanpatriciodelujan.com

Colegio San Pedro Apostol

Av Piamonte s/n, CP: X5016DQB, Córdoba
DP Coordinator Maria Clara Cunill
Languages Spanish
T: +54 3 51 4846584
W: www.sanpedroapostol.com

Colegio Santa María

Coronel Suárez 453, Salta 4400
DP Coordinator María Teran
Languages Spanish
T: +54 387 4213127
W: www.santamaria.edu.ar/

Colegio Tarbut

Rosales 3019, Olivos, Buenos Aires 1636
DP Coordinator Mateo García Haymes García Haymes
Languages Spanish
T: +54 11 4794 3444
W: www.tarbut.edu.ar

Dover High School

San Martín y Ruta 26, Ing Maschwitz, Buenos Aires 1623
DP Coordinator Rodrigo Negro
Languages English, Spanish
T: +54 93488 441106
W: www.dover.edu.ar

Escuela Goethe Rosario – 8222

España 440, Rosario, Santa Fe 2000
DP Coordinator Eduardo Palandri
Languages Spanish
T: +54 3 414 263024
W: goetherosario.com

Escuela Municipal Paula Albarracin de Sarmiento

Juan Bautista Alberdi 1227, Olivos, Buenos Aires
DP Coordinator Romina Biga
Languages Spanish
T: +54 11 4513 9873
W: empas.mvl.edu.ar

Escuela Normal Superior en Lenguas Vivas N°1

Córdoba 1951, Buenos Aires 1120
DP Coordinator Marcelina Gonzalez
Languages English
T: +54 11 48125602
W: ens1de1.buenosaires.edu.ar

Escuela Normal Superior en LV 'Sofia Broquen de Spangenberg'

Juncal 3251, Buenos Aires 1425
DP Coordinator Ursula Schroder
Languages Spanish
T: +54 114 807 2967/2966

Escuela Tecnica 32 DE 14 – Gral. Jose de San Martin

Teodoro Garcia 3899, Buenos Aires 1427
DP Coordinator Marisa Casares
Languages Spanish
T: +54 11 45519121
W: www.et32de14.com.ar

Escuela Técnica N°24 D.E. 17- Defensa de Buenos Aires

Ricardo Gutierrez 3246, Buenos Aires 1417
DP Coordinator Marcelo Saporito
Languages Spanish
T: +54 11 45019251
W: www.et24debsas.blogspot.com.ar

Escuela Técnica N°28 D.E. 10 República Francesa

Cuba 2410, Autónoma de Buenos Aires 1428
DP Coordinator Daniel Vena
Languages English
T: +54 11 47816881/31
W: www.et28.com.ar

Escuela Técnica N°29 D.E. 6 – Reconquista de Buenos Aires

Av. Boedo 760, Ciudad Autónoma de Buenos Aires 1218
DP Coordinator Margarita Sanabria
Languages Spanish
T: +54 11 49572920
W: www.buenosaires.gob.ar

Escuela Técnica N° 37 D.E. 11 – Hogar Naval Stella Maris
Pergamino 211, Ciudad Autónoma de Buenos Aires 1406
DP Coordinator Margarita González
Languages Spanish
T: +54 11 46123220
W: laboratorio37.blogspot.com.ar

Escuela Técnica N° 9 D.E. 7 Ingeniero Luis A. Huergo
Martin de Gainza 1050, Buenos Aires 1405
DP Coordinator Luciano Cocciro
Languages Spanish
T: +54 11 45826690
W: www.et9huergo.edu.ar

Holy Trinity College
Gascón 544, Mar del Plata 7600
DP Coordinator Valeria Tommasi de Ruival
Languages English, Spanish
T: +54 223 486 3471
W: www.trinity.esc.edu.ar

Instituto Ballester
San Martin 444, (1653) Villa Ballester, Buenos Aires 1653
DP Coordinator Sergio García
Languages Spanish
T: +54 11 4768 0760
W: www.iballester.esc.edu.ar

Instituto San Jorge
Godoy Cruz, Pedro J Godoy 1191, Mendoza 5547
DP Coordinator Marcela Carrizo
Languages Spanish
T: +54 2 614 287 247
W: colegiosanjorge.com.ar

Instituto Santa Brígida
Av Gaona 2068, C 1416DRV, Buenos Aires 1416DRV
DP Coordinator Diana Debenedetti
Languages Spanish
T: +54 1 145 811 268
W: www.santabrigida.esc.edu.ar

Instituto Wolfsohn
Roseti 50, Buenos Aires
DP Coordinator Maria Florencia Bacci
Languages English, Spanish
T: +54 11 4545 6020
W: wolfsohn.edu.ar

ISLANDS INTERNATIONAL SCHOOL
Amenábar St. 1840., Zip Code 1428, Buenos Aires
DP Coordinator Clotilde Alleva
Languages Spanish, English, Italian, Portuguese
T: +54 11 4787 2294
E: info@intschools.org
W: www.intschools.org/islands
See full details on page 516

NORTHERN INTERNATIONAL SCHOOL
Ruote 8 Km 61.5., Zip Code 1633. Pilar, Buenos Aires
DP Coordinator Marisa Zárate
Languages Spanish, English, Italian, Portuguese
T: +54 2322 49 1208
E: info@intschools.org
W: www.intschools.org/northern
See full details on page 535

NORTHLANDS SCHOOL
Olivos Site: Roma 1248, Olivos, Buenos Aires
DP Coordinator Alicia Olea
PYP Coordinator Joanne Gillan & Natalia Torlaschi
Languages English, Spanish
T: +54 11 4711 8400
E: admissionsolivos@northlands.edu.ar
W: www.northlands.edu.ar
See full details on page 536

NORTHLANDS SCHOOL NORDELTA
Nordelta site: Av de los Colegios 590, Nordelta, Buenos Aires B1670NNN
DP Coordinator Alicia Olea
PYP Coordinator Natalia Torlaschi
Languages English
T: +54 11 4871 2668/9
W: www.northlands.edu.ar

Orange Day School
Av. San Martín 1651/7, Ramos Mejia 1657
DP Coordinator María Penén Ramirez
Languages English, Spanish
T: +54 11 4464 7014
W: www.orangeschool.com.ar

Saint Mary of the Hills School
Xul Solar 6650, San Fernando, Buenos Aires 1646
DP Coordinator Gastón Arana
Languages Spanish
T: +54 11 4714 0330
W: www.stmary.edu.ar

Saint Mary of the Hills School Sede Pilar
Ruta 25 y Caamaño, Pilar, Buenos Aires 1644
DP Coordinator Mariana Xanthopoulos
Languages Spanish
T: +54 2304 458181
W: www.stmary.edu.ar

SOUTHERN INTERNATIONAL SCHOOL
Freeway Buenos Aires – La Plata Km 34., Zip Code 1884. Hudson, Berazategui, Buenos Aires
DP Coordinator Clotilde Alleva
Languages Spanish, English, Italian, Portuguese
T: +54 11 4215 3636
E: info@intschools.org
W: www.intschools.org/southern
See full details on page 545

St Francis School
Av. Benavidez 1326, Benavidez, Buenos Aires 1621
DP Coordinator Silvina Massa
Languages English
T: +54 11 2078 4200
W: saintfrancis.com.ar

St George's College – North
Los Polvorines, Buenos Aires
DP Coordinator Noelia Zago
PYP Coordinator Leda Spadaro
Languages English, Spanish
T: +54 (11) 4663 2494
W: www.stgeorges.edu.ar/north

St George's College – Quilmes
Guido 800, Quilmes, Buenos Aires CP 1878
DP Coordinator María Soledad Texidó
PYP Coordinator Mabel Orlando
Languages English, Spanish
T: +54 (11) 4350 7900
W: www.stgeorges.edu.ar/quilmes

St Mary's International College
Martin Garcia 1435 / 1236 / 1501, Ezeiza, Buenos Aires 1804
DP Coordinator Gloria María Morchio
Languages English, Spanish
T: +54 11 5075 0370
W: www.stmarys.edu.ar

St Matthew's College
Moldes 1469, Buenos Aires 1426
DP Coordinator Patricia Capecce
Languages Spanish, English
T: +54 11 4783 1110
W: www.smc.edu.ar

St Matthew's College North
Caamano 493, Pilar, Buenos Aires 1631
DP Coordinator Graciela Mouzo
Languages Spanish
T: +54 230 4693600
W: www.smcn.edu.ar

St Xavier's College
José Antonio Cabrera 5901, Buenos Aires 1414
DP Coordinator José Luis Goñi
Languages English
T: +54 114 777 5011/14
W: www.colegiosanjavier.com.ar

St. Andrew's Scots School
Roque Saenz Peña 601, Olivos, Buenos Aires 1636
DP Coordinator Diego Bertotto
Languages English
T: +54 11 4846 6500
W: www1.sanandres.esc.edu.ar

St. Catherine's Moorlands – Belgrano
Carbajal 3250, Buenos Aires 1426
DP Coordinator Roxana D'Amico
MYP Coordinator Mariela Buracco
Languages English, Spanish
T: +54 11 4552 4353
W: www.scms.edu.ar/es/belgrano

St. Catherine's Moorlands – Tortuguitas
Ruta Panamericana Km 38 Ramal Pilar, Tortuguitas, Buenos Aires 1667
MYP Coordinator Alejandro Elia
Languages English
T: +54 (348) 463 9000
W: www.scms.edu.ar/es/tortuguitas

St. John's School – Beccar
España 348/370, Beccar, Buenos Aires 1643
DP Coordinator Martín Russi
PYP Coordinator María Julieta Romero Vagni
Languages Spanish
T: +54 11 4513 4400
W: www.stjohns.edu.ar

St. John's School – Pilar
Panamericana Km. 48.800, Pilar, Buenos Aires 1629
DP Coordinator Luciano Cappuccio
Languages English, Spanish
T: +54 (0) 2304 667 667
W: www.stjohns.edu.ar

Sunrise School
Rio Negro, Casilla de Correo 79 (8324) Cipolletti, Río Negro
DP Coordinator Juan Manuel Ginez
Languages Spanish
T: +54 299 4786590

Villa Devoto School
Pedro Morán 4441, Buenos Aires 1419
DP Coordinator Roberto Mancuso
Languages English
T: +54 114 501 9419
W: www.vdevotoschool.edu.ar

Washington School
Avenida Federico Lacroze 2012, Ciudad Autónoma de Buenos Aires 1426
DP Coordinator Sonia Pino
PYP Coordinator Verónica Sartoni
Languages Spanish
T: +54 11 4772 8131
W: www.washingtonschool.edu.ar

Woodville School
Av de los Pioneros 2900, San Carlos de Bariloche 8400
DP Coordinator Andrew Schwartz
Languages Spanish, English
T: +54 2944 44 11 33
W: www.woodville.org

BAHAMAS

Lucaya International School
Chesapeake Drive, PO Box F-44066, Freeport
DP Coordinator Stephanie Doland
PYP Coordinator Erin Cordes
Languages English
T: +1 242 373 4004
W: www.lisbahamas.org

Lyford Cay International School
Lyford Cay Drive, PO Box N-7776, Nassau NB
CP Coordinator Timothy Connolly
DP Coordinator Michèle (Scullion) Mindorff
MYP Coordinator Giles Pinto
PYP Coordinator Katina Seymour
Languages English
T: +1 242 362 4774
W: www.lcis.bs

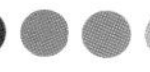

St Andrew's International School
PO Box EE 17340, Yamacraw Hill Road, Nassau, NP
DP Coordinator Ben Foley
PYP Coordinator Catherine Azikiwe
Languages English
T: +1 242 677 7800
W: www.standrewsbahamas.com

BARBADOS

The Codrington School
St John BB 20008
DP Coordinator Kirsty Thomas
MYP Coordinator Nicola Leedham
PYP Coordinator Jordana Carrington
Languages English
T: +1 246 423 2570
W: www.codrington.edu.bb

BERMUDA

Bermuda High School
19 Richmond Road, Pembroke HM08
DP Coordinator Catherine McMahon
Languages English
T: +441 295 6153
W: www.bhs.bm

SOMERSFIELD ACADEMY
107 Middle Road, Devonshire DV 06
DP Coordinator Kate Ross
MYP Coordinator Summer Wood Brice Pursell
Languages English
T: +1 441 236 9797
E: admissions@somersfield.bm
W: www.somersfield.bm
See full details on page 544

Warwick Academy
117 Middle Road, Warwick PG01
DP Coordinator Sara Jackson
Languages English
T: +1 441 236 1917/239 9452
W: www.warwick.bm

BOLIVIA

American International School of Bolivia
Casilla 5309, Cochabamba
DP Coordinator Ximena Aguilera
Languages English
T: +591 4 428 8577
W: www.aisb.edu.bo

Colegio Alemán Santa Cruz
Casilla 624, Av San Martin s/n, Santa Cruz
DP Coordinator Alexandra Kempff
Languages Spanish
T: +591 3 3326820
W: www.colegioaleman-santacruz.edu.bo

Saint Andrew's School
Casilla 1679, Av Las Retamas s/n La Florida, La Paz
DP Coordinator Ana Maria Garcia
PYP Coordinator Susana Guachalla
Languages English, Spanish
T: +591 22 79 24 84
W: www.saintandrews.edu.bo

BRAZIL

ABA Global School
Av. Rosa e Silva, 1510, Aflitos, Recife, Pernambuco PE 52050-245
PYP Coordinator Maria do Rozario Botelho
Languages English
T: +55 81 3427 8800
W: www.estudenaaba.com

American School of Brasília
SGAS 605, Conjunto E, Lotes 34/37, Brasília DF 70200-650
DP Coordinator Maria Sieve
Languages English
T: +55 61 3442 9700
W: www.eabdf.br

American School of Campinas – Escola Americana de Campinas
Rua Cajamar, #35, Campinas, São Paulo SP 13090-860
DP Coordinator Erika Bonet
Languages English
T: +55 19 21021006
W: www.eac.com.br

Associação Educacional Luterana Bom Jesus / IELUSC
Rua Princesa Isabel, 438, Joinville, Santa Catarina SC 89201-270
DP Coordinator Marcelli Mazzei Ramalho
Languages English
T: +55 47 3026 8000
W: www.ielusc.br

Beacon School
Rua Berlioz 245, Alto de Pinheiros, São Paulo SP 05467-000
PYP Coordinator Sonia Giglio
Languages English, Portuguese
T: +55 11 3021 0262
W: www.beaconschool.com.br

Centro Internacional de Educação Integrada
Estrada do Pontal 2093, Recreio dos Bandeirantes, Rio de Janeiro RJ 22790-877
DP Coordinator Tainá Silva Barbosa Lopes
PYP Coordinator Vanessa Vianna
Languages English
T: +55 21 2490 1673
W: www.ciei.g12.br

Chapel School – The American International School of Brazil
Rua Vigário João de Pontes, 537, Chácara Flora, São Paulo SP 04748-000
DP Coordinator Benjamin Vaughan
Languages English
T: +55 11 2101 7400
W: www.chapelschool.com

Colégio Miguel de Cervantes
Avenida Jorge João Saad, 905, São Paulo, Morumbí SP 05618-001
DP Coordinator Katia Pupo
Languages Portuguese, Spanish, English
T: +55 11 3779 1800
W: cmc.com.br

Colegio Positivo Internacional
Professor Pedro Viriato de Souza St 5300, Curitiba, Paraná PR 81280-330
DP Coordinator Karine Vairo
PYP Coordinator Michelline Ramos
Languages Portuguese, English
T: +55 (41) 3335 3535
W: www.colegiopositivo.com.br

Colégio Soka do Brasil
Avenida Cursino, 362, Saúde SP 04132-000
DP Coordinator Tania Sakuma
Languages English, Portuguese
T: +55 11 5060 3300
W: www.colegiosoka.org.br

Colégio Suíço-Brasileiro de Curitiba
Rua Wanda dos Santos Mallmann, 537, Jardim Pinhais, Pinhais, Paraná PR 83323-400
DP Coordinator Carlos Machado
Languages English
T: +55 41 3525 9100
W: www.chpr.com.br

Escola Americana de Belo Horizonte
Av. Professor Mario Werneck, 3002, Bairro Buritis, Belo Horizonte, Minas Gerais MG 30575-180
MYP Coordinator Jason Baxley
PYP Coordinator Judy Imamudeen
Languages English, Portuguese
T: +55 31 3378 6700
W: www.eabh.com.br

Escola Americana do Rio de Janeiro – Barra da Tijuca
Rua Colbert Coelho 155, Barra da Tijuca, Rio de Janeiro RJ 22793-313
DP Coordinator Scott Little
Languages English
T: +55 21 3747 2000
W: www.earj.com.br

ESCOLA AMERICANA DO RIO DE JANEIRO – GÁVEA
Estrada da Gávea 132, Gávea, Rio de Janeiro RJ 22451-263
DP Coordinator Flávia DiLuccio
Languages English
T: +55 21 2125 9000
E: admissions.gavea@earj.com.br
W: www.earj.com.br
See full details on page 504

Escola Beit Yaacov
Av Marques de Sao Vicente no 1748, Barra Funda, São Paulo SP 01139-002
DP Coordinator Renata Fogaça Bonacin
PYP Coordinator Alexandra Cunha
Languages English, Hebrew, Portuguese
T: +55 11 3611 0600
W: www.beityaacov.com.br

Escola Bilíngue Pueri Domus – Aldeia da Serra Campus
Estr. Dr. Yojiro Takaoka, 3900, Barueri, São Paulo SP 06423-150
DP Coordinator John Whittlesea
Languages English, Portuguese
T: +55 11 3512 2300
W: www.pueridomus.com.br

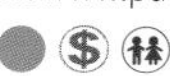

Escola Bilíngue Pueri Domus – Itaim Campus
Rua Itacema 214, Itaim Bibi, São Paulo SP 04530-050
DP Coordinator Ricardo Lourenco
Languages English, Portuguese
T: +55 11 3512 2300
W: www.pueridomus.com.br

ESCOLA BILÍNGUE PUERI DOMUS – VERBO DIVINO CAMPUS
Rua Verbo Divino 993-A, Chacara Sto. Antonio, São Paulo SP 04719-001
DP Coordinator Jason James
Languages English, Portuguese
T: +55 11 3512 2300
W: www.pueridomus.com.br
See full details on page 505

Escola Castanheiras
Alameda Castanheiras, 250, Res. Tres (Tambore), Santana de Parnaíba, São Paulo SP 06543-510
DP Coordinator Airton Pretini Junior
Languages English
T: +55 11 4 152 4600
W: www.escolacastanheiras.com.br

Escola Eleva – Botafogo
Rua General Severiano, 159, Botafogo, Rio de Janeiro RJ 22290-040
DP Coordinator Dulce Simas
Languages English, Portuguese
T: +55 21 4042 2492
W: escolaeleva.com.br

Escola Internacional de Alphaville
Av. Copacabana, 624, Cond. Empresarial 18 do Forte, Alphaville, Barueri SP 06472-001
PYP Coordinator Peter Rifaat
Languages English
T: +55 11 4134 6686
W: www.escolainternacional.com.br

Escola Internacional de Joinville
Rua Gothard Kaesemodel 833, Joinville, Santa Catarina SC 89203-400
DP Coordinator Anderson Madruga
PYP Coordinator Jamila Effting
Languages English
T: +55 47 34610500
W: eij.org.br

Escola Internacional UniSociesc Florianopolis
Rua Salvatina Feliciana dos Santos, 525, Florianópolis, Santa Catarina SC 88034-600
DP Coordinator Adriana Campbell
Languages English, Portuguese
T: +55 47 2111 2966
W: unisociesc.com.br/unidades/florianopolis-campus-ilh

Escola Suíço-Brasileira (ESB) by SIS Swiss International School
Rua Corréa de Araújo 81, Barra da Tijuca, Rio de Janeiro RJ 22611-060
DP Coordinator Rachel Guanabara
MYP Coordinator Soraia Dale-Harris
PYP Coordinator Aline Costa
Languages English
T: +55 21 33 89 20 89
W: www.swissinternationalschool.com.br

Escola Suíço-Brasileira de São Paulo
Rua Visconde de Porto Seguro 391, Alto da Boa Vista, São Paulo SP 04642-000
DP Coordinator Andreas Panse
Languages English
T: +55 11 5682 2140
W: www.esbsp.com.br

ESFERA ESCOLA INTERNACIONAL
Av Anchieta, 908 – Jardim Nova Europa, Sao José dos Campos, São Paulo SP 12242-280
MYP Coordinator Sandra Araujo
PYP Coordinator Melissa Therriault Zaramella
Languages English, Portuguese
T: +55 12 3322 1255
E: secretaria@escolaesfera.com.br
W: www.escolaesfera.com.br
See full details on page 506

Graded – The American School of São Paulo
Av. José Galante, 425, São Paulo SP 05642-000
DP Coordinator Carrie Giltner
Languages English
T: +55 11 3747 4800
W: www.graded.br

Gurilândia International School
Av. Cardeal Da Silva 1433, Federacao, Salvador, Bahia BA 40231-250
PYP Coordinator Denise Lima De Araújo Rocha
Languages English, Portuguese
T: +55 71 3336 6595
W: www.gurilandia.com.br

International School of Curitiba
Ave. Eugenio Bertolli, 3900, Sta. Felicidade, Curitiba, Paraná PR 82410-530
DP Coordinator Barbara Terrell
Languages English
T: +55 41 3525 7400
W: www.iscbrazil.com

Pan American School of Bahia
Av Ibirapitanga, Loteamento Patamares, s/n, Salvador, Bahia BH 41680-060
DP Coordinator Roberta Rodrigues
PYP Coordinator Mariane Munne
Languages English
T: +55 71 3368 8400
W: www.escolapanamericana.com

Pan American School of Porto Alegre
Av. João Obino 110, Petrópolis, Porto Alegre, Rio Grande do Sul RS 90470-150
MYP Coordinator Bruno Britto
PYP Coordinator Cassie Jo Koscianski
Languages English, Portuguese
T: +55 513 334 5866
W: www.panamerican.com.br

Red House International School
Rua Engenheiro Edgar Egidio de Souza 444, Pacaembu SP 01233-020
PYP Coordinator Denise Lam
Languages English
T: +55 11 2309 7999
W: www.redhouseschool.com.br

Saint Nicholas School
Av Eusébio Matoso 333, Pinheiros, São Paulo SP 05423-180
DP Coordinator Saulo Vianna
PYP Coordinator Stephen Eagles
Languages English
T: + 55 11 3465 9666
W: www.stnicholas.com.br

SIS Swiss International School Brasília
SGA/SUL, Quadra 905, cj B, Brasília DF 70390-050
PYP Coordinator Hayley Waghorn
Languages English
T: +55 61 34 43 41 45
W: www.swissinternationalschool.com.br/school-locations/brasilia

St Nicholas School – Alphaville Campus
Av. Honório Álvares Penteado, 5463, Tamboré, Santana de Parnaíba SP 06543-320
PYP Coordinator Jennifer Fletcher
Languages English, Portuguese
T: +55 11 3465 9658
W: stnicholas.com.br

ST. FRANCIS COLLEGE, BRAZIL
Rua Joaquim Antunes 678, Pinheiros, São Paulo SP 05415-001
DP Coordinator Sofie Muchardt Smith
MYP Coordinator Fabrice Bidaury
PYP Coordinator Gisele Caselli
Languages English, Portuguese
T: +55 11 3728 8050
E: office@stfrancis.com.br
W: www.stfrancis.com.br
See full details on page 547

ST. PAUL'S SCHOOL
Rua Juquiá 166, Jardim Paulistano, São Paulo SP 01440-903
DP Coordinator Ana Carolina Belmonte
Languages English
T: +55 11 3087 3399
E: head@stpauls.br
W: www.stpauls.br
See full details on page 548

THE BRITISH COLLEGE OF BRAZIL
Rua Álvares de Azevedo, 50, Chácara Flora, São Paulo SP 04671-040
DP Coordinator Mr. Ben Holman
Languages English
T: +55 11 5547 3030
E: info@britishcollegebrazil.org
W: www.britishcollegebrazil.org
See full details on page 553

THE BRITISH SCHOOL, RIO DE JANEIRO
Rua Real Grandeza 99, Botafogo, Rio de Janeiro RJ 22281-030
DP Coordinator Guy Smith & Leah Wilks
Languages English
T: +55 21 2539 2717
E: edu@britishschool.g12.br
W: www.britishschool.g12.br
See full details on page 554

The British School, Rio de Janeiro – Barra Site
Rua Mario Autuori, 100, Barra da Tijuca RJ 22793
DP Coordinator Leah Wilks
Languages English
T: +55 21 3329 2854
W: www.britishschool.g12.br

BRITISH VIRGIN ISLANDS

Cedar International School
Waterfront Drive, Kingston
DP Coordinator Elspeth Fraser
MYP Coordinator Sarah Dixon
PYP Coordinator Lesley Bayles
Languages English
T: +1 284 494 5262
W: cedar.vg

CANADA

Alberta

Annunciation Catholic Elementary School
9325-165 Street, Edmonton AB T5R 2S5
PYP Coordinator Ashley Jennings
Languages English
T: +1 780 484 4319
W: www.annunciation.ecsd.net

Archbishop Macdonald High School
14219-109 Ave., Edmonton AB T5N 1H5
DP Coordinator Jacqueline Sewell
MYP Coordinator Helen Grijo
Languages English
T: +1 780 451 1470
W: www.archbishopmacdonald.ecsd.net

Bellerose Composite High School
49 Giroux Road, St Albert AB T8N 6N4
DP Coordinator Clayton Beebe
Languages English
T: +1 780 460 8490
W: bchs.spschools.org

Bishop O'Byrne High School
333 Shawville Blvd SE, Suite 500, Calgary AB T2Y 4H3
DP Coordinator Brendan Bulger
Languages English
T: +1 403 500 2103
W: schools.cssd.ab.ca/bishopobyrne

Calgary French and International School
700-77th Street SW, Calgary AB T3H 5R1
DP Coordinator Christian Legault
Languages English, French
T: +1 403 240 1500
W: www.cfis.com

Coronation School
10925-139 Street, Edmonton AB T5M 1P8
PYP Coordinator Brittany Segin
Languages English
T: +1 780 455 2008
W: coronation.epsb.ca

Father Lacombe High School
3615 Radcliffe Drive SE, Calgary AB T2A 6B4
DP Coordinator Nadine Hindemith
Languages English
T: +1 403 248 9559
W: www.fatherlacombe.calgary.ab.ca/

Glenora School
13520-102 Avenue, Edmonton AB T5N 0N7
MYP Coordinator Laura Johnson
Languages English
T: +1 780 452 4740

Grande Prairie Composite High School
11202 – 104 Street, Grande Prairie AB T8V 2Z1
DP Coordinator Jay Smith
Languages English
T: +1 780 532 7721
W: www.gppsd.ab.ca/school/gpcomposite

Harry Ainlay High School
Harry Ainlay, 4350-111 Street, Edmonton AB T6J 1E8
DP Coordinator Dean Zuberbuhler
Languages English
T: +1 780 413 2700
W: www.ainlay.ca

Henry Wise Wood High School
910 – 75th Avenue SW, Calgary AB T2V 0S6
DP Coordinator Scott Garen
Languages English
T: +1 403 253 2261
W: www.cbe.ab.ca/b836

Holy Cross Académie Internationale
15120-104 Avenue, Edmonton AB T5P 0R5
MYP Coordinator Jana Psyrris
PYP Coordinator Edward Jean
Languages French, English
T: +1 780 489 1981
W: www.holycross.ecsd.net

Holy Trinity High School
7007-28th Avenue, Edmonton AB T6K 4A5
DP Coordinator Richard Downing
MYP Coordinator Kathryn Wojcicki
Languages English
T: +1 780 462 5777
W: www.holytrinity.ecsd.net

Jasper Place High School
8950-163 Street, Edmonton AB T5R 2P2
DP Coordinator Doug Chester
Languages English
T: +1 780 408 9000
W: jasperplace.epsb.ca

John G Diefenbaker High School
6620 – 4th Street NW, Calgary AB T2K 1C2
DP Coordinator Cheryl Sceviour
Languages English
T: +1 403 274 2240
W: www.cbe.ab.ca/b860

Lester B Pearson High School
3020 52nd Street NE, Calgary AB T1Y 5P4
CP Coordinator Tammy Lock
DP Coordinator Christine Hein
Languages English
T: +1 403 244 2278
W: www.schools.cbe.ab.ca

Lillian Osborne High School
2019 Leger Road NW, Edmonton AB T6R 0R9
DP Coordinator Jane Taylor
Languages English
T: +1 780 970 5249
W: lillianosborne.epsb.ca

Lindsay Thurber Comprehensive High School
4204-58th Street, Red Deer AB T4N 2L6
DP Coordinator David Smith
Languages English
T: +1 403 347 1171
W: lindsaythurber.rdpsd.ab.ca

Louis St Laurent
11230-43 Avenue, Edmonton AB T6J 0X3
DP Coordinator Nicole Schatz
MYP Coordinator Jocelyn Johnston
Languages English
T: +1 780 435 3964
W: www.louisstlaurent.ecsd.net

M.E. LaZerte School
6804 144 Ave, Edmonton AB T5C 3C7
DP Coordinator Diane Fischer
Languages English
T: +1 780 408 9800
W: www.melazerte.com

McNally High School
8440-105 Avenue, Edmonton AB T6A 1B6
DP Coordinator Laurel Usher
Languages English
T: +1 780 469 0442
W: mcnally.epsb.ca

Millarville Community School
130 Millarville Rd, Millarville AB T0L 1K0
PYP Coordinator Karla Davis
Languages English
T: +1 403 938 7832
W: millarville.fsd38.ab.ca

Old Scona Academic High School
10523-84th Avenue, Edmonton AB T6E 2H5
DP Coordinator Loretta Ng
Languages English
T: +1 780 433 0627
W: oldscona.epsb.ca

Prairie Waters Elementary School
201 Invermere Drive, Chestermere AB T1X 1M6
PYP Coordinator Breanna Baxter
Languages English
T: +1 403 285 6969
W: prairiewaters.rockyview.ab.ca

Ross Sheppard High School
13546-111th Avenue, Edmonton AB T5M 2P2
DP Coordinator Christine Mcgowan
Languages English
T: +1 780 448 5000
W: shep.epsb.ca

Salisbury Composite High School
#20 Festival Way, Sherwood Park AB T8A 4Y1
DP Coordinator Michelle Wyman
Languages English
T: +1 780 467 8816
W: www.salcomp.ca

Sir Winston Churchill High School, Calgary
5220 Northland Drive NW, Calgary AB T2L 2J6
DP Coordinator Brent Johnson
Languages English
T: +1 403 289 9241
W: schools.cbe.ab.ca/b857

St Albert Catholic High School
33 Malmo Drive, St Albert AB T8N 1L5
DP Coordinator Jill Stewart
Languages English
T: +1 780 459 7781
W: www.sachs.gsacrd.ab.ca

St Clement Catholic Elementary/Junior High School
7620 Mill Woods Road South, Edmonton AB T6K 2P7
MYP Coordinator Robin Cole
PYP Coordinator Robin Cole
Languages English
T: +1 780 462 3806
W: www.stclement.ecsd.net

St Edmund Elementary School
11712 130th Avenue, Edmonton AB T5E 0V2
MYP Coordinator Valentina Padovani
PYP Coordinator Laura Manucci
Languages English
T: +1 780 453 1596
W: stedmund.ecsd.net

St Joseph High School
10830-109 Street, Edmonton AB T5H 3C1
CP Coordinator Carla Cuglietta
DP Coordinator Christopher McGarity
Languages English
T: +1 780 426 2010
W: www.stjoseph.ecsd.net

St Mary's High School
111-18th Avenue SW, Calgary Catholic, Calgary AB T2S 0B8
DP Coordinator Cathy Harradence
Languages English
T: +1 403 500 2024
W: stmaryshs.calgary.ab.ca

St Thomas More Catholic Junior High School
9610 165 Street, Edmonton AB T5P 3S6
MYP Coordinator Chad Bryson
Languages English
T: +1 780 484 2434

St. Boniface Catholic Elementary School
11810-40 Avenue, Edmonton AB T6J 0R9
PYP Coordinator Courtney Repchuk
Languages English
T: +1 780 434 0294
W: www.stboniface.ecsd.net

Strathcona-Tweedsmuir School
RR 2, Okotoks AB T1S 1A2
DP Coordinator Chris Ruskay
MYP Coordinator Gabe Kemp
PYP Coordinator Cheryl Babin
Languages English
T: +1 403 938 4431
W: www.sts.ab.ca

Victoria School of the Arts
10210 – 108 Avenue, Edmonton AB T5H 1A8
CP Coordinator Wendy Plum
DP Coordinator Wendy Plum
MYP Coordinator Wendy Plum
PYP Coordinator Wendy Plum
Languages English
T: +1 780 426 3010
W: www.victoria-school.ca

Vincent J Maloney Catholic Junior High School
20 Mont Clare Place, St Albert AB T8N 1K9
MYP Coordinator Rebecca Scobie
Languages English
T: +1 780 458 1113
W: www.vjm.gsacrd.ab.ca

Western Canada High School
641-17 Avenue S.W., Calgary AB T2S 0B5
DP Coordinator Susan Rivers
Languages English
T: +1 403 228 5363
W: schools.cbe.ab.ca/b816

Westglen School
10950-127 Street, Edmonton AB T5M 0S7
MYP Coordinator Laura Johnson
Languages English
T: +1 780 454 3449
W: westglen.epsb.ca

Westminster School
13712-102 Avenue, Edmonton AB T5N 0W4
MYP Coordinator Laura Johnson
Languages English
T: +1 780 452 4343

Winston Churchill High School
1605-15th Avenue North, Lethbridge AB T1H 1W4
DP Coordinator Morgan Day
Languages English
T: +1 403 328 4723
W: wchs.lethsd.ab.ca

British Columbia

Abbotsford Middle School
33231 Bevan Avenue, Abbotsford BC V2S 0A9
MYP Coordinator Kelly Grant
Languages English
T: +1 604 859 7125
W: www.abbymiddle.com

Abbotsford Senior Secondary School
33355 Bevan Avenue, Abbotsford BC V2S 0E7
DP Coordinator Michael Keeley
Languages English
T: +1 604 853 3367
W: abbysenior.sd34.bc.ca

Alexander Academy
200-688 West Hastings Street, Vancouver BC V6B 1P1
DP Coordinator Spencer Todd
Languages English, French
T: +1 604 687 8832
W: www.alexanderacademy.ca

Aspengrove School
7660 Clark Drive, Nanaimo BC V0R 2H0
DP Coordinator Robert Ohly
MYP Coordinator J.O. Eriksson
PYP Coordinator Susan Riordan
Languages English
T: +1 250 390 2201
W: www.aspengroveschool.ca

Britannia Secondary School
1001 Cotton Drive, Vancouver BC V5L 3T4
DP Coordinator Veronica McGhee
Languages English
T: +1 604 713 8266
W: britannia.vsb.bc.ca

Brockton School
3467 Duval Road, North Vancouver BC V7J 3E8
DP Coordinator Brenda Ball
MYP Coordinator Karen Birchenall
PYP Coordinator Nichole Carrigan
Languages English
T: +1 604 929 9201
W: www.brocktonschool.com

Brookes Westshore
1939 Sooke Road, Victoria BC V9B 1W2
DP Coordinator Gary Ward
MYP Coordinator Linda Bayes
Languages English
W: westshore.brookes.org

Capilano Elementary School
1230 West 20th Street, North Vancouver BC V7P 2B9
PYP Coordinator David Andrews
Languages English
T: +1 604 903 3370
W: www.sd44.ca/school/capilano/Pages/default.aspx

Carson Graham Secondary School
2145 Jones Avenue, North Vancouver BC V7M 2W7
DP Coordinator Jennifer Tieche
MYP Coordinator Liz Thornhill
Languages English
T: +1 604 903 3555
W: carsongraham.ca

Cypress Park Primary School
4355 Marine Drive, West Vancouver BC V7V 1P2
PYP Coordinator Morikke Espenhain
Languages English
T: +1 604 981 1330
W: go45.sd45.bc.ca/schools/cypresspark/Pages/default.aspx

École Andre-Piolat
380 West Kings Road, North Vancouver BC V7L 2L9
MYP Coordinator Trâm Tran
Languages English
T: +1 604 980 6040
W: andrepiolat.csf.bc.ca

Ecole Cedardale Elementary
595 Burley Drive, West Vancouver BC V7T 1Z3
PYP Coordinator Kristina Hayes
Languages English
T: +1 604 981 1390
W: go45.sd45.bc.ca/schools/cedardale

École des Pionniers-de-Maillardville
3550, Wellington Street, Port Coquitlam BC V3B 3Y5
DP Coordinator Richard Hoole
MYP Coordinator Karine De Serres
Languages French
T: +1 604 552 7915
W: pionniers.csf.bc.ca

École Gabrielle-Roy
6887, 132 Rue, Surrey BC V3W 4L9
DP Coordinator Jean-Philippe Schall
Languages French, English
T: +1 604 599 6688
W: gabrielleroy.csf.bc.ca

École Secondaire Jules-Verne
5445 Baillie Street, Vancouver BC V5Z 3M6
DP Coordinator Louis-Philippe Surprenant
Languages French
T: +1 604 731 8378
W: julesverne.csf.bc.ca

École Victor-Brodeur
637 Head Street, Victoria BC V9A 5S9
DP Coordinator Joelle Briant
Languages French
T: +1 250 220 6010
W: brodeur.csf.bc.ca

Elsie Roy Elementary School
150 Drake Street, Vancouver BC V6Z 2X1
MYP Coordinator Amarit Marwaha
Languages English
T: +1 604 7135890

English Bluff Elementary
402 English Bluff Road, Delta BC V4M 2N2
PYP Coordinator Sarah Shove
Languages English
T: +1 604 943 0201
W: eb.deltasd.bc.ca

Fraser Valley Elementary School
20317 67 Ave., Langley BC V2Y 1P6
PYP Coordinator Natalie Morris
Languages English
T: +1 604 427 2282
W: www.fves.bc.ca

Garibaldi Secondary School
24789 Dewdney Trunk Road, Maple Ridge BC V4R 1X2
DP Coordinator Kyle Ludeman
Languages English
T: +1 604 463 6287
W: gss.sd42.ca

Glenlyon Norfolk School
801 Bank Street, Victoria BC V8S 4A8
DP Coordinator Angela Girard
MYP Coordinator Gina Simpson
PYP Coordinator Leanne Giommi
Languages English
T: +1 250 370 6801
W: www.mygns.ca
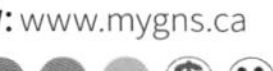

Hugh Boyd Secondary School
9200 No. 1 Road, Richmond BC V7E 6L5
MYP Coordinator Jane Leung
Languages English
T: +1 604 668 6615
W: www.hughboyd.com

Island Pacific School
671 Carter Road, Box 128, Bowen Island BC V0N 1G0
MYP Coordinator Amanda Szabo
Languages English
T: +1 604 947 9311
W: www.islandpacific.org

Johnston Heights Secondary School
15350-99 Avenue, Surrey BC V3R 0R9
MYP Coordinator Paul Jean Lavoie
Languages English
T: +1 604 581 5500
W: www.surreyschools.ca

King George Secondary School
1755 Barclay Street, Vancouver BC V6G 1K6
MYP Coordinator Anne Mackie
Languages English
T: +1 604 713 8999
W: kinggeorge.vsb.bc.ca

Lord Roberts Elementary School
1100 Bidwell Street, Vancouver BC V6G 2K4
MYP Coordinator Kay Shetty
Languages English
T: +1 604 713 5055
W: lordroberts.vsb.bc.ca

MEADOWRIDGE SCHOOL
12224 240th Street, Maple Ridge BC V4R 1N1
DP Coordinator Ms. Kristal Bereza
MYP Coordinator Mr. Scott Rinn
PYP Coordinator Mrs. Heather Nicholson
Languages English
T: +1 604 467 4444
E: admissions@meadowridge.bc.ca
W: www.meadowridge.bc.ca

See full details on page 528

Mountain Secondary School
7755-202 A Street, Langley BC V2Y 1W4
DP Coordinator Tina Costopoulos
Languages English
T: +1 604 888 3033
W: www.mssd35.bc.ca

MULGRAVE, THE INTERNATIONAL SCHOOL OF VANCOUVER
2330 Cypress Bowl Lane, West Vancouver BC V7S 3H9
DP Coordinator Kathryn Clark
MYP Coordinator Mike Olynyk
PYP Coordinator Janet Hicks & Shanaz Ramji
Languages English
T: +1 604 922 3223
E: admissions@mulgrave.com
W: www.mulgrave.com

See full details on page 530

New Westminster Secondary School
835 Eighth Street, New Westminster BC V3M 3S9
DP Coordinator James Janz
Languages English
T: +1 604 517 6220
W: nwss.ca

NorKam Secondary School
730 12th Street, Kamloops BC V2B 3C1
DP Coordinator Murray Williams
Languages English
T: +1 250 376 1272
W: nkss.sd73.bc.ca

Pacific Academy
10238 168th Street, Surrey BC V4N 1Z4
DP Coordinator David Rosborough
Languages English
T: +1 604 581 5353
W: www.pacificacademy.net

Parkland Secondary School
10640 McDonald Park Road, North Saanich BC V8L 5S7
DP Coordinator Erin Stinson
Languages English
T: +1 250 655 2700
W: parkland.sd63.bc.ca

Pearson College UWC
650 Pearson College Drive, Victoria BC V9C 4H7
DP Coordinator Sherry Crowther
Languages English
T: +1 250 391 2411
W: www.pearsoncollege.ca

Port Moody Secondary School
300 Albert Street, Port Moody BC V3H 2M5
DP Coordinator Sean Lenihan
Languages English
T: +1 604 939 6656
W: www.sd43.bc.ca/secondary/portmoody

Princess Margaret Secondary High School
120 Green Avenue W., Penticton, BC V2A 3T1
MYP Coordinator Christy Bevington
Languages English, French
T: +1 250 770 7620
W: www.sd67.bc.ca/school/princessmargaretsecondary

Queen Mary Community School
230 West Keith Road, North Vancouver BC V7M 1L8
PYP Coordinator Jen Aragon
Languages English
T: +1 604 903 3720
W: www.queenmary.ca

Richmond Secondary School
7171 Minoru Boulevard, Richmond BC V6Y 1Z3
DP Coordinator David Miller
Languages English
T: +1 604 668 6400
W: rhs.sd38.bc.ca

Rockridge Secondary School
5350 Headland Drive, West Vancouver BC V7W 3H2
MYP Coordinator Jennifer Towers
Languages English
T: +1 604 981 1300
W: go45.sd45.bc.ca/schools/rockridge/Pages/default.aspx

Seaquam Secondary School
11584 Lyon Road, Delta BC V4E 2K4
DP Coordinator Dhana Matthews
Languages English
T: +1 604 591 6166
W: www.deltasd.bc.ca/se

Semiahmoo Secondary School
1785 – 148th Street, Surrey BC V4A 4M6
DP Coordinator Karine Guezalova
Languages English
T: +1 604 536 6174
W: www.surreyschools.ca/schools/semi

SENPOKCHIN SCHOOL
1156 SenPokChin Blvd, Oliver BC V0H 1T8
PYP Coordinator Ms. Julie Shaw
Languages English, Nsyilxcen
T: +1 250 498 2019
W: www.senpokchin.ca

See full details on page 543

Sir Winston Churchill Secondary School, Vancouver
7055 Heather Street, Vancouver BC V6P 3P7
DP Coordinator Karen Puzio
Languages English
T: +1 604 713 8189
W: churchill.vsb.bc.ca

Southlands Elementary School
5351 Camosun Street, Vancouver BC V6N 2C4
PYP Coordinator Joanna Wood
Languages English
T: +1 604 713 5414
W: southlands.vsb.bc.ca

SOUTHPOINTE ACADEMY
1900 56th Street, Tsawwassen BC V4L 2B1
MYP Coordinator Christine Yang
PYP Coordinator Jaya Van Praagh
Languages English
T: +1 604 948 8826
E: admissions@southpointe.ca
W: www.southpointe.ca

See full details on page 546

Southridge School
2656 160th Street, Surrey BC V3S 0B7
MYP Coordinator Alison Ito
PYP Coordinator Jo-Ann Murchie
Languages English
T: +1 604 535 5056
W: www.southridge.bc.ca

St John's School
2215 West 10th Avenue, Vancouver BC V6K 2J1
DP Coordinator Christine Miklitz
MYP Coordinator Stephanie Brook
PYP Coordinator Leslie Morden
Languages English
T: +1 604 732 4434
W: www.stjohns.bc.ca

STRATFORD HALL
3000 Commercial Drive, Vancouver BC V5N 4E2
DP Coordinator Stefania Iacchelli
MYP Coordinator Mark Pulfer
PYP Coordinator Amanda Lempriere
Languages English
T: +1 604 436 0608
E: info@stratfordhall.ca
W: www.stratfordhall.ca

See full details on page 549

West Bay School
3175 Thompson Place, West Vancouver BC V7V 3E3
PYP Coordinator Morikke Espenhain
Languages English
T: +1 604 981 1260
W: go45.sd45.bc.ca/schools/westbay

West Vancouver Secondary School
1750 Mathers Avenue, West Vancouver BC V7V 2G7
DP Coordinator Joanne Pohn
Languages English
T: +1 604 981 1100
W: www.sd45.bc.ca

White Rock Christian Academy
2265 -152nd Street, Surrey BC V4A 4P1
DP Coordinator Jeff Weichel
MYP Coordinator John Bron
PYP Coordinator Emily Berry
Languages English
T: +1 604 531 9186
W: www.wrca.ca

Manitoba

Balmoral Hall School
630 Westminster Ave, Winnipeg MB R3C 3S1
PYP Coordinator Cathy Doerksen
Languages English
T: +1 204 784 1600
W: www.balmoralhall.com

Collège Louis-Riel
585 rue Saint-Jean-Baptiste, Winnipeg MB R2H 2Y2
DP Coordinator Benoît Pellerin
Languages French
T: +1 204 237 8927
W: www.louis-riel.mb.ca

Collège Sturgeon Heights Collegiate
2665 Ness Ave, Winnipeg MB R3J 1A5
DP Coordinator Jennifer Peters
Languages English
T: +1 204 888 0684
W: www.sjasd.ca/school/sturgeonheights

École secondaire Neelin High School
1020 Brandon Ave, Brandon MB R7A 1K6
DP Coordinator Trevor Beals
Languages English
T: +1 204 729 3180
W: www.bsd.ca/schools/Neelin

Kelvin High School
155 Kingsway, Winnipeg MB R3M 0G3
DP Coordinator Melani Decelles
Languages English
T: +1 204 474 1492
W: www.winnipegsd.ca/schools/kelvin

Miles MacDonell Collegiate
757 Roch Street, Winnipeg MB R2K 2R1
DP Coordinator Laura McMaster
Languages English
T: +1 204 667 1103
W: retsd.mb.ca/school/miles/Pages/default.aspx

New Brunswick

Ecole Mathieu-Martin
511 rue Champlain, Dieppe, Nouveau-Brunswick NB E1A 1P2
DP Coordinator Ronald LeBlanc
Languages French
T: +1 506 856 2791

École Sainte-Anne
715 rue Priestman, Fredericton NB E3B5W7
DP Coordinator Denis Gervais
Languages English
T: +1 506 453 3991
W: ecole.district1.nbed.nb.ca

Rothesay Netherwood School
40 College Hill Road, Rothesay NB E2E 5H1
DP Coordinator Jacqueline Albinati
Languages English
T: +1 506 847 8224
W: www.rns.cc

St John High School
170-200 Prince William Street, #8, Saint John NB E2L 2B7
DP Coordinator Tracy Lutz
Languages English
T: +1 506 658 5358
W: www.sjhigh.ca

Newfoundland and Labrador

Holy Heart of Mary High School
55 Bonaventure Avenue, St. John's NL A1C 3Z3
DP Coordinator Janet Toope
Languages English
T: +1 709 754 1600
W: www.holyheart.ca

Lakecrest Independent School
58 Patrick Street, St. John's NL A1E 2S7
PYP Coordinator Lisa Dove Major
Languages English
T: +1 709 738 1212
W: www.lakecrest.ca

Nova Scotia

Charles P. Allen High School
200 Innovation Dr., Bedford NS B4B 0G4
DP Coordinator Christopher Hall
Languages English
T: +1 902 832 8964
W: cpa.hrce.ca

Citadel High School
1855 Trollope Street, Halifax NS B3H 0A4
DP Coordinator Heather Michael
Languages English
T: +1 902 491 4444
W: www.qeh.ednet.ns.ca

Cobequid Educational Centre
34 Lorne Street, Truro NS B2N 3K3
DP Coordinator Jennifer Courish
Languages English
T: +1 902 896 5700
W: cec.ccrsb.ca

Cole Harbour District High School
2 Chameau Cresent, Dartmouth NS B2W 4X4
DP Coordinator Michael Jean
Languages English
T: +1 902 464 5220
W: www.coleharbourhigh.ednet.ns.ca

Dr John Hugh Gillis Regional High School
105 Braemore Avenue, Antigonish NS B2G 1L3
DP Coordinator Lindsay MacInnis
Languages English
T: +1 902 863 1620
W: www.drjohngillis.ednet.ns.ca

École du Carrefour
201A Avenue du Portage, Dartmouth NS B2X 3T4
DP Coordinator Simon Larose
Languages French
T: +1 902 433 7000
W: carrefour.ednet.ns.ca

Halifax Grammar School
945 Tower Road, Halifax NS B3H 2Y2
DP Coordinator Laura Brock
Languages English
T: +1 902 423 9312
W: www.hgs.ns.ca

Halifax West High School
283 Thomas Raddall Drive, Halifax NS B3S 1R1
DP Coordinator Joanne Des Roches
Languages English
T: +1 902 457 8900
W: www.hwhs.ednet.ns.ca

Horton High School
75 Greenwich Road S, Wolfville NS B4P 2R2
DP Coordinator Jason Fuller
Languages English
T: +1 902 542 6060
W: www.horton.ednet.ns.ca

King's-Edgehill School
11 King's-Edgehill Lane, Windsor NS B0N 2T0
DP Coordinator Derek Bouwman
Languages English
T: +1 902 798 2278
W: www.kes.ns.ca

Northumberland Regional High School
104 Alma Road, Westville NS B0K 2A0
DP Coordinator Christina Cameron
Languages English
T: +1 902 396 2750
W: nrhs.ccrsb.ca

Park View Education Centre
1485 King Street, Bridgewater NS B4V 1C4
DP Coordinator Charlotte Brooks
Languages English
T: +1 902 541 8200
W: www.pvec.ednet.ns.ca

Prince Andrew High School
31 Woodlawn Road, Dartmouth NS B2W 2R7
DP Coordinator Tracy Giffin
Languages English
T: +1 902 435 8452
W: www.pahs.ednet.ns.ca

Sydney Academy
49 Terrace Street, Sydney NS B1P 2L4
DP Coordinator Heather Urquhart
Languages English
T: +1 902 562 5464
W: sacademy.cbv.ns.ca

Yarmouth Consolidated Memorial High School
146 Forest Street, Yarmouth NS B5A 0B3
DP Coordinator Colleen Daley
Languages English
T: +1 902 749 2810
W: www.ycmhs.com

Ontario

Académie de la Capitale
1010 Morrison Dr Suite 200, Ottawa ON K2H 8K7
PYP Coordinator Melissa Hall
Languages English, French
T: +1 613 721 3872
W: www.acadecap.org

Académie Ste Cécile International School
925 Cousineau Road, Windsor ON N9G 1V8
DP Coordinator Laurie Bruce
Languages English
T: +1 519 969 1291
W: www.stececile.ca

Alexander Mackenzie High School
300 Major Mackenzie Dr. W., Richmond Hill ON L4C 3S3
DP Coordinator Nazila Reyhani
Languages English
T: +1 905 884 0554
W: www.yrdsb.ca/schools/alexandermackenzie.hs

Ancaster High School
374 Jerseyville Road West, Ancaster ON L9G 3K8
DP Coordinator Del Taylor
Languages English
T: +1 905 648 4468
W: www.hwdsb.on.ca/ancasterhigh

Ashbury College
362 Mariposa Avenue, Ottawa ON K1M OT3
DP Coordinator Shannon Howlett
Languages English
T: +1 613 749 5954
W: www.ashbury.ca

Assumption College Catholic High School
1100 Huron Church Road, Windsor ON N9C 2K7
DP Coordinator Elisa Houston
Languages English
T: +1 519 256 7801 EXT:278
W: sites.google.com/a/catholicboard.ca/acs-website

Bayview Secondary School
10077 Bayview Avenue, Richmond Hill ON L4C 2L4
DP Coordinator Lara Joffe
Languages English
T: +1 905 884 4453
W: www.bayview.ss.yrdsb.edu.on.ca

Bishop Macdonell Catholic High School
200 Clair Road West, Guelph ON N1L 1G1
DP Coordinator Amanda Belluz
Languages English
T: +1 519 822 8502
W: www.wellingtoncdsb.ca/school/bishopmacdonell/Pages/default.aspx

Branksome Hall
10 Elm Avenue, Toronto ON M4W 1N4
DP Coordinator Alena Oosthuizen
MYP Coordinator Owen Williams
PYP Coordinator Andrea Mills
Languages English
T: +1 416 920 9741
W: www.branksome.on.ca

Brockville Collegiate Institute
90 Pearl Street East, Brockville ON K6V1P8
DP Coordinator Cheryl Donovan
Languages English
T: +1 613 345 5641
W: www.bcirams.ca

Bronte College
88 Bronte College Court, 1444 Dundas Cres, Mississauga ON L5C 1E9
DP Coordinator Wynn Looi
Languages English
T: +1 905 270 7788
W: www.brontecollege.ca

Cameron Heights Collegiate Institute
301 Charles St. E., Kitchener ON N2G 2P8
DP Coordinator Julie Neeb
Languages English
T: +1 519 578 8330
W: chc.wrdsb.ca

Cardinal Carter Catholic High School
210 Bloomington Rd. W., Aurora ON L4G 0P9
DP Coordinator Derek Chan
Languages English
T: +1 905 727 2455
W: www.ycdsb.ca/cch

Cardinal Carter Catholic Secondary School
120 Ellison Ave., Leamington ON N8H 5C7
DP Coordinator Genevieve Cano
Languages English, French
T: +1 519 322 2804
W: sites.google.com/site/cougarscardinalcarter

Catholic Central High School
450 Dundas Street, London ON N6B 3K3
CP Coordinator Carla Mascherin Walton
DP Coordinator Carla Mascherin Walton
Languages English
T: +1 519 675 4431
W: www.ldcsb.on.ca

Cedarvale Community School
145 Ava Road, Toronto ON M6C 1W4
PYP Coordinator Dara Baek
Languages English
T: +1 416 394 2244
W: www.tdsb.on.ca

Chippewa Secondary School
539 Chippewa St. West, North Bay ON P1B 4R4
DP Coordinator Kim Larivee
Languages English
T: +1 705 475 2341
W: www.nearnorthschools.ca/chippewa

Cobourg Collegiate Institute
335 King Street East, Cobourg ON K9A 1M2
DP Coordinator Bruce LePage
Languages English
T: +1 905 372 2271
W: www.cobourgeast.ca

Collège Catholique Franco-Ouest
411 promenade Seyton, Nepean ON K2H 8X1
DP Coordinator Sophie Lapensée
MYP Coordinator Christine Leduc
Languages French
T: +1 613 820 2920
W: franco-ouest.ecolecatholique.ca

Collège catholique Mer Bleue
6401 chemin Renaud, Orléans ON K1W 0H8
CP Coordinator Valérie Labelle
DP Coordinator Valérie Labelle
MYP Coordinator Valérie Drouin
Languages French
T: +1 613 744 4022
W: mer-bleue.ecolecatholique.ca

Colonel By Secondary School
2381 Ogilvie Road, Ottawa ON K1J 7N4
DP Coordinator Lewis Harthun
Languages English
T: +1 613 745 9411
W: www.colonelby.com

Dr. G.W. Williams Secondary School
39 Dunning Ave., Aurora ON L4G 1A2
DP Coordinator Nicole Gordner
Languages English
T: +1 905 727 3131
W: drgwwilliams.ss.yrdsb.ca

Eastside Secondary School
275 Farley Avenue, Belleville ON K8N 4M2
DP Coordinator Kate Cockburn
Languages English
T: +1 613 962 8668
W: ess.hpedsb.on.ca

École élémentaire catholique Corpus Christi
362, avenue Hillside, Oshawa ON L1J 6L7
PYP Coordinator Dominique Perreault
Languages English
T: +1 905 728 0491
W: cc.csdccs.edu.on.ca

École élémentaire catholique Jean-Paul II
1001 avenue Hutchison, Whitby ON L1N 2A3
PYP Coordinator Pierre-Philippe David
Languages French
T: +1 905 665 5393
W: jpii.csdccs.edu.on.ca

École élémentaire publique L'Odyssée
1770, promenade Grey Nuns, Orléans ON K1C 1C3
PYP Coordinator Jacinthe Chapdelaine
Languages French
T: +1 613 834 2097
W: www.odyssee.cepeo.on.ca/Ecole

École élémentaire publique Michaëlle-Jean
11 chemin Claridge, Ottawa ON K2J 5A3
PYP Coordinator Sandra Sauvé
Languages English
T: +1 613 823 2288
W: www.michaelle-jean.cepeo.on.ca

École élémentaire publique Rose des Vents
1650, 2e Rue Est, Cornwall ON K6H 2C3
PYP Coordinator Samantha Sabourin
Languages French
T: +1 613 932 4183
W: www.rose-des-vents.cepeo.on.ca

École secondaire catholique E.J. Lajeunesse
600, avenue E.C. Row Ouest, Windsor ON N9E 1A5
DP Coordinator Mélanie Moir
Languages French
T: +1 519 972 0071
W: www.cscprovidence.ca

École secondaire catholique l'Essor
13605, Chemin St. Gregory, Tecumseh ON N8N 3E4
DP Coordinator Holly Dougall-Persichilli
Languages French
T: +1 519 735 4115
W: www.cscprovidence.ca

École secondaire catholique Monseigneur-de-Charbonnel
110, avenue Drewry, Toronto ON M2M 1C8
DP Coordinator Florence Kulnieks
Languages French
T: +1 416 393 5537
W: esmdc.csdccs.edu.on.ca

École secondaire catholique Père-René-de-Galinée
450, chemin Maple Grove, Cambridge ON N3H 4R7
MYP Coordinator Marie-Claude Malette
Languages French
T: +1 519 650 9444
W: esprdg.csdccs.edu.on.ca

École secondaire catholique Renaissance
700, chemin Bloomington, Aurora ON L4G 0E1
DP Coordinator Zinta Anna Amolins
MYP Coordinator Vincent Polsky
Languages French
T: +1 905 727 4631
W: esr.csdccs.edu.on.ca

École secondaire catholique Saint Frère André
330, avenue Lansdowne, Toronto ON M6H 3Y1
DP Coordinator Dumitru Trinca-Costica
Languages French
T: +1 416 393 5324
W: essfa.csdccs.edu.on.ca

École secondaire catholique Saint-Charles-Garnier
4101 rue Baldwin Sud, Whitby ON L1R 2W6
MYP Coordinator Mélanie Glasser
Languages French
T: +1 905 655 5635
W: esscg.csdccs.edu.on.ca

École secondaire catholique Sainte-Famille
1780, boulevard Meadowvale, Mississauga ON L5N 7K8
CP Coordinator Emmanuel Sincennes
DP Coordinator Emmanuel Sincennes
MYP Coordinator Alexandra Kalinin
Languages French
T: +1 905 814 0318
W: essf.csdccs.edu.on.ca

École secondaire catholique Sainte-Trinité
2600 Grand Oak Trail, Oakville ON L6M 0R4
DP Coordinator Barbara Nowak
MYP Coordinator Matthew Stewart
Languages French
T: +1 905 339 0812
W: esst.csdccs.edu.on.ca

IB AMERICAS

École secondaire Gaétan-Gervais
1075, McCraney Street East, Oakville ON L6H 1H9
DP Coordinator Emmanuelle Ritson
Languages English, French
T: +1 289 529 0065
W: gaetangervais.csviamonde.ca

École secondaire Hanmer
4800, Ave Notre-Dame, Hanmer ON P3P 1X5
DP Coordinator Michelle Jobin-Quenville
Languages French
T: +1 705 969 4402
W: esh.cspgno.ca

École secondaire Jeunes sans frontières
1445 Promenade Lewisham, Mississauga ON L5J 3R2
DP Coordinator Beatrice Khemiss
Languages French
T: +1 905 823 4424
W: www.jeunessansfrontieres.csdcso.on.ca

École secondaire Macdonald-Cartier
37, boulevard Lasalle ouest, Sudbury ON P3A 1W1
DP Coordinator Brigitte Marie Laing
Languages French
T: +1 705 566 7660
W: esmc.cspgno.ca

École secondaire publique Gisèle-Lalonde
500 Boulevard Millenium, Orléans ON K4A 4X3
DP Coordinator Caroline Joly
MYP Coordinator Pierrette Fequet
Languages English, French
T: +1 613 833 0018
W: www.gisele-lalonde.cepeo.on.ca

École secondaire publique L'Héritage
1111 chemin Montréal, Cornwall ON K6H 1E1
DP Coordinator Jasmine Bernier
MYP Coordinator Erin Baillie
Languages English
T: +1 613 933 3318

École secondaire publique Le Sommet
894, boul. Cécile, Hawkesbury ON K6A 3R5
DP Coordinator Chantal Lalonde
MYP Coordinator Chantal Lalonde
Languages French
T: +1 613 632 6059
W: lesommet.cepeo.on.ca

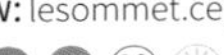

École Secondaire Publique Mille-Îles
72 Gilmour Avenue, Kingston ON K7M 9G6
DP Coordinator Stephanie Mailhot
MYP Coordinator Julie Soini
Languages French
T: +1 613 547 2556
W: www.mille-iles.cepeo.on.ca

École secondaire publique Odyssée
480, avenue Norman, North Bay ON P1B 0A8
DP Coordinator Luc Villeneuve
MYP Coordinator Luc Villeneuve
Languages French
T: +1 705 474 5500
W: cspne.ca/odyssee

École Secondaire Publique Omer-Deslauriers
159 Chesterton Dr, Nepean ON K2E 7E6
DP Coordinator Sophie Tchu-Ut-Gnon
MYP Coordinator Lise Gravelle
Languages French
T: +1 613 820 0992
W: omer-deslauriers.cepeo.on.ca

École secondaire Toronto Ouest
330, Avenue Lansdowne, Toronto ON M6H 3Y1
DP Coordinator Amy Morris
Languages French
T: +1 416 532 6592
W: ecolesecondairetorontoouest.csviamonde.ca

Elmwood School
261 Buena Vista Road, Ottawa ON K1M 0V9
DP Coordinator Jason Levesque
MYP Coordinator Alyson Bartlett
PYP Coordinator Kate Meadowcroft
Languages English
T: +1 613 749 6761
W: www.elmwood.ca

Erindale Secondary School
2021 Dundas Street West, Mississauga ON L5K 1R2
DP Coordinator Carolyn LaRoche
Languages English
T: +1 905 828 7206
W: schools.peelschools.org/sec/erindale

Father Michael McGivney Catholic Academy
5300 Fourteenth Avenue, Markham ON L3S 3K8
DP Coordinator Christine Gomes
Languages English
T: +1 905 472 4961
W: fmmh.ycdsb.ca

Georgetown District High School
70 Guelph Street, Georgetown ON L7G 3Z5
DP Coordinator Kyle Stewart
Languages English
T: +1 905 877 6966
W: www.georgetowndistricthighschool.com/ib

Glenforest Secondary School
3575 Fieldgate Drive, Mississauga ON L4X 2J6
DP Coordinator Daphne Habib
MYP Coordinator Doneen McLaren
Languages English
T: +1 905 625 7731
W: schools.peelschools.org/sec/glenforest

Glenview Park Secondary School
55 McKay Street, Cambridge ON N1R 4G6
DP Coordinator Colleen Caplin
Languages English
T: +1 519 621 9510
W: gps.wrdsb.on.ca

Harold M. Brathwaite Secondary School
415 Great Lakes Drive, Brampton ON L6R 2Z4
DP Coordinator Colin Parker
Languages English
T: +1 905 793 2155
W: www.hmbss.com

I E Weldon Secondary School
24 Weldon Road, Lindsay ON K9V 4R6
DP Coordinator Erin Matthew
Languages English
T: +1 705 324 3585
W: www.tldsb.on.ca/schools/iewss

Kenner CVI & Intermediate School
633 Monaghan Road South, Peterborough ON K9J 5J2
DP Coordinator Peter Mullins
Languages English
T: +1 705 743 2181
W: www.kenner.kprdsb.ca

Khalsa Community School
69 Maitland Street, Brampton ON L6S 3B5
MYP Coordinator Kiran Bedi
Languages English
T: +1 905 791 1750
W: khalsacommunityschool.com

Khalsa School Malton
7280 Airport Rd., Mississauga ON L4T 2H3
MYP Coordinator Meena Singh
Languages English
T: +1 905 671 2010
W: www.khalsaschoolmalton.com

King Heights Academy
28 Roytec Road, Woodbridge ON L4L 8E4
PYP Coordinator Kirti Pankaj
Languages English
T: +1 905 652 1234
W: kingheightsacademy.com

Kingston Collegiate & Vocational Institute
235 Frontenac Street, Kingston ON K7L3S7
DP Coordinator Helen Davis
Languages English
T: +1 613 544 4811

Korah Collegiate and Vocational School
636 Goulais Avenue, Sault Ste Marie ON P6C 5A7
DP Coordinator Ruth Koskenoja
Languages English
T: +1 705 945 7180
W: www.korahcvs.com

La Citadelle International Academy of Arts & Science
36 Scarsdale Road, North York, Toronto ON M3B 2R7
MYP Coordinator Denise Voinica
Languages English, French
T: +1 416 385 9685
W: www.lacitadelleacademy.com

Le Collège Français
100 rue Carlton, Toronto ON M5B 1M3
DP Coordinator Odin Cabrera
Languages French
T: +1 416 393 0175

Leamington District Secondary School
80 Oak St. W., Leamington ON N8H 2B3
DP Coordinator Lisa Jeffery
Languages English, French
T: +1 519 326 6191
W: www.publicboard.ca/school/ldss

Lo-Ellen Park Secondary School
275 Loach's Road, Sudbury ON P3E 2P8
DP Coordinator Julie Wuorinen
Languages English
T: +1 705 522 2320

London International Academy
365 Richmond Street, London, ON N6A 3C2
DP Coordinator Maggie Hanan
Languages English, Spanish
T: +1 519 433 3388
W: www.lia-edu.ca

Lynn-Rose Heights Private School
7215 Millcreek Drive, Mississauga ON L5N 3R3
DP Coordinator Lisa Little
MYP Coordinator Michelle Lau
PYP Coordinator Heidi Corley
Languages English
T: +1 905 567 3553
W: www.lynnroseheights.com

MacLachlan College
337 Trafalgar Road, Oakville ON L6J 3H3
PYP Coordinator Ashleigh Woodward
Languages English
T: +1 905 844 0372
W: www.maclachlan.ca

Maple High School
50 Springside Rd., Maple ON L6A 2W5
DP Coordinator Laura Harding
Languages English
T: +1 905 417 9444
W: maple.hs.yrdsb.ca

Merivale High School
1755 Merivale Road, Nepean ON K2G 1E2
DP Coordinator Lewis Harthun
Languages English, French
T: +1 613 224 1807
W: merivalehs.ocdsb.ca

Michael Power – St Joseph High School
105 Eringate Drive, Toronto ON M9C 3Z7
DP Coordinator Claudia Grilo
Languages English
T: +1 416 393 5529

Milliken Mills High School
7522 Kennedy Rd, Unionville ON L3R 9S5
DP Coordinator Natalie White
Languages English
T: +1 905 477 0072
W: www.yrdsb.ca/schools/millikenmills.hs

Milne Valley Middle School
100 Underhill Drive, Toronto ON M3A 2J9
MYP Coordinator Candice Masci
Languages English
T: +1 416 395 2700

Monarch Park Collegiate
1 Hanson Street, Toronto ON M4J 1G6
DP Coordinator Jacqueline Allen
Languages English
T: +1 416 393 0190
W: www.monarchparkcollegiate.ca

Nicholson Catholic College
301 Church Street, Belleville ON K8N 3C7
DP Coordinator Justin Walsh
Languages English
T: +1 613 967 0404
W: www.nccschool.org

NOIC ACADEMY
50 Featherstone Avenue, Markham ON L3S 2H4
DP Coordinator Mr. Pavle Milutinovic
Languages English
T: +1 905 472 2002
E: royhuang@neworientalgroup.org
W: noic.ca
See full details on page 533

Notre Dame Secondary School
2 Notre Dame Avenue, Brampton ON L6Z 4L5
DP Coordinator Gina Renda
Languages English
T: +1 905 840 2802
W: www.dpcdsb.org/NDAME/Guidance+Courses/IB+Program

Parkdale Collegiate Institute
209 Jameson Avenue, Toronto ON M6K 2Y3
DP Coordinator Miro Bartnik
Languages English
T: +1 416 393 9000
W: schools.tdsb.on.ca/parkdale

Regiopolis-Notre Dame Catholic High School
130 Russell Street, Kingston ON K7K 2E9
DP Coordinator James David
Languages English
T: +1 613 545 1902
W: alcdsb.on.ca/school/regi

Richland Academy
11570 Yonge Street, Richmond Hill, ON L4E 3N7
PYP Coordinator Joanne Pace
Languages English, French
T: +1 905 224 5600
W: www.richlandacademy.ca

RIDLEY COLLEGE
PO Box 3013, 2 Ridley Road, St Catharines ON L2R 7C3
DP Coordinator Kathy Anderson
MYP Coordinator Paul O'Rourke
PYP Coordinator Marcie Lewis
Languages English
T: +1 905 684 1889
E: admissions@ridleycollege.com
W: www.ridleycollege.com
See full details on page 541

Riverside Secondary School
8465 Jerome, Windsor ON N8S 1W8
DP Coordinator Derek Tomkins
Languages English, French
T: +1 519 948 4116
W: riversiderebels.ca

Robert Bateman High School
5151 New Street, Burlington ON L7L 1V3
DP Coordinator Jennifer Bright
Languages English
T: +1 905 632 5151
W: www.rbh.hdsb.ca

Sir Wilfrid Laurier Collegiate Institute
145 Guildwood Parkway, Scarborough ON M1E 1P5
DP Coordinator Inna Belozorovich
Languages English
T: +1 416 396 6820
W: www.sirwilfridlaurierci.ca

Sir Winston Churchill Collegiate and Vocational Institute
130 W. Churchill Drive, Thunder Bay ON P7C 1V5
DP Coordinator Clarke Loney
Languages English
T: +1 807 473 8100
W: churchill.lakeheadschools.ca

St Francis Xavier Secondary School
50 Bristol Road West, Mississauga ON L5R 3K3
DP Coordinator Eugene Ladna
Languages English
T: +1 905 507 6666
W: www.dpcdsb.org/STFXS

St John's – Kilmarnock School
2201 Shantz Station Road, Box 179, Breslau (Waterloo Region) ON N0B 1M0
DP Coordinator Lesa Currie
MYP Coordinator Carey Gallagher
PYP Coordinator Jennifer Wilkinson
Languages English
T: +1 519 648 2183
W: www.sjkschool.org

St Jude's Academy
2150 Torquay Mews, Mississauga ON L5N 2M6
DP Coordinator Leslie Roe-Etter
MYP Coordinator Melissa Chin
PYP Coordinator Marijana Haag
Languages English
T: +1 905 814 0202
W: www.stjudesacademy.com

St Robert Catholic High School
8101 Leslie Street, Thornhill ON L3T 7P4
DP Coordinator Andrea Steele
Languages English
T: +1 905 889 4982
W: www.strobertchs.com

St Thomas Aquinas Roman Catholic Secondary School
124 Dorval Drive, Oakville ON L6K 2W1
DP Coordinator Antonia Montanari
Languages English
T: +1 905 842 9494
W: sta.hcdsb.org

St. James Catholic Global Learning Centre
98 Wanita Rd, Mississauga ON L5G1B8
MYP Coordinator Steven Kelenc
PYP Coordinator Nicola Hughes
Languages English
T: +1 905 891 7619
W: dpcdsb.org/jamee

St. John Paul II Catholic Secondary School
685 Military Trail, Scarborough ON M1E 4P6
DP Coordinator Tracey Robertson
Languages English
T: +1 416 393 5531
W: www.tcdsb.org/schools/stjohnpaulii

St. Mary Catholic Academy
66 Dufferin Park Avenue, Toronto ON M6H 1J6
DP Coordinator Judite Calado Costa
Languages English
T: +1 416 393 5528
W: www.tcdsb.org/schools/stmarycatholicacademy

St. Paul Secondary School
815 Atwater Avenue, Mississauga ON L5E 1L8
DP Coordinator Anne Marie Miki
Languages English, French
T: +1 905 278 3994
W: www3.dpcdsb.org/pauls

Sunnybrook School
469 Merton Street, Toronto ON M4S 1B4
PYP Coordinator Michael Rossiter
Languages English
T: +1 416 487 5308
W: www.sunnybrookschool.com

TFS – CANADA'S INTERNATIONAL SCHOOL
306 Lawrence Avenue East, Toronto ON M4N 1T7
DP Coordinator Dr. Jennifer Elliott
MYP Coordinator Leslie Miller
PYP Coordinator Zein Odeh
Languages French, English
T: +1 416 484 6533
E: admissions@tfs.ca
W: www.tfs.ca
See full details on page 550

The Guelph Collegiate Vocational Institute
155 Paisley Street, Guelph ON N1H 2P3
DP Coordinator Angela Snell
Languages English
T: +1 519 824 9800
W: www.ugdsb.on.ca/gcvi

The Leo Baeck Day School
36 Atkinson Avenue, Thornhill ON L4J 8C9
MYP Coordinator Sheryl Faith
Languages English
T: +1 905 709 3636
W: www.leobaeck.ca

The York School
1320 Yonge Street, Toronto ON M4T 1X2
DP Coordinator Dawn Mcmaster
MYP Coordinator Dawn McMaster
PYP Coordinator Yochebel De Giorgio
Languages English
T: ADMISSIONS: +1 416 646 5275
SWITCHBOARD: +1 416 926 1325
W: www.yorkschool.com

TMS School
500 Elgin Mills Road East, Richmond Hill L4C5G1
DP Coordinator Theresa Hurley
MYP Coordinator Lisa Cantor
Languages English
T: +1 905 889 6882
W: www.tmsschool.ca

Town Centre Montessori Private Schools
155 Clayton Drive, Markham ON L3R 7P3
DP Coordinator Kenneth Huber
MYP Coordinator Leepy Hajra
PYP Coordinator Magdalena Therrien
Languages English
T: +1 905 470 1200
W: tcmps.com

Turner Fenton Secondary School
7935 Kennedy Road South, Brampton ON L6V 3N2
DP Coordinator Angela De Jong
MYP Coordinator Michael Langford
Languages English
T: +1 905 453 9220
W: www.turnerfenton.com

Upper Canada College
200 Lonsdale Road, Toronto ON M4V 1W6
DP Coordinator Colleen Ferguson
PYP Coordinator Dianne Jojic
Languages English
T: +1 416 488 1125
W: www.ucc.on.ca
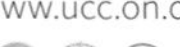  

Victoria Park Collegiate Institute
15 Wallingford Road, North York ON M3A 2V1
DP Coordinator Anna Macinnis
Languages English
T: +1 416 395 3310
W: victoriaparkci.ca

Walden International School
1030 Queen Street West, Brampton ON L6X 0B2
PYP Coordinator Shelley Charanduk
Languages English, French
T: +1 905 497 8890
W: www.waldeninternationalschool.com

Westdale Secondary School
700 Main Street West, Hamilton ON L8S 1A5
DP Coordinator Kim Parkes-Hallmark
Languages English
T: +1 905 522 1387
W: www.hwdsb.on.ca/westdale

Weston Collegiate Institute
100 Pine Street, York, Toronto ON M9N 2Y9
DP Coordinator Anne Dale
Languages English
T: +1 416 394 3250
W: www.westonci.ca

Wheatley School
497 Scott Street, St Catharines ON L2M 3X3
MYP Coordinator Isabel N. Machinandiarena
Languages English
T: +1 905 641 3012
W: www.wheatleyschool.com

White Oaks Secondary School
1330 Montclair Drive, Oakville ON L6K 1Z5
DP Coordinator Erin Davidson
Languages English
T: +1 905 845 5200
W: www.wossweb.com

William Grenville Davis Senior Public School
491 Bartley Bull Parkway, Brampton ON L6W 2M7
MYP Coordinator Andre Laferriere
Languages English
T: +1 905 459 3661
W: www.wgdavis.com

Windfields Junior High School
375 Banbury Road, North York ON M2L 2V2
MYP Coordinator Salima Kanani
Languages English
T: +1 416 395 3100
W: schools.tdsb.on.ca/windfields

Prince Edward Island

Charlottetown Rural High School
100 Raiders Road, Charlottetown PE C1E 1K6
DP Coordinator Philip Pierlot
Languages English
T: +1 902 368 6905
W: www.edu.pe.ca/rural

Colonel Gray High School
175 Spring Park Road, Charlottetown PE C1A 3Y8
DP Coordinator Angela MacCorquodale
Languages English
T: +1 902 368 6860
W: www.edu.pe.ca/gray

Quebec

Académie François-Labelle
1227 rue Notre Dame, Repentigny QC J5Y 3H2
PYP Coordinator Maryse Cadieux
Languages French
T: +1 450 582 2020
W: www.academiefrancoislabelle.qc.ca

Beurling Academy
6100 Boulevard Champlain, Verdun QC H4H 1A5
MYP Coordinator Fotini Papachronis
Languages English
T: +1 514 766 2357
W: beurling.lbpsb.qc.ca

Bishop's College School
80 Moulton Hill Road, PO Box 5001, Station Lennoxville, Sherbrooke QC J1M 1Z8
DP Coordinator Roxane Vigneault
Languages English
T: +1 819 566 0227
W: www.bishopscollegeschool.com

Carlyle Elementary School
109 Carlyle Avenue, Mount Royal QC H3R 1S8
PYP Coordinator Christina Mallozzi
Languages English
T: +1 514 738 1256
W: www.emsb.qc.ca/carlyle

Cégep de Rivière-du-Loup
80, rue Frontenac, Rivière-du-Loup QC G5R 1R1
DP Coordinator Jérémie Pouliot
Languages English
T: +1 418 862 6903
W: www.cegep-rdl.qc.ca

Cégep Garneau
1660 boulevard de l'Entente, Québec QC G1S 4S3
DP Coordinator Annie Jacques
Languages French
T: +1 418 688 8310 EXT:2372
W: www.cegepgarneau.ca

Children's World Academy
2241 Ménard, LaSalle QC H8N 1J4
PYP Coordinator Guy Walker
Languages English, French
T: +1 514 595 2043
W: cwa.lbpsb.qc.ca

Clearpoint Elementary School
17 Cedar Avenue, Pointe-Claire QC H9S 4X9
PYP Coordinator Marianne Brownie
Languages English, French
T: +1 514 798 0792
W: clearpoint.lbpsb.qc.ca

Collège André-Laurendeau
1111 rue Lapierre, Lasalle QC H8N 2J4
DP Coordinator Marie-Pier Blanchard
Languages French
T: +1 514 364 3320 EXT 160
W: www.claurendau.qc.ca

Collège Charlemagne
5000 rue Pilon, Pierrefonds, Montréal QC H9K 1G4
MYP Coordinator Luc Fortin
Languages French
T: +1 514 626 7060

Collège Charles-Lemoyne – Campus Longueuil
901, chemin Tiffin, Longueuil QC J4P 3G6
MYP Coordinator Cécile Leblanc
Languages English, French
T: +1 514 875 0505
W: www.monccl.com

Collège de l'Assomption
270 boulevard de l'Ange-Gardien, L'Assomption, Montréal QC J5Y 3R7
MYP Coordinator Hélène Pelland
Languages French
T: +1 450 589 5621
W: www.classomption.qc.ca

Collège de Valleyfield
169, rue Champlain, Salaberry-de-Valleyfield QC J6T1X6
DP Coordinator Mathieu Bélanger
Languages French
T: +1 450 373 9441
W: www.colval.qc.ca

Collège du Mont-Sainte-Anne
2100 Chemin de Sainte-Catherine, Sherbrooke QC J1N 3V5
MYP Coordinator Sébastien Rodrigue
Languages French
T: +1 819 823 3003
W: www.college-mont-sainte-anne.qc.ca

Collège Esther-Blondin
101 rue Sainte-Anne, Saint-Jacques QC J0K 2R0
MYP Coordinator Mélanie Martin
Languages French
T: +1 450 839 3672
W: collegeestherblondin.qc.ca

Collège Jean-de-Brebeuf
3200, chemin de la Côte-Sainte-Catherine, Montréal QC H3T 1C1
DP Coordinator Simon Fortin
MYP Coordinator Lyne Harvey
Languages French
T: +1 514 342 9342
W: www.brebeuf.qc.ca

Collège Jésus-Marie de Sillery
2047 chemin Saint-Louis, Québec City QC G1T 1P3
MYP Coordinator Christine Baillargeon
Languages French
T: +1 418 687 9250
W: www.collegejesusmarie.com

Collège Mont Notre-Dame de Sherbrooke
114 rue Cathédrale, Sherbrooke QC J1H 4MI
MYP Coordinator Nathalie Arès
Languages French
T: +1 819 563 4104
W: www.mont-notre-dame.qc.ca

Collège Notre-Dame-de-Lourdes
845 chemin Tiffin, Longueuil QC J4P 3G5
MYP Coordinator Marie-Josée Bellemare
Languages French
T: +1 450 670 4740
W: www.ndl.qc.ca

Collège Saint-Louis
275 36e Avenue, Lachine QC H8T 2A4
MYP Coordinator Denis Cadieux
Languages French
T: +1 514 855 4198
W: wp.csmb.qc.ca/college-saint-louis

Collège Saint-Maurice
630 rue Girouard Ouest, Saint-Hyacinthe QC J2S 2Y3
MYP Coordinator Elsa Würtele
Languages French
T: +1 450 773 7478 EXT:222
W: www.csm.qc.ca

Collège Saint-Paul
235 rue Ste-Anne, Varennes QC J3X 1P9
MYP Coordinator Sophie Laflamme
Languages French
T: +1 450 652 2941
W: www.college-st-paul.qc.ca

Collège Ville-Marie
2850 rue Sherbrooke Est, Montréal QC H2K 1H3
MYP Coordinator Catherine Roussety
Languages French
T: +1 514 525 2516
W: www.cvmarie.qc.ca

Courtland Park International School
1075 Wolfe, St-Bruno QC J3V 3K6
PYP Coordinator Grace Palmieri
Languages English
T: +1 450 550 2514
W: www.rsb.qc.ca

École Bois-Joli Sacré-Coeur
775 rue Sacré-Coeur Ouest, St-Hyacinthe QC J2S 1V2
PYP Coordinator Julie Bessette
Languages French
T: +1 450 774 5130
W: www.cssh.qc.ca/ecole_bois-joli_-_sacre-coeur/actualites.html

École Centrale
682 Principale, Saint-Joachim de Shefford QC J0E 2G0
PYP Coordinator Mathieu Lanoix
Languages French
T: +1 450 539 1816
W: www.centrale.csvdc.qc.ca

École Chabot et du l'Oasis
1666 Avenue De Lozère, Charlesbourg QC G1G 3L4
PYP Coordinator Caroline Giguère
Languages French
T: +1 418 624 3752

Ecole de la Baie Saint Francois
70 rue Louis VI Major, Salaberry De Valleyfield QC J6T 3G2
MYP Coordinator Daniel Hébert
Languages French
T: +1 450 371 2004
W: www.csvt.qc.ca/bsf

École de la Magdeleine
1100 boulevard Taschereau, La Prairie QC J5R 1W8
MYP Coordinator Maude Lemieux
Languages French
T: +1 514 380 8899
W: www.csdgs.qc.ca

École de l'Équinoxe
2949 boulevard de la Renaissance, Laval, QC H7L 0H3
PYP Coordinator Karine Bouffard
Languages English, French
T: +1 450 662 7000
W: delequinoxe.cslaval.qc.ca

École d'éducation internationale
720 rue Morin, McMasterville QC J3G 1H1
MYP Coordinator Geneviève Dubuc
Languages French
T: +1 450 467 4222
W: eei.csp.qc.ca

École d'éducation internationale de Laval
5075 boul du souvenir, Laval QC H7W 1E1
MYP Coordinator Étienne Jacques
Languages French
T: +1 450 662 7000 4300
W: eeil.cslaval.qc.ca

École d'éducation internationale Filteau-St-Mathieu
830 rue de Saurel, Sainte Foy QC G1X 3P6
PYP Coordinator Susie Goulet
Languages French
T: +1 418 652 2152
W: www.csdecou.qc.ca/filteau

École du Petit-Collège
9343 Rue Jean-Milot, LaSalle QC H8R 1Y7
PYP Coordinator Christine Renaud
Languages English, French
T: +1 514 748 4661

École du Sentier
1225 rue Victorin, Drummondville, QC J2C 7Z9
PYP Coordinator Marylène Bienvenue
Languages French
T: +1 819 850 1632
W: dusentier.csdc.qc.ca

École Évangéline
11845, boulevard de l'Acadie, Montréal QC H3M 2T4
MYP Coordinator Chantal Laporte
Languages French
T: +1 514 596 5280
W: www.csdm.qc.ca/evangeline

École Guy-Drummond
1475 avenue La Joie, Outremont QC H2V 1P9
PYP Coordinator Caroline Quevillon
Languages French
T: +1 514 270 4866

École Hubert-Maisonneuve
364 Rue Académie, Rosemère QC J7A 1ZA
MYP Coordinator Isabelle Bois
Languages French
T: +1 450 621 2003
W: sites.cssmi.qc.ca/hubert-maisonneuve
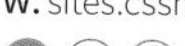

École internationale de Montréal
11 chemin Côte St-Antoine, Westmount, Montréal QC H3Y 2H7
MYP Coordinator Tammy Salamé
PYP Coordinator Cecile de Barbeyrac
Languages French
T: +1 514 596 7240
W: ecole-internationale.csdm.ca

École Internationale de Saint-Sacrement
1430 chemin Ste-Foy, Québec QC G1S 2N8
PYP Coordinator Bianka Lévesque
Languages French
T: +1 418 682 2619 EXT:3490
W: www.cscapitale.qc.ca/st-sacrement

École Internationale des Apprenants
4505 Boul Henri-Bourassa O, Saint-Laurent QC H4L 1A5
PYP Coordinator Adela Vintila
Languages French
T: +1 514 334 4153
W: ecoleia.ca

École internationale du Mont-Bleu
45 rue Boucher, Gatineau QC J8Y 6G2
PYP Coordinator Léticia Sanchez
Languages French
T: +1 819 777 5921
W: internationaledumontbleu.cspo.qc.ca

École internationale du Phare
405, rue Sara, Sherbrooke QC J1H 5S6
MYP Coordinator Stéphanie Dussault
Languages French
T: +1 819 822 5455
W: www.csrs.qc.ca/fr/internationale-du-phare

École Internationale du Village
19, rue Symmes, Gatineau QC J9H 3J3
PYP Coordinator Andrée-Anne Malette
Languages French
T: +1 819 685 2611
W: internationaleduvillage.cspo.qc.ca

École internationale Lucille-Teasdale
8350, boulevard Pelletier, Brossard QC J4X 1M8
MYP Coordinator Martin Laplante
Languages French
T: +1 450 465 6290
W: www.csmv.qc.ca

École internationale primaire de Greenfield Park
776 Cambell, Greenfield Park QC J4V 1YZ
PYP Coordinator Eloise Simoncelli-Bourque
Languages French
T: +1 450 672 0042

École internationale Saint-François-Xavier
8-A, rue Pouliot, Rivière-du-Loup QC G5R 3R8
PYP Coordinator Alexandre Gaudreau
Languages French, English, Spanish
T: +1 418 862 6901
W: web.cskamloup.qc.ca/sfx

École Jeanne-Mance
4240 rue de Bordeaux, Montréal QC H2H 1Z5
MYP Coordinator Isabelle Boyer
Languages English
T: +1 514 596 5815
W: jeanne-mance.csdm.qc.ca

École Joseph François Perrault
7540 rue François Perrault, Montréal QC H2A 1L9
MYP Coordinator Cathy-Anne Boiteau
Languages French
T: +1 514 596 4620

École La Dauversière
11 600 Boul. de l'Acadie, Montréal QC H3M 2T2
MYP Coordinator Cathy Cormier
Languages French
T: +1 514 596 5285
W: ladauversiere.csdm.ca

École La Vérendrye
3055, rue Mousseau, Montréal QC H1L 4W1
PYP Coordinator Gabrielle Bisson
Languages French
T: +1 514 596 4845
W: la-verendrye.csdm.ca

École Le tandem
605 rue Notre-dame Ouest, Victoriaville QC G6P 6Y9
MYP Coordinator Caroline Bilodeau
Languages French
T: +1 819 758 1534

École Les Mélèzes
393 de Lanaudière, Joliette QC J6E3L9
PYP Coordinator Caroline Beaulieu
Languages French
T: +1 450 752 4433
W: www.lesmelezes.qc.ca

École Marie-Clarac
3530 Boul Gouin Est, Montréal-Nord QC H1H 1B7
MYP Coordinator Annie Frenette
Languages French
T: +1 514 322 1160
W: www.ecolemarie-clarac.qc.ca

École Micheline-Brodeur
23 rue Sainte-Anne, Saint-Paul-d'Abbotsford QC J0E 1A0
PYP Coordinator Maxime Benoit
Languages English, French
T: +1 450 379 5674
W: brodeur.e.csdhr.qc.ca

École Monseigneur Robert
769 rue de lEducation, Québec QC G1E 1J2
PYP Coordinator Benoit-Olivier Marcoux
Languages French
T: +1 418 666 4490

École Notre-Dame-des-Neiges
4140, boulevard Gastonguay, Québec QC G2B 1M7
PYP Coordinator Gabrielle Prévost
Languages French
T: +1 418 686 4040 EXT:3300
W: www.cscapitale.qc.ca/nd-neiges

École Paul-Hubert
250, boulevard Arthur-Buies Ouest, Rimouski QC G5L 7A7
MYP Coordinator Martin Cote
Languages French
T: +1 418 724 3439
W: ph.csphares.qc.ca

École Père-Marquette
6030 rue Marquette, Montréal QC H2G 2Y2
MYP Coordinator Michel Clark
Languages French
T: +1 514 596 4128
W: pere-marquette.csdm.qc.ca

École Plein Soleil (Association Coopérative)
300, rue de Montréal, Sherbrooke QC J1H 1E5
PYP Coordinator François Normandeau
Languages French
T: +1 819 569 8359
W: www.pleinsoleil.qc.ca

École Pointe-Lévy
55 Rue des Commandeurs, Levis QC G6V 1P5
MYP Coordinator Manon Tessier
Languages French
T: +1 418 838 8402
W: www.pointe-levy.qc.ca

École Polyvalente Le Carrefour
125 Rue Self, Val d'Òr, Québec QC J9P 3N2
MYP Coordinator Éric Lunam
Languages French
T: +1 819 825 4670

École primaire d'éducation internationale
2750,boulevard des Forges, Trois-Rivières QC G8Z 1V2
PYP Coordinator Maryse Gélinas
Languages French
T: +1 819 379 6565
W: www.ecolepei.com

École primaire d'éducation internationale du secteur Est
175, rue Saint-Alphonse, Trois-Rivières QC G8T 7R8
PYP Coordinator Maryse Gélinas
Languages French
T: +1 819 840 4358
W: www.est.ecolepei.com

École Saint-Barthélemy
Pavillon Sagard, 7400 rue Sagard, Montréal QC H2E 2S9
PYP Coordinator Isabelle Crête
Languages French
T: +1 514 596 4858
W: www.csdm.qc.ca/st_barthelemy

École Saint-Édouard
376 chemin Knowlton, Lac Brome QC J0E 1V0
PYP Coordinator Catherine Olivier
Languages French
T: +1 450 243 6770
W: www.st-edouard.csvdc.qc.ca

École Saint-Jean
245, 2e Rue Ouest, Rimouski QC G5L 4Y1
MYP Coordinator Caroline Michaud
Languages French
T: +1 418 724 3381
W: ecole.csphares.qc.ca/st-jean

École Saint-Pierre et des Sentiers
1090 Château Bigot, Charlesbourg QC G2L 1G1
MYP Coordinator Manon Dufour
Languages French
T: +1 418 624 3757 EXT:0226
W: www.csdps.qc.ca

École Saint-Rémi
16 avenue Neveu, Beaconsfield QC H9W 5B4
PYP Coordinator Martine Gagnon
Languages English, French
T: +1 514 855 4206
W: saintremi.ecoleouest.com

École secondaire André-Laurendeau
7450 boulevard Cousineau, St-Hubert QC J3Y 3L4
MYP Coordinator Carole St-Amant
Languages French
T: +1 450 678 2080
W: andre-laurendeau.ecoles.csmv.qc.ca

Ecole Secondaire Armand-Corbeil

795 JF Kennedy Ouest, Terrebonne QC J6W 1X2
MYP Coordinator Samuel Jeannotte
Languages French
T: +1 450 492 3619 EXT:1112

École secondaire Bernard-Gariépy

2800 boulevard des Érables, Sorel-Tracy QC J3R 2W4
MYP Coordinator Michel Coulombe
Languages French
T: +1 450 742 5601

École secondaire Camille-Lavoie

500, Avenue des Métiers Sud, Alma QC G8B 3C4
MYP Coordinator Dominique Fortin
Languages French
T: +1 418 669 6062 EXT:6200
W: www.cslacst-jean.qc.ca

École Secondaire Cavelier-De LaSalle

9199 rue Centrale, LaSalle QC H8R 2JG
MYP Coordinator Josette Lévesque
Languages French
T: +1 514 595 2044

École secondaire Charles-Gravel

350 rue Saint-Gérard, Chicoutimi QC G7G 1J2
MYP Coordinator Audrey Morin
Languages French
T: +1 418 541 4343
W: www.csrsaguenay.qc.ca/charles-gravel

École secondaire de l'Île

255 rue Saint-Rédempteur, Gatineau QC J8X 2T4
MYP Coordinator Martin Seguin
Languages French
T: +1 819 771 6126

École secondaire De Mortagne

955 Boulevard De Montarville, Boucherville QC J4B 1Z6
MYP Coordinator Nathalie Phaneuf
Languages French
T: +1 450 655 7311
W: www.csp.qc.ca/ecolesweb/ecs117.htm

École secondaire de Neufchâtel

3600 avenue Chauveau, Neufchâtel QC G2C 1A1
MYP Coordinator Guylaine Plante
Languages French
T: +1 418 847 7300
W: www.cscapitale.qc.ca/neufchatel

École secondaire de Rivière-du-Loup

320 Rue Saint-Pierre, Rivière du Loup QC G5R 3V3
MYP Coordinator Justine Therrien
Languages French
T: +1 418 868 2233
W: www.cskamloup.qc.ca

École secondaire de Rochebelle

1095 de Rochebelle, Sainte Foy QC G1V 4P8
MYP Coordinator Karine Mercier
Languages French
T: +1 418 652 2167
W: www.derochebelle.qc.ca

École secondaire des Pionniers

1725, boulevard du Carmel, Trois-Rivières QC G8Z 3R8
MYP Coordinator Sylvie Gour
Languages French
T: +1 819 379 5822
W: despionniers.csduroy.qc.ca

École secondaire des Sources

2900 chemin Lake, Dollard-des-Ormeaux QC H9B 2P1
MYP Coordinator Inas Mourad
Languages French
T: +1 514 855 4208
W: www2.csmb.qc.ca/dessources/

École secondaire d'Oka

1700 Chemin Oka, Oka QC J0N 1E0
MYP Coordinator Mélanie Corneau
Languages French
T: +1 450 491 8410

École secondaire Dorval Jean XXIII

1301 avenue Dawson, Dorval QC H9S 1Y3
MYP Coordinator Mathieu Tremblay
Languages French
T: +1 514 855 4244

École secondaire Fernand-Lefebvre

265 de Ramezay, Sorel-Tracy QC J3P 4A5
MYP Coordinator Michel Coulombe
Languages French
T: +1 450 742 5901
W: www.cs-soreltracy.qc.ca/sec/esfl

École secondaire Grande-Rivière

100 rue Broad, Gatineau QC J9H 6A9
MYP Coordinator Annie Lavigne
Languages French
T: +1 819 682 8222 274
W: www.cspo.qc.ca

École secondaire Guillaume-Couture

70 Rue Philippe-Boucher, Levis QC G6V 1M5
MYP Coordinator Marianne Rhéaume
Languages French
T: +1 418 838 8550
W: ecgc.csdn.qc.ca

École secondaire Henri-Bourassa

6051 boul Maurice-Duplessis, Montréal-Nord QC H1G 1Y6
MYP Coordinator Francine Lalonde
Languages French
T: +1 514 328 3200 EXT:3210

École secondaire Hormisdas-Gamelin

580 rue Maclaren Est, Gatineau QC J8L 2W2
MYP Coordinator Marie-France Bastien
Languages French
T: +1 819 986 8511
W: www.cscv.qc.ca

École secondaire Jacques-Rousseau

444 rue Gentilly est, Longueuil QC J4H 3X7
MYP Coordinator Genevieve Lacroix
Languages French
T: +1 450 651 6800 EXT:467

École secondaire Jean-Baptiste-Meilleur

777 boul d`Iberville, Repentigny QC J5Y 1A2
MYP Coordinator Etienne Murray
Languages French
T: +1 450 492 3777
W: www.csaffluents.qc.ca/wjbm

École secondaire Jean-Jacques-Bertrand

255 rue Saint-André Sud, Farnham QC J2N 2B8
MYP Coordinator Julie Filion
Languages French
T: +1 450 293 3181 EXT:223

École secondaire Jeanne-Mance

45 avenue des Freres, Drummondville QC J2B 6A2
MYP Coordinator Mélanie Flamand
Languages French
T: +1 819 474 0753

École secondaire Joseph-François-Perrault

140 chemin Ste-Foy, Québec QC G1R 1T2
MYP Coordinator Sebastien Renald
Languages French
T: +1 418 686 4040 EXT:6011
W: www.cscapitale.qc.ca/jfperrault

École secondaire Kénogami

1954 Boulevard des Etudiants, Jonquière, Québec QC G7X 4B1
MYP Coordinator William Dumont
Languages French
T: +1 418 5423571

École secondaire La Courvilloise

2265 avenue Larue, Beauport QC G1C 1J9
MYP Coordinator François Couillard
Languages French
T: +1 418 821 4220
W: www.csdps.qc.ca

École secondaire La Voie

6755 rue Lavoie, Montréal QC H3W 2K8
MYP Coordinator Karine Laroche
Languages French
T: +1 514 736 3500
W: la-voie.csdm.ca

École secondaire Le tandem boisé

605 rue Notre-dame Est, Victoriaville QC G6P 6Y9
MYP Coordinator Marie-Eve Jutras
Languages French
T: +1 819 758 1534

École secondaire L'Envolée

549 rue Fournier, Granby QC J2J 2K5
MYP Coordinator Martin Nadeau
Languages French
T: +1 450 777 7536
W: www.envolee.csvdc.qc.ca

École secondaire Louis-Joseph-Papineau

378 Papineau, Papineauville QC J0V 1R0
MYP Coordinator Eric Lefrancois
Languages French
T: +1 819 427 6258
W: www.cscv.qc.ca/010/LJP/PPCS-LJP.html

École secondaire Louis-Philippe-Paré

235 boulevard Brisebois, Châteauguay QC J6K 3X4
MYP Coordinator Geneviève Allaire
Languages French
T: +1 514 380 8899 EXT:5480
W: lpp.csdgs.qc.ca

École secondaire Louis-Riel

5850 avenue de Carignan, Montréal QC H1M 2V4
MYP Coordinator Ronald Jean-Pierre
Languages French
T: +1 514 596 4134
W: www.louis-riel.csdm.qc.ca

École secondaire Monseigneur Euclide-Théberge
677 rue Desjardins, Marieville QC J3M 1R1
MYP Coordinator Patrick Mullen
Languages French
T: +1 450 460 4491
W: theberge.e.csdhr.qc.ca

École secondaire Mont Saint-Sacrement
200 boulevard Saint-Sacrement, Saint-Gabriel-de-Valcartier QC G0A 4S0
MYP Coordinator Jocelyne Boivin
Languages French
T: +1 418 844 3771 P35
W: www.mss.qc.ca

École secondaire Mont-Royal
50, avenue Montgomery, Ville Mont-Royal QC H3R 2B3
MYP Coordinator Linda Delarosbil
Languages French
T: +1 514 731 2761
W: www.ecolemont-royal.com

École secondaire Ozias-Leduc
525 rue Jolliet, Mont-Saint-Hilaire QC J3H 3N2
MYP Coordinator Guy Chatelain
Languages French
T: +1 450 467 0261

École secondaire Paul-Gérin-Lajoie-d'Outremont
475, avenue Bloomfield, Outremont, QC H2V 3R9
MYP Coordinator Christian Girouard
Languages French
T: +1 514 276 3746
W: www.paul-gerin-lajoie-doutremont.ca

École secondaire polyvalente de l'Ancienne-Lorette
1801 rue Notre-Dame, L'Ancienne-Lorette QC G2E 3C6
MYP Coordinator Mylène Bellavance
Languages French
T: +1 418 872 9836
W: www.csdecou.qc.ca/pal

École secondaire Rive-Nord
400 rue Joseph-Paquette, Bois des Filions QC J6Z 4P7
MYP Coordinator Pascale Gauthier
Languages French
T: +1 450 621 3686
W: sites.cssmi.qc.ca/rivenord

École secondaire Roger-Comtois
158 boulevard des Étudiants, Loretteville QC G2A 1N8
MYP Coordinator Raynald Dancause
Languages French
T: +1 418 847 7201

École secondaire Saint-Joseph de Saint-Hyacinthe
2875 Bourdages Nord, Saint-Hyacinthe QC J2S 5S3
MYP Coordinator Anne-Marie Rajotte
Languages French
T: +1 450 774 3775

École secondaire Saint-Luc
6300, chemin de la Côte, Saint-Luc, Montréal QC H3X 2H4
MYP Coordinator Chantal Filion
Languages French
T: +1 514 596 5920
W: st-luc.csdm.ca

École secondaire Serge-Bouchard
640, boulevard Blanche, Baie-Comeau QC G5C 2B3
MYP Coordinator Chantal Bérubé
Languages French
T: +1 418 589 1301
W: www.csestuaire.qc.ca/ecoles-secondaires

École secondaire St-Gabriel
8 Rue Tassé, Ste Thérèse QC J7E 1V3
MYP Coordinator Céline Chagnon
Languages French
T: +1 450 433 5445
W: sites.cssmi.qc.ca/stg

École Ste-Thérèse-de-l'Enfant-Jésus
700 9e rue, Saint-Jérôme QC J7Z 2Z5
PYP Coordinator Julie Dulong
Languages French
T: +1 450 438 8828
W: www.csrdn.qc.ca/ste-therese

École St-Noël
993 8e Avenue, Thetford Mines QC G6G 2E3
PYP Coordinator Lisa Vachon
Languages French
T: +1 418 335 9826
W: www.csappalaches.qc.ca

École Terre des jeunes
128 25e Avenue, St-Eustache QC J7P 2V2
PYP Coordinator Suzanne Allard
Languages French
T: +1 450 473 9219
W: sites.cssmi.qc.ca/tdj

École Val-des-Ormes
199 chemin de la Grande-Côte, Rosemère QC J7A 1H6
PYP Coordinator Nancy Prézeau
Languages French
T: +1 450 437 5770
W: www6.cssmi.qc.ca/vdo

École Wilfrid-Pelletier
8301 boulevard Wilfrid-Pelletier, Montréal (Anjou) QC H1K 1M2
PYP Coordinator Nathalie Fortier
Languages French
T: +1 514 352 7300
W: www.cspi.qc.ca/wp/

Heritage Regional High School
7445 Chambly Road, St Hubert QC J3Y 3S3
MYP Coordinator Angela Cavaliere
Languages English
T: +1 450 678 1070

Howard S Billings High School
210 McLeod, Chateauguay QC J6J 2H4
MYP Coordinator Paul Couture
Languages English
T: +1 450 691 3230
W: www.hsbillingsib.ca

John Paul I High School
8455 Pre-Laurin, St Leonard QC H1R 3P3
MYP Coordinator Valérie Barnabé
Languages English, French
T: +1 514 328 7171
W: www.emsb.qc.ca/johnpauli

JPPS-Bialik High School
6500 Kildare Road, Montreal QC H4W 3B8
MYP Coordinator Judy Stein
PYP Coordinator Marnie Stein
Languages English
T: +1 514 731 6456
W: www.jppsbialik.ca

Lakeside Academy
5050 Sherbrooke, Lachine QC H8T 1H8
MYP Coordinator Maude Daniel
Languages English
T: +1 514 637 2505
W: lakesideacademy.lbpsb.qc.ca

LaSalle Community Comprehensive High School
240-9th Avenue, LaSalle QC H8P 2N9
MYP Coordinator Julie Canty-Homier
Languages English
T: +1 514 595 2050
W: lcchs.lbpsb.qc.ca

Laurier Macdonald High School
7355 Boulevard Viau, St Leonard QC H1S 3C2
MYP Coordinator Valérie Barnabé
Languages English, French
T: +1 514 374 6000
W: www.lauriermacdonald.ca

Le Collège Saint-Bernard
25 avenue des Frères, Drummondville QC J2B 6A2
MYP Coordinator Marie-Eve Poulin
Languages French
T: +1 819 478 3330

L'École des Ursulines de Québec
4 rue du Parloir, CP 820, Haute – Ville, Québec QC G1R 4S7
PYP Coordinator Veronique Dussault
Languages French
T: +1 418 692 2612

L'Externat Saint-Jean-Eudes
650 avenue du Bourg-Royal, Charlesbourg, Québec City QC G2L 1M8
MYP Coordinator Louis-Philippe St-Charles-Bernier
Languages French
T: +1 418 627 1550
W: www.sje.qc.ca

LOWER CANADA COLLEGE
4090, avenue Royal, Montréal QC H4A 2M5
DP Coordinator Lisa Currie
Languages English
T: +1 514 482 9916
E: admissions@lcc.ca
W: www.lcc.ca
See full details on page 521

Marymount Academy
5100 Côte St-Luc Road, Montréal QC H3W 2G9
MYP Coordinator Ramin Khodaie
Languages English
T: +1 514 488 8144
W: www.emsb.qc.ca/marymount/

Michelangelo International Elementary School
9360 5e rue, Montréal QC H1E 1K1
PYP Coordinator Ida De Laurentiis
Languages English, French
T: +1 514 648 1218
W: michelangelomain.homestead.com

Pensionnat du Saint-Nom-de-Marie
628 chemin de la Côte, St Catherine, Outremont QC H2V 2C5
MYP Coordinator Chantal Gobeil
Languages French
T: +1 514 735 5261
W: www.psnm.qc.ca

Pierrefonds Comprehensive High School
13800 Pierrefonds Boulevard, Pierrefonds QC H9A 1A7
MYP Coordinator Caroline Clarke
Languages English
T: +1 514 626 9610

Polyvalente Chanoine-Armand-Racicot
940 boulevard de Normandie, St Jean-Sur-Richelieu QC J3A 1A7
MYP Coordinator Valérie Gosselin
Languages French
T: +1 450 348 6134
W: racicot.e.csdhr.qc.ca

Polyvalente de Charlesbourg
900, rue de la Sorbonne, Québec QC G1H 1H1
MYP Coordinator Cynthia Turcotte
Languages English, French
T: +1 418 622 7820
W: polyvalentedecharlesbourg.csdps.qc.ca

Polyvalente de Thetford Mines
561 rue St-Patrick, Thetford Mines QC G6G 5W1
MYP Coordinator Jean Gourdes
Languages French
T: +1 418 338 7832 EXT:1514

Polyvalente des Quatre-Vents
1099 boul Hamel, St-Félicien QC G8K 2R4
MYP Coordinator Marie-Andrée Plourde
Languages French
T: +1 418 275 4585
W: www.cspaysbleuets.qc.ca/pvq

Polyvalente Deux-Montagnes
500 chemin des Anciens, Deux-Montagnes QC J7R 6A7
MYP Coordinator Donald Prémont
Languages French
T: +1 450 472 3070

Polyvalente Hyacinthe-Delorme
2700 Avenue T D Bouchard, Saint-Hyacinthe QC J2S 7G2
MYP Coordinator Isabelle Guertin
Languages French
T: +1 450 773 8401

Polyvalente Le Carrefour
50 chemin de la Savane, Gatineau QC J8T 3N2
MYP Coordinator Sindy Poirier
Languages French
T: +1 819 568 9012
W: www.csdraveurs.qc.ca/carrefour

Polyvalente Marcel-Landry
365, avenue Landry, Saint-Jean-sur-Richelieu QC J2X 2P6
MYP Coordinator Jerome Bedard
Languages French
T: +1 450 347 1225
W: landry.e.csdhr.qc.ca

Polyvalente Saint Francois
228 Avenue Lambert, Beauceville QC G5X 3N9
MYP Coordinator Isabelle Roy
Languages French
T: +1 418 228 5541
W: psf.csbe.qc.ca

Polyvalente Saint-Jérôme
535 rue Filion, Saint-Jérôme QC J7Z 1J6
MYP Coordinator Chantal Dion
Languages French
T: +1 450 436 4330
W: www.psj.csrdn.qc.ca

Saint Lambert International High School
675 Green Street, St Lambert QC J4P 1V9
MYP Coordinator Kristen Witczak
Languages English
T: +1 450 671 5534
W: www.saintlambertinternational.ca

St Thomas High School
120 Ambassador, Pointe-Claire QC H9R 1S8
MYP Coordinator Amber Carlon
Languages English
T: +1 514 694 3770

Saskatchewan

Aden Bowman Collegiate Institute
1904 Clarence Ave S, Saskatoon SK S7J 1L3
DP Coordinator Jeff Speir
Languages English
T: +1 306 683 7600
W: www.spsd.sk.ca

Bedford Road Collegiate
722 Bedford Road, Saskatoon SK S7L 0G2
DP Coordinator Kim Buglass
Languages English
T: +1 306 683 7650
W: www.spsd.sk.ca/school/bedfordroad

Luther College High School
1500 Royal Street, Regina SK S4T 5A5
DP Coordinator Derek Frostad
Languages English
T: +1 306 791 9150
W: www.luthercollege.edu

North Battleford Comprehensive High School
1791-110th Street, North Battleford SK S9A 2Y2
DP Coordinator Josh Radchenko
Languages English
T: +1 306 445 6101
W: www.nbchs.north-battleford.sk.ca

CAYMAN ISLANDS

Cayman International School
PO Box 31364, 95 Minerva Drive, Camana Bay, Grand Cayman KY1-1206
DP Coordinator Sarah Dyer
Languages English
T: +1 345 945 4664
W: www.caymaninternationalschool.org

Prospect Primary School
169 Poindexter Road, P.O. Box 187, Grand Cayman KY1-1104
PYP Coordinator Charmaine Bravo
Languages English
T: +1 345 947 8889
W: schools.edu.ky/pps

Savannah Primary School
1659 Shamrock Rd., P.O. Box 435, Grand Cayman KY1-1502
PYP Coordinator Jessica Eden
Languages English
T: +1 345 926 8628
W: www.des.edu.ky/Savannah.cfm

Sir John A Cumber Primary School
PO Box 405, Grand Cayman KY1-1302
PYP Coordinator Annette Vaughan
Languages English
T: +1 345 949 3314
W: schools.edu.ky/jac

CHILE

Antofagasta International School
Avenida Jaime Guzmán Errázuriz, N° 04300, Antofagasta
PYP Coordinator Samantha Lonsdale
Languages English
T: +56 55 694900
W: www.ais.cl

Bradford School
Avada Luis Pateur 6335, Vitacura
DP Coordinator Hector Venegas Salgado
Languages English
T: +56 (2) 29 12 31 40
W: www.bradfordschool.cl

Colegio Alemán Chicureo
Av. Alemania 170, Piedra Roja, Chicureo
PYP Coordinator Maricarmen Rosenbaum
Languages Spanish
T: +56 223078962
W: www.dsch.cl

Colegio Alemán de Concepción
Camino El Venado 1075, Andalué, San Pedro de la Paz, Concepción VIII REGIÓN DEL BÍO BÍO
DP Coordinator Cristian Muñoz
Languages Spanish
T: +56 41 2140000
W: www.dsc.cl

Colegio Alemán de San Felipe de Aconcagua
60 CH N° 501 Panquehue, San Felipe
DP Coordinator Miriam Ramirez
Languages English, Spanish
T: +56 34 2 59 11 71
W: www.dssanfelipe.cl

Colegio Alemán de Temuco
Avenida Holandesa 0855, Temuco
DP Coordinator Leonardo Hernández Zapata
Languages Spanish
T: +56 45 963000
W: www.dstemuco.cl

Colegio Alemán de Valparaiso
Alvarez 2950, El Salto, Viña del Mar
DP Coordinator Rafael Yanez
Languages Spanish
T: +56 32 216 1531
W: www.dsvalpo.cl

Colegio Alemán Los Angeles
Casilla 367, Av. Gabriela Mistral 1360 (ex 1751), Los Ángeles
DP Coordinator Claudio Ibacache Soto
Languages Spanish
T: +56 43 2521111
W: www.dsla.cl

Colegio Alemán Puerto Varas
KM1,4 Camino Ensenada, Puerto Varas
PYP Coordinator Natalia Federici Maggi
Languages Spanish, German
T: +56 65 223 0450
W: www.dspuertovaras.com

Colegio Alemán St Thomas Morus
Casilla 16147, Correo 9, Providencia, Santiago de Chile 16147
DP Coordinator Carlos Obaid
Languages Spanish
T: +56 02 7291600
W: www.dsmorus.cl

Colegio Internacional SEK Chile
Avd Los Militares 6640, Las Condes, Santiago
DP Coordinator Marcela Gangas
Languages Spanish
T: +56 2 2127116
W: www.sekchile.com

Colegio Internacional SEK Pacifico
San Estanislao 50 Lomas de Montemar, Concón
DP Coordinator Paola de la Fuente Estay
PYP Coordinator Wilma Lizana
Languages English, Spanish
T: +56 32 2275700
W: www.sekpacifico.com

Colegio 'La Maisonnette'
Avda Luis Pasteur 6076, Vitacura, Santiago
DP Coordinator Oriana Martínez
Languages Spanish
T: +56 2 228162945
W: www.lamaisonnette.cl

Craighouse School
Casilla 20 007, Correo 20., Santiago
DP Coordinator Fernanda Silva
MYP Coordinator Leonora Cardemil
PYP Coordinator Barbara Atkinson
Languages English, Spanish
T: +56 2 227560218
W: www.craighouseschool.cl

Instituto Alemán Carlos Anwandter
Los Laureles 050, Casilla 2-D, Valdivia
DP Coordinator Sonia Videla
Languages Spanish
T: +56-63-2471100
W: www.dsv.cl

Instituto Alemán de Osorno
Los Carreras 818, Osorno
DP Coordinator Carla Sommer
MYP Coordinator Jaime Serón
PYP Coordinator Francisco Gálvez
Languages Spanish
T: +56 64 233 1800/1805
W: www.dso.cl

Instituto Alemán Puerto Montt
Bernardo Phillipi #350, Sector Seminario, Puerto Montt 5480000
PYP Coordinator Jose Silva
Languages Spanish
T: +56 65 2 252560
W: www.ialeman.cl

International School Nido de Aguilas
Casilla 162, Correo La Dehesa, Santiago
DP Coordinator Kurt Supplee
Languages English
T: +56 2 2339 8100
W: www.nido.cl

Liceo A 43 'Liceo Siete'
Monseñor Sótero Sanz 060, Santiago
DP Coordinator Isabel Villarroel
Languages Spanish
T: +56 2 2235 7921
W: www.liceosiete.cl

Mackay School
Vicuña Mackenna 700, Viña del Mar
DP Coordinator Silvio Bermudez Salas
MYP Coordinator Christian Vergara Palza
PYP Coordinator Humberto Poza Peralta
Languages English
T: +56 32 2386614
W: www.mackay.cl

Redland School
Camino El Alba 11357, Las Condes, Santiago 7600022
DP Coordinator Ruth Guzmán
MYP Coordinator Laura Wippell
PYP Coordinator Miguel Ramos
Languages Spanish
T: +56 2 29598500
W: www.redland.cl

Saint Gabriel's School
Avda Fco Bilbao 3070, Providencia, Santiago
DP Coordinator Laura Schiaffino
Languages Spanish
T: +56 22 462 5400
W: www.sangabriel.cl

SANTIAGO COLLEGE
Av. Camino Los Trapenses 4007, Lo Barnechea, Santiago
DP Coordinator Gustavo Paez
MYP Coordinator Angel Girano
PYP Coordinator Mónika Naranjo
Languages Spanish, English
T: +56 2 27338800
E: master@scollege.cl
W: www.scollege.cl/index.php/es/
See full details on page 542

St John's School
Fundo el Venado, San Pedro de la Paz, Concepción
DP Coordinator Gloria Soledad Guerrero Pastene
MYP Coordinator Melissa Vidal-MacKay
PYP Coordinator Alexandra Krumm
Languages English, Spanish
T: +56 41 2466440
W: www.stjohns.cl

St Margaret's British School For Girls
Casilla 392, Viña del Mar, Quinta Región
DP Coordinator Andrea Villalobos Danessi
Languages Spanish
T: +56 32 245 1700
W: www.stmargarets.cl

St Paul's School
Merced Oriente 54, Viña del Mar, Casilla 347
PYP Coordinator Mónica Pavez von Martens
Languages English, Spanish
T: (56 32) 314 2200
W: www.stpaul.cl

The Antofagasta British School
Pedro León Gallo 723, Antofagasta
DP Coordinator Cristian Daniel Retamales
MYP Coordinator Javier Silva
PYP Coordinator Gonzalo Carrasco
Languages English, Spanish
T: +56 55 598930
W: 2019.abs.school

The British School – Punta Arenas
Waldo Seguel 454, Punta Arenas
DP Coordinator José Antonio Vergara Rodríguez
MYP Coordinator Carolyn Rayment Mimica
PYP Coordinator Carolina Rees King
Languages Spanish, English
T: +56 61 2 22 33 81
W: www.britishschool.cl

The Mayflower School
Avda Las Condes 12 167, Las Condes, Santiago 668 2347
DP Coordinator Andrea Edwards Neut
PYP Coordinator Constanza Postigo Gaete
Languages Spanish
T: +56 22 3523100
W: www.mayflower.cl

Wenlock School
Casilla 27169, Correo 27, Santiago
DP Coordinator Marta Poblete
Languages Spanish
T: +56 223631803
W: www.wenlock.cl

COLOMBIA

Aspaen Gimnasio Iragua
Av. Calle 170, No. 76-55, Barrio San José de Bavaria, Bogotá, D.C.
DP Coordinator Yamid Guerra Pedroza
Languages Spanish
T: +57 (1) 667 95 00
W: www.iragua.edu.co

British International School
Apartado Aéreo 4368, Barranquilla, Atlántico
DP Coordinator Jose Donado Coronell
MYP Coordinator Guisella Pilonieta
Languages English
T: +57 (5) 359 92 43
W: www.britishschool.edu.co

Buckingham School
Cra 52 No 214 – 55, Bogotá, D.C.
DP Coordinator Aramis Vega arias
MYP Coordinator Elena Rokhas
PYP Coordinator Julieta Galeano León
Languages English, Spanish
T: +57 (1) 676 08 12
W: www.colegiobuckingham.edu.co

CIEDI – Colegio Internacional de Educación Integral
Km 3 vía Suba-Cota, Bogotá, D.C.
DP Coordinator Jorge Eduardo Baquero Cañas
MYP Coordinator Ernesto Campos
PYP Coordinator Mark Gaylor
Languages Spanish, English
T: +57 (1) 683 06 04
W: www.ciedi.edu.co

Colegio Abraham Lincoln
Av. Calle 170 # 65 31, Bogotá, D.C.
DP Coordinator Glenda Liliana Buitrago Ramirez
Languages Spanish
T: +57 (1) 742 31 66
W: www.abrahamlincoln.edu.co

Colegio Albania
Calle 15 3-00, Campamento de Mushaisa, Cerrejón La Mina, La Guajira
DP Coordinator Juan Carlos Tarazona Bautista
MYP Coordinator Juan Carlos Tarazona Bautista
PYP Coordinator Rubys Chinchia
Languages English, Spanish
T: +57 (5) 350 56 48
W: www.colegioalbania.edu.co

Colegio Alemán
Autopista al Mar poste 89 Electricaribe, Baranquilla, Atlántico
DP Coordinator Heidys María Navarro Escorcia
Languages Spanish
T: +57 (5) 359 85 20
W: www.colegioaleman.edu.co

Colegio Alemán Medellin
Cra 61 No 34 – 62, Itagüi, Antioquia
DP Coordinator Jaime Alonso López García
Languages Spanish
T: +57 (4) 281 88 11
W: www.colegioalemanmedellin.edu.co

Colegio Anglo-Colombiano
Apartado Aéreo 253393, Avenida 19 N° 152A-48, Santa Fé, Bogotá, D.C.
DP Coordinator Camila Rueda
MYP Coordinator Rusbel Martinez Rodriguez
PYP Coordinator Christianne Cowie
Languages English, Spanish
T: +57 (1) 259 57 00
W: www.anglocolombiano.edu.co

Colegio Británico – The British School
Call 18 # 142-255 (Esquina), La Viga, Pance, Cali, Valle del Cauca
DP Coordinator Edilson Sánchez Buitrago
Languages Spanish
T: +57 (2) 555 75 45
W: www.thebritishschoolcali.edu.co

Colegio Británico de Cartagena
Anillo Vial Km. 12, Cartagena, Bolívar 130001
DP Coordinator Adam Mcconnaughhay
Languages English, Spanish
T: +57 5 693 0982 83 84
W: www.colbritanico.edu.co/newcbc

Colegio Colombo Británico
Avenida La Maria 69 Pance, Pance, Cali, Valle del Cauca
DP Coordinator Juan Galindo Morales
MYP Coordinator Eleanor Alicia Cosh Lacouture
PYP Coordinator Claudia Fayad
Languages English, Spanish
T: +57 (2) 555 53 85
W: www.colombobritanico.edu.co

Colegio Colombo Gales
Avenida Guaymaral, Costado sur Aeropuerto, Bogotá, D.C.
DP Coordinator Nidia Elvira Gallego Vargas
Languages Spanish
T: +57 (1) 668 49 10
W: www.colegiocolombogales.edu.co

Colegio de Cambridge (Cambridge International School)
Vereda La Aurora, Municipio La Calera, Bogotá, D.C.
DP Coordinator Claudia Patricia Torres Bojacá
Languages Spanish
T: +57 (1) 593 18 90
W: www.colegiocambridge.edu.co

Colegio de Inglaterra – The English School
Calle 170 #15-68, Bogotá, D.C.
DP Coordinator Adam James Bennett
MYP Coordinator Lizbeth Santana
PYP Coordinator Kristine Ertl
Languages English, Spanish
T: +57 (1) 676 77 00
W: www.englishschool.edu.co

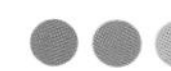

Colegio El Minuto de Dios Siglo XXI
Transversal 74 No 81 C – 05, Bogotá, D.C.
DP Coordinator William Rincón Mesa
Languages Spanish
T: +57 (1) 508 22 30
W: colegiosminutodedios.edu.co/sigloxxi

Colegio Gran Bretaña
Carrera 51 No 215-20, Bogotá, D.C.
DP Coordinator Gonzalo Serna Dimas
Languages English
T: +57 (1) 676 03 91
W: www.cgb.edu.co

Colegio Internacional Los Cañaverales
Carrera 29 No 10-500, Arroyohonfo, Vía Dapa Km 1 Yumbo, Yumbo, Valle del Cauca
DP Coordinator Carolina Avendaño Rodríguez
Languages English
T: +57 (2) 658 28 18
W: www.canaverales.edu.co

Colegio Los Tréboles
Vereda cerca de Piedra, Finca Santa Elena, Chía, Cundinamarca
DP Coordinator Clara Inés Díaz Rodríguez
Languages English, Spanish
T: +57 (1) 862 48 30
W: www.clt.edu.co

Colegio Mayor de los Andes
Kilómetro 3 vía Chía, Cajicá, Cundinamarca
DP Coordinator Adelina Nuñez Rojas
Languages Spanish
T: +57 (1) 866 29 56
W: www.colegiomayordelosandes.edu.co

Colegio Nueva Inglaterra (New England School)
Calle 218, No. 50-60, Bogotá, D.C.
DP Coordinator Natalia Castillo Castillo
Languages Spanish
T: +57 (1) 676 07 88
W: www.colegionuevainglaterra.edu.co

Colegio Nueva York
Calle 227 # 49-64 Urbanización el Jardín, Bogotá, D.C.
DP Coordinator Walter Mosquera
Languages English
T: +57 (1) 668 48 90
W: www.colegionuevayork.edu.co

Colegio San Viator – Sede Bogotá
Autopista Norte 209-51, Bogotá, D.C.
DP Coordinator Claudia Montaño
MYP Coordinator Jorge Rojas Luque
PYP Coordinator Diego Córdoba Prieto
Languages English
T: +57 (1) 676 09 97
W: www.sanviator.edu.co

Colegio San Viator – Sede Tunja
Av Universitaria 62 – 100, Tunja, Boyacá
DP Coordinator Fredy Hernando Contreras Moreno
Languages English, Spanish
W: www.sanviatortunja.edu.co

Colegio Tilatá
Kilómetro 9 vía La Calera, Bogotá, D.C.
DP Coordinator Paulo Lopez-Orellana
MYP Coordinator Diana Olivos Suarez
PYP Coordinator Marcela Castañeda
Languages English, Spanish
T: +57 (1) 592 14 14
W: www.colegiotilata.edu.co

Deutsche Schule – Cali / Kolumbien
Avenida Gualí N° 31, Barrio Ciudad Jardín, Cali, Valle del Cauca
DP Coordinator Carlos Rojas Padilla
Languages German, Spanish
T: +57 (2) 685 89 00
W: www.dscali.edu.co

Fundación Gimnasio Los Portales
Calle 212 No. 77- 20, Bogotá, D.C.
DP Coordinator Juan Pulido
MYP Coordinator Alirio Sneider Saavedra
PYP Coordinator Caroll Marulanda Guzmán
Languages English, Spanish
T: +57 (1) 676 40 55
W: www.losportales.edu.co

Fundación Nuevo Marymount
Calle 169B, No 74A-02, Bogotá, D.C.
DP Coordinator Liliana Manzanera
Languages English
T: +57 (1) 669 90 77
W: www.marymountschool.edu.co

Gimnasio Británico
Calle 21 No 9A-58, Avenida Chilacos, Chía, Cundinamarca
DP Coordinator Gabriel Alfredo Piraquive García
Languages English, Spanish, French
T: +57 (1) 861 50 84
W: www.gimnasio-britanico.edu.co

Gimnasio Campestre Los Cerezos
Vereda Canelón, Cajicá, Cundinamarca
DP Coordinator Marcia Malpica Ortiz
PYP Coordinator Ingrid Mogollón
Languages Spanish
T: +57 866 26 79
W: www.gimnasioloscerezos.edu.co

Gimnasio Campestre San Rafael
Sede Campestre, Km 6 vía Siberia, Tenjo, Cundinamarca
DP Coordinator Juan Antonio Alonso de Juan
Languages Spanish
T: +57 593 30 40
W: colegiosminutodedios.edu.co/sanrafael

Gimnasio de Los Cerros
Calle 119 N° 0-68, Usaquén, Santa Fé, Bogotá, D.C.
DP Coordinator Jorge Arango
Languages Spanish
T: +57 (1) 657 60 00
W: www.loscerros.edu.co

Gimnasio del Norte
Calle 207 N° 70 – 50, Bogotá, D.C.
DP Coordinator Mario Edwin Rueda Acosta
MYP Coordinator Adriana Rodríguez
PYP Coordinator Berta Gómez
Languages Spanish, English
T: +57 (1) 668 39 39
W: www.gimnasiodelnorte.edu.co

Gimnasio El Hontanar
Cra. 76 No. 150-26, Bogotá, D.C.
DP Coordinator Jaime Achury
Languages English, Spanish
T: +57 (1) 681 52 87
W: www.gimnasiohontanar.edu.co

Gimnasio Femenino
K7 #128-40, Bogotá, D.C.
DP Coordinator Fernando Rueda
MYP Coordinator Jimmy Pinilla Castillo
PYP Coordinator Gisela Toro López
Languages Spanish, English
T: +57 (1) 657 84 20
W: www.gimnasiofemenino.edu.co

Gimnasio Los Alcázares
Calle 63 Sur No 41-05 Sabaneta, Medellín, Antioquia
DP Coordinator Carlos Mejía
Languages Spanish
T: +57 (4) 305 40 00
W: www.alcazares.edu.co

Gimnasio Vermont
Cl 195 No 54-75, Bogotá, D.C.
DP Coordinator Claudia Aguirre
Languages Spanish
T: +57 (1) 674 80 70
W: www.gimnasiovermont.edu.co

International Berckley School
Km 5 – Vía al Mar, Poste 115, Barranquilla, Atlántico
DP Coordinator Sweney Giraldo
Languages Spanish
T: +575 354 81 31
W: ibs.edu.co

Jardín Infantil Tía Nora y Liceo Los Alpes
Av 8 Norte, No. 66-05 Urbanización Menga, Cali, Valle del Cauca
DP Coordinator Octavio Martínez
MYP Coordinator Ximena Rubio
PYP Coordinator Nini Johanna Ruiz Jaramillo
Languages Spanish, English
T: +57 (2) 665 41 20
W: www.jardintianorayliceolosalpes.edu.co

Knightsbridge Schools International Bogota
Calle 221 No 115-51, Bogotá, D.C.
DP Coordinator Deyanira Vargas Prieto
PYP Coordinator Andrea Roa
Languages English, Spanish
T: +57 (1) 676 29 02
W: www.ksi-bogota.com

Liceo Pino Verde
Vereda Los Planes kilometro, 5 Vía Cerritos Entrada 16, El Tigre, Pereira, Risaralda
DP Coordinator Rosa Damian Mesa
Languages English
T: +57 (6) 313 26 68
W: www.liceopinoverde.edu.co

New Cambridge School (Colegio Nuevo Cambridge)
Calle 32 N°22-140, Floridablanca, Bucaramanga, Santander
DP Coordinator Lia Buzeta
Languages English, Spanish
T: +57 (7) 638 61 52
W: cambridge.edu.co

Nuevo Gimnasio School
Kilometro 1 Autopista, Villavicencio, Meta
DP Coordinator Orlando Aguirre Urrutia
Languages English, Spanish
T: +57 310 801 52 83
W: www.nuevogimnasioschool.edu.co

The Victoria School
Calle 215 N° 50-60, Bogotá, D.C.
DP Coordinator María Bernal Baracaldo
MYP Coordinator Maria del Pilar Robles
PYP Coordinator Edna Esperanza Marin Steevens
Languages English, Spanish
T: +57 (1) 676 15 03
W: www.tvs.edu.co

Vermont School Medellín
Avenida Las Palmas Indiana Mall Km. 2 Vía La Fe, El Retiro, Antioquia
DP Coordinator Gerardo Franco
Languages English, Spanish
T: +57 (4) 520 60 60
W: vermontmedellin.edu.co

COSTA RICA

Academia Teocali
2.5 Km Norte de la Entrada Principal de Liberia, Carretera Interamericana Norte, Liberia, Guanacaste
DP Coordinator Jonathan Zuñiga Arrieta
Languages English
T: +506 2666 8780
W: www.academiateocali.ed.cr

Anglo American School
La Unión, 1 Km al norte de Sub Estación Electríca del ICE, Provincia de Cartago, Tres Rios, San Jose
DP Coordinator Ivannia Brenes Flores
Languages Spanish
T: +506 2279 2626
W: anglo.cr

Centro Educativo Futuro Verde
1 km este del Banco Nacional, Cóbano, Puntarenas 60111
DP Coordinator Stuart Millar
Languages English, Spanish
T: +506 2642 0291
W: www.futuro-verde.org

Centro Educativo Nueva Generacion
Sn Rafael de Heredia Del parqu 1 km al norte, Heredia 24-3015
DP Coordinator Nataly Campos
Languages English
T: +506 2237 8927
W: nuevageneracion.ed.cr/web

Colegio Bilingüe de Palmares
50 Metros sur Banco Popular, Palmares, Alajuela 215-4300
DP Coordinator Greivin Calderón Rodríguez
Languages Spanish
T: +506 2452 0157

Colegio de Bagaces
Contiguo al Gimnasio Municipal, Bag aces, Guanacaste
DP Coordinator Lelia Pineda Laguna
Languages Spanish
T: 506 2671 1116

Colegio Internacional SEK Costa Rica
Cipreses de Curridabat, San José 963 2050
DP Coordinator Geovanny Cordero Gutiérrez
Languages English, Spanish
T: +506 2 272 5464
W: www.sekcostarica.com

Colegio Los Ángeles
Calle Luisa, San José
DP Coordinator Carlos Darío Quirós Morales
Languages English, Spanish
T: +506 2232 0122
W: www.colegiolosangeles.ed.cr

Colegio Miravalle
800m al sur de la esquina sureste de los Tribunales de Justicia, Cartago
DP Coordinator Isaac Calvo Jiménez
Languages English, Spanish
T: +506 2552 7378
W: colegiomiravalle.com

Del Mar Academy
P.O. Box: 130, Nosara, Nicoya, Guanacaste 5233
DP Coordinator Genevieve Sehr
Languages English
T: +506 2682 1211
W: www.delmaracademy.com

European School
Heredia, San Pablo, P.O. Box: 177, Heredia
DP Coordinator Karen A Bye
Languages English
T: +506 2261 0717
W: www.europeanschool.com

Franz Liszt Schule
800 metros al sur de la gasolinera, Hermanos Montes a mano izq, Santa Ana, San José 10901
DP Coordinator Katelyn Tocci
Languages English, German
T: +506 2203 8128
W: www.fls.ed.cr

Golden Valley School
Del Lubricentro San Francisco 800 mts. Suroeste, Portones azules grandes a mano derecha, San Isidro, Heredia C.P. 40604
DP Coordinator Carlos Vega
Languages English, Spanish
T: +506 2268 9114
W: www.goldenvalleyschool.com

Instituto Dr. Jaim Weizman
100 norte, 100 oeste Compañía Nacional de Fuerza y Luz, Carretera Anonos, Mata Redonda, San José 4114-100
DP Coordinator Maria Gabriela Alfaro
Languages English, Spanish
T: +506 2220 1050

Instituto de Educación Dr. Clodomiro Picado Twight
De la Universidad de Costa Rica, Sede del Atlántico 150 metros al oeste, Turrialba, Cartago
DP Coordinator Jesús Alonso Quirós Paniagua
Languages Spanish
T: +506 25560025

International Christian School
San Miguel de Santo Domingo, Heredia
DP Coordinator Priscilla Diaz
Languages English, Spanish
T: +506 22411445
W: www.icscostarica.org

Iribó School
Del restaurante la casa de Doña, Lela 800 metros al sur, Curridabat, San José 662-2050 S
DP Coordinator Beatriz Vinueza
Languages Spanish
T: +506 4000 8989
W: iribo.org/site/

La Paz Community School
500 metros sur de la ferreteria, Buenaventura, Flamingo, Guanacaste 50309
DP Coordinator Martha Ortega
Languages English
T: +506 2654 4532
W: www.lapazschool.org

Liceo de Cariari
1Km al Norte de la Agencia del Banco Nacional de Costa Rica, Mano izquierda, carretera a Semillero, Pococi, Limón 70205
DP Coordinator Edgar Ruiz Contreras
Languages Spanish
T: +506 27677180

Liceo de Costa Rica
Calle 9, Avenida 18 y 20, San José
DP Coordinator Lucas Peraza Orellana
Languages Spanish
T: +506 221 3792

Liceo de Cot
100 mts norte y 500 este de Palí de Cot, Cot, Oreamuno, Cartago 30702
DP Coordinator Leonel Castro Rodríguez
Languages Spanish
T: +506 2536 6509
W: www.liceodecot.com

Liceo de Miramar
Costado Oeste del Cementerio Municipal, Miramar de Montes de Oro, Puntarenas 6-01-04
DP Coordinator Dilana Ramirez
T: +506 26 39 90 69
W: liceomiramar.com

Liceo de Moravia
San Rafael de Moravia, San José
DP Coordinator Lesly Carolina Ramírez Peña
Languages English
T: +506 22351336

Liceo de Poás
500 m Norte del Templo Católico, de San Pedro de Poás, Alajuela 24059
DP Coordinator José Francisco Víquez Castro
Languages Spanish
T: +506 2448 50 27
W: www.liceodepoas.ed.cr

Liceo de Puriscal
Costado oeste del nuevo, Templo Católico, Santiago de Puriscal, San José 214-6000
DP Coordinator Sally Sánchez Jiménez
Languages Spanish
T: +506 2416 5424 /6163
W: www.liceodepuriscal.ed.cr

Liceo de Tarrazú
Carretera a San Pablo de León Cortés, Barrio Santa Cecilia,, 200 metros este de Coopesantos R. L., San Marcos de Tarrazú, San José 8055
DP Coordinator Leonardo Vinicio Fonseca Hernández
Languages English
T: +506 25 46 60 12
W: tarrazu.edupage8.org

Liceo de Villarreal
200 metros Sur del centro de salud de Villarreal, Santa Cruz, Villarreal, Guanacaste 50309
DP Coordinator Siviany Piña Soto
Languages Spanish
T: +506 26530716

Liceo Gregorio José Ramirez Castro
200 m norte del plantel de MOPT, Montecillos de Alajuela, Alajuela
DP Coordinator Elenilzon Arroyo Bolaños
Languages Spanish
T: +506 2430 02 72
W: colegiogregoriojoseramirez.jimdo.com

Liceo Nuevo de Limón
Barrio La Colina, Contiguo a la Universidad de Costa Rica, Limón
DP Coordinator Andra Joyce Edwards Loban
Languages Spanish
T: +506 2758 09 80

Liceo Pacífico Sur
Principal hacia la Municipalidad de Osa, Cortés, Puntarenas
DP Coordinator Zaida Porras Santamaría
Languages Spanish

Liceo San Carlos
1 kilómetro al norte del parque de Ciudad Quesada, Quesada, Alajuela 21001
DP Coordinator Danny Gaitán Rodríguez
Languages English
T: +506 2460 0332

Liceo Santo Domingo
De la Clínica Dr. Hugo Fonseca, 150 Norte, San Vicente de Santo Domingo, Heredia 40302
DP Coordinator Osvaldo Molina Zamora
T: +506 2244 9549
W: www.liceosantodomingo.ed.cr

Liceo Sinaí
100 m E, de la Universidad Nacional, Sede Regional Brunca, San Isidro, Pérez Zeledón, San José
DP Coordinator Xédric Ureña Carvajal
Languages Spanish
T: +506 2770 66 69
W: www.liceosinai.com

Lighthouse International School
1 km north of the Guachipelin Tunnel, Escazú, San José 29028
DP Coordinator Amy Mishoe-Davenport
Languages English
T: +506 2215 2393
W: www.lis.ed.cr

Lincoln School
Barrio Socorro, Santo Domingo de Heredia
DP Coordinator Tucker Barrows
Languages English
T: +506 2247 6600
W: www.lincoln.ed.cr

Marian Baker School
PO Box 4269-1000, San José 1000
DP Coordinator Carolina Vargas
Languages English, Spanish
T: +506 2273 0024
W: www.mbs.ed.cr

Methodist School of Costa Rica
Sabanilla, Montes de Oca, San José 11502
DP Coordinator Guillermo Fernandez
Languages English, Spanish
T: +506 2280 1230
W: www.metodista.ed.cr

Pan-American School
632-4005 San Antonio de Belen, Heredia
DP Coordinator Henry Gutierrez
MYP Coordinator Henry Gutierrez
PYP Coordinator Andrea Barrantes
Languages English, Spanish
T: +506 2293 7393
W: www.panam.ed.cr

Saint Gregory School
San Juan de La Unión, Cartago
DP Coordinator Gabriela Leiva
Languages English, Spanish
T: +1 506 2279 4444
W: www.saintgregory.cr

Saint Mary School
Apartado 1471, Escazu 1250, San José ESCAZÚ 1250
DP Coordinator Carlos Mauricio Jurado Fernandez
Languages Spanish
T: +506 2215 2133
W: www.saintmary.ed.cr

St. Jude School
1.5 Kilometros al Oeste de Davivienda, Santa Ana, San José 488-6150
DP Coordinator Paula Forero
Languages Spanish
T: +506 2203 6474
W: www.stjude.ed.cr

The Blue Valley School
Apartado 1784-1250, Escazú, San José
DP Coordinator Patricia Prats
Languages English
T: +50 6 2215 2204
W: www.bluevalley.ed.cr

The British School of Costa Rica
PO Box 8184, San José 1000
DP Coordinator Sundey Christensen
Languages English
T: +506 2220 0131
W: www.thebritishschoolofcostarica.com

UWC Costa Rica
De la esquina sureste de la Iglesia Católica, 400m al norte, Santa Ana, San José 10901
DP Coordinator Ben Fugill
Languages Spanish, English
T: +506 22825609
W: www.uwccostarica.org

Yorkín School
800 metros sur y 200 metros este de la casa de Doña Lela, Lomas de Ayarco Sur, Curridabat, San José 11801
DP Coordinator Harold Molina Venegas
Languages Spanish
T: +506 4000 8900
W: yorkin.org/site

CURAÇAO

International School of Curaçao
PO Box 3090, Koninginnelaan z/n, Emmastad
DP Coordinator Suhasini Iyengar
Languages English
T: +599 9 737 3633
W: www.isc.cw

DOMINICAN REPUBLIC

Babeque Secundaria
Roberto Pastoriza #329, Ens. Naco, Distrito Nacional, Santo Domingo 10124
DP Coordinator Julissa Gomez
Languages Spanish
T: +1 809 567 9647
W: babequesecundaria.edu.do

Saint George School
C/ Porfirio Herrera #6, Ens. Piantini, Santo Domingo
DP Coordinator Rhayza Baptista de Hurtado
Languages English, Spanish
T: +1 809 562 5262
W: www.stgeorge.do

DUTCH CARIBBEAN

St Dominic High School
LB Scot Road # 209, South Reward, St Maarten
DP Coordinator Marie Richardson
Languages English
T: +1 721 548 4277
W: www.stdominichigh.com

ECUADOR

Academia Cotopaxi American International School
PO Box 17-11-6510, Quito, Pichincha
DP Coordinator Brian Voeller
PYP Coordinator Chanda Pinsent
Languages English
T: +593 (0)2 382 3270
W: www.cotopaxi.k12.ec

Academia Naval Almirante Illingworth
Ave José Gómez Gault KM 8 1/2, Vía Daule, Guayaquil, Guayas
DP Coordinator Rolando Álvarez Beltrán
Languages Spanish
T: +593 (0)4 3703300
W: www.anai.edu.ec

Ángel Polibio Chaves
Avenida el Maestro y Augusto Zavala, Barrio 13 de abril, San Miguel, Bolívar EC 020550
DP Coordinator Jhony Velasco Velasco
Languages Spanish
T: +593 (0)3 2989035
W: www.apch.edu.ec

Cardenal Carlos María de la Torre
Panamericana Norte S/N y Sucre, El Quinche, Quito, Pichincha EC 170907
DP Coordinator Irina Parra Taboada
Languages Spanish
T: +593 (0)2 387125
W: www.cdlt.edu.ec

Centro Educativo La Moderna
Km 2,5 Vía a Samborondón, Guayaquil, Guayas
DP Coordinator Harold Sojos
Languages English, Spanish
T: +593 42830581
W: www.lamoderna.edu.ec

Centro Educativo Naciones Unidas
Samborondón Km. 1 detrás del C.C. La Piazza, Samborondón, Guayas EC 092301
PYP Coordinator Valeria Galarza Alvarado
Languages English, Spanish
T: +593 (0)4 6018560
W: www.cenu.edu.ec

Col. Experimental e Inst. Superior Pedagógico Juan Montalvo
Gilberto Gatto Sobral Oe7-261, y Andrés de Artieda, Quito, Pichincha EC 170150
DP Coordinator Rocío Rubio
Languages Spanish
T: +593 02 2235180 / 250480

Colegio 24 de Mayo
María Angélica Carrillo y Abascal, Quito, Pichincha EC 170150
DP Coordinator Aquiles Vicente Pozo Vaca
Languages English, Spanish
T: +593 0222 60238
W: www.its24demayo.edu.ec

Colegio Alemán Humboldt de Guayaquil
Ciudadela Los Ceibos, Dr. Héctor Romero 216 y Av. Dr. José M. García Moreno, Guayaquil, Guayas EC 090904
DP Coordinator Nataniela Barreiro
Languages Spanish, German, English
T: +593 (0)4 2850260
W: www.cahgye.edu.ec

Colegio Alemán Stiehle Cuenca Ecuador
Autopista Cuenca – Azogues, Km 11,5, Sector Challuabamba, Cuenca, Azuay
DP Coordinator Susanna Wehner
Languages Spanish
T: +593 (0)7 4075646
W: www.casc.edu.ec

Colegio Americano De Guayaquil
Direccion General, Casilla 3304, Guayaquil, Guayas
DP Coordinator Whymper León Kuffó
Languages Spanish, English
T: +593 (0)4 3082 020
W: www.colegioamericano.edu.ec

Colegio Americano de Quito
Casilla 17-01-157, Quito, Pichincha
DP Coordinator David Weaver
MYP Coordinator Kara Latourell
PYP Coordinator Estela Proaño
Languages English
T: +593 (0)2 3976 300
W: www.fcaq.k12.ec

Colegio Bachillerato Machala
Avenida 25 de Junio y Edgar Córdova Polo, Machala, El Oro
DP Coordinator Laura Campoverde Romero
Languages Spanish
T: +593 (0)7 2935098
W: www.unidadmachala.tk

Colegio Balandra Cruz del Sur
Perimeter Road, The Prosperina, Guayaquil, Guayas
DP Coordinator Margarita Guillén Jiménez
Languages Spanish
T: +593 (0)4 285 0020
W: www.balandra.edu.ec

Colegio Becquerel
Tulipanes E12-50 y Los Rosales, Quito, Pichincha
DP Coordinator Ximena Del Pozo Espinosa
Languages Spanish
T: +593 (0)2 2257896
W: www.becquerel.edu.ec

Colegio Cap Edmundo Chiriboga
Av 9 de Octubre y Garcia Moreno, Riobamba, Chimborazo
DP Coordinator Ricardo Giovani Robles Rodríguez
Languages Spanish
T: +593 (0)3 295 3406

Colegio Católico José Engling
Calle Juan Montalvo s/n, Barrio La Dolorosa, Tumbaco, Quito, Pichincha EC 17172010
DP Coordinator Ana Cristina Sevilla
Languages English, Spanish
T: +593 (0)2 237 4329
W: www.jengling.org

Colegio de Bachillerato 27 de Febrero
Pablo Palacio y Kennedy, Loja
DP Coordinator Johnny Patricia Carrion Cabrera
Languages Spanish
T: +593 (0)7 2546370

Colegio de Bachillerato 8 de Noviembre
Calle Juan José Loayza y Segundo Figueroa, Piñas, El Oro EC 071050
DP Coordinator César Urgilés Paredes
Languages Spanish
T: +593 (0)7 2976015
W: www.ochodenoviembre.edu.ec

Colegio de Bachillerato Atacames
Via a Sua Entrada a la Unión de Atacames, Atacames, Esmeraldas
DP Coordinator Jackeline Salas Luna
Languages English
T: +593 (0)6 2731400
W: www.colegioatacames_cnta.edu

Colegio de Bachillerato Fiscal 5 de Agosto
Calle Simón Plata Torres, La Propicia N° 1, junto al Comando de la Policia Nacio+, Esmeraldas EC 080150
DP Coordinator Luisa Mercedes Mosquera Torres
Languages Spanish
T: +593 (0)6 2700593

Colegio de Bachillerato Limón
Ave. 12 de Diciembre, General Plaza, Limón Indanza, Morona Santiago EC 140351
DP Coordinator Enrique Guillermo Chalan Cabrera
Languages Spanish

Colegio de Bachillerato Macas
Hernando de Benavente, y Pedro Noguera, Macas, Morona Santiago
DP Coordinator Juan Quezada Orellana
Languages Spanish
T: +593 (0)7 2700214

Colegio de Bachillerato Manuela Garaicoa de Calderón
Av. 24 de Mayo y Camino al Valle, Cuenca, Azuay
DP Coordinator Nohemi Nauta
Languages Spanish
T: +593 (0)7 4096142

Colegio de Bachillerato Natalia Jarrín
Av. Natalia Jarrin N, 1201 y Vivar, Cayambe, Pichincha EC 170202
DP Coordinator Gonzalo Eduardo Cárdenas Arciniega
Languages Spanish
T: +593 (0)2 2360213
W: www.nataliajarrin.edu.ec

Colegio de Bachillerato 'Nelson Isauro Torres'
Av. Luis Cordero S/V Vía Ayora, Cayambe, Pichincha EC 170202
DP Coordinator Patricio Parra Escobar
Languages Spanish
T: +593 (0)2 2110243

Colegio de Bachillerato Ponce Enriquez
Av. 28 de Marzo y Bella Rica, Camilo Ponce Enriquez, Azuay EC 011550
DP Coordinator Jorge Luis Perez Apolo
Languages Spanish
T: +593 (0)7 2430004

Colegio de Bachillerato Técnico Rafael Vasconez Gómez
Calabí entre prolongación, de Cales Maria Zambrano y Zacarias Pérez, La Maná, Cotopaxi EC 050202
DP Coordinator Elva Rocio Tualumbo Valiente
Languages Spanish
T: +593 (0)3 2688112

Colegio de Bachillerato 'Victoria Vásconez Cuvi'
Felix Valencia 9-07 y Quito, Latacunga, Cotopaxi EC 050150
DP Coordinator Luis Ocaña Freire
Languages Spanish
T: +593 (0)3 2812 566

Colegio El Triunfo
Av. 8 de Abril y Asaad Bucaram (Esquina), El Triunfo, Guayas EC 090950
DP Coordinator Dairy Leones Stopper
Languages Spanish
T: +593 (0)4 2010050

Colegio Experimental Británico Internacional
Amagasí del Inca, Calle de las Nueces E18-21, y Las Camelias, Quito, Pichincha
DP Coordinator María Brioso Augustin
MYP Coordinator Andrea Proaño
PYP Coordinator Gabriela Gonzalez
Languages English, Spanish
T: +593 (0)2 3261254
W: www.colegiobritanico.edu.ec

Colegio Experimental Luis Cordero
Ingapirca y Rafael Maria Garcia, Azoguez, Cañar
DP Coordinator Sonia Ortega Vázquez
Languages Spanish
T: +593 7224 0067
W: colegioluiscordero.edu.ec

Colegio Fiscal Dr. Eduardo Granja Garces
Via al Valle de la Virgen secto 18, Calles Chile y Azuay, Pedro Carbo, Guayas EC 091450
DP Coordinator Marcia Cecilia Caicedo Gavilanez
Languages Spanish
T: +593 04 2704203

Colegio Fiscal el Empalme
KM 1 Via Quevedo, El Empalme, Guayas
DP Coordinator Wilson Germán Triana Litardo
Languages English
T: +593 04 2963900
W: colegionacionalelempalme.net

Colegio Fiscal Eloy Alfaro
Av. Luis Tufiño s/n y María Tixilema, Quito, Pichincha
DP Coordinator Saur Giovanny Montenegro Ruiz
Languages Spanish
T: +593 02 2990945
W: www.remq.edu.ec

Colegio Fiscal Guayaquil
Calle Gomez Rendon 1403 y Machala, Guayaquil, Guayas
DP Coordinator Jenny Margot Díaz Mendoza
Languages Spanish
T: +395 04 2373607
W: www.itsguayaquil.org

Colegio Fiscal Guillermo Ordoñez Gómez
Av. Francisco Pizarro Vía a Ballenita, Santa Elena
DP Coordinator Daniel Díaz Arévalo
Languages Spanish
T: +593 02 940539

Colegio Fiscal Marcelino Maridueña
Coop. 24 de octubre solar 11 manzana 2, Marcelino Maridueña, Guayas
DP Coordinator Martha Eugenia Velez Sanchez
Languages Spanish
T: +593 42720180
W: sites.google.com/site/uemarcelinomariduena

Colegio Fiscal Mixto 'Dr Teodoro Alvarado Olea'
Cdla Miraflores, Calle 8va y Las Brisas, Guayaquil, Guayas
DP Coordinator Dalia Rosemary Mora Argüello
Languages Spanish
T: +593 42203776

Colegio Fiscal Mixto 'Ismael Pérez Pazmiño'
Alborada 3era Etapa Ave José, María Roura entre Alameda 2 y 3, Guayaquil, Guayas EC 005934
DP Coordinator Blanca Lidia Ortiz Moreno
Languages Spanish
T: +59 34 2644562

Colegio Fiscal Mixto 'La Libertad'
Ciudadela San Vicente-Avenida 30, E/Calles 28 y 29, Santa Elena, La Libertad, Santa Elena EC 00593
DP Coordinator Elena Gonzalez Guzman
Languages Spanish
T: +593 429 34 443

Colegio Fiscal Nicolás Jiménez
Calle Tobias Godoy, y Av. Capitan Geovanny Calles, Quito, Pichincha
DP Coordinator Mónica Patricia Ramírez Pazmiño
Languages Spanish
T: +593 02 2065723

Colegio Fiscal 'Nueve de Octubre'
Av Palmeras entre Bolivar y Avda 25 de Junio, Machala, El Oro
DP Coordinator Maria Georgina Lapo Moreno
Languages Spanish
T: +593 7 293 0356

Colegio Fiscal Provincia de Tungurahua
Sauces 2 MZ.F 74-75, Guayaquil, Guayas EC 090112
DP Coordinator Lucrecia Elizabeth Valencia Mendoza
Languages Spanish
T: +593 09 88903912
W: www.instungurahua.edu.ec

Colegio Fiscal Rashid Torbay
Km1 1/2Via al Morro, Diagonal al Hospital de Playas, General Villamil, Playas, Guayas EC 092150
DP Coordinator Ruddy Tomalá Cruz
Languages Spanish
T: +593 02 76430

Colegio Fiscal Técnico Agropecuario Galo Plaza Lasso
Km.49.5 via Guayaquil – Santa Lucia., Daule, Guayas EC 090601
DP Coordinator Mercedes Hidalgo Arevalo
Languages Spanish
T: +593 (0)4 2798799

Colegio Fiscal Técnico El Chaco
26 de mayo y 12 de febrero, El Chaco, Napo EC 150450
DP Coordinator Angel Benigno Ojeda
Languages English
T: +593 062329188

Colegio Fiscal Tecnico Industrial Ancón
Av. del Petrolero N° 634, San José de Ancón, Santa Elena
DP Coordinator Cesar Jorge Soledispa Baque
Languages English
T: +593 04 2906238
W: www.colegioancon.com

Colegio Fiscal Técnico Valdivia
Via Sinchal Km 1, Valdivia, Parroquia Manglaralto, Santa Elena EC 241754
DP Coordinator Sixto Manzano Poveda
Languages English
T: +593 04 2941849
W: colegiovaldivia.webnode.es

Colegio Fiscal Vicente Rocafuerte
Vélez 2203 Y Lizardo García, Guayaquil, Guayas
DP Coordinator Susana Jessica Olea Acuña
Languages English
T: +593 04 2451276
W: www.colegiovicenterocafuerte.edu.ec

Colegio Fiscomisional Sagrado Corazón
Casilla No 65, Esmeraldas
DP Coordinator Lucetty Narcisa Quiñónez Ortiz
Languages Spanish
T: +59 306 272 8756

Colegio Fiscomisional 'San José'
Calle Juan Montalvo y Misión Josefina, Tena, Napo
DP Coordinator Blanca Coello Guijarro
Languages Spanish
T: +593 06 288 6241

Colegio Internacional Rudolf Steiner
Calle Francisco Montalvo Nro 212, y Av Mariscal Sucre, (Av Occidental), Sector Cochabampa, Quito, Pichincha
DP Coordinator Fernando Rojas Aguilar
MYP Coordinator Clara Santillan
PYP Coordinator María Gordillo
Languages Spanish
T: +593 2244 3315
W: www.colegiorudolfsteiner.edu.ec

Colegio Internacional SEK Ecuador
De los Guayacanes N51-69 y Carmen Olmo Mancebo, San Isidro de El Inca, Quito, Pichincha
DP Coordinator Verónica Tobar
MYP Coordinator Marcelo Pérez
PYP Coordinator Teresa Piedra
Languages English, Spanish
T: +593 2 2401 896
W: www.sekquito.com

Colegio Internacional SEK Guayaquil
Vía Salinas Km. 20.5, Guayaquil, Guayas EC 11373
DP Coordinator Hoover Mora
PYP Coordinator Marjorie Ladines
Languages Spanish, English
T: +593 4 3904794
W: www.sekguayaquil.com

Colegio Internacional SEK Los Valles
Eloy Alfaro S8-48 y De los Rosales, San Juan de Cumbayá, Quito, Pichincha EC 1717933
DP Coordinator Thula Dávila Egüez
PYP Coordinator Paula Contreras Puebla
Languages Spanish
T: +593 2 3566220
W: www.seklosvalles.ec

Colegio Intisana
Avenida Occidental 5329, y Marcos Joffre, Quito, Pichincha
DP Coordinator Diego Astudillo Cervantes
Languages Spanish
T: +593 2 2440 128
W: www.intisana.com

Colegio Johannes Kepler
Av. Simón Bolívar s/n Vía a Nayón, Sector Bosque Protector Bellavista, Quito, Pichincha EC 170511
DP Coordinator Fernando Torres Usechi
Languages Spanish
T: +593 2 394 4180
W: www.jkepler.edu.ec

Colegio Los Pinos
Calle Agustín Zambrano entre Vicente Pajuelo y Tomás Chariove, Quito, Pichincha EC 170104
DP Coordinator Pilar Costa de Martínez
Languages Spanish
T: +593 2 246 3189
W: www.colegiolospinos.ec

Colegio Miguel Moreno Ordoñez de Cuenca
Adolfo Peralta y Daniel Fernandez de Cordova Esq., Cuenca C. Cantonal, Azuay EC 010150
DP Coordinator Sandra Catalina Matovelle Jara
Languages Spanish
T: +593 07 2854585
W: miguelmorenoo.tk

Colegio Municipal Experimental 'Sebastián de Benalcázar'
RECTORADO, Irlanda E10-77 y Av 6 de Diciembre, Apartado Postal 17-01-25-37, Quito, Pichincha
DP Coordinator Ramón Humberto Flores Pozo
Languages Spanish
T: +593 2 243 5313

Colegio Nacional 26 de Noviembre
Av. Honorato Márquez S/N, Zaruma, El Oro
DP Coordinator Vladimir Carchi Cuenca
Languages Spanish
T: +593 7 2972178
W: www.colegio26denoviembre.net

Colegio Nacional 'Adolfo Valarezo'
Calles Carlos Román, y Adolfo Valarezo, Loja EC 110150
DP Coordinator Ramiro Lucio Sanmartín Acaro
Languages Spanish
T: +593 072571003

Colegio Nacional Alejo Lascano
Cotopaxi y Olmedo, Jipijapa, Manabí
DP Coordinator Geoconda Julissa Mendoza Tobar
Languages Spanish
T: +593 05 2600388
W: www.conal.edu.ec

Colegio Nacional Andrés Bello
Avenida de la Prensa, N71-79 y Pablo Picasso, Quito, Pichincha EC 170314
DP Coordinator Marlene Shuguli
Languages Spanish
T: +593 02 2596719
W: www.andresbello.edu.ec

Colegio Nacional 'Camilo Gallegos Toledo'
Rosendo Alvear y Vicente Velez, Gualaquiza, Morona Santiago EC 140201
DP Coordinator Héctor Caldas Condoy
Languages English
T: +593 0727 80164

Colegio Nacional Chordeleg
Juan Bautista Cobos y Gabriel Espinoza, Chordeleg, Azuay
DP Coordinator Maria Mercedes Lazo Carpio
Languages Spanish
T: +593 07222 3520

Colegio Nacional 'Cinco de Junio'
Av. cultura Calle Luis Arboleda, 593, Manta, Manabí
DP Coordinator Rocío Sornoza Mera
Languages Spanish
T: +593 2620866

Colegio Nacional Ciudad de Cuenca
Calle del Sauco Entre, la Azulina y Los Cerezos, Cuenca C. Cantonal, Azuay EC 010150
DP Coordinator Jaime Jose
Languages Spanish
T: +593 074089648
W: www.ciudaddecuenca.com

Colegio Nacional Conocoto
Calle Julio moreno S5-77, y Rosario de Alcazar, Conocoto, Quito, Pichincha EC 170156
DP Coordinator Pablo Quelal
Languages Spanish
T: +593 (0)2 2348807

Colegio Nacional Dr. Emilio Uzcátegui
Diego Céspedes y Moro Moro s/n, Quito, Pichincha
DP Coordinator Gabriela Soledad Vinueza Muñoz
Languages Spanish
T: +593 (0)2 623325

Colegio Nacional El Angel
José Benigno Grijalva 0398 y Quiroga, El Angel, Carchi EC 040301
DP Coordinator Hernan Rodrigo Valencia Montenegro
Languages English
T: +593 0629 77143
W: www.cna.webprosistem.com

Colegio Nacional Experimental Amazonas
Lauro Guerrero s/n y Luis Iturralde, Quito, Pichincha EC 170111
DP Coordinator Pablo Villavicencio
Languages English
T: +593 22612736
W: www.colegioamazonas.edu.ec

Colegio Nacional Experimental Ambato
Ave Humberto Albornoz, S/N y Vargas Torres, Ambato, Tungurahu EC 18001
DP Coordinator Anita Elizabeth López Rodríguez
Languages Spanish
T: +593 3 282 1776

Colegio Nacional Experimental María Angélica Idrobo
Calle a S/N barrio San Enrique de Velasco - El Condado, Quito, Pichincha EC 170150
DP Coordinator Elena Pazos
Languages English
T: +593 3393 293

Colegio Nacional Experimental Montufar
Av. Napo S6-381 y Miguel Cárdenas, Quito, Pichincha EC 52003
DP Coordinator José Licto García
Languages Spanish
T: +593 (0)2 3131380
W: www.colegiomontufar.edu.ec

Colegio Nacional Experimental Salcedo
Manuel María Salgado, y Mejía S/N, Salcedo, Cotopaxi EC 050550
DP Coordinator Germania Vilcaguano
Languages Spanish
T: +593 032 726 000
W: colegiosalcedo.webnode.es

Colegio Nacional Galápagos
Puerto Ayora-Isla Santa Cruz, Galápagos
DP Coordinator Wilson Villacís Manzano
Languages Spanish
T: +593 (0)5 2527259

Colegio Nacional General Píntag
Mariscal Sucre S/N y Antisana, Píntag, Quito, Pichincha EC 170176
DP Coordinator Santiago Haro
Languages Spanish
T: +593 (0)2 383447
W: www.remq.edu.ec

Colegio Nacional Guayllabamba
Av. Simón Bolívar 216 y El Aguacate, Barrio La Merced, parroquia Guayllabamba, Quito, Pichincha EC 170209
DP Coordinator Luis Fernando Reimundo Caiza
Languages Spanish
T: +593 (0)2 368 346
W: www.colegioguayllabamba.com

Colegio Nacional Huaca
8 de Diciembre y Aurelio Sierra S/N, Huaca, Carchi
DP Coordinator Jairo Prado
Languages Spanish
T: +593 06 2973032
W: www.colegiohuaca.edu.ec

Colegio Nacional José Julián Andrade
Carrera Montúfar 07-08 y Pichincha, San Gabriel, Carchi
DP Coordinator Sandra Puga
Languages Spanish
T: +593 602290112

Colegio Nacional Luis Napoleón Dillón
Avenida 9 de Octubre, 1680 y Berlín, Quito, Pichincha EC 170147
DP Coordinator Carmen Saquinga Chuto
Languages Spanish
T: +593 02 2564005
W: www.itsedillon.edu.ec

Colegio Nacional Machachi
Calle Simón Bolívar 1080 y el Hogar, Machachi, Pichincha
DP Coordinator Elena Barba
Languages Spanish
T: +593 2 231 6615

Colegio Nacional Mejía
Vargas N 13-93 y Arenas, Quito, Pichincha EC 170151
DP Coordinator Luis Gonzalo Araque Suárez
Languages Spanish
T: +593 02 2562841
W: www.inmejia.edu.ec

Colegio Nacional Mixto El Playon
Av. 12 de Febrero, Barrio San Francisco Del Playon, El Playon, Sucumbios EC 210551
DP Coordinator Alfonso Fernando Cuarán Ibarra
Languages English, Spanish
T: +593 062348017

Colegio Nacional Olmedo
Av Metropolitana KM 1 1/2, vía a Manta, Manabí, Portoviejo
DP Coordinator Rosa Daide Margarita Moreira Vera
Languages Spanish
T: +593 5 2934 763
W: cnolmedo.blogspot.co.uk

Colegio Nacional Palora
Av Cumandá s/n, Pakora, Morona Santiago
DP Coordinator Iván Zumba
Languages Spanish

Colegio Nacional Primero de Abril
Calle Hnas Páez Oriente, Latacunga, Cotopaxi
DP Coordinator Teresa Jara
Languages Spanish
T: +593 3 2801610

Colegio Nacional San José
Parroquia Guaytacama Via Saquisili, Latacunga, Cotopaxi EC 050150
DP Coordinator Marina Amparito Silva Montero
Languages Spanish
T: +593 0326 90217

Colegio Nacional Santa Isabel
Avenida Rafael Galarza, Santa Isabel, Azuay EC 010850
DP Coordinator Doris Neira Naranjo
Languages Spanish
T: +593 07 2270142
W: colegiosantaisabel.edu.ec

Colegio Nacional Tabacundo
Gonzales Suarez 558, y Juan Montalvo, Tabacundo, Pichincha
DP Coordinator Cesar Toapanta
Languages Spanish
T: +593 02 2365096

Colegio Nacional Técnico Agropecuario '26 de Febrero'
Vía Interoceánica e India Pau, Paute, Azuay
DP Coordinator Efren Escandon
Languages English
T: +593 0722 50200

Colegio Nacional Velasco Ibarra
Calle 10 de Agosto y Av. Macas, Guamote, Chimborazo EC 060650
DP Coordinator Pedro Javier Gaibor Urgilés
Languages Spanish
T: +593 03 2916141
W: www.velasco.edu.ec

Colegio Nacional Veracruz
Km. 7 vía Puyo-Macas, Puyo, Pastaza
DP Coordinator Nancio Enrrique Ajila Gia
Languages Spanish
T: +593 02 785005

Colegio Pomasqui
Av. Manuel Córdova Galarza, N1-189 y Manuela Sáenz, Quito, Pichincha EC 170177
DP Coordinator Carmen Alicia Guañuna Minango
Languages Spanish
T: +593 02 2351072
W: www.cnp.edu.ec

Colegio Réplica Vicente Rocafuerte
Cdla. Socio Vivienda, Lomas de la Florida, Guayaquil, Guayas
DP Coordinator Diana del Pilar Arnao Meza
Languages Spanish
T: +593 04 2491356

Colegio Santiago de Guayaquil
Calle Manuel Lopera, N5-210 e Itchimbía, Quito, Pichincha
DP Coordinator Catalina Molina Romero
Languages Spanish
T: +593 02 2571340

Colegio Séneca
Calle Juan Díaz y Paseo de la Universidad # 20, Urb. Iñaquito Alto, Quito, Pichincha EC 170523
DP Coordinator Paola Jaramillo
T: +593 22 922 544
W: www.seneca.edu.ec

Colegio Stella Maris
Avenida 6 y Calle 14, Manta, Manabí
DP Coordinator Valeria Sandoval Santacruz
Languages Spanish
T: +593 5 2611352
W: smaris.edu.ec

Colegio Técnico 12 de Febrero
Avenida Los Fundadores y Calle D, La Joya De Los Sachas, Orellana EC 220350
DP Coordinator Edwin Wilfrido Mantilla Barragan
Languages Spanish
T: +593 06 2898206

Colegio Técnico Agropecuario Leonardo Murialdo
Av. Rocafuerte 461 y Cosanga, Archidona, Napo EC 150350
DP Coordinator Wilson Plutarco Altamirano Castillo
Languages Spanish
T: +593 06 2889240

Colegio Técnico Cascales
Avenida Quito y Loja, El Dorado De Cascales, Sucumbios EC 210250
DP Coordinator Julio Hernando Chica Andrade
Languages English, Spanish
T: +593 062800176
W: www.cascales.edu.ec

Colegio Técnico Fiscomisional Ecuador Amazónico
Av. Jorge Mosquera y Eduardo Mariño, El Pangui, Zamora-Chinchipe EC 190650
DP Coordinator Fanny Elizabeth Diaz Bautista
Languages Spanish
T: +593 07 2310123

Colegio Técnico Humanístico Experimental Quito
Pedro Gual E1-65 y Pedro de Puelles, Chimbacalle, Quito, Pichincha EC 170125
DP Coordinator Marco Gonzalez
Languages Spanish
T: +593 02 2644846
W: www.colegioquito.edu.ec

Colegio Técnico Industrial Zumba
Av. del Colegio y 10 de Agosto, Zumba, Zamora-Chinchipe EC 190250
DP Coordinator Javier Bustamante
Languages Spanish
T: +593 07 2308034

Colegio Técnico Nacional Carmen Mora de Encalada
Ochoa León y Jubones, Pasaje, El Oro EC 070903
DP Coordinator Isidro Romero Fajardo
Languages Spanish
T: +593 07 2912060
W: www.colegiocarmenmorapasaje.comyr.com

Colegio Técnico Sucre
Av. Teodoro Gomez de la Torre, S14-72 y Joaquin Gutierrez, Quito, Pichincha EC 170148
DP Coordinator Diana Tumbaco
Languages Spanish
T: +593 02 2672433

Colegio Zoila Ugarte de Landívar
Avenida Zoila Ugarte de Landivar via a Caluguro, Frente a la Ciudadela los Helechos, Santa Rosa, El Oro EC 071201
DP Coordinator Holger Manuel Morocho Suriaga
Languages Spanish
T: +593 07 2945240

EMDI School
EMDI sector B, Parroquia Alangasi, Valle de los Chilos, Quito, Pichincha
DP Coordinator Enrique Segovia
Languages English, Spanish
T: +593 2278 8652
W: www.emdischool.edu.ec/pags/inicio/inicio.html

Institución Educativa Fiscal Benito Juárez
Aushyris Oe 3-207 y Jacinto Collaguazo, La Magdalena, Quito, Pichincha
DP Coordinator Mercedes Carola Aulestia Vivas
Languages Spanish
T: +593 02 2659244

Institución Educativa Fiscal 'Miguel de Santiago'
Borbon S-29 y Albeto Spencer, Quito, Pichincha
DP Coordinator Juan Pila Martínez
Languages Spanish
T: +593 02 22634867
W: sites.google.com/site/ctims2011

Instituto Consejo Provincial de Pichincha
Avenida Ajavì Oe 4-154 y Cardenal de la Torre, Quito, Pichincha
DP Coordinator Maura Cevallos Taimal
Languages Spanish
T: +593 02 2680166

Instituto Superior Tecnológico Daniel Alvarez Burneo
Av. Daniel Álvarez 12-51, Y Orillas Del Zamora, Loja EC 110141
DP Coordinator Geovana Jacqueline Aizaga Merino
Languages Spanish
T: +593 072570530
W: www.istdab.edu.ec

Instituto Tecnológico Cinco de Junio
Pinllopata OE1-389 y Moraspungo, Quito, Pichincha
DP Coordinator Luis Ernesto Flores
Languages Spanish
T: +593 02 2648261

Instituto Tecnologico Fiscomisional 'Nuestra Señora del Rosario'
9 DE Octubre y Eugenio Espejo, Catamayo, Loja EC 110301
DP Coordinator Narciza Quesada
Languages English
T: +593 0726 77024
W: www.tecnologicorosarista.edu.ec

Instituto Tecnológico Superior – Central Técnico
Gaspar de Villarroel, E6-125 e Isla Seymour, Casilla, Quito, Pichincha EC 1701-3698
DP Coordinator Mónica Liliana Martínez Obando
Languages Spanish
T: +593 02 449044
W: www.centraltecnico.edu.ec

Instituto Tecnológico Superior Angel Polibio Chaves
Jhonson City y Sucre, Guaranda, Bolívar EC 020150
DP Coordinator Mirian Leonor Patiño Ayala
Languages English
T: +593 32982158

Instituto Tecnológico Superior Primero de Mayo
Av. Ivan Riofrio E/22 de Noviembre y 13 de Abril, Yantzaza, Zamora-Chinchipe EC 190550
DP Coordinator Enma Rosario Castillo Bermeo
Languages English
T: +593 0723 00165
W: itspm.edu.ec

Instituto Tecnológico Tulcán
Rafael Arellano, 1853 y García Moreno, Tulcán, Carchi EC 040102
DP Coordinator Patricio Romeo Terán Montenegro
Languages Spanish
T: +593 06 2980422
W: www.institutotulcan.edu.ec

ISM Academy Quito
San Miguel de Anagaes, Quito, Pichincha EC 170124
DP Coordinator Sandra Acosta
MYP Coordinator Janeth León Barriga
Languages Spanish
T: +593 2 2414 198
W: www.ism.edu.ec

ISM International Academy
Calle Unión 886 y Ave Geovanny Calle, Sector Calderon, Quito, Pichincha
DP Coordinator Julio Quinteros
MYP Coordinator Llania Castro
Languages English, Spanish
T: +593 2 282 0549
W: www.ism.edu.ec

Liceo José Ortega y Gasset
Calle de los Cipreses N64-332 y Manuel Ambrosi, Quito, Pichincha EC 170309
DP Coordinator Víctor Regalado Bolaños
Languages Spanish
T: +593 22482976
W: www.gasset.edu.ec

Logos Academy
Km 14.5 Via a la Costa, Guayaquil, Guayas
DP Coordinator Mariella Coral
Languages Spanish
T: +59 34 390 0125
W: www.logosacademy.edu.ec

Ludoteca Elementary & High School, Padre Victor Grados
Av Simón Bolívar y Camino de los Incas # 5-6, Nueva Vía Oriental, Quito, Pichincha
DP Coordinator Roberto Rojas
MYP Coordinator Amparo Albán
PYP Coordinator Gloria Rebeca Bedon Criollo
Languages English, Spanish
T: +593 2 268 8142
W: ludoteca.edu.ec

The British School Quito
Via Cununyacu, Km 2.5 Tumbaco, PO Box 17-21-52, Quito, Pichincha
DP Coordinator Stefan Karakashian
Languages English
T: +593 2 2 374 649
W: www.britishschoolquito.edu.ec

U.E. Fiscomisional Inmaculada Stella Maris
Calle Pinzón Artesano y Cormorán, Isla Isabela, Galápagos EC 200250
DP Coordinator Jéssica Isabel Zeballos Torres
Languages Spanish
T: +593 05 2529126

Unidad Educativa – 12 de Febrero
Avenida del Ejercito y Marcelo Reyes, Zamora-Chinchipe EC 190102
DP Coordinator Carlos Enrique Izquierdo Samaniego
Languages Spanish
T: +593 07 2605126

Unidad Educativa – Babahoyo
Av. Enrique Ponce Luque, Km. 1.5 Via a Jujan, Babahoyo, Los Ríos
DP Coordinator Juan Carlos Morante Centeno
Languages English, Spanish
T: +593 05 2732244
W: www.institutobabahoyo.edu.ec

Unidad Educativa – El Carmen
Calle 9 de Octubre y Libertad, El Carmen, Manabí
DP Coordinator Erwin Muñoz Cevallos
Languages Spanish
T: +539 02 660117

Unidad Educativa 13 de Octubre
Av. Humberto González Álava, Km. 1 vía a Tosagua, Calceta, Manabí
DP Coordinator Josè Luis Rendon Chavarria
Languages Spanish
T: +593 05 2685183

Unidad Educativa '17 de Julio'
José Nicolás Hidalgo S/N, y Alfredo Gómez Jaime, Ibarra, Imbabura EC 100150
DP Coordinator Rodrigo Tapia Cevallos
Languages English, Spanish
T: +593 03 2640688
W: www.lotaip17dejulio.zobyhost.com

Unidad Educativa 24 de Mayo
Calle Juan de Dios Aviles Zarate No. 100, Ciudadela Santa Rosa, Quevedo, Los Ríos
DP Coordinator Nelson Bismark Naranjo Zuñiga
Languages Spanish
T: +593 05 2763886
W: www.colegio24demayo.ec

Unidad Educativa Abelardo Moncayo
Correo Central Atuntaqui, Atuntaqui, Imbabura
DP Coordinator Edison Patricio Rios Daza
Languages English
T: +593 62906135
W: www.colegioamoncayo.edu.ec

Unidad Educativa Alberto Einstein
Av Diego Vásquez de Cepeda N77-157 y Alberto Einstein, Casilla Postal 17-11-5018, Quito, Pichincha
DP Coordinator Kyle Kopsick
MYP Coordinator Jorge Grijalva
PYP Coordinator Juan Diego Reyes Villalva
Languages Spanish, English
T: +593 2 393 2570
W: www.einstein.k12.ec

Unidad Educativa Antonio Peña Celi
Barrio Belén Alto, Loja
DP Coordinator Maria Angelina Orellana Aguilar
Languages Spanish
T: +593 7 255 2010
W: www.apc.edu.ec

Unidad Educativa Atahualpa
Calle El Tejar y Avenida, 22 de Enero, Ambato, Tungurahua
DP Coordinator Narcisa Gardenia Rosero Núñez
Languages English
T: +593 03 2855812
W: www.colegioatahualpaambato.edu.ec

Unidad Educativa Atenas
Calle Gabriel Roman y Av. Pedro Vasconez, Yacupamba, Izamba, Ambato, Tungurahua EC 180156
DP Coordinator Esmeralda Quintanilla
Languages English, Spanish
T: +593 3 285 4297
W: www.atenas.edu.ec

Unidad Educativa Bernardo Valdivieso
Av Eduardo Kingman y Catamayo, Loja EC 110150
DP Coordinator Etna Martínez
Languages Spanish
T: +593 07 2570395
W: www.bernardovaldivieso.edu.ec

Unidad Educativa Bilingüe Delta
Kilómetro 12.5 Vía Puntilla-Samborondón, Guayaquil, Guayas
DP Coordinator Monica Macchiavello
Languages English, Spanish
T: +593 4 251 1266
W: www.uedelta.k12.ec

Unidad Educativa Bilingüe EducaMundo
Km 12 Av. León Febres-Cordero, Urb. Villa Club, entre las etapas Aura y Doral, Guayaquil, Guayas
DP Coordinator Alberto Ulises Ottati Baquero
Languages English, Spanish
T: +593 3725860
W: www.educamundo.edu.ec

Unidad Educativa Bilingüe Mixta Sagrados Corazones
El Oro 1219 y Avenida Quito, Guayaquil, Guayas
DP Coordinator Neyla Mora Rosales
Languages Spanish
T: +593 04 2440087
W: www.sscc.edu.ec

Unidad Educativa Bilingüe Nueva Semilla
Barrio Centenario Calle D and Argüelles, Guayaquil, Guayas
DP Coordinator Carolina Aldaz
Languages English
T: +593 4 2441174
W: www.nuevasemilla.com.ec

Unidad Educativa Bilingüe Nuevo Mundo
Km 2.5 Vía a Samborondón, Guayaquil, Guayas
DP Coordinator Brenda Estefanía Ortega Aviles
MYP Coordinator Fernando Castro
Languages English, Spanish
T: +593 4 2 830 095
W: www.nuevomundo.k12.ec

Unidad Educativa 'Bolívar'
Sucre y Argentina S/N, Tulcan, Carchi EC 040102
DP Coordinator Ivan Ramiro Mafla Argoti
Languages Spanish
T: +539 062980327
W: www.institutobolivar.edu.ec

Unidad Educativa Calasanz
Avenida Orillas del Zamora, s/n e Isidro Ayora, Loja EC 110150
DP Coordinator Beatriz Eugenia Ramón Ochoa
Languages Spanish
T: +593 07 2613750
W: www.calasanzloja.edu.ec

Unidad Educativa Caluma
Calle Tiwinza 776 y Condor Mirador, Coangos, Caluma, Bolívar EC 020650
DP Coordinator Isabel Fajardo Moràn
Languages English, Spanish
T: +593 03 2974142
W: colegiocaluma.jimdo.com

Unidad Educativa Camilo Ponce Enriquez
De Los Fresnos N55-129, y Guayacanes, Quito, Pichincha EC 145363
DP Coordinator Ricardo Mejia Rosero
Languages Spanish
T: +593 02 2407297

Unidad Educativa Carlos Cisneros
México 756 y Avenida La Paz, Riobamba, Chimborazo
DP Coordinator Hernán Uquillas Gallardo
Languages Spanish
T: +593 3 2 961 331

Unidad Educativa 'César Antonio Mosquera'
Calle Juan Montalvo y El Oro, Julio Andrade, Carchi
DP Coordinator Luis Guerrero
Languages Spanish
T: +593 95 959 6403
W: colegio-cam.blogspot.com

Unidad Educativa Chillanes
Eloy Alfaro y Santa Rita, Chillanes, Bolívar EC 020250
DP Coordinator Luis Alberto Barragán Velasco
Languages Spanish
T: +593 03 2978207
W: www.cnch.edu.ec

Unidad Educativa Cristo Rey
Calle Cristo Rey entre Sucre y Baquerizo Moreno, Portoviejo, Manabí EC 13010014
DP Coordinator Carlos Orozco
Languages Spanish
T: +593 052632558
W: www.cristorey.edu.ec

Unidad Educativa Dayuma
Via Auca KM 40, Parroquia Dayuma, Cantón, Francisco De Orellana
DP Coordinator Hernan Rodrigo Castañera Peña
Languages Spanish
T: +593 06 2370197
W: www.colegiodayuma.edu.ec

Unidad Educativa del Milenio – Cacique Tumbalá
Zumbahua Centro: Avenida Quilotoa y Pasaje Cóndor Matzi, Pujili, Cotopaxi EC 050450
DP Coordinator Mauricio Leonardo Zambrano Ruiz
Languages Spanish
T: +593 03 2672069

Unidad Educativa del Milenio Carlos Romo Dávila
Cdla. Walton García – Calle 29 de Abril, Flavio Alfaro, Manabí EC 130550
DP Coordinator David Fernando Alcivar Alcivar
Languages Spanish
T: +593 05 3019470

Unidad Educativa del Milenio Dr. Alfredo Raul Vera Vera
km 2.5 via Terminal Terrestre, (Pascuales) junto a la ciudadela, Cuidad del Río I, Guayaquil, Guayas
DP Coordinator Ana Vera Timbiano
Languages Spanish
T: +593 04 2157931
W: www.uemealfredovera.edu.ec

Unidad Educativa del Milenio Intercultural Bilingüe Chibuleo
Parroquia Juan Benigno Vela, Chibuleo San Francisco Km. 16, Ambato, Tungarahua EC 1801787
DP Coordinator Doris Borja
Languages Spanish
T: +593 03 2483007

Unidad Educativa del Milenio Licenciada Olga Campoverde
Ciudadela 16 de Julio, Velasco Ibarra y Amazonas, Huaquillas, El Oro EC 070750
DP Coordinator Maura Silvania Valencia Quezada
Languages Spanish
T: +593 07 2970800

Unidad Educativa del Milenio 'Nela Martínes Espinosa'
Cdla. Roberto isías – Calle 2da Sur y 16va Este, La Troncal, Cañar EC 030450
DP Coordinator Norma Cecilia Saula Guallpa
Languages English
T: +593 07 2423247

Unidad Educativa del Milenio Sayausi
Sayausi (Centro), Cuenca, Azuay EC 010165
DP Coordinator Miguel Montalvan Urgiles
Languages English, Spanish
T: +593 07 2370268

Unidad Educativa Dr. José María Velasco Ibarra
Panamericana Sur entre, Sáenz de Villaverde, El Guabo, El Oro EC 070650
DP Coordinator Roberto Carlos Moncada Alvarado
Languages Spanish
T: +593 7 2950328

Unidad Educativa Eloy Alfaro
Gonzalez Suarez entre Daniel Ojeda y Sucre, Cariamanga, Loja EC 110203
DP Coordinator Edwim Patricio Lima Celí
Languages Spanish
T: +593 07 2687127
W: www.galeon.com/colegioeloycalvas

Unidad Educativa Eloy Alfaro
Calle Panama y Rio Chilan 318, Coop. Las Palmas, Santo Domingo de los Tsáchilas EC 230102
DP Coordinator Jorge William Quishpe Viteri
Languages Spanish
T: +593 23701242

Unidad Educativa 'Émile Jaques-Dalcroze'
Calle Río Pastaza No 777 y Av Ilaló de los Chillos, San Rafael, Quito, Pichincha
DP Coordinator Sara Arroba Benítez
MYP Coordinator Andrea Torres Ramos
Languages Spanish
T: +593 2 2861 500
W: ejd.edu.ec

Unidad Educativa Eugenio Espejo
Avda. Universitaria Km. 1 1/2, Babahoyo, Los Ríos EC 120101
DP Coordinator Martha Marin Zambrano
Languages English
T: +593 05 2730070
W: www.ueee.edu.ec

Unidad Educativa Experimental Del Milenio Bicentenario
Calle E2d y Av. El Beaterio, Quito, Pichincha EC 170150
DP Coordinator Maribel Jessenia Coello Almagro
Languages English
T: +593 2269 8620
W: www.remq.edu.ec/colegiosremq/bicentenario

Unidad Educativa Experimental 'Manuala Cañizares'
Av 6 de diciembre N24-176, Quito, Pichincha
DP Coordinator Magaly Díaz Velasteguí
Languages Spanish
T: +593 02 223 0271

Ecuador

Unidad Educativa Experimental Pedro Fermín Cevallos
Bolívar 1-59 y Francisco Flor, Ambato, Tungurahua EC 180150
DP Coordinator Nancy Ortega Almeida
Languages English
T: +593 03 2421634

Unidad Educativa Experimental 'Teodoro Gómez de la Torre'
Av Teodoro Gómez 3-101 y Maldonado, Ibarra, Imbabura
DP Coordinator Sandra Hidalgo Padilla
Languages Spanish
T: +593 62950491
W: www.teodorogomez.edu.ec

Unidad Educativa Fanny de Baird
Calle Esmeralda y Rocafuerte, Parroquia Leonidas Plaza, Bahia de Caraquez, Manabí EC 131402
DP Coordinator Roque Gregorio Ureta Santos
Languages Spanish
T: +593 05 2398885

Unidad Educativa Federico González Suárez
Argentina S/N y Avenida Jose Antonio Ponton, Alausi, Chimborazo EC 060250
DP Coordinator Luis Edwin Quisatasi Cayo
Languages English
T: +593 03 2930092

Unidad Educativa Félix Granja
Matto Grosso S/N y Veintimilla, Simiatug, Bolívar EC020159
DP Coordinator Carmen Montes Garcés
Languages English, Spanish
T: +593 0322 23090

Unidad Educativa Fiscal – 15 de Octubre
Cotopaxi y Cinco de Junio, Jipijapa, Manabí 130650
DP Coordinator Maria Garcia Garcia
Languages Spanish
T: +593 05 2600330
W: www.uef15deoctubre.wix.com

Unidad Educativa Fiscal 23 de Octubre
Calle Manta y 13 de Octubre, Montecristi, Manabi 130902
DP Coordinator Nancy Cedeño Vera
Languages Spanish
T: +593 05 310451

Unidad Educativa Fiscal Aguirre Abad
Av. Dr. Luis Cordero, Entre Av. Sufragio Libre y Eloy Ortega, Guayaquil, Guayas
DP Coordinator Bety Valarezo
Languages Spanish
T: +953 04 2282240

Unidad Educativa Fiscal Dolores Sucre
km. 5.5 Via a Daule, Guayaquil, Guayas 090112
DP Coordinator Patricia Margarita Deleg Freire
Languages Spanish
T: +593 04 2650624
W: www.doloressucre.edu.ec

Unidad Educativa Fiscal Experimental del Milenio
Avenida Antonio Valdez, Via a Bayushig, Penipe C. Cantonal, Chimborazo 060950
DP Coordinator Jose Miguel Guadalupe Peñafiel
Languages Spanish
T: +593 032907380
W: www.uem-penipe.com

Unidad Educativa Fiscal 'Leonidas García'
Km 10.5 via Daule, Lotizacion Inmaconsa, Calle Casuarinas y Cedros, Guayaquil, Guayas 090112
DP Coordinator Hermelinda Calle
Languages Spanish
T: +583 04 2114001
W: www.leogar.edu.ec

Unidad Educativa Fiscal Portoviejo
Av. Universitaria entre Alajuela y, Francisco de Paula Moreira, Portoviejo, Manabi 130105
DP Coordinator Ximena Elizabeth Conce Bárcenas
Languages Spanish
T: +593 05 2631561
W: www.colegioportoviejo.edu.ec

Unidad Educativa Fiscal Réplica Guayaquil
Calle Pública entre Manglar, y Calle Pública, Manzana # 00782, Trinipuerto, Guayaquil, Guayas 090114
DP Coordinator Luis Nicolas Choez Pin
Languages Spanish
T: +593 09 99429558

Unidad Educativa Fiscal San Isidro
calle 9 de octubre y misioneros Vascos, Cantón Sucre, San Isidro, Manabí
DP Coordinator Fernando Argandoña Velasco
Languages Spanish
T: +593 05 2400085

Unidad Educativa Fiscal Sucre
Calle Padre Lasso, ingreso a la ciudad, Sucre – 24 de Mayo 131650
DP Coordinator Raquel Ines Macias Cedeño
Languages Spanish
T: +593 05 2344225

Unidad Educativa Fiscal Tosagua
Ciudadela Pensilvania Calle María Teresa Palma, Tosagua, Manabí 131550
DP Coordinator Maria Fernanda Giler Alcivar
Languages Spanish
T: +593 05 2330166
W: www.colegionacionaltosagua.edu.ec

Unidad Educativa Fiscal Uruguay
Calle 26 de Septiembre y Av. Schumacher, Portoviejo, Manabí 13-01-119
DP Coordinator Noralma Andrade Bravo
Languages Spanish
T: +593 05 2632297

Unidad Educativa Fiscal Veintiocho de Mayo
Avenida Carlos Julio Arosemena, KM. 3 1/2, Frente a Centro, Comercial Albán Borja, Guayaquil 090112
DP Coordinator Teresa de Jesús Peña Morán
Languages Spanish
T: +593 04 2202865
W: www.28demayo.edu.ec

Unidad Educativa Fiscomisional Don Bosco
Don Bosco e5-06 y Los Rios, Quito, Pichincha 170130
DP Coordinator Germania de Lourdes Araujo Arias
Languages Spanish
T: +593 02 2582278
W: www.donboscolatola.edu.ec

Unidad Educativa Fiscomisional Fray Bartolomé de las Casas
Parroquia Salasaca, Plaza Central, Pelileo, Tungurahua 180701
DP Coordinator Luis Germán Poveda Ortiz
Languages Spanish
T: +593 03 2748641

Unidad Educativa Fiscomisional Juan Bautista Montini
Avenida Carlos Acosta, San Francisco De Borja, Napo
DP Coordinator Blanca Maribel Agreda Ludena
Languages Spanish
T: +593 6 285 6221

Unidad Educativa Fiscomisional Juan Pablo II
Via Interoceanica Via Calmitoyaco, barrio Juan Montalvo, Loreto, Orellana 220450
DP Coordinator Amilcar Barney Ramírez Ruiz
Languages Spanish
T: +593 06 2893158

Unidad Educativa Fiscomisional Juan XXIII
Av. 6 de Diciembre y Jimmy Anchico, Esmeraldas, Quininde 080405
DP Coordinator María Narcisa Jiménez García
Languages Spanish
T: +593 06 2736180

Unidad Educativa Fiscomisional 'María Inmaculada'
Av. Rocafuerte 481 y Quijos, Archidona 5011449
DP Coordinator Marizza Edelina Jácome Alvarado
Languages Spanish
T: +593 06 2889142

Unidad Educativa Fiscomisional 'Pacífico Cembranos'
AV. Aguarico 439 y Del Coliseo, Nueva Loja
DP Coordinator Doris Azucena Sarango Lapo
Languages English
T: +593 062 366 136
W: www.pacifico.edu.ec

Unidad Educativa Fiscomisional Padre Miguel Gamboa
Calle Vicente Rocafuerte S/N y Av. Alejandro Labaka, Coca 220150
DP Coordinator Tito Vega Trujillo
Languages Spanish
T: +593 062 880 173
W: www.gamboa.edu.ec

Unidad Educativa Fiscomisional San Cristobal
Av. 12 de febrero y Guayaquil, Puerto Baquerizo Moreno, San Cristobal 200150
DP Coordinator Pablo Germanico Chicaiza Valladares
Languages English
T: +593 05 2520369

Unidad Educativa Fiscomisional San José de Calasanz – Cañar
Avenida Paseo de los Cañaris – Sector Guantug, Cañar EC030350
DP Coordinator Ivan Fernando Araujo Narvàez
Languages English
T: 05972235089
W: www.calasanzcanar.edu.ec

Unidad Educativa Fiscomisional San José de Calasanz – Loja
Avenida Reino de Quito, Saraguro, Loja EC111150
DP Coordinator Johana Arrobo Briceño
Languages Spanish
T: +593 7 220 0106
W: www.calasanz-saraguro.edu.ec

Unidad Educativa Fiscomisional Santa María del Fiat
Santuarion de Olón, Vía Puerto Lopez, Comuna Olón, Santa Elena 240108
DP Coordinator Juan Asencio Suárez
Languages Spanish
T: +593 04 2060105

Unidad Educativa Fiscomisional Santiago Fernández García
Velasco Ibarra street between October 14 and November 18, Cariamanga, Loja 110602
DP Coordinator Diana Coronel González
Languages Spanish
T: +593 (07) 2 687 368
W: uefsfg.marianosamaniego.edu.ec

Unidad Educativa Fiscomisional Verbo Divino
Avda Cándido Rada 301, y General Enriquez, Guaranda, Bolívar EC 020150
DP Coordinator Danilo Napoleon Cherres Arguello
Languages Spanish
T: +593 32980702
W: www.verbodivino.edu.ec

Unidad Educativa Gabriel Lopez
Av. Curaray y Juan Aguinda, Arajuno, Pastaza 160450
DP Coordinator Eduardo Tanguila Shiguango
Languages Spanish
T: +593 03 2780011

Unidad Educativa Guapán
Guapan Centro, Azogues, Cañar 030153
DP Coordinator Marta Alvarez Mendez
Languages Spanish
T: +593 07 2207005

Unidad Educativa Hipatia Cárdenas de Bustamante
Nicolas Joaquin de Arteta, OE 249 y Manuel Matheu, Quito, Pichincha 170530
DP Coordinator Oscar Portilla
Languages Spanish
T: +593 02 2406128

Unidad Educativa 'Hispano América'
Av. Bolivariana y Chimul, Ambato, Tungurahua EC 180104
DP Coordinator Natasha Bayas Lopez
Languages Spanish
T: +593 03 2520376
W: www.hispanoamerica.edu.ec

Unidad Educativa Ibarra
Av. Mariano Acosta 14-27, Ibarra, Imbabura 100150
DP Coordinator Elizabeth Muñoz
Languages English
T: +593 06 2644867

Unidad Educativa Internacional Pensionado Atahualpa
El Milagro, San Jose de Cananvalle S/N, Ibarra, Imbabura 100150
DP Coordinator Geovanna del Rocío Andrade Tapia
Languages Spanish
T: +593 6 2 542 115

Unidad Educativa 'Isabel de Godín'
Juan de Velasco S/N y Alfonso Villagomez, Riobamba, Chimborazo
DP Coordinator Mario Antonio Ruales Nuñez
Languages Spanish

Unidad Educativa José María Velasco Ibarra
Av. Los Chirijos y Av. Del Centenario, Esquina, Milagro, Guayas 091050
DP Coordinator Magdalena Ríos Idrovo
Languages Spanish
T: +593 09 042977976

Unidad Educativa Juan de Salinas
Av. Juan de Salinas S/N, Sangolqui, Pichincha 170501
DP Coordinator Laura Luna
Languages Spanish
T: +593 02 333801 (EXT:100)

Unidad Educativa Juan de Velasco
Av. Chimborazo 1156 y Cuba, Riobamba, Chimborazo 060150
DP Coordinator Rober Armando Yandún Martínez
Languages Spanish
T: + 593 03 2950693
W: www.juandevelasco.edu.ec

Unidad Educativa Julio Verne
De Los Nopales #58, Quito
DP Coordinator Lucia del Carmen Aguinaga Cáceres
Languages English, Spanish
T: +593 2280 7117
W: www.julioverne.edu.ec

Unidad Educativa Kleber Franco Cruz
Extension 25 de Junio y 9na Oeste, Machala, El Oro 070102
DP Coordinator Miriam Carmen Macas Aguilar
Languages English
T: +593 07 2935274
W: www.kleberfrancocruz.edu.ec

Unidad Educativa León Ruales
Av. León Ruales, 21-060 y González Suárez, Mira, Carchi 040450
DP Coordinator Lilian del Rosario Perez Goyes
Languages Spanish
T: +593 06 2280411
W: colegioleonruales.blogspot.com

Unidad Educativa Letort
Los Guayabos Nro E 13-05 y Farsalias, San Isidro del Inca, Quito
DP Coordinator Lucíá Carolina Pinzón Posada
MYP Coordinator María Fernanda Mármol Mazzini
PYP Coordinator Cristina Gomez
Languages Spanish
T: +593 2 326 0202
W: www.colegioletort.edu.ec

Unidad Educativa Liceo del Valle
km 1 vía a Pintag, Valle de los Chillos, Quito
DP Coordinator María de Lourdes Ochoa Delgado
MYP Coordinator Marta Salomé Moscoso Sánchez
PYP Coordinator Nathalia Vergara Uquillas
Languages Spanish
T: +593 2 2330703
W: www.liceodelvalle.edu.ec

Unidad Educativa Liceo Naval – VALM Manuel Nieto Cadena
Base Naval de Esmeraldas, Av. J.R. Coronel y calle Jaime Roldós, Esmeraldas
DP Coordinator Jose Jaramillo
Languages Spanish
T: +593 06 2727441
W: www.licesm.edu.ec

Unidad Educativa Liceo Naval de Guayaquil 'Cmdte. Rafael Andrade Lalama'
Av Pedro Menendez Gilbert, Base Naval Norte, Guayaquil, Guayas 9386
DP Coordinator Tatiana Lorena Vera Povea
Languages English
T: +593 04 2283438
W: www.liceonaval.mil.ec

Unidad Educativa Liceo Naval Jambelí
Av. Bolivar Madero Vargas #2330, Puerto Bolivar, Machala el Oro 070102
DP Coordinator Freddy Roberto Guañuna Castillo
Languages English
T: +593 07 2929885
W: www.liceonavaljambeli.edu.ec

Unidad Educativa Luis Rogerio González
Luis Cordero 702 y Cacique Tenemaza, Cañar, Azogues
DP Coordinator Lucila Palacios Valdivieso
Languages Spanish
T: +593 07 2240545
W: www.tecnologicolrg.edu.ec

Unidad Educativa Luz de América
Km. 23 Via a Quevedo, Margen Derecho, Santo Domingo de los Colorados, Santo Domingo de los Tsáchilas 230153
DP Coordinator Esperanza Monserrate Domínguez Osta
Languages Spanish
T: +593 02 2722231

Unidad Educativa 'Manta'
Calle 8 entre avenidas 27 y 28, Manta, Manabí EC 1305432
DP Coordinator Teófilo Mero Bermeo
Languages Spanish
T: +593 05 2622062

Unidad Educativa Maurice Ravel
Av. Cantabria OE2-18 y Av. Cacha (Sector San José de Morán), Quito 170155
DP Coordinator Ivan Oña Quizanga
Languages Spanish
T: +593 2 202 3508
W: mauriceravel.edu.ec

Unidad Educativa Militar Teniente Hugo Ortiz Garces
Ave. Francisco de Orellana Frente a Samanes 6, Guayaquil
DP Coordinator Jully Cecilia Campoverde Aguirre
Languages Spanish
T: +593 42212961
W: www.comilg.edu.ec

Unidad Educativa Monseñor Luis Alfonso Crespo Chiriboga
Avenida zumba, Barrio Celi Roman, Amaluza, Loja 110650
DP Coordinator Mario Agusto Sánchez Armijos
Languages Spanish
T: +593 02 653263

Unidad Educativa Monte Tabor Nazaret
Km 13.5 Via Samborondón, Guayaquil
DP Coordinator Ingrid Lozano Recalde
Languages English, Spanish
T: +593 4 259 0370
W: www.montetabornazaret.edu.ec

Unidad Educativa Nacional Napo
Barrio Napo Km. 1 1/2, Vía a Quito margen derecho, Nueva Loja, Sucumbíos 210150
DP Coordinator Germán Saito Robles Tandazo
Languages Spanish
T: 05962362352
W: www.unidadnapo.edu.ec

Unidad Educativa Nacional Tena
Av. Jumandy y GlorPalacios esquina, Barrio Las Palmas, Tena, Napo
DP Coordinator Verónica Emperatriz Valencia Coca
Languages Spanish
T: +503 06 2886278

Unidad Educativa Naval Comandante César Endara Peñaherrera
Pasaje El Prado, No. 1-192 y Av. González Suárez, Quito 170156
DP Coordinator María Fernanda Sánchez Villacís
Languages Spanish
T: +593 02 2343720
W: www.liceonaval-quito.mil.ec

Unidad Educativa Particular Bilingüe Ecomundo
Av. Juan Tanca Marengo Km 2, Guayaquil 90112
DP Coordinator Tannya Cardenas
MYP Coordinator Karrie Orellana
Languages English
T: +593 4 3703700 (EXT:115-118)
W: www.ecomundo.edu.ec

Unidad Educativa Particular Bilingüe Leonardo da Vinci
Vía a San Mateo Km. 2.4, a 100 metros de la Urbanización Ciudad del Mar, Manta EC130802
DP Coordinator Rubén Muñoz Pérez
Languages Spanish
T: +593 5 3 700 865
W: www.ueldv.edu.ec

Unidad Educativa Particular Bilingüe Liceo Panamericano
Km 3.5 vía Samborondon, Samborondon
DP Coordinator Nadia Salmon
Languages English
T: +593 42833900
W: www.liceopanamericano.edu.ec

Unidad Educativa Particular Bilingüe Martim Cererê
De Los Guayacanes N51-01, y Los Álamos, Quito, Pichincha 170150
DP Coordinator Zoili Noboa
Languages English, Spanish
T: +593 02 2405564
W: www.martimcerere.edu.ec

Unidad Educativa Particular Bilingüe Principito y Marcel Laniado de Wind
Avenida Luis Ángel León Roman y 1era Avenida 5ta, Machala, El Oro 07-01-835
DP Coordinator Diego Ayala Anzoátegui
Languages English
T: +593 72981881
W: www.ueprim.edu.ec

Unidad Educativa Particular Bilingüe Santo Domingo de Guzmán
Calle 5ta # 608 y Las Monjas (URDESA), Guayaquil 2260
DP Coordinator Isaac Augusto Caicedo Vera
Languages Spanish
T: +593 2 882 561
W: www.stodomingo.edu.ec

Unidad Educativa Particular Isaac Newton
Guayabos N50-120 y Los Álamos, Quito, Pichincha 170149
DP Coordinator Rosario Llerena
Languages Spanish
T: +593 22405001
W: www.isaacnewton.edu.ec

Unidad Educativa Particular Javier
Km 5.5 vía a la Costa, Guayaquil
DP Coordinator Natalia Patino
Languages Spanish
T: +593 4 2001590/3520/0724
W: www.uejavier.com

Unidad Educativa Particular La Salle
Av. Abdón Calderón S18 – 104, Conocoto, Quito, Pichincha EC 170156
DP Coordinator Diego Bastidas
Languages English, Spanish
T: +593 234 2115
W: www.lasalleconocoto.edu.ec

Unidad Educativa Particular Politécnico
Km 30.5 Vía Perimental, Campus Gustavo Galindo, Espol, 30,5 Via Perimetral, Guayaquil
DP Coordinator Linda García Muñoz
MYP Coordinator Yidda Marcial
PYP Coordinator Mónica Lasso Gallo
Languages Spanish
T: +593 4 226 9654
W: www.copol.edu.ec

Unidad Educativa Particular Redemptio
10 de Agosto 701 entre Colón y Juan Montalvo, Jipijapa, Manabí
DP Coordinator Gustavo Bykovsky Cañarte Gutiérrez
Languages English, Spanish
T: +593 5 2 600 475
W: www.redemptio.edu.ec

Unidad Educativa Particular 'Rosa de Jesús Cordero'
Parroquia Ricaurte, Sector el Tablón, Cuenca, Azuay 010162
DP Coordinator María José González
Languages Spanish
T: +593 7 2890503
W: www.catalinas.edu.ec

Unidad Educativa Particular San José la Salle Latacunga
Calle Quijano y Ordoñez 532, Y Av. General Maldonado, Latacunga, Cotopaxi EC 050104
DP Coordinator Elizabeth Cajas Morillo
Languages English
T: +593 32 807 884 / +593 32 801 333
W: www.lasallelatacunga.edu.ec

Unidad Educativa Paul Dirac
Av. Pedro Vicente Maldonado y la Cocha, Quito 170146
DP Coordinator Carmen Ramirez
Languages English, Spanish
T: +593 2 691 241 (EXT:1)
W: www.pauldirac.edu.ec

Unidad Educativa Pedro Vicente Maldonado
Primera Constituyente 24-50, entre Larrea y España, Riobamba, Chimborazo 060150
DP Coordinator Sandra Congacha León
Languages Spanish
T: +593 03 2960211
W: www.colegiomaldonado.edu.ec

Unidad Educativa Pública – Julio Moreno Espinosa
Avenida Quito 1222 y Chorrera del Napa, Santo Domingo de los Colorados, Santo Domingo de los Tsachilas 523-2
DP Coordinator Carlos López
Languages Spanish
T: +593 02 750361
W: www.ueducativajuliomoreno.edu.ec

Unidad Educativa 'Quince de Octubre'
Te Sucre s/n y Robles, Naranjal, Guayas
DP Coordinator Maria Esther Salcedo Montesdeoca
Languages Spanish
T: +593 09 93720734

Unidad Educativa Rafael Larrea Andrade
Calle Lopez N4 – 57 y Chile, Quito, Pichincha 170130
DP Coordinator Segundo Galo Lopez Guanoquiza
Languages Spanish
T: +593 02 2951330
W: sites.google.com/sitecolegiorafaellarrea

Unidad Educativa Riobamba
Avenida la Prensa, s/n y Canònigo Ramos, Riobamba, Chimborazo
DP Coordinator Carlos Aguirre Alarcon
Languages Spanish
T: +593 03 2306477

Unidad Educativa Sagrados Corazones de Rumipamba
Av. Atahualpa Oe1-20 y Av. 10 de Agosto, Quito, Pichincha 170521
DP Coordinator Marco Vinicio Duque Romero
Languages Spanish
T: +593 22 442 242
W: rumipamba.edu.ec

Unidad Educativa Saint Dominic School
César Davila N10-222 y Charles Darwin, Quito, Pichincha
DP Coordinator Santiago Andrango
Languages Spanish
T: +593 (0)2 3959960
W: www.saintdominic.edu.ec

Unidad Educativa Salesiana Cardenal Spellman
Mercadillo OE340 y Ulloa, Quito, Pichincha 17-03-125
DP Coordinator Alejandro Vinces
Languages Spanish
T: +593 3560 001/2/3
W: www.spellman.edu.ec

Unidad Educativa Salinas Innova
Av. Carlos Espinoza Larrea , via a salinas, Junto al centro de atención ciudadana, Salinas 241550
DP Coordinator Barbara Veronica Garnica Enderica
Languages Spanish
T: +593 4 277 5954
W: ueinnovaschool.edu.ec/wp

Unidad Educativa 'San Francisco de Asis'
entre Pío Jaramillo, Alvarado y Francisco de Orellana, Zamora-Chinchipe EC 190102
DP Coordinator Nube De Los Ángeles González Urgilé
Languages English
T: +593 7 260 5129

Unidad Educativa San Francisco de Sales

Av. Cristobal Colón E10-07 y Tamayo, Quito
DP Coordinator Andrea Sofía Narváez Ruano
Languages English, Spanish
T: +593 2903 861
W: frasales.edu.ec

Unidad Educativa San Jose La Salle

Tomás Martínez 501 y Baquerizo Moreno, Guayaquil EC 090150
DP Coordinator Luiggi Saenz de Viteri
Languages Spanish
T: +593 4 25 631 37
W: lasalleguayaquil.edu.ec

Unidad Educativa San Martín

Calle Sigsipamba S-2159 y Picoazá, Quito, Pichincha 170613
DP Coordinator Miriam Zambrano Macías
Languages Spanish
T: +593 (0)2 3080979
W: www.sanmartin.edu.ec

Unidad Educativa San Vicente Ferrer

Césalo Marin s/n y Álvaro Valladares, Puyo, Pastaza
DP Coordinator David Gonzalo Guano Ojeda
Languages Spanish
T: +5933 2885173

Unidad Educativa 'Santa Elena'

Santa Elena KM 2.5 Via Ancon, Santa Elena EC 241702
DP Coordinator Lupe Mercedes Llangari Morocho
Languages English
T: +593 04 2940533

UNIDAD EDUCATIVA SANTANA

Av. los Cerezos S/N y vía a Racar, Cuenca
DP Coordinator Xavier Tenorio Sánchez
Languages Spanish
T: +593 7 4121879
E: comunicacion@santana.edu.ec
W: www.santana.edu.ec
See full details on page 556

Unidad Educativa Santo Domingo de los Colorados

Vicente Rocafuerte 390 y Juan Montalvo, Santo Domingo, Santo Domingo de los Tsác
DP Coordinator Jorge Molina Cusme
Languages Spanish
T: +593 3700962
W: colegiosantodomingo.edu.ec

Unidad Educativa Sigchos

Av. Galo Troya Robayo N° 101, Ingreso a la Ciudad de Sigchos, Sigchos EC 050160
DP Coordinator Margarita Rocha Chasi
Languages Spanish
T: +593 03 2714243

Unidad Educativa Temporal Camilo Gallegos Dominguez

Vía San Luís sector el Paraíso, Biblián 030250
DP Coordinator Diego Joel Lliguichuzhca Dután
Languages Spanish
T: +593 07 2230245

Unidad Educativa Temporal Juan Bautista Vásquez

Azuay y Vía Oriente, Azogues, Cañar 030102
DP Coordinator Roosevelt Vicente Reyes Ordóñez
Languages Spanish
T: +593 072240464
W: www.juanbautistavasquez.edu.ec

Unidad Educativa Temporal Manuel Córdova Galarza

La Peñas/Baños, Cuenca 593
DP Coordinator Cristina Parra Duchi
Languages Spanish
T: +593 07 892475

Unidad Educativa Temporal Mariano Benítez

Calle 22 de Julio, No. 3-23 y Zopozopangui, San Pedro de Pelileo, Tungurahua 180701
DP Coordinator Susana del Rocío Zurita Lopez
Languages Spanish
T: +593 03 28711 41
W: colegionacionalmarianobenitez.blogspot.com

Unidad Educativa Terranova

Calle De Los Rieles 507, y Ave Simón Bolívar, San Juan Alto de Cumbayá, Quito
DP Coordinator Jose Hidalgo Carrillo
MYP Coordinator Jose Hidalgo Carrillo
PYP Coordinator María Victoria Dávila
Languages English, Spanish, French
T: +593 2 356 4000
W: www.colegioterranova.com.ec

Unidad Educativa Theodore W. Anderson

Av. Gaspar de Villarroel E5-35 e Isla Isabela, Quito 170104
DP Coordinator Ángel Benavides Peñafiel
Languages Spanish
T: +593 2 604 4738
W: www.twanderson.edu.ec

Unidad Educativa Tomás Moro

Av De Las Orquideas E13-120, y De Los Guayacanes, Quito
DP Coordinator Oswaldo Boada Sotomayor
MYP Coordinator Andrés Ruiz
PYP Coordinator Ana María Álvarez Maldonado
Languages Spanish
T: +593 2 2405357
W: www.tomasmoro.ec

Unidad Educativa Tumbaco

La Morita C/Tola Chica #3, Av. Universitaria y San Felipe, Tumbaco, Pichincha E12-183
DP Coordinator Yasnaia Diaz
Languages English
T: +593 0220 48391

Unidad Educativa Ventanas

Calle Jimmy Izquierdo y la R, Los Rios, Ventanas 052971250
DP Coordinator Enilfa Zoralla Mora Álvarez
Languages English, Spanish
T: +593 05 2971250

Unidad Educativo Bilingüe CEBI

Calle Modesto Chacón y Av. Pedro Vásconez Sevilla, Parroquia Izamba, Ambato
DP Coordinator Sandra Naranjo
MYP Coordinator Maria Eugenia Fierro Echeverria
PYP Coordinator Esthela Yolanda Razo Fiallos
Languages Spanish, English
T: +593 3 373 0370
W: www.cebi.edu.ec

Victoria Bilingual Christian Academy

Melchor de Valdez Oe-9240, Pbx: 253-6116, Quito, Pichincha 170528
DP Coordinator Sarah Catalina Ingman Bastidas
Languages Spanish
T: +593 (0)2 2536116
W: victoriaacademy.edu.ec

EL SALVADOR

Academia Britanica Cuscatleca

Apartado Postal 121, Santa Tecla, La Libertad
DP Coordinator Colin Hogan
Languages English
T: +503 2201 6222/6252/6261
W: www.abc.edu.sv

Colegio La Floresta

Estamos en el Km. 13 1/2, Carretera al Puerto de La Libertad
DP Coordinator Laura Calderón
Languages English
T: +503 2534 8800
W: www.lafloresta.edu.sv

Colegio Lamatepec

Carretera al Puerto de La Libertad Km 12.5, Calle Nueva a Comasauga Santa Tecla, La Libertad, San Salvador
DP Coordinator Daniel Guzmán
Languages English, Spanish
T: +503 2534 8900
W: www.lamatepec.edu.sv

Deutsche Schule – Escuela Alemana San Salvador

Calle del Mediterráneo, Jardines de Guadalupe, Antiguo Cuscatlán, San Salvador CA
DP Coordinator Beatriz Dreyer
Languages Spanish
T: +503 2243 4898
W: www.ds.edu.sv

GUATEMALA

Centro Escolar Campoalegre

35 Calle and 12 Av Final, Zona 11, Código 01011
DP Coordinator Angela María Gabriela Martínez Orti
Languages English, Spanish
T: +502 2380 3900
W: www.campoalegre.edu.gt

Centro Escolar 'El Roble'

11 Avenida Sur Final Zona 11, Guatemala City 01011
DP Coordinator Luis Fernando Micheo Hernández
Languages Spanish
T: +502 2387 7000
W: www.ceroble.edu.gt

Centro Escolar Entrevalles

Km. 16.8 Antigua Carretera a El Salvador, Santa Catarina Pinula
DP Coordinator Aida Camacho
Languages Spanish, English
T: +502 6685 4700
W: www.entrevalles.edu.gt

Centro Escolar Solalto

Km. 22.5 Carretera a Fraijanes, Fraijanes
DP Coordinator Juan Carlos Velásquez Valladares
Languages English, Spanish
T: +502 6686 0500
W: www.solalto.edu.gt

HONDURAS

The American School of Tegucigalpa
P.O. Box 2134, Tegucigalpa
DP Coordinator Daniel Dobbe
Languages English
T: +504 2276 8400
W: www.amschool.org

JAMAICA

American International School of Kingston
2 College Green Avenue, Kingston
DP Coordinator David Harvey
Languages English
T: +1 876 702 2070
W: www.aisk.com

Hillel Academy
PO Box 2687, 51 Upper Mark Way, Kingston 8
DP Coordinator Pauladene Steele
Languages English
T: +1 876 925 1980
W: hillelacademyjm.com/

MÉXICO

Alexander Bain Colegio
Barranca de Pilares 29, Colonia Tlacopac, San Angel C.P. 01760
PYP Coordinator Loren Karam Karam
Languages Spanish
T: +52 55 5595 0493
W: www.colegioab.mx

American College of Puebla
9 Poniente No. 2709, Col. La Paz, Puebla C.P. 72160
CP Coordinator Jorge Silva
DP Coordinator Cynthia Anderson
MYP Coordinator Sara Kent
PYP Coordinator Shannon Hickey
Languages English, Spanish
W: www.cap.edu.mx

American School Foundation of Chiapas
Blvd. Belisario Dominguez 5588-F, Fraccion Las Cinco Plumas, Terán, Tuxtla Gutierrez, Chiapas C.P. 29052
PYP Coordinator Aurora Topete
Languages English, Spanish
T: +52 961 671 5523
W: www.americanschool.edu.mx

Avalon International School
Av. San Jerónimo 1135, San Jerónimo de Lídice La Magdalena Contreras, Mexico D.F. C.P. 10200
PYP Coordinator Martha Alejandra Navarro Berea
Languages English, Spanish
T: +52 555 595 5582
W: avalon-school.mx

Bachillerato 5 de Mayo
Ave. del Trabajo # 6, Cuautlancingo, Puebla C.P. 72700
DP Coordinator Deborah Andena Casteñeda
Languages English
T: +52 222 2295500 EXT:2770
W: cmas.siu.buap.mx/portal_pprd/wb/b5mayo/inicio

Bachillerato Alexander Bain, SC
Las Flores 497, Tlacopac, San Ángel, México D.F C.P. 01049
DP Coordinator Beatriz Marquez Navarro
MYP Coordinator Ana Elia Hernández
Languages Spanish, English, French
T: +(5255) 5683 2911
W: www.bab.edu.mx

Bachillerato UPAEP Atlixco
Camino a la Uvera #2004, Ex-Hacienda La Blanca, 74365 Atlixco, Puebla
CP Coordinator Maria Leticia Ortiz Rosas
Languages English, Spanish
T: +52 244 445 1991
W: upaep.mx//prepa/atlixco

Bachillerato UPAEP Santa Ana
Avenida Tecpanxochitl 52 A, San Pedro Tlalcuapan, Chiautempan, Tlaxcala C.P. 90845
CP Coordinator Gerardo Arroyo Barillas
Languages English, Spanish
T: +52 246 46 496 33
W: upaep.mx/prepa/santa-ana

British American School S.C.
Fuente del Niño #16 Col. Tecamachalco, Naucalpan, Estado de México C.P. 53950
PYP Coordinator María Guadalupe Antimo Rivera
Languages English
T: +55 52 94 37 21
W: www.british.edu.mx

Centro de Educación Media de la Universidad Autónoma de Aguascalientes
Av de la Convencion Esq, Con Av Independencia S/N Fraccionamiento Norte, Aguascalientes, AGS C.P. 20020
DP Coordinator Rodrigo Ramirez Roa
Languages Spanish
T: +52 01 449 9 147708
W: www.uaa.mx/centros/cem/

Centro de Enseñanza Técnica y Superior – Campus Mexicali
Calzada del Cetys S/N, Colonia Rivera, Mexicali, Baja California C.P. 21259
DP Coordinator Alicia Hermosillo
Languages Spanish
T: +52 686 567 3704
W: www.cetys.mx

Centro de Ensenanza Tecnica y Superior – Campus Tijuana
Av. CETYS Universidad, No. 4 Fracc. El Lago, San Diego C.P. 22210
DP Coordinator Paulina Bueno
Languages Spanish
T: +52 664 903 1800
W: www.cetys.mx

Centro de Investigación y Desarrollo de Educación Bilingüe
Lázaro Cárdenas Al Ote, Sin Número, Unidad Mederos, Monterrey C.P. 64930
DP Coordinator Jorge Jesús López Castro
Languages Spanish
T: +52 818 3294180
W: cideb.uanl.mx

Centro Educativo Alexander Bain Irapuato
Enrique del Moral Domínguez 335, Ejido Lo de Juárez, 36630, Irapuato, Guanajuato
DP Coordinator María Elena Victoria Jardón
PYP Coordinator Atala Gamboa Ruiz
Languages Spanish, English
T: +52 462 114 2246
W: www.alexbain.edu.mx

Centro Educativo CRECER AC
Calle del Vecino No 3, Atlihuetzia, Yahuquehmecan, Tlaxcala C.P. 90459
PYP Coordinator Elsa Nina Rico Puebla
Languages English, Spanish
T: +52 24 646 13 148
W: www.crecer.edu.mx

Centro Escolar Instituto La Paz, SC
Av Plan de San Luis 445, Col Nueva Santa María, México City C.P. 02800
MYP Coordinator Maribel Sánchez
PYP Coordinator Maribel Sánchez
Languages Spanish, English
T: +52 55 55 56 66 46
W: www.institutolapaz.edu.mx

Churchill College
Moctezuma 125, Colonia San Pablo Tepetlapa, México DF C.P. 04620
DP Coordinator Isabel Rangel González
Languages English
T: +52 55 56 19 82 43
W: www.cc.edu.mx

Colegio Álamos
Acceso al Aeropuerto 1000, Colonia Arboledas, Santiago de Querétaro C.P. 76940
DP Coordinator Kevin Coll
Languages English, Spanish
T: +52 442 182 0222
W: www.colegioalamos.edu.mx

Colegio Alemán de Guadalajara
Av Bosques de los Cedros N°32, Las Cañadas, Zapopan, Jalisco C.P. 45132
DP Coordinator Patrick Weilandt
Languages Spanish
T: +52 33 3685 0136
W: www.colegioalemanguadalajara.edu.mx

Colegio Anglo de las Américas
Av. 5 de Febrero #1007, Col. Valle del Tecnológico, Lázaro Cárdenas, Michoacan C.P. 60950
PYP Coordinator Perla Ríos Ramos
Languages English, Spanish
T: +52 753 537 7274
W: www.colegioanglo.mx

Colegio Arji
Avenida México # 2, esquina Periférico, Colonia del Bosque, Villahermosa, Tabasco C.P. 86160
DP Coordinator Pablo Martinez Alvarez
MYP Coordinator Yocelin Priego
PYP Coordinator Ligia Teresa Balcázar Avilés
Languages English, Spanish
T: +52 993 3 510 250
W: www.arji.edu.mx

Colegio Atid AC
Av. Carlos Echanove #224, Col. Vista Hermosa Cuajimalpa, Mexico DF C.P. 05100
CP Coordinator Rachel Sayag
DP Coordinator Rachel Sayag
MYP Coordinator Noemi Dos Santos Andrade
PYP Coordinator Gustavo Mejía
Languages English, Spanish
T: +52 55 5814 0800
W: www.atid.edu.mx

Colegio Bilingüe Carson de Ciudad Delicias
Ave 50 Aniversario 1709, Delicias, Chihuahua C.P. 33058
PYP Coordinator Marcela Iveth Candelaria Ramos
Languages Spanish
T: +52 (639) 472 9340
W: www.colegiocarson.com

Colegio Bosques
Prol. Zaragoza No. 701, Fracc. Valle de las Trojes, Aguascalientes C.P. 20115
MYP Coordinator Aurora Esparza Arburúa
PYP Coordinator Manuel Macías Flores
Languages English, Spanish
T: +52 449 162 04 05
W: www.colegiobosques.edu.mx

Colegio Británico
Calle Pargo # 24, S.M. 3, Cancun, Quintana Roo C.P. 77500
DP Coordinator Silvia Ivette Luna Barra
PYP Coordinator Maria Cajigas
Languages English
T: +52 (998) 884 1295
W: www.cbritanico.edu.mx

Colegio Buena Tierra SC
Camino Viejo a San Mateo 273, San Salvador Tizatlalli, Metepec, Toluca C.P. 52172
PYP Coordinator Vanessa Suhaste Trejo
Languages Spanish, English
T: +52 722 271 2500
W: www.buenatierra.edu.mx

Colegio Celta Internacional
Libramiento Sur-Poniente Km 4+200, Colonia Los Olvera, Villa Corregidora, Querétaro C.P. 76902
CP Coordinator Claudia Edith Molleda Ortega
MYP Coordinator Alicia Silva
PYP Coordinator Nallely Wong
Languages English, Spanish
T: +52 442 227 36 00
W: www.celta.edu.mx

Colegio Ciudad de México
Campos Elíseos # 139, Col Polanco, Mexico D.F. C.P. 11560
DP Coordinator Sergio Morales
MYP Coordinator Sergio Morales
PYP Coordinator Maruja Esperante
Languages Spanish
T: +52 55 5254 4053
W: www.colegiociudad.edu.mx

Colegio Ciudad de Mexico – Plantel Contadero
Calle de la Bolsa 456, El Contadero, Cuajimalpa C.P. 05500
PYP Coordinator Ana Lilia Rueda Moreno
Languages Spanish
T: +52 58 12 06 10
W: www.colegiociudad.edu.mx/contadero.html

Colegio Discovery
Circuito Interior Norte Socorro Romero, Sánchez, No. 3525, Col. San Lorenzo, Tehuacán, Puebla
DP Coordinator Nayeli Hernandez Martinez
MYP Coordinator Violeta López Valerio
PYP Coordinator Carolina Lezama Olalde
Languages Spanish
T: +52 238 3820005
W: colegiodiscovery.edu.mx

COLEGIO EL CAMINO
Callejon del Jornongo #210, Colonia El Pedregal, Cabo San Lucas, B.C.S. C.P. 23453
DP Coordinator Ricardo Fumachi
PYP Coordinator Maria Ines Mayaudon
Languages English, Spanish
T: +52 624 143 2100 (EXT:112)
E: info@elcamino.edu.mx
W: www.elcamino.edu.mx
See full details on page 496

Colegio Fontanar
Camino al Fraccionamiento, Vista Real 119, Corregidora, Querétaro C.P. 76900
DP Coordinator María del Carmen Vargas Vázquez
Languages Spanish
T: +52 442 228 13 65
W: www.fontanar.edu.mx

COLEGIO HEBREO MAGUEN DAVID
Antiguo Camino a Tecamachalco #370, Lomas de Vista Hermosa, Mexico DF
DP Coordinator Susana Memun Zaga
MYP Coordinator Naomi Rojas
PYP Coordinator Graciela Silva Escobar
Languages Spanish, Hebrew, English
T: +52 (55) 52 46 26 00
E: chmd@chmd.edu.mx
W: www.chmd.edu.mx
See full details on page 497

Colegio Hebreo Monte Sinai AC
Av Loma de la Palma 133, Col Vista Hermosa, Cuajimalpa C.P. 05109
DP Coordinator Dalba Castello
MYP Coordinator Dalba Castello
PYP Coordinator Tania Navarro Elizalde
Languages Spanish, English
T: +52 55 52 53 01 68
W: www.chms.edu.mx

Colegio Hebreo Tarbut
Av. Loma del Parque 216, Colonia Lomas de Vista Hermosa, México D.F. C.P. 05100
MYP Coordinator Yemile Levy
PYP Coordinator Gabriela Rodriguez
Languages English, Spanish
T: +52 55 5814 0500
W: www.tarbut.edu.mx

Colegio Internacional de México
Río Magdalena 263, Colonia Tizapan San Ángel, Álvaro Obregón, Ciudad de México 01090
MYP Coordinator Susana Valenzuela Esquivel
PYP Coordinator María José Proaño
Languages English, Spanish
T: +52 55 55 50 01 01
W: www.colegiointernacional.edu.mx

Colegio Internacional Terranova
Av Palmira 705, Fracc. Desarrollo del Pedregal, San Luis Potosí C.P. 78295
DP Coordinator Enriqueta Pérez
MYP Coordinator Enrique Freeman
PYP Coordinator María Covarrubias Gómez
Languages Spanish
T: +52 444 8 41 64 22
W: www.terranova.edu.mx

Colegio La Paz de Chiapas
Carretera Tuxtla, Villaflores Nº 1170, Tuxtla Gutiérrez, Chiapas C.P. 29089
DP Coordinator Alejandra Fraguas Castañón
MYP Coordinator Ana Cecilia Toledo Palacio
Languages Spanish
T: +52 961 663 7000
W: www.colegio-lapaz.edu.mx

Colegio Linares AC
Marina Silva de Rodriguez 1301 Pte, Colonia centro Linares, Nuevo León C.P. 67700
DP Coordinator Norma Velasco
Languages Spanish
T: +52 821 212 0269
W: www.colegiolinares.edu.mx

Colegio Lomas Hill
Av. Veracruz 158, Cuajimalpa, México D.F. C.P. 05000
PYP Coordinator Mariana Resa Romo
Languages English
T: +52 55 5812 0818
W: www.lomashill.com

Colegio Madison Chihuahua
Fuente Trevi #7001, Fracc. Puerta de Hierro, Chihuahua, Chih C.P. 31205
PYP Coordinator Rossana Ortegón Alvarez
Languages English, Spanish
T: +52 614 430 1464
W: www.colegiosmadison.edu.mx/colegios-madison-chihuahua.htm

Colegio Maria Montessori de Monclova
Blvd Harold R Pape Nro 2002, Col Jardines del Valle, Monclova, Coah C.P. 25730
DP Coordinator Sara Aimee Montes de Oca Nolla
Languages Spanish
T: +52 866 633 2993
W: www.montessorimonclova.com

Colegio Monteverde
Av Santa Lucia No 260, Col Prados de la Montaña, Cualjimalpa, México D.F. C.P. 05610
DP Coordinator Andrea Ponce Toledo
Languages Spanish
T: +52 55 50819700
W: www.colegiomonteverde.edu.mx

Colegio Nuevo Continente
Nicolás San Juan 1141, Colonia Del Valle, México D.F. C.P. 03100
DP Coordinator Elisa Aizpuru González
Languages English, Spanish
T: +52 55 5575 4066
W: www.nuevocontinente.edu.mx

Colegio Olinca Altavista
Av Altavista No 130, Colonia San Angel, Delegación Álvaro Obregón, México D.F. C.P. 01060
PYP Coordinator María Isaura Ortiz Alvarez
Languages Spanish
T: +52 55 56160216
W: www.olinca.edu.mx

Colegio Suizo de México – Campus Cuernavaca
Calle Amates s/n, Col. Lomas de Ahuatlán, Cuernavaca, Morelos C.P. 62130
DP Coordinator Nora Smith
Languages English, Spanish
T: +52 777 323 5252
W: www.csm.edu.mx

México

Colegio Suizo de México – Campus México DF
Nicolás San Juan 917, Col del Valle, México D.F. C.P. 03100
DP Coordinator Aurelio Reyes
Languages English, Spanish
T: +52 55 55 43 78 62
W: www.csm.edu.mx

Colegio Suizo de México – Campus Querétaro
Circ. La Cima 901, Fracc. La Cima, Santiago de Querétaro C.P. 76146
DP Coordinator Pilar Eugenia Carrión Fajardo
Languages Spanish, German, English
T: +52 442 254 3390
W: www.csm.edu.mx

Colegio Vista Hermosa
Bachillerato, Av Loma de Vista Hermosa 221, Cuajimalpa, México D.F. C.P. 05100
DP Coordinator Ramón García Govea
MYP Coordinator Viviana Calleja
Languages Spanish
T: +52 55 50914630
W: www.cvh.edu.mx

COLEGIO WILLIAMS
Mixcoac Campus, Empresa 8, Col Mixcoac, Alcaldía Benito Juárez, México City CP 03910
DP Coordinator Laura Silva Rico
MYP Coordinator Erika Daniela Mendoza Pineda
PYP Coordinator María del Pilar González Mata
Languages Spanish
T: +52 55 1087 9797
E: kblum@colegiowilliams.edu.mx
W: www.colegiowilliams.edu.mx

See full details on page 498

Colegio Williams de Cuernavaca
Luna #32, Jardines de Cuernavaca, Cuernavaca, Morelos C.P. 62360
DP Coordinator Martha Alicia Nocetti Vilchis
MYP Coordinator Pedro López
PYP Coordinator María López Covarrubias
Languages English, Spanish
T: +52 (777) 3223640
W: www.cwc.edu.mx

Colegio Williams Unidad San Jerónimo
Presa Reventada No 53, Col San Jerónimo Lídice, Del. Magdalena Contreras, México D.F. C.P. 10400
PYP Coordinator Alejandra Silva Bringas
Languages Spanish, English
T: +52 55 1087 9797
W: www.colegiowilliams.edu.mx

Colegio Xail
Calle Xail No 10, Col. Lázaro Cárdenas, San Francisco de Campeche, Campeche C.P. 24520
MYP Coordinator Balbina Guadalupe Sosa Bautista
PYP Coordinator Susana Gómez Rodríguez
Languages Spanish
T: +52 981 813 0322
W: www.xail.edu.mx

Discovery School
Chilpancingo No 102, Colonia Vista Hermosa, Cuernavaca, Morelos 62290
PYP Coordinator Luz Gabriela Briseño Tellez
Languages English, Spanish
T: +52 777 318 5721
W: www.discovery.edu.mx

Educare Centro de Servicios Educativos S.C.
Norte 26 #498, Orizaba, Veracruz C.P. 94300
PYP Coordinator Verónica Avella Gamboa
Languages Spanish
T: +52 272 7241194
W: www.educarecentro.edu.mx

El Colegio Británico (Edron Academy)
Calz. Desierto de los Leones #5578, Col Olivar de Los Padres, México D.F. C.P. 1740
DP Coordinator Lorna Villasana
Languages English
T: +52 55 5585 1920
W: www.edron.edu.mx

Escuela Ameyalli SC
Calzada de las Águilas 1972, Axomiatla, México D.F. C.P. 01820
MYP Coordinator Irazi Navarro Alvarez
PYP Coordinator Irazí Navarro Álvarez
Languages English, Spanish
T: +52 55 12 85 70 20
W: www.ameyalli.edu.mx

Escuela John F. Kennedy
Av Sabinos 272, Jurica, Querétaro C.P. 76100
DP Coordinator Maria Regina Velazquez
MYP Coordinator Gabriel García Martínez
PYP Coordinator Christine Scharf
Languages English, Spanish
T: +52 442 218 0075
W: www.jfk.edu.mx

Escuela Lomas Atlas S.C.
Montañas Calizas #305, Lomas de Chapultepec, México D.F. C.P. 11000
PYP Coordinator Humberto Rodriguez Vega
Languages English
T: +52 55 55 20 53 75/20 37 25
W: www.lomasaltas.edu.mx

Escuela Mexicana Americana, A. C.
Gabriel Mancera 1611, Col. Del Valle, Mexico City C.P. 03100
DP Coordinator Eva Raquel López Jiménez
Languages English, Spanish
T: +52 55 240214
W: mexicanaamericana.edu.mx

Escuela Preparatoria Federal 'Lázaro Cárdenas'
Paseo de los Héroes #11161, Zona Rio. C.P. 22010
DP Coordinator Carlos Abel Eslava Carrillo
Languages Spanish
T: +1 52 664 686 12 97
W: www.lazarocardenas.edu.mx

Eton, SC
Domingo García Ramos s/n, Col. Prados de la Montaña, Santa Fe., Cuajimalpa de Morelos C.P. 05619
DP Coordinator Laura Alicia Salazar
MYP Coordinator Rosa María Olmos
Languages English, Spanish
T: +52 5 261 5800
W: www.eton.edu.mx

Formus
Cañón de la Mesa 6745, Monterrey, Nuevo León C.P. 64898
MYP Coordinator Aracely Garza Montes
Languages Spanish
T: +52 8317 8560
W: www.formus.edu.mx

GREENGATES SCHOOL
Av. Circunvalación Pte. 102, Balcones de San Mateo, Naucalpan, Edo. de México C.P. 53200
DP Coordinator David Grant
Languages English
T: +52 55 5373 0088
E: kuroda@greengates.edu.mx
W: www.greengates.edu.mx

See full details on page 510

Greenville International School
Prolongación Arco Noroeste s/n, Colonia González 1ra Sección, Villahermosa, Tabasco C.P. 86039
DP Coordinator Gerardo Ramírez
MYP Coordinator Gerardo Ramírez
Languages English
T: +52 993 310 8060
W: www.greenville.edu.mx

Instituto Alexander Bain SC
Cascada 320, Jardines del Pedregal
MYP Coordinator Beatriz Delia Marquez Navarro
PYP Coordinator Loxá Tamayo Márquez
Languages Spanish, English
T: +52 55 5595 6579
W: www.alexanderbain.edu.mx

Instituto Anglo Británico Campus Cumbres
Paseo de los leones 7001, Avenida Bosque de las Lomas, Valle de Cumbres, García, Nuevo León C.P. 66035
PYP Coordinator Mrs Alejandra Tijerina Reyna
Languages English, Spanish
T: +52 81 8526 2222
W: www.colegiosmadison.edu.mx/instituto-anglo-britanico-campus-cumbres.htm

INSTITUTO ANGLO BRITÁNICO CAMPUS LA FE
Av. Isidoro Sepúlveda #555, Col. La Encarnación, Apodaca, Nuevo León C.P. 66633
MYP Coordinator Ms. Elynn Vázquez Wong
PYP Coordinator Ms. Ana Laura Arellano Rodríguez
Languages English, Spanish
T: +52 8183 21 5000
E: contactus@iab.edu.mx
W: www.iab.edu.mx

See full details on page 512

Instituto Bilingüe Rudyard Kipling
Cruz de Valle Verde No 25, Santa Cruz del Monte, Naucalpan, Edo. de México C.P. 53110
DP Coordinator Magali Guerrero Olvera
MYP Coordinator Sandra Lorena Padró Torres
PYP Coordinator Silvia Garcia
Languages Spanish, English
T: +52 55 5572 6282
W: www.kipling.edu.mx

Instituto Cervantes, A.C.
Prol. León García # 2355, Col. General I. Martínez, San Luis de Potosí C.P. 78360
MYP Coordinator Marcela Robles Espinosa
PYP Coordinator Lorena Derreza Gallegos
Languages Spanish
T: +52 444 815 91 50
W: www.apostolica.mx

Instituto D'Amicis, AC
Camino a Morillotla s/n, Colonia Bello Horizonte, Puebla C.P. 72170
DP Coordinator Luis Jahir Mendoza
MYP Coordinator Adriana Cruz Hernández
PYP Coordinator Ma. Eugenia Tanus Diego
Languages Spanish, English
T: +52 222 303 2618
W: www.damicis.edu.mx

Instituto Educativo Olinca
Periférico Sur 5170, Col Pedregal de Carrasco, Delegación Coyoacán, 04700 México DF
DP Coordinator Julieta López Olalde
MYP Coordinator María Cristina Beltrán Aguerrebere
PYP Coordinator Claudia Ghigliazza & Isaura Ortiz
Languages Spanish, English, French
T: +52 55 5606 3113/5606 3371/5606 3510
W: www.olinca.edu.mx

Instituto Internacional Octavio Paz
Calle Internacional 63 Fracc. Las Brisas el Jaguey, Col. Las RedesChapala, Jalisco C.P. 45903
DP Coordinator Micaela Pérez Zaragoza
Languages English
T: +52 376 766 0903
W: www.iiop.edu.mx

Instituto Jefferson Internacional
Boulevard Jefferson No 666, Morelia, Michoacán C.P. 58080
DP Coordinator Vanya Nohemí Soto Maldonado
MYP Coordinator Valeria López Morales
PYP Coordinator Valeria López Morales
Languages Spanish
T: +52 443 3237967
W: jefferson.edu.mx

Instituto Kipling de Irapuato
Villa Mirador 5724, Villas de Irapuato, Irapuato, Gto C.P. 36670
MYP Coordinator Martha Sultane Caram Canavati
PYP Coordinator Diana Muttio Limas
Languages English, Spanish
T: +52 462 6230165
W: www.kiplingirapuato.edu.mx

Instituto Ovalle Monday – Plantel Secundaria
Guillermo Massieu Helguera 265, Col. Residencial La Escalera, Del. Gustavo A. Madero, México D.F. C.P. 07320
MYP Coordinator Laura Garcia
Languages Spanish
T: +52 5586 0316 (EXT:101)
W: www.ovallemonday.edu.mx

Instituto para la Educación Integral del Bachiller (INEDIB)
Calle 20 de Noviembre No. 310, San Mateo Oxtotitlán, Toluca, Estado de México C.P. 50100
PYP Coordinator Vicente Osorio Maldonado
Languages Spanish
T: +52 722 278 10 40
W: www.inedib.edu.mx

Instituto Piaget
Nubes 413, Col Jardines del Pedregal, México D.F. C.P. 01900
PYP Coordinator Mariana Mejía Fonseca
Languages English, Spanish
T: +52 555568 8881
W: www.institutopiaget.edu.mx

Instituto Sanmiguelense
Escuadrón 201, No. 10 Palmita de Landeta Km. 0.5, San Miguel de Allende, Guanajuato C.P. 37748
DP Coordinator Mayra Álvarez Soria
Languages Spanish
T: +52 415 154 8484
W: itses.edu.mx

Kipling Esmeralda
Av. Parque de los Ciervos No.1, Hacienda de Valle Escondido, Zona Esmeralda, Atizapan de Zaragoza, Edo de Mexico C.P. 52937
DP Coordinator Ariana Grimaldo Cardenas
MYP Coordinator Claudia García Ybarra
PYP Coordinator Irma Liliana Morales Lozano
Languages Spanish, English
T: +52 55 55726282
W: www.kiplingesmeralda.edu.mx

La Escuela de Lancaster A.C.
Av Insurgentes sur 3838, Col Tlalpan C.P. 14000
DP Coordinator Martha Susana García Ramírez
PYP Coordinator Caroline Horowitz
Languages English, Spanish
T: +52 5556 6697 96
W: www.lancaster.edu.mx

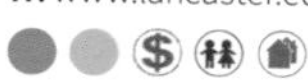

Liceo de Apodaca Centro Educativo
Ave. Virrey de Velazco No. 500, Nuevo León, Apodaca C.P. 66606
MYP Coordinator Monica Estrada
PYP Coordinator Monica Estrada
Languages English
T: +52 81 83862089
W: www.liceodeapodaca.edu.mx

Liceo de Monterrey
Humberto Junco Voigt #400, Col. Valle Oriente, San Pedro Garza García C.P. 66269
DP Coordinator Fátima Montes Villegas
Languages English, Spanish
T: +52 (81) 8748 4146
W: www.liceodemonterrey.edu.mx

Liceo de Monterrey – Centro Educativo
Col Sendero San Jeronimo, Monterrey, Nuevo Leon C.P. 64659
DP Coordinator Jose Ugalde Chavez
Languages Spanish
T: +1 8122 8900

Liceo Federico Froebel de Oaxaca SC
Ajusco No 100, Colonia Volcanes, Oaxaca C.P. 68020
DP Coordinator Nancy Villanueva Castillo
Languages English, Spanish
T: +52 951 5200 675
W: www.federicofroebel.edu.mx

MADISON CAMPUS MONTERREY
Marsella #3055, Col. Alta Vista, Monterrey, Nuevo León C.P. 64840
MYP Coordinator Perla Priscila Vargas Andrade
PYP Coordinator Ricardo Domínguez Gámez
Languages English, Spanish
T: +52 81 8359 0627
E: contacto@colegiosmadison.edu.mx
W: colegiosmadison.edu.mx/colegios-madison-monterrey.htm

See full details on page 523

MADISON INTERNATIONAL SCHOOL
Camino Real #100, Col. El Uro, Monterrey, Nuevo León C.P. 64986
MYP Coordinator Emerson García
PYP Coordinator Rolando De La Torre
Languages English, Spanish
T: +52 81 8218 7909
E: admisiones@mis.edu.mx
W: www.mis.edu.mx

See full details on page 524

Madison International School Campus Country-Mérida
Calle 24776 s/n, Chablekal, Merida, Yucatán C.P. 97300
DP Coordinator Peni Ganivatu
MYP Coordinator Fernando Ramírez
PYP Coordinator Kate Wade
Languages English, Spanish
T: +52 99 9611 9053
W: www.colegiosmadison.edu.mx/colegios-madison-merida.htm

Noordwijk International College
Blvd. del Mar #491, Fracc. Costa de Oro, Boca del Río, Veracruz C.P. 94299
MYP Coordinator José Angel Lozano Elizondo
PYP Coordinator Sandra Gamboa
Languages English, Spanish
T: +52 229 130 0714
W: www.noordwijk.com.mx

Orbis International School
Km 3.5 Carretera Aeropuerto #551, Colonia Rivera, Mexicali, Baja California C.P. 21220
PYP Coordinator Gabriela Coutino
Languages English
T: +52 686 565 0877
W: orbis.edu.mx

Peterson School – Lomas
Monte Himalaya 615, Lomas de Chapultepec, Miguel Hidalgo, México D.F. C.P. 11000
DP Coordinator Bella Cherem Picciotto
Languages Spanish
T: +52 5520 2213
W: www.peterson.edu.mx/lomas

Peterson School – Tlalpan
Carretera Federal a Cuernavaca, Km. 24 No. 6871, San Andrés Totoltepec, Tlalpan, México D.F. C.P. 14400
DP Coordinator Moisés Jesús Castillo Rojas
Languages Spanish
T: +52 3869 7040
W: www.peterson.edu.mx/tlalpan

Prepa UNI
Carretera Panamerican Km 269, Celaya, Guanajuato C.P. 38080
DP Coordinator Alejandra Nuñez
Languages Spanish
T: +52 461 61 39099
W: www.udec.edu.mx

Prepa UPAEP Angelópolis
Av. del Sol No. 5, Col. Concepción La Cruz, San Andrés Cholula, Puebla C.P. 72160
CP Coordinator Laura Mariana Hernández De la Torre
DP Coordinator Laura Mariana Hernández de la Torre
Languages Spanish
T: +52 222 225 2291
W: upaep.mx/prepa/angelopolis

Prepa UPAEP Cholula
Av. Forjadores No. 1804, Col Barrio de Jesús, San Pedro Cholula, Puebla C.P. 72760
CP Coordinator Claudia Yamilet Lomas Mendoza
DP Coordinator Claudia Yamilet Lomas Mendoza
Languages Spanish
T: +52 222 403 7373
W: upaep.mx/prepa/cholula

Prepa UPAEP Huamantla
Carr. Lib. Carr. México-Veracruz Kilómetro 147.5, Santa Clara, Huamantla, Tlaxcala C.P. 90500
CP Coordinator Yolanda Sánchez Flores
Languages Spanish
T: +52 247 472 2550
W: upaep.mx/prepa/huamantla

Prepa UPAEP Lomas
Circuito Mario Molina No. 15, Lomas de Angelópolis, San Andrés Cholula, Puebla C.P. 72828
CP Coordinator Alejandra Paola Anaya Salas
DP Coordinator Alejandra Paola Anaya Salas
Languages English, Spanish
T: +52 (0)1 222 5822102
W: upaep.mx/prepa/lomas

Prepa UPAEP Santiago
Av 9 Pte 1508, Barrio de Santiago, Puebla C.P. 72160
CP Coordinator Miguel Morales
DP Coordinator Miguel Morales
Languages Spanish
T: +52 222 246 8264
W: upaep.mx/prepa/santiago

Prepa UPAEP Sur
Calle Independencia No. 6339, Col. Patrimonio, Puebla C.P. 72470
CP Coordinator Claudia Verenice Sotelo Duarte
DP Coordinator Claudia Verenice Sotelo Duarte
Languages Spanish
T: +52 222 233 1342
W: upaep.mx/prepa/sur

Prepa UPAEP Tehuacán
Boulevard Tehuacán San Marcos No. 1700, Col. El Humilladero, Tehuacán, Puebla
CP Coordinator Francisco Javier Martínez Orea
Languages English, Spanish
T: +52 238 383 7800
W: upaep.mx/prepa/tehuacan

Tecnológico de Monterrey – Campus Ciudad de México
Calle del Puente #222, Col. Ejidos de Huipulco, Tlalpan, Distrito Federal C.P. 14380
DP Coordinator Adolfo Pedro Grovas Jaurena
Languages Spanish
T: +52 (55) 5483 2110
W: tec.mx/en/ciudad-de-mexico

Tecnológico de Monterrey – Campus Cumbres
Linces #1000, Col. Cumbres Elite, Monterrey, N.L. C.P. 64639
DP Coordinator Ada Verónica Chavarría Treviño
Languages Spanish, English
T: +52 (81) 8158 4622
W: tec.mx/en

Tecnológico de Monterrey – Campus Estado de México
Carretera Lago de Guadalupe, Km 3.5, Col. Margarita Maza de Juárez, Atizapán de Zaragoza, Estado de México C.P. 52926
DP Coordinator Paula Flores Kastanis
Languages Spanish, English
T: +52 (55) 5864 5714
W: tec.mx/en/estado-de-mexico

Tecnológico de Monterrey – Campus Eugenio Garza Lagüera
Topolobampo #4603, Valle de las Brisas, Monterrey, N.L. C.P. 64790
DP Coordinator Ana Isabel López Bernal
Languages Spanish
T: +52 (81) 8155 4490
W: tec.mx/en

Tecnológico de Monterrey – Campus Eugenio Garza Sada
Dinamarca #451 Sur Col Del Carmen, Monterrey, N.L. C.P. 64710
DP Coordinator Mónica Otálora
Languages Spanish, English
T: +52 (81) 8151 4264
W: tec.mx/en

Tecnológico de Monterrey – Campus Querétaro
Av. Epigmenio González #500, Fracc. San Pablo, Santiago de Querétaro C.P. 76130
DP Coordinator Christina Lee Norris González
Languages Spanish
T: +52 (442) 238 3208
W: tec.mx/en/queretaro

Tecnológico de Monterrey – Campus Santa Catarina
Morones Prieto No 290 Pte., Col Jesús M. Garza, Santa Catarina, N.L. C.P. 66180
DP Coordinator Rosalba Serrano Salinas
Languages Spanish, English
T: +52 (81) 8153 4045
W: tec.mx/en

Tecnológico de Monterrey – Campus Santa Fe
Av Carlos Lazo #100, Santa Fe, Delegación Alvaro Obregón C.P. 01389
DP Coordinator Mayte de Lassé Cañas
Languages Spanish, English
T: +52 (55) 9177 8131
W: tec.mx/en/santa-fe

Tecnológico de Monterrey – Campus Valle Alto
Carretera Nacional #8002 Km. 267.7, Col. La Estanzuela, Monterrey, N.L C.P. 64986
DP Coordinator Marcela Valero Cervantes
Languages English, Spanish
T: +52 (81)8228 5310
W: tec.mx/en

Tecnológico de Monterrey – Sede Esmeralda
Fracc. Conjunto Urbano, Col. Bosque Esmeralda, Manzana 7 Lote 1 y 2, Atizapán de Zaragoza, Estado de México C.P. 52930
DP Coordinator David Lee
Languages Spanish
T: +52 (55) 5864 5370 (EXT:2903)
W: tec.mx/en/esmeralda

Tecnológico de Monterrey – Sede Metepec
Av. Las Torres 1957 Ote., San Salvador Tizatlali, Metepec C.P. 52172
DP Coordinator Ernesto Solís Winkler
Languages Spanish, English
T: +52 (722) 271 5977
W: tec.mx/en

The American School Foundation, A.C.
Calle Sur 136-135, Colonia Las Americas, México D.F. C.P. 01120
DP Coordinator Lara Schupack
MYP Coordinator Kristen Leutheuser
PYP Coordinator Tara Munroe
Languages English, Spanish
T: +52 55 5227 4900
W: www.asf.edu.mx

The Churchill School
Felipe Villanueva No. 24, Col. Guadalupe Inn, Mexico City
MYP Coordinator Itzel Nava
PYP Coordinator Maria Garza Caligaris
Languages English
T: +52 55 50288800
W: www.churchill.edu.mx

Universidad de Monterrey Unidad Fundadores
Nova Scotia 109, between Av. Newfoundland and Av. General Mariano Escob+, Escobedo, Nuevo Leon C.P. 66054
CP Coordinator Lucía del Carmen Aguilar Pérez
DP Coordinator Homero de Jesús Treviño Villagómez
Languages Spanish
T: +52 (81) 8215 4151
W: www.udem.edu.mx

Universidad de Monterrey Unidad Valle Alto
Carretera Nacionala Salida Valle Alto Km1, Colonia Valle Alto, Monterrey, NL C.P. 64989
CP Coordinator Sara Esther Quiroga Ramírez
DP Coordinator María Aurora Tamez Elizondo
Languages English, Spanish
W: www.udem.edu.mx/Esp/Preparatoria/Pages/Unidad-Valle-Alto.aspx

Universidad Regiomontana Preparatoria Campus Centro
Matamoros # 430 Pte., Col. Centro, Monterrey, NL C.P. 64000
DP Coordinator Guillermo Acosta
Languages Spanish
T: +52 81 8220 4830
W: u-erre.mx

University of Monterrey
Av. Ignacio Morones Prieto 4500, Pte., 66238, San Pedro Garza García N.L. 66238
CP Coordinator Nabor Rodríguez Loera
DP Coordinator Rocío Ramírez Bolaños
Languages Spanish
T: 52 81 8215 1010
W: www.udem.edu.mx/prepaudem

Westhill Institute
Domingo Garcia Ramos No. 56, Col. Prados de la Montaña, Santa Fe, Cuajimalpa, Mexico City C.P. 05610
DP Coordinator Enrique Vargas
MYP Coordinator Enrique Vargas
PYP Coordinator Ktyall Malik
Languages English, Spanish, French
T: +52 55 8851 7000
W: www.westhillinstitute.edu.mx

Westhill Institute – Carpatos
Monte Carpatos 940, Lomas de Chapultepec, México D.F. C.P. 11000
PYP Coordinator Rocío Alvarez
Languages English, Spanish
T: +52 55 88517067
W: www.westhillinstitute.edu.mx/CampusCarpatos.html

NICARAGUA

Colegio Alemán Nicaragüense
Apartado 1636, Managua
DP Coordinator Hubert Luna Palacios
Languages Spanish, English
T: +505 2265 8449
W: www.coalnic.edu.ni/index.php/en/

Notre Dame School
Apartado 6092, Managua
DP Coordinator Carlos Ordoñez Mondragon
PYP Coordinator Silvia Vallecillo Ortega
Languages English
T: +505 22 760353
W: www.notredame.edu.ni

PANAMA

Boston School International
Ave. Arnulfo Arias Madrid Building. #727, Balboa, Ancón, Panama City
DP Coordinator Ruth Mendoza
PYP Coordinator Nairobys Rojas
Languages English
T: +507 833 8888
W: www.bostonschool.edu.pa

Colegio Isaac Rabin
Edificio 130, Ciudad del Saber
MYP Coordinator Sonia Martínez Robles
PYP Coordinator Marissa Rocha De Medina
Languages Spanish
T: +507 3170059
W: www.isaacrabin.com

International School of Panama
P.O. Box 0819-02588, Cerro Viento Rural, Panama City
DP Coordinator Nash Adamson
Languages English
T: +507 293 3000
W: www.isp.edu.pa

Knightsbridge Schools International Panama
Building 840, Andrews Blv., Panama Pacifico, Panama City
DP Coordinator Nelson Urrego
PYP Coordinator Yanisselly Norris
Languages English
T: +507 202 0877
W: www.ksi-panama.com

Metropolitan School of Panama
#104, Ave Vicente Bonilla, Ciudad del Saber, Clayton, Panama City
DP Coordinator Michael Foxmann
MYP Coordinator Dylan Carter
PYP Coordinator Erin Foxmann
Languages English
T: +507 317 1130
W: www.themetropolitanschool.com

PARAGUAY

Centro Educativo Arambé
Santísima Trinidad No 3.211, c/ Avda. Ita Ybaté (Zona Brítez Cue), Luque, Asunción
DP Coordinator Carolina Susana Bianco Wehrli
Languages Spanish
T: +595 21 694 662
W: www.arambe.edu.py

Colegio Goethe Asunción
Cnl Silva esq Tte Rocholl, Asuncion 232
DP Coordinator Anna Gabel
Languages Spanish
T: +595 21 606860
W: www.goethe.edu.py

Faith Christian School
Del Maestro 3471 c/ Soriano González, Barrio Herrera, Asunción
DP Coordinator Marisa Vaesken de Ramos
Languages English, Spanish
T: +595 21 620 5024
W: www.faith.edu.py

St Anne's School
Tte. Manuel Pino Gonzalez y Eulalio Facetti, Asunción
DP Coordinator Mirko Zayas
Languages English
T: +595 21 295649
W: www.sas.edu.py

PERU

Andino Cusco International School
Km 10.5 Carretera Cusco, Chinchero Distrito de Cachimayo, Anta, Cusco
DP Coordinator Bruno Vázquez Molinero
PYP Coordinator Emperatriz Yepez
Languages English, Spanish
T: +51 (84) 275135
W: www.andinoschool.edu.pe

André Malraux
Dirección:Batallón Concepción (antes San Francisco) N° 245, Urb. Sta. Teresa – Surco, Lima
DP Coordinator Ramiro Febres Tapia
Languages English
T: +51 1 275 4937
W: www.andremalraux.edu.pe

Asociación Colegio Mater Admirabilis
Avenida Arica 898, San Miguel, Lima
MYP Coordinator Fabiola Calero Coronel
Languages Spanish
T: +51 1 460 8306
W: www.maternet.edu.pe

Casuarinas International College
Av Jacarandá 391, Valle Hermoso – Monterrico, Lima
CP Coordinator Luis Felipe González del Riego
DP Coordinator Luis Felipe González del Riego
MYP Coordinator Norma Isabel Pagaza Sotelo
PYP Coordinator Claudia Santana Oliveros
Languages Spanish, English, French, Portuguese, Mandarin
T: +51 1 344 4040
W: www.casuarinas.edu.pe

Clemente Althaus
Jr, Cuzco, Prolongación 360, Cercado de Lima 15086
DP Coordinator Katherine Fernandez Alvarez
Languages Spanish
W: clementealthaus.edu.pe

Colegio Alpamayo
Calle Bucaramanga 145, Urb Mayorazgo, Lima
DP Coordinator Johan Fripp Anicama
Languages Spanish
T: +51 1 349 0111
W: www.alpamayo.edu.pe

Colegio Altair
Avenida La Arboleda 385, Urb. Sirius, La Molina, Lima 12
DP Coordinator Denise Llosa
MYP Coordinator Jimena La Rosa Massa
PYP Coordinator Maria Ines Ponce de Leon
Languages Spanish, English
T: +511 365 0298
W: www.altair.edu.pe

Colegio Anglo Americano Prescott
RUC: 20162560302, Av. Alfonso Ugarte N° 565, vCasilla Postal No 1036, Arequipa, Tingo 1036
DP Coordinator Patricio González Luna
MYP Coordinator Romina Ramos Solis
PYP Coordinator Katia Aíta
Languages English, Spanish
T: +51 54 232540
W: www.prescott.edu.pe

Colegio Champagnat
Av Prolongación Paseo de la, República 7930 – 7931, Lima SANTIAGO DE SURCO 33
DP Coordinator Humberto Lara Ceroni
PYP Coordinator Ana Elizabeth Gálvez Calderón
Languages Spanish
T: +511 519 0500
W: www.champagnat.edu.pe

Colegio de Alto Rendimiento de Amazonas
Jr. Amazonas Nro. 120, ISTP Perú-Japón, Distrito de Chachapoyas, Provincia de Chachapoyas 42
DP Coordinator Dante Javier Escobar Hurtado
Languages Spanish
T: +51 1 615 5800
W: www.minedu.gob.pe/coar

Colegio de Alto Rendimiento de Ancash
Sector Llacshahuanca, Recuay, Ancash 43
DP Coordinator Rosana Malpaso Morales
Languages Spanish
W: www.minedu.gob.pe/coar

Colegio de Alto Rendimiento de Apurímac
Jiron Tupac Amaru S/N, Pairaca, Chalhuanca 83, Apurímac
DP Coordinator Jaime Hugo Aquino Rodríguerz
Languages Spanish
T: +51 1 615 5800
W: www.minedu.gob.pe/coar

Colegio de Alto Rendimiento de Arequipa
Ca. Federico Barreto Nª 148, CEBA Nuestra Señora del Pilar, Arequipa 54
DP Coordinator Marina Josefina Vergara López
Languages Spanish
T: +51 1 615 5800 (EXT:26527)
W: www.minedu.gob.pe/coar

Colegio de Alto Rendimiento de Ayacucho
Jr. Mariano Ruiz de Castilla N° 150, Alameda Valdelirios, Distrito de Ayacucho, Provincia de Huamanga-Ay 05001
DP Coordinator Cosme Gerardo Palomino Cárdenas
Languages Spanish
T: +51 1 615 5800
W: www.minedu.gob.pe/coar

Colegio de Alto Rendimiento de Cajamarca
Jirón José Pardo No 103, Distrito Jesús, Cajamarca 00604
DP Coordinator Julio Trigoso Mori
Languages Spanish
T: +51 1 615 5800
W: www.minedu.gob.pe/coar

Colegio de Alto Rendimiento de Cusco
Sector Bellavista a 6 Km. del distrito de Anta, Distrito de Pucyura, Provincia de Anta Región 84
DP Coordinator Victor Humberto Rojas Pierta
Languages Spanish
T: +51 1 615 5800
W: www.minedu.gob.pe/coar

Colegio de Alto Rendimiento de Huancavelica
Jr. José Gabriel Condorcanqui S/N, CP Santa Ana, Huancavelica, Provincia de Huancavelica 67
DP Coordinator Jaime Artica
Languages Spanish
T: +51 1 615 5800
W: www.minedu.gob.pe/coar

Colegio de Alto Rendimiento de Huánuco
Centro Poblado Canchán, a 12 km de Huánuco, Huánuco 62
DP Coordinator Luis Ayala Marchan
Languages Spanish
T: +51 1 615 5800
W: www.minedu.gob.pe/coar

Colegio de Alto Rendimiento de Ica
Calle José María Mejía S/N, Nazca, Ica, 11401
DP Coordinator Luisa Angélica Loredo Valdéz
Languages Spanish
T: +51 1 615 5800
W: www.minedu.gob.pe/coar

Colegio de Alto Rendimiento de Junín
Ca. Huayna Capac, Cdra. 4 IESTP Jaime Cerrón Palomino, Chongos Bajo, Chupaca, Región Junín 64
DP Coordinator Alcides Roman Rivas
Languages Spanish
T: +51 1 615 5800 (EXT:26527)
W: www.minedu.gob.pe/coar

Colegio de Alto Rendimiento de La Libertad
Campamento San José Carretera Trujillo, Chimbote, Virú, Provincia de Virú Región 44
DP Coordinator Diana Rosales Murga
Languages Spanish
T: +51 1 615 5800
W: www.minedu.gob.pe/coar

Colegio de Alto Rendimiento de Lambayeque
Prolongación Bolognesi S/N, A media cuadra de la Av. José Leonardo Ortiz, Chiclayo 517414
DP Coordinator Jorge Luis Arrasco Alegre
Languages Spanish
T: +51 1 615 5800
W: www.minedu.gob.pe/coar

Colegio de Alto Rendimiento de Lima-Provincias
Av. 5 de Diciembre s/n Santa María, Huaura
DP Coordinator Félix Moisés Loza Rosadio
Languages Spanish
W: www.minedu.gob.pe/coar

Colegio de Alto Rendimiento de Loreto
Avenida Mariscal Cáceres con Pasaje Jorge Chávez S/N, Iquitos 16001, Maynas
DP Coordinator Luis Alberto Tulumba Villacrez
Languages Spanish
T: +51 1 615 5800
W: www.minedu.gob.pe/coar

Colegio de Alto Rendimiento de Madre de Dios
Av. Madre de Dios cuadra 4 esquina con, Jirón Ica, Tambopata 82
DP Coordinator Juan Eduardo Salvador Gloria
Languages Spanish
T: +51 1 615 5800
W: www.minedu.gob.pe/coar

Colegio de Alto Rendimiento de Moquegua
Prlg. Av. Mariano Lino Urquieta S/N, CP San Antonio, Distrito de Moquegua, Provincia de Mariscal Nie 53
DP Coordinator Reynaldo Arteta Ávila
Languages Spanish
T: +51 1 615 5800 (EXT:26527)

Colegio de Alto Rendimiento de Pasco
Jr. Joseph Albert Walijewski Szydlo Nro 201, Región de Pasco, Chontabamba, Provincia de Oxapampa 63
DP Coordinator Eduardo Verastegui Borja
Languages Spanish
T: +51 1 615 5800
W: www.minedu.gob.pe/coar

Colegio de Alto Rendimiento de Piura
Ca. Juan Velasco Alvarado S/N, AAHH Nueva Esperanza, CETPRO Bosconia, Distrito Veintiséis de Octubre, Provincia de Piura 73
DP Coordinator Maritza Quintana Carlin
Languages Spanish
T: +51 1 615 5800 (EXT:26527)
W: www.minedu.gob.pe/coar

Colegio de Alto Rendimiento de Puno
Av. Panamericana Nª943, a 17 km. de Puno- Carretera Chucuito, Seminario Ntra Señora de Guadalupe, Puno, Región Puno 51
DP Coordinator Isabel Mamani
Languages Spanish
T: +51 1 615 5800
W: www.minedu.gob.pe/coar

Colegio de Alto Rendimiento de San Martin
Jr. Pedro Pascasio Noriega Nª 061, IESPP Generalísimo José de San Martín, Distrito de Moyobamba, Región San Martín 42
DP Coordinator Percy Boza
Languages Spanish
T: +51 1 615 5800
W: www.minedu.gob.pe/coar

Colegio de Alto Rendimiento de Tacna
Sector Irrigación Copare, por la carretera Panamericana Sur, IE Norah Flores Tor+, Tacna, Región Tacna 52
DP Coordinator Freddy Edinson Jimenez Paredes
Languages Spanish
T: +51 1 615 5800
W: www.minedu.gob.pe/coar

Colegio de Alto Rendimiento de Tumbes
San Juan de la Vírgen s/n, Tumbes 72
DP Coordinator Efraín Villacorta Zárate
Languages Spanish
W: www.minedu.gob.pe/coar

Colegio de Alto Rendimiento de Ucayali
Psje. Huáscar S/N, PPJJ Micaela Bastidas, Departamento Ucayali, Calleria 61, Coronel Portillo
DP Coordinator Nancy Mely Del Aguila Pinedo
Languages Spanish
T: +51 1 615 5800
W: www.minedu.gob.pe/coar

Colegio Franklin Delano Roosevelt
The American School of Lima, Apartado 18-0977, Lima 18
DP Coordinator Robert Allan
Languages English, Spanish
T: +51 1 435 0890
W: www.amersol.edu.pe/index.asp

Colegio La Unión
Av. Cipriano Dulanto (ex La Mar) 1950, Pueblo Libre, Lima
DP Coordinator Miriam Palacios Velasquez
Languages English
T: +511 2610533
W: www.launion.edu.pe

Colegio León Pinelo
Calle Maimonides 610, San Isidro, Lima 27
DP Coordinator Yoana Kaliksztein Fihman
PYP Coordinator Silvia Kcomt
Languages Spanish
T: +51 1 2183040
W: www.lp.edu.pe

Colegio Los Álamos
Calle Estados Unidos 731, Jesús María, Lima 11
DP Coordinator César Chora Chamochumbi
Languages Spanish
T: +51 1 4631044
W: www.losalamos.edu.pe

Colegio Magister
Francisco de Cuéllar #686, Surco, Lima 33
DP Coordinator Giancarlo Belloni
Languages English, Spanish
T: +51 1 437 9029
W: www.magister.pe

Colegio Max Uhle
Av. Fernandini s/n, Sachaca, Arequipa
DP Coordinator Alejandro Gutiérrez Osorio
Languages Spanish
T: +51 54 232921
W: www.maxuhle.edu.pe

Colegio Mayor Secundario Presidente del Perú
Centro Vacacional de Huampaní, Carretera Central, Km 24.5, Chaclacayo, Lima
DP Coordinator José Hugo Nolasco Mayta
Languages Spanish
T: +51 1 223 0341
W: www.colegiomayor.edu.pe

Colegio Nuestra Señora del Pilar
Av Virgen del Pilar 1711, Cercado, Arequipa
DP Coordinator Ricardo Enríquez Cáceres
Languages Spanish
T: +5154226262
W: www.cnspilar.edu.pe

Colegio Peruano – Alemán Reina del Mundo
Avenida Rinconada del Lago 675, La Molina, Lima 12
DP Coordinator Luis Ernesto Gutierrez
Languages Spanish
T: +511 479 2191/+511 368 0495/+511 368 0496
W: www.rdm.edu.pe

Colegio Peruano Alemán Beata Imelda
Carretera Central Km. 29, Chosica, Lima 15
DP Coordinator Romina Ortiz Torres
Languages Spanish
T: +51 1 360 3119
W: www.cbi.edu.pe

Colegio Peruano Británico
Avda. Via Lactea 445, Monterrico, Santiago de Surco, Lima 33
DP Coordinator Magally Ramos Martínez
Languages English
T: +51 1 436 0151
W: www.britishschool.edu.pe

Colegio Pestalozzi (Colegio Suizo del Peru)
Casilla 18-1027, Aurora-Miraflores, Lima 18
DP Coordinator Karen Coral
Languages Spanish
T: +51 1 241 4218
W: www.pestalozzi.edu.pe

Colegio Sagrados Corazones 'Recoleta'
Av. Circunvalación del Golf 368, La Molina, Lima
DP Coordinator Lourdes Olano Vargas De Cieza
Languages Spanish
T: +51 1 702 2500
W: www.recoleta.edu.pe

Colegio Salcantay
Av Pío X11 261, Monterrico, Surco, Lima 33
DP Coordinator Rosa Elena Galagarza
Languages Spanish
T: +511 436 1226
W: www.salcantay.edu.pe

Colegio San Agustín
Av. Javier Prado Este 980 San Isidro, Lima 27
DP Coordinator Elizabeth Chavez Junes
PYP Coordinator Mercedes Varas Castillo
Languages Spanish
T: +51 1 616 4242 / +51 1 440 0320
W: www.sanagustin.edu.pe

Colegio San Agustín de Chiclayo
Km 8 Carretera Pimentel, Chiclayo, Lambayeque
DP Coordinator Patricia Quevedo Willys
Languages Spanish
T: +51 7 420 2948
W: www.sanagustinchiclayo.edu.pe

Colegio San Ignacio de Recalde
Calle Géminis 251 San Borja, Lima
DP Coordinator Patricia Loo Salas
Languages English
T: +511 2119430
W: www.sir.edu.pe

Colegio Santa Úrsula
Calle Salamanca N° 125, San Isidro, Lima
DP Coordinator Ana María Reyes Fajardo
Languages Spanish
T: +51 202 7430
W: www.santaursula.edu.pe

Colegio Santísimo Nombre de Jesús
Calle Mayorazgo 176, Urbanización Chacarilla del Estanque, San Borja, Lima
DP Coordinator Edwin Borda Meza
Languages English, Spanish
T: +511 372 1655
W: www.santisimo.edu.pe

Davy College
Avenida Hoyos Rubio 2684, Cajamarca
DP Coordinator David Utrup
Languages English, Spanish, French
T: +51 76 36 7501
W: www.davycollege.edu.pe

Euroamerican College
Parcela 183-187 Mz C, Fundo Casablanca, Pachacámac
DP Coordinator Carla Gloria Piscoya Salinas
PYP Coordinator Karina Munoz
Languages Spanish, English
T: +51 1 231 1617
W: www.euroamericano.edu.pe

Fleming College
P. O. Box 1310, Av. America Sur 3701, Trujillo
DP Coordinator Angel Alarcon
PYP Coordinator Sara Gosling
Languages English, Spanish
T: +51 44 284440
W: www.fleming.edu.pe

Hiram Bingham School
Paseo de la Castellana 919, Surco, Lima 33
DP Coordinator Martha Marengo
MYP Coordinator Carrie Rabel
PYP Coordinator Cinthya Estremadoyro
Languages English, Spanish
T: +51 1 271 9880
W: www.hirambingham.edu.pe

IE Pedro Ruiz Gallo
Av. Cdra 2 S/N Costado de la Clinica Maison de Sante, Distrito de Chorrillos
DP Coordinator Luz Rosas
Languages Spanish
T: +51 1 6514056
W: www.prg-chorrillos.com

Institución Educativa Fuerza Aérea Peruana José Quiñones
Av. Evitamiento S/N-Urb, Camacho, La Molina, Lima 12
DP Coordinator Patricia Aparicio Vargas
Languages Spanish
T: +51 1 4364595
W: www.diace.edu.pe

Institución Educativa Particular San Antonio de Padua
Av. Estados Unidos 569, Jesús María, Lima 11
DP Coordinator Jenny Polo Churrango
Languages Spanish
T: +51 1 6143600
W: www.sanantoniodepadua.edu.pe

Institución Educativa Privada Lord Byron
Calle Grande 250, Arequipa, Cayma
DP Coordinator Jeffrey Dagmar Fernández Castillo
Languages Spanish
T: +51 54 254976
W: www.lordbyron.edu.pe

Liceo Naval 'Almirante Guise'
Calle Monti 350, San Borja, Lima 41
DP Coordinator María Esther Huertas del Pino Saenz
Languages Spanish
T: +51 1 475 8055
W: www.lnag.edu.pe

Lord Byron School
Jr Viña del Mar 375-379, Urb. Sol de la Molina, 1era. Etapa, Lima 12
DP Coordinator Joselito Vallejos Avalos
MYP Coordinator Roxana Calderón
PYP Coordinator Roxana Ortega Tello
Languages English, Spanish
T: +511 4791717
W: www.byron.edu.pe

Markham College
Augusto Angulo 291, San Antonio - Miraflores, Lima 15048
DP Coordinator Guinevere Dyker
Languages English, Spanish
T: +51 1 315 6750
W: www.markham.edu.pe

Montessori International College
Maz. A Sub Lote 01A, Urb. Tecsup, Distrito Víctor Larco Herrera, Trujillo, La Libertad 13009
PYP Coordinator Kayleigh Poole
Languages Spanish, English
T: +51 44 340000
W: www.montessoricollege.edu.pe

Newton College
Av. Ricardo Elías Aparicio 240, Lima 12
DP Coordinator Chris Abbott
PYP Coordinator Kat Rymarz
Languages English
T: +51 1 207 9900
W: www.newton.edu.pe

Peruvian North American Abraham Lincoln School
Calle José Antonio, 475, Urb Parque de Monterrico, La Molina, Lima 12
DP Coordinator Brenda Yohana Caycho Avalos
MYP Coordinator Claudia Llarena San Blas
PYP Coordinator Karla Puente Garcia
Languages Spanish, English
T: +51 1 617 4500
W: www.abrahamlincoln.edu.pe

San Silvestre School Asociacion Civil
Apartado 18-0492, Miraflores, Lima 18
DP Coordinator Rafaela Antezana
Languages English
T: +51 1 2413334
W: www.sansilvestre.edu.pe

St George's College
Av General Ernesto Montagne 360, Urb La Aurora, Miraflores, Lima 18
DP Coordinator Luis Sifuentes Maldonado
Languages English, Spanish
T: +511 242 5747
W: www.sanjorge.edu.pe

Villa Alarife School
Jr. Alameda Don Augusto Mz D Lt 5, Urb. Los Huertos de Villa, Chorrillos, Lima
DP Coordinator María Luz Rojas Bonilla
T: +511 234 6969
W: villaalarife.edu.pe

PUERTO RICO

Robinson School
5 Nairn Street, San Juan 00907
DP Coordinator Yesenia Ramos
MYP Coordinator Carine Poinson Simon
PYP Coordinator Lorimar Ramirez
Languages English
T: +1 787 999 4600
W: www.robinsonschool.org

Puerto Rico

THE BALDWIN SCHOOL OF PUERTO RICO
PO Box 1827, Bayamón 00960-1827
DP Coordinator Mrs. Laura Maristany
MYP Coordinator Mrs. Cristina Castillo
PYP Coordinator Mrs. Sarah Loinaz
Languages English
T: +1 787 720 2421
E: admission@baldwin-school.org
W: www.baldwin-school.org
See full details on page 551
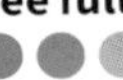

TRINIDAD & TOBAGO

The International School of Port of Spain
1 International Drive, Westmoorings, Port of Spain
MYP Coordinator Angela Shahien
PYP Coordinator Angela Shahien
Languages English
T: +1 868 633 4777
W: www.isps.edu.tt

URUGUAY

Colegio Stella Maris
Máximo Tajes 7357/7359, CP 11500 Montevideo 11500
DP Coordinator Maria Brossard Hitta
Languages English, Spanish
T: +598 2 600 0702
W: www.stellamaris.edu.uy

Escuela Integral Hebreo Uruguaya
Jose Benito Lamas 2835, Montevideo 11300
DP Coordinator Rosana Erosa
Languages Spanish
T: +598 2 708 1712
W: www.escuelaintegral.edu.uy

Escuela y Liceo Elbio Fernandez
Maldonado 1381, Montevideo 11200
MYP Coordinator Stella Arrieta
Languages English, Spanish
T: +598 2901 1254
W: www.elbiofernandez.edu.uy

International College
Blvr Artigas y Avda del Mar, Punta del Este, Maldonado
DP Coordinator Laura Cabrera
Languages English, Spanish
T: +598 42 228 888
W: www.ic.edu.uy

St Brendan's School
Av Rivera 2314, Montevideo CP 11200
CP Coordinator Maria del Rosario Rodríguez
DP Coordinator Maria del Rosario Rodríguez
MYP Coordinator Helena Sastre Abreu
PYP Coordinator Claudia Ourthe-Cabalè
Languages English, Spanish
T: +598 2409 4939
W: www.stbrendan.edu.uy

St Clare's College
California y los Médanos, Punta del Este, San Rafael 20000
DP Coordinator Josué Naranjo
Languages Spanish, English
T: +598 42 490200
W: www.scc.edu.uy

St Patrick's College
Camino Gigantes 2735, Montevideo 12100
MYP Coordinator Mary Evans
Languages Spanish
T: +598 2 601 3474
W: www.stpatrick.edu.uy

The British Schools, Montevideo
Máximo Tajes 6400, esq Havre, Montevideo 11500
DP Coordinator Florencia Paullier
PYP Coordinator Maria Fernanda Sobral
Languages English, Spanish
T: +598 2 600 3421
W: www.british.edu.uy

Uruguayan American School
Saldún de Rodríguez 2375, Montevideo 11500
DP Coordinator Gabriel Amaral
Languages English
T: + (598) 2600 7681
W: www.uas.edu.uy

Woodlands School
San Carlos de Bolivar s/n entre Havre y Cooper, Montevideo 11500
MYP Coordinator Fanny Bozzo Aldecosea
Languages Spanish
T: +59 82 604 27 14
W: www.woodlands.edu.uy

Woodside School
Mercedes y Louvre. Barrio Cantegril, 20100 Punta del Este, Maldonado
DP Coordinator Maria Jimena Popelka Casasnovas
Languages English, Spanish
T: +598 4225 2552

USA

Alabama

Auburn High School
405 South Dean Road, Auburn AL 36830
DP Coordinator Davis Thompson
Languages English
T: +1 334 887 4970
W: www.auburnschools.org/ahs

Central High School, Tuscaloosa
905 15th Street, Tuscaloosa AL 35401
DP Coordinator Jennifer Hines
Languages English
T: +1 205 759 3720
W: www.tuscaloosacityschools.com/domain/10

Charles A. Brown Elementary School
4811 Court J, Birmingham AL 35208
PYP Coordinator Vieshell Tatum
Languages English
T: +1 205 231 6860
W: www.bhamcityschools.org/page/67

Columbia High School
300 Explorer Boulevard, Huntsville AL 35806
CP Coordinator Karli LeCompte
DP Coordinator Karli LeCompte
Languages English
T: +1 256 428 7576
W: www.hsv.k12.al.us/schools/high/chs/index.htm

Columbia High School
300 Explorer Boulevard, Huntsville AL 35806
MYP Coordinator Paula Wilkinson
Languages English
T: +1 256 428 7576
W: www.hsv.k12.al.us/schools/high/chs/index.htm?1300716725182?1300716726521

Cornerstone Schools of Alabama
118 55th Street North, Birmingham AL 35212
PYP Coordinator Rebecca Stivender
Languages English
T: +1 205 591 7600
W: www.csalabama.org

Daphne High School
9300 Lawson Road, Daphne AL 36526
DP Coordinator Deborah Few
Languages English
T: +1 251 626 8787
W: www.daphnehs.com

Fairhope High School
One Pirate Drive, Fairhope AL 36532
DP Coordinator Darla Litaker
Languages English
T: +1 251 928 8309
W: www.fairhopehs.com

Hoover High School
1000 Buccaneer Drive, Hoover AL 35244
DP Coordinator Melissa Hamley
Languages English
T: +1 205 439 1200
W: www.hoover.k12.al.us

Jefferson County IB School
6100 Old Leeds Road, Birmingham AL 35210
DP Coordinator April Miller
MYP Coordinator Michael Cloninger
Languages English
T: +1 205 379 5356
W: jcib.jefcoed.com

John Herbert Phillips Academy
2316 7th Avenue North, Birmingham AL 35203
MYP Coordinator Jessica Jones Wedgeworth
PYP Coordinator Jessica Jones Wedgeworth
Languages English
T: +1 205 231 9500
W: www.bhamcityschools.org?

Johnnie R. Carr Middle School
1610 Ray Thorington Rd, Montgomery AL 36117
MYP Coordinator Joshua Farrow
Languages English
T: +1 334 244 4005
W: www.carr.mps-al.org

MacMillan International Academy
4015 McInnis Road, Montgomery AL 36116
PYP Coordinator Theresa Smith
Languages English
T: +1 334 284 7137
W: www.macmillan.mps-al.org

Murphy High School
100 South Carlen Street, Mobile AL 36606
CP Coordinator Sarah Woltring
DP Coordinator Rebecca Mullins
Languages English
T: +1 251 221 3186
W: www.murphy.mcs.schoolinsites.com

Phillips Preparatory School
3255 Old Shell Road, Mobile AL 36607
MYP Coordinator Andrea Woodbury
Languages English
T: +1 251 221 2286
W: phillipsprep.com

Providence Elementary School
10 Chalkstone Street, Huntsville AL 35806
PYP Coordinator Michele Spray
T: +1 256 428 7125
W: www.huntsvillecityschools.org/schools/providence-elementary

Ramsay Alternative High School
1800 13th Avenue South AL 35205
DP Coordinator Jonathan Barr
MYP Coordinator Jessica Jones Wedgeworth
Languages English
T: +1 205 231 7000
W: ramsayhigh.com

The Academy for Science and Foreign Language
3221 Mastin Lake Road, Huntsville AL 35810
MYP Coordinator Adam Landingham
PYP Coordinator Michele Spray
Languages English
T: +1 256 428 7000
W: www.huntsvillecityschools.org/schools/academy-science-foreign-language

Tuscaloosa Magnet Elementary School
315 McFarland Blvd. East, Tuscaloosa AL 35404
PYP Coordinator Mike Bissell
Languages English
T: +1 205 759 3655
W: blogs.tusc.k12.al.us/tmse

Tuscaloosa Magnet Middle School
315 McFarland Blvd. East, Tuscaloosa AL 35404
MYP Coordinator Lavanda Wagenheim
Languages English
T: +1 205 759 3653
W: www.tuscaloosacityschools.com

W H Council Traditional School
751 Wilkinson Street, Mobile AL 36603-1397
PYP Coordinator Mrs. E Danae Bowman
Languages English
T: +1 251 221 1139
W: council.mce.schoolinsites.com

W P Davidson High School
3900 Pleasant Valley Road, Mobile AL 36609
DP Coordinator Lydia Edmonds
Languages English
T: +1 251 221 3084
W: www.wpdavidson.org

Williams School
155 Barren Fork Blvd SW, Huntsville AL 35824
MYP Coordinator Christine King
PYP Coordinator Michele Spray
Languages English
T: +1 256 428 7540/5
W: www.huntsvillecityschools.org/schools/williams-middle

Alaska

Palmer High School
1170 West Arctic Avenue, Ma -Su Borough School District, Palmer AK 99645
DP Coordinator Nichelle Henry
Languages English
T: +1 907 746 8408

West Anchorage High School
1700 Hillcrest Drive, Anchorage AK 99517
DP Coordinator John Ruhlin
Languages English
T: +1 907 742 2610
W: www.asdk12.org/schools/west/pages

Arizona

Barry Goldwater High School
2820 West Rose Garden Lane, Deer Valley United School Dist, Phoenix AZ 85027
DP Coordinator Joseph Stempniewski
MYP Coordinator Joseph Stempniewski
Languages English
T: +1 623 445 3000
W: www.dvusd.org/domain/39

Betty H Fairfax High School
8225 South 59th Avenue, Laveen AZ 85339
DP Coordinator Elana Payton
Languages English
T: +1 602 764 9020
W: www.bettyfairfaxhs.org

Buckeye Union High School
1000 E. Narramore, Buckeye AZ 85326
DP Coordinator Joshua Stringham
Languages English, Spanish
T: +1 623 386 4423
W: www.buhsd.org/buckeye

Cactus Shadows High School
PO Box 426, Cave Creek AZ 85327-0426
DP Coordinator Jennifer Cento
Languages English
T: +1 480 575 2400
W: www.ccusd93.org/cshs

Canyon del Oro High School
25 West Calle Concordia, Oro Valley AZ 85704
DP Coordinator Amy Bomke
Languages English
T: +1 520 696 5560
W: www.amphi.com/cdo

Chandler High School
350 N. Arizona Ave., Chandler AZ 85225
CP Coordinator Melanie Mello
DP Coordinator Melanie Mello
MYP Coordinator Melanie Mello
Languages English
T: +1 480 812 7700
W: www.cusd80.com/chs

Cholla High Magnet School
2001 West Starr Pass Blvd, Tucson AZ 85713
DP Coordinator Kathryn Jensen
Languages English
T: +1 520 225 4000
W: edweb.tusd1.org/cholla

Desert Garden Montessori
5130 E. Warner Rd., Phoenix AZ 85044
MYP Coordinator Krista John
Languages English
T: +1 480 496 9833
W: desertgardenmontessori.org

Desert Mountain High School
12575 E Via Linda, Scottsdale Unified, Scottsdale AZ 85259
DP Coordinator Laura Kamka
Languages English
T: +1 480 484 7009
W: www.susd.org/schools/high/Desertmtn/

EDUPRIZE Schools
580 W Melody Ave., Gilbert AZ 85233
DP Coordinator Scott Greenhalgh
Languages English
T: +1 480 888 1610
W: www.eduprizeschools.net

Estrella Mountain Elementary School
10301 S. San Miguel Road, Goodyear AZ 85338
MYP Coordinator Michele Bove
PYP Coordinator Megan Deloff
Languages English
T: +1 623 327 2820
W: www.liberty.k12.az.us

Florence High School
1000 S. Main St, Florence AZ 85232
DP Coordinator Edward Callahan
Languages English
T: +1 520 866 3560
W: fhs.fusdaz.com

Ironwood High School
6051 W. Sweetwater Ave, Glendale AZ 85304
DP Coordinator Christine Kuczka
Languages English
T: +1 623 486 6400
W: www.peoriaunified.org/ironwood

Kyrene Middle School
1050 E Carver Rd, Tempe AZ 85284
MYP Coordinator Kathie Cigich
Languages English
T: +1 480 541 6600
W: www.kyrene.org/kyr

Madison Meadows Middle School
225 W. Ocotillo Rd, Phoenix AZ 85013
MYP Coordinator Victoria Coughlin
Languages English
T: +1 602 664 7610
W: www.madisonaz.org

Madison Simis Elementary School
7302 N. 10th Street, Phoenix AZ 85020
PYP Coordinator Melissa Powers
Languages English
T: +1 602 664 7300
W: www.madisonaz.org/simis-elementary

Mesa Academy of Advanced Studies
6919 East Brown Road, Mesa AZ 85217
MYP Coordinator Michael Spencer
Languages English
T: +1 480 308 7400
W: www.mpsaz.org/academy

Millennium High School
14802 W Wigwam Blvd, Goodyear AZ 85395
DP Coordinator Robert Schlosser
Languages English
T: +1 623 932 7200
W: www.aguafria.org

Mountain View Preparatory School
2939 Del Rio Drive, Cottonwood AZ 86326
PYP Coordinator Heather Langley
Languages English
T: +1 928 649 8144
W: www.cocsd.k12.az.us

Nogales High School
1905 N. Apache Blvd., Nogales AZ 85621
DP Coordinator Jennifer Valenzuela
Languages English
T: +1 520 377 2021
W: nhs.nusd.k12.az.us

North Canyon High School
1700 East Union Hills Drive, Phoenix AZ 85024
DP Coordinator Candace Davis
MYP Coordinator Candace Davis
Languages English
T: +1 623 780 4200
W: cmweb.pvschools.net/nchsweb

North High School
1101 E. Thomas Rd., Phoenix AZ 85014
DP Coordinator Estaban Flemons
Languages English
T: +1 602 826 4702
W: www.northhs.com

Quail Run Elementary School
3303 E. Utopia Rd., Phoenix AZ 85050
PYP Coordinator Dianna Rubey
Languages English
T: +1 602 449 4400
W: www.pvschools.net/qres

Rancho Solano Preparatory School
9180 E. Via de Ventura, Scottsdale AZ 85258
DP Coordinator Marco Garbarino
Languages English
T: +1 480 646 8200
W: www.ranchosolano.com

Summit Academy (7-8 Campus)
1550 Wets Summit Place, Chandler AZ 85224
MYP Coordinator Mary Roberts Winters
Languages English
T: +1 480 472 3430
W: www.mpsaz.org/summitacademy

Summit Academy (K-6 Campus)
1560 W Summit Place, Chandler AZ 85224
PYP Coordinator Camille Loudenbeck
Languages English
T: +1 480 472 3500
W: www.mpsaz.org/summitacademy

Tempe Academy of International Studies
3205 S. Rural Road, Tempe AZ 85282
MYP Coordinator Denise Dunwoody
Languages English
T: +1 480 730 7101
W: www.tempeschools.org

Tempe High School
1730 S Mill Avenue, Tempe AZ 85281
DP Coordinator James Michael Cooper
Languages English
T: +1 480 967 1661
W: www.tempeunion.org

The Odyssey Institute for Advanced and International Studies
6500 S Apache Rd, Buckeye AZ 85326
DP Coordinator Randy Hiatt
MYP Coordinator Becky Quigley
Languages English
T: +1 623 327 3111
W: www.theodysseyacademy.com

Verde Valley School
3511 Verde Valley School Road, Sedona AZ 86351
DP Coordinator Andy Gill
Languages English
T: +1 928 284 2272
W: www.vvsaz.org

Vista Verde Middle School
2826 E. Grovers Ave., Phoenix AZ 85032
MYP Coordinator Ian Connell
Languages English
T: +1 602 449 5300
W: www.pvschools.net/domain/44

Westwood High School
945 West 8th Street, Mesa AZ 85201
DP Coordinator Jacob Davis
MYP Coordinator Brian Buck
Languages English
T: +1 480 472 4400
W: www.mpsaz.org/westwood

Willow Canyon High School
17901 West Lundberg St, Surprise AZ 85388
DP Coordinator Jason Ward
Languages English
T: +1 623 523 8000
W: www.dysart.org

Arkansas

Bentonville High School
1801 SE J Street, Bentonville AR 72712
DP Coordinator Derek Miller
Languages English
T: +1 479 254 5100
W: bhs.bentonvillek12.org/pages/bentonville_hs

Hot Springs High School
701 Emory Street, Hot Springs AR 71913
CP Coordinator Shannon Geoffrion
DP Coordinator Shannon Geoffrion
MYP Coordinator Laura West
Languages English
T: +1 501 624 5286
W: www.hsprings.dsc.k12.ar.us

Hot Springs Middle School
701 Main Street, Hot Springs AR 71913
MYP Coordinator Laura West
Languages English
T: +1 501 624 5228

Park International Magnet School
617 Main Street, Hot Springs AR 71913
PYP Coordinator Kristal Brandon
Languages English
T: +1 501 623 5661
W: www.hssd.net

Springdale High School
1103 West Emma Avenue, Springdale AR 72764
DP Coordinator Carol Turley
Languages English
T: +1 479 750 8832
W: www.shs.springdaleschools.org

Walter Turnbow Elementary School
3390 Habberton Road, Springdale AR 72764
PYP Coordinator Alison Washkowiak
Languages English
T: +1 479 750 8785

Westwood Elementary School
1850 McRay Ave, Springdale AR 72762
PYP Coordinator Sharyn O'Hearn
Languages English
T: +1 479 750 8871
W: westwood.sdale.org

California

Academia Moderna Charter
2410 Broadway, Walnut Park CA 90255
PYP Coordinator Kaylene Rudd
Languages English
T: +1 323 923 0383
W: www.academiamoderna.org

ACE Charter High School
570 Airport Way, Camarillo CA 93010
CP Coordinator Laura Ochoa
Languages English, Spanish
T: +1 805 437 1410
W: www.acecharterhigh.org

Agoura High School
28545 W Driver Avenue, Agoura Hills CA 91301
DP Coordinator Jennifer Kestenbaum
Languages English
T: +1 818 889 1262
W: www.agourahighschool.net

Al-Arqam Islamic School & College Preparatory
6990 65th Street, Sacramento CA 95823
DP Coordinator Lula Abusalih
Languages English
T: +1 916 391 3333
W: www.alarqamislamicschool.org

Albert Einstein Academy Charter School
3035 Ash Street, San Diego CA 92102
MYP Coordinator Corie Julius
PYP Coordinator Michelle Guarino
Languages English
T: +1 619 795 1190
W: www.aeacs.org

Alice Birney Elementary School
4345 Campus Ave., San Diego CA 92103
PYP Coordinator Graciela Rosas
Languages English
T: +1 619 497 3500
W: www.sandi.net/birney

Alto International School
475 Pope St, Menlo Park CA 94025
DP Coordinator Alex Norwood
MYP Coordinator Chris Quinn
PYP Coordinator Christina Keller
Languages English, German
T: +1 650 324 8617
W: www.altoschool.org

Amelia Earhart Elementary School of International Studies
45-250 Dune Palms Road, Indio CA 92201
PYP Coordinator Kay Urmanski
Languages English
T: +1 760 200 3720
W: sites.google.com/a/desertsands.us/earhart

Anahuacalmecac International University Prep High School
4736 Huntington Drive South, Los Angeles CA 90032
MYP Coordinator Minnie Ferguson
PYP Coordinator Minnie Ferguson
Languages English
T: +1 323 225 4549 EXT:100
W: www.dignidad.org

Anahuacalmecac International University Preparatory
4736 Huntington Drive South, Los Angeles CA 90032
PYP Coordinator Minnie Ferguson
Languages English
T: +1 323 352 3148
W: www.dignidad.org

Andrew P Hill High School
3200 Senter Road, San Jose CA 95111-1399
DP Coordinator Michael Winsatt
Languages English
T: +1 408 347 4100
W: andrewphill.esuhsd.org

Armijo High School
824 Washington Street, Fairfield CA 94533
DP Coordinator Lisa Davis
Languages English
T: +1 707 422 7500
W: www.fsusd.org/armijo

Arroyo Elementary School
1700 E. 7th Street, Ontario CA 91764
PYP Coordinator Silvia Bustamante
Languages English
T: +1 909 985 1012
W: www.omsd.k12.ca.us

Arroyo Valley High School
1881 W Base Line, San Bernardino CA 92411
DP Coordinator Erik Sanchez
MYP Coordinator Dimitrios Chronopoulos
Languages English
T: +1 909 381 4295

Azusa High School
240 North Cerritos Avenue, Azusa CA 91702
DP Coordinator Robert Colera
Languages English
T: +1 626 815 3400
W: www.ahs-ausd-ca.schoolloop.com

Beechwood School
780 Beechwood Avenue, Fullerton CA 92835
MYP Coordinator Jason Lee
Languages English
T: +1 714 447 2850
W: beechwood.fullertonsd.org

Bel Aire Park Magnet School
3580 Beckworth Drive, Napa CA 94558
PYP Coordinator Stacey Abeyta
Languages English
T: +1 707 253 3775
W: bape-nvusd-ca.schoolloop.com

Benjamin Franklin Elementary School
77-800 Calle Tampico, La Quinta CA 92253
PYP Coordinator Christina Winchester
Languages English
T: +1 760 238 9424
W: sites.google.com/a/desertsands.us/franklin-elem

Berkeley High School
1980 Allston Way, Berkeley CA 94704
DP Coordinator Keldon Clegg
Languages English
T: +1 510 644 6120
W: www.bhs.berkeley.k12.ca.us

Bishop Amat Memorial High School
14301 Fairgrove Avenue, La Puente CA 91746
DP Coordinator Jolene Joseph Pudvan
Languages English
T: +1 626 962 2495
W: www.bishopamat.org

Blair High School
1135 S. Euclid Avenue, Pasadena CA 91106
CP Coordinator Karen Favor
DP Coordinator Karen Law
MYP Coordinator Maricela Brambila
Languages English
T: +1 626 396 5820
W: blair.pasadenausd.org

Bob Holcomb Elementary School
1345 W 48th St, San Bernardino CA 92407
PYP Coordinator Krista Bjur
Languages English
T: +1 909 887 2505
W: holcomb.sbcusd.com

Bon View Elementary School
2121 S. Bon View Avenue, Ontario CA 91761
PYP Coordinator Minerva De Leon
Languages English
T: +1 909 947 3932
W: www.omsd.net/bonview

Bonita Vista High School
751 Otay Lakes Road, Chula Vista CA 91913
DP Coordinator Jared Phelps
Languages English
T: +1 619 397 2000
W: bvh.sweetwaterschools.org

Burnett Academy
850 North Second Street, San Jose CA 95112
MYP Coordinator Jelani Canser
Languages English
T: +1 408 535 6267
W: sjusd.org/burnett

Cajon High School
1200 Hill Drive, San Bernardino CA 92407
DP Coordinator Matthew Reisenhofer
MYP Coordinator Matthew Reisenhofer
Languages English
T: +1 909 881 8120
W: www.sbcusd.k12.ca.us/index.aspx?nid=343

Caleb Greenwood Elementary School
5457 Carlson Drive, Sacramento CA 95819
PYP Coordinator Kelly Cordero Cordero
Languages English
T: +1 916 277 6266
W: www.scusd.edu/calebgreenwood

Canyon High School
220 S Imperial Highway, Anaheim Hills CA 92807
DP Coordinator Nancy Belinge
Languages English
T: +1 714 532 8000
W: www.canyonhighschool.org

Canyon Springs High School
23100 Cougar Canyon Rd., Moreno Valley CA 92557
DP Coordinator Christine Flores
T: +1 951 571 4760
W: canyonsprings.mvusd.net

Capistrano Valley High School
26301 Via Escolar, Mission Viejo CA 92692
DP Coordinator Dina Kubba
Languages English
T: +1 949 364 6100
W: www.cvhs.com/

Capuchino High School
1501 Magnolia Avenue, San Bruno CA 94066
DP Coordinator Martee Lopez-Schmitt
Languages English
T: +1 650 558 2700
W: www.chs.smuhsd.org

Carl Hankey K-8 School
27252 Nubles, Mission Viejo CA 92692
MYP Coordinator Kathy Beitz
PYP Coordinator Stacy Rumpf
Languages English
T: +1 949 234 5315
W: chhawks.schoolloop.com

Casita Center for Technology, Science & Math
260 Cedar Rd., Vista CA 92083
PYP Coordinator Jenny Chien
Languages English
T: +1 760 724 8442
W: cas.vistausd.org

Castle Park High School
1395 Hilltop Drive, Chula Vista CA 91911
DP Coordinator Robert Manroe
Languages English
T: +1 619 585 2000
W: cph.sweetwaterschools.org

Castle Rock Elementary School
2975 Castle Rock Road, Diamond Bar CA 91765
PYP Coordinator Kelly Howard
Languages English
T: +1 909 598 5006
W: www.castlerockknights.org

Cathedral City High School
69250 Dinah Shore Drive, Cathedral City CA 92234
DP Coordinator Ed Perry
Languages English
T: +1 760 770 0100
W: catcityhigh.com

Centennial High School
1820 Rimpau Avenue, Corona CA 92881-7405
DP Coordinator Colleen Lum
MYP Coordinator Jenna Rasmussen
Languages English
T: +1 951 739 5670
W: www.cnusd.k12.ca.us/cehs

Cesar E Chavez Middle School
6650 N Magnolia Avenue, San Bernardino CA 92407
MYP Coordinator Zackary Peters
Languages English
T: +1 909 886 2050
W: www.sbcusd.k12.ca.us/index.aspx?nid=344

Charter Oak High School
1430 E. Covina BLVD, Covina CA 91724
DP Coordinator Kathy Archer
Languages English
T: +1 626 915 5841
W: www.cousd.net/Domain/14

IB AMERICAS

Chatsworth Hills Academy
21523 Rinaldi St, Chatsworth CA 91311
PYP Coordinator Paulette Collins
Languages English
T: +1 818 998 4037
W: www.chaschool.org

Citrus Hill High School
18150 Wood Rd., Perris CA 92570
DP Coordinator Andrea Williamson
Languages English
T: +1 951 460 0400
W: citrushill.valverde.edu

Claremont High School
1601 North Indian Hill Blvd, Claremont CA 91711
DP Coordinator Natalie Sieg
Languages English
T: +1 909 624 9053
W: www.cusd.claremont.edu/~counsel/index2.html

Colfax High School
24995 Ben Taylor Rd, Colfax CA 95713
DP Coordinator Annette Udall
Languages English
T: +1 530 346 2284
W: sites.google.com/a/puhsd.k12.ca.us/colfax

Competitive Edge Charter Academy
34450 Stonewood Drive, Yucaipa CA 92399
MYP Coordinator Katherine Coutu
PYP Coordinator Jennifer Stahl
Languages English
T: +1 909 790 3207
W: ycjusd.ceca.schoolfusion.us

Cook Elementary School
875 Cuyamaca Ave., Chula Vista CA 91911
PYP Coordinator Denise Fimbrez
Languages English
T: +1 619 422 8381
W: schools.cvesd.org/schools/cook

Cooper Academy
2277 W. Bellaire Way, Fresno CA 93705
MYP Coordinator Jayne Day
Languages English
T: +1 559 248 7050
W: www.cooperacademyfresno.org

Cordova High School
2239 Chase Drive, Rancho Cordova CA 95670
CP Coordinator Amy Strawn
DP Coordinator Zandi Llanos
MYP Coordinator Amy Strawn
Languages English
T: +1 916 294 2450
W: www.fcusd.org/chs

Corona Fundamental Intermediate
1230 South Main Street, Corona CA 92882
MYP Coordinator Grace Bosquez
Languages English
T: +1 909 736 3321

Cyrus J Morris Elementary School
91785 E Calle Baja, Walnut CA 91789
PYP Coordinator Kelly Howard
Languages English
T: +1 909 594 0053
W: cjmorris.wvusd.k12.ca.us

Dailey Elementary Charter School
3135 N. Harrison Ave, Fresno CA 93704
PYP Coordinator Julia Cabrera
Languages English
T: +1 559 248 7060
W: fics.us/dailey

Damien High School
2280 Damien Avenue, La Verne CA 91750
DP Coordinator Christopher Arbizu
Languages English
T: +1 909 596 1946
W: www.damien-hs.edu

David Starr Jordan High School
6500 Atlantic Avenue, Long Beach CA 90805
DP Coordinator Esther Song
MYP Coordinator Deborah Wilk
Languages English
T: +1 562 423 1471
W: www.lbjordan.schoolloop.com

Del Mar High School
1224 Del Mar Avenue, San Jose CA 95128
DP Coordinator Jessica Olamit
Languages English
T: +1 408 626 3403
W: www.delmar.cuhsd.org

Diamond Bar High School
21400 East Pathfinder Rd, Diamond Bar CA 91765
DP Coordinator Margaret Ku
Languages English
T: +1 909 594 1405
W: www.walnutvalley.k12.ca.us/dbhs

Dos Pueblos High School
7266 Alameda Avenue, Goleta CA 93117
DP Coordinator Matt Moran
Languages English
T: +1 805 968 2541

Downtown Magnets High School
1081 W. Temple St, Los Angeles CA 90012
DP Coordinator Marilyn Watt
Languages English
T: +1 213 481 0371
W: www.downtownmagnets.org

Eagle Rock Junior/Senior High School
1750 Yosemite Drive, Los Angeles CA 90041
DP Coordinator Jonathan Malmed
MYP Coordinator Joseph Cohen
Languages English
T: +1 323 340 3500
W: www.erhs.la

EDGEWOOD HIGH SCHOOL
1625 W Durness, West Covina CA 91790
DP Coordinator Jennifer Zampiello
MYP Coordinator Manny Co
Languages English
T: +1 626 939 4600
E: jzampiello@wcusd.org
W: edgewoodib.wcusd.org
See full details on page 501

EDGEWOOD MIDDLE SCHOOL
1625 W. Durness St., West Covina CA 91790
MYP Coordinator Manny Co
Languages English
T: +1 626 939 4600
E: mco@wcusd.net
W: edgewoodib.wcusd.org
See full details on page 502

El Rancho High School
6501 S. Passons Blvd., Pico Rivera CA 90660
DP Coordinator Parvin Qureshi
Languages English, Spanish
T: +1 562 801 7500
W: www.erusd.k12.ca.us/elrancho

El Segundo Middle School
332 Center St., El Segundo CA 90245
MYP Coordinator Crystal Winner
Languages English, Spanish
T: +1 310 615 2690 EXT:1102
W: www.elsegundomiddleschool.org

El Sereno Middle School
2839 North Eastern Avenue, Los Angeles CA 90032
MYP Coordinator Rene Canales
Languages English
T: +1 323 224 4700
W: www.elserenoms.org

Ellen Ochoa Prep Academy
8110 Paramount Boulevard, Pico Rivera CA 90660
DP Coordinator Esmeralda Montoya
Languages English, Spanish
T: +1 562 801 7560
W: ochoaprep.erusd.org

Escuela Bilingüe Internacional
410 Alcatraz Avenue, Oakland CA 94609
MYP Coordinator Daniel Nube
PYP Coordinator Victoria Ladew
Languages English
T: +1 510 653 3324
W: www.ebinternacional.org

Fairmont Preparatory Academy
2200 West Sequoia Avenue, Anaheim CA 92801
DP Coordinator Michael Wheeler
Languages English
T: +1 714 999 5055
W: www.fairmontschools.com

Farmdale Elementary School
2660 Ruth Swiggett Drive, Los Angeles CA 90032
PYP Coordinator Christina Dominguez
Languages English
T: +1 323 222 6659
W: www.lausd.net

Foothill High School
19251 Dodge Avenue, Santa Ana CA 92705
DP Coordinator Josh Hermanson
Languages English
T: +1 714 730 7464
W: www.tustin.k12.ca.us/foothill

Frances E Willard Elementary Magnet School
301 South Madre Street, Pasadena CA 91107
PYP Coordinator Linda Wittry
Languages English
T: +1 626 793 6163
W: www.pusd.us

Franklin High School
4600 E Fremont St, Stockton CA 95215
DP Coordinator Sondra Knudsen
MYP Coordinator Emmanuel Calderon
Languages English
T: +1 209 933 7435
W: www.stocktonusd.net/franklin

French American International School & International High School
150 Oak Street, San Francisco CA 94102-5812
DP Coordinator Dina Srouji
Languages English
T: +1 415 558 2000
W: www.internationalsf.org

Fresno High School
1839 N Echo Avenue, Fresno CA 93704
CP Coordinator Kei Shabazz
DP Coordinator Kyra Orgill
MYP Coordinator Kyra Orgill
Languages English
T: +1 559 457 2793
W: go.fresnounified.org/fresno

Fullerton Union High School
201 E. Chapman Ave, Fullerton CA 92832
DP Coordinator Mark Henderson
Languages English
T: +1 714 626 3800
W: www.fullertonhigh.org

Gateway International School
900 Morse Avenue, Sacramento CA 95864
MYP Coordinator Deep Dhillon
PYP Coordinator Elizabeth Kaul
Languages English
T: +1 916 286 1985
W: gischarter.org

Glen A Wilson High School
16455 East Wedgeworth Drive, Hacienda Heights CA 91745
DP Coordinator Jinasha Udeshi
Languages English
T: +1 626 934 4401

Goethe International Charter School
12500 Braddock Dr, Los Angeles CA 90066
PYP Coordinator Angel Truong
Languages English, German
T: +1 310 306 3484
W: goethecharterschool.org

Granada High School
400 Wall Street, Livermore CA 94550
DP Coordinator Jon Cariveau
Languages English
T: +1 925 606 4800
W: www.granadahigh.com

Granada Hills Charter High School
10535 Zelzah Avenue, Granada Hills CA 91344
DP Coordinator Sean Lewis
Languages English
T: +1 818 360 2361
W: www.ghchs.com

Granite Bay High School
1 Grizzly Way, Granite Bay CA 95746
DP Coordinator Bernadette Cranmer
Languages English
T: +1 916 786 8676
W: granitebayhigh.org

Granite Hills High School
1719 East Madison Avenue, El Cajon CA 92021
DP Coordinator Matthew Davis
Languages English
T: +1 619 593 5500

Great Oak High School
32555 Deer Hollow Road, Temecula CA 92592
DP Coordinator January King
Languages English
T: +1 951 294 6450
W: gohs.tvusd.k12.ca.us

Grover Beach Elementary School
365 South Tenth Street, Grover Beach CA 93433
PYP Coordinator Petra Reynolds
Languages English
T: +1 805 474 3770
W: sites.google.com/a/lmusd.org/grover-beach

Guajome Park Academy
2000 North Santa Fe Avenue, Vista Unified School District, Vista CA 92083
CP Coordinator Judd Thompson
DP Coordinator Judd Thompson
Languages English
T: +1 760 631 5000
W: www.guajome.net

H. Allen Hight Elementary School
3200 North Park Dr., Sacramento CA 95835
PYP Coordinator Cody Worrall
Languages English
T: +1 916 567 5700
W: www.natomasunified.org/hah

H. Clarke Powers Elementary School
3296 Humphrey Road, Loomis CA 95650
PYP Coordinator Laurie Balsano
Languages English
T: +1 916 652 2635
W: www.powers.loomis-usd.k12.ca.us

Harding University Partnership School
1625 Robbins Street, Santa Barbara CA 93101
PYP Coordinator Lindsay Alker
Languages English
T: +1 805 965 8994
W: www.sbharding.org

Harriet G. Eddy Middle School
9329 Soaring Oaks Drive, Elk Grove CA 95758
MYP Coordinator Carolynn Puccioni
Languages English
T: +1 916 683 1302
W: hems.egusd.net

Harvest Middle School
2449 Old Sonoma Road, Napa CA 94558
MYP Coordinator Jenny Banta
Languages English
T: +1 707 259 8866
W: hms-nvusd-ca.schoolloop.com

Hawthorne Elementary School
705 W. Hawthorne, Ontario CA 91762
PYP Coordinator Elizabeth Alapizco
Languages English
T: +1 909 986 6582
W: www.omsd.k12.ca.us

Horace Mann School
55 North 7th Street, San Jose CA 95112
PYP Coordinator Julian Ramirez
Languages English
T: +1 408 535 6237
W: www.hme.ca.campusgrid.net

Hubert Howe Bancroft Middle School
323 N. Las Palmas Avenue, Los Angeles CA 90023
MYP Coordinator Terry Williamson
Languages English
T: +1 323 993 3400
W: bancroftmiddleschool.org

Inderkum High School
2500 New Market Drive, Sacramento CA 95835
DP Coordinator Jessica Downing
MYP Coordinator Theresa Quinby
Languages English
T: +1 916 567 5640
W: www.natomas.k12.ca.us/ihs

INTERNATIONAL CHILDREN'S ACADEMY
1046 South Robertson Blvd, Los Angeles CA 90035
PYP Coordinator Leyla Goldfinger
Languages English
T: +1 310 657 6798
E: info@icabh.org
W: www.icabh.org
See full details on page 513

INTERNATIONAL SCHOOL OF LOS ANGELES
1105 W. Riverside Drive, Burbank CA 91506
DP Coordinator John Lamphear
Languages English, French
T: +1 626 695 5159
E: admissions@lilaschool.com
W: www.internationalschool.la
See full details on page 515

International School of Monterey
1720 Yosemite Street, Seaside CA 93955
MYP Coordinator Paola Beletti
PYP Coordinator Paola Beletti
Languages English
T: +1 831 583 2165
W: ISMonterey.org

International School of the Peninsula
151 Laura Lane, Palo Alto CA 94303
PYP Coordinator Jacqueline Cody
Languages English, French
T: +1 650 251 8522
W: www.istp.org

James A Foshay Learning Center
3751 S. Harvard Blvd., Los Angeles CA 90018
MYP Coordinator Michael Laska
PYP Coordinator Danielle Mabry
Languages English
T: +1 323 373 2700
W: www.foshaylc.org

Jefferson Elementary School
3743 Jefferson Street, Carlsbad CA 92009
PYP Coordinator Laurel Ferreira
Languages English
T: +1 760 331 5500
W: jefferson.schoolloop.com

Joe Michell K-8 School
1001 Elaine Ave, Livermore CA 94550
MYP Coordinator Karen Marguth
PYP Coordinator Karen Marguth
Languages English
T: +1 925 606 4738
W: joemichell.schoolloop.com

John F Kennedy High School
8281 Walker Street, La Palma CA 90623
DP Coordinator Caylin Ledterman
Languages English
T: +1 714 220 4118

USA

John Glenn Middle School
79-655 Miles Avenue, DSUSD, Indio CA 92201
MYP Coordinator James Harper
Languages English
T: +1 760 200 3700
W: www.dsusd.k12.ca.us/schools/JGMS

John W. North High School
1550 Third St., Riverside CA 92507
DP Coordinator Christine Schive
Languages English
T: +1 951 788 7311
W: north.riversideunified.org

Jurupa Hills High School
10700 Oleander Avenue, Fontana CA 92337
DP Coordinator David Camberos
Languages English
T: +1 909 357 6300
W: www.jhills.org

Kate Sessions Elementary School
2150 Beryl Street, San Diego CA 92109
PYP Coordinator Jeffrey Corley
Languages English
T: +1 858 273 3111
W: www.sandiegounified.org/sessions

Kit Carson Middle School
5301 N Street, Sacramento CA 95819
DP Coordinator Shawn D'Alesandro
MYP Coordinator Shawn D'Alesandro
Languages English
T: +1 916 277 6750
W: www.kitcarson.scusd.edu

La Costa Canyon High School
1 Maverick Way, Carlsbad CA 92009
DP Coordinator Thea Chadwick
Languages English
T: +1 760 436 6136
W: lc.sduhsd.net

La Mirada Academy
3697 La Mirada Drive, San Marcos CA 92078
PYP Coordinator Yvonne Fojtasek
Languages English
T: +1 760 290 2000
W: lamiradaacademy.smusd.org

La Quinta High School
79-255 Westward Ho Drive, La Quinta CA 92253
DP Coordinator Elizabeth Van Dorn
Languages English
T: +1 760 772 4150
W: www.dsusd.k12.ca.us/schools/LQHS/

LA SCUOLA INTERNATIONAL SCHOOL
728 20th Street, San Francisco CA 94107
PYP Coordinator Douglas Lowney
Languages English, Italian And Spanish
T: +1 415 551 0000
E: admissions@lascuolasf.org
W: www.lascuolasf.org

See full details on page 518

Laguna Creek High School
9050 Vicino Drive, Elk Grove CA 95758
DP Coordinator Rod De Luca
MYP Coordinator Jose Oseguera
Languages English
T: +1 916 683 1339
W: www.lch.schoolloop.com

Laguna Hills High School
25401 Paseo de Valencia, Laguna Hills CA 92653
DP Coordinator Laurel Crossett
Languages English
T: +1 949 770 5447
W: www.svusd.org/schools/high-schools/laguna-hills

Letha Raney Intermediate
1010 West Citron Street, Corona CA 92882
MYP Coordinator Bronya Hamel
Languages English
T: +1 951 736 3221
W: www.cnusd.k12.ca.us/rais

Lexington Elementary School
19700 Old Santa Cruz Highway, Los Gatos CA 95033
PYP Coordinator Kristin Johnson
Languages English
T: +1 408 335 2150
W: www.lex.lgusd.k12.ca.us

Loomis Basin Charter School
5438 Laird Road, Loomis CA 95650
MYP Coordinator Lorena Brink
PYP Coordinator Justin VonSpreckelsen
Languages English
T: +1 916 652 2642
W: www.loomscharter.org

Luther Burbank High School
3500 Florin Road, Sacramento CA 95823
DP Coordinator Katherine Bell
Languages English
W: www.lutherburbankhs.com

Marco Antonio Firebaugh High School
5246 Martin Luther King Jr. Blvd, Lynwood CA 90262
DP Coordinator Omar Zúñiga
Languages English
T: +1 310 886 5200
W: fhs.lynwood.k12.ca.us

Maxwell Academy
733 Euclid Avenue, Duarte CA 91010
PYP Coordinator Johna Stienstra
Languages English
T: +1 626 599 5302
W: www.duarteusd.org/page/156

McKinleyville High School
1300 Murray Road, McKinleyville CA 95519
DP Coordinator Anne Sahlberg
Languages English
T: +1 707 839 6400
W: www.nohum.k12.ca.us/mhs/

Mira Loma High School
4000 Edison Avenue, San Juan Unified, Sacramento CA 95821
DP Coordinator David Mathews
MYP Coordinator Rachel Volzer
Languages English
T: +1 916 971 7973
W: www.sanjuan.edu/schools/miraloma.htm

Mission Bay High School
2475 Grand Ave., San Diego CA 92109
DP Coordinator Tracy Borg
Languages English
T: +1 858 273 1313
W: www.sandi.net/missionbay

Mission Viejo High School
25025 Chrisanta Drive, Mission Viejo CA 9269
DP Coordinator Sandra Hanneman
Languages English
T: +1 949 837 7722
W: www.svusd.k12.ca.us/Schools/mvhs

Modesto High School
First & H Street, Modesto City Schools, Modesto CA 95351
DP Coordinator Kerry Castellani
Languages English
T: +1 209 576 4404

Monterey High School
101 Herrmann Drive, Monterey CA 93940
DP Coordinator Elizabeth Desimone
MYP Coordinator Nikki Ahrenstorff
Languages English, Spanish
T: +1 831 392 3801
W: montereyhigh.mpusd.net

Montgomery High School
1250 Hahman Drive, Santa Rosa CA 95405
DP Coordinator Tracy Maniscalco
Languages English
T: +1 707 528 5512
W: www.montgomeryhighschool.com

Mount Vernon Elementary
8350 Mount Vernon Street, Lemon Grove CA 91945
PYP Coordinator Sylvia Echeverria
Languages English
T: +1 619 825 5613
W: lgsdmve.lgsd.k12.ca.us

Mt George Elementary School
1019 Second Avenue, Napa CA 94558
PYP Coordinator Colette Freeman
Languages English

Murrieta Valley High School
42200 Nighthawk Way, Murrieta CA 92562
DP Coordinator Alanna Fields
Languages English
T: +1 951 696 1408
W: www.murrieta.k12.ca.us

Natomas Middle School
3200 North Park Drive, Sacramento CA 95835
MYP Coordinator Cody Worrall
Languages English
T: +1 916 567 5540
W: natomasunified.org/nms

New Covenant Academy
3119 W 6th Street, Los Angeles CA 90020
DP Coordinator Joseph Chai
Languages English
T: +1 213 487 5437
W: www.e-nca.org

Newbury Park High School
456 Reino Road, Newbury Park CA 91320
DP Coordinator Deborah Dogançay
Languages English
T: +1 805 498 3676
W: dev.nphs.org

Newport Harbor High School
600 Irvine Avenue, Newport Beach CA 92663
DP Coordinator Alma Di Giorgio
Languages English
T: +1 949 515 6300
W: nhhs.schoolloop.com

Nogales High School
401 Nogales Street, Rowland Unified School Distric, La Puente CA 91744
DP Coordinator Clay Woodside
Languages English
T: +1 626 965 3437

Norte Vista High School
6585 Crest Avenue, Riverside CA 92503
DP Coordinator Shawn Marshall
Languages English
T: +1 951 351 9316
W: www.alvord.k12.ca.us/nortevista

Northcoast Preparatory Academy
285 Bayside Rd, 1761 11th St., Arcata CA 95518
DP Coordinator Amy Bazemore
Languages English
T: +1 707 825 1186
W: northcoastprep.org

Oakmont High School
1710 Cirby Way, Roseville CA 95661
DP Coordinator Jolie Geluk
Languages English
T: +1 916 782 3781
W: ohs.rjuhsd.us

Ocean Knoll Elementary School
910 Melba Road, Encinitas CA 92024
PYP Coordinator Sanjana Bryant
Languages English
T: +1 760 944 4351
W: www.eusd.net/ok

Ocean View High School
17071 Gothard St., Huntington Beach CA 92647
DP Coordinator Brandon Knight
Languages English
T: +1 714 848 0656
W: www.ovhs.info

ORANGEWOOD ELEMENTARY
1440 S. Orange Avenue, West Covina CA 91790
PYP Coordinator Ms. Jeanne Berrong
Languages English, Spanish
T: +1 626 939 4820
W: orangewood.wcusd.org
See full details on page 539

Pacific Beach Middle School
4676 Ingraham Street, San Diego CA 92109
MYP Coordinator Jennifer Sims
Languages English
T: +1 858 273 9070
W: www.sandiegounified.org/schools/pacific-beach-middle

Palmdale Learning Plaza
38043 Division Street, Palmdale CA 93551
MYP Coordinator Beverly Gonda
PYP Coordinator Beverly Gonda
Languages English
T: +1 661 538 9034
W: www.palmdalesd.org/lp

Pleasant Valley High School
1475 East Avenue, Chico CA 95926
DP Coordinator Beth Burton
Languages English
T: +1 530 891 3050
W: pvhs.chicousd.org

Prepa Tec Los Angeles High School
4210 E. Gage Ave., Bell CA 90201
DP Coordinator Kaylene Rudd
Languages English, Spanish
T: +1 323 800 2743
W: www.altapublicschools.org/prepatechighschool

Primary Years Academy
1540 N.Lincoln St, Stockton CA 95204
PYP Coordinator Hina Lee
Languages English
T: +1 209 933 7355
W: www.primaryyearsacademy.com

Quarry Lane School
6363 Tassajara Road, Dublin CA 94568
DP Coordinator Jyothi Kiran Hoskere
Languages English
T: +1 925 829 8000
W: www.quarrylane.org

Quartz Hill High School
6040 West Avenue L, Quartz Hill CA 93536
DP Coordinator Jeff Cassady
Languages English
T: +1 661 718 3100

Rancho Buena Vista High School
1601 Longhorn Drive, Vista CA 92081
DP Coordinator Melissa Neumann
Languages English
T: +1 760 727 7284
W: www.rbv-vistausd-ca.schoolloop.com

Ray Wiltsey Middle School
1450 E. "G" Street, Ontario CA 91764
MYP Coordinator Terri Bradley
Languages English
T: +1 909 986 5838
W: omsd.omsd.k12.ca.us/schools/DeAnza/Pages/default.aspx

Rio Mesa High School
545 Central Avenue, Oxnard CA 93030
CP Coordinator Ingrid Brennan
DP Coordinator Lori A Wrout
Languages English
T: +1 805 278 5500
W: www.ouhsd.k12.ca.us

Roosevelt Middle School
3366 Park Blvd., San Diego CA 92103
MYP Coordinator Deborah Christensen
Languages English
T: +1 619 293 4450
W: www.sandiegounified.org/roosevelt

Rowland High School
2000 S Otterbein Avenue, Rowland Heights CA 91748
DP Coordinator Stephen Ludlam
Languages English
T: +1 626 965 3448
W: www.rowlandhs.org

Royal High School
1402 Royal Avenue, Simi Valley CA 93065
DP Coordinator Kari Lev
Languages English
T: +1 805 306 4875 EXT:1
W: www.rhs.simi.k12.ca.us

Saddleback High School
2802 South Flower Street, Santa Ana CA 92707
DP Coordinator Dana Kassaei
Languages English
T: +1 714 569 6300
W: www.sausd.us/saddleback

San Clemente High School
700 Avenida Pico, San Clemente CA 92673
DP Coordinator Lisa Alizadeh
Languages English
T: +1 949 492 4165

San Diego High School of International Studies
1405 Park Boulevard, San Diego CA 92101
DP Coordinator Nirit Cohen-Vardi
Languages English
T: +1 619 525 7455
W: www.sandiegounified.org/sdhsis

San Jacinto High School
500 Idyllwild Drive, San Jacinto CA 92583
DP Coordinator Matthew Corum
Languages English
T: +1 951 654 7374
W: www.sanjacinto.k12.ca.us/sjhs

San Jacinto Valley Academy
480 N San Jacinto Avenue, San Jacinto CA 92583
DP Coordinator Jonathan Harrison
PYP Coordinator Kelly Perez
Languages English
T: +1 951 654 6113
W: www.sjva.net

San Jose High School
275 North 24th St., San Jose CA 95116-1109
CP Coordinator Gerson Sandoval
DP Coordinator Paul Da Silva
MYP Coordinator Salvatore Martinico
Languages English
T: +1 408 535 6320
W: www.sjusd.org/san-jose-high

Santa Clarita Valley International School
28060 Hasley Canyon, Castaic CA 91384
DP Coordinator Abbie Neall
Languages English
T: +1 661 705 4820
W: www.scvcharterschool.org

Santa Margarita Catholic High School
22062 Antonio Parkway, Rancho Santa Margarita CA 92688
DP Coordinator Maria D.S. Andrade Johnson
Languages English
T: +1 949 766 6000
W: www.smhs.org

Schools of the Sacred Heart
2222 Broadway, San Francisco CA 94115
DP Coordinator Devin DeMartini
Languages English
T: +1 415 563 2900
W: www.sacredsf.org

Scotts Valley High School
Principal, 555 Glenwood Drive, Scotts Valley CA 95066
DP Coordinator David Crawford
Languages English
T: +1 831 439 9555

Sequoia High School
1201 Brewster Avenue, Redwood City CA 94062
DP Coordinator Lisa McCahon
Languages English
T: +1 650 369 1411
W: www.sequoiahs.org

Shu Ren International School
1333 University Avenue, Berkeley CA 94702
PYP Coordinator Rebecca Zipprich
Languages English, Mandarin
T: +1 510 841 8899
W: www.shureninternationalschool.com

Sierra Elementary School
6811 Camborne Way, Rocklin CA 95677
PYP Coordinator Cynthia Brown
Languages English
T: +1 916 788 7141
W: ses.rocklinusd.org

Sonora High School
401 South Palm Street, Fullerton Joint Union, La Habra CA 90631
DP Coordinator Shannon Appenrodt
Languages English
T: +1 562 266 2013

South Hills High School
645 S. Barranca Street, West Covina CA 91791
DP Coordinator Marisol Marquez
Languages English
T: +1 626 974 6200
W: www.southhillshigh.com

Southwest High School
2001 Ocotillo Drive, El Centro CA 92243
DP Coordinator Cheryl Turner
Languages English
T: +1 760 336 4290
W: www.cuhsd.net

Spring Valley Academy
3900 Conrad Drive, Spring Valley CA 91977
MYP Coordinator Debra Lunamand
Languages English, Spanish
T: +1 619 668 5750
W: www.lmsvschools.org/springvalley

St. Mary's School
7 Pursuit, Aliso Viejo CA 92656
MYP Coordinator Jocelyn Williams
PYP Coordinator Lauren Sterner
Languages English
T: +1 949 448 9027
W: www.smaa.org

Stanley G Oswalt Academy
19501 Shadow Oak Drive, Walnut CA 91789
PYP Coordinator Robin Paerels
Languages English
T: +1 626 810 4109
W: oswalt.rowlandschools.org

Stockton Collegiate International Elementary School
321 E. Weber Ave, Stockton CA 95202
PYP Coordinator John Piasecki
Languages English
T: +1 209 390 9861
W: www.stocktoncollegiate.org

Stockton Collegiate International Secondary School
PO Box 2286, Stockton CA 95201
DP Coordinator Manuel Aguilar
MYP Coordinator Hauna Zaich
Languages English
T: +1 209 464 7108
W: www.stocktoncollegiate.org

Stowers Magnet School of International Studies
13350 Beach Street, Cerritos CA 90703
PYP Coordinator Kimberly Rath
Languages English
T: +1 562 229 7905
W: www.stowerselementary.org

Summit Charter Academy
1509 Lombardi Street, Porterville CA 93257
PYP Coordinator Shana Watson
Languages English
T: +1 559 788 6445
W: www.summitlombardi.org

Summit Charter Collegiate Academy
15550 Redwood Drive, Porterville CA 93257
MYP Coordinator Jenifer Sanders
Languages English, Spanish
T: +1 559 788 6440
W: www.summitcollegiate.org

Sunny Hills High School
1801 Warburton Way, Fullerton CA 92833
DP Coordinator Brian Wall
Languages English
T: +1 714 626 4213
W: www.sunnyhills.net

Sunnybrae Elementary School
1031 South Delaware Street, San Mateo CA 94402
PYP Coordinator Wynne Hegarty
Languages English
T: +1 650 312 7599
W: www.smfc.k12.ca.us/sunnybrae

Temescal Canyon High School
28755 El Toro Road, Lake Elsinore CA 92532
DP Coordinator Jason Garrison
Languages English
T: +1 951 253 7250
W: tch.leusd.k12.ca.us

The Healdsburg School
33H Healdsburg Avenue, Healdsburg CA 95448
PYP Coordinator Jami Trinidad
Languages English
T: +1 707 433 4847
W: www.thehealdsburgschool.org

Thomas Jefferson Elementary School
3770 Utah Street, San Diego CA 92104
PYP Coordinator Erin Knight
Languages English
T: +1 619 344 3300
W: www.sandiegounified.org/jefferson

Thomas Kelly Elementary School
6301 Moraga Drive, Carmichael CA 95608
PYP Coordinator Josh Costa
Languages English
T: +1 916 867 2401
W: www.sanjuan.edu/kelly

Trabuco Hills High School
27501 Mustang Run, Mission Viejo CA 92691
DP Coordinator Lindsay Casserly
Languages English
T: +1 949 768 1934

Tracy Joint Union High School
315 East 11th Street, Tracy Public Schools, Tracy CA 95376
DP Coordinator Rachel Hermann
Languages English
T: +1 209 830 3360
W: www.tracy.k12.ca.us/sites/ths/Pages/default.aspx

Troy High School
2200 East Dorothy Lane, Fullerton CA 92831
DP Coordinator Charlotte Kirkpatrick
Languages English
T: +1 714 626 4401
W: www.troyhigh.com

Valencia High School
500 N Bradford Avenue, Placentia CA 92870
DP Coordinator Fred Jenkins
Languages English
T: +1 714 996 4970

Villanova Preparatory School
12096 N. Ventura Avenue, Ojai CA 93023
DP Coordinator Brian Roney
Languages English
T: +1 805 646 1464
W: www.villanovaprep.org

Vista Academy of Visual and Performing Arts
600 N. Santa Fe Avenue, Vista CA 92083
PYP Coordinator Sharon Scott-Gonzalez
Languages English
T: +1 760 941 0880
W: vapa.vistausd.org

Vista Heights Middle School
23049 Old Lake Drive, Moreno Valley CA 92557
MYP Coordinator Susan Young
Languages English, Spanish
T: +1 951 571 4300
W: vistaheights.mvusd.net

Vista High School
1 Panther Way, Vista CA 92084
DP Coordinator Candice Kordis
Languages English
T: +1 760 726 5611
W: vhs.vistausd.org

Vista Magnet Middle School
151 Escondido Avenue, Vista CA 92084
MYP Coordinator Jennifer Eckle
Languages English
T: +1 760 726 2170 EXT:6195
W: www.vistamagnet.com

W.E. Mitchell Middle School
2100 Zinfandel Drive, Rancho Cordova CA 95670
MYP Coordinator Amy Strawn
Languages English
T: +1 916 635 8460
W: www.fcusd.org/mitchell

Walnut High School
400 N Pierre Rd, Walnut CA 91789
CP Coordinator Manette Idris
DP Coordinator Manette Idris
Languages English
T: +1 909 594 1333

Warren T. Eich Middle School
1509 Sierra Gardens Drive, Roseville CA 95661-4804
MYP Coordinator Lisa Shrider
Languages English
T: +1 916 771 1770
W: www.rcsdk8.org/apps/pages/?uREC_ID=89909&type=d

William F McKinley Elementary School
3045 Felton Street, San Diego CA 92104
PYP Coordinator Erin Knight
Languages English
T: +1 619 282 7694
W: www.sandiegounified.org/mckinley

Winston Churchill Middle School
4900 Whitney Avenue, Carmicheal CA 95608
MYP Coordinator Kristen Manchester
Languages English
T: +1 916 971 7324

Woodrow Wilson High School
4500 Multnomah Street, Los Angeles CA 90032
DP Coordinator Erica Welsh-Westfall
MYP Coordinator Desiree Palacios
Languages English
T: +1 323 276 1600
W: www.wilsonmules.org

Ybarra Academy of the Arts & Technology
1300 Brea Canyon Cut-off Road, Walnut CA 91789
PYP Coordinator Monica Gutierrez
Languages English, Spanish
T: +1 909 598 3744
W: ybarra.rowlandschools.org

Ygnacio Valley High School
755 Oak Grove Road, Concord CA 94518
DP Coordinator Carissa Weintraub
Languages English
T: +1 925 685 8414
W: yvhs.mdusd.org

Yosemite Union High School
50200 Road 427, Oakhurst CA 93644
DP Coordinator Arlene Aoki
Languages English
T: +1 559 683 4667
W: www.yosemiteusd.com

Colorado

Academy International Elementary School
8550 Charity Drive, Colorado Springs CO 80920
PYP Coordinator Michelle Lesseig
Languages English
T: +1 719 234 4000
W: academyinternational.asd20.org/Pages/default.aspx

Alameda International High School
1255 S. Wadsworth Blvd., Lakewood CO 80232
CP Coordinator Steve Houwen
DP Coordinator Merinda Sautel
MYP Coordinator Erin Murphy
Languages English
T: +1 303 982 8160
W: sites.google.com/a/jeffcoschools.us/alameda-hs

Alpine Elementary School
2005 Alpine Street, Longmont CO 80504
PYP Coordinator Carolyn Clifford
Languages English
T: +1 720 652 8140
W: aes.svvsd.org

Antelope Trails Elementary
15280 Jessie Drive, Colorado Springs CO 80921
PYP Coordinator Tia Guillan
Languages English
T: +1 719 234 4100
W: antelopetrails.asd20.org

Aspen High School
235 High School Road, Aspen CO 81611
DP Coordinator Eileen Knapp
Languages English
T: +1 970 925 3760
W: www.aspenk12.net/page/13

Aurora Hills Middle School
1009 S Uvalda, Aurora CO 80012
MYP Coordinator Sue Wagoner
Languages English
T: +1 303 341 7450
W: ahills.aurorak12.org

Avon Elementary School
PO Box 7567, W. Beaver Creek Blvd., Avon CO 0850
PYP Coordinator Holli Bishop
Languages English, Spanish
T: +1 970 328 2950
W: www.eagleschools.net/schools/avon-elementary

Bennett Elementary School
1125 Bennett Road, Fort Collins CO 80521
PYP Coordinator Sarah Shigemura
Languages English
T: +1 970 488 4750
W: ben.psdschools.org

Boulder Country Day School
4820 Nautilus Court North, Boulder CO 80301
MYP Coordinator Karen Morton
Languages English
T: +1 303 527 4931
W: www.bouldercountryday.org

Bradley International School
3051 S. Elm St., Denver CO 80222-7339
PYP Coordinator Jodie Leatherman
Languages English
T: +1 720 424 9468
W: bradley.dpsk12.org

Breckenridge Elementary School
312 S. Harris Street, PO Box 1213, Breckenridge CO 80424
PYP Coordinator Chloe Masseria
Languages English, Spanish
T: +1 970 368 1300
W: bre.summitk12.org

Brentwood Middle School
2600 24th Avenue Court, Greeley CO 80634
MYP Coordinator Andy Hartshorn
T: +1 970 348 3000
W: www.greeleyschools.org/domain/24

Brown International Academy
2550 Lowell Boulevard, Denver CO 80211
PYP Coordinator Melissa Capozza
Languages English
T: +1 720 424 9287
W: brown.dpsk12.org

Cache La Poudre Elementary School
3511 W. County Rd., Laporte CO 80535
PYP Coordinator Evan Netzer
Languages English
T: +1 970 488 7600
W: cpe.psdschools.org

Cache La Poudre Middle School
3511 W. County Rd. 54 G, La Porte CO 80535
MYP Coordinator Delhia Mahaney
Languages English
T: +1 970 488 7400
W: clp.psdschools.org

Centaurus High School
10300 E South Boulder Road, Lafayette CO 80026
DP Coordinator Johanna Wintergerst
Languages English
T: +1 720 561 7500
W: www.centaurushs.org

Central Elementary School
1020 4th Avenue, Longmont CO 80501
PYP Coordinator Hillary Simonson
Languages English
T: +1 303 776 3236
W: centrales.svvsd.org

Century Middle School
13000 Lafayette Street, Thornton CO 80241
MYP Coordinator Holly Jones
Languages English
T: +1 720 972 5240
W: century.adams12.org

Charles Hay World School
3195 S Layfayette Street, Englewood CO 80113
PYP Coordinator Matthew Palermo
Languages English
T: +1 303 761 2433
W: www.englewoodschools.net/charleshay

Cherokee Trail High School
25901 E Arapahoe Road, Aurora CO 80016
DP Coordinator Julian Jones
Languages English
T: +1 720 886 1900
W: www.cths.ccsd.k12.co.us

Corwin International Magnet School
1500 Lakeview Ave., Pueblo CO 81004
MYP Coordinator Cassie Pate
PYP Coordinator Jaime Quinn
Languages English
T: +1 719 549 7400
W: cims.pueblocityschools.us

Coyote Ridge Elementary School
7115 Avondale Road, Fort Collins CO 80525
PYP Coordinator Jennifer Bozic
Languages English
T: +1 970 679 9400
W: www.thompsonschools.org/coyoteridge

Dakota Ridge High School
13399 West Coal Mine Avenue, Littleton CO 80127
DP Coordinator Holly Davis
Languages English
T: +1 303 982 1970
W: jeffcoweb.jeffco.k12.co.us/high/dakota

Dillon Valley Elementary School
P.O. Box 4788, 0108 Deerpath, Dillon CO 80435
PYP Coordinator Gayle Westerberg
Languages English
T: +1 970 368 1400
W: www.summit.k12.co.us/dve

Discovery Canyon Campus
1810 North Gate Blvd, Colorado Springs CO 80921
DP Coordinator Andy Liddle
MYP Coordinator Alisa Schleder
PYP Coordinator Autumn Cave-Crosby
Languages English
T: +1 719 234 1800
W: www.asd20.org/dcc

Dos Rios Elementary School
2201 34th Street, Evans CO 80620
PYP Coordinator Amanda Abbood
Languages English
T: +1 970 348 1309
W: www.greeleyschools.org/dosrios

Douglas County High School
2842 Front Street, Castle Rock CO 80104
DP Coordinator Steven Fleet
MYP Coordinator Christine Veto
Languages English
T: +1 303 387 1004
W: www.dcsdk12.org

Dunn Elementary School
501 South Washington, Fort Collins CO 80521
PYP Coordinator Esther Croak
Languages English
T: +1 970 482 0450

Eagle Valley Elementary School
PO Box 780, Eagle CO 81631
PYP Coordinator Anita ortiz
Languages English, Spanish
T: +1 970 328 6981
W: www.eagleschools.net

East Middle School
1275 Fraser Street, Aurora CO 80011
MYP Coordinator Sue Sikorski
Languages English
T: +1 303 340 0660
W: east.aurorak12.org

Elkhart Elementary School
1020 Eagle Street, Aurora CO 80011
PYP Coordinator Stephanie Shiplet
Languages English
T: +1 303 340 3050
W: elkhart.aurorak12.org

Evans International Elementary School
1675 Winnebago Road, Colorado Springs CO 80915
PYP Coordinator Christine Dodson
Languages English
T: +1 719 495 5299
W: www.d49.org/school/ees

Fairview High School
1515 Greenbriar Blvd., Boulder CO 80305-7043
DP Coordinator Christopher Weber
Languages English
T: +1 720 561 3100
W: www.fairviewhs.org

Fountain International Magnet School
925 North Glendale Avenue, Pueblo CO 81001
PYP Coordinator Stephanie Burke
Languages English
T: +1 719 423 3050
W: www.fountainims.pueblocityschools.us

Frisco Elementary
PO Box 4820, Frisco CO 80443
PYP Coordinator Amy Hume
Languages English
T: +1 970 368 1500
W: www.summit.k12.co.us

Gateway High School
1300 S Sable Blvd, Aurora CO 80012
DP Coordinator Jason Dillon
MYP Coordinator Jason Dillon
Languages English
T: +1 303 755 7160
W: gateway.aurorak12.org

George Washington High School
655 South Monaco Street, Denver CO 80224
DP Coordinator Richard Maez
Languages English
T: +1 303 394 8620
W: gwhs.dpsk12.org

Global Intermediate Academy
7480 N. Broadway, Denver CO 80221
PYP Coordinator Lorina Gallardo
Languages English, Spanish
T: +1 303 853 1930
W: www.mapleton.us/site/Default.aspx?PageID=2768

Global Primary Academy
7480 N. Broadway, Denver CO 80221
PYP Coordinator Lorina Gallardo
Languages English, Spanish
T: +1 303 853 1930
W: www.mapleton.us/site/Default.aspx?PageID=21

Greeley West High School
2401 35th Avenue, Greeley CO 80634
DP Coordinator Marie Beach
MYP Coordinator Marie Beach
Languages English
T: +1 970 348 5400
W: www.west.greeleyschools.org

Harrison High School
2755 Janitell Road, Colorado Springs CO 80906
MYP Coordinator Bethany Danjuma
Languages English
T: +1 719 579 2080
W: www.hsd2.org/hhs

Hinkley High School
1250 Chambers Road, Aurora CO 80011
CP Coordinator Matthew Brown
DP Coordinator Matthew Brown
MYP Coordinator David Nickoloff
Languages English
T: +1 303 340 1500
W: hinkley.aurorak12.org

Horizon Middle School
1750 Piros Drive, Colorado Springs CO 80915
MYP Coordinator Jennifer McClain
Languages English
T: +1 719 574 7700
W: www.d49.org/schools/hms

INTERNATIONAL SCHOOL OF DENVER
7701 E. 1st Pl, Unit C, Denver CO 80230
MYP Coordinator Hope Forgey
Languages Chinese, English, French, Spanish
T: +1 303 340 3647
E: info@isdenver.org
W: www.isdenver.org
See full details on page 514

John F. Kennedy High School
2855 S. Lamar St., Denver CO 80227
DP Coordinator Alissa Warren
Languages English
T: +1 720 423 4300
W: jfk.dpsk12.org

King-Murphy Elementary School
425 Circle K Ranch Road, Evergreen CO 80439
PYP Coordinator Heather Zuckerman
Languages English
T: +1 303 670 0005
W: king-murphy.ccsdre1.org

Lakewood High School
9700 W. 8th Ave., Lakewood CO 80215
DP Coordinator Joellen Kramer
Languages English
T: +1 303 982 7096
W: sites.google.com/a/jeffcoschools.us/lhs

Leroy Drive Elementary School
1451 Leroy Drive CO 80233
PYP Coordinator Brianna Williams
Languages English
T: +1 720 972 5461
W: www.leroy.adams12.org

Lesher Middle School
1400 Stover Street, Fort Collins CO 80524
MYP Coordinator Jenna Ellingson
Languages English
T: +1 970 472 3800
W: les.psdschools.org

Liberty Point International School
484 S. Maher Dr., Pueblo West CO 81007
MYP Coordinator Kelly Jackson
Languages English
T: +1 719 547 3752
W: pwm.district70.org

Lincoln Middle School
1600 Lancer Drive, Fort Collins CO 80521
MYP Coordinator Julie Israelson
Languages English
T: +1 970 488 5700
W: lin.psdschools.org

Littleton High School
199 East Littleton Boulevard, Littleton CO 80121
DP Coordinator Claudia Anderson
Languages English
T: +1 303 347 7700
W: www.littleton.littletonpublicschools.net

Loveland High School
920 W 29th Street, Loveland CO 80538
DP Coordinator John Parks
MYP Coordinator John Parks
Languages English
T: +1 970 613 5209
W: www.lhs.thompson.k12.co.us

Lucile Erwin Middle School
4700 Lucerne Ave., Loveland CO 80538
MYP Coordinator Tané Leach
Languages English
T: +1 970 613 7600
W: thompson.k12.co.us/erwin

Mackintosh Academy
7018 S Prince Street, Littleton CO 80120
MYP Coordinator Sharon Muench
PYP Coordinator Sharon Muench
Languages English
T: +1 303 794 6222
W: www.mackintoshacademy.com

McAuliffe International School
2540 Holly Street, Denver CO 80207
MYP Coordinator Becky Middleton
Languages English
T: +1 720 424 1540
W: mcauliffe.dpsk12.org

McGraw Elementary School
4800 Hinsdale drive, Fort Collins CO 80526
PYP Coordinator Paul Schkade
Languages English
T: +1 970 223 0137

Mesa Middle School
365 North Mitchell Street, Castle Rock CO 80104
MYP Coordinator Sandy Browning
Languages English
T: +1 303 387 4750
W: www.dcsdk12.org/school/mesa-middle-school

Midland International Elementary School
2110 W Broadway, Colorado Springs CO 80904
PYP Coordinator Elizabeth Hudgens
Languages English
T: +1 719 328 4500
W: www.cssd11.k12.co.us/midland

Mountain Ridge Middle School
9150 Lexington Drive, Colorado Springs CO 80920
MYP Coordinator Shawn Reed Parsons
Languages English
T: +1 719 234 3200
W: mountainridge.asd20.org

Niwot High School
8989 E Niwot Road, Niwot CO 80503
DP Coordinator Elzbieta Towlen
Languages English
T: +1 303 652 2550
W: nhs.svvsd.org

North Middle School
301 North Nevada Avenue, Colorado Springs CO 80903
MYP Coordinator Adam Millman
Languages English
T: +1 719 328 5078

Northeast Elementary
1605 Longspeak Street, Brighton CO 80601
PYP Coordinator Jenny Ceretto
Languages English
T: +1 303 655 2550
W: www.sd27j.org/northeast

Northfield High School
5500 Central Park Blvd, Denver CO 80238
DP Coordinator Peter Wright
Languages English
T: +1 303 588 5989
W: northfield.dpsk12.org

Overland Trail Middle School
455 North 19th Ave., Brighton CO 80601
MYP Coordinator Christy Meredith
Languages English, Spanish
T: +1 303 655 4000
W: www.sd27j.org/domain/21

Palisade High School
3679 G Road, Palisade CO 81526
DP Coordinator Laura Meinzen
Languages English
T: +1 970 254 4800
W: www.phs.mesa.k12.co.us/

Patterson International School
1263 S Dudley St., Lakewood CO 80232
PYP Coordinator Ryan Livingston
Languages English
T: +1 303 982 8470
W: sites.google.com/a/jeffcoschools.us/patterson-es

Poudre High School
201 Impala Drive, Fort Collins CO 80521
DP Coordinator Cori Hixon
MYP Coordinator Katy Sayers
Languages English
T: +1 970 488 6000
W: phs.psdschools.org

Pueblo East High School
9 MacNeil Road, Pueblo CO 81001
DP Coordinator Dora Davis
MYP Coordinator Dora Davis
Languages English
T: +1 719 549 7222
W: east.pueblocityschools.us

Pueblo West High School
661 Capitstrano Drive, Pueblo West CO 81007
DP Coordinator Kati Wilson
MYP Coordinator Kati Wilson
Languages English
T: +1 719 547 8050
W: pwh.district70.org

Rampart High School
8250 Lexington Drive, Colorado Springs CO 80920
DP Coordinator Deirdre Mostica
MYP Coordinator Kari Kiser
Languages English
T: +1 719 234 2000
W: rampart.asd20.org

Ranch Creek Elementary School
9155 Tutt Blvd, Colorado Springs CO 80924
PYP Coordinator Diane Jensen
Languages English
T: +1 719 234 5500
W: www.asd20.org/rce

Ranch View Middle School
1731 Wildcat Reserve Parkway, Highlands Ranch CO 80129
MYP Coordinator Erin Isley
Languages English
T: +1 303 387 2300
W: sites.google.com/a/dcsdk12.org/ranch-view-middle-school

Range View Elementary School
700 Ponderosa Drive, Severance CO 80550
PYP Coordinator Shauna Curtis
Languages English
T: +1 970 674 6000
W: rv.weldre4.k12.co.us

Riffenburgh Elementary School
1320 East Stuart Street, Fort Collins CO 80525
PYP Coordinator Jennifer McCoy
Languages English
T: +1 970 488 7935
W: eweb.psdschools.org/schools/riffenburgh

Rifle High School
1350 Prefontaine Avenue, Rifle CO 81650
DP Coordinator Ann Conaway
Languages English
T: +1 970 665 7725
W: garfield-re2.riflehs.schoolfusion.us

Risley International Academy of Innovation
625 Monument Ave., Pueblo CO 81001-5706
MYP Coordinator Renee Schloss
Languages English
T: +1 719 549 7440
W: risley.pueblocityschools.us

Rock Ridge Elementary School
400 N Heritage Road, Castle Rock CO 80104
PYP Coordinator Pam Gutierrez
Languages English
T: +1 303 387 5150
W: www.dcsdk12.org/schools

Rockrimmon Elementary School
194 W Mikado Drive, Colorado Springs CO 80919
PYP Coordinator Leigh Ann Lawrentz
Languages English
T: +1 719 234 5200
W: www.asd20.org

Roxborough Primary and Intermediate School
8000 Village Circle West, Littleton CO 80125
PYP Coordinator Laura Maestas
Languages English
T: +1 303 387 6000
W: www.dcsdk12.org/school/roxborough-primary-and-intermediate-school

Sabin World Elementary School
3050 S Vrain Street, Denver CO 80236
PYP Coordinator Karen Carmean
Languages English
T: +1 720 424 4520
W: sabin.dpsk12.org

Sand Creek Elementary School
550 Sand Creek Drive, Colorado Springs CO 80916
PYP Coordinator Marika Gillis
Languages English
T: +1 719 579 3760
W: www.hsd2.org/Domain/15

Sand Creek High School
7005 North Carefree Circle, Colorado Springs CO 80922
DP Coordinator Nicole Sides
Languages English
T: +1 719 572 0924
W: d49.org/sandcreek

Semper Elementary School
7575 W 96th Ave., Westminster CO 80021
PYP Coordinator Molly James
Languages English, Spanish
T: +1 303 982 6460
W: semper.jeffcopublicschools.org

Silverthorne Elementary School
PO Box 1039, Silverthorne CO 80498
PYP Coordinator Ann-Mari Westerhoff
Languages English
T: +1 970 368 1600
W: summit.k12.co.us/schools/Silverthorne/silverthorne.html

Smoky Hill High School
16100 E. Smoky Hill Rd., Aurora CO 80015
DP Coordinator Michael Ady
MYP Coordinator Kathleen Fitzgerald
Languages English
T: +1 720 886 5300
W: smokyhill.cherrycreekschools.org

South Ridge Elementary School
1100 South Street, Castle Rock CO 80104
PYP Coordinator Marne Katsanis
Languages English
T: +1 303 387 5075
W: www.dcsdk12.org/school/south-ridge-elementary-school

Standley Lake High School
9300 W 104th Avenue, Westminster CO 80021
DP Coordinator Benjamin Thompson
Languages English
T: +1 303 982 3311
W: www.slhsgators.com

Summit Cove Elementary School
727 Cove Boulevard, Dillon CO 80435
PYP Coordinator Lesley Gregory
Languages English
T: +1 970 368 1700
W: www.summit.k12.co.us/sce

Summit High School
PO Box 7, Frisco CO 80443
DP Coordinator Nanci Morse
MYP Coordinator Douglas Blake
Languages English
T: +1 970 368 1100
W: www.summit.k12.co.us/

Summit Middle School
PO Box 7, Frisco CO 80443
MYP Coordinator Nelle Biggs
Languages English
T: +1 970 368 1100

Sunset Middle School
1300 S. Sunset Street, Longmont CO 80501
MYP Coordinator Alex Armstrong
Languages English
T: +1 303 776 3963
W: sms.svvsd.org

Swigert International School
3480 Syracuse Street, Denver CO 80238
PYP Coordinator Jamie Phillips
Languages English
T: +1 720 424 4800
W: swigert.dpsk12.org

Telluride Mountain School
Lawson Hill, 200 San Miguel River Dr., Telluride CO 81435
DP Coordinator Emily Durkin
Languages English
T: +1 970 728 1969
W: telluridemtnschool.org

Thornton High School
9351 North Washington Street, Thornton CO 80229
DP Coordinator Kristen McCloskey
MYP Coordinator Kelsey Barnes
Languages English
T: +1 720 972 4803
W: www.ad12.k12.co.us

Thornton Middle School
9451 Hoffman Way, Thornton CO 80229
MYP Coordinator Kim McLachlan
Languages English
T: +1 720 972 5160
W: thorntonm.adams12.org

Thunder Ridge High School
1991 West Wildcat Reserve Pkwy, Highlands Ranch CO 80129
DP Coordinator Donna Ferguson
MYP Coordinator Anne Morris
Languages English
T: +1 303 387 2000
W: www1.dcsdk12.org/secondary/trhs

Upper Blue Elementary School
PO Box 1255, 1200 Airport Road, Breckenbridge CO 80424
PYP Coordinator Toni Napolitano
Languages English
T: +1 970 368 1800
W: www.summit.k12.co.us/ube/site/default.asp

Westminster High School
6933 Raleigh Street, Westminster CO 80030
DP Coordinator Portia Curlee
Languages English
T: +1 720 542 5085
W: www.adams50.org/Domain/347

Wheeling Elementary
472 S Wheeling Street, Aurora CO 80012
PYP Coordinator Tricia Dutton Morato
Languages English
T: +1 303 344 8670
W: www.aps.k12.co.us/wheeling

Whittier International Elementary School
2008 Pine Street, Boulder CO 80302
PYP Coordinator Alysia Hayas
Languages English
T: +1 303 442 2282
W: www.bvsd.k12.co.us/schools/whittier/

William J Palmer High School
301 N. Nevada Ave., Colorado Springs CO 80903
DP Coordinator Carolyn Moyer
MYP Coordinator Carolyn Derr
Languages English
T: +1 719 328 5000
W: www.d11.org/palmer

Woodmen-Roberts Elementary School
8365 Orchard Path Road, Colorado Springs CO 80919
PYP Coordinator Laura Ayotte
Languages English
T: +1 719 234 5300
W: woodmenroberts.asd20.org

York International School
9200 York Street, Thornton CO 80229
MYP Coordinator Emelina Pacheco
PYP Coordinator Krystin Zwolinski
Languages English
T: +1 303 853 1600
W: www.mapleton.us

Connecticut

Brien McMahon High School
300 Highland Ave, Norwalk CT 06854
DP Coordinator Nicole Stockfisch
Languages English
T: +1 203 852 9488
W: bmhs.norwalkps.org

Charter Oak International Academy
425 Oakwood Avenue, West Hartford CT 06110
PYP Coordinator Kirsten Sanderson
Languages English
T: +1 860 233 8506
W: www.whps.org/school/charteroak

Cheshire Academy
10 Main Street, Cheshire CT 06410
DP Coordinator Jaimeson Anne Lynch
Languages English
T: +1 203 272 5396
W: www.cheshireacademy.org

Connecticut IB Academy
857 Forbes Street, East Hartford CT 06118
DP Coordinator Kathleen Simoneau
MYP Coordinator Michelle Galeota
Languages English
T: +1 860 622 5590
W: www.cibanet.org

Dr. Thomas S. O Connell Elementary School
301 May Rd, East Hartford CT 06118
PYP Coordinator Laurie Stock
Languages English
T: +1 860 622 5460
W: www.easthartford.org/page.cfm?p=8746

Global Communications Academy
85 Edwards Street, Hartford CT 06120
PYP Coordinator Kimberly Stone-Keaton
Languages English
T: +1 860 695 6020
W: www.hartfordschools.org

Guilford High School
605 New England Road, Guilford CT 06437
DP Coordinator Julia Chaffe
Languages English
T: +1 203 453 2741
W: ghs.guilfordps.org

International Magnet School for Global Citizenship
625 Chapel Road, South Windsor CT 06074
PYP Coordinator Katy Twyman
Languages English
T: +1 860 291 6001
W: www.crecschools.org/our-schools

King/Robinson Inter-District Magnet School
150 Fournier Street, New Haven CT 06511
MYP Coordinator Caterina Salamone
PYP Coordinator Caterina Salamone
Languages English
T: +1 203 691 2700

New Lebanon School
25 Mead Avenue, Greenwich CT 06830
PYP Coordinator Cheri Amster
Languages English
T: +1 203 531 9139
W: www.greenwichschools.org/NLS

Regional Multicultural Magnet School
1 Bulkeley Pl, New London CT 06320
PYP Coordinator Lynne Ramage
Languages English, Spanish
T: +1 860 437 7775
W: www.rmms.k12.ct.us

Rippowam Middle School
381 High Ridge Road, Stamford CT 06905
MYP Coordinator James Stanton
Languages English
T: +1 203 977 4410
W: www.rippowammiddle.org

Robert E Fitch Senior High School
101 Groton Long Point Road, Groton CT 06340
DP Coordinator Kelley Donovan
Languages English
T: +1 860 449 7200 EXT. 4507
W: www.groton.k12.ct.us

Rogers International School
202 Blachley Road, Stamford CT 06902
MYP Coordinator Virginia Maher
PYP Coordinator Virginia Maher
Languages English
T: +1 203 977 4562
W: www.rogersmagnetschool.org

Stamford High School
55 Strawberry Hill Avenue, Stamford CT 06902
DP Coordinator Tiffany Clark
Languages English
T: +1 203 977 4223
W: www.stamfordhigh.org

Sunset Ridge Middle School
450 Forbes St, East Hartford CT 06118
MYP Coordinator Daniel Hicks
Languages English
T: +1 860 622 5800
W: www.easthartford.org/page.cfm?p=7856

The International School at Dundee
55 Florence Road, Riverside CT 06878
PYP Coordinator Rosanna Sangermano
Languages English
T: +1 203 637 3800
W: www.greenwichschools.org/isd

The Metropolitan Learning Center Interdistrict Magnet School
1551 Blue Hills Avenue, Bloomfield CT 06002
DP Coordinator Caroline Alexopoulos
MYP Coordinator Emily Wright
Languages English
T: +1 860 242 7834
W: www.crec.org/magnetschools/schools/met/index.php

Valley Regional High School
256 Kelsey Hill Rd, Deep River CT 06417
DP Coordinator Maria Ehrhardt
Languages English
T: +1 860 526 5328
W: www.vrhs.reg4.k12.ct.us

Whitby School
969 Lake Avenue, Greenwich CT 06831
MYP Coordinator Shelley Castro
PYP Coordinator Diana Ljepoja
Languages English
T: +1 203 869 8464
W: www.whitbyschool.org

Delaware

John Dickinson High School
1801 Milltown Road, Wilmington DE 19808
DP Coordinator Geoffrey Ott
MYP Coordinator Valerie Morano
Languages English
T: +1 302 992 5500
W: www.johndickinsonhs.com

Mount Pleasant High School
5201 Washington St Extension, Wilmington DE 19809
DP Coordinator Leslie Carlson
MYP Coordinator Jeanne Beadle
Languages English
T: +1 302 762 7054
W: www.brandywine.schools.org/mphs

Sussex Academy
21150 Airport Road, Georgetown DE 19947
DP Coordinator Debbie Fees
Languages English
T: +1 302 856 3636
W: www.sussexacademy.org

Sussex Central High School
26026 Patriots Way, Georgetown DE 19947
DP Coordinator Kelly Deleon
Languages English
T: +1 302 934 3166
W: www.edline.net/pages/Sussex_Central_High_School

Talley Middle School
1110 Cypress Road, Wilmington DE 19810
MYP Coordinator Stefanie Feder
Languages English
T: +1 302 475 3976
W: brandywineschools.org/talley

Wilmington Friends School
101 School Road, Wilmington DE 19803
DP Coordinator Michael Benner
Languages English
T: +1 302 576 2900
W: www.wilmingtonfriends.org

District of Columbia

Alexander R. Shepherd Elementary School
7800 14th Street NW, Washington DC 20012
PYP Coordinator Avani Mack
Languages English
T: +1 202 576 6140
W: www.shepherd-elementary.org

Alice Deal Middle School
3815 Fort Drive, NW, Washington DC 20016
MYP Coordinator Caitlin Daniels
Languages English
T: +1 202 939 2010
W: www.alicedeal.org

Archbishop Carroll High School
4300 Harewood Road NE, Washington DC 20017
DP Coordinator Melanie Powell
Languages English
T: +1 202 529 0900 EXT:135
W: www.archbishopcarroll.org

Benjamin A Banneker Academic High School
800 Euclid Street NW, Washington DC 20001
DP Coordinator Raymond Kern
Languages English
T: +1 202 673 7325
W: www.benjaminbanneker.org

British International School of Washington
2001 Wisconsin Avenue NW, Washington DC 20007
DP Coordinator Pam Hayre
Languages English
T: +1 202 829 3700
W: www.biswashington.org

DC International School
1400 Main Drive NW, Washington DC 20012
CP Coordinator Shane Donovan
DP Coordinator Dean Harris
MYP Coordinator Dean Harris
Languages English, Spanish
T: +1 202 459 4790
W: www.dcinternationalschool.org

Eliot-Hine Middle School
1830 Constitution Ave NE, Washington DC 20002
MYP Coordinator Bess Davis
Languages English
T: +1 202 939 5380
W: www.eliothinemiddleschool.org

Friendship Public Charter School – Woodridge Campus
2959 Carlton Ave. NE, Washington DC 20018
PYP Coordinator Chastity Shipp
Languages English
T: +1 202 635 6500
W: www.friendshipschools.org/schools/woodridge

Mary McLeod Bethune Day Academy PCS
1404 Jackson Street NE, Washington DC 20017
PYP Coordinator Sanjay Singh
Languages English
T: +1 202 459 4710
W: www.mmbethune.org

National Collegiate Preparatory Public Charter High School
4600 Livingston Road SE, Washington DC 20032
DP Coordinator Thmaine S. Morgan
Languages English
T: +1 202 832 7737
W: www.nationalprepdc.org

Strong John Thomson Elementary School
1200 L Street NW, Washington DC 20005
PYP Coordinator Crystal Overstreet
Languages English
T: +1 202 898 4660
W: www.thomsondcps.org

Turner at Green Elementary School
1500 Mississippi Avenue SE, Washington DC 20032
PYP Coordinator Khadijah Shakir Hankton
Languages English
T: +1 202 645 3470
W: sites.google.com/a/dc.gov/turner-at-green-elementary-school

Washington International School
3100 Macomb Street NW, Washington DC 20008
DP Coordinator James Bourke
PYP Coordinator Stephanie Sneed
Languages English
T: +1 202 243 1800
W: www.wis.edu

Washington Yu Ying Public Charter School
220 Taylor St. NE, Washington DC 20017
PYP Coordinator Rebecca J Rosenberg
Languages English, Mandarin
T: +1 202 635 1950; +1 202 635 1960
W: www.washingtonyuying.org

Florida

Ada Merritt K-8 Center
660 SW 3 Street, Miami FL 33130
MYP Coordinator Andrew Alvarez
PYP Coordinator Jackeline Sanchez Jimenez
Languages English
T: +1 305 326 0791
W: adamerritt.dadeschools.net

Allen D Nease High School
10550 Ray Road, Ponte Vedra FL 32081
DP Coordinator Missy Kennedy
Languages English
T: +1 904 547 8300
W: www-nhs.stjohns.k12.fl.us

American Youth Academy
5905 E. 130th Ave, Tampa FL 33617
DP Coordinator Shabeah Usmanali
Languages English
T: +1 813 987 9282
W: www.ayatampa.org

Arthur I. Meyer Jewish Academy
5225 Hood Rd, Palm Beach Gardens FL 33418
MYP Coordinator Judy Edelman
Languages English
T: +1 561 686 6520
W: www.meyeracademy.org

Atlantic Community High School
2455 West Atlantic Ave, Palm Beach County, Delray Beach FL 33445
CP Coordinator Carlos Acosta
DP Coordinator Dr. David A Youngman
MYP Coordinator Jean Parlamento
Languages English
T: +1 561 243 1502
W: www.atlanticcommunityhighschool.com

Bhaktivedanta Academy
17414 NW 112th Blvd, Alachua FL 32615
MYP Coordinator Jaya Kaseder
Languages English
T: +1 386 462 2886
W: www.bhaktischool.org

Biscayne Elementary Community School
800 77th Street, Miami Beach FL 33141
PYP Coordinator Iris Garcia
Languages English, Spanish
T: +1 305 868 7727
W: www.biscaynees.org

Boca Prep International School
10333 Diego Drive South, Boca Raton FL 33428
DP Coordinator Elaine Chambart
MYP Coordinator Rachael Nassiri
PYP Coordinator Jodi-Kay Hylton-Senior
Languages English
T: +1 561 852 1410
W: www.bocaprep.net

Boyd H. Anderson High School
3050 NW 41st Street, Lauderdale Lakes FL 33309
DP Coordinator Marie Duperval
MYP Coordinator Marie Duperval
Languages English
T: +1 754 322 0200
W: www.browardschools1.com/boydanderson

Brandon Academy
801 Limona Road, Brandon FL 33510
DP Coordinator Dominick Giombetti
Languages English
T: +1 813 689 1952
W: www.brandon-academy.com

Brookside Middle School
3636 South Shade Avenue, Sarasota FL 34239
MYP Coordinator Lauren Haney
Languages English
T: +1 941 361 6472
W: sarasotacountyschools.net/schools/brookside

C Leon King High School
6815 North 56th Street, Tampa FL 33610
DP Coordinator Christian Finch
Languages English
T: +1 813 744 8333
W: www.sdhc.k12.fl.us/~king.high/

Cape Coral High School
2300 Santa Barbara Blvd, Cape Coral FL 33991
DP Coordinator Katelyn Uhler
Languages English
T: +1 239 574 6766
W: www.leeschools.net/schools/cch

Cardinal Newman High School
512 Spencer Drive, West Palm Beach FL 33409
DP Coordinator Theresa Fretterd
Languages English
T: +1 561 683 6266
W: www.cardinalnewman.com

Carrollton School of the Sacred Heart
3747 Main Highway, Miami FL 33133
DP Coordinator Caroline Gillingham-Varela
Languages English
T: +1 305 446 5673
W: www.carrollton.org

Carrollwood Day School
1515 W. Bearss Avenue, Tampa FL 33613
DP Coordinator Nancy Hsu
MYP Coordinator Sabrina McCartney
PYP Coordinator Lisa Vicencio
Languages English
T: +1 813 920 2288
W: www.carrollwooddayschool.org

Carver Middle School
101 Barwick Road, Delray Beach FL 33445
MYP Coordinator Nadia Stewart
Languages English
T: +1 561 638 2100
W: www.edline.net/pages/carver_middle_school

Carver Middle School
4500 W Columbia Street, Orlando FL 32811
MYP Coordinator Debbie Villar
Languages English
T: +1 407 296 5110
W: www.carvermiddle.ocps.net

Celebration High School
1809 Celebration Boulevard, Celebration FL 34747
DP Coordinator Aaron Foley
Languages English
T: +1 321 939 6600
W: www.celhs.k12.fl.us

Choctawhatchee Senior High School
110 Racetrack Road NW, Fort Walton Beach FL 32547
DP Coordinator Katherine White
Languages English
T: +1 850 833 3614
W: choctawindians.net

Clearwater Central Catholic High School
2750 Haines Bayshore Road, Clearwater FL 33760
DP Coordinator Alan Hamacher
Languages English
T: +1 727 531 1449
W: www.ccchs.org

Cocoa Beach Junior/Senior High School
1500 Minutemen Causeway, Cocoa Beach FL 32931
DP Coordinator Jocelyn Baldridge
MYP Coordinator Jocelyn Baldridge
Languages English
T: +1 321 783 1776
W: www.edline.net/pages/cocoa_beach_jshs

College Park Middle School
1201 Maury Road, Orlando FL 32804-3541
MYP Coordinator Wanda Alvarado
Languages English
T: +1 407 245 1800
W: collegeparkms.ocps.net

Conniston Community Middle School
673 Conniston Road, West Palm Beach FL 33405
MYP Coordinator Jeanette Machado
Languages English
T: +1 561 802 5477
W: www.edline.net/pages/conniston

Coral Gables Senior High School
450 Bird Road, Coral Gables FL 33146
DP Coordinator Diana Van Wyk
Languages English
T: +1 305 443 4871
W: www.cghs.dade.k12.fl.us

Coral Reef High School
10101 SW 152 Street, Miami FL 33157
DP Coordinator Kelli Wise
Languages English
T: +1 305 232 2044
W: coralreef.dadeschools.net

Corbett Preparatory School of IDS
12015 Orange Grove Drive, Tampa FL 33618
MYP Coordinator Jennifer Jagdmann
PYP Coordinator Linda Wenzel
Languages English
T: +1 813 961 3087
W: www.corbettprep.com

Cornerstone Learning Community
2524 Hartsfield Road, Tallahassee FL 32303
MYP Coordinator Karen Metcalf
Languages English
T: +1 850 386 5550
W: www.cornerstonelc.com

Cypress Creek High School
1101 Bear Crossing Drive, Orange County, Orlando FL 32824
DP Coordinator Helen Philpot
Languages English
T: +1 407 852 3400

Deerfield Beach High School
910 Buck Pride Way, Deerfield Beach FL 33441
DP Coordinator Kelly Caputo
MYP Coordinator Kelly Caputo
Languages English
T: +1 754 322 0650
W: www.deerfieldbeachhigh.net

Deerfield Beach Middle School
701 SE 6th Avenue, Deerfield Beach FL 33441
MYP Coordinator MJ Caputo
Languages English
T: +1 754 322 3300
W: www.deerfieldbeachmiddle.com

Deland High School
800 North Hill Avenue, Volusia, Deland FL 32724
DP Coordinator Lisa Nehrig
Languages English
T: +1 386 822 6909
W: www.volusia.k12.fl.us/schools/delandhigh/

Dr Mary McLeod Bethune Elementary School
1501 Avenue 'U', Riviera Beach FL 33404
PYP Coordinator Sherrita Crummell
Languages English
T: +1 561 882 7600
W: www.palmbeach.k12.fl.us/McLeodBethuneES

Dunbar High School
3800 E. Edison Avenue, Ft. Myers FL 33916
CP Coordinator Gayle Baisch
DP Coordinator Gayle Baisch
Languages English
T: +1 239 461 5322
W: dhs.leeschools.net

Dundee Elementary Academy
415 E Frederick Ave, Dundee FL 33838
PYP Coordinator Monica Crosthwaite
Languages English
T: +1 863 421 3316
W: dea.polk-fl.net

Dundee Ridge Academy
5555 Lake Trask Rd, Dundee FL 33838
MYP Coordinator Kerri Collins
Languages English
T: +1 863 419 3088
W: dra.polk-fl.net

Earlington Heights Elementary School
4750 NW 22nd Avenue, Miami FL 33142
PYP Coordinator Star Grimm
Languages English
T: +1 305 635 7505
W: earlingtonheightselem.dadeschools.net

Eastside High School
1201 South East 43rd Street, Gainesville FL 32641-7698
DP Coordinator Anne Koon
Languages English
T: +1 352 955 6704
W: www.ehs.sbac.edu

Fienberg-Fisher K-8 Center
1420 Washington Ave, Miami Beach FL 33139
MYP Coordinator Pierrela JeanBaptiste
PYP Coordinator Yessenia Cardoso
Languages English
T: +1 305 351 0419
W: www.fienbergfisherk8.com

Flagler Palm Coast High School
3265 Highway 100 East, Palm Coast FL 32164
DP Coordinator Roger M Tangney
Languages English
T: +1 386 437 7540
W: www.flagler.k12.fl.us

Forest Hill Community High School
3340 Forest Hill Boulevard, West Palm Beach FL 33405
CP Coordinator Saara Saarela-Vening
DP Coordinator Saara Saarela-Vening
MYP Coordinator Barbara Malone
Languages English
T: +1 561 540 2400

Forest Park Elementary School
1201 SW 3rd Street, Boynton Beach FL 33435
PYP Coordinator Simone Green
Languages English
T: +1 561 292 6900
W: www.edline.net/pages/forest_park_es

Fort Myers High School
2635 Cortez Boulevard, Fort Myers FL 33901
DP Coordinator Susan Postma
Languages English
T: +1 239 334 2167
W: www.lee.k12.fl.us/schools/fmh/home.asp

Frank C Martin Elementary School
14250 Boggs Drive, Miami FL 33176
MYP Coordinator Leidis Arechavaleta
PYP Coordinator Leidis Arechavaleta
Languages English
T: +1 305 238 3688
W: www.fcmartin.dadeschools.net

Franklin Academy – Cooper City Campus
6301 S. Flamingo Road, Cooper City FL 33330
MYP Coordinator Rachel Franco
Languages English
T: +1 954 780 5533
W: cc.franklin-academy.org

Franklin Academy – Pembroke Pines (K-12) Campus
5000 SW 207th Terrace, Pembroke Pines FL 33332
DP Coordinator Astrid Rivera-Ortiz
MYP Coordinator Maria Neumann
Languages English
T: +1 954 315 0770
W: pphs.franklin-academy.org

Franklin Academy – Pembroke Pines (K-8) Campus
18800 Pines Blvd, Pembroke Pines FL 33029
MYP Coordinator Kathy Ross
Languages English, Spanish
T: +1 954 703 2294
W: pp.franklin-academy.org

Franklin Academy – Sunrise Campus
4500 NW 103 Ave, Sunrise FL 33351
MYP Coordinator Alicia Glenn
Languages English, Spanish
T: +1 754 206 0850
W: sun.franklin-academy.org

Freedom 7 Elementary School of International Studies
400 4th Street South, Cocoa Beach FL 32931
PYP Coordinator Jennifer Noe
Languages English
T: +1 321 868 6610
W: www.freedom.es.brevard.k12.fl.us

Gateway High School
93 Panther Paws Trail, Osceola School District, Kissimmee FL 34744
DP Coordinator Heather Piper
Languages English
T: +1 407 935 3600

Glenridge Middle School
2900 Upper Park Road, Orlando FL 32814
MYP Coordinator Matthew Astone
Languages English
T: +1 407 623 1415
W: www.ibatwphs.org

G-Star School of the Arts for Motion Pictures & Broadcasting
2065 Prairie Road, Building J, Palm Springs FL 33406
DP Coordinator Emily Snedeker
Languages English
T: +1 561 967 2023
W: www.gstarschool.org

Gulf High School
5355 School Road, New Port Richey FL 34652
DP Coordinator Cheryl Macri
Languages English
T: +1 727 774 3300
W: www.gulfhigh.org

Gulliver Academy Middle School
12595 Red Road, Coral Gables FL 33156
MYP Coordinator Juan Carlos Garcia
Languages English
T: +1 305 665 3593
W: www.gulliverschools.org

Gulliver Preparatory School
6575 North Kendall Drive, Miami FL 33156
DP Coordinator Jan Patterson
Languages English
T: +1 305 666 7937
W: www.gulliverschools.org

Haines City High School
2800 Hornet Drive, Haines City FL 33844
DP Coordinator Crystal Young
Languages English
T: +1 863 419 3371
W: www.hainescityhighschool.com

Heights Elementary School
15200 Alexandria Court, Fort Myers FL 33908
PYP Coordinator Michelle Edwards
Languages English
T: +1 239 481 1761
W: het.leeschools.net

Herbert A Ammons Middle School
17990 SW 142 Avenue, Miami FL 33177
MYP Coordinator David Wilson
Languages English
T: +1 305 971 0158
W: ammons.dadeschools.net

Hillsborough High School
5000 Central Avenue, Tampa FL 33603
DP Coordinator Trisha Fitzgerald
Languages English
T: +1 813 276 5620
W: www.sdhc.k12.fl.us

Homestead Middle School
650 N.W. 2nd Avenue, Homestead FL 33030
MYP Coordinator Elizabeth Juste
Languages English
T: +1 305 247 4221
W: homesteadmiddle.org

Howard Middle School
1655 NW 10th Street, Ocala FL 34475
MYP Coordinator Allison Laplante
Languages English
T: +1 352 671 7225
W: www.marionschools.net/hms

International Baccalaureate School at Bartow High School
1270 South Broadway Avenue, Bartow FL 33830
DP Coordinator Katherine Marsh
Languages English
T: +1 863 534 0194

J. Colin English Elementary School
120 Pine Island Rd., N. Fort Myers FL 33903
PYP Coordinator Brian Taylor
Languages English
T: +1 239 995 2258
W: jce.leeschools.net

J.H. Workman Middle School
6299 Lanier Avenue, Penacola FL 32504
MYP Coordinator Michael Burton
Languages English
T: +1 850 494 5665
W: jhwms-ecsd-fl.schoolloop.com

Jackson Middle School
6000 Stonewall Jackson Road, Orlando FL 32807
MYP Coordinator Lynne Newsom Newsom
Languages English
T: +1 407 249 6430
W: www.stonewalljackson.ocps.net

James B. Sanderlin PK-8
2350 22nd Avenue South, St Petersburg FL 33712
MYP Coordinator Katherine Gilson
PYP Coordinator Kristen Herman
Languages English
T: +1 727 552 1700
W: www.sanderlinib.com

James S Rickards High School
3013 Jim Lee Road, Leon District Schools, Tallahassee FL 32301-7057
DP Coordinator Joe Williams
Languages English
T: +1 850 488 1783

Jewett Middle Academy
601 Ave T NE, Winter Haven FL 33881
MYP Coordinator Paulette Waldon
Languages English
T: +1 863 291 5320
W: schools.polk-fl.net/jewettacademy

John A Ferguson Senior High School
15900 SW 56th Street, Miami FL 33185
DP Coordinator Denise Graham
Languages English
T: +1 305 408 2700
W: www.fergusonhs.org

John F Kennedy Middle School
1901 Avenue 'S', Riviera Beach FL 33404
MYP Coordinator Joshua Wade
Languages English
T: +1 561 845 4502
W: www.edline.net/pages/John_F_Kennedy_Middle_School

Jones High School
801 South Rio Grande Avenue, Orlando FL 32805
DP Coordinator Kyra Brown
MYP Coordinator Michelle Allen
Languages English
T: +1 407 835 2300
W: www.jones.ocps.net

Kids Community College Southeast Campus
11519 McMullen Road, Riverview FL 33569
PYP Coordinator Lisa Briggs
Languages English
T: +1 813 699 4600
W: www.kidscc.org

Lake Wales High School
1 Highlander Way, Lake Wales FL 33853
DP Coordinator Anuj Saran
Languages English
T: +1 863 678 4222
W: www.lakewaleshigh.com

Lake Weir High School
10351 SE Maricamp Road, Ocala FL 34472
DP Coordinator Samantha Roberts
Languages English
T: +1 352 671 4820
W: www.marion.k12.fl.us/schools/lwh

Lamar Louise Curry Middle School
15750 SW 47th Street, Miami FL 33185
MYP Coordinator Iran Miranda
Languages English
T: +1 305 222 2775

Land O'Lakes High School
20325 Gator Lane, Land O'Lakes FL 34639
DP Coordinator Evette Striblen
Languages English
T: +1 813 794 9400

Largo High School
410 Missouri Ave N, Largo FL 33770
DP Coordinator Alec Liem
Languages English
T: +1 727 588 9158
W: www.largo-hs.pcsb.org

Lauderdale Lakes Middle School
3911 Northwest 30 th Avenue, Lauderdale Lakes FL 33309
MYP Coordinator Jeana Louis
Languages English
T: +1 954) 497 3900

Lawton Chiles Middle Academy
400 North Florida Avenue, Lakeland FL 33801
MYP Coordinator Susie Kallan
Languages English
T: +1 863 499 2742
W: www.lcmaknightsonline.com

Lecanto High School
3810 W Educational Path, Lecanto FL 34461
DP Coordinator Darrick Buettner
Languages English
T: +1 352 746 2334
W: www.citrus.k12.fl.us/lhs

Lexington Middle School
16351 Summerlin Road, Fort Myers FL 33908
MYP Coordinator Tiffany Sanders
Languages English
T: +1 239 454 6130
W: lxm.leeschools.net

Liberty Magnet Elementary School
6850 81st Street, Vero Beach FL 32967
PYP Coordinator Jamie Lunsford
Languages English
T: +1 772 564 5300
W: www.indian-river.K12.fl.us

Lincoln Avenue Academy
1330 North Lincoln Avenue, Lakeland FL 33805
PYP Coordinator Holly Wallace
Languages English
T: +1 863 499 2955
W: lincolnavenuejaguars.weebly.com

Lincoln Elementary Magnet School
1207 E Renfro Street, Plant City FL 33563
PYP Coordinator Michelle Arn
Languages English
T: +1 813 757 9329
W: lincoln.mysdhc.org

Lincoln Park Academy
1806 Avenue I, St Lucie County, Fort Pierce FL 34950
DP Coordinator Carol Kuhn
MYP Coordinator Carol Kuhn
Languages English
T: +1 772 468 5474
W: www.stlucie.k12.fl.us/LPA

Louise R Johnson Middle School
2121 26th Avenue East, Bradenton FL 34208
MYP Coordinator Kemira Denlea
Languages English
T: +1 941 741 3344
W: www.edline.net/pages/sdmcjohnsonms

Louise R. Johnson K-8 School of International Studies
2121 26th Avenue East, Bradenton FL 34208
PYP Coordinator Shana Berg
Languages English
T: +1 941 741 3344
W: www.manateeschools.net/johnson

Macfarlane Park Elementary Magnet School
1721 North MacDill Avenue, Tampa FL 33607
PYP Coordinator Angela Hartle
Languages English
T: +1 813 356 1760
W: macfarlanepark.mysdhc.org

IB AMERICAS

Mariner Middle School
425 Chiquita Blvd N., Cape Coral FL 33993
MYP Coordinator James Kroll
Languages English
T: +1 239 772 1848
W: mrm.leeschools.net

Maynard Evans High School
4949 Silver Star Road, Orlando FL 32808
DP Coordinator John Harrell
MYP Coordinator John Harrell
Languages English
T: +1 407 522 3400
W: www.evanshs.ocps.net

Melbourne High School
74 Bulldog Boulevard, Melbourne FL 32901
CP Coordinator Jennifer Mason
DP Coordinator Jennifer Mason
Languages English
T: +1 321 952 5880
W: melbourne.hs.brevard.k12.fl.us

Memorial Middle School
2220 W 29th Street, Orlando FL 32805
MYP Coordinator Sara Kowalski
Languages English
T: +1 407 245 1810
W: www.memorial.ocps.net

Miami Beach Senior High School
2231 Prairie Avenue, Miami Beach FL 33139
DP Coordinator Carlos Rodriguez
Languages English
T: +1 305 532 4515
W: miamibeachhigh.schoolwires.com

Mildred Helms Elementary School
561 S. Clearwater-Largo Rd., Largo FL 33770-3294
PYP Coordinator Kimberly Dennison
Languages English, Spanish
T: +1 727 588 3569
W: www.pcsb.org/mildred-es

Miramar High School
3601 SW 89th Avenue, Miramar FL 33025
DP Coordinator John Lamb
Languages English
T: +1 754 323 1350
W: www.broward.k12.fl.us/miramarhigh

Morikami Park Elementary School
6201 Morikami Park Road, Delray Beach FL 33484
PYP Coordinator Amy Mercier
Languages English
T: +1 561 865 3960

Nautilus Middle School
4301 N. Michigan Ave., Miami Beach FL 33140
MYP Coordinator Lissette Burns
Languages English
T: +1 305 532 3481
W: nautilus.dadeschools.net

New Gate School
5237 Ashton Road, Sarasota FL 34233
DP Coordinator Maria Alvarez
Languages English
T: +1 941 922 4949
W: www.newgate.edu

New Renaissance Middle School
10701 Miramar Blvd., Miramar FL 33025
MYP Coordinator Vivien Robotis
Languages English, Spanish
T: +1 754 323 3500
W: www.browardschools.com/newrenaissance

North Beach Elementary School
4100 Prairie Avenue, Miami Beach FL 33140
PYP Coordinator Savitria Green
Languages English
T: +1 305 531 7666
W: northbeach.schoolwires.com

NORTH BROWARD PREPARATORY SCHOOL
7600 Lyons Road, Coconut Creek FL 33073
DP Coordinator Tamara Wolpowitz
Languages English
T: +1 954 247 0179
E: admissions@nbps.org
W: www.nbps.org
See full details on page 534

North Dade Middle School
1840 NW 157th Street, Miami Gardens FL 33054
MYP Coordinator Taneisha Webster
Languages English
T: +1 305 624 8415
W: ndms.dadeschools.net

North Miami Middle School
700 NE 137th St, North Miami FL 33161
MYP Coordinator Clifton Hamilton
Languages English
T: +1 305 891 3680
W: nmiamid.dadeschools.net

North Miami Senior High School
13110 NE 8 Avenue, North Miami FL 33161
DP Coordinator Rose Weintraub
Languages English
T: +1 305 891 6590
W: www.dadeschools.net

Oakcrest Elementary School
1112 NE 28th Street, Ocala FL 34470
PYP Coordinator Jill Atchley
Languages English
T: +1 352 671 6350
W: www.Marion.k12.fl.us/schools/oce

Pahokee Elementary School
560 E Main Place, Pahokee FL 33476
PYP Coordinator Cassandra Moreland
Languages English
T: +1 561 924 9705
W: www.edline.net/pages/pahokee_elementary_school

Pahokee Middle Senior High School
900 Larrimore Road, Pahokee FL 33476
DP Coordinator Aya Hasegawa
MYP Coordinator Sonia SOTO
Languages English
T: +1 561 924 6400
W: www.palmbeach.k12.fl.us/pahokeemiddlesrhigh

Palm Harbor University High School
1900 Omaha Street, Palm Harbor FL 34683
DP Coordinator Kimberly Barker
Languages English
T: +1 727 669 1131

Parkway Middle School
857 Florida Parkway, Kissimmee FL 34743
MYP Coordinator Katalina Dasilva
Languages English
T: +1 407 344 7000
W: www.pm.osceola.k12.fl.us

Paxon School for Advanced Studies
3239 Norman E Thagard Blvd., Jacksonville FL 32254-1796
DP Coordinator Krystal Culpepper
Languages English
T: +1 904 693 7583
W: www.duvalschools.org/psas

Pedro Menendez High School
600 State Road 206 West, St Augustine FL 32086
DP Coordinator Jonathan Higgins
Languages English
T: +1 904 547 8660
W: www-pmhs.stjohns.k12.fl.us

Pensacola High School
A and Maxwell Streets, Pensacola FL 32501
DP Coordinator Laura Nelms Brewer
Languages English
T: +1 850 595 1500
W: www.phstigers.org

Phillippi Shores Elementary School
4747 South Tamiami Trail, Sarasota FL 34231
PYP Coordinator Christina Slattery
Languages English
T: +1 941 361 6424
W: www.sarasota.k12.fl.us/pse

Pine View Elementary School
5333 Parkway Boulevard, Land O' Lakes FL 34639
PYP Coordinator Erin Greco
Languages English, Spanish
T: +1 813 794 0600
W: pves.pasco.k12.fl.us

Pine View Middle School
5334 Parkway Boulevard, Land O' Lakes FL 34639
MYP Coordinator Rebecca Cardinale
Languages English
T: +1 813 794 4800
W: pvms.pasco.k12.fl.us

Plantation High School
6901 NW 16th Street, Plantation FL 33313
DP Coordinator Joseph Chiarmonte
Languages English
T: +1 754 322 1850
W: www.plantationhigh.org

PLANTATION MIDDLE SCHOOL
6600 West Sunrise Blvd, Plantation FL 33313
MYP Coordinator Pamela Van Horn
Languages English
T: +1 754 322 4100
E: nicole.s.wilson@browardschools.com
W: browardschools.com/plantationmid
See full details on page 540

Ponce de Leon Middle School
5801 Augusto Street, Coral Gables FL 33146
MYP Coordinator Marlene Ramos
Languages English
T: +1 305 661 1611 EXT:2212
W: ponce.dadeschools.net

Port St Lucie High School
1201 S E Jaguar Lane, Port St Lucie FL 34952
DP Coordinator Caroline Whiddon-Miller
Languages English
T: +1 772 337 6770
W: www.stlucie.k12.fl.us/pslh

Ridgeview High School Academy for Advanced Studies
466 Madison Avenue, Clay County, Orange Park FL 32065
DP Coordinator Kristine Guha
Languages English
T: +1 904 213 5203
W: www.clay.k12.fl.us/rhs

Riverdale High School
2600 Buckingham Road, Fort Myers FL 33905
DP Coordinator Traci Budmayr
Languages English
T: +1 239 694 4141
W: www.lee.k12.fl.us/schools/rdh

Riverhills Elementary Magnet
405 S. Riverhills Drive, Temple Terrace FL 33617
PYP Coordinator Diana Favata
Languages English
T: +1 813 987 6911
W: riverhills.mysdhc.org

Riverview High School
One Ram Way, Sarasota FL 34231
CP Coordinator Amy Earl
DP Coordinator James R Minor
Languages English
T: +1 941 923 1484
W: www.riverviewib.com

Robinson High School
6311 S Lois Avenue, Tampa FL 33616-1617
DP Coordinator Amanda Batista
Languages English
T: +1 813 272 3006
W: www.robinsonhs.mysdhc.org

Robinswood Middle School
6305 Balboa Drive, Orlando FL 32818
MYP Coordinator Vernalee Bickerstaff
Languages English
T: +1 407 296 5140
W: www.ocps.net/lc/west/mro

Roland Park K-8 Magnet School
1510 N. Manhattan Ave, Tampa FL 33607
MYP Coordinator Adrienne Rundle
PYP Coordinator Adrienne Rundle
Languages English
T: +1 813 872 5212
W: rolandpark.mysdhc.org

Royal Palm Beach High School
10600 Okeechobee Blvd., Royal Palm Beach FL 33411
DP Coordinator Laurie Cotton
Languages English
T: +1 561 753 4000
W: rpbhs.org

Rutherford High School
1000 School Avenue, Springfield FL 32401
DP Coordinator Catherine Rutland
Languages English
T: +1 850 767 4500
W: www.bayschools.com/rhs

Samuel W. Wolfson High School
7000 Powers Ave., Jacksonville FL 32217-3398
DP Coordinator Brandi Benga
Languages English
T: +1 904 739 5265
W: www.duvalschools.org/wolfson

Sarasota Military Academy
801 N. Orange Avenue, Sarasota FL 34236
DP Coordinator Pamela Donehew
MYP Coordinator Lisa Currie
Languages English
T: +1 941 926 1700
W: www.sarasotamilitaryacademy.org

Sebastian River High School
9001 90th Avenue, Indian River, Sebastian FL 32958
DP Coordinator Jaime Sturgeon
Languages English
T: +1 772 564 4170
W: www.indian-river.k12.us/srhs/main.html

Sebastian River Middle School
9400 State Road 512, Sebastian FL 32958
MYP Coordinator Bradley Wright
Languages English
T: +1 772 564 5111
W: www.indian-river.k12.fl.us/srms

Sebring High School
3514 Kenilworth Boulevard, Sebring FL 33870
DP Coordinator Jo Anna Cochlin
Languages English
T: +1 863 471 5500
W: www.highlands.k12.fl.us/~shs

Seminole High School
2701 Ridgewood Avenue, Seminole, Sanford FL 32773-4916
DP Coordinator Donna Noll
Languages English
T: +1 407 320 5100
W: www.seminolehs.scps.k12.fl.us

South Dade Senior High School
28401 SW 167 Ave., Homestead FL 33030
DP Coordinator Elena Delgado
Languages English
T: +1 305 247 4244
W: sdshs.net

South Fork High School
10000 SW Bulldog Way, Stuart FL 34997-2799
DP Coordinator Kelly Riccardo
Languages English
T: +1 772 219 1840
W: sfhs.martinschools.org/pages/south_fork_high_school

South Pointe Elementary School
1050 4th Street, Miami Beach FL 33139
PYP Coordinator Celine Clark
Languages English
T: +1 305 531 5437
W: southpointe.schoolwires.com

Southeast High School
1200 37th Avenue East, Bradenton FL 34208
DP Coordinator Shelly Decesare
Languages English
T: +1 941 741 3366
W: www.edline.net/pages/sdmcsoutheasths

Southside Middle School
2948 Knights Lane E, Jacksonville FL 32216-5697
MYP Coordinator Kassandra Kieffer
Languages English
T: +1 904 739 5238
W: www.duvalschools.org/southside

Spring Park Elementary School
2250 Spring Park Road, Jacksonville FL 32207
PYP Coordinator Griffin Lyon
Languages English
T: +1 904 346 5640
W: www.duvalschools.org/springpark

Springstead High School
3300 Mariner Boulevard, Spring Hill FL 34609
DP Coordinator John Imhof
Languages English
T: +1 352 797 7010
W: www.hcsb.k12.fl.us/shs

Spruce Creek High School
801 Taylor Road, Port Orange FL 32127
DP Coordinator Karie Cappiello
Languages English
T: +1 386 322 6272
W: www.sprucecreekhigh.com

St Andrew's School
3900 Jog Road, Boca Raton FL 33434
DP Coordinator Catherine Jennings
MYP Coordinator Victor Rivera
PYP Coordinator Sabah Rashid
Languages English
T: +1 561 210 2000
W: www.saintandrews.net

St Ann Catholic School
324 North Olive Avenue, West Palm Beach FL 33401
MYP Coordinator Philomena Smith
PYP Coordinator Susan Demes
Languages English
T: +1 561 832 3676
W: www.stannwpb.org

St John Vianney Catholic School
500 84th Avenue, St Pete Beach FL 33706
MYP Coordinator Becky LLoyd
Languages English
T: +1 727 360 1113
W: www.sjvcs.org

St Petersburg High School
2501 Fifth Avenue North, St Petersburg FL 33713
DP Coordinator Kieonna Lane
Languages English
T: +1 727 893 1842
W: www.stpetehigh.com

St. Cecelia Interparochial Catholic School
1350 Court Street, Clearwater FL 33756
MYP Coordinator Leah Steele
PYP Coordinator Leah Steele
Languages English
T: +1 727 461 1200
W: www.st-cecelia.org

Stanton College Preparatory School
1149 West 13th Street, Jacksonville FL 32209
DP Coordinator Benjamin Nasrallah
Languages English
T: +1 904 630 6760
W: www.duvalschools.org/stanton

Strawberry Crest High School
4691 Gallagher Road, Dover FL 33527
DP Coordinator Tiffany Ewell
Languages English
T: +1 813 707 7522
W: strawberrycrest.mysdhc.org

Suncoast Community High School
1717 Avenue S, Riviera Beach FL 33404
CP Coordinator Liesel Winchester
DP Coordinator Maria Edgar
MYP Coordinator Brett Stubbs
Languages English
T: +1 561 882 3401
W: www.edline.net/pages/suncoast_high_school

Terry Parker High School
7301 Parker School Road, Jacksonville FL 32211
DP Coordinator Darcey Gray
Languages English
T: +1 904 720 1650
W: www.duvalschools.org/tphs

Thacker Avenue Elementary School for International Studies
301 N. Thacker Avenue, Kissimmee FL 34741
PYP Coordinator Elizabeth Ziegler
Languages English
T: +1 407 935 3540
W: taes.osceolaschools.net

THE BILTMORE SCHOOL
1600 S. Red Road, Miami FL 33155
PYP Coordinator Isbel Salgueiro
Languages English
T: +1 305 266 4666
E: info@biltmoreschool.com
W: www.biltmoreschool.com

See full details on page 552

The Discovery School
102 15th Street South, Jacksonville Beach FL 32250
PYP Coordinator Nita Hurley
Languages English
T: +1 904 247 4577
W: thediscoveryschool.org

The Roig Academy
8000 SW 112 St, Miami FL 33156
PYP Coordinator Gustavo Roig
Languages English, Spanish
T: +1 305 235 1313
W: www.roigacademy.com

Treasure Island Elementary School
7540 East Treasure Drive, North Bay Village FL 33141
PYP Coordinator Obi Lawrence
Languages English
T: +1 305 865 3141
W: www.treasureislandschool.com

Union Academy Magnet School
1795 East Wabash Street, Bartow FL 33830
MYP Coordinator Deborah Draper
Languages English
T: +1 863 534 7435
W: schools.polk-fl.net/ua

University High School
11501 Eastwood Drive, Orange County, Orlando FL 32817
DP Coordinator Leonardo Calderon
Languages English
T: +1 407 482 8700

Vanguard High School
7 NW 28th Street, Ocala FL 34475
DP Coordinator Stephanie DeVilling
Languages English
T: +1 352 671 4900
W: www.marionschools.net/vhs

Venice High School
1 Indian Ave., Venice FL 34285
CP Coordinator Melanie Ritter
DP Coordinator Kathleen Jones
Languages English
T: +1 941 488 6726
W: sarasotacountyschools.net/schools/venicehigh

Walker Middle Magnet School
8282 North Mobley Road, Odessa FL 33556
MYP Coordinator Cassie Schroeder
Languages English
T: +1 813 631 4726
W: walker.mysdhc.org

Westward Elementary School
1101 Golf Avenue, Palm Beach, West Palm Beach FL 33401
PYP Coordinator Bernadette Beneby-Coleman
Languages English
T: +1 561 802 2130
W: www.edline.net/pages/westward_elementary/

William T Dwyer High School
13601 N Military Trail, Palm Beach Gardens FL 33418
DP Coordinator Susan Mulligan
Languages English
T: +1 561 625 7858
W: www.edline.net/pages/William__T__Dwyer_High_School

Williams Middle Magnet School for International Studies
5020 N 47th Street, Tampa FL 33610
MYP Coordinator Joyce Hoehn-Parish
Languages English
T: +1 813 744 8600
W: www.williams.mysdhc.org/

Wilton Manors Elementary School
2401 NE 3rd Avenue, Wilton Manors FL 33305
PYP Coordinator Lori Goldsmith
Languages English
T: +1 754 322 8950
W: www.broward.k12.fl.us/wiltonmanorselem

Windermere Preparatory School
6189 Winter Garden, Vineland Road, Windermere FL 34786
DP Coordinator Anne Lyng
Languages English
T: +1 407 905 7737
W: www.windermereprep.com

Winter Park High School
2100 Summerfield Road, Winter Park FL 32792
CP Coordinator Donald Blackmon
DP Coordinator Donald Blackmon
Languages English
T: +1 407 622 3212

Winter Springs High School
130 Tuskawilla Road, Winter Park FL 32708
DP Coordinator Courtney Doherty
Languages English
T: +1 407 320 8750
W: www.winterspringshs.scps.k12.fl.us

Georgia

4/5 Academy at Fifth Avenue
101 5th Avenue, Decatur GA 30030
PYP Coordinator Shannon Stewart
Languages English
T: +1 404 371 6680
W: fifthavenue.csdecatur.net

A.L. Burruss School
325 Manning Road, Marietta GA 30064
PYP Coordinator Kristen Green
Languages English
T: +1 770 429 3144
W: alburruss.marietta-city.org

Academy of Richmond County
910 Russell Street, Augusta GA 30904
CP Coordinator Scott Guinn
DP Coordinator Scott Guinn
Languages English
T: +1 706 737 7152
W: www.rcboe.org/arc

Alpharetta High School
3595 Webb Bridge Road, Alpharetta GA 30005
DP Coordinator Frank Fortunato
Languages English
T: +1 470 254 7640
W: school.fultonschools.org/hs/alpharetta

Atlanta International School
2890 North Fulton Drive, Atlanta GA 30305
DP Coordinator Adam Lapish
MYP Coordinator Maria Del Carmen Samanes Gajate
PYP Coordinator Leonie Ley-Mitchell
Languages English
T: +1 404 841 3840
W: www.aischool.org

Atlanta Neighborhood Charter School
820 Essie Ave, Atlanta GA 30316
MYP Coordinator Somer Hobby
Languages English
T: +1 678 904 0051
W: atlncs.org

Avondale Elementary School
10 Lakeshore Drive, Avondale Estates GA 30052
PYP Coordinator Kim L Siddiqui
Languages English
T: +1 678 676 5202
W: www.avondalees.dekalb.k12.ga.us

Beecher Hills Elementary School
2257 Bollingbrook Drive, SW, Atlanta GA 30311
PYP Coordinator Tiffany Harvey
Languages English
T: +1 404 802 8300
W: www.atlanta.k12.ga.us/Domain/316

Benjamin H Hardaway High School
2901 College Drive, Columbus GA 31906
CP Coordinator Ashley Snow
DP Coordinator Ashley Snow
Languages English
T: +1 706 649 0748

Bolton Academy Elementary School
2268 Adams Dr., Atlanta GA 30318
PYP Coordinator Monica Veiga Varner
Languages English
T: +1 404 802 8350
W: www.atlanta.k12.ga.us/domain/1979

Burke County High School
1057 Burke Veterans Parkway, Waynesboro GA 30830
CP Coordinator June Powell
Languages English
T: +1 706 554 6691
W: bchs.burke.k12.ga.us

Campbell High School
5265 Ward Street, Cobb County, Smyrna GA 30080
DP Coordinator Daniel Penick
Languages English
T: +1 678 842 6850
W: www.cobbk12.org/campbellhs

Campbell Middle School
3295 South Atlanta Road, Smyrna GA 30080
MYP Coordinator Jacquelyne Bosarge
Languages English
T: +1 678 842 6873
W: www.cobbk12.org/campbellms/

Carrollton High School
202 Trojan Drive, Carrollton GA 30117
DP Coordinator Noah Brewer
Languages English
T: +1 770 834 7726
W: chs.carrolltoncityschools.net

Centennial High School
9310 Scott Road, Roswell GA 30076
DP Coordinator Andrea Prewitt
Languages English
T: +1 470 254 4230
W: school.fultonschools.org/hs/centennial

Central High School, Macon
2155 Napier Avenue, Macon GA 31204
DP Coordinator Joshua Mccorkle
Languages English
T: +1 478 779 2300
W: www.bcsdk12.net/domain/110

Clubview Elementary School
2836 Edgewood Road, Columbus GA 31906
PYP Coordinator Kimberly Schorr
Languages English
T: +1 706 565 3017
W: www.clubviewschool.net

Coastal Middle School
4595 US Highway 80 East, Savannah GA 31410
MYP Coordinator Deborah Looye
Languages English
T: +1 912 395 3950

D. M. Therrell High School
3099 Panther Trail SW, Atlanta GA 30311
CP Coordinator Sarah Talluri
Languages English
T: +1 404 802 5300
W: www.atlantapublicschools.us/domain/1327

Dalton High School
1500 Manly Street, Dalton GA 30720
CP Coordinator Christina Siefert
DP Coordinator Christina Siefert
Languages English
T: +1 706 278 8757
W: www.dalton.k12.ga.us/dhs

Decatur High School
310 N. McDonough St., Decatur GA 30030
CP Coordinator Duane Sprull
DP Coordinator Cheryl Nahmias
MYP Coordinator Debra LeDoux
Languages English
T: +1 404 370 4170
W: dhs.csdecatur.net

Deerwood Academy
3070 Fairburn Road, Atlanta GA 30331
PYP Coordinator Erica Wynn
Languages English
T: +1 404 802 3300
W: www.apskids.org/deerwood

Douglas County High School
8705 Campbellton Street, Douglasville GA 30134
DP Coordinator Grant Fossum
Languages English
T: +1 770 651 6500
W: douglascounty.dch.schoolinsites.com

Druid Hills High School
1798 Haygood Drive NE, Atlanta GA 30307
DP Coordinator Anne Bracewell
Languages English
T: +1 678 874 6300
W: www.dekalb.k12.ga.us/~druidhills/

Druid Hills Middle School
3100 Mount Olive Drive, Decatur GA 30033
MYP Coordinator Kim Colossale
Languages English
T: +1 678 874 7602
W: www.druidhillsms.dekalb.k12.ga.us

Dublin High School
1127 Hillcrest Parkway, Dublin GA 31021
DP Coordinator Amber Donnell
Languages English
T: +1 478 277 4107
W: www.dublinschools.net/dublinscioto_home.aspx

E Rivers Elementary School
8 Peachtree Battle Avenue, Atlanta GA 30305
PYP Coordinator Nicole Cheroff
Languages English
T: +1 404 802 7050
W: www.erivers-elem.org

Fernbank Elementary School
157 Heaton Park Dr, Atlanta GA 30307
PYP Coordinator Elisabeth Beckwith
Languages English
T: +1 678 874 9302
W: www.fernbankes.dekalb.k12.ga.us

Garden Hills Elementary School
285 Sheridan Drive, Atlanta GA 30305
PYP Coordinator Krista L. Reilly
Languages English
T: +1 404 842 3103
W: www.gardenhillselementary.com

Heards Ferry Elementary School
6151 Powers Ferry Road, Sandy Springs GA 30339
PYP Coordinator Stephanie Soldo
Languages English
T: +1 470 254 6190
W: school.fultonschools.org/es/heardsferry

High Meadows School
1055 Willeo Road, Roswell GA 30188
PYP Coordinator Kathryn McElvaney
Languages English
T: +1 770 993 2940
W: www.highmeadows.org

High Point Elementary School
520 Greenland Rd NE, Sandy Springs GA 30342
PYP Coordinator Elizabeth Roberts
Languages English
T: +1 470 254 7716
W: school.fultonschools.org/es/highpoint

International Charter School of Atlanta
1335 Northmeadow Parkway, Suite 100, Roswell GA 30076
PYP Coordinator Severine Plesnarski
Languages English, French
T: +1 470 222 7420
W: www.icsatlanta.org

International Community School
2418 Wood Trail Lane, Decatur GA 30033
PYP Coordinator Aliya Jafri
Languages English
T: +1 404 499 8969
W: www.intcomschool.org

International Studies Elementary Charter School
2237 Cutts Drive, Albany GA 31705
PYP Coordinator Amber Davis
Languages English
T: +1 229 431 3384

Johnson High School
3305 Poplar Springs Road, Gainesville GA 30507
DP Coordinator Holly Wilson
Languages English
T: +1 770 536 2394
W: www.hallco.org/johnsonhs

Lake Forest Elementary School
5920 Sandy Springs Circle, Sandy Springs GA 30328
PYP Coordinator Caitlin Vanker
Languages English
T: +1 470 254 8740
W: school.fultonschools.org/es/lakeforest

Lake Forest Hills Elementary School
3140 Lake Forest Drive, Augusta GA 30909
PYP Coordinator Crystal Coleman
Languages English
T: +1 706 737 7317
W: www.rcboe.org/lakeforesthills

Lakeside High School
533 Blue Ridge Drive, Evans GA 30809
DP Coordinator Stacey Brown
Languages English
T: +1 706 863 0027
W: edline.net/pages/lakeside_hs

Langford Middle School
3019 Walton Way, Augusta GA 30909
MYP Coordinator Thaddeaus Mohler
Languages English
T: +1 706 737 7301
W: www.rcboe.org/langford

Marietta High School
1171 Whitlock Avenue, Marietta GA 30064
CP Coordinator Debbie Woolard
DP Coordinator Debbie Woolard
MYP Coordinator Kelly Herrero
Languages English
T: +1 770 428 2631
W: www.marietta-city.k12.ga.us/mhs

Marietta Middle School
121 Winn Street, Marietta GA 30064
MYP Coordinator Jill Sims
Languages English
T: +1 770 422 0311
W: www.marietta-city.k12.ga.us/mms

Marietta Sixth Grade Academy
340 Aviation Road, Marietta GA 30060
MYP Coordinator Tamara Edwards
Languages English
T: +1 770 429 3115
W: www.marietta-city.k12.ga.us

Marshpoint Elementary School
135 Whitemarsh Island Road, Savannah GA 31410
PYP Coordinator Deborah Looye
Languages English
T: +1 912 898 4000
W: www.marshpointelementary.com

Martin Luther King Jr High School
3991 Snapfinger Road, Lithonia GA 30038
DP Coordinator Hanifah Ali
Languages English
T: +1 678 874 5402
W: www.dekalb.ga.us/~mlking/

Martin Luther King, Jr. Middle School (GA)
545 Hill Street SE, Atlanta GA 30312
MYP Coordinator Shekela Edwards
Languages English
T: +1 404 802 5400
W: www.atlantapublicschools.us/page/8440

Maynard Holbrook Jackson High School
801 Glenwood Ave SE, Atlanta GA 30316
CP Coordinator Yusef King
DP Coordinator Yusef King
MYP Coordinator Debra Ross
Languages English
T: +1 404 802 5200
W: www.atlanta.k12.ga.us/domain/3508

Midvale Elementary School
3836 Midvale Road, Tucker GA 30084
PYP Coordinator Ashley Little
Languages English
T: +1 678 874 3402
W: www.dekalb.k12.ga.us/~midvale

Montessori Academy Sharon Springs
2830 Old Atlanta Road, Cumming GA 30041
DP Coordinator Carmen Serghi
Languages English, Spanish
T: +1 770 205 6277
W: montessoriacademysharonsprings.com

Morgan County High School
1231 College Drive, Madison GA 30650
DP Coordinator Lisa Hamilton
Languages English
T: +1 706 342 2336
W: www.morgan.k12.ga.us/mchs

Morris Brandon Elementary School
2741 Howell Mill Road, Atlanta GA 30327
PYP Coordinator Samuel De Carlo
Languages English
T: +1 770 350 2153
W: www.morrisbrandon.com

Norcross High School
5041 Staverly Lane, Norcross GA 30092
DP Coordinator Dan Byrne
MYP Coordinator Elizabeth O'Halloran
Languages English
T: +1 770 448 3674
W: www.norcrosshigh.org

North Atlanta High School
4111 Northside Parkway, Atlanta GEORGIA 30327
CP Coordinator Danielle Costarides
DP Coordinator Danielle Costarides
MYP Coordinator Nikia Showers
Languages English
T: +1 404 802 4700
W: www.atlanta.k12.ga.us/domain/3377

North Hall High School
4885 Mt Vernon Road, Gainesville GA 30506
DP Coordinator Lori Barrett
Languages English
T: +1 770 534 1080
W: nhhs.hallco.org

Notre Dame Academy, GA
4635 River Green Parkway, Duluth GA 30096
DP Coordinator Daniel Jewitt
MYP Coordinator Katherine Costello
PYP Coordinator Kelly Jenkins
Languages English
T: +1 678 387 9385
W: www.ndacademy.org

Peachtree Elementary School
5995 Crooked Creek Road, Peachtree Corners GA 30092
PYP Coordinator Brian Ginley
Languages English
T: +1 770 448 8710
W: www.peachtreees.org

Pinckneyville Middle School
5440 West Jones Bridge Road, Norcross GA 30092
MYP Coordinator Varonica Donham
Languages English
T: +1 770 263 0860
W: www.pinckneyvillemiddle.org

Ralph J. Bunche Middle School
1925 Niskey Lake Rd SW, Atlanta GA 30331
MYP Coordinator Kennette Blackman
Languages English
T: +1 404 802 6700
W: www.atlantapublicschools.us/bunche

Renfroe Middle School
220 W. College Ave., Decatur GA 30030
MYP Coordinator Kristen Karably
Languages English
T: +1 404 370 4440
W: renfroe.csdecatur.net

Richards Middle School
2892 Edgewood Road, Columbus GA 31906
MYP Coordinator Kimberly M. Casleton
Languages English
T: +1 706 569 3697
W: richardsmcsdga.com

Ridgeview Middle School
5340 S Trimble Road, Atlanta GA 30342
MYP Coordinator Andrea von Biberstein
Languages English
T: +1 404 843 7710
W: www.ridgeviewmiddleschool.com

Riverwood International Charter School
5900 Heards Drive NW, Atlanta GA 30328
DP Coordinator Diane Kopkas
MYP Coordinator Andrea von Biberstein
Languages English
T: +1 404 847 1980
W: www.riverwoodics.org

Salem Middle School
5333 Salem Road, Lithonia GA 30058
MYP Coordinator Anne Marion
Languages English
T: +1 678 676 9402
W: www.dekalb.k12.ga.us/salem

Sarah Smith Elementary School
4141 Wieuca Road, NE, Atlanta GA 30342
PYP Coordinator Karla Lamar
Languages English
T: +1 404 802 3880
W: www.sarahsmithelementary.com

Sawyer Road Elementary School
840 Sawyer Road, Marietta GA 30062
PYP Coordinator Jill Baker
Languages English
T: +1 770 429 9923
W: www.marietta-city.k12.ga.us/sawyerroad

Shiloh High School
4210 Shiloh Road, Snellville GA 30039
DP Coordinator Kirsten Menosky
Languages English
T: +1 770 972 8471
W: www.shilohhighschool.org

Shiloh Middle School
4285 Shiloh Road, Snellville GA 30039-6146
MYP Coordinator Stacee Brown
Languages English
T: +1 770 972 3224
W: shilohms.com

Sol C Johnson High School
3012 Sunset Blvd, Savannah GA 31404
CP Coordinator Lisa Campbell
DP Coordinator Jason Buelterman
MYP Coordinator Amanda Fanelli
Languages English
T: +1 912 395 6400
W: internet.savannah.chatham.k12.ga.us/schools/jhs

South Forsyth High School
585 Peachtree Parkway, Forsyth County, Cumming GA 30041
CP Coordinator Tera Graham
DP Coordinator Kevin Denney
Languages English
T: +1 770 781 2264
W: www.forsyth.k12.ga.us

Southwest Middle School
6030 Ogeechee Road, Savannah GA 31419
MYP Coordinator Craig Daughtry
Languages English
T: +1 912 395 3540
W: swms.sccpss.com

St Andrew's School
601 Penn Waller Road, Savannah GA 31410
DP Coordinator Tiffany Phillips
Languages English
T: +1 912 897 4941
W: www.saintschool.com

Summerour Middle School
585 Mitchell Road, Norcross GA 30071
MYP Coordinator Syretheal Glover
Languages English
T: +1 770 448 3045
W: www.gwinnett.k12.ga.us/summerourms

Sutton Middle School
2875 Northside Drive NW, Atlanta GA 30305
MYP Coordinator Joshua Sturtevant
Languages English
T: +1 404 802 5600
W: www.suttonmiddleschool.org

Tucker High School
5036 Lavista Road, Tucker GA 30084
DP Coordinator Amanda Xiques
Languages English
T: +1 678 874 3702
W: www.dekalb.k12.ga.us/~tucker

Tucker Middle School
2160 Idlewood Road, Tucker GA 30084
MYP Coordinator Eric Knapp
Languages English
T: +1 678 875 0902
W: www.dekalb.k12.ga.us/tuckerms

Valdosta High School
3101 N Forrest Street, Valdosta GA 31601
DP Coordinator Betsy McTier
Languages English
T: +1 229 333 8540
W: www.gocats.org/vhs

Victory World Christian School
5905 Brook Hollow Parkway, Norcross GA 30071
PYP Coordinator Deborah Fulkerson
Languages English, Spanish
T: +1 678 684 2030
W: vwcs.org

Warren T Jackson Elementary School
1325 Mt Paran Road, Atlanta GA 30327
PYP Coordinator Bria Pete
Languages English
T: +1 404 802 8800
W: www.wtjackson.org

Wesley International Academy
211 Memorial Drive, Atlanta GA 30312
MYP Coordinator Richard Pavone
PYP Coordinator Richard Pavone
Languages English
T: +1 678 904 9137
W: www.wesleyacademy.org

West Hall High School
5500 McEver Road, Oakwood GA 30566
CP Coordinator Anna Jackson
DP Coordinator Anna Jackson
Languages English
T: +1 770 967 9826
W: www.hallco.org/whhs

Westlake High School, Atlanta
2400 Union Road, Atlanta GA 30331
DP Coordinator Jenelle Wingfield
Languages English
T: +1 470 254 6400
W: www.westlakehs.org

Windsor Forest High School
12419 Largo Drive, Savannah GA 31419
CP Coordinator Jody Ranous
DP Coordinator Jody Ranous
MYP Coordinator Jennifer Dobbins
Languages English
T: +1 912 395 3400
W: internet.savannah.chatham.k12.ga.us/schools/wfhs

Hawaii

Aina Haina Elementary School
801 W. Hind Drive, Honolulu HI 96821
PYP Coordinator Trisha Shipman-Lameier
Languages English
T: +1 808 377 2419
W: www.ainahaina.k12.hi.us

Haha`ione Elementary School
595 Pepeekeo Street, Honolulu HI 96825
PYP Coordinator Shannon Goo
Languages English
T: +1 808 397 5822
W: www.hahaionees.org

Henry J Kaiser High School
511 Lunalilo Home Road, Honolulu HI 96825
CP Coordinator Shareen Murayama
DP Coordinator Bradley Bogard
MYP Coordinator Kristie Yamamoto
Languages English
T: +1 808 394 1200
W: www.kaiser.k12.hi.us

Iroquois Point Elementary School
5553 Cormorant Avenue, Ewa Beach HI 96706
PYP Coordinator Thomasina Simmons
Languages English
T: +1 808 499 6500
W: www.k12.hi.us/~iroquois

Island Pacific Academy
909 Haumea Street, Kapolei HI 96707
DP Coordinator Andrew Marchetto-Ryan
Languages English
T: +1 808 674 3523
W: www.ipahawaii.org

James Campbell High School
91-980 North Road, Ewa Beach HI 96706
DP Coordinator Jo-Hannah Liz Valdez
Languages English
T: +1 808 689 1200
W: www.campbellhigh.org

Kamiloiki Elementary School
7788 Hawaii Kai Drive, Honolulu HI 96825
PYP Coordinator Amber Stanley
Languages English
T: +1 808 397 5800
W: www.kamiloikielementary.org

Koko Head Elementary School
189 Lunalilo Home Road, Honolulu HI 96825
PYP Coordinator Jared Kagihara
Languages English
T: +1 808 397 5811
W: kokoheadschool.org

Le Jardin Academy
917 Kalanianaole Highway, Kailua HI 96734
DP Coordinator Lindsey Schiffler
MYP Coordinator Kristina Quint
PYP Coordinator Lori Shigehara
Languages English
T: +1 808 261 0707
W: www.lejardinacademy.org

Mid-Pacific Institute
2445 Kaala Street, Honolulu HI 96822
DP Coordinator Kymbal Roley
Languages English
T: +1 808 973 5020
W: www.midpac.edu

Niu Valley Middle School
310 Halemaumau Street, Honolulu HI 96821
MYP Coordinator Gwen Lee
Languages English
T: +1 808 377 2440
W: niuvalleymiddle.org

Idaho

Alturas International Academy
151 N Ridge Avenue, Idaho Falls ID 83402
PYP Coordinator Dayna Crose
Languages English, Spanish
T: +1 208 522 5145
W: www.alturasacademy.org

North Star Charter School
1400 N Park Lane, Eagle ID 83616
DP Coordinator Danica Hare
Languages English
T: +1 208 939 9600
W: www.northstarcharter.org

Renaissance High School
1307 East Central Drive, Meredian ID 83642
CP Coordinator Andrew Hunter
DP Coordinator Andrew Hunter
Languages English
T: +1 208 350 4380
W: www.westada.org/domain/58

Riverstone International School
5493 Warm Springs Avenue, Boise ID 83716
DP Coordinator Jami Whitmer
MYP Coordinator Damon Brown
PYP Coordinator James Hamilton
Languages English
T: +1 208 424 5000
W: www.riverstoneschool.org

Sage International School of Boise
457 E Parkcenter Blvd, Boise ID 83706
CP Coordinator Guy Falconer
DP Coordinator Faith Hansen
MYP Coordinator Mimi Trevino
PYP Coordinator Kadie Johnson
Languages English
T: +1 208 343 7243
W: www.sageinternationalschool.org

Illinois

Academy for Global Citizenship
4647 West 47th Street, Chicago IL 60632
PYP Coordinator Meredith McNamara
Languages English
T: +1 312 316 7373
W: www.agcchicago.org

Agassiz Elementary School
2851 N. Seminary Ave., Chicago IL 60657
MYP Coordinator Michele McNally
Languages English
T: +1 773 534 5725
W: agassizschool.org

Andrew Carnegie Elementary School
1414 East 61st Place, Chicago IL 60637
MYP Coordinator Franci Boateng
Languages English
T: +1 773 535 0882
W: www.carnegie.cps.edu

Back of the Yards College Preparatory High School
2111 West 47th Street, Chicago IL 60609
CP Coordinator Dawn Cox
DP Coordinator Dawn Cox
MYP Coordinator Matthew D'Agostino
Languages English
T: +1 773 520 1774
W: www.boycp.org

Barnard Elementary School
10354 S. Charles Street, Chicago IL 60643
MYP Coordinator Jeri Sparks
Languages English
T: +1 773 535 2625
W: barnardelementary.weebly.com

Beacon Academy
622 Davis St., Evanston IL 60201
DP Coordinator Hayley Ropiequet
Languages English
T: +1 224 999 1177
W: www.beaconacademyil.org

Benito Juarez Community Academy
1450 – 1510 W Cermak Rd, Chicago IL 60608
DP Coordinator Alfredo Peralta
MYP Coordinator Santiago Marquez
Languages English
T: +1 773 534 7030
W: www.benitojuarez.net

Bogan Computer Technical High School
3939 West 79th Street, Chicago IL 60652
DP Coordinator Maureen Waters
MYP Coordinator Maureen Waters
Languages English
T: +1 773535 8138
W: www.boganhs.org

British International School of Chicago, South Loop
161 W. 9th Street, Chicago IL 60605
DP Coordinator Rebecca Allister
Languages English
T: +1 773 599 2472
W: www.bischicagosl.org

Bronzeville Scholastic Institute
4934 South Wabash Avenue, Chicago IL 60615
DP Coordinator Sarah Collins
MYP Coordinator Sarah Collins
Languages English
T: +1 773 535 1101
W: www.bronzevillescholastic.org

Carl Schurz High School
3601 N. Milwaukee Ave, Chicago IL 60641
DP Coordinator Lori Kingen-Gardner
MYP Coordinator Lori Kingen-Gardner
Languages English
T: +1 773 534 3420
W: www.schurzhs.org

Christian Ebinger Elementary School
7350 West Pratt Avenue, Chicago IL 60631
MYP Coordinator Jill Randinelli
Languages English
T: +1 773 534 1070
W: ebingerschool.org

Coretta Scott King Magnet School
1009 Blackhawk Drive, University Park IL 60466
PYP Coordinator Shannon Bruns
Languages English
T: +1 708 672 2651
W: www.cm201u.org/CSK

Crete-Monee Middle School
635 Olmstead Ln, University Park IL 60484
MYP Coordinator Christina Flores Colbert
Languages English, Spanish
T: +1 708 367 2400

David G. Farragut Career Academy High School
2345 S. Christiana Avenue, Chicago IL 60623
DP Coordinator Emily Brightwell
MYP Coordinator Emily Brightwell
Languages English
T: +1 773 534 1300
W: www.farragutcareeracademy.org

Daystar Academy
1550 S. State St., Chicago IL 60605
MYP Coordinator Alison Good
Languages English, Spanish
T: +1 312 791 0001
W: www.daystaracademy.org

DePaul College Prep
3633 North California Avenue, Chicago IL 60618
DP Coordinator Heidi Bojorges
Languages English
T: +1 773 539 3600
W: www.depaulprep.org

Dr. Edward Alexander Bouchet International Academy
7355 S. Jeffery Boulevard, Chicago IL 60649
MYP Coordinator Franchesca Little
PYP Coordinator Tina Franklin-Bertrand
Languages English, Spanish
T: +1 773 535 0501
W: www.bouchet-brynmawr.cps.k12.il.us

Edward K. Duke Ellington Elementary School
243 N Parkside Ave, Chicago IL 60644
MYP Coordinator Anna Baskin-Tines
Languages English
T: +1 773 534 6361
W: www.ellingtoncps.weebly.com

Elizabeth Sutherland Elementary School
10015 South Leavitt Avenue, Chicago IL 60643
MYP Coordinator Meredith Parker
Languages English
T: +1 773 535 2580

Esmond Elementary School
1865 W Montvale Avenue, Chicago IL 60643
MYP Coordinator Bernika Green
Languages English
T: +1 773 535 2650

Francisco I Madero Middle School
3202 West 28th Street, Chicago IL 60623
MYP Coordinator Wendy Preciado
Languages English
T: +1 773 535 4466

Frazier International Magnet School
4027 West Grenshaw Street, Chicago IL 60624
MYP Coordinator Rhori Edwards
PYP Coordinator Rhori Edwards
Languages English
T: +1 773 534 6880
W: www.fraziermagnet.org

GEMS World Academy Chicago
350 E. South Water St., Chicago IL 60601
DP Coordinator Tracey Wood
MYP Coordinator Melissa Cuculich
PYP Coordinator Taneal Sanders
Languages English
T: +1 312 809 8910
W: www.gemschicago.org

George Washington High School
3535 East 114th Street, Chicago IL 60617
DP Coordinator Mike Pestich
MYP Coordinator Mike Pestich
Languages English
T: +1 773 535 6430

German International School Chicago
1447 West Montrose Ave, Chicago IL 60613
PYP Coordinator Katharina Koch
Languages English
T: +1 773 880 8812
W: www.germanschoolchicago.com

Gwendolyn Brooks Middle School
325 S Kenilworth Ave, Oak Park IL 60302
MYP Coordinator Christiana Harrington
Languages English
T: +1 708 524 3050
W: www.op97.org/brooks

Hansberry College Prep
8748 S. Aberdeen St., Chicago IL 60620
DP Coordinator Matthew Wienclawski
Languages English
T: +1 773 729 3400
W: hansberrycollegeprep.noblenetwork.org

Helen C. Peirce School of International Studies
1423 W. Bryn Mawr, Chicago IL 60660
MYP Coordinator Kimberly Lebovitz
PYP Coordinator Kimberly Lebovitz
Languages English
T: +1 773 534 2440
W: peirce.cps.edu

Henry R Clissold School
2350 West 110th Place, Chicago IL 60643
MYP Coordinator Deborah Turner-Blum
Languages English
T: +1 773 535 2560
W: www.clissoldschool.org

Holy Family Catholic Academy
2515 Palatine Road, Inverness IL 60067
PYP Coordinator Laura Clark
Languages English
T: +1 847 907 3452
W: holyfamilycatholicacademy.net

USA

Homewood-Flossmoor High School District 233
999 Kedzie Avenue, Flossmoor IL 60422
DP Coordinator Matthew Knoepke
Languages English
T: +1 708 799 3000
W: www.hfhighschool.org

Hubbard High School
6200 South Hamlin Avenue, Chicago IL 60629
DP Coordinator Jean Brown
Languages English
T: +1 773 535 2403

Hyde Park Academy
6220 South Stoney Island Ave, Chicago IL 60637
CP Coordinator Katharine Braggs
DP Coordinator Katharine Braggs
MYP Coordinator Rosette Edinburg
Languages English
T: +1 773 535 0882

Ida B Wells Preparatory Elementary Academy
249 E 37TH St, Chicago IL 60653
MYP Coordinator Rozetta Toney
Languages English
T: +1 773 535 1204
W: wellsprepelementary.com

Iles School
1700 South 15th Street, Springfield IL 62703
PYP Coordinator Tiffany Burris
Languages English
T: +1 217 525 3226
W: www.springfield.k12.il.us/schools/iles

Irvin C. Mollison Elementary
4415 South King Drive, Chicago IL 60653
MYP Coordinator Shelagh Jackson
Languages English
T: +1 773 535 1804
W: www.mollisonelementary.com

James B McPherson Elementary School
4728 N Wolcott, Chicago IL 60640
MYP Coordinator Marianne Turk
Languages English
T: +1 773 534 2625

John F. Kennedy High School
6325 West 56th Street, Chicago IL 60638
CP Coordinator James Clarke
DP Coordinator James Clarke
MYP Coordinator Allison Wika
Languages English
T: +1 773 535 2325
W: www.kennedyhschicago.org

John Fiske Elementary
6020 S Langley Avenue, Chicago IL 60637
MYP Coordinator Kiyana Grayer
Languages English
T: +1 773 535 0990
W: fiskeelementary.org

John L Marsh Elementary School
9810 South Exchange Avenue, Chicago IL 60617
MYP Coordinator Armando Avila
Languages English
T: +1 773 535 6430

John M Smyth Magnet School
1059 West 13th Street, Chicago IL 60608
MYP Coordinator Donnell White
PYP Coordinator Debra Ellis
Languages English
T: +1 773 534 7180
W: www.smyth.cps.k12.il.us

Jones-Farrar Magnet School
1386 South Kiwanis Drive, Freeport IL 61032
PYP Coordinator Carmen Madigan
Languages English
T: +1 815 232 0610
W: www.freeport.k12.il.us

Jose de Diego Community Academy
1313 N Claremont, Chicago IL 60622
MYP Coordinator Kenya Hodges-Walker
Languages English
T: +1 773 534 4451
W: josedediego.org

Josephinum Academy
1501 North Oakley Boulevard, Chicago IL 60622
DP Coordinator Anne Ross
Languages English
T: +1 773 276 1261
W: www.josephinum.org

Joshua D Kershaw Elementary
6450 S Lowe Avenue, Chicago IL 60621
MYP Coordinator Karen Jones
PYP Coordinator Aileen Lopez
Languages English
T: +1 773 535 3050
W: www.kershawmagnet.org

Kate Starr Kellogg Elementary School
9241 S Leavitt Street, Chicago IL 60643
MYP Coordinator Diane Pajkos
Languages English
T: +1 773 535 2590
W: kellogg.cps.edu

Legacy Academy of Excellence Charter School
4029 Prairie Road, Rockford IL 61102
MYP Coordinator Lynn Victorov
Languages English
T: +1 815 961 1100
W: www.legacy-academy.com

LINCOLN PARK HIGH SCHOOL
2001 North Orchard Street, Chicago IL 60614
CP Coordinator Mary Enda Tookey
DP Coordinator Mary Enda Tookey
MYP Coordinator Theresa McCormick
Languages English
T: +1 773 534 8149
E: lpibprogram@aol.com
W: www.lincolnparkhs.org
See full details on page 520

Locke Elementary School
2828 North Oak Park Avenue, Chicago IL 60634
MYP Coordinator Edgar Valentin
Languages English
T: +1 773 534 3300
W: www.lockeschool.org

Lycée Français de Chicago
1929 W Wilson Ave, Chicago IL 60640
DP Coordinator Sebastien Tourlouse
MYP Coordinator Sebastien Tourlouse
Languages English, French
T: +1 773 665 0066
W: www.lyceechicago.org

Mansueto High School
2911 W. 47th Street, Chicago IL 60632
DP Coordinator Thomas Evans
Languages English
T: +1 773 349 8200
W: nobleschools.org/mansueto

Marie Sklodowska Curie Metropolitan High School
4959 South Archer Avenue, Chicago IL 60632
CP Coordinator Alexandra Rake
DP Coordinator Sharyl Barnes
MYP Coordinator Jasmine Dorner
Languages English
T: +1 773 535 2100
W: www.curiehs.com

Marquette Elementary School
3939 West 79th Street, Chicago IL 60652
MYP Coordinator Michael Marzano
Languages English
T: +1 773 535 2174

Moos Elementary School
1711 N. California Ave, Chicago IL 60647
MYP Coordinator Teena Van Dyke
Languages English
T: +1 773 534 4340
W: www.mooselementary.org

Morgan Park High School
1744 West Pryor, Chicago IL 60643
CP Coordinator Morgan Mudron
DP Coordinator Morgan Mudron
MYP Coordinator Tim Gronholm
Languages English
T: +1 773 535 2550
W: www.cs.iit.edu/~morganpk

Nicholas Senn High School
5900 Glenwood Avenue, Chicago IL 60660
DP Coordinator Claire Saura
MYP Coordinator Lauren Lucchesi
Languages English
T: +1 773 534 2365

Oscar DePriest Elementary School
139 South Parkside Avenue, Chicago IL 60644
MYP Coordinator Tanya Bateson
Languages English
T: +1 773 534 6800
W: depriestschool.org

Oscar F Mayer Elementary School
2250 N Clifton Avenue, Chicago IL 60614
MYP Coordinator Jill Kittinger
Languages English
T: +1 773 534 5535
W: www.mayer.cps.k12.il.us

Percy Julian Middle School
416 S Ridgeland Ave, Oak Park IL 60302
MYP Coordinator Jennifer DeBruin
Languages French, Spanish
T: +1 708 524 3040
W: www.op97.org/julia

Pritzker College Prep
4131 W. Cortland Avenue, Chicago IL 60639
DP Coordinator Samantha Corvino
Languages English
T: +1 805 215 2616
W: pritzkercollegeprep.org

Prosser Career Academy
2148 N Long Avenue, Chicago IL 60639
CP Coordinator Jessica Stephenson
DP Coordinator Jessica Stephenson
Languages English
T: +1 773 534 3200
W: www.prosseracademy.org

Proviso Mathematics & Science Academy
8601 W. Roosevelt Rd, Forest Park IL 60130
DP Coordinator Rebecca Tanaka
Languages English
T: +1 708 338 4100
W: pmsa.pths209.org

Pulaski International School of Chicago
2230 W McLean Ave, Chicago IL 60647
MYP Coordinator Rosabel Sanchez
PYP Coordinator Rosabel Sanchez
Languages English
T: +1 773 534 4390
W: www.pulaskischool.org

Richard Edwards School
4815 S Karlov Avenue, Chicago IL 60632
MYP Coordinator Arturo Jurado
Languages English
T: +1 773 535 4878
W: edwardsschool.cps.k12.il.us

Richwoods High School
6301 N. University Street, Peoria IL 61614
DP Coordinator Travis Bowlby
Languages English
T: +1 309 693 4400
W: www.peoriapublicschools.org/richwoods

Roald Amundsen High School
5110 N Damen Avenue, Chicago IL 60625
CP Coordinator Colleen Murray
DP Coordinator Colleen Murray
MYP Coordinator Irwin Lim
Languages English
T: +1 773 534 2320

Roberto Clemente Community Academy
1147 N. Western Avenue, Chicago IL 60622
CP Coordinator Andrea Kulas
DP Coordinator Andrea Kulas
MYP Coordinator Chris Oakes
Languages English
T: +1 773 534 4000
W: www.rccachicago.org

South Shore International College Prep
1955 E. 75th Street, Chicago IL 60649
CP Coordinator Donna Delmonico
DP Coordinator Donna Delmonico
MYP Coordinator Sarah Gomez
Languages English
T: +1 773 535 8350
W: www.southshoreinternational.org

St. Matthias School
4910 N. Claremont Ave, Chicago IL 60625
MYP Coordinator Jennifer Reckamp
Languages English
T: +1 773 784 0999
W: www.stmatthiasschool.org

Steinmetz College Prep High School
3030 North Mobile Avenue, Chicago IL 60634
DP Coordinator Nancyanne Ferrarini
MYP Coordinator Rachel Rezny
Languages English
T: +1 773 534 3030
W: steinmetzcollegeprep.org

The Ogden International School of Chicago
1250 W Erie, Chicago IL 60642
DP Coordinator John McGinnis
MYP Coordinator Sara Fliehman Levinstein
PYP Coordinator Sara Schneeberg
Languages English
T: +1 773 534 0866
W: www.ogdenschool.org

Thomas Kelly High School
4136 South California Avenue, Chicago IL 60632
DP Coordinator Elisabeth Morrison
Languages English
T: +1 773 535 4915
W: www.schools.cps.k12.il.us/kelly/

Thornridge High School
15000 Cottage Grove, Dolton IL 60419
DP Coordinator Jason Curl
Languages English
T: +1 708 271 4403
W: www.district205.net/thornridge

Thornton Township High School
15001 S. Broadway, Harvey IL 60426
DP Coordinator Bradley Ablin
Languages English
T: +1 708 225 4102
W: www.district205.net/thornton

Thornwood High School
17101 South Park Avenue, South Holland IL 60473
DP Coordinator Cerelia Hampton
Languages English
T: +1 708 225 4700
W: www.district205.net/thornwood

Trinity College Preparatory High School
7574 West Division Street, River Forest IL 60305
DP Coordinator Rose Crnkovich
Languages English
T: +1 708 771 8383
W: www.trinityhs.org

Wildwood IB World Magnet School
6950 N Hiawatha, Chicago IL 60646
MYP Coordinator Tammy Kreydick
PYP Coordinator Tammy Kreydick
Languages English
T: +1 773 534 1187
W: www.wildwoodworldmagnet.org

William H. Seward Communication Arts Academy
4600 S. Hermitage, Chicago IL 60609
MYP Coordinator Lorel Madden
Languages English
T: +1 773 535 4890
W: seward.cps.edu

William Howard Taft High School
6530 West Bryn Mawr Avenue, Region 1 Area 19, Chicago IL 60631
CP Coordinator Lauren Zucchero
DP Coordinator Irene Kondos
MYP Coordinator Fakhira Chander
Languages English
T: +1 773 534 1000

Indiana

Allisonville Elementary School
4900 E 79th Street, Indianapolis IN 46228
PYP Coordinator Pamela Weiger
Languages English
T: +1 317 845 9441
W: av.msdwt.k12.in.us

Benjamin Bosse High School
1300 Washington Avenue, Evansville IN 47714
DP Coordinator Michele Hays
Languages English
T: +1 812 477 1661
W: www.evscschools.com/bosse

Carmel High School
520 East Main Street, Carmel IN 46032
DP Coordinator Kathleen Overbeck
Languages English
T: +1 317 846 7721
W: carmelhighschool.net

Cathedral High School
5225 East 56th Street, Indianapolis IN 46226
DP Coordinator Gary Spurgin
Languages English
T: +1 317 542 1481
W: www.gocathedral.com

Center for Inquiry School 2
725 N. New Jersey Street, Indianapolis IN 46202
MYP Coordinator Christine Snow
PYP Coordinator Christine Snow
Languages English
T: +1 317 226 4202
W: www.myips.org/cfi

Center for Inquiry School 27
545 E. 19th Street, Indianapolis IN 46202
PYP Coordinator Karen Sullivan
Languages English
T: +1 317 226 4227
W: www.myips.org/cfi

Center for Inquiry School 70
510 46th Street, Indianapolis IN 46205
PYP Coordinator Karla Reilly
Languages English, Spanish
T: +1 317 226 4270
W: www.myips.org/cfi

Center for Inquiry School 84
440 E. 57th Street, Indianapolis IN 46220
MYP Coordinator Rachel Green Sharpe
PYP Coordinator Rachel Green Sharpe
Languages English
T: +1 317 226 4284
W: www.myips.org/cfi

Central Middle School
303 E. Superior St, Kokomo IN 46901
MYP Coordinator Chantel Sullivan
Languages English
T: +1 765 454 7000
W: www.kokomoschools.com

Chesterton High School
2125 S 11th Street, Chesterton IN 46304
DP Coordinator Rebecca Uehling
Languages English
T: +1 219 983 3730
W: www.duneland.k12.in.us/chs

Childs Elementary School
2211 S. High Street, Bloomington IN 47401
PYP Coordinator Kris Stewart
Languages English
T: +1 812 330 7756
W: www.mccsc.edu/childs

USA

Clearwater Elementary School
3575 E 79th St., Indianapolis IN 46240
PYP Coordinator Jessica Murphy
Languages English
T: +1 317 259 5465
W: cw.msdwt.k12.in.us

Crooked Creek Elementary School
2150 Kessler Blvd W Drive, Indianapolis IN 46228
PYP Coordinator Kelly Ouattara
Languages English
T: +1 317 259 5478
W: cc.msdwt.k12.in.us

Eastwood Middle School
4401 East 62nd St., Indianapolis IN 46220
MYP Coordinator Anat Pinsky
Languages English
T: +1 317 259 5401
W: ew.msdwt.k12.in.us

Fishers High School
13000 Promise Road, Fishers IN 46038
DP Coordinator Jennifer Gabbard
Languages English
T: +1 317 915 4290
W: hse.k12.in.us/fhs

Floyd Central High School
6575 Old Vincennes Road, Floyd Knobs IN 47119
DP Coordinator Karen Mayer-Sebastian
Languages English
T: +1 812 542 3005
W: fchs.nafcs.k12.in.us

Fox Hill Elementary School
802 Fox Hill Drive, Indianapolis IN 46228
PYP Coordinator Emily Dickerson
Languages English
T: +1 317 259 5371
W: fh.msdwt.k12.in.us

Goshen High School
401 Lincolnway East, Goshen IN 46526
DP Coordinator Theresa Collins
Languages English
T: +1 574 533 8651
W: ghs.goshenschools.org

Greenbriar Elementary School
8201 Ditch Road, Indianapolis IN 46260
PYP Coordinator Katherine Sorrell
Languages English
T: +1 317 259 5445
W: www.msdwt.k12.in.us

Guerin Catholic High School
15300 Gray Road, Noblesville IN 46062
DP Coordinator Meaghan Neman
Languages English
T: +1 317 582 0120
W: www.guerincatholic.org

International School of Indiana
4330 N. Michigan Road, Indianapolis IN 46208
DP Coordinator Gabriel Evans
MYP Coordinator Marithe Benavente-Llamas
PYP Coordinator Stacy Gruen
Languages English
T: +1 317 923 1951
W: www.isind.org

James R. Watson Elementary
901 Eckhart Avenue, Auburn IN 46706
PYP Coordinator Michelle Wagner
Languages English
T: +1 260 920 1014
W: jrw.dekalbcentral.net

John Adams High School
808 South Twyckenham Blvd, South Bend IN 46615
DP Coordinator Rebecca Hernandez
Languages English
T: +1 574 283 7700
W: www.sbcsc.k12.in.us

Kokomo High School
2501 S. Berkley Road, Kokomo IN 46902
CP Coordinator Christa Jordan
DP Coordinator Leslie G. Fatum
MYP Coordinator Lori Magnuson
Languages English
T: +1 765 455 8040
W: www.kokomoschools.com

Lafayette Park Elementary School
919 N. Korby, Kokomo IN 46901
PYP Coordinator Marcy Brown
Languages English
T: +1 765 454 7060
W: www.kokomoschools.com

Lawrence Central High School
7300 East 56th Street, Indianapolis IN 46226
DP Coordinator Kathleen Legge
Languages English
T: +1 317 454 5301

Lawrence North High School
7802 Hague Road, Indianapolis IN 46256
DP Coordinator Jason Floyd
Languages English
T: +1 317 964 7700
W: lawrencenorth.ltschools.org

New Albany High School
1020 Vincennes St, New Albany IN 47150
DP Coordinator John Buerger
Languages English
T: +1 812 542 8506
W: nahs.nafcs.k12.in.us

Nora Elementary School
1000 East 91st Street, Indianapolis IN 46240
PYP Coordinator Kelli Glassley
Languages English
T: +1 317 844 5436
W: www.msdwt.k12.in.us

North Central High School
1801 E 86th St., Indianapolis IN 46240
DP Coordinator Andrew Hodson
MYP Coordinator Jocelyn Sisson
Languages English
T: +1 317 259 5301
W: www.nchs.cc

Northridge High School
57697-1 Northridge Drive, Middlebury IN 46540
DP Coordinator Tracy Wogoman
Languages English
T: +1 574 825 2142
W: ww.mcsin-k12.org

Northview Middle School
8401 Westfield Boulevard, Indianapolis IN 46240
MYP Coordinator Chad Hyatt
Languages English
T: +1 317 259 5421
W: nv.msdwt.k12.in.us

Pike High School
5401 West 71th street, Indianapolis IN 46268
DP Coordinator Danielle D. Vohland
Languages English
T: +1 317387 2600
W: www.pike.k12.in.us

Shortridge High School
3401 N. Meridian Street, Indianapolis IN 46208
CP Coordinator Jessica Carlson
DP Coordinator Mel Coryell
MYP Coordinator Garret Merle
Languages English
T: +1 317 226 2810
W: www.myips.org/shs

Signature School
610 Main Street, Evansville IN 47708
DP Coordinator Shannon Hughes
Languages English
T: +1 812 421 1820
W: www.signature.edu

South Side High School, Fort Wayne
3601 S Calhoun St., Fort Wayne IN 46807
DP Coordinator Kara Fultz
Languages English
T: +1 260 467 2600
W: www.fortwayneschools.org/schools/school_pages.php?school=0309

Spring Mill Elementary School
8250 Spring Mill Road, Indianapolis IN 46260
PYP Coordinator Julie Lowe
Languages English
T: +1 317 259 5462
W: sm.msdwt.k12.in.us

Sycamore Elementary School
1600 E. Sycamore St., Kokomo IN 46901
PYP Coordinator Julie Walker
Languages English
T: +1 765 454 7090
W: www.kokomoschools.com

Templeton Elementary
1400 S. Brenda Lane, Bloomington IN 47401
PYP Coordinator Laura Hall
Languages English
T: +1 812 330 7735
W: www.mccsc.edu/templeton

University Elementary School
1111 N. Russell Road, Bloomington IN 47408
PYP Coordinator Mary D'Eliso
Languages English
T: +1 812 330 7753
W: www.mccsc.edu/domain/21

Valparaiso High School
2727 North Campbell Street, Valparaiso IN 46383
DP Coordinator Veronica Tobon
Languages English
T: +1 219 531 3070
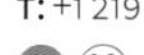

Westlane Middle School
1301 W. 73rd Street, Indianapolis IN 46260
MYP Coordinator Leigh Muller
Languages English
T: +1 317 259 5412
W: wl.msdwt.k12.in.us

Iowa

Brody Middle School
2501 Park Avenue, Des Moines IA 50321
MYP Coordinator Timm Pilcher
Languages English
T: +1 515 242 8443
W: brody.dmschools.org

Carter Lake Elementary
1000 Willow Dr, Carter Lake IA 51510
PYP Coordinator Erin Schoening
Languages English
T: +1 712 347 5876
W: www.cb-schools.org/domain/83

Central Academy
1912 Grand Avenue, Des Moines IA 50309
DP Coordinator Isaac Steven Pedelty
Languages English
T: +1 515 242 7888
W: ca.dmschools.org

College View Elementary School
1225 College Road, Council Bluffs IA 51503
PYP Coordinator Erin Schoening
Languages English
T: +1 712 328 6452
W: www.cbcsd.org

East High School
214 High Street, Waterloo IA 50703
DP Coordinator Ellen Shay
Languages English
T: +1 319 433 1800
W: easthigh.waterloo.k12.ia.us

Goodrell Middle School
3300 East 29th Street, Des Moines IA 50317
MYP Coordinator Christy Kuhl
Languages English
T: +1 515 242 8444

Herbert Hoover High School
4800 Aurora Ave., Des Moines IA 50310
MYP Coordinator Holly Meagher
Languages English
T: +1 515 242 7300
W: old.dmps.k12.ia.us/schools/3Hoover/index.htm

Hubbell Elementary School
800 42nd Street, Des Moines IA 50312
PYP Coordinator Kathleen Enos
Languages English
T: +1 515 242 8414
W: www.dmps.k12.ia.us/schools/1Hubbell/index.html

Meredith Middle School
4827 Madison Ave., Des Moines IA 50310
MYP Coordinator Holly Meagher
Languages English
T: +1 515 242 7250
W: old.dmps.k12.ia.us/schools/2Meredith/index.htm

Merrill Middle School
5301 Grand Avenue, Des Moines IA 50312
MYP Coordinator Danielle Taylor
Languages English
T: +1 515 242 8448
W: merrill.dmschools.org

Moore Elementary School
3716 50th Street, Des Moines IA 50310
PYP Coordinator Laura Manroe
Languages English
T: +1 515 242 8426
W: moore.dmschools.org

Park Avenue Elementary School
3141 SW 9th Street, Des Moines IA 50315
PYP Coordinator Katie Pilcher
Languages English
T: +1 515 242 8429
W: www.dmps.k12.ia.us/schools/1parkavenue

Stowe Elementary School
1411 East 33rd Street, Des Moines IA 50317
PYP Coordinator Tricia McCarty
Languages English
T: +1 515 242 8435
W: www.dmps.k12.ia.us/schools/1stowe/index.htm

Walnut Street School
901 Walnut Street, Des Moines IA 50309
PYP Coordinator Leslie Barnhizer
Languages English
T: +1 515 242 8438
W: walnutstreet.dmschools.org

West High School
425 E. Ridgeway Avenue, Waterloo IA 50702
DP Coordinator Ellen Shay
Languages English
T: +1 319 433 1800
W: www.waterloo.k12.ia.us/schoolsites/westhigh

Kansas

Campus High School
2100 W. 55th St. South, Wichita KS 67217
DP Coordinator Lisa Wehkamp
Languages English
T: +1 316 554 2236
W: Usd261.com

Hutchinson High School
810 East 13th St, Hutchinson KS 67501
CP Coordinator Todd Ray
DP Coordinator Todd Ray
Languages English
T: +1 620 615 4100
W: www.usd308.com/node/14

Shawnee Mission East High School
7500 Mission Road, Shawnee Mission KS 66208-4298
DP Coordinator Monique Goodeyon
Languages English
T: +1 913 993 6600
W: smeast.smsd.org

Shawnee Mission North High School
7401 Johnson Drive, Overland Park KS 66202
DP Coordinator Jonathan Durham
Languages English
T: +1 913 993 6900
W: smnorth.smsd.org

Shawnee Mission Northwest High School
12701 West 67th Street, Shawnee KS 66216
DP Coordinator Amy Walker
Languages English
T: +1 913 993 7200
W: smnorthwest.smsd.org

Sumner Academy of Arts and Science
1610 N 8th Street, Kansas City KS 66101
CP Coordinator Edward Gunter
DP Coordinator Paula Biggar
Languages English
T: +1 913 627 7200
W: www.kcksumner.schoolloop.com

Washburn Rural High School
5900 SW 61st Street, Topeka KS 66619
DP Coordinator Nick Bowling
Languages English
T: +1 785 339 4100
W: www.wrhs.net

Wichita High School East
2301 East Douglas, Wichita KS 67211
DP Coordinator Michael Boykins
Languages English
T: +1 316 973 7289
W: www.east.usd259.org/

Kentucky

Atherton High School
3000 Dundee Road, Louisville KY 40205
DP Coordinator Theresa Beckley
Languages English
T: +1 502 485 8202
W: schools.jefferson.kyschools.us/high/atherton

Highland Middle School
1700 Norris Place, Louisville KY 40205
MYP Coordinator Stacey Irvin
Languages English
T: +1 502 485 8266
W: highlandmiddle.com

Holmes High School
2500 Madison Ave., Covington KY 41014
DP Coordinator Tony Magner
Languages English
T: +1 859 655 9545
W: www.covington.kyschools.us/1/home

Sacred Heart Academy
3175 Lexington Road, Louisville KY 40206
DP Coordinator Candace Kresse
Languages English
T: +1 502 897 6097
W: www.sacredheartschools.org

Sacred Heart Model School
3107 Lexington Road, Louisville KY 40206
MYP Coordinator Tricia Forde
Languages English
T: +1 502 896 3931
W: sacredheartschools.org

Tates Creek Elementary School
1113 Centre Parkway, Lexington KY 40517
PYP Coordinator Lisa Johnson
Languages English
T: +1 859 381 3606
W: tces.fcps.net

Tates Creek High School
1111 Centre Parkway, Lexington KY 40517
DP Coordinator John Hatfield
Languages English
T: +1 859 381 3620
W: www.tchs.fcps.net

Tates Creek Middle School
1105 Centre Parkway, Lexington KY 40517
MYP Coordinator Kelly Sirginnis
Languages English
T: +1 859 381 3052
W: www.tcms.fcps.net

Whitney M Young Elementary School
3526 West Muhammad Ali Boulevard, Louisville KY 40212
PYP Coordinator Mary Jo Wimsatt
Languages English
T: +1 502 485 8354
W: www.jefferson.kyschools.us/schools/profiles/young-elementary

Louisiana

BATON ROUGE INTERNATIONAL SCHOOL
5015 Auto Plex Drive, Baton Rouge LA 70809
DP Coordinator Ms. Xiaoping Liu
MYP Coordinator Ms. Aareena Dhillon
Languages English, French, Spanish, Chinese, Portuguese
T: +1 225 293 4338
E: info@brisla.com
W: www.brintl.com

See full details on page 494

Hammond Eastside Elementary Magnet School
45050 River Road, Hammond LA 70401
MYP Coordinator Stephanie Ciresi
PYP Coordinator Katherine Johnson
Languages English
T: +1 985 474 8660
W: www.tangischools.org/heems

Hammond High Magnet School
45168 River Road, Hammond LA 70401
CP Coordinator Deirdra Disher
DP Coordinator Deirdra Disher
Languages English
T: +1 985 345 7235
W: www.tangischools.org/hhms

International High School of New Orleans
727 Carondelet Street, New Orleans LA 70130
DP Coordinator Cody Bourque
Languages English
T: +1 504 613 5703
W: www.ihsnola.org

John Ehret High School
4300 Patriot Street, Marrero LA 70072
DP Coordinator Angela Becnel
Languages English
T: +1 504 340 7651
W: ehret.jppss.k12.la.us

L. H. Marrero Middle School
Marrero Middle 4100 Seventh St., Marrero LA 70072
MYP Coordinator Juliet Lieberman
Languages English
T: +1 504 341 5842
W: www.jpschools.org/marrero

Louisiana State University Laboratory School
45 Dalrymple Drive, Baton Rouge LA 70803-0501
DP Coordinator Candence Robillard
Languages English
T: +1 225 578 9147
W: www.uhigh.lsu.edu

Morris Jeff Community School
3368 Esplanade Ave, New Orleans LA 70119
DP Coordinator Carmen Mack
MYP Coordinator Ryan Ruyle
PYP Coordinator Laura Krebs
Languages English
T: +1 504 373 6200
W: www.morrisjeffschool.org

Riverdale High School
240 Riverdale Drive, Jefferson LA 70121
DP Coordinator Monique Pontiff
Languages English
T: +1 504 833 7288
W: riverdalehigh.jppss.k12.la.us

Riverdale Middle School
3900 Jefferson Hwy, Jefferson LA 70121
MYP Coordinator Debbie Jo Guillot
Languages English
T: +1 504 828 2706
W: www.riverdalemiddle.jppss.k12.la.us

Maine

Academia Fórum
3 Canal Plaza, Suite 600, Portland ME 04101
DP Coordinator John Keffer
Languages Spanish
T: +1 207 553 2327
W: www.forumacademy.org

FOXCROFT ACADEMY
975 West Main Street, Dover-Foxcroft ME 04426
DP Coordinator Donna Newhouse
Languages English
T: +1 207 564 8351
E: admissions@foxcroftacademy.org
W: www.foxcroftacademy.org

See full details on page 507

Gray-New Gloucester High School
10 Libby Hill Road, Gray ME 04039
DP Coordinator Bobbie-Jo Thibodeau
Languages English
T: +1 207 657 9306
W: www.msad15.org

Greely High School
303 Main Street, Cumberland ME 04021
DP Coordinator Vanessa Gribbin
Languages English
T: +1 207 829 4805
W: www.msad51.org

Kennebunk High School
89 Fletcher Street, Kennebunk ME 04043
DP Coordinator William Putnam
Languages English
T: +1 207 985 1110
W: www.rsu21.net/khs

Ocean Avenue Elementary School
150 Ocean Avenue, Portland ME 04103
PYP Coordinator Patricia Sprague
Languages English
T: +1 207 874 8180
W: oceanavenue.portlandschools.org

The Middle School of the Kennebunks
60 Thompson Road, Kennebunk ME 04043
MYP Coordinator Stacy Knappe
Languages English
T: +1 207 467 8004
W: www.rsu21.net/msk

Maryland

Albert Einstein High School
11135 Newport Mill Road, Kensington MD 20895
DP Coordinator Kimberly Becraft
Languages English
T: +1 301 929 2200

Annapolis High School
2700 Riva Road, Annapolis MD 21401
DP Coordinator Patricia Newgent
MYP Coordinator Jay Koller
Languages English
T: +1 410 266 5240
W: www.annapolishighschool.org

Annapolis Middle School
1399 Forest Drive, Annapolis MD 21403
MYP Coordinator Domenick Chiddo
Languages English
T: +1 410 267 8658
W: www.aacps.org/page/1213

Archbishop Spalding High School
8080 New Cut Road, Severn MD 21144
DP Coordinator Angela Bentzley
Languages English
T: +1 410 969 9105
W: www.archbishopspalding.org

Baltimore City College
3220 The Alameda, Baltimore MD 21218
DP Coordinator Ndaneh Smart-Smith
MYP Coordinator Sarah Jeanblanc
Languages English
T: +1 410 396 6557
W: www.baltimorecitycollege.us

BALTIMORE INTERNATIONAL ACADEMY
4410 Frankford Avenue, Baltimore MD 21206
MYP Coordinator Henriette Sindjui
PYP Coordinator Henriette Sindjui
Languages Spanish, Mandarin, Arabic, Russian, French
T: +1 410 426 3650
E: elokounia@bcps.k12.md.us
W: www.baltimoreinternationalacademy.org

See full details on page 493

Bethesda Chevy Chase High School
4301 East West Highway, Bethesda MD 20814
DP Coordinator Michelle Dean
MYP Coordinator Caitlyn Trimble
Languages English
T: +1 240 497 6300
W: www.montgomeryschoolsmd.org

Central High School
200 Cabin Branch Road, Capitol Heights MD 20743
DP Coordinator Shaun Devlin Shepard
Languages English
T: +1 301 499 7080
W: www1.pgcps.org/central

College Gardens Elementary School
1700 Yale Place, Rockville MD 20850
PYP Coordinator Michael Dushel
Languages English
T: +1 301 279 8470
W: www.mcps.k12.md.us/schools/collegegardenses

Crossland High School
6901 Temple Hill Road, Temple Hills MD 20748
DP Coordinator Melissa Boyd
Languages English
T: +1 301 449 4800
W: www.pgcps.org/crossld

IB AMERICAS

Dwight D Eisenhower Middle School
13725 Briarwood Drive, Laurel MD 20708
MYP Coordinator Steve Mellen
Languages English
T: +1 301 497 3620
W: www1.pgcps.org/dwightdeisenhower

Eastport Elementary School
420 Fifth Street, Annapolis MD 21403
PYP Coordinator Corinne Codjoe
T: +1 410 222 1605
W: www.eastportelementaryschoolmd.com

Edgewood High School
2415 Willoughby Beach Road, Edgewood MD 21040
DP Coordinator Jamie Childs
Languages English
T: +1 410 612 1500
W: www.hcps.org/schools/high/edgewood.aspx

Francis Scott Key Middle School
910 Schindler Drive, Silver Spring MD 20903
MYP Coordinator Beth Hester
Languages English
T: +1 301 422 5600
W: www.mcps.k12.md.us/schools/fskms

Frank Hebron-Harman Elementary School
7660 Ridge Chapel Road, Hanover MD 21076
PYP Coordinator Karina Colon
Languages English
T: +1 410 859 4510
W: www.aacps.org/domain/1426

Frederick Douglass High School
8000 Croom Road, Upper Marlboro MD 20772
DP Coordinator Kim Watson
MYP Coordinator Letty Maxwell
Languages English
T: +1 301 952 2400
W: www1.pgcps.org/douglass

Germantown Elementary School
1411 Cedar Park Road, Annapolis MD 21401
PYP Coordinator Erika Boltz
Languages English
T: +1 410 222 1615
W: www.aacps.org/html/schol/Elementary/Gertowes.asp

James Madison Middle School
7300 Woodyard Road, Upper Marlboro MD 20772
MYP Coordinator Dana Blair
Languages English
T: +1 301 599 2422
W: www.pgcps.org/~jmadison

John F Kennedy High School
1901 Randolph Road, Silver Spring MD 20902
DP Coordinator Kia Patrice Davis
Languages English
T: +1 301 929 2100
W: www.mcps.k12.md.us/schools/kennedyhs

Julius West Middle School
651 Great Falls Road, Rockville MD 20850
MYP Coordinator Krista Fiabane
Languages English
T: +1 301 279 3979
W: www.montgomeryschoolsmd.org

Kenwood High School
501 Stemmers Run Road, Essex MD 21221
DP Coordinator Tara Funkhouser
Languages English
T: +1 410 887 0153
W: kenwoodhs.bcps.org

Laurel High School
8000 Cherry Lane, Laurel MD 20707
DP Coordinator Allen Diewald
Languages English
T: +1 301 497 2050
W: www.pgcps.org/laurelhs

MacArthur Middle School
3500 Rockenbach Road, Fort Meade MD 20755
MYP Coordinator Vanessa Facer
Languages English
T: +1 410 679 0032
W: www.aacps.org/aacps/mams/index.asp

Manor View Elementary School
2900 Macarthur Road, Fort Meade MD 20755
PYP Coordinator Marcia Ross
Languages English
T: +1 410 518 6473
W: www.aacps.org/aacps/manorves/index.asp

Martin Luther King, Jr. Middle School (MD)
13737 Wisteria Dr., Germantown MD 20874
MYP Coordinator Jennifer Scavullo
Languages English
T: +1 301 353 8080
W: www.montgomeryschoolsmd.org/schools/mlkms

MARYLAND INTERNATIONAL SCHOOL
6135 Old Washington Road, Elkridge MD 21075
DP Coordinator Nikki Tanner
MYP Coordinator Nikki Tanner
PYP Coordinator Emily Seppa
Languages English
T: +1 410 220 3792
E: info@marylandinternationalschool.org
W: www.marylandinternationalschool.org

See full details on page 525

Maya Angelou French Immersion School
2000 Callaway Street, Temple Hills MD 20748
PYP Coordinator Alphonse Talon
Languages English
T: +1 301 702 3950
W: www1.pgcps.org/mayaangelou

Meade Senior High School
1100 Clark Road, Ft Meade MD 20755
DP Coordinator Jennifer Quinn
MYP Coordinator Jenna Lerro
Languages English
T: +1 410 674 7710
W: www.meadesenior.org

Melwood Elementary School
7100 Woodyard Road, Upper Marlboro MD 20772
PYP Coordinator Stephanie Major
Languages English
T: +1 301 599 2500
W: www1.pgcps.org/melwood

Mercy High School Baltimore
1300 E. Northern Parkway, Baltimore MD 21239
MYP Coordinator Kathryn Adelsberger
Languages English, Spanish
T: +1 410 433 8880
W: mercyhighschool.com

Monarch Global Academy
430 Brock Bridge Road, Laurel MD 20724
PYP Coordinator Beth Ann Matthews
Languages English
T: 301-886-8648
W: www.monarchacademy.org/global

Montgomery Village Middle School
19300 Watkins Mill Road, Germantown MD 20886
MYP Coordinator Wendy Farmer
Languages English
T: +1 301 840 4660
W: montgomeryschoolsmd.org/schools/mvms

Mount Washington School
1801 Sulgrave Avenue, Baltimore MD 21209
MYP Coordinator Sarah Martin
Languages English
T: +1 410 396 6354
W: mountwashingtonschool.org

Neelsville Middle School
11700 Neelsville Church Road, Germantown MD 20876
MYP Coordinator David Alhadeff
Languages English
T: +1 301 353 8064
W: montgomeryschoolsmd.org/schools/neelsvillems

Newport Mill Middle School
11311 Newport Mill Road, Kensington MD 20895
MYP Coordinator Benjamin Legarreta
Languages English
T: +1 301 929 2244
W: www.mcps.k12.md.us/schools/newportmillms

North Hagerstown High School
1200 Pennsylvania Ave, Hagerstown MD 21742
CP Coordinator Chris Downs
DP Coordinator Kevin G Jackson
MYP Coordinator Chris Downs
Languages English
T: +1 301 766 8238
W: wcpsmd.com/schools/high-schools/north-hagerstown-high

Old Mill High School
600 Patriot Lane, Millersville MD 21108
DP Coordinator Virginia Sutherin
MYP Coordinator Vikki Romanoski
Languages English
T: +1 410 969 9010
W: www.oldmillhs.org

Old Mill Middle School North
610 Patriot Lane, Millersville MD 21108
MYP Coordinator Kysha Egungbemi
Languages English
T: +1 410 969 5950
W: www.oldmillnorth.org

USA

Our Lady of Good Counsel High School
17301 Old Vic Boulevard, Olney MD 20832
DP Coordinator Megan Dean
Languages English
T: +1 240 283 3200
W: www.olgchs.org

Overlook Elementary
401 Hampton Road, Linthicum MD 21090
PYP Coordinator Marcia Ross
Languages English
T: +1 410 222 6585
W: www.aacps.org/page/1170

Parkdale High School
6001 Good Luck Road, Riverdale MD 20737
DP Coordinator Erycka Constant
Languages English
T: +1 301 513 5700

Richard Montgomery High School
250 Richard Montgomery Drive, Rockville MD 20852
DP Coordinator Nancy Shay
MYP Coordinator Molly Clarkson
Languages English
T: +1 301 279 8400
W: montgomeryschoolsmd.org/schools/rmhs

Roberto Clemente Middle School
18808 Waring Station Road, Germantown MD 20874
MYP Coordinator Liz Gall
Languages English
T: +1 301 284 4750
W: montgomeryschoolsmd.org/schools/clementems

Rockville High School
2100 Baltimore Road, Rockville MD 21805
CP Coordinator Laurie Ainsworth
DP Coordinator Laurie Ainsworth
Languages English
T: +1 301 517 8105
W: www.montgomeryschoolsmd.org/schools/rockvillehs

Saint James Academy
3100 Monkton Road, Monkton MD 21111
MYP Coordinator Nina Theofiles
Languages English
T: +1 410 771 4816
W: www.saintjamesacademy.org

Seneca Academy
15601 Germantown Road, Darnestown MD 20874
PYP Coordinator Carol Schnatz
Languages English
T: +1 301 869 3728
W: www.senecaacademy.org

Seneca Valley High School
19401 Crystal Rock Drive, Germantown MD 20874
DP Coordinator Natasha Ezerski
Languages English
T: +1 301 353 8000
W: www.senecavalleyhighschool.com

Silver Creek Middle School
3701 Saul Road, Kensington MD 20895
MYP Coordinator Renee Hill
Languages English
T: +1 240 740 2200
W: www.montgomeryschoolsmd.org/schools/silvercreekms

Silver Spring International Middle School
313 Wayne Avenue, Silver Spring MD 20910
MYP Coordinator Molly Dougherty
Languages English
T: +1 301 650 6544
W: www.mcps.k12.md.us/schools/ssims

South Shore Elementary School
1376 Fairfield Loop Rd, Crownsville MD 21032
PYP Coordinator Erika Boltz
Languages English
T: +1 410 222 3865
W: www.aacps.org/aacps/southses/index.asp

Southgate Elementary School
290 Shetlands Ln, Glen Burnie MD 21061
PYP Coordinator Heather Giustiniani
Languages English
T: +1 410 222 6445
W: www.aacps.org/html/schol/Elementary/Southges.asp

Springbrook High School
201 Valley Brook Drive, Silver Spring MD 20904
DP Coordinator Amanda Trivers
MYP Coordinator John Weinshel
Languages English
T: +1 301 989 5700
W: www.mcps.k12.md.us/schools/springbrookhs

St. Francis of Assisi
3617 Harford Rd, Baltimore MD 21218
MYP Coordinator Mary Carol Lidinsky
Languages English
T: +1 410 467 1683
W: www.sfa-school.org

St. Timothy's School
8400 Greenspring Ave, Stevenson MD 21153
DP Coordinator Ghada Jaber
MYP Coordinator Ghada Jaber
Languages English
T: +1 410 486 7400
W: www.stt.org

Stemmers Run Middle School
201 Stemmers Run Rd, Essex MD 21221
MYP Coordinator Nicole Boyd
Languages English
T: +1 443 809 0177

Suitland High School
5200 Silver Hill Road, Forestville MD 20747
DP Coordinator Kamilah Williams
Languages English
T: +1 301 817 0500
W: www1.pgcps.org/suitlandhs

Sunset Elementary School
8572 Ft. Smallwood Road, Pasadena MD 21122
PYP Coordinator Molly Courtien
Languages English
T: +1 410 222 6478
W: www.aacps.org/Page/1204

Tarbiyah Academy
6785 Business Pky, Elkridge MD 21075
PYP Coordinator Hagar Aboubakr
Languages English
T: +1 844 827 2492
W: www.tarbiyahacademy.com

The Academy of the Holy Cross
4920 Strathmore Avenue, Kensington MD 20895
DP Coordinator Casey Robertson
Languages English
T: +1 301 929 6459
W: www.academyoftheholycross.org

The Boys' School of St Paul's Parish
PO Box 8100, Brooklandville MD 21022-8100
DP Coordinator Andrew Mezeske
Languages English
T: +1 410 825 4400
W: www.stpaulsschool.org

The Calverton School
300 Calverton School Rd, Huntingtown MD 20639
DP Coordinator Susan Dice
Languages English
T: +1 410 535 0216
W: www.calvertonschool.org

Thomas Jefferson Elementary
605 Dryden Drive, Baltimore MD 21229
PYP Coordinator Tracy Taylor
Languages English
T: +1 410 396 0534

Tracey's Elementary School
20 Deale Road, Tracys Landing MD 20779
PYP Coordinator Corinne Codjoe
Languages English
T: +1 410 222 1633
W: www.aacps.org/page/1205

Urbana High School
3471 Campus Drive, Ijamsville MD 21754
DP Coordinator Jessica McBroom
Languages English
T: +1 240 236 7600

Watkins Mill High School
10301 Apple Ridge Road, Gaithersburg MD 20879
CP Coordinator Lisa Ingram
DP Coordinator Lisa Ingram
MYP Coordinator Samuel Lee
Languages English
T: +1 301 840 3959

Westland Middle School
5511 Massachusetts Avenue, Bethedsa MD 20816
MYP Coordinator Rachel Johns
Languages English
T: +1 301 320 6515

Massachusetts

Abby Kelley Foster Charter Public School
10 New Bond Street, Worcester MA 01606
DP Coordinator Kelly Davila
Languages English
T: +1 508 854 8400
W: www.akfcs.org

British International School of Boston
416 Pond Street, Boston MA 02130
DP Coordinator Karen McWilliam
Languages English
T: +1 617 522 2261
W: www.bisboston.org

Brockton High School
470 Forest Ave, Brockton MA 02301
DP Coordinator Todd Erickson
Languages English
T: +1 508 580 7633
W: www.bpsma.org/schools/brockton-high-school

Eagle Hill School
242 Old Petersham Road, P.O. Box 116, Hardwick MA 01037
DP Coordinator Jason Przypek
Languages English
T: +1 413 477 6000
W: www.eaglehill.school

International School of Boston
45 Matignon Road, Cambridge MA 02140
DP Coordinator John Bray
Languages English
T: +1 617 499 1459
W: www.isbos.org

Joseph F Plouffe Academy
150 Clinton Street, Brockton MA 02302
MYP Coordinator Bonnie Brady
Languages English
T: +1 508 894 4301
W: www.brocktonpublicschools.com

Josiah Quincy Upper School
152 Arlington Street, Boston MA 02116
DP Coordinator Kristina Danahy
MYP Coordinator Jessica Tsai
Languages English
T: +1 617 635 8940
W: bostonpublicschools.org/jqus

Kensington International School
31 Kensington Avenue, Springfield MA 01108
PYP Coordinator Sheree Nolley
Languages English
T: +1 413 787 7522
W: www.springfieldpublicschools.com/schools/kensington

Mystic Valley Regional Charter School
770 Salem Street, Malden MA 02148
DP Coordinator Jonathan Keating
Languages English
T: +1 781 388 0222
W: www.mvrcs.org

Nauset Regional High School
100 Cable Road, Eastham MA 02642
DP Coordinator Amy Roberts
Languages English
T: +1 508 255 1505
W: www.nausetschools.org/page/537

NOTRE DAME ACADEMY, MA
1073 Main Street, Hingham MA 02043-3996
DP Coordinator Kate Carter
Languages English
T: +1 781 749 5930
E: admissions@ndahingham.com
W: www.ndahingham.com
See full details on page 538

Pioneer Valley Chinese Immersion Charter School
317 Russell Street, Hadley MA 01035
DP Coordinator Mary MacPherson
Languages English
T: +1 413 582 7040
W: www.pvcics.org

Provincetown Schools
12 Winslow Street, Provincetown MA 2657
MYP Coordinator Richard Gifford
PYP Coordinator Elizabeth Francis
Languages English
T: +1 508 487 5000
W: www.provincetownschools.com

Quabbin Regional High School
800 South Street, Barre MA 01005
DP Coordinator Jason Gilmartin
Languages English
T: +1 978 355 4651
W: www.qrsd.org/our-schools/high-school/

Snowden International School
150 Newbury Street, Boston MA 02116
DP Coordinator Denise Bylaska
Languages English
T: +1 617 635 9989
W: www.snowdeninternationalschool.org

Stoneleigh-Burnham School
574 Bernardston Road, Greenfield MA 01301
DP Coordinator Miriam Przybyla-Baum
Languages English
T: +1 413 774 2711
W: www.sbschool.org

Sturgis Charter School
Administration, 427 Main Street, Hyannis MA 02601
DP Coordinator Cynthia Gallo
Languages English
T: +1 508 778 1782
W: www.sturgischarterschool.com

THE NEWMAN SCHOOL
247 Marlborough Street, Boston MA 02116
DP Coordinator Andrew Nagy
Languages English
T: +1 617 267 4530
E: admissions@newmanboston.org
W: www.newmanboston.org
See full details on page 555

Wareham High School
7 Viking Drive, Wareham MA 02571
DP Coordinator Ashlie Yates-Paquin
Languages English
T: +1 508 291 3510
W: www.warehamps.org

Woodrow Wilson Elementary School
169 Leland St, Framingham MA 01702
PYP Coordinator Heather Flugrad
Languages English, Portuguese
T: +1 508 626 9164
W: www.framingham.k12.ma.us/wilson

Michigan

Adams Elementary School
1005 Adams Drive, Midland MI 48642
PYP Coordinator Robin Harshman-Rogers
Languages English
T: +1 989 923 6037
W: ade.midlandps.org

Adrian High School
785 Riverside Avenue, Adrian MI 49221
DP Coordinator Michelle Ratering
Languages English
T: +1 517 263 2115
W: www.theadrianmaples.com

Algonac High School
5200 Taft Road, Clay Township MI 48001
DP Coordinator Miechelle Landrum
Languages English
T: +1 810 794 4911 EXT:1202
W: www.algonac.k12.mi.us/schools/algonac_high_school/index.html

Bloomfield Hills High School
3456 Lahser Road, Bloomfield Hills MI 48302
DP Coordinator Jessica Lupone
MYP Coordinator Cathy McDonald
Languages English
T: +1 248 341 5700
W: www.bloomfield.org/schools/bloomfield-hills-high-school

Bloomfield Hills Middle School
4200 W Quarton Road, Bloomfield Hills MI 48304
MYP Coordinator Kathy Janelle
Languages English
T: +1 248 341 6000
W: www.bloomfield.org

Cass Technical High School
2501 Second Ave., Detroit MI 48201
DP Coordinator Sherise Hedgespeth
Languages English
T: +1 313 263 2079
W: casstech.schools.detroitk12.org

Central Academy
2459 South Industrial Hwy, Ann Arbor MI 48104
PYP Coordinator Nahla Attar
Languages English
T: +1 734 822 1100
W: centralacademy.net

Charyl Stockwell Preparatory Academy
1032 Karl Greimel Drive, Brighton MI 48116
DP Coordinator Matthew Stewart
T: +1 810 225 9940
W: www.csaschool.org

Chestnut Hill Elementary School
3900 Chestnut Hill Drive, Midland MI 48642
PYP Coordinator Amy Sabourin
Languages English
T: +1 989 923 6634
W: che.midlandps.org

City High Middle School
1400 Fuller Avenue NE, Grand Rapids MI 49505
DP Coordinator Jesse Antuma
MYP Coordinator Jesse Antuma
Languages English
T: +1 616 819 2380
W: www.grpublicschools.org/city/

Clarkston High School
6093 Flemings Lake Road, Clarkston MI 48346
DP Coordinator Rebecca Kroll
Languages English
T: +1 248 623 3600
W: sites.google.com/a/clarkston.k12.mi.us/chs/

Clear Lake Elementary School
2085 W. Drahner, Oxford MI 48371
PYP Coordinator Stephanie Niemi
Languages English
T: +1 248 969 5200
W: www.oxfordschools.org

Conant Elementary School
4100 West Quarton Road, Bloomfield Hills MI 48302
PYP Coordinator Nicholas Russo
Languages English
T: +1 248 341 7000
W: www.bloomfield.org/schools/conant-elementary-school

Daniel Axford Elementary School
74 Mechanic Street MI 48371
PYP Coordinator Rita Flynn
Languages English
T: +1 248 969 5050
W: www.oxfordschools.org

De La Salle Collegiate
14600 Common Road, Warren MI 48088
DP Coordinator Eric Wynn
Languages English
T: +1 586 778 2207
W: www.delasallehs.com

Detroit Country Day School
22305 West 13 Mile Road, Beverly Hills MI 48025-4435
DP Coordinator Jonathan Porter
Languages English
T: +1 248 646 7717
W: www.dcds.edu

Detroit Edison Public School Academy
1903 Wilkins, Detroit MI 48207
DP Coordinator Kimberly Bland
MYP Coordinator Kimberly Bland
Languages English
T: +1 313 833 1100
W: www.detroitedisonpsa.org

Dexter High School
2200 North Parker Road, Dexter MI 48130
DP Coordinator Debora Marsh
Languages English
T: +1 734 424 4240
W: dexterschools.org

East Grand Rapids High School
2211 Lake Drive SE, Grand Rapids MI 49506
DP Coordinator Heather McKinney-Rewa
Languages English
T: +1 616 235 7555
W: egrhs.egrps.org

East Hills Middle School
2800 Kensington Road, Bloomfield Hills MI 48304
MYP Coordinator Julia Beattie
Languages English
T: +1 248 341 6200
W: easthills.bloomfield.org

Fenton High School
3200 W Shiawassee Avenue, Fenton MI 48430
DP Coordinator Kelly Boike
Languages English
T: +1 810 591 2600
W: www.fenton.k12.mi.us

Franklin High School
31000 Joy Road, Livonia MI 48150
DP Coordinator Sunshine Weber
Languages English
T: +1 734 744 2655
W: franklin.livoniapublicschools.org

Genesee Academy
9447 Corunna Road, Swartz Creek MI 48473
MYP Coordinator Hana Sankari
Languages English
T: +1 810 250 7557
W: www.gaflint.org

Handley Elementary School
224 N Elm Street, Saginaw MI 48602
PYP Coordinator Kathy Gonzales
Languages English
T: +1 989 399 4250
W: www.spsd.net/handley

Harrison High School
29995 W. 12 Mile Road, Farmington Hills MI 48334
DP Coordinator Kevin Miesner
Languages English
T: +1 1 248 426 2918
W: www.farmington.k12.mi.us/hhs

Helen Keller Elementary School
1505 N Campbell Road, Royal Oak MI 48067
PYP Coordinator Kara Daunt
Languages English
T: +1 248 542 6500
W: www.royaloakschools.com/portal/keller

Herbert Henry Dow High School
3901 North Saginaw Road, Midland MI 48640
DP Coordinator Sarah Pancost
Languages English
T: +1 989 923 5382
W: www.dhs.mps.k12.mi.us

Heritage High School
3465 N Center Road, Saginaw MI 48603
DP Coordinator Brian Blaine
Languages English
T: +1 989 799 5790
W: www.stcs.org

Hillside Middle School
774 N. Center St., Northville MI 48167
MYP Coordinator William Lambdin
Languages English
T: +1 248 344 8493
W: hillside.northvilleschools.org

Huda School and Montessori
32220 Franklin Road, Franklin MI 48025
MYP Coordinator Aamna Saleem
Languages English
T: +1 248 626 0900
W: www.hudaschool.org

Huron High School
2727 Fuller Road, Ann Arbor MI 48105
CP Coordinator Carrie James
DP Coordinator Anna Fleury
MYP Coordinator Todd Newell
Languages English
T: +1 734 994 2040
W: www.a2schools.org/huron

International Academy
1020 East Square Lake Road, Bloomfield Hills MI 48304
DP Coordinator Sarah Fairman
MYP Coordinator Sarah Fairman
Languages English
T: +1 248 341 5900
W: www.iatoday.org

International Academy of Macomb
42755 Romeo Plank Road, Clinton Township MI 48038
DP Coordinator Susan Meyer
MYP Coordinator Rene Ribant-Amthor
Languages English
T: +1 586 723 7200
W: www.iamacomb.org

Kalkaska Middle School
1700 Kalkaska Road, Kalkaska MI 49646
MYP Coordinator Collette Sabins
Languages English
T: +1 231 258 4040
W: www.kpschools.com

Kingsbury Country Day School
5000 Hosner Road, Oxford MI 48370
PYP Coordinator Andrea Bristol
Languages English
T: +1 248 628 5000
W: www.kingsburyschool.org

Lakeville Elementary School
1400 Lakeville Road, Oxford MI 48371
PYP Coordinator Christine Vince
Languages English
T: +1 248 969 1850
W: www.oxfordschools.org

Lansing Eastern High School
220 North Pennsylvania Ave, Lansing MI 48912
DP Coordinator Emily Oberlitner
Languages English
T: +1 517 325 6500
W: www.lsd.k12.mi.us

Leland Public School
P.O. Box 498, 200 N. Grand Ave, Leland MI 49654
MYP Coordinator Joanna Aldridge
PYP Coordinator Paula Kelly
Languages English
T: +1 231 256 9857
W: www.lelandpublicschools.com

Leonard Elementary School
335 East Elmwood, Leonard MI 48367
PYP Coordinator Christine Vince
Languages English
T: +1 248 969 5300
W: www.oxfordschools.org/section_display.cfm?section_id=12

Lincoln Elementary School
158 S. Scott St, Adrian MI 49221
PYP Coordinator Natasha Wetzel
Languages English
T: +1 517 265 8544
W: www.theadrianmaples.com

Lone Pine Elementary
3100 Lone Pine Road, Orchard Lake MI 48323
PYP Coordinator Stephanie Olson
Languages English
T: +1 248 341 7300
W: lonepine.bloomfield.org

Mark Twain School for Scholars
12800 Visger Street, Detroit MI 48217-1056
PYP Coordinator Madeleine Karcz
Languages English
T: +1 313 386 5530
W: detroitk12.org/schools/twain

Meads Mill Middle School
16700 Franklin Rd., Northville MI 48168
MYP Coordinator Sandra Brock
Languages English
T: +1 248 344 8435
W: meadsmill.northvilleschools.org

Middle School at Parkside
2400 Fourth Street, Jackson MI 49203
MYP Coordinator Jennifer Oswalt
Languages English
T: +1 517 841 2300
W: www.jpsk12.org/parkside

Midland High School
1301 Eastlawn Drive, Midland MI 48642
DP Coordinator Kelly Murphy
Languages English
T: +1 989 923 5181
W: mhs.midlandps.org

Mill Creek Elementary School
9039 Old M-72, Williamsburg MI 49690
PYP Coordinator Kim Ranger
Languages English
T: +1 231 267 9955
W: erschools.com/millcreek

Mitchell Elementary School
3550 Pittsview Dr., Ann Arbor MI 48108
PYP Coordinator Wendy Rothman
Languages English
T: +1 734 997 1216
W: www.a2schools.org/mitchell

Northville High School
45700 Six Mile Road, Northville MI 48168
DP Coordinator James Davis
MYP Coordinator Sandra Brock
Languages English
T: +1 248 344 3800
W: nhs.northvilleschools.org

Norup International School
14450 Manhattan, Oak Park MI 48237
MYP Coordinator Jennifer Wilcox
PYP Coordinator Jennifer Wilcox
Languages English
T: +1 248 837 8300
W: www.berkley.k12.mi.us/index.asp?school=37&name=Norup%20School

Notre Dame Preparatory School & Marist Academy
1300 Giddings Road, Pontiac MI 48340
DP Coordinator Katrina Sagert
MYP Coordinator Katherine Thomas
PYP Coordinator Paul Frank
Languages English
T: +1 248 373 5300
W: www.ndpma.org

Novi High School
24062 Taft Road, Novi MI 48375
DP Coordinator Alaina Brown
Languages English
T: +1 248 449 1500
W: www.novi.k12.mi.us/hs

Owosso High School
765 East North Street, Owosso MI 48867
MYP Coordinator Lance Little
Languages English
T: +1 989 723 8231
W: www.owosso.k12.mi.us

Owosso Middle School
219 North Water Street, Owosso MI 48867
MYP Coordinator Lance Little
Languages English
T: +1 989 723 3460
W: www.owosso.k12.mi.us

Oxford Elementary School
109 Pontiac Street, Oxford MI 48371
PYP Coordinator Rita Flynn
Languages English
T: +1 248 969 1850
W: oxfordschools.org/index.cfm

Oxford High School
745 North Oxford Road, Oxford MI 48371
DP Coordinator Nicole Barnett
MYP Coordinator Molly Darnell
Languages English
T: +1 248 969 5101
W: oxfordschools.org/index.cfm

Oxford Middle School
1420 Lakeville Road, Oxford MI 48371
MYP Coordinator Molly Darnell
Languages English
T: +1 248 969 1800
W: oxfordschools.org/index.cfm

Plymouth Elementary School
1105 East Sugnet Rd, Midland MI 48642
PYP Coordinator Jen Servoss
Languages English
T: +1 989 923 7616
W: pme.midlandps.org

Plymouth High School
8400 Beck Road, Canton MI 48187
DP Coordinator Casey Swanson
Languages English
T: +1 734 582 6936
W: pcep.pccs.k12.mi.us

Portage Central High School
8135 South Westnedge Avenue, Portage MI 49002
DP Coordinator Eric Lancaster
Languages English
T: +1 269 323 5255
W: www.portageps.org

Portage Northern High School
1000 Idaho Avenue, Portage MI 49024-1233
DP Coordinator Rick Searing
Languages English
T: +1 269 323 5455
W: www.portageps.org/high_schools/Northern

Post Oak Magnet School
2320 Post Oak Lane, Lansing MI 48912
PYP Coordinator Ann Jones
Languages English
T: +1 517 755 1610
W: www.edline.net/pages/post_oak_school

Raisinville Elementary School
2300 North Raisinville Road, Monroe MI 48162
PYP Coordinator Kelly Davis
Languages English
T: +1 734 265 4800
W: www.monroe.k12.mi.us/res

Royal Oak High School
1500 Lexington Blvd., Royal Oak MI 48073
DP Coordinator Leah Barnett
MYP Coordinator Lindsey Belzyt
Languages English
T: +1 248 435 8500
W: www.royaloakschools.org/high-school

Royal Oak Middle School
709 N. Washington Ave, Royal Oak MI 48067
MYP Coordinator Lindsey Belzyt
Languages English
T: +1 248 541 7100
W: www.royaloakschools.org/middle-school

Scarlett Middle School
3300 Lorraine St, Ann Arbor MI 48108
MYP Coordinator Ryan Soupal
Languages English
T: +1 734 997 1220
W: www.a2schools.org/scarlett

Sharp Park Academy
766 Park Road, Jackson MI 49203
PYP Coordinator Elaine Themm
Languages English
T: +1 517 841 2860
W: www.jpsk12.org/sharppark

Siebert Elementary School
5700 Siebert Street, Midland MI 48640
PYP Coordinator Amy Sabourin
Languages English
T: +1 989 923 7835
W: sbe.midlandps.org

Southfield High School for the Arts and Technology
24675 Lahser Road, Southfield MI 48033
DP Coordinator Angela Mallory
Languages English
T: +1 248 746 8600
W: www.southfieldk12.org/schools/hs/southfield-high-school

Spring Lake High School
16140 148th Avenue, Spring Lake MI 49456
DP Coordinator Ann Henke
Languages English
T: +1 616 846 5500
W: springlakeschools.org/high

Thompson K-8 International Academy
16300 Lincoln Drive, Southfield MI 48076
MYP Coordinator Angela Mallory
PYP Coordinator Angela Mallory
Languages English
T: +1 248 746 7400
W: www.southfieldk12.org/schools/elem/thompson-k-8-international-academy

Utica Academy for International Studies
c/o Heritage Junior High School, 37400 Dodge Park Rd, Sterling Heights MI 48312
DP Coordinator Christopher Layson
Languages English
T: +1 586 797 3100
W: uais.uticak12.org

Walled Lake Western High School
600 Beck Road, Walled Lake MI 48390
DP Coordinator Ami Friedman
Languages English
T: +1 248 956 4400
W: www.wlcsd.org/Western.cfm

Washtenaw International High School
510 Emerick, Ypsilanti MI 48198
DP Coordinator Daniel Giddings
MYP Coordinator Jessica Garcia
Languages English
T: +1 734 994 8100 EXT:1263
W: www.wihi.org

West Hills Middle School
2601 Lone Pine Road, West Bloomfield MI 28323
MYP Coordinator Jennifer Teal
PYP Coordinator Jennifer Teal
Languages English
T: +1 248 341 6100
W: westhills.bloomfield.org

West Ottawa High School
3685 Butternut Drive, Holland MI 49424
DP Coordinator Corban Van Dam
Languages English
T: +1 616 994 5001
W: www.westottawa.net

Woodcrest Elementary School
5500 Drake Street, Midland MI 48640
PYP Coordinator Robin Harshman-Rogers
Languages English
T: +1 989 923 7940
W: wce.midlandps.org

Minnesota

Annunciation Catholic School
525 W 54th St, Minneapolis MN 55419
PYP Coordinator Sheila Loschy
Languages English
T: +1 612 823 4394
W: annunciationmsp.org/school

Anwatin Middle School
256 Upton Ave. S., Minneapolis MN 55405-1997
MYP Coordinator Sarah Wernimont
Languages English, Spanish
T: +1 612 668 2450
W: anwatin.mpls.k12.mn.us

Aquila Elementary School
8500 W 31st Street, St Louis Park MN 55426
PYP Coordinator Olivia Tolzin
Languages English
T: +1 952 928 6500
W: www.slpschools.org/aq

Bancroft Elementary School
3829 13th Ave So, Minneapolis MN 55407
PYP Coordinator Susan Francis
Languages English
T: +1 612 668 3550
W: bancroft.mpls.k12.mn.us

Benjamin E. Mays Magnet School
560 Concordia Ave., St Paul MN 55103
PYP Coordinator Stacy Klage
Languages English
T: +1 651 325 2400
W: benmays.spps.org

Central High School, St Paul
275 Lexington Pkwy N, St Paul MN 55105
DP Coordinator Ethan Cherin
MYP Coordinator Sarah Arneson
Languages English
T: +1 651 744 4900
W: central.spps.org

Champlin Park High School
6025 109th Avenue North, Champlin MN 55316
CP Coordinator Chris Baker-Raivo
DP Coordinator Ashley Brown
Languages English
T: +1 763 506 6800
W: www.anoka.k12.mn.us/cphs

Elizabeth Hall International Elementary School
1601 Aldrich Avenue North, Minneapolis MN 55411
PYP Coordinator Lindsey Rettmann
Languages English
T: +1 612 668 2650
W: hall.mpls.k12.mn.us

Fridley High School
6000 West Moore Lake Drive, Fridley MN 55432
CP Coordinator Jessica Baker
DP Coordinator Jessica Baker
MYP Coordinator Kari Reiter
Languages English
T: +1 763 502 5600
W: www.fridley.k12.mn.us

Fridley Middle School
6100 West Moore Lake Drive, Fridley MN 55432
MYP Coordinator Carol Neilson
Languages English
T: +1 763 502 5400
W: www.fridley.k12.mn.us

Global Academy
4065 Central Ave NE, Columbia Heights MN 55421
PYP Coordinator Melissa Storbakken
Languages English
T: +1 763 404 8200
W: www.globalacademy.us

Grand Rapids Senior High School
800 Conifer Drive, Grand Rapids MN 55744
DP Coordinator Dale Christy
Languages English
T: +1 218 327 5760
W: www.isd318.org

Great River School
1326 Energy Park Drive, St Paul MN 55108
DP Coordinator Lindsey Weaver
Languages English
T: +1 651 305 2780
W: www.greatriverschool.org

Harding High School
1540 E. Sixth Street, St Paul MN 55106
DP Coordinator Erik Brandt
MYP Coordinator Jake Lindeman
Languages English
T: +1 651 793 4700
W: harding.spps.org

Hayes Elementary School
615 Mississippi Street NE, Fridley MN 55432
PYP Coordinator Kirsten Wickman
Languages English
T: +1 763 502 5200
W: www.fridley.k12.mn.us

Hazel Park Preparatory Academy
1140 White Bear Avenue, St. Paul MN 55106
MYP Coordinator Lynette Scott
PYP Coordinator Lynette Scott
Languages English
T: +1 651 293 8970
W: hppa.spps.org

Highland Park Elementary School
1700 Saunders Ave., St Paul MN 55116
PYP Coordinator Michelle Strecker
Languages English
T: +1 651 293 8770
W: highlandel.spps.org

Highland Park Middle School
975 S Snelling Ave., St Paul MN 55116
MYP Coordinator Linda Jones
Languages English
T: +1 651 293 8950
W: highlandms.spps.org

Highland Park Senior High School
1015 Snelling Ave S, Saint Paul MN 55116
DP Coordinator Jason Schlukebier
MYP Coordinator Marissa Bonk
Languages English
T: +1 651 293 8940
W: highlandsr.spps.org

Hopkins North Junior High School
10700 Cedar Lake Rd., Minnetonka MN 55305
MYP Coordinator Angela Wilcox
Languages English, French, German, Spanish
T: +1 952 988 4800
W: www.hopkinsschools.org/schools/hopkins-north-junior-high

Hopkins West Junior High School
3830 Baker Road, Hopkins MN 55305
MYP Coordinator Jennifer Poncelet
Languages English
T: +1 952 988 4401
W: www.hopkinsschools.org/schools/hopkins-west-junior-high

International Spanish Language Academy
5959 Shady Oak Road, Minnetonka MN 55343
PYP Coordinator Karen Speich
Languages English, Spanish
T: +1 952 746 6020
W: isla-academy.org

Kaposia Education Center
1225 First Avenue South, South St Paul MN 55075
PYP Coordinator Ryan Higbea
Languages English
T: +1 651 451 9260
W: kaposia.sspps.schoolfusion.us

Lakes International Language Academy
246 11th Avenue SE, Forest Lake MN 55025
DP Coordinator Sarah Ray
MYP Coordinator Natalie Kainz
PYP Coordinator Amy Mueller
Languages Spanish, Mandarin
T: +1 651 464 0771
W: www.mylila.org

Lakeview Elementary School
4110 Lake Drive North, Robbinsdale MN 55422
PYP Coordinator Molly James
Languages English
T: +1 763 504 4100
W: lve.rdale.org

Lincoln Center Elementary School
357 9th Avenue North, South St Paul MN 55075
PYP Coordinator Diane Tiffany
Languages English
T: +1 651 457 9426
W: lincoln.sspps.schoolfusion.us

Matoska International
2530 Spruce Place, White Bear Lake MN 55110
PYP Coordinator Kirsten McPherson
Languages English
T: +1 651 653 2847
W: www.whitebear.k12.mn.us/mis/index.html

Minnetonka High School
18301 Highway 7, Minnetonka MN 55345
DP Coordinator Laura Herbst
Languages English
T: +1 952 401 5703
W: www.minnetonka.k12.mn.us/mhs

Northeast College Prep
300 Industrial Blvd. NE, Minneapolis MN 55413
PYP Coordinator Joanna Waggoner-Norquest
Languages English
T: +1 612 248 8240
W: www.northeastcollegeprep.org

Northeast Middle School
2955 Hayes Street North East, Minneapolis MN 55418
MYP Coordinator Angela Evenson
Languages English
T: +1 612 668 1500
W: www.northeast.mpls.k12.mn.us

Park Center Senior High School
7300 Brooklyn Boulevard, Brooklyn Park MN 55443
DP Coordinator Michael Cassidy
MYP Coordinator Jon Eversoll
Languages English
T: +1 763 569 7600
W: www.district279.org/sec/pcsh

Park High School
8040 80th Street South, Cottage Grove MN 55016
DP Coordinator Lisa Martineau
Languages English
T: +1 651 768 3701
W: www.sowashco.k12.mn.us/phs

Patrick Henry Senior High School
4320 Newton Ave N, Minneapolis MN 55412
CP Coordinator Kazuko Shiba
DP Coordinator Chad Owen
MYP Coordinator Natalie Tourtelotte
Languages English
T: +1 612 668 2000
W: henry.mpls.k12.mn.us

Peter Hobart Primary Center
6500 West 26th Street, St Louis Park MN 55416
PYP Coordinator Anne LaLonde-Laux
Languages English
T: +1 952 928 6600
W: www.slpschools.org.ph

Ramsey Middle School
1700 Summit Ave., St Paul MN 55105
MYP Coordinator Elisabeth Fontana
Languages English
T: +1 651 293 8860
W: ramsey.spps.org

Rice Elementary
200 NE Third Avenue, Rice MN 56367
PYP Coordinator Nancy Davis
Languages English
T: +1 320 393 2177
W: www.isd47.org/rice

Robbinsdale Cooper High School
8230-47th Avenue North, New Hope MN 55428
DP Coordinator Kari Christensen
MYP Coordinator Kari Christensen
Languages English
T: +1 763 504 8501
W: www.rdale.k12.mn.us/chs/ib/

Robbinsdale Middle School
3730 Toledo Ave. N., Robbinsdale MN 55422
MYP Coordinator Jennifer Holtgrewe
Languages English
T: +1 763 504 4801
W: rms.rdale.org

Robert Louis Stevenson Elementary School
6080 East River Road, Fridley MN 55432
PYP Coordinator Veronica Mathison
Languages English
T: +1 763 502 5300
W: www.fridley.k12.mn.us/schools/RLStevensonElem/RLStevensonElem.html

Rochester Arts and Sciences Academy
400 5th Avenue SW, Rochester MN 55902
PYP Coordinator Brianna Zabel
Languages English
T: +1 507 206 4646
W: www.rasamn.org

Rochester Montessori School
5099 7th Street NW, Rochester MN 55901
MYP Coordinator Bre Scheer
Languages English
T: +1 507 288 8725
W: www.rmschool.org

Roosevelt High School
4029 28th Avenue South, Minneapolis MN 55406
CP Coordinator Nicole Lamb
DP Coordinator Robyn Cook
MYP Coordinator Marika Belusa
Languages English
T: +1 612 668 4800
W: roosevelt.mpls.k12.mn.us

Saint John's Preparatory School
1857 Watertower Road, Collegeville MN 56321
DP Coordinator Martina Talic
Languages English
T: +1 320 363 3315
W: www.sjprep.net

Sanford Middle School
3524 42nd Avenue S., Minneapolis MN 55406
MYP Coordinator Ann Mack
Languages English
T: +1 612 668 4900
W: sanford.mpls.k12.mn.us

Scandia Elementary School
14351 Scandia Trail North, Scandia MN 55073
PYP Coordinator Emily Stegmeir
Languages English
T: +1 651 982 3301
W: sc.forestlake.k12.mn.us

South St. Paul Secondary
700 North Second Street, South St Paul MN 55075
DP Coordinator Conrad Anderson
MYP Coordinator Melissa Miller
Languages English
T: +1 651 457 9408
W: southp.schoolwires.net/domain/8

Southwest High School
3414 West 47th Street, Minneapolis MN 55410
CP Coordinator Maria Kimmes
DP Coordinator Lisa Ledman
MYP Coordinator Jocelyn Lovick
Languages English
T: +1 612 668 3036
W: southwest.mpls.k12.mn.us

St Louis Park Middle School
2025 Texas Avenue North, St. Louis Park MN 55426
MYP Coordinator Mia Waldera
Languages English
T: +1 952 928 6300
W: www.slpschools.org/domain/12

St Louis Park Senior High School
6425 W 33nd Street, St Louis Park MN 55426
DP Coordinator Jennifer Magdal
Languages English
T: +1 952 928 6107
W: www.slpschools.org

Susan B Anthony Middle School
5757 Irving Avenue South, Minneapolis MN 55419
MYP Coordinator Casey Strecker
Languages English
T: +1 612 668 3240
W: anthony.mpls.k12.mn.us

Susan Lindgren Elementary School
4801 West 41st Street, St Louis Park MN 55416
PYP Coordinator Ila Saxena
Languages English
T: +1 952 928 6700
W: www.slpschools.org/sl

Thomas Edison High School
700 22nd Ave. NE, Minneapolis MN 55418
DP Coordinator Max Athorn
MYP Coordinator Sharon Cormany
Languages English
T: +1 612 668 1300
W: edison.mpls.k12.mn.us

Washburn High School
201 West 49th St., Minneapolis MN 55419
DP Coordinator Aaron Percy
Languages English
T: +1 612 668 3400
W: washburn.mpls.k12.mn.us

Whittier International Elementary School
315 West 26th Street, Minneapolis MN 55404
PYP Coordinator Libby Dominguez
Languages English
T: +1 612 668 4170
W: whittier.mpls.k12.mn.us

Mississippi

Barack H. Obama Magnet
750 N. Congress Street, Jackson MS 39202
PYP Coordinator Beth West Roach
Languages English
T: +1 601 960 5333
W: www.jackson.k12.ms.us/obama

Jim Hill High School
2185 Coach Fred Harris Drive, Jackson MS 39204
DP Coordinator Larry Thurman
MYP Coordinator Tracee Thompson
Languages English
T: +1 601 960 5354
W: jimhill.jpsms.org

Northwest Magnet Middle School
7020 Highway 49N, Jackson MS 39213
MYP Coordinator Kimberly Smith
Languages English
T: +1 601 960 8700

Ocean Springs High School
PO Box 7002, Ocean Springs MS 39566
DP Coordinator Lamenda Hase
Languages English
T: +1 228 875 0333
W: www.ossdms.org/oshs/0main/index.html

Missouri

Academie Lafayette
6903 Oak Street, Kansas City MO 64113
MYP Coordinator Jessica McDowell
Languages French
T: +1 816 361 7735
W: www.academielafayette.org

Boyd Elementary School
1409 N. Washington Ave., Springfield MO 65802
PYP Coordinator Jamie Quirk
Languages English
T: +1 417 523 1500
W: boyd.spsk12.org

Camdenton High School
662 Laker Pride Road, Camdenton MO 65020
DP Coordinator Jody Welsh
Languages English
T: +1 573 346 9232
W: camdentonschools.schoolwires.net/chs

Central High School
2602 Edmond Street, St Joseph MO 64501
DP Coordinator Shawna Gilliland
Languages English
T: +1 816 671 4080
W: www.sjsd.k12.mo.us/Schools/Central/index.htm

Central High School, Springfield
423 E. Central St., Springfield MO 65802
CP Coordinator Donita Cox
DP Coordinator Melissa Morgan
MYP Coordinator Gretchen Teague
Languages English
T: +1 417 523 9600
W: central.spsk12.org

Eugene Field Elementary School
2120 E. Barataria, Springfield MO 65804
PYP Coordinator Jamie Quirk
Languages English
T: +1 417 523 4800
W: field.spsk12.org

Lee's Summit High School
400 Blue Parkway, Lee's Summit MO 64063
CP Coordinator Tammi Krones
DP Coordinator Vickie Metzler
Languages English
T: +1 816 986 2000
W: www.leesummit.k12.mo.us

Lee's Summit North High School
901 NE Douglas, Lee's Summit MO 64086
CP Coordinator Robert Rossiter
DP Coordinator Robert Rossiter
Languages English
T: +1 816 986 3005
W: www.leesummit.k12.mo.us/lsnhs/

Lee's Summit West High School
2600 SW Ward Road, Lee's Summit MO 64082
CP Coordinator Christy Dabalos
DP Coordinator Christy Dabalos
Languages English
T: +1 816 986 4000

Lincoln College Preparatory Academy
2111 Woodland Ave., Kansas City MO 64108
DP Coordinator Christopher Jennens
Languages English
T: +1 816 418 3000
W: www.kcpublicschools.org/domain/10

Lindbergh High School
5000 S. Lindbergh Blvd., St Louis MO 63126
DP Coordinator Miranda Gelven
Languages English
T: +1 314 729 2410
W: go.lindberghschools.ws/domain/8

Metro Academic & Classical High School
4015 McPherson Avenue, St Louis MO 63108
DP Coordinator Sharleta Williams
Languages English
T: +1 314 534 3894

North Kansas City High School
620 East 23rd Avenue, North Kansas City School Distr, North Kansas City MO 64116
CP Coordinator Chad Lower
DP Coordinator Jane Reed
Languages English
T: +1 816 413 5900
W: www.nkcsd.k12.mo.us

Ozark High School of Ozark R-6 School District
1350 West Bluff Drive, Ozark MO 65721
DP Coordinator Sara Floyd
Languages English
T: +1 417 582 5701
W: www.ozark.k12.mo.us/hs/index.htm

Pipkin Middle School
1215 N. Boonville, Springfield MO 65802
MYP Coordinator Elizabeth Troutman
Languages English
T: +1 417 523 6000
W: pipkin.spsk12.org

Raymore-Peculiar High School
PO Box 789, Peculiar MO 64078
DP Coordinator Steve Meek
Languages English
T: +1 816 892 1400
W: www.raypec.k12.mo.us

Rountree Elementary School
333 E. Grand St., Springfield MO 65804
PYP Coordinator Nicki Foltz
Languages English
T: +1 417 523 4900
W: rountree.spsk12.org

Montana

Big Sky High School
3100 South Ave. West, Missoula MT 59804
DP Coordinator Cameron Johnson
Languages English
T: +1 406 728 2401
W: www.mcpsmt.org/bigsky

Flathead High School
644 4th Avenue West, Kalispell Public Schools, Kalispell MT 59901
DP Coordinator Kelli Higgins
Languages English
T: +1 406 751 3462
W: www.sd5.k12.mt.us

Hellgate High School
900 South Higgins Avenue, Missoula MT 59801
DP Coordinator Christine Hiller-Claridge
Languages English
T: +1 406 728 2402
W: www.mcpsmt.org/hellgate

Lewis and Clark Elementary School
2901 Park Street, Missoula MT 59801
PYP Coordinator Kari Henderson
Languages English
T: +1 406 542 4035
W: www.mcpsmt.org/lewisclark

Lone Peak High School
45465 Gallatin Road, Gallatin Gateway MT 59730
DP Coordinator Marlo Mitchem
Languages English
T: +1 406 995 4281
W: www.bssd72.org/lone-peak-high-school

McCluer North High School
705 Waterford Drive, Florissant MO 63033
DP Coordinator Mark Forbes
Languages English
T: +1 314 506 9200
W: www.fergflor.org/mccluer-north-high

Missoula International School
1100 Harrison Street, Missoula MT 59802
MYP Coordinator Jeffrey Kessler
PYP Coordinator Patricia Cano
Languages Spanish, English
T: +1 406 542 9924
W: www.mismt.org

Ophir Elementary School
45465 Gallatin Road, Gallatin Gateway MT 59730
PYP Coordinator Marlo Mitchem
Languages English, Spanish
T: +1 406 995 4281
W: www.bssd72.org/ophir-elementary

Nebraska

Bess Streeter Aldrich Elementary
506 N 162nd Avenue, Omaha NE 68118
PYP Coordinator Jodi Fidone
Languages English
T: +1 402 715 2020
W: aldrich.mpsomaha.org

Black Elk Elementary
6708 S 161st Ave, Omaha NE 68135
PYP Coordinator Nicole Beins
Languages English, Spanish
T: +1 402 715 6200
W: blackelk.mpsomaha.org

Central High School
124 North 20th Street, Omaha NE 68102
DP Coordinator Cathy Andrus
MYP Coordinator Paul Nielson
Languages English
T: +1 402 557 3300
W: www.ops.org/high/central

Lewis and Clark Middle School
6901 Burt Street, Omaha NE 68132
MYP Coordinator Lisa Tingelhoff
Languages English
T: +1 402 557 4300
W: www.ops.org/middle/lewisandclark

Lincoln High School
2229 J Street, Lincoln NE 68510
DP Coordinator J.P. Caruso
Languages English
T: +1 402 436 1301
W: lhs.lps.org

Millard North High School
1010 S 144th Street, Millard Public Schools, Omaha NE 68154
DP Coordinator Amber Ripa
MYP Coordinator Elizabeth Swedlund
Languages English
T: +1 402 715 1411
W: www.mps.mnhs.schoolfusion.us

Millard North Middle School
2828 South 139th Plaza, Omaha NE 68144
MYP Coordinator Katharine Hadan
Languages English
T: +1 402 715 1280
W: nms.mpsomaha.org

Nevada

Basic Academy of International Studies
400 N. Palo Verde Dr., Henderson NV 89015
CP Coordinator Donna Rorer
DP Coordinator Michael Thorsteinson
MYP Coordinator Michael Thorsteinson
Languages English
T: +1 702 799 8000
W: www.basicacademy.org

Brown Junior High School
307 N. Cannes St, Henderson NV 89015
MYP Coordinator Erika Benedict
Languages English
T: +1 702 799 8900
W: www.brownjhs.org

Clarence A. Piggott Academy of International Studies
9601 Red Hills Drive, Las Vegas NV 89117
PYP Coordinator Tara Albidrez
Languages English
T: +1 702 799 4450
W: www.clarencepiggott.org

Earl Wooster High School
1331 East Plumb Lane, Reno NV 89502
CP Coordinator Dustin Coli
DP Coordinator Jennifer Lienau
MYP Coordinator Nikki Grose
Languages English
T: +1 775 333 5100
W: www.washoe.k12.nv.us/wooster

Green Valley High School
460 Arroyo Grande Blvd., Henderson NV 89014
DP Coordinator Angelique Callicoat
Languages English
T: +1 702 799 0950
W: greenvalleyhs.org

Kit Carson International Academy
1735 North D. Street, Las Vegas NV 89106
PYP Coordinator Robert Mitchell
Languages English
T: +1 702 799 7113
W: www.kitcarsoncougars.org

Palo Verde High School
333 Pavilion Center Drive, Las Vegas NV 89144
DP Coordinator Amy Reed
Languages English
T: +1 702 799 1450
W: www.paloverde.org

Roy W. Martin Middle School
200 N. 28th St., Las Vegas NV 89101
MYP Coordinator Jennifer Cain
Languages English
T: +1 702 799 7922
W: roymartinms.org

Sandy Searles Miller Academy for International Studies
4851 East Lake Mead Blvd, Las Vegas NV 89115
PYP Coordinator Lynn Tyrell
Languages English
T: +1 702 799 8830
W: www.ccsd.net/schools/sandymiller

Sheila Tarr Academy of International Studies
9400 W. Gilmore Ave., Las Vegas NV 89129
PYP Coordinator Tracy Baldwin
Languages English, Spanish
T: +1 702 799 6710
W: tarracademy.weebly.com

Spring Valley High School
3750 Buffalo Drive, Las Vegas NV 89147
DP Coordinator Anthony Gebbia
MYP Coordinator Anthony Gebbia
Languages English
T: +1 702 799 2580
W: www.springvalleyhs.com

Valley High School
2839 S Burnham Ave., Las Vegas NV 89169
DP Coordinator Andrew Magness
MYP Coordinator Daniel O'Brien
Languages English
T: +1 702 799 5450
W: www.valleyhs.vegas

Vaughn Middle School
1200 Bresson Avenue, Reno NV 89502
MYP Coordinator Linda Hunt
Languages English
T: +1 775 333 5160
W: www.washoeschools.net/vaughn

Walter Johnson Academy of International Studies
7701 Ducharme Ave, Las Vegas NV 89145-4937
MYP Coordinator Kirsten Lewis
Languages English
T: +1 702 799 4480
W: schools.ccsd.net/johnson

New Hampshire

Bedford High School
47 Nashua Road, Bedford NH 03110
DP Coordinator Jon Cannon
Languages English
T: +1 603 310 9000
W: www.sau25.net/highschool/BHShome.htm

NEW HAMPTON SCHOOL
70 Main Street, New Hampton NH 03256
DP Coordinator Jennifer McMahon
Languages English
T: +1 603 677 3401
E: admission@newhampton.org
W: www.newhampton.org

See full details on page 532

New Jersey

Bergen County Academies
200 Hackensack Avenue, Hackensack NJ 07601
DP Coordinator Michelle Pinke
Languages English
T: +1 201 343 6000 EXT:3385
W: www.bergen.org

Biotechnology High School
5000 Kozloski Road, Freehold NJ 07728
DP Coordinator Linda Rogers
Languages English
T: +1 732 431 7208
W: www.bths.mcvsd.org

Donovan Catholic
711 Hooper Ave, Toms River NJ 08753
DP Coordinator Kathleen D'Andrea
Languages English
T: +1 732 349 8801
W: donovancatholic.org

Dr. Orlando Edreira Academy, School 26
631-657 Westminster Avenue, Elizabeth NJ 07208
MYP Coordinator William Clark
PYP Coordinator David Reeseg
Languages English
T: +1 908 436 5970
W: edreira.epsnj.org/pages/dr__orlando_edreira_academy_no

East Side High School
238 Van Buren St, Newark NJ 07105
DP Coordinator Albert Moussab
Languages English
T: +1 973 465 4900
W: www.nps.k12.nj.us/EAS

Fort Lee High School
3000 Lemoine Ave, Fort Lee NJ 07024
DP Coordinator Brandon Barron
Languages English
T: +1 201 585 4675
W: fortlee-boe.net

Freehold Township High School
281 Elton Adelphia Rd, Freehold NJ 07728
DP Coordinator Michael Dillon
Languages English
T: 732-431-8460
W: www.frhsd.com/freeholdtwp

Hatikvah International Academy Charter School
7 Lexington Avenue, East Brunswick NJ 08816
MYP Coordinator Amanda Rosenberg
Languages English
T: +1 732 254 8300
W: hatikvahcharterschool.com

Howell High School
405 Squankum-Yellowbrook Road, Farmingdale NJ 07727
DP Coordinator Kristine Jenner
Languages English
T: +1 732 919 2131
W: www.frhsd.com

International High School
200 Grand Street, Paterson NJ 07501
DP Coordinator Catherine Forfia-Dion
Languages English
T: +1 973 321 2280
W: ihs-pps-nj.schoolloop.com

Learning Ladders
35 Hudson Street, Jersey City NJ 07302
PYP Coordinator Cherry Estrada
Languages English
T: +1 201 885 2960
W: www.learningladdersnj.com

Linden High School
121 W St Georges Avenue, Georges Avenue, Linden NJ 07036
DP Coordinator Anthony Fischetti
Languages English
T: +1 908 486 5432

Morris Knolls High School
50 Knoll Drive, Rockaway NJ 07866
DP Coordinator Scott Gambale
Languages English
T: +1 973 664 2200
W: www.mhrd.k12.nj.us/mk

Newark Academy
91 South Orange Avenue, Livingston NJ 07039
DP Coordinator Neil Stourton
Languages English
T: +1 973 992 7000
W: www.newarka.edu

Princeton Junior School
90 Fackler Road, Princeton NJ 08540
PYP Coordinator Catherine Blas
Languages English
T: +1 609 924 8126
W: www.princetonjuniorschool.org

Princeton Montessori School
487 Cherry Valley Road, Princeton NJ 08540
MYP Coordinator Michelle Jacob
Languages English
T: +1 609 924 4594
W: www.princetonmontessori.org

Red Bank Regional High School
101 Ridge Road, Little Silver NJ 07739
DP Coordinator Lisa Boyle
Languages English
T: +1 732 842 8000
W: www.rbrhs.org

Rosa International Middle School
485 Browning Lane, Cherry Hill NJ 08003
MYP Coordinator George Zografos
Languages English
T: +1 856 616 8787
W: rosa.chclc.org

Salem High School
205 Walnut Street, Salem NJ 08079
DP Coordinator Jordan Pla
Languages English
T: +1 856 935 3800
W: www.salemnj.org

Science Park High School
260 Norfolk Street, Newark NJ 10703
DP Coordinator Mary Garripoli
Languages English
T: +1 973 733 8787
W: www.nps.k12.nj.us/SCI/site/default.asp

Shore Regional High School
132 Monmouth Park Highway, West Long Branch NJ 07764
DP Coordinator Vanessa Miano
Languages English
T: +1 732 222 9300 EXT 210
W: www.shoreregional.org

Solomon Schechter Day School of Bergen County
275 McKinley Ave, New Milford NJ 07646
MYP Coordinator Jennifer Coxe
Languages English
T: +1 201 262 9898
W: www.ssdsbergen.org

The Red Oaks School
340 Speedwell Ave., Morristown NJ 07960
MYP Coordinator Nelyda Miguel
Languages English
T: +1 973 998 9424
W: www.redoaksschool.org

Waterfront Montessori
150 Warren St., Suite 108, Jersey City NJ 7302
MYP Coordinator Deanna Richardson
Languages English
T: +1 201 333 5600
W: www.waterfrontmontessori.com

West Morris Central High School
259 Bartley Road, Chester NJ 07930
CP Coordinator Erin Feltmann
DP Coordinator Debbie Gonzalez
Languages English
T: +1 908 879 5212
W: www.wmchs.org

West Morris Mendham High School
65 East Main Street, Mendham NJ 07945
CP Coordinator Lindsay Schartner
DP Coordinator Laura Pereira
Languages English
T: +1 973 543 2501
W: www.wmmhs.org

World of ABC
159 2nd St, Jersey City NJ 07302
PYP Coordinator Courtney Bode
Languages English
T: +1 201 963 5555
W: www.worldofabc.com

YINGHUA INTERNATIONAL SCHOOL
25 Laurel Avenue, Kingston NJ 08528-0088
PYP Coordinator Ms. Wen-Lin Su
Languages English, Chinese
T: +1 609 375 8015
E: admissions@yhis.org
W: yhis.org

See full details on page 562

New Mexico

Corrales International School
5500 Wilshire Ave NE, Albuquerque NM 87113
MYP Coordinator Sheley Wimmer
PYP Coordinator Ana Perea
Languages English
T: +1 505 344 9733
W: corralesis.org

Cottonwood Classical Preparatory School
1776 Montano Road NW, Building 3, Los Ranchos de Albuquerque NM 87107
DP Coordinator Meghan Lowe
Languages English
T: +1 505 998 1021
W: www.cottonwoodclassical.org

Desert Academy
7300 Old Santa Fe Trail, Santa Fe NM 87505
DP Coordinator Annette Kaare-Rasmussen
MYP Coordinator Annette Kaare-Rasmussen
Languages English
T: +1 505 992 8284 (EXT:22)
W: www.desertacademy.org

Mandela International Magnet School
1720 Llano St, Santa Fe NM 87505
DP Coordinator Jessie Gac
MYP Coordinator Holly Call
Languages English
T: +1 505 467 3370
W: mims.sfps.info

NAVAJO PREPARATORY SCHOOL
1220 West Apache Street, Farmington NM 87401
DP Coordinator Donna Fernandez
Languages English
T: +1 505 326 6571
E: sbecenti@navajoprep.com
W: www.navajoprep.com

See full details on page 531

New Mexico International School
8650 Alameda Blvd NE, Albuquerque NM 87122
PYP Coordinator Cynthia Pedrotty
Languages English
T: +1 505 503 7670
W: nmis.org

Sandia High School
7801 Candelaria NE, Albuquerque NM 87110
DP Coordinator Derek Maestas
Languages English
T: +1 505 294 1511
W: www.sandiamatadors.com

The International School at Mesa del Sol
2660 Eastman Crossing SE, Albuquerque NM 87106
PYP Coordinator Rebecca Mattingly
Languages English
T: +1 505 508 3295
W: www.tisnm.org

UWC-USA
State Rte 65, Montezuma NM 87731
DP Coordinator Alexis Mamaux
Languages English
T: +1 505 454 4252
W: www.uwc-usa.org

New York

Albany High School
700 Washington Avenue, Albany NY 12203
DP Coordinator Leah Evans
Languages English
T: +1 518 475 6200
W: ahs.albany.k12.ny.us

Archbishop Walsh Academy
208 North 24th Street, Olean NY 14760
DP Coordinator Danielle Michel
Languages English
T: +1 716 372 8122
W: www.stcswalsh.org

Baccalaureate School for Global Education
34-12 36th Avenue, Astoria NY 11106
DP Coordinator Jaime Meisler
Languages English
T: +1 718 361 5275
W: www.bsge.org

Ballston Spa High School
220 Ballston Avenue, Ballston Spa NY 12020
DP Coordinator Nicole Stehle
Languages English
T: +1 518 884 7150
W: www.bscsd.org/domain/87

Bay Shore High School
155 Third Avenue, Bay Shore NY 11706
DP Coordinator Jonathan Nelson
Languages English
T: +1 631 968 1157
W: www.bayshoreschools.org

BELA Charter School
125 Stuyvesant Ave., Brooklyn NY 11221
DP Coordinator Tyler Griffin
Languages English
T: +1 347 473 8830
W: www.belahs.org

Binghamton High School
31 Main Street, Binghamton NY 13905
CP Coordinator Steve McGovern
DP Coordinator James Gill
MYP Coordinator Mark Ward
Languages English
T: +1 607 762 8200
W: bhs.binghamtonschools.org

Bloomfield Elementary School
45 Maple Avenue, Suite B, Bloomfield NY 14469
PYP Coordinator Kathryn Taylor
Languages English
T: +1 585 657 6121
W: bloomfieldcsd.org

Bloomfield High School
PO Box 250, Oakmount Avenue, East Bloomfield NY 14469
DP Coordinator Travis Geary
Languages English
T: +1 585 657 6121
W: www.bloomfieldcsd.org

Boerum Hill School for International Studies
284 Baltic Street, Brooklyn NY 11201
DP Coordinator Rebecca Crawford
MYP Coordinator Emily Brandt
Languages English
T: +1 718 330 9390
W: www.K497.org

Bronx Early College Academy
250 East 164th Street, Bronx NY 10456
CP Coordinator Kathy Briceno-Paul
DP Coordinator Kathy Briceno-Paul
Languages English
T: +1 718 681 8287
W: www.beca324.org

BROOKLYN ARTS AND SCIENCE ELEMENTARY SCHOOL
443 St. Marks Ave., Brooklyn NY 11238
PYP Coordinator Christina Soriano
Languages English
T: +1 718 230 0851
E: brooklynartselementary@gmail.com
W: www.brooklynartselementary.org
See full details on page 495

Brooklyn Friends School
375 Pearl Street, Brooklyn, New York NY 11201
DP Coordinator Peter Prince
Languages English
T: +1 718 852 1029
W: www.brooklynfriends.org

Brooklyn Prospect Charter School
80 Willoughby Street, Brooklyn NY 11201
DP Coordinator Jamie Vaughan
Languages English
T: +1 718 722 7634
W: www.brooklynprospect.org

Canandaigua Academy
1 Academy Circle, Canandaigua NY 14424
DP Coordinator Keith Pedzich
Languages English
T: +1 585 396 3802

Churchville-Chili Senior High School
5786 Buffalo Road, Churchville NY 14428
DP Coordinator Kelley Fahy
Languages English
T: +1 585 293 4540
W: www.cccsd.org/senior_high.cfm

City Honors School
186 E North Street, Buffalo NY 14204
DP Coordinator Elissa Morganti Banas
MYP Coordinator James Moses
Languages English
T: +1 716 816 4230
W: www.cityhonors.org

Clarkstown High School North
151 Congers Road, New City NY 10956-6272
DP Coordinator Andrea Miranda
Languages English
T: +1 845 639 6500
W: www.ccsd.edu/Domain/19

Clarkstown Senior High School South
31 Demarest Mill Road, West Nyack NY 10994
DP Coordinator Melina Balducci-Flugger
Languages English
T: +1 845 624 3400
W: www.ccsd.edu/south

Commack High School
1 Scholar Lane, Commack NY 11725-1297
DP Coordinator Susan Shapiro
Languages English
T: +1 631 912 2106
W: www.commack.k12.ny.us/chs

Commack Middle School
700 Vanderbilt Parkway, Commack NY 11725
MYP Coordinator Kristen Kornweiss
Languages English
T: +1 631 858 3500
W: www.commack.k12.ny.us

Corning-Painted Post High School
201 Cantigney St., Corning NY 14830
DP Coordinator Kristie Radford
MYP Coordinator Cathy Honness
Languages English
T: +1 607 654 2988
W: www.corningareaschools.com/1/home

Corning-Painted Post Middle School
35 Victory Highway, Painted Post NY 14870
MYP Coordinator Cathy Honness
Languages English
T: +1 607 654 2966
W: www.corningareaschools.com/2/home

CULTURAL ARTS ACADEMY CHARTER SCHOOL AT SPRING CREEK
1400 Linden Blvd, Brooklyn NY 11212
PYP Coordinator David Mercaldo, MEd
Languages English, Spanish
T: +1 718 683 3300
E: caacs@caa-ny.org
W: www.culturalartsacademy.org
See full details on page 499

Curtis High School
105 Hamilton Avenue, Staten Island NY 10301
CP Coordinator Elaine Carrol
DP Coordinator Kathleen Francis
Languages English
T: +1 718 390 1800
W: sites.google.com/a/curtishs.org/home/Home

Dobbs Ferry High School
505 Broadway, Dobbs Ferry NY 10522
DP Coordinator Marion Halberg
MYP Coordinator Jennifer Hickey
Languages English
T: +1 914 693 7645
W: www.dfsd.org/hs

Dobbs Ferry Middle School
505 Broadway, Dobbs Ferry NY 10522
MYP Coordinator Jennifer Hickey
Languages English
T: +1 914 693 7640
W: www.dfsd.org/ms

Durand Eastman Intermediate School
95 Point Pleasant Road, Rochester NY 14622
PYP Coordinator Kathleen VanEps
Languages English
T: +1 585 339 1350
W: www.eastiron.org/schools/de

DWIGHT SCHOOL
291 Central Park West, New York NY 10024
CP Coordinator Jaya Bhavnani
DP Coordinator Liz Hutton
MYP Coordinator Shelby Levin
PYP Coordinator Brittany Dallal
Languages English
T: +1 212 724 6360
E: admissions@dwight.edu
W: www.dwight.edu
See full details on page 500

East Irondequoit Middle School
155 Densmore Road, Rochester NY 14609
MYP Coordinator Terry Reynolds
Languages English
T: +1 585 339 1586
W: www.eastiron.org

East Middle School
167 E Frederick Street, Binghamton NY 13904
MYP Coordinator Mark Ward
Languages English
T: +1 607 762 8300
W: www.binghamtonschools.org

Eastridge High School
2350 East Ridge Road, Rochester NY 14622
CP Coordinator Andrew Walter
DP Coordinator Terry Reynolds
Languages English
T: +1 585 339 1450
W: www.eicsd.k12.ny.us

EF ACADEMY NEW YORK
582 Columbus Avenue, Thornwood NY 10594
DP Coordinator Gabriela Deambrosio
Languages English
T: +1 914 495 6028
E: iaadmissionsny@ef.com
W: www.ef.edu/academy
See full details on page 503

FRENCH-AMERICAN SCHOOL OF NEW YORK
320 East Boston Post Road, Mamaroneck NY 10543
DP Coordinator Françoise Monier
Languages English, French
T: +1 914 250 0000
E: admissions@fasny.org
W: www.fasny.org
See full details on page 508

Global Community Charter School
2350 Fifth Avenue, New York NY 10037
PYP Coordinator Marisa Gaudiosi
Languages English
T: +1 646 360 2363
W: www.globalcommunitycs.org

Greenville Central School District
Route 81, PO Box 129, Greenville NY 12083
DP Coordinator Kendall Fritze
Languages English
T: +1 518 966 5190
W: www.greenville.k12.ny.us

Harlem Village Academies High
35 West 124th Street, New York NY 10027
DP Coordinator Meredith Dryden
Languages English
T: +1 646 812 9200
W: www.harlemvillageacademies.org/high-school

Harrison High School
255 Union Avenue, Harrison NY 10528
DP Coordinator Christopher Tyler
Languages English
T: +1 914 630 3095
W: www.harrisoncsd.org

Hauppauge High School
PO Box 6006, Hauppauge NY 11788
DP Coordinator Ellen Ryan
Languages English
T: +1 631 761 8302
W: www.hauppauge.k12.ny.us

Helendale Road Primary School
220 Helendale Road, Rochester NY 14609
PYP Coordinator Cheryl Jakobovic
Languages English
T: +1 585 339 1330
W: www.eastiron.org/schools/hr

Highview School
200 North Central Avenue, Hartsdale NY 10530
PYP Coordinator Erin Power
Languages English
T: +1 914 946 6946
W: www.greenburgh.k12.ny.us

Hilton High School
400 East Avenue, Hilton NY 14468
DP Coordinator Tim Ackroyd
MYP Coordinator Steve Cudzilo
Languages English
T: +1 585 392 1000

Horizons-on-the-Hudson Magnet School
137 Montgomery Street, Newburgh NY 12550
PYP Coordinator Robert Glowacki
Languages English
T: +1 845 563 3725
W: horizons.newburghschools.org

International School of Brooklyn
477 Court Street, Brooklyn, New York NY 11231
MYP Coordinator Katie Rogers
PYP Coordinator Muriel Stallworth
Languages English, French, Spanish
T: +1 718 369 3023
W: www.isbrooklyn.org

Ivan Green Primary School
800 Brown Road, Rochester NY 14622
PYP Coordinator Allison Pryor
Languages English
T: +1 585 339 1310
W: www.eastiron.org/schools/ig

James A Beneway High School
6200 Ontario Center Road, Ontario Center NY 14520
DP Coordinator Ryan VanAllen
Languages English
T: +1 315 524 1050
W: www.wayne.k12.ny.us

John Adams High School
101-01 Rockaway Blvd, Ozone Park NY 11417
DP Coordinator Jennifer Finkel
Languages English
T: +1 718 322 0500
W: www.johnadamsnyc.org

Jordan-Elbridge Middle School
19 N. Chappell Street, Jordan NY 13080
MYP Coordinator Paul Farfaglia
Languages English
T: +1 315 689 8520
W: www.jecsd.org

Joseph C Wilson Foundation Academy
200 Genesee Street NY 14611
MYP Coordinator Lori Locker
Languages English
T: +1 585 463 4100
W: secondary.rcsdk12.org/wilsoncommencement/site

Joseph C Wilson Magnet High School
501 Genesee Street, Rochester NY 14611
DP Coordinator Theresa Sarkis-Kruse
MYP Coordinator Nickole Lobdell
Languages English
T: +1 585 328 3440
W: www.rcsdk12.org/wilsoncommencement

Kenmore East High School
350 Fries Road, Tonawanda NY 14150
DP Coordinator Paul Lasch
Languages English
T: +1 716 874 8402
W: www.kenton.k12.ny.us/kentonkehs

Kenmore West High School
33 Highland Parkway, Buffalo NY 14223
DP Coordinator Laura Howse Howse
Languages English
T: +1 716 874 8401
W: www.kenton.k12.ny.us/kentonkwhs

Khalil Gibran International Academy
362 Schermerhorn Street, Brooklyn NY 11217
DP Coordinator Jennifer DeFilippo
Languages English
T: +1 718 237 2502
W: www.teachingandlearning.net

Kildonan
425 Morse Hill Road, Amenia NY 12501
MYP Coordinator John Dunford Jr.
Languages English
T: +1 845 373 8111
W: www.kildonan.org

Knowledge & Power Preparatory Academy (KAPPA) International
500 East Fordham Road, Bronx, New York NY 10458
DP Coordinator Samantha Heiderscheid
Languages English
T: +1 718 933 1247

LA SCUOLA D'ITALIA GUGLIELMO MARCONI
12 East 96th Street, New York NY 10021
DP Coordinator Dr. Beatrice Paladini
Languages English, Italian
T: +1 212 369 3290
E: admissions@lascuoladitalia.org
W: www.lascuoladitalia.org
See full details on page 517

Laurelton Pardee Intermediate School
600 Pardee Road, Rochester NY 14609
PYP Coordinator Jason Dejohn
Languages English
T: +1 585 339 1370
W: www.eastiron.org/schools/lp

Lee F Jackson Elementary School
2 Saratoga Road, White Plains NY 10607
PYP Coordinator Valarie Williams
Languages English
T: +1 914 948 2992
W: www.greenburgh.k12.ny.us

LÉMAN MANHATTAN PREPARATORY SCHOOL
41 Broad Street, New York NY 10004
DP Coordinator Ms. Lucy Alexander
Languages English
T: +1 212 232 0266
E: admissions@lemanmanhattan.org
W: www.lemanmanhattan.org
See full details on page 519

Link IB World School
51 Red Hill Road, New City NY 10956
PYP Coordinator Lauren Haugh
Languages English
T: +1 845 6243494
W: www.ccsd.edu/Domain/11

Locust Valley High School
99 Horse Hollow Road, Locust Valley NY 11560
DP Coordinator Angela Manzo
Languages English
T: +1 516 277 5105
W: www.lvcsd.k12.ny.us

Long Beach High School
322 Lagoon Drive West, Lido Beach NY 11561
DP Coordinator Christine Graham
Languages English
T: +1 516 897 2013
W: www.lbeach.org

Long Beach Middle School
239 Lido Boulevard, Lido Beach NY 11561
MYP Coordinator Eliot Lewin
Languages English
T: +1 516 897 2162
W: www.lbeach.org

LYCEUM KENNEDY FRENCH AMERICAN SCHOOL
225 East 43rd Street, New York NY 10017
DP Coordinator Dr. Vera Pohland
Languages French, English
T: +1 212 681 1877
E: lkadmissions@lyceumkennedy.org
W: www.lyceumkennedy.org
See full details on page 522

Massena Central High School
84 Nightengale Avenue, Massena NY 13662
DP Coordinator Jan Normile
Languages English
T: +1 315 764 3710
W: mcs.k12.ny.us

Merton Williams Middle School
200 School Lane, Hilton NY 14468
MYP Coordinator Steve Cudzilo
Languages English
T: +1 585 392 1000 (EXT: 30)
W: www.hilton.k12.ny.us/merton-williams.htm

Millbrook High School
70 Church Street, Millbrook NY 12545
DP Coordinator Georgia Herring
Languages English
T: +1 845 677 2510
W: millbrookcsd.org/highschool

Mott Hall Bronx High School
1595 Bathgate Avenue, Bronx, New York NY 10457
DP Coordinator Catherine Friesen
Languages English
T: +1 718 466 6800

MOTT HALL SCIENCE AND TECHNOLOGY ACADEMY
250 East 164th Street, Bronx, New York NY 10456
MYP Coordinator Ms. Yoshie Otomo
Languages English, Spanish
T: +1 718 293 4017
E: MHSTAIB@motthallsta.org
W: www.motthallsta.org
See full details on page 529

North Shore High School
450 Glen Cove Avenue, Glen Head NY 11545
DP Coordinator Kerri Titone
Languages English
T: +1 516 277 7801
W: www.northshoreschools.org

Northport High School
154 Laurel Hill Road, Northport NY 11768
DP Coordinator Wayne Jensen
Languages English
T: +1 631 262 6654
W: web.northport.k12.ny.us/NorthportHigh.cfm

Northwood Elementary School
433 North Greece Road, Hilton NY 14468
MYP Coordinator Kirk Ashton
Languages English
T: +1 585 392 1000 EXT:45
W: hilton.k12.ny.us/northwood.htm

Odyssey Academy
750 Maiden Lane, Rochester NY 14615
DP Coordinator Orlando Marrero
Languages English
T: +1 585 966 5200
W: www.greece.k12.ny.us/odyssey.cfm

Palmyra-Macedon High School
151 Hyde Parkway, Palmyra NY 14454
DP Coordinator Pamela Wagner
MYP Coordinator Pamela Wagner
Languages English
T: +1 315 597 3420
W: www.palmaccsd.org/high.cfm

Palmyra-Macedon Middle School
163 Hyde Parkway, Palmyra NY 14522
MYP Coordinator Pamela Wagner
Languages English
T: +1 315 597 3450
W: www.palmaccsd.org/Middle.cfm

Pelham Middle School
28 Franklin Place, Pelham NY 10803
MYP Coordinator Sean Llewellyn
Languages English
T: +1 914 738 8190
W: pms.pelhamschools.org

Pierson High School
200 Jermain Avenue, Sag Harbor NY 11963
DP Coordinator Michael Edward Guinan
Languages English
T: +1 631 725 5302
W: www.sagharborschools.org

Pine Street School
25 Pine Street, New York NY 10005
PYP Coordinator Jefferson Smith
Languages English, Spanish, Mandarin
T: +1 212 235 2325
W: www.pinestreetschool.com

Port Chester High School
One Tamarack Road, Port Chester NY 10573
DP Coordinator Juan Sanchez
Languages English
T: +1 914 934 7950
W: shs.portchesterschools.org/home.aspx

Portledge School
355 Duck Pond Road, Locust Valley NY 11560-2499
DP Coordinator Trish Rigg
Languages English
T: +1 516 750 3100
W: www.portledge.org

Putnam Valley High School
146 Peekskill Hollow Road, Putnam Valley NY 10579
DP Coordinator Vincent DeGregorio
Languages English
T: +1 845 526 7847
W: pvcsd.org/index.php/hs

Queensbury High School
409 Aviation Rd, Queensbury NY 12804
DP Coordinator Marnie DeJohn
Languages English
T: +1 518 824 4601
W: www.queensburyschool.org

Quest Elementary School
225 West Ave, Hilton NY 14468
PYP Coordinator Andrea Geglia
Languages English
T: +1 585 392 1000 (6100)
W: www.hilton.k12.ny.us/QE.htm

Red Hook Central High School
103 West Market Street, Red Hook NY 12571
DP Coordinator Michael McCrudden
Languages English
T: +1 845 758 2241 EXT3247
W: www.redhookcentralschools.org

Richard J Bailey Elementary School
33 West Hillside Avenue, White Plains NY 10607
PYP Coordinator Lenore Rotanelli
Languages English
T: +1 914 948 2992
W: bailey.greenburghcsd.org/pages/richard_j__bailey_school

Saint Edmund Preparatory High School
2474 Ocean Avenue, Brooklyn, New York NY 11229
DP Coordinator Kate Jones
Languages English
T: +1 718 743 6100
W: www.stedmundprep.org

Schenectady High School
1445 The Plaza, Schenectady NY 12308
DP Coordinator Patricia Embree
Languages English
T: +1 518 370 8190

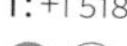

Somers High School
PO Box 620, 120 Primrose Street, Lincolndale NY 10540
DP Coordinator Alison Scanlon
Languages English
T: +1 914 248 8585
W: www.somersschools.org/domain/8

South Side High School
140 Shepherd Street, Rockville Centre NY 11570
DP Coordinator Elizabeth Nisler
Languages English
T: +1 516 255 8834
W: www.sshs.rvcschools.org

South Side Middle School
67 Hillside Avenue, Rockville Centre NY 11570
MYP Coordinator Darcy Gilchrist
Languages English
T: +1 516 255 8978
W: www.edline.net/pages/southside_middle_school

Stanley Makowski Early Childhood Center
1095 Jefferson Avenue, Buffalo NY 14208
PYP Coordinator Dawn DiNatale
Languages English
T: +1 716 816 4180

The British International School of New York
20 Waterside Plaza, New York NY 10010
MYP Coordinator Ann Marie Hourigan
PYP Coordinator Alicia Gibson
Languages English
T: +1 212 481 2700
W: www.bis-ny.org

The Brooklyn Latin School
325 Bushwick Ave, 4th floor, Brooklyn, New York NY 11206
DP Coordinator Michelle Capasso
Languages English
T: +1 718 366 0154
W: www.brooklynlatinschool.org

The Clinton School
10 East 15th Street, New York NY 10003
DP Coordinator Lauren Pournaras
Languages English
T: +1 212 524 4360
W: theclintonschool.net

The High School for Enterprise, Business, and Technology
850 Grand St, Brooklyn NY 11211
DP Coordinator Erwin Lara
Languages English, Spanish
T: +1 718 387 2800
W: www.ebtbrooklyn.com

Thomas J Corcoran High School
919 Glenwood Avenue, Syracuse NY 13207
DP Coordinator Carrianne Kirby
Languages English
T: +1 315 435 4321
W: www.syracusecityschools.com

United Nations International School
24-50 Franklin D Roosevelt Drive, New York NY 10010
DP Coordinator Luz Garcelon
Languages English
T: +1 212 684 7400
W: www.unis.org

Vestal High School
205 Woodlawn Drive, Vestal NY 13850
DP Coordinator Sally Lowenstein
Languages English
T: +1 607 757 2281
W: www.vestal.stier.org/highschool_home.aspx/

Victor Central High School
953 High Street, Victor NY 14564
DP Coordinator Karl Dubash
Languages English
T: +1 585 924 3252
W: www.victorschools.org

Village Elementary School
100 School Lane, Hilton NY 14468
MYP Coordinator Steve Cudzilo
Languages English
T: +1 585 392 1000 (EXT: 51)
W: www.hilton.k12.ny.us

West Islip High School
1 Lions Path, West Islip NY 11795
DP Coordinator James Gilmartin
Languages English
T: +1 631 893 3250
W: www.wi.k12.ny.us

West Middle School
West Middle Avenue, Binghamton NY 13905
MYP Coordinator Mark Ward
Languages English
T: +1 607 763 8400
W: www.binghamtonschools.org

WESTLAKE MIDDLE SCHOOL
825 West Lake Drive, Thornwood NY 10594
MYP Coordinator Dr. Susan Cowles-Dumitru
Languages English
T: +1 914 769 8540
E: amungioli@mtplcsd.org
W: wms.mtplcsd.org

See full details on page 559

Woodlands Middle School
475 West Hartsdale Avenue, Hartsdale NY 10570
MYP Coordinator Katherine Tovar
Languages English
T: +1 914 761 6052
W: www.greenburghcsd.org/domain/157

Yonkers Middle/High School
150 Rockland Avenue, Yonkers NY 10705
DP Coordinator Marcella Lentine
Languages English
T: +1 914 376 8191
W: www.yonkerspublicschools.org/ymhs

Young Diplomats Magnet Academy
134 West 122nd Street, New York NY 10473
PYP Coordinator Iffat Hossain
Languages English, French
T: +1 212 678 2908
W: www.ps242.com

North Carolina

Albemarle Road Middle School
6900 Democracy Drive, Charlotte NC 28212
MYP Coordinator Kimberly Lynch
Languages English
T: +1 980 343 6420

Ben L Smith High School
2407 South Holden Road, Greensboro NC 27407
DP Coordinator Margaret Powers
Languages English
T: +1 336 294 7300
W: smith.gcsnc.com/pages/Smith_High

Broughton Magnet High School
723 St Mary's Street, Raleigh NC 27605
DP Coordinator David Brooks
Languages English
T: +1 919 856 7810
W: www.wcpss.net/broughtonhs

Burton Magnet Elementary School
1500 Mathison Street, Durham NC 27701
PYP Coordinator Amy Sanchez
Languages English
T: +1 919 560 3908
W: burton.dpsnc.net

Cedar Ridge High School
1125 New Grady Brown School Rd, Hillsborough NC 27278
DP Coordinator Crystal Medlin
Languages English
T: +1 919 245 4000
W: www.orange.k12.nc.us/crhs

Charlotte Country Day School
1440 Carmel Road, Charlotte NC 28226
DP Coordinator Stewart Peery
Languages English
T: 0017049434500
W: www.charlottecountryday.org

Clyde Erwin Elementary Magnet School
323 New River Drive, Jacksonville NC 28540
PYP Coordinator Amanda Reopelle
Languages English
T: +1 910 347 1261
W: clydeerwin.nc.oce.schoolinsites.com

Coddle Creek Elementary School
141 Frank's Crossing Loop, Mooresville NC 28115
PYP Coordinator Lindsey Mehall
Languages English
T: +1 704 439 4077
W: www.iss.k12.nc.us/coddlecreek

Concord High School
481 Burrage Road NE, Concord NC 28025
DP Coordinator Marie Deal
MYP Coordinator Marie Deal
Languages English
T: +1 704 786 4161
W: www.cabarrus.k12.nc.us/concordhs

Cotswold Elementary School
300 Greenwich Road, Charlotte NC 28211
PYP Coordinator Debra Grimm
Languages English
T: +1 980 343 6720
W: schools.cms.k12.nc.us/cotswoldes

East Garner Magnet Middle School
6301 Jones Sausage Road, Garner NC 27529
MYP Coordinator Joanne Edwards
Languages English
T: +1 919 662 2339
W: www.wcpss.net/eastgarnerms

East Mecklenburg High School
6800 Monroe Road, Charlotte NC 28212
CP Coordinator Heather Hays
DP Coordinator Heather Hays
MYP Coordinator Heather Hays
Languages English
T: +1 980 343 6430
W: schools.cms.k12.nc.us/eastmecklenburghs

Enloe Magnet High School
128 Clarendon Crescent, Raleigh NC 27610
DP Coordinator April Hoffman
Languages English
T: +1 919 856 7918
W: www.wcpss.net/enloehs

Farmington Woods Elementary School
1413 Hampton Valley Road, Cary NC 27511
PYP Coordinator Anna Norris Goodrum
Languages English
T: +1 919 460 3469

Ferndale Middle School
701 Ferndale Blvd, High Point NC 27262
MYP Coordinator Nicole Beaulieu
Languages English
T: +1 336 819 2855
W: ferndale.gcsnc.com/pages/Ferndale_Middle

Fox Road Magnet Elementary School
7101 Fox Road, Raleigh NC 27616
PYP Coordinator Martha Hayes
Languages English
T: +1 919 850 8845
W: www.wcpss.net/foxroades

Garner Magnet High School
2101 Spring Drive, Garner NC 27529
DP Coordinator Jon Sherwin
MYP Coordinator Amy Bennett
Languages English
T: +1 919 662 2379
W: www.wcpss.net/garnerhs

Grimsley High School
801 Westover Terrace, Greensboro NC 27408
DP Coordinator Ben Barnard
Languages English
T: +1 336 370 8184

Hairston Middle School
3911 Naco Road, Greensboro NC 27401
MYP Coordinator Shonda Foster
Languages English
T: +1 336 378 8280
W: hairston.gcsnc.com/pages/hairston_middle

Harding University High School
2001 Alleghany Street, Charlotte NC 28208
DP Coordinator Chemier Bufford
MYP Coordinator Chemier Bufford
Languages English
T: +1 980 343 6007
W: www.cms.k12.nc.us

Hickory Day School
2535 21st Ave NE, Hickory NC 28601
PYP Coordinator Alison Tompkins
Languages English
T: +1 828 256 9492
W: www.hickoryday.org

Hickory High School
1234 3rd St NE, Hickory NC 28601
DP Coordinator Amy Baker
Languages English
T: +1 828 322 5860
W: hickoryhigh.hickoryschools.net

High Point Central High School
801 Ferndale Blvd., High Point NC 27262
DP Coordinator Susan Grace Easton Fleenor
Languages English
T: +1 336 819 2825
W: www.gcsnc.com/high_point_central_high

Hillside High School
3727 Fayetteville Street, Durham NC 27707
DP Coordinator Angelia Euba McKoy
MYP Coordinator Keshetta Henderson
Languages English
T: +1 919 560 3925
W: www.hillside.dpsnc.net

Huntingtowne Farms Elementary School
2520 Huntingtowne Farms Lane, Charlotte NC 28210
PYP Coordinator Nancy Bullard
Languages English
T: +1 980 343 3625
W: www.cms.k12.nc.us/allschools/huntingtownefarms/

J. N. Fries Magnet Middle School
133 Stonecrest Circle, Concord NC 28027
MYP Coordinator Shanna Turner-Meehan
Languages English
T: +1 704 788 4140
W: www.cabarrus.k12.nc.us/fries

J.Y. Joyner Magnet Elementary School
2300 Lowden Street, Raleigh NC 27608
PYP Coordinator Sheryl Davis
Languages English, Spanish
T: +1 919 856 7650
W: www.wcpss.net/joyneres

Jacksonville High School
1021 Henderson Drive, Jacksonville NC 28540
CP Coordinator Beth Bailey
DP Coordinator Amber Lumley
Languages English
T: +1 910 989 2048
W: www.onslow.k12.nc.us/jhs

James E. Shepard Magnet Middle
2401 Dakota Street, Durham NC 27707
MYP Coordinator Patrice Fletcher
Languages English
T: +1 919 560 3938
W: www.dpsnc.net/shepard

JM Alexander Middle School
12010 Hambright Road, Huntersville NC 28078
MYP Coordinator Mary Kendrick
Languages English
T: +1 980 343 3830
W: schools.cms.k12.nc.us/jmalexanderms

John T. Hoggard High School
4305 Shipyard Boulevard, Wilmington NC 28403
DP Coordinator Christi Lea
Languages English
T: +1 910 350 2072
W: www.nhcs.net/hoggard

Kinston High School
2601 North Queen Street, Kinston NC 28501
DP Coordinator Joshua Bridges
Languages English
T: +1 252 527 8067

Lansdowne Elementary School
6400 Prett Court, Charlotte NC 28270
PYP Coordinator Robin Blacker
Languages English
T: +1 980 343 6733
W: schools.cms.k12.nc.us/lansdownees

Lee County High School
1708 Nash Street, Sanford NC 27330
DP Coordinator Wendy Bryan
Languages English
T: +1 919 776 7541
W: www.lee.k12.nc.us/Domain/17

Legette Blythe Elementary School
12202 Hambright Rd, Huntersville NC 28078
PYP Coordinator Erik Hoover
Languages English
T: +1 980 343 5770
W: schools.cms.k12.nc.us/blythees

Marie G. Davis K-8 School
3351 W Griffith St., Charlotte NC 28203
PYP Coordinator Sallie Davis
Languages English
T: +1 980 343 0006
W: mariegdavis.wearecms.com

Marvin Ridge High School
2825 Crane Road, Waxhaw NC 28173
DP Coordinator Lindsey Arant
Languages English
T: +1 704 290 1520
W: mrhs.ucps.k12.nc.us

Millbrook High School
2201 Spring Forest Road, Raleigh NC 27615
DP Coordinator Loren Baron
MYP Coordinator Ashley Davis
Languages English
T: +1 919 850 8787
W: mhs.wcpss.net

Morganton Day School
305 West Concord Street, Morganton NC 28655
PYP Coordinator Teresa Cape
Languages English
T: +1 828 437 6782
W: www.morgantondayschool.com

Mount Mourne School
1431 Mecklenburg Highway, Mooresville NC 28115
MYP Coordinator Elisabeth White
Languages English
T: +1 704 892 4711
W: www.iss.k12.nc.us/domain/1964

Myers Park High School
2400 Colony Road, Charlotte NC 28209
DP Coordinator Katie Willett
MYP Coordinator Katie Willett
Languages English
T: +1 704 343 5800
W: www.tolerancematters.org

North Mecklenburg High School
11201 Old Statesville Road, Huntersville NC 28078
DP Coordinator Amy Pasko
MYP Coordinator Amy Pasko
Languages English
T: +1 980 343 3840

Northview School
625 Carolina Avenue, Statesville NC 28677
MYP Coordinator Elisabeth White
Languages English
T: +1 704 873 7354
W: www.iss.k12.nc.us/domain/1227

Northwood Elementary School
818 W Lexington Avenue, High Point NC 27262
PYP Coordinator Iris Ellington
Languages English
T: +1 336 819 2920
W: www.gcsnc.com

Northwoods Park Middle School
904 Sioux Drive, Jacksonville NC 28540
MYP Coordinator Shanta' Cooks
Languages English
T: +1 910 347 1202
W: northwoodspark.nc.ocm.schoolinsites.com

Paisley Magnet School
1400 Grant Street, Winston-Salem NC 27105
MYP Coordinator Amy Pantano
Languages English
T: +1 336 727 2775
W: www.paisleyms.org

Parkland High School
1600 Brewer Road, Winston-Salem NC 27127
CP Coordinator Laurel Lokant
DP Coordinator Laurel Lokant
Languages English
T: +1 336 771 4700
W: www.parklandmagneths.com

Phoenix Academy
7847 Clinard Farms Road, High Point NC 27265
MYP Coordinator Michelle Hawthorne
Languages English
T: 3368481870
W: www.pahp.com

Piedmont Open Middle School
1241 East 10th Street, Charlotte NC 28204
MYP Coordinator Maranda Thornburg
Languages English
T: +1 980 343 5435
W: www.cms.k12.nc.us/allschools/piedmont/index.htm

Ralph L Fike High School
500 Harrison Drive, Wilson NC 27893
DP Coordinator Rhonda Meszaros
Languages English
T: +1 252 399 7905

Randolph Middle School
4400 Water Oak Road, Charlotte NC 28211
MYP Coordinator Sarah Graboyes
Languages English
T: +1 980 343 6700
W: www.cms.k12.nc.us

Ranson Middle School
5850 Statesville Road, Charlotte NC 28269
MYP Coordinator Shanniska Howard
Languages English
T: +1 980 343 6800
W: schools.cms.k12.nc.us/ransonMS/Pages/Default.aspx

Reidsville High School
1901 South Park Drive, Reidsville NC 27320
DP Coordinator Wayne Knight
Languages English
T: +1 336 349 6361
W: www.rock.k12.nc.us

Rocky Mount High School
1400 Bethlehem Road, Rocky Mount NC 27803
DP Coordinator Michael Morris
Languages English
T: +1 252 977 3085
W: rmhs.nrms.org

Smith Magnet Elementary School
1101 Maxwell Drive, Raleigh NC 27603
PYP Coordinator Kellie Vanek
Languages English
T: +1 919 662 2458
W: smithes.wcpss.net

Smithfield-Selma High School
700 Booker Dairy Rd., Smithfield NC 27577
DP Coordinator Cynthia Hutchings
Languages English
T: +1 919 934 5191
W: johnston.k12.nc.us/sss

South Iredell High School
299 Old Mountain Road, Statesville NC 28677
CP Coordinator Rachael Moyer
DP Coordinator Rachael Moyer
MYP Coordinator Nicole Jones
Languages English
T: +1 704 528 4536
W: iss.schoolwires.com/southhigh/site/default.asp

South View High School
4184 Elk Road, Cumberland County, Hope Mills NC 28348
DP Coordinator Dawn Curle
Languages English
T: +1 910 425 8181

Speas Global Elementary School
2000 W. Polo Road, Winston-Salem NC 27106
PYP Coordinator Katryna Jacober
Languages English, Spanish
T: +1 336 703 4135
W: www.wsfcs.k12.nc.us/domain/5628

Statesville Road Elementary
5833 Milhaven Road, Charlotte NC 28213
PYP Coordinator Susan Patterson
Languages English
T: +1 980 343 6815
W: www.cms.k12.nc.us/allschools/statesvillerd

The British International School of Charlotte
7000 Endhaven Lane, Charlotte NC 28277
DP Coordinator Julie Tombs
Languages English
T: +1 704 341 3236
W: www.britishschoolofcharlotte.org

The Montessori School of Raleigh
408 Andrews Chapel Road, Durham NC 27703
DP Coordinator Kevin McLean
Languages English, Spanish
T: +1 919 848 1545
W: msr.org

Waldo C Falkener IB Elementary School
3931 Naco Road, Greensboro NC 27401
PYP Coordinator Kinza Brechka
Languages English
T: +1 336 370 8150
W: www.gcsnc.com

Walter Hines Page High School
201 Alma Pinnix Drive, Greensboro NC 27405
DP Coordinator Liana Blue
Languages English
T: +1 336 370 8200
W: www.gcsnc.com/page

Walter M. Williams High School
1307 South Church Street, Burlington NC 27215-4919
DP Coordinator Neil Schledorn
Languages English, Spanish
T: +1 336 570 6161
W: www.abss.k12.nc.us/wwh

Weddington Hills Elementary School
4401 Weddington Rd, Concord NC 28027
PYP Coordinator Mary Hooks
Languages English
T: +1 704 795 9385
W: www.cabarrus.k12.nc.us

West Charlotte High School
2219 Senior Drive, Charlotte NC 28216
DP Coordinator LaDawna Robinson
Languages English
T: +1 980 343 6060
W: www.cms.k12.nc.us/allschools/westchar

Ohio

Bassett Elementary School
2155 Bassett Road, Westlake OH 44145
PYP Coordinator Deb Wadden
Languages English
T: +1 440 835 6330
W: www.wlake.org/our-schools/bassett-elementary

Beaumont School
3301 North Park Boulevard, Cleveland Heights OH 44118
DP Coordinator Ann Hoelzel
Languages English
T: +1 216 321 2954
W: www.beaumontschool.org

Boulevard Elementary School
14900 Drexmore Road, Shaker Heights OH 44120
PYP Coordinator Jennifer Goulden
Languages English
T: +1 216 295 4020
W: www.shaker.org/boulevardschool_home.aspx

Campus International High School
3100 Chester Ave, Cleveland OH 44114
DP Coordinator Sarah Schneider
MYP Coordinator Maria Vazquez-Listenbee
Languages English
T: +1 216 838 8100
W: www.clevelandmetroschools.org/cihs

Campus International School
3000 Euclid Ave, Cleveland OH 44115
MYP Coordinator Sheila Orourke
PYP Coordinator Sheila Orourke
Languages English
T: +1 216 431 2225
W: www.csuohio.edu/campusinternational

Canterbury Elementary School
2530 Canterbury Road, Cleveland Heights OH 44118
PYP Coordinator Melissa Garcar Garcar
T: +1 216 371 7470
W: www.chuh.org/canterburyelementary_home.aspx
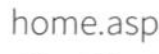

Case Elementary School
400 W. Market St., Akron OH 44303
PYP Coordinator Jennifer Victor
Languages English
T: +1 330 873 3350
W: akronschools.com/school/Case+Elementary

Central Academy of Ohio
2727 Kenwood Blvd, Toledo OH 43606
PYP Coordinator Karen Rayner
Languages English
T: +1 419 205 9800
W: www.ohiocentralacademy.net

IB AMERICAS

Columbus Alternative High School
2632 McGuffey Road, Columbus OH 43211
DP Coordinator Alice Webb
Languages English
T: +1 614 365 6006
W: www.cahs.ccsoh.us

Discovery School
855 Millsboro Rd, Mansfield OH 44903
PYP Coordinator Simon Clark
Languages English
T: +1 419 756 8880
W: www.discovery-school.net

Dublin Coffman High School
6780 Coffman Road, Dublin OH 43107-1099
DP Coordinator Eric Bringardner
Languages English
T: +1 614 764 5900
W: www.dublincoffman.com

Dublin Jerome High School
8300 Hyland-Croy Road, Dublin OH 43016
DP Coordinator Karen Kendall-Sperry
Languages English
T: +1 614 873 7377
W: www.dublinjerome.net

Dublin Scioto High School
400 Hard Road, Dublin OH 43016-8349
DP Coordinator Eric Bringardner
Languages English
T: +1 614 718 8300
W: scioto.dublin.k12.oh.us

Eastwood Elementary School
198 East College Street, Oberlin OH 44074
PYP Coordinator Cheryl Lawrie
Languages English
T: +1 440 775 3473
W: eastwood.oberlinschools.net

Fairfax Elementary School
3150 Fairfax Road, Cleveland Heights OH 44118
PYP Coordinator Leslie Garrett
Languages English
T: +1 216 371 7480
W: www.chuh.org

Fairmont High School
3301 Shroyer Road, Kettering OH 45429
DP Coordinator Darren McGarvey
Languages English
T: +1 937 499 1601
W: www.kettering.k12.oh.us

Fernway Elementary School
17420 Fernway Road, Shaker Heights OH 44120
PYP Coordinator Jean Reinhold
Languages English
T: +1 216 295 4040
W: shaker.org/about/schools/elementary/fernway/

Firestone High School
333 Rampart Avenue, Akron OH 44313
DP Coordinator Judith Harrison
Languages English
T: +1 330 873 3315
W: www.akron.k12.oh.us

GlenOak High School
1801 Schneider Street NE, Canton OH 44721
DP Coordinator Emily Palmer
Languages English
T: +1 330 491 3800
W: www.plainlocal.org/17/home

Kent State University Child Development Center
775 Loop Rd., Kent OH 44242
PYP Coordinator Rochelle Hostler
Languages English
T: +1 330 672 2559
W: www.kent.edu/ehhs/centers/cdc

Lakewood Catholic Academy
14808 Lake Avenue, Lakewood OH 44107
MYP Coordinator Eileen Murphy
Languages English
T: +1 216 521 0559
W: www.lakewoodcatholicacademy.com

Langston Middle School
150 North Pleasant Street, Oberlin OH 44074
MYP Coordinator Kristin Miller
Languages English, Spanish, Mandarin
T: +1 440 775 7961
W: langston.oberlinschools.net

Litchfield Middle School
470 Castle Blvd, Akron OH 44313
MYP Coordinator Sandra Cline
Languages English
T: +1 330 761 2775
W: www.akronschools.com

Lomond Elementary School
17917 Lomond Boulevard, Shaker Heights OH 44122
PYP Coordinator Shifa Isaacs
Languages English
T: +1 216 295 4050
W: www.shaker.org

McKinley Elementary School
602 Plum Street, Fairport Harbor OH 44077
PYP Coordinator Sabrina Rowan
Languages English
T: +1 440 354 5400
W: www.fhevs.org/mckinley

Mercer Elementary School
23325 Wimbledon Road, Shaker Heights OH 44122
PYP Coordinator Maria Baker
Languages English
T: +1 216 295 4070
W: www.shaker.org

Monticello Middle School
3665 Monticello Blvd., Cleveland Heights OH 44121
MYP Coordinator Leslie Garrett
Languages English
T: +1 216 371 6520
W: chuh.org/schools/monticello

Notre Dame Academy, OH
3535 W Sylvania Avenue, Toledo OH 43623
DP Coordinator Angela Joseph
Languages English
T: +1 419 475 9359
W: www.nda.org

Oberlin High School
281 North Pleasant Street, Oberlin OH 44074
DP Coordinator Rebecca Lahetta
MYP Coordinator Kristin Miller
Languages English
T: +1 440 774 1295
W: ohs.oberlinschools.net

Onaway Elementary School
15600 Parkland Boulevard, Shaker Heights OH 44120
PYP Coordinator Denise Brown
Languages English
T: +1 216 295 4080
W: www.shaker.org/onawayschool_home.aspx

Princeton High School
11080 Chester Road, Princeton City Schools, Cincinnati OH 45246
DP Coordinator Michele Ritzie
Languages English
T: +1 513 864 1500
W: www.phs.princeton.k12.oh.us

Prospect Elementary School
36 South Prospect Street, Oberlin OH 44074
PYP Coordinator Donna Shurr
Languages English
T: +1 440 774 4421
W: prospect.oberlinschools.net

Resnik Community Learning Center
65 N. Meadowcroft Dr., Akron OH 44313
PYP Coordinator Lori Wammes
Languages English, French
T: +1 330 873 3370
W: resnikclc.akronschools.com

Roxboro Elementary School
2405 Roxboro Road, Cleveland Heights OH 44106
PYP Coordinator Melissa Garcar Garcar
Languages English
T: +1 216 371 7115
W: www.chuh.org

Roxboro Middle School
2400 Roxboro Road, Cleveland Heights OH 44106
MYP Coordinator Melissa Garcar Garcar
Languages English
T: +1 216 320 3500
W: www.chuh.org

Shaker Heights High School
15911 Aldersyde Drive, Shaker Heights OH 44120
DP Coordinator John Moore
MYP Coordinator Molly Miles
Languages English
T: +1 216 295 4200
W: www.shaker.org/highschool_home.aspx

Shaker Heights Middle School
20600 Shaker Blvd, Shaker Heights OH 44122
MYP Coordinator Addie Tobey
Languages English
T: +1 216 295 4100
W: www.shaker.org/middleschool_home.aspx

Springfield High School
701 East Home Road, Springfield OH 45504
DP Coordinator Bill Slagle
Languages English
T: +1 937 342 4100
W: www.spr.k12.oh.us/

St Edward High School
13500 Detroit Avenue, Lakewood OH 44107
DP Coordinator Nicholas Kuhar
MYP Coordinator Nicholas Kuhar
Languages English
T: +1 216 221 3776
W: sehs.net

USA

Tri-County International Academy
c/o Wooster H.S., 515 Oldman Road, Wooster OH 44691
DP Coordinator Victoria Birk
Languages English
T: +1 330 345 4000 EXT:3004
W: www.ib.tricountyesc.org

Upper Arlington High School
1650 Ridgeview Road, Upper Arlington OH 43221
CP Coordinator Cynthia Ballheim
DP Coordinator Cynthia Ballheim
Languages English
T: +1 614 487 5200
W: www.uaschools.org

Westerville South High School
303 South Otterbein Avenue, Westerville OH 43081
DP Coordinator Bill Heinmiller
Languages English
T: +1 614 797 6000
W: www.wcsoh.org/south

Westlake High School
27200 Hilliard Blvd., Westlake OH 44145
DP Coordinator Matthew Planisek
Languages English
T: +1 440 250 1260
W: www.westlake.k12.oh.us

Woodbury Elementary School
15400 South Woodland Road, Shaker Heights OH 44120
MYP Coordinator Addie Tobey
Languages English
T: +1 216 295 4150
W: www.shaker.org/woodburyschool_home.aspx

Worthington Kilbourne High School
1499 Hard Road, Columbus OH 43235
DP Coordinator Jeannie Goodwin
Languages English
T: +1 614 883 2550
W: www.worthington.k12.oh.us/schools/wkhs

Oklahoma

Booker T Washington High School
1514 E. Zion St., Tulsa OK 74106
DP Coordinator Sharon Lazdins
MYP Coordinator Joyelle Payne
Languages English
T: +1 918 925 1000
W: btw.tulsaschools.org

Classen School of Advanced Studies
1901 North Elison Street, Oklahoma City OK 73106
DP Coordinator Mitch McIntosh
Languages English
T: +1 405 587 5400
W: www.okcps.org/domain/80

George Washington Carver Magnet Middle School
624 E Oklahoma Place, Tulsa OK 74106
MYP Coordinator Emily Baker
Languages English
T: +1 918 595 2939

Jenks West Elementary School
205 East B. Street, Jenks OK 74037
PYP Coordinator Cathryn McCarthy
Languages English
T: +1 918 299 4415
W: www.jenksps.org

Oregon

Bend Senior High School
230 NE 6th Street, Bend OR 97701
DP Coordinator Andria Lindsey
Languages English
T: +1 541 383 6293
W: www.bend.k12.or.us/bendhigh

Bonny Slope Elementary School
11775 NW McDaniel Road, Portland OR 97229
PYP Coordinator Jennifer Oordt
Languages English
T: +1 503 672 3775
W: www.beaverton.k12.or.us/bonny_slope

Cedar Park Middle School
11100 SW Park Way, Portland OR 97225
MYP Coordinator Amy Hattendorf
Languages English
T: +1 503 672 3620
W: www.beaverton.k12.or.us/cedar_park

Cleveland High School
3400 SE 26 Ave, Portland OR 97202
DP Coordinator Jennifer Wiandt Owens
Languages English
T: +1 503 916 5120

Dr Martin Luther King Jr Elementary School
4906 NE 6th Avenue, Portland OR 97211
PYP Coordinator Paige Thomas
Languages English
T: +1 503 916 6155
W: www.king.pps.k12.or.us

Elmonica Elementary School
16950 SW Lisa Street, Beaverton OR 97006
PYP Coordinator Kathy Leahy
Languages English
T: +1 503 356 2080
W: www.beaverton.k12.or.us/schools/elmonica

Eugene International High School
400 East 19th Avenue, Eugene OR 97401
DP Coordinator Steven Smith
Languages English
T: +1 541 687 3196
W: www.schools.4j.lane.edu/ihs/

Findley Elementary
4155 NW Saltzman Road, Portland OR 97229
PYP Coordinator Amber McLandrich
Languages English
T: +1 503 356 2100
W: www.beaverton.k12.or.us/schools/findley

French American International School
8500 NW Johnson Street, Portland OR 97229-6780
MYP Coordinator Anne Prouty
PYP Coordinator Kathlin Gabaldon
Languages English, French
T: +1 503 292 7776
W: www.faispdx.org

German International School of Portland
3900 SW Murray Blvd, Beaverton OR 97005
PYP Coordinator Stefanie Amann
Languages German, English
T: +1 503 626 9089
W: www.gspdx.org

Gresham High School
1200 North Main Street, Gresham OR 97030-3899
DP Coordinator Alan Simpson
Languages English
T: +1 503 674 5500
W: www.ghs.gresham.k12.or.us

Hillsboro High School
3285 SE Rood Bridge Road, Hillsboro OR 97123
DP Coordinator Ashley Clemens
Languages English
T: +1 503 844 1980
W: schools.hsd.k12.or.us/hilhi

Hiteon Elementary
13800 SW Brockman Road, Beaverton OR 97008
PYP Coordinator Traci Chelf
Languages English
T: +1 503 356 2140
W: www3.beaverton.k12.or.us/hiteon

International School of Beaverton
17770 SW Blanton Street, Beaverton OR 97007
DP Coordinator Amy Schuff
MYP Coordinator Kristin Hayward
Languages English
T: +1 503 259 3800
W: www.beaverton.k12.or.us/isb

Lincoln High School
1600 SW Salmon St., Portland OR 97205
DP Coordinator Kim Bliss
Languages English
T: +1 503 916 5200
W: www.pps.net/domain/136

McKinley Elementary School
1500 NW 185th Ave., Beaverton OR 97006
PYP Coordinator Michael Vieira
Languages English
T: +1 503 533 1845
W: beaverton.k12.or.us/McKinley

Meadow Park Middle School
14100 SW Downing Street, Beaverton OR 97006
MYP Coordinator Kristin Mccartney
Languages English, Spanish
T: +1 503 672 3660
W: www.beaverton.k12.or.us/meadow_park

Mountainside High School
12500 SW 175th Avenue, Beaverton OR 97007
DP Coordinator Brooke Mayo
Languages English
T: +1 503 356 3500
W: www.beaverton.k12.or.us/schools/mountainside

Nellie Muir Elementary School
1800 W Hayes St, Woodburn OR 97071
PYP Coordinator Mary Parra
Languages English, Spanish
T: +1 503 981 2670
W: woodburn.nmes.schoolfusion.us

Newport High School
322 NE Eads Street, Newport OR 97365
DP Coordinator Jody Hanna
Languages English
T: +1 541 265 9281
W: www.lincoln.k12.or.us/newporths

North Eugene High School
200 Silver Lane, Eugene OR 97404
CP Coordinator Taylor Madden
DP Coordinator Taylor Madden
Languages English
T: +1 541 790 4500
W: nehs.4j.lane.edu

Oregon Trail Academy
36520 SE Proctor Rd, Boring OR 97009
DP Coordinator Kasshawna Knoll
MYP Coordinator Erik Ofstie
PYP Coordinator Kasshawna Knoll
Languages English
T: +1 503 668 4133
W: oregontrailschools.com/ota

Pilot Butte Middle School
1501 N.E. Neff Road, Bend OR 97701
MYP Coordinator Karen Corson
Languages English
T: +1 541 355 7520
W: www.bend.k12.or.us/education/school/school.php?sectionid=97

Raleigh Park Elementary
3670 SW 78th Ave., Portland OR 97225
PYP Coordinator Stephanie Wollmuth
Languages English
T: +1 503 356 2500
W: www.beaverton.k12.or.us/schools/raleigh-park

Rex Putnam High School
4950 SE Roethe Road, Milwaukie OR 97267
DP Coordinator Traci Clarke
Languages English
T: +1 503 353 5860
W: www.nclack.k12.or.us/putnam

Ridgewood Elementary School
10100 SW Inglewood Street, Portland OR 97225
PYP Coordinator Mocalina Shearer
Languages English
T: +1 503 259 7535
W: www.beavton.k12.or.us/ridgewood

Sabin School
4013 NE 18 Avenue, Portland OR 97212
PYP Coordinator Sacha Luria
Languages English
T: +1 503 916 6181
W: www.pps.k12.or.us/schools/sabin

Seven Peaks School
19660 SW Mountaineer Way, Bend OR 97702
MYP Coordinator Hope Macauley
Languages English
T: +1 541 382 7755
W: www.sevenpeaksschool.org

Skyline School
11536 NW Skyline Blvd, Portland OR 97231
MYP Coordinator Melissa Dunn
PYP Coordinator Melissa Dunn
Languages English
T: +1 503 916 5412
W: www.pps.k12.or.us/schools/skyline

South Salem High School
1910 Church Street SE, Salem OR 97302
DP Coordinator Jennifer Harris-Clippinger
Languages English
T: +1 503 399 3252
W: www.southsaxons.com

Southridge High School
9625 SW 125th Street, Beaverton OR 97008
CP Coordinator Natalie Ballard Strauhal
DP Coordinator Celeste Colasurdo
Languages English
T: +1 503 259 5400
W: www.beavton.k12.or.us/southridge

Sunset High School
13840 NW Cornell Road, Portland OR 97229
DP Coordinator Jill Boeschenstein
Languages English
T: +1 503 259 5050

The International School
025 SW Sherman Street, Portland OR 97210
PYP Coordinator Kelly Rogers
Languages Chinese, Japanese, Spanish
T: +1 503 226 2496
W: www.intlschool.org

Tigard High School
9000 SW Durham Rd., Tigard OR 97224
DP Coordinator Michael Savage
Languages English
T: +1 503 431 5400
W: www.ttsdschools.org/ths

Tualatin High School
22300 SW Boones Ferry Rd, Tualatin OR 97062
DP Coordinator Lisa Lacy
Languages English
T: +1 503 431 5600
W: www.ttsdschools.org/tuhs

Valley Inquiry Charter School
5774 Hazel Green Road, Salem OR 97305
PYP Coordinator Jesse Payne
Languages English
T: +1 503 399 3150
W: valleyinquiry.salemkeizer.net

Vernon School
2044 N.E. Killingsworth Street, Portland OR 97211
MYP Coordinator Tarehna Wicker
PYP Coordinator Tarehna Wicker
Languages English
T: +1 503 916 6415
W: www.pps.k12.or.us/schools-c/profiles/?id=284

West Tualatin View Elementary
8800 SW Leahy Road, Portland OR 97225
PYP Coordinator Brooke Bailey
Languages English
T: +1 503 356 2510
W: www.beaverton.k12.or.us/schools/west-tv

Willamette High School
1801 Echo Hollow Road, Eugene OR 97402
DP Coordinator Jade Starr
Languages English
T: +1 541 689 0731
W: www.bethel.k12.or.us/schools/whs

Woodburn High School
1785 N Front Street, Woodburn OR 97071
DP Coordinator Doug Peterson
Languages English
T: +1 503 981 2600

Pennsylvania

Barack Obama Academy of International Studies
515 N. Highland Avenue, Pittsburg PA 15206
DP Coordinator Joseph Ehman
MYP Coordinator Michael Chapman
Languages English
T: +1 412 622 5980
W: www.pps.k12.pa.us/page/143

Boyce Middle School
1500 Boyce Road, Upper St Clair PA 15241
MYP Coordinator Christina Caragein
Languages English
T: +1 412 833 1600

Central High School
1700 W Olney Avenue, Philadelphia PA 19141
DP Coordinator Aviva Hockfield
Languages English
T: +1 215 276 5262
W: www.centralhigh.net

Chambersburg Area Senior High School
511 South Sixth Street, Chambersburg PA 17201
DP Coordinator Jennifer Michael
Languages English
T: +1 717 261 3324
W: www.chambersburg.k12.pa.us

Cumberland Valley High School
6746 Carlisle Pike, Mechanicsburg PA 17050
DP Coordinator Amy Miller
Languages English
T: +1 717 506 3454
W: www.cvschools.org

Downingtown STEM Academy
335 Manor Avenue, Downingtown PA 19335
DP Coordinator Michael Sheehan
Languages English
T: +1 610 269 8460
W: www.dasd.org

Fort Couch Middle School
515 Ft Couch Road, Upper St Clair PA 15241
MYP Coordinator Andrew Bowers
Languages English
T: +1 412 833 1600

GEORGE SCHOOL
1690 Newtown Langhorne Rd, Newtown PA 18940-2414
DP Coordinator Kim McGlynn
Languages English
T: +1 215 579 6500
E: admission@georgeschool.org
W: www.georgeschool.org
See full details on page 509

George Washington High School
10175 Bustleton Avenue, Philadelphia PA 19116
DP Coordinator Maria Pacheco
Languages English
T: +1 215 961 2001
W: www.gwhs.phila.k12.pa.us

Harrisburg Academy
10 Erford Road, Wormleysburg PA 17043
DP Coordinator Maureen Smith
Languages English
T: +1 717 763 7811
W: www.harrisburgacademy.org

Harriton High School
600 North Ithan Avenue, Rosemont PA 19010
DP Coordinator Thomas O'Brien
Languages English
T: +1 610 658 3970
W: www.lmsd.org

Hill-Freedman World Academy
6200 Crittenden Street, Philadelphia PA 19138
DP Coordinator Thomas Emerson
MYP Coordinator Pamela Taylor
Languages English
T: +1 215 276 5260
W: webgui.phila.k12.pa.us/schools/h/hill-freedman

J P McCaskey High School
445 North Reservoir St, Lancaster PA 17602
CP Coordinator Kelly White
DP Coordinator Benjamin Deardorff
Languages English
T: +1 717 291 6211
W: www.lancaster.k12.pa.us

Lehigh Valley Academy Regional Charter School
1560 Valley Center Parkway, Suite 200, Bethlehem PA 18017
CP Coordinator Andrew Hall
DP Coordinator Andrew Hall
MYP Coordinator Jacob March
PYP Coordinator Kelly Eddinger
Languages English
T: +1 610 866 9660
W: www.lvacademy.org

Manheim Township High School
PO Box 5134, School Road, Lancaster PA 17606
DP Coordinator Larry Penner
Languages English
T: +1 717 560 3097
W: www.mtwp.net

Mayfair Elementary School
3001 Princeton Avenue, Philadelphia PA 19149
MYP Coordinator Matthew Braun
PYP Coordinator Jamie Neal
Languages English
T: +1 215 400 3280
W: mayfair.philasd.org

MERCYHURST PREPARATORY SCHOOL
538 East Grandview Boulevard, Erie PA 16504
DP Coordinator Paul Cancilla
Languages English
T: +1 814 824 2323
E: mditullio@mpslakers.com
W: www.mpslakers.com
See full details on page 526

Northeast High School
Cottman & Algon Avenues, Philadelphia PA 19111
DP Coordinator Bonnie Taylor
Languages English
T: +1 215 728 5018
W: www.nehs.phila.k12.pa.us

Owen J. Roberts High School
901 Ridge Road, Pottstown PA 19465
CP Coordinator William Richardson
Languages English, Spanish
T: +1 610 469 5100
W: www.ojrsd.com

Pan American Academy Charter School
2830 North American Street, Philadelphia PA 19133
MYP Coordinator Kelly Blocker
PYP Coordinator Kelly Blocker
Languages English, Spanish
T: +1 215 425 1212
W: www.panamcs.org

Philadelphia High School for Girls
1400 West Olney Avenue, Philadelphia PA 19141-2398
DP Coordinator Megan McNamara
Languages English
T: +1 215 276 5258
W: www.phila.k12.pa.us/schools/girlshigh

School Lane Charter School
2400 Bristol Pike, Bensalem PA 19020
DP Coordinator Avni Shah
MYP Coordinator Karen Schade
Languages English
T: +1 215 245 6055
W: www.schoollane.org

State College Area High School, Pennsylvania
650 Westerly Parkway, State College PA 16801
CP Coordinator Shelly Ishler
DP Coordinator Jennifer Schreiber
Languages English
T: +1 814 231 1111
W: www.scasd.org/schighschool

Streams Elementary School
1560 Ashlawn Avenue, Upper St Clair PA 15241
PYP Coordinator Rebecca Smith
Languages English
T: +1 412 833 1600
W: www.uscsd.k12.pa.us/Domain/542

Upper St. Clair High School
1825 McLaughlin Run Road, Upper St. Clair PA 15241
DP Coordinator Tanya Chothani
MYP Coordinator Sarah Susa
Languages English
T: +1 412 833 1600
W: uscsd.k12.pa.us/Domain/59

VINCENTIAN ACADEMY
8100 McKnight Road, Pittsburgh PA 15237
DP Coordinator Leslie Robbins
Languages English
T: +1 412 364 1616
E: admissions@vincentianacademy.org
W: www.vincentianacademy.org
See full details on page 557

William W Bodine High School for International Affairs
1101 North 4th Street, Philadelphia PA 19123
DP Coordinator Kelli Mackay
Languages English
T: +1 215 351 7332
W: www.phila.k12.pa.us/schools/bodine

Woodrow Wilson Middle School
1800 Cottman Ave., Philadelphia PA 19111
MYP Coordinator Carlos Frederick
Languages English
T: +1 215 728 5015
W: webgui.phila.k12.pa.us/schools/w/wilson

York Academy Regional Charter School
32 West North Street, PO Box 1787, York PA 17401
MYP Coordinator Carol Alvarnaz
PYP Coordinator Brooke Bray
Languages English
T: +1 717 801 3900
W: www.yorkarcs.org

York County School of Technology
2179 S. Queen St., York PA 17402
CP Coordinator Jody Kessinger
Languages English
T: +1 717 741 0820
W: www.ytech.edu

Young Scholars of Central PA Charter School
1530 Westerly Parkway, State College PA 16801
MYP Coordinator Baris Yilmaz
Languages English
T: +1 814 237 9727
W: www.yscp.org

Rhode Island

International Charter School
334 Pleasant St., Pawtucket RI 02860
PYP Coordinator Michelle Johnson
Languages English
T: +1 401 721 0824
W: internationalcharterschool.org

Prout School
4640 Tower Hill Road, Wakefield RI 02879
DP Coordinator Christopher Bromley
Languages English
T: +1 401 789 9262
W: www.theproutschool.org

South Carolina

A C Flora High School
1 Falcon Drive, Columbia SC 29204
CP Coordinator Virginia Tate
DP Coordinator Virginia Tate
Languages English
T: +1 803 738 7300
W: flora.richlandone.org

Aynor High School
201 Jordanville Road, Aynor SC 29511
DP Coordinator Renee Atkinson
Languages English
T: +1 843 488 7100
W: www.horrycountyschools.net/aynor_high_school

Berkeley High School
406 West Main Street, Moncks Corner SC 29461
DP Coordinator Katherine Batkins
Languages English
T: +1 843 899 8800
W: bcsdschools.net/BHS

Buist Academy for Advanced Studies
103 Calhoun Street, Charleston SC 29401
MYP Coordinator Sara Lyle
PYP Coordinator Sara Lyle
Languages English
T: +1 843 724 7750
W: buist.ccsdschools.com

Chandler Creek Elementary School
301 Chandler Road, Greer SC 29651
PYP Coordinator Jenny Dehlinger
Languages English
T: +1 864 355 2400
W: www.greenville.k12.sc.us/ccreek/

Christ Church Episcopal School
245 Cavalier Drive, Greenville SC 29607
DP Coordinator Amanda Beckrich
PYP Coordinator Terri Garvin
Languages English
T: +1 864 299 1522
W: www.cces.org

Concord Elementary School
2701 Calrossie Road, Anderson SC 29621
PYP Coordinator Monica Loftis
Languages English
T: +1 864 260 5105
W: www.anderson5.net/concord

E. L. Wright Middle School
2740 Alpine Road, Columbia SC 29223
MYP Coordinator Mannietea Freeman
Languages English
T: +1 803 736 8740
W: www.richland2.org/elwm

Fork Shoals Elementary School
916 McKelvey Road, Pelzer SC 29669
PYP Coordinator Amy Giles
Languages English
T: +1 864 243 5680
W: www.greenville.k12.sc.us/forksh

Fort Dorchester High School
8500 Patriot Boulevard, North Charleston SC 29420
DP Coordinator Loyda McClellan
Languages English
T: +1 843 760 4450

Greer High School
3032 East Gap Creek Road, Greer SC 29651
DP Coordinator Mary Smith
Languages English
T: +1 864 355 5819
W: www.greenville.k12.sc.us/greerhs

Hartsville High School
701 Lewellyn Avenue, Hartsville SC 29550
DP Coordinator Paula Alvarez
Languages English
T: +1 843 857 3700
W: hhs.dcsdschools.org

Heritage Elementary School
1592 Geer Highway, Traveler's Rest SC 29690
PYP Coordinator Ashley LaRoche
Languages English
T: +1 864 355 6000

Hilton Head Elementary School
30 School Road, Hilton Head Island SC 29926
PYP Coordinator Karen Perdue
Languages English
T: +1 843 342 4100
W: hhe.beaufort.k12.sc.us/pages/HiltonHeadIslandElementary

Hilton Head High School
70 Wilborn Road, Beaufort, Hilton Head Island SC 29926
CP Coordinator Mary Beth White
DP Coordinator Mary Beth White
MYP Coordinator Kristen Karszes
Languages English
T: +1 843 689 4801
W: www.beaufort.k12.sc.us

Hilton Head Island Middle School
55 Wilborn Road, Hilton Head Island SC 29926
MYP Coordinator Kathleen Harper
Languages English
T: +1 843 689 4500
W: hhm.beaufort.k12.sc.us

Irmo High School
6671 St Andrews Road, Columbia SC 29212
CP Coordinator Lauren Prochak
DP Coordinator Diane Padula
Languages English
T: +1 803 732 8100
W: www.lex5.k12.sc.us/ihs

James H Hendrix Elementary School
1084 Springfield Road, Boiling Springs SC 29316
PYP Coordinator Allison Watson
Languages English
T: +1 864 578 1288
W: www.spartanburg2.k12.sc.us/hes

James Island High School
1000 Fort Johnson Road, Charleston SC 29412
DP Coordinator Jennifer Smillie
Languages English
T: +1 843 762 2754
W: jichs.ccsdschools.com

Jesse Boyd Elementary School
1505 Fernwood Glendale Road, Spartanburg SC 29307
PYP Coordinator Jennifer Squires
Languages English
T: +1 864 594 4430
W: boyd.spartanburg7.org

Latta High School
618 N. Richardson St., Latta SC 29565
DP Coordinator Christy Berry
Languages English
T: +1 843 752 5751
W: www.dillon3.k12.sc.us/lhs

Lexington Elementary School
116 Azalea Drive, Lexington SC 29072
PYP Coordinator Lynn Dempsey
Languages English, Spanish
T: +1 803 821 4000
W: les.lexington1.net

Lexington High School
2463 Augusta Highway, Lexington SC 29072
DP Coordinator Sherry Walters
Languages English
T: +1 803 821 3400
W: www.lexington1.net/lhs/index.htm

Lexington Middle School
702 North Lake Drive, Lexington SC 29072
MYP Coordinator Lauren LaVenia
Languages English
T: +1 803 821 3700
W: lms.lexington1.net

Lowcountry Preparatory School
300 Blue Stem Drive, Pawleys Island SC 29585
DP Coordinator Abigail Van Hoewyk
Languages English
T: +1 843 237 4147
W: www.lowcountryprep.org

Lower Richland High School
2615 Lower Richland Blvd, Hopkins SC 29061
CP Coordinator Timoty Shipley
DP Coordinator Michelle Peay
Languages English
T: +1 803 695 3000
W: www.lowerrichland.com

Memminger Elementary School
20 Beaufain Street, Charleston SC 29401
PYP Coordinator Maggie McClary
Languages English
T: +1 843 724 7778
W: memminger.ccsdschools.com

Northwestern High School
2503 West Main Street, Rock Hill SC 29732
DP Coordinator Patti Tate
Languages English
T: +1 803 981 1200
W: www.rock-hill.k12.sc.us/domain/31

Orangeburg-Wilkinson High School
601 Bruin Parkway, Orangeburg SC 29115
DP Coordinator Alexander Tryciecky
Languages English
T: +1 803 534 6180, 6823

Richland Northeast High School
7500 Brookfield Road, Columbia SC 29223
CP Coordinator Frances Staniec
DP Coordinator Sonja Merriwether-Hawki
MYP Coordinator Sonja Merriwether-Hawkins
Languages English
T: +1 803 699 2800
W: www.richland2.org/rnh

Rock Hill High School
320 West Springdale Road, Rock Hill SC 29730
DP Coordinator Patricia Sanford
Languages English
T: +1 803 981 1300
W: www.rock-hill.k12.sc.us/schools/high/rhhs/default.htm

Rosewood Elementary
2240 Rosewood Drive, Rock Hill SC 29730
PYP Coordinator Kallie Cromer
Languages English
T: +1 803 981 1540
W: rw.rock-hill.k12.sc.us

Sara Collins Elementary School
1200 Parkins Mill Road, Greenville SC 29607
PYP Coordinator Carrie Johnson
Languages English
T: +1 864 355 3200

Socastee High School
4900 Socastee Boulevard, Myrtle Beach SC 29588
DP Coordinator Danny Wilson
Languages English
T: +1 843 293 2513
W: www.hcs.k12.sc.us/high/sh/

South Pointe High School
806 Neely Road, Rock Hill SC 29730
DP Coordinator Laura Hall
Languages English
T: +1 803 984 3558
W: rock-hill.k12.sc.us/schools/high/sphs

Southside High School
6630 Frontage Rd, Greenville SC 29605
DP Coordinator Julie McGaha
Languages English
T: +1 864 355 8700
W: www.greenville.k12.sc.us/shs

Spartanburg Day School
1701 Skylyn Drive, Spartanburg SC 29307
PYP Coordinator Katie Clayton
Languages English
T: +1 864 582 8380
W: www.spartanburgdayschool.org

Sullivan Middle School
1825 Eden Terrace, Rock Hill SC 29730
MYP Coordinator Rebecca Shackleford
Languages English
T: +1 803 981 1450
W: www.rock-hill.k12.sc.us

Sumter High School
2580 McCray's Mill Road, School District 17, Sumter SC 29154-6098
DP Coordinator Marie Mulholland
Languages English
T: +1 803 481 4480
W: www.district.sumter17.k12.sc.us

Travelers Rest High School
301 North Main Street, Travelers Rest SC 29690
DP Coordinator Dawn Strickland
Languages English
T: +1 864 355 0000
W: www.greenville.k12.sc.us/trest

Williams Middle School
1119 North Irby Street, Florence SC 29501
MYP Coordinator Josie Stratton
Languages English
T: +1 843 664 8162

Wilson High School
1411 Old Marion Highway, Florence SC 29506
DP Coordinator Brian Howell
MYP Coordinator Brian Howell
Languages English
T: +1 843 664 8440
W: www.fsd1.org/wilson

Windsor Elementary School
9800 Dunbarton Dr, Columbia SC 29223
PYP Coordinator Jennifer Boone
Languages English
T: +1 803 736 8723
W: www.richland2.org/we

Woodmont High School
2831 West Georgia Road, Piedmont SC 29673
DP Coordinator Emily Styer
Languages English
T: +1 864 355 8600

Tennessee

Antioch High School
1900 Hobson Pike, Antioch TN 37013
CP Coordinator Nekesha Burnette
DP Coordinator Tosha Mannings
Languages English
T: +1 615 641 5400
W: schools.mnps.org/antioch-high-school

Avery Trace Middle School
230 Raider Drive, Cookeville TN 38501
MYP Coordinator Jessica Etheredge
Languages English
T: +1 931 520 2200
W: www.averytraceraiders.com

Balmoral Ridgeway Elementary
5905 Grosvenor Avenue, Memphis TN 38119
PYP Coordinator Celeste Fraser
Languages English
T: +1 901 416 2128
W: www.scsk12.org/schools/balmoral.es/site/index.shtml/

Bearden Middle School
1000 Francis Road, Knoxville TN 37909
MYP Coordinator Shannon Siebe
Languages English
T: +1 865 539 7839
W: www.knoxschools.org/beardenms

Bellevue Middle School
655 Colice Jeanne Road, Nashville TN 37221
MYP Coordinator Catie Dougherty
Languages English
T: +1 615 662 3000
W: schools.mnps.org/bellevue-middle-prep

Bolton High School
7323 Brunswick Road, Arlington TN 38002
DP Coordinator Natasha Medford
Languages English
T: +1 901 873 8150
W: www.boltonhigh.org

Cookeville High School
1 Cavalier Drive, Cookeville TN 38506
DP Coordinator Julie Benjamin
Languages English
T: +1 931 520 2287
W: www.cookevillecavaliers.com

Eakin Elementary School
2500 Fairfax Avenue, Nashville TN 37212
PYP Coordinator Angela Assalone
Languages English
T: +1 615 298 8076
W: www.eakines.mnps.org

Franklin High School
810 Hillsboro Road, Franklin TN 37064
DP Coordinator Ray Scheetz
Languages English
T: +1 615 472 4468
W: www.wcs.edu/fhs

Germantown High School
7653 Old Poplar Pike, Germantown TN 38138
DP Coordinator Melinda Keller
Languages English
T: +1 901 756 2350
W: www.scsk12.org/SCS/high/Germantwon/index.htm

Goodlettsville Middle School
1460 McGavock Pike, Nashville TN 37216
MYP Coordinator Ashley Jackson
Languages English
T: +1 615 227 1042
W: goodlettsvillems.mnps.org

Hillsboro Comprehensive High School
3812 Hillsboro Road, Nashville TN 37215
CP Coordinator Shuler Pelham
DP Coordinator Sharon Humphrey
MYP Coordinator Kenyae Reese
Languages English
T: +1 615 298 8400

Hunters Lane High School
1150 Hunters Lane, Nashville TN 37207
DP Coordinator Sara Hoyal
MYP Coordinator Olivia Roller
Languages English
T: +1 615 860 1401
W: www.hunterslanehs.mnps.org

J T Moore Middle School
4425 Granny White Pike, Nashville TN 37204
MYP Coordinator Gary Hughes
Languages English
T: +1 615 298 8095
W: www.jtmoore.org

Julia Green Elementary School
3500 Hobbs Road, Nashville TN 37215
PYP Coordinator Kathy Harris
Languages English
T: +1 615 298 8082
W: www.juliagreen.org

Lausanne Collegiate School
1381 West Massey Road, Memphis TN 38120
DP Coordinator Rocio Rodriguez del Rio
MYP Coordinator Kim Thorpe
PYP Coordinator Erica McBride
Languages English
T: +1 901 474 1001
W: www.lausanneschool.com

Oak Forest Elementary
7440 Nonconnah View Cove, Memphis TN 38119
PYP Coordinator Timkia Bryant
Languages English
T: +1 901 416 2257
W: www.mcsk12.net/schools/oakforest.es/site/index.shtml

Oakland High School
2225 Patriot Drive, Murfreesboro TN 37130
DP Coordinator Ann Borombozin
Languages English
T: +1 615 904 3780
W: www.ohs.rcs.k12.tn.us

Ooltewah High School
6123 Mountain View Road, Ooltewah TN 37363
DP Coordinator Erica Hitchcox
Languages English
T: +1 423 498 6920
W: ohs.hcde.org

Ridgeway High School
2009 Ridgeway Road, Memphis TN 38119
DP Coordinator Amy Dorsey
Languages English
T: +1 901 416 8820
W: www.ridgewayhigh.org

Ridgeway Middle School
6333 Quince Road, Memphis TN 38119
MYP Coordinator Patrice Carter
Languages English
T: +1 901 416 1588
W: www.mcsk12.net/schools/ridgeway.ms/site/index.shtml

Signal Mountain Middle/High School
2650 Sam Powell Trail, Signal Mountain TN 37377
DP Coordinator Marquita Thomas
MYP Coordinator Melissa Bouldin
Languages English
T: +1 423 886 0880
W: www.smmhs.com

West End Middle School
3529 West End Avenue, Nashville TN 37205
MYP Coordinator Noelle Taylor
Languages English
T: +1 615 298 8425
W: ptso.westnest.net

West High School
3300 Sutherland Avenue, Knoxville TN 37919
DP Coordinator Valerie Schmidt-Gardner
MYP Coordinator Shannon Siebe
Languages English
T: +1 865 594 4477
W: wesths.knoxschools.org

Texas

Alcuin School
6144 Churchill Way, Dallas TX 75230
DP Coordinator Margaret Davis
MYP Coordinator Joanne Chatlos
Languages English
T: +1 972 239 1745
W: www.alcuinschool.org

Allen High School
300 Rivercrest Boulevard, Allen TX 75002
DP Coordinator Shelly Holmes
Languages English
T: +1 972 727 0400
W: www.allenisd.org/allenhs

Alonzo De Leon Middle School
4201 North 29th St, McAllen TX 78504
MYP Coordinator Kimberly Alaniz
Languages English
T: +1 956 632 8800
W: deleon.mcallenisd.org

Amarillo High School/AISD
4225 Danbury Drive, Amarillo TX 79109
DP Coordinator Phillip Miller
Languages English
T: +1 806 326 2000
W: ahsamaisd.sharpschool.com

Anderson Mill Elementary School
10610 Salt Mill Hollow, Austin TX 78750
PYP Coordinator Jan Zimmern
Languages English
T: +1 512 428 3700
W: www.roundrockisd.org/andersonmill

Andress High School
5400 Sun Valley Dr., El Paso TX 79924
DP Coordinator Frances Morales
Languages English
T: +1 915 236 4000
W: andress.episd.org

Arlington High School
818 W Park Row, Arlington TX 76013
DP Coordinator Christine B. Fougerousse
Languages English
T: +1 682 867 8100
W: www.aisd.net/arlington-high-school

Arthur Kramer Elementary IB World School
7131 Midbury Drive, Dallas TX 75230
PYP Coordinator Kim West
Languages English
T: +1 972 794 8300
W: www.dallasisd.org/domain/540

Austin Eco Bilingual School (Austin EBS) USA
8707 Mountain Crest Dr, Austin TX 78735
PYP Coordinator Adriana Rodriguez
Languages English
T: +1 512 299 5731
W: www.austinbilingualschool.com

Baker Middle School
3445 Pecan Street, Corpus Christi TX 78411
MYP Coordinator Marlo Bazan
Languages English
T: +1 361 878 4600
W: baker.ccisd.us

Barbara Bush Middle School
515 Cowboys Parkway, Irving TX 75063
MYP Coordinator Christina Flatt
Languages English
T: +1 972 968 3700
W: bush.cfbisd.edu

Bellaire High School
5100 Maple Street, Houston ISD, Bellaire TX 77401
DP Coordinator Ann Linsley
Languages English
T: +1 713 295 3704
W: www.houstonisd.org/bellairehigh

Benjamin Franklin International Exploratory Academy
6920 Meadow Road, Dallas TX 75230
MYP Coordinator James Bryan
Languages English
T: +1 972 502 7100
W: www.dallasisd.org/franklin

Borman Elementary School
1201 Parvin St., Denton TX 76205
PYP Coordinator Heather Thornburg
Languages English
T: +1 940 369 2500
W: www.dentonisd.org/bormanes

Briargrove Elementary School
6145 San Felipe, Houston TX 77057
PYP Coordinator Quinetta Sampy
Languages English, Spanish
T: +1 713 917 3600
W: www.houstonisd.org/briargrovees

Briarmeadow Charter School
3601 Dunvale Rd, Houston TX 77063-5707
PYP Coordinator Jamie Hrabovsky
Languages English
T: +1 713 458 5500
W: www.houstonisd.org/briarmeadow

Briscoe Elementary School
2015 S. Flores St., San Antonio TX 78204
PYP Coordinator Cari Richter
Languages English, Spanish
T: +1 210 228 3305
W: schools.saisd.net/page/112.homepage

British International School of Houston
2203 North Westgreen Boulevard, Katy TX 77449
CP Coordinator D Lifton
DP Coordinator Mr. Ian McHugh
Languages English
T: +1 713 290 9025
W: www.bishouston.org

Caldwell Heights Elementary
4010 Eagles Nest, Round Rock TX 78665
PYP Coordinator Elizabeth Petty
Languages English
T: +1 512 428 7300
W: caldwellheights.roundrockisd.org

Calhoun Middle School
709 Congress Street, Denton TX 76201
MYP Coordinator Chris Slocum
Languages English
T: +1 940 369 2400
W: www.dentonisd.org/calhounms

CC Mason Elementary
1501 N. Lakeline Blvd, Cedar Park TX 78613
PYP Coordinator Ashley Swindle
Languages English
T: +1 512 570 5500
W: mason.leanderisd.org

Cesar E. Chavez High School
8501 Howard Dr., Houston TX 77017
CP Coordinator Jason Busby
DP Coordinator Rebecca Rice
Languages English
T: +1 713 495 6950
W: www.houstonisd.org/chavez

Chandler Oaks Elementary
3800 Stone Oak Drive, Round Rock TX 78681
PYP Coordinator Elizabeth Petty
Languages English
T: +1 512 704 0400
W: chandleroaks.roundrockisd.org

Coppell High School
185 West Parkway Blvd, Coppell TX 75019
DP Coordinator Michael Brock
Languages English
T: +1 214 496 6100
W: www.coppellisd.com/chs

Coronado High School
100 Champions Place, El Paso TX 79912
DP Coordinator Leslie Harris
Languages English
T: +1 915 236 2000
W: coronado.episd.org

Cunae International School LLC
5655 Creekside Forest Drive, Spring TX 77389
DP Coordinator Maria Jose Ferrer Garay
PYP Coordinator Maria Jose Ferrer Garay
Languages English
T: +1 281 516 3770
W: www.doortomyschool.com

Dallas International School
17811 Waterview Pkwy, Dallas TX 75252
DP Coordinator Zahra Boudaoui
Languages English
T: +1 469 250 0001
W: www.dallasinternationalschool.org

Daniel Ortiz Middle School
6767 Telephone Road, Houston TX 77061-2056
MYP Coordinator Tina Garcia
Languages English
T: +1 713 845 5650
W: www.houstonisd.org/page/79424

Denton High School
1007 Fulton Street, Denton TX 76201
DP Coordinator Beth Hughes
MYP Coordinator Crystal Sullivan
Languages English
T: +1 940 369 2000
W: www.dentonisd.org/dentonhs

Dove Elementary
1932 Dove Road, Grapevine TX 76051
PYP Coordinator Tanya Kellerman
Languages English, Spanish
T: +1 817 251 5700
W: des.gcisd.net

Dr. Pablo Perez Elementary School
7801 N. Main Street, Mc Allen TX 78504
PYP Coordinator Marla Skretta
Languages English
T: +1 956 971 1125
W: perez.mcallenisd.org

Durham Elementary School
4803 Brinkman Street, Houston TX 77018
PYP Coordinator Lisa Knupp
Languages English, Spanish
T: +1 713 613 2527
W: www.houstonisd.org/Domain/12141

Dwight D Eisenhower High School
7922 Antoine Drive, Houston TX 77088
DP Coordinator Mary Williams
Languages English
T: +1 281 878 0900

E A Murchison Middle School
3700 North Hills Drive, Austin TX 78731
MYP Coordinator Jana Tucker
Languages English
T: +1 512 414 3254

Edgar Allan Poe Elementary School
5100 Hazard Street, Houston TX 77098
PYP Coordinator Sara Williams
Languages English
T: +1 713 535 3780
W: www.houstonisd.org/poees

Eisenhower Ninth Grade School
3550 W Gulf Bank Road, Houston TX 77088
MYP Coordinator Shameka Garner
Languages English
T: +1 281 878 7700
W: www.aldine.k12.tx.us/schools/specific_campus.cfm?Campus Number=84

El Dorado High School
12401 Edgemere, El Paso TX 79938
DP Coordinator Paulina Hernandez
Languages English
T: +1 915 937 3200
W: www.schools.sisd.net/edhs

Esprit International School
4890 W Panther Creek Dr, The Woodlands TX 77381
PYP Coordinator Rosemary Brumbelow
Languages English
T: +1 281 298 9200
W: www.espritinternationalschool.com

Forest Park Middle School
1644 North Eastman Road, Longview TX 75601
MYP Coordinator Megan Burns
Languages English
T: +1 903 446 2510
W: www.lisd.org/forestpark/fpjump.htm

Francisca Alvarez Elementary School
2606 Gumwood Avenue, McAllen TX 78501
PYP Coordinator Marisela Chapa
Languages English
T: +1 956 971 4471
W: alvarez.mcallenisd.org

Garland High School
310 South Garland Avenue, Garland TX 75040
DP Coordinator Rebeckah Tisdale
Languages English
T: +1 972 494 8492
W: www.garlandowls.com

Geneva Heights Elementary School
2911 Delmar Avenue, Dallas TX 75206
PYP Coordinator Rhonda Barnwell
Languages English
T: +1 972 749 7400
W: www.dallasisd.org/relee

Graciela Garcia Elementary School
1002 W. Juan Balli Road, Pharr TX 78577
PYP Coordinator Tracy Lynn Southwell
Languages English, Spanish
T: +1 956 354 2790
W: www.psjaisd.us/garciaes

Grandview Hills Elementary
12024 Vista Parke Drive, Austin TX 78726
PYP Coordinator Ashley Swindle
Languages English
T: +1 512 434 7266
W: grandviewhills.leanderisd.org

Grisham Middle School
10805 School House Lane, Austin TX 78750
MYP Coordinator Dana Browning
Languages English
T: +1 512 428 2650
W: www.roundrockisd.org/grisham

Harry Stone Montessori Academy
4747 Veterans Dr., Dallas TX 75216
MYP Coordinator Megan Capshaw
Languages English
T: +1 972 794 3400
W: www.dallasisd.org/stone

Harvard Elementary School
810 Harvard Street, Houston TX 77007-1607
PYP Coordinator Heather Moore
Languages English
T: +1 713 867 5210
W: www.harvardschool.org

Headwaters School
801 Rio Grande, Austin TX 78701
DP Coordinator Paul Cronin
Languages English
T: +1 512 480 8142
W: headwaters.org

Heights High School
413 East 13th Street, Houston TX 77008-7021
CP Coordinator Cristina Bagos
DP Coordinator Cristina Bagos
MYP Coordinator Cristina Bagos
Languages English
T: +1 713 865 4400
W: www.houstonisd.org/heights

Hernandez Middle School
1901 Sunrise Road, Round Rock TX 78664
MYP Coordinator Emilee Hinegardner
Languages English
T: +1 512 424 8800
W: roundrockisd.org/schools/middle-schools/hernandez

Herrera Elementary School
525 Bennington, Houston 77511
PYP Coordinator Melody Vizi
Languages English, Spanish
T: +1 713 696 2800
W: www.houstonisd.org/herreraelem

Hillcrest High School
9924 Hillcrest Road, Dallas TX 75230
DP Coordinator Jeri Smith
Languages English
T: +1 972 502 6800
W: www.dallasisd.org/hillcrest

Hirschi Math-Science Magnet School
3106 Borton Lane, Wichita Falls TX 76306-6952
DP Coordinator Linda Fain
MYP Coordinator Linda Fain
Languages English
T: +1 940 716 2800
W: www.wichitafalls.hirschi.groupfusion.net

Huffman Elementary School
5510 Channel Isle Drive, Plano TX 75093
PYP Coordinator Amy Moore
Languages English, Spanish
T: +1 469 752 1900
W: www.pisd.edu/huffman

Humble High School
1700 Wilson Road, Humble TX 77338
DP Coordinator Sherrill Rene Lane
Languages English
T: +1 281 641 8129
W: www.humbleisd.net/hhs

Hutchinson Middle School
3102 Canton Ave, Lubbock TX 79410
MYP Coordinator Toby Klameth
Languages English
T: +1 806 219 3800
W: hutchinson.lubbockisd.org

IDEA College Prep Brownsville
4395 Paredes Line Road, Brownsville TX 78526
DP Coordinator Abigail Molina
T: +1 956 832 5150
W: ideapublicschools.org/our-schools/idea-brownsville

IDEA College Preparatory McAllen
201 N. Bentsen Rd., McAllen TX 78501
DP Coordinator Travis Lester
Languages English
T: +1 956 429 4100
W: ideapublicschools.org

IDEA College Preparatory South Flores
6919 South Flores Street, San Antonio TX 78221
DP Coordinator Valerie Trevino
Languages English, Spanish
T: +1 210 239 4150
W: www.ideapublicschools.org/our-schools/idea-south-flores

IDEA Donna
401 S. 1st St., Donna TX 78537
DP Coordinator Dikla Medina
Languages English
T: +1 956 464 0203
W: www.ideapublicschools.org/our-schools/idea-donna

IDEA Frontier
2800 S. Dakota Ave, Brownsville TX 78521
DP Coordinator Carlos Coronado
Languages English
T: +1 956 541 2002
W: ideapublicschools.org/our-schools/idea-frontier

Imagine International Academy of North Texas
2860 Virginia Parkway, McKinney TX 75071
DP Coordinator Hannah Nayakanti
MYP Coordinator Pamela Hinterscher
PYP Coordinator Kim Wood
Languages English
T: +1 214 491 1500
W: www.imaginenorthtexas.org

International School of Texas
4402 Hudson Bend, Austin TX 78734
PYP Coordinator Eleanor Mitchell
Languages English
T: +1 512 351 3403
W: www.internationalschooloftexas.com

J. L. Everhart Elementary
2919 Tryon Rd, Longview TX 75602
PYP Coordinator Nastascia Horton
Languages English
T: +1 903 758 5622
W: www.lisd.org

J.L. Long Middle School
6116 Reiger Avenue, Dallas TX 75214
MYP Coordinator Mary Ochoa
Languages English
T: +1 972 502 4700
W: www.dallasisd.org/Long

James Bowie High School
2101 Highbank Drive, Arlington TX 76018
DP Coordinator Amy Hayes
Languages English
T: +1 682 867 4500
W: www.aisd.net/bowie

James S Hogg Middle School
1100 Merrill Street, Houston TX 77009
MYP Coordinator Daniella Andrade
Languages English
T: +1 713 802 4700
W: www.houstonisd.org

Joel C. Harris Middle School
325 Pruitt Ave., San Antonio TX 78204
MYP Coordinator Amanda McKay
Languages English, Spanish
T: +1 210 228 1220
W: www.saisd.net/schools/harris047

Judson High School
9142 FM Road 78, Converse TX 78109
DP Coordinator Alexis Mcjilton
Languages English
T: +1 210 945 1100
W: school.judsonisd.org//judsonhigh.cfm

Killeen High School
500 N. 38th Street, Killeen TX 76543-4161
DP Coordinator Keina Cook
Languages English
T: +1 254 336 7208
W: killeenhighschool.wix.com/khsib

KIPP University Prep
4343 W. Commerce Street, San Antonio TX 78237
DP Coordinator Jonathan Villegas-Caine
Languages English
T: +1 210 290 8720
W: kippsa.org/our-schools/kipp-university-prep

Kirby Junior High – World Academy
1715 Loop 11, Wichita Falls TX 76306
MYP Coordinator Tami Davis
Languages English
T: +1 940 716 2900

Klein Oak High School
22603 Northcrest Drive, Spring TX 77389
DP Coordinator Linda Garner
Languages English, Spanish
T: +1 834 484 5000
W: kleinoak.kleinisd.net

L C Anderson High School
8403 Mesa Drive, Austin TX 78759
DP Coordinator Jill Spencer
Languages English
T: +1 512 414 2538
W: www.andersononline.org

Lamar Academy
1009 N 10th Street, McAllen TX 78501
DP Coordinator Andrea Gutierrez
MYP Coordinator Andrea Gutierrez
Languages English
T: +1 956 632 3222
W: lamar.mcallenisd.org

Lamar High School
3325 Westheimer Road, Houston TX 77098-1003
CP Coordinator David Munoz
DP Coordinator Alexander Brahm
MYP Coordinator Dennis Gillespie
Languages English
T: +1 713 522 5960
W: www.houstonisd.org/lamarhs

Lamar High School
1400 Lamar Blvd West, Arlington TX 76012
DP Coordinator Kathy Hitt
Languages English
T: +1 682 867 8300
W: w2.aisd.net/aisd/lamar

Lanier Middle School
2600 Woodhead, Houston TX 77098-1534
MYP Coordinator Kathleen Rhymes
Languages English
T: +1 713 942 1900
W: www.houstonisd.org/domain/3518

Las Colinas Elementary
2200 Kinwest Parkway, Irving TX 75063
PYP Coordinator Allison Elliott
Languages English
T: +1 972 968 2200
W: lascolinas.cfbisd.edu

Lawrence D Bell High School
1601 Brown Trail, Hurst TX 76054
DP Coordinator Nancy Shane
Languages English
T: +1 817 282 2551
W: www.hebisd.edu

Leander High School
3301 South Bagdad Road, Leander TX 78641
DP Coordinator Shawn Doctor
Languages English
T: +1 512 435 8000

Liberty Middle School
1212 S Fir Street, Pharr TX 78577
MYP Coordinator Chriselda Stevenson
Languages English
T: +1 956 354 2610
W: liberty.psjaisd.us

Lincoln Middle School
500 Mulberry Ave., El Paso TX 79932
MYP Coordinator Karen Reid
Languages English, Spanish
T: +1 915 236 3400
W: www.episd.org/lincoln

Longview High School
PO Box 3268, Longview TX 75606
DP Coordinator Beverly Coker
Languages English
T: +1 903 663 1301
W: www.lisd.org/lhs

Lubbock High School
2004 19th Street, Lubbock TX 79401
DP Coordinator Erin Castle
Languages English
T: +1 806 766 1444
W: www.lubbockhigh.com

Luther Burbank High School
1002 Edwards Street, San Antonio TX 78204
DP Coordinator Angela Meyer
MYP Coordinator Syuna Hawkins
Languages English
T: +1 210 532 4241 EXT:103

Magnolia High School
14350 FM 1488, Magnolia TX 77354
DP Coordinator Derek Parsons
Languages English
T: +1 281 356 3572
W: mhs.magnoliaisd.org

Magnolia West High School
42202 FM 1774, Magnolia TX 77354-0426
DP Coordinator Jeremy Day
Languages English
T: +1 281 252 2550
W: mwhs.magnoliaisd.org

Mark Twain Elementary School
7500 Braes Blvd, Houston TX 77025
PYP Coordinator Kathleen Blakeslee
Languages English
T: +1 713 295 5230

Massey Ranch Elementary School
3900 Manvel Road, Pearland TX 77584
PYP Coordinator Jennifer Hoot
Languages English
T: +1 281 727 1700
W: www.pearlandisd.org/masseyranch.cfm

Meridian School
2555 North IH-35, Round Rock TX 78664
DP Coordinator Stela Holcombe
MYP Coordinator Kristen Machczynski
PYP Coordinator Leah Lieurance
Languages English
T: +1 512 660 5232
W: www.mwschool.org

Morehead Middle School
5625 Confetti Dr., El Paso TX 79912
MYP Coordinator Angel Cesar Carmona
Languages English, Spanish
T: +1 915 236 3500
W: morehead.episd.org

Mountainview Elementary School
5901 Bishop Drive, Waco TX 76710
PYP Coordinator Ashlee Brewster
Languages English
T: +1 254 772 2520
W: www.wacoisd.org/mountainview

Nadine Kujawa Education Center
7007 Fallbrook, Houston TX 77086
PYP Coordinator Andrea Ross
Languages English
T: +1 281 878 1530
W: www.aldine.k12.tx.us

Newton Rayzor Elementary School
1400 Malone Street, Denton TX 76201
PYP Coordinator Linda Marquez-Gavilanes
Languages English
T: +1 940 369 3700
W: www.dentonisd.org/newtonres

Nolan Richardson Middle School
11350 Loma Franklin Dr., El Paso TX 79934
MYP Coordinator Marisa Marin
Languages English, Spanish
T: +1 915 236 6650
W: www.episd.org/richardson

North Hills Preparatory
606 East Royal Lane, Irving TX 75039
DP Coordinator Katherine Biela
MYP Coordinator Nicolau Pereira
PYP Coordinator Julie Hills
Languages English
T: +1 972 501 0645
W: www.northhillsprep.org

Northline Elementary
821 E Witcher Ln, Houston TX 77076-4818
PYP Coordinator Brenda Sanchez
Languages English
T: +1 713 696 2890
W: www.houstonisd.org/northline

Odessa High School
1301 Dotsy Ave., Odessa TX 79763
DP Coordinator Melissa Roth
Languages English
T: +1 432 456 0029
W: www.ectorcountyisd.org/ode

Peebles Elementary School
1800 WS Young Drive North, Killeen TX 76543
PYP Coordinator Lynn Hobson
Languages English
T: +1 254 336 2120
W: www.killeenisd.org

Pinkerton Elementary
260 Southwestern Blvd., Coppell TX 75019
PYP Coordinator Marnie Ward
Languages English
T: +1 214 496 6800
W: www.coppellisd.com/pinkerton

Plano East Senior High School
3000 Los Rios Boulevard, Plano TX 75074
DP Coordinator Karen Stanton
Languages English
T: +1 469 752 9000
W: www.k-12.pisd.edu/schools/planoeast/ib/ib.htm

Preston Hollow Elementary School
6423 Walnut Hill Lane, Dallas TX 75230
PYP Coordinator Araceli Hernandez
Languages English
T: +1 972 794 8500
W: www.dallasisd.org/prestonhollow

R E Good Elementary School
1012 Study Lane, Carrollton TX 75006
PYP Coordinator Allison Elliott
Languages English
T: +1 972 968 1900
W: www.cfbisd.edu/schools/goo/index.htm

Ramirez Elementary School
702 Ave. T, Lubbock TX 79401
PYP Coordinator Amber Faske
Languages English
T: +1 806 219 6500
W: ramirez.lubbockisd.org

Ranchview High School
8401 E Valley Ranch Parkway, Irving TX 75063
DP Coordinator Leslie Yager
MYP Coordinator Leslie Yager
Languages English
T: +1 972 968 5000
W: ranchview.cfbisd.edu

River Oaks Elementary School
2008 Kirby Drive, Houston TX 77019
PYP Coordinator Jana Bomersbach
Languages English
T: +1 713 942 1460
W: www.es.houstonisd.org/riveroakses

Robert E Lee High School
411 ESE Loop 323, Tyler TX 75703
CP Coordinator Terence Ryan
MYP Coordinator Stephanie Bilimoria
Languages English
T: +1 903 262 2625
W: www.tylerisd.org/Schools/REL

Roberts Elementary School
6000 Greenbriar Drive, Houston TX 77030
PYP Coordinator Kristina Tran
Languages English
T: +1 713 295 5272
W: www.houstonisd.org/robertselem

Rockwall High School
901 Yellowjacket Lane, Rockwall TX 75087
DP Coordinator Michelle Ghormley
Languages English
T: +1 972 771 7339
W: rockwallisd.com

Rockwall-Heath High School
801 Laurence Drive, Heath TX 75032
DP Coordinator Penny Harris
Languages English
T: +1 972 772 2474
W: rockwallisd.com

Roscoe Wilson Elementary School
2807 25th Street, Lubbock TX 79410
PYP Coordinator Amber Faske
Languages English
T: +1 806 766 0922
W: rwilson.lubbockisd.org

Sam Houston High School
2000 Sam Houston Drive, Arlington TX 76014
DP Coordinator Poppy Moore
Languages English
T: +1 682 867 8200
W: www.aisd.net/sam

Samuel Clemens High School
1001 Elbel Road, Schertz TX 78154
DP Coordinator Veronica Riordan
Languages English
T: +1 210 945 6100
W: www.scuc.txed.net

Sci-Tech Preparatory
6405 S IH 35 Frontage Rd, Austin TX 78744
DP Coordinator Kiwonda Riley
Languages English
T: +1 512 438 7325
W: waysideschools.org/stp

Scott Elementary School
2301 West Ave. P, Temple TX 76504
PYP Coordinator Chelsea Molton
Languages English
T: +1 254 215 6222
W: scott.tisd.org

Shotwell Middle School
6515 Trail Valley Way, Houston TX 77086
MYP Coordinator Peggy Tomme
Languages English
T: +1 281 878 0960
W: www.aldine.k12.tx.us/schools

South Texas Business Education & Technology Academy
510 S. Sugar Road, Edinburg TX 78539
DP Coordinator Victoria Marin
Languages English
T: +1 956 383 1684
W: www.stisd.net/beta.html

Spicewood Elementary School
11601 Olson Drive, Austin TX 78750
PYP Coordinator Jessica Oates
Languages English
T: +1 512 428 3600
W: www.roundrockisd.org

St Anthony Academy
3732 Myrtle Street, Dallas TX 75215
PYP Coordinator Qynthia Sanders
Languages English
T: +1 214 421 3645
W: www.saadallas.org

Stony Point High School
1801 Tiger Trail, Round Rock TX 78664
DP Coordinator Andi Brosché
Languages English
T: +1 512 428 7000
W: roundrockisd.org/schools/high-schools/stony-point

Sylvan Rodriguez Elementary
5858 Chimney Rock, Houston TX 77081
PYP Coordinator Minerva Gonzalez
Languages English
T: +1 713 295 3870
W: es.houstonisd.org/rodriguezes

Tanglewood Middle School
5215 San Felipe, Houston TX 77056-3605
MYP Coordinator Tal Gribbins
Languages English
T: +1 713 625 1411
W: www.houstonisd.org/grady

Temple High School
415 North 31st Street, Temple TX 76504
DP Coordinator Sharon Goldman
Languages English
T: +1 254 215 7000
W: ths.tisd.org

The Awty International School
7455 Awty School Lane, Houston TX 77055-7222
DP Coordinator Isabel Van Dyck
Languages English
T: +1 713 686 4850
W: www.awty.org

The Magellan International School
7938 Great Northern Boulevard, Austin TX 78757
MYP Coordinator Nicolas Puga
PYP Coordinator Julieta Carrillo
Languages English, Spanish
T: +1 512 782 2327
W: www.magellanschool.org

The Post Oak School
4600 Bissonnet Street, Bellaire TX 77401
DP Coordinator James Quillin
Languages English
T: +1 713 661 6688
W: www.postoakschool.org

The School at St. George Place
5430 Hidalgo St., Houston TX 77056
PYP Coordinator Maxine Adams
Languages English
T: +1 713 625 1499
W: www.schoolatstgeorgeplace.com

The Village School
13077 Westella Drive, Houston TX 77077
DP Coordinator Kerri Peters
Languages English
T: +1 281 496 7900
W: www.thevillageschool.com

The Westwood School
14340 Proton Road, Dallas TX 75244
DP Coordinator Gail Macalik
Languages English
T: +1 972 239 8598
W: www.westwoodschool.org

The Woodlands Preparatory School
27440 Kuykendahl Road, Tomball TX 77375
DP Coordinator Yixing Chen
MYP Coordinator Yixing Chen
PYP Coordinator Paola Borja
Languages English
T: +1 281 516 0600
W: www.woodlandsprep.org

Theodore Roosevelt Elementary School
4801 S 26th St, McAllen TX 78503
PYP Coordinator Christian A. Trevino
Languages English, Spanish
T: +1 956 971 4424
W: roosevelt.mcallenisd.org

Thomas Jefferson High School
723 Donaldson Ave., San Antonio TX 78201
DP Coordinator David Garcia
Languages English, Spanish
T: +1 210 438 6570
W: www.saisd.net/schools/jefferson007

Travis B. Bryan High School
3450 Campus Drive, Bryan TX 77802
DP Coordinator Sarah Patterson
Languages English
T: +1 979 209 2400
W: bryanhs.bryanisd.org

Travis Science Academy
1551 S. 25th Street, Temple TX 76504
MYP Coordinator Kimberly Demaree
Languages English
T: +1 254 215 6300
W: travis.tisd.org

Trinity High School
500 North Industrial, Euless TX 76039
DP Coordinator William Wells
Languages English
T: +1 817 571 0271
W: www.hebisd.edu

Uplift Grand Preparatory
300 E Church St., Grand Prairie TX 75050
DP Coordinator Grace Kirkland
MYP Coordinator Elizabeth Coughenour
PYP Coordinator Yvonne Cooper
Languages English, Spanish
T: +1 972 854 0600
W: www.upliftgrand.org

Uplift Hampton Preparatory
8915 S. Hampton Road, Dallas TX 75232
DP Coordinator Kendra Langley
MYP Coordinator Yalea Baughman
PYP Coordinator Miessa Bradley
Languages English
T: +1 972 421 1982
W: www.hamptonprep.org

Uplift Heights Preparatory
2650 Canada Dr., Dallas TX 75212
DP Coordinator Chelsea Rink
MYP Coordinator Kate Simpson
PYP Coordinator Rachel McCann
Languages English
T: +1 214 442 7094
W: www.uplifteducation.org/Domain/729

Uplift Infinity Preparatory
1401 S. MacArthur Street, Irving TX 75060
DP Coordinator Jesus Sesma
MYP Coordinator Sarah Stroube
PYP Coordinator Shannon Wright
Languages English
T: +1 469 621 9200
W: www.infinityprep.org

Uplift Luna Preparatory
2020 N. Lamar St., Dallas TX 75202
DP Coordinator Benjamin Higgins
MYP Coordinator Catherine Woodiel
PYP Coordinator Maria Pacailler
Languages English
T: +1 214 442 7882
W: www.upliftluna.org

Uplift Meridian Preparatory
1801 South Beach Street, Fort Worth TX 76105
PYP Coordinator Ann Wilson
Languages English
T: +1 817 288 1700
W: upliftmeridianprep.org

Uplift Mighty Preparatory
3700 Mighty Mite Drive, Fort Worth TX 76105
DP Coordinator Jordan Pratt
MYP Coordinator Wesley Kline
PYP Coordinator Juan Jimenez
Languages English
T: +1 817 288 3800
W: www.upliftmightyprep.org

Uplift Peak Preparatory
4600 Bryan Street, Dallas TX 75204
DP Coordinator Deborah Korthof
MYP Coordinator Sarah Boykins
PYP Coordinator Melissa Curran
Languages English
T: +1 214 276 0879
W: www.upliftpeak.org

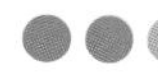

Uplift Pinnacle Preparatory
2510 South Vernon Ave, Dallas TX 75224
PYP Coordinator Octavia Silas
Languages English
T: +1 21 444 26100
W: pinnaclepreparatory.org

Uplift Summit International Preparatory
1305 North Center Street, Arlington TX 76011
DP Coordinator Tobias Rather
MYP Coordinator Tamara Phillips
PYP Coordinator Danielle Erbert
Languages English
T: +1 817 287 5121
W: www.summitinternationalprep.org

Uplift Triumph Preparatory
9411 Hargrove Dr., Dallas TX 75220
PYP Coordinator Sarah Santoyo
Languages English, Spanish
T: +1 972 590 5100
W: www.uplifteducation.org/triumph

Vandegrift High School
9500 McNeil Dr., Austin TX 78750
DP Coordinator Sherilyn Georgoulis
Languages English
T: +1 512 570 2300
W: vhs.leanderisd.org

W B Ray High School
1002 Texan Trail, Corpus Christi TX 78411
DP Coordinator Lorinda Hamilton
MYP Coordinator Lorinda Hamilton
Languages English
T: +1 361 878 7300
W: ray.ccisd.us

Walter W Fondren Middle School
6333 South Braeswood Blvd, Houston TX 77096
MYP Coordinator Melodye Montgomery
Languages English
T: +1 713 778 3360
W: www.houstonisd.org

Westchester Academy for International Studies
901 Yorkchester, Houston TX 77079
CP Coordinator Sara Sebesta-Camano
DP Coordinator Suzanne Acord
MYP Coordinator Cheryl Wegscheid
Languages English
T: +1 713 251 1800
W: wais.springbranchisd.com

Western Hills High School
3600 Boston Avenue, Fort Worth TX 76133
DP Coordinator Karen Hiller
Languages English
T: +1 817 871 2000
W: schools.fwisd.org/westernhills

WESTLAKE ACADEMY
2600 J.T. Ottinger Road, Westlake TX 76262
DP Coordinator Dr. James Owen
MYP Coordinator Terri Watson
PYP Coordinator Alison Schneider
Languages English
T: +1 817 4905757
E: info@westlakeacademy.org
W: www.westlakeacademy.org
See full details on page 560

Westwood High School
12400 Mellow Meadow, Austin TX 78750
DP Coordinator Stephanie Childress
Languages English
T: +1 512 464 4000
W: westwood.roundrockisd.org

William B. Lipscomb Elementary School
5801 Worth Street, Dallas TX 75214
PYP Coordinator Alicia McCowan
Languages English
T: +1 972 794 7300
W: www.dallasisd.org/lipscomb

William Wharton K-8 Dual Language Academy
900 West Gray Street, Houston TX 77019
PYP Coordinator Patricia Selin
Languages English, Spanish
T: +1 713 535 3771
W: www.houstonisd.org/whartondla

Williams Preparatory
1750 Viceroy Drive, Dallas TX 75235
DP Coordinator Matthew King
MYP Coordinator Young Lee
PYP Coordinator Judith Meyer
Languages English
T: +1 214 276 0352
W: www.williamsprep.org

Windsor Park Elementary School
4525 South Alameda Street, Corpus Christi TX 78412
PYP Coordinator Susan Ames
Languages English
T: +1 361 994 3664
W: windsorpark.ccisd.us

Woodlawn Academy
1717 W. Magnolia Ave, San Antonio TX 78201
MYP Coordinator Maxwell Ituah
PYP Coordinator Ana Femath
Languages English
T: +1 210 438 6560
W: schools.saisd.net/page/175.homepage

Woodrow Wilson High School
100 S Glasgow, Dallas TX 75214
DP Coordinator Kelly Renea Ritchie
Languages English
T: +1 972 502 4400
W: www.woodrowwildcats.org

Utah

Bountiful High School
695 South Orchard Drive, Bountiful UT 84010
DP Coordinator Luisa (Vickie) Ludwig
Languages English
T: +1 801 402 3900
W: www.davis.k12.ut.us/Domain/7221

Channing Hall
13515 South 150 East, Draper UT 84020
MYP Coordinator Jane Kilby
PYP Coordinator Jane Kilby
Languages English
T: +1 801 572 2709
W: www.channinghall.org

Clearfield High School
931 South 1000 East, Clearfield UT 84015
DP Coordinator Connie Kearl
Languages English
T: +1 801 408 8200
W: www.davis.k12.ut.us/domain/7356

Hawthorn Academy
9062 S 2200 W, West Jordan UT 84088
PYP Coordinator Candalyn Mettmann
Languages English
T: +1 801 282 9066
W: www.hawthornacademy.org

Highland High School
2166 South 1700 East, Salt Lake City UT 84106
DP Coordinator Kyle Bracken
Languages English
T: +1 801 484 4343
W: highland.slcschools.org

Hillcrest High School
7350 South 900 East, Midvale UT 84047
CP Coordinator John Olsen
DP Coordinator John Olsen
Languages English
T: +1 801 256 5484

Midvale Middle School
7852 S Pioneer St, Midvale UT 84047
MYP Coordinator Shelley Allen
Languages English
T: +1 801 826 7300
W: www.canyonsdistrict.org/midvale-middle

Ogden High School
2828 Harrison Blvd, Ogden UT 84403
DP Coordinator Kelly Boren
Languages English
T: +1 801 737 8700
W: www.ohs.ogden.k12.ut.us

Providence Hall Charter School
4557 West Patriot Ridge Drive, Herriman UT 84096
DP Coordinator Melissa McPhail
MYP Coordinator Odette Desmarais
PYP Coordinator Kimberly Andersen
Languages English
T: +1 801 727 8260
W: www.providencehall.com

Skyline High School
3251 East 3760 South, Salt Lake City UT 84109
DP Coordinator Christopher Krueger
Languages English
T: +1 385 646 5420 / IB: +1 385 646 9588
W: www.graniteschools.org/hs/skyline

Walden School of Liberal Arts
4266 N University Avenue, Provo UT 84604
DP Coordinator Lara Candland
Languages English
T: +1 801 623 1388
W: www.waldenschool.us

Weber High School
430 West Weber High Drive, Pleasant View UT 84414
DP Coordinator Marcia Kloempken
Languages English
T: +1 801 476 3700
W: whs.wsd.net

West High School
241 North 300 West, Salt Lake City UT 84103
CP Coordinator Shannon Wilson
DP Coordinator Shannon Wilson
Languages English
T: +1 801 578 8500
W: west.slcschools.org

Vermont

Long Trail School
1045 Kirby Hollow Road, Dorset VT 05251
DP Coordinator Kelley Swarthout
Languages English
T: +1 802 867 5717
W: www.longtrailschool.org

Middlebury Union High School
73 Charles Avenue, Middlebury VT 05753
DP Coordinator Cindy Atkins
Languages English
T: +1 802 382 1500
W: www.acsdvt.org/muhs

The Dover School
9 Schoolhouse Road, East Dover VT 05341
PYP Coordinator Alison Sullivan
Languages English
T: +1 802 464 5386
W: www.doverschool.net

Virginia

Academy for Discovery at Lakewood
1701 Alsace Avenue, Norfolk VA 23509
MYP Coordinator Judy Gulledge
Languages English
T: +1 757 628 2477
W: www.npsk12.com/afdl

Annandale High School
4700 Medford Drive, Annandale VA 22003
DP Coordinator Linda Bradshaw
MYP Coordinator Meagan Padgett
Languages English
T: +1 703 642 4100
W: annandalehs.fcps.edu

Antietam Elementary School
12000 Antietam Rd, Woodbridge VA 22192
PYP Coordinator Nancy Blake
Languages English
T: +1 703 497 7619
W: antietames.pwcs.edu

Atlee High School
9414 Atlee Station Road, Mechanicsville VA 23116
DP Coordinator Wendy Edelman
Languages English
T: +1 804 723 2100

Belvedere Elementary School
6540 Columbia Pike, Falls Church VA 22101
PYP Coordinator Bridget Louder
Languages English
T: +1 703 916 6800
W: www.fcps.edu/BelvedereES/

Brooke Point High School
1700 Courthouse Road, Stafford VA 22554
DP Coordinator Julie Stemple-Hoover
Languages English
T: +1 540 658 6080
W: stafford.brooke.schoolfusion.us

Buckland Mills Elementary School
10511 Wharfdale Place, Gainesville VA 20155
PYP Coordinator Amy Hardt
Languages English
T: +1 703 530 1560
W: Bucklandmillses.schools.pwcs.edu

Chimborazo Elementary School
3000 East Marshall Street, Richmond VA 23223
PYP Coordinator David Peck
Languages English
T: +1 804 780 8392
W: web.richmond.k12.va.us/ces/Home.aspx

Clarke County High School
627 Mosby Blvd, Berryville VA 22611
DP Coordinator Thom Potts
Languages English
T: +1 540 955 6130
W: cchs.clarke.k12.va.us

Edgar Allen Poe Middle School
7000 Cindy Lane, Annandale VA 2203
MYP Coordinator Michelle Sue Peters
Languages English
T: +1 703 813 3800
W: www.fcps.edu/poems

Ellen Glasgow Middle School
Fairfax County Public Schools, 4101 Fairfax Parkway, Alexandria VA 22312
MYP Coordinator Chinoyerem (Nonye) Oladimeji
Languages English
T: +1 703 813 8700
W: www.fcps.edu/glasgowms/ibmyp

Ellis Elementary School
10400 Kim Graham Lane, Manassas VA 20109
PYP Coordinator Sheryl Solow
Languages English
T: +1 703 365 0287
W: ellises.pwcs.edu

Fairfield Middle School
5121 Nine Mile Road, Henrico VA 23223
MYP Coordinator Leah Wiedenhoft
Languages English
T: +1 804 328 4020
W: www.henrico.k12.va.us/ms/fairfield

Fred M. Lynn Middle School
1650 Prince William Parkway, Woodbridge VA 22191
MYP Coordinator Greg Patterson
Languages English
T: +1 703 494 5157
W: lynnms.pwcs.edu

Galileo Magnet High School
230 South Ridge Road, Danville VA 24541
DP Coordinator Kathy Shanks
Languages English
T: +1 434 773 8186
W: web.dps.k12.va.us/galileo

Gar-Field Senior High School
14000 Smoketown Road, Woodbridge VA 22192
CP Coordinator Michelle Schneider
DP Coordinator Brian Bassett
MYP Coordinator Della Gordon
Languages English
T: +1 703 730 7000
W: www.IBatGF.com

George C Marshall High School
7731 Leesburg Pike, Falls Church VA 22043
DP Coordinator Matthew Axelrod
Languages English
T: +1 703 714 5402
W: www.fcps.edu/marshallhs

George H Moody Middle School
7800 Woodman Road, Richmond VA 23228
MYP Coordinator April Craver
Languages English
T: +1 804 261 5015
W: schools.henrico.k12.va.us/moody

George M. Hampton Middle School
14800 Darbydale Avenue, Woodbridge VA 22193
MYP Coordinator Della Gordon
Languages English
T: +1 703 670 6166
W: hamptonms.pwcs.edu

George Mason High School
7124 Leesburg Pike, Falls Church VA 22043
DP Coordinator Daniel Coast
MYP Coordinator Alicia Miller
Languages English
T: +1 703 248 5500
W: www.fccps.org/o/gmhs

Granby High School
7101 Granby Street, Norfolk VA 23505
DP Coordinator Rebecca Gardner
Languages English
T: +1 757 451 4110
W: www.nps.k12.va.us/Schools/GranbyHS

Green Run Collegiate
1700 Dahlia Drive, Virginia Beach VA 23456
CP Coordinator Rianne Patricio
DP Coordinator Rianne Patricio
MYP Coordinator Tonia Waters
Languages English
T: +1 757 648 5350
W: www.greenruncollegiate.com

Hampton High School
1491 W Queen Street, Hampton City Schools, Hampton VA 23669
DP Coordinator Chris Fredericks
Languages English
T: +1 757 825 4430
W: www.sbo.hampton.k12.va.us

Hanover High School
10307 Chamberlayne Road, Mechanicsville VA 23116
DP Coordinator Jessica Orth
Languages English
T: +1 804 723 3700
W: hanover.k12.va.us/hhs

Henrico High School
302 Azalea Avenue, Richmond VA 23227
DP Coordinator Priscilla Biddle
MYP Coordinator Priscilla Biddle
Languages English
T: +1 804 228 2700
W: schools.henrico.k12.va.us/henrico

Holmes Middle School
6525 Montrose Street, Alexandria VA 22312
MYP Coordinator Donna Starace
Languages English
T: +1 703 658 5900
W: holmesms.fcps.edu

Hugh Mercer Elementary School
2100 Cowan Blvd, Fredericksburg VA 22401
PYP Coordinator Stephanie Teri
Languages English
T: +1 540 372 1115

James Monroe High School
2300 Washington Ave, Fredericksburg VA 22401
DP Coordinator Shawn Barnard
MYP Coordinator Quincy Crecelius Click
Languages English
T: +1 540 372 1100
W: www.cityschools.com/jamesmonroehighschool

James River Elementary School
8901 Pocahontas Trail, Williamsburg VA 23185
PYP Coordinator Amy Zrakovi
Languages English
T: +1 757 887 1768
W: www.wjcc.k12.va.us/jr/

James W Robinson, Jr Secondary School
5035 Sideburn Road, Fairfax County Public Schools, Fairfax VA 22032
DP Coordinator Wendy Vu
MYP Coordinator Amy Riddick
Languages English
T: +1 703 426 2100
W: www.fcps.edu/RobinsonSS

Jefferson Houston Prek-8 School
1501 Cameron Street, Alexandria VA 22314
MYP Coordinator Anthony Washington
PYP Coordinator Anthony Washington
Languages English, Spanish
T: +1 703 706 4400
W: www.acps.k12.va.us/houston/index.php

John Randolph Tucker High School
2910 North Parham Road, Henrico VA 23294
DP Coordinator Ellie Harper
MYP Coordinator Ellie Harper
Languages English
T: +1 804 527 4600
W: www.henrico.k12.va.us/HS/Tucker

Justice High School
3301 Peace Valley Lane, Falls Church VA 22044
DP Coordinator Jennifer Kresse-Rodríguez
MYP Coordinator Katherine Naughton
Languages English
T: +1 703 824 3900
W: justicehs.fcps.edu

Key Middle School
6402 Franconia Road, Springfield VA 22150
MYP Coordinator Danielle Danz
Languages English
T: +1 703 313 3900
W: keyms.fcps.edu

King Abdullah Academy
2949 Education Dr, Herndon VA 20171
DP Coordinator Jalaika Hasan
MYP Coordinator Deborah Mohammed
Languages Arabic, English
T: +1 571 351 5520
W: www.kaa-herndon.com

King's Fork High School
351 King's Fork Road, Suffolk VA 23434
DP Coordinator Stuart Jones
Languages English
T: +1 757 923 5240
W: www.spsk12.net/schools/kfhs

Lafayette Upper Elementary School
3 Learning Lane, Fredericksburg VA 22401
PYP Coordinator Katya Zablotney
Languages English
T: +1 540 310 0029
W: www.cityschools.com/lafayetteupperelementaryschool

Langston Hughes Middle School
11401 Ridge Heights Road, Reston VA 20191
MYP Coordinator Danna Hailfinger
Languages English
T: +1 703 715 3600

Lee High School
6540 Franconia Road, Fairfax county, Springfield VA 22150
CP Coordinator Stephanie Dawley
DP Coordinator Mariano Acevedo
MYP Coordinator Stephanie Bilimoria
Languages English
T: +1 703 924 8300
W: www.fcps.edu/LeeHS

Lee-Davis High School
7052 Mechanicsville Pike, Hanover County, Mechanicsville VA 23111-3629
DP Coordinator Lesa Berlinghoff
Languages English
T: +1 804 723 2200
W: www.hanover.k12.va.us

Lucille Brown Middle School
6300 Jahnke Road, Richmond VA 23225
MYP Coordinator Tracy S. Cady
Languages English
T: +1 804 319 3013
W: www.richmond.k12.va.us/lucilleib

Mark Twain Middle School
4700 Franconia Road, Alexandria VA 22310
MYP Coordinator Mary Ball
Languages English
T: +1 703 313 3700
W: www2.fcps.edu/twainms

Mary Ellen Henderson Middle School
7130 Leesburg Pike, Falls Church VA 22043
MYP Coordinator Alicia Miller
Languages English
T: +1 703 720 5702
W: www.fccps.org/o/meh

USA

Massanutten Military Academy
614 South Main Street, Woodstock VA 22664
CP Coordinator Hannah Watterson
Languages English
T: +1 540 459 2167
W: www.militaryschool.com

Meadowbrook High School
4901 Cogbill Road, Richmond VA 23234
DP Coordinator Tiffany Huff
Languages English
T: +1 804 743 3675
W: www.chesterfield.k12.va.us/Schools/Meadowbrook_HS

Midlothian High School
401 Charter Colony Parkway, Chesterfield County, Midlothian VA 23114
DP Coordinator Mark Spewak
Languages English
T: +1 804 378 2440
W: www.chesterfield.k12.va.us/Schools/Midlothian_HS

Mount Daniel Elementary
2328 North Oak Street, Falls Church VA 22046
PYP Coordinator Carrie Checca
Languages English
T: +1 703 248 5640
W: www.fccps.org/o/mde

Mount Vernon High School
8515 Old Mount Vernon Road, Alexandria VA 22309
CP Coordinator Berkeley McHugh
DP Coordinator Berkeley McHugh
MYP Coordinator Nikolas Short
Languages English
T: +1 703 619 3103
W: www.fcps.edu/MtVernonHS

Mountain View High School
2135 Mountain View Road, Stafford VA 22556
DP Coordinator Theresa Gaddy
Languages English
T: +1 540 658 6840
W: mountainview.groupfusion.net

N.B. Clements Junior High School
7800 Laurel Spring Road, Prince George VA 23875
MYP Coordinator Michelle Bowen
Languages English
T: +1 804 733 2730
W: schools.pgs.k12.va.us/clements

Oscar F Smith High School
1994 Tiger Drive, Chesapeake VA 23320
DP Coordinator Kerri Lancaster
Languages English
T: +1 757 548 0696
W: www.eclipse.cps.k12.va.us/Schools/OSH

Patrick Henry High School
12449 West Patrick Henry Road, Ashland VA 23005
DP Coordinator Megan Lindemann
Languages English
T: +1 804 365 8011

Plaza Middle School
3080 South Lynnhaven Road, Virginia Beach VA 23452
MYP Coordinator Catherine Susewind
Languages English
T: +1 757 431 4060
W: www.plazams.vbschools.com

Prince George High School
7801 Laurel Spring Road, Prince George VA 23875
MYP Coordinator Michelle Bowen
Languages English
T: +1 804 733 2720
W: schools.pgs.k12.va.us/pghs

Princess Anne High School
4400 Virginia Beach Boulevard, Virginia Beach VA 23462-3198
DP Coordinator Helen T Cox
MYP Coordinator Helen T Cox
Languages English
T: +1 757 473 5000
W: www.princessannehs.vbschools.com

Randolph Elementary School
1306 S Quincy Street, Arlington VA 22204
PYP Coordinator Shannon Quinn
Languages English
T: +1 703 228 5830

Rosa Parks Elementary School
13446 Princedale Drive, Woodbridge VA 22193
PYP Coordinator Colbi Money
Languages English
T: +1 703 580 9665
W: pwcs.edu/rosaparkses

Saint Mary's Catholic School
9501 Gayton Road, Richmond VA 23229
MYP Coordinator Carole Forkey
Languages English
T: +1 804 740 1048
W: www.saintmary.org

Salem High School
400 Spartan Drive, Salem VA 24153
DP Coordinator Chris Wilkes
Languages English
T: +1 540 387 2437
W: www.salem.k12.va.us

South Lakes High School
11400 South Lakes Drive, Reston VA 20191
CP Coordinator Susan Brownsword
DP Coordinator Marie Turner
MYP Coordinator Daina Lieberman
Languages English
T: +1 703 715 4500

Spotsylvania High School
6975 Courthouse Road, Spotsylvania VA 22551
DP Coordinator Jennifer Navarrete
Languages English
T: +1 540 582 3882
W: www.spotsyschools.us/shs

St Michael's Episcopal School
8706 Quaker Lane, Richmond VA 23235
MYP Coordinator Leslie Eckmann
Languages English
T: +1 804 272 3514
W: stmschool.net

Stonewall Jackson High School
8820 Rixlew Lane, Manassas VA 20109
CP Coordinator Herman Hruska
DP Coordinator Katie Hodgson
MYP Coordinator Alaina Lynard
Languages English
T: +1 703 365 2900
W: stonewallhs.pwcs.edu/home

Stonewall Middle School
10100 Lomond Drive, Manassas VA 20109
MYP Coordinator Jeanine Fox
Languages English
T: +1 703 361 3185
W: www.stonewallms.schools.pwcs.edu

Stuart M Beville Middle School
4901 Dale Boulevard, Woodbridge VA 22193-4700
MYP Coordinator Patricia Kramolisch
Languages English
T: +1 703 878 2593
W: www.pwcs.edu/beville/

Thomas Alva Edison High School
5801 Franconia Road, Alexandria VA 22310
DP Coordinator Megan Garnett
MYP Coordinator Heather Browne
Languages English
T: +1 703 924 8007
W: www.fcps.k12.va.us/EdisonHS

Thomas Jefferson Elementary
601 South Oak Street, Falls Church VA 22046
PYP Coordinator Carrie Checca
Languages English
T: +1 703 248 5661
W: www.fccps.org/o/tje

Thomas Jefferson High School
4100 West Grace Street, Richmond VA 23230
DP Coordinator Melissa Johnston
MYP Coordinator Tracy S. Cady
Languages English
T: +1 804 780 6028
W: www.richmond.k12.va.us./ib_jefferson

Thomas Jefferson Middle School
125 S Old Glebe Road, Arlington VA 22204
MYP Coordinator Christopher "Kip" Malinosky
Languages English
T: +1 703 228 5900
W: www.apsva.us/jefferson

Trinity Episcopal School
3850 Pittaway Road, Richmond VA 23235
DP Coordinator Marti Truman
Languages English
T: +1 804 272 5864
W: www.trinityes.org

Tuckahoe Middle School
9000 Three Chopt Road, Henrico VA 23229
MYP Coordinator Marie Wilcox
Languages English
T: +1 804 673 3720
W: tuckahoems.henricoschools.us

Walker-Grant Middle School
One Learning Lane, Fredericksburg VA 22401
MYP Coordinator Quincy Crecelius Click
Languages English
T: +1 540 372 1145
W: www.cityschools.com/walkergrantmiddleschool

Walt Whitman Middle School
2500 Parkers Lane, Alexandria VA 22306
MYP Coordinator Dana Bayer
Languages English
T: +1 703 660 2400

Warwick High School
51 Copeland Lane, Newport News VA 23601
DP Coordinator Jason Hollar
Languages English
T: +1 757 591 4700
W: warwick.nn.k12.va.us

Washington-Lee High School
1301 N Stafford St, Arlington VA 22201
DP Coordinator Julie Cantor
Languages English
T: +1 703 228 6200
W: washingtonlee.apsva.us

York High School
9300 George Washington, Memorial Highway, Yorktown VA 23692
DP Coordinator Kevin Valliant
Languages English
T: +1 757 898 0354
W: www.edline.net/pages/YHS

Washington

A C Davis High School
212 South 6th Avenue, Yakima WA 98902
DP Coordinator Diane Main
Languages English
T: +1 509 573 2501
W: www.yakimaschools.org/davis

Alderwood Elementary School
3400 Hollywood Avenue, Bellingham WA 98225
PYP Coordinator Gretchen Stiteler
Languages English
T: +1 360 676 6404
W: alderwood.bellinghamschools.org

Annie Wright Schools
827 N Tacoma Avenue, Tacoma WA 98403
DP Coordinator Emily Lynn
MYP Coordinator Angelica Calcote
PYP Coordinator Jennifer Bills
Languages English
T: +1 253 272 2216
W: www.aw.org

Beach Elementary School
3786 Centerview Rd, Lummi Island WA 98262
PYP Coordinator Mark Hall
Languages English
T: +1 360 383 9440
W: www.ferndalesd.org/beach

Bellevue Children's Academy
14600 NE 24th St., Bellevue WA 98007
PYP Coordinator Amy Knapp
Languages English
T: +1 425 649 0791
W: www.bcacademy.com

Birchwood Elementary School
3200 Pinewood Avenue, Bellingham WA 98225
PYP Coordinator Melanie Haines
Languages English
T: +1 360 676 6466
W: birchwood.bellinghamschools.org

Capital High School
2707 Conger Avenue, Olympia WA 98502
DP Coordinator Ken Joling
Languages English
T: +1 360 753 8880
W: capital.osd.wednet.edu

Carl Cozier Elementary School
1330 Lincoln St., Bellingham WA 98229
PYP Coordinator Monica Savory
Languages English
T: +1 360 676 6410
W: carlcozier.bellinghamschools.org

Cedar Heights Middle School
2220 Pottery Ave, Port Orchard WA 98366
MYP Coordinator Jennifer Knowles
Languages English
T: +1 360 874 6020
W: cedarheights.skschools.org

Chief Sealth International High School
2600 SW Thistle, Seattle WA 98126
CP Coordinator Teresa Cairns
DP Coordinator Allison Hays
Languages English
T: +1 206 252 8550
W: chiefsealthhs.seattleschools.org

Columbia River High School
800 North West 99th Street, Vancouver WA 98665
DP Coordinator Julie A Nygaard
Languages English
T: +1 360 313 3900
W: portalsso.vansd.org/portal/page/portal/Building_Pages/COLUMBIA_RIVER_HIGH_SCHOOL

Discovery Middle School
800 E. 40th Street, Vancouver WA 98663
MYP Coordinator Sarah Puddy
Languages English
T: +1 360 313 3300
W: disco.vansd.org

Eastern Senior High School
1700 East Capitol Street NE, Washington DC 20003
DP Coordinator Elizabeth Braganza
Languages English
T: +1 202 698 4500
W: www.easternhighschooldc.org

Edmunds-Woodway High School
7600 212th St South West, Edmonds WA 98026
DP Coordinator David Quinn
Languages English
T: +1 425 431 7900
W: www.school.edmonds.wednet.edu/ewhs/

Giaudrone Middle School
4902 S Alaska Street, Tacoma WA 98408
MYP Coordinator Anthony Costa
Languages English
T: +1 253 571 5810
W: www.tacoma.k12.wa.us/sites/schools/giaudrone/Pages/Default.aspx

Harrison Preparatory School
9103 Lakewood DR SW, Lakewood WA 98499
DP Coordinator Erika Cox
MYP Coordinator Erika Cox
Languages English
T: +1 253 583 5419
W: www.edline.net/pages/Harrison_Preparatory_School/

Henry Foss High School
2112 South Tyler Street, Tacoma WA 98405
DP Coordinator Casey Silbaugh
Languages English
T: +1 253 571 7300
W: www.tacoma.k12.wa.us/foss

Idlewild Elementary School
10806 Idlewild Rd. SW, Lakewood WA 98499
PYP Coordinator Dori Zukowski
Languages English
T: +1 253 583 5290
W: www.edline.net/pages/Idlewild_Elementary_School

Inglemoor High School
15500 Simonds Rd NE, Kenmore WA 98028
DP Coordinator Amy Monaghan
Languages English
T: +1 425 408 7200
W: www.nsd.org/inglemoor

Ingraham High School
1819 North 135th Street, Seattle WA 98133-7709
DP Coordinator Guy Thomas
Languages English
T: +1 206 252 3923

Interlake High School
16245 NE 24th St., Bellevue WA 98008
DP Coordinator Teresa Cairns
Languages English
T: +1 425 456 7200
W: bsd405.org/interlake

Kennewick High School
500 S. Dayton Street, Kennewick WA 99336
DP Coordinator Ashley Williams
Languages English
T: +1 509) 222-7100
W: kennewick.ksd.org

Kent-Meridian High School
10020 SE 256th Street, Kent WA 98031
DP Coordinator Beth Shoemaker
Languages English
T: +1 253 373 7405

Kilo Middle School
4400 S. 308th St, Auburn WA 98001
MYP Coordinator Scott Schumeier
Languages English
T: +1 253 945 4700
W: schools.fwps.org/kilo

Liberty Bell Junior-Senior High School
24 Twin Lakes Rd, Winthrop WA 98862
MYP Coordinator Anne Andersen
Languages English
T: +1 509 996 2215
W: methow.org/schools/liberty-bell-jr-sr-high

McCarver Elementary
2111 S. J St, Tacoma WA 98405
PYP Coordinator Christel Elliott
Languages English
T: +1 253 571 4900
W: www.tacoma.k12.wa.us

Methow Valley Elementary
18 Twin Lakes Rd, Winthrop WA 98862
PYP Coordinator Anne Andersen
Languages English
T: +1 509 996 2186
W: methow.org/methow-valley-elementary-school

Mount Rainier High School
22450 19th Avenue S, Des Moines WA 98198
DP Coordinator Veronica Fairchild
MYP Coordinator Kevin Rawie
Languages English
T: +1 206 631 7000
W: www.highlineschools.org

Northern Heights Elementary
4000 Magrath Road, Bellingham WA 98226
PYP Coordinator Jayme Rios
Languages English
T: +1 360 647 6820
W: northernheights.bellinghamschools.org

Orchard Heights Elementary
2288 Fircrest Dr SE, Port Orchard WA 98366
PYP Coordinator Kimberly Powell
Languages English
T: +1 360 443 3530
W: orchardheights.skschools.org

PRIDE Schools
811 E Sprague Ave, Suite C, Spokane WA 99202
MYP Coordinator Stephanie Gronholz
Languages English, Spanish
T: +1 509 309 7680
W: prideschools.org

Rainier Beach High School
8815 Seward Park Avenue S WA 98118
DP Coordinator Steven Miller
Languages English
T: +1 206 252 6350
W: rainierbeachhs.seattleschools.org

Renton High School
400 S Second Street, Renton WA 98057
DP Coordinator Malcolm Robert Montgomery Collie
Languages English
T: +1 425 204 3400
W: renton.rentonschools.us

Saint George's School
2929 W. Waikiki Road, Spokane WA 99208
DP Coordinator Elizabeth Tender
Languages English
T: +1 509 466 1636 EXT:331
W: www.sgs.org

Skyline High School
1122 228th Avenue SE, Issaquah School District, Sammamish WA 98075-6914
CP Coordinator Stephania Gullikson
DP Coordinator Chris Wilder
Languages English
T: +1 425 837 7700
W: www.shs.issaquah.wednet.edu

Soundview School
6515 196th Street SW, Lynnwood WA 98036
MYP Coordinator Erin Armstrong
Languages English
T: +1 425 778 8572
W: www.soundview.org

South Charleston High School
One Eagle Way, South Charleston WA 25309
DP Coordinator Edward Booten
Languages English
T: +1 304 766 0352

South Kitsap High School
425 Mitchell Ave, Port Orchard WA 98366
CP Coordinator Michelle Duchene
DP Coordinator Michelle Duchene
Languages English
T: +1 360 874 5600
W: www.skitsap.wednet.edu/domain/31

Sumner High School
1707 Main Street, Sumner WA 98390
DP Coordinator Monica Swigart
Languages English
T: +1 253 891 5500
W: www.sumner.wednet.edu

Thomas Jefferson High School
4248 S. 288th Street, Auburn WA 98001
CP Coordinator Jennifer McKay
DP Coordinator Kailey Harem
MYP Coordinator Shari Winslow
Languages English
T: +1 253 945 5600
W: www.fwps.org/tjhs

Totem Middle School
26630 40th Avenue S., Kent WA 98032
MYP Coordinator Liz Andrade
Languages English
T: +1 253 945 5100
W: www.fwps.org/tot

Wade King Elementary School
2155 Yew Street Road, Bellingham WA 98229
PYP Coordinator Hana Anderson
Languages English
T: +1 360 647 6840
W: wadeking.bellinghamschools.org

West Sound Academy
16571 Creative Drive NE, Poulsbo WA 98370
DP Coordinator Catherine Freeman
Languages English
T: +1 360 598 5954
W: www.westsoundacademy.org

Willows Preparatory School
12280 NE Woodinville-Redmond Rd, Redmond WA 98052
MYP Coordinator Grant Norcross
Languages English
T: +1 425 649 0791
W: www.willowsprep.com

Wisconsin

Academy of Accelerated Learning
3727 South 78th Street, Milwaukee WI 53220
PYP Coordinator Renee Bast
Languages English
T: +1 414 604 7300
W: www2.milwaukee.k12.wi.us/aal

Bay Port High School
2710 Lineville Road, Green Bay WI 54313
DP Coordinator Chad McAllister
Languages English
T: +1 920 662 7000
W: bayporthssd.weebly.com

Casimir Pulaski High School
2500 W Oklahoma Ave, Milwaukee WI 53215
MYP Coordinator Christine Lemon
Languages English, Spanish
T: +1 414 902 8900
W: www5.milwaukee.k12.wi.us/school/pulaski

Catholic Memorial High School
601 East College Avenue, Waukesha WI 53186
CP Coordinator John Burke
DP Coordinator John Burke
Languages English
T: +1 262 542 7101
W: www.catholicmemorial.net

Chappell Elementary School
205 N Fisk Street, Green Bay WI 54303
PYP Coordinator Jackie Brosteau
Languages English
T: +1 920 492 2630
W: www.gbaps.org/ES/Chappell

Darrell Lynn Hines College Preparatory Academy of Excellence
7151 North 86th Street, Milwaukee WI 53224
PYP Coordinator Monica Carrington
Languages English
T: +1 414 358 3542

Franklin Middle School
1233 Lore Lane, Green Bay WI 54303
MYP Coordinator Jennifer Burgraff
Languages English
T: +1 920 492 2670
W: www.greenbay.k12.wi.us/franklin

Green Bay West High School
966 Shawano Avenue, Green Bay WI 54303
DP Coordinator Stephane Bielen
MYP Coordinator Andrew Evenson
Languages English
T: +1 920 492 2730
W: www.greenbay.k12.wi.us/west/

Green Lake School
612 Mill Street, PO Box 369, Green Lake WI 54941
DP Coordinator Patricia Priske
MYP Coordinator Mary Hunter
PYP Coordinator Katie James
Languages English
T: +1 920 294 6411
W: www.glsd.k12.wi.us

Holy Family School
1204 S. Fisk Street, Green Bay WI 54304
MYP Coordinator Steve Gromala
Languages English
T: +1 920 494 1931
W: holyfamilygreenbay.com

Jefferson Lighthouse Elementary
1722 West Sixth Street, Racine WI 53404
PYP Coordinator Colleen Strain
Languages English
T: +1 262 664 6900
W: jefferson.racine.k12.wi.us

Jerome I Case High School
7345 Washington Avenue, Racine WI 53406
CP Coordinator Patty Hammes
DP Coordinator Nicola Malacara
Languages English
T: +1 262 619 4200
W: www.rusd.org/case

Lincoln High School
1433 South Eighth Street, Manitowoc WI 54220
DP Coordinator Rachael George
Languages English
T: +1 920 663 9602
W: www.manitowocpublicschools.org

Lowell Elementary School
4360 S. 20th Street, Milwaukee WI 53221
PYP Coordinator Janet Key
Languages English
T: +1 414 304 6600
W: www5.milwaukee.k12.wi.us/school/lowell.html

MacDowell Montessori School
6415 W Mount Vernon Avenue, Milwaukee WI 53216
DP Coordinator Nicholas Beermann
Languages English
T: +1 414 256 8300
W: www5.milwaukee.k12.wi.us/school/macdowell/

Madison Country Day School
5606 River Road, Waunakee WI 53597
DP Coordinator Mark Childs
Languages English
T: +1 608 850 6000
W: www.madisoncountryday.org

McKinley Middle School
2340 Mohr Avenue, Racine WI 53405
MYP Coordinator Stephanie Skaarnes
Languages English
T: +1 262 664 6150
W: www.rusd.org/mckinley

Notre Dame de la Baie Academy
610 Maryhill Drive, Green Bay WI 54303
DP Coordinator Matthew Schultz
Languages English
T: +1 920 429 6100
W: www.NotreDameAcademy.com

Oconomowoc High School
641 East Forest Street, Oconomowoc WI 53066-3888
CP Coordinator Carrie Schultz
DP Coordinator Carrie Schultz
Languages English
T: +1 262 560 3100
W: www.oasd.k12.wi.us

Ronald Reagan High School
4965 South 20 Street, Milwaukee WI 53221
CP Coordinator Jamie Gonzalez
DP Coordinator David Walker
MYP Coordinator Teri Knight
Languages English
T: +1 414 304 6100
W: www.milwaukee.k12.wi.us/pages/mps/school/highs/reagan

Roosevelt Elementary
3322 Roosevelt Road, Kenosha WI 53142
PYP Coordinator Leah Ebener
Languages English
T: +1 262 359 6097
W: roosevelt.kusd.edu

Rufus King International School – High School Campus
1801 West Olive Street, Milwaukee WI 53209
DP Coordinator Daniel Gatewood
MYP Coordinator Laura Lewandowski
Languages English
T: +1 414 267 0705
W: www.rkhs.org

Rufus King International School – Middle School Campus
121 E Hadley St, Milwaukee WI 53212
MYP Coordinator Vanetta Collins
Languages English
T: +1 414 616 5200
W: www5.milwaukee.k12.wi.us/school/rkims

St. Joan Antida High School
1341 N. Cass Street, Milwaukee WI 53202
CP Coordinator Cynthia McLinn
DP Coordinator Susan Kosiboski
Languages English
T: +1 414 272 8423
W: www.saintjoanantida.org

Wausau East High School
2607 N 18th Street, Wausau WI 54403
DP Coordinator Darlene Beattie
Languages English
T: +1 715 261 0650
W: www.wausau.k12.wi.us/east/

Wauwatosa Catholic
1500 Wauwatosa Avenue, Wauwatosa WI 53213
MYP Coordinator Karen Scharrer-Erickson
PYP Coordinator Karen Scharrer-Erickson
Languages English
T: +1 414 258 9977
W: www.wauwatosacatholic.org

Wedgewood Park International School
6506 W Warnimont Avenue, Milwaukee WI 53220
MYP Coordinator Megan Kuczmarski
Languages English
T: +1 414 604 7800

West Ridge Elementary School
1347 S. Emmertsen Road, Racine WI 53406
PYP Coordinator Ruth Adamczyk
T: +1 262 664 6200
W: www.rusd.org/westridge

Wyoming

Cheyenne East High School
2800 E Pershing Blvd, Cheyenne WY 82001
DP Coordinator Jonathon Lever
Languages English
T: +1 307 771 2663 EXT 108
W: www.east.laramie1.org/

Journeys School
700 Coyote Canyon Road, Jackson WY 83001
DP Coordinator David Porter
Languages English
T: +1 307 733 3729
W: www.journeysschool.org

Natrona County High School
930 Elm Street, Casper WY 82601
DP Coordinator Marvin Birzer
Languages English
T: +1 307 253 1700

VENEZUELA

Colegio Integral El Avila
Centro de Artes Integradas, Urb. Terrazas del Avila, La Urbina Norte, Caracas 1073
DP Coordinator Carmen Winkler
Languages Spanish
T: +58 243.58.20
W: www.elavila.org

Colegio Internacional de Caracas
Calle Colegio, entre Los Samanes y Las Minas de Baruta, Caracas 1080
DP Coordinator Mike East
MYP Coordinator Mike East
Languages English, Spanish
T: +58 212 945 0444
W: cic-caracas.org

Colegio Los Campitos
Ruta C, Urbanización Los Campitos, Prados del Este, Miranda
DP Coordinator Margot Peña
Languages Spanish
T: +58 212 977 1768

Colegio Moral y Luces 'Herzl-Bialik'
Final Ave. Los Chorros, SEDE CLUB HEBRAICA (Frente al INAM), Los Chorros CARACAS 1071
DP Coordinator Naily Gamboa
Languages English
T: +58 212 273 6894/6807
W: www.secmyl.edu.ve

Escuela Bella Vista
67th Street between Av. 3D and 3E "La Lago" sector, Macaracaibo, Zulia 4001
DP Coordinator Anthony Varga
Languages English
T: +58 261 794 0000
W: www.ebv.org.ve

Escuela Campo Alegre
Final Calle La Cinta, Las Mercedes, Caracas
DP Coordinator Matthew Sheets
Languages English
T: +58 212 993 3922
W: www.ecak12.com

Instituto Educacional Juan XXIII
Calle San Enrique No 85-70, Trigal Centro, Valencia, Estado Carabobo 2002
CP Coordinator Jorge Bolivar Manzano
DP Coordinator Elkys Sequera
Languages English, Spanish
T: +58 241 8425732
W: www.juanxxiii.e12.ve

Liceo Los Robles
Urbanización el Doral Norte, Calle 34 esquina con Avenida, Fuerzas Armadas, Mar, Estado Zulia 4002
DP Coordinator Jesús Antonio Vilchez Chávez
Languages Spanish
T: +58 0261 7421833
W: losroblesenlinea.com.ve

The British School Caracas
PO Box 668708, c/o Jet International 489, Miami FL 33166, USA
DP Coordinator Peter O'Reilly
Languages English
T: +58 212 265 58 70
W: www.tbscaracas.com

WASHINGTON ACADEMY
Calle C, Urb. Colinas de Valle Arriba, Caracas 1080
DP Coordinator Dr. José Ruggiero
MYP Coordinator Prof. Gianna De Sena
Languages Spanish, English
T: +58 212 9757077
E: academiawashington@aw.edu.ve
W: www.washington.academy
See full details on page 558

VIRGIN ISLANDS (US)

Virgin Islands Montessori School & Peter Gruber International Academy
6936 Vessup Lane, St Thomas VI 00802
DP Coordinator Matthew Stocking
MYP Coordinator Alexandra Silva
Languages English
T: +1 340 775 6360
W: www.vimontessori.com

IB AMERICAS

Appendices

1. Addresses of all IB Offices
2. Location of IB World Schools
3. Diploma Programme Subjects Offered in 2020 (May and November sessions)
4. IB Associations Around the World
5. University Acknowledgement
6. University Scholarships for IB Diploma Holders

1. Addresses of all IB Offices

IB FOUNDATION OFFICE

International Baccalaureate
Route des Morillons 15
Grand – Saconnex, Genève
CH – 1218
SWITZERLAND

IB GLOBAL CENTRES

Africa, Europa, Middle East

IB Global Centre, The Hague
Churchillplein 6
2517 JW
The Hague
The Netherlands

IB Global Centre, Cardiff
Peterson House, Malthouse Avenue
Cardiff Gate
Cardiff, Wales
CF23 8GL
United Kingdom

Americas

IB Global Centre, Washington DC
7501 Wisconsin Avenue, Suite 200 West
Bethesda, Maryland 20814
USA

Asia – Pacific

IB Global Centre, Singapore
600 North Bridge Road,
#21 – 01 Parkview Square,
Singapore 188778
Republic of Singapore

2. Location of IB World Schools

Location (as of November 2019)	IB World Schools	Number of Programmes				Total number of Programmes
		PYP	MYP	DP	CP	
ALBANIA		9	3	3	3	3
ANDORRA			1	1	1	
ANGOLA		3	1	1	1	1
ANGUILLA			1	1	1	
ANTIGUA AND BARBUDA			1	1	1	
ARGENTINA		68	6	2	60	61
ARMENIA		5	1	1	3	3
AUSTRALIA	195	136	47	77	3	263
AUSTRIA		23	5	4	14	16
AZERBAIJAN		13	4	2	7	7
BAHAMAS	3	3	1	3	1	8
BAHRAIN	12	1	1	12	1	15
BANGLADESH	6	5	2	6	1	14
BARBADOS		3	1	1	1	1
BELGIUM	9	3	4	9	1	17
BERMUDA		3	4	1	3	
BOLIVIA		3	4	1	3	
BOSNIA AND HERZEGOVINA		3	4	1	3	
BOTSWANA		4	2	1	1	2
BRAZIL		53	18	5	30	40
BRITISH VIRGIN ISLANDS		3	1	1	1	1
BRUNEI DARUSSALAM			2	2	2	
BULGARIA		8	9	1	8	
BURKINA FASO			1	1	1	
CAMBODIA		8	3	2	3	4
CAMEROON		6	1	1	4	4
CANADA	383	93	157	186	6	442
CAYMAN ISLANDS		4	4	3	1	
CHILE		48	15	8	25	30
CHINA	169	89	45	115	2	251
COLOMBIA		74	15	14	45	45
COSTA RICA		49	1	1	47	47
CROATIA		6	1	2	3	4
CUBA			1	1	1	
CURACAO			1	1	1	
CYPRUS			4	4	4	
CZECH REPUBLIC	15	1	1	15	1	18
DENMARK		25	5	4	16	19
DOMINICAN REPUBLIC			2	2	2	
ECUADOR		302	16	17	269	270
EGYPT	29	12	7	23	1	43
EL SALVADOR			4	4	4	
ERITREA			1	1	1	
ESTONIA		11	4	3	4	5
ETHIOPIA		3	4	1	3	
FIJI		5	2	1	2	2
FINLAND	21	3	4	17	1	25

Location (as of November 2019)	IB World Schools	Number of Programmes				Total number of Programmes
		PYP	MYP	DP	CP	
FRANCE		25	5	2	18	18
GABON		5	2	1	2	3
GEORGIA		6	2	2	2	2
GERMANY	84	27	14	79	7	127
GHANA		11	2	3	6	6
GREECE		26	5	6	15	19
GUAM			1	1	1	
GUATEMALA			4	4	4	
GUERNSEY			1	1	1	
HONDURAS			1	1	1	
HONG KONG	66	40	12	33	6	91
HUNGARY			7	7	7	
ICELAND			1	1	1	
INDIA	173	96	39	138	1	274
INDONESIA	57	33	17	43	3	96
IRAQ		10	5	2	3	6
IRELAND		6	1	1	4	5
ISLAMIC REPUBLIC OF IRAN		9	3	3	3	6
ISLE OF MAN			1	1	1	
ISRAEL		3	4	1	3	
ITALY		58	18	13	27	36
IVORY COAST		3	3	1	2	
JAMAICA			2	2	2	
JAPAN		101	36	17	48	73
JERSEY		1	2	1	1	
JORDAN	19	9	9	18	2	38
KAZAKHSTAN		19	7	8	4	9
KENYA	7	3	2	6	1	12
KUWAIT		6	2	2	2	3
KYRGYZSTAN		4	1	1	2	2
LATVIA		8	3	2	3	5
LEBANON		22	7	2	13	17
LESOTHO			1	1	1	
LITHUANIA		8	1	1	6	7
LUXEMBOURG			4	4	4	
MACAU			2	2	2	
MADAGASCAR		1	2	1	1	
MALAWI		3	1	1	1	1
MALAYSIA	36	10	20	20	1	51
MALI			1	1	1	
MALTA			2	2	2	
MAURITIUS	5	2	1	3	1	7
MEXICO	122	60	41	79	15	195
MONACO			1	1	1	
MONGOLIA		5	1	1	3	3
MONTENEGRO		3	1	1	1	1
MOROCCO		15	2	9	4	13
MOZAMBIQUE		5	2	1	2	3
MYANMAR			2	2	2	
NAMIBIA		1	2	1	1	
NEPAL		4	2	1	1	3
NEW ZEALAND		34	18	3	13	27
NICARAGUA		2	3	1	2	

Location (as of November 2019)	IB World Schools	Number of Programmes				Total number of Programmes
		PYP	MYP	DP	CP	
NIGER			1	1	1	
NIGERIA		4	4	1	3	
NORWAY	41	18	16	25	1	60
OMAN		9	5	1	3	6
PAKISTAN		45	20	8	17	30
PALESTINIAN TERRITORY		3	1	1	1	2
PANAMA		11	4	2	5	6
PAPUA NEW GUINEA			1	1	1	
PARAGUAY			4	4	4	
PEOPLE'S DEMOCRATIC REPUBLIC LAO		3	1	1	1	1
PERU	70	14	8	69	2	93
PHILIPPINES		24	4	1	19	20
POLAND		67	12	11	44	53
PORTUGAL	11	2	3	10	1	16
PUERTO RICO		6	2	2	2	2
QATAR		34	10	9	15	17
REPUBLIC OF KOREA	13	9	8	11	1	29
REPUBLIC OF NORTH MACEDONIA		4	4	2	2	
ROMANIA		10	3	2	5	6
RUSSIAN FEDERATION		73	26	23	24	49
RWANDA			1	1	1	
SAUDI ARABIA		30	13	5	12	19
SENEGAL			4	4	4	
SERBIA		8	2	2	4	4
SINGAPORE	36	19	8	27	2	56
SINT MAARTEN			1	1	1	
SLOVAKIA		7	1	2	4	4
SLOVENIA		6	1	2	3	4
SOLOMON ISLANDS			1	1	1	
SOUTH AFRICA		3	4	1	3	
SPAIN	128	24	19	124	1	168
SRI LANKA		3	1	1	1	1
SUDAN		4	2	1	1	2
SWAZILAND			1	1	1	
SWEDEN	37	10	13	29	2	54
SWITZERLAND	51	14	10	46	4	74
TAIWAN		15	2	5	8	8
THAILAND	25	13	6	20	1	40
THE DEMOCRATIC REPUBLIC OF THE CONGO			2	2	2	
THE NETHERLANDS	23	6	13	19	2	40
TIMOR – LESTE		1	2	1	1	
TOGO		4	1	1	2	2
TRINIDAD AND TOBAGO		1	2	1	1	
TUNISIA		3	1	1	1	2
TURKEY		100	36	14	50	76
UGANDA		6	2	1	3	4
UKRAINE		7	3	1	3	4
UNITED ARAB EMIRATES	48	27	17	42	13	99
UNITED KINGDOM	127	10	15	93	45	163
UNITED REPUBLIC OF TANZANIA		15	6	4	5	6
UNITED STATES	1848	578	523	945	120	2166
UNITED STATES VIRGIN ISLANDS		1	2	1	1	
URUGUAY	11	2	4	8	1	15

Location (as of November 2019)	IB World Schools	Number of Programmes				Total number of Programmes
		PYP	MYP	DP	CP	
UZBEKISTAN		3	1	1	1	1
VENEZUELA		13	2	10	1	10
VIETNAM		23	6	4	13	13
ZAMBIA		5	2	1	2	2
ZIMBABWE		3	1	1	1	1
Grand Total	**5183**	**1789**	**1362**	**3436**	**253**	**6840**

Does not include European Platform nor MYP Partner Schools

3. Diploma Programme Subjects offered in 2020 (May and November sessions)

Group 1 – Studies in language and literature
Language A: literature HL
Language A: literature SL
Language A: language and literature HL
Language A: language and literature SL
Literature and performance SL

Group 2 – Language acquisition
Language B HL
Language B SL
Language *ab initio* SL
Classical languages HL
Classical languages SL

Group 3 – Individuals and societies
Business management HL
Business management SL
Economics HL
Economics SL
Environmental systems and societies SL
Geography HL
Geography SL
Global politics HL
Global politics SL
History HL: History of Africa and the Middle East
History HL: History of the Americas
History HL: History of Asia and Oceania
History HL: History of Europe
History SL
ITGS HL
ITGS SL
Philosophy HL
Philosophy SL
Psychology HL
Psychology SL
Social and cultural anthropology HL
Social and cultural anthropology SL
World religions SL

Group 4 – Sciences
Biology HL
Biology SL
Chemistry HL
Chemistry SL
Computer science HL
Computer science SL
Design technology HL
Design technology SL
Environmental systems and societies SL
Nature of Science (Pilot) SL
Physics HL
Physics SL
Sports, exercise and health science HL
Sports, exercise and health science SL

Group 5 – Mathematics
Mathematics: Analysis and approaches HL
Mathematics: Analysis and approaches SL
Mathematics: Applications and interpretation HL
Mathematics: Applications and interpretation SL
Further mathematics HL (last assessment 2020)
Mathematical studies SL (last assessment 2020)
Mathematics HL (last assessment 2020)
Mathematics SL (last assessment 2020)

Group 6 – The arts
Dance HL
Dance SL
Film HL
Film SL
Literature and performance SL
Music HL
Music SL
Theatre HL
Theatre SL
Visual arts HL
Visual arts SL

Core requirements
Creativity, activity, service
Extended essay, or
World studies extended essay
Theory of knowledge

Interdisciplinary subjects
Environmental systems and societies SL
Literature and performance SL

School based syllabuses

Art History (Individuals and societies)
Astronomy (Sciences)
Brazilian Social Studies (Individuals and societies) (also examined in November session)
Classical Greek & Roman Studies (Individuals and societies)
Food science and technology (Sciences)
Marine Science (Sciences)
Modern History of Kazakhstan (Individuals and societies)
Political Thought (Individuals and societies)
Turkey in the 20th Century (Individuals and societies)
World Arts and Cultures (Individuals and societies)

Languages offered in group 1 – studies in language and literature

Language A: literature

Afrikaans A (Nov only)
Albanian A (May only)
Amharic A (May only)
Arabic A (May only)
Belarusian A (ending 2020)
Bengali A (May only)
Bosnian A (May only)
Bulgarian A (May only)
Catalan A (May only)
Chinese A
Croatian A (May only)
Czech A (May only)
Danish A (May only)
Dutch A (May only)
English A
Estonian A (May only)
Filipino A (May only)
Finnish A (May only)
French A
German A
Hebrew A (May only)
Hindi A (May only)
Hungarian A (May only)
Icelandic A (May only)
Indonesian A
Italian A (May only)
Japanese A
Korean A
Latvian A (May only)
Lithuanian A (May only)
Macedonian A (May only)
Malay A (May only)
Modern Greek A (May only)
Nepali A (May only)
Norwegian A (May only)
Persian A (May only)
Polish A (May only)
Portuguese A (May only)
Romanian A (May only)
Russian A (May only)
Serbian A (May only)
Sesotho A (May only)
Sinhalese A (ending 2020)
SiSwati A (SL, November only)
Slovak A (May only)
Slovene A (May only)
Spanish A
Swahili A (May only)
Swedish A (May only)
Thai A (May only)
Turkish A
Ukrainian A (May only)
Urdu A (May only)
Vietnamese A (May only)
Welsh A (May only)

Language A: language and literature

Arabic A (May only)
Chinese A
Dutch A (May only)
English A
French A
German A
Indonesian A
Italian A (May only)
Japanese A (May only)
Korean A (May only)
Modern Greek A (May only)
Norwegian A (May only)
Portuguese A
Russian A (May only)
Spanish A
Swedish A (May only)
Thai A (May only)

Literature and performance

English

Language B

Arabic B (May only)
Chinese B – Cantonese
Chinese B – Mandarin
Danish B (May only)
Dutch B (May only)
English B
Finnish B (May only)
French B
German B
Hebrew B (SL only, May only)
Hindi B (May only)
Indonesian B
Italian B
Japanese B
Korean B (May only)
Malay B (SL, Nov only)
Norwegian B (May only)
Portuguese B (Nov, SL only)
Russian B (May only)
Spanish B
Swahili B (May only)
Swedish B (May only)
Tamil B (SL, Nov only)

Language *ab initio*

Arabic *ab initio* (May only)
Danish (May 2020, May only) *ab initio*
English *ab initio*
French *ab initio*
German *ab initio* (May only)
Indonesian *ab initio* (Nov only)
Italian *ab initio* (May only)
Japanese *ab initio*
Malay *ab initio* (May only)
Mandarin *ab initio*
Russian *ab initio* (May only)
Spanish *ab initio*
Swahili *ab initio* (May only)
Swedish (Mat 2020, May only)

Classical languages

Classical Greek (English) May only
Latin (English and Spanish)

Language B Notes:
Malay SL and Tamil SL are available only in the November session. Therefore, any candidate registered for a May session wishing to take Malay SL or Tamil SL must be additionally registered for a November session (usually, but not necessarily, in the preceding year). They must take all Malay SL or Tamil SL assessment components (written assignment, internal assessment, paper 1 and paper 2) in that November session.

4. IB Associations Around the World

Associations of IB World Schools

Associations of IB World Schools are groupings of IB World Schools who come together in order to provide mutual support in a variety of ways and who have been recognized by the International Baccalaureate Organization (IB). These associations are organized in various ways, sizes and constituencies, depending on their local circumstances and provide a forum for school collaboration, hold periodic meetings and share best practices among members.

The IB works closely with the recognized Associations of IB World Schools who play a key role in supporting IB World Schools. Much like IB World Schools themselves, each Association is an independent entity that is not run or managed by the IB but may choose to formalize its relationship with the IB, provided it meets certain criteria, by means of a recognition agreement and licence.

Associations can be an indispensable resource for schools discovering the IB for the first time, offer a wealth of IB experience and support, and are often active at district, state or government level raising awareness of all IB programmes within their area of representation. They may also, working in concert with their regional IB office, assist in negotiations with governments for acceptance of all IB programmes and with universities for recognition for the Diploma Programme.

Benefits of being an association of IB World Schools

The IB raises the profile of Associations by featuring them on its website, inviting their representatives to regional meetings, and permitting their use of a specially created logo for use under licence on their websites and in publicity to denote their status.

Recognized Associations have similar rights to IB World Schools in their use of IB materials, but can attend more IB meetings and have more routes to advice from the IB's regional offices.

How to become recognized as an association of IB World Schools

Groups of schools who wish to be recognized by the IB as an Association should contact their IB regional office. Contact information for the regional offices can be found on the IB website.

Recognized Associations are situated throughout the world in all three regions.

In addition to recognized Associations, there are many other formal and informal groups, coalitions and loose networks of IB World Schools at work in many areas of the world that are not recognized by the IB as Associations. This may be because they are newly formed or that they do not yet meet the recognition criteria. The IB criterion that they are an official entity may make recognition difficult in some countries where the rules of association prevent this.

IB – recognized Associations
IB Americas

Canada			
Name	**Area covered**	**Contact**	**Website**
Alberta Association of IBWS (ABIBS)	Alberta	President: Sue Rivers	www.abibs.ca
Atlantic Canadian AIBWS	Nova Scotia, New Brunswick, Newfoundland, Prince Edward Island, Bermuda	President: Beth Macmichael	
British Columbia AIBWS	British Columbia	Chair: Jennifer Towers	www.bcaibws.ca
IB Schools of Ontario (IBSO)	Ontario	Executive Director: Charlene Landry – Kyte	www.ibschoolsofontario.ca
Prairie AIBWS	Manitoba, Saskatchewan	Chair: Jennifer Peters Associate: Kim Buglass (SK)	paibws.org
Société des Écoles du Monde du BI du Québec et de la Francophonie (SEBIQ)	Quebec	Director General: Charles Vien Chair of the Board: Pierre Duclos	www.sebiq.ca/index_en.htm

United States

Name	Area covered	Contact	Website
Arizona AIBWS (AZIBS)	Arizona	Chair: Jake Davis	www.azibs.org
California AIBWS (CAWS)	California	Executive Director: Robin Oliver	www.c – aws.org
Florida League of IB Schools (FLIBS)	Florida	Executive Director: Ralph Cline President: Anuj Saran	flibs.org
AIBWS of Georgia	Georgia	President: Kevin Denney	ibgeorgia.org
Illinois Association of IB World Schools (IIBS)	Illinois	President: Rebecca Allister	www.ilibschools.org
Guild of US North East AIBWS (GIBS)	Maine, New York, New Jersey, Connecticut, Rhode Island, Massachusetts, New Hampshire, Vermont, Pennysylvania (east)	President: Jim Meyer	gibsib.org
Hoosier AIBWS	Indiana	President: Leslie Fatum	sites.google.com/site/ibhibs/home
Louisiana Association of IB World Schools	Louisiana	Executive Director: Cherissa Vitter	sites.google.com/a/selu.edu/libs/home
North Carolina AIBWS	North Carolina	President: Loren Baron	ibsnc.org
Northwest AIBWS NIBA	Alaska, Washington, Oregon, Montana, Idaho	Executive Director: Guy Thomas	sites.google.com/site/nwaibws
Michigan AIBWS IBSOM	Michigan	President: Jason Rubel	www.ibsom.org
Mid – Atlantic AIBWS IB – MA	DC, Virginia, Maryland, Delaware	President: Brian Bassett Executive Director: John L Day	www.ibmidatlantic.org
Midwest AIBWS MIBS	Nebraska, Kansas, Oklahoma, Missouri, Iowa	President: Amber Ripa	www.midwestibschools.org
Minnesota AIBWS (MNIB)	Minnesota	Executive director: Jon Peterson President: Kurt Carlson	www.mnibschools.org/home
Nevada Association of IB World Schools NAIBWS	Nevada	President: Ben Feinstein	www.naibws.org
Ohio AIBWS	Ohio	President: Cynthia Ballheim	www.ohioib.org
Rocky Mountain AIBWS IBARMS	Wyoming, Colorado	Executive Director: Jan Lotter President: Melissa Capozza	www.ibarms.org
IB Schools of South Carolina SCIBS	South Carolina	President: Diane Padula	www.southcarolinaib.org
Tennessee AIBWS TIBA	Tennessee	Executive Director: Emily Munn Deputy Director: Kelly Chastain	sites.google.com/site/tennesseeibschools
Association of Texas IBWS TIBS	Texas	Executive Director: Karen Phillips President: Kelly McBride	www.texasibschools.org
AIBWS of Utah	Utah	President: Connie Kearl	
Wisconsin AIBWS (WAIBWS)	Wisconsin	President: Jennifer Burgraff	ibwisconsin.org

Latin America

Name	Area covered	Contact	Website
Asociación Chilena del Bachillerato Internacional (ACHBI)	Chile	President: Lorna Prado	

Asociación de Colegios del Bachillerato Internacional del Rio de la Plata (ACBIRP)	Argentina	President: Paula Manzitti	
Asociación Ecuatoriana de Colegios con Bachillerato Internacional B.I. (ASECCBI)	Ecuador	President: Whymper León Kuffó	www.aseccbi.org.ec
Asociación Mexicana de Colegios Autorizados por la Organización del Bachillerato Internacional (IBAMEX)	Mexico	President: Isela Consuegra Gamón	www.amexcaobi.org.mx
Asociación de Colegios del BI de Costa Rica (ASOBITICO)	Costa Rica	President: Lilliana Lloyd	asobitico.org
Asociación Andina de Colegios de Bachillerato Internacional (AACBI)	Colombia	Executive Director: Luis Eduardo Rivas Garzon President: Robert Tomalin	www.aacbi.org.co
Asociación de Colegios IB Perú (ASCIBP)	Peru	President Alberto Pool	www.ascibp.net
Asociación de Colegios Del Mundo BI de Venezuela (COMUBIVE)	Venezuela	President: Jorge Luis Bolivar	
Brazil AIBWS (BAIBS)	Brazil	President: Shirley Hazell	
Uruguay AIBWS (AUCBI)	Uruguay	President; Jimena Taboada	

IB Africa, Europe and the Middle East

Name	Area covered	Contact	Website
Asociacion de Colegios BI en España (ACBIE)	Spain	Head: Jose Varela Núñez Deputy: Silvino Corada	
Asociacion Ibérica de Colegios de BI (ASIBI)	Spain	Head: Concepcion Pinedo Gurría Deputy: Jorge Mejias	www.asibi.org
Association of Central European Schools (ACES)	Eastern Europe	Head: Peter MJ Murphy	aces – ib.org
IB Schools in Greece Association (IBSIGA)	Greece	Head: Zoi Geitona	ibsiga.wordpress.com
IB Schools in Turkey	Turkey	Head: Mine Erim	
IB World School Association in Morocco (AEBIM)	Morocco	Head: Hayat Cherrouk	www.aebim.org
IB World Schools in Italy (IBSIWA)	Italy	Head: Anthony Allard	www.aibwsi.it
The IB Schools Association of Commonwealth of Independent States (IBSA)	CIS (incl Russia)	Head: Oleg Babyonyshev Deputy: Natalia Barinova	ibsa.su
IB Schools and Colleges Association (IBSCA)	United Kingdom	Head: Richard Markham	www.ibsca.org.uk
Association of IB World Schools in Pakistan (IBPAK)	Pakistan	Head: Wafaa Abdul Ghaffar Deputy: Azra Tahir	ibpak.pk
Norwegian IB Schools (NIBS)	Norway	Head: Mikael Sjøholm Deputy: Øivind Sørlie	

The Association of Swedish IB Schools (ASIB)	Sweden	Head: Johan Ahlqvist Deputy: Gilles Kennedy	www.swedishibschools.se
The Association of IB World Schools in Lebanon	Lebanon	Head: Mona Majzoub Deputy: Mrs. Samar Darazi	

IB Asia – Pacific

Name	Area covered	No. of member schools	Contact	Website
IB Association of Japan	Japan	57	Damian Rentoule	www.ibaj.or.jp
IB Association of World Schools for South Korea Resource Centre Society	South Korea		Kevin A. Skeoch	
IB Schools Australia	Australia, New Zealand, Fiji and Papua New Guinea, South – West Pacific Islands	173	Ashley Coats	www.ibaustralasia.org
The Association of International Schools of India	South Asia	106	Anuradha Monga	www.taisindia.org

Informal groupings of IB World Schools

The IB does not formally recognize all groups of IB World Schools. A group must have first formed itself into a formal or legal entity to meet the recognition criteria. There are, nevertheless, informal networks of schools in various parts of the world that make valuable contributions to supporting schools in their programme development. Their scope and activities vary from group to group and each operates independently of the IB regional office, which offers them its own support.

5. University Acknowledgement

The IB Diploma is a passport to higher education. Universities around the world welcome the unique characteristics of IB Diploma Programme students and recognize the way in which the programme helps to prepare students for higher education. IB students routinely gain admission to some of the best universities in the world. Most of these institutions have established recognition policies for the IB Diploma Programme.

The following list contains the names of the universities that according to IB records have a stated IB recognition policy. This list is not necessarily complete as other universities may recognize the IB Diploma but have not alerted the IB to their recognition policy.

Please note that this listing is accurate as of 2019. For more information, please see the University policy index at **ibo.org/university-admission/recognition-of-the-ib-diploma-by-countries-and-universities**

ANTIGUA AND BARBUDA

University of Health Sciences Antigua

ARGENTINA

Escuela Superior Técnica del Ejército Argentino
ESEADE – Instituto Universitario
Instituto Tecnológico de Buenos Aires (ITBA)
Instituto Universitario CEMIC
International Buenos Aires Hotel & Restaurant School (IBAHRS
Lincoln University College
Ott College
Pontificia Universidad Católica Argentina
Universidad Abierta Interamericana
Universidad Argentina de la Empresa
Universidad Austral
Universidad Blas Pascal
Universidad de Belgrano
Universidad de San Andrés
Universidad del CEMA
Universidad del Salvador
Universidad del Salvador – Campus "Nuestra Señora del Pilar"
Universidad Favaloro
Universidad Maimónides
Universidad Siglo 21
Universidad Torcuato Di Tella

AUSTRALIA

Academy of Design Australia
Australian Catholic University
Australian Defence Force Academy
Australian National University
Billy Blue College of Design
Blue Mountains Hotel School (Leura Campus)
Bond University
Campion College Australia
Central Queensland University
Charles Darwin University
Charles Sturt University (CSU)
Curtin University
Deakin University
Edith Cowan University
Flinders University
Griffith University
International College of Hotel Management
International College of Management, Sydney
James Cook University
La Trobe University
Macquarie University
Melbourne Institute of Business and Technology
Murdoch University
Queensland Institute of Business and Technology
Queensland University of Technology
QUEENSLAND UNIVERSITY OF TECHNOLOGY
Raffles College of Design and Commerce
Royal Melbourne Institute of Technology (RMIT)
SkillsTech Australia
Southern Cross University
Southern Queensland Institute of TAFE
Swinburne University of Technology
Sydney Institute of Business and Technology (SIBT)
TAFE Queensland Brisbane
The Australian National University
The Bremer Institute of TAFE
The University of Adelaide
The University of New South Wales
The university of Notre dame Australia
The University of Queensland
The University of Sydney
Tropical North Queensland Institute of TAFE
University of Adelaide
University of Ballarat
University of Canberra
University of Melbourne
University of New England
University of New South Wales (UNSW)
University of Notre Dame Australia (Sydney)
University of South Australia
University of Southern Queensland
University of Tasmania (UTAS)
University of Technology Sydney
University of the Sunshine Coast
University of Western Australia
University of Western Sydney
University of Wollongong
Victoria University
William Angliss Institute

AUSTRIA

Innsbruck Medical University
Johannes – Kepler – Universität Linz
Karl – Franzens Universität Graz
Leopold – Franzens – Universität Innsbruck
Technische Universität Graz
Universität Wien (University of Vienna)
University of Applied Sciences Wiener Neustadt
Webster University – Vienna campus

AZERBAIJAN

Khazar University

BAHRAIN

RCSI – Medical University of Bahrain

BELGIUM

Facultés Universitaires Saint – Louis
Ghent University (Universiteit Gent)
International Management Institute (IMI)
Universite Catholique de Louvain
Université de Liège
Université Libre de Bruxelles
Universiteit Antwerpen (University of Antwerp)

Universteit Antwerpen – RUCA
Vesalius College v.z.w.

BOSNIA AND HERZEGOVINA

University of Sarajevo

BRAZIL

FIA Business School
Pontificia Universidade Catolica de Sao Paulo
Pontifícia Universidade Catolica do Paraná

BULGARIA

American University in Bulgaria

CAMBODIA

Panha Chiet University

CANADA

Acadia University
Alberta College of Art & Design
Algonquin College
Ambrose University College
Bishop's University
Bishop's University
Booth University College
Brandon University
Brescia University College
Brock University
Camosun College – Interurban Campus
Camosun College – Lansdowne Campus
Canadian Mennonite University
Canadian Merit Scholarship Foundation
Cape Breton University
Capilano University
Carleton University
Centennial College
College of New Caledonia
Concordia University
Concordia University – Montréal
Concordia University College of Alberta
Dalhousie University
DeVry Institute of Technology – Calgary
Douglas College
École Polytechnique de Montréal
Faculte Saint – Jean of the University of Alberta
Glendon College
Grant MacEwan University
HEC Montréal
Huron University College
King's University College – Alberta
King's University College – Ontario
Kwantlen Polytechnic University
Lakehead University
Lakeland College – Alberta
Langara College
Laurentian University
McGill University
McGill University – Faculty of Medicine
McMaster University
Medicine Hat College
Memorial University of Newfoundland
Mount Allison University
Mount Royal University
Mount Saint Vincent University
Nipissing University
Nova Scotia Agricultural College
Nova Scotia College of Art and Design
Ontario College Application Service (OCAS)
Prairie Bible College
Queen's University
Quest University Canada
Red Deer College
Rocky Mountain College – Calgary
Royal Military College of Canada
Ryerson University
Saint Mary's University – Halifax
Sheridan College
Simon Fraser University
St. Francis Xavier University
St. Jerome's University
St. Mary's College – Alberta
St. Paul University
St. Thomas University
St. Thomas University – Fredericton
Taylor University College & Seminary
The University of British Columbia
Thompson Rivers University
Trent University
Trinity Western University
Tyndale University College & Seminary
Université de Moncton
Université de Montréal
Université de Saint – Boniface
Université du Québec a Montréal
Université Laval
University of Alberta
University of British Columbia
University of British Columbia
University of Calgary
University of Guelph
University of King's College
University of Lethbridge
University of Manitoba
University of Manitoba – Faculty of Medicine
University of New Brunswick (all campuses)
University of Northern British Columbia
University of Ontario Institute of Technology
University of Ottawa
University of Ottawa – Faculty of Medicine
University of Prince Edward Island
University of Regina
University of Saskatchewan
University of St. Michael's College
University of the Fraser Valley
University of Toronto
University of Victoria
University of Waterloo
University of Western Ontario – Western University
University of Windsor
University of Winnipeg
Vancouver Island University
Western University
Wilfrid Laurier University
York University

CHILE

Pontificia Universidad Católica de Chile
Universidad Adolfo Ibañez
Universidad Andrés Bello
Universidad Católica de Valparaíso
Universidad Central de Chile
Universidad de Artes, Ciencias y Comunicación, UNIACC
Universidad de La Serena
Universidad de Viña del Mar
Universidad del Bío – Bío
Universidad del Desarrollo
Universidad Diego Portales
Universidad Finis Terrae
Universidad Gabriela Mistral
Universidad Internacional SEK Chile
Universidad La República
Universidad Mayor
Universidad Metropolitana de Ciencias de la Educación
Universidad San Sebastián
Universidad Técnica Federico Santa María

CHINA

New York University Shanghai
Raffles Design Institute (Shanghai)
Shanghai International Studies University
The University of Nottingham Ningbo, China
University of Michigan – Shanghai Jiao Tong University Joint Institute

COLOMBIA

Colegio de Estudios Superiores de Administración
Escuela de Ingeniería de Antioquía

Instituto de Ciencias de la Salud
Politécnico Grancolombiano
Pontificia Universidad Javeriana
Universidad Antonio Nariño
Universidad de Bogotá Jorge Tadeo Lozano
Universidad de la Sabana
Universidad del Norte de Barranquilla
Universidad del Rosario – Bogotá, Colombia
Universidad EAFIT
Universidad Externado de Colombia
Universidad ICESI
Universidad Pontificia Bolivariana

COSTA RICA

Universidad de Costa Rica
Universidad Internacional de las Américas

CZECH REPUBLIC

Anglo – American University
University of Economics, Prague
University of Ostrava
University of South Bohemia
Univerzita Karlova (Charles University in Prague)

DENMARK

Aalborg University
Aarhus University
Business Academy Aarhus
Business Academy Aarhus, University of Applied Sciences
Business Academy Copenhagen North
Copenhagen Business School
IT University of Copenhagen
Metropolitan University College
Roskilde University
The Royal Danish School of Pharmacy
The Technical University of Denmark
The University of Copenhagen
University of Southern Denmark

DOMINICAN REPUBLIC

Instituto Tecnológico de Santo Domingo

ECUADOR

Blue Hill College
Pontificia Universidad Católica del Ecuador
Universidad Casa Grande
Universidad de Especialidades Espíritu Santo (UEES)
Universidad de las Américas
Universidad del Pacífico – Escuela de Negocios
Universidad Internacional SEK Ecuador
Universidad San Francisco de Quito
Universidad Santa María de Chile – Campus Guayaquil
Universidad Tecnológica Ecotec
UNIVERSIDAD TECNOLOGICA EMPRESARIAL DE GUAYAQUIL

EGYPT

The American University in Cairo

EL SALVADOR

Universidad Albert Einstein
Universidad Dr. José Matías Delgado
Universidad Tecnológica

ESTONIA

Tallinn University
Tallinn University of Technology (TUT)
Tartu Ülikool

FIJI

University of the South Pacific

FINLAND

Åbo Akademi
Hanken School of Economics
Helsinki Metropolia University of Applied Sciences
Helsinki School of Economics and Business Administration
Helsinki University of Technology
North Karelia University of Applied Sciences
Tampere University of Technology
University of Eastern Finland
University of Helsinki (Helsingin yliopisto)
University of Jyväskylä
University of Kuopio
University of Oulu
University of Tampere
University of Turku
University of Vaasa

FRANCE

ECAM Lyon
Grenoble Graduate School of Business (GGSB)
Institut National des Sciences Appliquées de Lyon
Institut Paul Bocuse
NEOMA Business School
Sciences Po
The American University of Paris
univeristé de poitiers
Université de Bretagne Occidentale
Université de Franche – Comté
Université de Paris VII
Université de Paris X Nanterre
Université Joseph Fourier Grenoble I
Université Panthéon – Assas Paris II
Université Pierre Mendes France Grenoble II
University of Poitiers

GERMANY

ACCADIS Bildung GmbH
Albert – Ludwigs – Universität Freiburg
Ausländerstudienkolleg (ASK) Konstanz
Bard College Berlin, A Liberal Arts University gGmbH
Bayerische Julius – Maximilians – Universität Würzburg
Bucerius Law School/Hochschule für Rechtswissenschaften
Christian – Albrechts – Universität zu Kiel
Eberhard – Karls – Universität Tübingen
Fachhochschule Hannover (FHH)
Frankfurt School of Finance and Management
Freie und Hansestadt Hamburg
Friedrich – Schiller – Universität Jena
Globe Business College Munich
Hochschule Konstanz University of Applied Sciences (HTWG)
HTW Berlin – Hochschule für Technik und Wirtschaft Berlin
Humboldt – Universität zu Berlin
IUBH School of Business and Management
Jacobs University
Jacobs University Bremen
Johann Wolfgang Goethe – Universität Frankfurt
Karlsruhe University of Applied Sciences
Munich Business School – MBS
Ruprecht – Karls – Universität Heidelberg
Technische Universität Hamburg – Harburg
Technische Universität München
Touro College Berlin
Universitaet des Saarlandes
Universität der Künste Berlin
Universität Hamburg
Universität zu Köln
University of Applied Management
University of Applied Sciences Würzburg – Schweinfurt
WHU – Otto Beisheim School of Management

GHANA

Ashesi University
University of Science and Technology

GREECE

American College of Thessaloniki (ACT)
The American College of Greece
University of Patras

GUATEMALA

Universidad del Valle de Guatemala
Universidad Francisco Marroquín
Universidad Rafael Landívar

HONG KONG

City University of Hong Kong
HKU SPACE – Centre for Degree Programmes
Hong Kong Baptist University
Hong Kong Design Institute
Hong Kong Institute of Vocational Education (IVE), VTC
Hong Kong Shue Yan University
Hong Kong University of Science and Technology
Lingnan University
Raffles School of Continuing Education, Hong Kong
Technological and Higher Education Institute of Hong Kong (THEi), VTC
The Chinese University of Hong Kong
The Hong Kong Academy for Performing Arts
The Hong Kong Institute of Education
The Hong Kong Polytechnic University
The Hong Kong University of Science and Technology
Tung Wah College
University of Hong Kong

HUNGARY

Eszterházy Károly College
Janus Pannonius University
McDaniel College Budapest
Nemzetközi Üzleti Föiskola (International Business School)
Pecs University Medical School
Semmelweis University of Medicine
University Medical School of Debrecen

ICELAND

University of Iceland

INDIA

Ahmedabad University
All India Institute of Medical Sciences (AIIMS)
Amity University
Andhra University
Anna University
Association of Indian Universities
Bangalore University
Bharathidasan University
Birla Institute of Technology & Science (Pilani)
BML Munjal University
Centre for Environmental Planning and Technology (CEPT) University, Ahmedabad
Christ University
Council of Architecture
D. Y. Patil Vidyapeeth, Pune
Delhi Technological University (formerly Delhi College of Engineering)
Dhirubhai Ambani Institute of Information and Communication Technology
FLAME – Foundation for Liberal AndManagement Education
Guru Gobind Singh Indraprastha University
HR College of Commerce & Economics affiliated to University of Mumbai
IILM – Institute of Integrated Learning in Management
Indian Institute of Science
Indian Institute of Science Education and Research (IISER)
Indian Institute of Space Science & Technology, Thiruvananthapuram
Indian Institute of Space Science and Technology
Indian Institutes of Technology
Indian School of Business and Finance(ISBF)
Indraprastha Institute of Information Technology
International Institute of Information Technology, Hyderabad
Jadavpur University
Jawaharlal Nehru University
K C College, affiliated to University of Mumbai
KIIT University (Kalinga Institute of Industrial Technology)
Kishinchand Chellaram College (K C College, affiliated to University of Mumbai)
Kurukshetra University
Lady Shri Ram College for Women affiliated to University of Delhi
Maharashtra State Board of Secondary and Higher Secondary Education
Mizoram Board of School Education
Narsee Monjee Institute of Management studies
National Institute of Design
National Institute of Open Schooling
National Law School of India University
Nirma University of Science & Technology, Gandhinagar
Osmania University
Punjab University, Chandigarh
Rajiv Gandhi University of Health Sciences, Karnataka
Russell Square International College
Shiv Nadar University
Sri Venkateswara College, affiliated to University of Delhi
St Xavier's College
Symbiosis International University
The Maharaja Sayajirao University of Baroda
Universal Business School
University of Calcutta
University of Delhi
University of Hyderabad
University of Kerala
University of Madras
University of Mumbai
Vellore Institute of Technology (VIT)
Visvesvaraya Technological University (VTU)

INDONESIA

Gandhi Institute of Business and Technology
Institut Teknologi Harapan Bangsa – International Program
MIBT Indonesia
Universitas Pelita Harapan

IRELAND

National College of Ireland
National University of Ireland (NUI), Galway
National University of Ireland (NUI), Maynooth
Royal College of Surgeons in Ireland
University College Cork
University College Dublin
University of Dublin – Trinity College

ISRAEL

Hebrew University of Jerusalem
Interdisciplinary Center (IDC) Herzliya
Technion – Israel Institute of Technology
Tel Aviv University

ITALY

Accademia Italiana Florence
Bocconi University
ESCP Europe Business School

Humanitas University
John Cabot University
Libero Instituto Universitario Carlo Cattaneo
Lorenzo de' Medici
The American University of Rome
Università Cattolica del Sacro Cuore
Universitádegli Studi Firenze

JAPAN

Aichi Gakuin Daigaku (Aichi Gakuin University)
Aichi Gakusen Daigaku (Aichi Gakusen University)
Aichi Kenritsu Daigaku (Aichi Prefectural University)
Aichi Kenritsu Kango Daigaku (Aichi Prefectural College of N
Aichi Kyoiku Daigaku (Aichi University of Education)
Ajia Daigaku (Asia University)
Akita Daigaku (Akita University)
Akita Prefectural University
Aomori Koritsu Daigaku (Aomori Public College)
Aoyama Gakui Gakuin Daigaku (Aoyama Gakuin University)
Asahi Daigaku (Asahi University)
Asahikawa Daigaku (Asahikawa University)
Asahikawa Ika Daigaku (Asahikawa Medical College)
Atomi Gakuen Joshi Daigaku (Atomi College)
Azabu Daigaku (Azabu University)
Baika Joshi Daigaku (Baika Women's College)
Baiko Jo Gakuin Daigaku (Baiko Jo Gakuin University)
BBT University
Beppu Daigaku (Beppu University)
Bukkyo Daigaku (Bukkyo University)
Bunkyo Daigaku (Bunkyo University)
Chiba Daigaku (Chiba University)
Chiba Keizai Daigaku (Chiba Keizai University)
Chiba Prefectural University of Health Sciences
Chubu Daigaku (Chubu University)
Chuo Daigaku (Chuo University)
Chuo Gakuin Daigaku (Chuogakuin University)
Daito Bunka Daigaku (Daito Bunka University)
Denki Tsushin Daigaku (The University of Electro Communications)
Dokkyo Daigaku (Dokkyo University)
Doshisha University
Ehime Daigaku (Ehime University)
Ferisu Joshigakuin Daigaku (Ferris University)
Fukui Daigaku (Fukui University)
Fukui Kenritsu Daigaku (Fukui Prefectural University)
Fukuoka Daigaku (Fukuoka University)
Fukuoka Joshi Daigaku (Fukuoka Women's University)
Fukuoka Kenritsu Daigaku (Fukuoka Prefectural University)
Fukushima Kenritsu Ika Daigaku (Fukushima Medical University)
Fukuyama City University
Future University Hakodate
Gakushuin Daigaku (Gakushuin University)
Gifu Keizai Daigaku (Gifu Keizai University)
Gufu Daigaku (Gifu University)
Gunma Daigaku (Gunma University)
Gunma Prefectural College of Health Sciences
Gunma Prefectural Women's University
Hakuo Daigaku (Hakuoh University)
Hamamatsu Ika Daigaku (Hamamatsu University School of Medici
Hannan Daigaku (Hannan University)
Heisei Kokusai Daigaku (Heisei International University)
Hijiyama Daigaku (Hijiyama University)
Himeji Dokkyo Daigaku (Himeji Dokkyo University)
Himeji Kogyo Daigaku (Himeji Institute of Technology)
Hirosaki Gakuin Daigaku (Hirosaki Gakuin College)
Hirosaki University
Hiroshima Daigaku (Hiroshima University)
Hiroshima Jogakuin Daigaku (Hiroshima Jogakuin University)
Hiroshima Joshi Daigaku (Hiroshima Women's University)
Hiroshima Kenritsu Daigaku (Hiroshima Prefectural University
Hiroshima Kogyo Daigaku (Hiroshima Institute of Technology)
Hitotsubashi Daigaku (Hitotsubashi University)
Hokkaido Daigaku (Hokkaido University)
Hokkaido Joho Daigaku (Hokkaido Information University)
Hokkaido Kyoiku Daigaku (Hokkaido University of Education, K
Hokkaido Tokai Daigaku (Hokkaido Tokai University)
Hokkaigakuen Daigaku (Hokkai – Gakuen University)
Hokusei Gakuen Daigaku (Hokusei Gakuen University)
Hosei Daigaku (Hosei University)
Hyogo Kenritsu Kango Daigaku (College of Nursing Art and Sci
Hyogo Kyoiku Daigaku (Hyogo University of Teacher Education)
Ibaraki Kirisutokyo Daigaku (Ibaraki Christian College)
International Christian University
International College of Liberal Arts (Yamanashi Gakuin University)
Ishikawa Prefectural University
Iwate Prefectural University
Iwate University
Jissen Joshi Daigaku (Jissen Women's University)
Jochi Daigaku Ichigaya Kyampasu
Jochi Daigaku Yotsuya Kyampasu
Josai Daigaku (Josai University)
Josai Kokusai Daigaku (Josai International University)
Joshi Bijutsu Daigaku (Women's College of Fine Arts)
Kagawa Daigaku (Kagawa University)
Kagoshima Daigaku (Kagoshima University)
Kagoshima Joshi Daigaku (Kagoshima Women's College)
Kanagawa Daigaku (Kanagawa University)
Kanagawa University of Human Services
Kanazawa College of Art
Kanazawa Daigaku (Kanazawa University)
Kanoya Taiiku Daigaku (National Institute of Fitness and Spo
Kansai Daigaku (Kansai University)
Kansai Gaikokugo Daigaku (Kansai Gaidai University)
Kanto Gakuin Daigaku (Kanto Gakuin University)
Kassui Joshi Daigaku (Kassui Women's University)
Kawamura Gakuen Joshi Daigaku (Kawamura Gakuen Woman's Univ,
Keiai Daigaku (Keiai University)
Keio Gijuku Daigaku (Keio University)
Keio University Shonan Fujisawa Campus
Keisen Jogakuen Daigaku (Keisen Jogakuen College)
Keiwa Gakuen Daigaku (Keiwa College)
Kinjo Gakuin Daigaku (Kinjo Gakuin University)
Kinki Daigaku (Kinki University)
Kitami Kogyo Daigaku (Kitami Institute of Technology)
Kitasato Daigaku (Kitasato University)
Kobe Daigaku (Kobe University)
Kobe Gakuin Daigaku (Kobe Gakuin University)

Kobe Geijutsu Koka Daigaku (Kobe Design University)
Kobe Jogakuin Daigaku (Kobe College)
Kobe Kokusai Daigaku (Kobe International University)
Kobe Shoka Daigaku (Kobe University of Commerce)
Kobe Shosen Daigaku (Kobe University of Mercantile Marine)
Kobeshi Gaikokugo Daigaku (Kobe City University of Foreign S
Kochi Daigaku (Kochi University)
Kochi University of Technology
Kokugakuin Daigaku (Kokugakuin University)
Kokushikan Daigaku (Kokushikan University)
Komazawa Daigaku (Komazawa University)
Konan Daigaku (Konan University)
Koshien Daigaku (Koshien University)
Kumamoto Daigaku (Kumamoto University)
Kumamoto Kenritsu Daigaku (Prefectural University of Kumamoto)
Kushiro Public University of Economics
Kwansei Gakuin University
Kyorin Daigaku (Kyorin University)
Kyoritsu Joshi Daigaku (Kyoritsu Women's University)
Kyoto Daigaku (Kyoto University)
Kyoto Gaikokugo Daigaku (Kyoto University of Foreign Studies
Kyoto Gakuen Daigaku (Kyoto Gakuen University)
Kyoto Kogei Sen'i Daigaku (Kyoto Institute of Technology)
Kyoto Prefectural University of Medicine
Kyoto Seika Daigaku (Kyoto Seika University)
Kyoto Tachibana Joshi Daigaku (Kyoto Tachibana Women's Unive
Kyushu Daigaku (Kyushu University)
Kyushu Geijutsu Koka Daigaku (Kyushu Instutute of Design)
Kyushu Kogyo Daigaku (Kyushu Institute of Technology)
Kyushu Sangyo Daigaku (Kyushu Sangyo University)
Kyushu Tokai Daigaku (Kyushu Tokai University)
Maebashi Institute of Technology
Matsuyama Shinonome Joshi Daigaku (Matsuyama Shinonome Colle
Meiji Daigaku (Meiji University)
Meiji Gakuin Daigaku (Meiji Gakuin University)
Meijo Daigaku (Meijo University)
Meikai Daigaku (Meikai University)
Mejiro Daigaku (Mejiro University)
Mie Daigaku (Mie University)
Miyazaki Daigaku (Miyazaki University)
Miyazaki Koritsu Daigaku (Miyazaki Municipal University)
Momoyama Gakuin Daigaku (St. Andrew's University)
Morioka Daigaku (Morioka College)
Muroran Kogyo Daigaku (Muroran Institute of Technology)
Musashi Daigaku (Musashi University)
Musashi Kogyo Daigaku (Musashi Institute of Technology)
Nagaoka Gijutsu Kagaku Daigaku (Nagaoka University of Technology)
Nagasaki Daigaku (Nagasaki University)
Nagoya Gakuin Daigaku (Nagoya Gakuin University)
Nagoya Institute of Technology
Nagoya Shiritsu Daigaku (Nagoya City University)
Nagoya University, International Programs
Nakamura Gakuen Daigaku (Nakamura Gakuen University)
Nanzan Daigaku (Nanzan University)
Nara Joshi Daigaku (Nara Women's University)
Nara Prefectural University
Nara Sangyo Daigaku (Nara Sangyo University)
Naruto Kyoiku Daigaku (Naruto University of Education)
National Fisheries University
Nihon Daigaku (Nihon University)
Nihon Fukushi Daigaku (Nihon Fukushi University)
Niigata College of Nursing
Niigata Daigaku (Niigata University)
Niigata Sangyo Daigaku (Niigata Institute of Technology)
Niimi College
Nippon Bunri Daigaku (Nippon Bunri University)
Nippon Veterinary and Life Science University
Nishinippon Kogyo Daigaku (Nishinippon Instutute of Technolo
Notorudamu Seishin Joshi Daigaku (Notre Dame Seishin Univers
NUCB
Obihiro Chikusan Daigaku (Obihiro University of Agriculture
Obirin Daigaku (Obirin University)
Ochanomizu University
Oita Daigaku (Oita University)
Oita University of Nursing and Health Sciences
Okayama Kenritsu Daigaku (Okayama Prefectural University)
Okayama University
Okinawa Kokusai Daigaku (Okinawa International University)
Okinawa Prefectural College of Nursing
Okinawa Prefectural University of Arts
Osaka City University
Osaka Daigaku (Osaka University)
Osaka Denki Tsushin Daigaku (Osaka Electro – Communication Uni
Osaka Furitsu Daigaku (Osaka Prefecture University)
Osaka Gaikokugo Daigaku (Osaka University School of Foreign Studies)
Osaka Joshi Daigaku (Osaka Women's University)
Osaka Kogyo Daigaku (Osaka Institute of Technology)
Osaka Kokusai Daigaku (Osaka International University)
Osaka Kyoiku University
Otaru Shoka Daigaku (Otaru University of Commerce)
Otemon Gakuin Daigaku (Otemon Gakuin University)
Otsuma Joshi Daigaku (Otsuma Women's University)
Ou Daigaku (Ohu University)
Prefectural University of Hiroshima
Puru Gakuin Daigaku (Pool Gakuin University)
Reitaku Daigaku (Reitaku University)
Rikkyo Daigaku (Rikkyo University)
Rissho Daigaku (Rissho University)
Ritsumeikan Asia Pacific University
Ritsumeikan Daigaku (Ritsumeikan University)
Ruteru Gakuin Daigaku (Japan Lutheran College)
Ryukyu Daigaku (University of the Ryukyus)
Ryutsu Kagaku Daigaku
Saga Daigaku (Saga University)
Saga Ika Daigaku (Saga Medical School)
Saitama Prefectural University
Saitama University
Sanno Daigaku (Sanno College, Isehara)
Sapporo City University
Sapporo Daigaku (Sapporo University)
Sapporo Kokusai Daigaku (Sapporo Kokusai University)
Seigakuin Daigaku (Seigakuin University)
Seikei Daigaku (Seikei University)
Seinan Gakuin Daigaku (Seinan Gakuin University)
Seisen Joshi Daigaku (Seisen University)
Seishin Joshi Daigaku (University of the Sacred Heart)
Seitoku Daigaku (Seitoku University)
Senshu Daigaku (Senshu University)

Setsunan Daigaku (Setsunan University)
Shibaura Kogyo Daigaku (Shibaura Institute of Technology)
Shiga Daigaku (Shiga University)
Shiga Kenritsu Daigaku (The University of Shiga Prefecture)
Shikoku Daigaku (Shikoku University)
Shimane Daigaku (Shimane University)
Shimonoseki Shiritsu Daigaku (Shimonoseki City University)
Shinshu Daigaku (Shinshu University)
Shitennoji Kokusai Bukkyo Daigaku (International Buddhist Un
Shizukoka Kenritsu Daigaku (University of Shizuoka)
Shizuoka Daigaku (Shizuoka University)
Shizuoka University of Art and Culture
Shotoku Gakuen Gifu Kyoiku Daigaku
Shujitsu Joshi Daigaku (Shujitsu Women's University)
Shukutoku Daigaku (Shukutoku University)
Soai Daigaku (Soai University)
Soka Daigaku (Soka University)
Sophia University
Sugiyama Jogakuen Daigaku (Sugiyama Jogakuen University)
Surugadai Daigaku (Surugadai University)
Suzuka Kokusai Daigaku (Suzuka International University)
Takachiho Shoka Daigaku (Takachiho University)
Takasaki Keizai Daigaku (Takasaki City University of Economics)
Takushoku Daigaku (Takushoku University)
Tamagawa Daigaku (Tamagawa University)
Teikyo Daigaku (Teikyo University)
Tenri Daigaku (Tenri University)
Tezukayama Daigaku (Tezukayama University)
The University of Tokyo
Tohoku Gakuin Daigaku (Tohoku Gakuin University)
Tohoku Geijutsu Koka Daigaku (Tohoku University of Art and Design)
Tohoku University
Tokai Daigaku (Tokai University)
Tokoha Gakuen Daigaku (Tokoha – Gakuen University)
Tokoha Gakuen Hamamatsu Daigaku (Tokoha – Gakuen Hamamatsu University)
Tokushima Daigaku (The University of Tokushima)
Tokyo Daigaku (The University of Tokyo)
Tokyo Gaikokugo Daigaku (Tokyo University of Foreign Studies
Tokyo Gakugei Daigaku (Tokyo Gakugei University)
Tokyo Joshi Daigaku (Tokyo Woman's Christian University)
Tokyo Junshin Joshi Daigaku (Tokyo Junshin Women's Univ.)
Tokyo Kasei Daigaku (Tokyo Kasei University)
Tokyo Kasei Gakuin Daigaku (Tokyo Kasei Gakuin University)
Tokyo Kasei Gakuin Tsukuba Joshi Daigaku
Tokyo Keizai Daigaku (Tokyo Keizai University)
Tokyo Kogei Daigaku (Tokyo Polytechnic University)
Tokyo Kogyo Daigaku (Tokyo Institute of Technology)
Tokyo Kokusai Daigaku (Tokyo International University)
Tokyo Medical and Dental University
Tokyo Nogyo Daigaku (Tokyo University of Agriculture)
Tokyo Noko Daigaku (Tokyo University of Agriculture and Technology)
Tokyo Seitoku Daigaku (Tokyo Seitoku University)
Tokyo Shosen Daigaku (Tokyo University of Mercantile Marine)
Tokyo Suisan Daigaku (Tokyo University of Fisheries)
Tokyo Toritsu Daigaku (Tokyo Metropolitan University)
Tokyo University of Foreign Studies
Tokyo University of Science (Tokyo Rika Daigaku)
Tottori Daigaku (Tottori University)
Toyama Daigaku (Toyama University)
Toyama Ika Yakka Daigaku (Toyama Medical and Pharmaceutical
Toyo Daigaku (Toyo University)
Toyo Eiwa Jogakuin Daigaku (Toyo Eiwa Women's University)
Toyohashi Gijutsu Kagaku Daigaku (Toyohashi University of Technology)
Truro & Penwith College
Tsukuba Daigaku (University of Tsukuba)
Tsukuba Kokusai Daigaku (Tsukuba International University)
Tsukuba University of Technology
Ueno Gakuen Daigaku (Ueno Gakuen University)
University of Fukui
University of Hyogo
University of Nagasaki
Utsunomiya Daigaku (Utsunomiya University)
Wakayama Daigaku (Wakayama University)
Wako Daigaku (Wako University)
Waseda Daigaku (Waseda University)
Yamagata University
Yamaguchi Daigaku (Yamaguchi University)
Yamaguchi Prefectural University
Yamanashi Daigaku (Yamanashi University)
Yamanashi Ika Daigaku (Yamanashi Medical University)
Yamanashi Prefectural University
Yokkaichi Daigaku (Yokkaichi University)
Yokohama Kokuritsu Daigaku (Yokohama National University)
Yokohama Shiritsu Daigaku (Yokohama City University)

JORDAN

Ministry of Education
The University of Jordan

KENYA

Strathmore University
University of Nairobi

KOREA, REPUBLIC OF

Ghent University Global Campus
Korea Advanced Institute of Science and Technology (KAIST)
Seoul National University
Yonsei University

LEBANON

American University College of Science and Technology
American University of Beirut
University of Balamand

LESOTHO

National University of Lesotho

LITHUANIA

Vilnius University

MALAYSIA

Heriot – Watt University Malaysia
Manipal International University
Monash University Malaysia
Newcastle University Medicine Malaysia
Sunway University
Universiti Tenaga Nasional
University College of Technology Sarawak
University of Malaya
University of Reading Malaysia

MALTA

American University of Malta
University of Malta

MAURITIUS

African Leadership University
Charles Telfair Institute

MEXICO

Benemérita Universidad Autónoma de Puebla
Escuela Bancaria y Comercial, S.C.
Instituto Tecnológico y de Estudios Superiores de Monterrey
Universidad Autónoma de Baja California
Universidad de las Américas, Puebla
Universidad de Monterrey (UDEM)

NETHERLANDS

Delft University of Technology
Eindhoven University of Technology TUE
Erasmus University Rotterdam
HAS University of Applied Sciences
Hogeschool InHolland
Leiden University
Leiden University College The Hague
Nyenrode Business Universiteit
Open University of the Netherlands
Rotterdam Business School, Rotterdam University of Applied Sciences
Rotterdam Business School/ Rotterdam University
Rotterdam School of Management, Erasmus University
The Hague University of Applied Sciences
University College Groningen
University College Maastricht
University College Utrecht
University of Amsterdam
University of Groningen
University of Nijmegen
University of Twente
Utrecht University
VHL University of Applied Sciences
Wageningen Agricultural University
Webster University the Netherlands
Wittenborg University of Applied Sciences

NEW ZEALAND

Auckland University of Technology
Lincoln University
Massey University
University of Auckland
University of Canterbury
University of Otago
University of Waikato
Victoria University of Wellington

NICARAGUA

Ave María College of the Americas
Universidad Americana (UAM)
Universidad Centroamericana de Nicaragua
Universidad Nacional Autónoma de Nicaragua, León

NORWAY

BI Norwegian Business School
Høgskulen i Volda
NHH Norwegian School of Economics
Norwegian School of Management
The Norwegian University of Science and Technology (NTNU)
University of Bergen
University of Oslo
University of Stavanger
University of Tromsö

PAKISTAN

Aga Khan University
Lahore University of Management Sciences

PANAMA

Universidad Santa María La Antigua

PARAGUAY

Universidad Americana
Universidad Católica "Nuestra Señora de la Asunción"
Universidad Columbia del Paraguay
Universidad del Norte

PERU

Escuela Naval del Perú
Instituto Peruano de Publicidad
Pontificia Universidad Católica del Perú
The Pontifical Catholic University of Peru
Universidad Científica del Sur
Universidad de Lima
Universidad de Piura
Universidad de San Martín de Porres
Universidad ESAN
Universidad Femenina del Sagrado Corazón (UNIFE)
Universidad Nacional Agraria La Molina
Universidad Nacional de Ingeniería
Universidad Nacional Federico Villarreal
Universidad Peruana Cayetano Heredia
Universidad Peruana de Ciencias Aplicadas
Universidad Privada del Norte
Universidad Ricardo Palma
Universidad San Ignacio de Loyola

PHILIPPINES

Ateneo de Manila University
De La Salle University
Enderun Colleges
Southville International School and Colleges
The University of the Philippines
University of Santo Tomas

POLAND

Kasimir Pulaski Technical University of Radom
Medical University of Gdansk
Poznan University of Technology
Technical University of Lodz
Technical University of Lublin
The Catholic University of Lublin
University of Gdansk
University of Lodz
Warsaw University of Technology
Wroclaw University

PORTUGAL

Escola Superior de Design (IADE)
Instituto Superior Técnico (IST)
Universidade Católica Portuguesa

QATAR

University of Calgary – Qatar

RUSSIAN FEDERATION

Lomonosov Moscow State University
Plekhanov Russian Academy of Economics

SINGAPORE

Curtin Singapore
East Asia Institute of Management (EASB)
James Cook University (JCUS)
KAPLAN Singapore
Management Development Institute of Singapore (MDIS)
National Institute of Education
National University of Singapore
PSB Academy Campus
SIM Global Education
Singapore Institute of Management
Singapore Institute of Technology
Singapore Management University

Singapore University of Technology & Design
Yale – NUS College

SLOVENIA

University of Ljubljana

SOUTH AFRICA

Rhodes University
University of Cape Town
University of Johannesburg
University of Natal
University of Port Elizabeth
University of South Africa (UNISA)
University of Witwatersrand

SPAIN

ESADE Business School
EU Business School
IE University
La Salle Campus Barcelona – Ramon Llull University
Saint Louis University – Madrid Campus
Toulouse Business School – Barcelona
UIC Barcelona (Universitat Internacional de Catalunya)
Universidad Camilo Jose Cela
Universidad Carlos III de Madrid
Universidad Católica San Antonio de Murcia – UCAM
Universidad Europea de Madrid
University Ceu Cardenal Herrera – Valencia
University of Navarra

SWAZILAND

University of Swaziland

SWEDEN

Chalmers University of Technology
Göteborg University
Handelshögskolan i Stockholm
Högskolan i Skövde
Högskolan Väst (University West)
Karolinska Institutet
Linköpings universitet
Lund University
The Royal Institute of Technology
Umeå University
University of Skövde
University of Stockholm
Uppsala University

SWITZERLAND

AGSB – The American Graduate School of Business
Ecole hôtelière de Lausanne
Ecole polytechnique fédérale de Lausanne
Eidgenössische Technische Hochschule Zürich (ETH Zürich)
FHNW Pädagogische Hochschule
Franklin University Switzerland
Glion Institute of Higher Education
Hochschule für Gestaltung & Kunst Luzern
International University in Geneva(IUG)
Les Roches Global Hospitality Education
Universität Basel
Universität Bern
Universität Freiburg / Université de Fribourg
Universitat Luzern
Universität Zürich
Université de Genève
Université de Lausanne
Université de Neuchâtel
University IFM
Webster University Geneva

THAILAND

King Mongkut's Institute of Technology Ladkrabang
Raffles Design Institute (Bangkok)

TURKEY

Middle East Technical University Northern Cyprus Campus
Özyegin University

UNITED ARAB EMIRATES

American University of Sharjah
Dubai Aerospace Enterprise University
French Fashion University Esmod
Heriot – Watt University, Dubai Campus
Middlesex University Dubai
MODUL University Dubai
RAK Medical and Health Sciences University
The Emirates Academy of Hospitality Management

UNITED KINGDOM

Aberystwyth University
Amity University [IN] London
Anglia Ruskin University
Aston University
Bangor University
Brunel University
Cardiff Metropolitan University
Cardiff University
City University
Colchester Institute
Courtauld Institute of Art
Coventry University
De Montfort University
Heriot – Watt University
Hult International Business School
Imperial College London
Keele University
Kent Institute of Art and Design
King's College London
Kingston University
Lancaster University
Leeds Beckett University
Liverpool Hope University
Liverpool John Moores University
London Metropolitan University
London School of Economics and Political Science
Loughborough University
Manchester Metropolitan University
Middlesex University
Napier University
New College of the Humanities
Northumbria University
Nottingham Trent University
Oxford Brookes University
Oxford University
Queen's University Belfast
Regent's University London
Richmond, The American International University in London
Robert Gordon University
Royal Free Hospital School of Medicine
Royal Holloway University of London
School of Pharmacy
SOAS University of London
St George's, (University of London)
St. Bartholomew's & Royal London School Medicine & Dentistry
Staffordshire University
Suffolk New College
Swansea Institute of Higher Education
Swansea University
The Royal Veterinary College
The University of Aberdeen
The University of Cambridge
The University of Edinburgh
The University of Reading
University College London
University of Bath
University of Bedfordshire
University of Birmingham
University of Bradford
University of Brighton (formerly Brighton Polytechnic)
University of Bristol
University of Buckingham
University of Buckingham, Faculty of International Studies
University of Central Lancashire

University of Chester
University of Chichester
University of Derby
University of Dundee
University of Durham
University of East Anglia
University of East London
University of Edinburgh
University of Essex
University of Exeter
University of Glamorgan
University of Glasgow
University of Greenwich – Avery Hill
University of Huddersfield
University of Hull
University of Kent
University of Leeds
University of Leicester
University of Liverpool
University of Reading
University of Salford
University of Sheffield
University of South Wales, Newport
University of Southampton
University of St Andrews
University of Stirling
University of Strathclyde
University of Surrey
University of Sussex
University of the West of England, Bristol
University of Ulster
University of Wales, Lampeter
University of Warwick
University of Westminster
University of Winchester
University of Wolverhampton
University of York
Unviersity of Sussex
Warrington Collegiate Institute
West Herts College

UNITED STATES

Abilene Christian University
Academy of Couture Art
Adams State University
Adelphi University
Agnes Scott College
Albany College of Pharmacy and Health Sciences
Albion College
Albright College
Alfred University
Allegheny College
Alliant International University
Alma College
Alverno College
Alvin Community College
American International University in London – Boston
American Medical College Application Service (AMCAS)
American River College
American University
American University in Cairo – US Office
American University of Paris – US Office
Amherst College
Anderson University – Indiana
Andrews University
Angelo State University
Anne Arundel Community College
Antioch College
Appalachian State University
Arcadia University
Arizona State University
Arizona State University – – Tempe
Arizona Western College
Arkansas Tech University
Armstrong Atlantic State University
Art Institute of Atlanta
Art Institute of California – Los Angeles
Art Institute of California – Orange County
Art Institute of Fort Lauderdale
Art Institute of Pittsburgh
Art Institute of Washington
Asbury University
Ashford University
Ashland University
Atlantic Union College
Auburn University – Auburn campus
Augsburg College
Augustana College – Illinois
Augustana College – South Dakota
Austin College
Austin Community College
Averett University
Avila University
AZTransfer (collective effort of all AZ public universities and community colleges)
Azusa Pacific University
Babson College
Baldwin Wallace University
Ball State University
Baptist College of Florida
Bard College
Barnard College
Barry University
Barton College
Bastyr University
Bates College
Baylor University
Beach College
Belhaven University
Bellarmine University
Bellevue College
Belmont Abbey College
Belmont University
Beloit College
Bemidji State University
Benedictine College
Bennett College
Bennington College
Bentley University
Berea College
Berklee College of Music
Berry College
Bethany College – Kansas
Bethany College – West Virginia
Bethany Lutheran College
Bethany University – Santa Cruz
Bethel College – Mishawaka
Bethel College – North Newton
Bethel University – St. Paul
Bethune – Cookman University
Biola University
Birmingham – Southern College
Blue Ridge Community College
Bluffton University
Bob Jones University
Boise State University
Boston College
Boston University
Bowdoin College
Bowling Green State University
Bradford College
Bradley University
Brandeis University
Brenau University
Brevard College
Brevard Community College – Cocoa Campus
Brewton – Parker College
Bridgewater College
Bridgewater State University
Brigham Young University – Hawaii
Brigham Young University – Idaho
Brigham Young University – Utah
Brigham Young University – Hawaii
Brown University
Bryan College
Bryant University
Bryn Mawr College
Bucknell University
Buena Vista University
Butler University
Cabarrus Collee of Health Sciences
Cal Poly Pomona
Caldwell University
California College of the Arts
California Institute of Technology
California Institute of the Arts
California Lutheran University
California Polytechnic State University, San Luis Obispo
California State University – Bakersfield
California State University – Chico
California State University – Dominguez Hills

California State University – East Bay
California State University – Fresno
California State University – Fullerton
California State University – Long Beach
California State University – Los Angeles
California State University – Northridge
California State University – Sacramento
California State University – San Bernardino
California State University – San Marcos
California State University – Stanislaus
California State University, Fullerton
California State University, Long Beach
Calvin College
Campbell University
Canisius College
Capital University
Cardinal Stritch University
Carleton College
Carlow University
Carnegie Mellon University
Carroll College
Carroll University
Carson – Newman University
Carthage College
Case Western Reserve University
Catawba College
Catholic University of America
Cedar Crest College
Cedarville University
Centenary College of Louisiana
Central College
Central Methodist University
Central Piedmont Community College
Central Texas College
Central Washington University
Centre College
Chaminade University of Honolulu
Champlain College
Chapman University
Charleston Southern University
Chatham University
Chemeketa Community College
Chicago State University
Chowan University
Christian Brothers University
Christopher Newport University
Citadel, The – Military College of South Carolina
Claremont McKenna College
Clarion University of Pennsylvania
Clark Atlanta University
Clark University
Clarke College
Clarkson University
Clearwater Christian College
Clemson University
Cleveland Institute of Art
Cleveland Institute of Music
Coastal Carolina University
Coe College
Coker College
Colby College
Colby – Sawyer College
Colgate University
College for Creative Studies
College of Charleston
College of Eastern Utah
College of Idaho, The
College of Mount St. Joseph
College of Mount St. Vincent
College of New Jersey
College of Notre Dame of Maryland
College of Saint Benedict – Saint John's University
College of Saint Elizabeth
College of Santa Fe
College of St. Scholastica
College of the Atlantic
College of the Holy Cross
College of William and Mary
College of Wooster
Collin College – Central Park Campus
Colorado Christian University
Colorado College
Colorado Community College System
Colorado Mesa University
Colorado Mountain College
Colorado School of Mines
Colorado State University
Colorado State University – Fort Collins
Colorado State University – Pueblo
Columbia College
Columbia College – Chicago
Columbia College – Columbia, MO
Columbia College – South Carolina
Columbia College Chicago
Columbia University – Columbia College Undergraduate Admission
Columbia University – Fu Foundation School of Engineering
Columbus State Community College
Columbus State University
Community College of Baltimore County – Essex
Concordia College
Concordia College – Moorhead
Concordia College – New York
Concordia University – Chicago
Concordia University – Irvine
Concordia University – Nebraska
Concordia University – Portland
Concordia University – St. Paul
Connecticut College
Converse College
Cooper Union for the Advancement of Science & Art
Corban University
Corcoran College of Art & Design
Cornell College
Cornell University
Cornell University – College of Engineering
Cornell University – School of Hotel Administration
Cottey College
Covenant College
Creighton University
Crossroads College
Crown College
CUNY – Queens College
Culver – Stockton College
Curry College
D'Youville College
Dallas Baptist University
Dallas Christian College
Dana College – Nebraska
Dartmouth College
Davidson College
Daytona State College
De Anza College
Defiance College
Delaware Valley College
Delta College
Denison University
DePaul University
DePauw University
Dickinson College
Doane College
Dominican University
Dominican University – River Forest
Dominican University of California
Dordt College
Drake University
Drew University
Drexel University
Drury University
Duke University
Duquense University
Duquesne University
Earlham College
East Carolina University
East Tennessee State University
Eastern Connecticut State University
Eastern Kentucky University
Eastern Michigan University
Eastern Oregon University
Eastern Washington University
Eckerd College
Edgewood College
El Centro College
Elizabethtown College
Elmhurst College
Elmira College
Elms College
Elon University

Embry – Riddle Aeronautical University – Daytona Beach
Emerson College
Emmanuel College – Boston
Emory and Henry College
Emory University
Emporia State University
Endicott College
Erskine College
Eureka College
Evangel University
Evergreen State College
Fairfield University
Fashion Institute of Technology – SUNY
Ferris State University
Ferrum College
Flagler College
Flathead Valley Community College – Kalispell
Florida Atlantic University – Boca Raton
Florida Atlantic University – Wilkes Honors College
Florida College
Florida Gulf Coast University
Florida Institute of Technology
Florida International University
Florida Memorial University
Florida Scholarships
Florida Southern College
Florida State College at Jacksonville
Florida State University
Fordham University
Fordham University (all campuses)
Fort Hays State University
Francis Marion University
Franciscan Missionaries of Our Lady University
Franciscan University of Steubenville
Franklin and Marshall College
Franklin College
Franklin Pierce University
Fresno Pacific University
Friends University
Front Range Community College – Westminster Campus
Frostburg State University – Maryland
Furman University
Gardner – Webb University
Geneva College
George Fox University
George Mason University
George Washington University
Georgetown College
Georgetown University
Georgia Baptist College of Nursing of Mercer University
Georgia College and State University
Georgia Institute of Technology
Georgia Southern University
Georgia State University
Germanna Community College
Gettysburg College
Golden Gate University
Gonzaga University
Gordon College – Georgia
Gordon College – Massachusetts
Goshen College
Goucher College
Grace College and Seminary
Graceland University
Grand Canyon University
Grand Valley State University
Greensboro College
Grinnell College
Grossmont College
Grove City College
Guilford College
Gulf Coast State College
Gustavus Adolphus College
Gwynedd Mercy University
Hamilton College
Hamline University
Hampden – Sydney College
Hampshire College
Hampton University
Hanover College
Hardin – Simmons University
Harding University
Harford Community College
Hartwick College
Harvard University
Harvey Mudd College
Hastings College
Haverford College
Hawaii Pacific College
Hawaii Pacific University
Heidelberg University
Hendrix College
High Point University
Hillsborough Community College – Brandon Campus
Hillsdale College
Hillsdale Free Will Baptist College
Hiram College
Hobart and William Smith Colleges
Hofstra University
Hollins University
Holy Names University
Hood College
Hope College
Hope International University
Houghton College
Houston Baptist University
Howard Community College – Maryland
Howard University
Humboldt State University, a California State University Campus
Huntingdon College
Huntington University
Hutchinson Community College
Illinois College
Illinois Institute of Technology
Illinois State University
Illinois Wesleyan University
Indian River State College
Indiana University – Purdue University at Indianapolis
Indiana University – Purdue University Fort Wayne
Indiana University – South Bend
Indiana University Bloomington
Indiana Wesleyan University
Iona College
Iowa State University
Iowa State University of Science and Technology
Ithaca College
Jacksonville University
James Madison University
John Brown University
John Carroll University
John Jay College of Criminal Justice (City University of New York)
Johns Hopkins University
Johnson & Wales University – Charlotte
Johnson & Wales University – Denver
Johnson & Wales University – North Miami
Johnson & Wales University – Providence
Johnson C. Smith University
Judson University – Illinois
Juniata College
Kalamazoo College
Kansas State University
Kansas Wesleyan University
Kaplan University
Keene State College
Kennesaw State University
Kent State University
Kentucky Wesleyan College
Kenyon College
Kettering University
King College
King's College – Pennsylvania
Knox College
Kutztown University of Pennsylvania
La Salle University
La Sierra University
Lafayette College
LaGrange College
Laguna College of Art and Design
Lake City Community College
Lake Forest College
Lander University
LaRoche College
Lasell College
Lawrence Technological University
Lawrence University
Lebanon Valley College
Lee University

Lees – McRae College
Lehigh University
Lehman College – The City University of New York
Lenoir – Rhyne University
Lesley University
LeTourneau University
Lewis and Clark College
Lincoln Memorial University
Linfield College
Linfield College – McMinnville
Linfield College – Portland
Lipscomb University
Livingstone College
Loma Linda University
Lone Star College – CyFair
Lone Star College – Kingwood
Lone Star College – Montgomery
Lone Star College – North Harris
Lone Star College – Tomball
Long Island University – Global
Long Island University at Riverhead
Long Island University – C.W.Post Campus
Longwood University
Loras College
Louisburg College
Louisiana State University – Baton Rouge
Loyola Marymount University
Loyola University – Chicago
Loyola University – Maryland
Loyola University Chicago
Loyola University Maryland
Loyola University New Orleans
Luther College
Lynchburg College
Lynn University
Lyon College
Macalester College
MacMurray College
Macon State College
Madonna University
Manchester College
Manhattan College
Manhattanville College
Marian University – Indiana
Marietta College
Marist College
Marlboro College
Marquette University
Mars Hill College
Mars Hill University
Marshall University
Mary Baldwin College
Maryland Institute College of Art (MICA)
Marymount California University
Marymount Manhattan College
Marymount University
Maryville College
Marywood University
Massachusetts College of Art and Design
Massachusetts College of Pharmacy and Health Sciences – Boston
Massachusetts Institute of Technology
Master's College, The
Mayville State University
McDaniel College
McMurry University
Menlo College
Mercer University
Mercyhurst University
Meredith College
Merrimack College
Messiah College
Methodist University
Metropolitan Community College – Blue River
Metropolitan Community College – Longview
Metropolitan Community College – Maple Woods
Metropolitan Community College – Omaha
Metropolitan Community College – Penn Valley
Metropolitan State University – St. Paul
Metropolitan State University of Denver
Miami Dade College
Miami University of Ohio
Michigan State University
Michigan Technological University
Mid – America Nazarene University
Middle Georgia State College
Middle Tennessee State University
Middlebury College
Midwestern State University
Millersville University
Milligan College
Millikin University
Mills College
Millsaps College
Milwaukee School of Engineering
Minerva Schools at KGI
Minneapolis College of Art and Design
Minneapolis Community and Technical College
Minnesota State University – Moorhead
Minnesota West Community and Technical College
Mississippi College
Mississippi Colleges and Universities
Mississippi State University
Missouri Southern State University – Joplin
Missouri State University
Missouri University of Science & Technology
Missouri University of Science and Technology
Missouri Western State University
Molloy College
Monmouth College
Monmouth University
Monroe Community College – Rochester
Montana State University Billings
Montana State University Bozeman
Montgomery College – Rockville
Montreat College
Moody Bible Institute
Moravian College
Morehouse College
Morgan State University
Mount Holyoke College
Mount St. Mary's College – Los Angeles
Mount St. Mary's University – Emmitsburg
Mount Union College
Mountain Empire Community College
Muhlenberg College
Multnomah Bible College and Biblical Seminary
Muskingum College
N.C. Wesleyan College
National American University – Rapid City
Nazareth College of Rochester
NCAA – Eligibility Center
Nebraska Wesleyan University
New College of Florida
New England College
New Jersey Institute of Technology
New Mexico Highlands University
New York Film Academy
New York Institute of Technology
New York University
New York University – Tisch School of the Arts
Newberry College
Niagara University
Norfolk State University
North Carolina Agricultural and Technical State University
North Carolina State University
North Central College
North Central University
North Dakota State University
North Dakota University System
North Greenville University
North Hennepin Community College
North Park University
Northeastern University
Northern Arizona University
Northern Illinois University
Northern Kentucky University
Northern Michigan University
Northern Virginia Community College – Alexandria

Northern Virginia Community College – Annandale
Northern Virginia Community College – Manassas
Northern Virginia Community College – Medical Ed. Campus
Northern Virginia Community College – Woodbridge
Northland College
Northwest Christian University
Northwest Missouri State University
Northwest Nazarene University
Northwest University
Northwestern University
Notre Dame de Namur University
Oakland University
Oberlin College
Occidental College
Oglethrope University
Ohio Dominican University
Ohio Northern University
Ohio State University
Ohio University
Ohio Valley University
Ohio Wesleyan University
Okaloosa – Walton Community College
Oklahoma Baptist University
Oklahoma Christian University
Oklahoma City University
Oklahoma State University
Old Dominion University
Olin College of Engineering
Olivet Nazarene University
Oral Roberts University
Oregon Institute of Technology
Oregon State University
Otis College of Art & Design
Ottawa University – Kansas
Ouachita Baptist University
Oxford College of Emory University
Pace University – Pleasantville
Pacific Lutheran University
Pacific Union College
Pacific University
Palm Beach Atlantic University
Palm Beach State College
Palomar College
Paradise Valley Community College
Park College (see Park University)
Park University
Pasco – Hernando State College – West Campus
Paul Smith's College
Pennsylvania State University – University Park
Pensacola Junior College
Pepperdine University
Pfeiffer University
PharmCAS
Piedmont College
Pine Manor College
Pittsburg State University
Pitzer College
Point Loma Nazarene University
Point Park University
Pomona College
Portland State University
Prairie View A&M University
Presbyterian College
Prince George's Community College
Princeton University
Principia College
Providence College
Purdue University, West Lafayette
Queens University of Charlotte
Quincy University
Quinnipiac University
Radford University
Ramapo College of New Jersey
Randolph College – Lynchburg
Randolph – Macon College – Ashland
Reed College
Regent University
Regis College
Regis University
Rensselaer Polytechnic Institute
Rhodes College
Rice University
Rider University
Ringling College of Art and Design
Ripon College
Roanoke College
Robert Morris University
Roberts Wesleyan College
Rochester Institute of Technology
Rockford University
Rockhurst University
Rocky Mountain College – Billings
Roger Williams University
Rollins College
Roosevelt University
Rose – Hulman Institute of Technology
Rosemont College
Rowan University
Russell Sage College
Rutgers – The State University of New Jersey
Rutgers – The State University of New Jersey
Rutgers University – – Newark
Sacred Heart University
Saginaw Valley State University
Saint Anselm College
Saint Augustine's University
Saint Edward's University
Saint Joseph's University
Saint Louis University
Saint Louis University – MO
Saint Martin's University
Saint Mary's College of California
Saint Mary's College – Notre Dame
Saint Mary's College of California
Saint Mary's University of Minnesota
Saint Michael's College
Saint Paul College – Minnesota
Saint Vincent College
Salem College
Salem – Teikyo University
Salisbury University
Salt Lake Community College
Salve Regina University
Sam Houston State University
Samford University
San Diego State University
San Diego State University – Imperial Valley Campus
San Francisco Art Institute
San Francisco State University
San Jacinto College
San Joaquin Delta College
San Jose State University
Santa Clara University
Santa Fe College
Sarah Lawrence College
Savannah College of Art and Design – Atlanta
Savannah College of Art and Design – Savannah
Schiller International University
School of the Art Institute of Chicago
School of the Museum of Fine Arts
Schreiner University
Scripps College
Seattle Pacific University
Seattle University
Seminole State College – Sanford Campus
Seton Hall University
Sewanee – University of the South
Shaw University
Shenandoah University
Shepherd University
Shimer College
Shorter University
Siena College
Sierra Nevada College
Simmons College
Simpson College
Skidmore College
Slippery Rock University
Smith College
Soka University of America
South Dakota School of Mines and Technology
South Dakota State University
South Georgia College
South University – Pittsburgh
Southeast Missouri State University
Southeastern Louisiana University
Southeastern University
Southern Adventist University
Southern Connecticut State University
Southern Illinois University – Carbondale

Southern Methodist University
Southern Nazarene University
Southern New Hampshire University
Southern Oregon University
Southern Polytechnic State University
Southern Utah University
Southern Vermont College
Southern Virginia University
Southwest Baptist University
Southwest Minnesota State University
Southwestern Assemblies of God University
Southwestern College – California
Southwestern University
Spelman College
Spring Arbor University
Spring Hill College
St Mary's College – Indiana
St. Andrews Presbyterian College
St. Andrews University
St. Bonaventure University
St. Catherine University
St. Cloud State University
St. Edward's University
St. John Fisher College
St. John's College
St. John's College – Maryland
St. John's College – New Mexico
St. John's University – Queens Campus
St. Johns College
St. Joseph's College – Brooklyn Campus
St. Lawrence University
St. Mary's College of Maryland
St. Mary's University – San Antonio
St. Mary's University – Texas
St. Norbert College
St. Olaf College
Stanford University
State University of New York – Brockport
State University of New York College at Plattsburgh
State University of New York Polytechnic Institute
Stephen F. Austin State University
Stephens College
Stetson University
Stonehill College
Stony Brook University
SUNY – Alfred State College
SUNY – Binghamton University
SUNY – Buffalo State College
SUNY – College at Brockport
SUNY – College at Cortland
SUNY – College at Fredonia
SUNY – College at Geneseo
SUNY – College at Old Westbury
SUNY – College at Oneonta
SUNY – College at Oswego
SUNY – Maritime College
SUNY – New Paltz
SUNY – Purchase College
SUNY – Ulster County Community College
SUNY – University at Albany
SUNY – University at Buffalo
SUNY Adirondack
SUNY Cortland
SUNY OSWEGO (State University of New York at OSWEGO)
Suffolk University
Sul Ross State University – Alpine
Susquehanna University
Swarthmore College
Sweet Briar College
Syracuse University
Tabor College
Tacoma Community College
Tallahassee Community College
Tarleton State University
Taylor University – Fort Wayne
Taylor University – Indianapolis
Taylor University – Upland
Teikyo Post University
Temple University
Tennessee Technological University
Texas A&M University – College Station
Texas A&M University – Commerce
Texas A&M University – Corpus Christi
Texas A&M University – Galveston
Texas A&M University – Kingsville
Texas A&M University – Commerce
Texas Christian University
Texas Lutheran University
Texas State University
Texas State University San Marcos
Texas Tech University
Texas Wesleyan University
Texas Woman's University
The College of Saint Rose
The Evergreen State College
The George Washington University
The New School
The New School for Liberal Arts – Eugene Lang College
The New School – Social Research
The University of New Mexico
The University of Southern Mississippi
The University of Texas at Austin
The University of Texas at San Antonio
The University of Tulsa
Thomas More College
Tiffin University
Toccoa Falls College
Tougaloo College
Towson University
Transylvania University
Trevecca Nazarene University
Trinity Christian College
Trinity College
Trinity International University
Trinity University
Troy University
Truman State University
Tufts University
Tulane University
Tulsa Community College
Tusculum College
UCBerkekey
Union College
Union College – Kentucky
Union College – New York
Union University
United States Air Force Academy
United States International University
United States Military Academy
United States Naval Academy
University at Albany – – SUNY
University of Advancing Technology
University of Akron
University of Alabama
University of Alabama – Tuscaloosa
University of Alabama at Birmingham
University of Alabama in Huntsville
University of Alaska – Anchorage
University of Alaska – Fairbanks
University of Alaska Southeast – Juneau
University of Alaska Southeast – Ketchikan
University of Arizona
University of Arizona – Tucson
University of Arkansas
University of Arkansas at Fayetteville
University of Arkansas at Little Rock
University of Baltimore
University of California – Berkeley
University of California – Davis
University of California – Irvine
University of California – Los Angeles
University of California – Merced
University of California – Office of the President
University of California – Riverside
University of California – San Diego
University of California – San Francisco
University of California – San Francisco, School of Dentistry
University of California – Santa Cruz
University of California – – Merced
University of California, Berkeley
University of California, Irvine
University of California, Office of the President
University of California, Santa Barbara
University of California – – Riverside
University of Central Florida
University of Central Missouri

University of Central Oklahoma – Edmond
University of Charleston
University of Chicago
University of Cincinnati
University of Colorado at Boulder
University of Colorado at Colorado Springs
University of Colorado Denver
University of Connecticut
University of Dallas
University of Dayton
University of Delaware
University of Denver
University of Dubuque
University of Evansville
University of Florida
University of Georgia
University of Georgia – Athens
University of Hartford
University of Hawaii – Hilo
University of Hawaii – Manoa
University of Hawaii – Manoa
University of Houston
University of Idaho
University of Illinois at Chicago
University of Illinois at Urbana Champaign
University of Illinois at Urbana – Champaign
University of Indianapolis
University of Iowa
University of Kansas
University of Kentucky
University of Louisville
University of Maine
University of Maine at Fort Kent
University of Maine at Orono
University of Mary Washington
University of Maryland
University of Maryland – Baltimore County
University of Maryland – University College
University of Maryland, College Park
University of Massachusetts
University of Massachusetts – Boston
University of Massachusetts – – Lowell
University of Memphis
University of Miami
University of Michigan
University of Michigan – Ann Arbor
University of Michigan – Dearborn
University of Michigan – Flint
University of Minnesota – Crookston
University of Minnesota – Duluth
University of Minnesota – Morris
University of Minnesota, Twin Cities
University of Mississippi
University of Missouri
University of Missouri – Columbia
University of Missouri – Kansas City
University of Missouri, Columbia
University of Mobile
University of Montana
University of Montana – Montana Tech
University of Montevallo
University of Mount Olive
University of Nebraska – Omaha
University of Nebraska – Lincoln
University of Nebraska – Omaha
University of Nevada – Las Vegas
University of Nevada – Reno
University of New Hampshire
University of New Haven
University of New Mexico
University of New Mexico – Albuquerque
University of New Orleans
University of North Carolina at Asheville
University of North Carolina at Chapel Hill
University of North Carolina at Charlotte
University of North Carolina at Greensboro
University of North Carolina at Pembroke
University of North Carolina at Wilmington
University of North Carolina Greensboro
University of North Carolina School of the Arts
University of North Dakota
University of North Florida
University of North Georgia
University of North Texas
University of Northern Arizona
University of Northern Colorado
University of Northern Iowa
University of Northwestern – St. Paul
University of Notre Dame
University of Oklahoma – Norman
University of Oregon – Eugene
University of Pennsylvania
University of Pittsburgh
University of Pittsburgh – McGowan Institute of Regenerative Medicine
University of Portland
University of Puget Sound
University of Redlands
University of Rhode Island
University of Richmond
University of Rochester
University of San Diego
University of San Francisco
University of Scranton
University of South Alabama
University of South Carolina – Beaufort
University of South Carolina – Columbia
University of South Carolina – Lancaster
University of South Carolina – Salkehatchie
University of South Carolina – Upstate
University of South Florida
University of South Florida – St Petersburg
University of South Florida – Tampa
University of Southern California
University of Southern Indiana
University of Southwestern Louisiana
University of St. Francis
University of St. Francis – Illinois
University of St. Mary
University of St. Thomas – Minnesota
University of St. Thomas – St. Paul
University of St. Thomas – Houston
University of St. Thomas – Minnesota
University of Tampa
University of Tennessee – Chattanooga
University of Tennessee – Knoxville
University of Texas – Pan American
University of Texas – Dallas
University of Texas at Arlington
University of Texas at Austin
University of Texas at Dallas
University of Texas at El Paso
University of Texas at San Antonio
University of Texas at Tyler
University of Texas of the Permian Basin
University of The Sciences in Philadelphia
University of Toledo
University of Tulsa
University of the Arts
University of the Pacific
University of the South – Sewanee
University of Utah
University of Vermont
University of Virginia
University of Virginia's College at Wise
University of Washington
University of Washington – Seattle
University of Washington – Tacoma
University of Washington Bothell
University of West Alabama
University of West Florida
University of West Georgia
University of Wisconsin – Eau Claire
University of Wisconsin – Green Bay
University of Wisconsin – HELP Program
University of Wisconsin – La Crosse
University of Wisconsin – Madison
University of Wisconsin – Milwaukee
University of Wisconsin – Oshkosh

University of Wisconsin – Parkside
University of Wisconsin – Richland
University of Wisconsin – River Falls
University of Wisconsin – Stevens Point
University of Wisconsin – Stout
University of Wisconsin – Whitewater
University of Wisconsin – Madison
University of Wisconsin – Superior
University of Wyoming
Universityof Detroit Mercy
Ursinus College
Utah State University
Utah Valley University
Utica College
Valdosta State University
Valencia College – all campuses
Valencia College – East Campus
Valparaiso University
Vanderbilt University
Vanguard University of Southern California
Vassar College
Villanova University
Virginia Commonwealth University
Virginia Military Institute
Virginia Polytechnic Institute & State University
Virginia State University
Virginia Wesleyan College
Virginia Western Community College
Viterbo University
Wabash College
Wagner College
Wake Forest University
Warner Pacific College
Warren Willson College
Washingotn and Lee University
Washington & Jefferson College
Washington and Lee University
Washington College
Washington State University
Washington State University – Pullman
Washington University in St. Louis
Wayland Baptist University – Phoenix Campus
Wayne State University
Webster University
Wellesley College
Wesleyan College
Wesleyan College – Macon
Wesleyan University
Wesleyan University – Middletown
West Chester University
West Chester University of Pennsylvania
West Texas A&MUniversity
West Virginia University
West Virginia Wesleyan College
Western Carolina University
Western Illinois University
Western International University – Arizona
Western Kentucky University
Western Michigan University
Western Oregon University
Western Texas College
Westminster College
Westminster College – Salt Lake City
Westmont College
Whatcom Community College
Wheaton College
Wheaton College – Illinois
Wheaton College – Massachusetts
Wheeling Jesuit University
Whitman College
Whittier College
Whitworth University
Wichita State University
Widener University
Willamette University
William Jessup University
William Jewell College
William Peace University
William Smith College
William Woods University
Williams College
Wingate University
Winona State University
Winston – Salem State University
Winthrop University
Witman College
Wittenberg University
Wofford College
Worcester Polytechnic Institute
Wright State University
Xavier University
Xavier University – Cincinnati
Xavier University of Louisiana
Yakima Valley Community College
Yale University
Young Harris College
Youngstown State University

URUGUAY

Universidad Católica del Uruguay
Universidad de la República
Universidad ORT Uruguay

VENEZUELA

Instituto Experimental de Tecnología y Agricultura
Universidad Tecnológica del Centro – UNITEC

ZIMBABWE

University of Zimbabwe

6. University Scholarships for IB Diploma Holders

As of December 2019

The following universities offer scholarships for recipients of the IB diploma. They are listed by country.

AUSTRALIA

SP Jain Center for Management
Deakin University
Murdoch University
Bond University
Curtin University
Edith Cowan University
Macquarie University
Griffith University
Monash University
University of Newcastle
University of Queensland
University of Wollongong
University of Technology Sydney
University of Southern Queensland
University of South Australia
University of Notre Dame
University of New South Wales
University of Newcastle
University of Melbourne
University of Adelaide
Australian National University
University of Sydney
University of Western Australia
Queensland University of Technology
RMIT University Melbourne
La Trobe University
James Cook University
University of Canberra

CANADA

Acadia University, NS
Bishop's University, QC
Brandon University, MB
Brescia University College, ON
Brock University, ON
Cape Breton University, NS
Collège universitaire de Saint-Boniface, MB
Concordia University College of Alberta, AB
Dalhousie University, NS
EduNova IB Entrance Scholarship Program
Huron University College, ON
Memorial University of Newfoundland, NF
Mount Allison University, NB
Mount Saint Vincent, NS
Nova Scotia Agricultural College, NS
Nova Scotia College of Art and Design, NS dub
Red Deer College, AB
Saint Mary's University, NS
Simon Fraser University, BC
St. Francis Xavier University, NS
St. Thomas University, NB
Trent University, ON
Trinity Western University, BC
Université Sainte-Anne, NS
Université de Moncton, NB
Université de Montréal QC
University of Alberta, AB
University of British Columbia, BC
University of Calgary, AB
University of King's College, NS
University of Manitoba, MB
University of New Brunswick (Fredericton), NB
University of New Brunswick (St. John), NB
University of Prince Edward Island, PEI
University of Regina, SK
University of Saskatchewan, SK
University of Toronto, ON
University of Victoria, BC
University of Waterloo, ON
University of Western Ontario, ON
University of Windsor, ON
University of Winnipeg, SK
Wilfred Laurier University, ON
York University, ON

FRANCE

American University of Paris

GERMANY

Jacobs University Bremen
International University of Bremen

HONG KONG

Hong Kong Polytechnic University
University of Hong Kong
Savannah College of Arts and Design – Hong Kong
City University of Hong Kong
Chinese University of Hong Kong
Hong Kong University of Science and Technology
Hong Kong Academy for Performing Arts
The Education University of Hong Kong

INDONESIA

FLAME University
Christ University
Amity University
Universitas Pelita Harapan
BINUS University

JAPAN

International Christian University
Tokyo International University
Nagoya University of Commerce and Business
BBT University
Kwansei Gakuen University
Ritsumeikan Asia Pacific University
Tsukuba University
Yokohama National University
Keio University
Waseda University
Hokkaido University
Nagoya University
Tohoku University
Tokyo Institute of Technology
Osaka University
Kyoto University
University of Tokyo
Sophia University
Temple University
Meiji University
Okayama University

MALAYSIA

University of Reading Malaysia
Taylor's University
Monash University Malaysia
Sunway University
Swinburne University of Technology Sarawak Campus
Heriot-Watt University Malaysia
Universiti Tunku Abdul Rahman
UCSI University
University of Nottingham Malaysia
RCSI & UCD Malaysia (formerly Penang Medical College)
International Medical University
New Zealand
Auckland University of Technology
Massey University
Lincoln University
University of Auckland
University of Canterbury
University of Otago
University of Waikato
Victoria University of Wellington

SINGAPORE

SP Jain Center for Management
Nanyang Academy of Fine Arts

Embry-Riddle Aeronautical University
National University of Singapore
Singapore Management University
Nanyang Technological University
Lasalle College of Arts
Singapore University of Technology and Design
Singapore University of Social Sciences

SPAIN

IE University
La Salle – Ramon Llull University

THAILAND

King Mongkut University of Technology
Mahidol University International College

TURKEY

Bahçeşehir University
Beykent University
Doğuş University
Işık Üniversity
İstanbul Bilgi University
İstanbul Kültür University
İstanbul Sabahattin Zaim University
İstanbul Şehir University
İzmir Ekonomi University
İzmir Üniversitesi
Kadir Has University
Koç University
Maltepe University
Okan University
Özyeğin University
Sabancı University
TED University
Türk Hava Kurumu University
Üsküdar University
Yeditepe University

UNITED ARAB EMIRATES

SP Jain Center for Management

UNITED KINGDOM

City University London
King's College London
University of Kent
University of Liverpool
University of Nottingham
University of Reading
University of Roehampton
University of Sheffield

UNITED STATES

American International College, MA
American University of Paris, US Office
Benedictine University, IL
Bowling Green State University-Bowling Green, Ohio
College of Idaho, ID
Concordia College-Moorhead, MN
Davis United World College Scholar Program, USA (91 institutions)
Defiance College, IN
Drew University, NJ
Drury University, MO
Florida Atlantic University – Wilkes Honors College, FL
Florida Bright Futures Scholarship Program, FL
Florida Gulf Coast University, FL
Georgetown College, KY
Grand Canyon University, AZ
High Point University, NC
Illinois Institute of Technology, IL
Meredith College, NC
Methodist University, MI
Michigan Technological University, MI
Middle Tennessee State University, TN
Midwestern State University, TX
Missouri State University, MO
Missouri Western State University, MO
Monmouth College- Monmouth, Illinois
Montana State University – Bozeman, MT
Murray State University- Murray KY
New College of Florida, FL
New England College, ME
New York Film Academy – Los Angeles, CA
Northern Arizona University, AZ
Northwestern Missouri State University, MO
Oregon State University, OR
Otterbein College, OH
Pacific University, OR
Queens University of Charlotte-Charlotte, NC
Saint Michael's College
Savannah College of Art & Design – Savannah, GA
Savannah College of Art & Design – Atlanta, GA
Simmons College Boston, MA
Simpson College, IA
Southern Methodist University, TX
St. Lawrence University, NY
St. Mary's College of Maryland, MD
St. Mary's University – San Antonio, TX
Stetson University, FL
Temple University, PA
Texas Tech University, TX
Texas State University San Marcos, TX
Transylvania University Lexington, KY
United States Government: Academic Competitiveness Grant (ACG)
United States Government: National SMART Grant (NSG)
University of Alabama, AL
University of Arizona, AZ
University of Bridgeport, CT
University of Dallas, TX
University of Dubuque, IA
University of Florida, FL (for UWC IB diploma holders)
University of Nebraska-Lincoln, NE
University of North Florida, FL
University of North Texas, TX
University of Oregon, OR
University of Rochester, NY
University of Tampa, FL
University of Texas at Tyler, TX
University of Texas – Pan American, TX
University of Tulsa, OK
University of Wisconsin - Superior, WI
Utica College, OK
Wabash College, IN
Western Oregon University, OR
Western Washington University, WA
William Jewell College, MO
Whitworth University, WA
Winthrop University, SC
Wittenberg University, OH
Worcester Polytechnic Institute, MA

VIETNAM

British University Vietnam
Ho Chi Minh City University of Technology
Hong Bang International University
RMIT University Vietnam
Ton Duc Thang University

Please note

- The scholarships vary in size. Some are modest, others are substantial. Please check universities' web sites and contact university officials for more detailed information about a particular scholarship.
- The IB diploma is recognized by universities worldwide. These universities, including those that do not offer scholarships for IB students, often look favourably on applications from IB graduates. They may offer other types of scholarships for which IB graduates are encouraged to apply.
- In many cases, universities with low tuition fees do not offer scholarships of any type because financial assistance is unnecessary. However, they may recognize the IB diploma and even be particularly interested in IB students.
- The list is not exhaustive and is regularly revised as new information is received from universities.
- The IB does not in any way endorse the universities listed.

Index

An index of all IB World Schools listed alphabetically.

B

C

D

E

F

I

J

K

P

Q

R

S

T

U

V

Z